The Bowker Annual

Library and Book Trade Almanac™

2003 | 48th Edition

Editor Dave Bogart
Consultant Julia C. Blixrud

 **Information Today, Inc.**

Published by Information Today, Inc.
Copyright © 2003 Information Today, Inc.
All rights reserved

International Standard Book Number 1-57387-165-6
International Standard Serial Number 0068-0540
Library of Congress Catalog Card Number 55-12434

Information Today, Inc.
143 Old Marlton Pike
Medford, NJ 08055-8750
Phone: 800-300-9868 (customer service)
              800-409-4929 (editorial queries)
Fax: 609-654-4309
E-mail (orders): custserv@infotoday.com
Web Site: www.infotoday.com

Printed and bound in the United States of America

ISBN 1-57387-165-6

$199.00

9 781573 871655   59999

Contents

Part 1
Reports from the Field

Part 4
Research and Statistics

Part 5
Reference Information

Part 6
Directory of Organizations

Directory of Library and Related Organizations

Directory of Book Trade and Related Organizations

Preface

This 48th edition of the *Bowker Annual* chronicles another year of change and challenge as national and global events, and ever-advancing technology, affect every aspect of the information world.

Heightened national security concerns since the terrorist attacks of September 11, 2001, pose hard questions and demand difficult decisions. The complexities of presenting and handling electronic information pervade all facets of the industry. And, meanwhile, the roles of the library, the librarian, and the publisher continue to be redefined.

As always, we have assembled a blend of expert analysis and practical information to keep the information professional up to date.

Our Special Reports in this edition look at five areas of immediate interest.

- Restrictive changes in the way government information is disseminated, enacted in the name of "homeland security," are the topic of Harold Relyea and Elaine Halchin, who question whether U.S. citizens will settle for "information lite."
- Looking at the development of "electronic government," Relyea and Henry B. Hogue examine how choices have been made, and will continue to be made, about what information should be available to the general public and in what form.
- Library portals: Are they "the updated embodiment of how a library delivers on its mission, or a faddish manifestation of a library's will to survive"? Brian E. C. Schottlaender and Mary E. Jackson provide an overview.
- The complex question of digital rights management—and its implications for scholars, libraries, and publishers—is explored by Grace Agnew and Mairéad Martin.
- Recruitment and retention of library staff is a growing concern as the profession "ages" at the same time that the supply of qualified graduates is falling. Pat Hawthorne co-led an ACRL task force studying the issue, and its findings are detailed here.

Also in Part 1, our News of the Year section offers experts' articles on developments in public libraries, school libraries, and publishing. Reports from a score of federal agencies and libraries and national and international organizations round out the section.

The year's legislation and regulations affecting libraries and those affecting publishing are examined in Part 2, which also includes reports from grant-making and funding programs.

Part 3 contains professional information for librarians, including help in finding employment, reports on placements and salaries, and lists of the year's winners of scholarships and awards.

A wealth of research and statistics makes up Part 4, from descriptions of noteworthy research projects to detailed data on library acquisition expenditures, prices of materials, and book title output.

Reference information in Part 5 includes lists of the year's bestselling books, most lauded books, and recommended books, the year's top literary prizes, and such practical information as how to obtain an ISBN, ISSN, or SAN.

Part 6 is our directory of library and publishing organizations at the state, national, and international levels, and includes a multiyear calendar of upcoming events.

Putting all this together is the work of many hands. We are grateful to all those who contributed articles, assembled statistics and reports, and responded to our requests for information. Particular thanks are due Consulting Editor Julia C. Blixrud and Contributing Editor Catherine Barr.

We are confident that you will find this edition of the *Bowker Annual,* like its predecessors, a valuable and handy resource. As always, we welcome your comments and suggestions for future editions.

Dave Bogart
Editor

Part 1
Reports from the Field

News of the Year

LJ News Report:
Victories Muted by Money Worries

Library Journal Staff

The economic repercussions of the September 11, 2001 attacks—which took a toll on libraries in 2001—were compounded in 2002 by a continued economic slump. It wasn't the most auspicious time to launch a salaries initiative, but American Library Association (ALA) President Maurice J. Freedman found much support among the rank and file.

The legacy of September 11, including an increased emphasis on public safety and the ominous (yet unclear) impact of the USA Patriot Act, blunted even a clear victory for libraries, the successful litigation against the Children's Internet Protection Act (CIPA). The concentration on 9/11 issues, combined with political deadlock, meant a slow-moving Congress. Library champions at the state and federal levels confronted revenue shortfalls and political gridlock, but they maintained support for library funding, freedom of expression, easy access to information, and the field's cherished exemptions to copyright. Libraries have traditionally been a bipartisan concern, and while fiscal support fell with the economic decline, library use exploded anew, just as the fruits of a library building boom—such as new main libraries in cities like Nashville and Memphis—became evident. As libraries served more people directly, they became more visible to politicians of all persuasions. After all, library users, of all American constituencies, are among the most likely to be voters.

Budget Woes

Many libraries were hurting, even those with ample funds for construction. The Seattle Public Library, beneficiary of a $196.4 million bond issue and a hefty amount of private fund-raising, found itself so short on operating funds that it closed twice during the year. In traditionally well-funded Ohio, libraries lost 7 to 8 percent in state aid. This led to cuts in materials budgets and talk of branch closures as well as new proposals to raise revenue.

Adapted from *Library Journal*, December 2002. Contributors to the article were Andrew Albanese, Associate Editor; John Berry, Editor-in-Chief; Lynn Blumenstein and Susan DiMattia, Contributing Editors; Brian Kenney, Senior Editor, *netConnect*; Norman Oder, Senior News Editor; and Michael Rogers, Senior Editor, *InfoTech*.

In Ohio, at least, libraries were not singled out; most state agencies were cut 15 percent. In some cases, notably state library agencies in Washington, Minnesota, and Virginia, libraries were targeted. Governor Gary Locke tried to close the Washington State Library (WSL), but a compromise moved WSL under the aegis of the secretary of state. Locke later slashed the library's budget 17 percent. In Minnesota, the state library agency was decimated, and librarians around the state have organized to restore the Office of Library Development and Services.

Academic libraries were under pressure as well. Public universities encountered shrinking state budgets, and private ones contended with shrinking endowments. In Missouri, for example, state funding for higher education—about 12 percent of the state budget—was cut nearly 37 percent, and libraries felt the pinch. The passage of a huge bond issue in California was good news.

President Bush's budget for Library Service and Technology Act (LSTA) funds contained only a modest increase for fiscal year (FY) 2002–2003. Library advocates placed more hope in a five-year reauthorization of LSTA. Before September 11, 2001, ALA called for $500 million; after that, advocates looked to the $350 million proposed in the Senate. However, after the Democrats lost the Senate in November 2002, the number seemed likely to be closer to the $300 million proposed in the House.

Forecast for 2003: Libraries will probably face more budget constraints, necessitating hard decisions and creative revenue ideas.

Salaries and Recruitment

In the areas of salaries and recruitment, rhetoric outpaced performance. Though Freedman catapulted the salary issue to the forefront, the initiative met not just a lagging economy but also bureaucratic roadblocks; ALA's new Allied Professional Association, organized in part to spur salaries, barely got off the ground. (In better news for ALA, the new executive director, Keith Fields, presided over a smooth transition.)

A healthy new union contract at the Los Angeles Public Library suggested progress. Still, the Minneapolis Public Library's stalled search for a director proved that a salary capped at $120,000 isn't attractive—one finalist, Multnomah County's Ginnie Cooper, instead went to the Brooklyn Public Library for some $80,000 more.

The salaries issue remained shackled to the subject of recruitment. Though salaries for 2001 graduates sprang back to beat inflation, as shown in *Library Journal*'s annual salary survey, and enrollment is growing, a good number of graduates opt for higher-paying jobs outside the library field. And the profession is graying.

However, having a librarian in the White House helped: First Lady Laura Bush gave library recruitment its biggest boost in many years via a $10 million initiative for library education. The funding, managed by the Institute of Museum and Library Services, targeted an assortment of recruitment methods, with library schools required to partner with public libraries. This pilot program, if successful, will continue throughout the Bush administration.

Forecast for 2003: Despite the economic downturn, the salaries issue won't go away, and ALA President-Elect Carla Hayden will be pressured by the rank and file to take up the salaries banner.

Privacy Under Pressure

How much did 9/11 change library procedures? At the Public Library Association conference in Phoenix in March 2002, Leigh Estabrook, director of the Library Research Center, University of Illinois at Urbana-Champaign, reported on a survey of U.S. public libraries conducted three to four months after the terrorist attacks. Some 39 percent of the 1,028 libraries responding, especially the larger ones, had reviewed building security. Seven percent reported monitoring patrons' Internet use, and nearly 15 percent saw circumstances in which privacy could be compromised.

More than 4 percent—a weighted average as opposed to the initial report of 8 percent—said that local or federal law enforcement agencies had requested information about patrons.

That doesn't necessarily mean those authorities were acting under expanded powers granted by the USA Patriot Act. How much law enforcement has used those new powers isn't clear. The Freedom to Read Foundation, ALA's sibling organization, along with three other groups, filed a lawsuit October 24 under the Freedom of Information Act (FOIA) to learn how many subpoenas have been issued to libraries, bookstores, and newspapers.

A branch of the Charlotte-Glades Library System in Florida was evacuated for three hours on July 29 after a sheriff's volunteer reported an Internet user he deemed suspicious to local police, who then found chemicals of unknown origin in the visitor's backpack. The chemicals turned out to be paint thinner and jewelry cleaner, and the homeless man was surfing a Web site about an ancient battery, not bombs. This proved an isolated case of—take your pick—vigilantism or excessive post-9/11 caution.

Forecast for 2003: Pressures on privacy—and dissent—may increase if the country goes to war. Still, a substantial mainstream constituency, especially on consumer issues, has emerged for privacy.

Libraries and the Law

Internet Filtering

CIPA would have required libraries receiving federal funds for Internet access to filter "harmful to minors" material from all terminals as well as obscenity and child pornography—essentially mandating filtering throughout the library.

If the May 3 legal decision overturning CIPA was clear-cut, based on legitimate speech blocked because of "the crudeness of filtering technology," the societal question was not. The three-judge federal panel noted that the trial record demonstrated that many minors seek to access pornography at the library. The case has been appealed by the Justice Department to the Supreme Court.

In the CIPA case, some prominent librarians testified for filtering—a sign of the lack of consensus within librarianship. Still, in May, the National Research Council issued a report that concluded that neither filters nor any other quick fix supplies the answer.

Copyright

After years of seeing the pendulum swing away from fair use and toward the interests of the content industry, librarians logged progress on copyright. In October, the Supreme Court heard *Eldred* v. *Ashcroft*, a challenge to Congress's latest 20-year copyright extension. Though the court may lack the basis to overturn the extension, the justices seemed troubled by Congress's approach to copyright issues. Reps. Rick Boucher (D-Va.) and Zoe Lofgren (D-Calif.) introduced bills that would reverse some of the draconian elements of the sweeping Digital Millennium Copyright Act (DMCA) of 1998.

Government Information

In addition, a string of government proposals may significantly impact public access to government information. These efforts include the closing of PubSCIENCE, the Department of Energy's database of abstracts and texts in the physical sciences, and the discarding of paper copies of the public's collection of paper patents at the U.S. Patent and Trademark Office. A proposal to allow government agencies to bypass the Government Printing Office (GPO) has also disturbed librarians.

Forecast for 2003: Expect a decision on CIPA and a fight over GPO. UCITA —a proposed uniform law for software transactions that would enshrine shrinkwrap licenses—lurks in state legislatures. The copyright issue will remain an uphill battle, but growing public recognition of the concerns should help the library community.

Virtual Reference Reaches Forward

Libraries around the country began new virtual reference services, and others expanded. In June the Library of Congress (LC), in partnership with the Online Computer Library Center (OCLC), launched its national service QuestionPoint. Both LSSI, Inc., which offers software and outsourced service, and 24/7 Reference, the first cooperative service, reported growth. The types of service expanded as well. In Ohio, CLEVNET's KnowItNow24x7 partnered with local healthcare providers to offer medical information. LSSI recently began to offer chat services in Spanish.

While usage statistics are reported to be rising, services must prove their value, even as librarians serve patrons outside their local jurisdiction or school. Librarians acknowledge they must do more to attract users, such as installing persistent buttons on a library or institution's Web site. Session transcripts provide a new level of accountability, and although the digital transaction allows personalization, privacy may be compromised.

Commercial reference providers have come and mostly gone in the past few years, but two new entrants may have more staying power. In April Google unveiled Google Answers, in which "more than 500 carefully screened researchers" answer questions. Also, the not-for-profit Wondir Foundation, with an advisory board including two prominent librarians, is developing a new service to connect "people with questions" to experts and enthusiasts.

Forecast for 2003: As more people use the Web, librarians will continue to move services as well as collections online. Expect increased pressure from nonlibrary reference providers.

E-Books Repositioned

E-books have gone through an almost opposite evolution from CD-ROMs, which were successfully translated into Web-based products. Designed initially for consumers, digitized books failed to find readers, and many big publishing houses quickly folded their e-book tents.

Software developers in the library market, however, learned from the mistakes made by print publishers. OCLC's purchase in the closing days of 2001 of the bankrupt netLibrary, which had a solid product but a poor business model, heralded a second act: e-books as a reference resource. After that, ABC-CLIO began releasing all its titles simultaneously in paper and e-books. Recently, Gale signed a 50 e-title deal with netLibrary and hopes to release all its titles in both formats.

Some titles may still work as e-books, or Adobe Systems believes so: The company released Content Server 3.0 to enable secure distribution of PDF-based e-books. Titles from major publishers range across nonfiction categories and include some fiction.

While libraries continued to expand their electronic collections—such as LC's National Digital Library Program and the University of Virginia's Electronic Text Center—vendors also brought significant content to the market this year. ProQuest completed the digitization of the first two titles in its Historical Newspapers program: the *New York Times* and *Wall Street Journal*.

Gale, which is currently digitizing the London *Times* all the way back to 1785, last year announced an ambitious digital publishing program: the Eighteenth Century, in cooperation with the British Library and others.

Forecast for 2003: With such major players pushing ahead, we should see additional vendors digitizing materials or mounting e-book programs.

Distance Ed and the "L" Word

More and more library education programs accredited by ALA offered some or all courses online. Some still require students to take a portion of their courses face-to-face, while others allow students to complete all studies online, including orientation sessions.

Some faculty prefer distance education, since it liberates them from inconvenient classroom schedules and limitations. Others, however, complain that teaching online requires much more work and that students lack support and resources they would get on campus. Still, distance ed has made librarianship accessible to new blood and in some cases has dramatically increased minority enrollment.

Librarians debated the proper positioning of library education programs. Practitioners still complained when programs dropped the "L" (library) word from their names. Library educators, such as Dean Mike Eisenberg of the University of Washington's recently renamed Information School, became defensive. They said the carping by practicing librarians hurt the programs both on campus and in the field, since librarianship remained central to their curricula. Practitioners held that since most of the graduates still work in libraries, the programs should keep *library* in their names. Some urged ALA to make it a requirement for accreditation, though the ALA Council rejected such a resolution at the annual conference.

Forecast for 2003: Expect more debate on the "L" word, as well as closer examination of distance ed.

Special Librarians: Mixed Message

Did special librarians gain ground? A Factiva report concluded that the search for free business information on the Web isn't worth it, implying that special expertise is needed to use fee-based resources. Still, an Outsell research report verified that average budgets of corporate information centers are at pre-2001 levels and that those running them must serve more users and provide higher-value services.

While one out of four survey respondents have reached executive or director ranks, there are fewer specialized librarians overall. As the head of one prestigious corporate library in New York City said, it is an employer's market because so many experienced people are out of work.

Such turmoil was reflected within the Special Libraries Association (SLA). In January, SLA's new executive director, Roberta Shaffer, following on earlier staff cuts, announced a plan for staff reassignments. In February, after only five months on the job, she resigned. The process to hire a permanent executive director did not begin in earnest until November 2002.

Members voiced strong exception when, at the Winter Meeting, the SLA board proposed taking on sweeping powers. After the protest, members agreed to a milder bylaws revision. A branding/name change initiative was stalled, suggesting it would be hard to find a name to appeal to the diverse members. Membership in SLA fell in 2002, while associations for law and medical librarians remained solid.

Forecast for 2003: Special librarians will have to acquire expanded competencies, reassert their worth, and do more with less.

Scholarly Innovation

As in previous years, journal prices went up, monograph sales declined, and librarians confronted ever-tightening budgets. But as digital technology reshapes the way scholars, students, and researchers work, creative, library-driven solutions are emerging.

The past year saw the launch of the Massachusetts Institute of Technology's DSpace institutional repository, which aims to "capture, distribute, and preserve" campus intellectual output, and the Association of Research Libraries' efforts to promote other alternative publishing models. Also, pioneering e-book efforts included the American Council of Learned Societies' history monograph program and the Columbia University Press/American Historical Association's Gutenberg-e project, which publishes monographs on the Web.

SPARC, which supports increased competition in scientific journal publishing, expanded to SPARC Europe, with the hiring of its first director, David Prosser, formerly of Oxford University Press.

Forecast for 2003: Change is coming slowly but steadily, so look for more innovation and partnerships.

The Year in K–12 Libraries:
School Librarians Redefine Themselves

Walter Minkel

Technology Editor, *School Library Journal*

Few years have been as tumultuous as 2002 in K–12 librarianship. President George W. Bush's "No Child Left Behind" legislation, the sinking national economy, and the continued fuss and furor over the Internet were only the backdrop. School librarians had five major issues of their own to cope with:

- The shortage of new librarians
- The drive to collaborate with other teachers
- The necessity to become partners with principals and other administrators
- The continuing campaign to find statistics that quantify school librarians' importance
- The increasing recognition of information literacy as the fundamental goal of the school librarian

The Background

No Child Left Behind

When President Bush signed the law establishing his "No Child Left Behind" (NCLB) campaign on January 8, 2002, he pleased many people, angered others, and made many American educators—particularly educators in public schools—nervous. The NCLB Web site (http://www.nclb.gov) described the central goal of the act as the "development of rigorous state accountability systems to ensure that every child meets the highest possible standards." The states would set up standards in all major curriculum areas that every child would be expected to meet. Every child in every school would be tested frequently to meet these standards. Every child would learn to read by the third grade. If schools continually failed to produce children who did not pass the tests, and were identified as "low performing" schools, children from those schools could be given the option of transferring to other schools—including private schools. Principals of low-performing schools could be subject to loss of their jobs.

Some educators saw the establishment of standards and testing, and particularly of testing plans or "accountability systems" that could lead to children moving to private religious schools, as an erosion of the division of church and state, and as an attack on public education. Bush's policies, critics say, could cause many at-risk students to abandon their schools even though there might be no convenient alternative school nearby (such as a charter school or religious school) that had any space for them.

Many public schools that serve at-risk children suffer from a lack of funding and a lack of classroom space. Los Angeles' 49 regular high schools, for example, have classroom space for about 145,000 students yet must house 165,000, and that number is supposed to grow to 200,000 by 2005. The quality of education in such crowded conditions is bound to suffer at the same time that the federal government is requiring stricter testing.

Layoffs, Cost-Cutting

The stagnation of the economy led to job layoffs and cost-cutting in many schools—and therefore in school libraries—nationwide. States, counties, and cities suffered sinking tax revenues between 2000 and 2002 and had to deal with significant budget cuts during the 2001–2002 school year. Many of them had surplus funds left over from the booming economy of the late 1990s to soften the blow, but during the 2002–2003 school year, schools were hit with enormous deficits in both local and state taxes, and the cuts for 2003–2004 may be much worse. The school district budget in Fresno, California, for example, was cut by $4.1 million in 2002–2003, but faced a $30 million budget cut for the next year. Hiring freezes were in place in many districts nationwide. At the same time, the state of Michigan announced that the 2003 fiscal year state budget would need to be cut by $280 million, and that early estimates for 2004 indicated a deficit of up to $2 billion.

Cuts of this magnitude were bound to affect school libraries. At Hale Middle School in Vermont's Nashoba Regional School District, librarian positions were eliminated and the school library only remained open with the help of 27 parent volunteers. The library's entire materials budget was cut as well. All elementary librarians and their assistants were cut from the Springfield, Illinois, school district budget and were replaced in many schools by volunteers.

Continuing Impact of the Internet

If you asked any school librarian in 2002 what single phenomenon had wrought the greatest change in his or her job, the reply would probably be "The Internet, definitely." If students were told to do research for an assignment without any restrictions, most went first to an Internet search tool such as Google or Yahoo. Librarians everywhere noted that students had little interest in looking first in a catalog for a book, then finding the book, and then searching the index or table of contents for the assigned information when they could simply sit in front of a screen, type one or two words into a search box, and have hundreds or thousands of answers stack up in front of them.

Librarians noticed as well that many teachers were not skilled Internet users and tended to believe that their students knew more than they did. But librarians also found that many students had no idea how to formulate a search or evaluate the quality of information resources they found online.

The nearly ubiquitous filtering of the Internet in K–12 schools—ordered by Congress under 2000's Children's Internet Protection Act (CIPA), which took full effect in the summer of 2002—was an area of concern for many educators and freedom-of-information activists. Internet filtering services, such as Smart-Filter, WebSense, and Bess, were ostensibly required to prevent young people from being exposed to pornography or pedophiles online. But a 2002 study by California's Kaiser Family Foundation demonstrated that when such filtering mechanisms were set at their highest level of restriction—at which sites that deal with the use of tobacco, for instance, are blocked as well as pornography sites—they also blocked 24 percent of appropriate Web sites on health issues.

The Major Issues

Shortage of New Librarians

The average librarian in the United States in 2002 was 45 years old, and almost 50 percent of the nation's professional librarians planned to retire in the next 12 years. And about 25 percent of America's 76,807 school libraries didn't have a certified librarian. There was one school librarian for every 953 students—not a good ratio. Although school librarians have active, challenging jobs—spending much of their day on their feet, helping students mine both books and the Internet for the correct tidbit of information for an assignment—the profession didn't seem to be attracting many new education graduates.

What should the school library profession do to turn things around? One of the most effective ways has been to bring teachers into the ranks of librarians. Della Curtis, director of library services at Baltimore County (Maryland) Public Schools, established in 1997 a School Library Media Cohort with Towson University that gives practicing teachers in Baltimore County and several other nearby counties the opportunity to train as library media specialists. The program is a tough one and includes training in the Information Power national school library standards, information literacy skills training, and library management courses. Curtis says that some teachers have applied for the program because they are burned out on classroom teaching and think being a librarian will be an easier job. She warns them that they should know that being a librarian may be the hardest job in the school.

There are similar programs in other parts of the country. Examples are the Metro Cohort at the University of Colorado at Denver and another at the University of Washington in Seattle. The boom in distance learning has also allowed teachers far from a school with a library media program to take the courses they need to become librarians.

The Need for Collaboration with Teachers

School librarians have always worked with teachers, but more and more experts in library media services say that school librarians must become activists in their schools. They need to take the information literacy curriculum to the teachers and invite them to work together on classroom assignments instead of waiting for the teachers to come to the library. Michael Eisenberg, dean of the University of Washington School of Information, says, "In many communities, some media specialists are passive and complain about how few teachers work with them. I ask them, 'What are you doing to change that?'"

The lack of collaboration is felt most intensely by librarians in elementary schools, who often feel they are relegated to the task of babysitting. Elementary school librarians are frequently on "fixed" schedules, which means that classes are scheduled to come to the library at particular times, whether or not the class has an immediate need to use the library. The time that the class spends in the library is often the teacher's planning period, with the result that the teacher often doesn't come to the library with the class.

Librarians on flexible schedules have opportunities to spend more time with classes doing research assignments. The American Association of School Librarians continues to hold up flexible librarian schedules as the ideal, but because teacher contracts often require that the school provide teachers with a planning period, sending the kids to the library is often the easiest solution.

The Need to Become Partners with Administrators

Every school librarian must be sure to let his or her principal know exactly what is happening in the library on a regular basis, says Eisenberg, who is one of the creators of the Big6, a widely used approach to teaching information literacy skills. To make his idea of improving communication between principals and school librarians a reality, the Seattle Public Schools invited him to create a training program for the city's media specialists.

Eisenberg's proposal redefines the notion of a school librarian. He or she is (or should be called) a "teacher-librarian," and plays three roles in the life of the school: as an information-literacy teacher for students and staff, a reading advocate, and an information manager who selects the school's print and electronic resources and trains everyone in the school how to use them effectively. The librarian's role as a teacher needs to be stressed. But to build this kind of image, the librarian has to be certain that the principal knows everything he or she does. "[Librarians] need to talk about how many research lessons they presented, how many books they booktalked, and detail the collaborations they've had with teachers," Eisenberg says.

He gave the Seattle school librarians forms that they could give to their principals every ten weeks, in which the librarians detailed all their activities, emphasizing those in which they served students directly. Laura Grosvenor, a librarian at Seattle's Kimball Elementary School, sent these reports to Principal Barbara Nielsen, and Nielsen says that when she read them she realized just how much teaching Grosvenor did.

Quantifying School Librarians' Importance

Eisenberg wants librarians to point out how much teaching they do, because many school board members and school district superintendents don't know much about what the librarians in their district really do. Most librarians haven't been very good at keeping statistics about their activities, instead using anecdotes about students who return to the school years later to tell the librarian how much he or she meant to them as proofs of the librarian's value. Anecdotes no longer serve as justification to principals and board members making tough budget decisions; they want hard numbers that demonstrate how a school librarian helps students get better scores on their statewide tests.

Since 1990 Keith Curry Lance of the Colorado State Library has been coordinating research projects that do just that, and in 2002 he completed two studies that include new findings. Lance and colleague Marcia Rodney have determined in studies for states including Colorado, Alaska, Pennsylvania, and Texas that test scores are higher in schools with a librarian with the freedom to collaborate with teachers. Two new studies in Michigan and New Mexico continue the trend. Lance's surveys over the past five years have also confirmed that schools with adequate library collections, higher numbers of computers that can access library resources, and librarians who teach students how to use the school's licensed databases (such as EBSCOhost or GaleNet) have higher test scores than those that do not. (See the Library Research Service site at http://www.LRS.org.)

Increasing Recognition of Information Literacy

The school librarian has always contributed to making and keeping students literate. But the definition of "literate" has changed over the past decade, and justifying the school librarian in a time of tight budgets often centers on how well he or she contributes to a student's information literacy level. "Information literacy" is often defined as how well a student can find and use information effectively in all media, including books, video, audio, and electronic sources. Many states— among them Colorado, Ohio, Oklahoma, and Rhode Island—have included information literacy standards among those all students must meet.

Teachers have complained over the past five years about a rise in Internet-based plagiarism. Material, they say, is simply too easy to find over the Web, too easy to copy from a Web site, and too easy to paste into a word processor; it can become part of a student's report without even being read fully.

The increasing sloppy and plagiaristic use of the Internet by K–12 student researchers has led to changes in the way teachers make assignments and in how school librarians are teaching students to use online resources. Many of the "classic" assignments every librarian knows well—the president report, the country report, and the animal report, for example—are prone to copying and pasting. Marcia Jensen, a media specialist at Davenport West High School in Iowa, says that teachers, with the librarian's collaboration, should be designing assignments that encourage students to do something with the information they find. She says she "would have the students [record] the information they located in the search portion of the report on a large class graph, instead of making a report." The teacher could then have the students ask each other questions: What does my animal eat? What kind of teeth do the meat-eaters have? What kind do the plant-eaters have? The librarian will locate, or show the students how they can locate, the proper materials—whether books, Web sites, or another medium—to answer these kinds of questions. Students who copy and paste are barely thinking; assignments must change into activities that force the students to think about essential questions.

All of these issues are reshaping what the school librarian has become and will become in the next few years. Attention will need to be paid to increasing both the numbers and the perceived role of school librarians, and the continuing push to make all students both print-literate and information-literate offers school librarians and their professional organizations ample raw material to stress how critical literacy has become in the 21st century.

Publishing in 2002: Few Trends Emerge from a Year of Ups and Downs

Jim Milliot

Senior Editor, Business and News, *Publishers Weekly*

Unlike the stormy year of 2001, which was dominated by the demise of electronic publishing and downsizing at many traditional publishing companies, 2002 was a relatively calm year, a year that Association of American Publishers President and CEO Pat Schroeder described as "difficult to get a handle on."

Indeed, while the last decade has seen the rise and fall of electronic publishing, the explosion in online book sales, the growth of superstores, and consolidation among publishing companies, there was no issue or trend that stood out in 2002. Many industry members were satisfied with tweaking their existing operations, usually by upgrading their technical infrastructure, in a bid to improve profits.

The biggest news of the year came in December when Barnes & Noble, the nation's largest bookstore chain, announced it had reached a preliminary agreement to acquire Sterling Publishing. The $115 million purchase gives a major boost to Barnes & Noble's publishing operations and is a significant step in the company's vertical integration strategy that calls for it not only to be a major player in bookselling but in distribution and publishing as well. The news of the purchase was met with a great amount of angst among publishers—particularly those who publish in Sterling's segments of crafts, hobbies, gardening and how-to—who were concerned that Barnes & Noble will give preferential treatment to Sterling titles while shelf space for their titles will be limited.

Another acquisition with industry-wide ramifications occurred in January 2002 when Advanced Marketing Services (AMS), the major supplier of books to warehouse clubs, paid $37 million to buy Publishers Group West (PGW), the largest exclusive distributor of independent publishers. Publishers distributed by PGW were hopeful that the greater financial resources of AMS would help get their titles into more outlets, while AMS viewed the deal as a way to broaden its own distribution capabilities as part of its plan to lessen its dependence on the warehouse club business.

While PGW found a new home at AMS, two of its competitors went out of business in the year. In April the LPC Group filed for Chapter 11 bankruptcy and closed its doors several months later. LPC represented more than 85 publishers, including some of the country's largest graphic novel publishers. In July Seven Hills Book Distributors faxed a letter to its small-publisher clients informing them that because of a dismal spring season the company was closing its operations. Distributor problems were not limited to the United States. General Publishing, a major Canadian publisher and parent company of General Distribution Services (GDS), filed for bankruptcy in May. GDS represented nearly 200 publishers, including a number of U.S. houses, and despite attempts to revive the business it shut down its operations later in the year.

Things were relatively stable in the retail sector, although late in the year FAO, Inc., parent company of the multimedia chain Zany Brainy, filed for

Chapter 11 and announced it planned to close 55 of Zany Brainy's 169 outlets in 2003. Earful of Books, a fledgling chain devoted solely to the sale and rental of spoken-word audio books, went out of business in June.

Staff Reductions

The end of 2001 did not bring an immediate stop to layoffs or downsizing in different segments of the industry, although the reductions in 2002 were not on the scale of those in the previous year. Random House, whose various divisions began trimming their staffs late in 2001, continued that practice into the new year. Random made cuts in its children's book group, Crown Book Group, and in its sales force, while also closing its five-person West Coast publicity office. Later in the year it cut another nine jobs in its children's group. Globe Pequot Press, hurt by the slowdown in sales in its largest segment, travel books, laid off 13 people in January 2002, while the international travel publisher Lonely Planet cut 81 positions from its U.S. operations in March. Travel books was one of the publishing segments most affected by the September 11, 2001, terrorist attacks. Computer books was another segment where sales were soft in 2001 and 2002. The weak market prompted Haights Cross Communications to close its computer book subsidiary Coriolis Group and led to layoffs at a number of other computer book publishers including O'Reilly & Associates and Pearson's computer book division. Soft sales of computer books, as well as other technology titles, hastened the integration of Fatbrain.com, an online retailer focused on the corporate and technology markets, into Barnes&Noble.com's operation in the early part of 2002. Barnes&Noble.com, which acquired Fatbrain in September 2000, closed Fatbrain.com's California office, eliminating about 50 positions, and brought all functions into its New York headquarters.

Two companies involved with electronic publishing that managed to survive in 2001 continued to scale back in 2002. Questia, the Web site aimed at providing information for college students, laid off 40 employees in February, leaving the firm with only a 28-person staff. InterTrust Technologies, a pioneer in the development of Digital Rights Management, went through several rounds of layoffs in 2002 before it was sold late in the year to a consortium headed by Sony and Philips.

Other layoffs were scattered throughout the industry. Simon & Schuster cut 20 positions, about 2 percent of its staff, in February, and trimmed four editorial spots in November as part of its decision to reduce the number of adult titles. Reader's Digest, still struggling to improve the results in its U.S. books and home entertainment division, eliminated 80 positions in April. Perseus Group folded Counterpoint Press into its Basic Books subsidiary in April, laying off six employees, including Counterpoint founder Jack Shoemaker. Shoemaker later re-emerged with a new imprint at Avalon. In a somewhat similar move, Penguin took over the operations of Prentice Hall Press from its sister company, Pearson Education, and in the process did away with 15 positions. In November Bookspan cut 10 spots in various departments.

The unkindest cut for publishers and booksellers alike came in April when TV talk show queen Oprah Winfrey announced she was ending her six-year-old

Oprah's Book Club. Over the course of its existence, the club had brought attention—and huge sales—to the work of dozens of noted authors including Maya Angelou, Ernest J. Gaines, Barbara Kingsolver, Wally Lamb, and Joyce Carol Oates. To help fill the void left by the cancellation of Oprah's club, several TV shows, including "Good Morning America," "The Today Show," and "Live with Regis and Kelly," introduced their own clubs, although no new effort was able to generate the sales power of Oprah's picks.

Mergers and Acquisitions

While Barnes & Noble's purchase of Sterling created the most buzz in the industry in 2002, the year's biggest deal was the acquisition of Houghton Mifflin by the investment firms Thomas H. Lee Partners and Bain Capital. The group paid $1.66 billion to Vivendi to acquire Houghton Mifflin. Vivendi had acquired Houghton Mifflin for $2.2 billion in 2000, but was forced to divest the company, along with several other assets, to pay down its large debt.

Another significant purchase was Reader's Digest's $760 million acquisition of Reiman Publications. Based in Wisconsin, Reiman publishes magazines and books on cooking, gardening, and country living.

The high prices paid for Houghton Mifflin and Reiman were the exceptions in 2002, a year in which strategic and niche acquisitions dominated. Two deals that brought more scale to mid-sized publishers were the Perseus Group's purchase of Running Press and F&W Publications' $120 million acquisition of Krause Publications. The latter deal united two of the country's largest hobby-and-crafts publishers, while Perseus's purchase of Running Press brought a greater trade presence to a company that has focused mainly on the scholarly and serious nonfiction categories.

Other strategic acquisitions by small and mid-sized companies included Lerner Publishing Group's purchase of Kar-Ben Copies, Red Wheel Weiser's acquisition of Conari Press, the purchase of Sheed & Ward by Roman & Littlefield, and Creative Publications' purchase of Two-Can Publishing, a deal that added a school and library component to Creative's more retail-oriented line. The Langenscheidt Publishing Group added to its presence in the travel market with the purchase of the publishing assets of Berlitz International. In a couple of deals that brought two religion publishers together, Continuum International acquired the Moorehouse Group, while Baker Book House acquired Bethany House. Gallery Press, a small fine arts publisher, expanded its presence in that field with the purchase of Hudson Hills Press. In one of the more unusual deals of the year, the small publisher Sleeping Bear Press sold its assets to three different parties. The Gale Group bought the company's children's titles; John Wiley acquired 50 turf management and golf architecture books, and a Sleeping Bear employee group acquired the remaining assets, which were composed primarily of golf and sports books.

Wiley's purchase of some of Sleeping Bear's books was one of several niche purchases by the company that also included the purchase of teacher-education titles from Prentice Hall Direct as well as the acquisitions of British publisher A&M Publishing and German publisher GIT Verlag. Other companies that made multiple purchases in the year included ProQuest, which bought the digital textbook publisher MetaText, as well as the custom publishing assets of Courier Corp. and online content provider bigchalk.com. Scholastic added four companies during the year with the largest purchase the $43 million acquisition of Klutz, the children's multimedia publisher. Scholastic also paid $7.5 million for Baby's First Book Club, and $6 million for Teacher's Friend Publications. In addition, Scholastic bought a 15 percent stake in the British children's book distributor Book People. Advanced Marketing Services also made moves in Britain, acquiring the distribution companies H. I. Marketing Ltd. and Airlift Book Company to complement its purchase earlier in the year of Publishers Group West. Random House made two small purchases: its Ballantine Book Group acquired the military book publisher Presidio, while its Alfred A. Knopf division bought the U.K.-based Everyman Publishers. Simon & Schuster acquired Distican, its long-time distributor in Canada.

An investment banking firm, Quad Ventures, entered the publishing industry with its purchase in September of Troll Communications. A month later a second investor paid $7.5 million for a stake in Troll.

People

A number of high-profile industry leaders had changes in their job descriptions in 2002. The most dramatic change came in the summer with the surprise forced resignation of Thomas Middelhoff as CEO of Bertelsmann, the parent company of Random House and co-owner of Bookspan. Middelhoff was replaced by Gunter Thielen. Random House had its own executive changes, highlighted by the departure of Phyllis Grann after a six-month stint as vice chair of the company. Grann quickly joined the board of advisers at the private equity firm Leeds, Weld where she joined former Simon & Schuster chair Jon Newcomb, who had resigned from the Simon & Schuster position earlier in the year.

Other personnel changes at Random House included the departure of Craig Virden as head of the company's children's publishing group where he was succeeded by Chip Gibson, who had headed Crown Publishers. Jenny Frost replaced Gibson at Crown. Late in the year, George Pfhul, Random House president, returned to Germany where he was named CEO of both Verlagsgruppe Random House and Random House Continental Europe.

David Wan resigned as president of the Penguin Group to take over as president and CEO of Harvard Business School Publishing Corp. John Makinson, director of finance for Penguin parent company Pearson, was named chairman of Penguin and later in the year added the role of CEO. (At the end of 2002, Pearson changed the name of its U.S. division, Penguin Putnam, to Penguin USA). Houghton Mifflin also had a change in leadership when Hans Gieskes was named CEO to replace the retiring Nader Darehshori. At Houghton Mifflin's trade and reference group, Theresa Kelly was picked to succeed Wendy Strothman as head of the division.

The major change in bookselling was the promotion of Steve Riggio to CEO of Barnes & Noble, succeeding his brother Len, who remained chairman. Marie Toulantis took over from Steven Riggio as CEO of Barnes&Noble.com. In the middle of the year, Michael Berry resigned as president of Barnes & Noble

Bookstores. At rival Borders Group, Greg Josefowicz officially took the reins as chairman, succeeding the retiring Bob DiRomualdo. Kathryn Winkelhaus resigned as president of merchandising and distribution.

The educational publishing world had a number of shifts in the upper management ranks in 2002. After more than a year's search, Pat Tierney, the president of Thomson Financial, was appointed to the newly created post of CEO of Reed Elsevier's Harcourt Education subsidiary. Reed had been looking to fill that position since it completed the acquisition of Harcourt in 2001. Tierney was replaced at Thomson Financial by David Shaffer, who had headed up Thomson Learning. Shaffer's position at Thomson Learning was taken by Ron Schlosser. Back at Harcourt, Jan Spalding was promoted to president of Harcourt School Publishers, succeeding the retiring Steve Gandy. Another educational-publishing powerhouse, the McGraw-Hill Companies (MHC), appointed Henry Hirschberg president of McGraw-Hill Education, replacing Bob Evanson, who retired. Sari Factor was named president of MHC's Macmillan/McGraw-Hill K–6 publishing division. The changing of the guard at John Wiley involved Peter Wiley succeeding his brother Brad Wiley as chairman.

The managerial merry-go-round even reached into university press publishing where Ellen Faran replaced MIT Press's longtime director Frank Urbanowski. Faran had been at Houghton Mifflin. Yale University Press tabbed John Donatich, publisher of Basic Books, to succeed John Ryden as press director. Liz Maguire was named to succeed Donatich at Basic. Trinity University announced that it was reviving its press and named Barbara Ras, former executive editor at the University of Georgia Press, to head the effort.

The illustrated book market suffered a loss in June when pioneer Paul Gottlieb died of a heart attack. The head of Harry Abrams for more than 20 years, Gottlieb had just taken over the leadership at the Aperture Foundation. At Abrams, Steve Parr was named CEO.

Outside mainstream publishing, Kirby Best replaced Ed Marino as president of Lightning Source, the on-demand publisher. iUniverse, the print on-demand subsidy publisher, overhauled its operations by closing its corporate documents business, shutting down its California office, and laying off 36 employees, including company president Doug Bennett. Henry Yuen resigned as chairman of Gemstar. Yuen was best known for his advocacy of e-books, although the company's e-book projects suffered from the same problems as all other e-book publishers. Jeff Abraham was named the new executive director of the Book Industry Study Group. Michael Cairns was named president of R. R. Bowker, and Andrew Grabois was appointed Bowker's senior director of publisher relations and content development.

Bestsellers

The top-selling books of the year came from both new and old sources. While the bestsellers in hardcover fiction included books written by such popular authors as John Grisham (*The Summons, Skipping Christmas*) and James Patterson (*The Beach House*), the two longest-running titles on the *Publishers Weekly* hardcover fiction chart were two debut fiction works, *The Nanny Diaries* by Emma

McLaughlin and Nicola Kraus and *The Lovely Bones* by Alice Sebold. In hardcover nonfiction, while how-to/self improvement remained a popular category, 16 books related to the September 11 attacks appeared on the *PW* list. Seven titles with a conservative bent also made the charts led by *Bias: A CBS Insider Exposes How the Media Distorts the News* by Bernard Goldberg and *Slander: Liberal Lies About the American Right,* which had runs of 17 and 15 weeks, respectively, on the *PW* charts.

A total of 421 books hit the *PW* bestseller lists in 2002, down slightly from the 433 that made the charts in 2001. As usual, Random House commanded the most bestsellers, although its 64 titles that made the hardcover list represented a 4.8 percent decline in market share from 2001 to 25.2 percent. Its 63 trade paperback and mass market paperback bestsellers were even with 2001. Penguin Putnam's share of hardcover bestsellers fell 3.1 percent in 2002 to 14.9 percent, while Simon & Schuster's market share rose by 0.9 percent to 13 percent. The Time Warner book group and Holtzbrinck (St. Martin's, Holt, FSG) posted gains in the year with Time Warner's market share up 3.2 percent to 12.7 percent and Holtzbrinck's presence increasing 4.2 percent to 7.5 percent. In paperback, the largest shifts came at Penguin, whose share dropped 11.6 percent to 12.7 percent, while Time Warner's share of the paperback market rose 6.3 percent to 16.3 percent.

Copyright and First Amendment

The annual conference of the American Library Association (ALA) in Atlanta highlighted the most pressing copyright and First Amendment issues confronting the industry in the year. One copyright issue that has divided the industry, the Copyright Extension Act of 1998, moved into the Supreme Court in the autumn when the justices heard oral arguments in *Eldred* v. *Ashcroft.* The lawsuit was brought on behalf of Eric Eldred, who distributed public domain books on the Internet and challenged the main provisions of the copyright act that extended copyright protection by 20 years to 70 years plus life of the author and 95 years plus life for corporations. The lawsuit was backed by ALA and opposed by most, though not all, members of the Association of American Publishers (AAP). To no one's surprise, the Supreme Court upheld the copyright extension in a 7–2 decision handed down in early January 2002.

Another copyright issue that pitted industry members against one another— in this case authors and e-book publishers against traditional publishers—came to a less decisive conclusion at the end of 2002. In an out-of-court settlement, Random House dropped the lawsuit filed in 2001 against e-book publisher Rosetta Books that the giant publisher had filed in 2001 charging the start-up with copyright infringement for publishing e-book versions of Random's print titles. Rosetta agreed to pay a licensing fee for publishing the e-books.

The Margaret Mitchell estate and Houghton Mifflin reached their own out-of-court settlement over Houghton's publication of *The Wind Done Gone,* a parody of *Gone With the Wind.* The Mitchell estate had filed suit in 2001 charging that *The Wind Done Gone* infringed the copyright of *Gone With the Wind.* Under the agreement, Houghton continued to publish the book with the label "An

Unauthorized Parody." Both sides also maintained the correctness of their respective legal positions.

A long-running privacy and First Amendment issue was settled in April when the Colorado Supreme Court blocked an attempt by local prosecutors to force the Tattered Cover Book Store to turn over the records of customers' book purchases in a case they were investigating. But booksellers couldn't take long to savor the victory as the passage of the USA Patriot Act put new pressure on booksellers and libraries to turn over their records regarding book purchases and book loans. The law also prevents booksellers and librarians from disclosing any order they receive from government investigators. After congressional hearings about the application of the law failed to generate sufficient information from the Justice Department, a coalition of free-speech advocates filed suit against the department demanding that it release more information about how the USA Patriot Act was being applied.

ALA and other free-speech advocates won a victory in June when a three-judge federal panel in Philadelphia threw out the Children's Internet Protection Act (CIPA), which would require libraries to use software that filters out pornographic content. The government appealed the Philadelphia ruling and in November the U.S. Supreme Court agreed to hear the case. In May, the Supreme Court had returned a decision challenging the Child Online Protection Act (COPA) to the Third District. COPA, passed in 1998, aimed to regulate adult content on the Internet. While the high court found the community standards can apply to the Internet, it suggested that there could be deeper First Amendment problems with the law.

Sales

Sales in the critical holiday selling season failed to hit expectations at the major bookstore chains and at many independent bookstores. Sales at Barnes & Noble rose 1.3 percent over the holiday period, but sales at stores opened for at least one year fell 3 percent at superstores and 11.5 percent at Dalton. At the Borders Group, comparable store sales fell 2.5 percent at its superstore group and 6.3 percent at Waldenbooks. At the nation's third-largest bookstore chain, Books-A-Million, holiday sales fell 2.7 percent with comparable store sales down 6.9 percent. Sales patterns at chain stores and independents both consisted of a slow start to the season followed by a busy last week that wasn't strong enough to boost sales to projected levels.

At the two major online bookstores, the news was better. Sales by Amazon.com's books/music/video group rose 12 percent in the fourth quarter and 11 percent for the year. Part of the success at Amazon in 2002 resulted from the sale of used books by third parties using Amazon's Web site. The practice drew protests from authors and publishers, who do not benefit from the sale of the used items, but Amazon has no intention of ending the service, which grew at a rapid rate during the year. At Barnes & Noble.com, sales were up 4.5 percent for the full year.

After rising by less than 1 percent in 2001, total book publishing sales rose 5.5 percent, to $26.87 billion, in 2002, according to preliminary estimates released by the Association of American Publishers. The sales figures contained one major surprise—unexpected strength in the adult trade segment. Sales in the adult hardcover segment increased 11.8 percent, to $2.93 billion, while sales of trade paperbacks increased 12.1 percent to $2.16 billion. Both segments were coming off two consecutive years of declining sales. Sales in the children's segments were not nearly as strong. Hardcover sales, rebounding from a 22.7 percent decline in 2001, rose 3.1 percent to $957.2 million. Paperback sales, which increased 17.9 percent in 2001, fell 1.3 percent in 2002 to $876.3 million. The gains posted by publishers are at odds with most reports from bookstores. Barnes & Noble and Borders Group had sales growth in the low single digits while the Census Bureau reported that retail bookstore sales rose only 1.5 percent in the year. The discrepancy can be partially explained by two factors. Heavy discounting by bookstores lowered their sales while not affecting publishers' receipts, and more books were sold through nontraditional outlets, including the Internet, where book sales posted solid growth for the year. Other segments that had strong gains in 2002 were higher education, where sales rose 12.4 percent to $3.9 billion, and mass market paperback, which had a 11.7 percent increase to $1.73 billion. The professional publishing segment recovered from a weak 2001 to post an 8.5 percent increase in 2002 to $5.14 billion. Book clubs had a solid year with sales ahead 9.7 percent to $1.46 billion. The increased demand for school testing drove up sales of standardized tests by 7.2 percent to $268.2 million. With fewer state adoptions on the calendar, the 5 percent decline in el-hi sales, to $4.07 billion, came as no surprise. The 3.3 percent decline in religion sales was due entirely to softer sales in the "other" category (which includes fiction and nonfiction works), which fell 5.8 percent to $933 million. Bible sales rose 4.5 percent to $329.2 million. University presses struggled in 2002 and sales were down 3.8 percent to $392.6 million. And the 5.8 percent decline in sales in the mail order segment, to $333.5 million, reflects continuing weakening in that category.

Federal Agency and
Federal Library Reports

Library of Congress

Washington, DC 20540
202-707-5000, World Wide Web http://www.loc.gov

Audrey Fischer
Public Affairs Specialist

The Library of Congress was established in 1800 to serve the research needs of the U.S. Congress. For more than two centuries, the library has grown both in the size of its collection (now totaling more than 126 million items) and in its mission. As the largest library in the world and the oldest federal cultural institution in the nation, the Library of Congress serves not only Congress but also government agencies, libraries around the world, and scholars and citizens in the United States and abroad. At the forefront of technology, the library now serves patrons on-site in its three buildings on Capitol Hill in Washington, D.C., and worldwide through its highly acclaimed Web site.

In 2002 the library continued to implement the new Integrated Library System (ILS), achieved record-high production of cataloging data, and played a leadership role in the development of online reference services. During the year the library celebrated the 25th anniversary of the Center for the Book [see the following article—*Ed.*] and the Juilliard String Quartet's 40th anniversary as the library's quartet-in-residence. In October the library sponsored the second National Book Festival on the Capitol grounds.

Second National Book Festival

Building on the success of last year's inaugural National Book Festival, the library organized and sponsored a second annual National Book Festival on October 12, 2002, on the West Lawn of the Capitol and the National Mall. Hosted once again by First Lady Laura Bush, the event drew a crowd estimated at 45,000—a considerable increase from last year's estimated 30,000 visitors.

The event, which was free and open to the public, featured more than 70 award-winning authors, illustrators, and storytellers, including mystery writers Mary Higgins Clark and David Baldacci, storytellers Carmen Deedy and Waddie Mitchell, and poets Billy Collins and Luci Tapahonso. Historian and author David McCullough delivered the concluding address in the History and Biography Pavilion. In addition to author readings and book discussions, the festival featured presentations by the storytellers; book sales and signings; appearances by children's storybook characters; a conservation clinic with demonstrations and advice on preserving books, family letters, and albums; and performances representing a wide range of America's musical traditions. Players from the National Basketball Association's and Women's National Basketball Association's "Read to Achieve" program—among them Jerry Stackhouse, Stacey Dales-Schuman, Bob Lanier, and Tamika Williams—also took part.

Response to Terrorism

The terrorist attacks of September 11, 2001, and their aftermath had a profound effect on the Library of Congress, forcing it to balance its mission to serve Congress and the nation with the need to secure its staff, visitors, buildings, and collections. The library revised evacuation plans and improved emergency communication with the staff as well as with local and national law enforcement agencies. While the library experienced a temporary decline in visitors and in-person reference immediately following the attacks, the number of requests received by e-mail and telephone, along with hits on its Web site, rose sharply as the library implemented alternative methods for making its resources available to the public.

The discovery of anthrax in the Hart Senate Office Building complex led to a decision to close the library for precautionary environmental testing October 18–24, 2001. No evidence of anthrax was found, but U.S. postal service to the library was suspended until early March 2002 in order to implement new methods for handling and irradiating the mail. This five-month interruption of mail delivery was felt most sharply in units that receive mail directly. Congress approved a supplemental appropriation of $39.1 million in emergency security funds that allowed the library to process mail off-site, pay for staff overtime and contractors to process the mail backlog, and pay for hazardous materials training and testing. These funds also covered the cost of establishing an off-site alternative computer facility to secure the library's electronic resources, to procure special freezers and other supplies to preserve waterlogged materials in the event of water damage, and to address a $7.5 million shortfall in fee receipts by the U.S. Copyright Office, which receives (mostly through the mail) approximately two thirds of its budget from fees for services.

In addition to safeguarding its staff and collections, the library drew on its vast resources to provide Congress and the nation with timely information on terrorism and related subjects. Within hours of the September 11 attacks, the library began documenting and recording for posterity both the incidents and the world-wide response to them. For example, the Serial and Government Publications Division began to build a collection of thousands of U.S. and foreign newspapers containing reports and photographs of the tragedy and its aftermath. The Prints and Photographs Division began a focused campaign to collect a broad range of pictorial images that both factually documented and creatively interpreted the attacks. The Geography and Map Division searched for maps and geographic information to satisfy requests from Congress, federal agencies, and the public for up-to-date and accurate cartographic information ranging from maps of countries in the Middle East to aerial views of Ground Zero in Manhattan. The library's six overseas offices (Cairo, Rio de Janeiro, Nairobi, Islamabad, New Delhi, and Jakarta) also played a critical role in acquiring material documenting the events from an international perspective.

Apart from its acquisitions activities, which continue, the library also launched several special projects to document the events of September 11. The American Folklife Center sponsored a September 11, 2001, Documentary Project, which encouraged folklorists across the nation to record on audiotape the national response to the attacks. The library also launched a September 11 Web Archive in collaboration with the Internet archive WebArchivist.org and the Pew Internet and American Life Project. Between September 11 and December 2001, the Internet Archive collected and indexed 40,000 Web sites and 500 million Web pages. Yahoo! named the September 11 Web Archive (http://september11.archive.org) its Site of the Year.

The national crisis highlighted the library's vast international resources and the expertise of its area specialists, whose knowledge of the languages and cultures of the Muslim world was critical in providing much-needed assistance to members of Congress, the executive branch, the media, and the general public. The library's Near East Section was flooded with requests for information about Afghanistan, Osama bin Laden, Islamist groups, and Muslim countries. A search of the library's collection by one Arab World area specialist led to the discovery and translation of a 93-page book written by Osama bin Laden and published in Cairo in 1991. Titled (in translation) *Battles of the Lion Den of the Arab Partisans in Afghanistan,* the work describes how bin Laden and the Mujahedeen fighters planned and executed major attacks against the occupying Soviet army in Afghanistan during the 1980s.

Other key discoveries in the library's collection included a unique two-volume English translation of Afghanistan's laws within the Library of Congress Law Library's collection of more than 2.4 million items as well as a 1999 Federal Research Division report titled "The Sociology and Psychology of Terrorism: Who Becomes a Terrorist and Why?" that predicted that members of al Qaeda could conceivably crash an aircraft into the Pentagon, CIA headquarters, or the White House. (The report is on the library's Web site at http://www.loc.gov/rr/frd/Sociology-Psychology%20of%20Terrorism.htm.)

The library's year-long effort to document the terrorist attacks culminated with a multimedia exhibition, "Witness and Response: September 11 Acquisitions at the Library of Congress," which opened in the Great Hall of the Thomas Jefferson Building on September 7, 2002, to mark the first anniversary of the tragedy. A series of lectures and concerts was held in conjunction with the exhibition.

Security

Ensuring the safety of the library's staff members, visitors, collections, facilities, and computer resources continued to be a major priority. During the year the library made progress in implementing its security enhancement plan, a multiyear program of physical security upgrades. Under one of the three major components of the plan, the library is consolidating its two police communications centers in the Madison and Jefferson buildings into one state-of-the-art Police Communications Center in the Jefferson Building. Construction of the center began at the end of January 2002, with completion anticipated by the end of June 2003. Under the second major component of the plan, the library will expand entry and perimeter security to include additional X-ray machines and detection equipment, security upgrades of building entrances, exterior monitoring cameras and lighting, and garage and parking lot safeguards. Work moved forward on this initiative, with a goal of completing this phase of the library's perimeter security plan by the end of 2003. The third component of the plan was completed in 2001 with the hiring and training of 46 new police officers and five police administrative personnel. In 2002 the new Police Administrative Unit functions were consolidated, ensuring a smooth transition of administrative functions from the Office of Security's support staff.

The library continued to safeguard its information systems resources through the implementation of technology solutions and computer security awareness training for the staff. An internal penetration study initiated by the Inspector General's Office revealed no significant holes in the library's network of computer defenses. Additional firewalls were implemented and virtual private network connections, providing secure access from remote sites, were extended locally and to the library's overseas offices.

Budget

The Library of Congress received a total of $525,837,000 in appropriations for fiscal year (FY) 2002 under four separate public laws. The Legislative Branch Appropriations Act of 2002 (P.L. 107-68), signed by the president on November 12, 2001, appropriated $486,762,000, including authority to spend $34,714,000 in receipts. Of amounts appropriated to the Architect of the Capitol under the 2001 Consolidated Appropriations Act (P.L. 106-554), signed by the president on December 21, 2000, $1,390,000 was transferred to the library to enhance physical security. The Department of Defense and Emergency Supplemental Appropriations Act of 2002 (P.L. 107-117), signed by the president on January 10, 2002, appropriated an additional $30,185,000 to enable the library to respond to the September 11 terrorist attacks and the Capitol Hill anthrax incident. The Supplemental Appropriations Act of 2002 for Further Recovery From and Response to Terrorist Attacks on the United States (P.L. 107-206), signed by the president on August 2, 2002, appropriated an additional $7.5 million to the Copyright Office to make up for lost receipts due to the anthrax incident. The total $39.1 million that the library received in emergency supplemental funding in FY 2002 also supported new and expanded security-related activities such as revised mail-processing procedures and the establishment of an off-site alternative computer center to secure the library's electronic resources. This supplemental funding was in addition to funds provided in other legislative branch agencies' budgets that also supported library-related projects (e.g., the Architect of the Capitol's budget).

Development

During 2002 the library's fund-raising activities brought in a total of $10.3 million, representing 736 gifts from 613 donors. These gifts, including $1.7 million received through the library's Planned Giving Program, were made to 74 library funds and consisted of $4.1 million in cash gifts, $5.8 million in new pledges, and $390,000 in in-kind gifts. Private gifts supported a variety of new and continuing programs throughout the library, including exhibitions, acquisitions, symposia, and other scholarly programs, as well as the second annual National Book Festival. The charter sponsors of the festival were AT&T, the *Washington Post,* and WorkPlace USA, and the patrons were the James Madison Council, Open Russia Foundation, PBS, and Target. Those donors, along with others, gave $1.6 million to support the festival.

In addition to the book festival, the James Madison Council continued to provide substantial support for a number of library initiatives throughout the year. Gifts from members totaled $2.4 million, bringing the council's total support to the library since 1990 to $145.6 million. The contributions received during the year provided support for the Center for the Book; a publication on the history of the U.S. House of Representatives to be written by Robert Remini, professor emeritus at the University of Illinois at Chicago; the activities of the Phillips Society, a friends group of the Geography and Map Division; and a number of new acquisitions.

Legislative Support to Congress

Law Library

Serving Congress is the library's highest priority. During the year, the Congressional Research Service (CRS), along with other library service units, ensured timely congressional access to the library's resources, both personnel and collections. CRS delivered nearly 800,000 research responses to members of Congress and committees. CRS developed an electronic briefing book on election reform and continually updated the electronic briefing book on the subject of terrorism.

Congress turned increasingly to the online Legislative Information System (LIS), as evidenced by a 20 percent increase in system use from the previous level. A new LIS Alert service was offered that notifies users by e-mail when bills are introduced and provides updates on their status. In addition, an LIS disaster-recovery server was tested and software was developed to detect inadvertent or unauthorized alteration of legislative files.

Law Library staff answered more than 2,000 requests from congressional users and produced 578 written reports for Congress. In response to congressional interest in the approaches to antiterrorist strategies undertaken by legislatures around the world, the Law Library compiled several multinational antiterrorist studies, including a 347-page comprehensive analysis of antiterrorist legislation, regulations, and enforcement initiatives covering 24 European jurisdictions.

The Law Library also made progress on the Global Legal Information Network (GLIN), an online parliament-to-parliament cooperative exchange of laws and legal materials from some 40 countries and institutions. Seventeen of these jurisdictions contributed records themselves, and the records of an additional 23 countries were entered by Law Library staff. Legal analysts in the Law Library added 2,663 laws to the GLIN database, covering 23 jurisdictions. The GLIN Web site was accessed more than 400,000 times during the year.

Copyright Office

The U.S. Copyright Office provided policy advice and technical assistance to Congress on important copyright laws and related issues such as the Digital Millennium Copyright Act (DMCA), the setting of royalty rates for Webcasting, distance education, and Copyright Arbitration Royalty Panel (CARP) reform. The Copyright Office also responded to numerous congressional inquiries about domestic and international copyright law and registration and recordation of works of authorship.

Congressional Relations Office

In addition to assisting members of Congress and their staff in making use of the library's collections, services, and facilities, the Congressional Relations Office, along with other library offices, worked with member and committee offices on current issues of legislative concern such as e-government, digital storage and preservation, the construction of a Capitol Visitors Center, and documenting the experiences of the nation's veterans and the history of the House of Representatives.

Digital Projects and Planning

Strategic Planning

Established in 2001 and funded with an appropriation of $99.8 million from Congress, the library's Office of Strategic Initiatives continued planning for the development and implementation of a National Digital Information Infrastructure and Preservation Program (NDIIPP). The goal of NDIIPP is to encourage shared responsibility for digital content and to seek national solutions for the continuing collection, selection, and organization of historically significant cultural materials regardless of evolving formats; the long-term storage, preservation, and authentication of those collections; and rights-protected access for the public to the digital heritage of the American people.

Internet Resources

The library continued to expand its electronic services to Congress and the nation through its award-winning Web site. An online monthly magazine, *Wise Guide,* was added to point newcomers to the many educational and useful resources on the site in a user-friendly and visually appealing way. During the year more than 2 billion transactions were recorded on all of the library's computer systems—a 50 percent increase over the previous year. The following are selected resources available on the library's Web site:

Online Catalog. The library continued to provide global access to its online public catalog (OPAC). The site recorded more than 287 million transactions during the year—an average of more than 24 million transactions a month, up from 19 million a month the previous year.

American Memory. At year's end, 7.8 million American historical items were available on the American Memory Web site. Fourteen multimedia historical collections were added to the American Memory Web site during the year, bringing the total to 116. Nine existing collections were expanded by more than 380,000 digital items. Use of the American Memory online collections increased from 28.5 million transactions a month in 2001 to 38.8 million a month in 2002.

America's Library. Work continued to expand the content and features available on America's Library, an interactive Web site for children and families that draws upon the library's online resources. The site has won numerous awards and is one of the most popular online offerings of the library. America's Library logged more than 154 million transactions during the year, an average of nearly 13 million transactions a month.

THOMAS. The public legislative information system known as THOMAS continued to be a popular resource, with nearly 13 million transactions logged on average each month. Two new features, Presidential Nominations and Treaties, were added. The Status of Appropriations table, a frequently updated and heavily used resource, was redesigned.

Global Gateway. Formerly known as International Horizons, Global Gateway—a project to foster international collaboration for joint digitization efforts and provide access to the library's global resources—was expanded during the year. The site now includes (1) Meeting of Frontiers, a bilingual Russian-English Web site showcasing materials from the Library of Congress and partner libraries in Russia and Alaska; and (2) Spain, the United States and the American Frontier: Historias Paralelas, a bilingual Spanish-English Web site initially including the Library of Congress, the National Library of Spain, and the Biblioteca Colombina y Capitular of Seville. A third component of the site, The Atlantic World: America and the Netherlands, is under way and is scheduled for release in summer 2003. This collaborative digital effort between the library and the Koninklijke Bibliotheek, the national library of the Netherlands, will focus on explorations by the Dutch in the Americas and Dutch influence on American culture.

Online Exhibitions. Seven new library exhibitions were added to the Web site in 2002, bringing the total to 41, and three continuing exhibitions were updated. This feature allows users who are unable to visit the library in person to view many of its past and current exhibitions online.

Collections

During 2002 the size of the library's collections grew to more than 126 million items, an increase of nearly 2 million over the previous year. This figure included nearly 29 million cataloged books and other print materials, 56 million manuscripts, 13.5 million microforms, nearly 4.9 million maps, more than 5 million items in the music collection, and 13.7 million visual materials.

Integrated Library System

The year was one of transition for the new integrated library system as it evolved from a project to a permanent operational part of the library. The system performs library functions such as circulation, acquisitions, and serials check-in, and also provides access to the library's online public catalog. A number of major system upgrades brought stability to the system and reduced downtime. Monograph and serials holdings conversion projects on ILS continued during the year.

Arrearage Reduction/Cataloging

The Cataloging Directorate and Serial Record Division achieved record-high production in 2002. Staff cataloged 310,235 bibliographic volumes on 291,749 bibliographic records, at an average cost of $94.58 per record (compared with $122.60 the previous year). Cataloging staff also created 41,776 inventory records for arrearage items. With the library serving as the secretariat for the international Program for Cooperative Cataloging (PCC), approximately 350 PCC member institutions created 162,363 new name authorities (a 13 percent increase over 2001 production); 10,044 new series authorities (a 6.7 percent increase); 3,165 subject authorities (a 20 percent increase); 2,551 LC Classification proposals (a 25 percent increase); 30,160 bibliographic records for serials (a 50 percent increase); and 82,014 bibliographic records for monographs (a 12 percent increase).

Secondary Storage

Linked to the library's arrearage reduction effort is the development of secondary storage sites to house processed materials and to provide for growth of the collections through the first part of the 21st century. With support from Congress, the library opened the first module of a climate-controlled, high-density book storage facility at Fort Meade, Maryland, on November 18. The facility is projected to extend the life of the collections by several centuries. The first module has a capacity of 1.2 million volumes, leaving room on the 100-acre building site for 13 more storage modules.

The library continued to plan for the construction of a National Audio-Visual Conservation Center in Culpeper, Virginia, to house and preserve its extensive multimedia collections. During the summer, the library developed an investment and program cost model and drafted a cost requirements plan for the entire facility over a five-year period. A 36,000-square-foot temporary storage site in Elkwood, Virginia, was acquired by the Packard Humanities Institute for the temporary storage of the library's film and video materials previously stored in the Culpeper facility pending the completion of the National Audio-Visual Conservation Center.

Important Acquisitions

The library receives millions of items each year from copyright deposits, federal agencies, and purchases, exchanges, and gifts. Notable acquisitions during the year included new additions by the Jefferson Library Project to reconstruct the collection in the original catalog of Thomas Jefferson's library, made possible through funding from the Madison Council, the library's private-sector advisory body. Other major acquisitions made possible by the Madison Council included additional funding toward the purchase of the only extant copy of the 1507 map of the world by Martin Waldseemüller that gave "America" its name; 69 autograph letters of 15th President James Buchanan; and more than 100 digital photographic prints documenting the September 11, 2001, attacks on the World Trade Center.

The library also acquired the following significant items and collections in 2002:

- A manuscript from the 1720s containing selections from three operas by George Frideric Handel
- The papers of former Secretary of Defense and Secretary of Energy James Schlesinger
- A total of 58 documentary photographs of the destruction of September 11, 2001, at the Pentagon and the Shanksville, Pa., crash site taken by news agency photographers
- The Thomas Kane library of materials about Ethiopia, including 200 Ethiopian manuscripts and 12 Ethiopian magic scrolls, some 2,500 works in Amharic, Tigrinya, Ge'ez, and other Ethiopian languages, and more than 3,500 titles in English and other European languages
- *Takvim-ut-Tevarih* by Katip Chelebi (1733), one of the first books printed by Muslims using movable type
- *Sisitan,* the first newspaper issued in Afghanistan, beginning in 1902

In addition, approximately 30,000 Web sites were acquired through the MINERVA Web preservation project, a collaboration among the Library of Congress, the Internet Archive, and WebArchivist.org. As part of the project, event-based Web site collections were developed, including those related to September 11, 2001, the 2002 Olympics, and the 2002 midterm election.

Reference Service

In addition to serving Congress, the library provides reference service to the public in its 21 reading rooms and through its Web site. During the year, library staff handled more than 775,000 reference requests that were received in person, on the telephone, or through written and electronic correspondence. Nearly 1.3 million items were circulated for use within the library.

Digital Reference

During the year the Public Service Collections Directorate launched Question-Point, a new online reference service, in collaboration with the Online Computer Library Center (OCLC). QuestionPoint provides library users with access to a growing collaborative network of reference librarians in the United States and worldwide, around the clock, through their local libraries' Web sites. The responding library's staff member answers the question online or forwards it to another participating library. This service, which is available to libraries by subscription, is free for library patrons. The Ask a Librarian service, by which a question can be submitted and answered within five business days via an interactive form on the Library of Congress Web site, was initiated in April 2002. In the first six months, the service received 20,000 queries directed to the 20 teams listed on the Ask a Librarian Web page. The service, which is supported by the QuestionPoint software, includes a live chat feature that enabled researchers to consult a reference librarian in real time via e-mail.

Copyright

The U.S. Copyright Office received 526,138 claims to copyright in 2002. Of these, it registered 521,041 claims. The office responded to more than 358,000 requests from the public for copyright information. The library's collections and exchange programs received 896,504 copies of works from the Copyright Office, with a net worth of $31,302,048. This included 390,150 items received from publishers under the mandatory deposit provisions of the copyright law. The office also continued major initiatives to re-engineer its core business processes and use information technology to increase the efficiency of operations and the timeliness of public services.

National Library Service for the Blind and Physically Handicapped

Established by an act of Congress in 1931, the National Library Service for the Blind and Physically Handicapped (NLS) has grown to a program that supplies nearly 23 million recorded discs and braille materials to approximately 500,000 readers through a network of 140 cooperating libraries around the country. During the year NLS made substantial progress toward its goal of developing a digital talking book to replace obsolete audio cassette equipment. NLS worked with other organizations over a five-year period to develop a national standard for a digital talking book; the standard was adopted on March 6, 2002. Under the sponsorship of the Industrial Designers Society of America, NLS held a national design competition, challenging undergraduate students to design a prototype digital talking book player. A panel of six judges evaluated 146 submissions from 28 design schools and announced the winners in June. A display featuring the six winning entries was on view in the library's James Madison Building from October through December 2002.

John W. Kluge Center

The John W. Kluge Center was established in the fall of 2000 with a gift of $60 million from John W. Kluge, president of Metromedia and founding chairman of the James Madison Council. Located within the Office of Scholarly Programs (OSP), the center's goal is to bring qualified senior scholars to the Library of Congress, where they can make wide-ranging use of the institution's resources to promote scholarship. In July 2002 the renovation of the Jefferson Building north curtain was completed, and the Kluge Center moved permanently into that space. The new facilities accommodate OSP staff, as well as 30 Kluge Fellows and 11 chair holders and senior scholars.

During the year competitions were held for five residential fellowship programs and by year's end 25 scholars had been selected as Kluge Fellows, Kluge Library of Congress Staff Fellows, Library of Congress International Studies Fellows (Mellon and Luce Foundations), and Rockefeller Fellows in Islamic Studies. The inaugural Henry Alfred Kissinger Lecture on foreign affairs, which was given by former Secretary of State Henry Kissinger himself, addressed the changes in U.S. policies as a result of the September 2001 terrorist attacks. The lecture was cybercast on the library's Web site and published as a brochure. The

Kissinger endowment also provides a grant for a ten-month research appointment at the library. Aaron Friedberg of Princeton University served as the first Kissinger Scholar in Foreign Policy and International Relations in 2001–2002. On September 2, 2002, Klaus W. Larres of Queen's University, Belfast, Northern Ireland, became the second scholar to occupy the Kissinger chair.

Publications and Exhibitions

The Library of Congress Publishing Office produced more than 30 books, calendars, and other products describing the library's collections in 2002, many in cooperation with trade publishers. These included three companion exhibition books. The release of *Beginnings: World Treasures of the Library of Congress* marked a new series of titles to coincide with the continuing World Treasures exhibition. Published in association with Third Millennium Publishing, and with text by historian Michael Roth, *Beginnings* includes 145 color illustrations that mirror the items included in the companion exhibition. *Roger L. Stevens Presents,* published in conjunction with an exhibition of the same title, includes five essays about Stevens' life and career as a theatrical producer, arts administrator, and real estate entrepreneur. An exhibition with the same title (May 16–September 7) also honored Stevens.

Featuring text by child psychologist Robert Coles, *When They Were Young: A Photographic Retrospective of Childhood from the Library of Congress* was published by the library in cooperation with Kales Publishing as a companion to a library exhibition. The exhibition (September 26–March 22) featured images of children during the past 150 years by photographers Dorothea Lange, Jack Delano, and Marion Post Wolcott.

A companion book to the 2001 exhibition "The Floating World of Ukiyo-e: Shadows, Dreams, and Substance" received honorable mention for design excellence from the American Association of Museums.

The library presented five new major exhibitions in the Thomas Jefferson Building in 2002. "Witness and Response: September 11 Acquisitions at the Library of Congress" (September 7–November 2) marked the anniversary of the terrorist attacks by displaying selections from the collections that the library amassed, and is still receiving.

The library mounted an exhibition titled "Margaret Mead: Human Nature and the Power of Culture" (November 30–May 31) to celebrate the centennial of the birth of the noted anthropologist.

The exhibition "American Beauties: Drawings from the Golden Age of Illustration" (June 27–November 2) showcased 19 early-20th-century drawings of women selected from recent acquisitions and graphic art in the library's Cabinet of American Illustration and the Swann Collection of Caricature and Cartoon in the Prints and Photographs Division.

In keeping with conservation and preservation standards, two rotational changes were made in the continuing "American Treasures of the Library of Congress" exhibition, three in "World Treasures of the Library of Congress," and two in the "Bob Hope Gallery of American Entertainment." Three major exhibitions that toured nationally and internationally during the year were "The Work of Charles and Ray Eames: A Legacy of Invention," "Sigmund Freud: Conflict and Culture," and "Religion and the Founding of the American Republic."

Literary Events, Concerts, Symposia

A variety of lectures, symposia, concerts, and literary events were held at the library throughout the year, and many were cybercast on the library's Web site.

The Books & Beyond lecture series centered on the importance of books and reading. The series featured such authors as Andrew Carroll discussing his compilation *War Letters: Extraordinary Correspondence from American Wars,* accompanied by guest readers Supreme Court Chief Justice William J. Rehnquist, U.S. Senator Chuck Hagel, former Senator Bob Dole, and ABC reporter Sam Donaldson.

The library launched a new lecture series titled Luminary Lectures @ Your Library. The inaugural lecture featured Judith Krug, director of the American Library Association's Office for Intellectual Freedom.

During the year, the library sponsored a number of symposia on such topics as Abraham Lincoln, gospel music, and the Islamic world. A major symposium, "The Civil War and American Memory," brought together historians, biographers, and other Civil War scholars November 12–14 to consider important questions arising from that war.

The library's 2002 concert season featured many classical performances in the Coolidge Auditorium by ensembles such as the Juilliard String Quartet and the Beaux Arts trio. The season also included a series of programs titled "Six by Sondheim," each focusing on a musical by composer Stephen Sondheim. On April 24 the library presented guitarist Eddie Pennington in the first concert of a new outdoor series of traditional music and dance titled "Homegrown: The Music of America." The series is sponsored by the library's American Folklife Center, the Kennedy Center Millennium Stage, and the Folklore Society of Greater Washington.

Billy Collins was appointed to serve a second term as the Library's Poet Laureate Consultant in Poetry. In this position, he continued to promote "Poetry 180," a Web site designed to encourage the appreciation and enjoyment of poetry in America's high schools.

Preservation

During 2002 the library preserved 1,126,598 items at a total cost of $11,205,276. The average per-item cost was $9.95. The library took action to preserve its collections by

- Deacidifying 150,000 books, thereby achieving the second-year goal of a five-year contract that would enable the library to deacidify 1 million books
- Installing a flat sheet mass deacidification treater that will rescue 1 million books and 5 million manuscripts over a five-year period

- Providing 30,000 hours of conservation for custodial division collections, including 220 items selected for inclusion on the American Memory Web site
- Completing the first year of a five-year preventive preservation initiative
- Completing the first year of a multiyear project to determine the life expectancy of compact discs
- Preservation microfilming of 2,334,737 exposures (4.7 million pages)
- Working in partnership with other organizations to develop a National Digital Information and Infrastructure Preservation Program to sort, acquire, describe, and preserve electronic materials

The American Folklife Center (AFC) continued its mandate to "preserve and present American folklife" through a number of outreach programs. "Save Our Sounds," a joint program with the Smithsonian Institution and supported by the White House Millennium Council's "Save America's Treasures" program, seeks to preserve a priceless heritage of sound recordings housed at the two institutions.

AFC continued to gather veterans' stories for the congressionally mandated Veterans History Project (VHP). Established in 2000, the program's purpose is to record and preserve first-person accounts of armed services personnel who served during wartime. By year's end, AFC had acquired more than 3,200 multiformat collections from veterans of all 20th-century U.S. armed conflicts. AFC worked with the American Folklore Society and the Oral History Association to train volunteers to conduct interviews. As of early 2003, 25 workshops had been held in 14 states. With the help of AARP, a principal supporter of VHP, the project produced a five-minute promotional video that was sent to all 450 partner organizations and members of Congress. On June 6, 2002, a program to mark the 56th anniversary of D-Day was held on the deck of the *USS Intrepid* in New York harbor. The program, which was attended by about 500 people, resulted in many pledges to participate in VHP.

National Film Registry

The library continued its commitment to preserving the nation's film heritage. The 25 films listed below were named to the National Film Registry in 2002, bringing the total to 350. The library works to ensure that the films listed on the registry are preserved either through its motion picture preservation program or through collaborative ventures with other archives, motion picture studios, and independent filmmakers.

Alien (1979)
All My Babies (1953)
The Bad and the Beautiful (1952)
Beauty and the Beast (1991)
The Black Stallion (1979)
Boyz N the Hood (1991)

Theodore Case Sound Tests: Gus Visser and His Singing Duck (1925)
The Endless Summer (1966)
From Here to Eternity (1953)
From Stump to Ship (1930)
Fuji (1974)
In the Heat of the Night (1967)
Lady Windermere's Fan (1925)
Melody Ranch (1940)
The Pearl (1948)
Punch Drunks (1934)
Sabrina (1954)
Star Theatre (1901)
Stranger Than Paradise (1984)
This Is Cinerama (1952)
This Is Spinal Tap (1984)
Through Navajo Eyes (series) (1966)
Why Man Creates (1968)
Wild and Wooly (1917)
Wild River (1960)

Additional Sources of Information

Library of Congress telephone numbers for public information:

Main switchboard (with menu)	202-707-5000
Reading room hours and locations	202-707-6400
General reference	202-707-5522
	(TTY 202-707-4210)
Visitor information	202-707-8000
	(TTY 202-707-6200)
Exhibition hours	202-707-4604
Reference assistance	202-707-6500
Copyright information	202-707-3000
Copyright hotline (to order forms)	202-707-9100
Sales shop (credit card orders)	888-682-3557

Center for the Book

John Y. Cole
Director, Center for the Book
Library of Congress, Washington, DC 20540
World Wide Web http://www.loc.gov/cfbook

On December 11, 2002, Librarian of Congress James H. Billington hosted a luncheon to celebrate the Center for the Book's 25th anniversary and the approval of its 50th state affiliate. Simultaneously, he honored his predecessor as Librarian of Congress, Daniel J. Boorstin, who established the center in 1977.

The Center for the Book is one of the Library of Congress's most dynamic and visible educational outreach programs. Since 1977 it has used the prestige and resources of the Library of Congress to stimulate public interest in books, reading, literacy, and libraries and to encourage the study of books and the printed word. This mission is carried to the states and the nation through the center's network of affiliated centers in 50 states and the District of Columbia and its reading promotion partnerships with more than 90 national educational and civic organizations.

The Center for the Book is a successful public-private partnership. The Library of Congress supports its four full-time positions, but all of its projects, events, and publications are funded primarily through contributions from individuals, corporations, and foundations, or transfers of funds from other government agencies.

Highlights of 2002

- Reaching the goal of 50 affiliated state centers through the addition of Hawaii, Iowa, New Jersey, New York, South Dakota, Rhode Island, Delaware, and New Hampshire to the center's network of state affiliates
- Major contributions to the second National Book Festival on Oct. 12, 2002, specifically the festival's author and reading promotion programs
- Sponsorship of more than 50 events at the Library of Congress and around the country that promoted books, reading, literacy, and libraries, as well as the National Book Festival
- Continuation of "Telling America's Stories," the Library of Congress's national reading-promotion campaign, which is chaired by First Lady Laura Bush
- Cosponsorship of the publication of three books: *Books, Libraries, Reading, and Publishing in the Cold War* (Oak Knoll Press and the Center for the Book); *Collectors & Special Collections: Three Talks* (Library of Congress); and *Perspectives on American Book History: Artifacts and Commentary* (University of Massachusetts Press)
- Conclusion of a two-year exchange project with Russian librarians and reading promoters that helped stimulate the creation of 22 "reading cen-

ters" in libraries throughout Russia funded by the Open Society Institute (Soros Foundation–Moscow)

Themes

The center establishes national reading promotion themes to stimulate interest and support for reading and literacy projects that benefit all age groups. The themes—used by state centers, national organizational partners, and hundreds of schools and libraries across the nation—remind Americans of the importance of books, reading, and libraries in today's world. The center's current three-year reading-promotion theme, "Telling America's Stories," launched in January 2001, is cosponsored with the library's American Folklife Center. Individuals, families, schools, libraries, civic and educational organizations, and businesses are invited to consult the campaign brochure and the center's Web site for ideas on how to participate.

Reading Promotion Partners

The partnership program includes more than 90 civic, educational, and governmental organizations that work with the center to promote literacy and reading by using themes and ideas developed by the center and other groups. On March 18, 2002, representatives of more than 45 partner organizations gathered at the Library of Congress to describe their organizations' activities and learn about other reading and literacy programs. During the year the center cosponsored projects with many of its organizational partners, including the American Antiquarian Society, the American Library Association, the library's Favorite Poem Project, Friends of Libraries U.S.A., the International Reading Association, KIDSNET, the National Coalition for Literacy, and Reading Is Fundamental, Inc.

State Centers

When James H. Billington became Librarian of Congress in 1987, the Center for the Book was linked to the states through formal affiliations with 10 state centers for the book. In December 2002 the center celebrated the addition of New Hampshire, its 50th state affiliate, which is located at the New Hampshire State Library.

Each state center has an institutional home: a state library, a large public library system, a university, or a state humanities council. The other new 2002 affiliates are Hawaii, at the Hawaii State Library; Iowa, at the State Library of Iowa; New Jersey, at Rutgers University; New York, at Syracuse University; South Dakota, at the South Dakota Humanities Council; Rhode Island, at Providence Public Library; and Delaware, at the Delaware State Library.

State centers work with the Center for the Book to promote books, reading, and libraries as well as the state's own literary and intellectual heritage. The most popular state programs are state book festivals, statewide book awards, and the creation of state literary maps and state author databases. Each center also develops and funds its own operations and statewide projects, using its partnership with the Library of Congress judiciously as both incentive and leverage. State centers are required to renew their affiliations every three years, outlining in their applications past accomplishments as well as future programming and funding plans. Renewals are for three-year periods. Twenty-two state centers and the District of Columbia center were renewed during 2002.

On May 1, 2002, state center representatives participated in an idea-sharing session at the Library of Congress marked by spirited discussion about several topics, including the popular "one book" community reading projects, book awards programs, and "Letters About Literature" awards programs. The highlight was the presentation of the 2002 Boorstin Center for the Book Award to the Connecticut Center for the Book. The Boorstin Award, supported by an endowment established in 1987 by retired Librarian of Congress Boorstin and his wife, Ruth, recognizes and supports achievements of specific state centers. The award includes a cash prize of $5,000. The Connecticut Center for the Book was recognized for the success of its annual World of Words program and other innovative and cooperative projects that stimulate interest in books and reading throughout Connecticut.

Projects

The Center for the Book continued to administer the Viburnum Foundation's program for supporting family literacy projects in rural public libraries. During the year, the foundation awarded 48 grants to small rural libraries in ten states. Regional workshops were sponsored by the Center for the Book in Columbia, South Carolina, August 14–16, and in Scottsdale, Arizona, September 25–27. These workshops provide training for representatives of the rural libraries and communities that received the grants.

"Letters About Literature," a student essay contest sponsored in association with the Weekly Reader Corporation, concluded another record-breaking year in number of entries and involvement by affiliated state centers. More than 24,000 students wrote letters to their favorite authors and 36 state centers honored statewide winners. Information on "Letters About Literature 2002" was made available on the center's Web site, including contest guidelines and an entry coupon.

The center's annual "River of Words" project, an environmental art and poetry contest for young people, culminated on April 27, 2002, with an awards ceremony and display of winning art works at the Library of Congress.

The Center for the Book made major contributions to the success of the second National Book Festival, which was held on October 12, 2002, on the West Capitol grounds and the National Mall. The First Lady hosted the event, which was organized and sponsored by the Library of Congress. The Carnegie Corporation of New York and AT&T made grants to the center to support, through its state center network, events in 22 states that promoted the National Book Festival. The center shaped and carried out the festival's author program, which featured presentations in five pavilions by more than 60 award-winning authors and illustrators. Drawing on its partnership networks, it organized, promoted, and enlisted participation in two "reading promotion" pavilions that highlighted book, reading, literacy, and library promotion around the country, the "Let's Read America" pavilion, and the Pavilion of the States.

An international project developed by the center with the Open Society Institute (Soros Foundation–Moscow) and the institute's Pushkin Library Mega-project included a series of exchange visits between Russian librarians and U.S. librarians and reading promoters. In 2001 the Open Society Institute announced its intention to create reading centers in libraries throughout Russia. As part of the project, two delegations of Russian regional librarians visited several libraries in the United States in trips organized by the Center for the Book. In 2002 the Soros Foundation announced that it would establish reading centers in 22 libraries throughout Russia. In June 2002 Center for the Book Director John Y. Cole led a U.S. delegation of seven librarians to visit St. Petersburg and Moscow and attend a conference, "Reading World and World of Reading." Librarians from the 22 new Russian reading centers joined their U.S. colleagues at the conference to exchange ideas and make plans for continuing the cooperative project.

Outreach

Several publicity efforts throughout the year highlighted the Center for the Book's forthcoming 25th anniversary on Oct. 13, 2002. Articles summarizing the center's activities during its first quarter-century appeared in a "CFB at 25" series in the Library of Congress *Information Bulletin,* and "CFB at 25" pins were distributed at library and scholarly conferences in which the center participated.

Director Cole publicized the Center for the Book and its activities through presentations in 14 states and at international library and book history conferences in Russia and Great Britain.

The scope and use of the center's Web site continued to expand dramatically during 2002. Established and maintained by Program Officer Maurvene D. Williams, the Web site describes Center for the Book projects, affiliations, and events. It also provides information about organizations that promote books, reading, literacy, and libraries as well as descriptions of book festivals and other literary events in the United States and abroad. Sections added to the Web site in 2002 included descriptions of more than 90 "One Book" community reading projects across the nation, and information about the national Center for the Book/Viburnum Foundation Family Literacy Project. The number of hits increased sharply to 445,313, compared with 306,045 in 2001.

Seven issues of the newsletter *Center for the Book News* were produced in 2002. The annual spring edition of the state center handbook was issued, supplemented by a 21-page document, *State Center Highlights—What's Happened Since Last Year's Meeting.* The Library of Congress issued 32 press releases about Center for the Book activities, and a two-page "News from the Center for the Book" feature appeared in all 2002 issues of the Library of Congress *Information Bulletin.* The library's weekly staff newsletter, *The Gazette,* publicized most of the center's public lectures and programs.

Events

Sponsorship of events, symposia, and lectures—at the Library of Congress and elsewhere—is an important Center for the Book activity. Through such special events, the center brings diverse audiences together on behalf of books and reading and publicizes its activities nationally and locally. Among events in 2002 were 17 talks at the Library of Congress in the center's "Books & Beyond" series featuring authors of newly published books that highlight Library of Congress collections or programs; each was cosponsored by a division or office.

Two other programs of special interest were the second Library of Congress Rare Book Forum, cosponsored by the Rare Book and Special Collections Division and featuring scholar Christopher de Hamel discussing the Library's copy of the Giant Bible of Mainz, and a program marking the inauguration of a new series of paperbound "Armed Services Editions" originally published during World War II and distributed to U.S. servicemen and servicewomen overseas. In 1983 the Center for the Book sponsored a program celebrating the 40th anniversary of the original Armed Services Editions.

Many of the center's programs at the Library of Congress are now available on the center's Web site, along with information about the dozens of events sponsored each year by affiliated state centers.

Federal Library and Information Center Committee

Library of Congress, Washington, DC 20540
202-707-4800
World Wide Web http://lcweb.loc.gov/flicc

Susan M. Tarr
Executive Director

Highlights of the Year

During fiscal year (FY) 2002, the Federal Library and Information Center Committee (FLICC) continued to carry out its mission "to foster excellence in federal library and information services through interagency cooperation and to provide guidance and direction for FEDLINK."

Information Policy Forum

FLICC's annual information policy forum, "Homeland Security: Impact of Policy Changes on Government Information Access," focused on the changes resulting from enhanced homeland security and their impact on access to federal information by those both inside and outside government. The keynote speaker for the event was Viet Dinh, assistant attorney general for the Office of Legal Policy at the Department of Justice. His talk was followed by a morning panel discussion on agency initiatives featuring Patrice McDermott, assistant director, Office of Government Relations, American Library Association; Nancy Blair, chief librarian, U.S. Geological Survey Library and U.S. Geological Survey Security Task Force; and W. Russell Neuman, senior policy analyst, Technology Division, Office of Science and Technology Policy, Executive Office of the President. Rep. Thomas M. Davis, III (R-Va.), began the afternoon session with the congressional keynote address, which was followed by another panel discussion involving June Daniels, senior systems analyst, Foreign Affairs Systems Integration Program, Department of State; Kurt Molholm, administrator, Defense Technical Information Center; and Francis Buckley, superintendent of documents, Government Printing Office. Peter Swire, visiting professor of law, George Washington University Law School, offered his perspective and summary of the day to conclude the forum. [For more on this topic, see the Special Report "Homeland Security and Information Management" later in Part 1—Ed.]

Working Groups

The FLICC working groups completed an ambitious agenda in FY 2002. Among their activities, they

- Selected FLICC awards recipients for 2001 and offered the fourth annual FLICC Awards to recognize the innovative ways in which federal libraries, librarians, and library technicians fulfill the information demands of government, business, scholarly communities, and the public
- Identified the federal library and information center context for content management and homeland security

- Established parameters and developed a management education series for current and potential federal library managers
- Met with the Office of Personnel Management to identify ways to enhance federal library recruitment
- Addressed issues on disaster planning and recovery, endangered federal collections, professional competencies, outsourcing, metrics and performance evaluation, benchmarking, e-government legislation, and other information science policy issues

Attorney–Librarian Meetings Continue

FLICC also continued its collaboration with the Library of Congress general counsel in a series of meetings between federal agency legal counsels and agency librarians. Now in their fourth year, these forums grew out of the recognition that federal attorneys and librarians face many of the same questions in applying copyright, privacy, the Freedom of Information Act (FOIA), and other laws to their agencies' activities in the electronic age—with regard both to using information within an agency and to publishing the agency's own information. The meetings have enhanced the relationship between agency attorneys and librarians and have helped them develop contacts with their counterparts at other agencies. This year's series featured discussions on licensing electronic publications, FOIA policy and the Trade Secrets Act, and legal challenges to Internet filtering in public libraries.

Federal Library Survey

In the absence of an updated census of federal libraries and information centers by the National Center for Education Statistics (NCES), FLICC endorsed membership participation in the annual Outsell, Inc., survey of "content deploying functions" in industry, academia, and the public sector. More than 100 federal librarians participated in the survey. According to Outsell, which focuses exclusively on the information content industry, the survey indicated that government information professionals serve significantly more users than their colleagues in corporations and academic libraries, and that they spend much less per user. The results also showed that while some government libraries have been progressive in their approach to digital content, they have been slower to make a transition to new business models.

Busy Year for FEDLINK

FLICC's cooperative network, FEDLINK, continued to enhance its fiscal operations while providing its members with $56.6 million in transfer-pay services and $38.1 million in direct-pay services, saving federal agencies approximately $10.3 million in vendor volume discounts and approximately $7.6 million more in cost avoidance. FEDLINK exceeded FY 2002 revenue targets by 5.5 percent.

To meet the requirements of the Fiscal Operations Improvement Act of 2000 (P.L. 106-481), which created new statutory authority for FEDLINK's fee-based activities, FEDLINK governing bodies and staff members developed a new five-year business plan that takes advantage of the increased opportunities of FEDLINK's authority as a revolving fund. The business plan outlines FEDLINK's new business processes, audiences, market position and message, staffing, and resources, while projecting fiscal goals including capitalization, anticipated expenditures, and revenues through 2006. During the first fiscal year of the five-year plan, FEDLINK made significant progress on 20 of the plan's 39 recommendations, including expanded vendor offerings, reduced barriers, improved marketing, and enhanced systems.

FEDLINK also developed and implemented its pilot Direct Express program. This will enable FEDLINK customers to place FY 2003 orders directly with five commercial information services vendors; the FEDLINK fee, included in the vendor prices, will be remitted to FEDLINK by the vendor on a quarterly basis. EBSCO Publishing (online services only), Gale Group, LexisNexis, ProQuest, and West Group will be the first vendors to offer their services under this streamlined process. Their product and service offerings will continue to include electronic database publications, document delivery services, associated print publications, and specialized access options.

FY 2002 saw continued improvements to the FEDLINK program with the addition of new procurement and procedural options as well as innovative educational initiatives, including workshops and seminars on Library of Congress subject headings, serial holdings, descriptive and cartographic cataloging, virtual reference, library assessment and benchmarking, and knowledge management. The program also expanded its consortial purchasing opportunities, renewed substantial vendor discounts, and established new basic ordering agreements with a variety of vendors of publications, electronic resources, and other products and services.

Systems staff members began an ambitious implementation of the new FEDLINK financial system, which entered a preliminary testing phase late in summer 2002.

Staff members also sponsored 29 seminars and workshops for 1,233 participants and conducted 38 OCLC, Internet, and related training classes for 415 students.

FEDLINK also continued to customize and configure software and support services for electronic invoicing and to increase online access to financial information for member agencies and vendors.

Continuing financial management efforts ensured that FEDLINK successfully passed the Library of Congress financial audit of FY 2001 transactions performed by Clifton Gunderson, LLP.

FLICC and FEDLINK programs continue to thrive in the facilitative leadership (FL) environment. The FL tools consistently provide approaches and techniques that involve FEDLINK staff and members in the planning process, resulting in streamlined, efficient, and cost-effective program actions.

FLICC Quarterly Membership Meetings

In addition to regular FLICC Working Group updates and reports from FLICC/FEDLINK staff members, each FLICC quarterly meeting included a special meeting focus on a new or developing trend in federal libraries. The first quarterly meeting featured Joanne Gard Marshall, dean and professor, School of Information and Library Science, University of North Carolina at Chapel Hill, speaking on "Competencies and Continuing Educational Needs of Federal Information Professionals"; the second meeting included a presentation by Denise Davis, director of statistics and surveys, National Commission on Libraries and Information Science (NCLIS), on "Metrics and Library Performance"; the third meeting's focus was a presentation by Roberta Shaffer, founder and principal of the KnowLedge Group, on "Speaking Up: Basic Tips for Getting What You Want Through Internal Lobbying"; and the fourth meeting included Marjorie Gildenhorn, director, Information Services, U.S. Department of the Treasury, who spoke on "Strategic Planning for Federal Information Services."

FLICC Executive Board

The FLICC Executive Board (FEB) focused its efforts on a number of initiatives related to professional development. Early in the year, the board redefined its annual awards program to further delineate federal library community efforts by the size of the institution in an effort to encourage both small and large federal libraries and information centers to compete for the awards.

FEB also supported Institute of Museum and Library Services (IMLS) efforts to increase expanded recruitment and educational efforts for librarians, and discussed with IMLS representatives specifics for federal librarian recruitment.

A more immediate issue for FEB was a focus on developments regarding the FAIR Act, the Commercial Activities Panel, and changes to Office of Management and Budget's A-76 memorandum. In addition to surveys of FLICC members and presentations on the topic, FEB also met formally with Robert Tobias, distinguished adjunct professor, American University, and member of the government's Commercial Activities Panel (CAP), to discuss CAP recommendations related to definitions of "inherently governmental" and modified procedures for competitive sourcing, particularly as related to federal libraries and information centers.

FEB took a leadership role in the developing issues of homeland security, content and knowledge management, bibliographic control, digital reference, and preservation. The board also advised the Department of Defense on planning the future of the Pentagon Library, and the Department of Labor on replacing its library director, and endorsed federal library and information center community support of the Library of Congress Veterans History Project and the National Book Festival.

FLICC Working Groups

Awards Working Group

To honor the many innovative ways in which federal libraries, librarians, and library technicians fulfill the information demands of government, business, research, scholarly communities, and the public, the Awards Working Group administered a series of national awards for federal librarianship. The award winners for FY 2002 were

- Federal Library/Information Center of the Year: The National Defense University Library, for outstanding, innovative, and sustained achievements during the fiscal year in fulfilling its organization's mission, fostering innovation in its services, and meeting the needs of its users.

- Federal Librarian of the Year (tie): Pamela Dawes, director, Haskell Library, Haskell Indian Nations University, Lawrence, Kansas; and Lynne C. Tobin, chief, Reference Library, National Imagery and Mapping Agency, Bethesda, Maryland, for their achievements during the fiscal year in the advancement of library and information sciences, the promotion and development of services in support of the agency's mission, and demonstrated professionalism as described in the Special Libraries Association's Competencies for Special Librarians in the 21st Century.

- Federal Library Technician of the Year: Leslie Yeakley, library technician, Defense Technical Information Center, Fort Belvoir, Virginia, for service excellence in support of the information center's mission, exceptional technical competency, and flexibility in adapting work methods and dealing with change during the fiscal year. Patricia E. Tellman, library technician, Base Library, Naval Air Station, Fort Worth, Texas, received honorable mention.

At the annual FLICC Forum on Federal Information Policies in March 2002, the Deputy Librarian of Congress presented the individual award winners with a certificate and an engraved crystal award in the shape of a book honoring their contributions to the field of federal library and information service and the institutional winner with a framed, hand-painted certificate for display.

Budget and Finance Working Group

The Budget and Finance Working Group developed the FY 2003 FEDLINK budget and fee structure in the winter quarter. The group developed an online budget questionnaire for FEDLINK members and used the results to verify assumptions for the budget for the 2003 fiscal year. This year also marked the first time the membership voted on the budget electronically by reviewing the information online and printing out official ballots. The final budget for FY 2002 kept membership fees for transfer-pay customers at FY 2002 levels: 7.75 percent on accounts up to $300,000 and 7.0 percent on amounts exceeding $300,000. Direct-pay fees also remained at FY 2002 levels. Library of Congress officials approved the budget in September 2002.

Content Management Working Group

After a hiatus related to the merger with the Chief Information Officers' Knowledge Management Working Group, the FLICC Content Management Working Group convened in September to plan a lunchtime discussion series that began with the topic of taxonomies and a day-long event in December 2002 to look at information technology disaster planning and recovery in federal libraries and information centers.

Education Working Group

The FLICC Education Working Group sponsored 29 programs for 1,233 participants during FY 2002 in the areas of licensing, portals, Web cataloging, electronic resources, knowledge management, disaster recovery, virtual reference, and performance measures. In addition, the FLICC Orientations to National Libraries and Information Centers and brown-bag luncheon discussions continued throughout the year.

The working group responded to the agenda developed for the December 2001 FLICC membership focus group sessions by dividing into three subgroups to carry out their charge. The initial result was the development of a management seminar series that will debut in FY 2003. The working group also initiated a revision to its Web-based *Handbook of Federal Librarianship,* for release in early 2003.

Nominating Working Group

The FLICC Nominating Working Group oversaw the 2002 election process for FLICC rotating members, FLICC Executive Board members, and the FEDLINK Advisory Council. Librarians representing a variety of federal agencies agreed to place their names in nomination for these positions. For the first time, the nominating process included a listing of eligible FEB candidates, which resulted in the largest nomination pool to date.

Personnel Working Group

Because of the high percentage of federal librarians approaching retirement age and the importance of refreshing the civil service with young, energetic information managers, the Personnel Working Group turned its focus to federal library recruitment. Meetings with Office of Management and Budget officials reinforced the working group's efforts on recruitment, and members began developing a slate of potential recruitment marketing and promotion efforts. The group started its promotional campaign by preparing a leaflet on federal librarianship for the Library of Congress National Book Festival.

Preservation and Binding Working Group

The Preservation and Binding Working Group set disaster planning and recovery as its educational priority. The centerpiece of its efforts was a special disaster-recovery program in the spring that featured Pentagon Library employees who related their experiences during and after the terrorist attacks of September 11, 2001, and detailed recovery activities. They completed a statement of work on preservation services for rare books, flat paper, and microfilming, which was published for industry comment before FEDLINK invites vendors to submit proposals. The group also advised the U.S. Government Printing Office on needed revisions to its binding contract requirements, which are scheduled for recompetition in FY 2003.

Publications and Education Office

In FY 2002 FLICC supported an ambitious publication schedule, producing six issues of *FEDLINK Technical Notes* and three issues of the *FLICC Quarterly Newsletter.*

FLICC streamlined and targeted materials to support the FEDLINK program more efficiently, including the FY 2003 *FEDLINK Registration Pamphlet* and five FEDLINK Information Alerts. FLICC also produced the minutes of the four FY 2002 FLICC Quarterly Meetings and bimonthly FLICC Executive Board meetings, as well as all FLICC Education Program promotional and support materials.

FLICC and FEDLINK staff members worked throughout 2002 to revise and update the FLICC/FEDLINK Web site. After extensive work with focus groups, concept mappers, designers, advisers, and colleagues, staff members were poised to release the new site at the end of FY 2002. FLICC expanded its distance-learning efforts to include event video series on the FLICC Forum, the FLICC awards program, and the spring FEDLINK Membership Meeting. Videos on Direct Express and on alternatives to the standard interagency agreement process debuted in late summer. The new site also contains a variety of information resources, FEDLINK member information, links to vendors and other members, listings of membership and minutes of various FLICC working groups and governing bodies, access to account data online, awards program information, event calendars, and an online training registration system that is updated nightly. FLICC staff members converted all publications, newsletters, announcements, alerts, member materials, meeting minutes, and working group resources into HTML and PDF formats, uploading current materials within days of being printed. Staff completed an extensive initiative to update the numerous Web links throughout the Web site, and links are now maintained on an established cycle.

In collaboration with FEDLINK Network Operations, publications staff continued to expand the Web site, offering resources including OCLC usage analysis reports, pricing data, and many new documents such as the FY 2003 budget questionnaire and ballot and a variety of training resources. Staff members also worked with the Library of Congress Contracts and Logistics Division to make electronic versions of FEDLINK's requests for proposals available online for prospective vendors.

Publications staff continued to support the Member Services Unit and its Online Registration/Online Interagency Agreement (IAG) system. This year, the system also includes a sample IAG, a sample alternative-purchasing vehicle, and a "determinations and findings" document supporting use of the program.

In conjunction with the Education Working Group, FLICC offered a total of 29 seminars, workshops, and lunchtime discussions to 1,233 members of the federal library and information center community. Multi-day institutes looked at Web cataloging, descriptive cataloging, serial holdings, and knowledge management; one-day sessions offered hands-on and theoretical information on metadata, Web portals, managing and preserving electronic resources, advanced Web searching, disaster recovery, Library of Congress subject headings, and virtual reference. FLICC was also host to three General Counsel forums on licensing electronic publications, FOIA policy and the Trade Secrets Act, and legal challenges to Internet filtering in public libraries.

FLICC demonstrated its ongoing commitment to library technicians' continuing education by hosting satellite downlinks to a popular teleconference, "Soaring to . . . Excellence," sponsored by the College of DuPage. Following the success of previous programs, FLICC held the sixth annual Federal Library Technicians Institute. This week-long summer institute again focused on orienting library technicians to the full array of library functions in the federal sector. Federal and academic librarians joined FLICC professionals to discuss various areas of librarianship, including acquisitions, cataloging, reference, and automation.

FLICC continued to improve its multimedia distance-learning initiative through increased use of upgraded equipment and software to produce high-quality, edited educational programs. This year, the spring FEDLINK Membership Meeting joined the FLICC Forum and the FLICC Awards Ceremony as part of both a cybercast and online video production effort, and three FLICC Quarterly Meetings were recorded for members unable to attend.

FEDLINK

In FY 2002 FEDLINK (the Federal Library and Information Network) managers and professional staff members outlined steps to improve processes, to better market the program to federal libraries and their partner contracting officers and chief information officers, and to expand the number and types of services that libraries and information centers can procure via the FEDLINK program. They quantified these steps in the FEDLINK five-year business plan, which paid special attention to helping the government build and improve digital libraries. Staff members also began industry research to understand the current market and best practices in the field. Early explorations suggest that there are limited data specific to the federal marketplace. During this first year, staff members concentrated on identifying new services to support effective use of the Web. Working with FLICC/FEDLINK governing bodies, with the Content Management Working Group, and with attendees at reference programs, staff members sought further insight into how federal libraries might best use such services.

FEDLINK continued to give federal agencies cost-effective access to an array of automated information retrieval services for online research, cataloging, and interlibrary loan. FEDLINK members also procured print serials, electronic journals, books and other publications, CD-ROMs, and document delivery via Library of Congress/FEDLINK contracts with more than 100 major vendors. The program obtained further discounts for customers through consortia and enterprise-wide licenses for journals, aggregated information retrieval services, and electronic books.

The FEDLINK Advisory Council met 11 times during the fiscal year. In addition to their general oversight activities, council members advised FEDLINK managers on priorities for the first year of the five-year business plan, provided valuable insight into trends in the information industry, and supported adoption of the FY 2003 budget. They also provided extensive feedback on the redesign of the FLICC/FEDLINK Web site.

The annual Fall FEDLINK Membership Meeting featured an update on the General Accounting Office opinion about FEDLINK's revolving fund, a report from FLICC's 2000 Information Center of the Year—the Patent and Trademark Office Technical Information Center, and reports from librarians affected by the Pentagon terrorist attack. At the Spring FEDLINK Membership Meeting, Robert Newlen, head, Legislative Relations Office, and Jill Ziegler, management specialist, Congressional Research Service (CRS), explained their Visual Identity Project to redesign the CRS logo and other visual aspects of their publications.

For the first time, this annual meeting was cybercast via the FLICC/FEDLINK Web site.

FEDLINK/OCLC Network Activity

Both FEDLINK/OCLC Users Group meetings, held in November and May, provided in-depth presentations on OCLC's expanded Web services: OCLC has improved both cataloging and interlibrary loan interfaces via the Web and added more functionality to FirstSearch to increase its connections to full text and to improve libraries' ability to integrate it with their other Web-based systems. Other reports at the meetings indicated that the Government Printing Office will continue to participate in OCLC's pilot project to build a digital archiving system and that FEDLINK will continue to assist federal libraries in their participation in the pilot stage of QuestionPoint, the Library of Congress-OCLC cooperative digital reference system.

FEDLINK staff supplemented these biannual meetings with six regular articles in *FEDLINK Technical Notes,* postings on electronic lists, extensive telephone consultations, and e-mail. They visited 16 member libraries to provide in-depth demonstrations of OCLC services and to consult on workflow and best practices, demonstrations, and lectures at several agency meetings such as the Army Library Institute, the Military Librarians Workshop, a U.S. Army Europe Libraries meeting, and the Geological Survey Library Consortium Meeting.

Training Program

The 2002 FEDLINK training program included 31 on-site training classes for 251 students and seven off-site programs for 164 participants. In the United States and Europe, staff members supplemented the basic Web-searching courses by adding a course on searching the alternative ("dark") Web. Robert Ellett, Jr., chief of cataloging at the Armed Forces Staff Members College, taught Advanced Cataloging and Authorities. OCLC courses emphasized the use of Web interfaces in cataloging and interlibrary loan.

FEDLINK also emphasized using training agreements so that FEDLINK customers could fund training accounts for OCLC and other workshops held by sister networks such as Amigos, BCR, CAPCON, NYLINK, Michigan Library Consortium, OCLC Western, and Palinet. FEDLINK also brokered the Computers in Libraries conference at a discounted rate for 282 attendees, saving the government $80,000.

Procurement Program

FEDLINK maintained an open Request for Proposal for online retrieval services that attracted responses from Bright Planet, *The Economist,* Inside Washington Publishers, Linguistics Systems, *The Nation* Digital Archives, Rapsheet.com, and Standard and Poor's IMS. An open season for books and other monograph publications resulted in agreements with eight additional companies: Books Research, Inc., Complete Book & Media Supply, Inc., Delmar Learning/Thomson, EBSCO Information Services, Econo-Clad Books/Sagebrush Corporation, G+L Wissenschaftliche Buchhandlung GmbH—Scientific Booksellers, Midwest Library Service, and Research Periodicals & Books Services, Inc.

Staff members collaborated with the Preservation Working Group on a Request for Proposals for preservation services that was scheduled for early in FY 2003.

FEDLINK Fiscal Operations

FEDLINK Vendor Services

Total FEDLINK vendor service dollars for FY 2002 totaled $56.6 million for transfer-pay customers and $38.1 million for direct-pay customers. Database retrieval services represented $19.5 million and $25.7 million spent, respectively, by transfer-pay and direct-pay customers. Within this service category, online services composed the largest procurement for transfer-pay and direct-pay customers, representing $18.2 million and $25.6 million, respectively. Publication acquisition services represented $30.0 million and $12.3 million, respectively, for transfer-pay and direct-pay customers. Within this service category, serials subscription services composed the largest procurement for transfer-pay and direct-pay customers, representing $22.4 million and $12.0 million, respectively. Library support services represented $7.1 million and $74,000, respectively, for transfer-pay and direct-pay customers. Within this service category, bibliographic utilities constituted the largest procurement area, representing $5.1 million and $74,000 for transfer-pay and direct-pay customers, respectively.

Accounts Receivable and Member Services

FEDLINK processed FY 2002 registrations from federal libraries, information centers, and other federal offices for a total of 584 signed FY 2002 IAGs. In addition, FEDLINK processed 2,473 IAG amendments (1,140 for FY 2002 and 1,333 for prior-year adjustments) for agencies that added, adjusted, or ended service funding. These IAGs and IAG amendments represented 9,018 individual service requests to begin, move, convert, or cancel service from FEDLINK vendors. For FY 2002 alone, FEDLINK processed $56.6 million in service dollars for 2,315 transfer-pay accounts and $38.1 million in service dollars for 124 direct-pay accounts. Included in the above member-service transactions were 924 member requests to move prior-year (no-year and multi-year) funds across fiscal-year boundaries. These no-year and multi-year service request transactions represented an additional contracting volume of $6.6 million, comprising 1,551 delivery orders.

The FEDLINK Fiscal Hotline responded to a variety of member questions ranging from routine queries about IAGs, delivery orders, and account balances to complicated questions regarding FEDLINK policies and operating procedures. In addition, the FLICC Web site and e-mail contacts continued to offer FEDLINK members and vendors 24-hour access to fiscal operations. Staff members continued to schedule appointments with FEDLINK member agencies and FEDLINK vendors to discuss complicated account problems, and assigned senior staff members to concentrate on resolving complex current and prior-year situations. FEDLINK's online financial service system, ALIX-FS, maintained current and prior-year transfer-pay accounts in FY 2002 and continued to provide members early access to their monthly balance information throughout the fiscal year.

Budget and Revenue

During FY 2002 FEDLINK revenue from signed IAGs exceeded first-year business plan goals by 5.5 percent ($247,000). Program fee revenue will likely exceed obligations by $66,000, markedly better than the proposed FY 2002 budget position, which was predicated on a deficit of $142,000. Program expenditure obligations were expected to be approximately $78,000 less than the budget because of delays in hiring program staff members. As FY 2002 ended, FEDLINK fee revenue was approximately 10.4 percent above FY 2001 levels for the same period. The increase in fee revenue is primarily attributed to a 9.5 percent increase in transfer-pay service procurement activities compared with the previous fiscal year. The increase in transfer-pay service procurement activities accounts for the total increase in FEDLINK fee revenue.

Business Plan Development and Implementation

In support of developing the FEDLINK business plan, fiscal operations managers worked diligently to complete required analyses of customer and vendor market participation. In addition, the fiscal managers proposed marketing plans to improve FEDLINK business and developed financial forecasts of business activity for program initiatives.

Fiscal staff members prepared a detailed historical analysis of customer participation and spending patterns regarding library products and services, and drafted a marketing plan. Staff members also prepared the detailed five-year forecast of program expenditures (personal and nonpersonal), service dollars by product category for transfer and direct pay, and management reserves and contingency plans. Fiscal Operations staff worked on a number of business plan initiatives:

Recruit vendors to fill gaps in products/services (e.g, Quick Wins): FEDLINK recruited several online and book vendors to fill immediate service requirements of FEDLINK customers. New vendors continued to join the program throughout FY 2002.

Improve processes and remove barriers: For the first time, customers registered up until the penultimate day of the fiscal year to take advantage of procurement opportunities under the revolving fund. FEDLINK also expanded its online registration options so that in FY 2003 customers can procure FEDLINK services with a purchase order, military interdepartmental purchase requisition, or alternative customer agency document authorizing the transfer/obligation of member funds.

Develop an alternative business model similar to that used by GSA: Staff members were actively involved in the creation of the Direct Express pilot program, development of the contract solicitation, and the recruitment of online vendors. The work entailed redefining contract requirements in solicitation and collaborating with the Library of Congress Financial Services Directorate to set up the central accounting system to monitor and record financial results using revenue source codes for vendors' quarterly payments to the library. These electronic transfers will require minimal manual intervention and will eliminate problems associated with check receipts. Finally, staff members collaborated with the library's contracts office to develop a standard quarterly reporting model for participating vendors.

Implement amendment processing (e.g., money moves, add funds, refunds): FEDLINK staff members and the library's Information Technology Services completed the work for amendment processing, including adding accounts-payable vendor verification in the online IAG registration system.

Carryover of annual funds for the Revolving Fund (P.L. 106-481): Staff members consulted with senior library managers and congressional relations staff members to put the carryover initiative on the library's legislative agenda for 2003.

In response to local mail delivery problems, FEDLINK worked to give Washington, D.C., area customers their statements in a portable document format. Staff members scanned statements and invoices to e-mail to customers or set up Web files for customers whose network firewalls prevented delivery of executable files. To improve the efficiency of this process, FEDLINK and Library of Congress IT staff set up customer files on the library's Web server. FEDLINK will eventually migrate all of its customers to this method of receiving statements. Short-term response to mail delays included creating a 90-day additional grace period for IAG bill collections; faxing IAGs and supporting documentation between customers and the library, and encouraging FEDLINK customers to move to electronic funds transfer.

FLICC Systems Office

FEDLINK chose Oracle Financials as the software package to replace its DOS-based SYMIN Fiscal Management System. The basic software provides general ledger, accounts payable, and accounts receivable capabilities. FEDLINK worked with an outside consultant to complete the system design and configuration. On the consultant's recommendation, FEDLINK also added the Oracle Purchasing and Discoverer Reports modules to the initial purchase.

Staff members and consultants worked together to install, configure, and interface the package to outside systems. The software is in its final tuning and testing phase with staff members intending to parallel test Oracle with the SYMIN system in the second quarter of FY 2003.

While developing the Oracle replacement system, staff members reconfigured SYMIN to allow processing under revolving-fund requirements with changes made to account codes needed for interface with the library's financial management system and to fee-calculation routines to eliminate charging additional fees to customers making no-year money moves.

Staff members installed the Windows 2000 Operating System on approximately half of the FLICC/FEDLINK workstations with the remaining installations scheduled for early FY 2003.

National Agricultural Library

U.S. Department of Agriculture, NAL Bldg., 10301 Baltimore Ave.,
Beltsville, MD 20705-2351
E-mail agref@nal.usda.gov
World Wide Web http://www.nal.usda.gov

Len Carey
Public Affairs Officer

The National Agricultural Library (NAL), established within the U.S. Department of Agriculture (USDA) when the department was created in 1862, is the primary resource in the United States for information about food, agriculture, and natural resources.

Congress assigned to the library the responsibilities to

- Acquire, preserve, and manage information resources of agriculture and allied sciences
- Organize agricultural information and information products and services
- Provide agricultural information and information products and services within the United States and internationally
- Plan, coordinate, and evaluate information and library needs related to agricultural research and education
- Cooperate with and coordinate efforts toward development of a comprehensive agricultural library and information network
- Coordinate the development of specialized subject information services among the agricultural and library information communities

In 1969 NAL moved from downtown Washington, D.C., to nearby Beltsville, Maryland. The library's 15-story Abraham Lincoln Building, on the grounds of USDA's Henry A. Wallace Beltsville Agricultural Research Center, is named in honor of the president who created the Department of Agriculture and signed many of the major laws affecting agriculture.

Today, NAL employs about 170 librarians, information specialists, computer specialists, administrators, and clerical personnel, supplemented by about 80 contract staff, volunteers, and cooperators from NAL partnering organizations. The library's expert staff, leadership in delivering information services, collaborations with other U.S. and international agricultural research and information organizations, extensive collection of agricultural information, AGRICOLA database, and advanced information technology infrastructure make it the world's foremost agricultural library.

NAL is an electronic gateway to a widening array of scientific literature, printed text, and images in agriculture. It maintains more than 40,000 Web pages and delivers more than 40 million direct customer services each year throughout the world via its Web site (http://www.nal.usda.gov) and other Internet-based services. NAL also works with other agricultural libraries and institutions to advance open and democratic access to information about agriculture and the nation's agricultural knowledge. NAL is the U.S. node of the international agricultural information system, and therefore a way for the world to access U.S. agricultural libraries and information resources.

NAL's eight national information centers are specialized gateways to science-based information in key areas of agriculture, including alternative farming systems (see http://www.nal.usda.gov/afsic), animal welfare (http://www.nal.usda.gov/awic), food and nutrition (http://www.nal.usda.gov/fnic), food safety (http://www.nal.usda.gov/fs), invasive species (http://www.invasivespecies.gov), rural revitalization (http://www.nal.usda.gov/ric), technology transfer (http://www.nal.usda.gov/ttic), and water quality (http://www.nal.usda.gov/wqic). These centers provide targeted information services in collaboration with other organizations throughout government to provide timely, accurate, comprehensive, and in-depth coverage within their subject areas.

The Collection

NAL manages an immense collection of information and databases about agriculture. The breadth, depth, size, and scope of the library's collection—more than 3.5 million items on 48 miles of shelves, dating from the 16th century to the present, covering all aspects of agriculture and related sciences, and including special "one-of-a-kind" items not available elsewhere—make it an irreplaceable resource for agricultural researchers, policy makers, regulators, and scholars. The NAL collection includes the most extensive set of materials anywhere on the history of agriculture in the United States, and is the most complete repository of U.S. Department of Agriculture publications. The library acquires more than 19,000 serial titles annually.

NAL's AGRICOLA (AGRICultural OnLine Access) bibliographic database contains more than 4 million citations to agricultural literature with links to the full text of many publications. From AGRICOLA's World Wide Web site (http://www.nal.usda.gov/ag98), NAL provides a broad base of users with no-cost access to this information.

NAL is nationally known as a leader in preservation of publications in print, digital, and other formats to ensure long-term access to agricultural information, and has led development of policies and procedures for preserving Department of Agriculture digital publications. The library is known for its expertise in preservation of microforms.

NAL's technology leadership in partnership with others can be seen in the newly implemented distributed architecture for managing agricultural information through the Agriculture Network Information Center (AgNIC) alliance. AgNIC (http://www.agnic.org) is a discipline-specific, distributed network on the Internet, providing quality agricultural information selected by a coalition involving NAL, land-grant universities, and other institutions.

Under NAL leadership, AgNIC was established by an alliance of agricultural organizations that included Cornell University, Iowa State University, the University of Arizona, and the University of Nebraska, Lincoln. In 1995 NAL established the AgNIC Web site with a calendar of events and a database of agriculture resources. During the following year AgNIC partners added subject-specific sites including agricultural statistics, animal science, plant science, range management, rural information, and food and nutrition. In 1997 "online reference" was added as a partner requirement for each subject. In 2002 AgNIC gained two new members, bringing the partnership to 42, and offered 40 subject-specific sites, with more than five additional subject sites expected by the end of 2003. The AgNIC partners' annual meeting in April 2002 drew more than 52 participants, including participants from Mexico and Costa Rica. Plans for AgNIC's future include an emphasis on developing a portal interface, developing content for each subject site, populating the new database, increasing subject coverage by increasing membership, continuing to expand coverage to include non-English languages, and a focus on locating funding resources.

NAL is a national and international authority on managing agricultural information and is known for its expertise in development and use of a thesaurus or controlled vocabulary, a critical component of effective electronic information systems. Such expertise positions the library to innovate both in promoting new technologies and in managing agricultural information.

Information Management

NAL is the bibliographic authority on managing agricultural information, both nationally and internationally, and an authority on the development and use of controlled vocabulary for agriculture. Its strong foundation and experience in collection development, implementation of bibliographic control standards, and systems for information retrieval uniquely position NAL to define and develop new models for identifying, organizing, preserving, and providing access to the vast quantities of agricultural information available digitally on the Internet and elsewhere. The collective expertise of the NAL staff and the vast array of print and digital information present in the national collection offer opportunity for collaboratively developing and testing innovative methods of creating and linking agricultural research information.

During the Year

Interagency Panel Assessment

In August 2002 USDA Under Secretary Joseph L. Jen issued, for 30 days of public comment, the report of an Interagency Panel for Assessment of the National Agricultural Library. The panel was appointed in October 2000 to review the activities of NAL and make recommendations about NAL's management and staff, programs, and operations. The panel's October 2001 report set forth a broad vision for NAL and 28 specific recommendations. In November 2002 USDA's National Agricultural Research, Extension, Education, and Economics Advisory Board reviewed and considered the public comments. The board advises the secretary of agriculture and the department's land-grant university partners on relevant policies and priorities and their effectiveness. The board chair later wrote Secretary of Agriculture Ann Veneman to endorse the report's recommendations and recommend their adoption.

Young named NAL Director

On June 3 Peter R. Young was appointed NAL director. Young most recently had been chief of the cataloging distribution service and acting chief of the Asian Division at the Library of Congress.

"We are extremely pleased to have Peter at the helm of the National Agricultural Library," Under Secretary Jen said. "His wealth of experience in the international library and information arenas will be an asset in serving the needs of USDA's global agricultural research and education communities."

Young has also held professional positions in college, university, research, and public libraries. From 1990 to 1997 he was executive director of the U.S. National Commission on Libraries and Information Science (NCLIS), an independent federal agency established in 1970 to advise the president and Congress on library and information services and policies. Earlier, he was an academic library administrator at Rice University, Franklin and Marshall College, and American University, and served as assistant director of the Grand Rapids (Michigan) Public Library. He served as a film-library specialist with the U.S. Army's 25th Infantry Division from 1968 to 1970 and was awarded three bronze star medals for meritorious achievement directing a Special Services Library in Cu Chi, Vietnam. Young holds a bachelor's degree in liberal arts from the College of Wooster in Wooster, Ohio, and a master's degree in library science from Columbia University's School of Library Service. He succeeds NAL Director Pamela Q. J. Andre, who retired in June 2001.

New Integrated Library Management System

In April 2002 NAL selected the Voyager integrated library management system produced by Endeavor Information Systems to organize, manage, and provide access to the library's extensive collection. NAL Associate Director Sally Sinn said the Voyager system offers NAL a fully integrated, multi-tiered client-server system, with software modules that allow digital information management and enhanced content linking. "This means local and remote information resources will be easily accessible from a single point of access in our online public access catalog, and that it will be easier for us to manage all facets of NAL's operations," Sinn said. The Voyager system will be fully implemented at NAL in the summer of 2003.

NAL Helps Establish Science Web Site

NAL was one of 14 scientific and technical information organizations from 10 major science agencies collaborating in 2002 to create science.gov (http://www.science.gov), a government online source of reliable information about science and technology from federal government organizations.

Science.gov is intended for the educational and library communities, business people, researchers, and anyone with an interest in science. Users can find more than 1,000 government science information resources, including technical reports, journal citations, databases, federal Web sites, and fact sheets. The service is free of charge and no registration is required.

Support for building the science.gov gateway came from CENDI, an interagency committee of senior managers of federal science and technology information programs. NAL Deputy Director Eleanor Frierson served as co-chair of the interagency group that created science.gov. Federal organizations participating in science.gov are the Departments of Agriculture, Commerce, Defense, Education, Energy, Health and Human Services, and Interior, along with the Environmental Protection Agency, National Aeronautics and Space Administration, and National Science Foundation.

Digital Desktop Library for USDA

In November 2002 NAL launched a digital desktop library for USDA for a pilot year. Secretary Veneman celebrated the launch of "DigiTop" in January 2003 at NAL's USDA headquarters reference center.

To create DigiTop, NAL combined funding from USDA agencies to acquire USDA-wide licenses to more than 7,000 electronic journals, newspapers, key databases, statistics, and other important digital information resources. "DigiTop gives USDA people access to electronic information about agriculture and a lot of other subjects 24 hours a day," NAL Director Young said. "It offers new and more efficient solutions consistent with e-government goals, showing the good things that can happen when USDA agencies collaborate."

National Library of Medicine

8600 Rockville Pike, Bethesda, MD 20894
301-496-6308, 888-346-3656, fax 301-496-4450
E-mail publicinfo@nlm.nih.gov
World Wide Web http://www.nlm.nih.gov

Robert Mehnert
Director, Office of Communications and Public Liaison

The National Library of Medicine (NLM), a part of the U.S. Department of Health and Human Services' National Institutes of Health in Bethesda, Maryland, is the world's largest library of the health sciences. NLM has two buildings with 420,000 total square feet. The older building (1962) houses the collection, public reading rooms, exhibition hall, and library staff and administrative offices. The adjacent 10-story Lister Hill Center Building (1980) contains the main computer room, auditorium, audiovisual facility, offices, and research laboratories.

The library's collections contain more than 6 million books, journals, audiovisuals, and historical materials. The library's mission has expanded over the years from primary responsibility for a physical collection and today encompasses

- An extensive Web site (http://www.nlm.nih.gov) that is the hub of an online international biomedical information network serving scientists, health professionals, and the public
- Two major research and development components, the Lister Hill National Center for Biomedical Communications and the National Center for Biotechnology Information
- A program concerned with developing information resources in environmental health, toxicology, and hazardous substances
- A program of extramural grants for library and information services and for research and training in medical informatics

The library's constantly expanding collections, extensive responsibilities, and rapidly growing staff in the area of molecular biology have combined to overcrowd its existing physical plant. Plans have been drawn up for an expanded facility, and NLM is hopeful that relief is in sight.

Databases

The library's major database, MEDLINE, contains more than 12 million references and abstracts from the worldwide journal literature from the early 1960s to the present. The database expands at a rate of about 500,000 citations a year. Available free on the Web, MEDLINE is searched using NLM's unique access system, PubMed. Each day the database is queried more than 1.3 million times by 220,000 users. This, when combined with the use of other NLM databases, amounts to more than 500 million searches a year, making the databases the world's most widely used medical information resource. The library provides many additional information resources through its Web site; for example, unified access to its catalog holdings, a database of historical images, and a variety of information services in such areas as toxicology, environmental health, and molecular biology.

To make MEDLINE/PubMed even more useful, NLM has introduced links between the references and publisher Web sites so that users can retrieve the full text of articles. Today more than 3,400 of the 4,600 publications indexed for the database have such links. Where links are not available, PubMed allows libraries to display information about print holdings available to their institutional users. Users far from a library can utilize the feature known as Loansome Doc to order an article from a library in the National Network of Libraries of Medicine. A recent improvement is a text version of PubMed for users who require special adaptive equipment to access the Web. This has had the additional benefit of making the system much more accessible for those using hand-held devices.

NLM is extending its reference databases back in time. OLDMEDLINE contains hundreds of thousands of citations to articles from international biomedical journals published from 1957 through 1965. There is important research in these articles—on smallpox and tuberculosis, for instance—and to have this information available through online searching is a boon to today's scientists and public health officials. NLM has also converted to electronic form the mammoth *Index-Catalogue of the Library of the Surgeon General's Office,* the premier resource for the history of medicine in the 19th century.

Another NLM Web information service, intended primarily for the general public, is MEDLINEplus, introduced in October 1998. This is an easily consulted and authoritative source of health information from the National Institutes of Health (NIH) and other reliable organizations. MEDLINEplus usage has been growing rapidly, doubling in the past year to a rate of more than 120 million page hits a year.

The main features of MEDLINEplus are

- Almost 600 "health topics," from Abdominal Pain to Yeast Infections
- Consumer-friendly information about thousands of prescription and over-the-counter drugs
- An illustrated medical encyclopedia and medical dictionaries
- Directories of hospitals and health professionals
- A daily health news feed from major print media
- Interactive and simply presented tutorials (with audio and video) about diseases and medical procedures

The MEDLINEplus health topics also have links to a database of ongoing and planned scientific studies, ClinicalTrials.gov (http://clinicaltrials.gov). Developed by NLM for NIH, this database is a registry of some 6,600 protocol records sponsored by NIH and other federal agencies, the pharmaceutical industry, and non-profit organizations in more than 70,000 locations, mostly in the United States and Canada but also in some 70 other countries. ClinicalTrials.gov includes a statement-of-purpose for each study, together with the recruiting status, the criteria for patient participation in the trial, the location of the trial, and specific contact information. The clinical trials site hosts more than 8,000 visitors daily.

NLM has been working with the National Institute on Aging to create NIHSeniorHealth.gov (http://nihseniorhealth.gov). Accessible from MEDLINEplus, the new site contains information in a format that is easily usable by senior citizens. At present NIHSeniorHealth.gov contains information on Alzheimer's Disease and exercise for older adults, but it will soon be expanded to include more topics of special interest to seniors as other NIH institutes contribute to it. NLM is working on adapting special software that would allow the visually impaired to more easily use the site and hear Web pages read.

Like MEDLINE, MEDLINEplus is a constantly evolving system. Links are checked daily and new health topics added weekly. In the days following the September 11, 2001, terrorist attacks, entries on anthrax, smallpox, and other bioterrorism-related subjects were quickly compiled and were heavily accessed. A Spanish-language version of MEDLINEplus was introduced in September 2002. In 2003 MEDLINEplus will carry links to local resources in North Carolina. "NC Health Info" was created at the University of North Carolina with funds provided by NLM. It may serve as a prototype for other states that want to provide local links to Web sites for hospitals, physicians, nursing homes, support groups, health screening clinics, and other services.

Another information resource is the Profiles in Science Web site (http://profiles.nlm.nih.gov). This site uses innovative digital technology to make available the manuscript collections of prominent biomedical scientists. The documents have been donated to NLM and contain published and unpublished materials, including books, journal volumes, pamphlets, diaries, letters, manuscripts, photographs, audio tapes, and other audiovisual resources. Presently the database features the archives of nine prominent American biomolecular researchers; added in 2002 were Linus Pauling and Donald Fredrickson. NLM also recently made available the Reports of the Surgeon General (1964–2000).

A new offering by NLM in 2002 was Tox Town. This is a Web site (http://toxtown.nlm.nih.gov) intended for a general audience that uses color, graphics, sound, and animation to add interest to learning about connections among chemicals, the environment, and the public's health. In its first release, Tox Town gives information about eight chemicals and 11 locations (for example, home, office, school, park) in an imaginary small town. Among the toxic substances are asbestos, lead, and radon. There are plans to include more toxic substances and add new scenes, such as an urban community and a farming region.

Outreach

A major challenge to the library lies in reaching both the scientific community and the general public to let them know that the tax dollars devoted to biomedical research have resulted in information that can be applied to clinical care and to public health. To help bring this about, NLM has funded hundreds of outreach projects with members of the National Network of Libraries of Medicine. The network was created by NLM in the 1960s to ensure that all U.S. health professionals had good information services available to them. Today it includes more than 5,000 regular and affiliate members. The regular members are libraries with health sciences collections, primarily in hospitals and academic health sciences centers; the affiliate members, including some small hospitals, public libraries, and community organizations, provide health information service but have little or no physical collection of health-related literature.

Eight regional medical libraries are funded by NLM as the backbone of the National Network of Libraries of Medicine. In 2002 NLM and these eight libraries decided to define uniform national measures of the network's success in reaching two outreach objectives: (1) improving health information access via public libraries and (2) connecting local public health departments to health information services. Individual outreach projects will continue to have project-specific evaluation measures. In addition to basic contracts with the eight regional medical libraries, NLM funds subcontracts for four centers that serve the entire network: the National Training Center and Clearinghouse at the New York Academy of Medicine, the Electronic Funds Transfer System at the University of Connecticut, the Outreach Evaluation Resource Center at the University of Washington, and the National Outreach Mapping Center at Indiana University in Indianapolis.

Today many network members are also serving the general public, and NLM is supporting them as they work with their public library counterparts and with churches, municipal and state agencies, and other organizations that have frequent contact with the public. They will provide new electronic health information services for all citizens in a community, from middle schools serving low-income and educationally underserved students to shopping malls and senior centers. There are special outreach projects to underserved groups such as Native Americans and isolated rural populations.

Exhibitions

Late in 2002 NLM installed "Dream Anatomy," an exhibition focusing on anatomy, medicine, and the artistic imagination. The exhibition, which will run through July 2003, features rare anatomical books and illustrations from the NLM collection, as well as 20th and 21st century art, holograms, and interactive displays that draw upon the Visible Human Project datasets (described in detail below).The *New York Times, Washington Post, Lancet,* and *Journal of the American Medical Association,* among other publications, have carried extensive stories about the exhibition.

The next major exhibition at NLM will be "Changing the Face of Medicine: The Rise of America's Women Physicians," scheduled to open in fall 2003.

"Frankenstein: Penetrating the Secrets of Nature," a popular exhibition created by and originally displayed at NLM several years ago, has been re-created in a traveling version that the American Library Association (ALA) is showing around the country with funding from the National Endowment for the Humanities. ALA solicited proposals from public, academic, and medical libraries interested in hosting the exhibit and was surprised by the high number of applications. Beginning in fall 2002, four copies of the exhibit were being shown at more than

80 libraries. Hosting libraries present a variety of public programs related to science, medicine, and the humanities in conjunction with the exhibit. Rutgers University Press published the catalog of the exhibition.

NLM worked with the British Library to add Vesalius's *De Humani Corporis Fabrica* to "Turning the Pages," a program developed by the British Library that uses computer animation, high-quality digitized images, and touch-screen technology to simulate that action of turning the pages of rare books. Both the original work by Vesalius and the "Turning the Pages" version, augmented with interactive links to additional related resources such as the Visible Humans, are featured in the "Dream Anatomy" exhibition. "Turning the Pages"—with *De Humani Corporis Fabrica* and a second rare book, Elizabeth Blackwell's *A Curious Herbal*—is on display in the NLM Visitors Center and in the History of Medicine Reading Room. Several more rare volumes will be added.

Research and Development

NLM remains on the cutting edge of research and development in medical informatics—the intersection of computer technology and the health sciences. It does this both through a program of grants and contracts to university-based researchers and through research and development conducted by NLM's own scientists. The library was a leader in the High Performance Computing and Communications initiative of the 1990s and is working to ensure that the health sciences are prepared to take full advantage of the Next Generation Internet. The library has two R&D components: the National Center for Biotechnology Information and the Lister Hill National Center for Biomedical Communications.

R&D conducted by the library has resulted in many advances in biomedical communications—the original development of MEDLINE in the late 1960s, document preservation techniques, innovative methods of providing copies of journal articles to remote users, development of the Unified Medical Language System, sophisticated databases and algorithms for searching gene sequences, and projects related to telemedicine and to the development of an electronic patient record.

Visible Human Project

One project that has been much reported in the media is the Visible Human Project, the creation of two immense (50-gigabyte) data sets, one male and one female, of anatomical MRI, CT, and photographic cryosection images. These data sets, licensed to more than 1,700 individuals and institutions in 43 countries, are being used in a wide range of educational, diagnostic, treatment planning, virtual reality, artistic, mathematical, and industrial applications. A Web site version of a head and neck atlas titled "Functional Anatomy of the Visible Human: Version 1.0, The Head and Neck," has been developed with support by NLM. The atlas is designed in educational modules covering the topics of mastication, deglutition, phonation, facial expression, extraocular motion, and hearing. A number of tools have been developed for using the atlas, including basic anatomical structure identification, a model builder, orthogonal plane browser, and links to the PubMed Web site for automatic keyword searches of the literature.

National Digital Mammography Archive

In the area of telemedicine, NLM has funded the National Digital Mammography Archive as part of the Next Generation Internet initiative. Under this program, doctors at four university hospitals can retrieve and view digital mammography images online. The hospitals each hope to save up to $1 million a year by not having to depend on film. If this project succeeds, the hope is to extend it to hospitals throughout the nation. Because the digital images are large files, the total volume of data being transferred would be staggering and would constitute a real challenge for "next generation" data networks.

Scalable Information Infrastructure

The newest initiative is to develop a Scalable Information Infrastructure. The purpose is to encourage the development of health-related applications of scalable, network-aware, wireless, geographic information systems and identification technologies in a networked environment. The initiative focuses on situations that require or greatly benefit from the application of these technologies in health care, medical decision making, public health, large-scale health emergencies, health education, and biomedical, clinical, and health services research. Projects must involve the use of test-bed networks linking one or more of the following: hospitals, clinics, health practitioners' offices, patients' homes, health professional schools, medical libraries, universities, medical research centers and laboratories, or public health authorities. NLM is reviewing a number of applications for support and will make awards in 2003.

GenBank

In the area of molecular biology, NLM's National Center for Biotechnology Information creates and maintains systems for storing, analyzing, and retrieving information on molecular biology and genetics. The center produces the largest database of public DNA sequence information, GenBank. This database is growing rapidly with contributions received from scientists around the world and now contains more than 15 million sequences and more than 14 billion base pairs from more than 100,000 species. It is accessed on the Web 200,000 times each day by some 50,000 researchers.

National Center for Biotechnology Information

In 2002 NLM's National Center for Biotechnology Information (NCBI) introduced a new, clearly written "About NCBI" section to its home page. This is noteworthy because—at a level that can be understood by a lay person—the site introduces researchers, educators, students, and the public to NCBI's role in organizing, analyzing, and disseminating information in the rapidly growing fields of molecular biology and genetics. One popular section is "A Science Primer," which introduces genome mapping, molecular modeling, and other topics. Another is the "Model Organism Guide," which explains key NCBI model-organism resources, mammalian and nonmammalian. "Databases and Tools" gives concise descriptions of all publicly available NCBI resources.

Administration

The director of the National Library of Medicine, Donald A. B. Lindberg, M.D., is guided in matters of policy by a board of regents consisting of 10 appointed and 11 ex officio members. Appointed as regents in 2002 were Ernest L. Carter of Howard University, A. Wallace Conerly, Sr., of the University of Mississippi, and Thomas Detre of the University of Pittsburgh. The most urgent subject discussed by the regents continues to be the need for more space for the library's increasing collections and the expanding programs associated with NCBI.

Table 1 / Selected NLM Statistics*

Library Operation	Volume
Collection (book and nonbook)	7,255,000
Items cataloged	21,400
Serial titles received	20,350
Articles indexed for MEDLINE	502,000
Circulation requests processed	711,900
For interlibrary loan	373,300
For on-site users	338,600
Computerized searches (all databases)	382,000,000
Budget authority	$283,792,000
Staff	684

*For the year ending September 30, 2002

United States Government Printing Office

North Capitol and H Sts. N.W., Washington, DC 20401
202-512-1991
E-mail asherman@gpo.gov
World Wide Web http://www.gpo.gov

Andrew M. Sherman
Director, Office of Congressional and Public Affairs

The Government Printing Office (GPO) is part of the legislative branch of the federal government and operates under the authority of the public printing and documents chapters of Title 44 of the U.S. Code. Created primarily to satisfy the printing needs of Congress, today GPO is the focal point for printing, binding, and information dissemination for the entire federal community. In addition to Congress, approximately 130 federal departments and agencies—representing more than 6,000 government units—rely on GPO's services. Congressional documents, Supreme Court decisions, federal regulations and reports, IRS tax forms, and U.S. passports are all produced by or through GPO.

Traditionally, GPO's mission was accomplished through production and procurement of ink-on-paper printing. Today, after more than a generation of experience with electronic printing systems, GPO is at the forefront in providing government information through a wide range of formats, including printing, microfiche, CD-ROM, and online technology through GPO Access (http://www.gpo.gov/gpoaccess).

GPO's central office facility is in Washington, D.C. Nationwide, GPO maintains 14 regional printing procurement offices; six satellite procurement facilities; a field printing office; a major distribution facility in Pueblo, Colorado; a nationwide network of bookstores; and a retail sales outlet at its publications warehouse in Laurel, Maryland.

This report focuses on GPO's role as the disseminator of government information in print and electronic formats.

Superintendent of Documents

GPO's documents programs, overseen by the Superintendent of Documents, disseminate one of the world's largest volumes of informational literature. In fiscal year (FY) 2002 GPO distributed 30,538,671 government publications in tangible print, microform, and electronic formats. In addition, approximately 31 million documents were downloaded each month from GPO Access. With the average size of these documents at about 49 kilobytes, and 2 kilobytes equaling roughly one typewritten page, the average size of a document retrieved from GPO Access was about 24.5 typewritten pages. The cost was less than a cent per retrieval.

Library Programs Service

The Library Programs Service (LPS) administers two major programs: the Federal Depository Library Program (FDLP) and the Cataloging and Indexing Program

(C&IP). In addition, it manages the distribution component of the International Exchange Program of the Library of Congress.

LPS achieves its mission to provide timely, permanent, no-fee public access to federal government publications by

- Coordinating a network of libraries that assist the public in using FDLP collections of government publications
- Creating and maintaining tools to identify, describe, locate, and obtain publications
- Maintaining permanent collections of government publications

These functions are accomplished through the basic operations of LPS:

- Acquiring, classifying, and cataloging government publications in all formats
- Disseminating government publications in all formats
- Assuring permanent public access to all publications in FDLP collections, with particular attention to archiving online government publications
- Inspecting depository libraries for compliance with statutory requirements
- Providing continuing education and training opportunities to depository library personnel

About 60 percent of new FDLP titles distributed to libraries or made directly accessible to the public are available online.

Changes for LPS in 2003 include revamping the workforce to deal with the challenges of electronic information and moving toward the acquisition of an integrated library system (ILS).

FDLP Publication Dissemination

Government publications are generally furnished to federal depository libraries solely in online electronic format. However, the 43 publications on the list of "Essential Titles for Public Use in Paper Format" and other titles meeting certain criteria will be distributed as paper publications as long as they are published in that format.

Table 1 / Distribution of Publications by FDLP, FY 2001–2002

Medium	FY 2001	FY 2002
Online (GPO Access)	15,235	10,931
Online (other agency sites)	7,630	9,654
Paper (includes USGS maps)	9,522	8,307
Microfiche	4,726	5,525
CD-ROM, DVD	480	483
Total	37,593	34,900

Cataloging: Gateway to the E-FDLP

With the advent of a more-electronic FDLP, the LPS cataloging staff has expanded the range of its cataloging and locator services efforts, moving beyond the traditional *Monthly Catalog* as its principal output. Cataloging now also functions as a gateway for bringing online titles into the FDLP electronic collection and then disseminating them under the program's auspices. The Cataloging and Indexing Program provides access to online as well as tangible resources through bibliographic control. GPO's online catalog can be searched at http://www.access.gpo.gov/catalog.

Federal Depository Libraries

Fifty-two regional federal depository libraries, roughly one per state, receive copies of every physical title disseminated by LPS and maintain those copies in perpetuity. Regional depositories back up the other depositories in their service areas to answer inquiries, supply copies of desired publications, and provide advice and expertise on depository operations.

A total of 1,236 selective depository libraries choose the kinds of publications they wish to receive based on the needs of their local constituencies. A selective library must retain the publications it selects for a minimum of five years, and may then dispose of those publications, subject to the statutory requirements and directions of their regional library.

LPS is moving toward approval of electronic-only depository library collections through a pilot project that will run through fall 2003. If approved, "virtual" depositories could select only those items available in online format and still maintain their status in the FDLP system. LPS is working with several institutions to develop an evaluative framework to ascertain the needs of their immediate user communities and congressional districts.

Information Withdrawn from FDLP

In the aftermath of the September 11, 2001, terrorist attacks, several agencies reviewed their public information based on a heightened need for national security. GPO takes seriously any federal agency's request to restrict access to government information previously made public. However, GPO has a duty under the law to cooperate with federal agencies in the appropriate distribution of the official information they publish. Since the terrorist attacks, only one agency has requested that the Superintendent of Documents withdraw a document from depository libraries. All agency withdrawal requests are handled in accordance with law and established policy.

New FDLP Promotional Campaign

A GPO working group has developed an updated marketing strategy to increase awareness of FDLP among various constituencies. The new marketing plan features the theme "U.S. Government Information: Make the Connection at a Federal Depository Library."

GPO has produced posters, bookmarks, brochures, and other FDLP promotional materials aimed primarily at reaching the various constituencies via the library community. One- and two-column filler articles and a radio spot have been made available to the media. Librarians can request new posters, bookmarks, brochures, advertisements, and other FDLP promotional materials from the FDLP Desktop Web site at http://www.access.gpo.gov/su_docs/fdlp/pr/order.html.

Digital Archiving

GPO has always guaranteed permanent public access to physical products in the FDLP via the regional depository libraries, and is equally committed to such access for online products.

LPS uses three approaches to providing permanent public access:

- Digital archiving using partner sites through contractual partnership agreements with depository libraries and/or publishing agencies
- Digital archiving on GPO servers
- Developing a processing tool kit of software for archiving digital objects and an off-site archival storage capability with the Online Computer Library Center, Inc. (OCLC)

GPO and OCLC have completed the first phases of testing a system to locate, identify, process, describe, and archive electronic publications. The Web Document Digital Archive Pilot Project includes several other partners, including the state libraries of Connecticut, Michigan, Arizona, and Ohio, and the University of Edinburgh in Scotland. The system incorporates a mix of new and existing solutions in an effort to refine and integrate LPS workflow and routines for processing and storing e-titles for the long term.

Partnerships

A guiding principle for LPS is that a system of shared responsibility for building capacity, storing, disseminating, and preserving government information will produce the greatest benefit in return for resources invested. The goal of establishing partnerships with agencies, depository libraries, and other organizations builds on the successful model of FDLP sharing responsibility for access and preservation.

Partnerships take various forms. Six libraries provide services or tools for locating government information or managing depository library collections. Nine partners manage content with specific permanent public access safeguards contractually defined. Among these are depository libraries, including the University of Illinois at Chicago, which hosts Department of State material; Indiana University, which hosts an online server for publications previously distributed in FDLP on unstable floppy disk media; and the University of North Texas, which houses the Cybercemetery, a site that collects and preserves the Web sites of government agencies and commissions that have ceased operation. Several government agencies, including the National Renewable Energy Laboratory and the National Library of Medicine, maintain agreements through which GPO is assured that Web content will be maintained on agency servers permanently while relieving GPO of the burden of capturing and archiving their content.

In late 2002 the U.S. Census Bureau, GPO, and the Case Western Reserve University Libraries (CWRU) began a content partnership. CWRU will operate a site specifically geared to depository libraries offering the 2000 Census Summary Files for download by file transfer protocol (ftp).

Outreach and Continuing Education

In 2003 LPS staff will attend and make presentations at the major library association conferences as well as at state and regional meetings. LPS also hosts the Depository Library Council to the Public Printer meetings, which will be held in Reno, Nevada, in April 2003 and in Arlington, Virginia, in October. The annual Federal Depository Conference is held in conjunction with the fall council meeting. Its proceedings are posted at http://www.access.gpo.gov/su_docs/fdlp/pubs/proceedings.

Council meetings and the conference provide information on new federal information products, especially new electronic products, as well as discussions on wide-ranging topics of interest to the depository library community.

LPS also hosts the annual six-day Interagency Depository Seminar, scheduled for May 27–June 4, 2003, at which LPS staff and information professionals from a variety of federal agencies train newly appointed depository library staff in the use of government information products.

GPO Access

GPO Access (http://www.gpo.gov/gpoaccess) provides free public access to electronic information products from all three branches of the federal government, as established by the Government Printing Office Electronic Information Access Enhancement Act of 1993 (P.L. 103-40). GPO Access now contains almost 2,800 separate databases in more than 80 applications. The dynamic GPO Access collection now totals more than 234,000 titles: approximately 142,000 titles on its servers and more than 92,000 titles through links to other federal government Web sites.

Additions and Improvements to Web Pages and Applications

For each new year or session of Congress, new databases, such as the 2002 Federal Register database, are added to existing applications on GPO Access. Several other applications were also made available in FY 2002, and improvements were made to the way users find and retrieve documents. The following is a list of significant enhancements to the Web site:

- *Cannon's Precedents of the House of Representatives* is a comprehensive study of the precedents of the House from 1908 to 1936 by Clarence Cannon, Clerk at the Speaker's Table. These documents are the second half of an 11-volume series containing selected rulings made by the chair between 1789 and 1936. Volumes 1 to 5 are titled *Hinds' Precedents of the House of Representatives* and were published in 1907. *Cannon's Precedents,* volumes 6 to 11, were published in 1936.

- *Riddick's Senate Procedure: Precedents and Procedures* is the revised edition of the Senate Procedure: Precedents and Procedures last published in 1981. More than 1,000 procedures and precedents have been researched, analyzed, and incorporated into the previous edition to produce this volume. This edition contains all current precedents and related standing rules and statutory provisions through the end of the 101st Congress.
- Two Independent Counsel Reports were released via GPO Access: *Final Report of the Independent Counsel In Re: Madison Guaranty Savings & Loan Association Regarding Monica Lewinsky and Others* and *The Final Report of the Independent Counsel In Re: Madison Guaranty Savings & Loan Association (The Madison Guaranty/Whitewater Investigation).*
- Changes were made to the Senate, House, and Executive Reports application on GPO Access. The application now includes the ability to search within a single Congress or across multiple Congresses.

New Hosted Web Sites

GPO hosts Web sites for 19 federal agencies as well as a number of online federal publications. Recent additions include

U.S. Capitol Police. The mission of the U.S. Capitol Police is to provide the congressional community and visitors with a full range of police services. The organization was created by Congress in 1898. The site offers information on career opportunities with the organization, such as minimum requirements, benefits, and basic training. Those interested in becoming a U.S. Capitol police officer can register online for the entry-level examination.

Millennial Housing Commission. This commission was created in September 2000 and was terminated in August 2002. Its mission was to identify, analyze, and develop recommendations that highlight the importance of housing, improve the housing delivery system, and provide affordable housing for the American people, including recommending possible legislative and regulatory initiatives.

Office of Independent Counsel Donald C. Smaltz—In Re: Secretary of Agriculture Alphonso Michael Espy. This site includes information solely on the investigation involving matters relating to former Secretary of Agriculture Alphonso Michael Espy.

U.S. Government Online Bookstore

In FY 2002 a number of enhancements were made to the U.S. Government Online Bookstore, available through GPO Access at http://bookstore.gpo.gov. These enhancements improved customers' ability to locate and purchase sales publications, as well as the quality of services received by customers using e-commerce.

The various applications on the Online Bookstore have been integrated so that customers can easily navigate between search and browse applications, add items to their shopping carts, and submit orders online. For instance, customers can now perform a search in the Sales Product Catalog (SPC) database, add an item to their shopping cart, and then go to the Browse a Topic page and search for additional items. Additionally, enhancements have been made so that the browse applications (such as the Browse a Topic pages, CD-ROM list, and Subscriptions Catalog) that exist on static HTML Web pages now work with existing servers to pull current price and availability status on a daily basis. Also, while the Online Bookstore has safeguarded a customer's personal information through online encryption since 1999, the service was recently changed so that users do not have to enter a secure environment until they have finished shopping and must enter personal information to complete their orders.

Each shopping cart is assigned a unique GPO order number that customers can use when contacting GPO's Order Division with questions about their orders. Also, a detailed transaction receipt is provided after each order submission and a copy of the transaction receipt is sent to the customer's e-mail address if the address has been provided on the online order form. In addition, customers can now choose the American Express payment option when placing orders online.

Future enhancements planned for the Online Bookstore include improved online ordering for international customers, providing third-party handoff orders for those who are unable to directly purchase from the U.S. Government Online Bookstore, and enabling customers to request special shipping options (e.g., Federal Express) online when they place their orders. Additionally, plans are under way to hire a consultant to assist GPO in developing a business case for procuring an e-commerce software solution for the "next generation" of the U.S. Government Online Bookstore.

Audio E-book

In FY 2002 GPO worked closely with the U.S. General Services Administration (GSA) to publish an audio e-book version of the Federal Architecture and Infrastructure Committee of the U.S. Chief Information Officers (CIO) Council publication *Extending Digital Dividends: Public Goods and Services That Work for All.* The audio e-book on CD-ROM accompanied the print publication and was the first e-book available for sale through the Superintendent of Documents and distributed through FDLP.

STAT-USA Partnership with the Department of Commerce

STAT-USA, an agency in the Economics and Statistics Administration, U.S. Department of Commerce, delivers vital economic, business, and international trade information produced by the U.S. government. GPO worked with STAT-USA to improve the availability and usability of information in the depository community, including free access to all federal depository libraries. To further assist the depository community, GPO and STAT-USA staff members worked together in creating a special insert for the GPO Access Training Manual. The project has given GPO staff the necessary instruction and knowledge base to conduct successful training on and promotion of STAT-USA.

Promotional Publications

Throughout FY 2002 changes were made to the GPO Access Training Manual in addition to the special insert covering STAT-USA. All updates to the manual are posted on the GPO Access help page. More than 30 pages were changed, including URL updates; new diagrams for tracking legislation, regulations, and federal publications; and updated U.S. Government Online Bookstore information.

GPO Access staff designed and developed new promotional publications containing information about the various products and services of GPO Access, the U.S. Government Online Bookstore, and Ben's Guide to U.S. Government for Kids. The publications were designed to function both as brochures and promotional/instructional posters. They are primarily distributed at trade shows and conferences, but copies are also available to federal depository libraries, members of Congress, and other interested parties.

Finding Aids

GPO Access provides a number of free tools to assist users in searching or browsing for government information. GPO Access Finding Aids act as a portal to information available on government Web sites. They can be used to conduct government-wide searches, locate government publications online and in print, and find agency Web sites based on broad subject areas. A complete list of finding aids can be found at http://www.gpo.gov/gpoaccess/tools.html.

GPO Access Redesign

Since the redesign of GPO Access in April 1999, GPO has been collecting user feedback by various methods—usability testing, focus groups, surveys, and comments received by the GPO Access User Support Team. As a result, a critical analysis of GPO Access is being conducted in an effort to improve the site's design and functionality.

Usability testing was conducted on current and redesigned GPO Access pages in a dedicated usability lab at the U.S. Department of Labor's Bureau of Labor Statistics. The usability tasks were designed to test the navigation and functionality of a proposed new look and feel for GPO Access pages. Two rounds of testing were conducted with federal depository librarians and the general public. The sessions were videotaped and observed, and analyses of the tapes were conducted. Valuable feedback was gained and, based on the suggestions received, adjustments were made to the new look and feel.

Search Engine Reports

One of the most popular ways for users to find the resources available via GPO Access is through major Internet search engines and directories. As a result, GPO is working to improve the visibility of GPO Access pages in such engines and directories. The eighth search engine report was completed in October 2002. Based on the current keywords and criteria being used, this report revealed that search engines are doing better at indexing GPO Access pages than previously.

Since the last iteration of the search engine report, research was conducted on the latest trends in the search engine industry. This research is necessary to further the goals of the reports and to make the findings reflect actual usage. Information gathered during the research process has led to a modification of the baseline reports. This modification will include several areas of consideration, including the removal of any search engines that are no longer operating their own directories (such as Excite and WebCrawler). Other search engines will be added to supplement the current list of engines examined in the evaluations, such as Teoma, Wisenut, and other engines that are new or have gained popularity.

In addition to the modification of the list of search engines, the keywords used will be altered to more accurately reflect current usage. Information from Web logs, user surveys, and other resources, such as the Overture Search Term Suggestion Tool (service provided on http://www.overture.com), will provide adequate data on what search terms and search engines are being used to find GPO Access and associated applications.

The report is available via the Federal Bulletin Board at http://fedbbs.access. gpo.gov/access.htm under GPO Access Search Engine Project Report. The next iteration of this report will be completed in 2003.

GPOLISTSERV

Users can register to receive e-mail notification when new publications become available for sale from the Superintendent of Documents through the "New Titles by Topic E-mail Alert Service." Anyone can sign up for one or more of the following lists free of charge: business publications, elementary and secondary education, defense and security, health care, military history, federal statistics, employment and occupations, and travel and tourism. Additionally, in response to the depository library community's request, the FDLP "Electronic Only Titles Available for Sale" list is now available. This list enables subscribers to receive notification when federal depository library publications have migrated to an electronic format and are available for purchase in tangible format from the U.S. Government Online Bookstore. Additional lists will be added in the future.

Training Classes, Demonstrations, and Trade Shows

The continued and rapid growth of GPO Access translated into a number of requests for training classes, demonstrations, and trade shows to educate users about electronic products and services available through the Superintendent of Documents. By combining multiple activities in the course of one trip, GPO was able to cover the widest possible geographic area within budget constraints. Recent sessions were conducted in Morgantown, West Virginia; Charleston, South Carolina; New Brunswick, New Jersey; Palm Springs, California; and Salt Lake City, Utah.

Methods of Access

To serve a large base of users with varying technological capabilities, GPO Access supports a wide range of information dissemination technologies, from the latest Internet applications to dial-up modem access. Methods compatible with technologies to assist users affected by the Americans with Disabilities Act are also available. To accommodate people without computers, nearly 1,300 federal depository libraries throughout the country have public-access workstations for GPO Access usage.

Section 508

In 1998 President Clinton signed the Workforce Investment Act into law. This act amended Section 508 of the Rehabilitation Act of 1973 to include accessibility requirements for electronic and information technology. Section 508 now requires that electronic and information technology used by the federal government, including its Web sites, be made as accessible for people with disabilities as it is for people without disabilities. GPO continues to ensure that existing pages on GPO Access are Section 508-compliant and that future pages will be created specifically with these accessibility standards in mind.

GPO Access Usage Statistics

GPO uses document retrievals for gauging Web site usage because they represent units of actual content delivered to users. Document retrievals indicate the number of downloads both of documents within databases and files outside databases that have been identified as containing government information content. The more than 33 million retrievals in March 2002 propelled total usage of GPO Access to more than 1.5 billion documents retrieved since the service premiered in 1994. The average number of monthly retrievals from GPO Access measures more than 1.5 terabytes in size and is equivalent to more than 759 million typewritten pages.

Recognition

The success of GPO Access is evident not only in usage statistics, but also in commendations that GPO Access received from organizations, publications, and other Web sites.

The GPO E-mail Alert Service was noted in the National Coordinating Committee Washington Update. As noted in the *NCC Washington Update,* Vol. 8, No. 7, February 19, 2002, by Bruce Craig of the National Coordinating Committee for the Promotion of History (NCCPH)

> GPO Announces E-mail Alert Service: The U.S. Government Printing Office has initiated a program, New Titles by Topic E-mail Alert Service, that allows users of government documents the advantage of notification when new publications are released and available to the public. This new service is a convenient way for scholars, historians, and others to find out about the latest military history publications from the U.S. Government. Subscribers can receive free e-mail announcements on new military history publications from all branches of the armed forces. Military history publications include valuable reading material, posters, and CD-ROMs on military topics ranging from the American Revolution through the Vietnam War. Additional information is available by joining a free online service at: http://bookstore.gpo.gov/alertservice.html. Readers may also want to visit the complete military history collection at the U.S. Online Government Bookstore at http://bookstore.gpo.gov/sb/sb-098.html.

The Catalog of U.S. Government Publications was mentioned in *PC World* magazine, July 2002, in the article titled "Search Gems: Sites for Special Searches":

> **Gov granddaddy.** This catalog of U.S. government publications might overwhelm you with information. The Web site has copies of all federal agency reports from 1994.

The complete *PC World* article is available at http://www.pcworld.com/features/article/0,aid,97431,pg,13,00.asp.

User Support

The GPO Access User Support Team provides assistance to GPO Access users via e-mail, phone, and fax. User Support Team members answer inquiries about GPO's electronic products, provide assistance in searching for and locating federal information products, and offer technical support for these products. On average, the team received more than 6,000 inquiries a month during FY 2002.

The team's hours of availability are Monday through Friday, 7:00 A.M. to 5:30 P.M., EST, except federal holidays. The team can be reached by e-mail, phone, or fax: e-mail gpoaccess@gpo.gov, telephone 888-293-6498 (toll-free) or 202-512-1530, fax 202-512-1262

Ben's Guide to U.S. Government for Kids

Ben's Guide to U.S. Government for kids (http://bensguide.gpo.gov) is a free service of GPO's Superintendent of Documents. As the educational component of GPO Access, Ben's Guide strives to introduce and explain the workings of the three branches of the federal government. Through the use of primary source materials, grade-appropriate explanations, and a stimulating site design, Ben's Guide not only increases the public's access to and knowledge of the federal government, but also is intended to make learning fun.

The site is broken down into four grade levels—K–2, 3–5, 6–8, and 9–12—and also provides an area for parents and educators. The material in each of these sections is specifically tailored to its intended audience. Ben's Guide includes resources such as historical documents and information on the legislative and regulatory processes, elections, and citizenship. The site also features learning activities and a list of federal Web sites designed for students, parents, and educators.

Sales

The Superintendent of Documents' sales program currently offers approximately 9,000 government publications on a wide array of subjects. These are sold principally via mail, telephone, fax, electronic and e-mail orders, and through GPO bookstores. The program operates on a cost-recovery basis. Publications for sale include books, forms, posters, pamphlets, maps, CD-ROMs, computer diskettes, and magnetic tapes. Subscription services for both dated periodicals and basic-and-supplement services (involving an initial volume and supplemental issues) are also offered.

Express service, which includes priority handling and Federal Express delivery, is available for orders placed by telephone for domestic delivery. Orders placed before noon EST for in-stock publications and single-copy subscriptions will be delivered within two working days. Some quantity restrictions apply. Call the telephone order desk using the toll-free number 866-512-1800 (202-512-1800 within the Washington, D.C., area) for more information.

Consumer-oriented publications are also either sold or distributed at no charge through the Consumer Information Center, in Pueblo, Colorado, which GPO operates on behalf of the General Services Administration.

New Sales Program Products

The sales program continues its efforts to conclude cooperative ventures to obtain, promote, and sell products not printed or procured by GPO, as well as products produced by federal agencies in cooperation with other parties. Ongoing projects with the Department of Commerce's Bureau of Export Administration, the Central Intelligence Agency, the Defense Acquisition Agency, the Department of State, the Library of Congress, the National Imaging and Mapping Agency, and the General Services Administration are continuing. Ventures under development include new partnerships with the Patent and Trademark Office.

Product Information

The U.S. Government Online Bookstore (http://bookstore.gpo.gov) is the single point of access for all government information products available for sale from GPO. A search interface with the Sales Product Catalog, a guide to current government information products offered for sale through the Superintendent of Documents and updated every working day, is part of the main page interface. Advanced search options are also available. Another feature on the main page is a "pop-up box" that enables customers to "Browse a Topic." This list of topics is based on the approximately 160 Subject Bibliographies available through the online bookstore. Customers can also browse the Special Collections on the U.S. Government Online Bookstore, including CD-ROMs, electronic products, the subscriptions catalog, and the Federal Consumer Information Center. Special collections include a list of federal tax products, emergency response publications, and a catalog of regulatory and legal publications. The Online Bookstore also provides information on the locations of GPO bookstores and complete ordering information.

Items purchased from the U.S. Government Online Bookstore are now assigned a unique GPO Order Number. Customers can reference this number when contacting GPO's Order Division with questions about their order. A detailed transaction receipt is provided after each order submission, and a copy of the transaction receipt is sent to the customer's e-mail address if provided on the online order form. In addition, customers can now choose the American Express payment option when ordering, in addition to VISA, MasterCard, and Discover/Novus.

GPO publishes a variety of free print catalogs covering hundreds of information products for sale on a vast array of subjects. The free catalogs include

- U.S. Government Information: new and popular information products of interest to the general public
- New Products: listing of new titles; distributed to librarians and other information professionals
- U.S. Government Subscriptions: periodicals and other subscription services

- Subject Bibliographies (SBs): approximately 160 lists, each containing titles relating to a single subject or field of interest
- Subject Bibliography Index: lists all SB subject areas
- Catalog of Information Products for Business: GPO's main catalog for business audiences

U.S. Government Subscriptions and Subject Bibliographies are also available via the Internet at http://www.access.gpo.gov/su_docs.

Customers can also register to receive e-mail updates when new publications become available for sale from the Superintendent of Documents through the New Titles by Topic E-mail Alert Service. Anyone can sign up for one or more of the lists free of charge. This service can be found at http://bookstore.gpo.gov/alertservice.html.

The sales program also lists its titles on Amazon.com, Barnesandnoble.com, and other online commercial book-selling sites.

GPO Bookstores

Publications of particular public interest are made available in GPO bookstores located in major cities throughout the United States. In addition, any bookstore can order any government information product currently offered for sale by the Superintendent of Documents and have it sent directly to a customer. Customers can order from any GPO bookstore by phone, mail, or fax. The addresses, hours, and a map of all bookstores currently in operation are available on GPO's Web site.

National Technical Information Service

Technology Administration
U.S. Department of Commerce, Springfield, VA 22161
800-553-NTIS (6847) or 703-605-6000
World Wide Web http://www.ntis.gov

Linda Davis
Marketing Communications

The National Technical Information Service (NTIS) serves as the nation's largest central source and primary disseminator of scientific, technical, engineering, and business information produced or sponsored by U.S. and international government sources. NTIS is a federal agency within the Technology Administration of the U.S. Department of Commerce.

Since 1945 the NTIS mission has been to operate a central U.S. government access point for scientific and technical information useful to American industry and government. NTIS maintains a permanent archive of this declassified information for researchers, businesses, and the public to access quickly and easily. Release of the information is intended to promote American economic growth and development and increase U.S. competitiveness in the world market.

The NTIS collection of approximately 3 million titles contains products available in various formats. Such information includes reports describing research conducted or sponsored by federal agencies and their contractors, statistical and business information, U.S. military publications, multimedia training programs, computer software and electronic databases developed by federal agencies, and technical reports prepared by research organizations worldwide. Approximately 60,000 new titles are added and indexed annually. NTIS maintains a permanent repository of its information products.

More than 200 U.S. government agencies contribute to the NTIS collection including the National Aeronautics and Space Agency, the Environmental Protection Agency, the Departments of Agriculture, Commerce, Defense, Energy, Health and Human Services, Interior, Labor, Treasury, Veterans Affairs, Housing and Urban Development, Education, Transportation, and numerous other agencies. International contributors include Canada, Japan, Britain, and several other European countries.

NTIS E-Government Virtual Library

NTIS offers Web-based access to the latest government scientific and technical research information products. Visitors to http://www.ntis.gov can search more than 750,000 NTIS database records dating back to 1990, free of charge. The new NTIS e-government initiative also provides links to documents at other government agency Web sites; downloading capability for technical reports, many free of charge, others for a nominal fee; and purchase of publications on customized CD-ROMs.

NTIS Database

The NTIS Database (listings of information products acquired by NTIS since 1964) offers unparalleled bibliographic coverage of U.S. government and world-wide government-sponsored research. Its contents represent hundreds of billions of research dollars and cover a range of important topics including agriculture, biotechnology, business, communication, energy, engineering, the environment, health and safety, medicine, research and development, science, space, technology, and transportation.

Most records include abstracts. Database summaries describe technical reports, data files, multimedia/training programs, and software. These titles are often unique to NTIS and generally are difficult to locate from any other source. The complete NTIS Database provides instant access to more than 2 million records.

Free 30-day trials of the NTIS Database are available through the GOV. Research_Center (http://grc.ntis.gov). The NTIS Database can be leased directly from NTIS, and can also be accessed through the following commercial services: Cambridge Scientific Abstracts, 800-843-7751, http://www.csa.com; DATA-STAR (DIALOG), 800-334-2564, http://www.dialog.com; EBSCO, 800-653-2726, http://www.epnet.com; Knowledge EXPRESS, 800-529-5337, http://www.knowledgeexpress.com; NERAC, 860-872-7000, http://www.nerac.com; Ovid Technologies, 800-950-2035, http://www.ovid.com; Questel-Orbit, 800-456-7248, http://www.questel.orbit.com; SilverPlatter Information, 800-343-0064, http://www.silverplatter.com; and STN International/CAS, 800-848-6533, http://www.cas.org. To access an updated list of organizations offering NTIS Database products, visit the NTIS Web site at http://www.ntis.gov/products/types/databases/commercial.asp.

To lease the NTIS Database directly from NTIS, contact the NTIS Subscriptions Department at 800-363-2068 or 703-605-6060. For more information, see http://www.ntis.gov/products/types/databases/ntisdb.asp.

Other Databases Available from NTIS

NTIS offers several valuable research-oriented database products.

FEDRIP

The Federal Research in Progress database (FEDRIP) provides access to information about ongoing federally funded projects in the fields of the physical sciences, engineering, and life sciences. FEDRIP's uniqueness lies in its structure as a nonbibliographic information source of research in progress. Project descriptions generally include project title, keywords, start date, estimated completion date, principal investigator, performing and sponsoring organizations, summary, and progress report. Record content varies depending on the source agency.

There are many reasons to search FEDRIP. Among these are to avoid research duplication, locate sources of support, identify leads in the literature, stimulate ideas for planning, identify gaps in areas of investigation, and locate individuals with expertise. For more information, see http://www.ntis.gov/products/types/databases/fedrip.asp.

AGRICOLA

One of the most comprehensive sources of U.S. agricultural and life sciences information, the Agricultural Online Access database (AGRICOLA) contains bibliographic records for documents acquired by the U.S. Department of Agriculture's National Agricultural Library (NAL). The complete database dates from 1970 and contains more than 4 million citations to journal articles, monographs, theses, patents, software, audiovisual materials, and technical reports related to agriculture.

AGRICOLA serves as the document locator and bibliographic control system for the NAL collection. The extensive file provides comprehensive coverage of newly acquired worldwide publications in agriculture and related fields. AGRICOLA covers the field of agriculture in the broadest sense. Subject headings include Agricultural Economics, Agricultural Education, Agricultural Products, Animal Science, Aquaculture, Biotechnology, Botany, Cytology, Energy, Engineering, Feed Science, Fertilizers, Fibers and Textiles, Food and Nutrition, Forestry, Horticulture, Human Ecology, Human Nutrition, Hydrology, Hydroponics, Microbiology, Natural Resources, Pesticides, Physiology, Plant and Animal, Plant Sciences, Public Health, Rural Sociology, Soil Sciences, Veterinary Medicine, and Water Quality. For more information on AGRICOLA, see http://www.ntis.gov/products/types/databases/agricola.asp.

AGRIS

The Agricultural Science and Technology database (AGRIS) depends on a cooperative system for collecting and disseminating information on the world's agricultural literature. More than 100 national and multinational centers take part in this effort. The information in AGRIS, much of which cannot be found elsewhere, includes government documents, technical reports, and nonconventional literature (documents not commercially available) from both developed and developing countries. References to citations for U.S. publications covered in the AGRICOLA database are not included in AGRIS. References to nonconventional literature contain information on where a copy can be obtained. For more information, see http://www.ntis.gov/products/types/databases/agris.asp.

Energy Science and Technology

The Energy Science and Technology database (EDB) is a multidisciplinary file containing worldwide references to basic and applied scientific and technical research literature. The information is collected for use by government managers, researchers at the national laboratories, and other research efforts sponsored by the U.S. Department of Energy. The results of this research are available to the public. Abstracts are included for records from 1976 to the present. EDB also contains the Nuclear Science Abstracts, a comprehensive abstract and index collection to the international nuclear science and technology literature for the period 1948 to 1976. Included are scientific and technical reports of the U.S. Atomic Energy Commission, U.S. Energy Research and Development Administration and its contractors, other agencies, universities, and industrial and research organizations. Approximately 25 percent of the records in the file contain abstracts. Nuclear Science Abstracts contains more than 900,000 bibliographic records. The entire EDB contains more than 3 million bibliographic records. For more information, see http://www.ntis.gov/products/types/databases/engsci.asp.

Immediately Dangerous to Life or Health Concentrations Database

The NIOSH (National Institute for Occupational Safety and Health) documentation for the Immediately Dangerous to Life or Health Concentrations (IDLHs) database contains air concentration values used by NIOSH as respirator selection criteria. This compilation is the rationale and source of information used by NIOSH during the original determination of 387 IDLHs and their subsequent review and revision in 1994. Toxicologists, persons concerned with use of respirators, industrial hygienists, persons concerned with indoor air quality, and emergency response personnel find this product beneficial. The database enables users to compare NIOSH limits to other limits and is important to those concerned with acute chemical exposures. For more information, see http://www.ntis.gov/products/types/databases/idlhs.asp.

NIOSH Manual of Analytical Methods Database

The NIOSH Manual of Analytical Methods Database (NMAM) is a compilation of methods for sampling and analysis of contaminants in workplace air, and in the bodily fluids of workers who are occupationally exposed to that air. These methods have been developed specifically to have adequate sensitivity to detect the lowest concentrations and sufficient flexibility of range to detect concentrations exceeding safe levels of exposure, as regulated by OSHA and recommended by NIOSH. The Threshold Values and Biological Exposure Indices of the American Conference of Governmental Industrial Hygienists are also cited. For more information, see http://www.ntis.gov/products/types/databases/nmam.asp.

NIOSH Pocket Guide to Chemical Hazards

The NIOSH Pocket Guide to Chemical Hazards (NPG) is intended as a quick and convenient source of general industrial hygiene information for workers, employers, and occupational health professionals. The NIOSH Pocket Guide presents in abbreviated tabular form key information and data on chemicals or substance groupings (such as cyanides, fluorides, and manganese compounds) that are found in the work environment. The industrial hygiene information found in NPG should help users recognize and control occupational chemical hazards. The information in NPG includes chemical structures or formulas, identification codes, synonyms, exposure limits, chemical and physical properties, incompatibilities and reactivities, measurement methods, recommended respirator selections, signs and symptoms of exposure, and procedures for emergency treatment. Industrial hygienists, industrial hygiene technicians, safety professionals, occupational health physicians and nurses, and hazardous material managers will find this database a versatile and indispensable tool. For more information, see http://www.ntis.gov/products/types/databases/npgfacts.asp.

NIOSHTIC

NIOSHTIC is a bibliographic database of literature in the field of occupational safety and health developed by NIOSH. The database has been static since 1998. It contains retrospective information, some dating back to the 19th century. Because NIOSH examines all aspects of adverse effects experienced by workers, much of the information contained in NIOSHTIC has been selected from sources that do not have a primary occupational safety and health orientation. NIOSHTIC subject coverage includes the behavioral sciences; biochemistry, physiology, and metabolism; biological hazards; chemistry; control technology; education and training; epidemiological studies of diseases/disorders; ergonomics; hazardous waste; health physics; occupational medicine; pathology and histology; safety; and toxicology. For more information, see http://www.ntis.gov/products/types/databases/nioshtic.asp.

Registry of Toxic Effects of Chemical Substances Database

The Registry of Toxic Effects of Chemical Substances (RTECS) is a database of toxicological information compiled, maintained, and updated by NIOSH. The program is mandated by the Occupational Safety and Health Act of 1970. The original edition, known as the Toxic Substances List, was published on June 28, 1971, and included toxicological data for approximately 5,000 chemicals. Since that time, the list has continuously grown and been updated. RTECS now contains more than 133,000 chemicals as NIOSH strives to fulfill the mandate to list "all known toxic substances . . . and the concentrations at which . . . toxicity is known to occur." RTECS is a compendium of data extracted from the open scientific literature. The data are recorded in the format developed by the RTECS staff and arranged in alphabetical order by prime chemical name. No attempt has been made to evaluate the studies cited in RTECS; the user has the responsibility of making such assessments. For more information, see http://www.ntis.gov/products/types/databases/rtecs.asp.

Specialized Online Subscriptions

Those wishing to expand their access to subject-specific resources through use of the Internet are likely to benefit from the NTIS online options highlighted below. Online subscriptions offer quick, convenient online access to the most current information available.

Government Research Center

GOV.Research_Center (GRC) is a collection of well-known government-sponsored research databases available on the World Wide Web via an online subscription service. Customers can subscribe to a single GRC database product or to several databases. The following databases made available at GRC by NTIS and the National Information Services Corporation (NISC) are searchable at the site using NISC's search engine Biblioline: NTIS Database, FEDRIP, NIOSHTIC, EDB, Nuclear Science Abstracts, AgroBase, AGRICOLA, and RTECS.

NTIS and NISC are constantly improving the content and features of GRC. Users can search across all databases within a subscription plan using only one search query. Limited day-pass access to the NTIS Database is available for a nominal fee.

For more information on GOV.Research_Center, see http://grc.ntis.gov.

World News Connection

World News Connection (WNC) is an NTIS online news service via the Internet. WNC provides English-language translations of time-sensitive news and information from thousands of non-U.S. media. Particularly effective in its coverage of local media, WNC provides the power to identify what is happening in a specific country or region. The information is obtained from speeches, television and radio broadcasts, newspaper articles, periodicals, and books, and the subject matter focuses on socioeconomic, political, scientific, technical, and environmental issues and events.

The information in WNC is provided to NTIS by the Foreign Broadcast Information Service (FBIS), a U.S. government agency. For more than 60 years, analysts from FBIS's domestic and overseas bureaus have monitored timely and pertinent open-source material, including gray literature. Uniquely, WNC allows subscribers to take advantage of the intelligence-gathering experience of FBIS.

WNC is updated every government-business day. Generally, new information is available within 24 to 72 hours of the time of original publication or broadcast.

Subscribers can conduct unlimited interactive searches and have the ability to set up automated searches known as profiles. When a profile is created, a search is run against WNC's latest news feed to identify articles relevant to a subscriber's area of interest. Once the search is completed, the results are automatically sent to the subscriber's e-mail address.

For WNC pricing and subscription information, see http://wnc.fedworld.gov.

U.S. Export Administration Regulations

The U.S. Export Administration Regulations (EAR) gives exporters the latest rules controlling the export of U.S. dual-use commodities, technology, and software. Step by step, EAR explains when an export license is necessary and when it is not; how to obtain an export license; policy changes as they are issued; new restrictions on exports to certain countries and of certain types of items; and where to obtain further help.

This information is now available through NTIS in three formats: looseleaf, CD-ROM, and online. A new e-mail update notification service is also available. For more information, see http://bxa.fedworld.gov.

Davis-Bacon Wage Determination Database

The Davis-Bacon Wage Determination Database subscription product contains wage determinations issued by the U.S. Department of Labor under the mandate of the Davis-Bacon Act and related legislation. The department determines prevailing wage rates for construction-related occupations in most counties in the United States. All federal government construction contracts and most contracts of more than $2,000 for federally assisted construction must abide by the Davis-Bacon structure. A variety of access plans are available. For more information, see http://davisbacon.fedworld.gov.

Service Contract Act Wage Determination Database

The Service Contract Act Wage Determination Database (SCA) contains unsigned copies of the latest wage determinations developed by the U.S. Department of Labor. These wage determinations, issued by the Wage and Hour Division in response to specific notices filed, set the minimum wage on federally funded service contracts. The database is updated each Tuesday with all wage determinations that were added or revised by the preceding Thursday.

For those federal agencies participating under a memorandum of understanding with the Wage and Hour Division, and meeting all requirements, SCA can be used in the procurement process. For all other users, the wage determinations are for information use only. They are not to be used to set prevailing wage rates on federal service contracts. These data form a convenient and accurate basis upon which rates can be compared by occupation and geography.

A variety of access plans are available. For more information, see http://servicecontract.fedworld.gov.

Special Subscription Services

NTIS Alerts

More than 1,000 new titles are added to the NTIS collection every week. NTIS Alerts were developed in response to requests from customers to search and tap into this fresh information. NTIS prepares a list of search criteria that is run against all new studies and R&D reports in 16 subject areas. An NTIS Alert provides a twice-monthly information briefing service covering a wide range of technology topics.

An NTIS Alert provides numerous benefits: efficient, economical, and timely access to the latest U.S. government technical studies; concise, easy-to-read summaries; information not readily available from any other source; contributions from more than 100 countries; and subheadings within each copy designed to identify essential information quickly.

For more information, call the NTIS Subscriptions Department at 703-605-6060 or see http://www.ntis.gov/new/alerts_printed.asp.

SRIM

Selected Research in Microfiche (SRIM) is an inexpensive, tailored information service that delivers full-text microfiche copies of technical reports based on a customer's needs. Customers choose from Standard SRIM Service (selecting one or more of the 380 existing subject areas) or choose Custom SRIM Service, which creates a new subject area created to meet their particular needs. Custom

SRIM requires a one-time fee; otherwise, the cost of Custom SRIM is the same as the Standard SRIM. Through this ongoing subscription service, customers receive microfiche copies of the new reports, pertaining to their field of interest, as NTIS obtains the reports.

For more information, see http://www.ntis.gov/products /srim.asp. Call the NTIS Subscriptions Department at 800-363-2068 or 703-605-6060 to order a SRIM subscription.

Also at NTIS

National Audiovisual Center

The National Audiovisual Center (NAC) makes the U.S. government's collection of federally sponsored or produced audiovisual and multimedia training and educational programs available to state and local governments, businesses, schools, and universities, as well as private individuals.

NAC's collection includes approximately 9,000 active titles covering 600 subject areas from more than 200 federal agencies. Included in the collection are language training materials, occupational safety and health training materials, fire service and law enforcement training materials, drug education programs for schools and industry, fine arts programs, and documentaries chronicling American history.

Call 703-605-6000 for assistance, or see http://www.ntis.gov/products/types/audiovisual/index.asp.

Federal Computer Products Center

The Federal Computer Products Center was established at NTIS to provide access to information in electronic formats. The current inventory of computer products includes more than 1,200 titles obtained since 1990 from hundreds of U.S. government agencies. They include datafiles and software on diskette, CD-ROM, and magnetic tape. The products cover a range of topics including banking, business, the environment, health care, health statistics, science, and technology. Most of the center's products are developed or sponsored by the federal government. However, NTIS does announce and distribute products developed by state governments and, in a few cases, by private-sector organizations. Examples of some of the center's titles include Stream Corridor Restoration, the SSA Death Master File, EPA Water Testing Methods, FDA's Food Code, North American Industry Classification System (NAICS), and the NOAA Dive Manual.

Full descriptions of the software and data available from NTIS can be found on the center's Web site at http://www.ntis.gov/products/types/computer.asp.

Homeland Security Information Center

NTIS is a resource for scientific and technical information related to homeland security. It provides a Web-based finding aid in the following homeland security categories: health and medicine, food and agriculture, biological and chemical warfare, preparedness and response, and safety training. For more information, see http://www.ntis.gov/hs.

NTIS FedWorld

Since 1992 NTIS FedWorld Information Technologies has served as the online locator service for a comprehensive inventory of information disseminated by the federal government. FedWorld helps federal agencies and the public to electronically locate federal government information, both information housed within the NTIS repository and information FedWorld makes accessible through an electronic gateway to other government agencies.

FedWorld is currently meeting the information needs of tens of thousands of customers daily, maximizing the potential of the Internet and the World Wide Web by offering multiple distribution channels for government agencies to disseminate information. Examples of electronic information available on FedWorld include EPA auto emissions information, federal job searches, and Supreme Court decisions. For more information, see http://www.fedworld.gov.

NTIS Customer Service

NTIS's automated systems keep it at the forefront when it comes to customer service. Electronic document storage is fully integrated with NTIS's order-taking process, which allows it to provide rapid reproduction for the most recent additions to the NTIS document collection. Most orders are filled and delivered anywhere in the United States in five to seven business days. Rush service is available for an additional fee.

Key NTIS Contacts for Ordering

Order by Phone

Sales Desk	800-553-6847
8:00 A.M.–6:00 P.M. Eastern time, Monday–Friday	or 703-605-6000
Subscriptions	800-363-2068
8:30 A.M.–5:00 P.M. Eastern time, Monday–Friday	or 703-605-6060
TDD (hearing impaired only)	703-487-4639
8:30 A.M.–5:00 P.M. Eastern time, Monday–Friday	

Order by Fax

24 hours a day, seven days a week	703-605-6900
To verify receipt of fax, call	703-605-6090
7:00 A.M.–5:00 P.M. Eastern time, Monday–Friday	

Order by Mail

National Technical Information Service
5285 Port Royal Road
Springfield, VA 22161

RUSH Service (available for an additional fee)	800-553-6847
	or 703-605-6000

Note: If requesting RUSH Service, please do not mail your order.

Order Via World Wide Web

Direct and secure online ordering   http://www.ntis.gov

Order Via E-Mail

24 hours a day   orders@ntis.gov

For Internet security, customers placing an order by e-mail can register their credit card in advance. To do so, call 703-605-6070 between 7:00 A.M. and 5:00 P.M. Eastern time, Monday through Friday.

National Archives and Records Administration

8601 Adelphi Rd., College Park, MD 20740
301-837-2000, World Wide Web http://www.archives.gov

Debra W. Leahy
Policy and Communications Staff

The National Archives and Records Administration (NARA), an independent federal agency, ensures for the citizen, the public servant, the president, Congress, and the courts ready access to essential evidence that documents the rights of American citizens, the actions of federal officials, and the national experience.

NARA is singular among the world's archives as a unified federal institution that accessions and preserves materials from all three branches of government. NARA assists federal agencies in documenting their activities, administering records management programs, scheduling records, and retiring noncurrent records to federal records centers. The agency also manages the presidential libraries; assists the National Historical Publications and Records Commission in its grant program for state and local records and edited publications of the papers of prominent Americans; publishes the laws, regulations, presidential documents, and other official notices of the federal government; and oversees classification and declassification policy in the federal government through the Information Security Oversight Office. NARA constituents include the federal government, a history-minded public, the media, the archival community, and a broad spectrum of professional associations and researchers in such fields as history, political science, law, library and information services, and genealogy.

The size and breadth of NARA's holdings are staggering. Together, NARA's facilities hold more than 26 million cubic feet (equivalent to more than 78 billion pieces of paper) of original textual and nontextual materials from the executive, legislative, and judicial branches of the federal government. Its multimedia collections include more than 93,000 motion picture films; nearly 5.7 million maps, charts, and architectural drawings; more than 207,000 sound and video recordings; more than 18 million aerial photographs; nearly 35 million still pictures and posters; and more than 3.7 billion electronic records.

Strategic Directions

NARA's strategic priorities are laid out in *Ready Access to Essential Evidence: The Strategic Plan of the National Archives and Records Administration, 1997–2007,* revised in 2000. Success for the agency as envisioned in the plan will mean reaching four strategic goals:

- Essential evidence will be created, identified, appropriately scheduled, and managed for as long as needed.
- Essential evidence will be easy to access regardless of where it is or where users are for as long as needed.

- All records will be preserved in an appropriate environment for use as long as needed.
- NARA's capabilities for making the changes necessary to realize its vision will continuously expand.

The plan lays out strategies for reaching these goals, sets milestone targets for accomplishments through 2007, and identifies measurements for gauging progress. The targets and measurements are further delineated in NARA's Annual Performance Plans.

The Strategic Plan and NARA's Annual Performance Plans and Reports are available on the NARA Web site at http://www.archives.gov/about_us/index. html or by calling the Policy and Communications Staff at 301-837-1850.

Records and Access

Internet

NARA's Web site provides the most widely available means of electronic access to information about NARA, including directions on how to contact the agency and do research at its facilities; descriptions of its holdings in an online catalog; direct access to certain archival electronic records; digital copies of selected archival documents; an online guide to researching family history in the 1930 census microfilm, including a searchable online database that helps locate specific rolls of microfilm to consult (http://1930census.archives.gov); an Internet Web form (http://www.archives.gov/global_pages/inquire_form.html) for customer questions, reference requests, comments, and complaints; electronic versions of *Federal Register* publications; online exhibits; and classroom resources for students and teachers.

NARA is continually expanding the kinds and amount of information available on the Web site and evaluating and redesigning the site to make it easier to use. For example, veterans and the next-of-kin of deceased veterans may now submit requests for their service records through a Web-based, interactive inquiry program (http://www.archives.gov/research_room/vetrecs). NARA also played a key role in a nationwide civics initiative called Our Documents (http://www.our documents.gov), which features 100 milestone documents drawn primarily from NARA's holdings, and has established a Web page providing access to federal rules open for public comment (http://www.archives.gov/federal_register/public_ participation/rulemaking_sites.html).

Electronic Access Project

As a result of NARA's Electronic Access Project, anyone, anywhere, with a computer connected to the Internet can search descriptions of NARA's nationwide holdings and view digital copies of some of its most popular documents. This is a significant piece of NARA's electronic access strategy as outlined in its Strategic Plan. The centerpiece of the project is the Archival Research Catalog (ARC), an online catalog of all NARA holdings that allows the public, for the first time, to use computers to search for information about all NARA holdings, including those in the regional archives and presidential libraries. It will take several years to complete the online catalog. At present, the catalog contains more than 610,000 descriptions of archival holdings and microfilm publications and 124,000 digital copies of high-interest documents. This represents about 20 percent of NARA's total holdings. The catalog is available on the Internet at http://www.archives.gov/research_room/arc.

Renovation and Re-encasement

On July 5, 2001, the Rotunda and exhibit halls of the National Archives Building in Washington, D.C., closed for renovation. When the renovation of the Rotunda is completed in September 2003, visitors will find the Charters of Freedom (the Declaration of Independence, the Constitution, and the Bill of Rights) displayed in new, state-of-the-art encasements. The re-encased documents will be easier to view for younger visitors and those using wheelchairs. For the first time, all four pages of the Constitution will be displayed. In the summer of 2004, the "National Archives Experience" is scheduled to open in the space surrounding the Rotunda and will showcase permanent and changing exhibits and interactive educational activities that will bring the records of America to life, letting visitors of all ages become "users" of the archives. Research facilities in the building also will be expanded and upgraded with the establishment of a new Genealogy and Community History Research Center.

During the renovation, the research areas of the building remain open. For more information about the renovation and Charters of Freedom re-encasement, see "The National Archives Experience" at http://www.archives.gov/national_archives_experience/index.html.

Archives Library Information Center

The Archives Library Information Center (ALIC) provides access to information on ready reference, American history and government, archival administration, information management, and government documents. ALIC is physically located in two traditional libraries in the National Archives Building in Washington, D.C., and the National Archives at College Park, Maryland. Customers also can visit ALIC on the Internet at http://www.archives.gov/research_room/alic, where they will find "Reference at Your Desk" Internet links, staff-compiled bibliographies and publications, an online library catalog, and more.

Government Documents

U.S. government publications are generally available to researchers at many of the 1,350 congressionally designated federal depository libraries throughout the United States. A record set of these publications also is part of NARA's archival holdings. Publications of the U.S. Government (Record Group 287) is a collection of selected publications of U.S. government agencies, arranged by the classification system (SuDoc System) devised by the Office of the Superintendent of Documents, U.S. Government Printing Office (GPO). The core of the collection is a library established in 1895 by GPO's Public Documents Division. By 1972, when NARA acquired the library, it included official publications dating from the early years of the federal government and selected publications produced for and by federal government agencies. Since 1972 the 28,000-cubic-foot collection has been augmented periodically with accessions of U.S. government publications selected by the Office of the Superintendent of Documents as a byproduct of its cataloging activity. As with the federal depository library collections, the holdings in NARA's Record Group 287 compose only a portion of all U.S. government publications.

NARA Publications

NARA publishes guides and indexes to various portions of its archival holdings; catalogs of microfilmed records; informational leaflets and brochures; general-interest books about NARA and its holdings that will appeal to anyone with an interest in U.S. history; more specialized publications that will be useful to scholars, archivists, records managers, historians, researchers, and educators; facsimiles of certain documents; and *Prologue,* a scholarly journal published quarterly. Some NARA publications are available through the National Archives Fax-on-Demand System described below. Some are also available on NARA's Web site at http://www.archives.gov/publications/online_publications.html. Many are available from NARA's Customer Service Center in College Park by telephoning the toll-free numbers 800-234-8861 or 866-272-6272 (the local telephone number is 301-837-2000) or faxing 301-837-0483. The NARA Web site's publications homepage (http://www.archives.gov/publications/index.html) provides more-detailed information about available publications and ordering details.

Fax-on-Demand

NARA customers can request faxed copies of select materials at any time by calling NARA's interactive fax retrieval system at 301-837-0990. By following the voice-activated instructions, customers will receive by fax copies of the materials stored digitally on the hard drive of an agency computer. Among the materials available by fax are brochures regarding NARA internships, NARA and federal government employment, and the semiannual Modern Archives Institute; published General Information Leaflets; other fact sheets about various NARA holdings, programs, and facilities (especially those located in Washington, D.C., and College Park and Suitland, Maryland, and at the National Personnel Records Center in St. Louis); instructions, forms, and vendor lists for ordering copies of records; and finding aids for some textual, audiovisual, and micrographic records. Instructions and a listing of currently available documents are found on NARA's Web site at http://www.archives.gov/fax_on_demand/fax_on_demand. html. Except for those customers who are making long-distance calls to Fax-on-Demand, there are no other charges for using this service.

Federal Register

The *Federal Register* is the daily newspaper of the federal government and includes proposed and final regulations, agency notices, and presidential legal documents. The *Federal Register* is published by the Office of the Federal Register and printed and distributed by GPO. The two agencies collaborate in the same way to produce the annual revisions of the *Code of Federal Regulations* (*CFR*). Free access to the full text of the electronic versions of the *Federal Register* and *CFR* is available through the GPO Access service, on the Internet at http://www. access.gpo.gov. In addition to these publications, the full text of other *Federal Register* publications is available through GPO Access, including the *Weekly Compilation of Presidential Documents, Public Papers of the President,* slip laws, *U.S. Statutes at Large,* and *United States Government Manual.* All of these publications also are maintained at all federal depository libraries. Public Law Electronic Notification Service (PENS) is a free subscription e-mail service available for notification of recently enacted public laws. The Federal Register Table of Contents Service (FEDREGTOC) is a free e-mail service available for delivery of the daily table of contents from the *Federal Register.* Publication information concerning laws, regulations, and presidential documents and services is available from the Office of the Federal Register (202-741-6000). Information about and additional finding aids for *Federal Register* publications also are available via the Internet at http://www.archives.gov/federal_register. Publications also can be ordered from GPO by writing to New Orders, Superintendent of Documents, Box 371954, Pittsburgh, PA 15250-7954.

Customer Service

Customers

NARA's Customer Service Plan, available free of charge in its research rooms nationwide and on its Web site (http://www.archives.gov/about_us/customer_ service/customer_service_plan.html), lists the many types of customers NARA serves and describes its standards for customer service. Few archives and records administrations serve as many customers as NARA. In fiscal year 2002 there were nearly 249,000 research visits to NARA facilities nationwide, including presidential libraries and federal records centers. At the same time, nearly 105,000 customers requested archival information by mail and by phone. NARA also served the executive agencies of the federal government, the courts, and Congress by providing records storage, reference service, training, advice, and guidance on many issues relating to records management. Federal records centers replied to more than 12 million requests for information and records, including more than 939,000 requests for information from military and civilian government service records provided by the National Personnel Records Center in St. Louis. NARA also provided informative public programs at its various facilities for more than 242,000 people. Exhibits in the presidential library museums were visited by more than 1.9 million people. NARA's customer service accomplishments are detailed in its Annual Performance Reports.

Customer Opinion

Among the specific strategies published in NARA's Strategic Plan is an explicit commitment to expanding the opportunities of its customers to inform NARA about information and services that they need. In support of that strategy, NARA continues to survey, hold focus groups, and meet with customers to evaluate and constantly improve services. NARA also maintains an Internet Web form (http://www.archives.gov/global_pages/inquire_form.html) to facilitate continuous feedback from customers about what is most important to them and what NARA might do better to meet their needs.

Grants

The National Historical Publications and Records Commission (NHPRC) is the grant-making affiliate of NARA. The Archivist of the United States chairs the commission and makes grants on its recommendation. The commission's 14 other members represent the president of the United States (two appointees), the U.S. Supreme Court, the U.S. Senate and House of Representatives, the U.S. Departments of State and Defense, the Librarian of Congress, the American Association for State and Local History, the American Historical Association, the Association for Documentary Editing, the National Association of Government Archives and Records Administrators, the Organization of American Historians, and the Society of American Archivists.

The commission carries out a statutory mission to ensure understanding of the nation's past by promoting nationwide the identification, preservation, and dissemination of essential historical documentation. The commission supports the creation and publication of eight Founding Era documentary editions and basic and applied research in the management and preservation of authentic electronic records, and it works in partnership with a national network of State Historical Records Advisory Boards to develop a national archival infrastructure. NHPRC grants help state and local governments and archives, universities, historical societies, professional organizations, and other nonprofit organizations establish or strengthen archival programs, improve training and techniques, preserve and process records collections, and provide access to them through finding aids and documentary editions of the papers of significant historical figures and movements in American history.

Administration

NARA employs approximately 3,000 people, of whom about 2,500 are full-time permanent staff members. For fiscal year 2003 NARA received a budget of $268,824,211, including $6,457,750 to support the National Historical Publications and Records Commission.

National Center for Education Statistics Library Statistics Program

U.S. Department of Education, Institute of Education Sciences
1990 K St. N.W., Washington, DC 20006

Adrienne Chute
Elementary/Secondary and Libraries Studies Division

In an effort to collect and disseminate more complete statistical information about libraries, the National Center for Education Statistics (NCES) initiated a formal library statistics program in 1989 that now includes surveys on academic libraries, public libraries, school library media centers, and state library agencies.* The Library Statistics Program (LSP) is administered and funded by NCES, under the leadership of Jeffrey Williams, acting program director. The U.S. National Commission on Libraries and Information Science (NCLIS) and the U.S. Bureau of the Census work cooperatively with NCES in implementing the program.

The four library surveys conducted by NCES are designed to provide comprehensive national data on the status of libraries. These surveys are used by federal, state, and local officials; professional associations; and local practitioners for planning, evaluation, and making policy, and to draw samples for special surveys. These data are also available to researchers and educators to analyze the state of the art of librarianship and to improve its practice.

The program's recently redesigned Web site (http://nces.ed.gov/surveys/libraries) provides links to data search tools, publications, and data files, with sub pages for each of the library surveys. Each of the sub pages links to highlights of the most recently published data, an explanation of what information is collected in the survey, details of new information that is coming up, and a Researchers and Respondents Corner.

This article describes the four library surveys.

Public Libraries

Descriptive statistics for more than 9,000 public libraries are collected and disseminated annually through a voluntary census, the Public Libraries Survey. The survey is conducted by NCES through the Federal-State Cooperative System (FSCS) for Public Library Data. In 2003 FSCS will complete its 15th data collection.

The Public Libraries Survey collects identifying information about public libraries and each of their service outlets, including street address, city, county, zip code, and telephone number. Additional identifying information is collected on public libraries, including library Web address, library mailing address, and e-mail and fax number of the library director. The survey collects data about public libraries, including data on staffing; type of legal basis; type of geographic boundary; type of administrative structure; type of interlibrary relationship; type

*The authorization for the National Center for Education Statistics to collect library statistics is included in the Education Sciences Reform Act of 2002 (P.L. 107-279), under Title I, Part C.
Note: Jeffrey Williams and Elaine Kroe of NCES contributed to this article.

and number of public service outlets; operating income and expenditures; size of collection; such service measures as reference transactions, interlibrary loans, circulation, public service hours, library visits, circulation of children's materials, and children's program attendance; and other data items. Newer data items on computers and the Internet include number of Internet terminals used by staff only, number of Internet terminals used by the general public, number of users of electronic resources in a typical week; access to electronic services, number of library materials in electronic format, operating expenditures for library materials in electronic format, and operating expenditures for electronic access.

The survey also collects several data items about outlets, including the location of an outlet relative to a metropolitan area, number of books-by-mail-only outlets, number of bookmobiles by bookmobile outlet, and square footage of the outlet.

Unit response typically has been more than 98 percent. The 50 states and the District of Columbia participate in data collection. Beginning in 1993, five outlying areas joined the FSCS for Public Library Data: Guam, Commonwealth of the Northern Mariana Islands, Republic of Palau, Puerto Rico, and the U.S. Virgin Islands. For the collection of fiscal year (FY) 2000 data, the respondents that provided publishable data were the more than 9,000 public libraries identified by state library agencies in the 50 states, the District of Columbia, and four of the five outlying areas: the Commonwealth of the Northern Mariana Islands, the Republic of Palau, the U.S. Virgin Islands, and Guam.

The first release of Public Libraries Survey data occurs approximately five months after data collection with the posting of the updated Public Library Peer Comparison Tool and the Public Library Locator on the LSP Web site. The data used in these Web tools are final but unimputed (imputation is a statistical means for providing an estimate for each missing data item). This is followed three months later by the release of an E.D. Tab (an NCES publication that presents data "highlights" followed by a succinct presentation of descriptive statistics, including tables) on the NCES Web site. Within a week of that release, the final imputed data file is released on the NCES Web site. The proportion of data that are imputed in the final file has been no more than 2 percent. [For a sampling of content from several recent E.D. Tabs, see "Highlights of NCES Surveys" in Part 4—*Ed.*]

Final imputed data files that contain FY 2000 data on nearly 9,000 responding libraries and identifying information about their outlets were made available in July 2002 on the LSP Web site. The FY 2000 data were also aggregated to state and national levels in the E.D. Tab *Public Libraries in the United States: FY 2000* and released in July 2002 on the LSP Web site. FY 2001 data and E.D. Tabs were expected to be released in early 2003.

The Public Library Peer Comparison Tool and the Public Library Locator have also been updated with FY 2000 data. FY 2001 data were expected to be available on these tools in early 2003.

The FSCS for Public Library Data is an example of the synergy that results from combining federal/state cooperation with state-of-the-art technology. The Public Libraries Survey was the first national NCES data collection in which the respondents supplied the data electronically. The data can also be edited and tabulated electronically at the state and national levels through NCES-developed software. All public library data collections have been made electronically. In addition, 49 states and two outlying areas submitted their FY 2001 data via the Internet.

Descriptive data on public libraries are collected via Windows-based data-collection software called WINPLUS. WINPLUS also collects identifying information on all known public libraries and their service outlets. The resulting universe file resource has been available for use in drawing samples for special surveys on such topics as literacy, access for the disabled, and library construction.

Efforts to improve Public Libraries Survey data quality are ongoing. For example, beginning with the FY 1995 data, most items with response rates below 100 percent have included imputations for nonresponding libraries. NCES also sponsored a series of six studies of the Public Libraries Survey including coverage, definitions, structure and organization, finance data, and staffing data. These studies were conducted by the Governments Division, U.S. Department of Commerce, Bureau of the Census. Over the years, the clarity of the Public Libraries Survey definitions, software, and tables has been significantly improved. In the past year, a strong and successful effort has been made to release data sooner.

At the state level and in the outlying areas, FSCS is administered by data coordinators, appointed by each state or outlying area's chief officer of the state library agency. FSCS is a working network. State data coordinators collect the requested data from public libraries and submit these data to NCES. NCES aggregates the data to provide state and national totals. An annual training conference is provided for the state data coordinators, and a steering committee that represents them is active in the development of the Public Libraries Survey and its data-entry software. Technical assistance to states is provided by state data coordinators, by NCES staff, by the Bureau of the Census, and by NCLIS. NCES also works cooperatively with NCLIS, the Bureau of the Census, the Institute for Museum and Library Service's Office of Library Programs, the Chief Officers of State Library Agencies (COSLA), the American Library Association (ALA), and the U.S. Department of Education's National Library of Education.

Completed Public Library Data Projects

A survey completed by NCES's Fast Response Survey System on the topic of public library programming for adults, including adults at risk, has been completed. The survey, conducted by Westat, covered programming for adult literacy instruction, family literacy, adults with physical disabilities, limited English-speaking, the elderly, and parents. The survey also asked about programming offered to adults for using the Internet. Data were collected from a sample of outlets nationwide in 2000 and early 2001 and the response rate was 97 percent. A report, *Programs for Adults in Public Library Outlets* (NCES-2003-010) by Laurie Lewis of Westat, was released on the NCES Web site and in print in November 2002.

In 2001 NCES published a trend analysis report for FY 1992–FY 1996 on 24 key variables from the Public Libraries Survey. As part of this project, FY 1992–1994 Public Libraries Survey data have been imputed for nonresponding libraries and were re-released on the LSP Web site in summer 2001. (FY 1995–FY 1996 have already been imputed.)

The Public Library Locator tool on the LSP Web site enables users to locate data about a public library or a public library service outlet in instances where the user knows some but not all of the information about the library. For example, if the city is known but not the library's name, the user can still locate the library and obtain most of the available Public Libraries Survey data about it, including identifying information, organizational characteristics, services, staffing, size of collection, income, and expenditures. To use this tool, see http://nces. ed.gov/surveys/libraries/liblocator.

LSP also released a Web-based Public Library Peer Comparison Tool on the Web site. Using this tool, a user can select a library of interest and search for a peer group of libraries by selecting key characteristics to define it (such as all other libraries in the same state with similar total operating expenditures), then view customized reports comparing the library of interest with its peers. These reports include bar charts, pie charts, rankings, data reports, and address/telephone reports. The user can also view reports on data for individual public libraries. To use this tool, see http://nces.ed.gov/surveys/libraries/publicpeer.

American Institutes for Research completed a project for NCES to develop two indices of inflation, an input cost index and a cost of services index. NCES published a report of the project in 1999 that presents and compares two approaches to measuring inflation for public libraries. One approach is based on a fixed "market basket" of the prices of library inputs, which yields a public library input cost index. The second approach is based on an econometric model of library services and costs, and yields a public library cost of services index.

Questions about public libraries have also been included as parts of other NCES surveys. For example, in 1996 questions about frequency of use and the purposes for which households use public libraries were included on NCES's National Household Education Survey (NHES). More than 55,000 households were surveyed to provide state- and national-level estimates on library items. A Statistics in Brief titled "Use of Public Library Services by Households in the United States: 1996" was released in July 1997 and is available on the NCES Web site. A CD-ROM and User's Manual were also made available in July 1997. NCES plans to update these data and add some additional survey questions; these data are expected to be available in early 2004.

Other Planned Public Library Data Projects

NCES has also fostered the use and analysis of FSCS data. A Data Use Subcommittee of the FSCS Steering Committee has been addressing the analysis, dissemination, and use of FSCS data, and several analytical projects recommended by this committee are under way.

NCES is developing a public library geographic mapping tool to be available on the Internet as part of NCES's Decennial Census School District 2000 project. This tool is an interactive online mapping system that integrates 2000 Decennial Census data with school district boundaries and school district data. The library part of this tool will be developed in phases over the next several years.

Additional information on public libraries is available from Adrienne Chute, Elementary/Secondary and Libraries Studies Division, National Center for Education Statistics, 1990 K St. N.W., Room 9091, Washington, DC 20006 (telephone 202-502-7328, e-mail adrienne.chute@ed.gov.

Academic Libraries

The Academic Libraries Survey (ALS) provides descriptive statistics on approximately 3,700 academic libraries in the 50 states, the District of Columbia, and the outlying areas of the United States. NCES surveyed academic libraries on a three-year cycle between 1966 and 1988. From 1988 to 1998, ALS was a component of the Integrated Postsecondary Education Data System (IPEDS), and was on a two-year cycle. Beginning with FY 2000, the Academic Libraries Survey is no longer a component of IPEDS but remains on a two-year cycle. IPEDS and ALS data can still be linked using the unit identification codes of the postsecondary education institutions. In aggregate, these data provide an overview of the status of academic libraries nationally and by state.

ALS collects data on libraries in the entire universe of degree-granting postsecondary institutions.

For a number of years, NCES used IDEALS, a software package for states to use in submitting ALS data to NCES. Beginning with the collection of FY 2000 data in fall 2000, ALS changed to a Web-based data collection system. FY 2002 data were collected from November 2002 to February 2003.

ALS has established a working group composed of representatives of the academic library community. Its mission is to improve data quality and the timeliness of data collection, processing, and release. NCES also works cooperatively with ALA, NCLIS, the Association of Research Libraries, the Association of College and Research Libraries, and academic libraries in the collection of ALS data.

ALS collects data on total library operating expenditures, full-time-equivalent (FTE) library staff, service outlets, total volumes held at the end of the academic year, circulation, interlibrary loans, public service hours, gate count, reference transactions per typical week, and online services. Academic libraries are also asked whether they offer library reference services by e-mail and electronic document delivery to patron's account-address. Beginning in FY 2000, questions about consortial services were added to the survey.

The E.D. Tab *Academic Libraries: 1998* was released on the NCES Web site in July 2001. A descriptive report of changes in academic libraries between 1990 and 1996, *The Status of Academic Libraries in the United States: Results from the 1996 Academic Library Survey with Historical Comparisons,* was released in May 2001. A technical report assessing the coverage of academic libraries through ALS was published in September 1999.

NCES has developed a Web-based peer analysis tool for ALS. It has a number of features similar to the Public Library Peer Comparison Tool and was updated in November 2002 with FY 2000 unimputed data.

Additional information on academic library statistics is available from Jeffrey Williams, Elementary/Secondary and Libraries Studies Division, National Center for Education Statistics, Room 9026, 1990 K St. N.W., Washington, DC 20006 (telephone 202-502-7476, e-mail jeffrey.williams@ed.gov).

School Library Media Centers

National surveys of school library media centers in elementary and secondary schools in the United States were conducted in 1958, 1962, 1974, 1978, 1986, 1994, and 2000. NCES plans to continue school library data collection once every four years.

NCES, with the assistance of the U.S. Bureau of the Census, conducted the School Library Media Centers Survey as part of the 1999–2000 Schools and Staffing Survey (SASS). The sample of schools surveyed consisted of 9,000 public schools, 3,500 private schools, and the 160 Bureau of Indian Affairs (BIA) schools in the United States. Data from the school library media center questionnaire will provide a national picture of school library staffing, collections, expenditures, technology, and services. These data can also be used to assess the status of school library media centers nationwide, and to assess the federal role in their support. An E.D. Tab and the data file for this survey were released in May 2002. The Bureau of the Census also completed a Technical Report for NCES, an "Evaluation of Definitions and Analysis of Comparative Data for the School Library Statistics Program," which was released in September 1998.

NCES has included some library-oriented questions on the parent and the teacher instruments of its new Early Childhood Longitudinal Study, Kindergarten Class of 1999. Some of the data from this study were released in 2000; see http://nces.ed.gov/ecls.

Additional information on school library media center statistics is available from Jeffrey Williams, Elementary/Secondary and Libraries Studies Division, National Center for Education Statistics, Room 9026, 1990 K St. N.W., Washington, DC 20006 (telephone 202-502-7476, e-mail jeffrey.williams@ed.gov).

State Library Agencies

The State Library Agencies Survey collects and disseminates information about state library agencies (StLAs) in the 50 states and the District of Columbia. A state library agency is the official unit of state government charged with statewide library development and the administration of federal funds under the Library Services and Technology Act (LSTA). StLAs' administrative and developmental responsibilities affect the operation of thousands of public, academic, school, and special libraries. StLAs provide important reference and information services to state governments, and sometimes also provide service to the general public. StLAs often administer state library and special operations such as state archives and libraries for the blind and physically handicapped, and the state Center for the Book.

The State Library Agencies Survey began in 1994 as a cooperative effort by NCES, COSLA, and NCLIS. The FY 2001 StLA survey collected data on the following: direct library services, adult literacy and family literacy, library development services, resources assigned to allied operations such as archive and records management, organizational and governance structure within which the agency operates, electronic networking, staffing, collections, and expenditures. These data are edited electronically. Prior to FY 1999 missing data were not imputed.

Beginning with FY 1999 data, however, national totals included imputations for missing data. Another change is that beginning with FY 1999 data the survey became a Web-based data collection system. The most recent data available are for FY 2001. Two FY 2001 data products were released on the Internet through the NCES Web site. An E.D. Tab, *State Library Agencies, Fiscal Year 2001,* with 30 tables for the 50 states and the District of Columbia, was released in October 2002. The survey database was also released in October 2002.

An evaluation study of the state library agency survey was released in the fall of 1999.

Additional information on the survey is available from Elaine Kroe, Elementary/Secondary and Libraries Studies Division, Room 9027, National Center for Education Statistics, 1990 K St. N.W., Washington, DC 20006 (telephone 202-502-7379, e-mail patricia.kroe@ed.gov).

How to Obtain Printed and Electronic Products

Under its library surveys, NCES regularly publishes E.D. Tabs that consist of tables, usually presenting state and national totals, a survey description, and data highlights. NCES also publishes separate, more in-depth studies analyzing these data.

Internet Access

Many NCES publications (including out-of-print publications) and edited raw data files from the library surveys are available for viewing or downloading at no charge through the Electronic Catalog on the NCES Web site at http://nces.ed.gov/pubsearch.

Ordering Printed Products

Many NCES publications are also available in printed format. To order one free copy of recent NCES reports, contact the Education Publications Center (ED Pubs) at

Internet: http://www.ed.gov/pubs/edpubs.html
E-mail: EdPubs@inet.ed.gov
Toll-free telephone: 877-4-ED-Pubs (877-433-7827)
TTY/TDD toll-free number: 877-576-7734
Fax: 301-470-1244
Mail: ED Pubs, P.O. Box 1398, Jessup, MD 20794-1398.

Many publications are available through the Educational Resources Information Clearinghouse (ERIC) system. These documents can be ordered from the ERIC Document Reproduction Service (EDRS) in three formats: paper, electronic (PDF), or microfiche. Orders can be placed with EDRS by phone at 800-443-3742 or 703-440-1400, by fax at 703-440-1408, or by e-mail at service@edrs.

com. For more information on services and products, visit the EDRS Web site at http://www.edrs.com.

Out-of-print publications and data files may be available through the NCES Electronic Catalog on the NCES Web site at http://nces.ed.gov/pubsearch or through one of the 1,400 Federal Depository Libraries throughout the United States. Use the NCES publication number included in the citations for publications and data files to quickly locate items in the NCES Electronic Catalog; use the GPO number to locate items in a Federal Depository Library.

National Education Data Resource Center

The National Education Data Resource Center (NEDRC) responds to requests for special tabulations of library data and other NCES survey data and provides assistance in obtaining data and publications over the Internet. These services are free of charge. Visit the NEDRC Web site at http://nces.ed.gov/partners/nedrc.asp or contact NEDRC, 1900 N. Beauregard St., Suite 200, Alexandria, VA 22311-1722 (telephone 703-845-3151, fax 703-820-7465, e-mail nedrc@pcci.com).

National Commission on Libraries and Information Science

1110 Vermont Ave. N.W., Suite 820, Washington, DC 20005-3522
World Wide Web http://www.nclis.gov

Robert S. Willard
Executive Director

The National Commission on Libraries and Information Science (NCLIS) is an independent agency of the federal government established in 1970 to provide advice to the president, Congress, and other entities, public and private, regarding the library and information needs of the American public. To carry out its functions, NCLIS conducts hearings, studies, surveys, and analyses of these needs, appraises the adequacies and deficiencies of current library and information resources and research and development activities, and issues publications.

The year 2002 was a period in which the need for such an agency was questioned, but in the end, the continuing mission of the agency was clearly approved.

Regrettably, the commission's budget was reduced one-third, from $1.5 million to $1 million, resulting in personnel reductions and program cutbacks. However, NCLIS was able to continue routine operations, including providing advice on the reauthorization of the Library Services and Technology Act (LSTA) and Government Printing Office (GPO) management and operations. It also moved forward on two new initiatives: "Trust and Terror," a briefing on the role of libraries as communicators to the public in times following natural or man-made disasters, and planning for a global conference on information literacy.

NCLIS Members and Staff

NCLIS is composed of 16 members—the Librarian of Congress, the director of the Institute of Museum and Library Services, and 14 individuals appointed by the president of the United States and confirmed by the Senate. Members serve a five-year term (with an additional year allowable when a successor has not yet been named); generally, one-fifth of the commission is replaced each year. President Bush did not nominate new members during the period of reappraisal of the commission's role, and consequently a large number of vacancies have ensued.

Martha B. Gould (retired director of the Washoe County public library in Reno, Nevada) continued as chairperson. She served along with Rebecca T. Bingham (retired director of school libraries in Jefferson County, Kentucky), Joan R. Challinor (historian and chair of the advisory committee of the Arthur and Elizabeth Schlesinger Library on the History of Women in America), José-Marie Griffiths (professor of information science, library science, and telecommunications, University of Pittsburgh), Jack E. Hightower (former member of Congress and a retired justice of the Texas Supreme Court), and Bobby L. Roberts (director of the Central Arkansas Library System in Little Rock). The terms of office of Bingham and Griffiths expired on July 19, 2002. Winston Tabb continued to represent James H. Billington, the Librarian of Congress, until he took on the new role of dean of libraries at Johns Hopkins University; his successor at NCLIS is Nancy Davenport, director of acquisitions at the Library of Congress. Robert S. Martin (a library educator and former director and librarian of the Texas State Library and Archives Commission) is, as director of the Institute of Museum and Library Services (IMLS), an ex officio member of the commission.

Robert S. Willard, a former commissioner, continued as the NCLIS executive director. Rosalie Vlach, director of legislative and public affairs, left NCLIS in April as a consequence of the budget reduction. By the end of the year, the two remaining members of the professional staff—Judith Russell, the deputy director, and Denise Davis, director of statistics and surveys—were also departing NCLIS. Ms. Davis, whose efforts had significantly improved the NCLIS Library Statistics Program, took a leadership position with the State Library of Oregon. Ms. Russell, whose library career included time as director of the Federal Depository Library Program, returned to GPO as the Superintendent of Documents, responsible for GPO's sales and library programs and the highest ranking woman in that agency's history. Robert Molyneux, a library school professor from the University of South Carolina–Columbia, joined the NCLIS staff to carry on the work of the Library Statistics Program. Madeleine McCain became director of operations for NCLIS.

Members of the commission convened twice in Washington in 2002. In June they evaluated nominations for the National Award for Library Services and recommended exceptional nominees to the director of IMLS. They also participated in a joint meeting with members of the National Museum Services Board. In October they reviewed ongoing NCLIS projects and attended the White House ceremony at which the national awards were presented by First Lady Laura Bush.

NCLIS Mission Reappraisal

In early 2002, for the second year in a row, the Office of Management and Budget (OMB) proposed that Congress no longer provide funding for NCLIS. This proposal was accompanied with the suggestion that "other agencies" could perform the work of the commission, although details were not provided how this reassignment would be accomplished. It was claimed that this move would save $1 million (which calculated at one-third of a penny for each American). This proposal clearly seemed to reflect a lack of understanding of the unique role of the commission to advance the national policy of library and information services for all Americans that was articulated in the law establishing the commission in 1970 (P.L. 91-345).

In February, responding to an invitation from Congress, NCLIS Chairperson Gould testified before the House Appropriations Subcommittee on Labor, Health and Human Services, and Education. She disputed the proposal to eliminate the commission and instead called for funding it at $2.8 million, the level unanimously supported by commissioners at a meeting in 2001. She also proposed minor technical amendments to improve the operation of the commission. Gould focused on the commission's effort to improve school libraries as one example of how the agency accomplishes its work. Also testifying was Commissioner

Hightower, who addressed the need for information in the moments following an emergency or disaster. He provided another example of the commission's work: the preparation of a briefing for public officials explaining how libraries can serve as trusted sources of information in times of crisis if the necessary planning and preparation have occurred beforehand.

In the more extensive testimony that NCLIS submitted for the record and in answers to follow-up questions that members of the appropriations subcommittee submitted to the commission, the case for the continued operation of NCLIS was put forward. A discussion of the legislative history of the commission made clear the ambitious role Congress had in mind for NCLIS. A 30-year summary of commission activities illustrated the breadth and depth of NCLIS concerns. An examination of the commission's independence demonstrated the essential importance of having a body free of outside influence, an independence that would be lost if NCLIS's functions were incorporated into one or more "other agencies" as proposed by OMB.

Support for the commission was articulated by a number of groups. When America's librarians visited Washington on National Library Legislative Day in May 2002 to discuss library needs with their senators and representatives, the commission's budget was among their priorities. Library associations and industry groups joined in the effort to support NCLIS. More than a dozen members of Congress signed a letter to the chairman of the House appropriations subcommittee urging full funding of NCLIS at the requested level of $2.8 million.

Congress did not conclude its consideration of most funding bills until long after the new fiscal year began on October 1, 2002. Instead, temporary measures, bills known as "continuing resolutions," provided stopgap funding for most federal agencies, including NCLIS. It was not until the beginning of the calendar year that funding for fiscal year (FY) 2003 was finally provided. For the second year, Congress rebuffed the proposal to eliminate NCLIS and instead appropriated $1 million for the agency.

The beginning of 2003 brought additional good news for the commission. OMB acknowledged that it did not intend to recommend the discontinuation of NCLIS and instead proposed "level funding" of $1 million in the budget for FY 2004. Shortly thereafter, the Office of Presidential Personnel began the process of identifying individuals for appointment to the vacancies on the commission.

Support for Executive and Legislative Branches

Because of the reduction in its budget, the commission was unable to continue to examine government information policy as it relates to creation, dissemination, and permanent accessibility of electronic government information. No further work was accomplished on the NCLIS report "A Comprehensive Assessment of Public Information Dissemination," which had been prepared the previous year and which recommended policies and procedures for strengthening the dissemination infrastructure of government information. However, the commission did establish a working relation with Bruce James, President Bush's nominee to be Public Printer (the head of the Government Printing Office). Executive Director Willard appeared at James's Senate nomination hearing and submitted testimony from Chairperson Gould in which she expressed the commitment of the commission to work with James on information policy issues. In a separate matter later in the year, Willard filed a statement with OMB regarding a proposed policy that was designed to allow federal agencies to procure printing from sources other than GPO despite a statutory requirement to the contrary.

National Information Activities

Also because of the budgetary reduction, NCLIS was forced to reduce its activities regarding school libraries. The commission had examined the status of school libraries, and their roles in student achievement and in promoting literacy and information literacy, in an April 2001 hearing in Cincinnati, Ohio. NCLIS deferred publishing the transcript of the hearing, *School Librarians: Knowledge Navigators Through Troubled Times,* which had been planned for 2002. However, the transcript was provided to IMLS Director Martin, who reviewed it in preparation for a June White House conference on school libraries convened by the First Lady. Commissioner Bingham represented NCLIS at this conference.

The commission provided advice to Congress on the reauthorization of the Library Services and Technology Act (LSTA), which provides federal financial support to libraries. After the Education and the Workforce Committee of the House of Representatives approved legislation, NCLIS expressed its full support and urged the Senate to take similar steps. Later, NCLIS also urged the House leadership to schedule floor action on the bill. (The legislation did not advance during 2002, but the House approved the measure in early March 2003 and similar action was expected in the Senate.)

Major effort was put into production of "Trust and Terror," an audiovisual briefing on the role libraries can take in providing needed information to the public in the immediate aftermath of a man-made or natural disaster. Under the leadership of former Commissioner Marilyn Gell Mason, Commissioner Griffiths, and Commission Vice-Chair Challinor, NCLIS developed a script and a computer slideshow designed for librarians and their governing boards as well as other public policymakers. This production was previewed before librarians in various organizations, such as the American Library Association (ALA) and the Chief Officers of State Library Agencies, and was modified based on the comments received. A brochure to accompany the briefing was also prepared. Challinor presented the briefing at a session of the International Federation of Library Associations and Institutions (IFLA) in Glasgow and arranged for the brochure to be available in French and Spanish as well as English.

Toward the end of the year, broadcaster Walter Cronkite recorded the narration for "Trust and Terror" and a more advanced computer presentation was produced. The production was recorded on CD-ROM with the intention to distribute the CDs in early 2003.

NCLIS/NCES Library Statistics Program

NCLIS believes strongly that in order for policy advice to be useful, it must be based on solid fact. The commission has long maintained an important statistical function, and despite its reduced budget this program was maintained at previous levels and even expanded into some new areas.

The commission had a significant presence at several research and statistics committee meetings of ALA and its divisions, as well as participation in a variety of state library conferences. NCLIS also continued its participation, initiated in late 2001, with the European Union library statistics project, LibEcon. NCLIS, through the participation of Denise Davis, its director of statistics and surveys, also remained actively involved in U.S. and international library standards activities.

NCLIS continued its support of the NCLIS/IMLS/NISO cosponsored project Developing National Data Collection Models for Public Library Network Statistics and Performance Measures. NCLIS hosted a forum in New Orleans on January 18, 2002, to bring the information community together to work toward the common goal of consistent and meaningful electronic use-measure reporting.

Fiscal Year 2002 marked the 15th consecutive year of cooperation between the commission and the National Center for Education Statistics (NCES) in implementing the Library Statistics Program (LSP). NCLIS serves as liaison to the library community, organizes meetings and professional development workshops, supports in-state training and technical assistance, monitors trends, and advises NCES on policy matters.

The following events occurred as part of the continuing improvement of LSP: Steering committee meetings for the Federal State Cooperative System (FSCS) survey, March, June, and September 2002; State Library Agency (STLA) survey, March and September 2002; Academic Library survey advisory committee meeting, January and June 2002; School Library Media Center survey task group meetings, June and September 2002; and the annual training workshop and orientation for new state data coordinators, December 2002.

There were several landmark projects for LSP. Foremost is the improvement of timeliness of reporting state-level data to the federal library data system. States approved a revised calendar for reporting data and moving the training workshop to the fall. These modifications improve the synchronicity of the processes between state collection and federal analysis and publication, thereby shortening the total collection-to-publication cycles.

The State Library Agency Survey Steering Committee undertook an ambitious project of analyzing Library Services and Construction Act (LSCA) and LSTA funding over a ten-year period. The working paper, *The Impact of Federal Funding on State Library Agencies: The LSCA to LSTA Transition,* was prepared by Bruce Kingma, School of Information Studies, Syracuse University. Kingma concluded that "LSTA funding not only increased the amount of federal dollars that were available for library services but generated a significant increase in state, local and other non-federal support to state libraries."

International Activities

NCLIS completed its 17th year of cooperation with the Department of State to coordinate and monitor proposals for International Contributions for Scientific, Educational and Cultural Activities (ICSECA) funds and to disburse the funds.

The commission continues to be an active participant in IFLA. However, because of reduced funding, only one commissioner, Challinor, attended the August 2002 IFLA General Conference in Glasgow.

The commission continued to host a number of visits to its office by delegations of librarians from other nations, usually under the auspices of the State Department. Executive Director Willard traveled to Minsk, Belarus, at the request of the State Department to participate in the 80th anniversary celebrations of the Belarus National Library and to speak to a number of library groups.

NCLIS carried on its work in preparation for an International Leadership Conference on Information Literacy planned in partnership with UNESCO and the National Forum on Information Literacy. Information literacy is the ability to recognize when information is needed and to locate, evaluate, organize, and use information effectively. It is believed that an information-literate public is a key component in national economic development. The commission originally hoped that a planning session of three dozen experts could be scheduled to take place in Prague in April 2002, but because of both budgetary restrictions and serious flooding in the Czech Republic, the meeting was indefinitely postponed. However, the invited experts were all requested to prepare papers on various aspects of information literacy, and these works are available on the commission's Web site. It is hoped that the meeting will take place in 2003. The output from such a meeting would provide input for the World Summit on the Information Society, scheduled to take place in Geneva in December 2003; the invited experts would also sketch out preliminary plans for the proposed International Leadership Conference to be held in 2004 or 2005.

Publications

Because of the reduction in the NCLIS budget and the resultant departure of the staff person responsible for publications, NCLIS, with little exception, did not produce printed publications during 2002. A number of documents related to the NCLIS budget and various programs were produced and made available on the commission's Web site.

The following became available in 2002.

Fiscal Year 2003 Appropriations Hearing. Electronic at http://www.nclis.gov/ news/FY2003.Appropriations.Hearing.Compilation.withQandA.pdf. Also partially available in the printed record of the Hearings of the Subcommittee on the Departments of Labor, Health and Human Services, Education, and Related Agencies for 2003, Part 6, pp. 381–425, 485–513.

The Impact of Federal Funding on State Library Agencies: The LSCA to LSTA Transition, prepared by Bruce Kingma, School of Information Studies, Syracuse University. 2002. Electronic only at http://www.nclis.gov/statsurv/ surveys/stla/reports/StLA.Policy.Paper2.2002.pdf.

Library Statistics Cooperative Program. 2002 (brochure). Electronic at http:// www.nclis.gov/statsurv/LSP_Brochure_2002.pdf.

Trust and Terror, New Demands for Crisis Information Dissemination and Management. 2002 (brochure). Also produced in Spanish as *Confianza . . .*

y Terror, Nuevas Demandas para la Diseminación y Gestión de Información de Crisis and in French as *Confiance . . . et Terreur. Nouveaux Besoins en Matière de Diffusion et Gestion de l'Information de Crise.*

Trust and Terror, New Demands for Crisis Information Dissemination and Management. 2002 (CD-ROM with accompanying brochure).

Generally, copies of NCLIS print publications are available free in limited quantities from the NCLIS office until supplies are exhausted. Electronic versions are available on the commission's Web site. In addition, selected reports, hearing testimony, comments on various matters before Congress and the administration, news releases, and other items are also on the Web site.

National Library of Education

U.S. Department of Education
400 Maryland Ave. S.W., Washington, DC 20202
202-219-1001, fax 202-219-0955
World Wide Web http://www.ed.gov/NLE

Christina Dunn

National Library of Education
202-219-1012, e-mail christina.dunn@ed.gov

The National Library of Education (NLE) began operation under Public Law 103-227, Educational Research, Development, Dissemination and Improvement Act of 1994, part of the Goals 2000: Educate America Act. This legislation gave the NLE three primary functions:

- To provide a central location within the federal government for information about education
- To provide comprehensive reference services on education issues to employees of the Department of Education and its contractors and grantees, other federal employees, and members of the public
- To promote greater cooperation and resource sharing among providers and repositories of education information in the United States

To carry out these functions, the legislation further charged NLE with four missions:

- Becoming a principal center for the collection, preservation, and effective utilization of research and other information related to education and to the improvement of educational achievement
- Striving to ensure widespread access to NLE's facilities and materials, coverage of all education issues and subjects, and quality control
- Having an expert library staff
- Using modern information technology that holds the potential to link major libraries, schools, and educational centers across the Untied States into a network of national education resources

Organization and Funding

NLE is organized into three divisions. The Reference and Information Services and Collection Development and Technical Services divisions make up the U.S. Department of Education (ED) Reference Center; the ERIC Program Division oversees all aspects of the ERIC program, including the 16 ERIC Clearinghouses and three support components. In 2002 NLE had a budget of $11.5 million, with $10.5 million supporting ERIC and $1 million supporting other functions. The ERIC program is covered in a separate report. [See the following article, "Educational Resources Information Center"—*Ed.*]

The Office of the NLE Director oversees the National Education Network (NEN). During 2002 three other programs that had operated under this office were moved to more appropriate organizations within the department. ED Pubs, the one-stop publications distribution center for the department, was moved to the Office of Management, which provides agency-wide support services. U.S. Network for Education Information, which provides a centrally coordinated mechanism for disseminating U.S. education information abroad, was placed with other international programs in the Office of the Under Secretary. The National Clearinghouse for Educational Facilities—created in 1997 as an information resource for people who plan, design, build, operate, and maintain K–12 schools—was moved to the newly created Office of Safe and Drug-Free Schools.

ED Reference Center

The ED Reference Center provides general and legislative reference and statistical information services in response to inquiries received by phone, mail, fax, and Internet. It offers interlibrary loan of NLE materials; identifies, selects, and acquires monographs and serials in education and related fields; maintains special collections of resources, such as Department of Education-published documents; provides electronic bibliographic and full-text access to education and related databases, books, and serials; provides orientation and specialized training in the use of the library and its collections; and serves as a depository library in the Government Printing Office's Federal Depository Library Program.

In 2002 NLE made a concerted effort to improve the quality of information services to Department of Education staff, moving reference staff into program offices where they are directly accessible to researchers; creating a portals service of relevant Web sites; and increasing access to desktop resources, especially electronic databases and journals.

The ED Reference Center can be reached by e-mail at library@ed.gov or by telephone at 202-205-5015 or toll-free at 800-424-1616. It is open from 9:00 A.M. to 5:00 P.M. weekdays, except federal holidays.

Collections

NLE's primary collections include its reference, circulating, serials, and microforms collections. While the circulating collection largely includes books in the field of education published since 1965, it also covers such related areas as law, public policy, economics, urban affairs, sociology, history, philosophy, psychology, and library and information science. Current periodical holdings number around 800 English-language print and electronic journals, including most of the primary journals indexed by the *Current Index to Journals in Education* (*CIJE*) and *Education Abstracts.*

In addition, the center holds historical collections of Department of Education publications and documents, spanning more than 100 years, related to federal education legislation. Other historical collections include documents and archives of the former National Institute of Education and the former U.S. Office of Education, including reports, studies, manuals, statistical publications, speeches, and policy papers. Together, these collections represent a resource covering the history of the U.S. Department of Education and its predecessor agencies.

Services

Reference and Information Services responds to public inquiries, about 90 percent of which continue to be submitted by e-mail. Information is provided in three major areas: the U.S. Department of Education Web site; U.S. Department of Education programs and statistics; and other current education-related issues such as charter schools, school violence, educational reform movement, student achievement, and testing. During 2002 NLE received nearly 20,000 requests for information. It also continued to cooperate with AskERIC, an Internet-based reference service operated by the ERIC Clearinghouse on Information and Technology at Syracuse University, answering questions on federal education statistics and the U.S. Department of Education.

In addition to handling reference inquiries, staff provide instruction and orientation, prepare pathfinders on current topics of department interest, develop finding aids, locate Web sites for reliable education information, and identify experts on various education research topics. While the center serves customers from all over the world, major emphasis is on meeting Department of Education staff's information needs.

National Education Network

The mission of the National Education Network (NEN), which is managed through the NLE director's office, is to provide and support comprehensive access to education information, promote effective access for users of education information, and sustain the development and preservation of education information. It is a collaborative partnership of entities that have as part of their mission the collection, production, and/or dissemination of education information. Representatives to the network's executive committee are from a broad spectrum, including college and university libraries, ERIC and other clearinghouses, publishers of educational resources, K–12 schools, and associations concerned with education.

The NEN Executive Committee, appointed by NLE, meets twice annually to plan and discuss NEN activities. In 2002 it continued to develop the NEN Education Materials Exchange Registry, a service allowing institutions to identify education-related materials that they would like to acquire or donate; and "Ask NEN," a question-answering service for education information professionals.

Reauthorization

The National Library of Education was reauthorized under Title I of Public Law 107-279, Education Sciences Reform Act of 2002, which was signed into law on November 5, 2002. The new legislation maintains NLE's relationship with the U.S. Department of Education's research function, placing it in the newly established Institute of Education Sciences. There the NLE will be under the National

Center for Education Evaluation and Regional Assistance. Further, the new legislation refines and streamlines the responsibilities of the NLE to encompass

- Collecting and archiving information, including products and publications developed through, or supported by, the Institute of Educational Sciences; and other relevant and useful education-related research, statistics, and evaluation materials and other information, projects, and publications that are consistent with scientifically valid research or the priorities and mission of the institute; and developed by the department, other federal agencies, or entities
- Providing a central location within the federal government for information about education
- Providing comprehensive reference services on matters related to education to employees of the Department of Education and its contractors and grantees, other federal employees, and members of the public
- Promoting greater cooperation and resource sharing among providers and repositories of education information in the United States

Educational Resources Information Center

ERIC Program Office
National Library of Education
U.S. Department of Education
400 Maryland Ave. S.W., Washington, DC 20202
World Wide Web http://www.eric.ed.gov

Christina Dunn

National Library of Education

The Educational Resources Information Center (ERIC) has been providing ready access to education literature since 1966 when it was established by the U.S. Department of Education to improve American education by increasing and facilitating the use of educational research and information to improve practice in learning, teaching, educational decision making, and research, wherever and whenever these activities take place.

The primary audience for ERIC includes teachers, librarians, school and college administrators, educational researchers, educational policymakers, instructors and students in teacher preparation programs, parents, and the media and business communities as they relate to education.

At the heart of ERIC is the largest education database in the world, containing more than 1 million bibliographic records. Contributing to the database's development are 16 subject-oriented clearinghouses and three support services—ACCESS ERIC, ERIC Document Reproduction Service (EDRS), and the ERIC Processing and Reference Facility. These components, known as the ERIC System, are managed by the National Library of Education's ERIC Program Office.

ERIC is currently in an evolutionary stage, transitioning from a system relying on paper and microfiche to a digital network. Recent accomplishments have pushed this change forward. For example, publication in paper of the monthly ERIC indexes, *Resources in Education (RIE)* and *Current Index to Journals in Education (CIJE)*, was ended in December 2001; now customers search the database electronically at http://www.eric.ed.gov for new accessions to education literature. To further improve quality control for accessions, a new processing technology was implemented that collectively feeds data from the ERIC Clearinghouses to the ERIC Facility, where the database is made accessible via the Internet. As these changes directly affect ERIC users, including libraries, part of this report describes the improvements in editorial tools and error checking along with the advantages in processing speed.

ERIC Database

In 2001 the ERIC System launched a major re-engineering effort called the ERIC Data Validation and Processing System (EDVAPS). Staff at the ERIC Processing and Reference Facility customized software to create an online data-entry system

Note: Much of this report is taken from the *ERIC Annual Report 2002: Summarizing the Recent Accomplishments of the Educational Resources Information Center,* prepared for the U.S. Department of Education by Lynn Smarte and Heather Starcher of ACCESS ERIC.

that automates data input and validation and streamlines document processing. The ERIC Clearinghouses now catalog, abstract, and index directly into this new Web-based system, which offers many quality control features, including

- Error and duplicate checking
- Online access to descriptors and identifiers with cut-and-paste routines
- Spell-check
- Online access to various editorial help tools

EDVAPS brings immediate and significant benefits to ERIC users by

- Improving the timeliness of information with database updates moving from monthly issues to continuous updates, making full-text documents more readily available
- Improving the accuracy of database cataloging and indexing so information retrieval is more exact

The new system accepts uploads of various digital file formats, including PDF, HTML, XML, video, and audio, moving ERIC from a largely paper-based system to an electronic system that provides more comprehensive coverage of education-related material.

In addition, EDVAPS enables ERIC to capture metadata pertaining to the expanding variety of educational materials. The user interface of the system can incorporate metadata schemes to automatically code and field new and developing forms of content such as pre-prints, digital media, and multimedia. This feature allows users to search and accurately retrieve a wider variety of education resources captured by ERIC.

Database Growth

In 2001 a total of 32,099 new records were added to the ERIC database: abstracts of 12,436 documents and abstracts of 19,663 journal articles. The entire bibliographic database, covering the period 1966–2001, contains 448,312 abstracts of documents and 628,868 abstracts of journal articles, totaling 1,077,180 records.

The database is built by the 16 ERIC Clearinghouses, which acquire and select articles and documents in their scope areas; catalog, abstract, and index them; and send them to the central ERIC Processing and Reference Facility. The facility performs final editing and combines records from all clearinghouses into the database.

ERIC currently indexes about 1,140 education-related journals. The clearinghouses catalog the journals in their scope areas and add new journals when appropriate. Many journals are indexed cover to cover, whereas others are indexed selectively. Journal articles compose approximately 60 percent of the ERIC database.

Documents other than journal articles compose approximately 40 percent of the database. ERIC systematically acquires most documents via acquisition arrangements with information providers such as universities and other research organizations, associations, commercial publishers, and state and local education agencies. In 2001 the ERIC Facility and the clearinghouses had a total of 2,678 such arrangements in place.

In addition to these standing acquisitions arrangements, ERIC aggressively solicits education-related material from new sources and accepts unsolicited documents for review. However, inclusion of submitted documents in the ERIC database is not automatic; all documents are evaluated by subject-matter experts at the ERIC Clearinghouses. A document selected for ERIC must be clearly linked to the process or practice of education. In addition, it is evaluated for quality of content, including contribution to knowledge, significance, relevance, newness, innovativeness, effectiveness of presentation, thoroughness of reporting, relation to current priorities, timeliness, authority of source, intended audience, and comprehensiveness. All documents must meet standards for legibility and reproducibility, and must be available from either the ERIC Document Reproduction Service (EDRS) or another source.

Database Content

ERIC catalogs bibliographic records in its database by describing records according to type of publication. In 2001 more than 80 percent of the documents and articles entered in the database were categorized as research/technical reports, descriptive reports, evaluative/feasibility reports, guides (including administrative and teaching guides), speeches, conference papers, viewpoints, or books.

Documents produced or funded by the U.S. Department of Education are given special priority in the database. The ERIC Facility reports that 1,516 department documents were entered into the database in 2001—approximately 12 percent of all documents entered.

In 2001 the highest numbers of document entries into the database came from three scope areas: adult, career, and vocational education (1,146 documents); higher education (1,042 documents); and reading, English, and communication (1,003 documents). The largest numbers of journal articles were processed in the scope areas of educational and information technology (1,862 articles), higher education (1,692 articles), and counseling and student services (1,675 articles).

Database Access

The ERIC database is available for public access on the Internet at http://www. eric.ed.gov. In fact, Internet accessibility is a major factor influencing how information from ERIC affects U.S. education. Teachers, researchers, and others interested in education can search ERIC at more than 1,000 public and university libraries as well as at Federal Depository Libraries. In addition to Internet accessibility, the entire database is available through commercial database subscription services and on CD-ROM. Currently, six online vendors and three CD-ROM vendors offer access to the ERIC database, including the ERIC Processing and Reference Facility, which offers a CD-ROM subscription for $100 a year. Three ERIC host organizations provide access to the database: the ERIC Clearinghouse on Assessment and Evaluation (http://searcheric.org), the ERIC Clearinghouse on Information and Technology (http://ericit.org/searcheric.shtml), and EDRS (http://www.edrs.com/webstore/search.cfm).

Because the ERIC database is accessible in so many ways, it is impossible to gather complete statistics on how many searches are executed each year. However, the three ERIC host organizations reported a combined total of 7,040,593 ERIC searches conducted in 2001—an average of 586,716 searches a month.

Document Delivery

The ERIC Document Reproduction Service (EDRS) provides access to full-text copies of ERIC documents. In 2001 the ERIC E*Subscribe service, which provides access to electronically releasable ERIC documents by subscription, more than doubled its customer base, growing from 438 at the beginning of the year to a year-end total of 1,032 customers.

E*Subscribe's customers include four-year colleges and universities (60 percent); K–12 institutions (16 percent); public libraries (14 percent); community colleges (7 percent); and nonprofit and corporate libraries (3 percent). This service provides direct access to electronic copies of more than 87,000 publications (nearly 95 percent of the releasable ERIC documents produced since 1993) to more than 9 million students, faculty, and other customers. Users at subscribing institutions can search the ERIC database and download ERIC documents in Adobe's Portable Document Format (PDF). A total of 655,086 ERIC documents were downloaded in electronic format in 2001.

Despite the interest in the E*Subscribe electronic subscription service, EDRS continues to fill on-demand orders for paper, microfiche, and electronic copies of ERIC documents. In 2001 customers ordered 38,962 copies of ERIC documents. Of these requests, 47 percent were for paper copies, 36 percent were for electronic copies, and 17 percent were for microfiche.

ERIC Products

In addition to building the ERIC database, the ERIC Clearinghouses analyze and synthesize literature in their areas of expertise and create research reviews, bibliographies, interpretive studies of high-interest topics, digests, and other publications that meet the information needs of the wide spectrum of ERIC users. In 2001 the clearinghouses and ACCESS ERIC produced 468 information products, with many resulting from partnerships among ERIC Clearinghouses and professional associations, private publishers, academic institutions, and other organizations. All clearinghouse products are reviewed by two subject matter experts prior to publication.

Over the years, the ERIC Digests have proved to be one of ERIC's most popular products. In 2001 the ERIC Clearinghouses produced 146 ERIC Digests. These two-page summaries cover the most current information available on specific education issues and topics. Topics are determined by examining research trends in documents and articles acquired for the database, questions most frequently asked by ERIC customers, and suggestions from the National Clearinghouse Committees. Several types of digests are available including overviews, fact sheets, issues (defining and describing a controversial topic), practice applications, research findings, syntheses of syntheses, and resource summaries. The complete text of more than 2,300 ERIC Digests can be found on online and CD-ROM versions of the database.

Other products include peer-reviewed electronic journals, virtual libraries, and numerous specialized directories. The clearinghouses continue to collaborate with ACCESS ERIC to produce the *ERIC Review,* a free journal for practitioners that reports critical trends and issues in education.

User Services

Consistent with its mission to increase and facilitate the use of educational research and information on educational practice, ERIC provides extensive user services to the public. These include reference and retrieval services, access to Internet resources, literature searches, bibliographies, identification of popular documents, and referrals to other sources of information.

Since 1987 the ERIC program has committed itself to reaching and serving more-diverse audiences. In addition to researchers and graduate students, ERIC serves teachers, policymakers, journalists, parents, students, and the general public. ERIC staff receive and answer requests via toll-free phone calls, faxes, mail, and e-mail as well as in person at clearinghouses and conferences. The chart below shows user statistics for 2001.

How Users Contacted ERIC in 2001

Method	Number	Percent
E-mail*	100,758	65.2
Phone	32,345	21.0
Letters/Fax	17,433	11.3
Visits	3,908	2.5
Total	154,444	100.0
Web hits	415,510,276	

*The e-mail category includes 34,571 AskERIC requests.

Anyone can send an education-related question to askeric@askeric.org and expect to receive a reply within two business days. During 2001 a total of 34,571 customers received responses to AskERIC requests that included ERIC database citations and relevant online resources. In October 2001 AskERIC introduced AskERIC Live!, a chat reference service that allows online users to ask questions that are answered immediately by AskERIC reference specialists. A transcript of the session is e-mailed to the questioner when the real-time chat is over. In its first two months of operation, 390 questions were addressed via AskERIC Live!

The ERIC system responds to user requests by answering queries; sending out materials such as ERIC Digests, newsletters, and bibliographies; searching the ERIC database and other ERIC-produced databases and directories for relevant information; and providing referrals to other education-related organizations. ERIC Clearinghouses are contacted by a broad spectrum of users, with most users being faculty and students from either K–12 or postsecondary schools.

The gateway to all ERIC Web sites is the ERIC Systemwide site at http://www.eric.ed.gov. The site links to all clearinghouse and component Web sites, and provides access to the ERIC Database, ERIC Calendar of Education-Related

Conferences, and the ERIC Slide Show, which provides an overview of ERIC products and services, as well as tips on searching the ERIC database.

Together, the ERIC Web sites received more than 415 million hits in 2001. Resources available on these sites include

- Full-text virtual libraries
- Special directories
- Records being processed for the ERIC database
- Pre-selected searches and expert search strategies on hot topics

ERIC Clearinghouses

The ERIC system includes 16 clearinghouses. Following is key information about each clearinghouse and a brief explanation of its scope. Several clearinghouses have associated adjunct clearinghouses that receive funding from sponsors outside the ERIC system. Adjuncts perform some or all of the following functions in their subject areas: identifying and acquiring significant literature for the ERIC database, providing reference and referral services, providing technical assistance, maintaining or contributing to Web sites, and producing publications.

ERIC Clearinghouse on Adult, Career, and Vocational Education

Ohio State University
1900 Kenny Rd.
Columbus, OH 43210-1090
Tel. 800-848-4815, ext. 2-7069 (toll-free) or 614-292-7069
TTY/TDD 614-688-8734
Fax 614-292-1260
E-mail ericacve@osu.edu
World Wide Web http://ericacve.org

Scope: All levels and settings of adult and continuing, career, and vocational/technical education, including school-to-work, tech prep, technology education, corrections education, employment and training programs, youth employment, work experience programs, education/business partnerships, entrepreneurship, adult retraining, and vocational rehabilitation for individuals with disabilities. Adult education information spans basic literacy training through professional skill upgrading and includes career education resources for experience-based education and career awareness, decision making, development, and change.

ERIC Clearinghouse on Assessment and Evaluation

University of Maryland, College Park
Department of Measurement, Statistics, and Evaluation
1129 Shriver Laboratory
College Park, MD 20742
Tel. 800-464-3742 (toll-free) or 301-405-7449
Fax 301-405-8134

E-mail ericae@ericae.net

World Wide Web http://ericae.net

Scope: Tests and other measurement devices; methodology of measurement and evaluation; application of tests, measurement, and evaluation in educational projects or programs; research design and methodology in the area of assessment and evaluation; and learning theory.

ERIC Clearinghouse for Community Colleges

University of California at Los Angeles
3051 Moore Hall
P.O. Box 951521
Los Angeles, CA 90095-1521
Tel. 800-832-8256 (toll-free) or 310-825-3931
Fax 310-206-8095
E-mail ericcc@ucla.edu
World Wide Web http://www.gseis.ucla.edu/ERIC/eric.html

Scope: Development, administration, and evaluation of two-year public and private community and junior colleges, technical institutes, and two-year branch university campuses; and information about two-year college students, faculty, staff, curricula (including distance education), programs, financing, support services, libraries, community services, linkages between two-year colleges and business/industrial organizations, and articulation of two-year colleges with secondary and four-year postsecondary institutions.

The Adjunct ERIC Clearinghouse on Entrepreneurship Education is sponsored by the Center for Entrepreneurial Leadership, Ewing Marion Kauffman Foundation.

ERIC Clearinghouse on Counseling and Student Services

University of North Carolina at Greensboro
School of Education
201 Ferguson Building
P.O. Box 26170
Greensboro, NC 27402-6170
Tel. 800-414-9769 (toll-free) or 336-334-4114
Fax 336-334-4116
E-mail ericcass@uncg.edu
World Wide Web http://ericcass.uncg.edu

Scope: Preparation, practice, and supervision of counselors, psychologists, therapists, and student personnel specialists at all educational levels and in all settings; theoretical development of counseling and student services; assessment and diagnosis procedures, such as testing and interviewing and the analysis and dissemination of the resultant information; outcomes analysis of counseling interventions; group and casework; nature of pupil, student, and adult characteristics; identification and implementation of strategies that foster student learning and achievement; personnel workers and their relation to career planning, family consultations, and student services activities; identification of effective strategies for enhancing parental effectiveness; and continuing preparation of counselors and therapists in the use of new technologies for professional renewal and the implications of such technologies for service provision.

ERIC Clearinghouse on Disabilities and Gifted Education

Council for Exceptional Children
1110 N. Glebe Rd.
Arlington, VA 22201-5704
Tel. 800-328-0272 (toll-free) or 703-264-9475
TTY/TDD 800-328-0272
Fax 703-620-2521
E-mail ericec@cec.sped.org
World Wide Web http://ericec.org

Scope: All aspects of special education and gifted education as well as the development of people with disabilities and those who are gifted; identification, assessment, and intervention and enrichment in special settings and in inclusive settings; learning, developmental, and physical disabilities; behavioral and emotional disorders; mental retardation; outstanding intellectual or creative ability in any area of achievement; referral, student evaluation, early intervention programs, early childhood special education, social integration, individualized education programs, individualized family service plans, school-to-work transition, and vocational and lifelong education; and employment, rehabilitation, applications of technology, physical accessibility, differentiated curriculum, acceleration, and leadership development. Further, the scope encompasses populations that are at risk (abused or medically fragile), low incidence, adjudicated, culturally and linguistically diverse, or economically disadvantaged, to the extent that these risk factors relate to disabilities and/or giftedness.

The Adjunct ERIC Clearinghouse on Early Intervention and Early Childhood Special Education is sponsored by the U.S. Department of Education, Office of Special Education Programs.

ERIC Clearinghouse on Educational Management

5207 University of Oregon
Eugene, OR 97403-5207
Tel. 800-438-8841 (toll-free) or 541-346-5043
Fax 541-346-2334
E-mail eric@eric.uoregon.edu
World Wide Web http://eric.uoregon.edu

Scope: Leadership, management, and structure of public and private education organizations at elementary and secondary school levels; practice and theory of administration; federal, state, and local education law, policy making, and governance; pre-service and in-service preparation of administrators; administrative tasks and processes, including planning, financing, and staffing education organizations; methods and varieties of organization, including organizational change and improvement; school–community relationships; and the social context of education organizations.

ERIC Clearinghouse on Elementary and Early Childhood Education

University of Illinois at Urbana-Champaign
Children's Research Center
51 Gerty Drive
Champaign, IL 61820-7469
Tel. 800-583-4135 (toll-free) or 217-333-1386
TTY/TDD 800-583-4135
Fax 217-333-3767
E-mail ericeece@uiuc.edu
World Wide Web http://ericeece.org
National Parent Information Network http://npin.org

Scope: Physical, cognitive, social, educational, and cultural development of children from birth through early adolescence; prenatal factors, parents, parenting, and family relationships that relate to education; learning theory research and practice related to the development of young children, including the preparation of teachers; interdisciplinary curriculum (including the project approach) and mixed-age teaching and learning; educational, social, and cultural programs and services for children; the child in the context of the family and the family in the context of society; and theoretical and philosophical issues pertaining to children's development and education.

The Adjunct ERIC Clearinghouse for Child Care is sponsored by the Child Care Bureau; Administration for Children, Youth, and Families; U.S. Department of Health and Human Services.

ERIC Clearinghouse on Higher Education

George Washington University
Graduate School of Education and Human Development
1 Dupont Circle N.W., Suite 630
Washington, DC 20036-1183
Tel. 800-773-3742 (toll-free) or 202-296-2597
Fax 202-452-1844
E-mail eric-he@eric-he.edu
World Wide Web http://www.eriche.org

Scope: All major junctures or levels, including entry to college, environment, outcomes of college, graduate or professional education, and international higher education; people, including administrators, faculty, students, external constituencies, and governance officers; processes (including instruction, learning, planning, and governance) and issues at colleges and universities providing higher education (that is, four-year degrees and beyond), including technology, legal issues, public relations, diversity, and methodology.

The Adjunct ERIC Clearinghouse on Educational Opportunity is sponsored by the U.S. Department of Education, Office of Higher Education Preparation and Support.

ERIC Clearinghouse on Information and Technology

Syracuse University
621 Skytop Rd., Suite 160
Syracuse, NY 13244-5290
Tel. 800-464-9107 (toll-free) or 315-443-3640
Fax 315-443-5448
E-mail eric@ericit.org or askeric@askeric.org
World Wide Web http://www.ericit.org
AskERIC http://www.askeric.org

Scope: All aspects of information technology related to education, covering educational technology and library and information science at all levels; and instructional design, development, and evaluation pertaining to educational technology and the media of educational communication: computers, the Internet, telecommunications, audio and video recordings, and other multimedia materials pertaining to teaching and learning. The focus is on the operation and management of information services for education-related organizations.

ERIC Clearinghouse on Languages and Linguistics

Center for Applied Linguistics
4646 40th St. N.W.
Washington, DC 20016-1859
Tel. 800-276-9834 (toll-free) or 202-362-0700
Fax 202-363-7204
E-mail eric@cal.org
World Wide Web http://www.cal.org/ericcll

Scope: Languages and language sciences and all aspects of second-language instruction and learning in all commonly and less commonly taught languages, including English as a second language; bilingualism and bilingual education; cultural education in the context of second-language learning, including intercultural communication, study abroad, and international education exchange; and all areas of linguistics, including theoretical and applied linguistics, sociolinguistics, and psycholinguistics.

The Adjunct ERIC Clearinghouse for ESL Literacy Education is sponsored by the U.S. Department of Education, Office of Vocational and Adult Education.

ERIC Clearinghouse on Reading, English, and Communication

Indiana University
Smith Research Center
2805 E. 10th St., Suite 140
Bloomington, IN 47408-2698
Tel. 800-759-4723 (toll-free) or 812-855-5847
Fax 812-856-5512
E-mail ericcs@indiana.edu

World Wide Web http://eric.indiana.edu

Scope: Reading, English, and communication (verbal and nonverbal), preschool through college; educational research and instructional development in reading, writing, speaking, and listening; identification, diagnosis, and remediation of reading problems; speech communication (including forensics), mass communication, interpersonal and small group interaction, interpretation, rhetorical and communication theory, speech sciences, and theater; preparation of instructional staff and related personnel; all aspects of reading behavior, emphasizing physiology, psychology, sociology, and teaching; instructional materials, curricula, tests/ measurement, and methodology at all levels of reading; the role of libraries and other agencies in fostering and guiding reading; and diagnostics and remedial reading services in schools and clinical settings. The clearinghouse also covers preparation of reading teachers and specialists and includes guidelines in these subject areas for related agencies and for parents.

ERIC Clearinghouse on Rural Education and Small Schools

AEL, Inc.
1031 Quarrier St.
P.O. Box 1348
Charleston, WV 25325-1348
Tel. 800-624-9120 (toll-free) or 304-347-0400
TTY/TDD 304-347-0448
Fax 304-347-0467
E-mail ericrc@ael.org
World Wide Web http://www.ael.org/eric

Scope: Programs, practices, and economic, cultural, social, and other factors pertaining to the education of rural residents, American Indians, Alaska Natives, Mexican Americans, and migrants; educational practices and programs in all small schools; and outdoor and experiential education.

The Adjunct ERIC Clearinghouse on Rural Mathematics Education is sponsored by the ACCLAIM Research Initiative funded by the National Science Foundation.

ERIC Clearinghouse on Science, Mathematics, and Environmental Education

Ohio State University
1929 Kenny Rd.
Columbus, OH 43210-1080
Tel. 800-276-0462 (toll-free) or 614-292-6717
Fax 614-292-0263
E-mail ericse@osu.edu
World Wide Web http://www.ericse.org

Scope: Science, mathematics, and environmental education at all levels, including the development of curriculum and instruction materials; teachers and teacher education; learning theory and outcomes, including the impact of parameters such as interest level, intelligence, values, and concept development on learning in these fields; educational programs; research and evaluative studies; media applications; and computer applications.

ERIC Clearinghouse on Social Studies/Social Science Education

Indiana University
Social Studies Development Center
2805 E. 10th St., Suite 120
Bloomington, IN 47408-2698
Tel. 800-266-3815 (toll-free) or 812-855-3838
Fax 812-855-0455
E-mail ericso@indiana.edu
World Wide Web http://ericso.indiana.edu

Scope: All levels of social studies and social science education; the contributions of history, geography, and other social science disciplines; applications of theory and research to social science education; education as a social science; comparative education (K–12); and content and curriculum materials pertaining to such social topics as law-related education, ethnic studies, bias and discrimination, aging, and women's equity. Music and art education are also covered.

Adjunct clearinghouses include the Adjunct ERIC Clearinghouse for International Civic Education, sponsored by the Center for Civic Education, and the Adjunct ERIC Clearinghouse for U.S.-Japan Studies, sponsored by the Japan Foundation Center for Global Partnership.

ERIC Clearinghouse on Teaching and Teacher Education

American Association of Colleges for Teacher Education
1307 New York Ave. N.W., Suite 300
Washington, DC 20005-4701
Tel. 800-822-9229 (toll-free) or 202-293-2450
Fax 202-457-8095
E-mail query@aacte.org
World Wide Web http://www.ericsp.org

Scope: School personnel issues at all levels, including teacher recruitment, selection, licensing, certification, training, pre-service and in-service preparation, evaluation, retention, and retirement; theory, philosophy, and practice of teaching; curricula and general education not specifically covered by other clearinghouses; and organizational, administrative, financial, and legal issues pertaining to teacher education programs and institutions. The clearinghouse also covers all aspects of health, physical, recreation, and dance education.

The Adjunct ERIC Clearinghouse on Clinical Schools is sponsored by the Ford Foundation.

ERIC Clearinghouse on Urban Education

Teachers College, Columbia University
Institute for Urban and Minority Education
Main Hall, Room 303, Box 40
New York, NY 10027-6696
Tel. 800-601-4868 (toll-free) or 212-678-3433
Fax 212-678-4012
E-mail eric-cue@columbia.edu
World Wide Web http://eric-web.tc.columbia.edu

Scope: Programs and practices in urban public, parochial, and independent schools; the education of African Americans, Hispanics/Latinos (excluding Mexican Americans), Asian Americans, and other ethnic groups and immigrant students in urban schools; educational equity; multicultural, antibias, conflict resolution, and violence-prevention education; parent and community involvement in urban schools; urban economic and social conditions affecting education; and public- and private-sector policies to improve urban education.

The Adjunct ERIC Clearinghouse on Homeless Education is sponsored by the National Center for Homeless Education at SERVE, the Regional Educational Laboratory for the Southeast.

ERIC Support Components

ACCESS ERIC

Aspen Systems Corporation
2277 Research Blvd., 4M
Rockville, MD 20850
Tel. 800-538-3742 (toll-free) or 301-519-5157
Fax 301-519-6760
E-mail accesseric@accesseric.org
World Wide Web http://www.eric.ed.gov

ACCESS ERIC coordinates ERIC's outreach and systemwide dissemination activities, develops new ERIC publications, and provides general reference and referral services. Publications and directories include *A Pocket Guide to ERIC, All About ERIC, The ERIC Review,* the online *ERIC Calendar of Education-Related Conferences,* and the online *Directory of ERIC Resource Collections.* ACCESS ERIC also maintains the ERIC systemwide Web site where visitors can view the monthly and weekly systemwide newsletters, as well as the introductory tutorial on ERIC services and the ERIC Slide Show.

ERIC Document Reproduction Service (EDRS)

DynEDRS, Inc.
7420 Fullerton Rd., Suite 110
Springfield, VA 22153-2852
Tel. 800-443-3742 (toll-free) or 703-440-1400
Fax 703-440-1408
E-mail service@edrs.com
World Wide Web http://www.edrs.com

EDRS produces and sells electronic, microfiche, and paper copies of documents abstracted in the ERIC database. Back collections of ERIC documents, annual subscriptions, cumulative indexes, and other ERIC products also are available from EDRS. Users can order ERIC documents by toll-free phone, fax, mail, or e-mail (service@edrs.com); through the EDRS Web site (http://www.edrs.com); or from commercial online vendors including Dialog Corporation and OCLC.

ERIC Processing and Reference Facility

Computer Sciences Corporation
4483-A Forbes Blvd.
Lanham, MD 20706
Tel. 800-799-3742 (toll-free) or 301-552-4200
Fax 301-552-4700
E-mail info@ericfac.piccard.csc.com
World Wide Web http://ericfacility.org

The ERIC Processing and Reference Facility is the central editorial and computer processing agency that coordinates document-processing and database-building activities for ERIC. The facility performs acquisition, lexicographic, and reference functions, and maintains systemwide quality control standards. The facility also prepares and maintains the Thesaurus of ERIC Descriptors, the ERIC Database Master File for distribution to database vendors, the ERIC Source Journal Index, the ERIC Identifier Authority List, ERIC Ready References, and sells the ERIC-on-NISC CD-ROM.

National Association and Organization Reports

American Library Association

50 E. Huron St., Chicago, IL 60611
312-944-6780, 800-545-2433
World Wide Web http://www.ala.org

Maurice J. Freedman
President

Founded in 1876, the American Library Association (ALA) is the oldest, largest, and most influential library association in the world. The association membership comprises primarily librarians but also includes library trustees, publishers, and other interested people from every U.S. state and many nations. The association serves public, state, school, and academic libraries, plus special libraries for people working in government, commerce and industry, the arts, the armed services, hospitals, prisons, and other institutions. Membership in fiscal year 2002 was nearly 64,000.

The mission of ALA is to provide leadership for the development, promotion, and improvement of library and information services and the profession of librarianship in order to enhance learning and ensure access to information for all. Key action areas include diversity, education and continuous learning, equity of access, intellectual freedom, and 21st-century literacy. ALA is a 501(C)(3) charitable and educational organization.

The association has 11 member divisions, each focused on a different area of special interest. They are the American Association of School Librarians (AASL), the Association for Library Trustees and Advocates (ALTA), the Association for Library Collections and Technical Services (ALCTS), the Association for Library Service to Children (ALSC), the Association of College and Research Libraries (ACRL), the Association of Specialized and Cooperative Library Agencies (ASCLA), the Library Administration and Management Association (LAMA), the Library and Information Technology Association (LITA), the Public Library Association (PLA), the Reference and User Services Association (RUSA), and the Young Adult Library Services Association (YALSA).

ALA is the nation's leading advocate for high-quality library and information services. The association maintains a close working relationship with more than 70 other library associations in the United States, Canada, and other countries, and works closely with organizations concerned with education, research, cultural development, recreation, and public service.

ALA's headquarters is in Chicago. The association maintains a legislative office and Office for Information Technology Policy in Washington, D.C., and an editorial office in Middletown, Connecticut, for *Choice,* a review journal for academic libraries.

Campaign for America's Librarians

The inauguration of ALA President Maurice J. Freedman at the 2002 ALA Annual Conference set in motion an initiative called the Campaign for America's Librarians: Advocating for Better Salaries and Pay Equity for All Library Workers. The initiative provided further stimulus for the efforts of the ALA-Allied Professional Association (ALA-APA), established to help improve status, pay equity, and salaries for librarians and library workers. The initiative has four major goals:

- To gather and analyze currently available resources and research regarding the status and salaries of librarians and library workers
- To encourage new research and the development of resources, tools, and structures that will help librarians and library workers achieve pay equity and salaries comparable to their worth
- To emphasize the Campaign for America's Librarians as a component of public awareness and advocacy efforts of ALA, using library staff and officials, funding agencies, and the public as advocates
- To help library workers to organize, including the use of unions as one mechanism, to achieve better salaries and pay equity for all library workers

Freedman's presidency also saw the launch of the ALA Campaign to Save America's Libraries, a public-awareness effort focused on the impact of library funding cuts nationwide.

"Librarians and our users cannot afford to be quiet about drastic cuts forcing libraries to close their doors earlier, lay off experienced library staff, eliminate periodicals collections, and reduce programs and services," Freedman said. "These cuts are deeper than those sustained even in the Great Depression, and they are affecting library services in schools, college and university campuses, and communities everywhere."

Freedman also pledged to use his ALA presidency to fight for

- Unfettered and unfiltered access to information in all formats
- Programs and funding to ensure the recruitment, education, and retention of a diverse library work force, including active support of the ALA Spectrum Scholarship Fund
- Continued fair use of databases and software
- Free access to and continued support of the widest possible publication and dissemination of government information
- Programs and funding to support early childhood initiatives and family literacy

- School libraries in their struggle against externally imposed Internet filters and censorship
- Promotion of collaboration between school and public libraries and librarians
- Continued recognition that libraries are physical as well as virtual places
- Keeping the "L" in library education by requiring ALA-accredited schools to teach library administration, services, and principles

Freedman also was committed to promoting ALA's programs and goals through an extensive media campaign that included numerous op-ed pieces, radio and print interviews, and local and national television appearances.

White House Conference on School Libraries

First Lady Laura Bush held the first-ever White House Conference on School Libraries June 4, 2002. The conference spotlighted research that ties academic achievement to strong school library programs. Education, library, government, and philanthropic leaders from across the country, including AASL Executive Director Julie Walker and AASL 2001–2002 President Helen Adams, took part. Walker was named to the national advisory committee for the nonprofit Laura Bush Foundation for America's Libraries, which will provide grants to help school libraries extend their collections.

@ Your Library

The Campaign for America's Libraries, trademarked "@ your library," took hold in libraries nationwide in 2002 with the message that libraries are dynamic places of opportunity that bring their patrons the world.

Thanks to the efforts of state chapters and state libraries, as well as regional cooperatives and associations, the campaign is now reaching approximately 10,000 libraries nationwide. Public, school, academic, and special libraries joined the campaign to enhance their existing marketing efforts, to promote new services, and to act as advocates for new programs and increased funding. Statewide efforts, including advocacy training, conferences, and special initiatives, were planned under the @ your library banner in 25 states.

The campaign's global presence increased during the year. Thirteen countries—Armenia, Australia, Azerbaijan, Bulgaria, Canada, Georgia, Iceland, Italy, Japan, Kazakhstan, Mexico, South Korea, and Turkey—joined the campaign. The @ your library brand was made available online for use by the global library community.

New Partners and Initiatives

A number of national partnerships and initiatives helped extend the outreach of the @ your library campaign. The first was "Drive to Read @ your library," sponsored by ALA and Morningstar Foods. Launched at the Indianapolis Motor

Speedway, the program aims to spur interest in reading among America's teens. More than 900 libraries participated in the first year of the program.

Woman's Day magazine joined ALA for "Put It in Writing @ your library," designed to encourage aspiring writers to use the resources of their local library. During National Library Week 2002, eight libraries hosted sold-out writer workshops, and *Woman's Day* launched a national essay contest for unpublished women writers, receiving nearly 1,000 entries.

Also during National Library Week, ALA launched "Rediscover America @ your library" to show that "libraries are needed now more than ever." The Rediscover America initiative was a response to the terrorist attacks of September 11, 2001, and carried the message that libraries are a resource for community dialogue on topics of national importance.

ALA also teamed up with Major League Baseball in a partnership called "Join the Major Leagues @ your library," designed to promote information literacy. Dave Roberts and Alex Cora of the Los Angeles Dodgers joined Sharon Robinson (daughter of baseball legend Jackie Robinson and vice president for educational programming of Major League Baseball), ALA President John W. Berry, and hundreds of children at an opening event at the County of Los Angeles Public Library/Culver City Library and at Dodgers Stadium in May 2002.

To cap a successful year of new campaign partnerships, ALA received a major cash sponsorship from Wells Fargo Home Mortgage. As a result, "The Path to Homeownership Begins @ your library" was unveiled in July at the Mount Pleasant branch of the District of Columbia Public Library. U.S. Secretary of Housing and Urban Development Mel Martinez and Derek Parra, program spokesperson (and first Mexican American to win a medal in the Olympics), joined members of the library community for the ceremony. The program is designed to promote home ownership among low- to moderate-income families and minorities. Administered by ALA's Reference and User Services Association, the program includes new online reference materials and free home-ownership workshops in 10 U.S. cities.

For more information about the campaign and how to get involved in partnership activities, see http://www.ala.org/@yourlibrary.

Office for Intellectual Freedom

Internet Filtering Battle

The ALA Office for Intellectual Freedom (OIF) and the ALA Washington Office were key players as ALA pressed its arguments against the federal Children's Internet Protection Act (CIPA) in 2001–2002.

The Children's Internet Protection Act (CIPA) and the Neighborhood Children's Internet Protection Act (NCIPA) went into effect on April 20, 2001. These laws place restrictions on the use of funding that is available through the Library Services and Technology Act (LSTA), Title III of the Elementary and Secondary Education Act, and on the Universal Service discount program known as the E-rate (P.L. 106-554). These restrictions take the form of requirements for Internet "safety policies" and technology that blocks or filters certain material from being accessed through the Internet.

On March 20, 2001, ALA filed a federal lawsuit on behalf of public libraries and library patrons seeking to overturn CIPA. The complaint, filed in the U.S. District Court for the Eastern District of Pennsylvania, held that the government cannot constitutionally place such restrictions on public libraries. CIPA, the lawsuit said, violates the First and Fifth Amendments because it makes access to funding and rate discounts for Internet use in public libraries contingent on the acceptance of content and viewpoint restrictions on constitutionally protected speech, burdening the right of libraries, their patrons, and those speaking on the Internet to communicate and receive protected speech.

On May 31, 2002, a three-judge panel of the Third Circuit Court of Appeals in the Eastern District of Pennsylvania agreed that government agencies cannot withhold funds on the ground that a public library has failed to install mandatory filters on every computer. The court held that "because of the inherent limitations in filtering technology, public libraries can never comply with CIPA without blocking access to a substantial amount of speech that is both constitutionally protected and fails to meet even the filtering companies' own blocking criteria."

Specifically, the court ruled that CIPA Sections 1712(a)(2) and 1721(b) were invalid under the First Amendment and permanently enjoined the government from enforcing those provisions. The Justice Department, acting on behalf of the Federal Communications Commission and the Institute of Museum and Library Services, appealed the decision to the Supreme Court, which scheduled arguments for March. For more information, visit the ALA CIPA Web site, http://www.ala.org/cipa. [See also the article "Legislation and Regulations Affecting Libraries in 2002" in Part 2—*Ed.*]

Antiterrorism Measures Cause Concern

The September 11 attacks heightened concerns about library patron confidentiality and access to information. In response, OIF developed "Confidentiality and Coping with Law Enforcement Inquiries: Guidelines for the Library and its Staff" (http://www.ala.org/alaorg/oif/guidelineslibrary.html) and Web resources addressing "FBI in Your Library" (http://www.ala.org/alaorg/oif/fbiinyour library.html), the Terrorism Information and Prevention System (TIPS) (http://www.ala.org/alaorg/oif/tips.html), and the USA Patriot Act (http://www.ala.org/alaorg/oif/usapatriotact.html).

OIF completed its Interpretation of the Library Bill of Rights on privacy, which was adopted by the ALA Council on June 19, 2002. The interpretation, along with questions and answers on privacy and confidentiality, can be found at http://www.ala.org/alaorg/oif/privacyinterpretation.html.

Banned Books Week

Banned Books Week 2002, with the theme "Let Freedom Read: Read a Banned Book," was observed September 21–28. Author Studs Terkel led a gathering of more than 20 authors, artists, columnists, and librarians on the front steps of ALA headquarters in Chicago in a "read-out" of banned books.

This was the 20th annual celebration of the anticensorship event, which is cosponsored by the American Booksellers Association, the American Booksellers Foundation for Free Expression, ALA, the American Society of Journalists and

Authors, the Association of American Publishers, and the National Association of College Stores. Dates for the event in 2003 are September 20–27.

Washington Office

ALA has dealt extensively with problems caused by added restrictions on access to government information brought about largely as a result of the September 11 terrorist attacks. A number of federal agencies removed information from their public Web sites following the attacks as part of antiterrorism efforts. The Washington Office has been working with the American Association of Law Libraries, the Association of Research Libraries, and other public interest organizations to encourage agencies to talk with their constituencies about the criteria they are using to review materials for dissemination on their Web sites and to restore access to these materials as quickly as possible (see http://www.ala.org/washoff/patriot.html).

Office for Information Technology Policy

The ALA Office for Information Technology Policy (OITP) presented two programs at the 2002 ALA Annual Conference to promote its Information Commons project. The programs, "Our Common Wealth: Libraries, Copyright, and the Fate of the Information Commons" and "The Creative Commons," were part of an effort to explore the importance of establishing and protecting a vital public domain of creative works and finding a middle ground in the current copyright debates. The programs highlighted the importance of a robust public media space of commercial, amateur, and fringe expression versus a closed, centralized system controlled by large commercial interests. OITP launched a Web site (http://www.info-commons.org) that includes papers generated from the project as well as book reviews, interviews, and commissioned articles on Information Commons issues.

The OITP E-book Task Force hosted a forum at which librarians and representatives of the e-book industry, both technologists and publishers, were able to conduct informal, off-the-record discussions. Participants shared views about the roles libraries will or can play in providing access to e-books and ways to improve mutual understanding of the key issues and opportunities e-book technology presents. Participants also worked to design an action plan, and four projects were identified: development of new business models that would better serve libraries; development of a model e-book license; a report on e-books in libraries, including user needs assessment; and an examination of ways in which ALA can play a larger role in the development of e-book standards. Participants asked that OITP continue to support their work with staff resources and more funding, if it is needed and available.

E-rate Examination

On April 5, 2002, ALA filed comments with the Federal Communications Commission (FCC) concerning a proposed FCC rule that would streamline the e-rate program, which provides discounted telecommunications rates to libraries and schools. ALA supported increasing the funding cap; allowing libraries alternative ways to establish their discount levels; broadening the definition of and revising the categories of eligible services; revising the priority schedule for discount eligibility; eliminating disincentives for consortia; and recognizing the role of state coordinators in reducing the administrative costs of the Universal Service Administrative Company's Schools and Libraries Division (SLD) and increasing the efficiency of the program as a whole. At an OITP-hosted retreat in Warrenton, Virginia, in February 2002, the ALA E-rate Task Force, SLD staff and board members, and FCC staff discussed the e-rate program, methods for improving communications among the various groups, and priorities for the coming year.

National Library Legislative Day

National Library Legislative Day 2002 events brought more than 450 librarians and friends of libraries from 47 states to Capitol Hill to speak with their representatives and senators about issues of concern to the library community. The event, cosponsored by the District of Columbia Library Association and ALA, is held each May to bring librarians, library trustees, board members, and other library friends to Washington. As part of the event, the Friends of Libraries U.S.A. (FOLUSA) gives an annual public service award to a member of Congress who provides leadership on and demonstrates commitment to important library issues. The 2002 recipient of the FOLUSA award was Sen. Olympia Snowe (R-Maine).

[For more on the activities of the Washington Office, see the article "Legislation and Regulations Affecting Libraries in 2002" in Part 2—*Ed.*]

Programs and Partners

'Frankenstein' Exhibition

The ALA Public Programs Office partnered with the National Library of Medicine (NLM) to develop "Frankenstein: Penetrating the Secrets of Nature," a traveling exhibition for libraries. The exhibition encourages audiences to examine the intent of Mary Wollstonecraft Shelley's novel *Frankenstein* and to discuss Shelley's and their own views about personal and societal responsibility in relation to science and other areas of life. Launched in October 2002, the exhibition is scheduled to visit 80 libraries across the country by December 2005.

In addition to the exhibition, participating libraries are hosting interpretive and educational programs that help audiences examine Shelley's novel and how it uses scientific experimentation as metaphor to comment on cultural values, especially the importance of exercising responsibility toward individuals and the community in all areas of human activity, including science. The exhibition is made possible by major grants from the National Endowment for the Humanities (NEH) and NLM. The traveling version of the exhibition is based on an exhibition produced by NLM in 1997–1998.

StoryLines America

StoryLines America completed its third season in fall 2002 with a series of radio programs that aired on participating National Public Radio stations in Illinois, Indiana, Iowa, Michigan, Minnesota, Missouri, Ohio, and Wisconsin. StoryLines

Midwest featured 13 weekly, one-hour radio shows, each focusing on an outstanding example of literature from the region. Books, discussion guides, supplemental reading lists, and tapes of all radio programs were made available to patrons at participating libraries. StoryLines Midwest was supported by a major grant from NEH, with additional funding from Barnes & Noble, Inc.

Steinbeck Centennial Project

The ALA Public Programs Office partnered with the Steinbeck Centennial in 2001–2002 to offer $500 grants to libraries to present public programs on the life and work of novelist John Steinbeck. Grants were awarded to 108 libraries in 39 states to present programs such as lectures by Steinbeck scholars, panel discussions featuring scholars or writers familiar with the themes portrayed in Steinbeck's works (such as rural poverty, migration, oceanography and ecology, and World War II and the Vietnam War), screenings of films based on Steinbeck's works, scholar- or teacher-led book discussion groups, and discussions of the differences and similarities between the book and film versions of Steinbeck's works. Major support for the Steinbeck Centennial Project was provided by NEH. The Steinbeck Centennial was coordinated by the Mercantile Library of New York, the Center for Steinbeck Studies at San Jose (California) State University, and the National Steinbeck Center in Salinas, California.

Film Discussion Series

The ALA Public Programs Office and National Video Resources partnered to present two film discussion series in 2001–2002. The first, "Presidents, Politics, and Power: American Presidents Who Shaped the 20th Century," was presented at 20 public libraries in 2002. "Presidents, Politics, and Power" used documentary films and text to engage the public in a study of the nation's strongest leaders. Participating libraries received a package of films and related materials; using these, each library hosted a six-week program to discuss the individuals portrayed in the films, which included award-winning documentaries on Theodore Roosevelt, Franklin D. Roosevelt, Harry Truman, Lyndon Johnson, Richard Nixon, and Ronald Reagan. A scholar with expertise in American history led each program. The series was funded by a major grant from NEH.

The second series, "Research Revolution: The Laboratory and the Shaping of Modern Life," sought to increase the public's understanding of the scientific discovery and technological transformations that took place in the 20th century. Fifty libraries were selected as pilot sites for this series, and the participating libraries started presenting the series in fall 2002. Major support for "Research Revolution" was provided by the National Science Foundation.

Prime Time Family Reading Time

The Public Programs Office partnered with the Louisiana Endowment for the Humanities to present the third national expansion of Prime Time Family Reading Time, a reading, discussion, and storytelling series based on illustrated children's books. Prime Time is designed to help families bond by reading and learning together; it teaches parents and children to read and discuss humanities topics and helps them choose books and become active public library users.

Fifteen libraries in 10 states participated in this round of the Prime Time initiative. Nearly 6,000 people have participated in more than 200 Prime Time programs in 25 states and the Virgin Islands. Major funding for Prime Time is provided by NEH.

LIVE! @ Your Library

LIVE! @ your library continued its three-year initiative, providing grant opportunities and programming support for libraries to present theme-based cultural programming for adult and family audiences. In 2001–2002, LIVE! grants totaling more than $243,600 were awarded to 145 libraries and partnering organizations in 47 states and territories. LIVE! @ your library programs were also held at a number of national library and literary events, including readings by such distinguished authors and poets as Pearle Cleage, Colman Barks, Terrence Cheng, Kwame Dawes, Terry Kay, and Kate Rushin, on the LIVE! @ your library Reading Stage at the ALA Annual Conference.

LIVE! @ your library receives major support from the National Endowment for the Arts, the Wallace-Reader's Digest Funds, the John S. and James L. Knight Foundation, and NEH. For more information, visit http://www.ala.org/publicprograms/live.

Planned Giving Program

The ALA Development Office launched the ALA Planned Giving Program in fall 2001. The charitable giving initiative was created to allow members to plan for the long-term needs of ALA or any of its units. During the first year of the program, the development office hosted its first annual seminar on changes in estate and gift tax laws at the 2002 ALA Midwinter Meeting. The ALA Legacy Society was established in spring 2002 to recognize donors who have included ALA as a beneficiary in their estate plans.

Conferences and Workshops

2002 Midwinter Meeting

At the 2002 ALA Midwinter Meeting, held in New Orleans January 18–23, the ALA Council responded to legislation passed by Congress in the wake of the September 11 terrorist attacks by unanimously approving a resolution affirming the principle of intellectual freedom. However, several other resolutions dealing with the nation's response to the attacks were voted down. The likely effects of the antiterrorism laws on libraries were also the focus of two well-attended sessions offered by ALA's Washington Office.

ALA President John W. Berry presented a program titled "Gatekeepers of the Internet: Balancing Access and Control in a Networked World," featuring Deborah Hurley of Harvard University and James J. O'Donnell of the University of Pennsylvania, who explored the challenges librarians are certain to face over access to information. For the first time, the President's Program was available as a Web cast.

Author and radio commentator Andrei Codrescu delivered the third annual Arthur Curley Lecture. His topic was censorship and repression under totalitarian regimes.

Registration totaled 11,853 attendees and exhibitors, of whom 4,314 registered on-site.

2002 Annual Conference

The 2002 ALA Annual Conference June 13–19 in Atlanta may be best remembered for its strong lineup of speakers. At the Opening General Session, art critic Robert Hughes delivered a scathing denunciation of the "patriotic correctness" unleashed in the United States following the terrorist attacks of September 11, and a call to librarians to "guard your liberties!" Said Hughes, "To confine the contents of a library in any way is to commit a kind of vandalism."

Activist and author Michael Moore thanked librarians for rescuing his latest book, *Stupid White Men* (HarperCollins), which the publisher had slated for cancellation in the face of the patriotic zeal set off by the terrorist attacks. An onslaught of e-mails from members of the library profession convinced the publisher to release it, and the book went on to top the bestseller lists.

Journalist Barbara Ehrenreich closed the conference by talking about her research for her recent book *Nickel and Dimed,* in which she personally took a number of entry-level jobs to determine whether it was possible to survive on entry-level wages. Ehrenreich tied her findings to the salaries paid to many professionals, including librarians.

The Opening General Session also saw the awarding of honorary memberships, ALA's highest honor, to E. J. Josey, librarian, educator, and cofounder of ALA's Black Caucus, and to Seymour Lubetzky, cataloging theorist and father of AACR2.

The more than 2,000 programs and meetings that made up the conference drew 21,130 attendees, including 250 from 50 other countries.

Other Conferences

Nearly 8,000 people attended the Public Library Association's ninth National Conference held March 12–16, 2002, in Phoenix, setting a new registration record for PLA and for all ALA division conferences to date. The conference, with more than 100 programs, preconferences, talk tables, author luncheons, and a bustling exhibits hall, drew praise from both exhibitors and attendees and helped increase PLA membership to more than 10,000. The conference featured other "firsts" for ALA division conferences: The entire program was available for downloading to a personal digital assistant, and two programs were videotaped and now are available as Web casts on PLA's Web site. Also for the first time, the PLA conference featured a "post-conference program." PLA provided travel grants for international librarians to attend the postconference program, "What Makes a Leader? Key Competencies for Public Library Leaders in the 21st Century," which was cosponsored by the Bertelsmann Foundation and the Phoenix Public Library.

Ten institutions participated in ACRL's Best Practices in Information Literacy Invitational Conference in Atlanta June 11–13. The purpose of the conference was to bring together librarians, faculty, and administrators involved in model programs to collaborate on further development of best-practice characteristics. As a result of the conference, a series of composite models for best practices will be developed.

More than 900 librarians, library supporters, and exhibitors converged on Fort Lauderdale August 13–16 to attend "Culture Keepers V: Access," the fifth national conference of African-American librarians hosted by the Black Caucus of ALA. Hugh B. Price, president of the National Urban League and a member of President Bush's Education Transition Team, was the John C. Tyson Memorial Lecture luncheon speaker.

Publishing

ALA's membership magazine, *American Libraries,* is published 11 times a year. Coverage of the effects of the September 11 terrorist attacks dominated the news during 2002. Other major themes were public relations, continuing education, librarian salaries, around-the-clock reference services, and the effects of the war on terrorism on free speech and privacy. In addition to *American Libraries,* ALA personal members are eligible to receive weekly library news updates by e-mail. *American Libraries'* classified job ads continue to be among the most widely consulted in the profession, the online version seeing more than 55,500 hits in a single month. *American Libraries'* Web site is at http://www.ala.org/alonline.

American Libraries, in cooperation with Library Video Network, produced a one-hour video documentary titled *Loss and Recovery: Librarians Bear Witness to September 11, 2001.* The video, which consists of interviews with librarians who were in or near the World Trade Center on September 11, premiered at the ALA Annual Conference in Atlanta and is available for $20 from Library Video Network (http://www.lvn.org).

Booklist, now in its 97th year of consecutive publication, continued to expand its content by adding more features to the publication's staple fare, reviews of books and media for public and school libraries. With bibliographies, author interviews, "read-alike" columns, and other book-related features, *Booklist* has aimed to become as valuable to readers' advisors as it has been to collection-development staff. Recent special issues devoted to women's history, biography, and horror fiction were added to a regular schedule of featured topics including black history, science and technology, mystery fiction, and poetry. In 2002 *Booklist* continued to sponsor two important book awards for young adults, both administered by YALSA: the Michael L. Printz Award and the Alex Awards.

Book Links, a *Booklist* publication, continued to refine its back-to-basics approach to connecting educators to quality children's literature. In a new initiative, editors published several articles tying books to national education standards, and greater effort was made to include audiobooks and Web sites relating to curricular themes in the magazine. In addition, editor Laura Tillotson traveled across the country giving in-service presentations to educators at conferences and schools on incorporating literature into the curriculum and promoting *Book Links'* mission.

In April 2002 *Choice* launched the new Site License Edition of ChoiceReviews.online. Like its older sibling, the Password Edition of ChoiceReviews.online launched in April 1999, the Site License Edition offers subscribers around-the-clock access to the more than 90,000 reviews in the *Choice* database. The Site License Edition uses IP ranges rather than passwords to control access. As a result, access is automatically available to any and all authorized users on a subscribing institution's network.

Choice's newest licensing agreement is with Baker & Taylor. Under the terms of this agreement, announced in July 2002, *Choice* reviews are now available through the Content Café, Baker & Taylor's enriched content library service. Like *Choice's* earlier alliance with Syndetic Solutions, the new agreement enables libraries with enhanced Web OPACs to add full-text *Choice* reviews to their online card catalog.

The staff of ALA TechSource used fiscal year 2002 to plan for changes in its publications. After several months of consideration following input from the unit's informal advisory group and the ALA Publishing Committee, *Library Systems Newsletter* had new authors as of the September 2002 issue and a new name effective with the January 2003 issue—it is now *Smart Libraries Newsletter.* The change also involved revising the newsletter's format and putting a new focus on digital libraries and electronic resources. The newsletter's mission—to provide useful, vital coverage of library technology in practice—has not changed.

Library Technology Reports is available in print or as an online subscription. Topics in 2002 included "Librarian's Guide to Copyright for Shared and Networked Resources," "Building and Optimizing Library Web Services," "Strategies for Measuring and Interpreting E-Use," "Establishing and Maintaining Live Online Reference Service," "Metadata and Its Applications," and "How to Plan and Implement a Library Portal."

Library Technology Reports began to accept advertising in 2002, through Benson, Coffee & Associates. For more information on *TechSource, Smart Libraries Newsletter,* or *Library Technology Reports,* see http://www.techsource.ala.org.

During 2002 ALA Graphics created powerful collateral support for ALA initiatives. Graphics featured the @ your library campaign for Teen Read Week. A Teen Read Week poster and other materials were introduced using the theme "Get Graphic @ your library." Celebrities Britney Spears, Salma Hayek, LeVar Burton, Coolio, Mike Mussina, Marion Jones, and the Indigo Girls donated their time for the celebrity READ poster series using the @ your library brand.

In response to the previous year's successful "Lord of the Rings" poster series, ALA Graphics used another exclusive image from the motion picture for a new poster and bookmark titled "Moving Words." Featuring the Ringwraiths, it highlights the graphic process of turning words into pictures.

To celebrate Library Card Sign-up Month in September, ALA Graphics introduced the "Get Carded @ your library" poster and bookmark targeted at teenagers.

ALA Graphics introduced a new tagline to the READ poster series, Read to Your Hero. Featuring a member of the New York Fire Department reading to a young friend, this was one of the most successful posters of 2002.

Other introductions included the ALA 2002 Awards Poster Set; bilingual "Read Please/Lea Por Favor!" clothing for babies and toddlers; a multilingual poster, bookmark, and notecards featuring more than 20 languages; and a number of gifts and incentives that promote libraries, literacy, and reading.

The ALA Online Store, with ALA Graphics (http://www.alastore.ala.org) and ALA Editions, continued its successful collaboration with its partners and divisions with new products and publications.

ALA Editions, in a year that exceeded expectations, published 29 new titles and enjoyed strong backlist sales led by AASL's *Information Power*. Prominent among projects developed in collaboration with partners in the divisions were OIF's *Intellectual Freedom Manual*, sixth edition; PLA's *Staffing for Results: A Guide to Working Smarter;* and YALSA's *New Direction for Library Service for Young Adults*. Publications commissioned independently with authors included *Developing a Compensation Plan for Libraries* and *Licensing Digital Content*.

Leadership

Keith Michael Fiels, formerly director of the Massachusetts Board of Library Commissioners, took office July 31, 2002, as ALA's executive director. Fiels has more 15 years of senior-level administrative experience in the state library arena as well as years of work in public and school libraries. He has been an ALA member since 1976 and has been active in ALA committees and divisions as well as various state library associations. Fiels succeeds William R. Gordon, who retired in August.

Patricia McCleary was named marketing manager, products and promotions, effective July 13, 2002; Patrice McDermott was named assistant director, Office of Government Relations, in the ALA Washington Office, effective December 3, 2001; Lorraine Olley became executive director of LAMA on September 17, 2001; Stephanie Orphan was appointed Web developer and editor of *C&RL News,* a publication of ACRL, on December 10, 2001; Mary Jane Petrowski became assistant director of ACRL on January 17, 2002; Cindy Welch became deputy executive director of YALSA on April 22, 2002; and Judith King, director of professional development for AASL and YALSA, resigned on October 31, 2002.

Maurice J. ("Mitch") Freedman, director of the Westchester (New York) Library System, was inaugurated as ALA president at the 2002 Annual Conference in Atlanta in July. Carla D. Hayden, executive director of the Enoch Pratt Free Library in Baltimore, became ALA president-elect in the 2002 election and will be inaugurated at the 2003 Annual Conference in Toronto. Her presidential focus will be equity of access with an emphasis on recruitment, retention, and the securing of adequate resources to maintain excellent library services.

The ALA Council elected three new executive board members at the 2002 ALA Midwinter Meeting: Kathleen E. Bethel, African American Studies librarian at Northwestern University in Evanston, Illinois; Nancy Davenport, director for acquisitions at the Library of Congress; and Barbara K. Stripling, director of the Astor Center for Public School Libraries, New Visions for Public Schools, New York. They began their three-year terms in July 2002 and will serve until the 2005 Annual Conference. Stripling was first elected to the board in January 2001 to complete the unexpired term (through June 2002) of board member Liz Bishoff, who was elected ALA Treasurer.

Grants and Contributions

Verizon made a $430,000 grant to ALA's Office for Literacy and Outreach Services (OLOS), marking year three of Verizon's commitment to ALA, libraries, and literacy. This made possible the interactive Web site Buildliteracy.org (http://www.Buildliteracy.org), a tool for new and existing urban literacy coalitions funded by Verizon through OLOS. It was promoted to library and literacy communities with support of a team of technical and research professionals, led by Dale P. Lipschultz, OLOS literacy officer. Content is provided by ALA, the National Alliance of Urban Literacy Coalitions, the National Institute for Literacy, and public libraries across the country.

The Institute of Museum and Library Services awarded $1.8 million in July 2002 to seven universities and colleges to recruit and educate students in library and information science. The awards also fund advanced training, especially in digital technologies, for professional librarians. The grant recipients will match the awards with an additional $1.7 million.

For the third consecutive year, 3M, in cooperation with AASL, donated $1.5 million in 3M Detection Systems to approximately 100 middle and high school library media centers in the United States through the 3M Salute to Schools program. The program will be offered again in 2003.

ALSC received a $50,000 grant from the W. K. Kellogg Foundation to produce and disseminate a brochure for parents featuring a list of recommended books by and about Latinos. ALSC is also collaborating with REFORMA, the National Association to Promote Library and Information Services to Latinos and the Spanish Speaking, in this effort. Free copies of the brochure were mailed to ALSC, REFORMA, and National Association of Bilingual Education members. In addition to the bilingual book list for children, the brochure also features tips for parents on how, when, and why to read to very young children, and ideas for encouraging reading in older children. ALSC provided tips for librarians and other community-service staff on using the brochure. The brochure and additional information on the annual El dia de los ninos/El Dia de los libros events can be found online at http://www.ala.org/alsc/eldia.html.

The PLA board voted during the 2002 ALA Annual Conference to contribute $100,000 to the ALA Spectrum Scholarship Endowment to award scholarships to minority students. Meanwhile, ALSC extended free one-year memberships to Spectrum scholars interested in youth services. Bound to Stay Bound Books, Inc., increased its funding, enabling ALSC to offer one more scholarship for a total of four Bound to Stay Bound scholarships. In honor of ALA's retiring executive director, the William R. Gordon Scholarship to benefit the Spectrum Initiative was established. The Spectrum Initiative's major emphasis is on recruiting applicants and awarding scholarships to African American, Latino/Hispanic, Asian/Pacific Islander, Native American, and Alaskan native students for graduate programs in library and information studies.

PLA and the Freedom to Read Foundation pledged $100,000 each and the ALSC earmarked $25,000 to support ALA as it prepared to argue its case before the U.S. Supreme Court against the Children's Internet Protection Act (CIPA). Donations to the legal defense fund from ALA member leaders brought total support to almost $250,000.

Other Highlights

ACRL created a joint task force with the Association of Research Libraries to look at recruitment issues facing the profession. The goal of this task force is to develop fresh strategies for recruiting and advancing a new generation of talent for the profession of academic librarianship to succeed in the 21st century. ACRL also launched a media campaign to underscore to members of the higher education community the continued vitality and value of academic and research libraries. These messages are aimed at campus decision-makers and profile the value and strength of librarians and libraries in meeting the knowledge demands of faculty and students. Four advertisements using the theme "exciting things happen @ your library" were placed in the *Chronicle of Higher Education* during the year. They featured quotes from administrators, faculty members, and students from a variety of post-secondary institutions about the importance of librarians on their campuses.

ASCLA successfully completed "Roads to Learning," a learning-disability initiative for public libraries. The project goal was to encourage linkages among libraries, community organizations, and service providers to improve service to people with learning disabilities, their families, professionals, and other interested parties. "Roads to Learning" ran from 1996 to 2001 with $633,000 in funding provided by the Tremaine Foundation. The final report can be found at http://www.ala.org/ascla/rtl_final_report.html.

RUSA celebrated its 30th anniversary. RUSA was formed in 1972 with the merger of the Reference Services and Adult Services divisions. One highlight of the anniversary year was the "Future of Reference Initiative" program presented at the 2002 ALA Annual Conference, at which five reference experts shared their predictions on what the future holds. The text of their papers is available at http://www.ala.org/rusa/forums/index.html.

The ALA Library collaborated with other units of ALA to prepare a quick pathfinder to resources for coping with patron inquiries in the aftermath of the September 11 terrorist attacks. This short document, first included as one of the FAQs on the ALA home page, has developed into more complete files of resources offered by ALSC, YALSA, and the ALA Public Programs Office.

The library continued its service to ALA staff, ALA members, and library colleagues and friends around the world by responding to more than 8,000 inquiries, half of which were received via e-mail. The library celebrated National Library Week by hosting a staff coffee break and running a trivia contest using the library's resources.

The Office for Human Resource Development and Recruitment (HRDR) sent out about 725 career packets in 2002, and more than 200 employers used ALA placement services (including those at the Midwinter Meeting and Annual Conference). The placement center listed about 600 jobs and about 600 registered job-seekers. HRDR also collaborated with AASL, ALSC, and YALSA to develop a new youth services recruitment brochure.

Beginning with a program at the ALA Annual Conference, YALSA began changing the face of library service for teens. The changes are explored in a new publication, *New Directions for Library Service to Young Adults,* reflecting an emphasis on positive youth development and long-range planning. By integrating more youth participation into every level of library planning and by urging libraries toward more collaboration with community organizations, the division hopes that the next generation will become better educated about the importance of libraries in their communities.

Building members was a key focus of ALTA President Gail Dysleski in 2001–2002, and the organization launched a direct-mail marketing campaign in support of this effort. ALTA has also been working with ALA Chapter Relations and a marketing firm to recruit new ALA/ALTA advocate members.

PLA developed a number of products to aid in the ongoing effort to recruit public librarians into the profession. The association has developed a comprehensive recruitment Web site (http://www.pla.org/projects/recruit.html) that contains testimonials from librarians on why they chose public librarianship, educational requirements, scholarships information and links, salary data, and an informative look at the public library world titled "Public Library Fast Facts."

Leaders, members, and staff of PLA embarked on a planning process that will lead to the completion of a long-range strategic plan for the organization. The plan takes into account all member input as well as ideas from the National Conference focus groups, and was presented to the PLA board at the 2002 ALA Annual Conference.

Continuing ALA's commitment to diversity, the ALA Office for Diversity began sponsorship in 2002 of an Annual Diversity Research Grant program to address critical gaps in the knowledge of diversity issues within library and information science. The winning research proposals of the inaugural three $5,000 grants were "Integrating Diversity into Library School Curriculum," submitted by Lorna Peterson, associate professor at the University at Buffalo/State University of New York; "Strategies for Promoting Mentoring Among Minorities," submitted by Ashley E. Bonnette, bibliographic instruction/distance learning librarian, Edith Garland Dupre Library, University of Louisiana at Lafayette; and "From the Inside Out: Collaborating for Recruitment, Outreach, and Diversity Through the Promotion of Literacy," submitted by Rosi Andrade, research associate, Community Outreach Project on AIDS in Southern Arizona, Southwest Institute for Research on Women, University of Arizona, and Cheryl Knott Malone, associate professor, School of Information Resources and Library Science, University of Arizona.

In June 2002, the Council Committee on Minority Concerns and Cultural Diversity changed its name to the Council Committee on Diversity (COD). The committee's charge was also revised to reflect more accurately its work as it relates to the Office for Diversity, ALA Council mandates, and ALA member diversity issues. For more information on COD, see http://www.ala.org/diversity/cod.

The Public Information Office (PIO) was busy throughout 2001–2002 with ALA's legal challenge to the Children's Internet Protection Act (CIPA). Daily tracking of the case was followed by weeks of news and editorial coverage that largely favored ALA's position against the act. The *New York Times* devoted two full pages to covering how different libraries approach the issue of Internet filtering. PIO estimates that more than 23 million people learned of ALA and its efforts to fight CIPA.

Following Past President Berry's focus on librarian recruitment and diversity, PIO worked with ORS and HRDR to develop a press kit and subsequently launch a national media outreach effort. A June 2002 Associated Press story discussed the growing need for librarians and salary concerns. Other main topics during the year were the USA Patriot Act, Banned Books Week, and National Library Week.

The ALA Committee on Accreditation and the Office for Accreditation completed revision of the documents that support the library science program accreditation process; the new documents are available at http://www.ala.org/alaorg/oa/ap3.html. The Committee on Accreditation conducted comprehensive reviews of nine programs during the year.

More than 160 librarians participated in the fifth year of the ALA-Feria Internacional del Libro (FIL) Free Pass Program to the Guadalajara Book Fair, which provides an opportunity to review and buy the latest in Spanish-language materials from around the world at discounted rates. ALA-FIL Free Pass participants buy about a million dollars' worth of Spanish-language materials at the fair.

Association of American Publishers

71 Fifth Ave., New York, NY 10010
212-255-0200, fax 212-255-7007

50 F St. N.W., Washington, DC 20001
202-347-3375, fax 202-347-3690

World Wide Web http://www.publishers.org

Judith Platt
Director, Communications/Public Affairs

The Association of American Publishers (AAP) is the national trade association of the U.S. book publishing industry. The association was created in 1970 through the merger of the American Book Publishers Council, a trade publishing group, and the American Educational Publishers Institute, an organization of textbook publishers. AAP's more than 300 corporate members include most of the major commercial book publishers in the United States as well as smaller and medium-sized houses, not-for-profit publishers, university presses, and scholarly societies.

AAP members publish hardcover and paperback books in every field, including general fiction and nonfiction; poetry; children's books; textbooks; Bibles and other religious works; reference works; scientific, medical, technical, professional, and scholarly books and journals; computer software; and a range of electronic products and services, such as online databases and CD-ROMs.

AAP also works closely with some 2,000 smaller regional publishers through formal affiliations with the Publishers Association of the West, the Publishers Association of the South, the Florida Publishers Association, the Small Publishers Association of North America, and the Evangelical Christian Publishers Association.

AAP policy is set by a board of directors elected by the membership for four-year terms, under a chair who serves for two years. There is an executive committee composed of the chair, vice chair, secretary, and treasurer, and a minimum of two at-large members. Management of the association, within the guidelines set by the board, is the responsibility of AAP's president and CEO, Pat Schroeder.

AAP maintains two offices, in New York and Washington, D.C.

Highlights of 2002

Among the highlights of the year in publishing:

- Book sales totaled $25.36 billion in 2001, a disappointing 0.1 percent increase over 2000, according to figures released by AAP in February 2002
- Bob Evanson of McGraw-Hill took over chairmanship of the AAP board
- Following up on the success of the 2001 event, a second "Get Caught Reading Day" on Capitol Hill in March 2002 and a third event in June

drew more than 100 members of the House and Senate to get their pictures taken with their favorite books

- First Lady (and former librarian) Laura Bush joined the ranks of Get Caught Reading celebrities
- Free-speech champion Barney Rosset, founder of Grove Press, won the Curtis Benjamin Award
- AAP President Schroeder wrote to New York Mayor Michael Bloomberg decrying proposed cuts in library funding
- AAP received the 2002 Access Award from the American Foundation for the Blind for its work in helping to meet the needs of blind and vision-impaired students
- Yale University Press received the PSP Division's R. R. Hawkins Award for *Lichens of North America*
- AAP took the lead on a legal brief urging the federal courts to nullify an executive order limiting access to presidential records
- Capping two years of cooperative effort, AAP welcomed introduction of legislation to help blind students obtain up-to-date instructional materials
- The International Freedom to Publish Committee established a new award, in honor of human rights activist Jeri Label, to benefit publishers who have suffered political persecution
- AAP joined authors and booksellers in protesting Justice Department secrecy in exercising USA Patriot Act search warrants for library and bookstore records
- NBC's "Today Show" received AAP Honors for advancing the cause of American books and authors
- A new AAP/National Education Association survey revealed nationwide shortages of textbooks
- AAP announced the creation of a new task force and initiative to serve the Latino book market

Government Affairs

AAP's Washington office is the industry's front line on matters of federal legislation and government policy. The office keeps AAP members informed about developments on Capitol Hill and in the executive branch to enable the membership to develop consensus positions on national policy issues. AAP's government affairs professionals serve as the industry's voice in advocating the views and concerns of American publishers on questions of national policy.

An AAP Government Affairs Council strengthens communications between the Washington office and the AAP leadership. The council comprises individuals designated by AAP board members to speak on behalf of their houses in formulating positions on legislative issues requiring a rapid response. [See "Legislation and Regulations Affecting Publishing in 2002" in Part 2—*Ed.*]

Communications/Public Affairs

The Communications and Public Affairs program is AAP's voice, informing the trade press and other media, the AAP membership, and the general public about AAP's work to promote the cause of American publishing. Through the program's regular publications, press releases and advisories, op-ed pieces, and other means, AAP expresses the industry's views and provides up-to-the-minute information on subjects of concern to its members.

AAP's public affairs activities include outreach and cooperative programs with such organizations as the Library of Congress's Center for the Book, the Arts Advocacy Alliance (supporting the National Endowment for the Arts and other federal arts programs), PEN American Center and its International Freedom to Write Program, and a host of literacy and reading promotion efforts including an early childhood literacy initiative, Reach Out and Read.

In addition to its traditional print distribution, the AAP newsletter *AAP Monthly Report* is published online at http://www.publishers.org, the association's Web site.

BookExpo America

AAP is a cosponsor of BookExpo America (BEA), the premiere English-language book event. BookExpo 2002 was held in New York May 3–5. Among the highlights was a concert by the Rock Bottom Remainders, a rock band whose members include bestselling authors Dave Barry, Stephen King, and Amy Tan, to benefit the First Amendment work of the American Booksellers Foundation for Free Expression (ABFFE) and the Get Caught Reading campaign.

At BEA, the Curtis Benjamin Award for Creative Publishing was presented to Barney Rosset, founder of Grove Press and publisher of the first unexpurgated U.S. edition of the D. H. Lawrence novel *Lady Chatterley's Lover.* In part because of that, Rosset is thought to have done more than perhaps any other individual to break down the walls of literary censorship in America.

AAP also joined with ABFFE and the Freedom to Read Foundation in sponsoring a program on freedom of speech in the aftermath of the September 11, 2001, terrorist attacks, "9/11: Civil Liberties in a Time of Crisis."

Get Caught Reading

In September First Lady Laura Bush became the newest celebrity "caught reading" as part of the continuing Get Caught Reading campaign. Mrs. Bush was caught reading *Long May She Wave: A Graphic History of the American Flag.* Her Get Caught Reading poster has been distributed to schools, libraries, and bookstores and used in advertising for the campaign.

AAP also offered new photos featuring comedian and actor Drew Carey (reading *Comedy Techniques for Writers and Performers*) and Spider Man reading a *The Hulk* comic book.

These celebrities joined more than 200 members of Congress who have been "caught reading" at events on Capitol Hill during the last year, as well as New

York Mayor Michael Bloomberg and celebrities Robin Williams, Derek Jeter, Whoopi Goldberg, Rosie O'Donnell, Sammy Sosa, Dolly Parton, Jane Seymour, Jake Lloyd, Vernon Jordan, Clifford the Big Red Dog, Donald Duck, and the Rugrats, who have all lent their support to the campaign, now in its third year. New posters feature mountaineer Eric Weihenmayer, who is blind, caught reading a book in braille, and actress Patty Duke, famed for her portrayals of Helen Keller and her teacher Annie Sullivan, sharing a braille book with a blind student.

Get Caught Reading posters were among the most popular souvenirs at the second annual National Book Festival in October, organized by the Library of Congress and hosted by the First Lady.

Materials were distributed at a Get Caught Reading booth at the Harlem Book Fair in New York in July, and at the "New York Is Book Country" street fair in September. The Get Caught Reading celebrity ads have appeared in many newspapers and magazines, all of which have donated the ad space. Among the publications that ran ads in 2002 were *TV Guide, USA Today,* the *New York Times, People, Better Homes & Gardens, Seventeen, Time Out New York, Rosie Magazine,* and *National Geographic.*

As in past years, teachers, librarians, and booksellers across the United States creatively used Get Caught Reading materials to stage their own events and encourage their students and patrons to get caught reading. AAP has received photographs of the events and letters too numerous to count, and continues to support these "reading ambassadors" with posters and ideas.

Copyright

The AAP Copyright Committee coordinates efforts to protect and strengthen intellectual property rights and to enhance public awareness of the importance of copyright as an incentive to creativity. The committee monitors intellectual property legislation in the United States and abroad, and serves as an advisory body to the board of directors in formulating AAP policy on legislation and compliance activities, including litigation. The committee coordinates AAP's efforts to promote understanding of and compliance with U.S. copyright law on America's college and university campuses. Bob Bolick (McGraw-Hill) chaired the committee in 2002.

At the direction of the Copyright Committee, AAP provided amicus support in several important copyright cases in 2002.

In August AAP was joined by a number of creative artists, including photographer Richard Avedon and playwright David Mamet, in filing an amicus brief to the U.S. Supreme Court in *Eldred* v. *Ashcroft,* a case challenging the constitutionality of the 1998 Copyright Term Extension Act (CTEA), which lengthened the term of existing and future copyrights by 20 years.

During the legislative process leading up to enactment of CTEA, AAP did not take a position for or against the legislation as public policy since there were strong voices within the AAP membership on both sides of the issue. However, following filing of the legal challenge, AAP member publishers became deeply concerned over arguments put forward by the plaintiffs that CTEA violated the First Amendment and that the validity of copyright legislation should be determined on the basis of whether it promotes "the progress of science and the useful arts." The latter contention undermines Congress's authority to make policy judgments pursuant to the Copyright Clause of the U.S. Constitution and would call into question a host of important recent copyright legislation that publishers have sought and have actively supported, including the Digital Millennium Copyright Act and the No Electronic Theft (NET) Act.

The AAP amicus brief rejected the plaintiffs' argument that CTEA violates the First Amendment and that its enactment exceeds Congress's legislative powers. The brief argued that copyright itself is the engine of free expression and that, far from restricting free speech, copyright merely protects an author's form of expression. "The primary concern of the First Amendment is the free flow of ideas," the brief pointed out, noting that "copyright does not restrain the exchange of an author's ideas, but merely prevents others from purloining an author's particular expression of those ideas." In addition to the AAP brief, other briefs were filed by content providers and organizations representing copyright-based industries. The Supreme Court heard the case on October 9, 2002.

In another important amicus effort, AAP joined with the Authors Guild in asking the U.S. Supreme Court to review and reverse a ruling by the U.S. Court of Appeals for the 10th Circuit in *Deseret Book Co.* v. *Jacobsen,* a copyright infringement case involving a work of fiction based in part on an unpublished World War II memoir. Maintaining that the 10th Circuit misapplied Supreme Court precedents regarding the treatment of verbatim quotes, and its own rulings regarding the treatment of fictional material, the brief argued that in holding that an author may be found liable for copyright infringement merely because a jury could find that factual elements in a work of fiction bear "too close" a resemblance to factual elements in a copyrighted factual work, the appellate court ruling is in direct conflict with established principles of copyright law. "If not reversed," the brief asserted, "that holding will have disastrous consequences for the entire publishing and broadcasting industry." The amicus brief pointed out that since facts cannot be copyrighted, "a de minimis appropriation of expressive elements from a copyrighted factual work does not give rise to a claim for infringement." In ruling to the contrary, the brief argued, the 10th Circuit has created "serious uncertainty for authors, publishers, and broadcasters," and its decision "will have a nationwide impact in an area of the law with profound First Amendment implications."

During the past year, the Copyright Committee continued its function of advising and supporting AAP staff with respect to participation in key proceedings and activities on copyright issues, including publisher participation in a wide-ranging distance-learning pilot project with the U.S. Department of Defense.

The Rights and Permissions Advisory Committee (RPAC), which operates under the aegis of the Copyright Committee, sponsors educational programs for rights and permissions professionals. Bonnie Beacher (McGraw-Hill) chaired the group in 2002. RPAC held a full-day conference in New York in May focusing on copyright basics, online piracy, copyright issues facing librarians, and document delivery. RPAC hosted a second program in July on *Eldred* v. *Ashcroft,* the copyright term extension challenge, which sought to present two opposing views of the case.

The mandate of the Copyright Education Committee (CEC), which also operates under the Copyright Committee umbrella, is to clarify copyright law and facilitate compliance in such areas as the production of college coursepacks, the use of copyrighted materials over networks, and the creation of digitized library holdings for instructional purposes. The CEC has been working with the Copyright Committee on a variety of research projects dealing with coursepacks, e-reserves, and other campus-related uses of copyrighted works that pose serious problems of infringement. Diann Korta (Pearson) chairs CEC.

Diversity/Recruit and Retain

AAP's Diversity/Recruit and Retain Committee assists member publishers in attracting and retaining talented staff, including individuals from all ethnic and social backgrounds and fields of study.

Finding a close alignment in mission and objectives, AAP's Diversity Committee and the Trade Committee's Recruit and Retain Task Force (RRTF) joined together early in 2002 under the chairmanship of Bridget Marmion (Houghton Mifflin). The newly combined group was named the Diversity/Recruit and Retain Committee and operates under the aegis of the Trade Executive Committee.

RRTF was launched in 2000 as part of the Trade Executive Committee's resolve to promote publishing on college campuses, to recent graduates, and to new publishing employees, as a viable and exciting career option offering expanding choices. RRTF created a Young-to-Publishing Group of junior-level employees who meet for lunch regularly to network with peers and to hear publishing professionals talk about the industry.

In 2002, in cooperation with the Association of American University Presses (AAUP), the Diversity/Recruit and Retain Committee provided grants to summer interns from the Publishing Certificate Program at City College of New York and from Howard University. The program at Howard, which provided 10 weeks' salary for two interns working at Howard University Press, along with travel expenses to attend the AAUP annual meeting, allowed the interns to participate in a host of activities connected to the publishing process, including weekly staff meetings. According to Howard University Press Director Kamili Anderson, the program was "an unequivocal success." Calling the experience a "win-win situation," Anderson noted that the interns' "efforts and enthusiasm filled critical gaps in the press's re-emerging publishing program."

Other highlights of the committee's activities in 2002 included the release of AAP's video "Voices of Diversity: The Power of Book Publishing" (produced by Kaufman Films), which speaks to students and professionals about the value and rewards of working in publishing and features interviews with well-known authors including Maya Angelou, Amy Tan, and Walter Mosley. AAP distributed more than 1,100 copies of the video in 2002, and continues to use it as an integral tool in its college outreach efforts.

Education Program

AAP's education program is designed to provide educational opportunities for publishing industry personnel. The most popular of these is the intensive "Introduction to Publishing" course. Usually given in the fall, the course is designed to provide entry-level employees with an overview of the industry. Other education programs have included seminars on issues related to work-for-hire and contracted services; financial issues for editors; and state, local, and federal tax developments affecting the publishing industry, the Internet, and new media.

Enabling Technologies

AAP's Enabling Technologies Committee (ETC) works to foster the development and implementation of technologies facilitating digital and print publishing. Companies from all segments of the industry (trade, professional and scholarly, K–12) participate. Evelyn Sasmor (McGraw-Hill) chaired the committee in 2002.

Throughout 2002 ETC continued its work to foster standards promoting the growth of the e-book industry. ETC representatives participated with an array of technology companies, libraries, users groups, and other constituents in the Open eBook Forum in an effort to establish industry-wide standards promoting robust usage features in digital rights management (DRM) products. In addition, ETC and the American Library Association (ALA) commissioned a White Paper (to be published early in 2003) analyzing numerous studies, reports, and testimonials of libraries, publishers, and other parties with an interest in the e-book industry to determine new features needed to make DRM products more attractive to consumers.

ETC continued to support the growing implementation of the Digital Object Identifier (DOI) for assignment to electronic content because of its powerful online linking capabilities. Noteworthy developments included reports that more than 6 million DOIs had been registered by CrossRef, a consortium of more than 150 scientific, technical, and medical (STM) journal publishers who link their articles together using DOIs; that McGraw-Hill Education registered 9,000 DOIs for its content through the DOI registration agency Content Directions; that the DOI was widely implemented in the U.S. Department of Defense distance-learning pilot project coordinated by Learning Objects Network; and that Content Directions entered into an agreement to issue DOIs for use across book publishing and electronic database programs at Gale (a division of the Thomson Corporation).

In late 2002 the AAP Board of Directors asked ETC to develop a position statement on whether the ISBN should be revised from a 10-digit to a 13-digit standard as recommended by the International Organization for Standardization (ISO). In December ETC hosted a panel discussion on the proposed change (sponsored by the National Information Standards Organization), which featured speakers from Barnes & Noble, R. R. Bowker, Random House, and the Uniform Code Council. Ed McCoyd, director of digital policy at AAP, has been asked to participate in the ISO working group on the revision of the standard.

Freedom to Read

The AAP Freedom to Read Committee works to protect intellectual freedom and the free marketplace of ideas, serving as the industry's early warning system on issues such as libel, privacy, school censorship, attacks on public libraries, reporters' privilege (confidentiality of source materials), the Internet and filtering technology, sexually explicit materials, third-party liability, and efforts to punish speech that "causes harm." The committee coordinates AAP's participation, as plaintiff or friend-of-the-court, in important First Amendment cases, and sponsors educational programs on free-speech issues of importance to publishers. AAP, through the committee, is a founding member of Media Coalition, a group of trade associations working together on censorship issues. Jane Isay (Harcourt) chaired the committee in 2002.

Working closely with allied organizations—ALA's Office for Intellectual Freedom (ALA/OIF), the American Booksellers Foundation for Free Expression (ABFFE), and PEN American Center—the committee actively fulfilled its educational mandate with a series of outstanding programs in 2002.

- In April the committee joined with PEN American Center and the Authors Guild Foundation to cosponsor a program on the Bush executive order limiting access to presidential papers and tapes. Moderated by Leonard Lopate, host of WNYC's "New York & Company," a panel of three presidential historians used the executive order as a springboard for a discussion of the role of primary source materials in the writing of history and biography. The panelists were Richard Reeves, author of highly regarded books on presidents Nixon and Kennedy; Robert Caro, who won a 2002 National Book Award for the second volume of his biography of Lyndon Johnson; and Pulitzer Prize-winning author, historian, and former Kennedy aide Arthur Schlesinger, Jr.

- In May, at BookExpo, the committee joined with ABFFE and the Freedom to Read Foundation to cosponsor an important program on the impact of the September 11, 2001, terrorist attacks on freedom of speech. Titled "9/11: Civil Liberties in a Time of Crisis," the program featured journalist and First Amendment advocate Nat Hentoff, *Harper's Magazine* publisher John R. ("Rick") MacArthur, and authors Barbara Kingsolver and Michael Moore.

- In June AAP joined with ALA's Intellectual Freedom Committee and ABFFE to sponsor a joint program at the ALA Annual Conference in Atlanta. Drawing inspiration from the previous spring's heated copyright battle over publication of *The Wind Done Gone,* a parody of *Gone With the Wind,* the program was entitled "Barry Trotter Done Gone: The Perils of Publishing Parody." A panel composed of Michael Gerber, author of *Barry Trotter and the Unauthorized Parody*; Wendy Strothman (Houghton Mifflin), publisher of *The Wind Done Gone*; and R. Bruce Rich, recognized authority on both intellectual property and First Amendment law (and counsel to the Freedom to Read Committee), explored the vital role of parody in the free marketplace of ideas.

For the publishing community, perhaps the most troubling aspect of the reaction to the September 11 terrorist attacks was embodied in Section 215 of the USA Patriot Act (the antiterrorism legislation passed by Congress shortly after the attacks), which gives the government expansive authority to conduct searches of homes and businesses pursuant to an investigation of terrorism. Section 215 poses a significant threat to the work of investigative journalists and authors who write about subjects that may be related to terrorism. It also threatens the privacy and First Amendment rights of library patrons and bookstore customers, whose reading choices and Internet usage patterns may be subject to disclosure. Under Section 215, a library or bookstore can be compelled to turn over information about patrons and customers, including borrowing records of a particular individual or a list of individuals who have borrowed or purchased a particular book or visited a particular Web site. The incursions on First Amendment-protected activities are particularly troubling because under the USA Patriot Act search warrants for books, journalists' interview notes, bookstore purchase records, library usage information, and similar materials can be obtained from a secret court, without an adversarial hearing or the need to show "probable cause," and are issued under a gag order. Denied the right to reveal the fact that such a warrant has been received, publishers, librarians, and booksellers are unable to defend their right to disseminate and the right of their patrons to receive constitutionally protected materials.

Factors such as the rapidity with which the USA Patriot Act was passed (a mere six weeks after the terrorist attacks) and the massive size (132 pages) and complexity of the act prevented the book community from immediately focusing its attention on the chilling effect of Section 215. To help raise awareness of these First Amendment concerns, the Freedom to Read Committee prepared a White Paper that was distributed at the ALA Annual Conference in Atlanta in June and at other gatherings. Titled "The Patriot Act and the First Amendment: Why the Book Community Is Concerned," the statement details the publishing community's specific concerns and urges publishers, librarians, authors, and booksellers to write to their members of Congress outlining these concerns and asking for congressional hearings to address them.

In August AAP, PEN American Center, and ABFFE sent a joint letter to House Judiciary Committee Chairman James Sensenbrenner (R-Wis.) and Representative John Conyers (D-Mich.), the committee's ranking Democrat, criticizing the Justice Department for refusing to tell Congress how many times it had used its power under the USA Patriot Act to force bookstores, libraries, and newspapers to reveal confidential records. As part of its oversight responsibilities, the House Judiciary Committee had requested this information in June but was stonewalled by the Justice Department.

The Freedom to Read Committee was involved in a number of important First Amendment fights in 2002:

- Leading a coalition of organizations representing publishers, authors, journalists, and historians in an amicus brief submitted February 28, 2002, AAP urged the U.S. District Court for the District of Columbia to nullify the Bush executive order on presidential records, calling it a "real, substantial, and immediate threat . . . to the integrity of the historical record and to the public interest." The brief was submitted in support of a legal challenge brought in November by the public interest group Public Citizen.

- The fact that state laws banning the dissemination, via the Internet, of materials harmful to minors have been held unconstitutional by federal courts in a growing number of states has not deterred state legislatures from continuing to enact such statutes. Guided by the Freedom to Read Committee, AAP joined in challenging these statutes in New York, New Mexico, Arizona, and Vermont. In 2002 both the Arizona and Vermont statutes were struck down as violations of the First Amendment and the Constitution's Commerce Clause (the New York and New Mexico laws had been previously declared unconstitutional on the same grounds). Undaunted, Ohio enacted its own Internet harmful-to-minors law, which was signed by the governor on May 6, 2002. On the same day, a coalition of plaintiffs including AAP filed suit challenging the Ohio law in federal court. Significantly, the challenge extended to Ohio's definition of "harmful to juveniles," the most sweeping in the nation, which included violence, foul language, nudity, and sexual content. As the complaint said, under this definition high school students could conceivably be denied the right to read such books as *Dead Man Walking, The Hot Zone,* and *A Time to Kill.* In September, without even having to reach the Internet issue, a federal judge found Ohio's definition of "harmful to juveniles" to be "substantially overbroad" and in violation of the First Amendment. In November AAP joined in challenging yet another state statute, this time in South Carolina.

- In February 2002, in an appeal that had been pending for more than two years, the California Supreme Court struck down California's "Son of Sam" law requiring convicted felons to surrender proceeds from the sale of their stories for books, movies, or magazine and newspaper articles to a victim-compensation trust fund. The California high court found the statute in violation of the First Amendment to the U.S. Constitution and Article 1 of the California Constitution. This was the first time since the U.S. Supreme Court's 1991 ruling striking down New York's "Son of Sam" law (*Simon & Schuster, Inc.* v. *Members of the New York State Crime Victims Board*) that a state supreme court had looked at the issue. The California court found that while it "imposes a content-based financial penalty on protected speech," the California statute, like its New York counterpart, "fails to satisfy strict scrutiny because it, too, is overinclusive." In 1999 AAP led an amicus effort urging the California Supreme Court to strike down the law.

- Opposing government secrecy at the local as well as the federal level, in February 2002 AAP joined a group of historians and journalists in protesting an arrangement made in the last day's of Rudy Giuliani's tenure as mayor of New York City under which all of the official records of Giuliani's eight years in office (including photographs, materials relating to the World Trade Center terrorist attacks, tapes, and papers) were turned over to a private group for prescreening and archiving under Giuliani's direction.

- In April 2002, in a ruling that affirmed "an individual's fundamental right to purchase books anonymously, free from government interference," the Colorado Supreme Court vindicated Tattered Cover Bookstore owner Joyce Meskis's two-year battle to resist turning over customer purchase records to law enforcement authorities. AAP had joined in a series of amicus briefs supporting Meskis. In its landmark decision, the Colorado Supreme Court held that search warrants targeting bookstore records represent such a serious threat to First Amendment-protected rights that they should be issued only after an adversarial hearing and a judicial determination that the law enforcement needs outweigh the constitutional harm.

- In May, in a lawsuit brought by ALA and the American Civil Liberties Union, a panel of three federal judges found the Children's Internet Protection Act (CIPA)—which mandates the use of filtering software on all public library computers as a condition for receiving federal funds, including e-rate Internet discounts—unconstitutional because it restricts library patrons' access to First Amendment-protected material. Although AAP was not a plaintiff in the suit, it is expected to provide amicus support before the U.S. Supreme Court.

- In spring 2002 AAP joined a diverse group of free-speech and civil liberties organizations and concerned parents in protesting the censorship of literary works used on the New York State Regents Examination in English Language Arts (which must be taken and passed by all public high school students in order to graduate). In a letter to New York State's commissioner of education, the groups said that in altering literary passages to conform to a standard of "political correctness," the regents engaged in "a form of censorship that distorts the content and meaning of the original work." Notwithstanding assurances that the practice would cease, the problem continued and bowdlerized literary passages appeared on exams given later in the year.

- In 2001 AAP, ABFFE, the ALA-affiliated Freedom to Read Foundation, and others joined in filing an amicus brief to the Supreme Court in *Ashcroft v. Free Speech Coalition,* a challenge to the Child Pornography Prevention Act (CPPA), on appeal from the 9th Circuit. CPPA broadened the definition of child pornography to criminalize images of adults who "appear to be" minors or images created totally by computer. On April 17, 2002, the Supreme Court voted 6–3 to find CPPA unconstitutionally overbroad and so far-reaching that it could chill mainstream works of artistic merit.

- In 2001 AAP had taken the lead in an amicus brief to the Supreme Court supporting a challenge to the Child Online Protection Act (COPA), Congress's second attempt to criminalize certain content on the Internet. The case went up from the 3rd Circuit, which had affirmed a lower court's preliminary injunction against COPA, but had done so on narrow grounds—the impossibility of establishing one "community standard" by which

Internet speech can be governed. In spring 2002, failing to find COPA unconstitutional solely on the community standard issue, the Supreme Court sent the case back to the 3rd Circuit for a fuller consideration of the First Amendment issues.

- In November 2002 AAP joined a group of media organizations and journalists' associations in asking the U.S. Supreme Court to review and reverse a California Supreme Court ruling that found that a corporate public relations campaign, including statements and letters to the press, was commercial speech that does not merit the highest level of First Amendment protection. The case, *Nike* v. *Kasky,* is seen as an important opportunity for the high court to clarify the commercial speech doctrine.

Higher Education

AAP's Higher Education Committee serves the needs and interests of AAP members that publish for the postsecondary educational market. The committee was chaired by John Isley (Pearson Education) in 2002.

The committee again coordinated AAP's participation at the National Association of College Stores (NACS) Annual Meeting and Campus Exposition, held in Los Angeles in the spring, as well as ConTEXT, the NACS trade show for textbooks. The committee continued its outreach to college stores to improve sell-through.

The committee also coordinated AAP member responses to state initiatives involving textbook accessibility for the blind and disabled, the cost of textbooks, and textbook rental programs.

It published its annual *AAP College Textbook Publishers Greenbook,* a resource that provides information on the college publishing industry for college store buyers.

The Higher Education Task Force, which operates under the umbrella of the Higher Education Committee, is a group of marketing specialists that focuses on issues such as the cost and accessibility of higher education instructional materials. Don Burden (McGraw-Hill) chairs the task force.

International Committee

The International Committee represents a broad cross-section of the AAP membership with interests in overseas markets. Deborah Wiley (John Wiley & Sons) chaired the committee in 2002.

The committee's International Sales Subcommittee focuses on issues relating to the export of mass market paperbacks. Composed of export sales directors from AAP member houses and chaired in 2002 by Chitra Bopardikar (McGraw-Hill), the subcommittee's major concerns are piracy, export, distribution, and currency issues associated with export sales to the U.S. military, overseas schools, hotels, bookstores, and airports. The group works to facilitate publisher/ bookseller/distributor dialogue at major book fairs.

International Copyright Protection

AAP conducts a vigorous international program designed to combat the world-wide problem of copyright piracy, increase fair access to foreign markets, and strengthen copyright law regimes in other countries. Deborah Wiley (John Wiley & Sons) chaired the committee in 2002.

Following the departure in the summer of 2001 of Susan Pai, who had been coordinating the program, AAP continued to consolidate gains resulting from the significant seizure of some 600,000 counterfeit English-language books in South Korea earlier in the year.

Under the interim directorship of Andrew Hoffman, the program initiated a new campaign against copyshops in Malaysia that bore fruit in the spring of 2002. Responding to pressure from AAP, in late May Malaysia's Ministry of Domestic Trade and Consumer Affairs mounted a series of raids against copyshops operating in the Kuala Lumpur area. The raids resulted in the seizure of hundreds of illegal copies of books and in the confiscation of a number of copy machines. One raid in late May highlighted the threat to publishers from the proliferation of increasingly sophisticated copying and binding technology. The raid uncovered hundreds of illegal copies bound to resemble the legitimate books, with good-quality laminated covers and glued spines, all of which were apparently created and assembled on the premises of one of the many copyshops that surround college campuses throughout Malaysia. In addition, the operators of the shop showed great sophistication in avoiding detection; they were careful to avoid reproducing trademarks and pages that would aid in identifying the owners of the copyright. This is not unusual; similar raids in Taiwan and Hong Kong have revealed comparable levels of organization and expertise in pirate operations.

At the instigation of AAP member companies, further raids were conducted in Malaysia, Hong Kong, and Taiwan at the beginning of the fall 2002 semester, with similar results. AAP and its members plan to press for additional raids in 2003, as well as for prosecution of the cases resulting from the 2002 enforcement actions.

Through its involvement in the International Intellectual Property Alliance (IIPA), AAP works with other U.S. copyright industries to mobilize U.S. government support for intellectual property protection among U.S. trading partners. AAP joined with other members of IIPA in providing information to the U.S. trade representative (USTR) to assist in USTR's annual Special 301 review of intellectual property protection around the world. In its filing, IIPA cited losses to the U.S. economy of an estimated $8.3 billion in 2001 as a result of copyright piracy in 70 countries.

According to figures provided by AAP, book piracy cost the industry an estimated $636.4 million in 2001. Photocopy piracy on and around college campuses, which has become increasingly sophisticated, accounts for a significant portion of publishers' intellectual property losses, along with continuing offset piracy in many regions. There is also growing evidence of technologically advanced commercial piracy operations, including Internet database piracy, being carried out by highly organized syndicates.

In October 2002 Patricia L. Judd, an attorney with a strong background in intellectual property and international law, formerly with the U.S. Patent and

Trademark Office, became AAP's director of international copyright enforcement. A month later she embarked on a three-week trip to Asia to meet with U.S. and local government officials, sales representatives of AAP member houses, local publishing groups, and attorneys working with AAP on piracy and counterfeiting issues. As a result of the information gathered, preparations began in November and December for strong enforcement and legal reform action in a number of the countries visited. Judd's arrival marks a re-energized phase in AAP's anti-piracy campaign.

International Freedom to Publish

AAP's International Freedom to Publish Committee (IFTP) defends and promotes freedom of written communication worldwide. The committee monitors human rights issues and provides moral support and practical assistance to publishers and authors outside the United States who are denied basic freedoms. IFTP carries on its work in close cooperation with other human rights groups, including Human Rights Watch and PEN American Center, and maintains its own Web site at http://www.iftpc.org. Nan Graham (Scribner) chaired the committee in 2002.

IFTP continued to provide Judith Krug, director of ALA's Office for Intellectual Freedom, with information on book censorship around the world. This listing of books that are banned in their own countries but available in the United States forms the new international section of the Banned Books Week Resource Guide published by ALA.

In spring 2002 IFTP established the Jeri Laber International Freedom to Publish Award, which will be given annually to a book publisher outside the United States who has demonstrated courage in the face of political persecution. The award is named in honor of human rights activist Jeri Laber, one of the founding members of IFTP, who has served as a consultant to AAP for the past 27 years directing the committee's work. In December the committee announced that it was actively seeking nominees for the first award, which carries a $10,000 cash prize.

In early March two members of IFTP, Nan Graham and Hal Fessenden (Viking Penguin), met in Istanbul with publishers, journalists, writers, human rights organizations, the Turkish Publishers Association, and others. The meetings focused on continuing action by the Turkish government to stifle free expression. Writers and journalists continue to be subject to legal action and imprisonment for criticizing the state and for advocating Kurdish issues and certain religious freedoms. The government has enacted new legislation requiring that all books be certified by the Ministry of Culture before publication. IFTP continues to closely monitor cases of censorship and harassment in Turkey.

The committee has followed with increasing concern the circumstances surrounding the imprisonment of Uzbek poet Madadali Makhmudov, a recipient of the Hellman-Hammet Award (given to writers who have suffered political persecution). IFTP's concerns were expressed in a letter to President Bush asking that he use his influence with the president of Uzbekistan on Makhmudov's behalf. The letter stated that "The United States now has influence and leverage in Uzbekistan that it did not have before the war on terrorism. We urge you to use your good offices to promote human rights and the rule of law there. An appeal for the release of Mr. Makhmudov would be a good start."

In communications with Nigerian authorities, the committee expressed outrage over the assassination of noted Nigerian publisher and author Chief Victor Nwankwo and distress that no serious investigation had been undertaken to identify and punish those responsible. AAP also called upon President Bush and Secretary of State Colin Powell to pressure the Nigerian government into actively pursuing the case. Nwankwo was managing director of one of Nigeria's major privately owned publishing companies, and the first African member of the International Publishers Association Executive Committee.

In 2002 IFTP continued to move ahead with an Iranian translation project undertaken with funding from the Open Society Institute to increase understanding of Iran and Iranian culture by making Iranian literature accessible in English. It is now commissioning English-language translations of excerpts from the works of six Iranian writers that will be circulated to American publishers for possible publication.

Postal

AAP's Postal Committee coordinates activity in the area of postal rates and regulations, monitors developments at the U.S. Postal Service (USPS) and the independent Postal Rate Commission, and intervenes on the industry's behalf in formal proceedings before the commission. The committee also directs AAP lobbying activities on postal issues. Paul DeGuisti (McGraw-Hill) chaired the committee in 2002.

Early in 2002, in response to the rate case that USPS filed the previous September, AAP and other major players in the mailer community reached agreement with USPS to settle rather than litigate the pending rate case, agreeing to the rates requested and setting June 2002 as their implementation date. The decision to reach a settlement was prompted by the realization that a refiling of the rate case would result in even steeper increases since the financially strapped USPS had suffered unprecedented drops in mail volume and staggering, unbudgeted security costs in the wake of the September 11 terrorist attacks and the subsequent anthrax incidents. It was agreed, however, that adopting the settlement would not establish any precedent nor bind any of the parties in future negotiations.

Long-awaited postal reform legislation was finally introduced in the House during the second session of the 107th Congress. Unfortunately, the bill never made it out of committee.

In December 2002 President Bush issued an executive order establishing the President's Commission on the United States Postal Service. The commission, composed of nine presidential appointees, will be charged with examining the current status of USPS and issuing a report, due at the end of July 2003, containing specific recommendations for legislative and administrative reform.

Professional/Scholarly Publishing

AAP's Professional/Scholarly Publishing Division (PSP) is composed of AAP members who publish books, journals, looseleaf, and electronic products in technology, science, medicine, business, law, humanities, the behavioral sciences, and scholarly reference. Professional societies and university presses also play an important role in the division. Pieter Bolman (Elsevier Science) chaired the division in 2002.

The 2002 PSP Annual Conference, "Eng@ging Our Customers," was held in Washington, D.C., in February, featuring guest speakers Richard Harrington, CEO, Thomson Corporation, and John Perry Barlow, cofounder and vice chairman, Electronic Frontier Foundation. Prior to the opening of the meeting, the division's Electronic Information Committee sponsored a preconference seminar, "Measuring Online Usage: For Whom, What, and Why." The division sponsors an awards program, open only to AAP/PSP members, to acknowledge outstanding achievements in professional, scholarly, and reference publishing. At the 26th annual PSP awards ceremony, the R. R. Hawkins Award for the outstanding professional/scholarly work of the year went to Yale University Press for *Lichens of North America*. In addition, book awards were presented in 32 subject categories, in design and production, and in journal and electronic publishing.

The PSP Journals Committee sponsored two roundtable discussions, "Online Submission and Peer Review" and "To Renew or Not to Renew . . . and What to Renew," as well as commissioning a booklet, *Explore the World of Professional and Scholarly Publishing*.

The Electronic Information Committee is at work developing its latest White Paper. As a direct result of the successful PSP satellite seminar at the PSP 2002 Annual Conference on usage statistics, the committee decided to move forward in preparing a White Paper that will serve as a primer to PSP publishers.

School Division

The School Division is concerned with publishing for the elementary and secondary school (K–12) market. The division works to enhance the role of instructional materials in the education process, to maintain categorical funding for instructional materials and increase the funds available for the purchase of these materials, to simplify and rationalize the process of state adoptions for instructional materials, and to generally improve the climate in which educational publishers do business. The division serves as a bridge between the publishing industry and the educational community, promoting the cause of education at the national and state levels and working closely with an effective lobbying network in key adoption states. Margery Mayer (Scholastic) chaired the division in 2002.

Two issues, implementing the federal No Child Left Behind legislation and state budget crises, dominated the agenda for the School Division in 2002 and in all likelihood will continue to do so in 2003.

With passage of the No Child Left Behind Act (NCLB) in late 2001, AAP spent considerable time and resources working with the U.S. Department of Education to develop regulations and obtain guidance to help implement this legislation, under which the federal government became a major factor in the K–12 publishing industry. NCLB created new mandates and provided substantial federal funds in the areas of reading and testing.

At the same time, many states were facing budget crises resulting from the combined effects of a slowdown in the economy and the aftermath of the terrorist attacks of September 11, 2001. AAP fought battles in numerous states to help maintain funding for instructional materials and were even successful in getting increased instructional materials funding in a few states. While sales of instructional materials for 2002 were down 5 percent nationwide, it is generally recognized that the situation would have been far worse without AAP's lobbying efforts.

Beginning in early 2002, AAP held numerous meetings with U.S. Department of Education Assistant Secretary Susan Neumann and other DOE officials on implementation of NCLB. AAP wrote to Secretary of Education Rod Paige seeking assurance that there was no "approved list" of reading programs for federal funding under the Reading First initiative. Those assurances were received in a letter from the secretary to AAP in April. Several months later, AAP again asked Paige for a clear statement that an analysis of reading assessments done by the University of Oregon did not constitute an official "approved list" of assessments for Reading First funding (both letters and DOE responses can be found on the AAP Web site).

In Florida AAP was successful in getting a $14.4 million increase in funding for instructional materials despite an ongoing budget crisis resulting from the economic slowdown. Also in Florida, AAP successfully headed off several attempts to eliminate categorical funding for instructional materials, as well as attempts to allow schools to purchase used textbooks with their state instructional materials funding.

In North Carolina, AAP succeeded in obtaining an exemption for educational publishers from the requirements of the state's new e-procurement system, including payment of a 1.75 percent marketing fee. AAP continues to closely monitor implementation of North Carolina's e-procurement system to ensure that publishers are not double-charged for doing business in the state.

North Carolina also issued new policy guidelines governing the way in which publishers handle putative errors in their instructional materials. AAP succeeded in negotiating a number of changes that render the policy less burdensome for publishers while insuring that instructional materials are accurate and free of factual errors.

For the third year, AAP successfully blocked legislation that would have eliminated New Mexico's adoption system for instructional materials and created the framework for eliminating categorical funding for textbooks.

In California AAP succeeded in securing $400 million in funding for instructional materials in the face of a budget deficit of more than $20 billion. AAP also won passage of AB 1781, a major restructuring of the way in which instructional materials are funded, which places this funding on a more secure footing.

The accessibility of instructional materials for students who are blind or otherwise print-disabled has been a major issue for AAP and its elementary and secondary education publishers for a number of years. On April 24 AAP joined with Senators Chris Dodd (D-Conn.) and Thad Cochran (R-Miss.) and Representatives Tom Petri (R-Wis.) and George Miller (D-Calif.) as they introduced the Instructional Materials Accessibility Act of 2002 (IMAA). AAP had worked for more than two years with various advocacy groups for the blind, including the American Foundation for the Blind, National Federation of the Blind, American Printing House for the Blind, and Recording House for the Blind and Dyslexic, to develop the IMAA legislation. Acknowledging AAP's leadership role in helping to create the IMAA legislation, the American Foundation for the Blind gave the association its 2002 Access Award.

In October AAP cosponsored, along with Harvard Law School's Berkman Center and the National Center for Accessing the General Curriculum, a two-day symposium on "Policy, Property, and Permissions: A Discussion of Accessible Curricular Materials." This groundbreaking meeting, attended by publishers, legal experts in intellectual property rights, and advocates for the visually impaired, produced creative thinking on ways in which to safeguard intellectual property rights and at the same time make copyrighted materials more accessible.

In 2002 AAP undertook two initiatives to increase awareness among public officials of the pressing need for more instructional materials funding. In cooperation with the National Education Association (NEA), AAP surveyed 1,100 classroom teachers on their views regarding the value and adequacy of instructional materials in their classrooms. The 2002 survey—a follow-up to the 1996 AAP/NEA survey, which had revealed a major, nationwide shortage of instructional materials—indicated that some progress has been made over the last six years, but confirmed the existence of a continuing "textbook deficit" in many schools. The complete survey results can be found on the AAP Web site.

AAP commissioned legal scholar and testing expert Susan E. Phillips to produce a policy paper titled "The Role of Instructional Materials in Providing Evidence of the Opportunity to Learn." The document shows that school officials, especially those with high-stakes tests, can reduce potential legal liability by insuring that their students are adequately supplied with instructional materials aligned with current state academic standards.

AAP lobbying efforts in New York State effectively helped to secure a $4.6 million increase in funding for instructional materials and defeated efforts to roll instructional materials funding into a block grant.

In Georgia, the state Board of Education adopted almost all of AAP's recommendations on implementing a new state law that requires an electronic version of all textbooks adopted in the state.

AAP hosted a highly successful "Reading Summit" in Washington, D.C., in September, bringing nearly 250 leading experts on reading from academia, government, and the private sector together with educational publishers to exchange ideas on ways to improve the teaching of reading to the nation's children.

Seeking to aid publishers in distributing their content in digital form, AAP and the National Association of Textbook Administrators (NASTA) created three working groups to review state adoption laws and regulations and to develop recommendations on adapting rules, originally written for print materials, to avoid unnecessarily restricting digital delivery of educational content. The objective of this initiative is to produce uniform standards for electronic delivery similar to the Manufacturing Standards and Specifications for Textbooks (MSST) for printed materials.

Also working with NASTA, AAP produced a White Paper on the "heavy backpack" problem. Last year California became the first state to pass a law mandating a limit on the size and weight of textbooks adopted in that state. New Jersey considered, but did not pass, similar legislation.

Trade Publishing

AAP's Trade Publishing group comprises publishers of fiction, general nonfiction, poetry, children's literature, religious, and reference publications, in hardcover, paperback, and electronic formats. Robert Miller (Hyperion) chaired the committee in 2002.

The committee's major areas of attention during the year included the formation of the Publishing for Latinos Task Force, overseeing AAP's Diversity/Recruit and Retain initiative, serving AAP's Smaller and Independent Publishers, and expanding the Get Caught Reading campaign. (These initiatives are discussed in detail in other sections of this report.)

The group also works on the AAP Honors program, nominating and electing a candidate from outside the publishing industry who has helped promote U.S. books and authors to be honored at the AAP Annual Meeting. The honoree in 2002 was NBC television's "Today Show" for its dedication to books and literacy as an integral part of the program.

AAP formed the Publishing for Latinos Task Force in response to the explosive growth in the Latino book market, both in English and in Spanish. The mission of the task force is to address issues that are of particular concern to publishers in this market and to heighten awareness and understanding—both among consumers and among those in the industry—of books published for the Latino market. This goal will be carried out in specific initiatives in 2003, which AAP plans to designate as The Year of Publishing for Latinos.

To continue its effort to help publishers find and retain a diverse pool of talented employees, the Trade Committee's Diversity Committee merged with its Recruit and Retain Task Force. The merged committee targets college students approaching graduation, individuals currently working in other industries who would like to change careers, and junior-level publishing employees who may be considering a move to a high-tech industry. Projects of this group include college campus outreach, a jobs Web site that will go live in 2003, and the Young to Publishing Group (YPG), which was established to facilitate networking among people who have worked in the book publishing industry for fewer than five years. YPG numbered more than 200 people at the end of 2002, with monthly brown-bag lunches hosted by AAP member houses that feature speakers on topics such as editing, sub-rights, literary agents, and other subjects pertaining to the industry.

AAP's Smaller and Independent Publishing (SIP) Committee held a seminar in conjunction with AAP's Annual Meeting in February, open to both AAP members and nonmembers, with panels addressing topics such as branding, publicity, and marketing. This group met throughout 2002 to discuss issues pertaining to the smaller-sized independent publishing house and to plan the SIP annual conference for 2003.

2002 Annual Meeting

Evanson, Friedman, Sargent Head AAP Board

The AAP membership has chosen Robert Evanson (McGraw-Hill Education), Jane Friedman (HarperCollins Publishers), and John Sargent (Holtzbrinck Publishers) as the association's officers for fiscal year 2002–2003, which began April 1, 2002. Evanson will serve a two-year term as AAP chairman, succeeding Robert Miller (Hyperion), with Friedman as vice chair, and Sargent as treasurer. Traditionally, the chair alternates between representatives of the trade and educational publishing communities.

As president of McGraw-Hill Education, Evanson heads a company whose educational and professional materials serve markets from kindergarten through higher education, generating $2.4 billion in revenue last year. A recipient of McGraw-Hill's Excellence in Management award, Evanson was instrumental in integrating Macmillan/McGraw-Hill School Publishing Company into the McGraw-Hill Companies.

Friedman, who was listed among *Vanity Fair*'s 200 "Women Legends, Leaders, and Trailblazers," is president and CEO of HarperCollins Publishers, a subsidiary of News Corporation. Under Friedman's leadership, HarperCollins had 93 adult and children's titles on the *New York Times* bestseller list last year. Before joining HarperCollins in 1997, she was executive vice president at Random House. With her election, which puts her in line to succeed Evanson in 2004, Friedman becomes only the second woman in AAP's 32-year history to occupy that post. (Joan Manley of Time-Life Books chaired the AAP board in 1975–1976.)

Sargent is CEO of Holtzbrinck, which owns three college publishers (Bedford, Freeman, and Worth) and five trade houses (Farrar Straus & Giroux, Henry Holt, Picador, St. Martin's Press, and TOR). Prior to joining Holtzbrinck, Sargent headed Dorling Kindersley USA and was president and publisher of the children's division of Simon & Schuster.

Business Meeting: FY 2002–2003 Budget

The membership approved an operating budget of $6,109,984 for fiscal year 2002–2003, with $4,010,684 allocated to Core Committees (including the three committees serving the Trade, Higher Education, and International constituencies) and $2,099,300 allocated to the two divisions ($1,442,800 for the School Division and $656,500 for Professional/Scholarly Publishing).

Other Highlights

Among other highlights of the meeting:

- Two members of Congress, Senator Max Cleland (D-Ga.) and House Democratic Whip Nancy Pelosi (D-Calif.), spoke movingly of their own love of books. Speaking with gratitude of his book-filled childhood, Senator Cleland quoted Helen Keller's observation that "books give us vision." Congresswoman Pelosi remarked on her penchant for giving to colleagues in Congress books she has enjoyed and found meaningful.

- Michael Parmentier, director of readiness, training policy, and programs for the Defense Department, reported on the Advanced Distributed Learning Initiative, a broad-ranging collaboration among government, academia, and the private sector to provide Web-based learning opportunities to military personnel worldwide. AAP is coordinating publisher participation in the initiative.

- Jocelyn Chadwick of Harvard University spoke of her efforts to encourage the inclusion of relevant and diverse literary voices in high school literary anthologies. As an expert on Mark Twain and as an African American, Chadwick has been particularly effective in advocating the need to keep Twain's work, especially *Huckleberry Finn,* in the classroom. Chadwick asked publishers to help classroom teachers by providing them with information they can use to counter attempts to censor controversial works.

- NBC "Today Show" correspondent Jamie Gangel, news anchor Ann Curry, and literary editor Andrea Smith were on hand to receive the 2002 AAP Honors for their work in promoting American books and authors. A video prepared for the occasion highlighted some of the more colorful author interviews on the show. Andrea Smith noted that some 200 books are featured each year on the program, mostly works of nonfiction and often involving celebrity or newsmaker authors. The "Today Show" designated the Susan G. Komen Foundation for Breast Cancer Research as the recipient of the $5,000 honors check.

- William J. Bennet, co-director of Empower America and former U.S. secretary of education, talked about the power of a book that "allows you to put yourself in the place of another human being."

- Best-selling author and lawyer Scott Turow, who serves as a member of a special Illinois commission on the death penalty, spoke about the public policy implications of capital punishment.

- The luncheon speaker, Disney CEO Michael Eisner, told his audience that the "common enemy" of digital piracy must be defeated. Coming straight from giving testimony before the Senate Commerce Committee, Eisner reported that he had urged Congress to press for the development of open technological standards to facilitate creation of private-sector solutions to protect digitally delivered content. He urged that these common standards be mandated for all digital media devices that handle creative content.

- Adobe CEO Bruce Chizen also addressed piracy, but from the point of view of a technology provider. Chizen noted that the business software industry will lose $12 billion to piracy this year, and that piracy of Adobe products will cost his company some $700 million. He expressed his uncertainty, however, about the wisdom of having Congress legislate solutions to complex technological problems of digital rights management. "Anyone who wants to steal will find a way to do so," Chizen said. "Our problem is keeping the honest people honest."

American Booksellers Association

828 S. Broadway, Tarrytown, NY 10591
914-591-2665, fax 914-591-2724
World Wide Web http://www.bookweb.org
E-mail info@bookweb.org

Michael Hoynes
Senior Marketing Officer

Founded in 1900, the American Booksellers Association (ABA) is a not-for-profit trade organization devoted to meeting the needs of its core members—independently owned bookstores—through education, information dissemination, and advocacy. ABA actively supports free speech, literacy, and programs that encourage reading. The association, headquartered in Tarrytown, New York, also hosts the annual ABA Convention in conjunction with the BookExpo America trade show each spring.

A major highlight of 2002 was the adoption of a revised strategic plan for 2003–2007. The strategic plan is titled "Independent Bookselling . . . Competing in a Changing World." Its key components follow.

Mission

The mission of the American Booksellers Association is to provide advocacy, opportunities for peer interaction, education, support services, and new business models that enable independent professional booksellers to compete successfully in a changing world.

Vision for 2007

Independent professional booksellers are skilled retail business people who, through innovation and success, are a vibrant, profitable, and growing force in a diverse marketplace. They are recognized as an influential and vital link among authors, readers, publishers, and the community.

Strategic Goals and Objectives

Goal I

To provide independent professional booksellers with access to the education, information, and business services they need to succeed in a changing world. *Objective IA*: To create an accessible education program that effectively meets the needs of independent professional booksellers. *Objective IB*: To provide independent professional booksellers with the timely information they need to compete successfully in a changing world. *Objective IC*: To provide independent booksellers with the tools they need to compete successfully in a changing world.

Goal II

To serve as the voice of independent professional booksellers and advocate on their behalf on issues such as free expression, trade practices, literacy, and community activism. *Objective IIA*: To defend free expression and First Amendment rights. *Objective IIB*: To maintain active vigilance in the arena of trade practices and achieve a more productive relationship with a growing number of vendors. *Objective IIC*: To encourage, with appropriate allies, literacy, a literary culture, and the development of new readers. *Objective IID*: To support community activism and help create alliances that promote independent bookselling and other independent businesses. *Objective IIE*: To identify and advocate members' interests on issues of public policy. *Objective IIF*: To create a strong public voice for independent bookselling by helping to build the market share and presence of current members and by developing new members.

Goal III

To promote the value of independent booksellers as a group through the Book Sense program and other cooperative activities. *Objective IIIA*: To increase the impact of the Book Sense program by expanding participation among new and existing ABA members and others. *Objective IIIB*: To keep Book Sense in tune with market developments and opportunities in order to further develop consumer awareness of the Book Sense brand among the reading public and to attract additional publisher support for the Book Sense program.

Goal IV

To foster development of new and enhanced business models, systems, and services. *Objective IVA*: To monitor development of new business models and technologies that will allow member bookstores to better operate according to sound business practices. *Objective IVB*: To investigate and incubate new business models that can help independent professional booksellers compete more profitably.

Highlights of 2002

ABA educational programs held in conjunction with BookExpo America were expanded to include a full day of workshops covering financial management, inventory management and control, and marketing.

In April booksellers celebrated an important victory in the fight to protect the privacy of bookstore customers when the Colorado Supreme Court ruled unanimously that Denver's Tattered Cover Book Store did not have to comply with a search warrant that sought a list of the titles purchased by one of its customers. The American Booksellers Foundation for Free Expression (ABFFE) organized national support for the Tattered Cover during its two-year battle and paid its legal costs.

ABFFE became increasingly concerned with the threat posed to First Amendment rights by the USA Patriot Act and other measures taken by the federal government to deal with international terrorism. In April it joined members of the Free Expression Network in issuing a statement at a Washington, D.C., press conference that featured remarks by two critics of the USA Patriot Act, Senator Russell Feingold (D-Wis.) and Representative Patsy Mink (D-Hawaii).

ABFFE later joined with the American Civil Liberties Union and other groups in filing a Freedom of Information Act (FOIA) request to determine how many times the FBI has examined bookstore and library records under Section 215 of the USA Patriot Act.

During the year, ABFFE also

- Convinced the University of California, San Diego, to drop plans to discipline two student groups, including a collective that runs a bookstore, for linking their university-supported Web sites to groups that the State Department lists as "foreign terrorist organizations; the university claimed that the links violated the USA Patriot Act's ban on providing "material support" to terrorist groups
- Opposed the Bush administration's effort to give a president, vice president, or their families the right to limit the release of papers that is now required by the Presidential Records Act
- Joined an amicus brief that helped persuade the U.S. Supreme Court to strike down the Child Pornography Prevention Act of 1996 because it widened the definition of child pornography beyond pictures of real minors to include adults posing as minors and thereby threatened to chill the dissemination of legitimate artistic work, including such films as *American Beauty* and *Traffic*
- Filed lawsuits in Ohio, Vermont, and South Carolina to overturn bans on the display of material that is "harmful to minors" on the World Wide Web
- Defended the University of Minnesota Press, which was under attack for its decision to publish *Harmful to Minors: The Perils of Protecting Children from Sex*
- Urged the New York Commissioner of Education to stop the censoring of literary passages used in the state's Regents proficiency examinations
- Successfully protested a California high school principal's decision to remove William Styron's novel *Sophie's Choice* from the shelves of the school library
- Cosponsored the 21st annual Banned Books Week in September, distributing nearly 1,000 free promotional kits to bookstores

Association of Research Libraries

21 Dupont Circle N.W., Washington, DC 20036
202-296-2296, e-mail arlhq@arl.org
World Wide Web http://www.arl.org

Duane E. Webster
Executive Director

The Association of Research Libraries (ARL) represents 124 research libraries that serve major research institutions in the United States and Canada. ARL's mission is to shape and influence forces affecting the future of research libraries in the process of scholarly communication. ARL programs and services promote equitable access to and effective use of recorded knowledge in support of teaching, research, scholarship, and community service. The association articulates the concerns of research libraries and their institutions, forges coalitions, influences information policy development, and supports innovation and improvement in research library operations. ARL operates as a forum for the exchange of ideas and as an agent for collective action.

ARL fulfills its mission and builds its programs through a set of strategic objectives. To meet these objectives, ARL resources are organized into a framework of programs and capabilities. Annually the ARL Board of Directors identifies the priorities the association staff and standing committees will address in the coming year. As outlined in the 2002 ARL Program Plan, the present priorities are to

- Provide leadership in advocacy and educational efforts within the North American and international research and educational communities to influence legislation, institutional policies, and individual practices in the areas of intellectual property, copyright, and information policy
- Encourage and support development of and access to institution-based repositories for the work of scholars and explore other strategies that could lead to more cost-effective models for managing scholarly communication in a global environment
- Develop new approaches and models for measuring and improving library service effectiveness, diversity, and leadership
- Promote tools, policies, and programs to ensure enduring, cost-effective, and integrated access to research materials from all parts of the world, in all formats, to readers working both near and at a distance from those resources, and, to the greatest extent possible, to support delivery of these resources and related services to the user's desktop
- Develop effective strategies to assist member libraries in recruiting and retaining talented staff in a changing demographic environment, including continuing to strengthen the curriculum of graduate library school programs to meet the challenges of the 21st century

Scholarly Communication

The Office of Scholarly Communication (OSC) undertakes activities to understand and influence the forces affecting the production, dissemination, and use of scholarly and scientific information. OSC seeks to promote innovative, creative, and affordable ways of sharing scholarly findings, particularly through championing evolving electronic techniques for recording and disseminating academic and research scholarship. OSC collaborates with others in the scholarly community to build a common understanding of the challenges presented by electronic scholarly communication and to generate strategies for transforming the system.

In early 2002 an ARL ad hoc task force met to review ARL's strategy for managing intellectual property in the best interests of the academic community and the public. The task force recommended that ARL promote "open access to quality information in support of learning and scholarship." Open access, in this context, refers to works created with no expectation of financial remuneration and available at no cost to the reader on the public Internet for purposes of education and research. The task force developed a five-year action agenda to promote open access. Activities were identified in seven major areas: education, advocacy, legal, legislative, new funding models, global alliances, and research. The task force also identified essential partners to engage in these efforts, including scholars and scientists, the higher education and library associations, university counsels, scholarly societies, and numerous others. As one of the first steps in implementing the action agenda, OSC created the Open Access Web site (http://www.arl.org/scomm/open_access/index.html), designed to encourage discussions among library staff, campus administrators, university counsels, faculty, and policymakers about open access and how its application in research institutions can provide a cost-effective way to disseminate and use information.

To promote the use of institutional repositories as a way to implement open access, ARL, the Scholarly Publishing and Academic Resources Coalition (SPARC), and the Coalition for Networked Information (CNI) held a one-day workshop in October on "Institutional Repositories: Creating an Infrastructure for Faculty–Institution Partnerships" that attracted over 250 participants. The workshop focused on the cultural and management dimensions of establishing an institutional repository to help academic and research library and IT directors begin planning for the implementation of repositories to house faculty works, such as articles, data sets, images, video, and courseware.

In February 2002 ARL signed on to the Budapest Open Access Initiative (BOAI), a movement to accelerate progress in the international effort to make research articles in all academic fields available on the public Internet at no cost to the user. Hundreds of individuals and organizations around the world, including scientists and researchers, universities, laboratories, libraries and library organizations, foundations, journals, publishers, and learned societies, have signed the initiative.

Representatives of ARL and the Association of American University Presses (AAUP) met in April 2002 to explore ideas and projects for strengthening the working relationships between research libraries and university presses. The group discussed the differences in financing between libraries and presses, identified areas of agreement and concern, and agreed to meet on a regular basis. The group also proposed developing a joint ARL/AAUP statement on the complementary roles of presses and libraries within scholarly communications and to investigate the viability of installing print-on-demand facilities in libraries.

Because both the publishing industry and the research community are global, OSC is working with colleagues in the new International Scholarly Communications Alliance (ISCA) to develop an agenda for addressing scholarly communications issues globally. In February 2002 research library associations in Australia, Canada, Europe, Japan, Hong Kong, New Zealand, Britain, and the United States announced they had formed an action-oriented global network that will collaborate with scholars and publishers to establish equitable access to scholarly and research publications.

To build a better understanding of the evolving publishing environment, OSC continues to track mergers and acquisitions in the scholarly publishing arena and continues its efforts with antitrust authorities to raise awareness of library concerns about the increased consolidation of the publishing industry. OSC is working to build a collaborative capacity for data collection and maintenance that will provide libraries with the information necessary to support antitrust arguments and advance other educational and advocacy initiatives related to scholarly communication. To begin developing such a dataset, ARL surveyed its members to gather information on prices and licensing terms for electronic journals.

Federal Relations and Information Policy

The Federal Relations and Information Policy program is designed to monitor activities resulting from the legislative, regulatory, or operating practices of international and domestic government agencies and other relevant bodies on matters of concern to research libraries. The program analyzes and responds to federal information policies and influences federal action on issues related to research libraries. It examines issues of importance to the development of research libraries and develops ARL positions on issues that reflect the needs and interests of members. Through the Canadian Association of Research Libraries (CARL), the program monitors Canadian information policies.

The ARL Board of Directors has identified intellectual property and copyright as a defining set of issues for the future of scholarly communications. While these issues have been a priority for some time, activity has been accelerated in recent years because of developments in the U.S. Congress, state legislatures, and the courts.

In 2002 the Federal Relations program represented ARL's interests in *Eldred* v. *Ashcroft,* a case that challenges the constitutionality of the 1998 Sonny Bono Copyright Term Extension Act (CTEA). ARL joined library associations and other national organizations in submitting an *amici curiae* brief asking the Supreme Court to rule that the extended term of protection for copyrighted works arising from CTEA is unconstitutional. The brief argued that CTEA exceeds the limits on protection authorized by the Constitution's copyright clause and causes substantial harm by perpetually keeping works under copyright protection, thereby limiting growth of the public domain. The Supreme Court heard arguments on the case in October, and in January the Court ruled 7–2 that CETA was not unconstitutional.

Results of the implementation of the Digital Millennium Copyright Act (DMCA) demanded considerable attention of the program during the past year. In October ARL joined the American Association of Law Libraries, the American Library Association (ALA), the Medical Library Association, and the Special Libraries Association to endorse the Digital Media Consumers' Rights Act of 2002 (DMCRA). This legislation is designed to recalibrate DMCA to safeguard the interests of the public and reaffirm fair use in a networked environment. DMCRA resolves key concerns regarding hardware and software that permit significant noninfringing uses, and it allows researchers to engage in scientific research on technological protection measures.

Digital rights management systems (DRMs) have emerged as a critical concern for libraries. The Federal Relations program is working with others in the library, education, high-tech, and consumer electronics communities to respond to the DRM legislation introduced in Congress. The program also worked with other library associations to promote the Technology Education and Copyright Harmonization Act (TEACH Act, S. 487) that was passed by Congress in summer 2002 and signed by the president in November. This legislation will allow faculty to use copyrighted works such as videos, music, images, and computer software in their online courses, in certain circumstances, without seeking permission from the copyright owners.

Antiterrorism Concerns

One of the key concerns of the library community has been the legislation to promote homeland security and restrict access to information that followed the terrorist attacks of September 11, 2001. ARL, with others in the library and higher education communities, worked extensively with House and Senate staff and met with representatives of the FBI, law enforcement, and the Office of Management and Budget (OMB) to discuss these measures. The program continues to monitor new legislation in this arena. The USA Patriot Act and related antiterrorism measures broadened the surveillance capabilities of law enforcement and contained new provisions governing criminal and foreign intelligence investigations. Many libraries have seen an increase in law enforcement inquiries as authorities have sought access to patron records, including electronic mail and other electronic communications. On May 30, 2002, the attorney general issued guidelines that expand the FBI's investigative powers and, on July 16, President Bush announced a "National Strategy for Homeland Security." To help libraries and educational institutions comply with proper search warrants, subpoenas, and wiretap requests from law enforcement officials, ARL, with others in the Shared Legal Capability, hosted a teleconference on the USA Patriot Act and related issues on December 11, 2002. The teleconference program reviewed the relevant laws, legislation, and initiatives; discussed the implications for libraries; reviewed possible scenarios; and offered tips for developing responses to government requests for information.

Collection Services

By focusing on both local and collaborative strategies, the Collections Services program enhances the availability of ARL member libraries' collections, regardless of their location. Over the years, the program's efforts have included improving the structures and processes for effective cooperative collection development, along with access to digital resources; collaboration with other organizations in collections-related projects, both in North America and internationally; attention to general issues of collections policies and budget management; and the promotion of government and foundation support for collections of national prominence in the United States and Canada.

In June 2001 a symposium was held at Brown University to explore the prospects and promise of special collections in the expanding electronic environment and articulate a long-term programmatic agenda for special collections in research libraries. A new ARL Special Collections Task Force was formed in late 2001 and charged to engage and advance the agenda that emerged from the symposium. This group, chaired by Joe Hewitt, University of North Carolina at Chapel Hill, brings together ARL directors and special collections librarians, including representatives of the ALA Rare Books and Manuscripts Section (RBMS) and the Society of American Archivists (SAA). The October 2002 task force meeting held at Yale focused on developing the following projects: a principles statement articulating the role and importance of special collections, a White Paper and conference on improving access to "hidden" and other special collections, a statement of need for extending the training and recruitment of curators for special collections, and identification of statistics and performance measures that better describe the role and contribution of special collections in research libraries.

The ARL Forum on Collections and Access for the 21st Century Scholar, held in October 2001, led to the creation of the Task Force on Collections and Access to advance the multifaceted agenda that emerged from the forum. Chaired by Shirley Baker, Washington University in St. Louis, the task force examined how research libraries' collection management and access services are responding to changes in research, teaching, and learning. Particular attention was given to the impact of the growing reliance by students and others in research institutions on using the Web to find information. ARL members were surveyed online in July and 60 libraries provided more than 150 examples of how they are responding to these changes. A new ARL standing committee, Collections and Access Issues, will be formed in 2003 by merging and updating the agendas of two previous distinct committees, the Access to Information Resources Committee and the Research Collections Committee.

In 1996 the Andrew W. Mellon Foundation awarded $450,000 to ARL to create the Association of American Universities (AAU)/ARL Global Resources Program (GRP). Originally intended to be a three-year grant, the funding stimulated and enabled more than five years of activity focused on improving access to international research materials through cooperative structures and the use of new technologies, and on generating increased communication within the scholarly community regarding future information needs. "The AAU/ARL Global Resources Program at a Crossroads," a comprehensive report that documented achievements, best practices, new challenges, and proposed next steps, was distributed and discussed at the 2002 ARL May Membership Meeting (http://www.arl.org/collect/grp/crossroads.html) and formed the basis of the final report to the Mellon Foundation.

A new phase of GRP is now taking shape. Dan Hazen, Harvard University, the ARL visiting program officer currently directing GRP, presented "The AAU/ARL Global Resources Program—Phase II: Discussion Document on Goals, Priorities, Operating Principles, Budget Requirements, and Desired Outcomes" to the ARL board and the Research Collections Committee during their meetings in October. This paper, which was also distributed to ARL's full membership, is available on the Web at http://www.arl.org/arl/proceedings/141. A new Global Resources Program Advisory Committee, chaired by Paul Mosher, University of Pennsylvania, held its initial meeting in February 2003. The program plans to foster several new projects, among them one on the Middle East and perhaps one on an interdisciplinary topic that will cut across geographic areas. New strategies for financial stability, along with new organizational alliances, are also under consideration. Ongoing activities include communications about and advocacy for international information needs in a variety of forums.

In November 2002 ARL joined with the Center for Research Libraries (CRL) to provide a forum for a select group of library and other academic professionals to explore the new dynamics and economics of cooperative collection development. The meeting explored how limited resources for acquisitions and the myriad challenges posed by e-journals, databases, and other digital materials for scholarly research are eliciting innovative new approaches to building collections in both electronic and hard copy.

Access and Technology

ARL's Access capability undertakes activities to support resource sharing among libraries in the electronic environment and to improve access to research information resources while minimizing costs for libraries. This capability works to strengthen interlibrary loan and document delivery performance, interoperability among library systems, cooperative cataloging programs, and policies that increase user access to information both on-site and remotely.

On May 1, 2002, ARL announced the launch of the Scholars Portal Project, a three-year collaboration between several ARL member libraries and Fretwell-Downing, Inc. (FD). The goal of the Scholars Portal Project is to provide software tools that allow an academic community to have a single point of access on the Web to find high-quality information resources and, to the greatest extent possible, deliver the information and related services directly to the user's desktop. Initially, the Scholars Portal Project will use FD's ZPORTAL and several related FD products to deliver cross-domain searching of licensed and openly available content in a range of subject fields and from multiple institutions. Over the course of the next three years, the project will expand to include other services that improve user access to and use of information resources, such as integration of the searching tool within the local online learning environment for a course and linkage to an around-the-clock digital reference service to consult with a reference librarian.

With the beginning of the Scholars Portal Project, the Scholars Portal Working Group disbanded and the Portal Applications Working Group was established. The new group fosters the definition and development of portals for research libraries and the communities they serve, and ensures ARL's presence in discussions of similar initiatives advocating the integration of information technology and content for the benefit of the academic and research communities. The working group also monitors how libraries are applying portal technology and seeks to identify common issues or barriers to successful implementations.

The Interlibrary Loan/Document Delivery (ILL/DD) Performance Measures Study was a two-year effort to measure the performance of ILL departments in 119 North American research and college libraries in 1995–1996. The study, funded by the Andrew W. Mellon Foundation, examined four performance measures: direct cost, fill rate, turnaround time, and user satisfaction. ARL plans to update, replicate, and expand this study to obtain current data on the performance of mediated and user-initiated ILL/DD operations in research and academic libraries. New to this study is the focus on the performance of user-initiated ILL/DD services. This 12-month project, undertaken as part of ARL's New Measures Initiative, began in September 2002.

The Access capability continues to support several projects of the AAU/ARL Global Resources Program (GRP). The German Resources Project operates as part of GRP. GRP members may subscribe to Xipolis, a collection of nine online German reference resources. Another activity was access to GBVdirekt/NA, a document delivery service focused on journal literature. Changes in GBV invoicing required ARL to advise German Project members to stop ordering via GBVdirekt/NA at the end of January 2002.

As of mid-August, 27 libraries had joined the AAU/ARL/National Coordinating Committee on Japanese Library Resources (NCC) Japan Journal Access Project to participate in the Global ILL Framework (GIF) initiative. Participants, including ARL and non-ARL libraries, have access to nearly 60 Japanese university and special libraries to obtain photocopies. North American participants use OCLC to place and receive orders, OCLC's ILL Fee Management (IFM) service to pay lending fees, and Ariel to send and receive documents. Japanese participants receive requests on the NACSIS ILL system, use IFM for payment, and use EPICWIN to send and receive articles. This is the third document delivery initiative between North American and Japanese libraries, but the first to use the International Standards Organization (ISO) ILL Protocol for communication of ILL requests between OCLC and NACSIS ILL systems. The first document delivery initiative with Waseda University now has 29 North American participants, including several non-ARL libraries.

Preservation

The Preservation capability pursues initiatives that support member libraries' efforts to provide enduring access to their research collections. Strategies include encouraging and strengthening broad-based participation in national preservation efforts in the United States and Canada, supporting development of preservation programs within member libraries, monitoring copyright and licensing developments to ensure support of preservation activities in the electronic environment, supporting effective bibliographic control of preservation-related processes, encouraging development of preservation information resources, and monitoring technological developments that may have an impact on preservation goals.

In response to the dramatic changes that have taken place in preservation over the past decade, the ARL board reasserted the importance of preservation as a fundamental responsibility of research libraries. The ARL statement, developed by the Preservation Committee and approved by the board at its May 2002 meeting, reaffirms the commitment of ARL members to preserving collections basic to an understanding of our intellectual and cultural heritage through an active stewardship that enables current and future consultation and use of library resources. The statement also reflects an appreciation of the difficulties faced by libraries in trying to effectively balance preservation needs and available resources. See http://www.arl.org/preserv/responsibility.html.

Approximately 150 people attended the March 2002 conference "Redefining Preservation, Shaping New Solutions, Forging New Partnerships" in Ann Arbor, Michigan, that was cosponsored by ARL and the University of Michigan Libraries. Attendees heard from 18 speakers over two days and participated in small group discussions. Fifteen high-priority actions were identified as needing national attention, and the ARL Preservation Committee met with preservation administrators from ARL libraries at the meeting's conclusion to discuss specific recommendations for ARL. In May 2002 representatives of ARL, the Library of Congress, the Council on Library and Information Resources (CLIR), and the National Endowment for the Humanities met to review the recommendations from the conference and suggest individual and collective strategies for action.

ARL has actively participated in an Institute of Museum and Library Services project with CLIR, the University Libraries Group, and the Regional Alliance for Preservation to research and document current conditions and challenges in preservation programs in American college and research libraries. The first phase of the project focused on collecting quantitative data on preservation and digitizing activities, and data on the institutional context for the non-ARL libraries represented in the group. The ARL Preservation Statistics survey served as the basis for this inquiry. The second phase of the project, designed to document preservation needs, involved visits to 20 representative libraries, including six ARL institutions.

In 2002 ARL published three compilations of data, covering the years 1998–1999, 1999–2000, and 2000–2001, that provide detailed information about preservation expenditures, conservation treatment and preservation reformatting, administration of preservation programs, and staffing patterns in ARL member libraries. Highlights from the 1999–2000 and the 2000–2001 ARL Preservation Statistics reports show that the fluctuation of preservation expenditures and staffing that ARL libraries have experienced over the past decade has continued. Expenditures for 113 ARL libraries were $92,276,777 in 2000–2001, reflecting a 7.5 percent increase from 1999–2000, and a slow, irregular increase of about $20 million over the last ten years. Total preservation staff increased to just over 1,800 full-time-equivalent (FTE) employees, the second time the staffing level has been more than 1,800 since the survey was revised in 1996–1997. After a rapid increase in 1998–1999, microfilming activity dropped just as sharply, stopping just short of a record low.

SPEC Kit 269, *Integrating Preservation Activities,* explored to what extent preservation activities have been integrated into research library operations by examining the many facets of mature preservation programs and determining how much activity takes place within, and how much outside, the purview of preservation departments. It examines which units participate in preservation activities in research libraries and the degree to which those activities are spread across the library. The survey—distributed to the 124 ARL member libraries in June 2002—asked whether levels of preservation activity have changed over the years, how staff and users are trained about preservation issues, and how preservation activity is evaluated. Sixty-nine libraries (56 percent) responded to the survey, and the findings indicate that the scope of research library preservation programs is expanding, the level of activity is increasing overall, and many of these activities are highly integrated across library operations—especially disaster planning and response, selection for treatment, policy development, and reformatting. Preservation activities are more integrated and more successful than five years ago in a significant number of libraries.

Diversity

The ARL Diversity Program supports and extends efforts within member institutions to promote and develop library staff and leaders who are representative of a diverse population. These efforts include the recruitment and retention of library personnel from a variety of backgrounds—particularly from groups traditionally underrepresented in the academic and research library work force—and the creation of professional development opportunities and networks that enhance climates conducive to diversity and help promote diverse leadership.

The diversity program administers two national programs: the Initiative to Recruit a Diverse Work Force and the Leadership and Career Development Program (LCDP). Both focus on the recruitment and retention of persons from diverse racial, ethnic, and national backgrounds. The Initiative to Recruit a Diverse Work Force grants stipends to students from minority backgrounds to assist in the completion of their MLS degree. Grantees agree to a minimum two-year working relationship with an ARL library upon graduation. Four MLS candidates, from a competitive pool, were selected in May 2002 to receive the award. They were chosen on the strength of their educational and professional credentials, breadth of developmental experiences, and essays articulating their desire to pursue professional careers in ARL libraries. An advisory group of deans from ARL and other libraries and the ARL Diversity Committee will continue to provide guidance and support for the program.

LCDP prepares talented mid-career minority librarians for leadership roles and positions in the research library community. Since it was launched in 1997–1998, the program has completed two successful offerings with a total of 38 participants. A combination of theory—presented by key leaders in the research library community—and experiential learning opportunities allow for exploration of critical issues facing leaders in the research library and higher education communities. LCDP participants attend two week-long leadership institutes. The institutes are intensive curriculum-based programs designed to intellectually engage the LCDP participants and focus on horizon issues in the library community. The 20 librarians in the 2001–2002 class, along with their faculty and mentors, celebrated the successful completion of the program with a closing ceremony at the ALA Annual Conference in Atlanta in June.

To increase the number of participants able to be accepted into each LCDP class, and to provide the opportunity for the involvement of the medical library community, ARL and the Medical Library Association (MLA) have entered into a formal partnership under which MLA will provide direct involvement of MLA staff and member leaders and a nominal contribution to the program's annual operating budget. MLA staff and representatives will work with ARL staff and the Leadership Committee to recruit potential LCDP applicants and mentors from MLA libraries.

Office of Leadership and Management Services

Over the past 30 years, the Office of Leadership and Management Services (OLMS) has successfully designed and facilitated effective and well-attended library staff development programs. OLMS products and services help research libraries serve their clientele through the strategic deployment of talented and well-trained individuals and through the use of timely and relevant information. The program stays abreast of innovations in library services, technologies, and methods while keeping current with the latest research findings in the areas of organizational structure, productivity, learning, and leadership development.

Public workshops give participants an opportunity to travel away from the workplace and learn in an intensive, retreat-like setting that also provides a valuable networking experience. In 2002 OLMS workshops, institutes, and presentations reached more than 1,600 library staff members. OLMS also consulted with staff and administrators on such activities as organizational climate assessment, organizational redesign, strategic planning, and values clarification. ARL member libraries hosted most of the public institutes, giving institute participants the chance to visit various libraries and allowing member libraries an opportunity to showcase their collections, facilities, and staff.

In response to the need for new leadership in academic health sciences libraries, OLMS worked with the National Library of Medicine and the Association of Academic Health Sciences Libraries to create a fellows program that will prepare emerging leaders in academic health sciences libraries. Fellows will have the opportunity to develop their knowledge and skills in a variety of learning settings, including exposure to leadership in a new environment, and will be paired with mentors who are academic health sciences library directors. The program design takes advantage of flexible scheduling and an online learning community to allow fellows to maintain their professional and personal lives.

The ARL/OLMS Second Human Resources Management Symposium, held in October 2002, focused on recruitment issues and innovations in academic libraries. More than 60 professionals, including human resources managers, staff development officers, associate directors and directors, and library school students, faculty, and placement officers, attended the meeting. The program featured guest presenters who shared current data on significant demographic changes in academic libraries and how those trends are affecting candidate pools and recruitment processes.

In April 2002 OLMS and the Association of College and Research Libraries cosponsored "Living the Future 4: Collaboratively Speaking, A Library Conference on Organizational Renewal," hosted by the University of Arizona Library. The meeting was devoted to discovery and dialogue on 21st-century initiatives in library organizational renewal.

The OLMS Information Services program publishes current information on operating practices and policies in its SPEC Kit series. These important resources serve as guides for libraries as they face ever-changing management problems. Through the OLMS Collaborative Research and Writing Program, participating librarians work with ARL staff to design the surveys, evaluate the responses, write the analysis, and edit the components of the completed SPEC Kit.

Six SPEC Kits were published in 2002: SPEC Kit 268, *Reference Service Statistics and Assessment*; SPEC Kit 269, *Integrating Preservation Activities*; SPEC Kit 270, *Core Competencies*; SPEC Kit 271, *Library Systems Office Organization*; SPEC Kit 272, *Insuring and Valuing Research Library Collections*; and SPEC Kit 273, *Chat Reference*. Potential authors are currently developing draft surveys for the 2003 SPEC Kits, and they will be posted to the Web site in early 2003.

The Online Lyceum, a collaborative partnership between ARL and Southern Illinois University–Carbondale Library Affairs Instructional Support Services, provides professional development opportunities through distance learning technology. The Online Lyceum specializes in the development of interactive, Web-based learning that provides critical content and instruction related to issues and trends in research libraries, including management skills and leadership development. In 2002 more than 250 library and information technology professionals took advantage of these online learning opportunities. Several new courses were developed, including "Licensing Review and Negotiation" and "Library Conflict Management" as well as a completely redesigned version of "Accessible Web Design." In addition, the Online Lyceum offered the final two courses, "Library Fund Development" and "Power Dynamics and Influencing Skills," of a three-course suite that supported the work of LCDP by allowing the program to expand its curriculum and facilitate continued learning between in-person institutes.

Statistics and Measurement

The Statistics and Measurement program describes and measures the performance of research libraries and their contributions to teaching, research, scholarship, and community service. Strategies to accomplish the objectives of the program include

- Collecting, analyzing, and publishing quantifiable information about library collections, personnel, and expenditures, as well as expenditures and indicators of the nature of research institutions
- Developing new ways to describe and measure traditional and networked information resources and services

- Developing mechanisms to assess the relationship among campus information resources, high-quality research, and the teaching and learning experience of students
- Providing customized, confidential analysis for peer comparisons
- Offering workshops on statistics and measurement issues in research libraries
- Sustaining a leadership role in the testing and application of academic research library statistics for North American institutions of higher education
- Collaborating with other national and international library statistics programs and accreditation agencies

In 2002 the Statistics and Measurement program continued its 40-year effort to collect and publish quantitative and descriptive statistics about ARL member libraries. In addition, the New Measures Initiative, begun in 1999, focused attention on a number of specific topics to measure and describe the library's contribution to teaching and learning and to research. This initiative has identified several research and development projects and secured funding to support two major projects: LibQUAL+, an effort to measure library service quality from the user's perspective, and E-Metrics, an effort to explore the feasibility of collecting data on the usage of electronic resources.

LibQUAL+ emerged from a pilot project spearheaded by Fred Heath and Colleen Cook of Texas A&M University Libraries. In October 2000 ARL and Texas A&M were awarded a grant from the Fund for the Improvement of Post-secondary Education (FIPSE) to continue development work on the LibQUAL+ instrument and service for three years. The goals of the project include the development of tools and protocols for evaluating library service quality, development of effective Web-based delivery mechanisms for those tools, identification of best practices in providing library service, and the establishment of an ongoing, cost-recovery, service-quality assessment program at ARL. The number of participating institutions expanded from 43 in 2001 to 164 in 2002. More than 78,000 users completed the spring 2002 survey, which included 25 questions. As LibQUAL+ enters its fourth year, and its last year under the financial support of the FIPSE grant, a number of new libraries and consortia are joining the project, enriching the mix of participants and more fully reflecting the wide range of North American library systems. Consortia representing public, military, and college libraries such as the New York Reference and Research Resources Councils (NY3Rs), Military Education Coordination Council, Oberlin Libraries Group, and the Network of Alabama Academic Libraries will participate in the project in 2003.

Another area of interest has been how to measure the collection and use of electronic resources. The ARL E-Metrics project, led by ARL member library directors Sherrie Schmidt, Arizona State University, and Rush Miller, University of Pittsburgh, was completed in three phases:

- An inventory of what libraries were already doing in this area and identification of any libraries that could provide best practices

- Identification and testing of data elements that could be collected and used as measures of electronic resources for trend analysis and benchmarking
- Analysis of the connection between the use of electronic resources and institutional outcomes.

The project documents, *Measures for Electronic Resources (E-Metrics),* are available as a five-part printed publication and online at http://www.arl.org/stats/newmeas/emetrics. Thirty-five ARL members expressed an interest in participating in the 2002 E-Metrics Pilot Project designed to further develop and test the proposed measures on electronic networked services and resources. Gordon Fretwell, University of Massachusetts, volunteered to coordinate project activities.

Project COUNTER (Counting Online Usage of NeTworked Electronic Resources), an international effort sponsored by ARL as part of the E-Metrics project, aims to develop a uniform code of practice for reporting publisher and vendor statistics to libraries. At a meeting on December 5, 2002, the COUNTER Steering Group agreed on the text of Release 1 of the COUNTER Code of Practice, which was published on the COUNTER Web site (http://www.project Counter.org) on January 14, 2003. There will be only one valid version of the Code of Practice at any given time, but different levels of compliance will be possible. Release 1 will focus on journals and databases, as these products are not only the most significant budget item for libraries but also have been available online for some time and have a core of well-accepted definitions and content structures. The Code of Practice will be systematically extended to cover other categories of publications, such as e-books. The project is actively supported by the international community of librarians and publishers and by their professional organizations.

The goal of the Higher Education Outcomes Research Review, another E-Metrics project, is to investigate strategies to assess the library's value to the community and to explore the library's impact on learning, teaching, and research. The Learning Outcomes Working Group has been focusing on (a) identifying assessment expertise on campuses, (b) working with national campus-wide surveys to identify which ARL institutions have participated in these efforts, and (c) working with the Standardized Assessment of Information Literacy Skills (SAILS) research team at Kent State University for further development of an instrument to measure information literacy skills. Doug Jones, University of Arizona, is currently working on a White Paper describing library contributions to research outcomes.

Office of Research and Development

The ARL Office of Research and Development (ORD) consolidates the administration of grants and grant-supported projects administered by ARL. The major goal within this capability is to identify and match ARL projects that support the research library community's mission with sources of external funding. Among the projects under way in 2002 were Knight Collaborative Roundtable, Scholars Portal Project, FIPSE funding for LibQUAL+, NSDL Digital Library Assessment Project, AAU/ARL Global Resources Program, and the ARL GIS Literacy Project.

Another initiative of ORD is the ARL Visiting Program Officer (VPO) program. This program provides an opportunity for a staff member in an ARL member library to assume responsibility for carrying out part or all of a project for ARL. It provides a visible professional development opportunity for an outstanding staff member and serves the membership as a whole by extending the capacity of ARL to undertake additional activities. Typically, the member library supports the salary of the staff person and ARL supports or seeks grant funding for travel or other project-related expenses. Depending on the nature of the project and the circumstances of the individual, a VPO may spend extended periods of time in Washington, D.C., or may conduct most of the project from his or her home library. In 2002 seven VPOs served as part of ARL: Dan Hazen, Harvard University; Judith Panitch, University of North Carolina, Chapel Hill; Susan Beck, Rutgers University; Gordon Fretwell, University of Massachusetts; Doug Jones, University of Arizona; and Brendan Rapple and Barbara Mento, Boston College.

Communications, External Relations, and Publications

The Communications, External Relations, and Publications capabilities are engaged in many activities that support ARL's objectives. These include acquainting ARL members with current, important developments of interest to research libraries; informing the library profession of ARL's position on these issues; influencing policy and decision makers within the higher education, research, and scholarly communities; educating academic communities about issues related to scholarly communication and research libraries; and providing the library community with information about activities with which research libraries are engaged. External relations with relevant constituencies are also carried out through all ARL programs.

Using print and electronic media as well as direct outreach, the communications program disseminates information about the association and its programs, positions, and services. It works to advance the interests of research libraries to the higher education and scholarly communities as well as to ARL member institutions. One of the goals of the program is to promote a better understanding of the issues confronting research libraries in the process of scholarly communication. The program supports ARL activities by promoting workshops, conferences, and publications, and responding to requests for information about ARL and research library issues from the press and community at large. The ARL-Announce listserv provides press releases, news items, and timely information about ARL and its member libraries to a wide range of subscribers. ARL sponsors more than 75 electronic discussion lists, both private and public. Archives for the lists are updated monthly and made available on the ARL server.

The publications program offers a full range of timely, accurate, and informative resources to assist library and higher education communities in their efforts to improve the delivery of scholarly communication. Print and electronic publications are issued from ARL programs on a regular basis. The association makes many of its titles available electronically via the World Wide Web; some are available in excerpted form for preview before purchase, and others are available in their entirety. Six issues of *ARL: A Bimonthly Report on Research Library Issues and Actions from ARL, CNI, and SPARC* were published in 2002. In

February 2002 a special issue was devoted to Open Access, and the April issue focused on the recruitment and retention of research librarians. The August issue highlighted institutional repositories and the Agriculture Network Information Center (AgNIC) Initiative, and an excerpt from the AAUP presidential address delivered by R. Peter Milroy (University of British Columbia Press) was the lead article in the October issue.

Celebrating Seventy Years of the Association of Research Libraries, 1932–2002 commemorated ARL's 70th anniversary. The publication featured a sweeping overview of the major issues that the association's programs addressed in its first 70 years as well as a brief history of the organization. Also included were a reprint of a speech by David Stam of Syracuse University, "Plus Ça Change: Sixty Years of the Association of Research Libraries"; a chronology of significant events; and a list of ARL members and leaders from 1932 to 2002.

The following publications were released in 2002: *ARL Annual Salary Survey 2001–2002*; *ARL Supplementary Statistics 2001–2002*; *ARL Academic Law Library Statistics 1998–1999, 1999–2000, 2000–2001*; *ARL Academic Health Sciences Library Statistics 1998–1999, 1999–2000, 2000–2001*; and *ARL Preservation Statistics 1998–1999, 1999–2000, 2000–2001*. *Proceedings of the 4th Northumbria International Conference on Performance Measurement in Libraries and Information Services* was published in August and included an overview, seven keynote papers, and 37 seminar papers. Each Northumbria conference has covered developments in measuring the increasingly electronic library environment, service quality from the user's perspective, and library users' changing needs.

Association Governance and Membership Activities

A total of 107 member institutions were represented at ARL's 140th Membership Meeting, "Building Capacities: New Strategies for Fund Raising and Recruitment," held in Santa Monica May 22–24, 2002. The meeting was cohosted by the University of California, Los Angeles, and the University of Southern California. Chaired by ARL President Paula Kaufman (University of Illinois at Urbana-Champaign), the meeting addressed two of the most challenging responsibilities of a research library leader: supplementing library budgets and successfully recruiting new staff.

ARL's 141st Membership Meeting, held in Washington, D.C., October 16–17, drew 112 member institutions. More than 40 former ARL directors and guests joined the celebration as the association marked its 70th anniversary. Digital preservation strategies and the open sharing of knowledge were the major themes of the meeting. On October 17, Fred Heath, Texas A&M University, began his term as ARL president. The board elected Sarah Thomas, Cornell University, as vice president/president elect, and the membership elected three new ARL board members: Rush Miller, University of Pittsburgh; Sherrie Schmidt, Arizona State University; and Paul Willis, University of South Carolina.

The 142nd Membership Meeting was scheduled for May 14–16, 2003, in Lexington, Kentucky, hosted by the University of Kentucky and the University of Louisville. The program focus is "A Community Commons: Libraries in the New Century." The fall Membership Meeting is set for October 14–17 in Washington, D.C.

Scholarly Publishing and
Academic Resources Coalition (SPARC)

21 Dupont Circle N.W., Suite 800
Washington, DC 20036
202-296-2296, e-mail sparc@arl.org
World Wide Web http://www.arl.org/sparc

Richard Johnson
SPARC Enterprise Director

The Scholarly Publishing and Academic Resources Coalition (SPARC) is a worldwide alliance of research institutions, libraries, and organizations that encourages competition in the scholarly communications market. SPARC introduces new solutions to scientific journal publishing and partners with publishers to bring top-quality, low-cost research to a greater audience. SPARC strives to return scholarship to the scholar, research to the researcher, and science to the scientist. SPARC's members, member affiliates, and endorsers can be found in North America, Europe, Asia, Australia, and New Zealand.

SPARC was established as an initiative of the Association of Research Libraries (ARL) to create competition in a dysfunctional scientific publishing market. In its several years of existence, SPARC has demonstrated not only that high-quality, affordable competitors to high-priced commercial journals can be created, but also that informed and motivated authors and editors can be effective agents for change. Today SPARC has nearly 200 members, plus a counterpart organization in Europe (SPARC Europe) with 40 additional members, partnerships with 25 different projects in three program areas, a groundbreaking institutional repositories initiative, and an extensive and effective publicity and education program.

Three strategic thrusts support SPARC's agenda to enhance broad and cost-effective access to peer-reviewed scholarship:

- *Expand competition in the journals marketplace.* SPARC seeks to introduce new competitive forces in the journals market as a means of controlling prices. The strategy promotes more effective journal price signaling to faculty and supports the start-up of affordable alternative journals.

- *Introduce alternatives to the subscription model.* The access-restricting subscription model of financing publication of research is an artifact of the print environment. SPARC encourages new business models that support open electronic access to research by recovering publication costs via means other than subscriptions (such as publication fees).

- *Disaggregate the core functions of scholarly publication.* As a means of squeezing cost inefficiencies out of the publishing process, this strategy envisions the logical separation of scholars' articles and the discrete services that enhance their value. SPARC supports the development of interoperable "open archives" of articles (e.g., institutional or disciplinary repositories) that interact with value-adding services such as peer review, linking, and searching as a new framework for scholarly communications with attractive long-term potential.

Since its formal launch in June 1998, SPARC has advanced its agenda by

- Demonstrating that new journals can successfully compete for authors and quickly establish quality
- Effectively showing that journal costs can be moderated by market forces
- Creating an environment in which editors and editorial board members claim more prominent roles in the business aspects of their journals
- Stimulating the development of increased publishing capacity in the not-for-profit sector and encouraging new players to enter the market
- Providing help and guidance to scientists and librarians interested in creating change
- Carrying the methods and message of change to international stakeholders

Publisher Partnership Programs

SPARC's publishing strategy is to partner with scholarly societies, university presses, and start-ups that are able to produce high-quality publications rather than to become a publisher in and of itself. To provide an incentive for publishers to offer library-friendly alternatives, most SPARC members commit to subscribe to SPARC partner journals as long as the titles fit into their collection profile. As its partnership projects have developed, SPARC has categorized its efforts into three programmatic areas: SPARC Alternatives, SPARC Leading Edge, and SPARC Scientific Communities.

SPARC Alternatives

SPARC Alternatives are the titles that were established to compete directly with high-priced STM (science, technology, and medicine) titles. The first partnership in this category was with the American Chemical Society (ACS). *Organic Letters,* SPARC's first collaborative effort with ACS, began publication in July 1999. Another high-profile SPARC Alternative is *Evolutionary Ecology Research (EER)*, a title founded by Michael Rosenzweig, a professor of ecology and evolutionary biology at the University of Arizona. In the mid-1980s, Rosenzweig had founded another title that had been subsequently bought and sold with significant price increases each time. Unhappy with the increases and the refusal of the publishers to take their concerns seriously, the entire editorial board resigned and in January 1999 launched their own independent journal at a fraction of the cost of the original title. Both of these titles have demonstrated that authors are very willing to submit papers to a new journal if it is edited by respected scholars in the field. Other SPARC partnerships are in fields such as geometry and topology, logic programming, machine learning, neuro-oncology, physical chemistry, crystal engineering, geochemistry, sensors, and vegetation science. Partner titles have been the result of both new start-ups and the movement of editorial boards to new publishing arrangements. In 2003 SPARC will move beyond the STM publishing arena with several publishing partnerships supporting affordable or open-access alternatives in economics, where journal prices are a growing problem.

Over the course of the year, partnerships and publishing initiatives in other areas of social sciences and the humanities will also be explored.

SPARC Leading Edge

To support the development of new models in scholarly publishing, SPARC's Leading Edge program publicizes the efforts of ventures that demonstrate promising open-access business models that look to alternatives to subscription fees for recovery of publication costs. Titles in this program include the *New Journal of Physics* (which charges fees to authors whose articles are accepted for publication), *Documenta Mathematica* (supported by the mathematics department of the University of Bielefeld in Germany), *Journal of Insect Science* (published by the library of the University of Arizona), and BioMed Central (supported via article-processing fees). In addition, several SPARC Alternative titles are open-access journals.

SPARC Scientific Communities

Scientific Communities projects are intended to support broad-scale aggregations of scientific content around the needs of specific communities of interest. Through these projects, SPARC encourages collaboration among scholars, their societies, and academic institutions. This program also helps to build capacity within the not-for-profit sector by encouraging academic institutions to develop electronic-publishing expertise and infrastructure and seeks to provide small societies and independent journals with alternative academic partners for moving into the electronic environment. Projects in this program include *eScholarship* from the California Digital Library, which is creating an infrastructure for the management of digitally based scholarly information; *Columbia Earthscape,* a collaboration among Columbia University's press, libraries, and academic computing services that integrates earth sciences research, teaching, and public policy resources; and *MIT CogNet,* an electronic community for researchers in cognitive and brain sciences that includes a searchable, full-text library of major reference works, monographs, journals, and conference proceedings, as well as job postings and threaded discussion groups. SPARC is also supporting Project Euclid, a venture of the Cornell University Library. This project is providing an infrastructure for Web publishing for independent journals in theoretical and applied mathematics and statistics. In 2002 SPARC partnered with Figaro, a European academic e-publishing initiative focused on the creation of an effective and affordable communication and publishing environment for scholars.

A particularly ambitious SPARC project is *BioOne,* a nonprofit, Web-based aggregation of peer-reviewed articles from dozens of leading journals in the areas of biological, environmental, and ecological sciences. It was officially launched in April 2001 and includes access to more than 50 titles. *BioOne* was conceived as an opportunity for societies, libraries, and the private sector for collaboration. It offers small, undercapitalized societies, members of the American Institute of Biological Sciences (AIBS) and others, a means to move to electronic publishing while maintaining financial viability. In addition to AIBS, collaborators include Allen Press, the Greater Western Library Alliance, the University of Kansas, and SPARC. The business plan calls for 50 percent of the revenues from sales to be returned to the societies based on an individual journal's relative size and use, with the other 50 percent covering the cost of operations.

Communication

A strong component of success for SPARC has been its ability to bring scholarly communication issues to the mainstream and scientific press. An aggressive media program was established early, and, through it, SPARC has developed key contacts with reporters, has placed targeted stories in a range of media outlets, issues frequent press releases, and responds quickly to information requests. More than 150 articles and news items recorded on the SPARC "In the News" Web page chronicle the work of SPARC and concerns about scholarly communication.

SPARC staff, steering committee members, and publishing partners travel extensively to speak at local, regional, national, and international meetings and conferences. A speakers' bureau provides SPARC members and others with assistance in arranging speakers for campus or society meeting events.

Other communication channels update members and interested observers with news about SPARC activities. *SPARC E-News* is a bimonthly newsletter that provides information on new partners, innovative developments in scholarly publishing outside SPARC's own programs, industry news, opinion pieces, and reviews of software or tools. A comprehensive Web site provides resources for those interested in scholarly communication issues and SPARC activities. With the Association of College and Research Libraries (ACRL), SPARC hosts a semiannual forum at American Library Association meetings to bring the issues and SPARC's work to a wider library audience. SPARC also exhibits at library conferences and provides materials for society conferences.

Advocacy and Education

In addition to raising awareness through its public relations work, SPARC has been engaged in specific programs and initiatives to encourage librarians and faculty to take an active part in changing the current system of scholarly communication.

Create Change

Supported by SPARC, ACRL, and the ARL Office of Scholarly Communications, the Create Change campaign is designed to aid faculty and librarians in advocating changes in scholarly communication. The Create Change Web site (http://www.createchange.org) includes descriptive information on scholarly communication issues with supporting data, advocacy planning tools for librarians, and sample letters and copyright agreements for faculty. The site also includes a database of the editors of the 100 most expensive journals. A printed brochure is available for purchase, and the text is available on the Web site for local adaptation. Many SPARC members have begun or are planning to begin a Create Change program on their campuses, representing a substantial number of contacts with scholars about the issues.

Declaring Independence

A key SPARC strategy for expanding scientist control over scientific communication is to encourage editorial boards to assert a broader role in determining journal business policies and practices. This is being advanced with the Declaring Independence initiative, launched by SPARC in collaboration with the Triangle Research Libraries Network. Declaring Independence encourages journal editorial boards to evaluate their current journals, and, if warranted, either work with the publisher to make changes or move the editorial board to an alternative publisher.

The main vehicles for carrying the Declaring Independence message are an instructive SPARC-developed handbook and corresponding Web site (http://www.arl.org/sparc/di). The handbook was mailed by SPARC to editorial board members of high-priced journals and distributed by library staff to editors as part of their scholarly communications campus outreach activities. The Declaring Independence themes and availability of the handbook and Web site also are promoted widely at meetings and conferences around the world, in SPARC publicity and articles, and at speaking engagements.

A companion to Declaring Independence, *Gaining Independence: A Manual for Planning the Launch of a Nonprofit Electronic Publishing Venture,* is available on the Web free of charge at http://www.arl.org/sparc/GI. It is a detailed, step-by-step guide leading readers through the creation of a business plan for start-up and early-stage electronic publishing ventures, including digital repositories and journals.

Gaining Independence helps universities, libraries, societies, and others conceive, plan, and implement alternatives to commercially published scholarly and scientific information. It provides background on relevant electronic-publishing models and focuses especially on areas of business planning that may be unfamiliar to those considering new communications initiatives. The manual includes sections on Situational Assessment and Strategic Response; Technology and Technical Considerations; Markets, Marketing, and Sales; Organization; Finances; and the Financial Plan and Operating Plan. A detailed appendix links readers to pertinent resources.

Institutional Repositories

In August 2002 SPARC released *The Case for Institutional Repositories: A SPARC Position Paper,* the first major articulation of the strategic rationale for the development of institution-based repositories for work created within institutional communities. The paper has elicited considerable international attention and has presaged surging interest by institutions in creating repositories.

SPARC also published the *SPARC Institutional Repository Checklist and Resource Guide,* a practical examination of the major issues that institutions and consortia need to address in implementing an institutional repository.

In October 2002 SPARC cosponsored meetings in Washington, D.C., and Geneva to encourage the development of institutional repositories.

SPARC Europe

As a means of extending outreach to scholars and libraries, SPARC and several European supporting organizations launched SPARC Europe in July 2001 (http://www.sparceurope.org). SPARC Europe is an alliance of European libraries, library organizations, and research institutions supporting solutions to the economic challenges facing the system of scientific-journal publishing. SPARC Europe facilitates competition in the European scientific journals marketplace and introduces advocacy initiatives tailored to the European research and library communities.

Several national organizations and institutions in Europe sponsor SPARC Europe, including the Consortium of University Research Libraries (CURL) and the Joint Information Systems Committee (JISC) in Britain; the Society of College, National and University Libraries (SCONUL) in Britain and Ireland; and UKB, the Netherlands Cooperative of Research Libraries, in collaboration with IWI, the SURF Foundation program for innovation in scientific information supply. Start-up of SPARC Europe was an initiative of LIBER, the European organization of research libraries.

In October 2002 David Prosser became the first director of SPARC Europe. Under his leadership, SPARC Europe will collaborate with the international SPARC organization based in Washington, D.C., but will develop Europe-focused initiatives under the direction of a European managing board. A European membership base supports this work.

Membership in SPARC Europe is open to national and academic libraries, library organizations, and research institutions in the region.

Open Access

SPARC and SPARC Europe have participated in the creation of the Budapest Open Access Initiative (BOAI), which aims to accelerate progress in the international effort to make research articles in all academic fields freely available on the Internet. SPARC and SPARC Europe are involved in BOAI because access to knowledge is the central purpose of scholarly communication. A system built on open access offers the prospect of being less expensive to operate and of better serving scholars, the scholarly process, and society. A number of SPARC's publishing partners have already achieved success as peer-reviewed open access journals. In support of this goal, SPARC is promoting development of e-journals supported by business models that enable open access to research and alternatives to subscriptions as a means of supporting scholarly communication. With support from the Open Society Institute, the SPARC Consulting Group developed two business-planning manuals for the launch of new open access journals and for the conversion of existing journals to open access. For more information, see http://www.soros.org/openaccess.

SPARC Consulting Group

In January 2002 SPARC launched the SPARC Consulting Group (SCG), a network of specialized consultants who will provide in-depth business, financial, and strategic consulting services on a fee basis to universities and university presses, not-for-profit learned societies, and other academic and not-for-profit organizations. Already, SCG has been engaged to work on major projects for the American Anthropological Association, Project Euclid, and the Open Society Institute.

Priorities for 2003

Encourage Adoption of Open Access Models

Promoting and aiding the adoption of open access scholarly communication models is SPARC's top priority for 2003. Efforts will cluster around three areas: open access advocacy and education, deployment of institutional repositories, and demonstration of open access journal publishing models.

Support Community-Based Digital Publishing in the Social Sciences and Humanities

In 2003 SPARC will move beyond the STM publishing arena with several publishing partnerships supporting affordable or open access alternative journals in economics, where journal prices are a growing problem. Over the course of the year, partnerships and publishing initiatives in other areas will also be explored.

Encourage and Enhance the Viability of New Library-Friendly Publishing Ventures

In this period of acute pressure on higher education budgets, it will be important to ensure that new alternative publishing ventures maintain momentum and secure a stable base of ongoing support. SPARC will address this need through development of practical Web and print resources on topics including marketing, business planning, and building awareness, as well as through the efforts of the SPARC Consulting Group.

Expand Grass-Roots Scholarly Communications Advocacy Efforts

SPARC will collaborate with and support initiatives by ACRL's new scholarly communications program to carry campus scholarly communications advocacy to an expanded audience. SPARC will also continue support of campus advocacy events by offering consultation services to libraries that are planning scholarly communication programs and providing SPARC speakers.

Propel SPARC's Agenda Internationally

SPARC's incubation of the SPARC Europe organization will continue during 2003. SPARC will provide transition support to the new SPARC Europe director and close, ongoing communication and coordination of activities. The SPARC Enterprise Director serves on the SPARC Europe board and works closely with the European organization's director and board.

In addition, SPARC will continue to build ties with organizations in Japan that are championing changes in scholarly publishing.

Raise Awareness of the Adverse Impact of Consolidation in the Journals Publishing Industry

SPARC also continues to support an ARL-led project to document the adverse impact of corporate consolidation in the journals industry. A White Paper on the topic will be published in 2003.

Governance

The working group that established SPARC was determined that SPARC be a lean and agile organization. Its focus was to be on developing partnerships and projects, not on issues of governance or membership. However, as it reached a level of maturity and membership, it was agreed that a more formal structure was needed. The appointed SPARC Steering Committee that had guided SPARC since early 1998 decided that it should replace itself with a democratically elected body that would ensure a mechanism for continually renewing its leadership. A new steering committee consisting of seven members with staggered terms was elected in fall 1999 to take office in January 2000. In 2001 the committee adjusted its membership again to ensure that it included official representatives from Canada and SPARC Europe. The steering committee meets at least twice a year in person and conducts other business through regularly scheduled conference calls.

Several categories of membership are available: full, consortia, and supporting members (extending worldwide; European members belong to SPARC Europe).

Council on Library and Information Resources

1755 Massachusetts Ave. N.W., Suite 500, Washington, DC 20036-2124
202-939-4754, fax 202-939-4765
World Wide Web http://www.clir.org

Kathlin Smith
Director of Communications

The Council on Library and Information Resources (CLIR) is an independent, nonprofit organization dedicated to improving the management of information for research, teaching, and learning. CLIR works to expand access to information, however recorded and preserved, as a public good.

CLIR's agenda is framed by a single, important question: What is a library in the digital age?

Rapid changes in technology, evolving intellectual-property legislation, new modes of scholarly communication, and new economic models for information provision have all contributed to a new information environment for libraries. In partnership with other organizations, CLIR helps create services that expand the concept of "library," and it supports the providers and preservers of information.

CLIR is supported by fees from sponsoring institutions, grants from public and private foundations, contracts with federal agencies, and donations from individuals. CLIR's board establishes policy, oversees the investment of funds, sets goals, and approves strategies for their achievement. The program staff of CLIR develops projects and programs in response to the broad charges of the CLIR board. CLIR's current activities reflect its concern with six themes: resources for scholarship, preservation awareness, digital libraries, economics of information, leadership, and international developments. (In the summary that follows, CLIR's international activities are described in the relevant sections, rather than under a separate heading.)

Resources for Scholarship

In 2002 CLIR emphasized work that will help it better understand the needs and aspirations of scholarly-information users, whether in the digital or analog realm. CLIR also supported work that will examine models of shared repositories for printed materials, a key recommendation issued by CLIR's Task Force on the Artifact in Library Collections in its report of November 2001.

Analysis of Studies of Users and Usage

CLIR, the Digital Library Federation (DLF), and many other organizations have recently undertaken studies of users and usage of electronic resources. The topic is important to both librarians and publishers, whose roles are affected as users go directly to the Web for the scholarly resources they need.

CLIR commissioned Carol Tenopir, professor of library and information science at the University of Tennessee, Knoxville, to review the studies undertaken to date, and to summarize their purposes and findings in a single document.

Tenopir, working with Donald King, research professor in the School of Information Sciences at the University of Pittsburgh, has studied changes in scholarly communication over the past several decades. CLIR expects to publish the report in summer 2003.

Shared Repositories for Imprints

With support from CLIR, the Center for Research Libraries (CRL) is doing a survey and analysis of different models of shared repositories for printed materials. CRL is gathering information about repositories that serve as secondary storage, as consortial repositories, and as repositories that hold materials of last resort. The survey will become the basis for a report that CLIR will write with CRL to describe the promises and challenges of managing more effectively collections of imprints that are of high research value but are little used. The report is scheduled for release in the first half of 2003.

Preservation Awareness

As the information landscape has changed, so, too, has the context in which libraries make decisions about what to keep for future scholarly use, in what form to make it available, how to ensure that it remains fit for use, and who is responsible for maintaining it.

State of Preservation in American Academic Libraries

CLIR joined forces with the Association of Research Libraries (ARL), the University Libraries Group (ULG), and the Regional Alliance for Preservation to examine the state of preservation programs in American academic libraries. The examination involved preservation educators and representatives of leading liberal arts colleges, land grant institutions, and the American Library Association. The Institute of Museum and Library Services (IMLS) funded the work.

The study was based on a survey of 68 institutions including members of ULG, non-ARL land grant institutions, and liberal arts colleges belonging to what is known informally as the Oberlin Group. The survey was designed to obtain data from these libraries comparable to information on ARL members that appears in *ARL Preservation Statistics for 2000–2001*. To obtain qualitative data to supplement the survey findings, project staff members conducted extensive on-site interviews at 20 institutions representing ARL, ULG, and Oberlin Group, as well as a number of non-ARL land grant institutions.

The report, published in December 2002, underscores the challenges facing preservation in a changing information landscape. They include the challenge of integrating the preservation of analog and digital materials, and the challenge of including preservation in libraries' strategic planning. The report concludes with a series of six recommendations developed by the project's advisory committee, and a list of ways in which concerned parties can act on this guidance.

National Digital Information Infrastructure and Preservation Program

In 2002 CLIR helped support a national initiative that addresses the long-term preservation of digital content. The initiative, known as the National Digital Information Infrastructure and Preservation Program (NDIIPP), was mandated by Congress in legislation passed in December 2000. The Library of Congress (LC) was charged with leading the effort to develop a digital preservation infrastructure that will provide persistent, rights-protected access to digital content. LC contracted with CLIR to organize key activities in the planning phase of this work. The centerpiece was the preparation of a master plan, completed in September 2002, that describes the year-long process of fact finding and analysis and sets forth a framework within which to proceed. CLIR expects to continue its planning work with LC in areas that concern the academic and research library communities.

Preserving Web-based Scholarship

In April 2002 CLIR convened a group of digital librarians and archivists, humanities scholars, private and government funding officials, publishers, and technologists to explore issues in archiving primary digital resources of high scholarly value. The meeting focused on materials that are not intended for publication and may, therefore, not fall naturally into the collecting scope of research libraries. The aim of the meeting, funded by the Alfred P. Sloan Foundation, was to engage key stakeholders in the consideration of born-digital scholarship. Participants looked intensively at several Web sites created by scholars that collect primary resources—e-mails, multimedia objects, databases—and are intended to serve in the future as primary documentation of a given subject. Few data creators are preparing these resources in formats that are easily managed by a digital repository, and many of the most interesting resources are created outside the purview of a library or other institution with a preservation mandate. A report, based on discussions at the meeting, will be published in 2003.

The State of Digital Preservation: An International Perspective

In April 2002 CLIR hosted the first in a new series of international symposia that will address key issues in digital libraries, economics of information, and resources for scholarship. The series, supported by a grant from Documentation Abstracts, Inc. (DAI), is called the DAI Institutes for Information Science. The inaugural symposium drew more than 150 individuals from around the world to discuss strategies for digital preservation. A volume of conference proceedings was published in July.

Web-Based Preservation Tutorial

With support from the Henry Luce Foundation, CLIR commissioned Cornell University Library to produce a Web-based tutorial on preservation for developing countries in Southeast Asia. The tutorial includes a self-assessment that allows libraries and archives to evaluate their level of preservation, an instructional narrative, a resource guide, and a technical glossary. The narrative has four major sections: management and planning, preservation, building capacity, and supporting the effort. A list of local suppliers of conservation materials and equipment is provided in the resource guide, while terms in the glossary are offered in the vernacular. The tutorial is found at http://www.librarypreservation.org.

Preservation in the 21st Century

CLIR's work in 2002 has shown that the preservation requirements of the 21st century will demand active and educated involvement by data creators, publishers, and distributors working closely with libraries and archives. Plans are under way for an invitational meeting in 2003 titled "Redefining Preservation in the 21st Century." It will bring together scholars, library directors, university administrators, publishers, and representatives of the legal and preservation communities to examine the assumptions that have informed preservation practice to date and to discuss the implications of the changed environment for new forms of cooperation. This initiative to reconceptualize preservation for the 21st century is a first step toward understanding the complete life cycle of scholarly resources and offering opportunities for all library staff to see their particular role in the preservation process.

Digital Libraries

CLIR is committed to fostering the development of digital libraries as a resource for research and learning. Its aim is to help policymakers, funding organizations, and academic leaders understand the social and institutional investments in digital libraries that are needed to organize, maintain, and provide access to a growing body of digital materials for scholarly purposes.

Digital Library Federation

The Digital Library Federation (DLF) is CLIR's major effort in digital libraries. DLF is a consortium of 34 leading research libraries and related agencies, sponsored by CLIR, that are developing online collections and services. DLF's work in 2002 was split between activities that support strategic thinking about the library and scholarly communication, and activities of technical working groups that advance the collective ability to describe, share, protect, and use digital content in libraries and classrooms.

Enabling Strategic Planning. Increasingly, DLF is engaging in work that supports strategic planning for the rapidly changing library and scholarly landscape. DLF's largest undertaking in this area was its work with the research firm Outsell, Inc. on a study titled "Dimensions and Use of the Scholarly Information Environment." More than 3,200 faculty members, graduate students, and undergraduate students in varying disciplines from almost 400 public and private institutions were surveyed for the study, which documents how academic users find and use information, and their attitudes toward the library. CLIR and DLF published an introduction to the data set and 158 selected data tables in November

2002. The full set of 659 data tables provided by Outsell can be found at http://www.diglib.org/pubs/scholinfo.

Improving Interoperability. In 2002 DLF supported major initiatives that further its members' ability to share digital library contents across institutions, such as the Open Archives Initiative, and to describe information about them in a manner that greatly eases large-scale, multi-institutional aggregation, such as the Metadata Encoding and Transmission Standard (METS). Both the Open Archives Initiative and METS have solved real problems and have been adopted by dozens of DLF and non-DLF institutions in the United States and abroad. Work continued in the description of visual images for online delivery (with the Visual Resources Association) and on shared tools for the creation and delivery of online archival guides (for example, Encoded Archival Description). DLF also worked with the Online Computer Library Center (OCLC) to develop a registry of existing digitized books and journals, to avoid duplication of digitizing effort.

DLF laid the groundwork to pursue the following projects in 2003:

- A registry of information about the computer formats of digital objects. This registry would record the technical details of the file formats (TIFF, PDF, and so forth) in which content is stored. The registry is intended to support digital preservation programs, and would be useful, for example, when files have been preserved that belong to a program that is no longer readily available.
- A common XML standard for recording license requirements and rights-management issues for commercially licensed databases, journals, and the like. Often, this information is kept on desktop computers, on paper in filing cabinets, or just in human memory. The University of Washington will lead an endeavor to provide libraries and vendors with a common way of expressing this information that can be shared.

Economics of Information

As the role of the library is redefined, economic issues assume even greater importance. Economics of information is a theme that cuts across all program activities at CLIR.

Redesigning Library Services and Processes

In 2002 CLIR began planning workshops that will focus on redesigning library services and processes. A group of chief information officers (CIOs) from liberal arts colleges will collaborate with economic consultants to study how current work can be restructured to provide liberal arts colleges with the time and resources they need to take on the important tasks connected with the digital transformation. The CIOs of liberal arts colleges are uniquely positioned to understand the sometimes overlapping or duplicative tasks carried out by the libraries and information technology divisions on their campuses. It is hoped that this project will offer guidance to other institutions that want to rethink the nature of their work at a time of tight budgets.

The Library as Place for Teaching and Research

CLIR has provided support for Scott Bennett, Yale University librarian emeritus, to conduct a study of the academic library as a space for teaching and learning. The study, which is being cosponsored by the Council on Independent Colleges, focuses on the academic needs that motivate library renovation and new construction, and attempts to understand the interplay between traditional needs (such as shelving for the collections) and emerging needs (such as space for collaborative learning). CLIR will publish the report in 2003.

Leadership

The library of the future will require information professionals who have both discipline-specific and technical skills. CLIR's leadership activities are designed to cultivate a large cadre of individuals who are prepared to work in collaboration with faculty and administrators to design information products and services appropriate for the new environment.

Frye Leadership Institute

The annual Frye Leadership Institute—jointly sponsored by CLIR, EDUCAUSE, and Emory University—brings together individuals from libraries, information technology divisions, and faculty departments in all types of academic institutions to focus on changes in higher education and on the role of information services in academia.

The third Frye Institute was held at Emory University June 2–14, 2002. Forty-three applicants were selected for participation. During the first week, presidents, provosts, business officers, and other administrative officers offered their views on the state of higher education today and the challenges confronting colleges and universities. In the second week, faculty members, researchers, financial officers, library and information technology leaders, and training specialists addressed such issues as intellectual property and copyright, technological advances in teaching and research, scholarly communication, and funding.

Nearly 150 librarians, information technologists, and teaching faculty from a wide range of academic institutions have completed the Frye Institute. The goal is to build a corps of some 500 individuals by the end of the decade.

The Robert W. Woodruff Foundation provides the primary support for the Frye Leadership Institute, and IMLS and the Andrew W. Mellon Foundation provide supplemental funding. The Patricia Battin Scholarship Fund makes participation possible by individuals whose institutions cannot afford to support their attendance.

Scholarly Communication Institute

In March 2002 the Andrew W. Mellon Foundation awarded a grant to CLIR to develop, in collaboration with Dartmouth College, a Scholarly Communication Institute. The institute will provide an opportunity for individuals who are leading developments in scholarly communication to study, plan, and organize institutional and discipline-based strategies for advancing the state of scholarly communication. Over time, the institute will develop a cadre of leaders who can serve as mentors to the next generation of individuals who aspire to work in the area of scholarly communication. The first institute, to be held in July 2003, will be an invitational session for university administrators, scholars, and scholarly communication innovators who will be asked to help articulate the desirable futures for scholarly communication and create a curriculum that will be used for subsequent sessions. After 2003 the institute will be open to all applicants on a competitive basis.

Working Group of Librarians and Publishers

CLIR collaborated with the Scholarly Publishing Division of the Association of American Publishers to create a Working Group of Librarians and Publishers that is exploring mutual concerns about the effects of digital technology developments. In meetings that began in January 2002, librarians and publishers have, among other things, shared results of studies they have conducted separately of electronic information use.

Meetings of Chief Information Officers

In 2002 CLIR organized two meetings of chief information officers from liberal arts colleges. These individuals, who oversee combined library and computing services, had expressed to CLIR a need for a forum in which their issues are treated as an integrated whole. Common areas of concern include organizational relationships and planning models; staffing, staff training, and role issues; and specific services such as merged or adjacent reference and instructional technology desks, courseware management systems, and networking. CLIR will continue to facilitate the work of this group as it refines its agenda in 2003.

Academic Library Advisory Committee

The six-member Academic Librarians Advisory Committee met twice in 2002. The group's main focus was the use of course management software and its impact on libraries—specifically the lack of connection between libraries and developers of course management systems.

Outreach

In 2002 CLIR continued efforts to reach new audiences through the publication of articles and columns in a broad range of magazines and journals. *Trusteeship* magazine, in its September/October 2002 issue, published an article by CLIR President Deanna Marcum titled "The Disintegrating Paper Trail." The article calls attention to preservation needs in academic libraries. *Trusteeship,* published by the Association of Governing Boards of Universities and Colleges, reaches presidents and chief academic officers as well as board members.

The March/April 2002 issue of *EDUCAUSE Review* debuted a new column titled "E-Content" edited by Marcum. Her inaugural article explained the column's purpose, which is to deal with issues about the content that new information technologies deliver. Subsequent columns focused on the need for integrating library resources with course-management software, the JSTOR

Scholarly Journal Archive use study, and the IMLS principles for good digital libraries. Marcum will serve as the column's editor for two years.

Annals of the History of Computing published, in its July–September 2002 issue, an article by Marcum titled "Automating the Library: The Council on Library Resources," about the council's historical contributions to the development of library automation. The council became part of CLIR several years ago.

In April 2002 CLIR conducted a survey of readers of *CLIRinghouse,* the one-sheet monthly bulletin aimed at campus executives, to learn whether readers wished to continue receiving it. Of 211 presidents, chancellors, and chief academic officers who responded, more than three-fifths said they did. Of 625 librarians who responded, more than four-fifths said they did. Accordingly, CLIR decided to continue publishing *CLIRinghouse* for at least 12 more months, although on a bimonthly basis.

CLIR Publications

In 2002 CLIR published the following:

Reports

Council on Library and Information Resources. *CLIR Annual Report 2001–2002* (October 2002).

Council on Library and Information Resources. *The State of Digital Preservation: An International Perspective, Proceedings of the First DAI Institute in Information Science* (July 2002).

Council on Library and Information Resources and Library of Congress. *Building a National Strategy for Digital Preservation: Issues in Digital Media Archiving* (April 2002).

Friedlander, Amy. *Dimensions and Use of the Scholarly Information Environment: Introduction to a Data Set Assembled by the Digital Library Federation and Outsell, Inc.* (November 2002).

Greenstein, Daniel, and Suzanne Thorin. *The Digital Library: A Biography* (September 2002).

Kenney, Anne R., and Deirdre Stam. *The State of Preservation Programs in American College and Research Libraries: Building a Common Understanding and Action Agenda* (December 2002).

Lougee, Wendy. *Diffuse Libraries: Emergent Roles for the Research Library in the Digital Age* (August 2002).

Troll Covey, Denise. *Use and Usability Assessment: Library Practices and Concerns* (January 2002).

Newsletters

CLIR Issues, nos. 25–30.
CLIRinghouse, nos. 5–13.

Scholarships and Awards

Mellon Fellowships for Dissertation Research

In April 2002 CLIR announced the first recipients of the Mellon Dissertation Fellowships for doctoral research in original resources. These fellowships are designed to enable humanities scholars early in their careers to spend up to 12 months in archives, libraries, museums, and other repositories (including private collections) to develop their research abilities. With funding from the Andrew W. Mellon Foundation, CLIR awarded 11 fellowships of up to $20,000 each to graduate students who are working in little-known collections, using primary sources in creative or nontraditional ways, or working in repositories that are not in a position to offer fellowships.

The 2002 recipients and their institutions and fields were Sinan Antoon, Harvard University, Arabic literature; Brenda Foley, Brown University, interdisciplinary studies (history, theater, women's studies); Christiane Gruber, University of Pennsylvania, art history; Angela Herren, CUNY Graduate Center, pre-Columbian art history; Drew Hopkins, Columbia University, cultural anthropology; Daniel Neely, New York University, ethnomusicology; Susan Pearson, University of North Carolina, Chapel Hill, U.S. history; Alisha Rankin, Harvard University, history of medicine; Maria Rose, New York University, musicology; Natalie Rothman, University of Michigan, anthropology and history; and Paula Saunders, University of Texas at Austin, anthropology.

Bill and Melinda Gates Foundation Access to Learning Award

In November 2001 CLIR began administering the annual Bill and Melinda Gates Foundation Access to Learning Award. The award is given to a library, library agency, or comparable organization outside the United States for efforts to expand free public access to information, computers, and the Internet for all people. Colombia's BibloRed (Capital Network of Public Libraries) received the award in 2002. BibloRed was recognized for its success in providing free and innovative access to information for the citizens of Bogotá, particularly those in low-income areas. The library will use the US$1 million award to expand its services. An international advisory committee of librarians and information technology experts reviews the applications and selects the recipient. The award is presented each year at the annual meeting of the International Federation of Library Associations and Institutions (IFLA).

Zipf Fellowship

The 2002 A. R. Zipf Fellowship in Information Management was awarded to Miles James Efron, a Ph.D. student in Information Science at the University of North Carolina, Chapel Hill. Efron is the sixth recipient of the Zipf Fellowship. His research focuses on how statistical methods can be used to map information spaces to enable better access to information.

The Zipf Fellowship is awarded annually to the graduate student in some field of information management or systems who best represents the ideals of Al Zipf, for whom the fellowship is named. Kent Smith of the National Library of

Medicine chairs the selection committee. Other members are Christine Borgman, Martin Cummings, Billy Frye, Deanna Marcum, and Rena Zipf.

Patricia Battin Scholarship

The third annual Patricia Battin Scholarship was awarded in June 2002 to Candice Scott, director of W. M. Logan Library and Information Technology Services, Schreiner University. Established in 1999 by friends and family of Patricia Battin, the scholarship provides financial assistance for participants in the Frye Leadership Institute whose institutions cannot afford to support their attendance.

International Reports

International Federation of Library Associations and Institutions

Box 95312, 2509 CH The Hague, Netherlands
31-70-314-0884, fax 31-70-383-4827, e-mail ifla@ifla.org
World Wide Web http://www.ifla.org

Beacher Wiggins

Acting Associate Librarian for Library Services, Library of Congress
Library of Congress Representative, IFLA Standing Committee on Bibliography

The International Federation of Library Associations and Institutions (IFLA) is the preeminent international organization representing librarians, other information professionals, and library users. During 2002 IFLA marked its 75th anniversary, broadened participation in the federation's governance, fostered the integration of digital technologies into an enormous range of library activities, and promoted equitable access to digital content and information without regard to barriers of poverty, handicap, or geographic isolation.

68th General Conference

The 68th IFLA Council and General Conference, held in Glasgow, Scotland, August 18–24, 2002, had as its theme "Libraries for Life: Democracy, Diversity, Delivery." Unlike most recent IFLA conferences, the Glasgow conference was hosted and organized by a single organization, the Chartered Institute of Library and Information Professionals (CILIP), Britain's chief library professional association, and its business arm CILIP Enterprises. The conference attracted more than 4,700 registrants from more than 120 nations. The original decision to establish IFLA was taken in Edinburgh, Scotland, in 1927. In keeping with this return to roots, the conference subtheme was "Building on the Past—Investing in the Future."

Irish poet Seamus Heaney, 1995 winner of the Nobel Prize for Literature, delivered the keynote address, "Stiles and Stacks, Old and New," in which he stressed the need for libraries and librarians to reinvent themselves if they are to preserve world cultural heritage and civilized values in the digital age. Cultural outings included visits to Dunfermline, the birthplace of Scottish American industrialist and library benefactor Andrew Carnegie (1835–1919).

The Social Responsibilities Discussion Group finished its work at the Glasgow conference. The discussion group submitted 13 recommendations, which were adopted without dissent by the IFLA Council to be considered for implementation during the federation's next planning cycle. The recommendations call for

- Creating a research program on rural library development in coordination with national library agencies
- Promoting adult basic education skills as a component of library and information school curricula
- Promoting literacy training as a basic library service
- Opposing fees for basic services and working with commercial information providers to establish a standard price structure for publicly supported libraries, based on ability to pay
- Developing socially responsible library school curricula
- Promoting research into the education and training needs of Southern Hemisphere countries
- Assisting in formatting local content for electronic resources
- Promoting policies and developing programs that equalize access to the Internet
- Promoting greater resource sharing between the "information rich" and the "information poor"
- Advocating and developing strategies for library associations to use in establishing policies conducive to creating information infrastructures offering equitable, adequate, and reliable communications for all
- Monitoring how various library associations are addressing "information gap" issues
- Continuing to work toward putting the concerns of Third World librarianship at the center of IFLA's program and activities

The council unanimously adopted two other sweeping declarations of principle at the conference. The Glasgow Declaration on Libraries, Information Services and Intellectual Freedom calls upon "libraries and information services and their staff to uphold and promote the principles of intellectual freedom and to provide uninhibited access to information." The IFLA Internet Manifesto deems a freely accessible Internet "essential to unrestricted access to information" and states that access to the Internet and all of its resources should be consistent with the United Nations Universal Declaration of Human Rights. The council also forwarded the Internet Manifesto to the UNESCO Inter-Governmental Council for its endorsement.

The General Conference featured an update session on copyright and other legal matters that covered national implementations of the European Copyright Directive; United States copyright issues, including new laws restricting or criminalizing the use of circumvention technologies; copyright issues in South Africa; and the impact on libraries of international trade treaties. A separate session considered the worldwide problem of repatriation of library materials removed from their original countries, with three case studies involving Iceland, Russia, and Mexico. The National Libraries Section also highlighted legal deposit and copyright laws.

The international nature of the General Conference afforded the opportunity to offer satellite meetings and workshops to information professionals from around the world, many from countries where the information profession and publishing industry are not well developed or operate under censorship or other government restrictions. Satellite meetings included Using Market Research to Improve Customer Satisfaction (Glasgow), 18th Conference of Parliamentary Librarians (London), Gateways to the Changing Landscape of Art Information (Glasgow), Informing Government: Government Library and Information Services in the Information Age (London), and Statistics in Practice—Measuring and Managing (Loughborough, England). The Conference of Directors of National Libraries also met in conjunction with the 68th IFLA Conference, and the Fifth World Conference on Continuing Professional Education for the Library and Information Professions took place in Aberdeen, Scotland.

Grants and Awards

IFLA continues to collaborate with corporate partners and national libraries to maintain programs and opportunities that would otherwise not be possible, especially for librarians and libraries in developing countries. For instance, the IFLA/OCLC Early Career Development Fellowships have been awarded since 1999 to bring five library and information science professionals from countries with developing economies who are in the early stages of their careers to the United States for four weeks of intensive experience in librarianship. In 2003 the fellows, announced in Glasgow, will be from Turkey, India, Mauritius, South Korea, and Vietnam.

The Bill and Melinda Gates Foundation 2002 Access to Learning Award was presented to BibloRed, the integrated public library network in Bogotá, Colombia. This award, managed by the Council on Library and Information Resources, is given annually to a library, library agency, or comparable organization outside the United States that has been innovative in providing free public access to information. The award includes a grant of up to $1 million to help the recipient develop new initiatives and expand outreach.

The U.S. IFLA 2001 National Organizing Committee announced the Fellowships for the Americas program at the 2002 Conference. The program will use net revenues from the Boston conference in 2001 to provide grants for 15 librarians from North, South, and Central America and the Caribbean to attend the next two IFLA General Conferences. All of these awards were likely to assume greater importance as DANIDA, the international development agency of Denmark, withdrew its funding of both study and travel grants from IFLA.

The Digital Present

The interdependence of libraries with digital (electronic) content was evident throughout the conference. President-elect Kay Raseroka of Botswana announced that the theme for her presidency would be "Bridging the Digital Divide." She held a brainstorming session in Glasgow at which it was noted that "Ongoing technological progress potentially widens the gap between the information rich and the information poor world-wide. . . Technology of itself, however, will not resolve social and cultural policy issues of access to information." Nearly 200 IFLA registrants discussed how to ensure that closing the gap would be a public-policy priority. They identified the need for stronger advocacy for library and information rights with government agencies and funding bodies, and also saw a need to continue simplifying IFLA's complex structure and to improve relationships between the IFLA organization and individual members.

The president-elect's planning group solicited further comment from members via e-mail and prioritized the numerous recommended actions for presentation to the IFLA Governing Board in March 2003.

Membership

IFLA has approximately 1,700 members in 155 countries. Established in Edinburgh in 1927, it has been registered in the Netherlands since 1971 and has headquarters at the Koninklijke Bibliotheek (Royal Library) in The Hague. Although IFLA did not hold a General Conference outside Europe and North America until 1980, there has since been steadily increasing participation from Asia, Africa, South America, and Australia. The federation now maintains regional offices for Africa (in Dakar, Senegal), Asia and Oceania (in Bangkok), and Latin America (in Rio de Janeiro). The organization has five working languages—English, French, German, Russian and Spanish—and offers five membership categories: international library associations, national library associations, institutions, and personal and student affiliates. Association and institution members have voting rights in the IFLA General Council and may nominate candidates for IFLA offices; personal affiliates have no voting rights, but may run for any office. In 2001, for a four-year trial period, IFLA began offering student affiliate memberships at reduced rates, with the aim of broadening participation and enhancing the stability and continuity of the organization by attracting affiliate members early in their careers. In addition, approximately 30 corporations in the information industry have formed a working relationship with IFLA as Corporate Partners, providing financial and "in-kind" support. The United Nations Educational, Scientific and Cultural Organization (UNESCO) has given IFLA formal associate relations status, the highest level of relationship accorded to nongovernmental organizations by UNESCO.

Personnel, Structure, and Governance

Ross Shimmon has been secretary general of IFLA since May 1999. Sjoerd M. J. Koopman continues as coordinator of professional activities, an IFLA headquarters position.

The current president of IFLA is Christine Deschamps, director, Bibliothèque de l'Université Paris V—René Descartes, who completed a first four-year term at the 2001 General Conference in Boston and was reelected, unopposed, for a second two-year term that will run through August 2003. Kay Raseroka, director of library services at the University of Botswana, was chosen as president-elect and began her two-year term as president-elect at the conclusion of the

Boston conference. Derek Law, Information Resources Directorate, University of Strathclyde, Scotland, was elected treasurer. This was the first time that IFLA had an elected president-elect and the first time that IFLA's president and other officers were elected by postal or electronic ballot, under the revised IFLA Statutes and Rules of Procedure.

Under the revised statutes, which took effect in 2001, IFLA's Executive and Professional Boards were combined in a new Governing Board. The new 21-member board (plus the secretary general, ex officio) is responsible for the federation's general policies, management and finance, and external communications. The current members, in addition to Deschamps, Raseroka, Law, and Shimmon, are Sissel Nilsen (Norway), Alex Byrne (Australia), Ana Maria Peruchena Zimmerman (Argentina), Ingrid Parent (Canada), Jianzhong Wu (China), Claudia Lux (Germany), Sally McCallum (United States), Ellen Tise (South Africa), and Jerónimo Martinez (Spain), plus the chair and members of the Professional Committee (formerly Professional Board). Their terms of service began at the conclusion of the Boston conference and will run for two years.

The Governing Board delegates responsibility for overseeing the direction of IFLA between board meetings, within the policies established by the board, to the six-member IFLA Executive Committee that includes the president, president-elect, treasurer, chair of the Professional Committee, two members of the Governing Board (elected every two years by members of the board from among its elected members), and IFLA's secretary general, ex-officio. The first elected Governing Board members of the Executive Committee are Parent and Tise.

The IFLA Professional Committee monitors the planning and programming of professional activities carried out by IFLA's two types of bodies: professional groups—eight divisions, more than 50 sections, and discussion groups—and core activities (formerly called core programs). The Professional Committee is composed of one elected officer from each division plus a chair elected by the incoming members, the coordinator of professional activities (Koopman), and two elected members of the Governing Board (currently Lux and Wu). Winston Tabb, dean of university libraries and director of the Sheridan Libraries, Johns Hopkins University, chairs the Professional Committee.

The eight divisions of IFLA and their representatives on the Professional Committee are: Division I, General Research Libraries (Cristóbal Pasadas Ureña, Spain); Division II, Special Libraries (John Meriton, Britain); Division III, Libraries Serving the General Public (John Day, United States); Division IV, Bibliographic Control (Ia McIlwaine, Britain); Division V, Collections and Services (Mary E. Jackson, United States); Division VI, Management and Technology (Wanda Dole, United States); Division VII, Education and Research (Marian Koren, Netherlands); and Division VIII, Regional Activities (Rashidah Begum bt. Fazal Mohamed, Malaysia). Each division has interest sections such as Statistics and Evaluation, Library Theory and Research, and Management and Marketing; other sections focus on particular types of libraries or parts of the world.

To continue streamlining IFLA's organizational structure, in 2002 the roundtables were discontinued. Eight were restructured as sections within the divisions, bringing the total number of sections to 53; one former roundtable, National Centres for Library Services, became a separate organization with consultative status.

The core activities are Advancement of Librarianship (ALP), Universal Bibliographic Control and International MARC (UBCIM), Universal Availability of Publications (UAP), and Preservation and Conservation (PAC). In addition, Freedom of Access to Information and Freedom of Expression (FAIFE) and Copyright and Other Legal Matters (CLM) are functionally core activities although their place in the IFLA governance structure is different. Each of these six activities is supported and hosted by a European library or agency: Bibliothèque Nationale de France (PAC), British Library (UAP, CLM), Deutsche Bibliothek (UBCIM), Uppsala University Library (ALP), and DANIDA, the Danish international development agency (FAIFE). The Universal Dataflow and Telecommunications (UDT) core program closed in December 2001, DANIDA withdrew support of FAIFE in 2002, and UBCIM and UAP were due to close in early 2003 as staff at their host libraries retired. Questions of funding and support for the core activities thus loomed large, and the Governing Board is considering how to continue the vital work they perform.

Canada's Libraries in 2002: A Year of Partnerships

Karen G. Adams
Director of Library Services and Information Resources
University of Alberta Libraries

Canada continued to develop strategies in support of the knowledge-based economy in 2002, with emphasis during the year on research and innovation. A sub-theme was the growth of the information and communications technology sector and its dispersal across all sectors of the economy.

Although libraries are, by virtue of Canada's constitution (the British North America Act), a provincial matter, issues around information policy, research, and information and communications technology (ICT) expansion kept libraries engaged with the federal government on a variety of matters, from new funding to partnerships in library Web sites.

If one were to seek a theme to describe the mode of operation underlying the activities reported here, it would be partnerships: between institutions; resulting from mergers; funding and creating digital services; across types of libraries; with for-profit organizations; with not-for-profit organizations; and through consortia at local, regional, and national levels. Looking at library Web sites across the country, one notes the continuance of traditional services, along with the establishment of both emerging and mature electronic services. It is the latter category that most frequently generates the collaboration.

In spite of the expected negative effect on the Canadian economy of the September 11, 2001, terrorist attacks, the nation's gross domestic product (GDP) grew 4.1 percent from October 2001 to October 2002,[1] and the country's mood was relatively positive. As a result, it appeared early in 2003 that libraries also experienced modest growth, with cutbacks an exception rather than the norm. It should be noted that the crisis in Canada's school libraries was identified in 2002; it was not created during 2002.

Canadian libraries continue to value universal access to information, a goal underlying concerns with national information policy, with access to broadband networks outside large urban centers, with the state of library services to First Nations (aboriginal) communities, and with library service to Canadians with print disabilities.

Federal Information Policy Issues

Copyright

The federal government continues to work on copyright legislation in preparation for implementation of its obligations under the World Intellectual Property Organization (WIPO) treaties and to make the legislation more appropriate to the digital environment. A group of national associations representing users and creators of copyrighted content came together as the Copyright Forum. Present forum members are the Association of Canadian Community Colleges, the Association of Universities and Colleges of Canada, l'Association pour l'Avancement des Sciences et des Techniques de la Documentation, the Bureau of Canadian Archivists, the Canadian Association of Law Libraries, the Canadian Association of University Teachers, the Canadian Association of Research Libraries (CARL), the Canadian Library Association (CLA), the Canadian Museums Association, the Canadian School Boards Association, the Canadian Teachers' Federation, the Copyright Consortium of the Council of Ministers of Education, and the Council of Administrators of Large Urban Public Libraries.

In April and May of 2002, forum members focused on the government's consultation meetings on digital copyright issues. The digital issues under discussion were the right of making available technological protection measures, rights management information, and liability of Internet service providers.

Then, without having dealt with these digital issues, it became clear that the government's next agenda item was to be the Section 92 review required by the Copyright Act (". . . a report on the provisions and operation of this Act, including any recommendations for amendments to this Act . . ."). Forum members provided individual input to the review, with CLA commenting under five broad categories: clarifying existing provisions, responding to technological innovation, ensuring reasonable access, international trends, and administration of copyright. The government released its report, "Supporting Culture and Innovation: Report on the Provisions and Operation of the Copyright Act," in early October, and the next step will be the referral of the document to a parliamentary committee so that priorities for action can be established. The library community remains concerned that the government must ensure balanced legislation between the access rights of users and the controls available to rights holders.[2, 3]

General Agreement on Trade in Services

CLA continues to express concerns over the potential impact of the General Agreement on Trade in Services (GATS) on the not-for-profit sector, including education and libraries. These concerns include the potential for the private sector to challenge library activities such as lending videotapes, providing training in computers, and providing public access to the Internet. GATS makes the distinction between services provided by governments and those provided by the public sector. CLA is seeking to ensure that the government understands the unique position of the not-for-profit sector, which is often mandated and partially funded by government and the public sector, and may provide services that appear to be also provided by the commercial sector, but is not itself "government." CLA is further concerned that community-based organizations such as libraries become unintentionally included in the relationships created by GATS.[4]

Depository Services Program

The government has had a robust program of providing its publications in all formats to libraries holding depository status, with the Depository Services Program (DSP) receiving feedback from an advisory committee drawn from the library community. In recent years, with the decentralization of government publishing, the library community has watched carefully as DSP has been moved through different reporting relationships. In fall 2002 Communication Canada, the department responsible for DSP, announced suddenly that it was moving the program into its publishing operation. The move included a change in the leadership of the program after many years of stability and success. Librarians conducted a letter-writing campaign expressing their concerns about the future of DSP; ironically, this campaign followed a campaign of congratulations to the government on the program's 75th anniversary, celebrated earlier in the year. Many of the letters in the fall included the suggestion that the program be moved to the National Library of Canada. The government's response declared its purpose to be ". . . to alleviate any fears you might have . . ." but did not indicate that changes to the original announcement were under consideration.[5]

Library Book Rate

Another program funded by the government to support the mailing of printed materials between libraries, and between libraries and their patrons, has been continued after an additional review. These reviews have seen the library community seeking to include nonprint formats in the preferential rate, and the government seeking to minimize its financial commitment. The new agreement provides pricing that increases 13.1 percent over the next three years, and provides for a study of the use of the rate.[6]

National Issues

The Research Agenda

Research libraries were pleased with the July 2002 announcement of one-time funding of $30 million to 39 universities to provide infrastructure support for new faculty and their research. Libraries were included as an appropriate use of the funding, with each university making its own decision as to how to manage its own award. In general, libraries either received a share of the infrastructure funds for specific purposes or received increased operating budgets. Lobbying to renew the program on an ongoing basis followed.

Innovation Strategy

The federal government launched its Innovation Strategy in February 2002 with two companion documents: *Achieving Excellence: Investing in People, Knowledge, and Opportunity* and *Knowledge Matters: Skills and Learning for Canadians*. Both academic and public libraries, and their associations, found opportunity to comment on the value that they bring to the innovation agenda and to note new opportunities in response to the government's agenda.[7, 8]

Health libraries, through associations such as the Canadian Health Libraries Association, also provided input to the federal government's Commission on the Future of Health Care in Canada, with a focus on the need for a national network of libraries for health, building on existing initiatives in the absence of a national library of medicine for Canada.[9]

Services to First Nations

In February 2002 the Saskatchewan government released its report on library services to First Nations and Métis people, *Information Is for Everyone.* The report proposes strategies for bringing service to all Saskatchewan residents, including those living on reserve lands, and for achieving library use by aboriginal people that is proportionate to their population. Forty-six recommendations touch areas ranging from having a storytelling week to training aboriginal people to participate in the library work force.[10]

In the same month, the Ontario Library Association (OLA) established the Grace Buller Scholarship for Indigenous Peoples. The scholarship will enable indigenous young people to pursue studies at the University of Toronto's Faculty of Information Studies. OLA also sponsored First Nations Public Library Week to promote resources and services to aboriginal communities and fielded proposals targeted at improving library services in 25 aboriginal communities.[11, 12]

School Libraries

The May Summit on School Libraries gave further weight to fears that Canada's school libraries are in crisis, the result of funding cutbacks at the provincial and municipal levels. A survey of schools in Ontario found them reporting one teacher-librarian for every 1,064 students; 59 percent of schools reported having a teacher-librarian, compared with 80 percent in 1997–1998. The Canadian Coalition for School Libraries was formed to address the problem through advocacy with provincial education ministers. Coalition membership includes the Canadian School Library Association, the Association of Canadian Publishers, People for Education, and the Canadian Association of Children's Librarians, as well as writers, academics, and parents. National Librarian Roch Carrier is the honorary chair.[13, 14]

Projected Shortage of Librarians

The University of Alberta is leading development of a research proposal to conduct a comprehensive study of library human resources in Canada, premised in part on the projected shortage of librarians in all sectors of the profession. The proposal outlines an in-depth study of the eight elements that the literature raises in the context of the impending human resource shortage in librarianship: recruitment, retention, remuneration, repatriation, rejuvenation, reaccreditation, retirement, and restructuring (the "Eight Rs"). Supporting partners at the time this report was prepared included CLA, the Council of Administrators of Large Urban Public Libraries, CARL, the Association of Professional Librarians of New Brunswick, and the University of Alberta.

Mergers

In October the federal government announced a merger of great interest. Minister of Canadian Heritage Sheila Copps announced the creation of the Library and Archives of Canada, combining the 50-year-old National Library of Canada

(NLC) and the National Archives of Canada. As of early 2003, the governance and organizational structures were still to be announced. CLA responded with cautious optimism while acknowledging the leadership role that NLC has played in building equitable access to library service for all Canadians. CLA also requested a meeting with the minister, and reiterated its support for an appropriate building for the new agency.[15, 16] [For more information, see the following article, "A Golden Celebration: The National Library of Canada at 50"—*Ed.*]

In a similar vein, new legislation in Quebec in March 2002 merged the existing Bibliothèque Nationale du Québec (BNQ) with the new Grande Bibliothèque du Québec (GBQ). The new GBQ results from discussions between the Quebec government and the City of Montreal beginning in 1996, and is scheduled to open in late 2004 with the collections of the former Bibliothèque Nationale and the Bibliothèque Centrale of the City of Montreal, as well as newly acquired materials in support of its dual mandate: to preserve Quebec's documentary heritage and to make that heritage and other collections accessible to the public. While construction of the new physical site is under way, the Web site has already merged and brings together news of GBQ with the catalog and digital collections of BNQ.[17]

Continuing the trend initiated by the Ontario government with cities such as Toronto and Ottawa, the Quebec government merged the City of Montreal and 27 surrounding municipalities. The Bibliothèque de Montréal, with a central location and 54 branches, became the largest French-language public library on the continent in 2002.[18]

Studying the Digital Divide

Given the large landmass of Canada and the number of rural and remote communities, it is no surprise that the "digital divide" is a concern to Canadians. The federal government had initially promised to ensure that broadband access be available to all Canadian homes and businesses by 2004, but scaled back those plans in its most recent budget and extended its deadline to 2005. Canadian Advanced Technology Alliances has noted that 4,700 out of 6,000 communities in Canada (or 22 percent of the population) do not have high-speed Internet access. In spite of those limitations, a study by Ipsos-Reid reported that high-speed Internet access in Canadian households has doubled since 2000. Statistics Canada reported that while the digital divide is shrinking slowly, there continues to be a gap between those with the highest and lowest incomes, with growth in Internet use being attributed to middle-income households. There was also an urban-rural digital divide, as well as gaps based on level of education, family type, and age. In another study, Statistics Canada found that in 2001 small Canadian communities still had limited access to high-speed cable Internet, even though such access overall had increased substantially.[19, 20, 21, 22]

A Statistics Canada survey of Internet use found that some 232,000 households that had regularly used the Internet said they no longer did, citing as the most common reason having "no need" for the Internet. Others dropped out because it was too expensive, or because they had lost access to a computer. The statistics are comparable to findings in the United States.[23]

A study of Canadian student use of computers conducted by researchers at the Canadian Research Institute for Social Policy found that students use computers mainly for accessing information on the Internet, communication, word-processing, and games. The study also confirmed the existence of a digital divide for students, based on socioeconomic status.[24]

Ekos made available the results of its study "Rethinking the Information Highway for 2002." The study is a comprehensive research initiative examining how the digital revolution is transforming the environment of companies and governments. Libraries were interested to find that, overall, more than one in two Canadians have accessed the Internet from a public place, and for those who have done so, the library is the first choice of public access location.[25]

The Conference Board of Canada's *Connectedness Index* placed Canada second only to the United States in use of information and communications technology, but noted three areas in Canada requiring improvement: broadband services, content, and wireless.[26]

CARL received funding from the Social Sciences and Humanities Research Council to study some of the questions around scholarly communication in Canada. The project, "Optimizing the Transformation of Knowledge Dissemination: Towards a Canadian Research Strategy," will look at such questions as

- What is the current state of scholarly communication in Canada?
- How are external drivers transforming knowledge dissemination within the current system of scholarly communication?
- Is there a need for a specific Canadian research strategy to facilitate the adaptation of the scholarly communication system to this new dynamic environment?
- If so, what should that strategy be?[27]

Innovations and Initiatives

Broadband Networks

In September federal Minister of Industry Allan Rock launched the government's $105 million Broadband for Rural and Northern Development Program. The program reflects federal commitment to establishing the infrastructure of a broadband network in Canada by 2005, with special emphasis on rural and remote areas, the far north, and aboriginal communities, where waiting for the private sector to build the network is not a solution.[28]

The Alberta SuperNet intends to connect all libraries, universities, school boards, hospitals, provincial government buildings, and regional health authorities across the province through a broadband network. The number of communities with high-speed Internet access will rise from 30 to 422.[29]

Similarly, in Saskatchewan, SaskTel announced that it will expand its high-speed Internet service to another 191 communities, up from 46 and resulting in 71 percent of the population having access to this service. At the same time, funding from the Canada-Saskatchewan Infrastructure Program was announced to enable the extension of high-speed Internet access to 162 public libraries across the province.[30]

The Quebec government made funding available for preliminary studies by schools and municipalities, with the goal of making broadband networks available throughout the province. Addressing the barrier posed by the limited amount of French-language information available on the Internet, the federal government also made funding available through its Francommunautés Virtuelles program. The program supports the development of French-language applications and content on the Internet. One of the national projects involves designing a Web site offering information content, a forum for telecollaboration, a training workshop for librarians, a guide, promotional material, and entertaining learning activities for youth on the safe use of resources on the Internet. French-speaking employees in public libraries will thus have access to public educational tools and professional training.[31]

In British Columbia, Industry Canada's Community Access Program provided support for 34 new public access sites in libraries, schools, and community sites across the Okanagan Valley. A multitype relationship including the Prince George Public Library and City Hall, the Regional Hospital, and the University of Northern British Columbia has brought high-speed connectivity (200 times faster than was available) to that city.[32]

At the same time, the province's Premier's Technology Council released a report, responding in part to recommendations made by the British Columbia Library Association, recommending that public access to the Internet be expanded to every community in the province, and that the broadband infrastructure be improved.[33]

Services

Working through the four academic regional consortia (Council of Prairie and Pacific University Libraries, Ontario Council of University Libraries, Conférence des Recteurs et des Principaux des Universités du Québec, and Council of Atlantic University Libraries/Conseil des Bibliothèques Universitaires de l'Atlantique), Canadian university libraries have extended in-person borrowing privileges to faculty, staff, and students from other participating universities. Reciprocal borrowing privileges are determined by each lending library. There are some exceptions for undergraduate students.[34]

Vancouver Public Library became the first library in the world to offer a service that provides its patrons with same-day access to international newspapers. Newspapers are laser-printed at the library using PDF files supplied by NewspaperDirect, a British Columbia company that is an innovator in electronic newspaper delivery. Available titles come from Spain, South Korea, France, the Philippines, Britain, and the United States.

Vancouver Public Library also launched a new book club for men only.[35]

Surrey (British Columbia) Public Library opened a new computer-based language-learning lab to help patrons use self-teaching software to improve English skills. Users are also able to access the site through the Internet. Surrey also offered lessons in Internet and basic computer skills.[36]

In an effort to minimize barriers for users, Woodstock (Ontario) Public Library has installed Web-4-All, an assertive technology combining hardware and software that can quickly configure a public access computer to accommodate a user's special needs and then return to a standard setting for the next user.[37]

The Canadian National Institute for the Blind has put its catalog online with a Web interface, and included the collections of other libraries such as Britain's National Library for the Blind and NLC.[38]

The University of British Columbia is testing a unique method of displaying the contents of its catalog in a visual interface, intended to improve the results of inexact (no specific author or title) searches.[39]

Prince Rupert Public Library in British Columbia launched a new Web site based on open-source software (Linux and GNU) over the summer, and is looking for an OPAC that can function effectively on this platform.[40]

In partnership with Southampton City Libraries in Britain and Eastern Regional Libraries in Australia, the Vaughn (Ontario) and Surrey (British Columbia) Public Libraries began offering Global Librarian, an around-the-clock e-mail reference service. In Surrey it is available from Monday at 9:00 A.M. to Saturday 3:30 P.M. local time, excluding public holidays.[41]

Toronto Public Library received Ontario government funding of $1.4 million to develop its Virtual Reference Library of subject guides, digital collections and online services. The library serves all residents of Ontario and its public libraries.[42]

New Brunswick Library Services launched its New Brunswick Virtual Reference Library/Bibliothèque de Référence Virtuelle du Nouveau-Brunswick, a provincewide service organizing free Web sites in both English and French.[43]

In Ottawa, Sm@rtLibrary, one component of the SmartCapital project, began building a one-stop portal for Ottawa residents to access the collections and services of the region's libraries. The project currently includes the Canada Institute for Scientific and Technical Information, Carleton University Library, NLC, Ottawa Public Library, and the University of Ottawa Library Network.[44]

Ontario's Oxford County Library unveiled a new Internet Portal for children, with Interactive features including a joke engine and ask-a-librarian service.[45]

Pictou-Antigonish Regional Library in Nova Scotia launched its virtual public library in January, enabling patrons across the region to apply for library cards, search for materials, request materials, read electronic journals, e-mail reference requests, and access the Web site (which includes local history on the lobster industry). The electronic library is the result of a partnership among LibraryNet, Human Resources Development Canada, and the Nova Scotia Technology and Science Secretariat. Pictou-Antigonish is also a partner with Human Resources Development Canada in offering employment insurance registration from its Web site.[46]

Consumer health initiatives continued to grow, with the Nova Scotia Health Network going live. The network is a Web-based consumer health information service that provides links to quality information, health organizations in the province, articles from health and wellness magazines, drug information, a link to the Canadian Health Network, and an ask-a-librarian service.[47]

Windsor (Ontario) Public Library launched the Windsor Essex County Health Gateway to provide local residents with one-stop access to health services and to serve as prototype for the Windsor Essex Smart Communities WEconnect project.[48]

The University of Alberta initiated its PDA Zone service, providing access to resources and library services that are available for users of handheld devices known as Personal Digital Assistants (PDAs).[49]

Literacy

London (Ontario) Public Library received $200,000 from a television station to establish North America's first library-based media literacy center, the CHUM Television Media Literacy Centre. Print, electronic, and audiovisual materials will support users to develop an informed and critical understanding of screen-based media. The center is housed in the new central library.[50]

Girl Guides of Canada/Guides du Canada, in an effort to help girls become more critical users of the technology and to encourage them to become more involved in the online world of kids, has partnered with the Media Awareness Network to develop the You Go Girl in Technology (YGGT) Internet literacy project.[51]

Building the Canadian Digital Library

Windsor Public Library added to its digital exhibits a new site, iCity: Historic Sites of Windsor. The site uses Geographic Information Systems (GIS) software to track the history, geography, and architecture of the city's historic Walkerville district. As the site is developed, researchers will be able to trace the history of a block of land by beginning with current information. This site is the result of a partnership among the library, the University of Windsor, and the Ontario Ministry of Tourism, Culture, and Recreation. This site complements its bilingual local history site, Settling Canada's South.[52]

The Canadian National Site Licensing Project (CNSLP), a digital library initiative established by the Canadian research library community to enhance the capacity for research and innovation in Canada by increasing published scholarly content available to academic researchers, added to its existing relationships with the American Chemical Society, the American Mathematical Society, Elsevier Science/Academic Press, the Institute for Scientific Information, the Institute of Physics Publishing, the Royal Society of Chemistry, and Springer-Verlag by establishing a new relationship with Elsevier to bring access to the nearly 1,700 e-journals on the ScienceDirect platform to the CNSLP academic library community.

The Ontario Council of University Libraries (OCUL) unveiled the Ontario Information Infrastructure Project in 2002. The project comprises four strategies: providing access to scholarly information by centrally mounting and delivering information resources licensed through OCUL, providing interlibrary loan and document delivery, providing integrated access through a "scholar's portal," and licensing electronic content.[53]

With partial funding from the Canada Foundation for Innovation, six universities are establishing the Text Analysis Portal for Research (TAPoR), which will build a unique human and computing infrastructure for text analysis across the country by establishing six regional centers to form one national text-analysis research portal. Participants include the University of Victoria, the University of

Alberta, McMaster University, the Université de Montréal, the University of Toronto, and the University of New Brunswick.[54]

Use of one of Canada's digital collections, Early Canadiana Online, was the subject of a second study by Joan Cherry and Wendy Duff of the University of Toronto's Faculty of Information Studies. Findings were that the user group and its use of the collections remained similar to the previous study. The study also provides useful information on user preferences for those developing digital sites for general use and for teaching and research.[55]

The Ontario Digital Library continued to move closer to the reality of its vision: a digital network of high-quality information resources and services, including provincewide licensing of electronic resources for all types of libraries. In February 2002 the concept was presented to the provincial government in a proposal titled "To Create the Ontario Digital Library," which recommended the establishment of a multitype library organization to be run by a board.[56]

The Canadian National Institute for the Blind announced a $33 million fundraising campaign to support digitization of its entire collection of 60,000 alternate format materials and create the world's first Internet library portal for the blind, in a process that uses a single digital file to create materials in multiple formats.[57]

The University of Calgary and Université Laval launched Our Roots/Nos Racines, a comprehensive coast-to-coast record of Canadian local histories being compiled and made available to students of history everywhere via the World Wide Web.[58]

The Canadian Association of Research Libraries (CARL) began work on its Institutional Repositories Pilot Project, Online Resource Portal in July with 13 initial participating universities. The purpose of the project is fivefold: to increase the visibility of institutional and Canadian content, especially with most journal articles being published outside Canada; to enhance the current scholarly publishing environment, in support of the Scholarly Publishing and Academic Resources Coalition (SPARC) position of repositories serving as a complement to the publishing system; to experiment with content, format, and software systems; to showcase interoperability in the Canadian context; and to speed up the learning process by exchanging best-practice information. CARL subsequently sponsored a symposium, "Research Innovation and Scholarship: The Role of Open Access Publishing," in support of the project and related initiatives.[59]

Conclusion

In 2002 Canadian libraries continued expansion of their Web sites, digital collections, and electronic services without abandoning traditional collections and services. Web sites continued to bring information about traditional services and programs, as well as emerging electronic versions of those services and programs, to the communities the libraries served. Partnership relations, many of them nontraditional in terms of bringing together different types of libraries, and sometimes-distant geographies, supported these developments. A national digital collection available to all began to emerge through local, regional, and national activities.

Supplemental Bibliography

1. http://www.statcan.ca/Daily/English/021224/d021224a.htm
2. http://strategis.ic.gc.ca/SSG/rp00863e.html
3. http://www.cla.ca/issues/copyright.htm
4. http://www.cla.ca/issues/correspondence.htm
5. http://www.cla.ca/issues/dsp_response.htm
6. http://www.cla.ca/issues/lbr.htm
7. http://www.innovationstrategy.gc.ca/cmb/innovation.nsf/MenuE/InnovationStrategy
8. http://www.cla.ca/issues/innovation.htm
9. http://www.chla-absc/news/romanow.html
10. http://www.lib.sk.ca/staff/minaboriginal/ablib/ablibfinal.html
11. http://www.accessola.com/about/awards/buller.html
12. http://www.accessola.org/action/issues/indigenouspeoples
13. http://www.peopleforeducation.com/librarycoalition
14. http://www.peopleforeducation.com/reports/library/library2.pdf
15. http://www.canadianheritage.gc.ca/newsroom/news_e.cfm?Action=Display&code=2N0227E
16. http://www.cla.ca/issues/nlc_nac_merger.htm
17. http://www.bnquebec.ca
18. http://www2.ville.montreal.qc.ca/biblio
19. http://www.cata.ca/cata/news/April242002.cfm
20. http://www.ipsos-reid.com/media/dsp_displaypr_cdn.cfm?id_to_view=1491
21. http://www.statcan.ca/Daily/English/021001/d021001e.htm
22. http://www.statcan.ca/Daily/English/020903/d020903a.htm
23. http://www.statcan.ca/Daily/English/020611/d020611b.htm
24. http://www.cmec.ca/stats/pcera/RSEvents02/Bcorbett_OEN.pdf
25. http://www.ekos.com/studies/highway.asp
26. http://www.conferenceboard.ca/kmeb/abstracts/connectedness_new.htm
27. http://www.carl-abrc.ca/projects/RDI/1page_summary.htm
28. http://broadband.gc.ca/index_e.asp
29. http://www.albertasupernet.ca
30. http://www.gov.sk.ca/newsrel/releases/2002/05/16-364.html
31. http://francommunautes.ic.gc.ca
32. http://www.city.pg.bc.ca/pages/media2002/nov12_2002.html
33. http://www.bcla.bc.ca/news/index.html
34. http://www.carl-abrc.ca/frames_index.htm
35. http://www.vpl.ca/branches/LibrarySquare/prl/menwithbooks.html
36. http://www.spl.surrey.bc.ca
37. http://www.woodstock.library.on.ca
38. http://visucat.cnib.ca:8000
39. http://www.library.ubc.ca/home/visual
40. http://www.princerupertlibrary.ca
41. http://www.spl.surrey.bc.ca
42. http://www.culture.gov.on.ca/culture/english/index.html

43. http://www1.gnb.ca/0003/vrl-brv/000.asp
44. http://www.smartcapital.ca/PDFs_presentations/Smart_Library_Presentation.html
45. http://kids.ocl.net
46. http://parl.ns.ca
47. http://www.nshealthnetwork.ca
48. http://www.weconnect.org/health
49. http://www.library.ualberta.ca/pdazone/index.cfm
50. http://www.londonpubliclibrary.ca/news/news.php?article_uid=145
51. http://www.girlguides.ca/technology
52. http://www.windsorpubliclibrary.com/digi/icity
53. http://www.ocul.on.ca/OIIstrategicprograms.html
54. http://huco.ualberta.ca/Tapor
55. http://informationr.net/ir/7-2/paper123.html
56. http://www.accessola.org/action/issues/ontariodigitallibrary
57. http://www.cnib.ca/eng/about/news/campaign_kickoff.htm
58. http://www.ourroots.ca/e/home.asp
59. http://www.carl-abrc.ca/frames_index.htm

A Golden Celebration:
The National Library of Canada at 50

Mary Jane Starr

Director General, Communications
National Library of Canada
395 Wellington St., Ottawa ON K1A 0N4
613-996-7490, fax 613-991-9871, e-mail mary-jane.starr@nlc-bnc.ca

On January 1, 2003, the National Library of Canada (NLC) celebrated its 50th anniversary. The library was created to gather, protect, and make accessible to the citizens of Canada all that is published in Canada; to bridge the information gap in a country that is vast in size and was limited in the information resources within its borders.

Fifty years later, NLC is on the threshold of a new era in providing timely and comprehensive information to all Canadians. The creation of a new institution—the Library and Archives of Canada—as announced by the minister of Canadian Heritage on October 2, 2002, heralds a renewed investment in Canadian culture.

Canada's national library is very young; one of the youngest in the world. But it has built a collection of almost 20 million items: books, magazines, authors' manuscripts, music CDs and sound recordings, software, and electronic documents. This collection reflects the creative output of Canada—the nation's stories, history, and music. With partner libraries across Canada, NLC has built a robust network of interlibrary loan services and the National Union Catalog (the AMICUS database), which provides information on the items in the collections of more than 1,300 libraries nationwide, in both of Canada's official languages (English and French).

NLC reports to Parliament through the minister of Canadian Heritage, whose portfolio also includes the National Archives of Canada, the Canada Council for the Arts, federal museums, the Canadian Broadcasting Corporation, the National Film Board, and Parks Canada. Together these institutions and agencies document, reflect, and inspire the Canadian experience.

1950–1968: The Lamb Years

In 1883 Canada's first prime minister, Sir John A. Macdonald, made a statement in Parliament on the need for a national library. Seventy years and two world wars later, in 1949, the concerted lobbying of librarians, archivists, scholars, and those urging national cultural development through the Royal Commission on National Development in the Arts, Letters, and Sciences finally brought results. The commission's recommendations were strongly influenced by the positions of the Canadian Library Association (CLA), the Association des Bibliothécaires de Langue Française, the Royal Society of Canada, the Canadian Historical Association, and many other groups.

In its report, published in 1951, the commission noted that Canada was "the only civilized country in the world lacking a National Library"[1] and recommended that a national library be established without delay. Prime Minister William Lyon Mackenzie King finally became convinced of the necessity of a national library to advance and preserve Canada's culture and to meet the needs of researchers. One of the winning ploys in attracting the prime minister's attention was made by Elizabeth Homer Morton, the first executive director of CLA (1946). CLA was engaged in the microfilming of old Canadian newspapers— many in a desperate, crumbling state—wherever they could be found. A microfilm set of the *Colonial Advocate*—edited from 1824 to 1834 by King's grandfather, William Lyon Mackenzie—was assembled and presented to the prime minister. The actual presentation of the microfilm was made by W. Kaye Lamb, a historian from British Columbia. Lamb had administrative experience in both archives and libraries in his native province. When he was named dominion archivist in 1948, he accepted the position on the condition that he could also take an active role in paving the way for a national library.

The precursor of the National Library of Canada, the Canadian Bibliographic Centre, opened on May 1, 1950, scarcely 16 months after Lamb arrived in Ottawa. Its two purposes were to identify, collect, and record publications written by Canadians and items published in Canada or about Canada, and to compile a catalog of the holdings of the major libraries in every region of the country. In fact, unlike many of its counterparts, NLC began primarily as a set of services, delivered at first without a collection from crowded quarters in successive archives buildings. (From the outset, the administration of NLC and the National Archives of Canada has been highly integrated.)

The national bibliography, *Canadiana,* was compiled from a number of sources, including the copyright collection of the Library of Parliament, and it moved quickly from being a bimonthly publication to appearing monthly in 1951. Initially, the union catalog consisted of copies of the cards of special, university, and large public libraries, photographed with a 35-millimeter camera in cities and towns across Canada. Later these same institutions submitted extra copies of their own catalog cards for filing in the union catalog.

There were urgent reasons for embarking on the national union catalog. Canada was a book-poor country at a time when the education system was expanding greatly. Looking forward slightly, a study completed in 1957 showed that 109 cities in the United States possessed research, college, and public libraries that together had a total of more than 500,000 volumes; at the same time, only five Canadian cities had libraries that in the aggregate had more than half a million volumes. Moreover, the book collections of the libraries in these American cities amounted to 289,000,000 volumes, whereas in 1957 the national union catalog, reflecting the contents of the great majority of the larger Canadian reference and research collections in Canada, listed 7,000,000 volumes.[2]

Legislation to create NLC was introduced and passed in the House of Commons in May 1952. Subsequently, the legislation was passed without amendment by the Senate in June, received royal assent, was proclaimed in December, and came into force on January 1, 1953.

NLC came into being with Lamb holding the dual positions of national librarian and dominion archivist. The national librarian serves at the pleasure of the governor in council—that is, the Governor General of Canada (the head of state) acting by and with the advice of the Queen's Privy Council for Canada. (In practical terms, the appointment is arranged by the prime minister, who is the head of government.)

The primary responsibilities of the library were to compile and maintain the national union catalog, to compile and publish the national bibliography, and to dispose of surplus books. The act also established the National Library Advisory Council (later Board), gave NLC responsibility for coordinating the library services of federal government departments, and contained provisions for the legal deposit of every book published in Canada. The library's staff drew up the legal deposit regulations for books, which have since been revised to include periodicals, microforms, CDs and videos, and multimedia items.

Closely associated with NLC's bibliographical work was the filming of rare original publications. NLC began filming the items listed in Marie Tremaine's *Bibliography of Canadian Imprints, 1751–1800,* a project involving the cooperation of institutions and collectors in Canada, the United States, and Britain. By 1956 nearly 800 titles were on 21 reels of film, and positive prints were available for purchase.

As he added staff and services, Lamb also acquired—through transfer, gift, and purchase—a number of collections of foreign publications, including the library of the British musicologist Percy Scholes, and approximately 300,000 titles from the Library of Parliament. To manage this expansion, a new building was required. Prime Minister Lester B. Pearson presided in Canada's centennial year (1967) over the opening of a new building, shared by NLC and the archives, near Parliament Hill in Ottawa.

Publishing complemented collecting in the early years of the NLC. In addition to the listings of new books, pamphlets, and federal and provincial publications in the monthly issues of *Canadiana,* the library published works that contributed to knowledge of earlier Canadian publications and texts on subjects not covered by the national bibliography. Examples are varied: Olga Bishop's *Publications of the Government of Nova Scotia, Prince Edward Island, New Brunswick: 1758–1952*; *Canadian Graduate Theses, 1952*; and Gerhard Lomer's *Stephen Leacock: A Check-list and Index of His Writings.* The library also gave annual support for printing the *Canadian Index to Periodicals and Documentary Films* compiled by the Canadian Library Association.

In his inaugural speech as president of CLA in 1947, Lamb urged the library community to "make it our business to see that the big things we try to do on a national scale reach right down to the people at the cross-roads." [3] Up until his retirement in 1968, he never wavered in his belief that interlibrary cooperation and the promotion of Canadiana formed the basis on which services at the national level improve library and information services in local and rural communities across the country.

1968–1983: The Sylvestre Years

In June 1968 Guy Sylvestre—journalist, writer, critic, private secretary to Prime Minister Louis St. Laurent, and associate parliamentary librarian—was appointed Canada's second national librarian. Sylvestre noted that the library operated in four spheres: as a library proper, as a federal government institution, as part of the national information network, and as a player and partner on the international scene. In his vision, NLC would expand its Canadian collections and its inheritance from the Library of Parliament into a research collection in the social sciences, humanities, and arts, with emphasis on Canadian studies. Indeed, the 1969 revision of the National Library Act committed NLC to strengthening and extending its service and heritage roles, among them, the Canadian Book Exchange Centre, where books surplus to one library could be acquired by another library in need of those titles.

To complement the existing reference, location, and interlibrary loan services, Sylvestre appointed a number of subject specialists for collections in areas such as music, rare books, literary manuscripts, and children's literature. He attracted major gifts, notably the collection of rare Hebraica and Judaica of Jacob M. Lowy, Montreal collector and philanthropist. He also established a number of specialized services: the Library Documentation Centre, to support the library profession, and the Multilingual Biblioservice, to assist public libraries with collections for the increasingly diverse and growing immigrant population. To address the need for cooperation and concerted action within the community of federal libraries across Canada, Sylvestre established the Council of Federal Libraries.

A wave of technological advances prompted Sylvestre to set up a series of task forces and committees with representatives from across Canada to move Canadian library cooperation to automated systems. Within the library, the national bibliography and the union catalog for interlibrary loan needed to be automated, expanded, and updated. To achieve a coherent network, the systems had to be based on international standards that would allow for the exchange of records from diverse sources across Canada and from institutions such as the Library of Congress and the British Library, and for their integration into cooperative databases, as well as for retrieval of information through both English- and French-language search strategies. Sylvestre set up national task groups to study Canadian cataloging standards, the Canadian MARC (MAchine-Readable Cataloguing) formats, and the nature and needs of the national union catalog.

Between 1976 and 1979, with the assistance of the Canada Institute for Scientific and Technical Information, which serves as the national science library for Canada, NLC acquired, tested, and adapted the Dortmunder Bibliothekssystem (DOBIS) from the University of Dortmund in Germany. In January 1984 the DOBIS system was made available to libraries across the country to search for cataloging copy and locations for interlibrary loan requests. The cataloging and search modules of the system were used by NLC and a number of federal libraries well into the 1990s.

To serve Canadian information needs, NLC published three classifications series based on the Library of Congress classification schedules—F 5000 (which became FC and includes works on Canadian history), KE (Canadian law), and PS 8000 (Canadian literature)—and instituted the Cataloguing-in-Publication (CIP) program for Canada. Specific Canadian subject headings to identify those areas of publishing output that are distinctively Canadian in context and meaning were established, and NLC began working with Université Laval to produce the Répertoire de Vedettes-matière, the French-language equivalents for terms that appear in the Canadian subject headings as well as those in the Library of Congress subject headings. The Office of Library Resources began gathering information for a national inventory of research collections in the humanities and social sciences; the results were documented in *Research Collections in Canadian Libraries* (1972 and 1974). Subsequently, a subject approach was taken to identify collections' strengths, and volumes in the series were also dedicated to federal libraries and official publications.

In its first 25 years, NLC had grown from a staff of 14 and a budget of C$76,608 to a staff of 490 and a budget of C$14,939,000 in 1979–1980. However, Sylvestre believed that greater development was still needed. *The Future of the National Library of Canada* (1979) laid out the Sylvestre blueprint for the development of the bibliographic, communications, and resource networks needed to achieve his vision. Briefs were solicited, statistics on public and university libraries gathered, and a literature search conducted. The resulting report caused quite a stir in the Canadian library community. One reason was that Sylvestre argued for the transfer of some activities, responsibilities, and collections (such as maps, literary manuscripts, and music archives of all sorts) from the National Archives to NLC. A second reason was that he recommended the transfer of the Canada Institute for Scientific and Technical Information from its home at the National Research Council to NLC. Sylvestre also argued that separate accommodations should be found for the national archives, that the library's administrative services should be separated from the joint services provided by the national archives, and that the headquarters building of the library should be expanded to house the staff and collections. None of these recommendations was implemented, however, although the archives and the library did rationalize a number of their collections in the 1980s and 1990s under the leadership of the next national librarian, Marianne Scott.

From the early 1980s, NLC extended its cultural presence in Ottawa through enhanced exhibition and public programming. These activities were at first based on the library's special collections and the collaboration of foreign embassies. National initiatives—many of which were focused on Canadian studies, the preservation of the published heritage, and better tools for resource sharing—were put in place. They involved, for example, a national program for the preservation and accessibility of Canadian newspapers; the expansion of the national theses publishing program; the extension of legal deposit to new formats; a limited retrospective conversion of the Canadian union catalog and a major expansion of the database with machine-readable records; and the development of a union catalog and register of alternate format materials (initially braille, audiocassette, and large print).

Beyond Canada's borders, Sylvestre initiated staff exchanges and regular meetings with counterparts at the Library of Congress to discuss issues such as standards, interlibrary loan services, and cultural celebrations, and he also promoted strong relations with the U.S. library community through membership in the Association of Research Libraries (dating from 1971). The national librarian and his senior staff made notable contributions to the development of library services through the International Federation of Library Associations and Institutions (IFLA), and NLC took a lead role in establishing the international standard numbering systems for monographs and serials. Sylvestre led the Canadian delegation to the UNESCO Programme d'Information Générale meetings and prepared its *Guidelines for National Libraries* (1987). His commitment to the functions of national libraries led him, in 1974, to encourage the creation of a new international organization within IFLA, the Conference of Directors of National Libraries.

1984–1999: The Scott Years

Sylvestre retired in November 1983, and many of the national initiatives and programs begun under his tenure became the focus of the third national librarian, Marianne Scott, who was appointed in February 1984. As the first professionally trained librarian in the position (she had experience in academic libraries through her career as law librarian and director of libraries at McGill University in Montreal from 1953 to 1984) and a former president of CLA, she emphasized the importance and value of getting into the community to meet representatives of other libraries, which were at that time the primary users of the services of NLC.

Scott's dream was that all Canadians would be served as close to home as possible through the collections, services, expertise, and systems of a multisectoral library network. Early in her tenure, however, it became evident that the economic climate in Canada had changed. So, using her knowledge of the community and her experience in working with groups, she made it her mission to consolidate the gains made by NLC and Canadian libraries in the years of expansion.

As formulated in *Orientations: A Planning Framework for the 1990s* (1988), the responsibilities of NLC were threefold: the collection, preservation, and promotion of the nation's published heritage; the development of Canadian library services; and support for national resource sharing. Central to this threefold mission was the library's mandate to acquire, preserve, and make accessible Canada's published heritage. Confronted with increasing amounts of published information in various media, rising costs of materials, and the initial phases of government fiscal restraint, the staff realized that the library would have to focus its collecting efforts on Canadiana and limit its collections to the social sciences and humanities. To this end, the library expanded the application of legal deposit to microforms, video recordings, and compact discs and broadened its arrangements with other government agencies for the deposit of official publications. The library also struck an agreement with the National Archives of Canada that recognized the library's prerogative to collect manuscript and archival materials in Canadian music and Canadian literature, including publishing and the book arts and illustrations for children's literature.

To improve access to information, NLC staff concentrated on protocols and programs that would allow for the most efficient and effective sharing of Canadian collections and services, and the library continued to practice leadership in international standards and best practices through its work with a number of organizations, including the International Standards Organization, the International Serials Data System (ISDS), CONSER, the North American Plan for Collection Inventories, and the North American Interlibrary Loan and Document Delivery Project.

NLC had assumed a leadership role in the Canadian cataloging community with the establishment in 1974 of the Canadian Committee on Cataloguing, which is a constituent member of the Joint Steering Committee for Revision of

Anglo-American Cataloguing Rules. In 1991 NLC joined the Library of Congress, the British Library, CLA, the American Library Association, and the (British) Library Association as a member of the Anglo-American Cataloguing Rules Committee of Principals, the body responsible for overseeing the development of cataloging practice in the English-speaking world.

During the 1990s NLC focused on a multilayered preservation strategy and plan. At that time Canada led the world in the use of a mass deacidification system for both archival and published materials. Originally designed as a prototype for the national archives, this system was used extensively until 2000 to deacidify NLC's collections of current and retrospective works. The library initiated a coordinated preservation program to extend the life of its collections, including sound recordings. To address the problem of brittle paper, NLC took a lead in influencing the federal government to adopt a permanent paper policy for official publications. NLC's own publications have been printed on permanent paper since 1990.

Greater emphasis on Canadiana and on preservation at the library brought to light gaps in the comprehensiveness of the collections. Retrospective Canadiana items have been bought or acquired through gifts, and the microform collections have been strengthened through the Canadian Institute for Historical Microreproductions, established with the support of NLC in 1978. The special collections in music and literature were strengthened to include manuscript materials of major Canadian authors such as Carol Shields and Michael Ondaatje and musical archives of classical and popular musicians including Glenn Gould and Oscar Peterson. The collection relating to the study of Canadian society was enhanced by the transfer of print collections from the national archives and the Library of Parliament, as well as by major gifts from individual Canadians.

As part of its responsibility to promote Canada's published heritage, NLC focused its public programming events on its Canadian collections and on Canadian writers and musicians (the renowned Glenn Gould 1988 exhibition is an example). Traveling exhibitions and participation in book fairs brought increased awareness of the collections.

Since 1984, and particularly during the five-year Program Review of the Government of Canada in the mid-1990s, NLC experienced some severe budget cuts. The National Library Advisory Board was abolished, and the department shrank in size by more than 20 percent; both salary and operating dollars were significantly reduced. The book budget was reduced by almost 50 percent, and some of the specialized services, including the Library Documentation Centre and the Multilingual Biblioservice, were reorganized or eliminated. To improve efficiencies, NLC tackled automation in acquisitions, circulation, and collection management (modules not developed in DOBIS), and began planning for the successor to DOBIS, a relational database with client-server software called AMICUS. Special funding for technological developments and the library's first grant program accounted for the rise in expenditures to a peak of C$47,095,000 in 1993–1994. There had already been a decline in the base funding, however.

Between 1991 and 1996 NLC participated in the federal government's Interdepartmental Strategy for the Integration of Persons with Disabilities. With extra funds from the federal government, this group awarded matching grants to 120 Canadian libraries for the purchase of devices to assist print-disabled users and partial funding to 14 publishers for publication of 56 large-print titles. The total amount awarded by the library through a peer selection process was C$1.37 million.

Scott made her mark in her tireless effort to enhance local access to library services for all Canadians and in her preservation and promotion of Canadiana, including digital collections (in 1997, the NLC established the Canadian Initiative on Digital Libraries). Within the community, she received support from the Friends of the National Library and the Council of the Jacob M. Lowy Collection. Within the government, she supported and defended the federal library system and used every opportunity to underscore the importance of well-organized government information and management of electronic information. On the international scene, her work in IFLA and UNESCO continues to be recognized. Scott retired in September 1999 after 15 years in her position.

1999 to the present: The Carrier Years

Throughout its history, NLC has had a close relationship with the national archives. In 1998 the minister of Canadian Heritage, through whom both institutions report to Parliament, commissioned John English of the History Department at the University of Waterloo to review the roles of the National Archives of Canada and the National Library of Canada. The report of this consultation was made available to the public in the summer of 1999, after which two appointments were made: Ian E. Wilson as national archivist and Roch Carrier as national librarian.

Internationally known as an author and a household name in Canada for his short story *Le Chandail d'Hockey* (*The Hockey Sweater*) (1984), Carrier brought to his position knowledge of the academic world through his teaching, management experience as a senior administrator of the Collège Militaire Royal, and experience in cultural administration as director of the Canada Council for the Arts from 1993 to 1997. His particular challenge has been to increase the public's awareness of NLC and its services, and Carrier has traveled extensively in Canada to promote the library and its collections, its services, and the expertise of its staff.

He has taken on the vital issue of preservation of the published heritage, and he is speaking out on the need for appropriate facilities to ensure the long-term accessibility of the national newspaper collection in particular. The more than 70 incidents involving the library's collections in the last decade underscore the urgent nature of this situation.

Carrier has made literacy and school libraries in Canada his priorities as well. He makes time to visit schools, to talk with teachers and school librarians, and, most importantly, children. The perspectives gained from these encounters are shaping the library's programs and services such as the Read Up On It, the International Forum on Canadian Children's Literature (June 2003), and the Kids' Page on the NLC Web site.

Under Carrier's leadership, the library has worked in close collaboration with the national archives, other agencies for which the Department of Canadian Heritage is responsible (including museums, the Canadian Broadcasting Corporation, and the Canada Council for the Arts), and partners not only in the library sector but also in other sectors across Canada. NLC has launched an aggressive access agenda, first through the Digital Library of Canada, which is developing Canadian Web content; second by removing the barrier of user fees from the AMICUS services (now at more than 25 million bibliographic records and 43 million holdings, including Canadiana records), and third by advocating an inclusive approach to library services for all Canadians. To this end, NLC is currently developing resources and programs for aboriginal peoples, multicultural communities, and print-disabled users.

Announcement of the creation of the Library and Archives of Canada heralds a new era in access to information about Canada and Canadians. It underscores the government's intent to ensure that Canadians participate fully in the world of the 21st century in which innovation and knowledge will be key critical factors to success.

Core Library Services

The National Library and Archives of Canada

- Builds and preserves a comprehensive collection of published Canadiana to serve as an information and cultural resource for Canadians now and in the future
- Builds a bibliographic database to serve as a comprehensive record of Canadian publishing output, to facilitate access to the collection, and to assist libraries, the book trade, and other information providers in identifying, acquiring, promoting, and making available Canadian materials
- Provides reference, research, and referral services on-site, by telephone, and via the Web site, to Canadians and Canadian libraries using the library's Canadiana collection, several collections of wider scope supporting Canadian studies, and staff expertise
- Sponsors exhibitions, readings, lectures, concerts, and other events in order to provide Canadians with the opportunity to explore, understand, and appreciate their cultural heritage
- Facilitates public access to information about its own holdings as well as the holdings of other libraries in Canada
- Promotes reading and literacy via the annual Read Up On It kit and support to literacy initiatives
- Works with libraries throughout Canada to develop and implement policies, procedures, standards, products, and systems that support the sharing of information resources among libraries in order to optimize the delivery of library services to all Canadians
- Coordinates cooperative library services among the departments and agencies of the federal government
- Provides strategic policy and professional support for library development and coordination both in Canada and at the international level

- Has acquired a worldwide reputation, in bodies such as the International Organization for Standardization (ISO), for its leadership role in the development of standards for the exchange of bibliographic data, the preservation of library materials, the application of information technology to library services, and the promotion of universal and equitable access to basic information services, especially in the developing world

NLC By the Numbers

- The NLC Web site has more 8 million visits annually.
- The collection has nearly 20 million items (books, periodicals, sound and video recordings, microforms, and electronic documents) representing 3 million unique titles.
- The database for Canadiana, the national bibliography, has more than 2 million records representing 250 years of Canadian publishing.
- The AMICUS database contains more than 25 million records of items in the library's collections as well as holdings currently reported by 450 Canadian libraries.
- More than 1,300 Canadian libraries and other information institutions use the AMICUS service to search for materials for their clients.
- NLC has 460 staff members.
- The collections are housed in eight separate facilities in the national capital region.

Notes

1. Canada. Royal Commission on National Development in the Arts, Letters, and Sciences, Report (Ottawa: Edmond Cloutier, 1951), p. 101.
2. Report of the National Librarian 1957 (Ottawa: Queen's Printer, 1957), p. 10.
3. W. Kaye Lamb, "A Mandate for the Future," *Proceedings,* June 24–26, 1947, Second Conference, Vancouver (Ottawa: Canadian Library Association/Association Canadienne des Bibliothèques, 1947), p. 41. Speech delivered June 26, 1947.

Special Reports

Homeland Security and Information Management

Harold C. Relyea

Specialist in American National Government
Congressional Research Service

L. Elaine Halchin

Analyst in American National Government
Congressional Research Service

The terrorist attacks of September 11, 2001, prompted rethinking about various aspects of the internal security—frequently described as homeland security—of the United States. The public availability of information of seemingly potential value to those who might perpetrate a so-called terrorist incident is one such area of rethinking and continuing concern.

Thus far, the concept of homeland security, although defined in the national strategy for homeland security published in July 2002, provides little policy guidance in the form of criteria for determining the potential value of information to terrorists.[1] Various actions, nonetheless, have been taken since the September 11 attacks to regulate or manage information thought to be of possible value to terrorists. Moreover, it seems likely that further efforts in this regard will be made, if for no other reason than that the Homeland Security Act of 2002 authorizes the president, when prescribing and implementing procedures facilitating the sharing of relevant and appropriate "homeland security information" among federal agencies, as well as appropriate state and local government personnel, to also "identify and safeguard homeland security information that is sensitive but unclassified."[2] The phrase "sensitive but unclassified" is not explained or defined in the legislation.

Provided here is an overview of various information management developments that have occurred in the aftermath of, and in response to, the attacks of September 11 and the continued effort to maintain homeland security. George W. Bush was not quite eight months into his presidency when the attacks occurred. It must be borne in mind that he arrived at the office with his own information-management agenda, one that called for a reassessment of security classification policy and practice, which was initiated prior to the spectacular terrorist events, and one that probably would have resulted in some modification of operative Freedom of Information Act (FOIA) administration even if the attacks had not occurred. Before the prevailing security classification arrangements could be overhauled, the president found it necessary to extend such authority to classify to the secretary of health and human services, the head of the Environmental Protection Agency, and the secretary of agriculture as a consequence of the important roles their entities play in preparations to combat biological and chemical terrorism.[3]

The Bush administration's FOIA policy, which undoubtedly was being formulated prior to the September 11 attacks, was issued in an October 12, 2001, memorandum from the attorney general to the heads of all federal departments and agencies.[4] The memorandum appeared to ignore the act's presumptive right of records access and seemed to regard the application of its exemptions to the rule of disclosure as mandatory rather than permissive. The memorandum assured readers that the Department of Justice and "this Administration," in addition to being "committed to full compliance with the Freedom of Information Act," were "equally committed to protecting other fundamental values that are held by our society," including "safeguarding our national security, enhancing the effectiveness of our law enforcement agencies, protecting sensitive business information and, not least, preserving personal privacy." The attorney general encouraged each agency "to carefully consider the protection of all such values and interests when making disclosure determinations under the FOIA." Furthermore, the agencies were told, when "making these decisions, you should consult with the Department of Justice's Office of Information and Privacy when significant FOIA issues arise, as well as with our Civil Division on FOIA litigation matters." Readers were assured that "the Department of Justice will defend your decisions unless they lack a sound legal basis or present an unwarranted risk of adverse impact on the ability of other agencies to protect other important records."

The new policy was not well received by users of the act—journalists and public interest organizations, among others—or by at least one congressional overseer. In its March 2002 version of *A Citizen's Guide on Using the Freedom of Information Act,* the House Committee on Government Reform pointedly noted that "the statute requires Federal agencies to provide the fullest possible disclosure of information to the public." Continuing, it said:

> The history of the act reflects that it is a disclosure law. It presumes that requested records will be disclosed, and the agency must make its case for withholding in terms of the act's exemptions to the rule of disclosure. The application of the act's exemptions is generally permissive—to be done if information in the requested records requires protection—not mandatory. Thus, when determining whether a document or set of documents should be withheld under one of the FOIA exemptions, an agency should withhold those documents only in those cases where the agency reasonably foresees that disclosure would be harmful to an interest protected by the exemption. Similarly, when a requestor asks for a set of documents, the agency should release all documents, not a subset or selection of those documents. *Contrary to the instructions issued by the Department of Justice on October 12, 2001, the standard should not be to allow the withholding of information whenever there is merely a "sound legal basis" for doing so.*[5]

It was also in March that a memorandum from White House Chief of Staff Andrew H. Card, Jr., to the heads of executive departments and agencies reminded recipients that they and their entities had "an obligation to safeguard Government records regarding weapons of mass destruction." It was accompanied by guidance from the Information Security Oversight Office and the Justice Department's Office of Information and Privacy, in the words of the Card memo, "for reviewing Government information in your department or agency regarding weapons of mass destruction, as well as other information that could be misused to harm the security of our Nation and the safety of our people." The guidance directed the agencies "to safeguard sensitive but unclassified information related to America's homeland security." Failing to define such information, it disingenuously stated that "the Freedom of Information Act recognizes the concept by authorizing agencies to withhold from public disclosure several categories of 'sensitive but unclassified' information." It also advised the agencies to follow the attorney general's October 12, 2001, memorandum "by giving full and careful consideration to all applicable FOIA exemptions," and made certain in a question-and-answer exchange that they understood that the Bush administration wanted them to remove from their Web sites information "regarding weapons of mass destruction, as well as other information that could be misused to harm the security of our Nation and the safety of our people."[6]

Web Site Information Removal

Protecting information that enemies could use against the United States is not a new idea. "Loose lips might sink ships" was emblazoned on posters during World War II, reminding military personnel and civilians alike that the country's foes could glean useful information from overhearing casual conversations.

The federal government's current endeavors at safeguarding information, however, differs from earlier efforts, which focused on protecting information about military forces, weapons, and capabilities. Concern has broadened to include public information—information that, prior to the terrorist attacks, was notable primarily because of its value to citizens, not terrorists. Moreover, with government increasingly relying upon the Internet to disseminate information, the larger phenomenon of electronic government, or e-government, is considered, by some, to be part of the security problem.[7]

Through this popular and convenient medium, public information, including information possibly useful to terrorists, is available to everyone who has access to a computer and the Internet, whether at home, the office, a public library, a kiosk, or an Internet café. Though many sources of information exist, the very features that make the Internet a valuable tool for citizens also make it a useful device for terrorists. It contains a tremendous amount of information on a plethora of subjects, and the material is available virtually in one place. Though the scope, quality, and usefulness of information can vary from Web site to Web site, overall the information is comprehensive, detailed, and current. Text is often supplemented by graphics that range from photographs and diagrams to video and interactive displays. The extensive volume of information would be difficult to navigate if not for the search capability. Useful for finding information on a single, specific topic, the search function also aids users in finding and aggregating information from different sources and on a variety of topics.

The federal government has responded in several ways to the possibility that compromising information resides on government Web sites. Federal agencies have removed or modified information; have established firewalls around, or limited access to, some data; or, in cases where old information is of no use, have not provided updates.[8]

While the Bush administration had not previously issued any policy on agency Web sites, Attorney General John Ashcroft's October 2001 memorandum on FOIA and White House Chief of Staff Card's March 2002 memorandum, accompanied by the guidance jointly prepared by the Information Security Oversight Office and the Justice Department's Office of Information and Privacy, sent this message to agencies: "When in doubt, leave it (information) out."

Two federal entities, the Federal Bureau of Investigation (FBI) and the Office of the Secretary of Defense, have issued guidance on Web site information management. In an advisory dated January 17, 2002, the FBI provided its guidance to agencies on Web site content. Cautioning that information technology has made it easy for Internet users to retrieve "arcane and seemingly isolated information quickly," the advisory reports that "infrastructure related information available on the Internet is being accessed from sites around the world." A series of questions listed in the advisory attempts to aid government officials in evaluating their agencies' Web sites, including[9]

1 Has the information been cleared and authorized for public release?
2 Does the information provide details concerning enterprise safety and security?
   Are there alternative means of delivering sensitive security information to the intended audience?
3 Are any personal data posted (such as biographical data, addresses, etc.)?
4 How could someone intent on causing harm misuse this information?
5 Could this information be dangerous if it were used in conjunction with other publicly available data?
6 Could someone use the information to target your personnel or resources?

In a January 2003 message, Secretary of Defense Donald Rumsfeld cautioned subordinate commands that Defense Department (DOD) Web sites are likely targets of the nation's enemies, mentioned that 1,500 instances of improper posting of information had occurred over the past year, and reminded subordinate commands of DOD policies on Web site information management. Specific guidance for Web site owners advised them to

• Verify that there is a valid mission need to disseminate the information to be posted
• Apply the OPSEC [operations security] review process
• Limit details
• Use the required process for clearing information for public dissemination
• Protect information according to its sensitivity
• Ensure reviewing officials and webmasters are selected and have received appropriate training in security and release requirements in support of DOD Web policy[10]

Many federal agencies have taken steps to remove, or secure, information on their Web sites following September 11, 2001. Early examples were the Bureau of Transportation Statistics, which restricted access to its National Transportation Atlas Data Base; the Environmental Protection Agency, which removed from its Web site a database with information on chemicals used at 15,000 industrial sites around the country that had been compiled from risk management plans filed with the agency by industries; and the Nuclear Regulatory Commission, which, after briefly closing its Web site, returned with a "bare bones" version.[11] The Government Printing Office ordered federal depository libraries to destroy a CD-ROM containing government survey data on reservoirs and dams in the United States, and other depository holdings were reportedly under scrutiny for similar action.[12] These and other limitations, such as the National Aeronautics and Space Administration's restriction of public access to many of its Web sites, have been chronicled by OMB Watch, a public interest organization.[13] Among the military organizations, the Navy no longer updates tracking information on the movements of its aircraft carriers; the Army has eliminated some of its Web sites, made others available only to individuals using military servers, or has relocated them to Army Knowledge On-line, a Web portal "that provides multiple levels of access for different Army users."[14]

With each agency and executive department responsible for its own Web sites, it is difficult to know exactly what information has been removed from government sites or placed behind firewalls. By one account, no one in government knows. The executive director of OMB Watch has expressed amazement "that a nonprofit organization like OMB Watch has become the basis for [reporting] what kind of information was restricted."[15] There is no doubt, though, that the effects are extensive. Steven Aftergood, who directs the project on secrecy of the Federation of American Scientists, has observed that public information, previously considered "an unalloyed good," has come to be viewed as a possible threat in the aftermath of the September 2001 terrorist attacks. "'That will affect future disclosure policies, which will affect the nature of public policy,' he said. There are always constraints on information in wartime, but in the war on terrorism, 'it is governmentwide in ways we haven't seen before.'"[16]

Sensitive But Unclassified

The federal government has long maintained security classification arrangements for creating official secrets. Presidentially mandated procedures for classifying information were first prescribed in 1940 with E.O. 8381.[17] While information could be protected if its disclosure "might endanger national security" or "would impair the effectiveness of governmental activity in the prosecution of the war," allowance also was made for restricting information "the disclosure of which should be limited for reasons of administrative privacy."[18] A fourth level of protection—*Top Secret*—was authorized in 1950, largely to bring American classification levels into parallel with those of overseas allies.[19] However, a 1951 revision of the system limited the application of all four levels of classification to national security protection; "administrative privacy" was no longer a basis for security classification.[20] Two years later, the three-tiered classification system was introduced.[21] The *Restricted* level was eliminated, probably because it was being confused with *Restricted Data* prescribed for protection by the Atomic Energy Act of 1946.[22]

If there were those in the federal bureaucracy who were seeking some basis short of security classification to protect information, those efforts were obstructed in 1966 by FOIA.[23] The statute contained nine exemptions to its rule of records disclosure, but discretion to protect information thought to be somehow sensitive or administratively private was not permissible. In 1972, during hearings on the administration and operation of FOIA, congressional overseers pursued executive branch use of administrative markings and distribution labels as devices to restrict information access.[24] A decade later, when defense and security officials were deliberating over the security classification arrangements that would be prescribed by President Ronald Reagan in E.O. 12356, consideration was given, at one point, to reinstating a fourth level of protection just below the *Confidential* category.

The early years of the Reagan administration also saw the emergence of a policy to restrict, for reasons of national security, so-called dual-use scientific and technological information from unauthorized acquisition by the Soviet Union and its Warsaw Pact allies.[25] Dual use scientific and technological information is regarded to have both civilian and military applications or utility. Such information was regarded by defense and security officials to be "sensitive but unclassified." In fact, much of it, because it was privately generated and in private custody, was unclassifiable.[26] Consequently, other means were used to regulate the imparting of such information to foreign nationals. Primary among these were export controls under the Export Administration Act, the Arms Export Control Act, and their related regulations, and publication controls in research contracts and grant agreements.[27] For the academic and research communities, the controversy generated by such restrictions subsided in late 1985 with the issuance of National Security Decision Directive (NSDD) 189, which established a Reagan administration policy that, "to the maximum extent possible, the products of fundamental research remain unrestricted," and that "where the national security requires control, the mechanism for control of information gathered during federally-funded fundamental research in science, technology and engineering at colleges, universities and laboratories is classification."[28] For the high-technology business community, relief came later when export controls were relaxed somewhat due to a deepening trade deficit, the collapse of the Soviet Union, and the promotion of trade competitiveness.

The terrorist attacks of September 11 and new thinking about the internal security of the nation, or homeland security, prompted a return to the issue of identifying a category of sensitive information that should be protected under arrangements short of security classification. Section 892 of the Homeland Security Act of 2002 authorizes the president to prescribe and implement procedures by which relevant federal agencies shall share "homeland security information" with other federal agencies, as well as appropriate state and local government personnel. In so doing, the president is directed to "identify and safeguard homeland security information that is sensitive but unclassified."[29] The statute does not define the "sensitive but unclassified" concept. The section raises a number of questions concerning, among other considerations, information delivery and integrity arrangements, the need for and provision of personnel clearances, the detection and punishment of security breaches, and the associated costs for subnational governments, many of which are already financially challenged.[30] It seems unlikely that such information could be protected from disclosure pursuant to FOIA as it does not appear to fall clearly within any of that statute's exemptions.

Elsewhere, in section 208 of the E-Government Act of 2002, allowance is made for the modification or waiver of a required privacy impact assessment "for security reasons, or to protect classified, sensitive, or private information contained in an assessment."[31] What constitutes "sensitive" information for this section is not evident as the term is neither defined in the statute nor is its relationship, if any, explained to the "sensitive but unclassified" information mentioned in section 892 of the Homeland Security Act. Perhaps the president's information-sharing procedures required by the Homeland Security Act will prove to be instructive.

Scientific and Technical Information

As noted above, an active effort was made during the Reagan administration to prevent the unauthorized acquisition of so-called dual-use scientific and technological information—information having both civilian and military applications or utility—by the Soviet Union and its Warsaw Pact allies. A similar attempt to protect such information had been made during the Eisenhower administration.[32] To deny enemies scientific and technological information, national security controls were imposed as if the country were in a condition of declared war.

Such thinking was revived by the September 11 terrorist attacks. A technology—passenger aircraft—had been turned into a weapon. A month later, letters laced with anthrax made their appearance in government buildings. These events posed questions about the ready acquisition of scientific and technological products for use by terrorists. Similar concerns arose over the availability of scientific and technological information that might be of value to terrorists, either to create a harmful device or to position such an instrument so as to have the maximum damaging effect. There were also concerns, at least within the practitioner communities, that science and technology might be stifled by new, overreaching controls, or diverted, leaving the course of discovery interrupted and the quality of intellectual life distorted and impaired.

In January 2002 the Bush administration began withdrawing from public availability more than 6,600 technical documents of the Defense Technical Information Center dealing mainly with the production of germ and chemical weapons. The material was undergoing review by experts to determine if it could be again be made publicly accessible, in whole or with redactions. Scientific societies, such as the American Society of Microbiology, were being asked to limit some kinds of information published in research reports and professional journals. Also, consideration reportedly was being given to allowing some declassified records to be reclassified, a practice generally proscribed by the operative presidential policy order, E.O. 12958.[33]

In late May Congress completed action on the Public Health Security and Bioterrorism Preparedness and Response Act of 2002, which amended the Public Health Service Act to provide enhanced controls over certain biological agents and toxins. These included procedures governing the possession and use of such materials, such as required registration and security requirements for persons possessing, using, or transferring a listed agent or toxin.[34] Implementing regulations were issued in December.[35]

Such efforts to restrict information and communications have raised serious issues for the scientific and technological communities, not the least of which involve intent and specificity regarding the subject matter that is to be controlled. That scientists and technologists have a contribution to make to countering terrorism, and are willing to do so, was evident with the issuance of the National Research Council's report, *Making the Nation Safer,* in June 2002.[36] However, many are left with uncertainty about government control of "sensitive but unclassified" information, as was the case in the 1980s when this nebulous standard was initially introduced. To avoid government control of the publication and communication of their research results, many scientists and technologists and their university employers have declined to undertake security classified studies. In a June 2002 report, a faculty committee of the Massachusetts Institute of Technology (MIT) reaffirmed this position, recommending "that no classified research should be carried out on campus, that no student, graduate or undergraduate, should be required to have a security clearance to perform thesis research, and that no thesis research should be carried out in areas requiring access to classified materials." The committee was also unaccepting of "sensitive" and other restrictive designations for campus-based research, but remained supportive of the tradition of national security studies being performed in off-campus facilities on a security-classified basis. The report singled out the "sensitive but unclassified" category of protection, so troubling to many scientists and technologists, noting that "there is no consistent understanding or definition of what would constitute 'sensitive' information."[37]

Another concern for campus-based scientists and technologists, as the MIT faculty committee report indicates, is the possibility of greater limitations on the role of foreign students in research deemed by government officials to be in need of stricter regulation.[38] Such limitations might be imposed through visa controls, export regulations, research contract or grant conditions, or some categorical restriction such as "sensitive" information. Indeed, federal research dollars are being offered increasingly with clauses banning the involvement of unscreened foreign students and requiring official review of resulting reports prior to publication or public disclosure.[39] Many scientists believe such reviews are redundant in view of self-regulation exercised by many professional journals, and may unnecessarily prolong publication. For example, the American Society for Microbiology (ASM), according to its president, Ronald M. Atlas, has adopted specific policies and procedures for its journals to ensure that peer reviewers are alert to security concerns when examining submitted manuscripts. "Of the more than 6,000 papers ASM publishes each year," he writes, "a handful have raised specific concerns."[40]

In an October 18, 2002, joint statement, the presidents of the National Academies called for achieving "an appropriate balance between scientific openness and restrictions on public information. Restrictions are clearly needed," said the statement, "to safeguard strategic secrets; but openness also is needed to accelerate the progress of technical knowledge and enhance the nation's understanding of potential threats." Realization of a successful balance "demands clarity in the distinctions between classified and unclassified research," and the presidents felt it was "essential that these distinctions not include poorly defined categories of 'sensitive but unclassified' information that do not provide precise guidance on what information should be restricted from public access." The statement urged a close working relationship between the scientific, engineering, and health research community and the federal government "to determine which research may be related to possible new security threats and to develop principles for researchers in each field." It also called for government affirmance and maintenance of the general principle of NSDD 189 regarding federally funded fundamental research.[41]

Privacy Concerns

Another aspect of information management for maintaining homeland security involves the collection and perusal of massive amounts of personally identifiable information. One of the first legislative responses to the September 11 terrorist attacks was the USA Patriot Act, which was signed into law on October 26, 2001.[42] It was enacted to strengthen the ability of law enforcement officers to gather information on terrorist activity and suspects through enhanced authority for surveillance, communications tracking and interception, and easier access to personal records, such as those held by businesses and public libraries. The former appear to have had fewer reservations about making their records available for perusal than the latter, many librarians being distraught that patron records must be made available for examination, that state and local privacy protections may be overridden for such reviews, and that the occurrence of such inspections may not be publicly revealed.[43]

At the time the USA Patriot Act was being legislated, some thought the statute did not go far enough in granting new powers. Many months later, however, it came to be regarded by others as a clear threat to the privacy rights of Americans. In mid-December, the city council of Oakland, California, adopted a resolution opposing the act—the 19th American city to do so. Similar efforts are reportedly underway in more than 50 cities in 25 states.[44]

On June 6, 2002, just before President Bush proposed establishing a Department of Homeland Security, Attorney General Ashcroft began promoting the creation of a Citizen Corps program, initially called Volunteers in Police Service, to enlist private citizens to assist local police in various ways.[45] An iteration of this program followed shortly thereafter with Operation TIPS (Terrorism Information and Prevention System), an attempt by the Department of Justice to recruit letter carriers, utility workers, and others whose employment provided entry to private homes into a cadre of organized government informants. Such volunteers, as part of the effort at combating terrorism and securing the homeland, would report what they considered to be potential terrorist activities. These reports would be collected in a centralized database.[46]

Operation TIPS not only alarmed many Americans as an unauthorized, unwieldy domestic spying effort clearly invading personal privacy, but also ignored the many problems, including personal liability issues, already experienced with citizen informants.[47] Among those disturbed by the proposed program was the House manager of the president's Department of Homeland Security proposal, Majority Leader Dick Armey (R-Texas). His opposition was manifested in a new provision in the bill prohibiting implementation of Operation TIPS. He also added a section specifying that nothing in the legislation was to be construed as authorizing the development of a national identification system or card.[48] Both restrictions remained in the Homeland Security Act signed by the president.

Another antiterrorism effort shocked many Americans in mid-November 2002. First, news columns in the *New York Times* and, shortly thereafter, the *Washington Post* reported that the Defense Advanced Research Projects Agency (DARPA), a Pentagon entity, was funding the development of a computer system that would function as a vast electronic dragnet. Once operational, it would search personal information in databanks maintained by governments and private-sector organizations around the world in furtherance of identifying and apprehending terrorists. Heading the DARPA project, to the surprise of many, was retired Vice Admiral John M. Poindexter, a former national security adviser to President Reagan. He was the highest-ranking Reagan administration official to have been found guilty in the so-called Iran-Contra scandal—the secret sale of arms to Iran in the mid-1980s and the diversion of the resulting profits to the contra rebels in Nicaragua. Poindexter had escaped punishment when an appeals court overturned his conviction on five felony counts because his prosecution had been based upon testimony he had given before a congressional committee under a grant of immunity.[49]

Alarm bells were sounded nationally by syndicated columnist William Safire a few days after the news stories appeared. He clearly and concisely explained the implications of the DARPA computer system in terms of its use to invade a variety of personally identifiable records compiled on every American.[50] The Safire column and the public anxiety it generated brought the DARPA effort— increasingly referred to as Total Information Awareness (TIA), which was actually the name of the office headed by Poindexter—to the attention of Congress, which was fashioning the final version of the Homeland Security Act. Senator Charles E. Grassley (R-Iowa) asked the Pentagon's inspector general to review the TIA program and provide him with the results;[51] later, when a fiscal year 2003 omnibus funding bill was under consideration by the new 108th Congress, he and Senator Ron Wyden (D-Ore.) cosponsored an amendment making continued funding of the TIA effort contingent upon detailed reporting to, and approval by, Congress.[52] Nonetheless, privacy concerns have not abated because many other surveillance technologies are in active use for national security purposes.[53]

Institutional Relationships

A few weeks after the September 11 terrorist attacks, President Bush, in a memorandum October 5 to his secretaries of state, the treasury, and defense, and to the attorney general, the director of central intelligence, and the director of the FBI, set stringent limitations on the information their organizations might disclose to Congress "about the course of, and important developments in, our critical military, intelligence, and law enforcement operations." Only the recipients of the memorandum or officers expressly designated by them were authorized to brief members of Congress regarding classified or sensitive law-enforcement information, and the only members to be so briefed were the speakers of the House, the House minority leader, the Senate majority and minority leaders, and the chairs and ranking members of the House and Senate intelligence committees.[54] The restriction was greeted with bipartisan, bicameral protest.[55] Five days later, the president reversed himself and allowed intelligence briefings for a less limited group of congressional members.[56]

At the time of this attempt to limit congressional access to executive branch information, many in Congress were well aware that the president, as the head of a unitary executive, adhered to a strict doctrine of constitutional separation of powers, which resulted in his exercising prerogative powers over congressional requests for agency internal documents.[57] In July Vice President Richard B. Cheney had refused to comply with a demand letter from the General Accounting Office (GAO), an investigative arm of Congress, seeking the records of an energy task force he had chaired.[58] When GAO pressed its claim in court, government attorneys were successful in having the lawsuit dismissed.[59] In December, the Senate Committee on Environment and Public Works sought records from the Environmental Protection Agency concerning the development of air pollution policy, but, six months later, had received several hundred pages that committee staff reportedly described as "incomprehensible" and "unusable."[60] That same month, the president formally invoked executive privilege—a refusal to provide records to a coequal branch based upon the constitutional doctrine of separation of powers—against a House Committee on Government Reform subpoena for prosecution materials related to a 30-year-old organized crime case.[61] As the new year progressed, the administration grudgingly, in the face of a subpoena, provided the Senate Committee on Governmental Affairs records of White House contacts with the Enron Corporation.[62] In August the president sought to keep secret details of President Clinton's last-day pardons by invoking executive privilege in U.S. District Court in response to a lawsuit seeking access to the materials.[63]

It was also just after the beginning of 2002 that Tom Ridge, director of the Office of Homeland Security, began to become embroiled in controversy over his refusal to testify before congressional committees. Among the first to request his appearance were Senator Robert C. Byrd (D-W.Va.) and Senator Ted Stevens (R-Alaska), respectively the chairman and ranking minority member of the Committee on Appropriations. Ridge turned down their initial, informal invitation and later formal requests of March 15 and April 4.[64] When Ridge declined the request of Representative Ernest Istook, Jr. (R-Okla.), chairman of the House Appropriations Subcommittee on Treasury, Postal Service, and General Government, appropriations for the Executive Office of the President were threatened, prompting Ridge to offer to meet with Istook and other subcommittee members in an informal session.[65] Thereafter, Ridge arranged other informal briefings with members of the House Committee on Government Reform and a group of senators, and agreed to a similar session with members of the House Committee on Energy and Commerce. These informal meetings, however, did not appear to abate the controversy that Ridge's refusals to testify had generated.[66]

In August 2002 the Department of Justice rebuffed a letter from the chairman and ranking minority member of the House Committee on the Judiciary posing 50 questions on the department's exercise of its new antiterrorism powers. The department indicated it would send its responses to the House Permanent Select Committee on Intelligence, which had not sought the information and had no plans to conduct any oversight of the USA Patriot Act.[67] A few days later, the conflict escalated when the department refused to provide the Judiciary Committee a copy of an unclassified opinion issued by the special court that oversees secret intelligence warrants pursuant to the Foreign Intelligence Surveillance Act. As a consequence, the committee chair indicated he would subpoena the attorney general to obtain the information sought by the panel.[68] The department thereafter responded to the questions posed earlier, reportedly revealing that it had made relatively limited use of its new antiterrorism powers, but had found such authorities to be invaluable in key cases.[69]

Later, when signing the Homeland Security Act into law on November 25, 2002, President Bush, in his signing statement, proffered views regarding several provisions in the new law indicative of his adherence to a strict doctrine of constitutional separation of powers. For example, he noted that one section provided that voluntarily shared critical infrastructure information shall not be used or disclosed by any federal employee without the written consent of the person or entity submitting the information, except when disclosure of the information would be to Congress or the comptroller general. "The executive branch," he indicated, "does not construe this provision to impose any independent or affirmative requirement to share such information with the Congress or the Comptroller General and shall construe it in any event in a manner consistent with the constitutional authorities of the President to supervise the unitary executive branch and to withhold information the disclosure of which could impair foreign relations, the national security, the deliberative processes of the Executive, or the performance of the Executive's constitutional duties."[70]

Concerning a section providing for the preparation of reports by the Homeland Security Science and Technology Advisory Committee and their transmittal to Congress, the signing statement said this provision would be construed "in a manner consistent with the constitutional authorities of the President to supervise the unitary executive branch and to recommend for the consideration of the Congress such measures as the President judges necessary and expedient." Similarly, sections of the statute which "purport to require the submission of budget requests for the new Department to the Congress and to require such requests to be in a particular form" would be construed "in a manner consistent with the constitutional authority of the President to recommend for the consideration of the Congress such measures as the President judges necessary and expedient."[71]

E-Government Implications

As reflected in this overview, the information management steps taken by federal officials in furtherance of homeland security are bringing about a change in the balance between the security and the public availability of government information. For the foreseeable future, it appears that safeguarding the nation—an undertaking that has many components, including scrubbing potentially compromising information from government Web sites—will continue to trump other objectives and other values. As a result of the changes made to agency Web sites after September 11, less information is available to citizens. However, to vote responsibly, think independently, and act wisely, citizens need information about issues, government programs and policies, and the activities and decisions of public officials. Furthermore, the public and its surrogates, such as the press and consumer interest groups, need information to exercise watchful oversight over the people's government.

This new reality, in turn, may well affect public confidence in government. Generally, the American electorate appears to continue to trust the federal government in the aftermath of the September 11 attacks. In the long run, however, citizens may not be willing to settle for "information lite." Granted, some of the public information that has been removed from, or has been modified at, agency Web sites may still be available in other formats or venues, but the loss of convenience could translate into a loss of accessibility for some.

Less information may make it more difficult for citizens to hold government officials accountable for their decisions and actions. Members of the public may not know what questions to ask, or, if they are able to identify salient issues, they may not be able to obtain the details they need. Yet, these are two benefits—accountability and accessible information—that citizens expect to reap from electronic government. Hart-Teeter conducted a nationwide poll of adults in November 2001 for the Council for Excellence in Government. When asked to name the most important benefit of e-government, 30 percent of the respondents chose accountability and 17 percent selected greater access to information. The remaining respondents chose convenient services (15 percent) and cost-effectiveness (14 percent).[72]

Electronic government is hailed by some as a means to transform government. In the introduction to its report on e-government, the Council for Excellence in Government states

> Electronic government can fundamentally recast the connection between people and their government. It can make government far more responsive to the will of the people and greatly improve transactions between them. It can also help all of us to take a much more active part in the democratic process.[73]

However, the removal, or withholding, of what was once considered public information from agency Web sites may thwart the promise of e-government. In the aftermath of September 11, the situation may be one of relative deprivation: expectations may be higher than the information agency Web sites are delivering to the public. Even if the expectations of most people are met, the ongoing debate over the removal, or withholding, of information could well detract from the luster of e-government.

Until September 11, customer service was the focus of e-government; now, security is the focus, suggests Brookings Institution scholar Paul Light.[74] Agencies may experience heightened tension as they strive to balance the principle of open government with concerns about homeland security. Two groups of agency personnel would feel this tension most keenly, those "who aim to improve public access and those who try to maximize security."[75] Members of the former group could envision electronic government as an initiative designed to offer citizens the ultimate experience in customer service, where the public "can choose to get information, conduct transactions, or communicate with their elected representatives. . . . In short, [the public] can choose how and when to connect with government, with the ability to choose appropriate levels of privacy and security."[76] Personnel charged with protecting homeland security can, and do, see agency Web sites as information sources potentially useful to terrorists. Testifying at a congressional hearing in 1999, a National Volunteer Fire Council representative cautioned: "There [is] no reason to provide terrorists with a Home Shopping Network to the most hazardous sites in the country."[77]

Tension, and perhaps confusion, over the role or objectives of e-government may be fueled by the different messages sent by the Bush administration. While agencies have been changing Web site content and the attorney general has issued guidance on FOIA administration that encourages government personnel to err on the side of the nondisclosure of requested records, the administration continues, in other forums, to tout e-government and its own efforts in this area.

In early 2002 the Bush administration revamped the government's portal, Firstgov, and Mark Forman, associate director for information technology and e-government at the Office of Management and Budget (OMB), released a report titled "E-Government Strategy." It recounted the goals of the president's expanding e-government initiative:

- Make it easy for citizens to obtain service and interact with the federal government
- Improve government efficiency and effectiveness
- Improve government's responsiveness to citizens[78]

Work began on the strategy on August 9, 2001, with the launch of the E-Government Task Force. The report presents a vision and a strategy for e-government; identifies problems that have prevented government from fully realizing the potential of e-government; provides the task force's approach and findings; and discusses recommendations and an implementation strategy. No mention is made of the terrorist attacks, concerns that have arisen about the dissemination of public information on agency Web sites, agency efforts to protect information, or the effect such actions might have on the administration's vision for e-government. By publicly presenting two different views of e-government—as an avenue to potentially compromising information, and as a key means for improving customer service to citizens—the administration is certainly delivering a mixed message.

The Bush administration's plan for e-government is also at odds with the view of federal chief information officers (CIOs) regarding their responsibilities since September 11. The Information Technology Association of America (ITAA) conducted a study of federal CIOs between August and December 2001. At the beginning of its report on the results of this study, ITAA acknowledged that two major events affected the survey results: the transition to a new administration and the terrorist attacks. In writing about the latter event, ITAA said

The policies, guidance, organization and resources associated with winning this new war have yet to be played out. However, it is clear that the [federal] CIOs recognized that their role in this effort is of the highest priority. And within that role they recognize security is the focus. Each is addressing security primarily from answering the call for homeland security versus meeting requirements to provide a foundation for e-government.[79]

ITAA reported that security was one of the top three issues for almost every CIO. One consequence of the heightened emphasis on security was "an indication that the CIOs are putting their 'best' people on security at the indirect expense of e-government initiatives."[80] An implication of the ITAA survey results for e-government at the agency level is that security will be emphasized, not e-government as a customer-driven initiative. Moreover, as indicated by the ITAA results, resources likely will be shifted to security efforts. [For a detailed examination of e-government, see the following Special Report—*Ed.*]

Conclusion

Information management for reasons of homeland security is still evolving in terms of both policy and practice. Developments thus far clearly reflect a change in the balance between the security and the public availability of government information. Security is the dominant concern. Additional changes can be expected regarding, among other considerations, government Web site content, "sensitive but unclassified" information, and the status of electronic government, as well as some areas not examined here, such as the accessibility of certain kinds of information to the press. The "engine" in this information management is the executive in the federal government. Some regulatory initiatives in this regard have relied upon an expansion of older powers, such as security classification authority. Others have derived from new grants, such as broader information gathering pursuant to the USA Patriot Act, specifying biological agents and toxins to be controlled under the Public Health Security and Bioterrorism Preparedness and Response Act, and determining "sensitive but unclassified" information as prescribed by the Homeland Security Act.

During the latter half of the 20th century, it has been observed, presidents relied on two doctrines to justify executive initiatives in furtherance of national security: inherent presidential power and post hoc congressional ratification. The president's national security powers became powers to act in peacetime as if the country were at war.[81] Now, in the aftermath of the September 11 terrorist attacks, it is said that the nation is at war. Whether one agrees or disagrees with that determination, recent history would seem to recommend close attention to, and careful consideration of, the policies made and the actions taken in the name of homeland security.

Notes

1. See U.S. Office of Homeland Security, *National Strategy for Homeland Security* (July 2002), p. 2, where it is stated: "Homeland security is a concerted national effort to prevent terrorist attacks within the United States, reduce America's vulnerability to terrorism, and minimize the damage and recover from attacks that do occur."

2. 116 Stat. 2135 at 2253.

3. See Alison Mitchell, "Classified Information: Bush Gives Secrecy Power to Public Health Secretary," *New York Times,* December 20, 2001, p. B6; *Federal Register,* vol. 66, December 12, 2001, p. 64347; Ibid., vol. 67, May 9, 2002, p. 31109; Ibid., vol. 67, September 30, 2002, p. 61465.

4. U.S. Department of Justice, Office of the Attorney General, "The Freedom of Information Act," Memorandum for the Heads of all Federal Departments and Agencies, October 12, 2001; available at http://www.usdoj.gov/04foia/011012.htm.

5. U.S. Congress, House Committee on Government Reform, *A Citizen's Guide on Using the Freedom of Information Act and the Privacy Act of 1974 to Request Government Records,* 107th Congress, 2nd session, H. Rept. 107-371 (GPO, 2002), p. 3 (*emphasis added*).

6. White House Office, Chief of Staff, "Action to Safeguard Information Regarding Weapons of Mass Destruction and Other Sensitive Documents Related to Homeland Security," Memorandum for the Heads of Executive Departments and Agencies, March 19, 2002, accompanied by Information Security Oversight Office and Department of Justice, Office of Information and Privacy, "Safeguarding Information Regarding Weapons of Mass Destruction and Other Sensitive Records Related to Homeland Security," Memorandum for Departments and Agencies, undated; available at http://www.usdoj.gov/oip/foiapost/2002foiapost10.htm. The version available at this Web site does not include the question-and-answer clarifications accompanying the original documents.

7. The concept and development of electronic government are discussed in the following Special Report, Harold C. Relyea and Henry B. Hogue, "The Development of Electronic Government in the United States: The Federal Policy Experience."

8. Federal agencies are not alone in responding in this fashion. Michael Levi of the Federation of American Scientists (FAS) is reviewing documents posted on the FAS Web site and already has removed some items, such as satellite photographs of nuclear facilities. An Internet search engine enterprise, Google, is working with the government to remove information from its cache that government has removed from its Web sites. (Ariana Eunjung Cha, "Risks Prompt U.S. to Limit Access to Data," *New York Times,* February 24, 2002, p. A10.) In New York, Governor George Pataki's administration has issued a policy restricting what information state agencies may place on the Internet. (James C. McKinley, Jr., "State Pulls Data from Internet in Attempt to Thwart Terrorists," *New York Times,* February 26, 2002, p. A23).

9. U.S. Department of Justice, Federal Bureau of Investigation, National Infrastructure Protection Center, *Internet Content Advisory: Considering the Unintended Audience,* Advisory 02-001, January 17, 2002; available at http://www.nipc.gov/warnings/advisories/2002/02-OO1.htm.

10. U.S. Department of Defense, Office of the Secretary, "Web Site OPSEC Discrepancies," message to subordinate commands, January 14, 2003.

11. Guy Gugliotta, "Agencies Scrub Web Sites of Sensitive Chemical Data," *Washington Post,* October 4, 2001, p. A29; Robin Toner, "Reconsidering Security, U.S. Clamps Down on Agency Web Sites," *New York Times,* October 28, 2001, p. B4.

12. Eric Lichtblau, "Response to Terror; Rising Fears That What We Do Can Hurt Us," *Los Angeles Times,* part A, part 1, November 18, 2001, p. 1; also see Saragail Runyon Lynch, "GPO Recalls of Depository Documents," *Journal of Government Information,* vol. 22, January-February 1995, pp. 23–31.

13. OMB Watch, *The Post-September 11 Environment: Access to Government Information,* undated; available at http://www.ombwatch.org/article/articleprint/213/-1/104.

14. Hampton Stephens, "Security Concerns Prompt Army to Review Web Sites, Access," *Defense Information and Electronics Report,* October 26, 2001; available at http://www.fas.org/sgp/news/2001/10/dier102601.html.

15. Stephen Chiger, "Has Terrorism Curtailed E-Government?" *PC World.Com,* September 11, 2002; available at http://www.pcworld.com/resource/printable/article/0,aid,104796,00.asp.

16. William Matthews, "Walking a Fine Line on Web Access," *Federal Computer Week,* February 4, 2002, p. 44.

17. 3 C.F.R., 1938–1943 Comp., pp. 634–635.

18. Harold C. Relyea, "The Evolution of Government Information Security Classification Policy: A Brief Overview, 1775–1973," in U.S. Congress, Senate Committee on Government Operations, *Government Secrecy,* hearings, 93rd Congress, 2nd session (GPO, 1974), pp. 854–855.

19. E.O. 10104, 3 C.F.R., 1949–1953 Comp., pp. 298–299.

20. E.O. 10290, 3 C.F.R., 1949–1953 Comp., pp. 789–797.

21. E.O. 10501, 3 C.F.R., 1949–1953 Comp., pp. 979–986.

22. See 60 Stat. 766–768.

23. 5 U.S.C. 552.

24. See U.S. Congress, House Committee on Government Operations, *U.S. Government Information Policies and Practices—Security Classification Problems Involving Subsection (b)(1) of the Freedom of Information Act,* hearings, 92nd Congress, 2nd session (GPO, 1972), pp. 2283–2505, 2929–2937.

25. See Harold C. Relyea, *Silencing Science: National Security Controls and Scientific Communication* (Ablex, 1994).

26. Such private information might become subject to government protection if it was included in a patent application, which could become subject to a secrecy order under the Invention Secrecy Act (35 U.S.C. 181-188), or if it constituted *Restricted Data,* which could be confiscated and protected under the Atomic Energy Act (42 U.S.C. 2014(y), 2071, 2073, 2077, 2161, et seq.).

27. See 50 U.S.C. 2401 et seq.; 22 U.S.C. 2751 et seq.; 15 C.F.R. 730 et seq.; 22 C.F.R. 120 et seq.

28. The full text of NSDD-189 may be found in Relyea, *Silencing Science,* pp. 213–214.

29. 116 Stat. 2135 at 2253.

30. Among available criminal punishment authorities is 18 U.S.C. 641 governing stolen or misappropriated government property or records.

31. P.L. 107-347, section 208.

32. See Relyea, *Silencing Science,* p. 77.

33. William J. Broad, "U.S. Is Tightening Rules on Keeping Scientific Secrets," *New York Times,* February 17, 2002, pp. 1, 13.

34. 116 Stat. 594 at 637.

35. See *Federal Register,* vol. 67, December 13, 2002, pp. 76885–76905, 76907–76938.

36. See National Research Council, *Making the Nation Safer: The Role of Science and Technology in Countering Terrorism* (National Academy Press, 2002).

37. Ad Hoc Faculty Committee on Access to and Disclosure of Scientific Information, Massachusetts Institute of Technology, *In the Public Interest* (MIT, June 12, 2002), pp. ii–iv.

38. See Mark Clayton, "Password, Please," *Christian Science Monitor,* September 24, 2002, pp. 11, 14–16.

39. Associated Press, "Researchers' Dilemma: Grants With Strings," *Washington Times,* January 5, 2003, p. A4.

40. Ronald M. Atlas, "National Security and the Biological Research Community," *Science,* vol. 298, October 25, 2002, p. 753.

41. See National Academies, "Statement on Science and Security in an Age of Terrorism from Bruce Alberts, Wm. A. Wulf, and Harvey Fineberg, Presidents of the National Academies," October 18, 2002; available at http://www4.nationalacademies.org/news.nsf. 0a254cd9b53e0bc585256777004e74d3/64b44637d96e335385256ca70072dccb?Open Document; William J. Broad, "Security Measures: Researchers Say Science Is Hurt by Secrecy Policy Set Up by the White House," *New York Times,* October 19, 2002, p. A8.

42. 115 Stat. 272.

43. Concerning businesses, see Daniela Deane, "Legal Niceties Aside . . .," *Washington Post,* November 7, 2001, pp. E1, E6; Robert O'Harrow, Jr., "In Terror War, Privacy vs. Security," *Washington Post,* June 3, 2002, pp. A1, A6; John Schwartz, "Some Companies Will Release Customer Records on Request," *New York Times,* December 18, 2002, p. A16. Concerning libraries, see Adam Clymer, "Privacy: Librarians Get Advice on Handling Government Requests for Information on Readers," *New York Times,* December 12, 2002, p. A23; Laura Flanders, "Librarians Under Siege," *The Nation,* August 5/12, 2002, pp. 42–44; David E. Rosenbaum, "Questions of Confidentiality: Competing Principles Leave Some Professionals Debating Responsibility to Government," *New York Times,* November 23, 2001, p. B7.

44. Michael Janofsky, "Cities Wary of Antiterror Tactics Pass Civil Liberties Resolutions," *New York Times,* December 23, 2002, pp. A1, A13.

45. Jerry Seper, "Ashcroft Promotes Initiative for Volunteers to Aid Police," *Washington Times,* May 31, 2002, p. A6.

46. Bill Berkowitz, "AmeriSnitch," *The Progressive,* May 2002, pp. 27–28; Dan Eggen, "Ashcroft: No Database for TIPS," *Washington Post,* July 26, 2002, p. A10; Ellen Sorokin, "Planned Volunteer-Informant Corps Elicits '1984' Fears," *Washington Times,* July 16, 2002, p. A4.

47. See Ariana Eunjung Cha, "Citizen Tips on Terrorists: Leads or Liabilities?" *Washington Post,* June 19, 2002, pp. A8–A9.

48. Ellen Sorokin, "Security Bill Loses ID Card, Domestic Spies," *Washington Times,* July 19, 2002, p. A15.

49. John Markoff, "Intelligence: Pentagon Plans a Computer System That Could Peek at Personal Data of Americans," *New York Times,* November 9, 2002, p. A10; Robert O'Harrow, Jr., "U.S. Hopes to Check Computers Globally," *Washington Post,* November 12, 2002, p. A4.

50. William Safire, "You Are a Suspect," *New York Times,* November 14, 2002, p. A35.

51. Associated Press, "Grassley Wants Review of Database," *Washington Times,* November 24, 2002, p. A3.

52. See *Congressional Record,* vol. 149, January 23, 2003, pp. S1412–S1416 (daily edition); Adam Clymer, "Surveillance: Senate Votes to Curb Project to Search for Terrorists in Databases and Internet Mail," *New York Times,* January 24, 2003, p. A12.

53. See Michael Moss and Ford Fessenden, "New Tools for Domestic Spying, and Qualms," *New York Times,* December 10, 2002, pp. A1, A18; John Markoff and John Schwartz, "Many Tools of Big Brother Are Up and Running," *New York Times,* December 23, 2002, pp. C1, C4.

54. White House Office, "Disclosures to the Congress," Memorandum to the Secretary of State, Secretary of the Treasury, Secretary of Defense, Attorney General, Director of Central Intelligence, and Director of the Federal Bureau of Investigation, October 5, 2001.

55. See Dave Boyer, "Bush's Curbs on Classified Briefings Irk Congress, *Washington Times,* October 10, 2001, pp. A1, A8; Dana Milbank and Peter Slevin, "Bush Edict on Briefings Irks Hill," *Washington Post,* October 10, 2001, pp. A1, A4.

56. Joseph Curl and Dave Boyer, "Bush Resumes Hill Intelligence Briefings," *Washington Times,* October 11, 2001, p. A3.

57. See Ellen Nakashima and Dan Eggen, "White House Seeks to Restore Its Privileges," *Washington Post,* September 10, 2001, p. A2.

58. Dana Milbank, "Cheney Records Demanded," *Washington Post,* July 19, 2001, pp. A1, A4; Joseph Curl, "Cheney Refuses Demand by GAO," *Washington Times,* July 27, 2001, pp. A1, A16.

59. Adam Clymer, "Judge Says Cheney Needn't Give Data on Energy Policy to G.A.O.," *New York Times,* December 10, 2002, pp. A1, A25; Neeley Tucker, "Suit Versus Cheney Is Dismissed," *Washington Post,* December 10, 2002, pp. A1, A13.

60. Dana Milbank, "Growing Conflict Over Presidential Powers," *Washington Post,* December 15, 2001, p. A1; Eric Pianin, "Senators to Subpoena White House," *Washington Post,* June 24, 2002, p. A2.

61. Joseph Curl, "Bush Uses Privilege Power to Bar Hill from Probes," *Washington Times,* December 14, 2001, p. A4; Ellen Nakashima, "Bush Invokes Executive Privilege on Hill," *Washington Post,* December 14, 2001, p. A43.

62. See Mike Allen, "Subpoena Urged on Enron Records," *Washington Post,* May 18, 2002, p. A7; Mike Allen, "Panel Demands Enron Papers," *Washington Post,* May 23, 2002, pp. A1, A4; Richard A. Oppel, Jr., "White House to Supply New List of Enron Contacts," *New York Times,* May 25, 2002, pp. B1, B3; Mike Allen, "White House Gives Lieberman Limited Access to Enron Data," *Washington Post,* June 4, 2002, p. A2; Staff writer, "Senate Panel Gets Some Enron Data," *Washington Post,* June 5, 2002, p. A4.

63. George Lardner, Jr., "Bush Seeks Secrecy for Pardon Discussions," *Washington Post,* August 27, 2002, pp. A1, A7.

64. Dave Boyer, "Ridge Reluctant to Testify in Senate," *Washington Times,* February 27, 2002, p. A4; Alison Mitchell, "Congressional Hearings: Letter to Ridge Is Latest Jab in Fight Over Balance of Powers," *New York Times,* March 5, 2002, p. A8; Mark Preston, "Byrd Holds Firm," *Roll Call,* April 18, 2002, pp. 1, 26.

65. George Archibald, "Panel Ties Funding to Ridge Testimony," *Washington Times,* March 22, 2002, pp. A1, A14; George Archibald, "White House Mollifies House Panel," *Washington Times,* March 23, 2002, pp. A1, A4.

66. Bill Miller, "Ridge Will Meet Informally with 2 House Committees," *Washington Post,* April 4, 2002, p. A15; George Archibald, "Ridge Attends Private Meeting on Hill," *Washington Times,* April 11, 2002, p. A4; Elizabeth Becker, "Ridge Briefs House Panel, But Discord Is Not Resolved," *New York Times,* April 11, 2002, p. A17; Bill Miller, "From Bush Officials, a Hill Overture and a Snub," *Washington Post,* April 11, 2002, p. A27; Amy Fagan, "Democrats Irked by Ridge's Closed House Panel Meeting," *Washington Times,* April 12, 2002, p. A6; Stephen Dinan, "Ridge Briefing Called 'Stunt'" *Washington Times,* May 3, 2002, p. A9; Bill Miller, "On Homeland Security Front, a Rocky Day on the Hill," *Washington Post,* May 3, 2002, p. A25.

67. Adam Clymer, "Justice Dept. Balks at Effort to Study Antiterror Powers," *New York Times,* August 15, 2002, p. A14.

68. Dan Eggen, "Ashcroft Assailed on Policy Review," *Washington Post,* August 21, 2002, p. A2; Audrey Hudson, "Ashcroft Threatened with Hill Subpoena," *Washington Times,* August 21, 2002, p. A4.

69. Dan Eggen, "Justice Made Limited Use of New Powers, Panel Told," *Washington Post,* October 18, 2002, p. A11.

70. *Weekly Compilation of Presidential Documents,* vol. 38, November 25, 2002, pp. 2092–2093.

71. Ibid., p. 2093.

72. Council for Excellence in Government, *E-Government: To Connect, Protect, and Serve Us,* undated (released February 26, 2002); available at http://www.excelgov.org/techcon/0225poll.

73. Council for Excellence in Government, *E-Government, The Next American Revolution,* undated, p. 2 (released September 28, 2000); available at http://www.excelgov.org/egovpoll/lindex.htm.

74. Patricia Daukantas and Preeti Vasishtha, "New World Order Pits Security Against Web," *Government Computer News,* February 4, 2002, p. 1; available at http://www.gcn.com/21-3/news/17913-I.html.

75. Ibid.

76. Council for Excellence in Government, *E-Government, The Next American Revolution,* p. 5.

77. David Whitman, "A Highly Explosive Mixture," *U.S. News and World Report,* October 22, 2001, p. 32.

78. U.S. Office of Management and Budget, Associate Director for Information Technology and E-Government, *E-Government Strategy,* (February 27, 2002), p. 1; available at http://www.whitehouse.gov/omb/inforeg/egovstrategy.pdf.

79. Information Technology Association of America, *The Federal Information Age: Stakeholders, Customers, Citizens* (February 2002), p. 6; available at http://www.itaa.org/es/itaaciosurvey.pdf. QUERIED

80. Ibid., p. 7.

81. John Shattuck, "National Security a Decade After Watergate," *Democracy,* vol. 3, Winter 1983, pp. 61–62.

The Development of Electronic Government in the United States: The Federal Policy Experience

Harold C. Relyea

Specialist in American National Government
Congressional Research Service

Henry B. Hogue

Analyst in American National Government
Congressional Research Service

The term "electronic government" entered public discourse only a decade ago, but its roots can be traced back into the 19th century to the development, in American national government, of ways to record and communicate information in the furtherance of democratic governance. In more recent times, a series of technological, conceptual, and policy developments during the latter half of the 20th century converged to create the basis for contemporary e-government in the United States. Like earlier tools that were adapted by public administrators, digital computing and the Internet have also been adopted and developed to further governmental goals. As the federal government has adopted and adapted these tools, policy has been developed through statute and administrative directives. Through this process, elected officials have addressed traditional concerns raised by the use of these new technologies in government.

E-government has been touted as a means to increase the efficiency of, and public access to, government. At the same time, the arrival of e-government has raised concerns about the privacy of electronic transactions with government and the security of sensitive information held by government. Four good government goals—effective management, information access, privacy, and security—can sometimes be pursued in tandem with each other. In some cases, however, these goals are in tension with one another. For example, increased public access may lead to slower decision making, lower efficiency, or greater security risks.[1] Greater attention to individual privacy will almost certainly decrease efficiency and access. The resolution of these tensions in U.S. national government, through interwoven technological, conceptual, and policy changes, occurs in the context of an ever-evolving political environment, as the saliency of certain governmental concerns grows and that of others declines.

This overview begins with a brief description of the roots of electronic government in the mid- and late 20th century. It then examines policy developments in institutional and political contexts, tracking those developments in recent Congresses, the Clinton administration, and the current Bush administration.

Brief History

In the United States, e-government at the federal level may appear to have emerged, fully formed, in the late 20th century. However, its technological, conceptual, and policy roots can be traced to earlier periods in the nation's history.[2] Fundamentally, e-government is based in the needs of democratic government for accountability, through records creation, preservation, and accessibility, and for communication among elected officials, public administrators, and citizens. In the earliest days of the republic, existing technologies, such as the printing press, were employed for these purposes, and the national government enacted laws providing for the printing, distribution, and preservation of official documents and publications. In the mid-19th century, the telegraph extended the range and immediacy of governmental communications. By the beginning of the 20th century, the telephone was in use throughout government in Washington. Each of these technologies had broad application in the private sector as well. Many incremental technological developments contributed to the advent of e-government as it is known today. These steps included the development of digital computing, networked computers, the Internet, and the World Wide Web. The federal government, research universities (often through government funding), and the private sector contributed to this evolution. The development of computers was under way prior to World War II, and defense needs during the war focused resources and personnel on their further development. The Electronic Numerical Integrator and Computer (ENIAC), funded by the Army Ordnance Department to compute ballistic firing tables, was completed in the winter of 1944–1945. It was succeeded by the Electronic Discrete Variable Computer (EDVAC), also funded through the Army Ordnance Department. These early machines were very large, very expensive, very slow by today's standards, and dependent on the functioning of vacuum tubes, but they were able to do the high-speed calculations necessary for complex mathematical problems. Later generations of computers became smaller, cheaper, faster, more reliable, and had added memory.

The roots of the Internet lie in the development of computer networking, through federally funded projects, beginning in the 1960s. The precursor of the Internet, ARPANET, was developed with funding from the Advanced Research Projects Agency (ARPA, later renamed the Defense Advanced Research Projects Agency, or DARPA), a Pentagon research and development organization. Among other things, networking facilitated more efficient use of expensive computing resources by allowing networked computers to be shared. ARPANET became operational in 1969 and, during the 1970s, was accessible only to ARPA contractors. Electronic mail (e-mail), developed in early 1972, became the most popular use of ARPANET. Over time, computer networks were developed by other institutions as well. In the 1980s the National Science Foundation (NSF) created NSFNET, which provided the infrastructure foundation of the Internet. NSFNET evolved into a network of regional networks, which were, in turn, connected to institutional systems. The Internet continued to grow, and, for the most part, has been transferred from NSF management to the private sector.

By the early 1990s, the Internet was used by millions of people around the world. The broader use of the Internet has been facilitated by the creation of the World Wide Web. The Web, based in the document format Hypertext Markup Language (HTML), allowed for the use of the Internet by people with little technical knowledge or aptitude. The development of Web browsers and search engines, which help users navigate through the Web and search for information, further facilitated the spread of Internet utilization. Wireless Internet access, faster processing speeds, greater storage capacity, and other technological developments continue to make information storage and communication faster and easier.

Conceptual and technological developments have been entwined during the evolution of e-government. Undoubtedly, many participants on the technological side envisioned the potential future uses of their developments and applications, although they may not have published their ideas. Two visionaries who did commit their ideas to paper were Vannevar Bush and J. C. R. Licklider. Conceptual developments can also be found in writings of elected officials and government bureaucrats, as discussed further below.

Vannevar Bush, an engineer by training, taught at the Massachusetts Institute of Technology, served as a president of the Carnegie Institution of Washington, chaired the National Defense Research Committee, and served as the head of the Office of Scientific Research and Development under President Franklin D. Roosevelt. In 1939 Bush initially drafted an article concerning the problem of limited human memory and information overload; it was later accepted for publication in the *Atlantic Monthly* in 1945.[3] He envisioned a machine that could address these growing difficulties. As he conceived it, "every time one combines and records facts in accordance with established logical processes, the creative aspect of thinking is concerned only with the selection of the data and the process to be employed, and the manipulation thereafter is repetitive in nature and hence a fit matter to be relegated to the machines."[4] Such a machine, which he called a "memex," would act as "a sort of mechanical private file and library," enabling the user to store and retrieve information with ease. Ideally, the machine would, to the degree possible, imitate human cognition, operating through associative selection and retrieval. Bush foresaw the need for technological aids to human memory and processing, and the need to attend to the human–machine interaction in the development of those aids. The federal government, with its tremendous growth in size and complexity during the mid-20th century, was among those institutions that would come to rely on the realization of these ideas.

In a 1960 essay, "Man-Computer Symbiosis," Joseph Carl Robnett "Lick" Licklider, an experimental psychologist by training, forecast the development of a close cooperative relationship between humans and computers.[5] Like Bush, Licklider was interested in the ability of machines to aid humans in the thinking and decision-making processes. By the time of his essay, however, computers were already in use for some of the information storage and retrieval functions Bush had discussed, as well as for data processing. Licklider envisioned going beyond these functions "to let computers facilitate formulative thinking as they now facilitate the solution of formulated problems, and . . . to enable men and computers to cooperate in making decisions and controlling complex situations without inflexible dependence on predetermined programs."[6] Computers would aid formulative thinking by answering questions, producing simulated models, graphically displaying results, and drawing on past experience to extrapolate solutions for new situations. Humans would still set goals, formulate questions and hypotheses, and come up with the mechanisms, procedures, and models.

Licklider, together with his colleagues, also envisioned widespread communication between computers and between humans through computers. In 1962 he and Welden E. Clark published "On-Line Man-Computer Communication," widely regarded as one of the first conceptualizations of the Internet.[7] Licklider and Robert W. Taylor coauthored "The Computer as a Communication Device," which was published in 1968.[8] In this article, they saw the potential of linked computers to allow people, either in the same room or at a distance, to more clear-ly articulate their internal models during communication. In a group setting, each participant would have access not only to the content of the speaker's presentation but also to any data, models, or other information that might underlie that presen-tation, provided the speaker had stored it on his or her own computer. They also foresaw the linkage of multiple interactive networked communities into a "super-community" in which all members of all the communities would commonly share the data resources and programs of the supercommunity. The result would be a greater ability to express interests, ideas, and models at greater depth, with easier access to the underlying precepts, among greater numbers of people.

The actualization of these ideas has been so profound that present-day gov-ernment (and much of the rest of American society) could hardly be imagined without it. Governmental use of computers for data collection, processing, stor-age, and dissemination, and for assistance with modeling, decision making, and communication, is ubiquitous. As early as 1986, members of Congress were aware of this, as reflected in a report by the House Committee on Government Opera-tions.[9] The report observed that an "ongoing revolution in computer and telecom-munication technology [was] producing major changes in the way that the Federal Government collect[ed], maintain[ed], and disseminat[ed] information." It fur-ther noted that "Information and the ability to access it quickly and reliably have become a source of political and economic power."[10] While the report saw the potential for these changes to improve government, it also sounded a cautionary note concerning the potential for abuses to occur, particularly where such changes made obsolete existing practical limitations and legal structures govern-ing many aspects of the government information life cycle. A 1988 report by the Office of Technology Assessment (OTA) echoed some of these concerns, and highlighted the need for new policies and administrative arrangements to plan and manage an emerging electronic government phenomenon and make effective use of information technology (IT).[11]

In 1993 OTA published another report, which, among other things, pointed to the movement, by agencies, "beyond internal automation to the application of computers and telecommunications for delivering services and interacting with clients."[12] The report foresaw an inevitable increase in the use, by the federal government, of electronic delivery, largely in the furtherance of the good govern-ment management goals of efficiency, economy, and effectiveness. The report expressed concern about the lack of overall governmental strategy and vision in this area, however, and recommended that Congress take an active role in cor-recting this problem.

Also in 1993, the Clinton administration reform initiative, denominated the National Performance Review (NPR) and led by Vice President Al Gore, released its first report.[13] It was filled with recommendations to fulfill its title theme of "creating a government that works better and costs less." As part of its blueprint for improvement, the report called for an expansion of "electronic government," with more widespread and effective use of information technology to manage the operations and information of federal agencies and to deliver services. In the introduction to a later NPR report, released in February 1997, Vice President Gore expressed the NPR vision for electronic government more broadly.

> Taken together, the recommendations here paint a picture of the kind of government we should have as we begin the next century. It will be a government where all Americans have the opportunity to get services electronically and where, aided by technology, the productivity of government operations will be soaring.[14]

Technological developments have provided the means for the development of e-government, and conceptual developments have given that development direction. It has been the role of policy, as largely established by elected leaders, to resolve the inevitable tensions among the consequences and potential consequences of these developments in the federal government. In that forum, the striving for efficient, economical, effective, and productive government is measured against other concerns of democratic government, including access, privacy, and security.

Policy Developments

The evolution of electronic government has been guided and regulated by statutory and administrative policies that were operational before its occurrence and by new ones designed explicitly for it. In general, they seek to promote the use of new electronic information technology by government entities with a view to improving the efficiency and economy of government operations. Moreover, they are designed to ensure the proper application and management of these technologies and the systems they serve, as well as their protection from physical harm, and the security and privacy of their information. These policies are identified and discussed here in terms of management, access, privacy, and security considerations.

Management

Enacted largely to relieve the public from mounting federal information collection and reporting requirements, the Paperwork Reduction Act of 1980 (PRA) promoted coordinated information management activities on a governmentwide basis by the director of the Office of Management and Budget (OMB), and prescribed information management responsibilities for the executive agencies, as well.[15] The management focus of PRA was sharpened in 1986 with amendments that refined the concept of "information resources management" (IRM), defined as "the planning, budgeting, organizing, directing, training, promoting, controlling, and management activities associated with the burden, collection, creation, use, and dissemination of information by agencies, and includes the management of information and related resources such as automatic data processing equipment."[16] This key term and its subset concepts received further definition and explanation in the PRA of 1995,[17] making IRM a tool for managing the contribution of information activities to program performance, and for managing related resources, such as personnel, equipment, funds, and technology.[18]

The evolution of PRA reflects a continuing effort to manage electronic information and support IT more effectively. The PRA of 1995 specifies a full range of responsibilities for the director of OMB for all government information, regardless of form or format, throughout its life cycle. Regarding IT, the director, among other duties, is tasked with (1) developing and overseeing the implementation of policies, principles, standards, and guidelines for federal IT functions and activities, including periodic evaluations of major information systems; (2) overseeing the development and implementation of certain statutorily specified technology standards; (3) monitoring the effectiveness of, and compliance with, certain statutorily authorized technology directives; (4) coordinating the development and review by the OMB Office of Information and Regulatory Affairs (OIRA) of policy associated with federal procurement and acquisition of IT with the OMB Office of Federal Procurement Policy; (5) ensuring, through the review of agency budget proposals, IRM plans, and other means, both the integration of IRM plans with program plans and budgets for the acquisition and use of IT by each agency, and the efficiency and effectiveness of inter-agency IT initiatives to improve agency performance and the accomplishment of agency missions; and (6) promoting agency use of IT to improve the productivity, efficiency, and effectiveness of federal programs, including the dissemination of public information and the reduction of information collection burdens on the public. Similar responsibilities are specified for the agencies regarding government information throughout its life cycle. OMB guidance on PRA implementation-related policies is provided in Circular A-130.[19]

PRA was modified in 1996 by new procurement reform and IT management legislation, which had originated as two distinct bills that were subsequently combined into a single proposal that was attached to a Department of Defense appropriations authorization act. Division D of the statute was denominated the Federal Acquisition Reform Act of 1996;[20] Division E was titled the Information Technology Management Reform Act of 1996.[21] The two divisions were later denominated the Clinger-Cohen Act in honor of the House and Senate legislators who had proposed the original bills.[22]

The Clinger-Cohen Act makes each agency responsible for its own IT planning and acquisition, and requires the purchase of the best and most cost-effective technology available.[23] It also establishes chief information officer (CIO) positions in the departments and major agencies, and prescribes their qualifications and duties.

Following the enactment of PRA and the Clinger-Cohen Act, President Bill Clinton issued Executive Order 13011 on July 16, 1996, to improve federal IT management and promote a coordinated approach to its application and use across the executive branch.[24] The directive prescribes, as a matter of policy, that executive agencies significantly improve the management of their information systems, including the acquisition of IT, through compliance with PRA and the Clinger-Cohen Act; refocus IT management to support directly their strategic missions, implement an investment review process that drives budget information and execution for information systems, and rethink and restructure the way they perform their functions before investing in IT to support that work; establish clear accountability for IRM activities by creating agency CIOs with the visibility and management responsibilities necessary to advise agency heads on the design, development, and implementation of those information systems; and cooperate in the use of IT to improve the productivity of federal programs and to provide a coordinated, interoperable, secure, and shared governmentwide infrastructure that is provided and supported by a diversity of private-sector suppliers and a well-trained corps of IT professionals. Responsibilities for agency heads include effectively using IT to improve mission performance and service to the public, and strengthening the quality of decisions about the employment of information resources to meet mission needs through integrated analysis, planning, budgeting, and evaluation processes.

In 1998 amendments to the Rehabilitation Act of 1973 set requirements for federal agencies to procure, maintain, and use electronic and information technology that provides individuals with disabilities, including both federal employees and members of the public, with accessibility comparable to what is available to individuals without disabilities.[25] The Architectural and Transportation Barriers Compliance Board, known as the Access Board, was tasked with developing access standards to implement the new requirement. After some delay, these standards were issued on December 21, 2000, for agency compliance by June 2001.[26]

The Government Paperwork Elimination Act (GPEA) further amended PRA in 1998.[27] These amendments make the director of OMB responsible for providing governmentwide direction and oversight regarding "the acquisition and use of information technology, including alternative information technologies that provide for electronic submission, maintenance, or disclosure of information as a substitute for paper and for the use and acceptance of electronic signatures."[28] In fulfilling this responsibility, the director, in consultation with the National Telecommunications and Information Administration (NTIA) of the Department of Commerce, is tasked with developing procedures for the use and acceptance of electronic signatures by the executive departments and agencies. A five-year deadline is prescribed for the agencies to implement these procedures.[29] The statute provides that electronic records submitted or maintained in accordance with its procedures, "or electronic signatures or other forms of electronic authentication used in accordance with such procedures, shall not be denied legal effect, validity, or enforceability because such records are in electronic form."[30]

The convergence of computer and telecommunications technologies not only revolutionized the storage, retrieval, and sharing of information, but also, in the considered view of many, produced an information economy resulting from commercial transactions on the Internet. The federal government is a participant in e-commerce, and statutes such as GPEA, discussed above, reflect encouragement of this development.

Among the first initiatives in furtherance of government participation in e-commerce was the Clinton administration's June 15, 1995, unveiling of the U.S. Business Advisor, a new online computer service directly linking the federal government to American business.[31] An upgraded and improved version of the U.S. Business Advisor, providing users with one-stop electronic access to more than 60 different federal organizations that assist or regulate businesses, was announced on February 13, 1996.

On July 1, 1997, President Clinton released a report, *A Framework for Global Electronic Commerce*, expressing five operating principles that the administration would follow in fostering e-commerce, and designating lead federal agencies in key policy areas.[32]

- The private sector should lead.
- Governments should avoid undue restrictions on electronic commerce.

- Where government involvement is needed, its aim should be to support and enforce a predictable minimalist, consistent, and simple legal environment for commerce.
- Governments should recognize the unique qualities of the Internet.
- Electronic commerce on the Internet should be facilitated on a global basis.

In his remarks announcing the release of the report, the president indicated he was directing all federal department and agency heads to review the policies of their organizations that affect global electronic commerce with a view to assuring that they were consistent with the five core principles of the report.

In a November 29, 1999, memorandum to the heads of executive departments and agencies, President Clinton directed each federal agency, including independent regulatory agencies, to assist a working group on electronic commerce with identifying any provision of law administered by the agencies, and any regulation issued by them, that may impose a barrier to electronic transactions or otherwise impede the conduct of commerce online or by electronic means. They were also tasked with recommending how such laws or regulations might be revised to allow electronic commerce to proceed while maintaining protection of the public interest.

The heads of executive departments and agencies were informed of Clinton administration efforts to address the so-called digital divide in a December 9, 1999, presidential memorandum. The digital divide is a reference to the perceived disparity that results from portions of the population not having the ability to use IT due to a lack of access and/or skill. Among the actions directed, the memorandum indicated, were the development of a national strategy for making computers and the Internet accessible to all Americans; expansion of the federal community technology centers network to provide low-income citizens with access to IT; encouragement of the development of IT applications that would help enable low-income citizens to start and manage their own small businesses; and use of training to upgrade the IT skills of the American work force, particularly workers living in disadvantaged urban and rural communities.

A December 17, 1999, memorandum to the heads of executive departments and agencies directed them, among other actions, to make available online, by December 2000, to the maximum extent possible, the forms needed for the top 500 government services used by the public; to make transactions with the federal government performable online, with online processing, by October 2003; and to promote the use of electronic commerce, where appropriate, for faster, cheaper ordering on federal procurements.

The E-Government Act, signed into law on December 17, 2002, contains a number of management, privacy, security, and other innovations.[33] Management developments include establishment of an Office of Electronic Government (OEG) within OMB to promote, coordinate, and plan electronic government services and related information life cycle management. A CIO council and an E-Government Fund are statutorily mandated.[34] In addition to managing the e-government fund, the administrator of general services is tasked with creating and promoting a governmentwide program to encourage contractor innovation and excellence in facilitating the development and enhancement of electronic government services and processes. Among other responsibilities, agencies are to develop performance measures that demonstrate how electronic government enables progress toward their objectives, strategic goals, and statutory mandates. The act prescribes a system of Web sites for the federal courts, as well as their minimal information content, and promotes the use of Web sites, electronic submissions, and electronic docketing by regulatory agencies. Programs for federal IT work force development and public–private sector IT personnel exchange are also mandated.

Access

In 1966 Congress enacted the Freedom of Information Act[35] (FOIA) to replace the public information section of the Administrative Procedure Act (APA), which was found to be ineffective in providing the public with a means of access to unpublished executive agency records.[36] Subsection (a) of FOIA reiterates the requirements of the APA public information section that certain operational information—e.g., organization descriptions, delegations of final authority, and substantive rules of general policy—be published in the *Federal Register.*

Subsection (b) statutorily establishes a presumptive right of access by any person—individual or corporate, regardless of nationality—to identifiable, existing, unpublished records of federal agencies without having to demonstrate a need or even a reason for such a request. Subsection (b)(1)-(9) lists nine categories of information that may be exempted from the rule of disclosure. The burden of proof for withholding material sought by the public is placed upon the government. Denials of requests may be appealed to the head of the agency holding the sought records and ultimately pursued in federal court.

FOIA was subsequently amended in 1974, 1976, 1986, and 1996, the last modifications being the Electronic Freedom of Information Amendments (E-FOIA), which, among other changes, confirm the statute's applicability to records in electronic forms or formats, require that responsive materials be provided in the form or format sought by the requester, and mandate so-called electronic reading rooms that the public can access online to examine important and high-interest agency records.[37]

The E-Government Act authorizes the director of OMB, when promulgating guidance for agency Web sites, to require direct links to operational and other information made available to the public under subsections (a)(1) and (b) of FOIA.

Privacy

With the Privacy Act of 1974, Congress addressed several aspects of personal privacy protection.[38] First, it sustained some traditional, major privacy principles. For example, an agency shall "maintain no record describing how any individual exercises rights guaranteed by the First Amendment unless expressly authorized by statute or by the individual about whom the record is maintained or unless pertinent to and within the scope of an authorized law enforcement activity."[39]

Second, the statute gives an individual who is a citizen of the United States, or an alien lawfully admitted for permanent residence, access and emendation arrangements for records maintained on him or her by most, but not all, federal agencies. General exemptions in this regard are provided for systems of records maintained by the Central Intelligence Agency and federal criminal law enforcement agencies.

Third, the statute embodies a number of principles of fair information practice. For example, it sets certain conditions concerning the disclosure of personally identifiable information; prescribes requirements for the accounting of certain disclosures of such information; requires agencies to "collect information to the greatest extent practicable directly from the subject individual when the information may result in adverse determinations about an individual's rights, benefits, and privileges under Federal programs"; requires agencies to specify their authority and purposes for collecting personally identifiable information from an individual; requires agencies to "maintain all records which are used by the agency in making any determination about any individual with such accuracy, relevance, timeliness, and completeness as is reasonably necessary to assure fairness to the individual in the determination"; and provides civil and criminal enforcement arrangements.

Congress amended the Privacy Act in 1988 to regulate the use of computer matching—the computerized comparison of records for the purpose of establishing or verifying eligibility for a federal benefit program or for recouping payments or delinquent debts under such programs—conducted by federal agencies or making use of federal records subject to the statute. The amendments were denominated the Computer Matching and Privacy Protection Act of 1988.[40] Excepting matches performed for statistical, research, law enforcement, tax, and certain other purposes, the amendments regulate matches involving personally identifiable records maintained in a system of records subject to the Privacy Act. In order for matches to occur, a written matching agreement, effectively creating a matching program, must be prepared specifying details explicitly required by the amendments. Copies of such matching agreements are transmitted to congressional oversight committees and are available to the public upon request. Every agency conducting or participating in a matching program also must establish a Data Integrity Board, composed of senior agency officials, to oversee and coordinate program operations, including the execution of certain specified review, approval, and reporting responsibilities.

Frustration with industry's slow response to establishing Internet privacy protections for minors prompted the Clinton administration and Congress to enact the Children's Online Privacy Protection Act of 1998 (COPPA).[41] The statute requires the operator of a commercial Web site or online service targeted at children under the age of 13 to provide clear notice of information collection and use practices; to obtain verifiable parental consent prior to collecting, using, and disseminating personal information about children under 13; and to provide parents access to their children's personal information and the option to prevent its further use. On October 20, 1999, the Federal Trade Commission issued a final rule to implement COPPA, which went into effect on April 21, 2000.[42] The statute authorizes the commission to bring enforcement actions and impose civil penalties for violations of the rule.

A June 2, 1999, memorandum from the OMB director to the heads of executive departments and agencies directs the posting of clear privacy policies on federal Web sites and provides guidance for this action.[43] Such policies "must clearly and concisely inform visitors to the site what information the agency collects about individuals, why the agency collects it, and how the agency will use it." Also, they "must be clearly labeled and easily accessed when someone visits a web site," according to the memorandum. Agencies are reminded that, pursuant to the Privacy Act, they must protect an individual's right to privacy when they collect personal information.

A June 22, 2000, followup memorandum was issued by OMB after press disclosures that the National Drug Control Policy Office, an agency within the Executive Office of the President, was secretly tracking visitors to its Web site through the use of computer software known as "cookies."[44] Addressing this revelation, it said:

> Particular privacy concerns may be raised when uses of web technology can track the activities of users over time and across different web sites. These concerns are especially great where individuals who have come to government web sites do not have clear and conspicuous notice of any such tracking activities. "Cookies"—small bits of software that are placed on a web user's hard drive—are a principal example of current web technology that can be used in this way. The guidance issued on June 2, 1999, provided that agencies could only use "cookies" or other automatic means of collecting information if they gave clear notice of those activities.

> Because of the unique laws and traditions about government access to citizens' personal information, the presumption should be that "cookies" will not be used at Federal web sites. Under this new Federal policy, "cookies" should not be used at Federal web sites, or by contractors when operating web sites on behalf of agencies, unless, in addition to clear and conspicuous notice, the following conditions are met: a compelling need to gather the data on the site; appropriate and publicly disclosed privacy safeguards for handling of information derived from "cookies"; and personal approval by the head of the agency. In addition, it is Federal policy that all Federal web sites and contractors when operating on behalf of agencies shall comply with the standards set forth in the Children's Online Privacy Protection Act of 1998 with respect to the collection of personal information online at web sites directed to children.[45]

Another Internet privacy law, the Children's Internet Protection Act, requires schools and libraries that receive "E-rate" discounts, or reduced charges, for Internet access to certify to the Federal Communications Commission that they are using filters to block child pornography and obscene, hard-core pornography sites.[46] Other material, "inappropriate for minors," such as soft-core pornography, may be blocked as well. Opponents of the policy have contended that it is an unfunded mandate, a federal intrusion into family and local community matters, and a violation of First Amendment guarantees.[47] Anticipated court challenge of the new law by civil liberties and library organizations occurred in March 2001 when a lawsuit was filed in federal district court in Philadelphia.[48] On March 31, 2002, a federal district court panel unanimously declared the statute unconstitutional and enjoined its enforcement insofar as it applies to libraries.[49] At the time of this writing, the case was on appeal to the Supreme Court, with arguments set to begin in early March 2003.[50]

The E-Government Act requires the agencies, prior to developing or procuring IT, or initiating a new collection of information using IT that collects, maintains, or disseminates information that is in a personally identifiable form, to conduct a privacy impact assessment. This assessment, to be prepared in accordance with guidance issued by the director of OMB, provides a basis for evaluating the nature of the collection and attending considerations, such as sharing and security. The director of OMB is also directed to develop guidance for privacy notices on agency Web sites, consistent with the Privacy Act. Points to be addressed in the notices are specified in the E-Government Act.

Security

Recognizing the increasing use of computers by federal agencies and the vulnerability of computer-stored information, including personal information, to unauthorized access, Congress enacted the Computer Security Act of 1987.[51] The statute requires each federal agency to develop security plans for its computer systems containing sensitive information. Such plans are subject to review by the National Institute of Standards and Technology (NIST) of the Department of Commerce, and a summary, together with overall budget plans for IT, is filed with OMB. NIST is authorized to set security standards for all federal computer systems except those containing intelligence, cryptologic, or certain military information, or information specifically authorized under criteria established by an executive order or statute to be kept secret in the interest of national defense or foreign policy. Each federal agency is directed to provide all employees involved with the management, use, or operation of its computer systems with mandatory periodic training in computer security awareness and accepted computer security practice.

Concerned about the vulnerabilities of certain critical national infrastructures—including the telecommunications system—to physical and cyber attack, President Clinton, with E.O. 13010 of July 15, 1996, established the President's Commission on Critical Infrastructure Protection.[52] The temporary study panel was tasked with assessing the scope and nature of the vulnerabilities of, and threats to, critical infrastructures; determining what legal and policy issues are raised by efforts to protect critical infrastructures and assessing how these issues should be addressed; recommending a comprehensive national policy and implementation strategy for protecting critical infrastructures from physical and cyber threats and assuring their continued operation; and proposing any statutory or regulatory changes necessary to effect its recommendations. The commission produced 12 special topical reports and submitted its final report, offering many recommendations, on October 13, 1997.[53]

On May 22, 1998, the White House issued documents concerning Presidential Decision Directive 63 (PDD 63), a security classified policy instrument on critical infrastructure protection resulting from an interagency evaluation of the recommendations of the president's commission.[54] The directive mandated a National Coordinator for Security, Infrastructure Protection, and Counter-Terrorism; a National Infrastructure Protection Center at the Federal Bureau of Investigation, which recently was transferred to the new Department of Homeland Security; a National Infrastructure Assurance Council, composed of private-sector experts and state and local government officials, to provide guidance for a national plan for critical infrastructure protection; and a Critical Infrastructure

Assurance Office to provide support for the National Coordinator's work with government agencies and the private sector in developing a national plan for critical infrastructure protection. The centerpiece of the efforts launched with PDD 63 is a national plan to serve as a blueprint for establishing a critical infrastructure protection capability. Version one, the National Plan for Information Systems Protection, was unveiled on January 7, 2000.[55]

In late 2000 PRA was amended with new government information security requirements.[56] These provisions were subsequently replaced by comparable requirements specified in the E-Government Act of 2002.[57] With the exception of national security systems, the director of OMB is responsible for overseeing agency information security policies and practices. Each agency must develop, document, and implement an information security program, approved by the director of OMB, providing security for the information and information systems that support its operations and assets. In addition, each agency, in consultation with the director of OMB, must include in its performance plan required by the Government Performance and Results Act a description of the time periods and resources that are necessary to implement its security program.[58] Each agency is required to have an annual independent evaluation of its information security program and practices to determine their effectiveness.

Conclusion

The development of new information and communications technologies, interwoven with conceptual developments about the role of such technologies in people's lives and government activity, have contributed to the evolution of e-government. The use of these new tools has been further shaped in the federal government by policy choices reflected in statutes and administrative directives. Policy developments in this area can be seen as an attempt to address some of the concerns that often attend American government: realizing efficient, economical, and effective administration; providing citizens relatively unimpeded access to information about government policy, decision making, and operations; minimizing government intrusion into the private life of citizens and safeguarding personal information collected by government; and protecting the security of government information.

Familiarity with the evolution of e-government policy, past and future, is important to understanding contemporary information management in the federal government. During this evolution, choices have been made, and will continue to be made, about what information should be available to the general public, in what form it should be provided, and how much citizens will be protected from unauthorized release or interagency sharing of personal information. These choices are likely to vary over time, depending on the salience of different values under varying governing coalitions and within different political climates. The full impact of information management for maintaining homeland security on e-government operations and development, for example, remains to be seen and assessed.

For those whose role is to facilitate the public's retrieval of government information, the evolution of e-government policy and practice is crucial. The nuances of that policy influence not only access to government information, but also the ease with which it is obtained, and its overall accuracy and balance. Those who are striving to strengthen the links between citizens and their government are likely to find public access to government decision making processes and outcomes similarly influenced by policy developments in this area. Such professionals and interested parties likely will wish to maintain an active presence in the policy making process concerning the areas discussed in this report.

Notes

1. The implications of recent homeland security information management policies and practices for e-government are discussed in the preceding article, "Homeland Security and Information Management."

2. This history of the development of electronic government is provided in more detail in Harold C. Relyea and Henry B. Hogue, "A Brief History of the Emergence of Digital Government in the United States," in Alexei Pavlichev and G. David Garson, eds., *Digital Government: Principles and Best Practices,* (Idea Group Press, 2003).

3. Vannevar Bush, "As We May Think," *Atlantic Monthly,* vol. 176, July 1945, pp. 101–108; retrieved March 21, 2002, from http://www.theatlantic.com/unbound/flashbks/computer/bushf.htm.

4. Ibid.

5. J. C. R. Licklider, "Man-Computer Symbiosis," *IRE Transactions on Human Factors in Electronics,* vol. 1, 1965, pp. 4–11. Retrieved March 21, 2002, from http://memex.org/licklider.pdf.

6. Ibid.

7. J. C. R. Licklider and Welden E. Clark, "On-Line Man-Computer Communication," *Proceedings of the American Federation of Information Processing Societies,* vol. 21, 1962, pp. 113–128.

8. J. C. R. Licklider and Robert W. Taylor, "The Computer as a Communication Device," *Science and Technology,* vol. 76, 1968, pp. 21-31. Retrieved March 21, 2002, from http://memex.org/licklider.pdf.

9. U.S. Congress, House Committee on Government Operations, *Electronic Collection and Dissemination of Information by Federal Agencies: A Policy Overview,* 99th Congress, 2nd session, (H. Rept. 99-560), (GPO, 1986).

10. Ibid., p. 2.

11. U.S. Office of Technology Assessment, *Informing the Nation: Federal Information Dissemination in an Electronic Age,* (GPO, 1988).

12. U.S. Office of Technology Assessment, *Making Government Work: Electronic Delivery of Federal Services,* (GPO, 1993).

13. U.S. Office of the Vice President, *From Red Tape to Results: Creating a Government That Works Better and Costs Less, Report of the National Performance Review,* (GPO, 1993).

14. U.S. Office of the Vice President, *Access America: Reengineering Through Information Technology, Report of the National Performance Review and the Government Information Technology Services Board,* (GPO, 1997), p. 2.

15. 94 Stat. 2812; 44 U.S.C. 3501 et seq.

16. 100 Stat. 3341-336.

17. 109 Stat. 165-166.

18. See David Plocher, "The Paperwork Reduction Act of 1995: A Second Chance for Information Resources Management," *Government Information Quarterly,* vol. 13, no. 1, 1996, pp. 35–50.

19. See *Federal Register,* vol. 61, Feb. 20, 1996, pp. 6428–6453; the circular is also available from the OMB Web site at http://www.whitehouse.gov/OMB/inforeg/index.html under the heading "Information Policy and Technology."

20. 110 Stat. 642.

21. 110 Stat. 679.

22. 110 Stat. 3009-393; the sponsors, respectively, were Representative William F. Clinger, Jr. (R-Pa.) and Senator William S. Cohen (R-Maine).

23. 110 Stat. 186.

24. 3 C.F.R., 1996 Comp., pp. 202–209.

25. The Rehabilitation Act Amendments of 1998 constituted Title IV of the Workforce Investment Act of 1998, 112 Stat. 936; the electronic and information technology access requirement was appended to the Rehabilitation Act as section 508, 112 Stat 1203, at 29 U.S.C. 794(d); the Rehabilitation Act was originally enacted in 1973, 87 Stat. 355, at 29 U.S.C. 701 et seq.

26. Associated Press, "Guidelines to Force Federal Agencies to Redesign Web Sites," *Washington Times,* Dec. 22, 2000, p. A5.

27. See 112 Stat. 2681-749.

28. 44 U.S.C. 3504(a)(1)(B)(vi), as amended.

29. The final version of OMB procedures and guidance for implementing the GPEA was published in *Federal Register,* vol. 65, May 2, 2000, pp. 25508–25521, and a memorandum on the preparation and submission of agency plans to implement the statute was issued on July 25; both documents are available from the OMB Web site at http://www.whitehouse.gov/OMB/inforeg/index.html under the heading "Information Policy and Technology."

30. 112 Stat. 2681-751.

31. U.S. Business Advisor can be found at http://www.business.gov.

32. President's Information Infrastructure Task Force, *A Framework for Global Electronic Commerce* (July 1, 1997), available from the National Institute of Standards and Technology Web site at http://www.iitf.nist.gov/eleccomm/ecomm.htm.

33. P.L. 107-347.

34. These entities replace the CIO council established by E.O. 13011 and the e-gov fund proposed by President Bush in his February 2001 *Blueprint for New Beginnings: A Responsible Budget for America's Priorities* (GPO, 2001), which was realized in the Treasury and General Government Appropriations Act, 2002 (115 Stat. 537). The lack of a statutory authorization for the e-gov fund had been a concern of both congressional appropriations committees.

35. 80 Stat. 250; 5 U.S.C. 552.

36. 60 Stat. 237.

37. 110 Stat. 3048; 5 U.S.C. 552.

38. 88 Stat. 1896; 5 U.S.C. 552a.

39. 5 U.S.C. 552a(e)(7).

40. 102 Stat. 2507.

41. 112 Stat. 2681-728; 15 U.S.C. 6501-6506.

42. *Federal Register,* vol. 64, Nov. 3, 1999, pp. 59888–59915.

43. This memorandum is available from the OMB Web site at http://www.whitehouse.gov/ OMB/inforeg/index.html under the heading "Information Policy and Technology."

44. See John F. Harris and John Schwartz, "Anti-Drug Web Site Tracks Visitors," *Washington Post*, June 22, 2000, p. A23; Lance Gay, "White House Uses Drug-Message Site to Track Inquiries," *Washington Times*, June 21, 2000, p. A3.

45. This memorandum is available from the OMB Web site at http://www.whitehouse.gov/OMB/inforeg/index.htm under the heading "Information Policy and Technology."

46. 114 Stat. 2763A-335.

47. Cheryl Wetzstein, "New Measure Takes Aim at Obscene Sites on Web," *Washington Times*, Dec. 24, 2000, p. C2.

48. Associated Press, "Libraries Lodge Legal Challenge to Internet Filters," *Washington Times*, March 20, 2001, pp. B6, B10; Robert O'Harrow, Jr., "Curbs on Web Access Face Attack," *Washington Post*, March 20, 2001, p. A4; Cheryl Wetzstein, "ACLU, Library Group Sue to Stop Child Internet Protection Act," *Washington Times*, March 21, 2001, p. A3.

49. *American Library Association* v. *United States*, 201 F Supp. 2d 401 (E.D. Pa. 2002).

50. For developments in the case, see the Web site of the American Library Association at http://www.ala.org/cipa.

51. 101 Stat. 1724.

52. 3 C.F.R., 1996 Comp., pp. 198–202; according to E.O. 13010, a "cyber" attack involves "electronic, radio-frequency, or computer-based attacks on the information or communications components that control critical infrastructures."

53. President's Commission on Critical Infrastructure Protection, *Critical Foundations: Protecting America's Infrastructures* (GPO, 1997); this report and other related documents are available at http://www.ciao.gov/PCCIP/pccip_documents.htm.

54. A fact sheet, a White Paper, and a press briefing transcript on PDD 63 were initially provided by the White House; the full text of PDD 63 is now available at http://www.fas.org/irp/offdocs/pdd/pdd-63.htm.

55. The full text and executive summary of the national plan are available from the Critical Infrastructure Assurance Office Web site at http://www.ciao.gov in the "CIAO Document Library."

56. 114 Stat. 1654, 1654A-266.

57. The 2000 information security amendments to PRA were initially replaced by Title X of the Homeland Security Act, signed into law on Nov. 25, 2002 (P.L. 107-296), but these modifications were subsequently superseded by Title III of the E-Government Act, signed into law on Dec. 17, 2002 (P.L. 107-347).

58. The performance plan requirement can be found at 31 U.S.C. 1115.

Digital Rights Management:
Why Libraries Should Be Major Players

Grace Agnew

Mairéad Martin

Introduction

Digital Rights Management (DRM) can be simply defined as the documentation and administration of rights for the access to and use of digital works. Rights are managed through an agreement among two or more parties for the use of a specified digital work or collection of works. This agreement involves rights or permissions for access and use of a resource, including the right to view, copy, print, annotate, edit, reuse, own, and transfer ownership of the resource. Permissions can be limited by constraints or obligations that must be met in order to exercise a right, for example the payment of a fee or possession by the user of a required attribute, such as registration in a course or membership in an association.

At a minimum, a digital rights agreement involves three entities: the rights holder, who confers rights or permissions; the user, who exercises those rights; and the digital work (or resource). All three entities in a rights agreement must be authenticated for the agreement to be valid. The rights holder must be authenticated as owning or managing rights for a resource, and the user must be authenticated as possessing a required role or attribute or as having met a required obligation to obtain a right to use a resource. The authenticity and integrity of the resource is also critical to a rights transaction, since alteration of the resource can change the intellectual property rights and invalidate an agreement. A critical component of DRM is therefore the establishment and safeguarding of identity and the authenticity of that identity for all three entities in a rights agreement.

The most common parties to a digital rights agreement are the creator or owner of a work and the user of the work. Rights to digital works belong to the creator or owner of the work, while the user seeks to exercise one or more rights to the work. A common third party in a digital rights agreement, however, is the intermediary who distributes, leases, or administers access to creative works. The intermediary usually has contractual or legal obligations to manage rights of access and use for the work.

In the print world, intellectual property management was largely based on the principle of fair use of copyrighted materials and also on the principle of first sale, which stated that the right to use a work, or to transfer use of a work through gift or resale, belonged to the purchaser of the work. First sale of analog

Note: Grace Agnew is the associate university librarian for digital library systems at the Rutgers University Libraries. She is the coauthor of the books *Getting Mileage out of Metadata* and *The Online System Migration Guide* and the designer of the Moving Image Collections (MIC) portal. Mairéad Martin is assistant director for Middleware Systems Technology within the Division of Information Technology at the University of Wisconsin–Madison. The two co-chaired the National Science Foundation-funded Middleware Initiative and DRM workshop held in September 2002 at Georgetown University in Washington, D.C.

works referred to the physical, lawfully produced, copy of a work rather than its intellectual content, such as a physical book that a person might buy, read, and then sell to a secondhand bookstore or donate to a book sale. Copyright in the print world generally involved the copying and reuse of information from an analog work. Responsible use of a work in accordance with copyright was, and still remains, the responsibility of the user. Monitoring and tracking use of analog works was difficult. Discovering misuse generally required intensive human monitoring or serendipitous discovery.

Digital technologies have made it possible for anyone to be a creator and a publisher, able to share his or her works with a worldwide audience. However, digital technologies have also made it possible to readily capture, reuse, redistribute, or alter the intellectual property belonging to another, often without the original owner's knowledge. This technical ability to reuse a digital work without further reference to the copyright holder is seen as a serious threat to the profitability, and ultimately the viability, of commercial publishing for digital works.

In the early days of the Web, a tremendous amount of information was made available for access and use at no cost. Libraries expended considerable effort to identify authoritative information among the wealth of information on the Web for marketing to their users via catalog records, pathfinders, and Webliographies. As the Web has matured, it has become a marketplace for commercially distributed information with explicit constraints on access and use. The Web has also become a portal for the digital archives of libraries, museums, and other public-information agencies. DRM concerns libraries not just as distributors and intermediaries of information, but also as creators and owners of copyright-protected information.

Providing access to creative works is a core mission of libraries, and therefore rights management is a common library activity. Despite this fact, DRM is viewed by many in the library and research and educational communities as antithetical to the principles of information sharing upon which those communities depend. "Restrictive DRM"[1] is now emerging as a term to characterize DRM technologies that have come to dominate the DRM landscape—technologies that protect the rights of the copyright owner exclusively, that implement ex ante enforcements of those rights, thereby undermining fair use, and that also have the capacity to compromise the privacy of the end user. This direction in DRM technology development has been led by the film and music recording industries for the most part and has resulted in legislation, such as the Digital Millennium Copyright Act (DMCA),[2] that endorses that direction and reifies the features of restrictive DRM products. A backlash to this restrictive DRM trend is emerging, however, with collaboration among librarians, information technologists, copyright law experts, and others to define a different variety of DRM—one that is based on enabling access and supporting the rights of the user as much as the copyright owner.

Distaste for the restrictive features of some conventional instantiations of DRM aside, the model for DRM in research and education is obviously different from that of the film and recorded music industries and needs to be articulated. As applications in e-learning, digital library, and online collaboration mature, and with the recent emergence of institutional repositories and new scholarly publishing models, the need to add robust DRM features to these applications is recognized and being pursued. The research, education, and public-information sectors (e.g., libraries, archives, and museums) have many unique requirements that cannot be met by the current generation of "restrictive DRM" products. These include an accommodation of fair use and the "first sale" principle, both of which are key to the use of copyrighted materials in teaching, research, and the dissemination of information resources for the public good.

In research and education, an acceptable DRM model must provide support for the collaborative nature of many educational activities: collaborations that go across national boundaries and security domains, for example; support for the heterogeneous applications used in teaching and research today; and interoperability with existing infrastructure and applications. For public-information providers, such as public libraries and museums, service to users is based on a trust relationship built over several centuries of respect and safeguards for the privacy of users' identities and the confidentiality of their information use. Clearly, there is a need for a variety of DRM solutions to meet these requirements.

The passing of the Technology, Education and Copyright Harmonization (TEACH) Act in November 2002[3] also has implications for the use of DRM in education. TEACH redefines how educational institutions use copyrighted materials to support distance education, but also requires implementation of measures to control the use of that material. At institutions taking advantage of TEACH, the control measures that information technology officials will need to support could be interpreted as requiring the application of DRM technologies: access to copyrighted materials will need to be limited to enrolled students; provisions will need to be implemented to control content downstream so as to prevent storage and further dissemination; and instructional delivery systems must not interfere with the implementation of systems or code to control copyright.

Controlling access is the least problematic requirement. Preventing retention and retransmission of copyrighted materials opens the door to the application of DRM technologies. Many factors need to be weighed before institutions take that route, such as the "value" of the material, the possibility of acquiring permission for use from the copyright owner, and the possible compromises of user privacy that implementing a trusted DRM system may entail. The TEACH Act does not mandate the use of DRM technologies by any means, but it has intensified the debate on DRM in education.

Core DRM Concepts and Technologies

Rights management in the digital era involves the use of technologies to define, document, and broker agreements for rights to use a work. End-to-end rights management can involve authenticating all parties to the agreement: the rights holder, the end user, any intermediaries, and the work itself; administering constraints to use, such as payment in advance, page limits for printing, or display resolution; as well as the monitoring and tracking of use throughout the life of a digital rights agreement. Several core concepts and technologies are involved in the documentation and management of digital rights agreements.

Rights Data Model

A rights data model provides the conceptual framework for understanding and documenting all the entities involved in a rights agreement; the attributes of those entities; and the relationships between entities involved in rights agreements and transactions. A rights data model will support business models and scenarios of use specific to the community developing the model to enable common applications based on the model. Development of a rights data model for the research, education, and public-information domains is a necessary first step in the development of a rights expression language to support DRM in those domains.

Rights Data Dictionary

A rights data dictionary is a collection of standardized data elements required to identify entities and relationships in a rights transaction, including the rights or permissions extended to users of a work; the constraints on the exercise of those rights; the entities or agents involved in a rights transaction; the applications that manage the agreement and enable access to the work; and the storage devices housing the work. A rights data dictionary provides authoritative and unambiguous terms ("data elements") and definitions for those terms to enable shared understanding and collaborative rights applications within a community of users. It also ensures that a community identifies and documents the minimum concepts and entities required to model a rights environment and to develop a rights management application. A published rights data dictionary also enables interoperability across communities through the reuse of data elements or mapping between equivalent data elements. Many communities are currently developing rights data dictionaries as a necessary first step to developing a digital rights management implementation.

Rights Expression Language

A rights expression language (REL) communicates offers and agreements between rights holders and end users for the access and use of a specified digital resource. A REL communicates rights, conditions limiting the exercise of rights, and the context relevant to the rights transactions. The REL will express the business rules of the community engaged in DRM activities. A REL is both a required component and a facilitator for DRM applications that manage the exercise of rights transactions. It is standardized according to documented rules and employs one or more rights data dictionaries and a standard syntax for expression, such as XML.

Currently, two rights expression languages have emerged as front-runners in this arena, and their developers hope that they will be sufficiently flexible for reuse by different communities. XrML[4] (eXtensible Rights Markup Language) is an open-source language, currently in version 2.0 (2001-11-20). ContentGuard is the patent and license owner for XrML. XrML was developed from Xerox PARC's digital property rights language, which was first issued in 1996. XrML is expressed in XML and employs a core schema that documents core entities and agreements, and extension schemas that can be extended in a modular manner to customized applications for other communities. XrML is based on an e-commerce model and employs other XML-based standards and encryption technologies to provide an end-to-end hybrid description language and application suite that documents and administers rights transactions. XrML has been adopted by commercial software providers and the Open eBook Forum,[5] among others.

ODRL[6] (Open Digital Rights Language) was developed by Renato Ianella and IPR Systems, an information management consulting firm based in Australia. The current version is 1.1 (2002-08-08). ODRL is based on both commercial and archival business models. ODRL is being used by the mobile computing industry and also by COLIS[7] (Collaborative Online Learning and Information Services), a collaboration to build interoperable e-learning infrastructures among five universities in Australia. ODRL is also XML-based and modular in design to support extensibility to different communities and applications. Unlike XrML, ODRL is application-independent and does not dictate how rights are exercised or how constraints to rights are enforced.

In a digital repository, rights information should be tightly bound to descriptive and administrative metadata about a digital resource. Constraints on access to a digital resource, such as payment for access, can be a critical determining factor in selecting among resources listed in a search result. Descriptive and administrative metadata can clearly identify the resource and also the rights holder and the provenance documenting rights ownership for a resource—critical information for establishing a rights agreement. Both XrML and ODRL support the modular insertion of descriptive metadata from an XML-based schema such as Dublin Core to identify the resource as an entity in a rights agreement. A standard such as METS[8] (Metadata Encoding and Transmission Standard) plays an important role in a digital repository by binding rights metadata to other metadata that describe and manage the digital resource.

Additional XML-based expression languages that will likely complement the functionalities of a REL are SAML and XACML, both of which come from OASIS (Organization for the Advancement of Structured Information Standards). SAML (Security Assertion Markup Language), currently in version 1.0 (2002-11-12), is a language for securely sharing assertions about parties to a transaction across systems.[9] These assertions may represent an authentication or an authorization transaction for a subject, which may be the rights holder, an intermediary, or the end user, to enable resulting transactions such as access to a resource. XACML[10] (Extensible Access Control Markup Language) is an OASIS specification to provide standardized methods, expressed as XML, for attribute-based access to resources within a trusted environment. Attributes in this context of DRM are the characteristics of an entity, such as an end user, that satisfy the restrictions to access or use of a resource that the rights holder imposes. An example would be the requirement that a user must be a registered patron with a valid library ID for access to a public library's licensed electronic databases. A patron with a lapsed or blocked library registration may be authenticated as a library patron but lacks the attribute of a valid registration status required to access the databases.

DRM Reference Architecture

An end-to-end DRM system generally consists of a content server; a license server containing information about the identity of a user or device; identification of content and specification of rights to that content; a content packager, which essentially packages the content with metadata and rights specifications before distribution; a DRM controller that manages the integration of all of the aforementioned to enable distribution of content; and a client and rendering application on the user's side.[11]

Access Control

Identity management, authentication, and authorization are key components of access control, an essential feature of a DRM system. Identity management provides procedures for establishing and maintaining persistent identities for persons and organizations, including the authentication mechanism that establishes identity among trusted parties, the directory databases that document and store identities, and the mechanisms to ensure privacy and confidentiality for authenticated participants. Authentication establishes the validity of the entities referenced in a rights transaction, while authorization entails the management and exercise of rights or entitlements based on attributes or roles associated with each entity. Authentication is based on the use of identifiers, such as NetIDs, passwords, keys, and certificates, and can be centralized, application-based, or a combination of both.

Authorization is a more complex function, the challenges of which are partly responsible for the limited and restrictive nature of conventional DRM systems. Authorizations in these systems are typically nongranular—one time or pay-per-view—and based on static content, i.e., the user is not expected to interact with or modify the content, a view that does not support the dynamic nature of most digital content nor the collaborative and interactive nature of many research and educational activities. Higher education has the capacity to implement more sophisticated authorizations thanks to well-developed identity management and directory services nationally, and the fact that identity in higher education is tied to people, whereas identity in the commercial arena is typically tied to devices. Directory services in higher education may well form the foundation for the development of DRM systems in that arena.

An emerging project with promise in that respect is Shibboleth, from Internet2/MACE (Middleware Architecture Committee for Education). Shibboleth is "developing architectures, policy structures, practical technologies, and an open source implementation to support inter-institutional sharing of Web resources subject to access controls."[12] Shibboleth is based on core concepts of attribute-based access within a community of trust. Shibboleth is designed to support shared authentication and authorization mechanisms coupled with active privacy measures to control the release of identity information in a transaction. This is accomplished by sharing only the minimum information required to complete a rights transaction, such as a general attribute (e.g., "student in Chemistry 101") rather than the unique identity of the course enrollee. Shibboleth implementations are in development or experimental use at many large universities. Collaborative projects, such as the National Science Digital Library[13] (NSDL), a collaborative portal of digital materials to support science education, are extending Shibboleth to K–12 institutions, public libraries, and other public-information providers. The Federated DRM project[14] proposes expanding the Shibboleth architecture to include DRM functions, and is a first step in exploring how existing and emerging infrastructure on our campuses might be leveraged to implement DRM.

Encryption

Encryption algorithms are used to convert eye-readable information to a form that cannot be read or modified without decryption, and for conversion back to eye-readable form once the information has been decrypted. Encryption is used to ensure confidentiality and to ensure authenticity of digital information. Sometimes only a "signature" is encrypted, to authenticate an individual with regard to a rights agreement or a resource. XrML employs digital signatures to authenticate parties to a rights agreement. An encrypted message digest may also be created and attached to a resource to document that an unencrypted resource has not been altered. Keys combined with an algorithm are used to encrypt and decrypt information. Symmetric encryption uses a shared private key—to both encrypt information for sending and to decrypt information upon receipt. Asymmetric encryption uses two keys—a public key and a private key. The private key holder distributes public keys to those who are authorized to decrypt the encrypted resource.

Trust

Trust in digital rights management refers to a common understanding among parties that enables rights transactions to occur. This common understanding results from a shared business model, common rules and assumptions, shared standards, or shared technologies. "Trusted systems" refer to systems with shared underlying technologies that enforce policies by controlling the hardware and software required to enable or execute rights transactions. XrML requires trusted systems to function because the standards and protocols required to authenticate participants, enforce constraints, and enable rights are inherent in the language. ODRL, on the other hand, documents rights agreements without any assumptions about the technology used to enable and enforce rights.

DRM Standards Organizations and Players

There are currently multiple standards organizations and players operating in the DRM environment. The MPEG-21 Multimedia Framework,[15] a developing standard currently in design by the Motion Picture Experts Group, entails development of a comprehensive architecture for delivery of digital multimedia. This framework includes standardization of a REL (the basis of which is XrML) and the development of a rights data dictionary under development by the <indecs>rdd consortium,[16] a component of the <indecs> (Interoperability of Data in E-Commerce Systems) project. The OASIS Rights Language Technical Committee[17] is also using XrML as the foundation for its REL standardization activities and is endeavoring to develop a REL to support a variety of business models. The IEEE

Learning Technology Standards Committee issued a draft White Paper, *Towards a Digital Rights Expression Language Standard for Learning Technology,*[18] that delineates the needs and requirements for a REL to support e-learning applications. The goal of the Australian COLIS project, mentioned earlier, is to develop an open, standards-based e-learning system, including DRM functionalities. COLIS is using ODRL for rights expressions and integrating the REL into a content management system in the first phase of the COLIS project.

The Creative Commons Licensing Project was launched in December 2002 and "enables users to build and attach machine-readable licenses that dedicate at least some of the rights within a 'copyright' to the public."[19] Copyright owners can select online from a set of conditions under which they can license their work to be used—with or without attribution, for commercial use, or granting derivative use, for example. Alternatively, the copyright owner can choose to put the work into the public domain. The Creative Commons Licensing Project is a response to the perceived negative impact of restrictive DRM on access to information and focuses on an aspect of DRM that is perhaps most useful for libraries—the documentation, rather than the enforcement, of rights.

The major industry players in the DRM space include Microsoft, InterTrust, Sony, ContentGuard, Adobe, and Real Networks. Several early DRM companies suffered the same fate as other dot-com startups as DRM technologies had not had time to penetrate the market sufficiently to withstand the demise of the dot-com phenomenon. Meanwhile, the bigger players have recently been positioning themselves to leverage their DRM technologies to create "de facto" industry standards on the basis of market share. The bulk of DRM patents belong to ContentGuard (which is partially owned by Microsoft) and InterTrust, whose patents were licensed by Sony at the end of 2002. The patent issue is a particularly contentious one in the DRM arena and has the potential to seriously hinder the development of rights languages that might compete with XrML.[20]

Use of DRM in the Library Worlds

Most libraries apply some level of DRM to administer access to licensed commercial resources such as electronic journals and databases. Access to commercial resources may be constrained by password, digital certificates, or IP (Internet Protocol) ranges to limit access by device location. Libraries also apply access controls to copyright-protected digital resources such as scanned journal articles or book excerpts in an electronic reserves implementation.

As libraries develop a publishing presence on the Web, through digital library initiatives such as digital photograph or text archives, DRM has become an issue of greater importance. An important issue that most libraries with a digitization program must confront is the library's rights to create and share digital surrogates for items in the library's collection. Many deeds of gift did not provide for the eventual worldwide distribution of digital copies over the Web. In other cases, no deed of gift or documented chain of provenance exists. The need to document rights for analog source objects and their digital surrogates is an additional requirement for DRM systems in libraries, archives, and museums.

Even when a clear chain of provenance exists, and the right to publish a digital surrogate on the Web is clear, it remains important to document the copyright status of the resource and to provide clear attribution for the resource creators and other rights holders. Libraries may also want to protect digital resources from unauthorized reuse through common strategies, such as watermarking, or by providing low-resolution digital surrogates that lack sufficient quality for commercial reproduction.

Moving beyond basic strategies to control access or reproduction of resources requires an understanding of the enabling technologies for an end-to-end digital rights management solution, as well as a business model that supports the library's core mission and demonstrates a thorough understanding of the information needs of the library's users. As with many computer applications, a DRM implementation is a complex and unforgiving system. The "yes/no" world of computer bits works very well for straightforward aspects of a DRM implementation, such as limiting course reserves to registrants in a course, but not well at all for managing the wide range of digital resources that a library offers to its users. The flow of information is a central activity for any library. The implementation of a system that exists to restrict that flow of information should not be taken lightly. There are many serious issues to consider before developing a DRM implementation.

DRM Issues and Concerns

Many information management applications are beginning to bundle DRM implementations as core technologies within an applications suite. Web portal applications, content management systems, learning management systems, media asset management systems, and desktop software applications may have DRM implementations with different, even competing, technologies. Most libraries are part of larger institutions, such as a university or a county or city government. A first step in developing a DRM project is to discover what DRM solutions have already been implemented, generally by IT or administrative departments. At a minimum, the institution may have developed an authentication system, such as a directory-based identity management system.

It is also critical to understand the information ecology of the library's user community. A poorly designed DRM system can execute draconian controls over information resources, with the DRM administrators becoming "de facto" rights holders. Current commercial DRM applications apply primarily to commercial software and resources, which were developed as "works for hire" by employees who disclaim all ownership once the resource is offered for sale. By contrast, the creators of intellectual content in a university or public library setting identify strongly with their works and will not be willing to relinquish the right to dispose of their resources as they choose. There can also be serious legal and ethical concerns if a resource is not made available expeditiously, particularly in a medical or legal setting. Two simple examples can illustrate the dangers of a poorly implemented DRM system:

- Professor A writes a paper for prepublication, and it is placed in a digital repository. He references the paper in his curriculum vitae, which he sends to a university where he has applied for a more prestigious position. The search committee attempts to read the article to determine whether his scholarship warrants an interview, but is denied access by the DRM system in the repository.

- Instructor B obtains a lesson plan from the school's educational repository. The lesson plan is excellent in every respect, except that some of the information has been supplanted by new discoveries in the field. The instructor attempts to edit the dated information but is denied the right to edit the resource. The instructor who created the lesson plan is on sabbatical and thus not available to modify the permissions attached to the resource.

Two issues of great concern to the library community are the privacy and confidentiality of users accessing information. Privacy and confidentiality are concepts that are often viewed as synonymous. In actuality, privacy refers to safeguarding the identity of the information user, while confidentiality refers to the user's right to access information without that information use being observed or recorded. Many DRM implementations include tracking mechanisms to maintain control of a resource and to either prevent or monitor downstream use. "Downstream use" refers to the extending of rights to access and use a resource by the initial user to other users, generally without further reference to the rights holder. Monitoring and logging use of digital resources has been suggested as a means of documenting and enforcing the rights holder's interpretation of fair use, preventing or controlling downstream access, and enforcing other restrictions on use of the resource. Most emerging commercial DRM implementations, whether stand-alone or part of an application suite, such as a media asset management system, include monitoring and tracking of use. A library may be creating and maintaining resource usage logs that explicitly identify resource users, without intending to archive this information, simply because a feature of a system was not disabled or because the library did not make a conscious decision to wipe the log files rather than back them up along with other system files.

Conclusion

This overview has attempted to convey some of the complexity of the DRM arena. Currently, the DRM space is characterized by a number of emerging standards but few operational solutions. Current implementations exist primarily in the commercial world and support the simple paradigm that rights transactions are straightforward and consist of an offer from a single rights holder to provide access to a resource after a fee has been paid. DRM development has not kept pace with the applications that it will need to support.

For libraries, museums, universities, and other public-information providers, the managed but unimpeded flow of information has not only been the foundation but, in a real sense, defines those organizations. More than most institutions, libraries exist because it pleases their users to have libraries. Libraries recognize that a relationship of trust with their users is core to the continued existence of libraries and central to the well-being of both. Though very much in development, DRM has the potential to be the "deal breaker" for this relationship of trust. The library world has a window of opportunity to provide leadership or at least to participate in the development of DRM as an enabling technology that supports the rights of owners and users to share information to support the public good. That window is steadily shrinking.

DRM is a polarizing issue not because those who support open information wear white hats and those who support "pay-per-view" wear black. The economy of most nations is increasingly information-based, and a healthy economy benefits everyone. The danger of DRM lies in exclusive support for the simplistic "pay-per-view" paradigm of one-way information transfer, and a growing suite of standards and technologies to support that model, as well as the assumption that there is only way to do DRM. As DRM standards mature and their application is better understood, they can be either rejected or extended to support the complex, volatile, often ambiguous information flow that characterizes discovery, understanding, synthesis, and innovation. Melvin C. Kranzberg's first law of the history of technology is particularly applicable to the lively debate about digital rights management: "Technology is neither good nor bad, nor is it neutral."[21]

References

1. "Defining a Proactive Role for Libraries, Higher Education, and Commercial and Public Interest Allies in Developing Digital Rights Management (DRM) Technology." Workshop sponsored by the American Library Association, Association of Research Libraries, and Samuelson Law, Technology and Public Policy Clinic, University of California, Berkeley, January 9–10, 2003.

2. U.S. Copyright Office. *Digital Millennium Copyright Act of 1998: U.S. Copyright Office Summary.* Library of Congress, December 1998. http://www.loc.gov/copyright/legislation/dmca.pdf.

3. Crews, Kenneth D. *The Technology, Education and Copyright Harmonization (TEACH) Act.* American Library Association, 2003. http://www.ala.org/washoff/teach.html.

4. *XrML: The Digital Rights Language for Trusted Content and Services.* ContentGuard, 2000–2003. http://www.xrml.org.

5. *The Open eBook Forum <OeBF>* http://www.openebook.org.

6. The Open Digital Rights Language Initiative. http://odrl.net.

7. COLIS: Collaborative Online Learning and Information Services. http://www.colis.mq.edu.au.

8. Library of Congress. METS: Metadata Encoding and Transmission Standard Official Web Site. February 19, 2002. http://www.loc.gov/standards/mets.

9. Cover, Robin. *Security Assertion Markup Language (SAML).* Cover Pages Technology Reports. Last modified February 10, 2003. http://xml.coverpages.org/saml.html.

10. Cover, Robin. *Extensible Access Control Markup Language (XACML).* Cover Pages Technology Reports. Last modified February 25, 2003. http://xml.coverpages.org/xacml.html.

11. Rosenblatt, B., et al. *Digital Rights Management: Business and Technology.* John Wiley, 2001.

12. Internet2. Shibboleth Project. March 5, 2003. http://shibboleth.internet2.edu.

13. The National Science Digital Library: The Comprehensive Source for Science, Technology, Engineering, and Mathematics Education. http://nsdl.org/render.userLayoutRootNode.uP.

14. Martin, Mairéad, et al. "Federated Digital Rights Management: A Proposed DRM Solution for Research and Education" in *D-Lib Magazine* (July/August 2002) vol. 8, no. 7/8.

15. Bormans, Jan, and Keith Hill, eds., *MPEG21 Overview* vol. 5. International Organisation for Standardisation. ISO/IEC JTC1/SC29/WG11, Coding of Moving Pictures and Audio.(ISO/IEC JTC1/SC29/WG11/N5231). October 2002. http://mpeg.telecomitalialab.com/standards/mpeg-21/mpeg-21.htm.

16. <indecs>rdd Consortium. <indecs>rdd White Paper: A Standard Rights Data Dictionary. May 2002. http://www.rightscom.com/Indecs2RDD_White_Paper_May2002.pdf.

17. OASIS. OASIS Rights Language TC. Updated 15 November 2002. http://www.oasis-open. org/committees/rights.

18. Friesen, Norm, et al. "Towards a Digital Rights Expression Language Standard for Learning Technology." IEEE Learning Technology Standards Committee Digital Rights Expression Language Study Group. December 98, 2002 http://xml.coverpages.org/DREL-DraftREL.pdf.

19. The Creative Commons Licensing Project (March 6, 2003). http://creativecommons.org/license.

20. Giantsteps Media Technology Strategies *DRM Watch* (March 6, 2003). http://www.giantstepsmts.com/drmwatch.htm.

21. Kranzberg, Melvin. "The Information Age: Evolution or Revolution?" in B. R. Guile (ed.), *Information Technologies and Social Transformation.* National Academy of Engineering, 1985: 50.

The Current State and Future Promise
of Portal Applications

Brian E. C. Schottlaender
University Librarian
University of California, San Diego

Mary E. Jackson
Senior Program Officer for Access Services
Association of Research Libraries

Introduction

Library portals are new tools for discovering a range of diverse content, from resources freely available on the public Web to the online catalogs, abstracting and indexing databases, licensed journals, and special collections and archives that are the domain of the "deep" Web. In addition, portals offer a range of services that facilitate post-discovery information use.

However, an increasing number of library users are turning to Google or other commercial search engines for their information needs before they avail themselves of the resources their libraries provide. Why? Simply put, because they value simplicity. For some users, three mouse clicks is one click too many. The single, powerful search engine, simple search interface, and rapid result sets offered by Google and similar services are sufficient to satisfy many information needs. Users appear to prefer speed and ease of use to comprehensiveness of information. Librarians, for their part, continue to want to ensure that high-quality, library-vetted content can and will be discovered by their users and therefore are looking carefully at the usefulness of portals.

Defining a Portal

What is a portal? Many librarians and users think they know what "portal" means. The challenge for libraries is that everyone thinks it means something different. There is no consensus definition of a portal, even within the library community. In fact, portals have been defined and characterized in a variety of ways, including

- "Systems which gather a variety of useful information resources into a single, 'one stop' web page."[1]
- Access points that reach across deep and surface Web content.[2]
- Entry points to the Web.[3]
- System of integrated programs designed to make it easier for a user to find information.[4]
- A virtual library, with a range of services equal to those currently provided in the library.[5]
- Portals assemble a variety of useful information into a one-stop Web page, bringing about greater efficiency.[6]

Brian Schottlaender has described a portal as a structured entry point to the academic Web, an academic workbench, an academic platform, a "super discovery tool."[7] The focus in Schottlaender's latter characterization is on the word "super" because so many current discovery tools are not super. The Association of Research Libraries Scholars Portal Project group has described a portal as a tool to search Web resources, local catalogs, online journals, digitized resources, and links to supporting services such as online reference, course management tools, ILL software, and so forth. It goes on to characterize a portal as a "suite of Web-based services that will connect the higher education community as directly as possible with quality information resources that contribute to the teaching and learning process and that advance research."[8]

Finally, Mary Jackson's definition may be the most descriptive of all: "Google with 'good' content supported by a range of library services."[9]

So what, in sum, is a portal? It is a software application layer that sits between the resources and the presentation of those resources to the user. Portal software hides the differences of the various resources being searched. Portals federate or integrate resources and fuse the results from federated searches. Current portal software includes the presentation layer, but it is not required. Perhaps the success of Google and other commercial search engines can in part be attributed to their integration of resources and content in a manner transparent to the user; this, is unlike most library Web sites, which—while they may offer a range of content to users—require users to manually "fuse" search results for presentation.

What Functionality Is Included in a Portal?

The definitions above describe, or at least intimate, the core discovery functionality at the heart of a successful academic portal: the ability of portal users to carry out high-quality searches across a wide range of content. Additional functions an academic portal might ideally support include

- *Capture* (having discovered an information object, portal users should be able to capture it and bring it into their workspace)
- *Integrate* (the ability of portal users to integrate and contextualize information objects with other resources they have in their workspace)
- *Manipulate* (the ability of portal users to do things with their information objects: edit them, annotate them, add to them, combine them)
- *Distribute* (the ability of portal users to share information objects with others: send them to their colleagues, deposit them in archives, "publish" them)
- *Consult* (the ability of portal users to interact with others who study or teach in their areas of interest or who otherwise can inform their work)

Portal Features

Key portal features may be divided into two broad categories. One is the set of features/services aimed at and visible to users; the second is the underlying infrastructure services, invisible to users, that facilitate and support those features/services. User features and services include personalization; distributed searching; data harvesting; request and delivery services; reference services; integration, annotation, and collaboration services; alerting services; and recommender services. Underlying infrastructure services include configuration/customization, record fusion and enrichment, terminology services, resolution services, and directory services.

Personalization

The "MyLibrary" concept is being built into many portals. Users can select or modify the resources that will be checked, how results are displayed (for example, full-text first, from a specific journal, by date of publication), the features displayed on the screen (for example, add the weather or link to a stock quote feed), and their arrangement on the page. Users may opt to display advanced search screens as their default. Finally, personalization permits users to integrate portals with local e-mail systems, calendars, campus schedules, and so forth. Early experience from Boston College and Macalester College suggests that less than 10 percent of portal users presently take advantage of the personalization feature. Monash University in Australia discovered that of the nearly 7,000 users who participated in a trial of Fretwell-Downing's ZPORTAL software, only 15 new profiles, or sets of resources, were created.[10] It was not clear whether this was a problem with the instructions to set up new user profiles or whether users preferred to use the default profiles set up by the library. These findings are consistent with those reported by Ketchell.[11]

It is too early to determine whether the screens, features, and content have been well chosen by these libraries, or whether users are simply too busy to take the time to personalize their portal interfaces. Some portal products permit libraries to offer "multiple views" or permit "semi-personalization." Multiple-view portals allow content appropriate to a particular portal user group to display first, with additional, less-appropriate content moved to secondary screens.

Distributed Searching

Portals are designed to query two distinct streams of resources, regardless of format or location. That is, they provide access both to a universal stream of unrestricted resources available on the public Web and to local stream of "deep" Web resources, access to which is often restricted to local users by license or other agreement. Distributed searching of this range of content must support a variety of format, record syntaxes, and search standards (for example, Z39.50, http). Some users will prefer to limit searches by subject, format, or date; others will want to be as comprehensive as possible. Search results need to be merged, de-duped, sorted, and relevancy-ranked. Relevancy ranking across this diverse range of content will be a challenge as one resource may rank its citations from 1 to 100, a second from 1 to 10, and a third not at all.

A number of libraries are developing portals devoted to specific subjects. Many libraries have already developed subject indexes or guides for their Web sites, so expanding this approach into a portal environment is a natural outgrowth of their Web experience.

Data Harvesting

An alternative to searching is data harvesting. Although searching of remote catalogs or resources has been the primary discovery method to date, the emerging Open Archives' Metadata Harvesting Protocol permits libraries to search a repository of metadata and bring that content back to the user's desktop.

Request and Delivery Services

Portals are not simply discovery tools. Rather, when available and appropriate, they deliver full-text or other information objects directly to the user's desktop. One reason Google is so heavily used is because it both finds and delivers content, rather than simply presenting citations for items. Although many portal users will pursue only those results that actually include a document, some users may wish to obtain items not available in full text. In those cases, users will need a feature that permits them to place an interlibrary loan (ILL) request, submit a request for materials held in the user's local library, submit a request to a commercial document delivery firm, and so forth.

Reference Services

Portal users may wish to pursue reference queries after reviewing their search results. Portal reference services run the gamut from simple reference request forms e-mailed to local reference departments to tight integration with the growing number of virtual or online reference tools such as LSSI or Question Point. Lorcan Dempsey, OCLC's vice president for research, quipped at a recent conference that the integration of virtual reference and portals is "a mortal in a portal."[12]

Integration/Annotation/Collaboration

Portals support resource integration on the desktop in at least three dimensions: integration of search results, integration of retrieved content with other content already on the desktop, and integration of the portal itself with other academic applications, notably course or learning management systems such as Blackboard and WebCT and citation building tools such as EndNote and ProCite. From his or her institution's course management system (CMS), a student in need of a citation should be able to initiate a search of his or her library's electronic journals without leaving the CMS. Conversely, a student searching a library portal should be able to transfer a citation from a search result into a bibliography in EndNote or add a quote from an article in an electronic journal into a course assignment being written in Blackboard or WebCT.

Users increasingly expect to be able to annotate their search results and the documents retrieved by their searches and either save them on their desktops or forward them to other productivity applications. From highlighting to automated document naming to version control, the span of control users wish to assert over resources on their desktop is seemingly endless.

Some assert that portals "in any form are collaborative tools."[13] This is true in at least two dimensions: portals are products of collaboration for collaboration. Collaboration among librarians and information service providers in building and offering portal technology has allowed them to leverage the efforts already taking place in the commercial sector and in research libraries to offer clientele tailored access to electronic resources. It is essential, further, that librarians collaborate with their academic colleagues in portal development because it is they who will know best what primary content the portal should include and what shape that content should take. Users, finally, are looking increasingly to portals as a means to collaborate with others who study or teach in their areas of interest or who can otherwise inform their work. Features that might facilitate such collaboration are already available in the commercial arena, including whiteboarding, event notification, Web co-browsing, and threading and thread linking.

Alerting and Recommender Services

Some users turn to portals for alerts and recommendations of various kinds. Portals—particularly those portals that permit users to maintain profiles of specific resources to be searched—can alert users when new content is available in which they might be interested. Other portals may alert users when materials they have requested are received or when materials need to be returned.

Amazon.com's "customers who bought this book also bought" feature has popularized recommender services. While that feature is exemplary of services that focus on specific resources, other recommender services focus on search strings ("people who searched X also search Y"). Still others offer spelling correction ("did you mean X?").

Infrastructure Services

Configuration/Customization

Because libraries want to add content relevant to their local communities, portal software must be highly configurable or customizable. From the branding of the portal page to include the library's logo and institutional colors to the links to remote resources, portal software needs to reflect the institutional environment in which it is being used. Customization of portals permits libraries to impart their own "look and feel" to a commercial product. Sophisticated portals permit library staff to select the screen layout, make local decisions on fonts and colors, determine where the search bar is placed, select appropriate resources, determine the order in which the results are presented, select the content available to users who are not logged in, and enable or disable links to supporting services such as ILL order forms or online reference.

Record Fusion and Enrichment

Content is described using a variety of metadata schemata. MARC is well known in the library community as it is used in online catalogs for bibliographic description. Newer descriptive schemata include Dublin Core, Visual Resources Association (VRA) Core, Encoded Archival Description (EAD), and the Computer Interchange of Museum Information (CIMI) standard. Portals need to fuse results using all different schemata, and more.

Portals can provide a means by which libraries can enrich records in their online catalogs. MARC bibliographic records can, for instance, be pulled together in a portal with associated cover art for the materials they describe, along with tables of content, abstracts, links to commercial sites (such as alibris.com, abebooks.com, Amazon.com), and so forth.

Terminology Services

Libraries have spent decades developing controlled thesauri. The Library of Congress Subject Headings and the National Library of Medicine's MESH are two examples. Dentists and engineers should be able to search for the term *bridges* and each have results returned that are appropriate to their definition and use of the term. Crosswalks are being developed to deal with such similar, but not identical, terminology.

Resolution Services

Portals that incorporate the Open URL standard enable users to be directed to the "most appropriate copy," as the Open URL resolver offers users choices: full-text licensed content, online catalog if the item is not available in digital form, links to commercial document providers, links to ILL request forms, and so forth. As Madeleine McPherson notes, "hyper linking, dynamic multiple searching and open URLs make it possible to build rich information environments without forcing users to recognize or master the structures that are so important to librarians."[14]

Directory Services

Because libraries include licensed content in their portals, a portal must support authentication and authorization. Authentication is the process of confirming an identity of a user; authorization provides a set of privileges to a specific user group. In portals that require logins, a single sign-on encompasses both authentication and authorization. In the current Web environment, it is unfortunately still all too possible that a user will be required to sign in multiple times.

One of the biggest challenges associated with authentication and authorization is determining how and where to maintain current user information. Some portals permit libraries to develop a user database within the portal software itself. This, however, is not a desirable long-term strategy as it means keeping this user database in synch with the patron database in the library's integrated library system, the institution's authorized user files, or both. If the user database is maintained remotely, there are several standards that can be used to access patron information, including 3M's SIP2, NCIP, Kerberos, LDAP, http, SQL lookup, and Shibboleth. Others will no doubt emerge over the next several years. Authorizing remote users can be particularly vexing, as it requires integration (or at least interfacing) with the institution's proxy server.

Portals or Home Pages?

It is rare to discover a library without a home page. Many libraries have developed extensive lists of their electronic journals and other resources and posted them on their home pages. Some libraries have developed subject lists; others provide alphabetical lists of electronic journals. In both cases, users can search resources, but generally cannot search across titles or subject categories. These home pages permit users to undertake multiple, parallel searches of different content, but the challenge is directing a user to the most appropriate starting point.

Most often library home pages are built from the library perspective. They reflect, understandably enough, an approach to organizing content that is logical for librarians; hence, the alphabetical listing of electronic journals, for instance, is separate from either the online catalog or similar listings for Web sites. Portals, meanwhile, are more often designed with a user-centric view, pulling together content that a "typical" user might want to use.

Portals or Channels?

Libraries are not the only agencies developing portals in the academic environment. Is the library portal a parallel to the institutional portal, or is it a channel within the superordinate portal? Bernard W. Gleason views a portal as "a collection of many applications, which are treated as separate channels."[15] In a college or university setting, the institutional portal typically "sits on top of" other campus portals, speaks to both internal and external audiences, and focuses on providing access to campus information of broad interest, including news, administrative information for prospective and current faculty and students, staff directory information, and sports, alumni, and arts events. The library portal, meanwhile, is likely to be one of several "subordinate" campus portals (or channels) designed to speak to specific (usually internal) audiences. The library portal will typically focus on scholarly (and some recreational) content, while others will focus on business information, financial information, course and student information, and the like.

The Commercial Portal Marketplace

Portal application software is "hot." Many commercial firms offer portal products, but most are aimed at corporations and management of corporate intranet information. Library vendors are developing a range of products specifically aimed at the library community. Products such as Auto-Graphic's AGent, Blue Angel Technologies' MetaStar, Dynix's DigitalLink, Endeavor's EnCompass, Ex-Libris' MetaLib, Fretwell-Downing's ZPORTAL, Gaylord's Polaris PowerPAC, Innovative Interface's Millennium, the Library Corporation's YouSeeMore, MuseGlobal's Muse Search and Information Connection Engine, SIRSI's ibistro, VTLS's Chameleon iPortal, and WebFeat's Knowledge Prism are in varying stages of development and include varying features and functionality.[16] Alternatives to commercial products include various open source software developments such as North Carolina State University's MyLibrary[17] and JA-SIG's uPortal.[18] It is not the intent of this report to review software in the marketplace.

Portal Challenges in an Emerging Environment

Portal application software is not as yet mature. In fact, librarians themselves have not yet reached consensus on required or desired functionality. Instead they are approaching the vendor community with requirements to develop products with variant, and sometimes conflicting, features and functionality. The challenge for vendors is to build products that meet as many of these needs as possible, while that for librarians is to determine which product best matches their needs.

Portal software is unlikely to be of the monolithic "killer app" variety, but, rather, will more likely assemble—perhaps transparently—a range of productivity-enabling applications that will interoperate in a "killer app environment." How libraries might best integrate the range of applications into their local framework is unclear. The current environment requires each portal vendor to incorporate one or more of the invisible infrastructure services described above into its products. It is possible, and perhaps desirable, for third-party organizations or service bureaus to provide one or more of those infrastructure services to libraries, regardless of the particular portal application they are implementing. Why, for example, should each vendor build and maintain a patron database when it may be more effective to link to the institution's authentication and authorization service? The same question might be asked for a good many, if not all, of the infrastructural services described above.

Another challenge for libraries (and librarians) in the emerging environment is to be mindful that portal functionality/features they think desirable may not be those in which their patrons are interested. In light of the growing evidence that users prefer Google over library Web pages, it may, for instance, be tempting to add content in which users "should be" interested.[19] Users, however, may be perfectly satisfied with the first results they retrieve, irrespective of whether those results are for items in which they "should be" interested.

Scalability is yet another challenge. Will a portal ever have enough content to satisfy all its potential users? There are no clear guidelines for what is involved in maintaining a comprehensive portal with a range of supporting services, in terms of financial commitment, staff resources, or software development. Moreover, while the cost of implementing a portal may be known, the staff cost involved in that initial implementation is often underestimated. Beyond initial implementation, maintenance costs are largely unknown and almost certainly higher than libraries estimate them to be.

Portal content needs to be searched using a variety of extant and emerging standards: Z39.50, http, OpenURL, and proprietary search tools for some sites. The challenge is how to determine which standard should be used when a resource can be accessed via multiple standards—Z39.50 and http, for example. Z39.50 is criticized for its lack of precision compared with searching the native interface of an online catalog. Moreover, Z39.50 only works as well as local implementation will allow. On the other hand, a Z39.50 search may well be preferable to the labor-intensive configuration required to search a remote resource using a Web search engine. It is likely that, in the short term, both Z39.50 and http will be needed, and time alone will tell how portals use each.

Portals, finally, introduce real tradeoffs between personalization and privacy. In order to personalize a portal environment, an individual will need to describe himself or herself in some detail. Search histories of resources, if maintained in the portal software, may be even more telling than the circulation histories libraries so carefully eliminate from patron records.

Scholars Portal Project

The Scholars Portal Project is a collaboration between several member libraries of the Association of Research Libraries (ARL) and Fretwell-Downing, Inc. (FD) to develop a suite of scholarly productivity tools and services designed to facilitate an academic user's wish to integrate, manipulate, exploit, and explore the academic content universe. Current participants include the University of Southern California, University of California–San Diego, Dartmouth College, University of Arizona, Arizona State University, University of Utah, and Iowa State University.

The three-year project will test with one vendor's products the vision articulated by the ARL Scholars Portal Working Group.[20] FD products being used in the project include ZPORTAL, Z2Web, Z'MBOL, and OL2. FD is contributing development resources to permit the participants to enhance the products in ways that meet their needs. It is hoped that the collaborative partnership approach to the project will strengthen its outcome. Although the initial focus is on cross-domain searching, the participants expect to integrate the portal with their online learning environments, digital reference services, interlibrary loan requesting systems, and so forth.

By the end of 2002 all participants had the software installed and had received training. Participants have begun to identify Web sites and Z39.50 targets to be added to their portals. Rather unexpectedly, the range of targets and Web sites was far greater than anticipated, and the amount of overlap in resources considered desirable among the participants far lower. In two separate exercises, participants listed the resources they wanted to see added. Approximately 80 percent of the titles submitted were unique to one institution, or at least unique in terms of top priority or initial subject approach.

Portal Functionality Provided by ARL Libraries

The Scholars Portal Project is not the only portal initiative under way in the ARL institutions. In February 2002 ARL surveyed its member libraries to identify the state of current or planned research library applications of portals. Recognizing that there are many definitions and views of library portals, the ARL survey sought responses from libraries that offered portals that include (1) search engine tools that offer the user the capability to search across multiple sources and integrate the results of those searches, and (2) at least one kind of supporting service for the user (such as requesting retrieval or delivery of nondigital material, online reference help, and so forth).[21]

Of the 77 responses, 16 were close enough to the definition to be analyzed. Several others offered portals, but not as defined by the survey. Most of the libraries developed their portals locally, suggesting that many libraries may be upgrading or expanding existing Web sites rather than introducing a completely new portal. Portals may emerge from library Web sites as those sites become more database-driven. The target audience for most library portals is the general university community.

The features and functionality provided by these 16 portals varied somewhat. Most portals permit users to limit searches, while some eliminate duplicate results. A wide variety of materials are available. Both local and remote content is accessible, including e-books, e-journals, the local online catalog, licensed resources, research guides/finding aids, and freely available Web resources. The selection of content is most often the responsibility of individual bibliographers, collection development officers, or other library staff with selection responsibility.

The ability to submit online reference questions is the most common supporting service available in the portals, followed closely by ILL requests or automated retrieval of locally owned material. Only three libraries provide access to institutional services, an indication that library portals are still being developed independently of the institutional portal.

ARL asked respondents to identify features and functionality that they plan to add to their portals. Examples of desired enhancements include more personalization, navigation by subject through all resources, and customizing links to individual journal titles.

Although the majority of respondents to the survey indicated that they did not offer a portal in early 2002, about half were in the discussion or exploration phase. Because portal technology is so "hot," ARL repeated its survey in December 2002 with slight modifications. In an attempt to avoid definitional confusion, ARL members were asked whether their libraries provided cross-resource searching (a single search against multiple licensed materials, the Web, online catalogs, local databases, finding aids, and so forth); customized data mining of content or metadata; Web page personalization; and one or more supporting services such as online reference, links to learning management software, ILL systems, and so forth. Thirty-four ARL member institutions responded to this survey. It is possible, given the way the question was structured, that some of the 34 libraries do not consider their Web sites to be portals, although these sites are being enhanced to include features common in portals. Twenty-four of the 34 provided cross-resource searching, 6 supported data mining, 6 permitted users to personalize their Web pages, and 29 offered one or more supporting service. ILL was the most common, with 13 libraries providing that service, while 12 libraries offered online or virtual reference services.

Three definitions from these results illustrate the evolving nature of portals. Duke University defined a portal as a Web gateway to digital resources and services that provides a high level of seamless integration and that includes a feature-rich toolkit that enables user productivity along the entire scholarly communications spectrum. Boston College defined its portal as an interactive gateway to resources and services. The University of Connecticut envisions its portal serving as the premier point for the discovery and identification of high-quality information resources, regardless of format, in a single, intuitive, secure, and personalized gateway.

The Future of Portals

Are portals the updated embodiment of how a library delivers on its mission, or a faddish manifestation of a library's will to survive? Will portals become a preferred or even necessary library service? If we build them, will they come? These are questions with no ready answers. While it may not yet be clear whether and how libraries will ultimately embrace this new technology, it does seem very clear indeed that "one-stop-shopping" is most appealing to library users. Portals represent a very powerful tool for facilitating the interaction of people, activities, and resources; that is, specific user types (students, faculty, lifelong learners, and so forth) pursuing specific activities (searching, retrieving, integrating, manipulating, distributing) with specific and appropriate resources (print and nonprint, digital and nondigital, local and remote, and so forth). To the extent that portals continue to play this role in facilitating the management of an increasingly chaotic information environment, they are likely to thrive.

Notes

1. Michael Looney and Peter Lyman, "Portals in Higher Education." *Educause Review,* vol. 35, no. 4 (July/August 2000).

2. *Library Journal Academic Newswire* (Oct. 17, 2002) citing Clifford Lynch's closing remarks at the 2002 LITA Conference.

3. Sarah E. Thomas, "Abundance, Attention, and Access: Of Portals and Catalogs." Available at http://www.arl.org/newsltr/212/portal.html.

4. "What Is a Portal?" Available at http://www.portalking.com/portal.htm.

5. Mary E. Jackson, "The Advent of Portals." *Library Journal,* vol. 127, no. 15 (Sept. 15, 2002), p. 39.

6. Sylvia Charp, "Administrative and Instructional Portals." *The Journal* (September 2002). Available at http://www.thejournal.com/magazine/vault/A4122.cfm.

7. Brian E. C. Schottlaender, "The New Academic Platform: Beyond Resource Discovery." *Journal of Internet Cataloging,* vol. 5, no. 3 (2002), pp. 27–32.

8. "ARL Scholars Portal Working Group Final Report" (May 21, 2002). Available at http://www.arl.org/access/scholarsportal/final.html.

9. Mary E. Jackson, "The Advent of Portals." *Library Journal,* vol. 127, no. 15 (Sept. 15, 2002), p. 37.

10. David Groenewegen and Simon Huggard, "The Answer to All Our Problems?" Presentation at the Online 2003 Conference. Available at http://www.alia.org.au/conferences/online2003/conferencepapers/groenewegen.htm.

11. D. S. Ketchell, "Too Many Channels: Making Sense Out of Portals and Personalization." *Information Technology and Libraries,* vol. 19, no. 4 (December 2000), pp. 175–179.

12. Lorcan Dempsey's presentation at the Improved Access to Information Conference sponsored by the University of Oklahoma Libraries, March 6–7, 2003.

13. Amos Lakos, "Personalised Library Portals and Organisational Change." Available at http://dochost.rz.hu-berlin.de/eunis2001/e/Lakos/HTML/lakos.html.

14. Madeleine McPherson, "Position or Purpose: Situating the Library in a Webbed World." *Australian Academic & Research Libraries*, vol. 32, no. 3 (September 2001). Available at http://www.usq.edu.au/library/homepgs/mcpherso/AARL.htm.

15. Bernard W. Gleason, "Portal Technology Opportunities, Obstacles, and Options: A View from Boston College." In *Web Portals & Higher Education* by Richard N. Katz and Associates, Jossey-Bass, 2002, p. 90.

16. http://www.auto-graphics.com/ls_agent.html

    http://www.blueangeltech.com/products.html

    http://www.epixtech.com/about_us/press/2002/9870.asp

    http://encompass.endinfosys.com; http://www.exlibris-usa.com/MetaLib

    http://www.fdusa.com/products/zportal.html

    http://www.gis.gaylord.com/Polaris/PAC/PowerPAC.asp

    http://www.iii.com/products/millennium/index.shtml

    http://www.carl.org/tlccarl/products/pacs/youseemore.asp

    http://www.museglobal.com/Products/MuseSearch/index.html

    http://www.sirsi.com/sirsiproducts/ibistro.html; http://chaos.vtls.com/chameleon

    http://www.webfeat.org/prism.html

17. Keith Morgan and Tripp Reade, "Pioneering Portals: MyLibrary@NCState." *Information Technology and Libraries*, vol. 19, no. 4 (December 2000), pp. 191–198.

18. http://www.uportal.org/forum.

19. Amy Friedlander, "Dimensions and Use of the Scholarly Information Environment: Introduction to a Data Set Assembled by the Digital Library Federation and Outsell, Inc." Available at http://www.clir.org, and Pew Charitable Trusts, "The Internet Goes to College: How Students are Living in the Future with Today's Technology." Available at http://www.pewinternet.org.

20. ARL Scholars Portal Working Group Report (May 2001). Available at http://www.arl.org/access/scholarsportal/may01rept.html.

21. Karen A. Wetzel and Mary E. Jackson, "Portal Functionality Provided by ARL Libraries: Results of an ARL Survey." *ARL Bimonthly Report*, no. 222 (June 2002). Available at http://www.arl.org/newsltr/222/portalsurvey.html

Recruitment and Retention: A Professional Concern

Ad Hoc Task Force on Recruitment and Retention Issues

A Subcommittee of the Personnel Administrators and Staff Development Officers Discussion Group, Association of College and Research Libraries

Recruitment and retention of library staff moved into the spotlight as major professional issues in 2002. Dire predictions of massive retirements of librarians, an inadequate supply of MLS/MLIS graduates, increased competition from nonlibrary employers, less-than-competitive salaries, and a lingering image problem fueled discussion, debate, growing concern, and action within the profession.

Reports from all types of libraries seem to indicate that the demographic tidal wave of librarian retirements expected for several years has begun, and that the number of job openings is significantly higher than the number of available qualified candidates. Search committees and hiring officers report smaller applicant pools, longer searches, more unsuccessful searches, and increased competition for applicants both from other libraries and from nonlibrary employers.

Even with the bursting of the dot.com bubble, MLS/MLIS graduates continue to be recruited by the private sector at higher salaries. Salaries are increasing in libraries, but not quickly enough in most cases to recruit or retain highly qualified candidates or to be competitive with comparable professions. Also, image issues continue to linger, negatively impacting recruitment to the profession at large.

With the demand for library and information science graduates increasing and the supply of qualified librarians in decline, the labor gap has widened, and the profession has taken note.

The Profession's Response

In the past year, the issues of recruitment and retention took on new meaning and resulted in much discussion and a good deal of action by a number of professional library associations. National media coverage highlighted the growing shortage of librarians in all types of libraries and emphasized the increasing demand for these professionals in both library and nonlibrary settings.

The national coverage included such stories as "Librarian Slots Stack Up in State: Pay, Age, Image Take Toll in Schools" in the *Denver Post* November 11, 2002 (Whaley, 2002). The article documented the shortage of school librarians in Colorado (one third of the state's 1,437 schools do not have a school librarian) and the adverse impact on student performance. According to the article, nearly 50 percent of the United States' 125,000 librarians are expected to retire within 12 years.

This article was a collaborative effort by the members of the task force, which wrote a White Paper titled *Recruitment, Retention, and Restructuring: Human Resources in Academic Libraries,* published by ACRL in 2002. Members of the task force were William Black, Middle Tennessee State University; George Bynon (Co-Chair), University of California, Davis; Kathleen DeLong, University of Alberta; Pat Hawthorne (Co-Chair), University of California, Los Angeles; Ken Hood, University at Buffalo; Kurt Murphy, Arizona State University; Carol Olsen, Stanford University; Laine Stambaugh, University of Oregon; Teri R. Switzer, Auraria Library/University of Colorado at Denver; Diane Turner, Yale University; and Denise Weintraub, University of Chicago.

This was one of many articles about the profession's recruitment problems to appear in newspapers across the country. They told the story of a profession in which the median age is 47 and in which retirements are leaving huge gaps of expertise. Other articles told of the difficulty faced by school systems, public libraries, and colleges and universities in filling librarian positions.

In response, the American Library Association (ALA) launched a national public relations campaign designed to improve the image of the profession and to recruit diverse individuals to become librarians. ALA 2002 President John W. Berry made recruitment and retention a theme of his presidential year, giving interviews to media around the country about the need for more librarians, hosting a "national town hall" teleconference on the topic, and appointing a presidential task force to study the issues. ALA 2003 President Maurice J. Freedman has made pay equity and better salaries a platform of his presidential year, initiating programs and funding to encourage the recruitment, education, and retention of a diverse library work force.

The Public Library Association (PLA), a division of ALA, addressed the emerging shortage of public librarians in a report to its executive committee in January 2000. The report defined the issues related to public librarian recruitment and salaries and outlined a series of recommendations to address the "shortage of MLS librarians going into the field of public librarianship, and what can be done about it" (Public Library Association, 2000).

In 2002 the Personnel Administrators and Staff Development Officers Discussion Group of the Association for College and Research Libraries (ACRL) published a White Paper titled "Recruitment, Retention, and Restructuring: Human Resources in Academic Libraries." Written by an ad hoc task force of human resources officers in academic libraries, the White Paper provides an overview of the current situation in academic institutions and lists a large number of strategies that the various stakeholders might employ to address the issues and cope with the tightening labor market. The Association of Research Libraries (ARL) and ACRL also joined forces to appoint a joint task force to focus on recruitment and retention issues in academic libraries.

Also in 2002 the Canadian Association of Research Libraries (CARL), under the aegis of Ernie Ingles, University of Alberta, initiated a nationwide study of Canadian academic libraries designed to provide hard data on library work force supply and demand. Recently, CARL has been joined by other library associations—ranging from the Canadian Library Association and the Council of Administrators of Large Urban Public Libraries to provincial library associations—and expanded the study to identify trends in the library community as a whole, with the intention of developing a foundation of data that would support the development of a national human-resources strategy for the library profession in Canada. All library sectors in Canada acknowledge that there is much anecdotal evidence pointing to major staffing shortages and that these shortages are predicated upon a number of variables, the magnitude of their individual or compound effects completely unknown. Thus the study intends to examine library workers at all stages of their careers, as well as in library programs, and provide a comprehensive look at issues around recruitment, retention, rejuvenation, retirement, restructuring, remuneration, reaccreditation, and repatriation (of librarians working outside Canada or in the private sector)—the "Eight Rs" of human-resource planning in Canadian libraries.

The library staffing issue has also attracted attention in Washington, D.C. In early 2002 a $10 million initiative to fund a variety of programs to recruit librarians—including scholarships for graduate students in library and information science, distance-learning technology for training programs in underserved areas, and recruitment of librarians with diverse language skills—was announced by the White House. The Institute for Museum and Library Services (IMLS) will oversee the initiative, which is designed to increase the number of professionals and to enhance diversity within the profession.

In these actions and others, the emerging picture of a profession facing a crisis was evident. The factors contributing to the growing problem have been written about extensively in professional literature.

Large numbers of librarian retirements coupled with a flat number of MLS/MLIS graduates illustrate the mathematical component of the problem.

Retirements

Predictions of massive retirements of librarians from all segments of the profession have been appearing in the library literature since the mid-1990s. Based on data from various library surveys as well as U.S. Department of Labor census information, the library profession is clearly facing the potential loss to retirement of approximately 60 percent to 65 percent of all current librarians by the year 2020. In libraries of all types across North America, the predictions are beginning to become reality.

The Age Demographics of Academic Librarians: A Profession Apart (Wilder, 1995) provided a stark picture of academic librarians in terms of age. In comparison to similar professions, academic librarianship had significantly fewer individuals under the age of 30 and a higher percentage of individuals over the age of 45. In 1994 the group aged 45–49 was the largest single age group (23 percent) of the existing cohort of ARL librarians; by 2000, more than 20 percent (the largest percentage group) of the ARL librarian population was between 55 and 59 (Wilder, 2002). According to Wilder, the ARL data indicates that the population of academic librarians in ARL libraries will reach its oldest point in 2005. The end result will be an enormous loss of professional expertise and leadership due to retirements. Wilder's (1995) research indicated that 16 percent of academic librarians could retire between 2000 and 2005, 24 percent between 2005 and 2010, and 27 percent between 2010 and 2020; overall that translates to a whopping 67 percent of academic librarians working in 1995 being eligible for retirement by 2020.

In November 2001 ALA's Office for Human Resource Development and Recruitment (HRDR) surveyed members of the Human Resources Section of the Library Administration and Management Association, a division of ALA. In one question, respondents were asked what percentage of librarians in their institutions was expected to retire in the coming five years. A total of 171 responded, and these were the results: 34 percent expected less than 5 percent of their librarians to retire; 22 percent expected 5 percent to 10 percent to retire; 22 percent expected 10 percent to 20 percent to retire; and 22 percent expected more than 20 percent to retire. This means that 5 percent to 20 percent of librarians in the libraries responding to this small survey will retire by 2006.

Using 1990 census data, ALA has developed an age profile of the profession—a profile that mirrors the ARL data and indicates that the trends identified by Wilder for academic librarians will be similar for the profession at large, thus affecting academic, public, school, and special libraries. In an *American Libraries* article (Lynch, 2002), the 1990 census data on 87,409 librarians showed that approximately 10 percent of librarians would reach age 65 between 2000 and 2004, 16 percent between 2005 and 2009, more than 20 percent between 2010 and 2014, and approximately 18 percent between 2015 and 2019. This demographic analysis shows that more than 60 percent of librarians currently employed will reach retirement age by 2020.

With most libraries expecting to lose up to 20 percent of their librarians to retirement and up to 65 percent of librarians eligible for retirement by 2020, the certain loss of veteran talent and expertise seems vast. While the personal decision to retire may or may not come at age 65, most available statistics indicate that less than 3 percent of the population works past the traditional retirement age of 65 (Wilder, 2002). The expected waves of retirements among Baby Boomers, coupled with fewer younger workers, will undoubtedly create tighter labor markets in many fields. In a 2001 report, the General Accounting Office predicted that the potential for acute labor shortages in all professions and industries would intensify as the supply of younger workers declined and the Baby Boomer generation aged and moved toward retirement. While the trend in recent years toward earlier retirements is understandable, it is also potentially disastrous in an aging society where people are healthier, life expectancy is rising, and labor shortages are predicted (Samuelson, 2002).

For the library profession, the predicted number of retirements of librarians paired with the larger trend of fewer younger workers is a complex problem.

Inadequate Supply of Graduates

A second contributing factor to the situation is the inadequate supply of MLS/MLIS graduates. While the number of jobs is increasing, the number of graduates available to hire is relatively stable. Such a labor gap is considered a supply issue; one that is exacerbated by the increasing demand for librarians in nonlibrary settings, because that demand further reduces the number of graduates available to library employers.

The increasing demand for librarians made national news following the release of a 2001 Bureau of Labor Statistics (BLS) report. The report noted high retirement rates and predicted growth of about 5 percent in the number of librarian job openings (about 7,000 more jobs in 2008 than in 1998). While the BLS report pointed out that the majority of librarian job openings would continue to be in public, school, college, and university libraries, it also noted that the expertise and skills of library and information science graduates made them more marketable, and, as a result, that librarians were being recruited by private-sector employers to work in nonlibrary settings, and that this competition was resulting in increased salaries (Crosby, 2000–2001).

Such publicity may increase the number of applicants to MLS/MLIS programs, but it does not guarantee a rise in the number of graduates. With a finite number of graduate library and information science programs and enrollment caps, the number of graduates has remained relatively flat in recent years. In Canada, while enrollment in library and information science programs shows a slight and recent increase, this follows years of sustained decline in the numbers of graduates.

Faced with a dramatic number of retirements across the profession, two aspects of the pipeline issue central to providing an adequate future work force have emerged: the decreasing number of graduate programs for library and information science and the relatively flat number of graduates produced annually by master's-level degree programs in library and information science. In the 1990s the closing of library school programs was a major topic within the profession. The issues surrounding the various closings included debate regarding the role of the professional school in a research university as well as the role of educators and practitioners in library education, in addition to discussion about curriculum (Marcum, 1991). Overall, the number of library schools declined from 68 in 1976 to 56 in 2002, a decrease of more than 17 percent. In addition, state budget deficits continue to have a negative effect on academic programs and a few graduate library science programs are newly threatened in recent months.

Fifty-six library schools—49 U.S. schools and 7 Canadian—report student-related data to the Association for Library and Information Science Education (ALISE) annually. The reports show total enrollment generally on the increase, although fluctuating, between 1996 and 2001. During this period, the highest enrollment was 22,883 in the fall of 2001 while the lowest level of enrollment was 18,699 in the fall of 1999, a difference of 4,184.

Table 1 / Enrollment in MLS/MLIS Programs, U.S. and Canada, 1996–2001

	Total Enrollment	Difference	Percentage
Fall 1996	19,206		
Fall 1997	18,901	- 305	-1.6 %
Fall 1998	19,984	+ 1,083	+ 5.7 %
Fall 1999	18,699	- 1,285	- 6.4 %
Fall 2000	21,115	+ 2,416	+ 12.9 %
Fall 2001	22,883	+ 1,768	+ 8.3 %

During the same period, the total number of degrees awarded (not just MLS/MLIS, but also bachelor's, master's, post-master's, and doctoral) increased by only 740. In recent years a number of library and information science programs have added an undergraduate program, most in information science. These programs seem to be attracting undergraduates interested in using the information science degree in a variety of settings. Initial anecdotal evidence indicates that graduates of bachelor's degree programs in information science generally do not seek employment in traditional library settings, but instead seek jobs in the private sector.

In examining ALISE's annual statistics, one of the most striking facts relates to the number of ALA-accredited master's degrees awarded. Over the last five academic years, the average number of such degrees awarded is 4,993 per academic year. The overall trend is that the number of degrees awarded is declining, from a high of 5,068 in 1996–1997 to 4,953 in 2000–2001. From year to year, the increase or decrease is less than 5 percent, illustrating the relatively flat number of ALA-accredited degrees awarded. These figures are illustrated in the table below.

Table 2 / Number of Information Science Degrees Awarded, 1996–2001

	Total (Bachelor's, Master's, Post-Master's, Doctoral)		Master's Degrees Only	
1996–1997	5,710	-171 / -2.9%	5,068	- 203 / -3.9%
1997–1998	5,835	+125 / +2.1%	5,024	-44 / -0.8%
1998–1999	6,071	+ 236 / +4%	5,046	+22 / +0.4%
1999–2000	5,999	-72 / -1.1%	4,877	-169 / -3.3%
2000–2001	6,450	+451 / +7.5%	4,953	+76 / +1.5%

Given the number of enrollments and degrees awarded, specifically ALA-accredited master's degrees, it is clear that the 56 existing library and information science programs will not be capable of producing the number of librarians needed between now and 2020 unless both total enrollment and total number of ALA-accredited master's degrees increases sharply and dramatically.

Competition, Salary, and Image

Additional factors that affect recruitment and retention issues include competition for library school graduates from other sectors, poor salaries, and a negative professional image.

Competition

Competition from nonlibrary employers is growing as the demand for the skills of librarians increases. During the 1980s and 1990s, special libraries created new job opportunities for librarians to work in a wide variety of industries and professions. The emergence of the World Wide Web has since created additional employment opportunities for librarians as Web designers and webmasters in both library and nonlibrary settings. The dot.com craze of the late 1990s attracted many new graduates to new information jobs and away from more traditional library settings. The emergence of new technologies and the increasing reliance on electronic information resources is likely to add to the demand for librarians as information professionals in many different settings, further accelerating the competition for the few graduates available.

Salaries

Salaries for librarians are increasing, but are still lower on average than salaries for other comparable professions requiring a master's degree (Wilder, 1995). An example was cited by PLA in its report "Recruitment of Public Librarians," which included a comparison of the salaries of public librarians with those of secondary school teachers in New York City. The unpublished study was based on census data and showed that "1.9 percent of librarians earned over $50,000 as compared to 12 percent of teachers. In both groups (librarians and teachers), the subjects were employed by local government and held master's degrees. Again for those persons in this study, the largest segment of librarians, 44.1 percent, fell into the $20,000 to $30,000 range salary, while the largest segment of teachers, 34.6 percent, fell into the $40,000 to $50,000 range. In this analysis, librarian salaries consistently and dramatically lagged behind teachers with comparable education" (Public Library Association, 2000).

According to *Library Journal*'s annual survey of placements and salaries, the average starting salary for 1997 was $30,270 and rose to $31,915 for 1998, an increase of 5.4 percent. In 1999 the average starting salary rose 6.5 percent to $33,976. The 2000 survey noted that the average starting salary was $34,871, an increase of 2.6 percent over 1999. Further increases in salaries are likely, given supply and demand factors.

Image

Image has always been a source of concern within the profession, and that concern is likely to continue. Despite all the changes of the past decade and the increasing complexity of professional work and new roles, many still feel that the negative stereotype of librarians hampers recruitment efforts to the profession.

Responses to the Labor Gap

When demand increases beyond available supply or supply falls below existing demand, a labor shortage occurs. With a relatively stable number of MLS/MLIS graduates and the predicted number of librarian retirements, a labor shortage is likely to become the reality for the library profession over the next decade. This shortage is likely to be caused by both supply and demand issues, making it more complex than a labor shortage caused by increased demand alone or one caused by reduced supply alone.

This labor shortage will exist in a diverse United States, which may make recruitment to the profession more difficult given the current demographics of the profession. Between 1995 and 2050, racial and ethnic minority populations are expected to account for 90 percent of the total growth of the U.S. population (Jones, 2000). With expected lower birthrates and the majority of growth predicted to be among minorities, it is obvious that efforts to recruit young people to the profession must focus on attracting minority librarians to serve user communities that will also be more diverse. Attracting diverse racial and ethnic minorities to a profession with negative stereotypes and low salaries will be a challenge. Higher salaries and increased job opportunities will need to be emphasized in outreach and marketing efforts to ensure that minority young people see the profession as one that has the potential to be both exciting and financially viable as a career.

This gap between the growing demand for librarians and the inadequate supply of qualified candidates is requiring a variety of responses from employers and the profession. One clear result of the labor gap has been the pressure on employers to offer higher salaries in order to attract and retain qualified and talented staff. The responses from library employers have been primarily in the areas of recruitment and retention, with some libraries also using restructuring to address the issues.

In the area of recruitment, employers are using a variety of creative strategies, among them

- Streamlining search procedures to shorten the search process
- Using current staff to assist in recruiting
- Moving to more active recruiting methods
- Hiring search firms
- Using new technologies and methods in recruiting to increase the size of applicant pools and decrease length of searches
- Sending support staff to graduate school to earn an MLS or MLIS
- Hiring librarians with credentials from other countries
- Using incentives to enhance offers to candidates
- Offering referral fees to current employees to identify qualified candidates

Developing new minority and residency programs to enhance diversity is another strategy used to attract a diverse pool of candidates so that libraries reflect the communities they serve.

Failed recruitments force libraries to seek other options and solutions such as outsourcing to get the work done. Libraries are also beginning to examine jobs more carefully and evaluating whether positions truly require an MLS/MLIS degree. In cases where the jobs do not require the degree, paraprofessionals or functional specialists (professionals from other fields such as systems, human resources, budget and fiscal operations, development) are being hired, thus creating a different type of work force in libraries, one that does not have a common professional training.

Retention for many employers has taken on new meaning in the competitive recruiting environment. In general, retention efforts usually focus on salary and other compensation, working conditions, and professional education and development. Libraries that have faced difficulty in filling vacant positions have become more willing to consider and enhance retention efforts to retain high-quality staff. Among retention efforts are

- Enhancing work environments and job descriptions
- Providing more professional-development opportunities
- Offering job rotations or exchanges or special projects
- Allowing flexible work schedules
- Increasing mentoring efforts
- Providing more leadership opportunities

In addition, some employers have been forced to offer higher salaries and incentives and to make generous counteroffers when competing employers recruit staff members, and some libraries are offering incentives for potential retirees to remain on the job either full-time or part-time.

Effective retention strategies must be customized to individuals and local labor markets. Retention strategies usually deal with the following factors: salary and benefits, position responsibilities, opportunities for growth and development, ability to move laterally to learn new skills or to make a career change, potential for promotion, quality of work life, relationships with supervisor and colleagues, work environment, and image or reputation of the employer. In many cases, retention strategies differ and reflect the individual's career level. Employees in their first or second job are more likely to be drawn to challenging and varied job duties, or to the potential to learn new skills or earn additional degrees, and may be more open to moving for a specific position or to work in a specific geographic area. Individuals who are at mid-career or in a senior-level position are going to be drawn by different incentives, such as higher salaries, increased responsibility, and flexibility, and may or may not be interested in relocating. Lifestyle factors and spouse and family are also more likely to be a consideration in a work force that remains dominantly female.

Retention strategies can also be customized to organizations and to play a role in long-term planning. Libraries should consider some form of succession planning and analyze their work force for leadership and administrative skills in light of future needs, and then offer training and development programs that prepare librarians and staff for positions that are likely to become available through retirements.

Use of Paraprofessionals

Libraries of all types have been using more paraprofessionals in a wider variety of roles to complete the day-to-day operational work while librarians move into more-managerial roles and focus on management and strategic planning. In some cases, positions that once required an MLS or MLIS have been conceptualized in a different way and the requirement for a MLS/MLIS dropped if not absolutely necessary. This has led, particularly in academic libraries, to the rise of the functional specialist, a trend that is changing the staffing patterns of many libraries.

Conclusion

Over the past decade, social, technological, economic, and political changes, and the speed of these changes, have created library working environments with new realities. Learning must continue over the entire span of a career. Jobs are no longer static; change is the new constant. Competencies are increasingly important.

In this new reality, recruitment and retention have clearly emerged as key professional issues. It is unclear, however, what the profession's responses will be or what the ultimate results of those responses and various initiatives will be. Given labor market demographics, the work force employed by libraries of all types will undoubtedly change significantly between now and 2020. The most likely scenario is one with fewer librarians with MLS/MLIS degrees leading and managing library staffs composed of nonlibrarian professionals and paraprofessionals who bring a variety of education, experience, expertise, skills, and diverse employment histories to libraries of all types.

References

Association for Library and Information Science Education. Library and Information Science Education Statistical Reports: 1997–2002. Available on the Web at http://ils.unc.edu/ALISE.

Boston Globe (2001). "Librarians in Demand as Job Needs Change." Reprinted in *Miami Herald* January 22, 2001, 43.

Carson, C. H. (1996, October 15). "Placements & Salaries '95: Beginner's Luck: A Growing Job Market." *Library Journal* 121 (17), 29–35.

Carson, C. H. (1997, October 15). "Placements & Salaries '96: Counting on Technology." *Library Journal* 122 (17), 27–33.

Crosby, O. (2000–2001, Winter). "Librarians: Information Experts in the Information Age." *Occupational Outlook Quarterly* 44 (4), 2–15.

General Accounting Office (2001, November). "Older Workers: Demographic Trends Pose Challenges for Employers and Workers." Report to the Ranking Minority Member, Subcommittee on Employer-Employee Relations, Committee on Education and the Workforce, House of Representatives. U.S. House of Representatives. Retrieved November 29, 2001, from http://www.gao.gov/new.items/d0285.pdf.

Gregory, V. L. (1999, October 15). "Placements & Salaries '98: Beating Inflation Now." *Library Journal* 124 (17), 33–42.

Gregory, V. L., and McCook, K. de la P. (1998, October 15). "Placements & Salaries '97: Breaking the $30K Barrier." *Library Journal* 123 (17), 32–38.

Gregory, V. L., and Wohlmulth, S. R. (2000, October 15). "Placements & Salaries '99: Better Pay, More Jobs." *Library Journal* 125 (17), 30–36.

Jones, D. (2000, February/March). "North American Demographic Shifts and the Implications for Minority Librarian Recruitment." *ARL: A Bimonthly Report on Research Library Issues and Actions from ARL, CNI, and SPARC* 208/209, 18–19.

Marcum, D. B. (1991). "Library Education: A Challenge for the 1990s." In *Bowker Annual Library and Book Trade Almanac* (pp. 83–89). 36th Edition. R. R. Bowker.

Lynch, M. J. (2002, March). "Reaching 65: Lots of Librarians Will Be There Soon." *American Libraries* 33 (3), 55–56.

Public Library Association Recruitment of Public Librarians Committee, American Library Association (January 2000). Report to the Executive Committee of the Public Library Association: Recruitment of Public Librarians. Retrieved January 6, 2003, from http://www.pla.org/projects/report.html.

Samuelson, R. J. (2002, December 16). "The 'Mature Worker' Glut." *Newsweek* 140 (25), 55.

Terrell, T., and Gregory, V. L. (2001, October 15). "Placements & Salaries 2000: Plenty of Jobs, Salaries Flat." *Library Journal* 126 (17), 34–40.

Weaver, G. (2001, July 30). "Library Group Steps Up Recruiting Efforts: Image, Lack of Degree Programs in the State Contribute to Shortage of Qualified Librarians." *Indianapolis Star*. Retrieved August 17, 2001, from http://www.starnews.com/print/articles/library30.html.

Whaley, Monte (2002, November 11). "Librarian Slots Stack Up in State: Pay, Age, Image Take Toll in Schools." *Denver Post*. Retrieved January 24, 2003 from http://www.denverpost.com/Stories/0,1413,36%257E53%257E983598%257E,00.html.

Wilder, S. J. (1995). *The Age Demographics of Academic Librarians: A Profession Apart*. Association of Research Libraries.

Wilder, S. J. (1996). "Generational Change and the Niche for Librarians." *Journal of Academic Librarianship* 22 (5), 385–386.

Wilder, S. J. (2000, February/March). "The Changing Profile of Research Library Professional Staff." *ARL: A Bimonthly Report on Research Library Issues and Actions from ARL, CNI, and SPARC* 208/209, 1–5.

Wilder, S. J. (2002, October 14). "The Demographics of Library Leadership." Presentation at ARL/OLMS Human Resources Symposium, Washington, D.C.

Zipkowitz, F. (1995, October 15). "Placements & Salaries '94: New Directions for Recent Grads." *Library Journal* 120 (17), 26–33.

Professional Resources

The issues of recruitment and retention within the library profession are generating a great deal of interest and concern. These articles, Web sites, and resources provide additional information.

AASL, ACRL, PLA Announce Cooperative Recruitment Effort
http://www.ala.org/news/v8n15/jobshadow.html

Become a Librarian
http://www.becomealibrarian.org

The Changing Profile of Research Library Professional Staff
http://www.arl.org/newsltr/208_209/chgprofile.html

New Hires in Research Libraries: Demographic Trends and Hiring Priorities
http://www.arl.org/newsltr/221/newhires.html

North American Demographic Shifts and the Implications for Minority Librarian Recruitment
http://www.arl.org/newsltr/208_209/demograph.html

Recruitment, Retention & Restructuring: Human Resources in Academic Libraries
http://www.ala.org/acrl/recruit-wp.html

Report to the Executive Committee of the Public Library Association: Recruitment of Public Librarians
http://www.pla.org/projects/report.html

Where Do the Next "We" Come from? Recruiting, Retaining, and Developing Our Successors
http://www.arl.org/newsltr/221/recruit.html

White House Proposed Initiative to Recruit and Educate Librarians
http://www.imls.gov/grants/library/lib_bdre.htm

Part 2
Legislation, Funding, and Grants

Legislation

Legislation and Regulations Affecting Libraries in 2002

Emily Sheketoff

Executive Director, Washington Office, American Library Association

Mary R. Costabile

Associate Director, Washington Office, American Library Association

The congressional year came to a close with the fiscal year (FY) 2003 appropriations bills still incomplete, and with the impetus for change and speedy process that was so evident in early 2002 having dissipated throughout the long, partisan summer.

Appropriators managed to report out and achieve passage of only two of the 13 bills, Defense Appropriations (P.L. 107-248) and Military Construction Appropriations (P.L. 107-249), both completed on October 23. While some hoped that the lame duck session of Congress after the November election—which returned the control of the Senate to the Republicans—would produce some appropriations results, only the Homeland Security Act of 2002 (P.L. 107-296) was enacted, along with a series of continuing resolutions to keep government up and running.

The Labor, Health and Human Services (HHS), and Education Appropriations bill was passed by the Senate Appropriations Subcommittee on July 18, 2002, as S. 2766 (S. Report 107-216), but never saw floor action. In the House, Rep. Ralph Regula (R-Ohio), chair of the House Labor HHS Education Appropriations Subcommittee, introduced a bill, H.R. 5329, that essentially contained President Bush's FY 2003 budget request. The bill was not reported out of subcommittee, nor was it voted on by the full House. (The Omnibus Appropriations Bill passed on February 13, 2003, is composed of all the remaining 11 bills not passed in 2002, and, whether passed by one or both houses or in conference, formed the basis for conference discussions.)

Members of the American Library Association staff who contributed to this article included Lynne Bradley, director, Office of Government Relations; Patrice McDermott, assistant director; Miriam Nisbet, legislative counsel; and Claudette Tennant, Internet policy specialist, Office of Information Technology Policy.

Funding

The president's budget submission for FY 2003 was presented on February 4, 2002. Included in the budget was an increase for education of $1.4 billion or 2.8 percent. The proposed budget was met with disappointment on the part of the education community, since many of the programs reauthorized by the No Child Left Behind legislation would be frozen at 2002 levels or not funded at all. In addition, because of a 12 percent increase in eligible Pell grant applicants, there would be a grant shortfall of approximately $1.3 billion. The president's budget suggested cuts in other education programs to fill the shortfall.

Library programs would be funded at $181,720,000, and the budget request included a presidential initiative of $10 million to recruit a new generation of librarians. First Lady Laura Bush announced this initiative a few weeks before the budget was released, saying she was aware of the fact that more than 40 percent of librarians are currently nearing or reaching retirement age. In addition, the Improving Literacy Through School Libraries line item would be funded again at $12.5 million. (More than 1,000 applications were received by September 2002, but only 101 grants were awarded by the Department of Education.)

The final appropriations numbers that appear below show a total of $243,889,000 for the Institute of Museum and Library Services, with $151,700,000 for state library grant programs and $29,022,000 for museum programs. The remainder included administration for both programs, the Native American and Native Hawaiian set-asides, and the National Leadership Program, which included the increase of $10 million for recruitment for librarians, as well as 120 congressional earmarks.

Improving Literacy Through School Libraries, part of the Reading First Initiative in the No Child Left Behind legislation, would receive $12,294,000; grant notification by the Department of Education began in March 2002.

Congress levied a 0.65 percent across-the-board cut on all discretionary programs, but not all numbers were available as this article was being written.

The Legislative Branch Appropriations bill, which had been ready for conference but was never completed, would allocate $528,759,000 for the Library of Congress, including $86,952,000 for the Congressional Research Service. The Superintendent of Documents office at the Government Printing Office (GPO) would be funded at $29,468,000. The Public Printer, Bruce James, was approved by the Senate in November and sworn into office on January 9, 2003. The Superintendent of Documents, Judy Russell, was appointed by James on January 6, 2003.

The National Commission on Libraries and Information Science (NCLIS) was funded at $1,010,000, a slight increase over its FY 2002 level.

Museum and Library Services Act of 2002

(Includes reauthorization of the Library Services and Technology Act)

H.R. 3784, the Museum and Library Services Act of 2002 was introduced in the House of Representatives on February 26, 2002. A hearing was held on the legislation on March 6 in the House Select Education Subcommittee, chaired by Rep. Pete Hoekstra (R-Mich.). Robert Martin, director of the Institute of Museum and Library Services (IMLS); Linda Yoder, director of the Nappanee (Indiana) Public

Table 1 / Funding for Federal Library and Related Programs, FY 2003
(amounts in thousands)

	Final FY 2002	FY 2003 Budget Request	Final FY 2003
GPO Superintendent of Documents	$27,954	$29,639	$29,468
Library of Congress	547,247	572,700	528,759
Institute of Museum and Library Services (IMLS)	243,889		
Library Services and Technology Act	207,219	182,600	208,733*
Museum Programs			28,637
National Agricultural Library	20,400	20,000	21,319
National Commission on Libraries and Information Science	1,495	0	1,010
National Library of Medicine (includes MLAA)	246,801	275,725	310,299
Library-Related Programs			
Department of Education			
Adult Education and Literacy	540,000	575,000	584,609
ESEA Title I, Education for Disadvantaged	9,788.6	10,980.6	7,125
ESEA Even Start	250,000	200,000	245,889
ESEA Educational Technology	872,096	722,500	694,669
ESEA Innovative Education Program Strategies (state grants)	385,000	385,000	384,168
ESEA 21st Century Community Learning Centers	845,600	1,000,000	991,675
Star Schools	27,500	0	27,291
Community Technology Centers	64,950	32,475	32,205
Special Education (IDEA) state grants	6,340,000	7,339,685	8,883,095
Institute of Education Sciences**			450,887
Educational Research	185,567	123,067	139,000
Educational Statistics	80,000	85,000	89,415
Educational Assessment	40,000	109,053	94,767
HEA Title III, Institutional Development	332,500	347,500	388,869
HEA Title IV-C, College Work Study	1,011,000	1,011,000	1,004,429
HEA Title VI, International Education	78,022	78,022	107,795
HEA Title X-A, Postsecondary Education Improvement Fund	146,687	51,200	171,614
Inexpensive Book Distribution (RIF)	23,000	24,000	25,288
Improving Literacy Through School Libraries	12,500	12,500	12,294
Reading First state grants	900,000	1,000,000	986,762
Early Reading First	75,000	75,000	73,767
Other Government Agencies			
IMLS Museum Grants	24,907	24,899	see note
NTIA Information Infrastructure Grants (TOP)	45,500	15,503	15,503
National Archives and Records Administration	209,393	244,247	249,875
National Endowment for the Arts	102,656	105,200	116,500
National Endowment for the Humanities	115,656	120,500	124,937
National Historical Publications and Records Commission	6,450	4,436	6,500

Note: There was an across-the-board cut of discretionary programs for FY 2003 of 0.65 percent. The figures above from the Department of Education, NEA, NEH, and the Institute of Museum and Library Services include the cut. The remaining numbers were unavailable.

*The FY 2003 appropriations bill is the first in which museum programs, traditionally funded in Interior appropriations, have joined library programs in being funded as one total appropriation for IMLS.

**Passage of P.L. 107-279, OERI reauthorization, created a newly named Institute of Education Sciences that takes the place of the Office of Educational Research and Improvement (OERI).

Library; and Lucille Thomas of the Brooklyn Public Library Board of Trustees testified on the legislation.

On March 20, the House Education and the Workforce Committee marked up H.R. 3784 and reported it out favorably (H. Report 107-395). The bill had 94 cosponsors, but was never voted on by the full House.

In the Senate, S. 2611 was introduced and gained 23 bipartisan Senate sponsors. A hearing was held on April 10 and Martin again testified, joined by David Macksam, director of the Cranston Public Library of Rhode Island. The bill was never voted on by the full Senate Health, Education, Labor and Pensions Committee.

National Library Legislative Day

National Library Legislative Day on May 6 and 7 drew more than 450 librarians, friends of libraries, and trustees. In 2002 the Delaware Library Association offered a continuing education seminar the weekend before Legislative Day. At the Tuesday morning May 7 briefing, Friends of Libraries USA (FOLUSA) gave its Congressional Award to Sen. Olympia Snowe (R-Maine) for her work in cosponsoring and supporting the e-rate telecommunications discounts for schools and libraries. Senator Snowe spoke on the importance of librarians and libraries. Sen. Jack Reed (D-R.I.) received a standing ovation for his tireless work to support school and public libraries.

OERI Reauthorization

The reauthorization and reorganization of the Office of Educational Research and Improvement (OERI) was signed by the president on November 5 (P.L. 107-279). The legislation creates an Institute of Education Sciences that replaces and reconstitutes OERI. It establishes within the institute a National Center for Education Research that will carry out research on successful state and local education reform activities, including increasing student achievement; on impacts and uses of technology in education; and on improved methods of mathematics and science teaching for use in elementary and secondary classrooms, including in low-performing schools. There will be at least eight national research and development centers, including the existing National Center for Education Statistics. A National Center for Education Evaluation and Regional Assistance will be established within the institute, and the ERIC Clearinghouses and regional educational laboratories will be under this department, as will the National Library of Education. Title III of the legislation authorizes the National Assessment of Educational Progress. Grover "Russ" Whitehurst, who has been in the field of education research for more than 30 years, has been named director of the institute.

On December 17, Secretary of Education Rod Paige announced the formation of two new offices, the Office of Innovation and Improvement (OII) (http://www.ed.gov/offices/OII) and the Office of Safe and Drug-Free Schools (http://www.ed.gov/offices/OSDFS/index.html). OII will administer about 25 discretionary grant programs, including the Technology Innovation Challenge Grants and the Teaching American History grant, as well as Star Schools and Reading Is Fundamental grants.

Copyright

Distance Education

After passing almost unanimously in the Senate in 2001, the Technology, Education and Copyright Harmonization (TEACH) Act, S. 487, was held up in the House Judiciary Committee until October 2002. The act was eventually passed by both houses of Congress as an amendment to the Justice Department reauthorization bill (H.R. 2215). According to Sen. Patrick Leahy (D-Vt.), one of the original sponsors of the TEACH Act, the language of this legislation is identical to that of the earlier TEACH Act that the Senate passed in June 2001 (CR S. 9889). The president signed H.R. 2215 on November 2, 2002.

The TEACH Act expands face-to-face teaching exemptions in the copyright law, allowing teachers and faculty to use certain copyrighted works in the "digital classroom" under certain conditions without prior permission from the copyright holder. The law is complex and details numerous responsibilities that must be met before educational institutions (including their libraries) can benefit from the exemptions. The American Library Association (ALA) Washington Office has created a TEACH Web site to help members understand the complexities of TEACH (www.ala.org/washoff/teach.html). In addition, ALA's Office for Information Technology Policy will offer an e-mail tutorial on distance education and copyright.

Database Protection

Proponents of database-protection legislation continued their efforts to introduce a bill in the fall, not only in the House, where intensive negotiating sessions have taken place over the past year and a half, but in the Senate as well. No bill was introduced in either house, however. ALA continues to insist that any database-protection bill must allow "fair use" of databases comparable to that under copyright law and permit downstream, transformative use of facts and government-produced data contained in a database.

Access to and Use of Technology

Proponents of legislation to permit copyright owners to control access to and downstream use of their products are aggressively pushing their agenda in Congress. The ALA Washington Office has been following several bills that would undermine the careful balances of the copyright law.

In July 2002 Rep. Howard Berman (D-Calif.) introduced H.R. 5211, a bill to "limit the liability of copyright owners for protecting their works on peer-to-peer networks." This bill permits a copyright owner to use a variety of technological remedies to "prevent infringement" of copyrighted works. Although an initial hearing occurred in September, no vote was held on this bill in 2002.

In August there was an effort to pass S. 2395, the Anticounterfeiting Amendments of 2002, introduced in April 2002 by Sen. Joseph Biden (D-Del.). The bill would create liability for trafficking in illicit "authentication features"—a holo-gram, watermark, certification, symbol, code, or other means of designating that the product to which the authentication feature is affixed is authentic. The bill could pose major problems for anyone exercising fair use. The bill passed out of the Judiciary Committee in July without hearings or a report. Just before the Senate's August recess, there was an effort to pass the bill by unanimous con-sent, but several senators, responding to concerns expressed by libraries and other diverse organizations, placed a "hold" on the bill. Negotiations continued to address concerns of a number of groups, including libraries. No final action occurred on this bill in 2002.

Fair Use

On October 3, shortly before the 197th Congress was scheduled to adjourn, Reps. Rich Boucher (D-Va.) and John Doolittle (R-Calif.) introduced the Digital Media Consumers' Rights Act (DMCRA), a bill that proposed three key changes to sec-tions of the flawed Digital Millennium Copyright Act (DMCA) of 1998. This bill would reaffirm fair use in the digital environment. Although it primarily focuses on the concerns of consumers, it is a first step in recognizing the rights of copy-right users and is a bill that libraries strongly support.

DMCRA (1) would bar the anticircumvention provision of Section 1201 of DMCA and prosecute only those individuals with intent to infringe as in the rest of the copyright law; (2) would not criminalize anticircumvention tools when the tools have substantial noninfringing uses; and (3) would broaden allowances for anticircumvention research.

It was expected that the bill would be reintroduced in 2003.

Also, on October 3, Rep. Zoe Lofgren (D-Calif.) introduced H.R. 5522, the Digital Choice and Freedom Act of 2002, signaling to Congress that copyright law needs to be recalibrated to restore consumer and public rights.

The following statement was provided by several library associations to Rep. Lofgren's office as the bill was introduced: "The introduction of the Digital Choice and Freedom Act of 2002 is yet another sign that Congress needs to reex-amine a number of key copyright issues in the digital age. We very much appre-ciate Representative Lofgren's strong interest in these issues and look forward to working with her and other members of Congress on these issues of critical importance to the library community."

E-Government and Access to Government Information

The major shift in focus on various e-government and government information access issues following the September 11, 2001, terrorist attacks continues. In some instances, actions by the Bush administration have caused concern. We said in this report last year that none of the actions removing or restricting public access to government appeared to have come from the administration; we cannot make that claim this year.

Restrictions of Access

In the immediate aftermath of the terrorist attacks, a number of federal government agencies removed information from their public Web sites. ALA, in conjunction with the American Association of Law Libraries (AALL) and the Association of Research Libraries (ARL) as well as other coalitions and groups such as OMB Watch, met with the Office of Management and Budget (OMB) to discuss these removals and to urge OMB and federal agencies to consult with their stakeholders when making such decisions. ALA and its allied organizations continue to push for this.

In early 2002 publications that had been widely available to the public—some for many years—were withdrawn from online access. The bibliographic information about them was also removed; not only can they not be obtained, but their very existence is obscured (at least on government sites). The Energy Department decided to suppress about 9,000 documents from its Information Bridge Web service. Many of these are scientific research papers from national labs that contain keywords such as "nuclear," "chemical," and "storage."

Also, the Defense Technical Information Center was told to remove thousands of documents from online public access. These are primarily old federal documents detailing the government's research on and production of biological weapons, generally between 1943 and 1969. While studies are planned to assess whether the documents should once again be made available to the public, the results are likely to be that documents that were never classified may now be, and documents that were declassified may be reclassified. Current federal policy generally bars the reclassification of formerly secret documents. This could, however, be changed by a new Executive Order, which is expected.

ALA and a number of other organizations submitted comments to the Department of Energy on its proposal to discontinue PubSCIENCE, a searchable gateway for the department's Web patrons. PubSCIENCE was discontinued as of November 4, 2002. While there were only seven comments in favor of ending PubSCIENCE, there were nearly 240 public comments, many from librarians and other PubSCIENCE users, pressing for continuance of the indexing service.

The Department of Education is in the process of "reevaluating" the material available on its Web site. As part of ALA's ongoing work to ensure permanent public access to government information, it joined several other groups (among them the National Education Association, the American Educational Research Association, and the National Knowledge Industry Association) in writing a letter requesting information about the department's intentions in reorganizing and/or removing key information from its public Web pages. The department has responded to concerns raised about the redesign with assurances that "files will not be deleted or removed, but rather simply moved to that particular section's archive."

On March 19, 2002, the acting director of the Information Security Oversight Office and the codirectors of the Justice Department's Office of Information and Privacy issued a "memorandum for the heads of executive departments and agencies" on "Safeguarding Information Regarding Weapons of Mass Destruction and Other Sensitive Records Related to Homeland Security." As a consequence, various documents that were in the Public Access Records File and available for public inspection and copying have been withdrawn.

The memorandum stated that it is intended to "provide guidance for reviewing Government information regarding weapons of mass destruction, as well as other information that could be misused to harm the security of our nation or threaten public safety. It is appropriate that all federal departments and agencies consider the need to safeguard such information on an ongoing basis and also upon receipt of any request for records containing such information that is made under the Freedom of Information Act (FOIA), 5 U.S.C. § 552 (2000)." It addresses three different kinds of information: classified information, previously unclassified or declassified information, and "sensitive but unclassified information." The third category of information is of greatest concern to ALA.

ALA and others have met with OMB about its plans to issue guidance on the "sensitive but unclassified" category presented in the March 19 memorandum.

ALA will be participating with other library organizations and public-interest groups to continue to monitor the implementation of the memorandum. The concern is that a broad range of information that is not otherwise subject to nondisclosure under FOIA will be withheld from public access and that these withholdings will be defended by the Justice Department.

Additionally, the new Homeland Security Act instructs the president to "identify and safeguard homeland security information that is sensitive but unclassified" (Section 892). As with the March 19 memorandum, no formal definition of the word "sensitive" is provided, opening the door for this provision to be used to justify expansive new restrictions on the disclosure of unclassified information.

As reported in this article last year, the National Archives has issued guidance to its components to carefully screen, and withhold and withdraw where already publicly available, documents that might have information on critical infrastructures, emergency plans, or government continuity plans. As of early 2003, only two documents (having to do with blueprints and security) had been withdrawn.

E-Government Act of 2002

On December 17, 2002, President Bush signed the E-Government Act of 2002 into law. A modified version of the legislation unanimously passed the House and Senate on November 15, 2002. This is legislation that the library community has been involved with since its initiation and in support of which Sharon Hogan (ALA 2001–2002 Committee on Legislation chair) testified in July 2001.

While the legislation has changed in a number of ways since then, its passage is a large step in the direction of better federal executive branch management of information over its life cycle, with public access being a key focus. The legislation creates a number of new opportunities for the public, libraries, and others concerned with information access to participate in the process. The bill also contains important provisions regarding the privacy implications of government information systems, "digital divide" concerns, and community technology centers. It also essentially codifies FirstGov as a service and authorizes funding for it.

While the bill remained mostly intact as it moved through the House and Senate, there were a few significant changes from the original Senate version, which the Senate passed on June 27, 2002. The addition of most interest to the library, privacy, and public-access communities is a new title, Title V, which ensures that data or information acquired by an agency under a pledge of confidentiality for exclusively statistical purposes shall not (1) be disclosed by an agency in an "identifiable form" (any representation of information that permits the identity of the respondent to be reasonably inferred by either direct or indirect means) to anyone not authorized by the law, nor (2) be used for any nonstatistical purpose.

OMB Memorandum M-02-07

On May 3, 2002, OMB issued Memorandum M-02-07 on "Procurement of Printing and Duplicating Through the Government Printing Office." This memo intends to allow agencies to procure printing of their publications outside the GPO system without requiring any waiver to do so. It instructs departments and agencies, in a footnote, that they shall continue to ensure that all government publications, as defined in 44 U.S.C. Part 19, are made available to the depository library program through the Superintendent of Documents.

The Joint Printing Committee (chaired by Sen. Mark Dayton, D-Minn.) held a hearing July 10 on GPO's role in government printing. Julia Wallace, head of the Government Publications Library at the University of Minnesota, testified on behalf of the library associations.

Separately, committee report language for the 2003 Treasury and General Government Appropriations Bill says that the committee "strongly opposes" OMB Memorandum M-02-07, and "directs the administration to abide the statutory requirement that printing be done through the GPO." This language has been carried over into the continuing resolutions.

On November 13, the Department of Defense, the General Services Administration, and the National Aeronautics and Space Administration, on behalf of the Federal Acquisition Regulations (FAR) Council, proposed that FAR be amended to relieve agencies from being required to use GPO for their printing.

ALA submitted joint comments on the proposed amendment to FAR on December 13, 2002.

On October 31, ALA sent a letter to the Office of Procurement in the Executive Office of the President in relation to its October 28, 2002, presolicitation notice seeking bids on the printing of the president's FY 2004 budget documents. In December it was announced that GPO would print the 2004 budget.

ALA, AALL, and ARL have held meetings with OMB and with congressional staff on this issue and will continue to work to ensure the vitality of the depository library program as a key point for ongoing public access to government information.

Critical Infrastructure Information

ALA's Washington Office has been actively engaged in promoting the public's "right to know" regarding information created and collected by or for the federal government. This concept is an expansion and strengthening of the long-standing principle that government should make this information available. The public's right to information has come under steady pressure and challenge since the September 11 terrorist attacks.

On November 22, 2002, Congress passed H.R. 5005, the Homeland Security Act of 2002, to create a Department of Homeland Security. It was signed into law (P.L. 107-296) by President Bush on November 25. Although ALA and the library community continued to work together with access-community coalitions and the environmental community and with the staffs of Sens. Joseph Lieberman (D-Conn.), Robert Bennett (R-Utah), Carl Levin (D-Mich.), and Leahy to prevent it, the law includes a provision (Sec. 204) that will create a broad exemption from FOIA. The provisions will (1) allow the private sector, on its own say-so, to designate a very broad array of voluntarily submitted information as prohibited from disclosure under this law; (2) prevent the public, other federal agencies, and state and local officials from having access to a wide range of information about risks and vulnerabilities in "infrastructures," including computer-related systems, physical plants and structures, and emergency services; (3) give immunity from civil litigation for such voluntarily disclosed information; and (4) criminalize disclosure of such information.

Official Secrets

No legislation arose in 2002 on the Official Secrets Act. This is largely due to the apparent success of ongoing, nonpublic discussions among representatives of the publishing community and representatives of the federal national security infrastructure. These discussions grew out of the previous successful efforts by the public-interest coalition to stop the legislation in 2001. With the change in committee leadership, however, what will happen in 2003 is uncertain.

Presidential Records

The Presidential Records Act (PRA) of 1978, declaring that the official records of a former president belong to the American people, was passed by Congress to ensure that the official records of a president are preserved and made publicly accessible. Under the act, as amended in 1989, the U.S. government asserts complete "ownership, possession, and control" of all presidential and vice presidential records. When a president leaves office, the Archivist of the United States is required to assume custody of the records and to make them available to the public "as rapidly and completely as possible."

The first presidential records to come under the act are those of former President Ronald Reagan. Those records should have become publicly available in February 2001, but for much of that year their release was delayed by the current administration. On November 1, 2001, President Bush issued an executive order to govern the review of former presidents' records for possible "executive privilege" claims. The executive order asserts an extremely expansive view of the scope of that privilege, stating that it includes not only the privilege for confidential communications with his advisers that has been recognized by the Supreme Court, but also the state secrets privilege, the attorney–client privilege and attorney work-product privileges, and the deliberative process privilege.

On November 28, 2001, Public Citizen, a nonprofit public-interest group, filed suit against the National Archives and Records Administration (NARA) and U.S. Archivist John Carlin to overturn E.O. 13233 and "to compel the release of presidential materials of former President Ronald Reagan that are in the custody of NARA and are being withheld in violation of the PRA."

In March 2002 the administration released 59,850 of the 68,000 pages from the Reagan papers originally identified by the archivist. A remaining 155 pages were released in July. During the discovery process, however, approximately 1,500 additional pages of the Reagan papers were identified. These are still under administration review and have not yet been released. The suit was awaiting court action in early 2003.

In October 2002 the House Committee on Government Reform unanimously approved legislation first introduced by Rep. Stephen Horn (R-Calif.) and cosponsored by 44 other legislators, including 37 Democrats, one Independent, and six Republicans that reinforces PRA's implementation.

In a letter to the committee, the White House attacked the bill as "unnecessary and inappropriate, and, more importantly, unconstitutional." The administration claimed that the Reagan presidential records had been released, showing that the bill was not needed. While the administration is correct about the Reagan-era records, the records of the first Bush administration are scheduled to be released in two years. Policy papers and "confidential advice" offered to the president by a number of high-profile public officials in the current administration, including Vice President Dick Cheney, Deputy Defense Secretary Paul Wolfowitz, and Secretary of State Colin Powell, will be subject to release.

The Washington Office worked to promote Representative Horn's legislation in the 107th Congress and will follow this issue in the 108th Congress and as it moves through the courts.

James Madison Award

Each year the James Madison Award is presented on Freedom of Information Day to recognize individuals or groups that have championed access to government information and the public's right to know. Last year marked the 36th anniversary of FOIA and the 13th year that ALA made this award in honor of President James Madison.

Freedom of Information Day is an annual event held on or near March 16, the birthday of James Madison. Madison is regarded as the Father of the Constitution and the foremost advocate for openness in government.

Last year's award was presented to Steven Garfinkel, an advocate for open public access to government information throughout his long career. In January 2002, after more than three decades in government service, Garfinkel retired as director of the Information Security Oversight Office where he oversaw the declassification of more than 800 million pages, the largest number of pages declassified in the history of the government's program.

Telecommunications and Technology

ALA and Broadband Legislation

There were numerous competing broadband bills in the 107th Congress. The chairs of both the Senate and House Commerce Committees each introduced their own bills. Other Commerce Committee leaders from both parties and on both sides of Congress had other proposals on the table.

These broadband proposals reflected the decades-long struggles between local and long-distance telephone companies, with a third industry mixed in— new entrants into the telephony and broadband marketplace, primarily cable television companies. As always, part of the debate centered on how much or how little regulation would be appropriate to promote broadband deployment. Inherent to the tug-of-war was the battle over who should "pay in" and who would "receive" funding from the universal service fund.

The various bills tended to reflect sympathy for one part of the larger marketplace over another. For example, House Committee on Energy and Commerce Chair Billy Tauzin (R-La.) sponsored H.R. 1542, which would have allowed the major operating companies to provide broadband on DSL lines while not requiring them to provide access to their networks to competitors. Sen. Fritz Hollings (D-S.C.) introduced S. 2448, which would provide tax credits, loans, and other financial incentives to those companies to build out more broadband with funding coming from the federal telephone excise tax. Meanwhile, Sen. John Breaux (D-La.), in S. 2430, would have had the Federal Communications Commission (FCC) establish guidelines for "regulatory parity" so that competitors could have access to existing networks to promote broadband deployment.

As it has done historically, ALA did not take a position on any of these "dueling broadband" bills. However, in monitoring these issues ALA remained concerned about accessibility and affordability issues related to universal service. Key questions included

- What is the impact of any particular proposal on Universal Service and the E-rate program?
- What public-interest provisions are included in any particular bill?
- Is there an impact on the "diversity of voices and ownership" issues?
- What is the impact on accessibility to all communities?
- What is the impact on affordability of broadband services for libraries?

Background

Representative Tauzin succeeded in getting his bill passed in the House in February 2002. Senator Hollings, his counterpart on the Senate Commerce Committee, continued his public opposition to Tauzin's proposal with his own version of broadband legislation.

Hearings were held in the Senate on "Tauzin-Dingell" as well as the Hollings alternative. Hollings consistently indicated that the Tauzin-Dingell bill would "go nowhere" in the Senate, so a standoff on this legislation was inevitable. None of these bills was passed in the 107th Congress.

Summary of Selected Bills

H.R. 1542: Tauzin-Dingell, the Internet Freedom and Broadband Deployment Act. Tauzin-Dingell, which passed the House in late February 2002, would have allowed local telephone operating companies to provide high-speed Internet services on DSL lines while not requiring them to provide competitors with access to their networks.

S. 2430: Breaux-Nickles, The Broadband Regulatory Parity Act of 2002. This bill would have given FCC exclusive jurisdiction over broadband regulation and directed FCC to develop new rules within four months (of passage of the bill), to assure that all providers had "regulatory parity" and function under the "same rules."

S. 2448: Hollings, the Broadband Telecommunications Deployment Act of 2002. This proposal sought to promote broadband deployment by providing grants and loans to encourage build out, especially in rural and underserved communities. Funding for the program would have come from the federal telephone excise tax. The bill also addressed research and pilot projects related to broadband, including wireless technology.

S. 2582: Lieberman, the National Broadband Strategy Act of 2002. Introduced in early June 2002, this bill proposed a "national strategy" for broadband deployment. It would have removed the federal government from regulatory authority over broadband, deferring instead to innovation and private sector/marketplace activities.

E-Rate

There were no specific legislative or political assaults on the E-rate (which provides telecommunications discounts for schools and libraries) in 2002, although anxiety over the filtering requirements of the Children's Internet Protection Act (CIPA) appeared to affect some participation in the program. ALA sought to increase library applications in the E-rate program and to encourage libraries to apply even as CIPA litigation was pending.

E-Rate: Notice of Proposed Rulemaking

The Federal Communications Commission (FCC), for the first time since it started dispersing E-rate discounts in 1998, has undertaken a comprehensive review of the program. On January 16, 2002, it adopted a Notice of Proposed Rulemaking (CC 02-6) seeking comments and answers to several questions regarding service eligibility; vendor participation; distribution of funds; and waste, fraud, and abuse. Comments were due April 5, 2002, followed by reply comments on May 6, 2002.

ALA, as well as many libraries and library consortia and networks across the country filed comments. The following are a sampling of the concepts supported by these comments:

- Allowing libraries alternative methods of establishing their discount levels
- Including new services in the definition of eligible services
- Increasing the funding cap

- Revising the categories of eligible services
- Revising the priority schedule for discount eligibility
- Eliminating disincentives for consortia
- Recognizing the role of the state coordinators in reducing the administrative costs of the program and increasing the efficiency of the program as a whole

While the e-rate did capture FCC's attention, its efforts were focused on rule changes for the program that were required in order to respond to court action on CIPA. By the end of the year, FCC had yet to produce any substantial orders responding to comments filed in the notice of proposed rulemaking.

CIPA Court Case

On May 31, 2002, a three-judge panel for the Eastern District of Pennsylvania held that Sections 1712(a)(2) and 1721 (b) of CIPA were unconstitutional because the mandated use of blocking technology on all library computers would result in blocked access to substantial amounts of constitutionally protected speech. The opinion, written by Chief Judge Edward R. Becker of the Third Circuit and joined by U.S. District Judges John P. Fullam and Harvey Bartle, III, stated, "we are constrained to conclude that the library plaintiffs must prevail in their contention that CIPA requires them to violate the First Amendment rights of their patrons, and accordingly is facially invalid."

The court permanently enjoined FCC and IMLS from enforcing the relevant sections of CIPA. As a result, public libraries were not required to install blocking or filtering technology on their computers in order to receive funds from either the E-rate or from Library Services and Technology Act (LSTA) grants.

However, the U.S. Justice Department appealed the District Court's ruling to the Supreme Court, and arguments before the Supreme Court were set to begin in March 2003.

E-rate: Fine-Tuning Discount Calculations

The E-rate program has provided an average of $62 million a year in discounts to libraries for telecommunications since its inception in 1998. While this support is substantial for the library community, it has never exceeded 4 percent of the total dollars available for schools and libraries through the E-rate program. Additionally, most libraries find it impossible to achieve the 90 percent discount level that would comfortably assure them of discounts for eligible internal connections that would allow them to distribute connectivity throughout larger library buildings.

In fall 2002 ALA became convinced that improvements could be made to the way discount calculations were being administered for libraries without requiring FCC to produce a new order or rulemaking. Careful reading of all the previous orders and regulations led ALA to propose to the E-rate fund administrator that libraries should be allowed to use National School Lunch Program totals for the districts in which they are located rather than using the weighted averages of all schools within a district. Since all the federal rules and regulations of the E-rate program supported this change, FCC announced that it would be in effect for the 2003 funding year.

Electronic Surveillance and Privacy

Electronic surveillance and privacy concerns pervaded ALA's Washington activities during 2002. Following passage of the USA Patriot Act in October 2001, there was technically no new similar legislation. However, other actions, such as the issuance of revised Attorney General's Guidelines to the FBI, raised major concerns within the library community about the impact of law enforcement investigations on the confidentiality of the uses of the library by patrons and community groups.

USA Patriot Act

During 2002 ALA continued to analyze and closely monitor the implementation of the USA Patriot Act. The implementation of the act was the focus of much concern, although the full potential impact continued to be hard to assess because of gag rules and confidentiality requirements for those receiving many kinds of court orders and warrants.

FBI Guidelines

Attorney General John Ashcroft announced revised guidelines for FBI investigations at the end of May. These new guidelines were not part of the USA Patriot Act, but an executive branch memorandum giving direction to the FBI. Provisions of the guidelines relate not just to terrorist investigations but "any criminal activity"—from drugs to white-collar crime to copyright infringement. These directives revise previous guidelines in several key ways including, but not limited to, extending the length of "preliminary" investigations from 90 days to a year without any indication of criminal activity, lifting restrictions on FBI data-gathering, and expressly allowing the FBI to use Web surfing and data-mining, long applied in the course of criminal investigations, before any criminal activity is suspected.

For example, the FBI had already been allowed to surf the Internet or utilize commercial data-mining services, but previously such searches had to be related to some investigation and had to be looking for some kind of criminal activity; they could not just go on a "fishing expedition."

In analyzing the guidelines, ALA worked extensively with the Center for Democracy and Technology (CDT) and other organizations to determine what implications these changes in the guidelines had for libraries in conjunction with concerns with the USA Patriot Act.

The FBI Guidelines are at http://www.usdoj.gov/ag/readingroom/general crimea.htm.

Accountability and Oversight

ALA focused on pushing for oversight of the act and monitoring implementation of the FBI guidelines. For example, the chairman and the ranking member of the House Committee on the Judiciary, Reps. F. James Sensenbrenner, Jr. (R-Wis.) and John Conyers (D-Mich.), wrote a letter to Attorney General Ashcroft requesting information from both Ashcroft and FBI Director Robert F. Mueller "concerning the Department of Justice's user of [the] new tools and their effectiveness." Specific questions were asked in their letter about whether Section 215 of the USA Patriot Act was ". . . used to obtain records from a public library, bookstore or newspaper." The full text of the letter is available at http://www. house.gov/judiciary/ashcroft061302.htm. Responses to the congressional inquiry were limited, and much of the information was classified and not available to the public, not even to most of Congress. Senators Leahy and Russell Feingold (D-Wis.) also submitted questions and received a similar response.

Terrorism Information and Prevention System (TIPS)

Operation TIPS was proposed by the Justice Department, which described it as "simply a reporting system—not a membership organization or recruiting activity." The proposed program would have enlisted "millions of American workers who, in the daily course of their work, are in a unique position to see potentially unusual or suspicious activity in public places," according to a Justice Department statement. The intent was to engage millions of truck drivers, letter carriers, train conductors, ship captains, utility employees, and others in a formal way to report "suspicious" activity.

The Department of Justice would have offered them ". . . training . . . in how to look out for suspicious and potentially terrorist-related activity." It would also have provided "a formal way to report" that activity "through a single and coordinated toll-free number." Following a great public outcry against the program (including opposition from the U.S. Postal Service) the program died and Congress refused to fund it.

The House bill creating the Department of Homeland Security did not include any mention of TIPS, but Rep. Dick Armey (R-Texas) introduced a floor amendment in the House that prohibited the program. Further, the House version of the bill creating the Department of Homeland Security contained a provision that "Any and all activities of the federal government to implement the proposed component program [TIPS] are hereby prohibited." The final version of the bill contained this provision, and TIPS is prohibited.

Other ALA E-SPY (Electronic Surveillance, Privacy and You) Activities

While closely monitoring and analyzing the above developments, ALA was heavily involved in providing information about the USA Patriot Act and related measures to ALA members and educating the library community about the Act's implications. There was approximately a 30 percent increase in invitations to speak at state library association conferences and similar venues, and the majority of the invitations requested ALA representatives to speak about the USA Patriot Act and related concerns. There was also much press activity on these privacy and surveillance issues, activity that was closely coordinated between ALA's Washington Office and its Office of Intellectual Freedom and Public Information Office.

Legislation and Regulations Affecting Publishing in 2002

Allan Adler

Vice President, Legal and Governmental Affairs
Association of American Publishers
50 F St. N.W., Suite 400
Washington, DC 20001

The Second Session of the 107th Congress focused primarily on homeland security following the September 11, 2001, terrorist attacks, the possibility of war in Iraq, and the midterm elections.

After months of debate, Congress successfully passed legislation that established the new Department of Homeland Security, a top priority for the Bush administration and many legislators. That effort, however, consumed an exorbitant amount of the legislative session. Another pressing issue for the administration that also whittled away a lot of legislative time was the resolution authorizing the use of military force against Iraq, which passed only weeks before the midterm election. Finally, the midterm election resulted in the Senate shifting from Democratic to Republican control, a significant change for many legislative interests but one that should not have a great impact on publishers' legislative interests.

The following is a review of the significant legislative activities that AAP's Washington office either monitored or participated in on behalf of AAP member publishers. The report focuses on legislative actions that affect book and journal publishing interests, primarily in the areas of intellectual property protection, freedom of expression, new technologies and "e-commerce," education, trade, and postal matters. The report serves to highlight some of the public policy issues that AAP expects to require publishers' attention in the 108th Congress.

Technology, Education and Copyright Harmonization (TEACH) Act

S. 487, enacted as Subtitle C, Title III, Division C of H.R. 2215, Public Law 107-273, November 2, 2002

As the desire to adjourn for election campaigning competed with congressional efforts to complete unfinished legislative work, the House and Senate Judiciary Committees decided to use the must-pass Justice Department appropriations authorization legislation (H.R. 2215) as a vehicle for enacting several noncontroversial pieces of legislation that had been held up between the two committees. One of these was the Technology, Education and Copyright Harmonization (TEACH) Act (S. 487), the carefully crafted Copyright Act amendments that the Association of American Publishers (AAP) forged through negotiations with the education and library communities to facilitate the use of copyrighted works in distance-education programs delivered via the Internet.

The TEACH Act was introduced in the first session of the 107th Congress by Sens. Orrin Hatch (R-Utah) and Patrick Leahy (D-Vt.), based on recommendations contained in a study conducted and issued by the U.S. Copyright Office under a mandate of the Digital Millennium Copyright Act (DMCA). The TEACH act broadens the existing copyright exemption for instructional broadcasting to encompass distance education delivered via digital networks. After weeks of intensive negotiations in which AAP and other copyright industry organizations, representatives of the education and library communities, and U.S. Copyright Office officials sought a consensus compromise on a digital distance-education bill, a revised version of S. 487 moved quickly through the Senate and the House Judiciary Subcommittee on Intellectual Property, the Courts and Internet in the spring and early summer of 2001.

Subsequently, however, the bill languished in the full House Judiciary Committee for more than a year because of political considerations that had nothing to do with its substance. Even after the House Judiciary Committee finally approved the bill in July 2002, the same murky political considerations resulted in the loss of an opportunity for quick House passage before the August recess. Only with the approach of adjournment, and the realization that a workable consensus compromise to a thorny set of copyright and education issues might be lost due to unreasonable inaction, were judiciary leaders in the House and Senate roused to the need to secure final passage of the legislation.

Despite the introduction of several bills containing proposals to amend DMCA or other copyright protections, the TEACH Act was one of only two substantive pieces of copyright legislation to be enacted during the 107th Congress. The other measure, a bill to resolve disputes over Webcasting music fees (H.R. 5469), was hastily crafted and enacted in the waning hours before adjournment.

E-Government Act of 2002

H.R. 2458, enacted as Public Law 107-347, December 17, 2002

Ensuring that citizens have adequate access to federal government services and information was a key bipartisan legislative goal for Congress and the Bush administration during the 107th Congress. Bills introduced by Sen. Joseph Lieberman (D-Conn.) and Rep. Jim Turner (D-Texas) sought to improve such citizen access through the Internet and to promote electronic government information policies, but they required substantial negotiations with the Bush administration before a compromise was reached on ambitious legislation to achieve these objectives and more.

Among other measures designed to strengthen governmentwide approaches to improving the use of information technology for government service delivery, efficiency, and effectiveness, the new act creates an Office of Electronic Government within the Office of Management and Budget and charges it with various responsibilities for enhancing public access to federal government information and services through the Internet. It also establishes an interagency Chief Information Officers Council and an interagency E-Gov Fund to promote innovative e-gov initiatives, including broader use of electronic signatures, development of a federal Internet portal, and improvement of federal workforce information technology skills. The act also provides a governmentwide, risk-based approach to information security management and a uniform approach for improving government statistical capabilities.

AAP and other content industry organizations were particularly concerned about the legislation as originally introduced in the Senate (S. 803) and approved by the Senate Governmental Affairs Committee because it contained language for a proposed "national digital library" that apparently would have permitted the federal government to make instructional materials and other copyrighted works freely available to the public on government Web sites. AAP worked successfully with Lieberman's staff to have this language removed from the legislation before the full Senate considered the bill.

S. 803 unanimously passed the Senate and was sent to the House in June. The House, however, took up a different bill (H.R. 2458), eventually incorporating most of the major provisions from S. 803 as passed by the Senate into the legislation. One of the changes from the Senate-passed version, permitting the administrator of the Office of Electronic Government to be appointed by the president without Senate confirmation, proved to be a key compromise that helped gain administration support for the legislation. Both houses passed H.R. 2458 in mid-November.

Trade Act of 2002

H.R. 3009, enacted as Public Law 107-210, August 8, 2002

Just before its August recess, Congress ended a divisive eight-year battle between the executive and legislative branches of the federal government by passing a bill (H.R. 3009) to restore "fast track" trade promotion authority to the president. The bill renewed the president's ability to enter into trade agreements that can be approved or rejected by Congress but not amended. Such authority had expired in 1993 during President Clinton's first term and was the subject of political stalemates in subsequent efforts to reenact it. AAP lobbied through the International Intellectual Property Alliance (IIPA) for restoration of this important authority, which helps to support continued growth in U.S. exports of copyrighted works and to combat international piracy of intellectual property.

On behalf of AAP and its other association members, IIPA also lobbied the Senate to include a number of trade amendments in an unintroduced Miscellaneous Tariffs bill. The amendments, primarily technical in nature, would have standardized intellectual property protection across trade programs, resulting in better copyright protection and enforcement globally for U.S. copyright industries. The United States Trade Representative (USTR) had signed off on the amendments and Senators Leahy and Hatch worked together to ensure that the amendments would be included in the final Senate Miscellaneous Tariffs bill. AAP sent a letter urging Rep. Charles Rangel (D-N.Y.), ranking member of the House Ways and Means Committee, to support the amendments if the bill passed the Senate and was taken up by the House before the end of the session. Unfortunately, neither the House nor the Senate took up the Miscellaneous tariffs bill before Congress adjourned in November.

Dot Kids Implementation and Efficiency Act of 2002

H.R. 3833, enacted as Public Law 107-317, December 4, 2002

With two previous efforts successfully challenged on First Amendment grounds, it was a top priority of some legislators in Congress to enact constitutional legislation that would help to avoid exposing children to pornography and pedophiles on the Internet. They succeeded in pushing through legislation that creates a new second-level domain within the United States country code domain to provide an online "safe haven" for children and their families.

As enacted, H.R. 3833 requires the domain name registry that operates the ".us" United States country code to also operate and maintain a ".kids.us" second-level domain that provides Internet access only to material that is both "suitable for minors" and "not harmful to minors." As a practical matter, the legal restrictions limit the subdomain to materials that would be appropriate for children under 13 years of age. Although statutorily responsible for establishing and operating the "child-friendly" second-level domain, Neustar (the registry selected to operate and maintain the ".us" Internet domain) is protected under the new law with "Good Samaritan" immunity under Section 230(C) of the Communications Act if material deemed inappropriate for children is found on the ".kids.us" subdomain.

The new act defines "suitable for minors" as any material that (1) "is not psychologically or intellectually inappropriate for minors" and (2) "serves the educational, information, intellectual, or cognitive needs of minors; or the social, emotional, or entertainment needs of minors." This definition, which combines language from the Supreme Court's decision in *Board of Education* v. *Pico* with language from the Children's Television Act of 1990 and its implementing regulations, is believed by the drafters to be broad enough to include good programming for children but narrow enough to avoid a constitutional challenge on vagueness grounds. The act's definition of "harmful to minors" was drafted to be consistent with the Supreme Court's *Ginsberg* and *Miller* decisions.

H.R. 3833 was passed in the House in May by a vote of 406–2. Just prior to adjournment in November, an amended version of the bill was passed by unanimous consent in the Senate and then approved by the House.

Digital Choice and Freedom Act of 2002

H.R. 5522

Digital Media Consumers' Rights Act

H.R. 5544

By introducing their respective bills to amend the Copyright Act just a week before the target adjournment date for the 107th Congress last October, Reps. Zoe Lofgren (D-Calif.) and Rick Boucher (D-Va.) let everyone know they were not positioning themselves to make an 11th-hour push for enactment of the proposed legislation, but were instead signaling their intentions to fire the first legislative shots across the collective bow of the copyright community for the new Congress beginning in 2003.

Lofgren and Boucher are probably the most vocal and best-known congressional critics of the Digital Millennium Copyright Act, which was enacted in 1998 without the limiting amendments that each of them unsuccessfully offered during consideration of the legislation in the House Judiciary Committee. Both style themselves as defenders of consumers' rights with respect to "fair use" and "first sale" limitations on the rights of copyright holders, and both are outspoken critics of DMCA's prohibitions regarding the circumvention of access and copy controls used by copyright holders to protect their rights with respect to copyrighted works in digital formats.

The respective bills proposed different means of achieving essentially the same key results, which would be to amend DMCA to permit the circumvention of technological access and use controls for noninfringing purposes, and to legalize tools that would facilitate such circumvention. Beyond addressing these matters, Lofgren's bill (H.R. 5522), which was originally cosponsored by Rep. Mike Honda (D-Calif.), proposed to establish a "digital first sale" doctrine for online transmissions of copyrighted works; permit the making and use of copies of digital works for "archival purposes"; permit private performances or displays of digital works on any digital media device; and make unenforceable any "nonnegotiable license terms" that apply to a digital work that is distributed to the public to the extent that such terms restrict or limit any limitation on the rights of copyright owners under copyright law. Lofgren, who has several major software companies among her constituents, excluded "computer programs" from the latter provision despite the fact that it is the software industry that most commonly imposes the kind of license terms that were otherwise targeted by her bill.

Beyond the circumvention provisions, Boucher's bill (H.R. 5544), originally cosponsored by Rep. John Doolittle (R-Calif.), proposed to address his criticism of copy-protected music CDs by empowering the Federal Trade Commission to make the advertising or sale of a "mislabeled" prerecorded music CD an "unfair and deceptive act or practice" if the CD is identified as an audio compact disc or fails to prominently disclose on its packaging that it is not an audio compact disc or might not be recordable or play properly on a personal computer or device capable of play or recording content from an audio compact disc. Although the bill was referred to the House Judiciary Committee with respect to its proposed amendments to the Copyright Act, the latter provision regarding the trade commission put that part of H.R. 5544 within the jurisdiction of the House Commerce Committee. Given the intense "turf" battles that have arisen between the two committees since their initial scrap over DMCA nearly five years ago, it is likely that the split jurisdiction would only have added to the obstacles that the bill would have faced from the copyright community if there had been any effort to advance the legislation toward enactment.

Child Obscenity and Pornography Prevention Act
H.R. 4623

In April 2002, by a vote of 6–3 in *Ashcroft* v. *Free Speech Coalition,* the Supreme Court struck down key portions of the Child Pornography Prevention Act (CPPA) as unconstitutionally overbroad and violative of First Amendment protections for creative works of artistic merit. The legislation, which was enacted in 1996, had broadened the existing statutory definition of "child pornography" to cover sexually explicit materials that were computer-generated, as well as visual depictions of adults who "appear to be" minors.

Immediately upon hearing of the court's decision, a number of members of Congress began working closely with the Department of Justice to craft revised legislation that would past constitutional muster. The collaboration produced the proposed "Child Obscenity and Pornography Prevention Act" (H.R. 4623), which was introduced by Rep. Lamar Smith (R-Texas). That legislation moved quickly through the House Judiciary Committee and was passed by the House in June. Only two members of the House, Bobby Scott (D-Va.) and Jerrold Nadler (D-N.Y.), voted against it, both citing unresolved First Amendment problems.

As passed by the House, H.R. 4623 would have criminalized as child pornography "a computer image or computer-generated image that is, or appears, virtually indistinguishable from that of a minor engaging in sexually explicit conduct." The new language deviated only slightly from the language struck down by the Supreme Court, which had banned any visual depiction that "is, or appears to be, of a minor engaging in sexually explicit conduct." Under H.R. 4623, it would have been illegal to offer, agree, attempt, or conspire to provide, sell, receive, or to produce, distribute, receive, or possess with intent to distribute or possess a visual depiction that is, or is virtually indistinguishable from, that of a pre-pubescent child engaging in such conduct. The legislation also barred the use of child pornography to facilitate offenses against minors.

On the Senate side, Jean Carnahan (D-Mo.) and Kay Bailey Hutchinson (R-Texas) introduced companion legislation (S. 2511), which was referred to the Senate Judiciary Committee. The committee's chairman and ranking member— Senators Leahy and Hatch, respectively—introduced their own legislation to address the Supreme Court's decision, the "Prosecutorial Remedies and Tools Against the Exploitation of Children Today Act of 2002" (S. 2520). Their bill would have prohibited the acts of pandering or soliciting anything represented to be obscene child pornography and any depictions of minors, or apparent minors, in sexual acts. S. 2520 also would have strengthened the existing record-keeping requirements for individuals who produce sexually explicit materials by requiring them to keep records confirming that no minors were used to produce the materials.

In mid-November the Senate Judiciary Committee quickly approved four technical amendments to S. 2520 and sent the bill to the Senate floor where, on the same day, it was passed by unanimous consent and sent to the House. However, it was too late for the House and Senate to work out differences between their respective passed bills before adjournment.

Consumer Technology Bill of Rights

H.J. Res. 116/S.J. Res. 51

In addition to the two "anti-DMCA" bills introduced by Representatives Boucher and Lofgren, respectively, in October, Sen. Ron Wyden (D-Ore.) and Rep. Chris Cox (R-Calif.) each introduced resolutions proposing to establish a "Consumer Technology Bill of Rights." Wyden and Cox were relatively new critics of the Digital Millennium Copyright Act, and members who had not been active on the issues were addressed in their resolutions. Both members stated in their press releases that the resolutions were introduced in anticipation of addressing the digital copyright issues in the 108th Congress.

Both resolutions were based on the so-called Consumer Bill of Rights set out by DigitalConsumer.org, a consumer rights organization that was started in 2001 with a membership made up of entrepreneurs, investors, and consumers who share a legislative goal of curtailing DMCA by enactment of broad, but explicit, "fair use" principles.

The two resolutions, introduced just weeks before the adjournment of the 107th Congress, advocate that consumers who have legally purchased copyrighted and noncopyrighted works would have the right to record or copy the digital content for noncommercial purposes. Both resolutions enumerate the following rights for consumers: (1) to record legally acquired video or audio for later viewing or listening ("time-shifting"); (2) to use legally acquired content in different places ("space-shifting"); (3) to archive or make backup copies of legally acquired content for use if the original copies are destroyed; (4) to use legally acquired content on the electronic device of the consumer's choice; (5) to translate legally acquired content into comparable formats; and (6) to use technology in order to achieve the rights enumerated in (1) through (5). The resolutions, if adopted, could have been viewed as committing Congress to revision of the anticircumvention provisions of DMCA, as well as other provisions in the Copyright Act.

Anticounterfeiting Amendments of 2002

S. 2395

In the 107th Congress, Sen. Joseph Biden (D-Del.) became actively involved in trying to combat piracy of U.S. intellectual property abroad. As chairman of the Senate Foreign Relations Committee, Biden held a hearing in February 2002 that focused on the growing problem of intellectual property theft abroad and resulted in the committee's issuance of a report, *Theft of American Intellectual Property: Fighting Crime Abroad and At Home,* that discusses "piracy" and "counterfeiting" as two types of intellectual property theft that constitute serious threats to U.S. publishers abroad.

In April 2002 Senator Biden introduced the Anticounterfeiting Amendments of 2002 (S. 2395) in an effort to address the growing problem of counterfeiting of U.S. products abroad. The legislation would have updated provisions in the

U.S. criminal code that currently criminalize trafficking in counterfeit documentation and packaging for software programs. S. 2395 would have expanded the law to include documentation and packaging for phonorecords, motion pictures, and other audiovisual works; added a prohibition for trafficking in illicit "authentication features" like watermarks and holograms; and provided aggrieved parties with a private cause of action against violators of the act. Unfortunately, "literary works" (including books) were not included in the bill as approved by the Senate Judiciary Committee in July of last year.

When AAP approached Senator Biden and his staff about revising the bill to cover "literary works," opposition surfaced from the library and educational communities based on their concerns about becoming targets of criminal prosecution for unintended violations of the anticounterfeiting prohibitions while engaging in certain routine uses of copyrighted works, such as interlibrary loans and online distance education. However, before this issue could be resolved, a separate controversy over the committee's amendment of the bill to make it cover works in digital form linked the anticounterfeiting measure to the ongoing battles over proposed "digital rights management" legislation and ensured that it would not be considered in the full Senate prior to the adjournment of the 107th Congress.

Instructional Materials Accessibility Act of 2002

S. 2246/H.R. 4582

After nearly two years of intensive negotiations and lobbying by AAP and representatives of the major advocacy groups for the blind, the Instructional Materials Accessibility Act (IMAA) was introduced in April 2002 by Sens. Chris Dodd (D-Conn.) and Thad Cochran (R-Miss.) and Reps. Tom Petri (R-Wis.) and George Miller (D-Calif.). The legislation was designed to create a national infrastructure to help K–12 students who are blind or have other print disabilities receive accessible versions of core classroom instructional materials in a timely manner.

The bill provided for the establishment of: (1) a standardized national electronic file format to be used for creating accessible versions of textbooks and other core instructional materials; (2) a central repository offering timely and convenient access to such files for producing accessible versions of such instructional materials; (3) necessary funding authorizations for the repository and capacity-enhancing training programs; and (4) statewide plans to ensure that students who are blind or have print disabilities have access to instructional materials in formats they can use at the same time such materials are provided to classmates who do not have such disabilities.

IMAA garnered broad support, with 22 cosponsors in the Senate and 88 in the House, and was the focus of a June hearing before the Senate Subcommittee on Children and Families that featured AAP President and CEO Pat Schroeder as one of the witnesses. But despite scheduling on several occasions for a full committee mark-up in the Senate, the bill saw no further action in the 107th Congress because of opposition from key Republican legislators and Bush administration officials.

In several meetings with the majority staff of the House Education Committee and the assistant secretary for special education and rehabilitation services at the Department of Education, Robert Pasternack, the bill's supporters were told that the administration and some Republican legislators opposed provisions in the bill that would preempt the states on the national file format issue, establish a central repository for conversion files, and require funding authorization for the repository and training programs.

Unwilling to negotiate revisions in the legislation, Pasternack announced in October that the Department of Education would award a $200,000 grant to the National Center on Accessing the General Curriculum at the Center for Applied Special Technology to establish an advisory panel with the goal of creating a voluntary national standard for accessible digital instructional materials for all disabled students in grades K–12. The proposed standard is to be published in the *Federal Register* for public comment at the end of 2003.

P2P Piracy Prevention Act

H.R. 5211

A number of bills introduced in the second session of the 107th Congress caused increased tension between the technology industries and content industries. The P2P Piracy Prevention Act (H.R. 5211), introduced by Reps. Howard Berman (D-Calif.) and Howard Coble (R-N.C.), the ranking member and chairman, respectively, of the House Intellectual Property Subcommittee, was no exception.

The introduction of H.R. 5211 added yet another layer to the ongoing debate over the use of technology to protect copyrights in digital environments. The legislation would have allowed a copyright owner to use "technological self-help measures" to protect copyrighted works against infringement through peer-to-peer (P2P) digital network exchanges. It also provided the copyright owner with safe harbors from trespass, privacy, and other possible legal barriers to such actions if a copyright owner first notified the Department of Justice of the specific technologies to be used. To protect against abusive self-help practices, however, the legislation barred a copyright owner from altering, removing, or corrupting any files or data on a P2P user's computer when deploying "technological self-help measures," and made copyright owners subject to civil damages suits for knowingly causing such results.

Opponents of the bill, including the computer hardware and software industries, as well as the library and educational communities and the usual other opponents of strong copyright protection, argued that the bill would allow copyright owners to "hack" into a user's computer and damage the computer and/or related files. Proponents of the bill argued that it provided strong protections against copyright owners who would abuse its authority, including more protections than are available under existing laws for computer users who are victims of abusive actions by copyright owners. The bill also granted authority to the U.S. attorney general to bar abusive copyright owners from future use of "self-help" measures.

Postal Accountability and Enhancement Act

H.R. 4970

United States Postal Service Commission Act of 2002

S. 2754

For most of the 107th Congress, AAP and others in the mailing community waited for Congress to introduce postal reform legislation. Both the Senate and House held hearings and AAP President and CEO Schroeder testified in July 2001 before the House Government Reform Committee on the immediate need for postal reform.

Legislation, however, was not introduced until the second session, when long-time reform advocate Rep. John McHugh (R-N.Y.) introduced the Postal Accountability and Enhancement Act (H.R. 4970). Unfortunately, this much-awaited postal reform legislation imploded when taken up by the House Government Reform Committee in June of last year. Despite cosponsorship from Committee Chair Dan Burton (R-Ind.) and ranking member Henry Waxman (D-Calif.), the bill was rejected by the committee by a 20–5 vote, with Representative Waxman withdrawing his support in apparent protest of the House Republican leadership's unwillingness to promise that the bill would be considered by the full House. Although complicated and watered down through negotiations among the cosponsors, the bill was generally supported by AAP and others in the mailing community as a much-needed first step toward addressing the current postal crises. United Parcel Service and the Teamsters led the opposition to the bill.

On the Senate side, in the absence of any pending reform legislation similar to the House bill, Sen. Susan Collins (R-Maine) introduced the United States Postal Service Commission Act of 2002 (S. 2754) in July. The bill would have created an 11-member Presidential Commission on the United States Postal Service (USPS) to be appointed by the president and charged with reporting to the president and Congress on its findings and recommendations for legislation and administrative action after conducting a 15-month study to determine how USPS should be restructured to ensure its future in the 21st century. S. 2754 was referred to the Senate Governmental Affairs Committee, but no further action was taken before the adjournment of Congress in November.

However, in December, President Bush issued an executive order establishing a President's Commission on the United States Postal Service composed of nine members appointed by the president for the purpose of examining the current state of USPS. By July 31, 2003, the commission is required to issue a report containing a "proposed vision" of the future of USPS and specific recommendations for legislative and administrative reform.

Presidential Records Act Amendments of 2002

H.R. 4187

In November 2001 President Bush issued Executive Order 13233 to give current and past presidents, as well as the current vice president and members of a former president's family, veto power over the release of presidential records. In April 2002 a bipartisan group of House members sought to overturn the executive order through enactment of the proposed Presidential Records Act Amendment of 2002.

Introduced by Rep. Steve Horn (R-Calif.), H.R. 4187 was referred to the House Committee on Government Reform with 22 original cosponsors, including Committee Chairman Burton and Ranking Member Waxman. On the day the bill was introduced, the committee heard testimony from a group of distinguished historians and presidential scholars expressing their opposition to the executive order and calling on Congress to nullify it.

The bill would have amended the Presidential Records Act (PRA) of 1978, which was enacted in response to public outrage over the secrecy abuses of the Nixon administration. PRA established permanent public ownership and governmental control of presidential records, setting forth procedures governing their preservation and making them publicly available 12 years after a president has left office. A review process provided in H.R. 4187 would have ensured compliance with the intent of PRA by imposing a firm time limit and procedure that must be followed for a president or former president to assert privilege claims. Specifically, the bill would have (1) nullified Executive Order 13233; (2) created a specific 40-day time limit for presidential review of records and assertion of any privilege claims; and (3) required immediate release of all records for which privilege had not been asserted.

But when the House Government Reform Committee marked up the bill in October, the committee adopted a substitute measure that watered down the review and privilege assertion requirements to make the legislation acceptable to the Bush administration. AAP and most other supporters of H.R. 4187 as introduced refused to support the substitute adopted by the committee, and no further action on the legislation was taken.

Whois Database Legislation

H.R. 4640

Accuracy of domain name registration data in the Whois Database maintained by the Internet Corporation for Assigned Names and Numbers (ICANN) is of critical importance to combating online copyright piracy. In an effort to address the problem of fraudulent data in the Whois database, Reps. Coble and Berman, chairman and ranking member, respectively, of the House Intellectual Property Subcommittee, introduced legislation in May 2002 that would have made it a criminal offense to knowingly provide false or misleading information when registering a domain name on the Internet.

The bill was introduced to address the concerns of many different groups and industries regarding inaccurate information in the Whois Database. The Whois Database is a publicly accessible Web site consisting of a number of information directories that provide contact information for registrants of "second level domains." The information available to the public is only the information that appears immediately to the left of the "dot" in an Internet address and after the "@" symbol. For example, in the address "smith@publishers.org,"

Whois data only reveals the party responsible for the second level domain registration of "publishers." Whois does not disclose any information regarding further subdomains to the left of the second level domain name, or any information to the right of ". org."

Opponents of the Whois database are concerned about privacy, claiming that many individuals provide false information to avoid entering sensitive personal information, such as home telephone numbers and addresses. The bill was narrowly drafted to address these concerns by focusing only on those individuals who "knowingly provide false or misleading information" with the intent to defraud. Accurate, publicly accessible information is essential to maintaining a useful Whois database. Many companies and individuals rely on the accuracy of the information provided to Whois to identify and locate parties responsible for operating sites involved in copyright piracy and trademark infringement. If the information is inaccurate, it makes it even more difficult for property owners to protect their property on the Internet.

Under the bill's provisions, a person found guilty of knowingly providing false and misleading domain information to a domain name registrar with the intent to defraud could be fined or imprisoned up to five years. It was anticipated that this bill would move quickly through the House of Representatives, but scheduled hearings were canceled and no further action took place before adjournment.

Security Systems Standards and Certification Act

S. 2048

The most controversial copyright protection bill to surface in the 107th Congress was clearly the proposed "Security Systems Standards and Certification Act" (S. 2048), which was introduced by Senate Commerce Committee Chairman Fritz Hollings (D-S.C.). Although AAP never took a formal position on the bill, its introduction created problems for copyright industries by pitting high-tech companies against the motion picture industry and splitting the pro-copyright coalition that had successfully worked to enact and defend the Digital Millennium Copyright Act over the last few years.

Senator Hollings and supporters of the legislation argued that, in order to speed up the rollout of digital TV broadcasting, copyrighted works such as motion pictures and television programming required necessary technological protections against unauthorized reproduction, distribution, and performance. S. 2048, if enacted, would have given the high-tech industries and the motion picture industries one year to reach a consensus on security system standards to protect digital content from piracy over the Internet and airwaves. At the end of that year, if the industries failed to come to an agreement on standards the Federal Communications Commission, along with the Register of Copyright, would have been required to mandate security standards and rules for all new "digital media devices."

The key issues to be addressed between the motion picture and high-tech industries were: (1) developing standards to adequately protect digital content over broadcast airwaves by establishing a "broadcast flag;" (2) plugging the "analog hole" to reduce piracy; and (3) limiting the distribution of unauthorized file sharing of copyrighted works on peer-to-peer networks.

However, shortly after Senator Hollings held a Commerce Committee hearing on the legislation in February 2002, the Senate Judiciary Committee held a hearing at which its chairman, Senator Leahy, made it clear that legislation such as S. 2048 would not advance in this Congress because he did not support government-mandated solutions for digital rights management, but instead preferred such technologies to be developed in the private sector. Although similar hearings were held in two separate subcommittees on the House side, legislation like S. 2048 was not introduced in the House.

The loud public debate over S. 2048 subsided considerably after the last of the four hearings, as it became clear that the committees with jurisdiction over copyright legislation did not support its approach to providing digital copyright protections. Although no further action took place on S. 2048, introduction of the bill did prod the high-tech and motion picture industries to make some progress in their meetings.

Intellectual Property Protection Restoration Act of 2001

S. 1611/S. 2031

As the result of a series of controversial 5–4 decisions by the U.S. Supreme Court in 1999, state entities that infringe the rights of intellectual property (IP) owners under federal statutory law may now assert a right of sovereign immunity under the 11th Amendment to avoid the injured party's claims for monetary damages in federal court.

This radical departure from prior U.S. law, permitting state entities to fully protect their own statutory IP rights from infringement while escaping any meaningful liability for violating the same statutory IP rights of others, poses a serious economic threat to all non-state IP rights holders. This includes authors as well as book and journal publishers, whose entire business enterprise hinges on their ability to enforce and protect the copyrights in works they create or acquire from others for publication.

In March 2002, following congressional hearings that highlighted the unfairness and risk that this extraordinary change in the legal landscape poses to copyright and other IP owners, Senators Leahy and Sam Brownback (R-Kans.) reintroduced a sovereign immunity bill (S. 2031) that Leahy had previously introduced without a Republican cosponsor, and Reps. Coble and Berman introduced a companion bill (H.R. 3204) in the House. Both bills proposed a "waiver" approach that attempted—within the limited authority left to Congress under the Supreme Court's constitutional rulings—to restore equal treatment in the application of federal statutory IP law to state entities and other parties. Under this approach, if states and state agencies wanted the ability to sue for damages when their own intellectual property rights were violated, the states would have to waive their immunity from damage liability for violating the intellectual property rights of others. States that failed to do so would lose their ability to enforce their own intellectual property rights through suits for monetary damages.

AAP and other organizations and IP-based industries actively supported the legislation, but plans to move the bill through committee to the Senate floor were thwarted when key committee members raised objections on behalf of state colleges and universities that feared losing the ability to protect their IP rights if their state legislatures failed to waive immunity. In addition, the National Governors Association and key state attorneys general voiced strong opposition to any legislation that would require states to waive the sovereign immunity that, in their view, had been rightfully restored by the high court's rulings.

Freelance Writers and Artists Protection Act of 2002

H.R. 4643

In response to the U.S. Supreme Court's decision in *New York Times* v. *Tasini,* Reps. John Conyers, Jr. (D-Mich.) and Chris Cannon (R-Utah) introduced the proposed Freelance Writers and Artists Protection Act of 2002 (H.R. 4643) in May 2002. The bill was referred to the House Judiciary Committee, but no further action was taken before Congress adjourned.

H.R. 4643 would have granted freelance writers and artists an antitrust exemption to engage in collective bargaining with publishers. Representative Conyers, in his explanation of the need for such legislation, characterized standard-form publishing agreements as inherently unfair contracts of adhesion, a comment AAP found extremely disturbing.

In addition to permitting collective bargaining, the bill would also have amended Section 412 (2) of the Copyright Act to permit the registration of a collective work to suffice as registration of the individual contributions to that work. This amendment would allow a publisher to be sued by a freelance writer based on the publisher's own copyright registration. The bill would also have addressed the theft of unpublished works. The Copyright Act currently authorizes criminal prosecution of individuals who willfully infringe on works for purposes of commercial advantage or private financial advantage, or whose willfully infringing reproduction or distribution activities involve works with a total retail value of more than $1,000. However, absent the ability to prove such purposes or retail value, the willful infringement of unpublished works would apparently not be subject to criminal prosecution, and the proposed amendment sought to rectify that situation.

AAP staff met with Representative Conyers' staff to raise book publishers' concerns about the bill, which really has little to do with the issues in the *Tasini* case, and about the scope of the proposed antitrust exemption, which AAP believes would unjustifiably cover authors' negotiations with book publishers.

Funding Programs and Grant-Making Agencies

National Endowment for the Humanities

1100 Pennsylvania Ave. N.W., Washington, DC 20506
202-606-8400, 800-634-1121
E-mail info@neh.gov, World Wide Web http://www.neh.gov

Thomas C. Phelps

The National Endowment for the Humanities (NEH) is an independent federal agency created in 1965. It is the largest funder of humanities programs in the United States.

Because democracy demands wisdom, NEH serves and strengthens the republic by promoting excellence in the humanities and conveying the lessons of history to all Americans. It accomplishes this mission by providing grants for high-quality humanities projects in four funding areas: preserving and providing access to cultural resources, education, research, and public programs.

NEH grants typically go to cultural institutions, such as museums, archives, libraries, colleges, universities, public television and radio stations, and to individual scholars. The grants

- Strengthen teaching and learning in the humanities in schools and colleges across the nation
- Facilitate research and original scholarship
- Provide opportunities for lifelong learning
- Preserve and provide access to cultural and educational resources
- Strengthen the institutional base of the humanities

Over the past 37 years, NEH has reached millions of Americans with projects and programs that preserve and study the nation's cultural heritage while providing a foundation for the future.

The endowment's mission is to enrich American cultural life by promoting the study of the humanities.

According to the National Foundation on the Arts and Humanities Act, "The term 'humanities' includes, but is not limited to, the study of the following: language, both modern and classical; linguistics; literature; history; jurisprudence; philosophy; archaeology; comparative religion; ethics; the history, criticism, and theory of the arts; those aspects of social sciences which have humanistic content and employ humanistic methods; and the study and application of the humanities to the human environment with particular attention to reflecting our diverse heritage, traditions, and history and to the relevance of the humanities to the current conditions of national life."

This act, adopted by Congress in 1965, provided for the establishment of the National Foundation on the Arts and the Humanities in order to promote progress and scholarship in the humanities and the arts in the United States. The act included the following findings:

- The arts and the humanities belong to all the people of the United States.
- The encouragement and support of national progress and scholarship in the humanities and the arts, while primarily matters for private and local initiative, are also appropriate matters of concern to the federal government.
- An advanced civilization must not limit its efforts to science and technology alone, but must give full value and support to the other great branches of scholarly and cultural activity in order to achieve a better understanding of the past, a better analysis of the present, and a better view of the future.
- Democracy demands wisdom and vision in its citizens. It must therefore foster and support a form of education, and access to the arts and the humanities, designed to make people of all backgrounds and wherever located masters of their technology and not its unthinking servants.
- It is necessary and appropriate for the federal government to complement, assist, and add to programs for the advancement of the humanities and the arts by local, state, regional, and private agencies and their organizations. In doing so, the government must be sensitive to the nature of public sponsorship. Public funding of the arts and humanities is subject to the conditions that traditionally govern the use of public money. Such funding should contribute to public support and confidence in the use of taxpayer funds. Public funds provided by the federal government must ultimately serve public purposes the Congress defines.
- The arts and the humanities reflect the high place accorded by the American people to the nation's rich cultural heritage and to the fostering of mutual respect for the diverse beliefs and values of all persons and groups.

What NEH Grants Accomplish

Interpretive Exhibitions

Interpretive exhibitions provide opportunities for lifelong learning in the humanities for millions of Americans. Since 1967 NEH has made more than 2,400 grants totaling nearly $194 million for interpretive exhibitions, catalogs, and public programs that are among the most highly visible activities supported by the agency. All 50 states and the District of Columbia will host more than 122 exhibitions over the next two years.

Renewing Teaching

Over the years, more than 20,000 high school teachers and nearly 30,000 college teachers have deepened their knowledge of the humanities through intensive summer study supported by NEH. It is estimated that more than 140,000 students benefitted from these better-educated teachers in the first year alone.

Reading and Discussion Programs

Since 1982 NEH has supported reading and discussion programs in libraries, in which people come together to discuss works of literature and history. The programs are facilitated by scholars in the humanities who provide thematic direction for the discussion programs. Using such texts and themes as "Work," "Family," "Diversity," and "Not for Children Only," these programs have attracted more than 1 million Americans to read and talk about what they've read.

Preserving the Nation's Heritage

The United States Newspaper Program is rescuing a piece of history by cataloging and microfilming 57 million pages from 133,000 newspapers dating from the early days of the republic. Another microfilming program has rescued the content of more than 860,000 brittle books.

Stimulating Private Support

More than $1.3 billion in humanities support has been generated by NEH's Challenge Grants program, which requires most recipients to raise $3 or $4 in nonfederal funds for every dollar they receive.

Presidential Papers

Ten presidential papers projects, from George Washington to Dwight D. Eisenhower, are underwritten by NEH. The Washington and Eisenhower papers have each leveraged more than $1.4 million in nonfederal contributions.

New Scholarship

NEH grants enable scholars to do in-depth study. Jack Rakove explored the making of the Constitution in his *Original Meanings,* while James McPherson chronicled the Civil War in his *Battle Cry of Freedom.* Both won the Pulitzer Prize.

History on Screen

Thirty-eight million Americans saw the Ken Burns documentary *The Civil War,* and 750,000 people bought the book. Through other films such as *Liberty!, Jazz,* and *The Invisible Man,* and film biographies of Theodore and Franklin Roosevelt, Andrew Carnegie, and Gen. Douglas MacArthur, Americans learn about the events and people that shaped the nation.

Library of America

Two million books have been sold as part of the Library of America series, a collection of the riches of our literature. Begun with NEH seed money, the 122 published volumes include the writings of Henry Adams, Edith Wharton, William James, Eudora Welty, and W. E. B. DuBois, as well as 19th- and 20th-century American poets.

Science and the Humanities

The scientific past is being preserved with NEH-supported editions of the letters of Charles Darwin, the works of Albert Einstein, and the 14-volume papers of Thomas A. Edison.

The Sound of Poetry

One million Americans use cassettes from the NEH-supported Voices and Visions series on poets. As a telecourse, Voices and Visions reached more than 200 colleges, 2,000 high schools, and 500 public libraries.

Learning Under the Tent

From California to Florida, state humanities councils bring a 21st-century version of Chautauqua to the public, embracing populations of entire towns, cities, even regions. Scholars portray significant figures such as Meriwether Lewis, Sojourner Truth, Willa Cather, Teddy Roosevelt, and Sacagawea, first speaking as the historic character and later giving audiences opportunities to ask questions. The give-and-take between the scholar/performer and the audiences provides an entertaining, energetic, and thought-provoking exchange about experiences and attitudes in the present and the past.

Technology and the Classroom

NEH's EDSITEment Web site (http://edsitement.neh.gov) assembles the best humanities resources on the Web. Online lesson plans help teachers use more than 50 Web sites to enhance their teaching. Schools across the country are developing curricula to bring digital resources to the classroom as part of the Schools for a New Millennium project.

Special Initiatives

We the People

We the People is an initiative launched by NEH to encourage the teaching, studying, and understanding of American history and culture. Under this initiative, NEH invites scholars, teachers, filmmakers, curators, librarians, and others to submit grant applications that explore significant events and themes in the nation's history and culture and that advance knowledge of the principles that define the United States.

Proposals responding to the initiative can take the form of

- New scholarship
- Projects to preserve and provide access to documents and artifacts
- Educational projects for every level, from kindergarten through college
- Public programs in libraries, museums, and historical societies, including exhibitions, film, radio, and Internet-based programs

NEH will accept We the People proposals for all programs and all deadlines. Proposals are expected to meet the guidelines of the program that best fits the character of the project. A list of programs and deadlines is available on the NEH Web site.

The three main components of "We the People" are a call for applications to NEH for projects designed to explore significant events and themes in the nation's history; an annual "Heroes of History" lecture by a scholar on an individual whose heroism has helped to protect America; and an "Idea of America" essay contest for high school juniors.

Plans include expanding We the People through a grant program to support projects that help schools and universities improve their teaching of American history, government, and civics. The Summer Seminar and Institutes program will be extended to offer teachers more opportunities to study significant texts. Exhibits on the "Idea of America" essay contest will travel to small and mid-sized communities. NEH will also convene an annual national conference on civics education, the state of historical knowledge, and ways to enhance the teaching of American history.

EDSITEment

EDSITEment, a joint project to share the best humanities Web sites with teachers and students, was launched in 1997 by NEH, the Council of the Great City Schools, WorldCom Foundation, and the National Trust for the Humanities. Users of EDSITEment now have access to more than 100 high-quality humanities sites, representing more than 50,000 files searchable through the EDSITEment search engine at http://www.edsitement.neh.gov.

Federal–State Partnership

The Office of Federal-State Partnership links NEH with the nationwide network of 56 humanities councils, which are located in each state, the District of Columbia, Puerto Rico, the U.S. Virgin Islands, the Northern Mariana Islands, American Samoa, and Guam. Each humanities council funds humanities programs in its jurisdiction. A contact list for all the state councils can be found below:

Directory of State Humanities Councils

Alabama

Alabama Humanities Foundation
1100 Ireland Way, Suite 101
Birmingham, AL 35205-7001
205-558-3980, fax 205-558-3981
http://www.ahf.net

Alaska

Alaska Humanities Forum
421 W. First Ave., Suite 300
Anchorage, AK 99501
907-272-5341, fax 907-272-3979
http://www.akhf.org

Arizona

Arizona Humanities Council
Ellis-Shackelford House
1242 N. Central Ave.
Phoenix, AZ 85004
602-257-0335, fax 602-257-0392
http://www.azhumanities.org

Arkansas

Arkansas Humanities Council
10800 Financial Centre Pkwy., Suite 465
Little Rock, AR 72211
501-221-0091, fax 501-221-9860
http://www.arkhums.org

California

California Council for the Humanities
312 Sutter St., Suite 601
San Francisco, CA 94108
415-391-1474, fax 415-391-1312
http://www.calhum.org

Colorado

Colorado Endowment for the Humanities
1490 Lafayette St., Suite 101
Denver, CO 80218
303-894-7951, fax 303-864-9361
http://www.ceh.org

Connecticut

Connecticut Humanities Council
955 S. Main St., Suite E
Middletown, CT 06457
860-685-2260, fax 860-704-0429
http://www.ctculture.org

Delaware

Delaware Humanities Forum
100 W. 10th St., Suite 1009
Wilmington, DE 19801
302-657-0650, fax 302-657-0655
http://www.dhf.org

District of Columbia

Humanities Council of Washington, D.C.
925 U St. N.W.
Washington, DC 20001
202-347-1732, fax 202-347-3350
http://wdchumanities.org

Florida

Florida Humanities Council
599 2nd St. S.
St. Petersburg, FL 33701-5005
772-553-3800, fax 772-553-3829
http://www.flahum.org

Georgia

Georgia Humanities Council
50 Hurt Plaza S.E., Room 1565
Atlanta, GA 30303-2915
404-523-6220, fax 404-523-5702
http://www.georgiahumanities.org

Hawaii

Hawaii Council for the Humanities
First Hawaiian Bank Bldg.
3599 Waialae Ave., Room 23
Honolulu, HI 96816
808-732-5402, fax 808-732-5402
http://www.hihumanities.org

Idaho

Idaho Humanities Council
217 W. State St.
Boise, ID 83702
208-345-5346, fax 208-345-5347
http://www.idahohumanities.org

Illinois

Illinois Humanities Council
203 N. Wabash Ave., Suite 2020
Chicago, IL 60601-2417
312-422-5580, fax 312-422-5588
http://www.prairie.org

Indiana

Indiana Humanities Council
1500 N. Delaware St.
Indianapolis, IN 46202
317-638-1500, fax 317-634-9503
http://www.ihc4u.org

Iowa

Humanities Iowa
100 Oakdale Campus, Northlawn
University of Iowa
Iowa City, IA 52242-5000
319-335-4153, fax 319-335-4154
http://www.humanitiesiowa.org

Kansas

Kansas Humanities Council
112 S.W. 6th Ave., Suite 210
Topeka, KS 66603
785-357-0359, fax 785-357-1723
http://www.kansashumanities.org

Kentucky

Kentucky Humanities Council
206 E. Maxwell St.
Lexington, KY 40508
859-257-5932, fax 859-257-5933
http://www.kyhumanities.org

Louisiana

Louisiana Endowment for the Humanities
938 Lafayette St., Suite 300
New Orleans, LA 70113
fax 504-529-2358
http://www.leh.org

Maine

Maine Humanities Council
674 Brighton Ave.
Portland, ME 04102-1012
207-773-5051, fax 207-773-2416
http://www.mainehumanities.org

Maryland

Maryland Humanities Council
11350 McCormick Rd., Suite 503
Hunt Valley, MD 21031-1002
410-771-0650, fax 410-771-0655
http://www.mdhc.org

Massachusetts

Massachusetts Foundation for the Humanities
66 Bridge St.
Northampton, MA 01060
413-584-8440, fax 413-584-8454
http://www.mfh.org

Michigan

Michigan Humanities Council
119 Pere Marquette Drive, Suite 3B
Lansing, MI 48912-1270
517-372-7770, fax 517-372-0027
http://michiganhumanities.org

Minnesota

Minnesota Humanities Commission
987 E. Ivy Ave.
St. Paul, MN 55106
651-774-0105, fax 651-774-0205
http://www.thinkmhc.org

Mississippi

Mississippi Humanities Council
3825 Ridgewood Rd., Room 311
Jackson, MS 39211
601-432-6752, fax 601-432-6750
http://www.ihl.state.ms.us/mhc/index.html

Missouri

Missouri Humanities Council
543 Hanley Industrial Court, Suite 201
St. Louis, MO 63144
314-781-9660, fax 314-781-9681
http://www.mohumanities.org

Montana

Montana Committee for the Humanities
311 Brantly Hall
University of Montana
Missoula, MT 59812-8214
406-243-6022, fax 406-243-4836
http://www.umt.edu/lastbest

Nebraska

Nebraska Humanities Council
Lincoln Center Bldg., Suite 225
215 Centennial Mall S.
Lincoln, NE 68508
402-474-2131, fax 402-474-4852
http://www.lincolnne.com/nonprofit/nhc

Nevada

Nevada Humanities Committee
1034 N. Sierra St.
Reno, NV 89507
775-784-6587, fax 775-784-6527
http://www.nevadahumanities.org

New Hampshire

New Hampshire Humanities Council
19 Pillsbury St.
Box 2228
Concord, NH 03302-2228
603-224-4071, fax 603-224-4072
http://www.nhhc.org

New Jersey

New Jersey Council for the Humanities
28 W. State St.
Trenton, NJ 08608
609-695-4838, fax 609-695-4929
http://www.njch.org

New Mexico

New Mexico Endowment for the Humanities
Onate Hall, Room 209
University of New Mexico
Albuquerque, NM 87131
505-277-3705, fax 505-277-6056
http://www.nmeh.org

New York

New York Council for the Humanities
150 Broadway, Suite 1700
New York, NY 10038
212-233-1131, fax 212-233-4607
http://www.nyhumanities.org

North Carolina

North Carolina Humanities Council
200 S. Elm St., Suite 403
Greensboro, NC 27401
336-334-5325, fax 336-334-5052
http://www.nchumanities.org

North Dakota

North Dakota Humanities Council
2900 Broadway E., Suite 3
Box 2191
Bismarck, ND 58502
701-255-3360, fax 701-223-8724
http://www.nd-humanities.org

Ohio

Ohio Humanities Council
695 Bryden Rd.
Box 06354
Columbus, OH 43206-0354
614-461-7802, fax 614-461-4651
http://www.ohiohumanities.org

Oklahoma

Oklahoma Humanities Council
Festival Plaza
428 W. California, Suite 270
Oklahoma City, OK 73102
405-235-0280, fax 405-235-0289
http://www.okhumanitiescouncil.org

Oregon

Oregon Council for the Humanities
812 S.W. Washington St., Suite 225
Portland, OR 97205
503-241-0543, fax 503-241-0024
http://www.oregonhum.org

Pennsylvania

Pennsylvania Humanities Council
325 Chestnut St., Suite 715
Philadelphia, PA 19106
215-925-1005, fax 215-925-3054
http://www.pahumanities.org

Rhode Island

Rhode Island Committee for the Humanities
385 Westminster St., Suite 2
Providence, RI 02903
401-273-2250, fax 401-454-4872
http://www.uri.edu/rich

South Carolina

Humanities Council of South Carolina
1308 Columbia College Drive
Box 5287
Columbia, SC 29250
803-691-4100, fax 803-691-0809
http://www.schumanities.org

South Dakota

South Dakota Humanities Council
Box 7050, University Station
Brookings, SD 57007
605-688-6113, fax 605-688-4531
http://web.sdstate.edu/humanities

Tennessee

Tennessee Humanities Council
1003 18th Ave. S.
Nashville, TN 37212
615-320-7001, fax 615-321-4586
http://tn-humanities.org

Texas

Texas Council for the Humanities
Banister Place A
3809 S. 2nd St.
Austin, TX 78704
512-440-1991, fax 512-440-0115
http://www.public-humanities.org

Utah

Utah Humanities Council
202 W. 300 N.
Salt Lake City, UT 84103-1108
801-359-9670, fax 801-531-7869
http://www.utahhumanities.org

Vermont

Vermont Council on the Humanities
200 Park St.
RR 1, Box 7285
Morrisville, VT 05661
802-888-3183, fax 802-888-1236
http://www.vermonthumanities.org

Virginia

Virginia Foundation for the Humanities and
  Public Policy
145 Ednam Drive
Charlottesville, VA 22903-4629
804-924-3296, fax 804-296-4714
http://www.virginia.edu/vfh

Washington

Washington Commission for the Humanities
615 2nd Ave., Suite 300
Seattle, WA 98104
206-682-1770, fax 206-682-4158
http://www.humanities.org

West Virginia

West Virginia Humanities Council
1310 Kanawha Blvd. E., Suite 800
Charleston, WV 25301
304-346-8500, fax 304-346-8504
http://www.wvhumanities.org

Wisconsin

Wisconsin Humanities Council
222 S. Bedford St., Suite F
Madison, WI 53703-3688
608-262-0706, fax 608-263-7970
http://www.danenet.org/whc

Wyoming

Wyoming Council for the Humanities
Box 3643, University Station
Laramie, WY 82071-3643
307-721-9244, fax 307-742-4914
http://www.uwyo.edu/special/wch

American Samoa

Amerika Samoa Humanities Council
Box 5800
Pago Pago, AS 96799
684-633-4870, fax 684-633-4873
(No Web address)

Guam

Guam Humanities Council
426 Chalan San Antonio

Center Pointe Bldg., Suite 101
Tamuning, Guam 96911
671-646-4461, fax 671-646-2243
http://www.guamhumanitiescouncil.org

Northern Mariana Islands

Northern Mariana Islands Council for the
Humanities
AAA-3394, Box 10001
Saipan, MP 96950
670-235-4785, fax 670-235-4786
http://cnmi.humanities.org.mp

Puerto Rico

Fundación Puertorriqueña de las
Humanidades
109 San Jose St., 3rd floor
Box 9023920
San Juan, PR 00902-3920
787-721-2087, fax 787-721-2684
http://www.fprh.org

Virgin Islands

Virgin Islands Humanities Council
5-6 Kongens Gade, Corbiere Complex
Suites 200B and 201B
St. Thomas, VI 00802
340-776-4044, fax 340-774-3972
http://www.vihumanities.org

NEH Overview

Division of Preservation and Access

Grants are made for projects that will create, preserve, and increase the availability of resources important for research, education, and public programming in the humanities.

Projects may encompass books, journals, newspapers, manuscript and archival materials, maps, still and moving images, sound recordings, and objects of material culture held by libraries, archives, museums, historical organizations, and other repositories.

Preservation and Access Projects

Support may be sought to preserve the intellectual content and aid bibliographic control of collections; to compile bibliographies, descriptive catalogs, and guides to cultural holdings; to create dictionaries, encyclopedias, databases, and other types of research tools and reference works; and to stabilize material culture collections through the appropriate housing and storing of objects, improved environmental control, and the installation of security, lighting, and fire-prevention systems. Applications may also be submitted for national and regional education and training projects, regional preservation field service programs, and research and demonstration projects that are intended to enhance institutional practice and the use of technology for preservation and access.

Proposals may combine preservation and access activities within a single project. Historically Black Colleges and Universities (HCBUs) with significant institutional collections of primary materials are encouraged to apply.

Eligible applicants:	Individuals, nonprofit institutions and cultural organizations, state agencies, and institutional consortia
Application deadlines:	May 15, July 1, and July 15, 2003
Contact:	202-606-8570, e-mail preservation@neh.gov

Division of Public Programs

This division fosters public understanding and appreciation of the humanities by supporting projects that bring significant insights of these disciplines to general audiences of all ages through interpretive exhibitions, radio and television programs, lectures, symposia, multimedia projects, printed materials, and reading and discussion groups.

Public Programs

Grants support consultation with scholars and humanities programming experts to shape an interpretive project; the planning and production of television and radio programs in the humanities intended for general audiences; the planning and implementation of exhibitions, the interpretation of historic sites, and the production of related publications, multimedia components, and educational programs; and the planning and implementation of projects through the use of books, new technologies, and other resources in the collections of libraries and archives in formats such as reading and discussion programs, lectures, symposia, and interpretive exhibitions of books, manuscripts, and other library resources.

Eligible applicants:	Nonprofit institutions and organizations including public television and radio stations and state humanities councils
Application deadlines:	Planning, scripting, implementation, production, February 3, April 7, September 16, and November 3, 2003; Consultation grants, April 7 and September 16, 2003
Contact:	202-606-8267, e-mail publicpgms@neh.gov

Division of Research Programs

Through fellowships to individual scholars and grants to support complex, frequently collaborative, research, the Division of Research Programs contributes to the creation of knowledge in the humanities.

Fellowships and Stipends

Grants provide support for scholars to undertake full-time independent research and writing in the humanities. Grants are available for a maximum of one year and a minimum of two months of summer study.

Eligible applicants:	Individuals
Application deadlines:	Fellowships, May 1, 2003; Summer Stipends, October 1, 2003
Contact:	202-606-8200 for Fellowships, 202-606-8551 for Summer Stipends, e-mail fellowships@neh.gov, stipends@neh.gov

Research

Grants provide up to three years of support for collaborative research in the preparation for publication of editions, translations, and other important works in the humanities, and in the conduct of large or complex interpretive studies including archaeology projects and the humanities studies of science and technology. Grants also support research opportunities offered through independent research centers and international research organizations.

Eligible applicants:	Individuals, institutions of higher education, nonprofit professional associations, scholarly societies, and other nonprofit organizations
Application deadlines:	Collaborative Research, November 3, 2003; Fellowships at Independent Research Institutions, September 1, 2003
Contact:	202-606-8200, e-mail research@neh.gov

Division of Education

Through grants to educational institutions, fellowships to scholars and teachers, and through the support of significant research, this division is designed to strengthen sustained, thoughtful study of the humanities at all levels of education and promote original research in the humanities.

Education Development and Demonstration

Grants, including "next semester" Humanities Focus Grants, support curriculum and materials development efforts; faculty study programs within and among educational institutions; and conferences and networks of institutions. NEH is interested in projects that help teachers use electronic technologies to enhance students' understanding of humanities subjects.

Eligible applicants:	Public and private elementary and secondary schools, school systems, colleges and universities, nonprofit academic associations, and cultural institutions, such as libraries and museums.

Application deadlines: Exemplary Education Projects, October 15, 2003;
                          Humanities Focus Grants, April 15, 2003
Contact: 202-606-8500, e-mail education@neh.gov

Schools for a New Millennium

Grants enable whole schools, in partnership with colleges and communities, to design professional development activities integrating digital technology into the humanities classroom.

Application deadlines: Implementation Grants, October 1, 2003
Contact: 202-606-8500, e-mail education@neh.gov

Seminars and Institutes

Grants support summer seminars and national institutes in the humanities for college and school teachers. These faculty development activities are conducted at colleges and universities across the country. Those wishing to participate in seminars submit their seminar applications to the seminar director.

Eligible applicants: Individuals, and institutions of higher learning
Application deadlines   Participants, March 1, 2003, for summer seminars
for seminars: in 2003; Directors, March 1, 2003, for summer seminars in 2004
Contact: 202-606-8463, e-mail sem-inst@neh.gov
Application deadline
for national institutes: March 1, 2003
Contact: 202-606-8463, e-mail sem-inst@neh.gov

Office of Challenge Grants

Nonprofit institutions interested in developing new sources of long-term support for educational, scholarly, preservation, and public programs in the humanities can be assisted in these efforts by an NEH Challenge Grant. Grantees are required to raise three or four dollars in new or increased donations for every federal dollar offered. Both federal and nonfederal funds may be used to establish or increase institutional endowments and thus guarantee long-term support for a variety of humanities needs. Funds may also be used for limited direct capital expenditures, where such needs are compelling and clearly related to improvements in the humanities.

Eligible applicants: Nonprofit postsecondary, educational, research, or cultural institutions and organizations working within the humanities
Application deadlines: February 3, May 1, and November 3, 2003
Contact: 202-606-8309, e-mail challenge@neh.gov

Institute of Museum and Library Services Library Programs

1100 Pennsylvania Ave. N.W., Washington, DC 20506
202-606-5527, fax 202-606-1077
World Wide Web http://www.imls.gov

Robert S. Martin
Director
Institute of Museum and Library Services

The Library Services and Technology Act (LSTA), Subchapter II of the Museum and Library Services Act of 1996, changed the federal administration of library programs by moving programs from the U.S. Department of Education to the newly formed Institute of Museum and Library Services (IMLS). The first LSTA grants were made in 1998. A total of $197,602,000 was available for library programs in fiscal year (FY) 2002. LSTA funds are administered by the Office of Library Services. The Office of Museum Services administers grants to museums.

The purposes of LSTA are

- To consolidate federal library service programs
- To stimulate excellence and promote access to learning and information resources in all types of libraries for individuals of all ages
- To promote library services that provide all users access to information through state, regional, national, and international electronic networks
- To provide linkages between and among libraries
- To promote targeted library service to people of diverse geographic, cultural, and socioeconomic backgrounds, to individuals with disabilities, and to people with limited functional literacy or information skills

Within IMLS, the Office of Library Services is responsible for the administration of LSTA. It is composed of the Division of State Programs, which administers the Grants to States Program, and the Division of Discretionary Programs, which administers the National Leadership Grant Program, the Native American Library Services Program, and the Native Hawaiian Library Services Program.

State-Administered Programs

Approximately 90 percent of the annual federal appropriation under LSTA is distributed through the State Grant Program to the state library administrative agencies according to a population-based formula. The formula consists of a minimum amount set by the law ($340,000 for the states and $40,000 for the Pacific Territories) and supplemented by an additional amount based on population. For 2002, the State Grant Program appropriation was $149,014,000 (Table 1). State agencies may use the appropriation for statewide initiatives and services. They may also distribute the funds through competitive sub-grants or cooperative agreements to public, academic, research, school, or special libraries. For-profit and federal libraries are not eligible applicants. LSTA state grant funds have been used to meet the special needs of children, parents, teenagers, the unemployed, senior citizens, and the business community, as well as adult learners. Many libraries have partnered with community organizations to provide a variety of services and programs including access to electronic databases, computer instruction, homework centers, summer reading programs, digitization of special collections, access to e-books and adaptive technology, bookmobile service, and development of outreach programs to the underserved. The act limits the amount of funds available for administration at the state level to 4 percent and requires a 34 percent match from nonfederal state or local funds. Grants to the Pacific Territories and Freely Associated States are funded under a Special Rule (20 USCA 9131(b)(3)) that authorizes a small competitive grants program in the Pacific. There are six eligible entities in two groups: the Pacific Territories (Insular areas) consisting of Guam, American Samoa, and the Commonwealth of Northern Mariana Islands; and the Freely Associated States, which includes the Federated States of Micronesia, the Republic of the Marshall Islands, and the Republic of Palau. The funds for this grant program are taken from the allotments for the Freely Associated States (Micronesia, Marshall Islands, and Palau), but not from the allotments to the territories. The three territories (Guam, American Samoa, and the Northern Mariana Islands) receive their allotments through the regular program and in addition may apply for funds under this program. Five entities (American Samoa, Guam, the Northern Mariana Islands, Micronesia, and the Marshall Islands) received a total of $224,879 in FY 2002. This amount included the set-aside of 5 percent because Pacific Resources for Education and Learning (PREL), based in Hawaii, facilitated the competition. PREL received the set-aside amount to administer parts of the program.

Priorities for funding that support the goals of LSTA are set by the individual State Library Administrative Agencies (SLAAs) based on needs they identify in the five-year plans they are required to submit to IMLS.

Table 1 / Funding for LSTA State Programs, FY 2002
Total Distributed to States: $149,014,000[1]

State	Federal Allocation[2] 66%	State Matching Fund 34%	Total
Alabama	$2,377,520	$1,224,783	$3,602,303
Alaska	627,240	323,124	950,364
Arizona	2,690,692	1,386,114	4,076,806
Arkansas	1,564,867	806,144	2,371,011
California	15,858,909	8,169,741	24,028,650
Colorado	2,310,701	1,190,361	3,501,062
Connecticut	1,900,321	978,953	2,879,274
Delaware	699,021	360,102	1,059,123
Florida	7,662,616	3,947,408	11,610,024
Georgia	4,090,772	2,107,367	6,198,139
Hawaii	895,088	461,106	1,356,194
Idaho	932,848	480,558	1,413,406
Illinois	6,030,124	3,106,428	9,136,552
Indiana	3,125,885	1,610,304	4,736,189
Iowa	1,680,748	865,840	2,546,588

Table 1 / Funding for LSTA State Programs, FY 2002 *(cont.)*

State	Federal Allocation[2] 66%	State Matching Fund 34%	Total
Kansas	1,571,747	809,688	2,381,435
Kentucky	2,191,810	1,129,114	3,320,924
Louisiana	2,387,542	1,229,946	3,617,488
Maine	924,129	476,066	1,400,195
Maryland	2,766,681	1,425,260	4,191,941
Massachusetts	3,248,954	1,673,704	4,922,658
Michigan	4,893,478	2,520,883	7,414,361
Minnesota	2,593,949	1,336,277	3,930,226
Mississippi	1,643,332	846,565	2,489,897
Missouri	2,903,547	1,495,767	4,399,314
Montana	753,357	388,093	1,141,450
Nebraska	1,124,046	579,054	1,703,100
Nevada	1,255,538	646,792	1,902,330
New Hampshire	906,198	466,829	1,373,027
New Jersey	4,195,187	2,161,157	6,356,344
New Mexico	1,173,429	604,494	1,777,923
New York	9,034,408	4,654,089	13,688,497
North Carolina	4,027,939	2,074,999	6,102,938
North Dakota	634,236	326,728	960,964
Ohio	5,541,647	2,854,788	8,396,435
Oklahoma	1,920,980	989,596	2,910,576
Oregon	1,907,576	982,691	2,890,267
Pennsylvania	5,966,788	3,073,800	9,040,588
Rhode Island	820,306	422,582	1,242,888
South Carolina	2,178,176	1,122,091	3,300,267
South Dakota	685,845	353,314	1,039,159
Tennessee	2,946,648	1,517,970	4,464,618
Texas	9,893,640	5,096,724	14,990,364
Utah	1,363,167	702,238	2,065,405
Vermont	618,945	318,850	937,795
Virginia	3,583,150	1,845,865	5,429,015
Washington	3,040,498	1,566,317	4,606,815
West Virginia	1,168,526	601,968	1,770,494
Wisconsin	2,797,465	1,441,118	4,238,583
Wyoming	566,235	291,697	857,932
District of Columbia	602,099	310,172	912,271
Puerto Rico	2,153,424	1,109,340	3,262,764
American Samoa	71,471	36,818	108,289
Northern Marianas	75,421	38,853	114,274
Guam	113,672	58,558	172,230
Virgin Islands	96,583	49,754	146,337
Pacific Territories[3]	224,879	115,846	340,725
Totals	$149,014,000	$76,764,788	$225,778,788

1. The amount available to states is based on the balance remaining after enacted allocations have been subtracted from the total appropriation as follows:

Library allocation, FY 2002	$197,602,000
Native Americans, Native Hawaiians	$2,941,000
National Leadership Grants	$40,605,000
Administration	$5,042,000
Total distributed to states	$149,014,000

2.Calculation is based on minimum set in the law (P.L.104-208, as amended by P.L.105-128 111 Stat 2548) and reflects appropriations enacted by P.L. 107-116. Data for the District of Columbia and the 50 states are from Bureau of Census (BOC) resident population as of April 1, 2000, which were made available by BOC on December 28, 2000. For the continental United States, BOC data can be accessed at the BOC Web site at http://www.census.gov/population/cen2000/tab02.xls. Data for Puerto Rico, American Samoa, the Northern Marianas, Guam, the Virgin Islands, and the Pacific Territories are from the BOC International database at http://www.census.gov/cgi-bin/ipc/idbrank.pl. Data are also available by telephone at 301-457-2422.

3.Total allotment (including administrative costs) for Palau, Marshall Islands, and Micronesia. Funds are awarded on a competitive basis and administered by Pacific Resources for Education and Learning.

Discretionary Programs

In 1998 IMLS also began administering the discretionary programs of LSTA. In FY 2002, $44,546,000* was allocated for the National Leadership Grant Program, the Native American Library Services Program, and the Native Hawaiian Library Services Grant Program. This includes $29,524,000 for directed grants.

The FY 2002 congressional appropriation for discretionary programs includes the following:

- National Leadership Grant Program: $11,081,000 for competitive programs
- Native American Library Services Program: $2,521,000
- Native Hawaiian Library Services Program: $420,000

The Native American Library Services Program provides opportunities for improved library services for an important part of the nation's community of library users. The program offers three types of support to serve the range of needs of Indian tribes and Alaska Native villages. The Native Hawaiian Library Services Program provides opportunities for improved library services to Native Hawaiians through a single award. The National Leadership Grant Program provides funding for innovative model programs to enhance the quality of library services nationwide. National Leadership Grants are intended to produce results useful for the broader library community.

National Leadership Grant Program

In 2002 IMLS awarded 46 National Leadership Grants totaling $12,013,000 using FY 2002 funding. This figure represents 3.75 percent of the LSTA appropriation for competitive programs, plus $1,000,000 from the IMLS Office of Museum Services to supplement funding for library and museum collaborations. A total of 188 applications requesting more than $49,939,021 were received. The projects funded were selected as innovative model projects in the field of library and information science in education and training, research and demonstration, preservation and digitization of library resources, and library and museum collaborations (Table 2).

*Includes $1,000,000 from the IMLS Office of Museum Services to supplement LSTA funding for library and museum collaborations.

The FY 2002 priorities for National Leadership Grant funding were

Education and Training

- Projects to help libraries take a leadership role in the education of lifelong learners in the 21st century
- Projects to attract individuals from diverse cultural backgrounds to the field of librarianship and information science and promote their success educationally and professionally
- Projects that implement innovative approaches to education and training and enhance the availability of professional librarians with advanced skills and specializations
- Projects that train librarians to enhance people's ability to use information effectively
- Projects that train librarians in outcome-based evaluation techniques

Proposals from graduate schools of library and information science to train doctoral students in outcome-based evaluation were particularly encouraged. Projects will be carried out in collaboration with IMLS.

Research and Demonstration

- Projects to help libraries take a leadership role in the education of lifelong learners in the 21st century
- Projects that conduct research and/or demonstrations to enhance library services through the effective and efficient use of new and appropriate technologies
- Projects that conduct research and/or demonstrations to enhance the ability of library users to make more effective use of information resources
- Projects that conduct research and/or demonstrations that will assist in the evaluation of library services, including economic, social, and cultural implications of services, and other contributions to a community
- Projects that conduct research and/or demonstrations that address how people find information, how they would prefer to find information, and how they benefit from information
- A project for development of a metadata agent to collect and broker metadata to other service providers in accordance with the Open Archives Initiative protocol
- Projects to add value to already-digitized collections as a demonstration of interoperability with the National Science Foundation's National Science Digital Library Program

Preservation or Digitization of Library Materials

- Projects to help libraries take a leadership role in the education of lifelong learners in the 21st century
- Projects that address the challenges of preserving and archiving digital media

- Projects that preserve and enhance access to valuable library resources useful to the broader community
- Collaborative projects to increase access to related collections, that provide evidence of good stewardship of materials in all formats, and that exemplify or help to develop standards and best practices for the creation and management of digital collections

Library and Museum Collaborations

- Projects to help museums and libraries take a leadership role in the education of lifelong learners in the 21st century
- Projects that develop, document, and disseminate model programs of cooperation between libraries and museums, with emphasis on how technology is used, education is enhanced, or the community is served
- Projects that support research and other activities to enhance interoperability, integration, and seamless access to digital library and museum resources

(text continues on page 358)

Table 2 / National Leadership Grant Awards, FY 2002

UCLA Film and Television Archive $112,619

The University of California at Los Angeles Film and Television Archive—in collaboration with the university's Department of Information Studies and the Department of Film, Television and Digital Media—will establish the first continuing-education program for individuals working in the moving-image archive field. The program will provide hands-on instruction in modern archival practice and will complement UCLA's new master's degree program in moving-image archive studies.

University of California at Los Angeles $196,055

UCLA will train eight professional librarians of diverse backgrounds in research, information technology, and policy to prepare them for future doctoral studies. It will award participants a post-MLIS certificate and will assist them in preparing study plans for doctoral programs.

Florida State University, Tallahassee $482,780

The university, in collaboration with the University of Illinois and the University of Washington, will develop "Project Athena" to recruit and educate LIS doctoral students interested in becoming the next generation of LIS educators. The program will include development of a model recruitment plan, a curriculum based on current innovations in higher education, and a strong assessment component.

Florida State University, Tallahassee $248,600

This two-year project introduces a network statistics training program. The program will instruct librarians on the intent and definition of network statistics and various methodologies for collecting statistics, assist libraries with developing management and collection plans and in-house staff training programs, and instruct librarians in outcomes-based evaluation of their networked services. It will also disseminate online materials via a library statistics clearinghouse.

Chicago Library System $80,000

The system will train 24 librarians nearing retirement to become consultant-coaches to 48 library staff most likely to move into management and specialized positions. The project will also create a Web-based learning resource to support coaching and staff retention efforts in the library profession.

Table 2 / National Leadership Grant Awards, FY 2002 *(cont.)*

University of Illinois $216,737

IMLS and the University of Illinois Graduate School of Library and Information Science will collaborate to develop a two-week institute to train students in the methods and application of outcome-based evaluation. The curriculum developed will be made freely available, and students who complete the pilot program will help to integrate outcomes assessment into library programs.

Louisiana State University, A&M, Baton Rouge $498,653

Louisiana State University, A&M—in collaboration with Auburn University, Georgia College and State University, the University of Kentucky, and the University of South Carolina—will develop a pilot program for professional education in archives management for students across the Southeast. The curriculum will be developed by a regional collaboration of archives educators and will be delivered via distance-education technology. Course materials will be made available for the use of other educators at the end of the project.

Rutgers University, New Brunswick, New Jersey $233,861

Rutgers University School of Communication, Information, and Library Studies, Rutgers University Libraries, and the Research Libraries of the New York Public Library will develop an online training program for library assistants in academic and research libraries. Course materials will be made available for the use of other online instructors at the end of the two-year project.

Research and Demonstration

University of California–Berkeley School of Information Management and Systems $241,643

In "Going Places in the Catalog," a two-year demonstration project, the School of Information Management and Systems and the university's Electronic Cultural Atlas Initiative will show how geographic location searching in library catalogs can be improved and extended to scholarly and educational resources in and beyond library catalogs. The project links online catalogs with online gazetteers and uses geographical map displays with latitudinal and longitudinal coordinates.

California Digital Library $374,736

In this two-year demonstration project, the California Digital Library, in partnership with the University of California–Berkeley Library, will create a model preservation repository for multi-institutional digital materials following the Open Archival Information System reference model. The project will also explore and report on issues related to repository operation and policies.

University of California–Riverside Library $249,581

The university—in a one-year demonstration project in conjunction with Librarians' Index to the Internet, the Internet Public Library, BUBL Information Service (originally Bulletin Board for Libraries), and the Virtual Reference Library—will research and create open source software tools to enhance functionality and interoperability in a collaborative portal system environment.

Division of Library and Information Services, Florida Department of State $86,561

In a 30-month demonstration project, the division will develop and demonstrate a modular, outcome-based evaluation training kit in print and Web-based formats, with the participation of and incorporating best practices from other states.

Florida State University, Tallahassee $249,081

In a two-year demonstration project, the university's GeoLib Program in its Florida Resources and Environmental Analysis Center and Information Use Management and Policy Institute will develop a nationwide public library database system linked to a digital base map, including data sets from the U.S. Census and the National Center for Education Statistics. The database will provide consolidated information on public libraries nationwide.

Table 2 / National Leadership Grant Awards, FY 2002 *(cont.)*

University of Illinois Urbana-Champaign Library $499,440

The library will create a collection-level registry of digital collections created with IMLS funding from 1998 to 2005 in this three-year research project, and will research, design, and implement a prototype item-level metadata repository service based on the Open Archives Initiative Metadata Harvesting Protocol.

Milton S. Eisenhower Library, Johns Hopkins University, Baltimore $229,352

In the Peabody Digital Audio Archives Project, the library will create a workflow management system prototype for digitizing an estimated 10,000 analog audio tapes and building a Web-accessible digital audio library. The two-year demonstration project will also develop audio segmentation software to automatically separate pieces and movements within a piece and establish a database for scientific studies on such topics as music information retrieval, tempo tracking, and performance style analysis.

University of Maryland Institute for Advanced Computer Studies, College Park $397,162

The institute, in partnership with the Internet Archive, will undertake a three-year research project to evaluate the impact the International Children's Digital Library can have on children, based upon research on ethnographic and demographic variables in children's use patterns and preferences, and upon the application of outcomes-based evaluation techniques to children's use of digital content.

Tufts University Digital Collections and Archives, Medford, Massachusetts $212,035

In this two-year demonstration project, "Boston Streets: Mapping Directory Data," Tufts will digitize 11 Boston city directories from 1865 to 1955 to incorporate contextual information about geographic locations featured in digital images of photographs using a geographic information system. The result will be a resource of visual information with associated spatial and other data.

University of Nebraska–Lincoln Libraries $245,723

"A Virtual Archive of Whitman's Manuscripts" is a two-year demonstration project in which the university libraries, in partnership with the University of Virginia, will create a finding aid to an estimated 70,000 Walt Whitman manuscripts located in more than 60 institutions. It will produce digital images of poetry drafts and a search interface, establish best practices for encoded archival description (EAD) implementation across collections, and develop a model for scholar–archivist collaboration.

State University of New York School of Informatics, Buffalo $177,668

In a 14-month research project, the School of Informatics will investigate the impact of youths' use of the Internet on their use of the public library. The project will sample students from schools in the Buffalo area and western New York State to determine which populations have access to digital information and how they are using it, and where students access the Internet. The results will suggest the likely impact of the Internet on the public library.

Syracuse University School of Information Studies, Syracuse, New York $483,507

In this three-year demonstration project, the school will develop and implement "S.O.S. (Situation variables, Outcome variables Strategy) for Information Literacy" a multimedia, Web-based teaching support system that will provide teaching strategies and materials for elementary and middle school library media specialists who provide information literacy skills instruction.

Kent State University Libraries, Kent, Ohio $252,418

Kent State Libraries will convert its Standardized Assessment of Information Literacy Skills (SAILS) instrument for measuring the impact of information literacy on student learning to a Computer Adaptive Test format in this three-year demonstration project. Researchers will test the tool with other institutions and create a results database that will allow for internal and external benchmarking of information literacy skills.

Drexel University College of Information Science and Technology
Philadelphia $233,056

The college will collaborate with the Free Library of Philadelphia in a three-year research project, "Everyday Information-Seeking Behavior of Urban Young Adults," to develop and

Table 2 / National Leadership Grant Awards, FY 2002 *(cont.)*

test tools for improving service provision to young adults by examining their information-seeking behaviors in their everyday lives.

University of Washington Information School, Seattle $249,996

In a two-year research project, "Approaches for Understanding Community Information Use," the school, in conjunction with the University of Michigan, will gather data to better understand the information-seeking behavior of consumers. It will also identify best practices in the provision of community information and community services.

Preservation or Digitization

Berkeley Art Museum Pacific Film Archive, University of California, Berkeley $149,884

The Berkeley Art Museum and Pacific Film Archive will research and report on new approaches to securing copyright permissions for digital copies of film-related documentation in this three-year project, which is part of "Cinefiles: Pacific Film Archive's Film Document Imaging Project."

Stanford University Libraries, Stanford, California $249,420

In a 17-month project, the libraries will digitize General Agreements on Tariffs and Trade (GATT) documents from GATT's inception in 1947 to 1986 and report on international intellectual property issues. The project will serve as a model for libraries wishing to digitize and provide access to large-scale and complex digital content.

Council of American Overseas Research Centers, Washington, D.C. $313,744

In the Middle East Research Journals Project, the council—in partnership with the American Center for Oriental Research, the American Institute for Maghrib Studies, the American Institute for Yemeni Studies, the American Research Center in Egypt, the Cyprus American Archeological Research Institute, and the W. F. Albright Institute of Archeological Research—will microfilm and catalog more than 2,200 Middle East research journals and digitize, index in a Web-accessible database, and provide document delivery on articles from the journals.

Florida Center for Library Automation, University of Florida, Gainesville $190,604

In this three-year project, the center will develop a "central digital archiving facility" for the libraries of Florida's public college and university system. It will identify costs of all aspects of archiving for cost-recovery purposes and serve as a model for the development of other central archiving facilities.

University of Kentucky Libraries, Lexington $210,237

In "Beyond the Shelf," a two-year project, the university libraries, in partnership with the Kentucky Virtual Library, will create a digital collection of 950 volumes from microfilm print masters, providing a model of a sustainable, high-production workflow for film-to-digital conversion.

Northeast Document Conservation Center, Andover, Massachusetts $213,700

In "Steal This Disaster Plan," a three-year project, the Northeast Document Conservation Center, in partnership with the Massachusetts Board of Library Commissioners, will create and disseminate an online training curriculum for library disaster planning based on a computerized tool for writing disaster plans.

Fogler Library, University of Maine, Orono, Maine $344,270

In "The Maine Music Box," the library, in partnership with the Bagaduce Music Lending Library and the Bangor Public Library, will undertake a two-year project to design and implement an interactive, multimedia digital music library linked to statewide public school music curriculum standards and consisting of images of scores with associated sound renditions, cover art, and lyrics. Users will be able to view, play, and print scores, and "manipulate" music by changing the key or the instrument.

*Walter P. Reuther Library and University Libraries, Wayne State University
Detroit, Michigan* $110,072

In a 14-month project, "The Urban Beat," the libraries will digitize images from the Detroit News photo collection dating from the late 19th century through 1980.

Table 2 / National Leadership Grant Awards, FY 2002 *(cont.)*

Michigan State University Library, East Lansing $486,016

In "The Making of Modern Michigan," Michigan State University Library—in partnership with the Library of Michigan, Michigan Library Consortium, University of Michigan, Wayne State University, the University of Detroit Mercy, Western Michigan University, Traverse Area District Library, and the Hiawathaland Library Cooperative—will undertake a two-year project to enhance a digital collection on Michigan history for use in the K–12 history curriculum. It will also create regional digitization centers and provide training to libraries in techniques, metadata standards, and copyright issues so that they can digitize their own unique collections.

John M. Echols Collection on Southeast Asia, Cornell University Library
Ithaca, New York $281,449

In "Images of Southeast Asia," the library will digitize text and illustrations taken from early Western travel narratives and first-person accounts of life in Southeast Asia before 1927.

Hoskins Library, University of Tennessee–Knoxville $245,722

In "Digital Access for WPA Photographs," the library—in partnership with the University of Kentucky's William S. Webb Museum of Anthropology and the University of Alabama's Alabama Museum of Natural History—will digitize and create an online database of information describing photographs taken by Works Progress Administration workers of archaeological projects conducted in preparation for the construction of the Tennessee Valley Authority dam in the 1930s.

State Historical Society of Wisconsin $202,596

In "Contact! Eyewitness Accounts of Early American Exploration," the State Historical Society of Wisconsin, in partnership with National History Day, will create a digital library containing full texts of approximately 150 exploration narratives and will distribute instructional guides to 40,000 teachers in the National History Day program.

Library Museum Collaboration

Tucson Botanical Gardens, Tucson, Arizona $220,536

Tucson Botanical Gardens, in partnership with the Tucson-Pima Public Library, will design and implement "Desert Connections," a program that will seek to raise awareness of and foster appreciation for desert plants and animals by encouraging homeowners to create "desert-friendly" lawns and gardens. Partners will develop interactive Web pages, public programs, educational materials, and a traveling exhibit for libraries and special events.

University of California–Merced $229,276

University of California at Merced Library, in collaboration with the Ruth and Sherman Lee Institute for Japanese Art at the Clark Center in the San Joaquin Valley region, will pilot a model of collaboration for developing significant online research collections through the use of Metadata Encoding and Transmission Standard (METS) encoding. As part of the three-year project, it will also digitize holdings of the institute, including 454 hanging scrolls and 46 folding screens.

California Digital Library $337,542

The library—in partnership with Bancroft Library, the Berkeley Art Museum and Pacific Film Archive, and the Phoebe Hearst Museum of Anthropology, as well as the Grunwald Center and the Graduate School of Education and Information Studies, Department of Information Studies at UCLA—will develop and complete a formal user evaluation of the Museums and the Online Archive of California (MOAC) test bed. The two-year research project will also develop evaluation tools that can be used by other digital libraries, and make general recommendations for the improvement of digital libraries based on the results.

Fort Lewis College Center of Southwest Studies, Durango, Colorado $104,361

The center, in partnership with the college's Reed Library and the Southern Ute Museum and Cultural Center, will develop a database of their institutional holdings. The collaboration will serve as a model for sharing artifact, archive, and library collections in rural, underserved communities that maintain native American collections and that are working within guidelines of the Native American Graves Protection and Repatriation Act.

Table 2 / National Leadership Grant Awards, FY 2002 *(cont.)*

Thomas J. Dodd Research Center at the University of Connecticut $498,770

The center—in collaboration with the Connecticut Historical Society, Mystic Seaport, New Haven Colony Historical Society, and the Connecticut State Library—will enhance an existing graphic database, "Connecticut History Online," with the goal of ultimately providing access to the holdings of both large and small institutions across the state.

Association of Children's Museums, Washington, D.C. $110,318

The association, in partnership with the Association for Library Service to Children and IMLS, will host a two-day leadership institute to examine the potential role of museums, libraries, nonprofits, and public broadcasting in forming community-based partnerships to promote early childhood learning.

University of Illinois, Champaign $241,348

The university, in collaboration with the Illinois Heritage Association and the Illinois State Library, will develop a multitrack digitization training program for museums and libraries of all sizes throughout Illinois and neighboring states. "Basics and Beyond" will include a range of training options from one-day workshops to an online course and hands-on training opportunities.

Indianapolis-Marion County Public Library, Indianapolis, Indiana $60,963

The library—in collaboration with the Greater Indianapolis Literacy League, Inc., and Conner Prairie Historic Site—will design and implement "Travels Across Time," a program to improve the reading skills of adult low-level-literacy students by facilitating educational experiences at a living history museum.

North Carolina Museum of Life and Science $247,027

The museum, in collaboration with the Durham County Library and Durham Public Schools, will develop "Discovery in Motion," a mobile science education exhibit for students between the ages of six and nine, while also creating service-learning opportunities for 24 inner-city teens.

Cornell University Library, Ithaca, New York $471,724

The library—in collaboration with the Museum of the City of New York, San Francisco Performing Arts Library and Museum, St. Petersburg (Russia) State Museum of Theater and Music, the Gertrude Stein Repertory Theater, and the University of Washington Libraries—will develop and test a metadata structure for the Global Performing Arts Database (GloPAD). The three-year project will also serve as the foundation for an international metadata standard for the performing arts.

University of Pittsburgh $242,157

The university, in collaboration with the Carnegie Museum of Art and the Historical Society of Western Pennsylvania, will create a Web portal for increasing access to "Historic Pittsburgh," a multi-institutional collection of visual images of and related descriptive information on the Pittsburgh region.

(continued from page 353)

Native American Library Services Program

In 2002 IMLS distributed $2,521,000 in grants for American Indian tribes and Alaska Native villages.

The Native American Library Services Program provides opportunities for the improvement of library services to Indian tribes and Alaska Native villages, the latter coming under the definition of eligible Indian tribes as recognized by the secretary of the interior. The program offers three types of support.

- Basic Library Services Grants, in the amount of $4,000, support core library operations on a noncompetitive basis for all eligible Indian tribes and Alaska native villages that apply for such support. IMLS awarded Basic Grants to 221 tribes in 28 states in 2002.

- Professional Assistance Grants, in the amount of $2,000, heighten the level of professional proficiency of tribal library staff. This noncompetitive program supports assessments of library services and provides advice for improvement. IMLS awarded Professional Assistance Grants to 52 tribes in 16 states in 2002.

- Enhancement Grants support new levels of library service for activities specifically identified under LSTA. In 2002 these competitive awards ranged from $76,941 to $150,000 (Table 3).

Of the 38 applications received, IMLS awarded 12 Enhancement Grants for a total of $1,569,000.

Table 3 / Native American Library Services Enhancement Grants, FY 2002

Arctic Slope Regional Corporation

Barrow, Alaska $149,964

This two-year project will digitize the microfilm of the *Tundra Times* newspaper, 1962–1997, create a full-text index to the articles with links to the scanned newspaper images, provide the Alaska Periodicals Index with 3,000 indexing records, and develop local talent in advanced library technology issues.

Chippewa Cree Indians of Rocky Boy's Reservation

Box Elder, Montana $147,882

This project will develop a children's learning center within an existing tribal college library by increasing the children's collection and purchasing computers, software, shelving, and audio/visual equipment.

Elk Valley Rancheria

Crescent City, California $76,941

This project will staff and outfit a new tribal library facility with new furniture, equipment, shelving, public access computers, and an automated circulation system.

Fort Belknap Indian Community

Harlem, Montana $143,443

Library services to children and adults will be expanded under this project through after-school and summer reading programs, increasing the children's and native American collections, conducting cultural enrichment programs for adults, and creating an electronic social-services information center on the library Web site.

Keweenaw Bay Indian Community

Baraga, Michigan $108,732

This project will support staffing and combine three small collections into one central library facility to establish a computer technology center; increase materials for the tribal college, vocational, and reading-readiness collections; and improve access for vision-impaired patrons, particularly elders.

Minnesota Chippewa Tribe/White Earth Band

White Earth, Minnesota $136,902

This one-year project will increase library staff, train staff, update collections, purchase furniture and equipment, establish Web sites, and automate collections at two tribal libraries.

Table 3 / Native American Library Services Enhancement Grants, FY 2002 *(cont.)*

Oglala Sioux Tribe

Kyle, South Dakota $150,000

This project will increase the collections of children's, young adult, and adult library materials in each of ten library centers and develop summer reading programs in two centers.

Pala Band of Mission Indians

Pala, California $119,507

This project hopes to preserve the Cupeño language and traditions by digitizing visual, audio, and print materials to develop language curriculum products and by offering language tutoring sessions given by tribal elders.

Pribilof Islands/St. Paul Library

St. Paul Island, Alaska $103,786

This project establishes a library annex as a community telecommunications center and provides staff to collaborate with local businesses and organizations to assess information needs, provide technical support and training for the annex users, establish electronic links between St. Paul and other Alaskan libraries, and investigate establishing a consortium with other libraries in the Bering Sea Region for sharing resources.

Pueblo of Jemez

Jemez Pueblo, New Mexico $141,646

This project will offer literacy programs for community members of various ages, provide tutoring sessions for elementary to college students, and continue the Jemez Library Consortium, which supports technology programs including curriculum-based computer classes for teachers, basic and advanced computer classes for community members, and development of a distance-learning program.

Pueblo of Santa Clara

Española, New Mexico $141,532

This project will improve Internet access and distance-education opportunities, provide technology training to seniors and Head Start students, establish a Web-based newsletter, provide multigenerational literacy programs, support a tribal language center, and expand a tribal digital archives initiative.

Rosebud Sioux Tribe

Rosebud, South Dakota $148,665

This project will enhance the library's print and electronic collections, increase staff, train staff to install and maintain a one-stop-shopping electronic information portal, and offer training sessions on electronic resources on and off site to a variety of user groups.

Native Hawaiian Library Services Program

The Native Hawaiian Library Services Program provides opportunities for improved library services for an important part of the nation's community of library users through a single grant to a Native Hawaiian organization, as defined in section 7207 of the Native Hawaiian Education Act (20 U.S.C. 7517).

In 2002 the Native Hawaiian Library Services Grant was awarded to ALU LIKE, Inc. of Honolulu, a private, nonprofit organization serving the Native Hawaiian community, in the amount of $420,000.

Evaluation of IMLS Programs

IMLS has taken a leadership role in evaluating the value of its programs through incorporating outcome-based measurement as a tool to document effectiveness of funded projects. Within the State-Administered Programs, IMLS has provided training in outcome-based evaluation (OBE). LSTA requires that each State Library Administrative Agency independently evaluate its LSTA activities prior to the end of the state LSTA five-year plan. In addition, IMLS is currently training all new National Leadership Grant recipients in OBE outcome-based evaluation and is presenting information about evaluation at state, regional, and national professional meetings. In 2002 IMLS made National Leadership awards to the Florida State Library to develop a model OBE toolkit for training LSTA state grant fund recipients in the use of OBE for project evaluation and to the University of Illinois at Urbana-Champaign for development of an OBE curriculum that can be used by graduate schools of library and information science to prepare library professionals as OBE evaluators.

In order to ensure that it is meeting current public and professional needs in library services, IMLS routinely seeks advice from diverse representatives of the library community, carries out studies of library practice, and evaluates its programs with the assistance of external consultants.

IMLS Conferences and Activities

The IMLS Web-Wise 2002 Conference on Libraries and Museums in the Digital World was held March 20–22 in Baltimore. The conference, which brought together over 300 participants, was cosponsored by Johns Hopkins University. The theme was Building Digital Communities. Conference participants included representatives of numerous federal agencies as well as museums and libraries of all types nationwide, graduate schools of library and information science, and departments of computer science. International participants included library and museums professionals from Canada, Europe, and Asia. Web-Wise papers are published in *First Monday,* a peer-reviewed e-journal on the Internet (http://www.firstmonday.dk) and are also available on the IMLS Web site at http://www.imls.gov/pubs/webwise2002/wbws02.htm. Compelling stories of the power of school libraries to make a difference in student achievement were presented at an invitational Conference on School Libraries hosted by First Lady Laura Bush on June 4, 2002. These papers are located at http://www.imls.gov/pubs/whitehouse0602/whitehouse.htm. IMLS also participated in the National Book Festival held in Washington, D.C., on October 12. On November 4–6, IMLS hosted "Making Connections," a conference for State Library Administrative Agencies focusing on the theme of connecting evaluation and implementation to the state LSTA five-year plans.

IMLS Web Site and Publications

The IMLS Web site (http://www.imls.gov) provides information on the various grant programs, national awards for library and museum service, projects funded, application forms, and staff contacts. The Web site also highlights model projects developed by libraries and museums throughout the country. Through an electronic newsletter, *Primary Source*, IMLS provides timely information on grant deadlines and opportunities. Details on subscribing to the IMLS newsletter are located on the Web site.

The following recent publications are available on Web site: *2003 Grant Award Program Brochure; Status of Technology and Digitization in the Nation's Museums and Libraries 2002 Report;* and *Sustaining Our Heritage—Commemorating the 25th Anniversary of the Museum Services Act.* In 2002 IMLS received the findings of a group it supported to examine issues relating to digital content creation and management. The "Framework of Guidance for Building Good Digital Collections," produced by the IMLS Digital Library Forum and available on the IMLS Web site, has been endorsed by the Chief Officers of State Library Agencies and the Digital Library Federation.

National Awards for Museum and Library Service

The National Award for Library Service was first presented in FY 2002. It honors U.S. libraries that have made a significant and exceptional contribution to their communities, seeking to recognize libraries that demonstrate extraordinary and innovative approaches to public service, reaching beyond the expected levels of community outreach and core programs generally associated with library services. The principal criterion for selection is evidence of the library's systematic and ongoing commitment to public service through exemplary and innovative programs and community partnerships.

Information about the award and upcoming deadlines appear on the IMLS Web site. The 2002 recipients received their awards from the First Lady at the White House Colloquium on Libraries, Museums, and Lifelong Learning on October 29, 2002. They were: Boundary County District Library, Bonners Ferry, Idaho; Bronx Zoo/Wildlife Conservation Society, Bronx, New York; Hartford Public Library, Hartford, Connecticut; Please Touch Museum, Philadelphia, Pennsylvania; Southern Alleghenies Museum of Art, Loretto, Pennsylvania; and Southwest Georgia Regional Library System, Bainbridge, Georgia.

IMLS Wins Award

Americans for the Arts gave special recognition to IMLS for 25 years of service at its seventh annual National Arts Awards on October 7 in New York City to launch National Arts and Humanities Month. The annual awards recognize those artists and arts supporters who exhibit exemplary national leadership and whose work demonstrates extraordinary artistic achievement. Segments of the awards ceremony were incorporated into a 30-minute documentary on arts leadership in America that aired on Bravo on January 19, 2003.

Part 3
Library/Information Science Education, Placement, and Salaries

Employment Sources on the Internet

Catherine Barr
Contributing Editor

The library and information science community has always actively shared information about job openings, with individual libraries, professional associations, library schools, and other organizations spreading the word through telephone "joblines" and fax services as well as through advertising in trade journals and use of employment agencies. This activity has naturally progressed to the Internet, and now the World Wide Web and a variety of online listservs and discussion groups have become some of the most useful—and current—resources for library and information professionals seeking jobs within and outside the library profession.

There are now hundreds of job-related sites of interest to library and information professionals. A search on Google in early 2003 for just the phrase "library jobline"—a term still used despite the fact that databases and text postings are now the norm—returned more than 1,500 hits, many of which were up-to-date sites or linked to up-to-date sites. This article makes no attempt to be all-inclusive, but aims instead to point readers to some of the most useful sites.

Many of the sites recommended simply list job openings; however, others also offer advice on searching for jobs, writing résumés, preparing for interviews, average salaries, and how to negotiate higher salaries.

Before spending a lot of time on any Web site, users should check that the site has been updated recently and that out-of-date job listings no longer appear. If a jobseeker has a particular location or specialized field in mind, he or she may find that the Directory of Organizations in Part 6 of this volume will provide a relevant Web address faster than starting to search on the Web.

Background Information

One particularly useful print resource, *The Information Professional's Guide to Career Development Online* (Information Today, Inc., 2001), has a companion Web site at http://www.lisjobs.com/careerdev. Both print and online versions present information on job hunting, networking, and online and continuing education. An article by the same authors—Rachel Singer Gordon and Sarah L. Nesbeitt—titled "Market Yourself Online!" appeared in the October/November 2001 issue of *Marketing Library Services*. The article presents practical advice on promoting yourself and your abilities on the Web; it is available at http://www.infotoday.com/mls/oct01/gordon&nesbeitt.htm.

The Winter 2000–2001 issue (vol. 44, no. 4) of *Occupational Outlook Quarterly* led with the article "Librarians: Information Experts in the Information

Age," which took an interesting and thorough look at the kinds of work performed by librarians and at future opportunities in the field. A PDF version is available at http://stats.bls.gov/opub/ooq/2000/winter/art01.pdf. "The Editor's Desk" column in the Jan. 4, 2001, issue of the Department of Labor's *Monthly Labor Review* forecast librarian employment growth in selected industries through 2008 (http://stats.bls.gov/opub/ted/2001/Jan/wk1/art03.htm).

General Sites/Portals

American Library Association: Library Employment Resources
http://www.ala.org/education
Maintained by the American Library Association (ALA).
Offering a combination of information and advice, this site links to library job ads in *American Libraries* (and its Hot Jobs Online, which is updated daily), *C&RLNews* and *C&RLNews*Net, and *LITA*. There are also links to ALA's conference placement service, to information about discrimination and unfair employment practices, and to listings of positions available at ALA itself. Particularly useful are How to Apply for a Library Job (http://www.tk421.net/howto.html) and compilations of salary surveys and library surveys.

Graduate School of Library and Information Science—Resources/Jobs
http://alexia.lis.uiuc.edu/gslis/resources/jobs.html
Maintained by the Graduate School of Library and Information Science at the University of Illinois at Urbana-Champaign.
An excellent, comprehensive site that would be a good starting place for anyone seeking library opportunities. It includes links to sites that have library and information science job postings, dividing them into the following categories: comprehensive, regional, school libraries/media centers, special types of libraries, information technology, and library schools. There are also lists of general employment sites that include library jobs, sources of employment overseas, and library listservs.

Library Job Postings
http://www.libraryjobpostings.org
Compiled by Sarah Nesbeitt of Booth Library, Eastern Illinois University, coauthor of *The Information Professional's Guide to Career Development Online* (Information Today, 2001).
Links to more than 275 library employment sites, with easy access by location and by category of job.

Lisjobs.com—Jobs for Librarians and Information Professionals
http://www.lisjobs.com
Maintained by Rachel Singer Gordon, author of the Computer Media column in *Library Journal* and coauthor of *The Information Professional's Guide to Career Development Online* (Information Today, 2001).
A searchable database of job listings and guide to online job resources in the United States and abroad. Jobseekers can also post résumés for a small fee. Also features an advice page.

The Riley Guide: Employment Opportunities and Job Resources on the Internet

http://www.rileyguide.com

Compiled by Margaret F. Dikel, MSLIS, a private consultant and co-author with Frances Roehm of *The Guide to Internet Job Searching* (McGraw-Hill, 2002).

A site rich in advice for the job seeker, from résumé writing and how to target a new employer to tips on networking and interviewing. Library and information job listings are found under Information Design, Delivery, & Management.

University of Missouri–Columbia: Library Job Listings

http://www.coe.missouri.edu/~career/library.html

Maintained by Career and Program Support, College of Education, University of Missouri–Columbia.

Presents links to sites that list library jobs. Includes many state joblines.

Professional Associations

General

Professional Associations in the Information Sciences

http://slisweb.sjsu.edu/resources/orgs.htm

Maintained by San José State University's School of Library and Information Science.

An excellent starting place that gives links to a large number of professional associations, from state, regional, and national library associations to specialized groupings.

Public

Public library openings can be found at all the sites listed above. The Public Library Association offers information on public librarianship—from educational requirements and salaries to testimonials from public librarians and the opportunity to participate in Job Shadow Day. The URL is http://www.pla.org/projects/recruit.html.

School

School library openings can be found at many of the sites listed above. Sites with interesting material for aspiring school librarians include

AASL: Career Development and Continuing Education

http://www.ala.org/aasl/education_menu.html

The American Association of School Librarians hosts this site. "Roles and Responsibilities of the School Library Media Specialist" is excerpted from Chapter 1, "The Vision," of *Information Power: Building Partnerships for Learning* (ALA/AECT, 1998). The section called School Librarianship as a Career includes a variety of useful resources.

Become a Librarian Who Serves Children and Young Adults
http://www.ala.org/hrdr/youth_recruit.html
The Association for Library Service to Children (http://www.ala.org/alsc) and the Young Adult Library Services Association (http://www.ala.org/yalsa) both link to this brochure describing the options for librarians interesting in working with young people.

General education sites usually include library openings. Among sites with nationwide coverage are

Education America
http://www.educationamerica.net
Library openings can be search by state(s).

K12Jobs.com
http://k12jobs.com/Home
Library jobs are found under Teaching.

Special and Academic

AALL Job Placement Hotline
http://aallhq.org/jobhotline
Maintained by the American Association of Law Librarians.

ASIS&T Jobline Online
http://www.asis.org/Jobline/index.html
Maintained by the American Society for Information Science and Technology.

Association for Library and Information Science Education: Job Postings
http://www.alise.org/cgi-bin/jobsee.cgi
Openings are organized under the following headings: Dean/Director Positions, Faculty Positions, Visiting/Summer Positions, and Other Positions.

Association of Research Libraries: Career Resources
http://db.arl.org/careers/index.html
In addition to job listings, there is a database of research library residency and internship programs. ARL's annual salary survey also appears on this site, as does the article "Careers in Research Libraries and Information Science: The Dynamic Role of the Research Librarian."

C&RL News Classified Advertising
http://www.ala.org/acrl/advert3.html
Online access to job postings placed in *C&RL News* and *C&RLNews*Net, organs of the Association of College and Research Libraries, a division of ALA.

Chronicle of Higher Education
http://chronicle.com/jobs
Access job openings from more than 1,140 institutions.

EDUCAUSE Job Posting Service
http://www.educause.edu/jobpost
EDUCAUSE member organizations post positions related to technology-based information resources, with a focus on higher education.

HigherEdJobs.com

http://www.higheredjobs.com
Published by Internet Employment Linkage, Inc. Access job openings from more than 730 institutions.

MLANet: Career

http://www.mlanet.org/career/index.html
The Medical Library Association offers much more than job listings here (medical librarian openings are listed by location in the Career Resources section). Among the additional offerings are career tips (for teens, college students, and postgraduate students and seekers of second careers) and brochures on medical librarianship.

Special Libraries Association: Jobs and Internships

http://www.ibiblio.org/slanews/index.html
Click on Jobs and Internships to find current listings.

Government

Library of Congress

http://www.loc.gov/hr/employment
Job openings plus fellowships, internships, and volunteer opportunities.

National Archives and Records Administration

http://www.archives.gov/careers/employment/employment.html
Employment, internships, and volunteering.

Miscellaneous

BUBL: Job Vacancies

http://bubl.ac.uk/news/jobs
Lists jobs in Europe and the United States, with an emphasis on Britain.

Exchanging Jobs

http://www.exchangingjobs.org
"A free matching service for people who work in libraries and the information field . . . specialties include job exchanges that can last for days, weeks, or even months." This service is not limited to the United States.

REFORMA Employment

http://www.reforma.org/refoempl.htm
REFORMA (The National Association to Promote Library and Information Services to Latinos and the Spanish-Speaking) collects job postings from listservs and direct mailings. The page is updated weekly. Knowledge of Spanish is required for some, but not all, jobs listed here.

Library Periodicals

American Libraries: Career Leads Online

http://www.ala.org/education/careerleads/careerleads.html

Access the ads from previous issues of *American Libraries* as well as new postings that are added daily. "Working Knowledge" is a monthly column about life on the job.

Feliciter
http://www.cla.ca/careers/careeropp.htm
The Canadian Library Association lists openings here; some may have already appeared in the association's publication *Feliciter*.

Library Journal/School Library Journal
http://libraryjournal.reviewsnews.com
http://slj.reviewsnews.com
Access to online job listings (which may not include all listings in the print edition) is under Tools and Services.

Employment Agencies/Commercial Services

A number of employment agencies and commercial services in the United States and abroad specialize in library-related jobs. Among those that keep up-to-date listings on their Web sites are

ASLIB
http://www.aslib.co.uk/recruit/index.html#
Lists jobs in Britain and around the world.

Free Pint
http://www.freepint.com
Lists jobs in Britain and around the world. Includes an archive of articles related to information science and librarianship.

Information Media Jobs
http://www.informationmediajobs.com

Library Associates
http://www.libraryassociates.com/jobs1.shtml

TPFL: The Information People
http://www.tfpl.com
Select an area of specialization and then permanent or temporary recruitment to access lists of jobs around the world.

Listservs

Many listservs allow members to post job openings on a casual basis.

LIBJOBS
http://www.ifla.org/II/lists/libjobs.htm
Managed by IFLANET. Subscribers to this list receive posted job opportunities by e-mail.

NASIGWeb Job Listings

http://www.nasig.org/jobs/list.htm

This site collects serials-related job openings posted on the following listservs: ACQNET, AUTOCAT, COLLIB-L, INNOPAC, LIBJOBS, LITA-L, PACS-L, SERIALST, SLAJOB, STS-L.

PUBLIB

http://sunsite.berkeley.edu/PubLib

Public library job openings often appear on this list.

slis_job

A list for students. Type *listproc@listproc.sjsu.edu* in the "To" field and type *subscribe slis_job Joe Smith* in the "Message" field to subscribe.

Placements and Salaries 2001:
Salaries Rebound, Women Break Out

Tom Terrell

Assistant Professor, School of Library and Information Science,
University of South Florida, Tampa

The economic outlook may be bleak, but *Library Journal*'s annual Placements and Salaries Survey shows librarians are still in demand. In fact, 2001 graduates of American Library Association (ALA)-accredited library and information science (LIS) schools report increased salaries and solid opportunities in traditional and new library positions. The average starting salary for 2001 LIS graduates was $36,818, a 5.49 percent increase over the 2000 average of $34,871. This rise substantially exceeds the rate of inflation (1.3 percent) and returns to the trend of 1998–1999, when LIS starting salaries outdistanced inflation.

Average salaries for men and women increased at similar rates, 5.98 percent for men and 5.37 percent for women. This is in sharp contrast with the last few years. Men's salaries jumped 12 percent in 1999 but less than 1 percent last year. Men still make better average starting salaries, $2,000 more per year than women. However, in comparison with previous years, women are increasingly scoring higher pay than men at the top end of the scale. A look at the average high salaries, by school, shows women outdistancing men on the high end in 20 of 33 schools that turned in a gender breakdown.

Job Trends

Table 1 shows the job status—both by region and in total—of those 1,223 graduates (of 1,397 total) who reported job status. Of those, 1,173 (95.9 percent) were employed in some library capacity.

Of those employed in libraries, 1,105 (94.2 percent) were in permanent or temporary professional positions, with the rest in nonprofessional positions. The percentage of graduates working in temporary professional jobs rose slightly. The 983 graduates working in full-time permanent professional positions represented 83.8 percent of those employed in libraries, as compared with 85 percent in 2000 and 83.5 percent in 1999.

Salaries Come Back

Table 8 lists placements and full-time salaries by school. An analysis of aggregate data reported in Table 2 and Table 5 reveals that the average 2001 professional salary for starting library positions increased by $1,917 over 2000.

The salary increase in 2001 (5.49 percent) more than doubles the percentage increase in 2000 (2.72 percent), returning to the levels of 1999 and 1998 (6.5 percent and 5.4 percent increases, respectively). While the Consumer Price Index

(text continues on page 378)

Adapted from *Library Journal*, October 15, 2002.

Table 1 / Status of 2001 Graduates,* Spring 2002

| Region | Number of Schools Reporting | Number of Graduates Responding | Graduates in Library Positions | | | | Graduates in Nonlibrary Positions | Unemployed or Status Unreported |
			Permanent Professional	Temporary Professional	Non-professional	Total		
Northeast	10	491	338	34	28	400	21	70
Southeast	11	229	184	19	6	209	6	14
Midwest	9	418	270	36	22	328	16	74
Southwest	5	89	70	10	4	84	3	2
West	4	143	104	16	6	126	4	13
Canada	2	27	17	7	2	26	—	1
Total	41	1,397	983	122	68	1,173	50	174

*Table based on survey responses from schools and individual graduates. Figures will not necessarily be fully consistent with some of the other data reported that came from individual graduates. Tables do not always add up, individually or collectively, since both schools and individuals omitted data in some cases.

Table 2 / Placements and Full-Time Salaries of 2001 U.S. Graduates/Summary by Region

| Region | Number of Placements | Number of Reported Salaries | | | Low | | High | | Average | | | Median | | |
		Women	Men	Total	Women	Men	Women	Men	Women	Men	All	Women	Men	All
Northeast	499	327	36	363	$16,500	$25,000	$75,000	$72,000	$36,755	$39,576	$37,325	$35,023	$38,500	$36,000
Southeast	180	127	37	164	14,000	24,000	80,000	54,275	34,513	36,774	34,963	32,600	34,001	33,000
Midwest	244	103	32	135	17,548	17,600	76,870	75,000	34,615	35,504	34,836	33,600	34,700	34,000
Southwest	76	37	37	74	21,000	23,000	73,000	72,000	35,438	38,939	36,137	34,662	36,540	35,000
West	116	87	19	106	18,000	25,000	85,000	75,000	41,371	41,031	41,389	40,000	38,000	40,000
Canada/Intl.*	30	22	6	28	NR	37,000	NR	37,000	NR	37,000	31,500	NR	37,000	31,500
Combined**	1,115	681	161	842	14,000	37,000	85,000	75,000	36,433	38,433	36,818	35,000	36,040	35,000

*All international salaries converted to American dollars based on conversion rates for August 1, 2002.
**U.S. results. This table represents only salaries reported as full-time. Comparison with other tables will show different numbers of placements. NR=not reported

Table 3 / 2001 Total Graduates and Placements by School

Schools	Graduates Women	Graduates Men	Graduates Total	Employed Women	Employed Men	Employed Total	Unemployed Women	Unemployed Men	Unemployed Total	Students Women	Students Men	Students Total
Alabama	22	5	27	18	4	22	4	1	5	—	—	—
Alberta	28	2	30	—	—	—	—	—	—	—	—	—
Arizona	35	7	42	14	5	19	—	—	—	—	—	—
California (UCLA)	30	14	44	3	0	3	—	0	3	—	—	—
Clarion	44	5	49	14	2	16	3	—	7	—	—	2
Dominican	71	15	86	—	—	80	—	—	1	—	—	—
Drexel	44	11	55	34	8	42	1	0	1	—	—	—
Florida State	—	—	—	21	7	28	2	0	2	—	—	—
Hawaii	28	7	35	5	1	6	1	0	1	1	1	2
Indiana	139	46	185	25	6	31	—	—	1	—	—	—
Iowa	20	7	27	16	8	24	1	0	1	—	—	—
Kentucky	—	—	—	16	4	20	—	—	4	—	—	—
Long Island	105	10	115	34	1	39	4	0	4	—	—	—
Louisiana State	50	13	63	—	—	—	—	—	8	—	—	—
Maryland	103	26	129	29	6	35	7	1	8	3	0	3
Michigan	61	33	94	—	—	50	—	—	—	—	—	5
N.C. Chapel Hill	31	14	45	22	5	27	—	—	—	—	—	—
N.C. Greensboro	63	10	73	9	7	16	—	—	—	—	—	—
North Texas	101	19	120	—	—	—	—	—	—	—	—	—

Oklahoma	39	7	46	14	2	16	3	0	3	—	—	—
Pittsburgh	77	29	106	11	6	17	2	1	3	—	—	—
Pratt	—	—	—	38	10	56	6	1	9	1	0	2
Rhode Island	51	9	60	19	4	24	0	1	1	0	1	1
Rutgers	—	—	0	30	5	36	1	0	1	—	—	—
San Jose	150	56	206	81	5	86	7	1	8	2	0	2
Simmons	173	36	209	126	26	152	4	2	6	—	—	—
South Carolina	—	—	—	24	4	29	—	—	—	—	—	—
South Florida	118	15	133	27	3	30	—	—	—	—	—	—
Southern Connecticut	63	8	71	17	3	20	3	0	3	—	—	—
Southern Mississippi	—	—	—	0	2	2	1	0	1	—	—	—
St. John's	16	8	24	6	2	8	0	2	2	—	—	—
Syracuse	55	15	70	19	3	25	3	0	3	—	—	—
Tennessee	76	10	86	—	—	—	—	—	—	—	—	—
Texas (Austin)	99	38	137	32	8	41	1	0	2	—	—	—
Texas Woman's	—	—	—	6	2	8	—	—	—	—	—	—
University at Albany	—	—	—	16	3	20	1	2	3	—	—	—
University at Buffalo	—	—	—	15	2	17	7	0	7	—	—	—
Washington	—	—	—	12	8	21	3	1	4	—	—	—
Wayne State	142	29	171	70	10	80	5	1	6	—	1	1
Western Ontario	64	38	102	20	5	25	1	1	2	1	0	0
Wisconsin–Madison	52	18	70	25	12	37	12	2	14	0	1	1
Total	2,150	560	2,710*	868	199	1,208	83	17	110	8	3	19

*Unknown status: 1,034 women, 308 men, with a total of 1,341

Table 4 / Placements by Type of Organization

Schools	Public			Elementary & Secondary			College & University			Special			Government			Library Co-op/Network			Vendor			Other			Total		
	Women	Men	Total	Women	Men	Total	Women	Men	Total	Women	Men	Total	Women	Men	Total	Women	Men	Total	Women	Men	Total	Women	Men	Total	Women	Men	Total
Alabama	4	2	6	4	0	4	6	1	7	3	1	4	—	—	6	—	—	6	1	0	1	—	—	—	18	4	34
Arizona	4	—	4	5	2	7	2	3	5	1	0	1	1	—	1	—	—	—	—	—	—	—	—	—	13	5	18
California (UCLA)	2	0	2	—	—	—	—	—	—	1	0	1	—	—	—	—	—	—	—	—	—	—	—	—	3	0	3
Clarion	8	1	9	2	0	2	2	1	3	—	—	—	1	0	1	—	—	—	—	—	—	1	0	1	14	2	16
Dominican	—	—	23	—	—	26	—	—	17	—	—	—	—	—	—	—	—	—	—	—	—	—	—	3	0	0	69
Drexel	10	2	12	3	0	3	12	2	14	4	4	8	1	—	1	—	—	—	2	0	2	2	0	2	34	8	41
Florida State	10	4	14	2	0	2	6	0	6	1	1	2	1	1	2	—	—	—	0	1	1	1	0	1	21	7	28
Hawaii	2	0	2	0	1	1	1	0	1	1	0	1	—	—	—	—	—	—	—	—	—	1	0	1	5	1	6
Indiana	10	1	11	6	0	6	5	2	7	1	1	2	—	—	—	—	—	—	1	0	1	2	2	4	25	6	31
Iowa	7	0	7	4	1	5	5	7	12	—	—	—	—	—	—	—	—	—	—	—	—	—	—	—	16	8	24
Kentucky	7	2	9	1	0	1	7	1	8	—	—	—	0	1	1	1	0	1	—	—	—	—	—	—	16	4	20
Long Island	12	—	13	15	—	18	2	1	3	2	0	2	1	—	1	—	—	—	—	—	—	2	0	2	34	1	39
Maryland	4	1	5	4	0	4	5	2	7	8	1	9	4	0	4	—	—	—	3	0	3	1	2	3	29	6	35
Michigan	6	2	8	2	0	2	6	6	12	5	2	7	—	—	—	—	—	—	—	—	—	10	12	22	29	22	51
N.C. Chapel Hill	3	0	3	0	1	1	16	3	19	—	—	—	3	1	4	—	—	—	—	—	—	—	—	—	22	5	27
N.C. Greensboro	2	1	3	1	0	1	4	6	10	2	0	2	—	—	—	—	—	—	—	—	—	—	—	—	9	7	16
Oklahoma	5	1	6	4	0	4	4	1	5	—	—	—	—	—	—	—	—	—	—	—	—	1	0	1	14	2	16

Pittsburgh	2	2	4	2	0	2	4	4	8	—	—	—	—	—	—	—	—	—	—	—	—	3	0	3	11	6	17
Pratt	19	1	24	7	0	8	4	3	8	0	3	5	0	1	1	—	—	1	0	1	1	8	1	9	38	10	56
Rhode Island	10	1	12	6	2	8	2	0	2	1	1	2	1	—	1	—	—	—	—	—	—	1	0	1	19	4	24
Rutgers	13	2	15	5	0	5	6	2	9	4	0	4	3	0	3	—	—	1	1	—	1	—	0	4	30	5	36
San Jose	30	5	35	14	7	21	18	3	21	12	0	12	2	2	4	—	1	1	—	2	5	11	1	12	81	15	96
Simmons	37	4	41	15	1	16	36	14	50	22	2	24	2	2	4	—	—	—	3	2	5	—	—	—	126	26	152
South Carolina	11	2	14	8	0	8	3	2	5	2	0	2	—	—	—	—	—	—	—	—	—	—	—	—	24	4	29
South Florida	12	2	14	7	0	7	8	1	9	—	—	—	—	—	—	—	—	—	—	—	—	—	—	—	27	3	30
S. Connecticut	6	1	7	7	0	7	3	1	4	1	1	2	1	1	2	—	—	—	—	—	—	—	—	—	17	3	20
S. Mississippi	—	—	—	—	—	—	2	—	2	—	—	—	—	—	—	—	—	—	—	—	—	—	—	—	0	2	2
St. John's	1	1	2	3	0	3	1	1	2	2	0	2	—	—	—	—	—	—	—	—	—	1	0	1	7	2	9
Syracuse	3	1	5	8	0	9	7	1	9	1	0	1	0	0	1	—	—	—	—	—	—	1	1	2	20	2	25
Texas (Austin)	4	2	6	7	1	8	15	4	19	5	0	5	1	0	1	—	—	—	—	—	—	1	1	2	32	8	41
Texas Woman's	0	1	1	1	0	1	5	1	6	—	—	—	—	—	—	0	—	—	—	—	—	—	—	—	6	2	8
Univ. at Albany	3	0	4	4	1	5	3	1	4	2	0	2	3	0	3	—	—	—	1	1	2	1	1	2	16	3	20
Univ. at Buffalo	3	0	3	6	0	6	5	2	7	—	—	—	—	—	—	—	—	—	—	—	—	1	0	1	15	2	17
Washington	4	1	6	0	1	1	4	5	9	0	1	1	—	—	—	—	—	—	—	—	—	4	0	4	12	8	21
Wayne State	35	3	38	17	3	20	12	5	17	3	0	3	—	—	—	—	—	—	—	—	—	1	0	1	68	11	79
Western Ontario	—	—	6	—	—	1	—	—	7	—	—	—	—	—	4	—	—	—	—	—	—	—	2	2	0	0	25
Wis.–Madison	4	1	5	5	1	6	11	8	19	2	0	2	1	—	2	1	—	1	—	0	1	2	0	2	25	11	37
Total	285	45	369	166	20	218	222	92	341	81	16	103	21	7	34	1	2	3	10	4	14	59	20	84	845	206	1,166

This table represents only placements reported by type. Some individuals omitted placement information, rendering some information unusable. Comparison with other tables will show different numbers of placements.

Table 5 / Average Salary Index Starting Library Positions, 1990–2001

Year	Library Schools*	Average Beginning Salary	Dollar Increase in Average Salary	Salary Index	BLS-CPI**
1990	38	$25,306	$725	143.03	130.7
1991	46	25,583	277	144.59	136.2
1992	41	26,666	1,083	150.71	140.5
1993	50	27,116	450	153.26	144.4
1994	43	28,086	970	158.74	148.4
1995	41	28,997	911	163.89	152.5
1996	44	29,480	483	166.62	159.1
1997	43	30,270	790	171.05	161.6
1998	47	31,915	1,645	180.38	164.3
1999	37	33,976	2,061	192.03	168.7
2000	37	34,871	895	197.26	175.1
2001	40	36,818	1,947	208.09	177.1

* Includes U.S. schools only.

**U.S. Department of Labor, Bureau of Labor Statistics, Consumer Price index, All Urban Consumers (CPI-U), U.S. city average, all items, 1982–1984=100. The average beginning professional salary for that period was $17,693.

(continued from page 372)

increased in 2001 by two points (or 1.3 percent), the *LJ* Salary Index rose 10.83 (or 2.72 percent).

Location still matters when it comes to pay. Higher average salaries are reported for the West and the Northeast in some traditional library positions (school, academic, special), as Table 7 indicates. The West is still home of significantly higher average salaries at all types of libraries, notably school libraries. The Northeast is consistently second in most categories except public libraries, where the Southwest offers a higher average salary.

Gender Splits

Men had higher average salaries in school, academic, and special libraries by 7.9 percent. However, women led men in average salary in public and government libraries by 0.4 percent and 0.6 percent.

The average difference between salaries of men ($36,433) and women ($34,433) was $2,000 (5.8 percent). Men made up almost 21 percent of the reported graduates. They showed up disproportionately in government (25 percent) and academic (29.5 percent) libraries and at vendors (30.8 percent). Men were represented least in public (11.6 percent), school (14.6 percent), and special (17.8 percent) libraries.

The high-tech "other" area rebounded. In 2001 the salaries for men, who made up 21.1 percent of the respondents, averaged $50,609, an increase of 10 percent. Salaries for women in these positions rose to $43,184, an increase of 6.8 percent. In 2000 salaries for men dropped 4.4 percent to $46,000, while those for women rose 4.5 percent, to $40,426.

Table 6 / Salaries of Reporting Professionals by Area of Job Assignment

Assignment	Number	Percent of Total	Low Salary	High Salary	Average Salary	Median Salary
Acquisitions	18	1.98	$22,000	$52,000	$36,036	$35,500
Administration	48	5.28	27,000	67,000	39,831	37,500
Archives	48	5.28	20,000	50,000	35,264	35,000
Automation/Systems	13	1.43	29,500	60,000	43,731	45,000
Cataloging and Classification	59	6.49	16,500	56,600	33,233	33,500
Circulation	24	2.64	18,000	60,000	32,166	31,500
Collection Development	13	1.43	29,000	41,000	36,000	37,000
Database Management	13	1.43	27,300	54,275	39,881	40,000
Government Documents	1	0.11	32,000	32,000	32,000	32,000
Indexing/Abstracting	5	0.55	36,000	48,000	41,250	40,500
Instruction	5	0.55	34,000	56,000	41,700	36,500
Interlibrary Loan	10	1.10	18,000	36,811	27,431	28,250
LAN Manager	3	0.33	27,000	52,399	39,800	40,000
Media Specialist	180	19.80	16,800	85,000	39,334	37,500
Reference/ Info Services	319	35.09	14,000	75,000	35,549	34,000
Solo Librarian	61	6.71	25,000	65,000	40,022	37,450
Telecomm.	2	0.22	26,297	45,000	35,649	35,649
Youth Services	86	9.46	17,500	50,243	33,708	33,300
Webmaster	1	0.11	55,000	55,000	55,000	55,000
Total	909	100.00	14,000	85,000	36,806	35,000

This table represents only placements reported by job assignment. Some individuals omitted placement information, rendering some information unusable. Comparison with other tables will show different numbers of placements.

Minority Data

Over 10 percent of those who got full-time permanent jobs identified themselves as members of a minority group. The largest group (39.5 percent) found jobs in public libraries, followed by 30.7 percent in academic libraries, 15.8 percent in K–12 media centers, and 5.3 percent in special libraries. For minority graduates, salaries increased $684, to $37,166 (1.9 percent), which is well below the 11.1 percent increase seen in 2000, but still higher than the overall average of $36,818. The "other" area offered minority graduates the highest salaries at $46,571, while special libraries ($41,656) offered salaries above the national average for all special libraries ($40,293), as did school library media centers, $40,772 to $39,371.

In general, institution type again had a significant impact on salaries. In spite of a healthy 5.3 percent increase, public libraries still offered the lowest average salary ($33,345, compared with $31,656 in 2000), followed by academic libraries ($35,883, compared with $33,380 the previous year, up 7.5 percent). All other institution types exceeded the overall salary of $36,818. School library salaries rose to $39,371 (up 7.2 percent) and government pay increased 7.6 percent to $39,538. Last year's leader, special libraries, increased 6.4 percent to $40,293,

(text continues on page 384)

Table 7 / Comparison of Salaries by Type of Organization

	Total Placements	Salaries		Low Salary		High Salary		Average Salary			Median Salary		
		Women	Men	Women	Men	Women	Men	Women	Men	All	Women	Men	All
Public Libraries													
Northeast	123	96	12	$16,500	$27,000	$52,399	$39,000	$33,374	$32,941	$33,269	$33,625	$32,000	$33,625
Southeast	60	46	10	14,000	24,000	67,000	54,000	31,676	32,557	31,820	30,125	31,184	30,484
Midwest	45	36	8	17,548	17,600	50,000	42,000	31,573	31,032	31,474	32,000	31,963	32,000
Southwest	17	12	4	27,912	29,000	49,000	41,000	35,212	35,070	34,931	34,662	35,140	34,424
West	33	26	3	18,000	26,000	51,700	45,100	38,149	38,033	38,137	40,000	43,000	40,000
All Public	278	216	37	14,000	17,600	67,000	54,000	33,358	33,210	33,345	33,000	32,000	33,000
School Libraries													
Northeast	81	71	3	24,646	37,000	65,000	56,000	38,908	49,333	39,500	38,000	55,000	38,750
Southeast	27	25	2	16,800	27,500	49,362	35,000	34,146	31,250	33,931	34,000	31,250	34,000
Midwest	35	30	5	23,000	33,000	76,870	75,000	37,721	48,603	39,275	34,368	43,000	35,000
Southwest	17	13	2	24,000	30,500	73,000	35,000	37,331	32,750	36,720	33,500	32,750	33,500
West	23	14	8	23,921	25,000	85,000	75,000	49,989	41,750	46,750	48,500	36,000	45,000
All School	183	153	20	16,800	25,000	85,000	75,000	38,864	42,646	39,371	37,000	39,000	37,100
College/University Libraries													
Northeast	106	65	30	20,000	25,100	60,000	58,000	35,546	40,748	37,189	35,000	40,000	35,000
Southeast	64	47	15	18,000	30,000	52,500	46,000	34,132	36,233	34,640	33,000	35,000	34,000
Midwest	45	30	15	23,180	22,000	45,000	41,150	33,838	33,185	33,620	34,000	34,700	34,000
Southwest	31	20	11	21,000	23,000	40,300	58,000	33,232	37,364	34,698	34,000	37,000	35,000
West	32	24	7	29,120	28,800	53,000	60,000	38,801	39,502	38,551	37,585	37,900	37,585
All Academic	278	186	78	18,000	22,000	60,000	60,000	35,014	37,800	35,883	34,000	38,000	35,000

Special Libraries												
Northeast	53	36	10	25,000	28,500	75,000	72,000	40,796	42,630	41,195	40,000	35,000	39,000
Southeast	11	9	2	22,000	41,250	53,000	52,000	37,295	46,625	38,991	36,656	46,625	40,000
Midwest	4	3	1	32,000	22,000	50,000	22,000	38,633	22,000	34,475	33,900	22,000	32,950
Southwest	4	4	—	30,000	—	39,000	—	34,050	—	34,050	33,600	—	33,600
West	14	13	1	28,000	50,000	52,800	50,000	40,653	50,000	41,320	40,000	50,000	40,500
All Special	86	65	14	22,000	22,000	75,000	72,000	39,768	42,254	40,293	39,000	38,125	39,500
Government Libraries												
Northeast	19	13	2	20,000	40,000	55,000	46,413	36,937	43,207	37,773	37,288	43,207	37,440
Southeast	7	4	3	27,900	34,000	72,400	46,000	46,364	39,000	43,208	42,578	37,000	37,000
Midwest	1	—	1	—	33,000	—	33,000	—	33,000	33,000	—	33,000	33,000
West	1	1	—	48,000	—	48,000	—	48,000	—	48,000	48,000	—	48,000
All Government	28	18	6	20,000	33,000	72,400	46,413	39,647	39,402	39,538	37,364	38,500	37,440
Library Cooperatives/Networks												
Southeast	2	1	1	36,000	47,000	36,000	47,000	36,000	47,000	$41,500	36,000	47,000	41,500
All Co-op./Networks	2	1	1	36,000	47,000	36,000	47,000	36,000	47,000	41,500	36,000	47,000	41,500
Vendors												
Northeast	11	6	4	32,000	27,300	51,800	45,000	44,358	36,075	41,045	47,175	36,000	42,000
Southeast	2	2	0	34,000	—	55,000	—	44,500	—	44,500	44,500	—	44,500
West	1	1	—	38,400	—	38,400	—	38,400	—	38,400	38,400	—	38,400
All Vendors	14	9	4	32,000	27,300	55,000	45,000	43,728	36,075	41,373	45,000	36,000	39,000
Other Organizations												
Northeast	21	15	3	32,000	40,000	53,000	55,000	40,547	46,000	41,456	40,000	43,000	40,000
Southeast	7	5	2	30,000	44,000	80,000	54,275	48,480	49,138	48,668	47,500	49,138	47,500
Midwest	4	2	1	36,800	56,600	60,000	56,600	48,400	56,600	51,133	48,400	56,600	56,600
Southwest	6	4	2	35,000	40,000	45,000	72,000	42,375	56,000	46,917	44,750	56,000	44,750
West	4	4	0	39,000	—	56,000	—	49,000	—	49,000	50,500	—	50,500
All Other	42	30	8	30,000	40,000	80,000	72,000	43,184	50,609	44,669	42,250	49,138	44,250

This table represents only salaries and placements reported by type and region. Some individuals omitted placement information, rendering some information unusable. Comparison with other tables will show different numbers of placements. Regions have been dropped where no data were reported.

Table 8 / Placements and Full-Time Salaries of Reporting 2001 Graduates*

Schools	Placements	Salaries		Low Salary		High Salary		Average Salary			Median Salary		
		Women	Men	Women	Men	Women	Men	Women	Men	All	Women	Men	All
Alabama	22	18	3	$22,000	$30,000	$40,300	$41,250	$32,590	$34,313	$32,903	$32,644	$33,000	$32,644
Arizona	19	14	5	28,000	23,000	53,000	58,000	36,135	37,750	36,539	34,712	35,000	35,000
California (UCLA)	3	3	0	40,000	—	48,185	—	43,180	—	43,180	41,356	—	41,356
Clarion	16	14	2	8,000	17,600	47,000	55,000	27,600	36,300	28,843	27,000	36,300	27,000
Dominican	87	—	—	—	—	—	—	—	—	—	—	—	—
Drexel	42	34	8	25,000	27,500	51,800	72,000	36,972	42,270	37,775	35,413	35,000	35,326
Florida State	28	21	7	20,000	32,000	52,500	54,275	34,135	41,779	35,899	30,000	39,350	32,430
Hawaii	6	5	1	30,000	56,000	80,000	56,000	47,755	56,000	49,129	44,000	56,000	47,850
Indiana	31	25	4	17,548	22,000	50,277	72,000	33,877	40,638	35,185	34,000	33,500	34,000
Iowa	24	16	8	15,000	23,000	37,000	41,150	28,562	33,851	30,510	32,000	34,000	32,000
Kentucky	20	16	4	26,297	33,000	42,500	41,000	32,956	35,731	33,511	32,448	34,463	33,463
Long Island	39	34	1	9,000	24,600	63,000	24,600	38,871	24,600	38,723	41,541	24,600	42,000
Maryland	35	29	6	17,500	24,000	72,400	55,000	39,130	38,667	39,051	38,000	39,000	38,000
Michigan	49	29	20	—	—	—	—	—	—	—	—	—	—
N.C. Chapel Hill	27	22	5	27,900	27,500	48,500	38,000	34,872	35,500	34,988	34,000	37,000	34,000
N.C. Greensboro	16	9	7	18,000	30,000	44,000	46,000	32,192	36,000	33,858	30,000	35,000	33,500
Oklahoma	16	14	2	24,000	29,000	50,000	40,000	31,400	34,500	31,843	30,500	34,500	30,500

Pittsburgh	17	11	6	12,000	15,000	60,000	41,000	32,904	32,382	32,720	34,000	34,326	34,000
Pratt	56	38	10	24,000	27,000	50,000	65,000	36,728	40,430	37,024	36,912	40,000	36,824
Rhode Island	24	19	4	23,000	31,000	55,000	56,000	31,846	43,950	33,828	30,514	44,400	31,000
Rutgers	36	30	5	29,500	15,000	75,000	46,000	40,536	33,400	39,368	37,450	36,000	37,000
San Jose	96	81	15	10,000	17,680	85,000	75,000	38,092	38,433	38,149	38,000	37,900	38,000
Simmons	152	126	26	14,500	25,100	58,500	50,000	33,625	35,478	33,902	33,000	34,500	33,000
South Carolina	29	24	4	10,608	30,368	67,000	54,000	34,567	41,467	35,431	33,306	40,750	34,153
South Florida	30	27	3	17,000	25,500	40,000	34,001	29,793	30,500	29,867	29,753	32,000	29,806
S. Connecticut	20	17	3	14,700	37,000	73,000	46,413	39,642	41,138	39,866	38,000	40,000	38,000
S. Mississippi	2	0	2	—	32,000	—	42,000	—	37,000	37,000	—	37,000	37,000
St. John's	9	7	2	28,000	39,000	50,000	40,000	39,200	39,500	39,267	39,000	39,500	39,000
Syracuse	25	19	3	27,000	35,000	50,900	52,000	36,837	41,000	37,756	36,500	36,000	36,500
Texas (Austin)	41	32	8	11,000	30,500	50,000	46,000	34,321	36,473	34,751	34,831	35,540	34,831
Texas Woman's	8	6	2	21,000	33,000	51,000	41,000	31,898	37,000	33,173	28,500	37,000	31,500
Univ. at Albany	20	16	3	14,000	37,000	55,000	58,000	33,489	45,000	35,214	34,000	40,000	35,000
Univ. at Buffalo	17	15	2	28,000	33,000	42,241	36,000	32,542	34,500	32,803	32,000	34,500	32,000
Washington	21	12	8	27,500	33,500	56,000	50,000	37,900	40,938	39,816	37,000	40,500	38,000
Wayne State	80	69	11	6,900	24,000	76,870	75,000	29,485	41,084	31,100	32,000	35,500	33,000
Western Ontario	25	—	—	—	—	—	—	—	—	25,521	—	—	—
Wis.–Madison	37	25	12	8,320	22,000	50,000	47,000	32,457	33,683	32,877	33,000	34,500	33,700

*This table only shows schools reporting data.

(continued from page 379)

while library cooperatives/networks averaged $41,500 (up from $37,617) with just two placements.

Vendors saw the only drop in average salary in 2001 at $41,373, down 9.8 percent from $42,250 in 2000. Additionally, the number of graduates reporting vendor placements declined from 30 in 2000 to 14 in 2001.

The "other" category is the leader. It includes many of the high-tech and dot-com positions filled by LIS graduates. There is increasing diversity of positions in this area. Some of the reported job titles include researcher for government agencies, data conversion/content management, and indexing and abstracting for documentary production. Only four respondents identified themselves as web-masters and five as database managers; two years ago these were the predominant placements for those working outside libraries. In 2001 they combine for just over 10 percent of the "other" category, which is now dominated by people doing traditional library work in nonlibrary settings. The 2001 average of $44,669 is up 6.9 percent from $41,778 in 2000. Placements in this area are also up from 24 in 2000 to 42 in 2001. This slight rebound may foreshadow recovery in the technology sector, or it may indicate the extent to which LIS students have expanded the boundaries of the profession.

Placements Competitive

Over two-thirds of the schools responded to inquiries about the availability of job openings: Seven noted an increase in the number of positions, five experienced a decrease, and the rest saw no change. The reported number of available positions listed at individual schools or their placement offices ranged from a low of 50 to a high of 6,700 potential jobs. Overall, these reports indicate a less optimistic placement picture than in 2000. For instance, one institution noted a 73 percent drop in the number of placement listings.

As in 2000, four schools indicated that in 2001 they had experienced less difficulty placing their graduates than during the previous year; one reported that it was harder; and 22 said the situation hadn't changed. Schools most commonly mentioned a harder sell to vendors, Web, and academic libraries. Several schools indicated that they experienced no noticeable increase or decrease by type of library or position.

Table 4 shows 2001 placements by type of organization. Reported college and university library placements (341) were down again from 2000 (363). Elementary and secondary library placements (218) continued the downward trend of 2000 (223). Public library placements (369) were up after falling in 2000 (340), compared with 1999 (458).

The Graduate Perspective

In a follow-up survey, about one-third of the 145 graduates contacted commented on the placement process and the preparation they received in library school. Tenacity in the hiring process was an important theme in 2001. One graduate summed up what new hires need: "People skills first and foremost—what [Daniel] Goleman calls 'emotional intelligence.' Web skills—particularly online searches and Internet homepage design experience—are at this point almost a given. Finally, strategic planning ability for people applying for managerial posts."

The need to master people skills, technology, and strategic planning was echoed by many graduates. Interaction with clients and colleagues is a major consideration in the hiring process. "Attitude first—general overall good 'people skills'—comfort level with putting the public first and serving the customer well," said one graduate.

Schools: Teach More Technology

Money and management issues came up frequently. One graduate wrote, "I also use the management skills I learned every minute . . . I do wish that we had spent a bit more class time on working around a budget and time constraints. In my small library I have a slim budget, and I spent my first four months learning how to prioritize. It becomes an issue not of what to buy but when to buy, as well as what is most cost-effective to buy." Another suggested, "Perhaps some segments of administration/management courses (especially those finance related) could be joint-taught by business school faculty."

In the area of customer service, reference skills are highly valued. One student felt a bit unprepared: "I wish that the reference courses I took could have provided some interaction with 'real' patrons. We focused a lot on sources (which was good), but we didn't get any practice in the reference interview." Another agreed: "We focused on print reference, and I needed more experience with electronic databases and evaluation of Internet sites. Dialog was the primary electronic source, and it would have been helpful to have spent time on other databases."

Technology and Web skills are more important than ever, and students want more training in school. One graduate wrote, "I felt adequately prepared for my position because I sought out technology courses. Still, I wasn't fully satisfied with my education in this regard. Library schools must, must, must integrate technology into their programs. They need to teach computer networking and programming as it relates to libraries." Another confirmed this sentiment, writing, "The more technology-oriented classes, such as info retrieval, info design/presentation, dBase management, and usability testing, were most useful."

Salary negotiations generated a range of responses again this year. Those working at public and school libraries generally face a predetermined salary schedule, while vendors and other private companies offer some room to negotiate. One graduate reported, "In a school you do not negotiate salary. It is a schedule that is based on years of experience and the degree that you hold." Another said, "I found the ranges to be negotiable. The job I took did not offer good health benefits, so I was able to negotiate a higher salary to compensate for the extra money I'd have to pay out to cover my prescriptions."

Finally, one new librarian summed up her job skills enthusiastically: "To be honest, there isn't a moment that goes by that I don't think about *something* I learned at library school."

Accredited Master's Programs in Library and Information Studies

This list of graduate programs accredited by the American Library Association is issued as a brochure, with additional detail, early in each calendar year. The brochure is available from the ALA Office for Accreditation. Regular updates appear on the Office for Accreditation's Web site at http://www.ala.org/alaorg/oa/lisdir.html. More than 200 institutions offering both accredited and nonaccredited programs in librarianship are included in the 55th edition of *American Library Directory* (Information Today, Inc., 2002).

Northeast: Conn., D.C., Md., Mass., N.J., N.Y., Pa., R.I.

Catholic University of America, School of Lib. and Info. Science, Washington, DC 20064. Peter Liebscher, Dean. Tel. 202-319-5085, fax 202-219-5574, e-mail cuaslis@cua.edu, World Wide Web http://slis.cua.edu. Admissions contact: Jason Papanikolas.

Clarion University of Pennsylvania, Dept. of Lib. Science, 840 Wood St., Clarion, PA 16214-1232. Andrea Miller, Chair. Tel. 814-393-2271, fax 814-393-2150, e-mail amiller@clarion.edu, World Wide Web http://www.clarion.edu/libsci.

Drexel University, College of Info. Science and Technology, 3141 Chestnut St., Philadelphia, PA 19104-2875. David E. Fenske, Dean. Tel. 215-895-2474, fax 215-895-2494, e-mail info@cis.drexel.edu, World Wide Web http://www.cis.drexel.edu. Admissions contact: Ray Campbell. Tel. 215-895-2485.

Long Island University, Palmer School of Lib. and Info. Science, C. W. Post Campus, 720 Northern Blvd., Brookville, NY 11548-1300. Michael E. D. Koenig, Dean. Tel. 516-299-2866, fax 516-299-4168, e-mail palmer@cwpost.liu.edu, World Wide Web http://www.liu.edu/palmer. Admissions contact: Rosemary Chu. Tel. 516-299-2487 or 516-998-2680, fax 516-299-4168 or 212-995-4072.

Pratt Institute, School of Info. and Lib. Science, Pratt Manhattan Center, 144 W. 14 St., New York, NY 10011. Marie L. Radford, Acting Dean. Tel. 212-647-7682, fax 202-367-2492, e-mail infosils@pratt.edu, World Wide Web http://www.pratt.edu/sils. Admissions contact: Virginia Papandrea.

Queens College, City Univ. of New York, Grad. School of Lib. and Info. Studies, 65-30 Kissena Blvd., Flushing, NY 11367. Marianne Cooper, Dir. Tel. 718-997-3790, fax 718-997-3797, e-mail gslis@qcunixl.qc.edu, World Wide Web http://www.qc.edu/GSLIS. Admissions contact: Virgil L. P. Blake. E-mail Virgil_Blake@qc.edu.

Rutgers University, Dept. of Lib. and Info. Science, School of Communication, Info., and Lib. Studies, 4 Huntington St., New Brunswick, NJ 08903-1071. Nicholas J. Belkin, Chair. Tel. 732-932-7917, fax 732-932-2644, e-mail scilsmls@scils.rutgers.edu, World Wide Web http://www.scils.rutgers.edu. Admissions contact: Carol C. Kuhlthau. Tel. 732-932-7916, e-mail kuhlthau@scils.rutgers.edu.

Saint John's University, Div. of Lib. and Info. Science, 8000 Utopia Pkwy., Jamaica, NY 11439. Sherry Vellucci, Dir. Tel. 718-990-2790, fax 718-990-2071, e-mail libis@stjohns.edu, World Wide Web http://www.stjohns.edu/academics/sjc/depts/dlis/index.html. Admissions contact: Wayne F. James. Tel. 718-990-2790, fax 718-990-5827.

Simmons College, Grad. School of Lib. and Info. Science, 300 The Fenway, Boston, MA 02115-5898. Michelle Cloonan, Dean. Tel. 617-521-2800, fax 617-521-3192, e-mail gslis@simmons.edu, World Wide Web http://www.simmons.edu/programs/gslis. Admissions contact: Judith Beals.

Tel. 617-521-2801, e-mail jbeals@ simmons.edu.

Southern Connecticut State University, School of Communication, Info., and Lib. Science, 501 Crescent St., New Haven, CT 06515. Edward C. Harris, Dean. Tel. 888-500-7278 (press 4) or 203-392-5781, fax 203-392-5780, e-mail lis@southernct.edu, World Wide Web http://www.southernct.edu/ departments/ils. Admissions contact: Mary E. Brown. E-mail brown@southernct.edu.

Syracuse University, School of Info. Studies, 4-206 Center for Science and Technology, Syracuse, NY 13244-4100. Raymond F. von Dran, Dean. Tel. 315-443-2911, fax 315-443-5673, e-mail vondran@syr.edu, World Wide Web http://www.istweb.syr. edu.

University at Albany, State Univ. of New York, School of Info. Science and Policy, 135 Western Ave., Draper 113, Albany, NY 12222. Philip B. Eppard, Dean. Tel. 518-442-5110, fax 518-442-5367, e-mail infosci@albany.edu, World Wide Web http://www.albany.edu/sisp.

University at Buffalo, State Univ. of New York, Dept. of Lib. and Info. Studies, Box 1020, Buffalo, NY 14260-1020. Judith Robinson, Chair. Tel. 716-645-2412, fax 716-645-3775, e-mail ub-lis@buffalo.edu, World Wide Web http://informatics.buffalo. edu/lis/index.asp.

University of Maryland, College of Info. Studies, 4105 Hornbake Lib. Bldg., College Park, MD 20742-4345. Bruce Dearstyne, Interim Dean. Tel. 301-405-2033, fax 301-314-9145, World Wide Web http: //www.clis.umd.edu. Admissions contact: Vicky H. Reinke. Tel. 301-405-2038, e-mail clisumpc@umdacc.umd.edu.

University of Pittsburgh, School of Info. Sciences, 505 IS Bldg., Pittsburgh, PA 15260. Ron Larsen, Dean. Tel. 412-624-5230, fax 412-624-5231, World Wide Web http:// www.sis.pitt.edu. Admissions contact: Ninette Kay. Tel. 412-624-5146, e-mail nkay@mail.sis.pitt.edu.

University of Rhode Island, Grad. School of Lib. and Info. Studies, Rodman Hall, 94 W. Alumni Ave., Suite 2, Kingston, RI 02881. W. Michael Havener, Dir. Tel. 401-874-2947, fax 401-874-4964, e-mail gslis@etal.uri.edu, World Wide Web http://www.uri.edu/artsci/lsc. Admissions contact: Jennifer Legate.

Southeast: Ala., Fla., Ga., Ky., La., Miss., N.C., S.C., Tenn., P.R.

Clark Atlanta University, School of Lib. and Info. Studies, 300 Trevor Arnett Hall, 223 James P. Brawley Dr., Atlanta, GA 30314. Arthur C. Gunn, Dean. Tel. 404-880-8697, fax 404-880-8977, e-mail agunn@cau.edu, World Wide Web http://www.cau.edu. Admissions contact: Gwendolyn Callaway.

Florida State University, School of Info. Studies, Tallahassee, FL 32306-2100. Jane B. Robbins, Dean. Tel. 850-644-5775, fax 850-644-9763, World Wide Web http:// www.lis.fsu.edu. Admissions contact: Don Latham. Tel. 850-644-8124, e-mail latham @lis.fsu.edu.

Louisiana State University, School of Lib. and Info. Science, 267 Coates Hall, Baton Rouge, LA 70803. Beth M. Paskoff, Dean. Tel. 225-578-3158, fax 225-578-4581, e-mail slis@lsu.edu, World Wide Web http://slis.lsu.edu. Admissions contact: Polly McKenzie.

North Carolina Central University, School of Lib. and Info. Sciences, Box 19586, Durham, NC 27707. Benjamin F. Speller, Jr., Dean. Tel. 919-560-6485, fax 919-560-6402, e-mail speller@slis.nccu.edu, World Wide Web http://www.slis.nccu.edu. Admissions contact: Lionell Parker. Tel. 919-560-5211, e-mail lparker@slis.nccu.edu.

University of Alabama, School of Lib. and Info. Studies, Box 870252, Tuscaloosa, AL 35487-0252. Joan L. Atkinson, Dir. Tel. 205-348-4610, fax 205-348-3746, World Wide Web http://www.slis.ua.edu.

University of Kentucky, College of Communications and Info. Studies, School of Lib. and Info. Science, 502 King Library Bldg., Lexington, KY 40506-0039. Timothy W. Sineath, Dir. Tel. 859-257-8876, fax 859-257-4205, e-mail tsineath@pop.uky.edu, World Wide Web http://www.uky.edu/ CommInfoStudies/SLIS. Admissions contact: Jane Salsman.

University of North Carolina at Chapel Hill, School of Info. and Lib. Science, CB 3360, 100 Manning Hall, Chapel Hill, NC 27599-3360. Joanne G. Marshall, Dean. Tel. 919-962-8366, fax 919-962-8071, e-mail info@ils.unc.edu, World Wide Web http://www.ils.unc.edu. Admissions contact: Lucia Zonn. E-mail zonn@ils.unc.edu.

University of North Carolina at Greensboro, Dept. of Lib. and Info. Studies, School of Education, Box 26170, Greensboro, NC 27402-6170. Lee Shiflett, Chair. Tel. 336-334-3478, fax 336-334-5060, e-mail br shaw@uncg.edu, World Wide Web http://www.uncg.edu/lis. Admissions contact: Jim V. Carmichael. Tel. 910-334-3478, e-mail Jim_Carmichael@uncg.edu.

University of Puerto Rico, Graduate School of Info. Science and Technologies, Box 21906, San Juan, PR 00931-1906. Consuelo Figueras, Dir. Tel. 787-763-6199, fax 787-764-2311, e-mail consuelof@compuserv.com. Admissions contact: Migdalia Dávila. Tel. 787-764-0000 ext. 3530, e-mail m_davila@rrpad.upr.clu.edu.

University of South Carolina, College of Lib. and Info. Science, Davis College, Columbia, SC 29208. Fred W. Roper, Dir. Tel. 803-777-3858, fax 803-777-7938, World Wide Web http://www.libsci.sc.edu. Admissions contact: Betsy Bailey. Tel. 803-777-5067, fax 803-777-0457, e-mail b bailey@gwm.sc.edu.

University of South Florida, School of Lib. and Info. Science, 4202 E. Fowler Ave., CIS 1040, Tampa, FL 33620-7800. Vicki L. Gregory, Dir. Tel. 813-974-3520, fax 813-974-6840, e-mail lis@luna.cas.usf.edu, World Wide Web http://www.cas.usf.edu/lis.

University of Southern Mississippi, School of Lib. and Info. Science, Box 5146, Hattiesburg, MS 39406-5146. Melanie J. Norton, Dir. Tel. 601-266-4228, fax 601-266-5774, World Wide Web http://www-dept.usm.edu/~slis.

University of Tennessee, School of Info. Sciences, 451 Communications and UEB, 1345 Circle Park Drive, Knoxville, TN 37996-0341. Elizabeth Aversa, Dir. Tel. 865-974-2148, fax 865-974-4967, World Wide Web http://www.sis.utk.edu. Admissions contact: Kristie Atwood. Tel. 865-974-2858, e-mail katwood@utk.edu.

Midwest: Ill., Ind., Iowa, Kan., Mich., Mo., Ohio, Wis.

Dominican University, Grad. School of Lib. and Info. Science, 7900 W. Division St., River Forest, IL 60305. Prudence W. Dalrymple, Dean. Tel. 708-524-6845, fax 708-524-6657, e-mail gslis@email.dom.edu, World Wide Web http://www.gslis.dom.edu, http://www.stkate.edu (College of St. Catherine). Admissions contacts: Elisa Topper (Dominican Univ.), Mary Wagner (College of St. Catherine).

Emporia State University, School of Lib. and Info. Management, Box 4025, Emporia, KS 66801. Robert Grover, Dean. Tel. 316-341-5203, fax 316-341-5233, World Wide Web http://slim.emporia.edu. Admissions contact: Mirah Dow. E-mail dowmirah@emporia.edu.

Indiana University, School of Lib. and Info. Science, Main Library 011, 1320 E. 10 St., Bloomington, IN 47405-3907. Blaise Cronin, Dean. Tel. 812-855-2018, fax 812-855-6166, e-mail slis@indiana.edu, World Wide Web http://www.slis.indiana.edu. Admissions contact: Rhonda Spencer.

Kent State University, School of Lib. and Info. Science, Box 5190, Kent, OH 44242-0001. William Caynon, Interim Dean. Tel. 330-672-2782, fax 330-672-7965, e-mail wcaynon@slis.kent.edu, World Wide Web http://web.slis.kent.edu. Admissions contact: Cheryl Tennant. E-mail ctennant@slis.kent.edu.

University of Illinois at Urbana-Champaign, Grad. School of Lib. and Info. Science, 501 E. Daniel St., Champaign, IL 61820. Linda C. Smith, Interim Dean. Tel. 217-333-3280, fax 217-244-3302, World Wide Web http://alexia.lis.uiuc.edu. Admissions contact: Valerie Youngen. Tel. 800-982-0914, 217-333-0734, e-mail vyoungen@uiuc.edu.

University of Iowa, School of Lib. and Info. Science, 3087 Library, Iowa City, IA 52242-1420. David Eichmann, Dir. Tel. 319-335-5707, fax 319-335-5374, World Wide Web http://www.uiowa.edu/~libsci.

Admissions contact: Jane Bradbury. E-mail slis@uiowa.edu.

University of Michigan, School of Info., 304 West Hall Bldg., 550 E. University Ave., Ann Arbor, MI 48109-1092. John L. King, Dean. Tel. 734-763-2285, fax 734-764-2475, e-mail si.admissions@umich.edu, World Wide Web http://www.si.umich.edu. Admissions contact: Yvonne Perhne.

University of Missouri–Columbia, School of Info. Science and Learning Technologies, 303 Townsend Hall, Columbia, MO 65211. John Wedman, Dir. Tel. 877-747-5868 (toll free), 573-882-1391, fax 573-884-2917, World Wide Web http://www.coe.missouri.edu/~sislt. Admissions contact: Paula Schlager. Tel. 573-884-2670, e-mail sisltnfo@coe.missouri.edu.

University of Wisconsin–Madison, School of Lib. and Info. Studies, Helen C. White Hall, 600 N. Park St., Madison, WI 53706. Louise S. Robbins, Dir. Tel. 608-263-2900, fax 608-263-4849, e-mail uw_slis@slis.wisc.edu, World Wide Web http://www.slis.wisc.edu. Admissions contact: Barbara Arnold. Tel. 608-263-2909, e-mail bjarnold@facstaff.wisc.edu.

University of Wisconsin–Milwaukee, School of Info. Studies, Bolton Hall 510, 3210 N. Maryland, Milwaukee, WI 53211. James H. Sweetland, Interim Dean. Tel. 414-229-4707, fax 414-229-6699, e-mail info@sois.uwm.edu, World Wide Web http://www.uwm.edu/dept/sois. Admissions contact: Twyla McGhee. Tel. 414-229-2902.

Wayne State University, Lib. and Info. Science Program, 106 Kresge Library, Detroit, MI 48202. Joseph J. Mika, Interim Dir. Tel. 313-577-1825, fax 313-577-7563, e-mail aa2500@wayne.edu, World Wide Web http://www.lisp.wayne.edu. Admissions contact: Yolanda Reader. E-mail af7735@wayne.edu.

Southwest: Ariz., Okla., Texas

Texas Woman's University, School of Info., Box 425438, Denton, TX 76204-5438. Laurie J. Bonnici, Dir. Tel. 940-898-2602, fax 940-898-2611, e-mail lbonnici@twu.edu, World Wide Web http://www.libraryschool.net.

University of Arizona, School of Info. Resources and Lib. Science, 1515 E. 1 St., Tucson, AZ 85719. Brooke Sheldon, Dir. Tel. 520-621-3565, fax 520-621-3279, e-mail sirls@u.arizona.edu, World Wide Web http://www.sir.arizona.edu.

University of North Texas, School of Lib. and Info. Sciences, Box 311068, NT Sta., Denton, TX 76203-1068. Philip M. Turner, Dean. Tel. 940-565-2445, fax 940-565-3101, e-mail pturner@unt.edu, World Wide Web http://www.unt.edu/slis. Admissions contact: Herman L. Totten. E-mail totten@lis.unt.edu.

University of Oklahoma, School of Lib. and Info. Studies, 401 W. Brooks, Norman, OK 73019-0528. Danny P. Wallace, Dir. Tel. 405-325-3921, fax 405-325-7648, e-mail slisinfo@lists.ou.edu, World Wide Web http://www.ou.edu/cas/slis. Admissions contact: Maggie Ryan.

University of Texas at Austin, Grad. School of Lib. and Info. Science, Austin, TX 78712-1276. Andrew Dillon, Dean. Tel. 512-471-3821, fax 512-471-3971, e-mail info@gslis.utexas.edu, World Wide Web http://www.gslis.utexas.edu. Admissions contact: Julie Hallmark. Tel. 512-471-3720, e-mail hallmark@gslis.utexas.edu.

West: Calif., Hawaii, Wash.

San Jose State University, School of Lib. and Info. Science, 1 Washington Sq., San Jose, CA 95192-0029. Blanche Woolls, Dir. Tel. 408-924-2490, fax 408-924-2476, e-mail office@wahoo.sjsu.edu, World Wide Web http://slisweb.sjsu.edu.

University of California, Los Angeles, Graduate School of Educ. and Info. Studies, Dept. of Info. Studies, Mailbox 951521, Los Angeles, CA 90095-1521. Virginia Walter, Chair. Tel. 310-825-8799, fax 310-206-3076, e-mail vwalter@ucla.edu, World Wide Web http://is.gseis.ucla.edu. Admissions contact: Susan Abler. Tel. 310-825-5269, fax 310-206-6293, e-mail abler@gseis.ucla.edu.

University of Hawaii, Lib. and Info. Science Program, 2550 The Mall, Honolulu, HI 96822. Peter Jacso, Program Chair. Tel. 808-956-7321, fax 808-956-5835, e-mail slis@hawaii.com, World Wide Web http://www.hawaii.edu/slis.

University of Washington, The Info. School, Mary Gates Hall, Suite 370, Box 352840, Seattle, WA 98195-2840. Michael B. Eisenberg, Dean. Tel. 206-543-1794, fax 206-616-3152, e-mail info@ischool.washington. edu, World Wide Web http://www.ischool. washington.edu.

Canada

Dalhousie University, School of Lib. and Info. Studies, Halifax, NS B3H 3J5. Bertrum H. MacDonald, Dir. Tel. 902-494-3656, fax 902-494-2451, e-mail slis@is. dal.ca, World Wide Web http://www. mgmt.dal.ca/slis. Admissions contact: Shanna Balogh. Tel. 902-494-2453, e-mail shanna@is.dal.ca.

McGill University, Grad. School of Lib. and Info. Studies, 3459 McTavish St., Montreal, PQ H3A 1Y1. Jamshid Beheshti, Dir. Tel. 514-398-4204, fax 514-398-7193, e-mail gslis@mcgill.ca, World Wide Web http://www.gslis.mcgill.ca. Admissions contact: Dorothy Carruthers.

Université de Montréal, Ecole de Bibliothéconomie et des Sciences de l'Information, C.P. 6128, Succursale Centre-Ville, Montreal, PQ H3C 3J7. Carol Couture, Dir. Tel. 514-343-7400, fax 514-343-5753, e-mail carol.couture@umontreal.ca, World Wide Web http://www.ebsi.umontreal.ca.

Admissions contact: Diane Mayer. E-mail diane.mayer@umontreal.ca.

University of Alberta, School of Lib. and Info. Studies, 3-20 Rutherford S., Edmonton, AB T6G 2J4. Alvin Schrader, Dir. Tel. 780-492-4578, fax 780-492-2430, e-mail slis@ualberta.ca, World Wide Web http://www.slis.ualberta.ca.

University of British Columbia, School of Lib., Archival, and Info. Studies, 1956 Main Mall, Room 831, Vancouver, BC V6T 1Z1. Terrance Eastwood, Acting Dir. Tel. 604-822-2404, fax 604-822-6006, e-mail slais@interchange.ubc.ca, World Wide Web http://www.slais.ubc.ca. Admissions contact: Admissions Secretary. Tel. 604-822-2404, e-mail slais.admissions @ubc.ca.

University of Toronto, Faculty of Info. Studies, 140 George St., Toronto, ON M5S 3G6. Lynne C. Howarth, Dean. Tel. 416-978-8589, fax 416-978-5762, e-mail howarth@fis.utoronto.ca, World Wide Web http://www.fis.utoronto.ca. Admissions contact: Pamela Hawes. E-mail Hawes@fis.utoronto.ca.

University of Western Ontario, Grad. Programs in Lib. and Info. Science, Middlesex College, London, ON N6A 5B7. Catherine Ross, Dean. Tel. 519-661-4017, fax 519-661-3506, e-mail fimsdean@julian.uwo.ca. Admissions contact: Tel. 519-661-2111, e-mail mlis@uwo.ca or phd @uwo.ca.

Library Scholarship Sources

For a more complete list of scholarships, fellowships, and assistantships offered for library study, see *Financial Assistance for Library and Information Studies*, published annually by the American Library Association. The document is also available on the ALA Web site at http://www.ala.org/hrdr/scholarship.html.

American Association of Law Libraries. (1) A varying number of scholarships of a minimum of $1,000 for graduates of an accredited law school who are degree candidates in an ALA-accredited library school; (2) a varying number of scholarships of varying amounts for library school graduates working on a law degree, non-law graduates enrolled in an ALA-accredited library school, and law librarians taking a course related to law librarianship; (3) the George A. Strait Minority Stipend of $3,500 for an experienced minority librarian working toward an advanced degree to further a law library career. For information, write to: Scholarship Committee, AALL, 53 W. Jackson Blvd., Suite 940, Chicago, IL 60604.

American Library Association. (1) The Marshall Cavendish Scholarship of $3,000 for a varying number of students who have been admitted to an ALA-accredited library school; (2) the David H. Clift Scholarship of $3,000 for a varying number of students who have been admitted to an ALA-accredited library school; (3) the Tom and Roberta Drewes Scholarship of $3,000 for a varying number of library support staff; (4) the Mary V. Gaver Scholarship of $3,000 to a varying number of individuals specializing in youth services; (5) the Miriam L. Hornback Scholarship of $3,000 for a varying number of ALA or library support staff; (6) the Christopher J. Hoy/ERT Scholarship of $3,000 for a varying number of students who have been admitted to an ALA-accredited library school; (7) the Tony B. Leisner Scholarship of $3,000 for a varying number of library support staff; (8) Spectrum Initiative Scholarships of $5,000 for 50 minority students admitted to an ALA-accredited library school. For information on all ALA scholarships, write to:

ALA Scholarship Clearinghouse, 50 E. Huron St., Chicago, IL 60611. Application can also be made online; see http://www.ala.org/hrdr/scholarship.html.

ALA/American Association of School Librarians. The AASL School Librarians Workshop Scholarship of $2,500 for a candidate admitted to a full-time ALA-accredited MLS or school library media program. For information, write to: ALA Scholarship Clearinghouse, 50 E. Huron St., Chicago, IL 60611, or see http://www.ala.org/hrdr/scholarship.html.

ALA/Association for Library Service to Children. (1) The Bound to Stay Bound Books Scholarship of $6,000 each for two students who are U.S. or Canadian citizens, who have been admitted to an ALA-accredited program, and who will work with children in a library for one year after graduation; (2) the Frederic G. Melcher Scholarship of $6,000 each for two U.S. or Canadian citizens admitted to an ALA-accredited library school who will work with children in school or public libraries for one year after graduation. For information, write to: ALA Scholarship Clearinghouse, 50 E. Huron St., Chicago, IL 60611, or see http://www.ala.org/hrdr/scholarship.html.

ALA/Association of College and Research Libraries and the Institute for Scientific Information. (1) The ACRL Doctoral Dissertation Fellowship of $1,500 for a student who has completed all coursework and submitted a dissertation proposal that has been accepted, in the area of academic librarianship; (2) the Samuel Lazerow Fellowship of $1,000 for a research, travel, or writing project in acquisitions or technical services in an academic or research library; (3) the ACRL and Martinus Nijhoff International West European Specialist Study Grant, which pays travel expenses, room, and board for a ten-day trip to Europe for an ALA member (selection is based on proposal outlining purpose of trip). For information, write to: Meredith Parets, ACRL/ALA, 50 E. Huron St., Chicago, IL 60611.

ALA/Association of Specialized and Cooperative Library Agencies. Century Scholarship of up to $2,500 for a varying number of disabled U.S. or Canadian citizens admitted to an ALA-accredited library school. For information, write to: ALA Scholarship Clearinghouse, 50 E. Huron St., Chicago, IL 60611, or see http://www.ala.org/hrdr/scholarship.html.

ALA/International Relations Committee. The Bogle Pratt International Library Travel Fund grant of $1,000 for a varying number of ALA members to attend a first international conference. For information, write to: Michael Dowling, ALA/IRC, 50 E. Huron St., Chicago, IL 60611.

ALA/Library and Information Technology Association. (1) The LITA/Christian Larew Memorial Scholarship of $3,000 for a student who has been admitted to an ALA-accredited program in library automation and information science; (2) the LITA/GEAC Scholarship in Library and Information Technology of $2,500 for a student who has been admitted to an ALA-accredited program in library automation and information technology; (3) the LITA/OCLC Minority Scholarship in Library and Information Technology of $2,500 for a minority student admitted to an ALA-accredited program; (4) the LITA/LSSI Minority Scholarship of $2,500 for a minority student admitted to an ALA-accredited program. For information, write to: ALA Scholarship Clearinghouse, 50 E. Huron St., Chicago, IL 60611, or see http://www.ala.org/hrdr/scholarship.html.

ALA/New Members Round Table. EBSCO/NMRT Scholarship of $1,000 for a U.S. or Canadian citizen who is a member of the ALA New Members Round Table. Based on financial need, professional goals, and admission to an ALA-accredited program. For information, write to: ALA Scholarship Clearinghouse, 50 E. Huron St., Chicago, IL 60611, or see http://www.ala.org/work/awards/scholars.html.

ALA/Public Library Association. The New Leaders Travel Grant Study Award of up to $1,500 for a varying number of PLA members with MLS degrees and five years' or less experience. For information, write to: Scholarship Liaison, PLA/ALA, 50 E. Huron St., Chicago, IL 60611.

American-Scandinavian Foundation. Fellowships and grants for 25 to 30 students, in amounts from $3,000 to $18,000, for advanced study in Denmark, Finland, Iceland, Norway, or Sweden. For information, write to: Exchange Division, American-Scandinavian Foundation, 58 Park Ave., New York, NY 10026.

Association for Library and Information Science Education. A varying number of research grants of up to $2,500 each for members of ALISE. For information, write to: Association for Library and Information Science Education, Box 7640, Arlington, VA 22207.

Association of Jewish Libraries. The May K. Simon Memorial Scholarship Fund offers a varying number of scholarships of at least $500 each for MLS students who plan to work as Judaica librarians. For information, write to: Sharona R. Wachs, Association of Jewish Libraries, 1000 Washington Ave., Albany, NY 12203.

Association of Seventh-Day Adventist Librarians. The D. Glenn Hilts Scholarship of $1,000 to a member of the Seventh-Day Adventist Church in a graduate library program. For information, write to: Ms. Wisel, Association of Seventh-Day Adventist Librarians, Columbia Union College, 7600 Flower Ave., Takoma Park, MD 20912.

Beta Phi Mu. (1) The Sarah Rebecca Reed Scholarship of $2,000 for a person accepted in an ALA-accredited library program; (2) the Frank B. Sessa Scholarship of $1,250 for a Beta Phi Mu member for continuing education; (3) the Harold Lancour Scholarship of $1,500 for study in a foreign country related to the applicant's work or schooling; (4) the Blanche E. Woolls Scholarship for School Library Media Service of $1,500 for a person accepted in an ALA-accredited library program; (5) the Doctoral Dissertation Scholarship of $2,000 for a person who has completed course work toward a doctorate; (6) the Eugene Garfield Doctoral Dissertation Scholarship of $3,000 for a person who has approval of a dissertation topic. For information, write to: Jane Robbins, Executive Director, Beta Phi Mu, Florida State University, SLIS, Tallahassee, FL 32306-2100.

Canadian Association of Law Libraries. The Diana M. Priestly Scholarship of $2,500 for a student with previous law library experience or for entry to an approved Canadian law school or accredited Canadian library school. For information, write to: Ann Rae, Chair, CALL/ACBD Scholarship and Awards Committee, Bora-Kaskin Law Library, University of Toronto, 78 Queens Park, Toronto, ON M5S 2C5.

Canadian Federation of University Women. (1) The Alice E. Wilson Award of $2,500 for three students enrolled in graduate studies in any field, with special consideration given to candidates returning to study after at least three years; (2) the Margaret McWilliams Pre-Doctoral Fellowship of $10,000 for a full-time student who has completed one full year of study at the doctoral level; (3) the CFUW Memorial/Professional Fellowship of $5,000 for a student enrolled in a master's program in science, mathematics, or engineering; (4) the Beverly Jackson Fellowship of $2,000 for a student over age 35 enrolled in graduate work at an Ontario University; (5) the 1989 Polytechnique Commemorative Award of $2,800 for a student enrolled in graduate studies related particularly to women; (6) the Bourse Georgette LeMoyne award of $2,500 for graduate study at a Canadian university where one of the languages of administration and instruction is French; (7) the Dr. Marion Elder Grant Fellowship of $9,000 for a full-time student at the master's or doctoral level (preference will be given to holders of an Acadia University degree); (8) the Margaret Dale Philp Biennial Award of $3,000 for graduate studies in the humanities or social sciences. For information, write to: Fellowships Program Manager, Canadian Federation of University Women, 251 Bank St., Suite 600, Ottawa, ON K2P

1X3, Canada (e-mail cfuwfls@rogers.com, World Wide Web http://www.cfuw.org).

Canadian Library Association. (1) The World Book Graduate Scholarship in Library and Information Science of $2,500; (2) the CLA Dafoe Scholarship of $3,000; and (3) the H. W. Wilson Scholarship of $2,000. Each scholarship is given to a Canadian citizen or landed immigrant to attend an accredited Canadian library school; the World Book scholarship can also be used for an ALA-accredited U.S. school; (4) the Library Research and Development Grant of $1,000 for a member of the Canadian Library Association, in support of theoretical and applied research in library and information science. For information, write to: CLA Membership Services Department, Scholarships and Awards Committee, 328 Frank St., Ottawa, ON K2P 0X8, Canada.

Catholic Library Association. (1) The World Book, Inc., Grant of $1,500 divided among no more than three CLA members for continuing education in children's or school librarianship; (2) the Rev. Andrew L. Bouwhuis Memorial Scholarship of $1,500 for a student accepted into a graduate program in library science. For information, write to: Jean R. Bostley, SSJ, Scholarship Chair, Catholic Library Association, 100 North St., Suite 224, Pittsfield, MA 01201-5109.

Chinese American Librarians Association. (1) The Sheila Suen Lai Scholarship; (2) the C. C. Seetoo/CALA Conference Travel Scholarship. Each scholarship offers $500 to a Chinese descendant who has been accepted in an ALA-accredited program. For information, write to: Meng Xiong Liu, Clark Library, San Jose State University, 1 Washington Sq., San Jose, CA 95192-0028.

Church and Synagogue Library Association. The Muriel Fuller Memorial Scholarship of $200 (including texts) for a correspondence course offered by the University of Utah Continuing Education Division. Open to CSLA members only. For information, write to: CSLA, Box 19357, Portland, OR 97280-0357.

Council on Library and Information Resources. The A. R. Zipf Fellowship in

Information Management of $8,000 is awarded annually to a U.S. citizen enrolled in graduate school who shows exceptional promise for leadership and technical achievement. For information, write to: Council on Library and Information Resources, 1755 Massachusetts Ave. N.W., Suite 500, Washington, DC 20036.

Sandra Garvie Memorial Fund. A scholarship of $1,000 for a student pursuing a course of study in library and information science. For information, write to: Sandra Garvie Memorial Fund, c/o Director, Legal Resource Centre, Faculty of Extension, University of Alberta, 8303 112th St., Edmonton, AB T6G 2T4, Canada.

Massachusetts Black Librarians' Network. Two scholarships of at least $500 and $1,000 for minority students entering an ALA-accredited master's program in library science, with no more than 12 semester hours toward a degree. For information, write to: Pearl Mosley, Chair, Massachusetts Black Librarians' Network, 27 Beech Glen St., Roxbury, MA 02119.

Medical Library Association. (1) The Cunningham Memorial International Fellowship of $6,000 plus travel expenses; (2) a scholarship of $5,000 for a person entering an ALA-accredited library program, with no more than one-half of the program yet to be completed; (3) a scholarship of $5,000 for a minority student for graduate study; (4) a varying number of Research, Development and Demonstration Project Grants of $100 to $1,000 for U.S. or Canadian citizens who are MLA members; (5) Continuing Education Grants of $100 to $500 for U.S. or Canadian citizens who are MLA members. For information, write to: Development Department, Medical Library Association, 65 E. Wacker Pl., Suite 1900, Chicago, IL 60601-7298.

Mountain Plains Library Association. (1) A varying number of grants of up to $600 each and (2) a varying number of grants of up to $150 each for MPLA members with at least two years of membership for continuing education. For information, write to: Joseph R. Edelen, Jr., MPLA Executive Secretary, I. D. Weeks Library, University of South Dakota, Vermillion, SD 57069.

REFORMA, the National Association to Promote Library Services to Latinos and the Spanish-Speaking. A varying number of scholarships of $1,000 to $2,000 each for minority students interested in serving the Spanish-speaking community to attend an ALA-accredited school. For information, write to: Ninfa Trejo, Main Library, University of Arizona, 1510 E. University, Tucson, AZ 85721.

Society of American Archivists. The Colonial Dames Awards, two grants of $1,200 each for specific types of repositories and collections. For information, write to: Debra Mills, Society of American Archivists, 521 S. Wells St., 5th fl., Chicago, IL 60607.

Southern Regional Education Board. A varying number of grants of varying amounts to cover in-state tuition for graduate or postgraduate study in an ALA-accredited library school for residents of Arkansas, Delaware, Georgia, Kentucky, Louisiana, Mississippi, Oklahoma, South Carolina, Tennessee, Virginia, and West Virginia. For information, write to: Academic Common Market, c/o Southern Regional Education Board, 592 Tenth St. N.W., Atlanta, GA 30318-5790.

Special Libraries Association. (1) Three $6,000 scholarships for students interested in special-library work; (2) the Plenum Scholarship of $1,000 and (3) the ISI Scholarship of $1,000, each also for students interested in special-library work; (4) the Affirmative Action Scholarship of $6,000 for a minority student interested in special-library work; and (5) the Pharmaceutical Division Stipend Award of $1,200 for a student with an undergraduate degree in chemistry, life sciences, or pharmacy entering or enrolled in an ALA-accredited program. For information on the first four scholarships, write to: Scholarship Committee, Special Libraries Association, 1700 18th St. N.W., Washington, DC 20009-2508; for information on the Pharmaceutical Stipend, write to: Susan E. Katz, Awards Chair, Knoll Pharmaceuticals Science Information Center, 30 N. Jefferson St., Whippany, NJ 07981.

Library Scholarship and Award Recipients, 2002

Library awards are listed by organization. For information on awarding organizations, see the preceding article, "Library Scholarship Sources."

American Association of Law Libraries (AALL)

AALL Educational Scholarships. *Winners*: (Type I: Library Degree for Law School Graduates) Dawn Chavez, Druet Klugh, Maryellen O'Brien; (Library Degree for Non-Law School Graduates) Ethel Leslie.

AALL/West Group George A. Strait Minority Scholarship. Awarded to college graduates with law library experience who are members of a minority group and are degree candidates in accredited library or law schools. *Winner*: Mary Thai.

James F. Connolly/LexisNexis Academic and Library Solutions Scholarship. Awarded to a law librarian who is interested in pursuing a law degree and who has demonstrated an interest in government publications. *Winner*: James Donovan.

Institute for Court Management Scholarship. To encourage law librarians to attend the Institute for Court Management. *Winner*: Kay Newman.

LexisNexis/John R. Johnson Memorial Scholarships. *Winners*: (Library Degree for Law School Graduates) Druet Klugh, Jennifer Sekula; (Library Degree for Non-Law School Graduates) Christine Kujawa, Heather Miller.

Meira Pimsleur Scholarship. *Donor*: Arthur W. Diamond Law Library, Columbia Law School. *Winner*: Andrew Evans.

American Library Association (ALA)

ALA/Information Today Library of the Future Award ($1,500). For a library, consortium, group of librarians, or support organization for innovative planning for, applications of, or development of patron training programs about information technology in a library setting. *Donor*: Information Today, Inc. *Winner*: Northwestern Regional Library, Elkin, North Carolina.

ALA Research Grant (up to $25,000). To support problem-based research for the library and information science profession. *Donor*: ALA. *Winner*: Not awarded in 2002.

Hugh C. Atkinson Memorial Award ($2,000). For outstanding achievement (including risk-taking) by academic librarians that has contributed significantly to improvements in library automation, management, and/or development or research. *Offered by*: ACRL, ALCTS, LAMA, and LITA divisions. *Winner*: Harold W. Billings.

Carroll Preston Baber Research Grant (up to $3,000). For innovative research that could lead to an improvement in library services to any specified group(s) of people. *Donor*: Eric R. Baber. *Winner*: Ethelene Whitmire, University of Wisconsin–Madison for "Faculty Research Productivity and Academic Library Resources and Services."

Beta Phi Mu Award ($500). For distinguished service in library education. *Donor*: Beta Phi Mu International Library Science Honorary Society. *Winner*: Leigh Stewart Estabrook.

Bogle/Pratt International Library Travel Fund Award ($1,000). To ALA member(s) to attend their first international conference. *Donor*: Bogle Memorial Fund. *Winner*: Ellen Bosman.

Bill Boyd Literary Award. See "Literary Prizes, 2002" by Gary Ink in Part 5.

David H. Clift Scholarship ($3,000). To worthy U.S. or Canadian citizens enrolled in an ALA-accredited program toward an MLS degree. *Winner*: Jason M. Stieber.

Melvil Dewey Medal. To an individual or group for recent creative professional achievement in library management, training, cataloging and classification, and the tools and techniques of librarianship.

Donor: OCLC/Forest Press. *Winner*: James F. Williams, II.

Tom and Roberta Drewes Scholarship ($3,000). To a library support staff person pursuing a master's degree. *Winner*: Mary H. Bass.

EBSCO/ALA Conference Sponsorship Award ($1,000). To enable ten librarians to attend the ALA Annual Conference. *Donor*: EBSCO Subscription Services. *Winners*: Sherri Baker, Laurel Bliss, Deborah Bruce, Tracy Kurasaka Brundage, Scott Collard, Whitney E. Davison-Turley, Genevieve A. C. Gallagher, Stacey Greenwell, Jennifer Masciadrelli, Beth Thomsett-Scott.

Equality Award ($500). To an individual or group for an outstanding contribution that promotes equality of women and men in the library profession. *Donor*: Scarecrow Press. *Winner*: Clara M. Chu.

Freedom to Read Foundation Roll of Honor Award. *Winners*: Candace D. Morgan, Joyce Meskis.

Elizabeth Futas Catalyst for Change Award ($1,000). To recognize and honor a librarian who invests time and talent to make positive change in the profession of librarianship. *Donor*: Elizabeth Futas Memorial Fund. *Winner*: Carla J. Stoffle.

Loleta D. Fyan Public Library Research Grant (up to $10,000). For projects in public library development. *Winner*: Not awarded in 2002.

Gale Group Financial Development Award ($2,500). To a library organization for a financial development project to secure new funding resources for a public or academic library. *Donor*: Gale Group. *Winner*: Haines Borough (Alaska) Public Library.

Mary V. Gaver Scholarship ($3,000). To a library support staff member specializing in youth services. *Winner*: Suzanne Dasaro.

Grolier Foundation Award ($1,000). For stimulation and guidance of reading by children and young people. *Donor*: Grolier Education Corporation, Inc. *Winner*: Mary D. Lankford.

Grolier National Library Week Grant ($4,000). To libraries or library associations of all types for a public awareness campaign in connection with National Library Week in the year the grant is awarded. *Donor*: Grolier Educational Cor-

poration. *Winner*: Omaha (Nebraska) Public Library.

Highsmith Library Literature Award ($500). To an author or coauthors who make an outstanding contribution to library literature issued during the three years preceding the presentation. *Donor*: Highsmith. *Winner*: John M. Budd for *Knowledge and Knowing in Library and Information Science: A Philosophical Framework* (Scarecrow Press).

Honorary ALA Membership. E. J. Josey, Seymour Lubetzky.

Miriam L. Hornback Scholarship ($3,000). To an ALA or library support staff person pursuing a master's degree in library science. *Winner*: Lucinda Moriarity.

Paul Howard Award for Courage ($1,000). To a librarian, library board, library group, or an individual who has exhibited unusual courage for the benefit of library programs or services. *Donor*: Paul Howard. *Winner*: Not awarded in 2002.

Christopher J. Hoyt/ERT Scholarship ($3,000). To worthy U.S. or Canadian citizens enrolled in an ALA-accredited program toward an MLS degree. *Winner*: Christopher S. Walter.

John Ames Humphry/OCLC/Forest Press Award ($1,000). To an individual for significant contributions to international librarianship. *Donor*: OCLC/Forest Press. *Winner*: Nancy R. John.

Tony B. Leisner Scholarship ($3,000). To a library support staff member pursuing a master's degree program. *Winner*: Brian W. McDonald.

Joseph W. Lippincott Award ($1,000). To a librarian for distinguished service to the profession. *Donor*: Joseph W. Lippincott, Jr. *Winner*: Ann K. Symons.

James Madison Award. To recognize efforts to promote government openness. *Winner*: Steven Garfinkel.

Marshall Cavendish Excellence in Library Programing Award ($5,000). Recognizes either a school library or public library that demonstrates excellence in library programming by providing programs that have community impact and respond to community need. *Winner*: Houston (Texas) Public Library.

Marshall Cavendish Scholarship ($3,000). To a worthy U.S. or Canadian citizen to begin an MLS degree in an ALA-accredited program. *Winner*: Jack M. Maness.

SIRSI Leader in Library Technology Grant ($10,000). To a library organization to encourage and enable continued advancements in quality services for a project that makes creative or groundbreaking use of technology to deliver exceptional services to its community. *Donor*: SIRSI Corporation. *Winner*: Portage County (Ohio) District Library.

Spectrum Initiative Scholarships ($5,000). Presented to minority students admitted to an ALA-accredited library school. *Winners*: Michelle Baildon, Ali Jamal Boyd, Maia Lani Daugherty, Erica Dean Glenn, Antonia Dugan, Andrew Evans, Maribel Garza, Morna Hilderbrand, Josue Hurtado, Elisia Johnson, Sarah Kostelecky, Jessica Langlois, Guadalupe Leyva, Nona Martin, Dominic Matthews, Michael McGrorty, Martin Muhammad, Annie Patrick, Don Pinanong, Maria Bey Pontillas, Nova Seals, Rekesha Spellman, Robert Vega, Pete Villasenor, Laura Ward, Gwen L. Williams, Pamela D. Williams.

H. W. Wilson Library Staff Development Award ($3,500). To a library organization for a program to further its staff development goals and objectives. *Donor*: H. W. Wilson Company. *Winner*: Newport News (Virginia) Public Library System.

World Book–ALA Goal Grant (up to $10,000). To ALA units for the advancement of public, academic, or school library service and librarianship through support of programs that implement the goals and priorities of ALA. *Donor*: World Book, Inc. *Winners*: Chapter Relations Office, Public Information Office, Public Awareness Committee, Pay Equity Committee, and Maurice J. Freedman, then president-elect of ALA, for the Campaign for America's Librarians.

American Association of School Librarians (AASL)

AASL ABC/CLIO Leadership Grant (up to $1,750). For planning and implementing leadership programs at state, regional, or local levels to be given to school library associations that are affiliates of AASL. *Donor*: ABC/CLIO. *Winner*: Nebraska Educational Media Association for "Leadership and Technology @ Your Library."

AASL/Baker & Taylor Distinguished Service Award ($3,000). For outstanding contributions to librarianship and school library development. *Donor*: Baker & Taylor Books. *Winner*: David Loertscher.

AASL Collaborative School Library Media Award ($2,500). For expanding the role of the library in elementary and/or secondary school education. *Donor*: Sagebrush Corporation. *Winners*: Anieta Trame, Sarah Knobloch, and Tim Condron, Mattoon (Illinois) Middle School.

AASL Crystal Apple Award. To an individual or group that has had significant impact on school libraries and students. *Winner*: U.S. Rep. Ralph Regula (R-Ohio).

AASL/Frances Henne Award ($1,250). To a school library media specialist with five or fewer years in the profession to attend an AASL regional conference or ALA Annual Conference for the first time. *Donor*: Greenwood Publishing Group. *Winner*: Laura Stiles.

AASL/Highsmith Research Grant (up to $5,000). To conduct innovative research aimed at measuring and evaluating the impact of school library media programs on learning and education. *Donor*: Highsmith, Inc. *Winner*: Linda Jordan and Diane Stanley for "Does Accelerated Reader Improve Children's Reading Ability and Achievement?"

AASL School Librarian's Workshop Scholarship ($3,000). To a full-time student preparing to become a school library media specialist at the preschool, elementary, or secondary level. *Donor*: Jay W. Toor, President, Library Learning Resources. *Winner*: Susan McQuaid.

Distinguished School Administrators Award ($2,000). For expanding the role of the library in elementary and/or secondary school education. *Donor*: SIRS-Mandarin, Inc. *Winner*: William Meuer, Norwood Park School, Chicago.

Information Technology Pathfinder Award ($1,000 to the specialist and $500 to the library). To library media specialists for innovative approaches to microcomputer applications in the school library media center. *Donor*: Follett Software Company.

Winners: Secondary, Ken Vesey; Elementary, not awarded in 2002.

Intellectual Freedom Award ($2,000, and $1,000 to media center of recipient's choice). To a school library media specialist who has upheld the principles of intellectual freedom. *Donor*: SIRS-Mandarin. *Winner*: Not awarded in 2002.

National School Library Media Program of the Year Award ($10,000 each in three categories). To school districts and a single school for excellence and innovation in outstanding library media programs. *Donor*: AASL and Follett Library Resources. *Winners*: Single school, James River High School, Midlothian, Virginia; Large school district, not awarded in 2002; Small school district, not awarded in 2002.

Association for Library Trustees and Advocates (ALTA)

ALA Trustee Citations. To recognize public library trustees for individual service to library development on the local, state, regional, or national level. *Winners*: Mary Lou Dewey, Glenna G. Kramer.

ALTA/Gale Outstanding Trustee Conference Grant Award ($750). *Donor*: Gale Group. *Winner*: Claire Gritzer.

ALTA Literacy Award (citation). To a library trustee or an individual who, in a volunteer capacity, has made a significant contribution to addressing the illiteracy problem in the United States. *Winner*: Beverly Conner.

ALTA Major Benefactors Honor Award (citation). To individuals, families, or corporate bodies that have made major benefactions to public libraries. *Winners*: Adele Whitenack Davis, Ann Johnson.

Association for Library Collections and Technical Services (ALCTS)

Hugh C. Atkinson Memorial Award. *See under* American Library Association.

Paul Banks and Carolyn Harris Preservation Award ($1,500). To recognize the contribution of a professional preservation specialist who has been active in the field of preservation and/or conservation for library and/or archival materials. *Donor*:

Preservation Technologies. *Winner*: Ellen McCrady.

Best of *LRTS* Award (citation). To the author(s) of the best paper published each year in the division's official journal. *Winners*: Bartley A. Burk and Laura D. Shedenhelm for "Book Vendor Records in the OCLC Database: Boon or Bane?"

Blackwell's Scholarship Award ($2,000 scholarship to the U.S. or Canadian library school of the recipient's choice). To honor the author(s) of the year's outstanding monograph, article, or original paper in the field of acquisitions, collection development, and related areas of resource development in libraries. *Donor*: Blackwell/North America. *Winner*: Richard Meyer for "A Tool to Access Journal Price Discrimination" in *College and Research Libraries,* May 2001.

Bowker/Ulrich's Serials Librarianship Award ($1,500). For demonstrated leadership in serials-related activities through participation in professional associations and/or library education programs, contributions to the body of serials literature, research in the area of serials, or development of tools or methods to enhance access to or management of serials. *Donor*: R. R. Bowker. *Winner*: Eric Lease Morgan.

First Step Award (Wiley Professional Development Grant) ($1,500). For librarians new to the serials field to attend ALA's Annual Conference. *Donor*: John Wiley & Sons. *Winner*: Susanna Flodin.

Leadership in Library Acquisitions Award ($1,500). For significant contributions by an outstanding leader in the field of library acquisitions. *Donor*: Harrassowitz Company. *Winner*: Rosann Bazirjian.

Margaret Mann Citation ($2,000 scholarship to the U.S. or Canadian library school of the winning author's choice). To a cataloger or classifier for achievement in the areas of cataloging or classification. *Donor*: Online Computer Library Center. *Winner*: Jean L. Hirons.

Esther J. Piercy Award ($1,500). To a librarian with fewer than ten years' experience for contributions and leadership in the field of library collections and technical services. *Donor*: Yankee Book Peddler. *Winner*: Lisa German.

Association for Library Service to Children (ALSC)

ALSC/Book Wholesalers Reading Program Grant ($3,000). To an ALSC member for implementation of an outstanding public library summer reading program for children. *Donor*: Book Wholesalers, Inc. *Winner*: Keene (New Hampshire) Public Library.

ALSC/Econo-Clad Literature Program Award ($1,000). To an ALSC member who has developed and implemented an outstanding library program for children involving reading and the use of literature, to attend an ALA conference. *Donor*: Econo-Clad Books. *Winner*: Katie O'Dell.

May Hill Arbuthnot Honor Lectureship. To invite an individual of distinction to prepare and present a paper that will be a significant contribution to the field of children's literature and that will subsequently be published in *Journal of Youth Services in Libraries*. *Winner*: Maurice Sendak.

Mildred L. Batchelder Award. See "Literary Prizes, 2002" by Gary Ink in Part 5.

Louise Seaman Bechtel Fellowship ($4,000). For librarians with 12 or more years of professional-level work in children's library collections, to read and study at the Baldwin Library/George Smathers Libraries, University of Florida (must be an ALSC member with an MLS from an ALA-accredited program). *Donor*: Bechtel Fund. *Winner*: Leslie Barban.

Bound to Stay Bound Books Scholarships (four awards of $6,000). For men and women who intend to pursue an MLS or advanced degree and who plan to work in the area of library service to children. *Donor*: Bound to Stay Bound Books. *Winners*: Sarah Dutelle, Jill Heritage, Melissa Kerrigan, Cami Kitzel.

Caldecott Medal. See "Literary Prizes, 2002" by Gary Ink in Part 5.

Andrew Carnegie Medal. To the U.S. producer of the most distinguished video for children in the previous year. *Donor*: Carnegie Corporation of New York. *Winner*: Dante Di Loreto and Anthony Edwards (Aviator Films) and Willard Carroll and Tom Wilhite (Hyperion Studio) for *My Louisiana Sky*.

Distinguished Service to ALSC Award ($1,000). To recognize significant contributions to, and an impact on, library services to children and/or ALSC. *Winner*: Phyllis J. Van Orden.

Frederic G. Melcher Scholarship ($6,000). To two students entering the field of library service to children for graduate work in an ALA-accredited program. *Winners*: Leigh Barnes, Stephanie Schott.

John Newbery Medal. See "Literary Prizes, 2002" by Gary Ink in Part 5.

Penguin Putnam Books for Young Readers Awards. To children's librarians in school or public libraries with ten or fewer years of experience to attend the ALA Annual Conference for the first time. Must be a member of ALSC. *Donor*: Penguin Putnam. *Winners*: Karen DeAngelo, Genevieve Gallagher, Michael Gorman, Jill Walker.

Robert F. Sibert Informational Book Award. To the author of the most distinguished informational book published during the preceding year. *Donor*: Bound to Stay Bound Books. *Winner*: Susan Campbell Bartoletti for *Black Potatoes: The Story of the Great Irish Famine, 1845–1850* (Houghton Mifflin).

Laura Ingalls Wilder Medal. To an author or illustrator whose works have made a lasting contribution to children's literature. *Winner*: Not awarded in 2002.

Association of College and Research Libraries (ACRL)

ACRL Academic/Research Librarian of the Year Award ($3,000). For outstanding contribution to academic and research librarianship and library development. *Donor*: Baker & Taylor. *Winner*: Shirley E. Phipps.

ACRL Doctoral Dissertation Fellowship ($1,500). To a doctoral student in the field of academic librarianship whose research has potential significance in the field. *Donor*: Institute for Scientific Information (ISI). *Winner*: Charlotte Ford.

ACRL EBSS Distinguished Education and Behavioral Sciences Librarian Award (citation). To an academic librarian who has made an outstanding contribution as an education and/or behavioral sciences librarian through accomplishments and service to the profession. *Winner*: Barbara E. Kemp.

ACRL WSS/Greenwood Career Achievement in Women's Studies Librarianship ($1,000). Honors distinguished academic librarians who have made outstanding contributions to women's studies through accomplishments and service to the profession. *Donor*: Greenwood Publishing Group. *Winner*: Joan Ariel.

ACRL WSS/Routledge Award for Significant Achievement in Women's Studies Librarianship ($1,000). *Winners*: Eri Fujieda, Meg Miner, Beth Stafford.

Hugh C. Atkinson Memorial Award. *See under* American Library Association.

Coutts Nijhoff International West European Specialist Study Grant (travel funding for up to 14 days' research in Europe). Supports research pertaining to West European studies, librarianship, or the book trade. *Sponsor*: Coutts Nijhoff International. *Winner*: James P. Niessen.

Miriam Dudley Instruction Librarian Award ($1,000). For contribution to the advancement of bibliographic instruction in a college or research institution. *Donor*: Elsevier. *Winner*: Randall Burke Hensley.

EBSCO Community College Learning Resources Leadership Award ($500). *Donor*: EBSCO Subscription Services. *Winner*: Cynthia Steinhoff.

EBSCO Community College Learning Resources Program Award ($500). *Donor*: EBSCO Subscription Services. *Winner*: St. Petersburg (Florida) College.

Excellence in Academic Libraries Awards ($3,000 plus travel expenses).To recognize an outstanding community college, college, and university library. *Donor*: Blackwell's Book Services. *Winners*: Anne Arundel (Maryland) Community College, Cornell University Library, Oberlin College.

Instruction Section Innovation in Instruction Award ($3,000). Recognizes and honors librarians who have developed and implemented innovative approaches to instruction within their institution in the preceding two years. *Donor*: LexisNexis. *Winner*: Ross T. LaBaugh.

Instruction Section Publication of the Year Award (citation). Recognizes an outstanding publication related to instruction in a library environment published in the preceding two years. *Winner*: Betsy Baker.

Marta Lange/CQ Award ($1,000). Recognizes an academic or law librarian for contributions to bibliography and information service in law or political science. *Donor*: *Congressional Quarterly*. *Winner*: Mary K. Fetzer.

Samuel Lazerow Fellowship for Research in Acquisitions or Technical Services ($1,000). To foster advances in acquisitions or technical services by providing librarians a fellowship for travel or writing in those fields. *Sponsor*: Institute for Scientific Information (ISI). *Winner*: Jeffrey Beall.

Katharine Kyes Leab and Daniel J. Leab Exhibition Catalog Awards (citations). For the best catalogs published by American or Canadian institutions in conjunction with exhibitions of books and/or manuscripts. *Winners*: (Category I–Expensive) *The Great Wide Open: Panoramic Photographs of the American West*, Huntington Library; (Category II–Moderately Expensive) *The Ecstatic Journey: Athanasius Kircher in Baroque Rome*, Dept. of Special Collections at the University of Chicago; (Category III–Inexpensive) *Cut and Paste–California Scrapbooks*, California Historical Society at the North Baker Research Library; (Category IV–Brochures) *Ruskin's Italy, Ruskin's England*, Pierpont Morgan Library Publications.

Oberly Award for Bibliography in the Agricultural Sciences ($350). Biennially, for the best English-language bibliography in the field of agriculture or a related science in the preceding two-year period. *Donor*: Eunice R. Oberly Fund. *Winner*: Not awarded in 2002.

K. G. Saur Award for Best *College and Research Libraries* Article ($500). To author(s) to recognize the most outstanding article published in *College and Research Libraries* during the preceding year. *Donor*: K. G. Saur Publishing. *Winner*: Susan Davis Herring.

K. G. Saur Award for Best *LIBRI* Student Paper ($500). See under K. G. Saur.

Association of Specialized and Cooperative Library Agencies (ASCLA)

ASCLA Century Scholarship (up to $2,500). For a library school student or students with disabilities admitted to an ALA-accredited library school. *Winner*: Christine Anne Baynes.

ASCLA Exceptional Service Award. *Winner*: Michael Gunde.

ASCLA Leadership Achievement Award. To recognize leadership and achievement in the areas of consulting, multitype library cooperation, and state library development. *Winner*: Stephen Prine.

ASCLA/National Organization on Disability Award for Library Service to People with Disabilities ($1,000). To institutions or organizations that have made the library's total service more accessible through changing physical and/or additional barriers. *Donor*: National Organization on Disability, funded by Aetna U.S. Healthcare. *Winner*: Dunellen (New Jersey) Public Library.

ASCLA Professional Achievement Award. To recognize professional achievement within the areas of consulting, networking, statewide service, and programs. *Winner*: Not awarded in 2002.

ASCLA Service Award (citation). For outstanding service and leadership to the division. *Winner*: Stephen Prine.

Francis Joseph Campbell Citation. For a contribution of recognized importance to library service for the blind and physically handicapped. *Winner*: Julie Klauber.

Ethnic and Multicultural Information and Exchange Round Table

David Cohen/EMIERT Multicultural Award. *Winners*: Brigid A. Cahalan, Fred J. Gitner, Irina A. Kuharets.

Gale Group/EMIERT Multicultural Award ($1,000). For outstanding achievement and leadership in serving the multicultural/multiethnic community. *Donor*: Gale Group. *Winner*: Linda Tse.

Exhibits Round Table

Friendly Booth Award (citation). *Cosponsor*: New Members Round Table. *Winners*:

First place, Library of Congress; second place, Sauder Manufacturing; third place, Reading Is Fundamental.

Christopher J. Hoy/ERT Scholarship ($3,000). To an individual or individuals who will work toward an MLS degree in an ALA-accredited program. *Donor*: Family of Christopher Hoy. *Winner*: Christopher S. Walter.

Kohlstedt Exhibit Award (citation). To companies or organizations for the best single, multiple, and island booth displays at the ALA Annual Conference. *Winner*: Not awarded in 2002.

Federal and Armed Forces Librarians Round Table (FAFLRT)

Federal Librarians Achievement Award. *Winner*: Dan O. Clemmer.

Adelaide del Frate Conference Sponsor Award. To encourage library school students to become familiar with federal librarianship and ultimately seek work in federal libraries; for attendance at ALA Annual Conference and activities of the Federal and Armed Forces Librarians Round Table. *Winner*: Mari-Jana O. Phelps.

Distinguished Service Award (citation). To honor a FAFLRT member for outstanding and sustained contributions to the association and to federal librarianship. *Winner*: Not awarded in 2002.

Gay, Lesbian, Bisexual, and Transgendered Round Table (GLBT)

GLBT Book Awards. To authors of fiction and nonfiction books of exceptional merit relating to the gay/lesbian experience. *Winners*: Moisés Kaufman and the Tectonic Theatre Project for *The Laramie Project* (Vintage), Barry Werth for *The Scarlet Professor: Newton Arvin, A Literary Life Shattered by Scandal* (Nan Talese/Doubleday).

Government Documents Round Table (GODORT)

James Bennett Childs Award. To a librarian or other individual for distinguished lifetime contributions to documents librarianship. *Winner*: Ridley Kessler, Jr.

CIS/GODORT/ALA Documents to the People Award ($2,000). To an individual, library, organization, or noncommercial group that most effectively encourages or enhances the use of government documents in library services. *Donor*: Congressional Information Service, Inc. (CIS). *Winner*: Andrea Sevetson.

Bernadine Abbott Hoduski Founders Award (plaque). To recognize documents librarians who may not be known at the national level but who have made significant contributions to the field of state, international, local, or federal documents. *Winner*: Not awarded in 2002.

Readex/GODORT/ALA Catharine J. Reynolds Award ($2,000). Grants to documents librarians for travel and/or study in the field of documents librarianship or area of study benefiting performance as documents librarians. *Donor*: Readex Corporation. *Winners*: Cathy Hartman and Valerie Glenn, John Walters.

David Rozkuszka Scholarship ($3,000). To provide financial assistance to an individual who is currently working with government documents in a library while completing a master's program in library science. *Winner*: Laura Sare.

Intellectual Freedom Round Table (IFRT)

John Phillip Immroth Memorial Award for Intellectual Freedom ($500). For notable contribution to intellectual freedom fueled by personal courage. *Winner*: Joyce Meskis, Tattered Cover Book Store.

Eli M. Oboler Memorial Award ($1,500). Biennially, to an author of a published work in English or in English translation dealing with issues, events, questions, or controversies in the area of intellectual freedom. *Donor*: Providence Associates, Inc. *Winner*: Marjorie Heins for *Not in Front of the Children: Indecency, Censorship, and the Innocence of Youth* (Hill and Wang).

SIRS State and Regional Achievement Award ($1,000). To an innovative and effective intellectual freedom project covering a state or region during the calendar year. *Donor*: Social Issues Resource Series, Inc.

(SIRS). *Winner*: LeRoy C. Merritt Humanitarian Fund.

Library Administration and Management Association (LAMA)

Hugh C. Atkinson Memorial Award. *See under* American Library Association.

John Cotton Dana Library Public Relations Awards. To libraries or library organizations of all types for public relations programs or special projects ended during the preceding year. *Donor*: H. W. Wilson Company. *Winners*: Baltimore County (Maryland) Public Library; Bowling Green (Kentucky) Public Library; Calgary Public Library, Alberta, Canada; Maryland State Department of Education, Division of Library Development Services; New York Public Library; North Suburban Library System, Wheeling, Illinois.

LAMA/AIA Library Buildings Award (citation). A biennial award given for excellence in architectural design and planning by an American architect. *Donor*: American Institute of Architects and LAMA. *Winner*: Not awarded in 2002.

LAMA Cultural Diversity Grant (up to $1,000). To support creation and dissemination of resources that will assist library administrators and managers in developing a vision and commitment to diversity. *Winners*: University of Notre Dame, University of Tennessee–Knoxville.

LAMA Leadership Award. *Winner*: Paul M. Anderson.

LAMA President's Award. *Winner*: SOLINET (Southeastern Library Network).

LAMA Recognition of Group Achievement Award. To honor LAMA committees or task forces, recognizing outstanding teamwork supporting the goals of LAMA. *Winner*: Not awarded in 2002.

LAMA/YBP Student Writing and Development Award. *Winner*: Emily Ranseen.

Library and Information Technology Association (LITA)

Hugh C. Atkinson Memorial Award. *See under* American Library Association.

LITA/Christian Larew Memorial Scholarship ($3,000). To encourage the entry of qualified persons into the library and information technology field. *Donor*: Electronic Business and Information Services (EBIS). *Winner*: Josue Hurtado.

LITA/Endeavor Student Writing Award ($1,000). For the best unpublished manuscript on a topic in the area of libraries and information technology written by a student or students enrolled in an ALA-accredited library and information studies graduate program. *Winner:* Rachel Mendez.

LITA/Gaylord Award for Achievement in Library and Information Technology ($1,000). *Donor*: Gaylord Bros., Inc. *Winner*: Sally McCallum.

LITA/Library Hi Tech Award ($1,000). To an individual or institution for a work that shows outstanding communication for continuing education in library and information technology. *Donor*: MCB University Press. *Winner*: Illinois OCLC Users Group.

LITA/LSSI Minority Scholarship in Library and Information Science ($2,500). To encourage a qualified member of a principal minority group to work toward an MLS degree in an ALA-accredited program with emphasis on library automation. *Donor*: Library Systems & Services, Inc. *Winner*: Pete Villasenor.

LITA/OCLC Frederick G. Kilgour Award for Research in Library and Information Technology ($2,000 and expense-paid attendance at ALA Annual Conference). To bring attention to research relevant to the development of information technologies. *Winner*: Carol C. Kuhlthau.

LITA/OCLC Minority Scholarship in Library and Information Technology ($3,000). To encourage a qualified member of a principal minority group to work toward an MLS degree in an ALA-accredited program with emphasis on library automation. *Donor*: OCLC. *Winner*: Michelle Baildon.

LITA/SIRSI Scholarship in Library and Information Technology ($2,500). To encourage the entry of qualified persons into the library automation field who demonstrate a strong commitment to the use of automated systems in libraries. *Winner*: Not awarded in 2002.

Library History Round Table (LHRT)

Phyllis Dain Library History Dissertation Award ($500). To the author of a dissertation treating the history of books, libraries, librarianship, or information science. *Winner*: Not awarded in 2002.

Donald G. Davis Article Award (certificate). For the best article written in English in the field of U.S. and Canadian library history. *Winner*: Carl Ostrowski.

Justin Winsor Prize Essay ($500). To an author of an outstanding essay embodying original historical research on a significant subject of library history. *Winner*: Marek Sroka.

Library Research Round Table (LRRT)

Jesse H. Shera Award for Distinguished Published Research ($500). For a research article on library and information studies published in English during the calendar year. *Winner*: Not awarded in 2002.

Jesse H. Shera Award for Excellence in Doctoral Research ($500). For completed research on an unpublished paper of 10,000 words or less on library and information studies. *Winner*: Not awarded in 2002.

Map and Geography Round Table (MAGERT)

MAGERT Honors Award (citation and cash award). To recognize outstanding contributions by a MAGERT personal member to map librarianship, MAGERT, and/or a specific MAGERT project. *Winner*: Johnnie Sutherland.

New Members Round Table (NMRT)

NMRT/EBSCO Scholarship ($1,000). To a U.S. or Canadian citizen to begin an MLS degree in an ALA-accredited program. Candidates must be members of NMRT. *Donor*: EBSCO Subscription Services. *Winner*: Roberta L. Carswell-Panjwani.

NMRT/3M Professional Development Grant. To NMRT members to encourage professional development and participation in national ALA and NMRT activities. *Donor*: 3M. *Winners*: Mary Mannix, Jenna Freedman, Tanzi Merritt.

Shirley Olofson Memorial Award ($1,000). To an individual to help defray costs of attending the ALA Annual Conference. *Winner*: Dru Henson-Hunt.

Office for Literacy and Outreach Services

Jean E. Coleman Library Outreach Lecture. *Winner*: Lotsee Patterson.

Estela and Raul Mora Award. *Winner*: El Paso (Texas) Public Library.

Public Library Association (PLA)

Advancement of Literacy Award (plaque). To a publisher, bookseller, hardware and/or software dealer, foundation, or similar group that has made a significant contribution to the advancement of adult literacy. *Donor*: *Library Journal*. *Winner*: Center for Literacy, Philadelphia.

Baker & Taylor Entertainment Audio Music/Video Product Grant ($2,500 worth of audio music or video products). To help a public library to build or expand a collection of either or both formats. *Donor*: Baker & Taylor Entertainment. *Winner*: Signal Mountain (Tennessee) Public Library.

Carnegie-Whitney Awards (up to $5,000). For the publication of bibliographic aids for research. *Donor*: James Lyman Whitney and Andrew Carnegie Funds. *Winners*: Born to Read, Association for Library Service to Children; *Librarianship and Information Science in the Islamic World 1966–1999: An Annotated Bibliography,* Sterling Coleman; Readmore Statewide Reading Project for the State of Missouri, Wicky Sleight, Kirkwood (Missouri) Public Library; Women's Studies Reading List, Adonna Fleming, James A. Michener Library, Greeley, Colorado; Right Here I See My Own Books: A Database of the Library in the Woman's Building of the World's Columbian Exposition, Chicago, Illinois, 1893, Wayne Wiegand, University of Wisconsin–Madison.

Demco Creative Merchandising Grant ($1,000). To a public library proposing a project for the creative display and merchandising of materials either in the library or in the community. *Donor*: Demco,

Inc. *Winner*: Isaac F. Umberhine Public Library, Richmond, Maine.

Excellence in Small and/or Rural Public Service Award ($1,000). Honors a library serving a population of 10,000 or less that demonstrates excellence of service to its community as exemplified by an overall service program or a special program of significant accomplishment. *Donor*: EBSCO Subscription Services. *Winner*: Wallowa County Library, Enterprise, Oregon.

Highsmith Library Innovation Award ($2,000). Recognizes a public library's innovative achievement in planning and implementation of a creative program or service using technology. *Winner*: Santa Fe Springs (California) City Library.

Allie Beth Martin Award ($3,000). Honors a librarian who, in a public library setting, has demonstrated extraordinary range and depth of knowledge about books or other library materials and has distinguished ability to share that knowledge. *Donor*: Baker & Taylor Books. *Winner*: Merle Jacob.

New Leaders Travel Grants (up to $1,500). To enhance the professional development and improve the expertise of public librarians by making their attendance at major professional development activities possible. *Donor*: GEAC, Inc. *Winners*: Jill Rourke, Katherine Clowers, Angela Meyer, Karen Yanetta.

Charlie Robinson Award ($1,000). Honors a public library director who, over a period of seven years, has been a risk-taker, an innovator, and/or a change agent in a public library. *Donor*: Baker & Taylor Books. *Winner*: Gary Strong.

Leonard Wertheimer Award ($1,000). To a person, group, or organization for work that enhances and promotes multilingual public library service. *Donor*: NTC Publishing Group. *Winner*: Not awarded in 2002.

Women's National Book Association/Ann Heidbreder Eastman Grant ($500 to $1,000). To a librarian to take a course or participate in an institute devoted to aspects of publishing as a profession or to provide reimbursement for such study completed within the past year. *Winner*: Debbie Abilock.

Reference and User Services Association (RUSA)

Virginia Boucher-OCLC Distinguished ILL Librarian Award ($2,000). To a librarian for outstanding professional achievement, leadership, and contributions to interlibrary loan and document delivery. *Winner*: Tom Delaney.

Dartmouth Medal. For creating current reference works of outstanding quality and significance. *Donor*: Dartmouth College, Hanover, New Hampshire. *Winner*: *The Oxford Encyclopedia of Ancient Egypt* (Oxford University Press).

Dun & Bradstreet Award for Outstanding Service to Minority Business Communities (BRASS) ($2,000). *Winner*: Queens Borough (New York) Public Library.

Dun & Bradstreet Public Librarian Support Award (BRASS) ($1,000). To support the attendance at the ALA Annual Conference of a public librarian who has performed outstanding business reference service and who requires financial assistance. *Winner*: Sandra G. Rizzo.

Gale Group Award for Excellence in Business Librarianship (BRASS) ($3,000). To an individual for distinguished activities in the field of business librarianship. *Donor*: Gale Group. *Winner*: Irwin D. Faye.

Gale Group Award for Excellence in Reference and Adult Services ($3,000). To a library or library system for developing an imaginative and unique library resource to meet patrons' reference needs. *Donor*: Gale Group. *Winner*: Not awarded in 2002.

Genealogical Publishing Company/History Section Award ($1,500). To encourage and commend professional achievement in historical reference and research librarianship. *Donor*: The Genealogical Publishing Company. *Winner*: Curt B. Witcher.

Margaret E. Monroe Library Adult Services Award (citation). To a librarian for impact on library service to adults. *Winner*: Marsha Spyros.

Bessie Boehm Moore/Thorndike Press Award ($1,000). To a library organization that has developed an outstanding and creative program for library service to the aging. *Winner*: Montclair (New Jersey) Public Library.

Isadore Gilbert Mudge–R. R. Bowker Award ($5,000). For distinguished contributions to reference librarianship. *Winner*: James P. Danky.

Reference Service Press Award ($2,500). To the author or authors of the most outstanding article published in *RUSQ* during the preceding two volume years. *Donor*: Reference Service Press, Inc. *Winner*: Catherine Sheldrick Ross and Kirsti Nilsen for "Has the Internet Changed Anything in Reference? The Library Visit Study, Phase 2."

John Sessions Memorial Award (plaque). To a library or library system in recognition of work with the labor community. *Donor*: AFL/CIO. *Winner*: Web Design Group, Allegheny County (Pennsylvania) Labor Council.

Louis Shores–Greenwood Publishing Group Award ($3,000). To an individual, team, or organization to recognize excellence in reviewing of books and other materials for libraries. *Donor*: Greenwood Publishing Group. *Winner*: Kathleen K. Piehl.

Thomson Financial Student Travel Award (BRASS) ($1,000). For a student enrolled in an ALA-accredited master's degree program to attend the ALA Annual Conference. *Donor*: Thomson Financial. *Winner*: Christy A. Donaldson.

Social Responsibilities Round Table (SRRT)

Jackie Eubanks Memorial Award ($500). To honor outstanding achievement in promoting the acquisition and use of alternative media in libraries. *Donor*: AIP Task Force. *Winner*: Zoia Horn.

Coretta Scott King Awards. See "Literary Prizes, 2002" by Gary Ink in Part 5.

Young Adult Library Services Association (YALSA)

Alex Awards. To the authors of ten books published for adults that have high potential appeal to teenagers. *Winners*: Geraldine Brooks for *Year of Wonders: A Novel of the Plague* (Viking); William Doyle for *An American Insurrection: The Battle of Oxford, Mississippi* (Doubleday); David Anthony Durham for *Gabriel's Story*

(Doubleday); Barbara Ehrenreich for *Nickel and Dimed: On (Not) Getting By in America* (Holt/Metropolitan); Leif Enger for *Peace Like a River* (Atlantic Monthly); Kobie Kruger for *The Wilderness Family: At Home with Africa's Wildlife* (Ballantine); Donna Morrissey for *Kit's Law* (Houghton/Mariner); Mel Odom for *The Rover* (Tor); Vineeta Vijayaraghavan for *Motherland* (Soho); Rebecca Walker for *Black, White and Jewish: Autobiography of a Shifting Self* (Putnam/Riverhead).

Baker & Taylor/YALSA Conference Grants ($1,000). To young adult librarians in public or school libraries to attend an ALA Annual Conference for the first time. Candidates must be members of YALSA and have one to ten years of library experience. *Donor:* Baker & Taylor Books. *Winners:* Linette Ivanovitch, Julie Halpern.

Book Wholesalers, Inc./YALSA Collection Development Grant ($1,000). To YALSA members who represent a public library and work directly with young adults, for collection development materials for young adults. *Winners:* Taralee Alcock, Willie Braudaway.

Margaret A. Edwards Award ($2,000). To an author whose book or books have provided young adults with a window through which they can view their world and which will help them to grow and to understand themselves and their role in society. *Donor: School Library Journal. Winner:* Paul Zindel.

Great Book Giveaway (books, videos, CDs, and audio cassettes valued at a total of $25,000). *Winner:* Bell County (Kentucky) Public Library System.

Frances Henne/YALSA/VOYA Research Grant ($500 minimum). To provide seed money to an individual, institution, or group for a project to encourage research on library service to young adults. *Donor: Voice of Youth Advocates. Winner:* Teri S. Lesesne.

Michael L. Printz Award. See "Literary Prizes, 2002" by Gary Ink in Part 5.

YALSA/Sagebrush Award ($1,000). For an exemplary young adult reading or literature program. *Donor:* Sagebrush Corporation. *Winner:* Patricia Suellentrop.

American Society for Information Science and Technology (ASIS&T)

ASIS&T Award of Merit. For an outstanding contribution to the field of information science. *Winner:* Karen Sparck Jones.

ASIS&T Best Information Science Book. *Winner:* Stuart Biegel.

ASIS&T/ISI Outstanding Information Science Teacher Award ($500). *Winner:* Deborah K. Barreau.

ASIS&T Research Award. For a systematic program of research in a single area at a level beyond the single study, recognizing contributions in the field of information science. *Winner:* Carol Tenopir.

ASIS&T Special Award. To recognize long-term contributions to the advancement of information science and technology and enhancement of public access to information and discovery of mechanisms for improved transfer and utilization of knowledge. *Winner:* Not awarded in 2002.

ASIS&T/UMI Doctoral Dissertation Award. *Winner:* Pamela Savage Knepshield.

James Cretsos Leadership Award. *Winner:* Suzanne Allard.

ISI Citation Analysis Research Grant. *Winner:* Chaomei Chen.

ISI Doctoral Dissertation Proposal Scholarship ($1,500). *Winner:* Joan Bartlett.

Pratt Severn Best Student Research Paper. *Winner:* Elizabeth Zogby.

Watson Davis Award. *Winner:* Thomas Hogan.

John Wiley & Sons Best JASIST Paper Award. *Winners:* Justin Zobel and Marcin Kaszkiel.

Art Libraries Society of North America (ARLIS/NA)

John Benjamins Award. To recognize research and publication in the study and analysis of periodicals in the fields of the fine arts, literature, and cross-disciplinary studies. *Winner:* Not awarded in 2002.

Andrew Cahan Photography Award ($750). To encourage participation of art information professionals in the field of photography through reference, research, or bibliographic work. *Winner*: James Soe Nyun.

Distinguished Service Award. Betty Jo Irvine.

Melva J. Dwyer Award. To the creators of exceptional reference or research tools relating to Canadian art and architecture. *Winner*: Joan Reid Acland for *First Nations Artists in Canada: A Biographical/Bibliographical Guide 1960 to 1999* (Gail and Stephen A. Jarislowsky Institute for Studies in Canadian Art).

Howard and Beverly Joy Karno Award ($1,000). To provide financial assistance to a professional art librarian in Latin America through interaction with ARLIS/NA members and conference participation. *Cosponsor*: Howard Karno Books. *Winner*: Maria Concepción Alexandrina Sepúlveda.

David Mirvish Books/Books on Art Travel Award (C$500). To encourage art librarianship in Canada. *Winner*: Kathy Zimon.

Gerd Muehsam Award. To one or more graduate students in library science programs to recognize excellence in a graduate paper or project. *Winner*: Alison Gilchrest.

Puvill Libros Award ($1,000). To encourage professional development of European art librarians through interaction with ARLIS/NA colleagues and conference participation. *Winner*: Selale Korkut.

Research Libraries Group Asia/Oceania Award ($1,000). To encourage professional development of art information professionals who reside in Asia/Oceania through interaction with ARLIS/NA colleagues and conference participation. *Winner*: Stephen O'Brien.

Research Libraries Group Travel Award ($1,000). To promote participation in ARLIS/NA by supporting conference travel for an individual who has not attended an ARLIS/NA Annual Conference. *Winner*: Sara Harrington.

Thames and Hudson Conference Attendance Award ($500). *Winner*: Marilyn Russell-Bogle.

H. W. Wilson Foundation Research Award. To support research activities by ARLIS/NA members in the fields of librarianship,

visual resources curatorship, and the arts. *Winners*: Roberto C. Ferrari for *The Letters of Simeon Solomon;* Sara Harrington for *Women's Work: The Valorization of Domestic Labor in American World War II Posters*.

George Wittenborn Memorial Book Award. For outstanding publications in the visual arts and architecture. *Winner*: Seymour Slive for *Jacob van Ruisdael: A Complete Catalogue of his Paintings, Drawings and Etchings* (Yale University Press).

Worldwide Books Award for Electronic Resources. *Winner*: Roberto C. Ferrari for the Simeon Solomon Research Archive Web Site.

Worldwide Books Publications Award. *Winners*: Lamia Doumato for "Opening the Door to Paradise: Bishop Theodorus and St. Thomas Imagery in Thirteenth Century Syria" in *Al-Masaq* (*Islam and the Medieval Mediterranean*), vol. 12, 2000; Elizabeth Broman for "Egyptian Revival Funerary Art in Green-Wood Cemetery" in *Markers: The Annual Journal of the Association for Gravestone Studies,* vol. XVIII, 2001.

Asian/Pacific American Librarians Association (APALA)

Asian/Pacific American Librarians scholarships. To enable LIS students to attend the organization's national conference. *Winners*: Eydie Detera, Todd Honma.

Association for Library and Information Science Education (ALISE)

ALISE Award for Teaching Excellence in the Field of Library and Information Science Education. *Winner*: Jerry D. Saye.

ALISE Bohdan S. Wynar Research Paper Competition. For a research paper concerning any aspect of librarianship or information studies by a member of ALISE. *Winner*: Not awarded in 2002.

ALISE Methodology Paper Competition ($500). *Winners*: Lisa M. Given and Hope A. Olson.

ALISE Pratt-Severn Faculty Innovation Award. *Winner*: Not awarded in 2002.

ALISE Professional Contribution to Library and Information Science Education Award. *Winner:* Toni Carbo.

ALISE Research Grant Awards (one or more grants totaling $5,000). *Winner*: Not awarded in 2002.

ALISE Service Award. *Winner*: Charles Curran.

Eugene Garfield/ALISE Doctoral Dissertation Awards ($500). *Winners*: Soo Young Rieh for "Information Quality and Cognitive Authority in the World Wide Web"; Bradley L. Taylor for "The Effect of Surrogation on Viewer Response to Expressional Qualities in Works of Art."

OCLC/ALISE Library and Information Science Research Grants (up to $15,000). *Winners*: Jane Greenberg, Lorna Peterson, Wonsik Shim.

Beta Phi Mu

Beta Phi Mu Award. *See under* American Library Association.

Eugene Garfield Doctoral Dissertation Fellowships ($3,000). *Winners*: Diane Kelly, Jinmock Kim, Ciaran Trace, Heiko Haubitz, Kelly Maglaughlin, Jeffery Pomerantz.

Harold Lancour Scholarship for Foreign Study ($1,500). For graduate study in a foreign country related to the applicant's work or schooling. *Winner*: Pat Kittelson.

Sarah Rebecca Reed Scholarship ($2,000). For study at an ALA-accredited library school. *Winner*: Eileen O'Connell.

Frank B. Sessa Scholarship for Continuing Professional Education ($1,250). For continuing education for a Beta Phi Mu member. *Winner*: Susannah Benedetti.

E. Blanche Woolls Scholarship ($1,500). For a beginning student in school library media services. *Winner*: Lena Michaud.

Bibliographical Society of America (BSA)

BSA Fellowships ($1,000–$2,000). For scholars involved in bibliographical inquiry and research in the history of the book trades and in publishing history. *Winners*: Barbara M. Benedict, Mark Brandon Bland, Joanne Filippone, Robert Byron Hamm, Jr., John N. King, Reginald Brian Parker, Catherine M. Rodriguez, Paul Jefferson Shaw, Robert W. Trogdon, Carola Wessel.

Canadian Library Association (CLA)

Olga B. Bishop Award ($100). To a library school student for the best paper on government information or publications. *Winner*: Not awarded in 2002.

CLA Award for the Advancement of Intellectual Freedom in Canada. *Winners*: Peter Carver, Nancy Fleming, Sarah Thring.

CLA Elizabeth Dafoe Scholarship ($3,000). *Winner*: Michele Hilton.

CLA Echo Award Program. *Winner*: Not awarded in 2002.

CLA/Information Today Award for Innovative Technology. *Donor*: Information Today, Inc. *Winner*: Windsor (Ontario) Public Library.

CLA Outstanding Service to Librarianship Award. *Donor*: R. R. Bowker. *Winners*: Paul Whitney, Gwynneth Evans.

CLA Research and Development Grant ($1,000). *Winner*: Not awarded in 2002.

CLA/3M Award for Achievement in Technical Services. *Winner*: University of Calgary Library.

CLA Student Article Award. *Winner*: Robin Bergart.

W. Kaye Lamb Award for Service to Seniors. *Winners*: Calgary Public Library, Western Counties Regional Library.

H. W. Wilson Scholarship ($2,000). *Winner*: Lise Doucette.

World Book Graduate Scholarship in Library Science ($2,500). *Winner*: Ross Gordon.

Canadian Association of College and University Libraries (CACUL)

CACUL Innovation Achievement Award ($1,500). *Winner*: Canadian National Site Licensing Project.

CACUL/Miles Blackwell Award for Outstanding Academic Librarian. *Winner*: Holly Melanson.

CACUL Workshop Incentive Grants. *Winners*: Kathy Plett, Doris Rauch, Trina Grover, Sandy Iverson, Karen Hunt, Jordana Heaton.

Community and Technical College Libraries (CTCL) Merit Award for Distinguished Service as a Public Library Trustee. For outstanding leadership in the advancement of public library trusteeship and public library service in Canada. *Winner*: Maureen Ellis Rudzik.

CTCL Award for Outstanding College Librarian. *Winner*: Seneca College Learning Resource Center.

CTCL Innovation Achievement Award. *Winner*: Laraine Tapak.

Canadian Association of Public Libraries (CAPL)

CAPL/Brodart Outstanding Public Library Service Award. *Winner*: Trudy Amirault.

Canadian Association of Special Libraries and Information Services (CASLIS)

CASLIS Award for Special Librarianship in Canada. *Winner*: Not awarded in 2002.

Canadian Library Trustees Association (CLTA)

CLTA/Stan Heath Achievement in Literacy Award. For an innovative literacy program by a public library board. *Donor*: ABC Canada. *Winner*: Winnipeg Public Library Board.

Canadian School Library Association (CSLA)

National Book Service Teacher-Librarian of the Year Award. *Winner*: Joanne Laforty.

Margaret B. Scott Award of Merit. For the development of school libraries in Canada. *Winner*: Not awarded in 2002.

Chinese-American Librarians Association (CALA)

CALA Distinguished Service Award. To a librarian who has been a mentor, role model, and leader in the fields of library and information science. *Winner*: Lai Xinxia.

CALA President's Recognition Award. *Winner*: Sally T. Tseng.

Huang Tso-ping and Wu Yao-yu Scholarship. *Winner*: Beverly Anmay Ku.

Sheila Suen Lai Scholarship ($500). To a student of Chinese nationality or descent pursuing full-time graduate studies for a master's degree or Ph.D. degree in an ALA-accredited library school. *Winner*: Fei Yu.

C. C. Seetoo/CALA Conference Travel Scholarship ($500). For a student to attend the ALA Annual Conference and CALA program. *Winner*: Yu Su.

Church and Synagogue Library Association (CSLA)

CSLA Award for Outstanding Congregational Librarian. For distinguished service to the congregation and/or community through devotion to the congregational library. *Winner*: Lillian Koppin.

CSLA Award for Outstanding Congregational Library. For responding in creative and innovative ways to the library's mission of reaching and serving the congregation and/or the wider community. *Winner*: St. John's Lutheran Church Library, Summit, New Jersey (Ruth Elizabeth Foreman, Librarian).

CSLA Award for Outstanding Contribution to Congregational Libraries. For providing inspiration, guidance, leadership, or resources to enrich the field of church or synagogue librarianship. *Winner*: Joyce

Troyer, Our Lady of Sorrows Catholic Church, Kansas City, Missouri.

Muriel Fuller Scholarship Award. *Winner*: Not awarded in 2002.

Helen Keating Ott Award for Outstanding Contribution to Children's Literature. *Winner*: Audrey Penn.

Pat Tabler Memorial Scholarship Award. *Winner*: Henry Jessie.

Coalition for Networked Information

Paul Evan Peters Award. To recognize notable and lasting international achievements related to high-performance networks and the creation and use of information resources and services that advance scholarship and intellectual productivity. *Winner*: Vinton Gray Cerf.

Paul Evan Peters Fellowship ($2,500 a year for two years). To a student pursuing a graduate degree in librarianship or the information sciences. *Winner*: Christopher Lee.

Council on Library and Information Resources

A. R. Zipf Fellowship in Information Management ($5,000). Awarded annually to a student enrolled in graduate school who shows exceptional promise for leadership and technical achievement. *Winner*: Miles James Efron.

International Federation of Library Associations and Institutions (IFLA)

Hans-Peter Geh Grant. To enable a librarian from the former Soviet Union to attend a conference in Germany or elsewhere. *Winner*: Not awarded in 2002.

Medical Library Association (MLA)

Estelle Brodman Award for the Academic

Medical Librarian of the Year. To honor significant achievement, potential for leadership, and continuing excellence at mid-career in the area of academic health sciences librarianship. *Winner*: Judith F. Burnham.

Lois Ann Colaianni Award for Excellence and Achievement in Hospital Librarianship. To a member of MLA who has made significant contributions to the profession in the area of overall distinction or leadership in hospital librarianship. *Winner*: Margaret Bandy.

Continuing Education Awards ($100–$500). *Winner*: Linda Collins.

Cunningham Memorial International Fellowship ($6,000). A six-month grant and travel expenses in the United States and Canada for a foreign librarian. *Winner*: Yuan Lin.

Louise Darling Medal. For distinguished achievement in collection development in the health sciences. *Winner*: Not awarded in 2002.

Janet Doe Lectureship. *Winner*: Jacqueline Donaldson Doyle.

EBSCO/MLA Annual Meeting Grant (up to $1,000). *Winners*: Sandra De Groote, Candice Benjes-Small, Verma Walker, Norma Walters.

Ida and George Eliot Prize. For an essay published in any journal in the preceding calendar year that has been judged most effective in furthering medical librarianship. *Donor*: Login Brothers Books. *Winner*: Not awarded in 2002.

Murray Gottlieb Prize. For the best unpublished essay submitted by a medical librarian on the history of some aspect of health sciences or a detailed description of a library exhibit. *Donor*: Ralph and Jo Grimes. *Winner*: Michael A. Flannery for "The Early Botanical Medical Movement as a Reflection of Life, Liberty, and Literacy in Jacksonian America."

Hospital Libraries Section/MLA Professional Development Grants. *Winners*: Not awarded in 2002.

ISI/Frank Bradway Rogers Information Advancement Award ($500). For an outstanding contribution to knowledge of health science information delivery. *Donor*:

Institute for Scientific Information (ISI). *Winner*: Not awarded in 2002.

ISI/MLA Doctoral Fellowship ($2,000). To encourage superior students to conduct doctoral work in an area of health sciences librarianship or information sciences. *Winner*: Not awarded in 2002.

Joseph Leiter NLM/MLA Lectureship. *Winner*: Francis S. Collins.

Lucretia W. McClure Excellence in Education Award. To an outstanding eduator in the field of health sciences librarianship and informatics. *Winner*: Ellen Gay Detlefsen.

John P. McGovern Award Lectureship. *Winner*: Seaborn Beck Weathers.

Medical Informatics Section/MLA Career Development Grant ($1,500). For up to two individuals to support a career development activity that will contribute to advancement in the field of medical informatics. *Winners*: Mary Linn Bergstrom, Marilyn Teolis.

MLA Award for Distinguished Public Service. *Winner*: U.S. Sen. Harry Reid (D-Nev.).

MLA/NLM Spectrum Scholarship ($5,000). For a minority student seeking to become a health sciences information professional. *Winner*: Michelle Baildon.

MLA President's Award. *Winner*: Not awarded in 2002.

MLA Research, Development, and Demonstration Project Grant ($100 to $1,000). *Winner*: Not awarded in 2002.

MLA Scholarship (up to $5,000). For graduate study in medical librarianship at an ALA-accredited library school. *Winner*: Shelagh Genuis.

MLA Scholarship for Minority Students (up to $5,000). *Winner*: Crystal Smith.

Marcia C. Noyes Award. For an outstanding contribution to medical librarianship. The award is the highest professional distinction of MLA. *Winner*: Robert M. Braude.

Rittenhouse Award. For the best unpublished paper on medical librarianship submitted by a student enrolled in, or having been enrolled in, a course for credit in an ALA-accredited library school or a trainee in an internship program in medical librarianship. *Donor*: Rittenhouse Medical Bookstore. *Winner*: Not awarded in 2002.

K. G. Saur (Munich, Germany)

K. G. Saur Award for Best *College and Research Libraries* Article. *See under* American Library Association, Association of College and Research Libraries.

K. G. Saur Award for Best *LIBRI* Student Paper ($500). To author(s) to recognize the most outstanding article published in *LIBRI* during the preceding year. *Donor*: K. G. Saur Publishing. *Winner*: Jennifer Wolfe Thompson.

Society of American Archivists (SAA)

C. F. W. Coker Award for Description. *Winners*: Not awarded in 2002.

Colonial Dames of America Scholarships (up to $1,200). To enable new archivists to attend the Modern Archives Institute of the National Archives and Records Administration. *Winners*: Ian Graham, Valerie J. Frey, Charity Anne Galbreath.

Distinguished Service Award. Recognizes outstanding service and exemplary contribution to the profession. *Winner*: Duke University.

Fellows' Posner Prize. For an outstanding essay dealing with a facet of archival administration, history, theory, or methodology, published in the latest volume of *American Archivist*. *Winner*: Terry Cook, for "The Imperative of Challenging Absolutes in Graduate Archival Education Programs: Issues for Educators and the Profession."

Philip M. Hamer–Elizabeth Hamer Kegan Award. For individuals and/or institutions that have increased public awareness of a specific body of documents. *Winner*: Vermont State Archives for its involvement in the state government Web site Continuing Issues of Government and Governance (http://vermont-archives.org/governance/govern.htm).

Oliver Wendell Holmes Award. To enable overseas archivists already in the United States or Canada for training to attend the SAA annual meeting. *Winner*: Not awarded in 2002.

J. Franklin Jameson Award. For individuals and/or organizations that promote greater public awareness of archival activities and programs. *Winners*: Joan Winters and Louise Addis of the Stanford Linear Accelerator Center.

Sister M. Claude Lane Award. For a significant contribution to the field of religious archives. *Winner*: Not awarded in 2002.

Waldo Gifford Leland Prize. For writing of superior excellence and usefulness in the field of archival history, theory, or practice. *Winner*: Richard J. Cox for *Managing Records for Evidence and Information* (Quorum Books, 2001).

Theodore Calvin Pease Award. For the best student paper. *Winner*: Reto Tschan for "A Comparison of Jenkinson and Schellenberg on Appraisal."

Harold T. Pinkett Minority Student Award. To encourage minority students to consider careers in the archival profession and promote minority participation in the Society of American Archivists. *Winner*: Petrina D. Jackson.

Preservation Publication Award. To recognize an outstanding work published in North America that advances the theory or the practice of preservation in archival institutions. *Winner*: Robert E. Schnare, Jr., for *Bibliography of Preservation Literature, 1983–1996* (Scarecrow Press).

SAA Fellows. Highest individual distinction awarded to a limited number of members for their outstanding contribution to the archival profession. *Honored*: Mark A. Greene, Elizabeth W. Adkins, Thomas J. Frusciano.

Special Libraries Association (SLA)

Mary Adeline Connor Professional Development Scholarship ($6,000). *Winner*: Not awarded in 2002.

John Cotton Dana Award. For exceptional support and encouragement of special librarianship. *Winner*: Mimi Drake.

Dow Jones 21st Century Competencies Award. *Winner*: Not awarded in 2002.

Factiva Leadership Award ($2,000). To an SLA member who exemplifies leadership as a special librarian through excellence in personal and professional competencies. *Winner*: Tom Fearon.

Steven I. Goldspiel Research Grant. *Sponsor*: Primark Corp. *Winner*: Deborah Barreau for "The New Information Professional: Vision and Practice."

Hall of Fame Award. To a member or members of the association at or near the end of an active professional career for an extended and sustained period of distinguished service to the association. *Winners*: Mary Dickerson, Richard Funkhouser, Elizabeth Eddison.

Honorary Membership. *Winner*: Not awarded in 2002.

Innovations in Technology Award ($1,000). To a member of the association for innovative use and application of technology in a special library setting. *Sponsor*: FIS. *Winner*: Gary Price.

International Special Librarians Day (ISLD) Award. *Winner*: Mary Howery.

Member Achievement Award. *Winner*: Michael Keating.

SLA Affirmative Action Scholarship ($6,000). *Winner*: Todd Honma.

SLA Diversity Leadership Development Award ($1,000). *Winners*: Suzan J. Lee, Jeffrey Mah.

SLA Fellows. *Honored*: Sandy Spurlock, Lynn McCay, Peter Moon, Charlene Baldwin-Reed.

SLA President's Award. *Winner*: Carol Ginsburg, Judy Field, Suzi Hayes, Tom Rink, Ethel Salonen, Barbara Semonche.

SLA Professional Award. *Winner*: Mary Ellen Bates.

SLA Public Relations Media Award. *Winner*: Not awarded in 2002.

SLA Student Scholarships ($6,000). For students with financial need who show potential for special librarianship. *Winners*: Donna Jean Cook, Farah Gheriss, Kari Anne Swanson.

Rose L. Vormelker Award. *Winner*: Billie Connor-Dominguez, Nettie Seaberry.

H. W. Wilson Company Award ($500). For the most outstanding article in the past year's *Information Outlook*. *Donor*: H. W. Wilson Company. *Winner*: Martha K. Heyman for "Building Successful Relationships with IT Professionals" (April 2001).

Part 4
Research and Statistics

Library Research and Statistics

Research on Libraries and Librarianship in 2002

Mary Jo Lynch
Director, Office for Research and Statistics, American Library Association

The year 2002 was a time of increasing fiscal trouble for the institutions that support library research, as for many other institutions in the United States. Research was done nonetheless, and much of it involved both library service and the Internet. Despite the bursting of the dot-com bubble, use of the Internet continues to climb. In late December, a survey by the Pew Internet and American Life Project found that the Internet has become a mainstream information tool.

Also in December, there were two announcements that bode well for the relationship between libraries and the Internet. The Institute of Museum and Library Services (IMLS) invited proposals to conduct a large national study of the information needs and expectation of users and potential users of online information, and of the effects of having such information. The study will provide data and recommendations about

- Content that should be made available online to meet information and enterprise needs of the public, using broad definitions of both *information* and *public*
- Mechanisms and resources necessary to efficiently and effectively connect users to that content

This is an important research initiative for the library community because it has the potential to alter public perceptions of how that community relates to the Internet.

Another announcement in December 2002 promises enhancement of that relationship. For several years now, libraries have spent increasing amounts of money and time on licenses to provide electronic periodicals and databases for use by library patrons. A few individual libraries have devised ways to generate meaningful statistics about how those services are used. But there are no valid state- or national-level statistics and none that can be used by researchers to compare one library with others. A major reason for that lack is the fact that publishers and other intermediaries do not provide comparable statistics to libraries. Several groups have been working on this for several years and a major breakthrough came in December with the Web posting of a "code of practice" from COUNTER: Counting Online Usage of NeTworked Electronic Resources (http://

www.projectcounter.org). This international initiative had its genesis in Britain and is supported by a number of organizations in the United States and elsewhere. Its goal is "to provide a single, international, extendible Code of Practice that allows the usage of online information products and services to be measured in a credible, consistent, and compatible way using vendor-generated data." By 2004 vendors are expected to be "COUNTER-compliant." This was done for reasons other than to facilitate research, but it will definitely prove useful to researchers.

Academic Libraries

In October 2002 preliminary results became available from a large-scale study of how information-usage patterns are changing among undergraduates, graduate students, and faculty members in U.S. academic institutions. *Dimensions and Use of the Scholarly Information Environment: Introduction to a Data Set Assembled by the Digital Library Federation and Outsell, Inc.* is available at http://www. clir.org/pubs/abstract/pub110abst.html. The data come from telephone interviews with 3,234 faculty members, graduate students, and undergraduate students in a range of disciplines from nearly 400 public and private institutions of varying sizes. In general, patterns vary depending on user group (faculty, graduate students, and undergraduate students) and activity (research, teaching, and coursework), but both print and online resources are used heavily by all three groups for all three activities. Online resources are often used through the library's Web site. The preliminary report was based on 158 selected data tables. The full set of 659 data tables is now available at the same site. Researchers are encouraged to use them or to consult the raw data tapes that will be deposited with the Inter-University Consortium for Political and Social Research (ICPSR).

A different but related study was described at the OCLC Symposium preceding the 2002 American Library Association (ALA) Annual Conference in Atlanta. The OCLC White Paper on the information habits of college students was called "How Academic Libraries Can Influence Students' Web-Based Information Choices." The study was done online for OCLC by Harris Interactive to find out how students use the Web to do course assignments, which role libraries play in that process, and how libraries can improve the service to students. Seventy-three percent of students reported using their library's Web site at least some of the time. During their last visit to the site, 67 percent used the full text of journal articles, 57 percent used the library catalog, and 51 percent used databases or indexes to journal articles. The majority of respondents (89 percent) used print resources from their campus library (see http://www2.oclc.org/oclc/pdf/printon demand/informationhabits.pdf).

A different aspect of academic library service was examined in an IMLS-funded study on "The State of Preservation Programs in American College and Research Libraries: Building a Common Understanding and Action Agenda" conducted by the Council on Library and Information Resources in cooperation with the Association of Research Libraries (ARL), the University Libraries Group (ULG), and the Regional Alliance for Preservation. Data for the study were collected by means of a paper survey and on-site interviews. The survey was conducted in 116 libraries, including 22 midsize universities belonging to

ULG, 20 major non-ARL land grant institutions (LG), and 75 liberal arts colleges belonging to what is known informally as the Oberlin Group (OG). The survey was designed to secure documentation from the ULG, OG, and LG libraries that was comparable to information on ARL members that appears in the ARL Preservation Statistics for 2000–2001.

After conducting the survey, project staff members made site visits to 20 institutions representing ARL, ULG, LG, and OG. The purpose of the visits was to collect qualitative information on attitudes, opinion, and emotions relating to the topic of preservation that would supplement the quantitative survey data. Results were used to develop a series of six recommendations to guide stakeholders (see http://www.pewinternet.org/reports/toc.asp?Report=80).

Public Libraries

The press release for National Library Week 2002 announced the results of two ALA-sponsored studies with good news about use of public libraries. One study, later reported in *American Libraries* with the title "Economic Hard Times and Public Library Use Revisited" (http://www.ala.org/alaorg/ors/econhardtimes. html), was prompted by calls to ALA in late 2001 asking for proof of the popular belief that library use goes up when the economy goes down. Librarians were seeing this happen locally and wanted evidence from other places. The ALA Office for Research and Statistics (ORS) worked with the staff at the Library Research Center (LRC) of the University of Illinois Graduate School of Library and Information Science to design a small study that would take a contemporary look at an old belief.

LRC contacted the 25 public libraries in the United States serving populations of 1 million or more and asked them to provide monthly data on circulation and visits for the last five years. Twenty-three agreed to cooperate and sent data. The visits data were not robust enough for statistical analysis. However, circulation data from 18 libraries were exactly what was needed. Using that data and the standard methodology of time series regression analysis, LRC found that circulation had increased significantly in all the months since March 2001, when the National Bureau of Economic Research pegged the beginning of the latest recession.

To measure the public's use of public libraries and opinion on messages in its "@ your library" campaign, ALA contracted with KRC Research and Consulting for telephone interviews with 1,000 people over the age of 18. Among other things, they found that

- 66 percent of all respondents reported using the public library at least once in the last year in person, by phone, or by computer
- 62 percent of respondents had a library card
- 91 percent of the total respondents believed libraries will exist in the future, despite the abundance of information available on the Internet

The questions and results have been posted at http://www.ala.org/pio/presskits/nlw2002kit/krc_data.pdf.

The KRC study found that 26 percent of people who visited the public library used the Internet while they were there. A study by the Library Research Service at the Colorado State Library examined that use by asking public libraries to distribute a nine-item questionnaire to patrons on two different days and at all times of those days. Funded by an LSTA grant, "Colorado Public Libraries and the 'Digital Divide' 2002" produced a detailed report with three key findings:

- Technology in public libraries spans all demographics and fulfills a highly demanded patron need.
- Technology have-nots are not limited to the poor or undereducated.
- Library patrons are teaching themselves new technology skills, communicating on a global level, and accessing online information on a wide variety of topics. With access to online information about education, health, employment, and volunteer opportunities, they are improving their quality of life and that of their communities.

The report is posted at http://www.lrs.org/documents/DD_2002/DDSR_W-appendix.pdf.

An unusual publication from ALA describes one aspect of what library patrons are doing online. *Online Community Information: Creating a Nexus at Your Library* by Joan C. Durrance and Karen E. Pettigrew is a unique combination of research report and how-to manual. The research was funded by a 1998 IMLS National Leadership Grant for "Help-Seeking in an Electronic World: The Role of the Public Library in Helping Citizens Obtain Community Information Over the Internet." IMLS has now funded a related study by the same study team. In "Approaches for Understanding Community Information Use," the team will gather data to better understand the information-seeking behavior of consumers. It will also identify best practices in the provision of community information and community services.

Youth and Libraries

Two other IMLS grants in the 2002 cycle focus on public library service to young adults. Two faculty members at the Drexel University College of Information Science and Technology, in collaboration with the Free Library of Philadelphia, will conduct a three-year research project titled "Everyday Information-Seeking Behavior of Urban Young Adults." In a smaller and shorter project, the School of Informatics at the State University of New York, Buffalo, will investigate the impact of youths' use of the Internet on their use of the public library. The project will sample students from schools in the Buffalo area and western New York state to determine which populations have access to digital information and how they are using it, and where students access the Internet.

IMLS also funded a three-year project with the University of Maryland to evaluate the impact the International Children's Digital Library can have on children, based on research on ethnographic and demographic variables in children's use patterns and preferences, and on the application of outcomes-based evaluation techniques to children's use of digital content.

The Children's Digital Library itself will be developed by a $3 million National Science Foundation grant to the same institution. Research issues surrounding scale, metadata, book readers, localization, and community-building will be addressed during this five-year project. In addition, intellectual property, copyright protection, and distribution issues are being explored with the help of stakeholders (e.g., authors, publishers, and librarians) who have come together as partners in this research effort. The results of this research will be disseminated in conference and journal papers, as well as through yearly workshops and a final book describing the children's personal experiences with the library. This research will be an important demonstration of new advances in digital libraries technologies for children and will lead to a critical discussion concerning rights management and access to copyrighted materials.

Another aspect of youth and the Internet will be explored by researchers at the McGill University Graduate School of Library and Information Studies. Using a three-year grant from Canada's Social Science and Humanities Research Council (SSHRC), Andy Large and Jamshid Beheshti will explore whether children can play a role in Web portal design, to what extent portals should be designed to meet the needs of specific ages and genders, the difference between a child's and an adult's design concept, and whether a design that children find attractive will also be as usable as that from a professional. The research will aid understanding of how children approach software design, as well as their specific opinions on portal design. It will elaborate portal design criteria from young users' perspectives and enable future portals to be constructed based on the cognitive processes of their users.

School Libraries

There were two important developments to note in the school library field in 2002. Many of the leading researchers in the field, plus more than 20 young scholars, met at the Elms Resort and Spa near Kansas City May 30–June 2 for another Treasure Mountain Research Institute. This was number 10 in a series of research retreats created in 1989 to provide researchers in the field of school library media studies an opportunity to share their research, gather ideas, and interact with practitioners. This time the organizers were Daniel Callison and Nancy Thomas, and the theme was "Assessment of Student Achievement and Information Literacy Education with Emphasis on Children and Youth in a Multicultural Context" (see http://slis.iupui.edu/TreasureMountain/description/index. htm). Proceedings will be published by Hi Willow Press in 2003 and plans are already under way for the next institute.

One of the speakers at the event was Keith Curry Lance, whose state studies have demonstrated a correlation between strong library media center programs and student achievement. Several state reports were described in this article last year. The Iowa report was released in 2002 (see http://www.aea9.k12.ia.us/aea_ statewide_study.pdf) and a Michigan study was in progress. At this writing, statistics are in the planning stages in California and Illinois.

The View from OCLC

Last year this article noted that the OCLC Office of Research had a new director, Lorcan Dempsey. The October 2002 issue of the *OCLC Newsletter* featured a long interview with Dempsey under the headline "Libraries Change Lives, and Research Changes Libraries." The interview describes five major themes in the current research agenda at OCLC:

- Metadata management and knowledge organization
- Content management
- Management intelligence
- Interoperability
- Systems and interaction design

At the end of the interview, Dempsey explained the double goal of his unit, "OCLC Research has an interesting dual role. We support OCLC products and services. We also act on behalf of the wider community. For many libraries, R&D activity is not possible. This means that we are keen to do work that at once benefits OCLC and the wider community" (see http://www.oclc.org/news/newsletter/oclcnewsletter258.pdf).

Awards That Honor Excellent Research

All active awards are listed along with the amount of the award, the URL for the award (if available), and the 2002 winners. If the award is annual but was not given in 2002, that fact is noted. General ALA awards are listed first, followed by units of ALA in alphabetical order, followed by other organizations in alphabetical order.

American Library Association

Library History Round Table

Donald G. Davis Article Award
http://www.ala.org/alaorg/ors/davis.html
Winner: Carl Ostrowski, Middle Tennessee State University
Project: "James Alfred Pearce and the Question of a National Library in Antebellum America," published in *Libraries and Culture,* vol. 35, no. 2, Spring 2000
Rationale: This article examines the origins of the debate over a national library and the role of Maryland Senator James Alfred Pearce in the resolution of the issue. It demonstrates how legal, social, and intellectual issues influenced key decisions, and offers new insights into the evolution of the Library of Congress as the nation's library.

Justin Winsor Prize ($500)
http://www.ala.org/alaorg/ors/winsor.html
Winner: Marek Sroka, University of Illinois at Urbana-Champaign
Project: "The Destruction of Jewish Libraries and Archives in Cracow (Krakow) during World War II"

Rationale: The author fills a significant gap in library history by documenting the destruction of a people's culture, intellectual capital, and memory. Very little has been written in English on the topic of Jewish libraries and archives in Poland and their destruction.

Library Research Round Table

Jesse H. Shera Award for Distinguished Published Research ($500)
http://www.ala.org/alaorg/ors/shera1.html
Not given in 2002.

Jesse H. Shera Award for Excellence in Doctoral Research ($500)
http://www.ala.org/alaorg/ors/shera2.html
Not given in 2002.

Association for Library Collections and Technical Services

One award, given annually by the Association for Library Collections and Technical Services (ALCTS) but not always for research, was given for research in 2002. The **Blackwell's Scholarship Award**—given annually to honor the author or authors of the year's outstanding monograph, article, or original paper in the field of acquisitions, collection development, and related areas of resource development in libraries—was given to Richard Meyer, dean and director of libraries at the Georgia Institute of Technology, for "A Tool to Assess Journal Price Discrimination" published in *College & Research Libraries* (*C&RL*) vol. 62, pp. 269–288. Meyer is one of the first researchers to apply empirical data to a major question in collection development. He builds on previous research, and uses sophisticated analysis to answer the question.

Association of College and Research Libraries

Another award, given by the Association of College and Research Libraries (ACRL) annually, but not always for research, was given for research in 2002. The **K. G. Saur Award for the Most Outstanding Article in** *College & Research Libraries* went to Susan Davis Herring for "Faculty Acceptance of the World Wide Web for Student Research" in the May 2001 issue of *C&RL*. The award committee noted that Herring's article "has implications for information literacy instruction, faculty course assignments, and students' ability to do effective research." The cash award of $500 is funded by K. G. Saur Publishing Company.

Library and Information Technology Association

Frederick G. Kilgour Award (with OCLC) ($2,000 plus expense-paid trip to ALA Annual Conference)
Winner: Carol C. Kuhlthau, School of Communications, Information, and Library Studies, Rutgers University
Rationale: Kuhlthau's research has led to the development of the Information Search Process (ISP) model that describes the stages a searcher goes through while seeking information. Her ISP model is among the most highly cited works in library and information science and it is one of the conceptualizations most often used by library and information science researchers. Her work carries on the tradition of Kilgour in its recognition of the centrality of the user in the development of responsive information systems.

American Society for Information and Technology (ASIS&T)

ASIS&T Award for Research in Information Science

http://www.asis.org/awards/research.htm
Winner: Carol Tenopir, School of Information Services, University of Tennessee, Knoxville
Rationale: Tenopir is an internationally known researcher with a history of innovative and influential work on databases, online searching, scholarly publishing, and other topics central to the interests of ASIS&T members.

ASIS&T/UMI Doctoral Dissertation Award

http://www.asis.org/awards/docdissumi.htm
Winner: Pamela Savage Knepshield
Project: "Mental Models: Issues in Construction, Congruency, and Cognition"

Pratt-Severn Best Student Research Paper Award

http://www.asis.org/awards/stdresearch.htm
Winner: Elizabeth Zogby, Drexel University
Project: "Representing Oral History: Challenges and Opportunities for Content-Based Retrieval"

Association for Library and Information Science Education (ALISE)

ALISE Methodology Paper Award

Winners: Lisa M. Given and Hope A. Olson
Project: "Data Preparation Using the Principles of Knowledge Organization: A Guiding Model for Quantitative, Qualitative, and Textual Research Methodologies"

ALISE–Bohdan S. Wynar Research Paper Competition

Not given in 2002

Eugene Garfield–ALISE Doctoral Dissertation Award ($500 for travel expenses plus 2002 conference registration and membership in ALISE for 2001–2002)

Winner: Soo Young Rieh, Rutgers University
Project: "Information Quality and Cognitive Authority in the World Wide Web"
Winner: Bradley L. Taylor, University of Michigan
Project: "The Effect of Surrogation on Viewer Response to Expressional Qualities in Works of Art"

Grants That Support Research

All active grants are listed with amount of the grant, the URL for the grant (if available), and the 2002 winners. If the grant was not given in 2002, that fact is noted. General ALA grants are listed first, followed by units of ALA in alphabetical order, followed by other organizations in alphabetical order.

American Library Association

ALA Research Grant ($25,000)

Not given in 2002.

Carroll Preston Baber Research Grant ($7,500)
http://www.ala.org/alaorg/ors/baber.html
Winner: Ethelene Whitmire, University of Wisconsin–Madison
Project: "Faculty Research Productivity and Academic Library Resources and Services." This study will examine the relationship between those variables by using two data sets available from the National Center for Education Statistics, the National Study of Postsecondary Faculty, and the Academic Library Survey. The researcher will run a series of multiple regressions using SPSS software to test a theoretical model of the relationship between faculty productivity and library resources.

American Association of School Librarians (AASL)

AASL/Highsmith Research Grant ($5,000)
http://www.ala.org/aasl/awardapps/highsmith.html
Winners: Linda Jordan and Diane Stanley
Project: "Does Accelerated Reader Improve Children's Reading Ability and Achievement?"

Association of College and Research Libraries (ACRL)

ACRL/ISI Doctoral Dissertation Fellowship ($1,500)
http://www.ala.org/acrl/doctoral.html
Winner: Charlotte Ford, Indiana University
Project: "An Exploration of the Differences Between Face-to-Face and Computer-Mediated Reference Interactions"

Samuel Lazerow Fellowship for Research in Acquisitions or Technical Services in Academic and Research Libraries ($1,000)
http://www.ala.org/acrl/lazerow.html
Winner: Jeffrey Beall, University of Colorado at Denver
Project: To study the impact of bibliographic errors on user access to items in online catalogs

Coutts Nijhoff International Western European Study Grant (4,500 Euros)
http://www.ala.org/acrl/nijhoff.html
Winner: James P. Niessen, Rutgers University
Project: "German Acquisitions in Hungarian Research Libraries: Cooperative Collection Development in the 20th Century"

Young Adult Library Services Association (YALSA)

Francis Henne/YALSA/VOYA Research Grant ($500)
http://www.ala.org/yalsa/awards/hennewinner2001.html
Winner: Teri S. Lesesne, Sam Houston State University
Project: "Project H.E.A.R: Help Encourage At-Risk Readers"

American Society for Information Science and Technology (ASIS&T)

ISI/ASIS&T Citation Analysis Research Grant ($3,000)
http://www.asis.org/awards/citation.isi.htm

Winner: Chaomei Chen, Drexel University

Project: "Tracing the Transfer of Knowledge." The intention of the research is to provide a set of streamlined analytical and visualization tools to the communities of information science and related disciplines and practitioners in order to stimulate more studies of three currently peripheral areas of knowledge transfer.

ISI Information Science Doctoral Dissertation Proposal Scholarship ($1,500 plus $500 toward travel or other expenses)

http://www.asis.org/awards/dscholarisi.htm

Winner: Joan Bartlett, University of Toronto

Project: Bartlett's proposal, titled "Capturing, Modeling, and Utilizing Bioinformatics Expertise," will use a task-analysis-like technique to reduce the complexity of doing bioinformatics analyses so that genomics data can be exploited by the typical bench scientists who may not have computing or genomics expertise.

Association for Library and Information Science Education (ALISE)

OCLC/ALISE Research Grant ($10,000 each)

http://www.oclc.org

Winner: Jane Greenberg, University of North Carolina at Chapel Hill

Project: "Optimizing Metadata Creation: A Model for Integrating Human and Automatic Processes." Greenberg's research will develop a model to facilitate the most efficient and effective means of metadata production by integrating human and automatic processes. Three tiers of metadata will be explored: that created by resource authors, by catalogers, and by automatic processing tools. Protocols will be established for collaboration between resource authors and professionals and for integrating these human metadata generation processes with automatic processes.

Winner: Wonsik Shim, Florida State University

Project: "Reification of Information Seeking Habits." This study will investigate innovative and effective methods of collecting information about undergraduate students' information-use habits and factors affecting them. In addition to two existing data-collection methods, online surveys and case studies, the study will use personal digital assistants (PDAs) to collect the raw data relating to user information behaviors as they occur in the natural settings.

Winner: Lorna Peterson, University at Buffalo, SUNY

Project: "Operationalizing Barriers in Dissemination of African Research and Scholarship." Peterson's research seeks to operationalize and measure the barriers in the dissemination of indigenous African scholarship at a case-study level. The intended outcome is to move beyond assertion of the problem to a measurement of the problem. This research will assist with the preservation, access, and dissemination of African scholarship while presenting opportunities for additional research and solutions.

Research Grant Award (one or more grants totaling $5,000)

http://www.alise.org/nondiscuss/Research_grant.html

Not given in 2002.

Medical Library Association (MLA)

ISI/MLA Doctoral Fellowship ($2,000)
http://mlanet.org/awards/grants/doctoral.html
Not given in 2002.

MLA Research, Development, and Demonstration Project Grant
http://mlanet.org/awards/grants/research.html
Not given in 2002.

Special Libraries Association

Steven I. Goldspiel Memorial Research Grant (up to $20,000)
http://www.sla.org/content/memberservice/researchforum/goldspiel/index.cfm
Winner: Deborah Barreau, University of North Carolina, Chapel Hill
Project: "The New Information Professional: Vision and Practice." The purpose
of Barreau's project is to examine a number of questions about new roles for the
information professional within a specific corporate domain, the newspaper industry. Typical of special libraries, newspaper libraries exist to serve the parent
organization, and professionals must constantly struggle with how best to do this.

Number of Libraries in the United States and Canada

Statistics are from *American Library Directory* (*ALD*) *2002–2003* (Information Today Inc., 2002). Data are exclusive of elementary and secondary school libraries.

Libraries in the United States

Public Libraries	16,598*
Public libraries, excluding branches	9,445†
Main public libraries that have branches	1,379
Public library branches	7,153
Academic Libraries	3,480*
Junior college	1,082
Departmental	169
Medical	5
Religious	5
University and college	2,398
Departmental	1,546
Law	165
Medical	238
Religious	199
Armed Forces Libraries	329*
Air Force	92
Medical	13
Army	145
Medical	28
Navy	88
Law	1
Medical	14
Government Libraries	1,326*
Law	416
Medical	198
Special Libraries (excluding public, academic, armed forces, and government)	9,170*
Law	1,045
Medical	1,776
Religious	603

Note: Numbers followed by an asterisk are added to find "Total libraries counted" for each of the three geographic areas (United States, U.S.-administered regions, and Canada). The sum of the three totals is the "Grand total of libraries listed" in *ALD*. For details on the count of libraries, see the preface to the 55th edition of *ALD—Ed.*

† Federal, state, and other statistical sources use this figure (libraries *excluding* branches) as the total for public libraries.

Total Special Libraries (including public, academic, armed forces,
and government)   10,452
    Total law   1,627
    Total medical   2,272
    Total religious   1,126
Total Libraries Counted(*)   30,903

Libraries in Regions Administered by the United States

Public Libraries   28 *
    Public libraries, excluding branches   9 †
    Main public libraries that have branches   3
    Public library branches   19
Academic Libraries   35 *
    Junior college   7
      Departmental   3
      Medical   0
    University and college   28
      Departmental   22
      Law   2
      Medical   1
      Religious   1
Armed Forces Libraries   2 *
    Air Force   1
    Army   1
    Navy   0
Government Libraries   7 *
    Law   2
    Medical   2
Special Libraries (excluding public, academic, armed forces,
and government)   15 *
    Law   5
    Medical   2
    Religious   0
Total Special Libraries (including public, academic, armed forces,
and government)   23
    Total law   9
    Total medical   5
    Total religious   2
Total Libraries Counted(*)   87

Libraries in Canada

Public Libraries   1,684 *
    Public libraries, excluding branches   680 †

Main public libraries that have branches	123
Public library branches	1,004
Academic Libraries	328*
Junior college	80
Departmental	21
Medical	0
Religious	2
University and college	248
Departmental	202
Law	15
Medical	19
Religious	27
Government Libraries	346*
Law	23
Medical	5
Special Libraries (excluding public, academic, armed forces, and government)	1,227*
Law	118
Medical	224
Religious	32
Total Special Libraries (including public, academic, and government)	1,318
Total law	156
Total medical	248
Total religious	100
Total Libraries Counted(*)	3,585

Summary

Total U.S. Libraries	30,903
Total Libraries Administered by the United States	87
Total Canadian Libraries	3,585
Grand Total of Libraries Listed	34,575

Highlights of NCES Surveys

Public Libraries

The following are highlights from the E.D. Tab publication *Public Libraries in the United States: Fiscal Year 2000,* released in July 2002. The data were collected by the National Center for Education Statistics (NCES). For more information on NCES surveys, see the article "National Center for Education Statistics Library Statistics Program" in Part 1.

Number of Public Libraries, Population of Legal Service Area, Service Outlets

- There were 9,046 public libraries (administrative entities) in the 50 states and the District of Columbia in fiscal year (FY) 1999.
- Ninety-seven percent of the total population of the states and the District of Columbia had access to public library services, and 3 percent did not.
- Eleven percent of the public libraries served 72 percent of the population of legally served areas in the United States; each of these public libraries had a legal service area population of 50,000 or more.
- Eighty-one percent of public libraries had one single direct service outlet (an outlet that provides service directly to the public). Nineteen percent had more than one direct service outlet. Types of direct service outlets include central library outlets, branch library outlets, and bookmobile outlets.
- A total of 1,505 public libraries (17 percent) had one or more branch library outlets, with a total of 7,337 branches. The total number of central library outlets was 8,883. The total number of stationary outlets (central library outlets and branch library outlets) was 16,220. Nine percent of public libraries had one or more bookmobile outlets, with a total of 907 bookmobiles.

Legal Basis and Interlibrary Relationships

- Fifty-five percent of public libraries were part of a municipal government, 11 percent were part of a county/parish, 1 percent were part of a city/county, 5 percent had multijurisdictional legal basis under an intergovernmental agreement, 10 percent were nonprofit association or agency libraries, 3 percent were part of a school district, and 8 percent were separate government units known as library districts. Six percent reported their legal basis as "other."
- Seventy-five percent of public libraries were members of a system, federation, or cooperative service, while 22 percent were not. Three percent served as the headquarters of a system, federation, or cooperative service.

Operating Income and Expenditures

- Seventy-eight percent of public libraries' total operating income of about $7.1 billion came from local sources, 13 percent from state sources, 1 percent from federal sources, and 9 percent from other sources, such as monetary gifts and donations, interest, library fines, and fees.

- Nationwide, the average total per capita operating income for public libraries was $27.20. Of that, $21.13 was from local sources, $3.45 from state sources, 17 cents from federal sources, and $2.44 from other sources.
- Per capita operating income from local sources was under $3.00 for 10 percent of public libraries, $3.00 to $14.99 for 41 percent of libraries, $15.00 to $29.99 for 31 percent of libraries, and $30.00 or more for 18 percent of libraries.
- Total operating expenditures for public libraries were $6.6 billion in FY 1999. Of this, 64 percent was expended for paid staff and 15 percent for the library collection.
- Thirty-four percent of public libraries had operating expenditures of less than $50,000, 40 percent expended $50,000 to $399,999, and 26 percent expended $400,000 or more.
- Nationwide, the average per capita operating expenditure for public libraries was $25.25. The highest average per capita operating expenditure in the 50 states and the District of Columbia was $46.41 and the lowest was $11.00.
- Expenditures for library collection materials in electronic format were 1 percent of total operating expenditures for public libraries. Expenditures for electronic access were 3 percent of total operating expenditures.

Staff and Collections

- Public libraries had a total of 127,890 paid full-time-equivalent (FTE) staff in FY 1999, or 12.18 paid FTE staff per 25,000 population. Of these, 23 percent, or 2.7 per 25,000 population, were librarians with an MLS degree from an ALA-accredited program (ALA-MLS) and 10 percent were librarians by title but did not have an ALA-MLS. Sixty-seven percent of the staff were in other positions.
- Nationwide, public libraries had 747 million books and serial volumes in their collections, or 2.8 volumes per capita. By state, the number of volumes per capita ranged from 1.7 to 5.0.
- Public libraries nationwide had 30 million audio materials and 19 million video materials in their collections.
- Nationwide, public libraries provided 5.1 materials in electronic format per 1,000 population (e.g., CD-ROMs, magnetic tapes, and magnetic disks).

Library Services

- Nationwide, 92 percent of public libraries had access to the Internet. Eighty-three percent of all public libraries made the Internet available to patrons directly or through a staff intermediary, 5 percent of public libraries made the Internet available to patrons through a staff intermediary only, and 4 percent of public libraries made the Internet available only to library staff.

- Ninety-seven percent of the unduplicated population of legal service areas had access to the Internet through their local public library.
- Nationwide, 78 percent of public libraries provided access to electronic services.
- Total nationwide circulation of public library materials was 1.7 billion, or 6.4 materials circulated per capita. The highest circulation per capita in the 50 states and the District of Columbia was 12.4 and the lowest was 2.7.
- Nationwide, 14 million library materials were loaned by public libraries to other libraries.
- Nationwide, reference transactions in public libraries totaled 295 million, or 1.1 reference transactions per capita.
- Nationwide, library visits in public libraries totaled 1.1 billion, or 4.3 library visits per capita.

Children's Services

- Nationwide, circulation of children's materials was 612 million, or 36 percent of total circulation. Attendance at children's programs was 48 million.

Academic Libraries

The following are highlights taken from the E.D. Tab publication *Academic Libraries 1998,* released in July 2001.

Services

- In 1998, 3,658 of the 4,141 two-year and four-year degree-granting postsecondary institutions in the United States reported that they had their own academic library. Of these 3,658 academic libraries, 97 percent responded to the survey.
- In FY 1998 general collection circulation transactions in the nation's academic libraries at degree-granting postsecondary institutions totaled 175.4 million. Reserve collection circulation transactions totaled 40.7 million.
- In FY 1998 academic libraries provided a total of about 9.2 million interlibrary loans to other libraries (both academic libraries and other types of libraries) and received about 7.7 million loans.
- Overall, the largest percentage of academic libraries (42 percent) reported having 60 to 79 hours of public service per typical week. However, 38 percent provided 80 or more service hours per typical week during the academic year. The percentage of institutions providing 80 or more public-service hours ranged from 6 percent in less than four-year institutions to 75 percent in doctorate-granting institutions. Twenty libraries reported that they were open 168 hours a week (24 hours 7 days a week).
- Taken together, academic libraries reported a gate count of about 16.2 million visitors per typical week (about 1.6 visits per total FTE enrollment).
- About 2.1 million reference transactions were reported in a typical week.

- Over FY 1998 about 438,000 presentations to groups serving about 7.4 million were reported.

Collections

- Taken together, the nation's 3,658 academic libraries at degree-granting postsecondary institutions held a total of 878.9 million paper volumes (books, bound serials, and government documents) at the end of FY 1998.
- The median number of paper volumes held per FTE student was 53.7 volumes. Median volumes held ranged from 18.5 per FTE in less than four-year institutions to 119.8 in doctorate-granting institutions.
- Of the total paper volumes held at the end of the year, 43 percent (376 million) were held at the 125 institutions categorized under the Carnegie Classification as Research I or Research II institutions. About 55 percent of the volumes were at those institutions classified as either Research or Doctoral in the Carnegie Classification.
- In FY 1998 the median number of paper volumes added to collections per FTE student was 1.5. The median number added ranged from 0.7 per FTE student in less than four-year institutions to 2.9 in doctorate-granting institutions.

Staff

- There was a total of 96,709 FTE staff working in academic libraries in 1998. Of these, 30,041 (31 percent) were librarians or other professional staff; 38,026 (39 percent) were other paid staff; 270 (less than 0.5 percent) were contributed services staff; and 28,373 (29 percent) were student assistants.
- Excluding student assistants, the institutional median number of academic library FTE staff per 1,000 FTE students was 5.6. The median ranged from 3.6 in less than four-year institutions to 9.1 in doctorate-granting institutions.

Expenditures

- In 1998 total expenditures for libraries at the 3,658 degree-granting postsecondary institutions totaled $4.6 billion. The three largest expenditure items for all academic libraries were salaries and wages, $2.31 billion (50 percent); current paper and electronic serial subscription expenditures, $974.9 million (21 percent); and paper books and bound serials, $514.0 million (11 percent).
- The libraries of the 570 doctorate-granting institutions (16 percent of the total institutions) accounted for $2.92 billion, or 64 percent of the total expenditure dollars at all academic libraries at degree-granting postsecondary institutions.
- In 1998 the median total operating expenditures per FTE student was $301.25 and the median for information resource expenditures was $84.98.

Electronic Services

- In FY 1998, 84 percent of degree-granting postsecondary institutions with an academic library had access from within the library to an electronic catalog of the library's holdings, 95 percent had Internet access within the library, and 54 percent had library reference service by e-mail both within the library and elsewhere on campus. Ninety-two percent had instruction by library staff on the use of Internet resources within the library.
- In FY 1998, 44 percent had technology within the library to assist persons with disabilities and 34 percent of academic libraries had access to this service from elsewhere on campus. Sixty-five percent provided services to distance-education students.
- Almost three-fourths (71 percent) had computers not dedicated to library functions for patron use inside the library. Fewer institutions (12 percent) had video/desktop conferencing by or for the library within the library and 19 percent had access from elsewhere on campus. Seventeen percent had satellite broadcasting by or for the library within the library and 23 percent had access from elsewhere on campus.
- Just under one-third (30 percent) had electronic document delivery by the library to a patron's account or address from within the library.

State Library Agencies

The following highlights are from the E.D. Tab publication *State Library Agencies: Fiscal Year 2000,* released in November 2001.

Governance

- Nearly all state library agencies (47 states and the District of Columbia) are located in the executive branch of government. In three states (Arizona, Michigan, and Tennessee), the agency is located in the legislative branch.
- Of the state library agencies located in the executive branch, almost two-thirds (31 states) are part of a larger agency, most commonly the state department of education (12 states). Six other state library agencies have direct connections to education through their locations within departments or agencies that include *education, college, university,* or *learning* in their titles.

Allied and Other Special Operations

- State library agencies in 14 states reported having one or more allied operations. Allied operations most frequently linked with state library agencies are the state archives (ten states) and the state records management service (ten states). Expenditures for allied operations totaled $23.4 million, or 2.3 percent of total expenditures.
- State library agencies in 15 states contracted with public or academic libraries in their states to serve as resource or reference/information ser-

vice centers. State library agencies in 21 states hosted or provided funding for a state Center for the Book.

Electronic Services and Information

Electronic Networks, Databases, and Catalogs

- Almost all state library agencies (48 states and the District of Columbia) planned or monitored the development of electronic networks. State library agencies in 42 states and the District of Columbia operated electronic networks. State library agencies in 46 states and the District of Columbia supported the development of bibliographic databases via electronic networks, and state library agencies in 44 states and the District of Columbia supported the development of full-text or data files via electronic networks.
- Almost all state library agencies (49 states) provided or facilitated library access to online databases through subscription, lease, license, consortial membership, or agreement.
- State library agencies in 42 states and the District of Columbia facilitated or subsidized electronic access to the holdings of other libraries in their states through Online Computer Library Center (OCLC) participation. More than half provided access via a Web-based union catalog (30 states) or Telnet gateway (26 states).
- State library agencies in 46 states had combined expenditures for statewide database licensing of more than $32.4 million. Of these, Texas had the highest expenditure ($3.1 million) and South Dakota the lowest ($5,000). All state library agencies with such expenditures provided statewide database licensing services to public libraries in their states, and at least two-thirds provided statewide database licensing services to each of the following user groups: academic, school, and special libraries, library cooperatives, and other state agencies.
- More than two-thirds (68 percent) of the total expenditures for statewide database licensing were from state funds; 31.8 percent were from federal sources. Of the states reporting statewide database-licensing expenditures, 16 states funded this activity with state dollars only, 16 states used federal dollars only, and 13 states used multiple funding sources.

Internet Access

- All state library agencies facilitated library access to the Internet in one or more of the following ways: training or consulting state or local library staff or state library end users in the use of the Internet; providing a subsidy to libraries for Internet participation; providing equipment to libraries to access the Internet; providing access to directories, databases, or online catalogs; and managing gopher/Web sites, file servers, bulletin boards, or listservs.
- Nearly all state library agencies (48 states) had Internet workstations available for public use, ranging in number from 2 to 4 (17 states); 5 to 9

(14 states); 10 to 19 (seven states); 20 to 29 (seven states); and 30 or more (three states). Louisiana reported the largest number of public-use Internet terminals (53).

- State library agencies in 32 states and the District of Columbia were applicants to the Universal Service Program (E-rate discount) established by the Federal Communications Commission under the Telecommunications Act of 1996 (P.L. 104-104).

Library Development Services

Services to Public Libraries

- All state library agencies provided the following types of services to public libraries: administration of Library Services and Technology Act (LSTA) grants; collection of library statistics; continuing education programs; and library planning, evaluation, and research. Nearly all state library agencies (49 to 50) provided consulting services, library legislation preparation or review, and review of technology plans for the E-rate discount program.
- Services to public libraries provided by more than three-quarters of state library agencies (41 to 47) were administration of state aid, interlibrary loan referral services, literacy program support, reference referral services, state standards or guidelines, statewide public relations or library promotion campaigns, and summer reading program support. About three-quarters of state library agencies (38) provided union list development.
- Two-thirds of state library agencies (33) provided OCLC Group Access Capability (GAC).
- Twelve state library agencies reported accreditation of public libraries, and 22 reported the certification of public librarians.

Services to Academic Libraries

- More than three-quarters of state library agencies (39 to 43) provided the following services to academic libraries: administration of LSTA grants, continuing education, and interlibrary loan referral services.
- More than two-thirds of state library agencies (36) provided reference referral services, 30 agencies provided consulting services, and 31 agencies provided union list development.
- No state library agency accredited academic libraries; only the state library agency of Washington State reported the certification of academic librarians.

Services to School Library Media Centers

- More than three-quarters of state library agencies provided continuing education (39 agencies) or interlibrary loan referral services (41 agencies) to school library media centers (LMCs).
- At least two-thirds of state library agencies provided administration of LSTA grants (35 agencies) or reference referral services (34 agencies) to

LMCs, and more than half of the agencies (30) provided consulting services.

- No state library agency accredited LMCs or certified LMC librarians.

Services to Special Libraries

- More than three-quarters of state library agencies (40 to 42) served special libraries through administration of LSTA grants, continuing education, and interlibrary loan referral.
- More than two-thirds of state library agencies (37) provided reference referral services to special libraries. About two-thirds provided consulting services (34 agencies) or union list development (33 agencies). More than half of state library agencies (26) provided library planning, evaluation, and research.
- Only the Nebraska state library agency accredited special libraries, and only Indiana, Nebraska, and Washington State reported certification of librarians of special libraries.

Services to Systems

- About two-thirds of state library agencies (33 to 36) provided the following services to library systems: administration of LSTA grants; consulting services; continuing education; interlibrary loan referral; library legislation preparation or review; and library planning, evaluation, and research.
- More than half of state library agencies (26 to 29) served library systems through administration of state aid, collection of library statistics, reference referral, state standards or guidelines, statewide public relations or library promotion campaigns, union list development, and review of technology plans for the E-rate discount program.
- Six state library agencies reported accreditation of library systems, and five reported certification of systems librarians.

Service Outlets

- State library agencies reported a total of 151 service outlets—53 main or central outlets, 77 other outlets (excluding bookmobiles), and 21 bookmobiles. The user groups receiving library services through these outlets, and the number of outlets serving them, included the general public (106 outlets), state government employees (101 outlets), blind and physically handicapped individuals (58 outlets), residents of state correctional institutions (34 outlets), and residents of other state institutions (22 outlets).

Collections

- The number of books and serial volumes held by state library agencies totaled 25.6 million. Three state library agencies had book and serial volumes of more than 2 million each: Tennessee and New York had 2.5 million volumes each, and Michigan had 2.3 million volumes. The number of book and serial volumes held by other state library agencies were

1,000,000 to 1,999,999 (four states); 500,000 to 999,999 (ten states); 200,000 to 499,999 (ten states); 100,000 to 199,999 (nine states); 50,000 to 99,999 (seven states); and under 50,000 (six states). The state library agencies in Maryland and the District of Columbia do not maintain collections.

- The number of serial subscriptions held by state library agencies totaled more than 98,000, with New York and Indiana holding the largest number (more than 11,000 each), followed by Connecticut (more than 10,000). The number of serial subscriptions held by other state library agencies were 5,000 to 9,999 (three states); 2,000 to 4,999 (five states); 1,000 to 1,999 (11 states); 500 to 999 (13 states); 100 to 499 (11 states), and under 100 (three states). The state library agencies in Maryland and the District of Columbia do not maintain collections.

Staff

- The total number of budgeted FTE positions in state library agencies was 4,053. Librarians with ALA-MLS degrees accounted for almost 1,262 of these positions, or 31.1 percent of total FTE positions; other professionals accounted for 18.8 percent of total FTE positions; and other paid staff accounted for 50 percent. Rhode Island reported the largest percentage (55 percent) of ALA-MLS librarians, and Virginia reported the smallest (12.5 percent).
- Most of the budgeted FTE positions (56.9 percent) were in library services; 16.5 percent were in library development; 11.5 percent were in administration; and 15.1 percent were in other services such as allied operations. More than two-thirds of the library development positions were for public library development.

Income

- State library agencies reported a total income of more than $1 billion in FY 2000. Most income was from state sources (84.6 percent), followed by federal sources (13.7 percent) and other sources (1.8 percent).
- State library agency income from state sources totaled $872.9 million, with more than two-thirds ($592.4 million) designated for state aid to libraries. In ten states, more than 75 percent of the state library agency income from state sources was designated for state aid to libraries, with Massachusetts having the largest percentage (96.8 percent). Six states (Hawaii, Idaho, New Hampshire, South Dakota, Vermont, and Wyoming) and the District of Columbia targeted no state funds for aid to libraries.
- Federal income totaled $141.1 million, with 94.7 percent from LSTA grants.

Expenditures

- State library agencies reported total expenditures of more than $1 billion in FY 2000. More than four-fifths (84.6 percent) of these expenditures were from state funds, followed by federal funds (14 percent) and funds from other sources (1.4 percent).

- In six states, more than 90 percent of total expenditures were from state sources. These states were Massachusetts (95.3 percent), Georgia (93.6 percent), Maryland (92.7 percent), New York (92.2 percent), and Rhode Island and Pennsylvania (91 percent each). The District of Columbia had the smallest percentage of expenditures from state sources (47.4 percent), followed by Utah (57.5 percent).

- Financial assistance to libraries accounted for 68.6 percent of total expenditures of state library agencies, and more than two-thirds of such expenditures were targeted to individual public libraries (46.9 percent) and public library systems (21.6 percent). Most of these expenditures were from state sources (87.9 percent); 11.9 percent were from federal sources.

- Thirteen state library agencies reported expenditures for allied operations. These expenditures totaled $23.4 million and accounted for 2.3 percent of total expenditures of state library agencies. Of states reporting such expenditures, Virginia reported the highest expenditure ($5.1 million) and West Virginia the lowest ($12,000).

- Thirty-five state library agencies had a combined total of $21.9 million in grants and contracts expenditures to assist public libraries with state or federal education reform initiatives. The area of adult literacy and family literacy accounted for 85 percent of such expenditures, and prekindergarten learning accounted for 15 percent. Expenditures were focused exclusively on prekindergarten learning projects in five states (Kentucky, Louisiana, Maryland, North Carolina, and Vermont) and exclusively on adult literacy and family literacy projects in eight states (California, Illinois, Indiana, Michigan, New Jersey, Rhode Island, West Virginia, and Wyoming).

Library Acquisition Expenditures, 2001–2002: U.S. Public, Academic, Special, and Government Libraries

The information in these tables is taken from *American Library Directory* (*ALD*) *2002–2003* (Information Today Inc., 2002). The tables report acquisition expenditures by public, academic, special, and government libraries.

The total number of libraries in the United States and in regions administered by the United States listed in this 55th edition of *ALD* is 30,990, including 16,626 public libraries, 3,515 academic libraries, 9,185 special libraries, and 1,333 government libraries.

Understanding the Tables

Number of libraries includes only those U.S. libraries in *ALD* that reported annual acquisition expenditures (3,862 public libraries, 1,751 academic libraries, 486 special libraries, 165 government libraries). Libraries that reported annual income but not expenditures are not included in the count. Academic libraries include university, college, and junior college libraries. Special academic libraries, such as law and medical libraries, that reported acquisition expenditures separately from the institution's main library are counted as independent libraries.

The amount in the *total acquisition expenditures* column for a given state is generally greater than the sum of the categories of expenditures. This is because the total acquisition expenditures amount also includes the expenditures of libraries that did not itemize by category.

Figures in *categories of expenditure* columns represent only those libraries that itemized expenditures. Libraries that reported a total acquisition expenditure amount but did not itemize are only represented in the total acquisition expenditures column.

Table 1 / Public Library Acquisition Expenditures

State	Number of Libraries	Total Acquisition Expenditures	Books	Other Print Materials	Periodicals/ Serials	Manuscripts & Archives	AV Equipment	AV Materials	Microforms	Electronic Reference	Preservation
							Categories of Expenditure (in U.S. dollars)				
Alabama	52	8,860,491	4,077,358	46,708	404,074	0	201,042	258,946	209,380	2,917,854	1,600
Alaska	22	1,203,587	603,997	12,032	188,186	0	11,779	54,081	7,500	61,628	2,420
Arizona	41	16,077,083	10,813,687	434,585	1,521,127	0	752,498	11,200	84,197	1,708,049	93,187
Arkansas	34	5,775,696	2,719,295	12,200	265,477	250	94,204	73,300	48,124	922,404	11,200
California	122	91,118,569	44,536,189	1,188,702	7,194,248	50,422	2,934,287	4,009,930	2,109,838	7,191,753	342,921
Colorado	50	37,503,543	14,184,094	4,928	1,431,452	0	102,824	988,320	76,143	1,300,154	9,884
Connecticut	112	16,792,912	7,452,710	682,027	1,092,229	5,400	472,054	342,608	174,165	1,211,401	84,969
Delaware	7	859,237	630,925	5,000	67,590	2,000	41,300	11,000	20,500	15,422	3,500
District of Columbia	3	13,877,283	1,582	1,539	466	0	0	0	0	0	0
Florida	81	51,425,680	27,506,848	651,581	4,344,259	41,424	1,980,429	948,996	277,202	2,621,570	39,411
Georgia	37	22,266,380	9,702,291	0	304,034	720	296,493	82,260	74,418	425,843	24,184
Hawaii	1	3,174,613	2,577,776	0	261,194	0	0	0	72,873	262,770	0
Idaho	34	2,549,794	965,702	37,756	79,691	0	53,555	51,053	9,356	538,003	2,829
Illinois	262	65,441,070	20,773,099	173,089	2,351,770	7,775	1,030,889	2,387,026	285,370	4,641,889	51,919
Indiana	114	58,721,709	16,469,740	139,250	2,190,386	0	947,541	2,495,396	322,767	1,543,059	188,482
Iowa	188	11,699,732	5,139,692	204,545	757,052	2,555	454,595	292,953	42,880	951,017	3,219
Kansas	95	9,911,575	5,999,182	101,239	1,532,744	450	682,318	94,670	61,631	600,558	1,700
Kentucky	58	10,090,316	4,134,448	32,021	285,039	0	356,640	225,449	56,492	438,290	9,851
Louisiana	35	10,929,389	6,412,040	55,258	1,135,766	1,300	175,004	539,738	70,551	120,939	15,300
Maine	67	2,227,217	1,472,864	5,643	239,060	950	89,276	50,108	18,488	152,028	6,543
Maryland	23	27,035,599	14,387,075	3,500	685,582	0	254,800	1,195,679	115,170	1,399,161	500
Massachusetts	164	27,379,577	14,118,097	522,818	2,319,082	8,885	1,247,307	588,346	173,070	959,628	18,110
Michigan	187	29,380,667	15,085,319	230,308	1,931,470	3,000	1,216,796	665,185	167,058	1,591,989	41,436
Minnesota	75	19,014,088	11,074,173	3,725,714	410,789	0	378,478	1,119,437	2,649	802,217	2,825
Mississippi	29	4,477,506	1,818,217	8,852	216,498	0	91,496	73,802	25,064	1,274,123	3,281

State											
Missouri	70	27,361,516	14,945,586	53,679	2,068,853	0	770,329	1,725,413	470,894	2,595,016	53,175
Montana	30	1,647,748	1,155,971	2,253	119,788	6,500	545	36,580	4,746	72,960	51,738
Nebraska	66	5,318,108	2,969,689	6,921	374,495	200	21,476	201,437	37,982	667,403	7,256
Nevada	8	11,311,699	722,556	67,181	153,696	0	24,000	3,660,600	72,752	208,500	3,000
New Hampshire	104	3,507,559	1,653,579	33,925	154,336	0	62,624	86,278	1,957	116,783	5,700
New Jersey	149	29,153,784	19,485,299	104,777	2,587,042	5,200	690,371	1,124,079	364,281	1,769,710	31,975
New Mexico	21	2,645,892	1,230,891	22,049	44,536	875	10,515	19,636	6,699	151,851	3,500
New York	283	65,986,187	37,394,501	374,818	5,172,239	8,500	1,313,906	1,668,125	545,468	4,226,718	114,782
North Carolina	68	16,966,778	5,354,735	20,248	496,758	7,643	141,405	295,825	113,321	468,193	4,463
North Dakota	20	1,435,667	645,918	70,085	154,535	0	32,300	21,084	12,794	125,751	1,500
Ohio	136	128,131,692	42,699,516	1,441,722	8,376,616	17,787	4,309,399	2,713,195	1,754,044	4,859,375	973,613
Oklahoma	25	6,427,510	2,040,530	6,692	1,034,947	0	124,246	290,280	17,522	253,697	6,001
Oregon	65	14,607,594	8,002,093	14,446	1,399,503	0	1,439,909	534,916	4,938	869,817	94,522
Pennsylvania	206	30,924,570	12,921,032	82,373	1,237,858	10,500	510,506	624,390	662,366	875,166	112,390
Rhode Island	23	3,484,665	1,945,870	2,000	215,523	750	40,905	204,606	27,192	587,410	9,001
South Carolina	29	12,855,418	8,069,081	43,746	1,068,526	1,000	594,905	904,433	300,012	794,168	26,635
South Dakota	30	1,882,831	1,268,711	1,268	248,827	530	26,473	48,622	29,310	259,664	646
Tennessee	49	9,740,692	6,664,412	47,403	904,017	11,000	170,587	401,924	24,934	879,853	78,317
Texas	195	32,591,673	17,869,986	347,653	3,526,566	1,000	656,734	772,460	284,532	1,626,071	54,527
Utah	17	15,615,264	6,385,918	8,708	642,002	0	1,495,460	600,254	21,800	575,568	19,400
Vermont	70	1,227,075	790,865	8,075	43,557	120	1,600	32,840	454	27,506	1,125
Virginia	62	19,859,514	10,980,307	76,221	1,284,331	162,664	318,578	833,496	171,386	900,764	521,992
Washington	33	15,611,700	6,480,615	218,935	432,157	0	340,841	1,094,661	1,503	665,842	113,261
West Virginia	27	3,050,082	2,098,278	192,113	191,114	0	17,832	74,366	13,100	135,462	12,972
Wisconsin	166	18,386,402	9,551,712	480,276	2,369,703	0	1,141,809	720,149	111,656	592,745	14,853
Wyoming	15	1,477,122	354,028	0	46,014	1,060	1,000	2,595	280	56,810	1,589
Northern Marianas	1	46,100	42,100	0	4,000	0	0	0	0	0	0
U.S. Virgin Islands	1	8,000	7,000	0	1,000	0	0	0	0	0	0
Total	3,862	1,029,056,155	466,387,179	12,006,862	65,561,804	360,460	28,123,860	35,251,727	9,560,809	58,014,552	3,277,204
Estimated % of Acquisition Expenditures			45.32	1.17	6.37	0.04	2.73	7.56	0.93	5.64	0.32

Table 2 / Academic Library Acquisition Expenditures

State	Number of Libraries	Total Acquisition Expenditures	Books	Other Print Materials	Periodicals/ Serials	Manuscripts & Archives	AV Equipment	AV Materials	Microforms	Electronic Reference	Preservation
Alabama	29	17,992,419	3,248,366	116,217	10,266,841	2,000	94,298	3,428	250,717	632,093	200,108
Alaska	5	1,949,349	540,099	35,748	702,989	0	17,549	0	76,501	351,604	84,526
Arizona	17	6,508,733	1,755,567	239,022	2,714,766	14,111	77,985	72,182	82,423	1,489,485	58,192
Arkansas	18	8,700,408	1,684,307	81,903	5,509,706	3,891	63,784	47,388	197,298	700,093	143,120
California	115	103,245,701	18,473,496	1,871,878	33,744,694	1,728	812,345	321,515	1,314,614	7,855,329	1,361,332
Colorado	22	19,072,773	3,933,979	31,151	10,120,099	0	18,236	7,695	127,798	703,306	164,891
Connecticut	27	34,437,022	8,396,028	60,070	14,132,225	1,000	93,471	82,947	201,112	1,450,180	217,759
Delaware	4	481,961	154,000	33,000	88,955	0	0	0	18,506	47,500	0
District of Columbia	13	22,306,085	2,529,542	816,226	8,122,286	20,531	39,058	634	199,306	896,016	193,041
Florida	46	50,040,856	13,494,365	1,890,017	18,575,037	8,165	343,362	222,909	7,090,764	5,863,471	702,132
Georgia	48	33,919,648	8,695,728	186,867	17,911,293	3,200	122,436	64,790	887,546	3,036,176	517,392
Hawaii	9	7,338,027	1,834,717	300	4,391,070	0	13,200	4,230	42,740	218,835	25,100
Idaho	8	7,359,919	1,885,976	88,976	4,772,769	500	59,924	1,489	107,793	280,118	162,359
Illinois	73	78,022,115	18,813,826	1,405,082	33,710,476	22,286	447,123	140,432	750,814	3,832,782	2,166,124
Indiana	35	30,665,923	7,163,420	0	18,311,505	1,096,796	173,947	36,507	228,521	1,670,761	263,811
Iowa	38	18,473,015	4,959,237	318,854	10,340,099	3,675	85,433	87,836	342,906	1,339,734	189,820
Kansas	33	10,701,713	2,689,006	7,382	5,588,838	5,548	20,151	47,960	116,454	913,346	203,063
Kentucky	30	27,875,368	6,795,695	67,023	16,061,718	36,117	92,979	87,100	893,482	1,941,943	557,421
Louisiana	20	15,913,489	2,185,443	245,475	7,655,074	8,070	60,048	5,460	159,265	606,483	77,485
Maine	13	7,417,924	1,768,465	0	4,210,193	10,247	29,418	3,500	145,998	534,496	181,879
Maryland	37	27,301,512	6,295,385	76,351	12,767,693	5,400	361,323	5,290	458,851	2,069,153	413,429
Massachusetts	61	79,219,101	12,282,076	1,157,694	31,842,460	5,000	402,597	124,281	1,157,785	5,714,251	623,431
Michigan	61	52,130,178	14,423,581	361,300	27,798,817	47,587	714,851	42,134	498,866	4,891,302	562,871
Minnesota	27	22,473,087	4,147,009	403,126	5,179,587	0	128,580	11,300	216,664	1,213,695	197,066
Mississippi	16	8,956,399	1,117,567	4,000	2,947,469	1,600	142,833	3,591	257,064	437,950	129,429
Missouri	48	35,121,377	4,657,766	1,325,020	10,996,482	4,502	64,386	107,097	363,559	3,621,266	435,968
Montana	13	5,324,261	1,201,548	100,653	3,227,872	21,252	46,121	154,998	137,918	112,237	17,825

Categories of Expenditure (in U.S. dollars)

State	Count									
Nebraska	20	12,526,450	2,293,657	35,862	4,012,705	40,300	69,459	26,624	117,864	521,285	99,288
Nevada	6	8,723,742	1,465,584	0	3,235,210	0	551	0	0	266,445	65,572
New Hampshire	13	7,892,159	1,345,340	43,833	3,809,475	0	20,897	9,804	50,815	782,585	79,198
New Jersey	27	31,241,323	7,334,459	513,533	8,856,262	318,962	83,944	46,939	1,071,990	1,681,724	1,035,268
New Mexico	19	15,364,337	7,608,980	107,839	5,860,659	0	30,941	11,514	127,597	939,747	239,678
New York	124	126,636,501	16,252,532	1,112,353	37,822,728	10,800	661,906	233,951	1,628,205	8,430,340	1,283,722
North Carolina	64	54,368,941	8,855,484	77,121	20,564,340	10,300	262,072	73,197	4,730,067	3,421,643	519,044
North Dakota	11	4,887,091	665,721	38,487	2,704,377	0	5,445	47,111	63,231	581,395	73,511
Ohio	65	57,759,717	9,001,701	202,688	16,103,136	19,400	447,260	154,289	740,575	3,574,038	670,818
Oklahoma	25	18,126,090	2,170,338	42,000	5,390,623	7,100	53,712	18,355	261,212	453,109	126,029
Oregon	30	17,081,415	3,689,991	144,794	5,676,474	0	157,280	64,954	274,751	1,311,616	187,682
Pennsylvania	90	88,478,646	14,935,245	247,755	25,073,607	27,671	341,097	330,724	1,443,008	5,459,536	805,857
Rhode Island	7	7,918,183	1,916,304	884,045	4,449,535	0	0	15,557	102,398	146,029	286,242
South Carolina	32	18,039,855	2,742,855	27,135	5,809,031	25,000	188,403	32,523	258,444	1,213,307	125,201
South Dakota	13	4,675,474	797,064		2,429,607	0	12,105	8,074	66,468	710,951	60,415
Tennessee	47	34,140,009	6,554,024	35,274	20,442,361	1,344	67,862	94,547	480,147	1,639,768	343,433
Texas	101	94,313,781	19,010,537	215,463	31,367,090	12,573	901,188	258,174	1,964,571	7,960,885	793,469
Utah	10	10,854,568	3,941,620	500	5,454,772	63,487	31,335	44,013	59,191	541,895	212,422
Vermont	15	7,921,061	1,907,425	21,040	4,170,371	200	63,810	13,500	72,691	695,866	149,306
Virginia	46	38,652,443	9,934,449	397,520	19,165,898	16,433	243,007	244,784	789,820	2,470,573	455,304
Washington	30	11,098,139	2,965,646	159,612	5,075,040	2,500	234,508	41,593	238,191	937,242	208,061
West Virginia	22	4,529,610	1,231,083	14,617	1,886,594	13,711	54,607	16,153	206,609	644,662	60,971
Wisconsin	46	23,804,754	8,773,678	33,060	10,510,012	30,107	241,819	172,029	593,312	2,143,600	302,200
Wyoming	5	3,841,379	565,057	1,000	2,749,871	0	26,628	18,107	0	66,805	71,137
American Samoa	1	5,000	1,000	0	3,000	0	0	1,000	0	0	0
Guam	3	799,652	235,221	0	424,781	0	12,090	15,350	43,210	7,500	0
Northern Marianas	1	117,399	74,000	0	14,340	0	9,564	11,495	0	8,000	0
Puerto Rico	11	6,299,909	794,600	7,545	2,276,247	500	51,000	10,000	20,111	593,693	6,400
U.S. Virgin Islands	1	56,484	0	0	0	0	0	0	0	0	0
Total	1,751	1,443,102,475	292,189,789	15,286,411	577,029,105	1,923,594	8,797,928	3,701,054	31,729,743	99,627,844	18,109,802
Estimated % of Acquisition Expenditures		20.25	1.06	39.99	0.13	0.61	1.27	2.20	6.90	1.25

Table 3 / Special Library Acquisition Expenditures

State	Number of Libraries	Total Acquisition Expenditures	Books	Other Print Materials	Periodicals/ Serials	Manuscripts & Archives	AV Equipment	AV Materials	Microforms	Electronic Reference	Preservation
Alabama	3	18,050	2,100	0	950	0	0	0	0	0	0
Alaska	2	15,030	4,350	850	7,200	0	630	1,500	0	500	0
Arizona	14	129,650	40,640	200	59,525	2,335	500	50	0	0	6,100
Arkansas	2	6,370	4,870	0	1,500	0	0	0	0	0	0
California	41	2,551,029	482,476	42,700	409,480	20,900	34,300	7,500	16,300	87,000	220,005
Colorado	10	81,520	25,350	0	6,898	0	4,355	4,000	250	250	1,800
Connecticut	11	192,292	51,374	383	42,436	47,500	702	0	1,000	11,000	19,239
Delaware	0	0	0	0	0	0	0	0	0	0	0
District of Columbia	12	1,351,606	198,317	100	212,325	200	500	0	30,000	46,100	14,000
Florida	23	435,934	121,281	6,250	107,053	6,750	7,000	4,000	5,300	8,500	10,100
Georgia	6	167,850	40,900	0	85,200	0	300	0	0	13,500	0
Hawaii	5	129,800	29,500	2,500	89,000	200	1,000	0	0	0	4,600
Idaho	1	4,000	1,000	0	500	500	1,000	500	0	0	500
Illinois	35	4,557,730	405,829	92,600	1,875,933	37,751	11,237	10,000	26,131	540,560	16,125
Indiana	6	63,200	31,150	0	3,500	0	0	0	1,000	1,000	700
Iowa	8	506,008	37,067	0	19,937	0	3,000	0	0	1,750	2,059
Kansas	6	87,375	27,200	0	43,375	100	3,000	0	7,500	5,050	850
Kentucky	3	27,267	14,857	0	9,406	0	469	0	0	0	1,500
Louisiana	3	8,500	6,900	0	0	0	0	0	0	0	0
Maine	5	31,809	6,873	6,000	5,700	1,000	0	0	0	0	1,424
Maryland	18	919,377	50,311	55,500	229,316	7,550	1,000	0	1,050	422,000	2,250
Massachusetts	23	1,528,995	481,387	31,465	217,260	5,500	480	16,000	500	333,000	56,667
Michigan	8	632,825	11,200	0	320,000	2,000	0	0	0	20,000	0
Minnesota	11	161,555	98,980	0	19,510	2,900	1,315	5,000	2,000	16,000	11,350
Mississippi	2	100,600	2,500	0	98,000	0	0	0	0	0	100

Missouri	13	3,597,106	358,159	2,900	3,020,955	720	500	600	204	57,458	97,527
Montana	4	111,800	21,050	3,000	62,750	4,000	0	0	7,000	14,000	0
Nebraska	6	30,678	17,026	500	6,800	2,000	1,500	0	2,102	0	0
Nevada	2	7,000	0	0	0	0	0	0	0	0	0
New Hampshire	7	510,100	15,000	4,000	2,500	5,000	8,000	0	2,000	0	15,000
New Jersey	13	834,762	69,900	4,000	69,250	12,000	6,550	6,500	2,000	24,200	24,000
New Mexico	4	85,900	37,900	4,000	18,000	0	0	0	500	21,000	2,500
New York	56	16,873,953	1,120,292	40,004	2,177,038	51,200	7,594	79,823	7,400	54,950	137,837
North Carolina	6	122,610	33,210	0	39,670	1,000	0	0	0	0	1,230
North Dakota	1	10,416	6,224	0	3,692	0	0	0	0	0	500
Ohio	28	1,541,286	269,869	7,078	840,375	2,900	16,495	26,935	5,154	79,067	21,689
Oklahoma	3	481,650	60,250	0	250,400	2,500	15,000	0	0	152,000	1,500
Oregon	6	79,000	19,200	0	46,750	0	0	0	50	13,000	0
Pennsylvania	19	890,242	57,212	25,600	267,337	0	625	2,000	1,100	53,136	50,650
Rhode Island	3	65,336	46,095	0	13,000	0	0	0	0	0	5,991
South Carolina	3	124,800	65,000	0	30,600	0	0	0	0	0	0
South Dakota	0	0	0	0	0	0	0	0	0	0	0
Tennessee	6	29,753	11,398	2,500	7,283	0	500	283	0	3,189	0
Texas	11	605,766	166,118	2,260	102,012	550	1,298	589	3,500	73,700	2,000
Utah	1	2,400	400	100	200	100	600	0	500	500	0
Vermont	3	8,100	400	0	0	0	0	0	0	0	500
Virginia	16	749,448	118,427	16,000	78,311	15,750	19,400	0	10,000	22,000	79,500
Washington	7	133,319	22,800	3,000	86,096	14,500	750	0	0	5,973	200
West Virginia	1	1,800	0	0	1,600	0	0	0	0	0	200
Wisconsin	8	238,265	77,250	200	111,870	2,000	1,595	1,000	0	43,900	50
Wyoming	0	0	0	0	0	0	0	0	0	0	0
Puerto Rico	1	2,500	0	0	0	0	0	0	0	0	2,500
Total	486	40,846,362	4,769,592	353,690	11,100,493	249,406	151,195	166,280	132,541	2,124,283	812,743
Estimated % of Acquisition Expenditures		11.68		0.87	27.18	0.61	0.37	3.49	0.32	5.20	1.99

Table 4 / Government Library Acquisition Expenditures

State	Number of Libraries	Total Acquisition Expenditures	Categories of Expenditure (in U.S. dollars)								
			Books	Other Print Materials	Periodicals/ Serials	Manuscripts & Archives	AV Equipment	AV Materials	Microforms	Electronic Reference	Preservation
Alabama	2	681,991	395,147	0	24,548	0	14,000	0	20,000	204,426	8,000
Alaska	2	72,050	14,000	5,000	32,050	0	10,000	0	0	11,000	0
Arizona	2	214,612	5,000	3,000	1,500	0	0	0	0	0	0
Arkansas	3	628,420	39,314	0	348,000	0	0	0	0	57,000	0
California	29	4,842,562	1,493,337	672,036	732,675	0	24,076	16,690	104,729	132,922	53,865
Colorado	4	204,800	52,500	4,000	58,500	0	0	0	0	37,800	0
Connecticut	0	0	0	0	0	0	0	0	0	0	0
Delaware	0	0	0	0	0	0	0	0	0	0	0
District of Columbia	3	2,707,784	36,000	0	20,000	0	0	0	37,000	23,000	5,000
Florida	7	548,000	141,400	700	201,900	3,000	0	28,500	15,000	10,000	500
Georgia	0	0	0	0	0	0	0	0	0	0	0
Hawaii	2	997,163	333,575	0	652,813	0	0	0	0	0	275
Idaho	1	60,000	4,000	0	36,000	0	0	0	10,500	0	0
Illinois	2	46,600	0	0	43,000	0	0	0	0	0	0
Indiana	2	119,000	50,000	0	0	0	0	0	0	0	0
Iowa	0	0	0	0	0	0	0	0	0	0	0
Kansas	2	679,857	300,640	231,927	101,169	0	0	0	0	37,556	8,565
Kentucky	0	0	0	0	0	0	0	0	0	0	0
Louisiana	5	4,114,686	13,745	0	45,440	0	0	0	0	16,000	0
Maine	2	390,161	4,000	0	75,000	0	0	0	0	6,000	0
Maryland	10	5,528,239	648,000	8,000	1,912,400	0	9,000	0	0	1,331,000	71,000
Massachusetts	8	919,668	128,072	0	0	0	0	0	0	0	0
Michigan	3	112,383	34,311	6,500	56,315	0	0	4,807	0	10,450	0
Minnesota	4	1,013,300	25,000	0	62,600	0	0	0	0	36,700	0

State											
Mississippi	2	132,500	2,500	0	0	0	0	0	0	0	0
Missouri	2	456,546	300,000	0	0	0	0	0	0	60,000	0
Montana	5	587,497	45,210	0	229,848	0	0	0	985	6,454	0
Nebraska	0	0	0	0	0	0	0	0	0	0	0
Nevada	3	899,028	650,893	0	68,217	0	4,549	0	4,878	121,127	3,651
New Hampshire	0	0	0	0	0	0	0	0	0	0	0
New Jersey	1	10,000	10,000	0	125,000	0	0	0	0	0	0
New Mexico	2	639,000	25,000	240,000	333,700	0	0	6,000	2,000	230,000	15,000
New York	12	2,509,210	1,286,770	0	25,800	0	2,630	29,000	2,900	84,948	15,300
North Carolina	3	481,100	407,000	300	0	0	0	0	5,000	7,000	0
North Dakota	0	0	0	0	0	0	0	0	0	0	0
Ohio	3	117,834	67,845	8,051	14,177	0	0	0	0	9,500	0
Oklahoma	1	5,695	565	0	1,830	0	0	0	0	3,300	0
Oregon	2	381,000	55,000	0	120,000	0	0	0	0	0	0
Pennsylvania	10	1,529,608	1,249,668	0	5,500	0	0	0	0	79,600	8,000
Rhode Island	2	890,598	666,034	0	58,272	0	0	111	4,000	162,181	0
South Carolina	3	56,212	13,839	0	36,848	0	250	0	0	5,275	0
South Dakota	0	0	0	0	0	0	0	0	0	0	0
Tennessee	3	290,679	0	0	0	140	0	4,759	0	0	0
Texas	5	625,147	404,643	0	74,794	0	0	0	0	1,500	128,072
Utah	2	249,700	30,200	0	211,500	0	0	0	0	2,000	6,000
Vermont	0	0	0	0	0	0	0	0	0	0	0
Virginia	4	254,947	50,350	0	30,233	0	0	4,663	0	5,400	109
Washington	1	10,000	3,000	0	7,000	0	0	0	0	0	0
West Virginia	0	0	0	0	0	0	0	0	0	0	0
Wisconsin	4	212,500	13,000	0	94,000	0	0	0	0	33,000	1,000
Wyoming	2	231,250	190,000	500	25,500	250	0	0	10,000	0	5,000
Total	165	34,451,327	9,189,558	1,180,014	5,866,129	3,390	64,505	94,530	216,992	2,725,139	329,337
Estimated % of Acquisition Expenditures			26.67	3.43	17.03	0.01	0.19	1.03	0.63	7.91	0.96

LJ Budget Report: A Precarious Holding Pattern

Norman Oder

Senior News Editor, *Library Journal*

Library usage rises in economic hard times, and that raises a paradox: The more libraries are needed, the less money there is to support them. Over the past five years, overall budgets have risen 33 percent (or nearly 7 percent each year), with materials budgets up 25 percent, and libraries are now in a precarious holding pattern.

According to *Library Journal*'s (*LJ*'s) annual budget survey, total budgets (see Table 1) will rise only 2.2 percent in fiscal year (FY) 2003, while salaries are expected to go up 2.9 percent. The average materials budget for FY 2003, will dip 2.1 percent, the first decline in the past five years. It's not that there is less demand for materials, but libraries have high fixed costs, mainly personnel, and the materials budget is often most vulnerable.

Of 1,800 libraries sent *LJ*'s Budget Survey 2002, 365 responded, a response rate of more than 20 percent. A notable segment reported continuing budget increases, often owing to a strong local economy or secure funding gained through a separate taxing district. For most, however, last year's wariness was borne out this year in local and state funding decreases. In several states, among them Arkansas, Colorado, and North Carolina, direct support for libraries—a relatively small percentage of total funding—declined. In Ohio, where large-scale state support has meant well-funded libraries, cuts were often painful. Elsewhere, reduced state revenues have in turn reduced aid to localities, which has had a ripple effect on libraries. Funding also has been pared in some cities, including New York, where the three library systems have absorbed a nearly 14 percent drop in FY 2002 and FY 2003.

Some Signs of Growth

Per capita funding for public libraries (PLs) continues to grow—it is projected to be $35.98 in FY 2003, a rise of more than $1 from the current $34.71. Three-quarters of respondents project an increase. Per capita circulation in FY 2002 was reported at 8.08, a slight increase from that reported in last year's survey, 8.06. However, respondents expect per capita circulation to rise to 8.45 in FY 2003.

Internet usage inside libraries rose even faster, by nearly 25 percent, and remote usage was up 45 percent in those libraries (about 60 percent) that measure such usage. Remote access grew fastest at larger libraries.

Staffing rose an average of 4.1 percent, but libraries reported a slight decrease in hours—a little less than 1 percent—to cope with diminished budgets. Several cut weekend or evening hours.

Adapted from *Library Journal*, January 2003

Table 1 / Projected Library Budgets (Averages) for Fiscal Year 2003*

Population Served	Total Budget 2002	Total Budget 2003	Change of Total Budget	Materials Budget 2002	Materials Budget 2003	Change of Materials Budget	Salary Budget 2002	Salary Budget 2003	Change of Salary Budget
Total Sample (weighted)	$6,101,000	$6,236,000	+2.21%	$847,000	$829,000	-2.1%	$3,734,000	$3,844,000	+2.9%
Under 10,000	168,000	171,000	1.79	25,000	25,000	0.0	102,000	105,000	2.94
10,000 to 24,999	660,000	680,000	3.03	88,000	90,000	2.27	399,000	414,000	3.76
25,000 to 49,999	1,774,000	1,868,000	5.30	277,000	285,000	2.89	1,078,000	1,132,000	5.01
50,000 to 99,999	2,343,000	2,433,000	3.84	309,000	311,000	0.65	1,419,000	1,481,000	4.37
100,000 to 499,999	6,719,000	6,926,000	3.10	984,000	971,000	-1.32	4,094,000	4,304,000	5.13
500,000 to 999,999	25,369,000	25,165,000	-0.80	3,661,000	3,495,000	-4.53	16,330,000	16,707,000	2.31
1 million or more	57,298,000	59,076,000	3.10	7,094,000	6,847,000	-3.48	33,785,000	33,785,000	0.00

*LJ mailed 1,800 questionnaires to public libraries in September 2002, with 365 responding, for an overall response rate of 20%.

Source: Library Journal Budget Survey, 2002

Larger Libraries Hit Hard

Larger libraries among survey respondents seemed to be suffering the most. Some libraries serving populations of 500,000 or more projected slight decreases in their total budgets, significant drops in their materials budgets (some 4 percent), and slight increases in salary money, the last a result of attrition and hiring freezes.

While the downward trend in fund raising reported last year continued, not all library segments suffered losses: the 34 largest libraries that reported—those serving populations of 500,000 or more—actually acknowledged a more than 15 percent increase in fund raising. Those libraries raised an average of $1.69 million.

Among libraries that reported a decline in fund raising, some of the same culprits as last year could be blamed: a slower economy and stock market losses. Libraries serving populations of 50,000 to 99,999 raised an average of $37,000, while the smallest libraries, serving populations under 10,000, raised an average of $5,000.

Grants and Gates

The survey respondents reported receiving an average of $273,900 in grants in the last fiscal year. State governments remained the largest source of grants (74 percent), followed by private foundations (40 percent), the federal government (34 percent), and individual gifts (13 percent). While two-thirds of the respondents said they had received Gates Learning Foundation monies, some 82 percent of that subset said the funds had run out, and only one-fifth of them had replaced the funds.

Of course, librarians have known that the Gates money is finite. In last year's report, more than half the respondents said they would try to increase their budgets, but this past year has not been the easiest in which to respond. Larger libraries—those serving populations of 500,000 or more—were more than twice as likely to have been able to replace their Gates subsidies.

Libraries reported they were most likely to spend grants on books and other materials (57 percent), technology/automation (50 percent), special projects (47 percent), staff/hours (26 percent), Internet/Web (24 percent), literacy programs/training (22 percent), and capital costs (16 percent).

Internet Costs

Internet-related expenditures continue to rise. Respondents reported that 4.6 percent of their budgets go to the Internet, a 28 percent increase from three years ago. Smaller libraries spent a disproportionate amount on new hardware, while large libraries spent more on staffing.

Only 20 percent of respondents—a number consistent with last year's survey—said they had to cut back on spending to pay for technology. Libraries expect their Internet expenditures for FY 2003 to be 7.9 percent above those of FY 2002.

The budget survey shows the importance of E-rate funds to libraries; 61 percent of respondents applied for the postal and telecommunications discounts, with an average award of $51,524. For the smallest libraries, the awards averaged $1,779 and for libraries serving populations of 25,000 to 49,999, the average was $5,809. Libraries serving 100,000 to 499,999 gained savings averaging $47,486, while libraries serving 500,000 or more expected to save an average of $294,194.

The Long View

Given the continued recession, few respondents were optimistic about the future. Still, library administrators taking the long view reminded us that library funding tends to flow in cycles; after lean years, the money has generally returned.

Local Progress Reports

Here is a fiscal snapshot of how public libraries are faring nationwide. Dollars represent total FY 2003 budget.

Serving fewer than 10,000

Danville-Center Township Public Library, IN ($530,000, up 5.2%)

With secure funding and a per capita budget over $54, this library west of Indianapolis stays open 63 hours a week. Its materials budget has remained static over five years, and some of that budget has been shaved to pay for technology.

Harwinton Public Library, CT ($105,000, up 2.4%)

Iconn.org, the state digital library, "has helped tremendously with reference costs." Now this northwest Connecticut library wants more affordable training for its staff. Per capita spending is over $20.

Langworthy Public Library, Hope Valley, RI ($110,000, down 10.9%)

Steady growth over five years has come to a screeching halt. Per capita spending remains over $31, but prospects are "very modest" for this library 24 miles from Providence.

Sebewaing Township Library, MI ($85,000, up 1.2%)

Situated near Lake Huron, this library relies heavily on local court fines from traffic, firearms, and hunting and fishing violations, as do many in Michigan. While "this is the only year [fines] haven't decreased," the future is insecure. Per capita spending is $18.

Serving 10,000–24,999

Ft. Morgan Public Library, CO ($478,675, up 15%)

The library's budget has been virtually static for the past five years, but sales tax revenues from a new Wal-Mart in this town 80 miles northeast of Denver will pay for the library's increased health and life insurance costs, as well as capital items added to the operating budget. Per capita spending is $35.

Milton-Union Public Library, OH ($535,538, down 23.2%)

The plunge in this budget comes about largely because of a building project the library paid for out of savings. Though state support for libraries has declined, this library outside Dayton has managed a static materials and salary budget, maintaining a solid $54 per capita figure.

Holbrook Public Library, MA ($295,238, unchanged)

Absorbing cuts of more than 10 percent in staff and hours, this library just 13 miles from Boston is bracing for less direct aid from the state as well as the ripple effect of lowered aid to municipalities; the forecast for

FY 2004 is a 10 percent budget cut. Per capita spending is $31.

Indianola Public Library, IA ($378,000, up 4.5%)

Circulation has increased 37 percent in four years in this town just south of Des Moines, and the library has been reasonably well supported. However, a city council efficiency committee recommendation that the library's materials budget be cut in half still hangs over the library's head. Per capita spending is over $29.

Serving 25,000–49,999

Indian Prairie Public Library, Darien, IL ($3.55 million, up 24%)

The library's expenditures increase 5 percent a year while its revenue increases 2 percent a year. Faced with a tax cap, this suburban Chicago library is tapping its reserves, which are projected to be exhausted by 2007. For the time being this library is still well funded, with a per capita budget over $64. The FY 2003 outlook includes an expansion project.

Moore Memorial Public Library, Texas City, TX ($875,000, up 4.2%)

With a per capita budget projected at $17, this library near Galveston struggles to maintain the status quo as property tax levels are being challenged and sales tax decreases are expected.

Saratoga Springs Public Library, NY ($4.1 million, up 4.9%)

Set in a college and resort town, the library enjoys a happy combination of strong public support, a stable tax base, and "district governance that protects us from radical budget cuts." Per capita spending will reach $84.

Shawano City-County Library, WI ($590,000, up 2.5%)

The future "looks bleak," reports this library in northeast Wisconsin, since it saw its 2003 budget hopes thwarted and since the state is in financial trouble. Per capita spending is $16.

Carnegie Public Library, Clarksdale, MS ($488,486, unchanged)

In this rural Mississippi Delta county, "people are leaving in droves." A trimmed materials budget—down 45 percent in five years—pays for technology. Per capita spending is $16.

Serving 50,000–99,999

Quincy Public Library, IL ($1.9 million, down 3.3%)

Located in west central Illinois, Quincy reports that it will increase fund raising and grant writing efforts to cover expected losses in state support. Per capita spending is under $14.

Pine Bluff/Jefferson County Public Library, AR ($1.04 million, up 2%)

Given that state aid has been cut by 90 percent, when this south Arkansas library added a branch this year it had to shorten hours at other locations to keep the system going. It has shifted its materials budget, cutting books and AV to offer electronic materials. Per capita spending is just over $12.

Parkersburg and Wood County Public Library, WV ($1.05 million, down 2.8%)

This library in the Mid-Ohio Valley has a stable base of funding, founded on property tax revenues from the city, county, and board of education, but the slight growth in the past few years is tailing off. Per capita spending nears $14.

Portsmouth Public Library, OH ($3 million, down 7.1%)

Salaries keep nudging up, but the library's total budget and materials budget have shrunk because of lowered state support, even as library use has increased. Internet usage in this south central Ohio library has nearly doubled in a year. Per capita spending is over $37.

Serving 100,000–499,999

New Orleans Public Library
($7.16 million, down 1.4%)

To make up for an increase in salaries and hospitalization costs, the library cut its materials budget more than 90 percent, from $265,000 to $25,258. The library will try to use state aid and foundation support to restore that money. Per capita spending is under $16.

Richland County Public Library, Columbia, SC
($17.11 million, up 3%)

State funding for all services has been cut by 35 percent over two years, with more cuts expected. County funding is stable, but there's little optimism for growth at *LJ*'s Library of the Year 2001. Gates money hasn't been replaced. Per capita spending is $40.

Pierce County Library System, WA
($15.35 million, up 4%)

A state ballot initiative on tax increases has made Washington State libraries wary; it reduces revenue to 1 percent inflation plus the value of new construction. The materials budget for this system outside Tacoma has gone down slightly. Per capita spending is $32.

Public Library of Johnston County and Smithfield, NC
($774,000, down 1.7%)

This rural library south of Raleigh has suffered cuts in state, county, and town funding; even more are expected in the next fiscal year. Per capita spending is under $7.

San Bernadino Public Library, CA
($2.52 million, unchanged)

The city's financial strictures for more than a decade cut into materials, staffing, and services, and influenced branch closings. Now

the library must face state budget cuts. With a per capita budget under $12, the outlook for future funding "is grim."

Serving 500,000–999,999

Ocean County Library, NJ
($25.1 million, up 8.7%)

With a per capita budget due to climb above $50, the library also gained a $13 million bond issue for expansion this past year. Growth in the tax base has allowed the library, located 60 miles south of New York City, to increase its budget even as the library tax has been lowered.

Carnegie Library of Pittsburgh
($22.2 million, up 0.5%)

"The fiscal situation can best be described as holding," reports the library, which did win a $14.5 million bond issue for renovations this past year. The library has trimmed building maintenance to help pay for technology. Per capita spending is $34.

Milwaukee Public Library
($21.7 million, up 0.9%)

The materials budget is shrinking a bit, though the library has managed to avoid cuts in hours or branch closings. The library may turn to fees for videos and other services in FY 2004. Per capita spending is over $36.

Cobb County Public Library, GA
($10 million, up 1%)

This northwest suburban Atlanta library is funded at less than $16 per capita, but a stable local fiscal situation should help it surmount state and regional economic trends.

San Jose Public Library, CA
($29.8 million, down 18%)

While the library has experienced steady growth over the past five years, the budget reduction anticipates a 10 percent cut in general fund revenues from the city, as well as a lowered materials budget after funding the new joint- use city-university library, opening this year. Per capita spending is over $32.

Serving 1 million or more

Phoenix Public Library
($30.6 million, down 0.3%)

The total budget has increased by 52 percent over five years, but it now faces a slowdown. The library did win a $33 million bond issue in 2001 for new branches and renovation. Per capita spending is $22.

San Diego Public Library
($36.7 million, up 11.9%)

The library's budget has increased nearly 90 percent over five years. While local funding is tight, the city council has agreed not to cut the library's operating budget unless a major reduction in tax revenues occurs. Per capita budget is $30. The city council has approved a $312 million expansion plan.

Fairfax County Public Library, VA
($27.8 million, up 6.5%)

The outlook for the next two fiscal years has not improved; revenue shortfalls are projected and all agencies in this suburban Washington, D.C., county have been asked to cut their budgets. Per capita spending is $27.

Chicago Public Library
($96.5 million, up 1.6%)

Library managers are looking for new funds to supplement a static materials budget. Per capita spending is over $33.

Las Vegas–Clark County Library District, NV ($52 million, up 3.2%)

The library's materials budget has more than doubled in five years, though budget expansion is tailing off. The library has to find new capital and operating funds to keep up with explosive local growth. Per capita spending is $36.

Price Indexes for Public and Academic Libraries

Research Associates of Washington
1200 North Nash St., No. 1112, Arlington, VA 22209
703-243-3399
World Wide Web http://www.rschassoc.com

Kent Halstead

A rise in prices with the gradual loss of the dollar's value has been a continuing phenomenon in the U.S. economy. This article reports price indexes measuring this inflation for public libraries, and for college and university academic libraries. (Current data for these indexes are published by Research Associates of Washington. See *Inflation Measures for Schools, Colleges and Libraries, 2001 Update.*) Price indexes report the year-to-year price level of what is purchased. Dividing past expenditures per user unit by index values determines if purchasing power has been maintained. Future funding requirements to offset expected inflation may be estimated by projecting the indexes.

A price index compares the aggregate price level of a fixed market basket of goods and services in a given year with the price in the base year. To measure price change accurately, the *quality* and *quantity* of the items purchased must remain constant as defined in the base year. Weights attached to the importance of each item in the budget are changed infrequently—only when the relative *amount* of the various items purchased clearly shifts or when new items are introduced.

Public Library Price Index

The Public Library Price Index (PLPI) is designed for a hypothetical *average* public library. The index together with its various subcomponents are reported in Tables 2 through 6. The PLPI reflects the relative year-to-year price level of the goods and services purchased by public libraries for their current operations. The budget mix shown in Table 1 is based on national and state average expenditure patterns. Individual libraries may need to tailor the weighting scheme to match their own budget compositions.

The Public Library Price Index components are described below together with sources of the price series employed.

Personnel Compensation

PL1.0 Salaries and Wages

PL1.1 *Professional librarians*—Median salary of professional librarians at medium and large size libraries. Six positions are reported: director/dean, deputy/

(text continues on page 461)

Note: Publication rights for the public and academic library price indexes reported here are for sale. The sale package consists of copyrights; computer software; written data collection, compilation, and layout instructions; and mailing lists. Interested parties are requested to call 703-243-3399.

Table 1 / Taxonomy of Public Library Current Operations Expenditures by Object Category, 1991–1992 estimate

Category	Mean	Percent	Distribution
Personnel Compensation			64.7
PL1.0 Salaries and Wages		81.8	
PL1.1 Professional librarians	44		
PL1.2 Other professional and managerial staff	6		
PL1.3 Technical staff (copy cataloging, circulation, binding, etc.)	43		
PL1.4 Support staff (clerical, custodial, guard, etc.)	7		
	100		
PL2.0 Fringe Benefits		18.2	
		100.0	
Acquisitions			15.2
PL3.0 Books and Serials		74.0	
PL3.1 Books printed	82		
PL3.1a Hardcover			
PL3.1b Trade paper			
PL3.1c Mass market paper			
PL3.2 Periodicals (U.S. and foreign titles)	16		
PL3.2a U.S. titles			
PL3.2b Foreign titles			
PL3.3 Other serials (newspapers, annuals, proceedings, etc.)	2		
	100		
PL4.0 Other Printed Materials		2.0	
PL5.0 Non-Print Media		22.0	
PL5.1 Microforms (microfiche and microfilm)	21		
PL5.2 Audio recordings (primarily instructional and children's content)	17		
PL5.2a Tape cassette			
PL5.2b Compact disk			
PL5.3 Video (TV) recordings (primarily books & children's content)	58		
PL5.3a VHS Cassette			
PL5.3b Laser disk			
PL5.4 Graphic image individual item use	2		
PL5.5 Computer files (CD-ROM, floppy disks, and tape)	2		
	100		
PL6.0 Electronic Services		2.0	
		100.0	
Operating Expenses			20.1
PL7.0 Office Operations		27.0	
PL7.1 Office expenses	20		
PL7.2 Supplies and materials	80		
	100		
PL8.0 Contracted Services		38.0	
PL9.0 Non-capital Equipment		1.0	
PL10.0 Utilities		34.0	
		100.0	100.0

Table 2 / Public Library Price Index and Major Component Subindexes, FY 1992 to 2001

1992=100 Fiscal year	Personnel Compensation		Acquisitions				Operating Expenses				Public Library Price Index^ (PLPI)
	Salaries and wages (PL1.0)	Fringe benefits (PL2.0)	Books and serials (PL3.0)	Other printed materials (PL4.0)	Non-print media (PL5.0)	Electronic services (PL6.0)	Office operations (PL7.0)	Contracted services (PL8.0)	Non-capital Equipment (PL9.0)	Utilities (PL10.0)	
1992	100.0	100.0	100.0	100.0	100.0	100.0	100.0	100.0	100.0	100.0	100.0
1993	102.5	104.8	102.0	102.9	75.3	101.9	99.2	102.6	101.8	101.5	101.6
1994	105.8	107.9	103.5	105.5	65.8	104.8	100.8	105.1	103.6	105.8	104.1
1995	110.5	110.6	105.6	107.7	64.8	108.5	102.6	107.7	105.7	103.8	107.3
1996	112.3	113.9	107.3	111.3	67.8	110.3	113.9	113.3	108.5	100.0	109.6
1997	114.6	116.1	111.1	118.5	69.5	110.3	113.3	114.1	110.3	113.7	112.7
1998	119.4	118.1	117.5	122.7	67.2	115.5	112.3	118.0	111.9	119.1	116.8
1999	123.6	121.4	118.0	125.7	68.8	119.2	110.4	121.4	113.5	107.7	118.9
2000	128.2	125.3	119.2	128.9	70.1	125.5	111.1	125.1	114.8	112.4	122.6
2001	133.3	128.1	118.3	132.9	72.1	131.2	116.9	130.5	116.6	148.4	128.8
1993	2.5%	4.8%	2.0%	2.9%	-24.7%	1.9%	-0.8%	2.6%	1.8%	1.5%	1.6%
1994	3.2%	3.0%	1.4%	2.5%	-12.6%	2.8%	1.6%	2.4%	1.7%	4.2%	2.5%
1995	4.4%	2.5%	2.1%	2.1%	-1.5%	3.5%	1.7%	2.5%	2.1%	-1.9%	3.0%
1996	1.6%	3.0%	1.6%	3.3%	4.7%	1.7%	11.1%	3.3%	2.6%	-3.6%	2.1%
1997	2.1%	1.9%	3.5%	6.5%	2.5%	0.0%	-0.5%	2.6%	1.7%	13.7%	2.9%
1998	4.2%	1.7%	5.7%	3.5%	-3.3%	4.7%	-0.9%	3.4%	1.4%	4.7%	3.6%
1999	3.5%	2.8%	0.4%	2.4%	2.3%	3.2%	-1.7%	2.9%	1.4%	-9.5%	1.8%
2000	3.7%	3.2%	1.0%	2.5%	1.9%	5.3%	0.6%	3.1%	1.2%	4.4%	3.1%
2001	4.0%	2.2%	-0.8%	3.1%	2.9%	4.5%	5.3%	4.3%	1.6%	32.0%	5.1%

^ PLPI weightings: See text.
Sources: See text.

457

Table 3 / Public Library Price Index, Personnel Compensation, FY 1992 to 2001

	Salaries and Wages							
1992=100	Professional librarians			Other professional & managerial (PL1.2)	Technical staff (PL1.3)	Support staff (PL1.4)	Salaries & wages index* (PL1.0)	Fringe benefits index (PL2.0)
Fiscal year	Medium size library~	Large size library~	Index^ (PL1.1)					
1992	100.0	100.0	100.0	100.0	100.0	100.0	100.0	100.0
1993	105.0	99.5	102.3	102.8	102.7	102.8	102.5	104.8
1994	109.2	102.7	106.0	105.7	105.7	106.0	105.8	107.9
1995	115.5	106.9	111.2	109.5	110.1	109.1	110.5	110.6
1996	113.7	108.9	111.3	112.9	113.2	112.1	112.3	113.9
1997	119.2	112.0	115.6	115.6	113.6	113.9	114.6	116.1
1998	123.2	118.2	120.7	121.3	118.1	117.9	119.4	118.1
1999	124.9	125.2	125.1	125.0	122.2	121.9	123.6	121.4
2000	133.2	126.6	129.9	131.2	126.3	126.4	128.2	125.3
2001	138.5	131.7	135.1	135.9	131.3	131.6	133.3	128.1
1993	5.0%	-0.5%	2.3%	2.8%	2.7%	2.8%	2.5%	4.8%
1994	4.0%	3.2%	3.6%	2.8%	2.9%	3.1%	3.2%	3.0%
1995	5.8%	4.1%	5.0%	3.6%	4.2%	2.9%	4.4%	2.5%
1996	-1.6%	1.9%	0.1%	3.1%	2.8%	2.7%	1.6%	3.0%
1997	4.8%	2.8%	3.9%	2.4%	0.4%	1.6%	2.1%	1.9%
1998	3.4%	5.5%	4.4%	4.9%	4.0%	3.5%	4.2%	1.7%
1999	1.4%	5.9%	3.6%	3.1%	3.5%	3.4%	3.5%	2.8%
2000	6.6%	1.1%	3.9%	5.0%	3.4%	3.7%	3.7%	3.2%
2001	4.0%	4.0%	4.0%	3.6%	4.0%	4.1%	4.0%	2.2%

~ medium size libraries have service areas from 25,000 to 99,999 population; large libraries, 100,000 or more.
^ Professional librarian salary weights: 50% medium libraries + 50% large libraries.
* Salaries and wages index weights: 44% professional librarians + 6% other professional + 43% technical staff +7% support staff.
Sources: See text.

Table 4 / Public Library Price Index, Books and Serials, FY 1992 to 2001

Books and Serials

1992=100	Books printed							Periodicals					Other serials (newspapers)		Books & Serials index** (PL3.0)	Other printed materials index (PL4.0)
	Hardcover		Trade paper		Mass market		Books printed index* (PL3.1)	United States		Foreign		Periodicals index~ (PL3.2)				
Fiscal year	Price^	Index (PL3.1a)	Price^	Index (PL3.1b)	Price^	Index (PL3.1c)		Price^	Index (PL3.2a)	Price^	Index (PL3.2b)		Price^^	Index (PL3.3)		
1992		100.0		100.0		100.0	100.0	$45.18	100.0	$117.71	100.0	100.0	$222.68	100.0	100.0	100.0
1993		101.5		102.1		103.4	101.6	48.12	104.0	125.70	105.1	104.1	229.92	103.3	102.0	102.9
1994		102.5		104.4		106.5	102.8	47.19	104.4	133.50	113.4	105.5	261.91	117.6	103.5	105.5
1995		103.9		107.1		108.8	104.3	48.36	108.8	143.78	122.6	110.5	270.22	121.3	105.6	107.7
1996		104.2		109.3		113.7	104.8	50.58	114.2	153.34	134.8	116.7	300.21	134.8	107.3	111.3
1997		107.1		116.1		126.7	108.3	52.76	118.9	164.46	144.5	122.0	311.77	140.0	111.1	118.5
1998	$12.55	114.0	$8.49	120.5	$3.40	135.5	115.0	54.79	123.3	174.05	153.2	126.9	316.60	142.2	117.5	122.7
1999	12.60	114.4	8.57	121.6	3.50	139.5	115.6	56.94	123.3	185.97	153.2	126.9	318.44	143.0	118.0	125.7
2000	12.73	115.6	8.81	125.0	3.57	142.3	117.0	58.90	123.3	196.37	153.2	126.9	324.26	145.6	119.2	128.9
2001	12.78	116.1	9.05	128.4	3.72	148.2	117.8	60.61	114.2	207.49	134.8	116.7	330.78	148.5	118.3	132.9
1993		1.5%		2.1%		3.4%	1.6%		4.0%		5.1%	4.1%		3.3%	2.0%	2.9%
1994		1.0%		2.2%		3.0%	1.2%		0.4%		7.9%	1.3%		13.9%	1.4%	2.5%
1995		1.4%		2.6%		2.2%	1.5%		4.2%		8.1%	4.7%		3.2%	2.1%	2.1%
1996		0.2%		2.1%		4.6%	0.5%		5.0%		10.0%	5.6%		11.1%	1.6%	3.3%
1997		2.8%		6.2%		11.4%	3.3%		4.1%		7.2%	4.5%		3.9%	3.5%	6.5%
1998		6.4%		3.8%		6.9%	6.2%		3.7%		6.0%	4.0%		1.5%	5.7%	3.5%
1999		0.4%		0.9%		2.9%	0.5%		0.0%		0.0%	0.0%		0.6%	0.4%	2.4%
2000		1.0%		2.8%		2.0%	1.2%		0.0%		0.0%	0.0%		1.8%	1.0%	2.5%
2001		0.4%		2.7%		4.2%	0.7%		-7.4%		-12.0%	-8.1%		2.0%	-0.8%	3.1%

^ Book and periodical prices are for calendar year. * Books printed index weights: 89.5% hardcover + 8.2% trade paper + 2.3% mass market.

~ Periodical index weights: 87.9% U.S. titles + 12.1% foreign titles.

^^ Other serials prices are for calendar year.

** Books & serials index weights: 82% books + 16% periodicals + 2% other serials.

Sources: See text.

Table 5 / Public Library Price Index, Non-Print Media and Electronic Services, FY 1992 to 2001

1992=100 Fiscal year	Microforms (microfilm) Index (PL5.1)	Audio recordings — Tape cassette Price^	Tape cassette Index (PL5.2a)	Compact disc Price^	Compact disc Index (PL5.2b)	Audio recordings index* (PL5.2)	Video — VHS cassette Price^	Index (PL5.3a)	Video index (PL5.3)	Graphic image (PL5.4)	Computer files (CD-ROM) Price^	Index (PL5.5)	Non-print media index* (PL5.0)	Electronic services index (PL6.0)
1992	100.0	$12.18	100.0			100.0	$199.67	100.0	100.0	100.0	$1,601	100.0	100.0	100.0
1993	104.3	11.73	96.3	$13.36	67.3	96.3	112.92	56.6	56.6	97.3	1,793	112.0	75.3	101.9
1994	107.9	8.20	67.3	14.80	74.6	67.3	93.22	46.7	46.7	108.4	1,945	121.5	65.8	104.8
1995	110.6	8.82	72.4	14.86	74.9	73.5	84.19	42.2	42.2	111.3	1,913	119.5	64.8	108.5
1996	128.0	7.96	65.4	16.43	82.8	70.1	83.48	41.8	41.8	114.5	1,988	124.2	67.8	110.3
1997	132.9	8.13	66.7	14.35	72.3	74.8	82.10	41.1	41.1	126.5	2,012	125.7	69.5	110.3
1998	138.9	8.31	68.2	12.65	63.7	70.3	72.31	36.2	36.2	129.1	2,007	125.4	67.2	115.5
1999	142.9	8.20	67.3	12.00	60.4	65.5	77.85	39.0	39.0	124.5	2,007	125.4	68.8	119.2
2000	145.6	8.20	67.3	12.00	60.4	63.9	80.00	40.1	40.1	142.7	2,037	127.2	70.1	125.5
2001	145.7	8.20	67.3			63.9	85.00	42.6	42.6	168.8	2,085	130.2	72.1	131.2
1993	4.3%		-3.7%			-3.7%		-43.4%	-43.4%	-2.7%		12.0%	-24.7%	1.9%
1994	3.5%		-30.1%		10.80%	-30.1%		-17.4%	-17.4%	11.4%		8.5%	-12.6%	2.8%
1995	2.5%		7.6%		0.04%	9.2%		-9.7%	-9.7%	2.7%		-1.6%	-1.5%	3.5%
1996	15.7%		-9.8%		10.60%	-4.6%		-0.8%	-0.8%	2.9%		3.9%	4.7%	1.7%
1997	3.8%		2.1%		-12.70%	6.6%		-1.7%	-1.7%	10.5%		1.2%	2.5%	0.0%
1998	4.5%		2.2%		-11.80%	-6.0%		-11.9%	-11.9%	2.1%		-0.2%	-3.3%	4.7%
1999	2.9%		-1.3%		-5.1%	-6.7%		7.7%	7.7%	-3.6%		0.0%	2.3%	3.2%
2000	1.9%		0.0%		0.0%	-2.5%		2.8%	2.8%	14.6%		1.5%	1.9%	5.3%
2001	0.1%		0.0%			0.0%		6.3%	6.3%	18.3%		2.4%	2.9%	4.5%

^ Prices are for immediate preceding calendar year, e.g., CY 1993 prices are reported for FY 1994.

* Audio recordings index weights: 50% tape cassette + 50% compact disk. Non-print media index weights: 21% microforms + 17% audio recordings +58% video + 2% graphic image + 2% computer files.

Sources: See text

Table 6 / Public Library Price Index, Operating Expenses, FY 1992 to 2001

1992=100 Fiscal year	Office Operations		Office operations index^ (PL7.0)	Contracted services index (PL8.0)	Noncapital equipment index (PL9.0)	Utilities index (PL10.0)
	Office expenses (PL7.1)	Supplies and materials (PL7.2)				
1992	100.0	100.0	100.0	100.0	100.0	100.0
1993	103.1	98.3	99.2	102.6	101.8	101.5
1994	107.3	99.2	100.8	105.1	103.6	105.8
1995	111.1	100.4	102.6	107.7	105.7	103.8
1996	117.8	112.9	113.9	111.3	108.5	100.0
1997	120.0	111.6	113.3	114.1	110.3	113.7
1998	123.1	109.5	112.3	118.0	111.9	119.1
1999	124.2	106.9	110.4	121.4	113.5	107.7
2000	127.8	106.9	111.1	125.1	114.8	112.4
2001	131.5	113.3	116.9	130.5	116.6	148.4
1993	3.1%	-1.7%	-.8%	2.6%	1.8%	1.5%
1994	4.1%	1.0%	1.6%	2.4%	1.7%	4.2%
1995	3.5%	1.2%	1.7%	2.5%	2.1%	-1.9%
1996	6.1%	12.4%	11.1%	3.3%	2.6%	-3.6%
1997	1.8%	-1.2%	-0.5%	2.6%	1.7%	13.7%
1998	2.6%	-1.9%	-0.9%	3.4%	1.4%	4.7%
1999	0.9%	-2.4%	-1.7%	2.9%	1.4%	-9.5%
2000	2.9%	-0.1%	0.6%	3.1%	1.2%	4.4%
2001	2.9%	6.0%	5.3%	4.3%	1.6%	32.0%

^ Office operations index weights: 20% office expenses + 80% supplies and materials.
Sources: See text.

(text continued from page 455)

associate/assistant director, department heads/coordinator/senior management, managers/supervisors, librarian non-supervisory, beginning librarian. Source: Mary Jo Lynch, *ALA Survey of Librarian Salaries*, Office for Research and Statistics, American Library Association, Chicago, IL, annual.

PL1.2 *Other professional and managerial staff* (systems analyst, business manager, public relations, personnel, etc.)—Employment Cost Index (ECI) for wages and salaries for state and local government workers employed in "Executive, administrative, and managerial" occupations, *Employment Cost Index*, Bureau of Labor Statistics, U.S. Department of Labor, Washington, DC.

PL1.3 *Technical staff* (copy cataloging, circulation, binding, etc.)—ECI as above for government employees in "Service" occupations.

PL1.4 *Support staff* (clerical, custodial, guard, etc.)—ECI as above for government employees in "Administrative support, including clerical" occupations.

PL2.0 Fringe Benefits

ECI as above for state and local government worker "Benefits."

Acquisitions

PL3.0 Books and Serials

PL3.1 *Books printed*—Weighted average of sale prices (including jobber's discount) of hardcover (PL3.1a), trade paper (PL3.1b), and mass market paperback books (PL3.1c) sold to public libraries. Excludes university press publications and reference works. Source: Baker & Taylor Books.

PL3.2 *Periodicals*—Publisher's prices of sales of approximately 2,400 U.S. serial titles (PL3.2a) and 115 foreign serials (PL3.2b) sold to public libraries. Source: *Serials Prices*, EBSCO Subscription Services, Birmingham, AL.

PL3.3 *Other serials* (newspapers, annuals, proceedings, etc.)—Average prices of approximately 170 U.S. daily newspapers. Source: Genevieve S. Owens, University of Missouri, St. Louis, and Wilba Swearingen, Louisiana State University Medical Center. Reported by Adrian W. Alexander, "Prices of U.S. and Foreign Published Materials," in *Bowker Annual*, R. R. Bowker.

PL4.0 *Other Printed Materials* (manuscripts, documents, pamphlets, sheet music, printed material for the handicapped, etc.)

No direct price series exists for this category. The proxy price series used is the Producer Price Index for publishing pamphlets and catalogs and directories, Bureau of Labor Statistics.

PL5.0 Non-Print Media

PL5.1 *Microforms*—Producer Price Index for micropublishing in microform, including original and republished material, Bureau of Labor Statistics.

PL5.2 *Audio recordings*

PL5.2a *Tape cassette*—Cost per cassette of sound recording. Source: Dana Alessi, Baker & Taylor Books, Bridgewater, NJ. Reported by Alexander in *Bowker Annual*, R. R. Bowker.

PL5.2b *Compact disk*—Cost per compact disk. Source: See Alessi above.

PL5.3 *Video (TV) recordings*

PL5.3a. *VHS cassette*—Cost per video. Source: See Alessi above.

PL5.4 *Graphic image* (individual use of such items as maps, photos, art work, single slides, etc.). The following proxy is used. Average median weekly earnings for the following two occupational groups: painters, sculptors, craft artists, and artist printmakers; and photographers. Source: *Employment and Earnings Series*, U.S. Bureau of Labor Statistics

PL5.5 *Computer files* (CD-ROM, floppy disks, and tape). Average price of CD-ROM disks. Source: Martha Kellogg and Theodore Kellogg, University of Rhode Island. Reported by Alexander in *Bowker Annual*, R. R. Bowker.

PL6.0 Electronic Services

Average price for selected digital electronic computer and telecommunications networking available to libraries. Source: This source has requested anonymity.

Operating Expenses

PL7.0 Office Operations

PL7.1 *Office expenses* (telephone, postage and freight, publicity and printing, travel, professional fees, automobile operating cost, etc.)—The price series used for office expenses consists of the subindex for printed materials (PL4.0) described above; Consumer Price Index values for telephone and postage; CPI values for public transportation; the IRS allowance for individual business travel as reported by Runzheimer International; and CPI values for college tuition as a proxy for professional fees.

PL7.2 *Supplies and materials*—Producer Price Index price series for office supplies, writing papers, and pens and pencils. Source: U.S. Bureau of Labor Statistics.

PL8.0 Contracted Services (outside contracts for cleaning, building and grounds maintenance, equipment rental and repair, acquisition processing, binding, auditing, legal, payroll, etc.)

Prices used for contracted services include ECI wages paid material handlers, equipment cleaners, helpers, and laborers; average weekly earnings of production or non-supervisory workers in the printing and publishing industry, and the price of printing paper, as a proxy for binding costs; ECI salaries of attorneys, directors of personnel, and accountants, for contracted consulting fees; and ECI wages of precision production, craft, and repair occupations for the costs of equipment rental and repair.

PL9.0 Non-Capital Equipment

The type of equipment generally purchased as part of current library operations is usually small and easily movable. To be classified as "equipment" rather than as "expendable utensils" or "supplies," an item generally must cost $50 or more and have a useful life of at least three years. Examples may be hand calculators, small TVs, simple cameras, tape recorders, pagers, fans, desk lamps, books, etc. Equipment purchased as an operating expenditure is usually not depreciated. Items priced for this category include PPI commodity price series for machinery and equipment, office and store machines/equipment, hand tools, cutting tools and accessories, scales and balances, electrical measuring instruments, television receivers, musical instruments, photographic equipment, sporting and athletic goods, and books and periodicals.

PL10.0 Utilities

This subindex is a composite of the Producer Price Index series for natural gas, residual fuels, and commercial electric power, and the Consumer Price Index series for water and sewerage services. Source: U.S. Bureau of Labor Statistics.

Academic Library Price Indexes

The two academic library price indexes—the University Library Price Index (ULPI) and the College Library Price Index (CLPI)—together with their various subcomponents are reported in Tables 8–12A. The two indexes report the relative year-to-year price level of the staff salaries, acquisitions, and other goods and services purchased by university and college libraries respectively for their current operations. Universities are the 500 institutions with doctorate programs responding to the National Center for Education Statistics, U.S. Department of Education, *Academic Library Survey*. Colleges are the 1,472 responding institutions with master's and baccalaureate programs.

The composition of the library budgets involved, defined for pricing purposes, and the 1992 estimated national weighting structure are presented in Table 7. The priced components are organized in three major divisions: personnel compensation; acquisitions; and contracted services, supplies, and equipment.

The various components of the University and College Library Price Indexes are described in this section. Different weightings for components are designated in the tables "UL" for university libraries, "CL" for college libraries, and "AL" for academic libraries (common for both types). Source citations for the acquisitions price series are listed.

UL1.0 and CL1.0 Salaries and Wages

AL1.1 *Administrators* consists of the chief, deputy associate, and assistant librarian, e.g., important staff members having administrative responsibilities for management of the library. Administrators are priced by the head librarian salary series reported by the College and University Personnel Association (CUPA).

AL1.2 *Librarians* are all other professional library staff. Librarians are priced by the average of the median salaries for circulation/catalog, acquisition, technical service, and public service librarians reported by CUPA.

AL1.3 *Other professionals* are personnel who are not librarians in positions normally requiring at least a bachelor's degree. This group includes curators, archivists, computer specialists, budget officers, information and system specialists, subject bibliographers, and media specialists. Priced by the Higher Education Price Index (HEPI) faculty salary price series as a proxy.

AL1.4 *Nonprofessional staff* includes technical assistants, secretaries, and clerical, shipping, and storage personnel who are specifically assigned to the library and covered by the library budget. This category excludes general custodial and maintenance workers and student employees. This staff category is dominated by office-type workers and is priced by the HEPI clerical workers price series reported by the BLS Employment Cost Index.

AL1.5 *Students* are usually employed part-time for near minimum hourly wages. In some instances these wages are set by work-study program requirements of the institution's student financial aid office. The proxy price series used for student wages is the Employment Cost Index series for non-farm laborers, U.S. Bureau of Labor Statistics.

AL2.0 Fringe Benefits

The fringe benefits price series for faculty used in the HEPI is employed in pricing fringe benefits for library personnel.

UL3.0 and CL3.0 Books and Serials

UL3.1a *Books printed, U.S. titles, universities.* Book acquisitions for university libraries are priced by the North American Academic Books price series reporting the average list price of approximately 60,000 titles sold to college and university libraries by four of the largest book vendors. Compiled by Stephen Bosch, University of Arizona.

CL3.1a *Books printed, U.S. titles, colleges.* Book acquisitions for college libraries are priced by the price series for U.S. College Books representing approximately 6,300 titles compiled from book reviews appearing in *Choice* during the calendar year. Compiled by Donna Alsbury, Florida Center for Library Automation.

AL3.1b *Foreign Books.* Books with foreign titles *and* published in foreign countries are priced using U.S. book imports data. Bureau of the Census, U.S. Department of Commerce.

AL3.2a *Periodicals, U.S. titles.* U.S. periodicals are priced by the average subscription price of approximately 2,100 U.S. serial titles purchased by college and university libraries reported by EBSCO Subscription Services, Birmingham, AL.

AL3.2b *Periodicals, Foreign.* Foreign periodicals are priced by the average subscription price of approximately 600 foreign serial titles purchased by college and university libraries reported by EBSCO Subscription Services.

AL3.3 *Other Serials* (newspapers, annuals, proceedings, etc.). Average prices of approximately 170 U.S. daily newspapers. Source: Genevieve S. Owens, University of Missouri, St. Louis, and Wilba Swearingen, Louisiana State University Medical Center. Reported by Bill Robnett, "Prices of U.S. and Foreign Published Materials," in *Bowker Annual*, R. R. Bowker.

AL4.0 Other Printed Materials

These acquisitions include manuscripts, documents, pamphlets, sheet music, printed material for the handicapped, and so forth. No direct price series exists for this category. The proxy price series used is the Producer Price Index (PPI) for publishing pamphlets (PC 2731 9) and catalogs and directories (PCU2741#B), Bureau of Labor Statistics, U.S. Department of Labor.

AL5.0 Non-Print Media

AL5.1 *Microforms.* Producer Price Index for micropublishing in microform, including original and republished material (PC 2741 797), Bureau of Labor Statistics.

AL5.2 *Audio recordings*

AL5.2a *Tape cassette*—Cost per cassette of sound recording. Source: Dana Alessi, Baker & Taylor Books, Bridgewater, NJ. Reported by Alexander in *Bowker Annual*, R. R. Bowker.

AL5.2b *Compact Disc*—Cost per compact disc. Source: See Alessi above.

AL5.3 *Video (TV) recordings*

PL5.3a *VHS cassette*—cost per video. Source: See Alessi above.

AL5.4 *Graphic image* (individual use of such items as maps, photos, art work, single slides, etc.). No direct price series exists for graphic image materials. Average median weekly earnings for three related occupational groups (painters, sculptors, craft artists; artist printmakers; and photographers) is used as a proxy. these earnings series are reported in *Employment and Earnings Series*, U.S. Bureau of Labor Statistics.

AL5.5 *Computer files* (CD-ROM floppy disks, and tape). Average price of CD-ROM disks; primarily bibliographic, abstracts, and other databases of interest to academic libraries. Source: Developed from *Faxon Guide to CD-ROM* by Martha Kellogg and Theodore Kellogg, University of Rhode Island. Reported by Alexander in *Bowker Annual*, R. R. Bowker.

AL6.0 Electronic Services

Average price for selected digital electronic computer and telecommunications networking available to libraries. The source of this price series has requested anonymity.

AL7.0 Binding/Preservation

In-house maintenance of the specialized skills required for binding is increasingly being replaced by contracting out this service at all but the largest libraries. No wage series exists exclusively for binding. As a proxy, the Producer Price Index (PPI) for bookbinding and related work (PC 2789) is used. Source: Bureau of Labor Statistics, U.S. Department of Labor.

AL8.0 Contracted Services

Services contracted by libraries include such generic categories as communications, postal service, data processing, and printing and duplication. The HEPI contracted services subcomponent, which reports these items, is used as the price series. (In this instance the data processing component generally represents the library's payment for use of a central campus computer service.) However, libraries may also contract out certain specialized activities such as ongoing public access cataloging (OPAC) that are not distinctively priced in this AL8.0 component.

AL9.0 Supplies and Materials

Office supplies, writing papers, and pens and pencils constitute the bulk of library supplies and materials and are priced by these BLS categories for the Producer Price Index, Bureau of Labor Statistics, U.S. Department of Labor.

AL10.0 Equipment

This category is limited to small, easily movable, relatively inexpensive and short-lived items that are not carried on the books as depreciable capital equipment. Examples can include personal computers, hand calculators, projectors, fans, cameras, tape recorders, small TVs, etc. The HEPI equipment price series has been used for pricing.

Table 7 / Budget Composition of University Library and College Library Current Operations by Object Category, FY 1992 Estimate

Category	University Libraries		College Libraries	
	Percent Distribution		Percent Distribution	
Personnel Compensation				
1.0 Salaries and wages.		43.4		47.2
1.1 Administrators (head librarian)		10		25
1.2 Librarians		20		15
1.3 Other professionals^		10		5
1.4 Nonprofessional staff		50		40
1.5 Students hourly employed		10		15
		100.0		100.0
2.0 Fringe benefits		10.6		11.5
Acquisitions				
3.0 Books and Serials		28.5		24.8
3.1 Books printed		35		47
3.1a U.S. titles	80		95	
3.1b Foreign titles	20		5	
3.2 Periodicals		60		48
3.2a U.S. titles	80		95	
3.2b Foreign titles	20		5	
3.3 Other serials (newspapers, annuals, proceedings, etc.)		5		5
		100.0		100
4.0 Other Printed Materials*		1.2		0.7
5.0 Non-Print Media		1.6		3.3
5.1 Microforms (microfiche and microfilm)		45		45
5.2 Audio recordings		5		5
5.2a Tape cassette				
5.2b Compact disc (CDs)				
5.3 Video (TV) VHS recordings		15		15
5.4 Graphic image individual item use~		5		5
5.5 Computer materials (CD-ROM, floppy disks, and tape)		30		30
		100.0		100.0
6.0. Electronic Services^^		4.0		3.5
Contracted Services, Supplies, Equipment				
7.0 Binding/preservation.		1.3		0.8
8.0 Contracted services**		4.4		3.1
9.0 Supplies and materials		3.1		2.6
10.0 Equipment (non-capital)#		1.9		2.5
		100.0		100

^ Other professional and managerial staff includes systems analyst, business manager, public relations, personnel, etc.
* Other printed materials includes manuscripts, documents, pamphlets, sheet music, printed material for the handicapped, etc.
~ Graphic image individual item use includes maps, photos, art work, single slides, etc.
^^Electronic services includes software license fees, network intra-structure costs, terminal access to the Internet, desktop computer operating budget, and subscription services.
** Contracted services includes outside contracts for communications, postal service, data processing, printing and duplication, equipment rental and repair, acquisition processing, etc.
# Relatively inexpensive items not carried on the books as depreciable capital equipment. Examples include microform and audiovisual equipment, personal computers, hand calculators, projectors, fans, cameras, tape recorders, and small TVs.
Source: Derived, in part, from data published in *Academic Libraries: 1992,* National Center for Education Statistics, USDE.

Table 8 / University Library Price Index and Major Component Subindexes, FY 1992 to 2001

1992=100 Fiscal year	Personnel Compensation		Acquisitions					Operating Expenses			University Library Price Index ULPI
	Salaries and wages (UL1.0)	Fringe benefits (AL2.0)	Books and serials (UL3.0)	Other printed materials (AL4.0)	Non-print media (AL5.0)	Electronic services (AL6.0)	Binding/preservation (AL7.0)	Contracted services (AL8.0)	Supplies and material (AL9.0)	Equipment (AL10.0)	
1992	100.0	100.0	100.0	100.0	100.0	100.0	100.0	100.0	100.0	100.0	100.0
1993	103.2	105.4	105.4	102.9	98.7	101.9	100.5	102.6	98.3	101.8	103.7
1994	106.5	110.5	111.4	105.5	100.8	104.8	101.2	106.2	99.2	103.6	107.7
1995	110.0	114.2	115.6	107.7	101.5	108.5	102.9	108.4	100.4	105.7	111.3
1996	113.4	115.8	122.3	111.3	108.9	110.3	107.1	112.4	112.9	108.5	115.8
1997	117.0	117.0	136.8	118.5	113.3	110.3	108.9	114.8	111.6	110.3	121.8
1998	120.7	122.1	144.4	122.7	115.3	115.5	112.8	118.6	109.5	111.9	126.7
1999	125.1	123.4	154.1	125.7	117.3	119.2	115.0	121.5	106.9	113.5	131.8
2000	129.9	131.5	164.5	128.9	120.0	125.5	116.9	125.5	106.9	114.8	138.2
2001	134.5	135.0	176.1	132.9	122.7	131.2	120.8	129.9	113.3	116.6	144.7
1993	3.2%	5.4%	5.4%	2.9%	-1.3%	1.9%	0.5%	2.6%	-1.7%	1.8%	3.7%
1994	3.1%	4.8%	5.7%	2.5%	2.1%	2.8%	0.7%	3.5%	0.9%	1.8%	3.9%
1995	3.4%	3.4%	3.8%	2.1%	0.7%	3.5%	1.7%	2.1%	1.2%	2.0%	3.3%
1996	3.2%	1.4%	5.8%	3.3%	7.3%	1.7%	4.1%	3.7%	12.5%	2.6%	4.0%
1997	3.1%	1.0%	11.8%	6.5%	4.0%	0.0%	1.7%	2.1%	-1.2%	1.7%	5.2%
1998	3.2%	4.4%	5.6%	3.5%	2.0%	4.7%	3.6%	3.3%	-1.9%	1.5%	4.0%
1999	3.6%	1.1%	6.7%	2.4%	1.4%	3.2%	2.0%	2.4%	-2.4%	1.4%	4.0%
2000	3.8%	6.5%	6.7%	2.5%	2.4%	5.3%	1.7%	3.3%	0.0%	1.1%	4.9%
2001	3.6%	2.7%	7.1%	3.1%	2.2%	4.5%	3.3%	3.4%	6.0%	1.6%	4.7%

Sources: See text.

Table 9 / College Library Price Index and Major Component Subindexes, FY 1992 to 2001

1992=100 Fiscal year	Personnel Compensation		Acquisitions					Operating Expenses			College Library Price Index CLPI
	Salaries and wages (CL1.0)	Fringe benefits (AL2.0)	Books and serials (CL3.0)	Other printed materials (AL4.0)	Non-print media (AL5.0)	Electronic services (AL6.0)	Binding/preservation (AL7.0)	Contracted services (AL8.0)	Supplies and material (AL9.0)	Equipment (AL10.0)	
1992	100.0	100.0	100.0	100.0	100.0	100.0	100.0	100.0	100.0	100.0	100.0
1993	103.5	105.4	107.1	102.9	98.7	101.9	100.5	102.6	98.3	101.8	104.2
1994	106.5	110.5	112.8	105.5	100.8	104.8	101.2	106.2	99.2	103.6	107.9
1995	110.0	114.2	114.9	107.7	101.5	108.5	102.9	108.4	100.4	105.7	110.9
1996	113.8	115.8	118.7	111.3	108.9	110.3	107.1	112.4	112.9	108.5	114.7
1997	117.5	117.0	131.2	118.5	113.7	110.3	108.9	114.8	111.6	110.3	119.9
1998	120.9	122.1	138.1	122.7	115.6	115.5	112.8	118.6	109.5	111.9	124.3
1999	125.1	123.4	146.6	125.7	117.3	119.2	115.0	121.5	106.9	113.5	128.8
2000	129.8	131.5	153.5	128.9	120.0	125.5	116.9	125.5	106.9	114.8	134.2
2001	134.4	135.0	162.6	132.9	122.7	131.2	120.8	129.9	113.3	116.6	139.7
1993	3.5%	5.4%	7.1%	2.9%	-1.3%	1.9%	0.5%	2.6%	-1.7%	1.8%	4.2%
1994	2.9%	4.8%	5.3%	2.5%	2.1%	2.8%	0.7%	3.5%	0.9%	1.8%	3.6%
1995	3.3%	3.4%	1.8%	2.1%	0.7%	3.5%	1.7%	2.1%	1.2%	2.0%	2.7%
1996	3.5%	1.4%	3.3%	3.3%	7.3%	1.7%	4.1%	3.7%	12.5%	2.6%	3.5%
1997	3.2%	1.0%	10.6%	6.5%	4.0%	0.0%	1.7%	2.1%	-1.2%	1.7%	4.6%
1998	2.9%	4.4%	5.2%	3.5%	2.0%	4.7%	3.6%	3.3%	-1.9%	1.5%	3.6%
1999	3.5%	1.1%	6.2%	2.4%	1.4%	3.2%	2.0%	2.4%	-2.4%	1.4%	3.7%
2000	3.7%	6.5%	4.7%	2.5%	2.4%	5.3%	1.7%	3.3%	0.0%	1.1%	4.1%
2001	3.6%	2.7%	6.0%	3.1%	2.2%	4.5%	3.3%	3.4%	6.0%	1.6%	4.2%

Sources: See text.

Table 10 / Academic Library Price Indexes, Personnel Compensation, FY 1992 to 2001

1992=100 Fiscal year	Administrators (head librarian) (AL1.1)	Librarians (AL1.2)	Other professional (AL1.3)	Non-professional (AL1.4)	Students hourly employed (AL1.5)	Salaries and Wages Indexes Universities* (UL1.0)	Colleges^ (CL1.0)	Fringe benefits index (AL2.0)
1992	100.0	100.0	100.0	100.0	100.0	100.0	100.0	100.0
1993	105.0	102.6	102.5	103.2	102.7	103.2	103.5	105.4
1994	107.3	106.0	105.6	106.6	105.4	106.3	106.5	110.5
1995	110.6	110.2	109.3	110.1	108.5	110.0	110.0	114.2
1996	116.3	113.6	112.5	113.3	111.8	113.4	113.8	115.8
1997	120.2	116.5	115.8	117.0	115.6	117.0	117.5	117.0
1998	121.6	120.1	119.7	121.2	119.9	120.7	120.9	122.1
1999	125.6	124.5	124.1	125.8	123.6	125.1	125.1	123.4
2000	130.1	129.2	128.7	130.8	127.7	129.9	129.8	131.5
2001	134.3	131.0	133.1	136.4	133.3	134.5	134.4	135.0
1993	5.0%	2.6%	2.5%	3.2%	2.7%	3.2%	3.5%	5.4%
1994	2.2%	3.3%	3.0%	3.3%	2.6%	3.1%	2.9%	4.8%
1995	3.1%	4.0%	3.5%	3.3%	3.0%	3.4%	3.3%	3.4%
1996	5.2%	3.1%	2.9%	2.9%	3.0%	3.2%	3.5%	1.4%
1997	3.4%	2.6%	3.0%	3.2%	3.4%	3.1%	3.2%	1.0%
1998	1.2%	3.1%	3.4%	3.6%	3.7%	3.2%	2.9%	4.4%
1999	3.3%	3.7%	3.6%	3.8%	3.1%	3.6%	3.5%	1.1%
2000	3.6%	3.8%	3.7%	3.9%	3.33%	3.8%	3.7%	6.5%
2001	3.2%	1.4%	3.5%	4.3%	4.4%	3.6%	3.6%	2.7%

* University library salaries and wages index weights: 10 percent administrators, 20 percent librarians, 10 percent other professionals, 50 percent nonprofessional staff, and 10 percent students.
^ College library salaries and wages index weights: 25 percent administrators, 15 percent librarians, 5 percent other professionals, 40 percent nonprofessional staff, and 15 percent students.
Sources: See text.

Table 11 / Academic Library Price Indexes, Books and Serials, FY 1992 to 2001

1992=100	Books Printed						Book indexes	
	North American		U.S. college		Foreign books		University* (UL3.1)	College^ (CL3.1)
Fiscal year	Price~	Index (UL3.1a)	Price~	Index (CL3.1a)	Price	Index (AL3.1b)		
1992	$45.84	100.0	$44.55	100.0	n.a.	100.0	100.0	100.0
1993	45.91	100.2	47.48	106.6		98.9	99.9	106.2
1994	47.17	102.9	48.92	109.8		96.7	101.7	109.2
1995	48.16	105.1	47.93	107.6		105.0	105.0	107.5
1996	49.86	108.8	48.17	108.1		108.3	108.7	108.1
1997	52.24	114.0	50.44	113.2		106.6	112.5	112.9
1998	53.12	115.9	51.33	115.2		99.9	112.7	114.5
1999	54.24	118.3	52.72	118.3		105.7	115.8	117.7
2000	56.30	122.8	52.04	116.8		101.9	118.6	116.1
2001	58.45	127.5	53.00	119.0		111.9	124.4	118.6
1993		0.2%		6.6%		-1.1%	-0.1%	6.2%
1994		2.7%		3.0%		-2.2%	1.8%	2.8%
1995		2.1%		-2.0%		8.6%	3.3%	-1.6%
1996		3.5%		0.5%		3.1%	3.5%	0.6%
1997		4.8%		4.7%		-1.6%	3.5%	4.4%
1998		1.7%		1.8%		-6.3%	0.2%	1.4%
1999		2.1%		2.7%		5.8%	2.8%	2.8%
2000		3.8%		-1.3%		-3.6%	2.4%	-1.4%
2001		3.8%		1.8%		9.8%	4.8%	2.2%

~ Prices are for previous calendar year, e.g., CY 1993 prices are reported for FY 1994.
* University library books printed index weights: 80 percent U.S. titles, 20 percent foreign titles.
^ College Library books printed index weights: 95 percent U.S. titles, 5 percent foreign titles.
Sources: See text.
n.a. = not available

Table 11A / Academic Library Price Indexes, Books and Serials, FY 1992 to 2001

| 1992=100 Fiscal year | Periodicals | | | | | | Other Serials (newspapers) | | Books and Serials Indexes | | Other printed materials index (AL4.0) |
| | U.S. titles | | Foreign | | Periodical indexes | | | | | | |
	Price~	Index (AL3.2a)	Price~	Index (AL3.2b)	University* (UL3.2)	College^ (CL3.2)	Price~	Index (AL3.3)	University** (UL3.0)	College^^ (CL3.0)	
1992	$125.86	100.0	$341.02	100.0	100.0	100.0	$222.68	100.0	100.0	100.0	100.0
1993	136.33	108.3	377.48	110.7	108.8	108.4	229.92	103.3	105.4	107.1	102.9
1994	145.64	115.7	408.70	119.8	116.5	115.9	261.91	117.6	111.4	112.8	105.5
1995	152.88	121.5	411.32	120.6	121.3	121.4	270.22	121.3	115.6	114.9	107.7
1996	159.46	126.7	475.94	139.6	129.3	127.3	300.21	134.8	122.3	118.7	111.3
1997	185.52	147.4	559.75	164.1	150.7	148.2	311.77	140.0	136.8	131.2	118.5
1998	201.37	160.0	599.35	175.8	163.1	160.8	316.60	142.2	144.4	138.1	122.7
1999	219.67	174.5	642.83	188.5	177.3	175.2	318.44	143.0	154.1	146.6	125.7
2000	239.46	190.3	691.33	202.7	192.8	190.9	324.26	145.6	164.5	153.5	128.9
2001	260.21	206.7	736.81	216.1	208.6	207.2	330.78	148.5	176.1	162.6	132.9
1993		8.3%		10.7%	8.8%	8.4%		3.3%	5.4%	7.1%	2.9%
1994		6.8%		8.3%	7.1%	6.9%		13.9%	5.7%	5.3%	2.5%
1995		5.0%		0.6%	4.1%	4.7%		3.2%	3.8%	1.8%	2.1%
1996		4.3%		15.7%	6.6%	4.9%		11.1%	5.8%	3.3%	3.3%
1997		16.3%		17.6%	16.6%	16.4%		3.9%	11.8%	10.5%	6.5%
1998		8.5%		7.1%	8.2%	8.5%		1.5%	5.6%	5.2%	3.5%
1999		9.1%		7.3%	8.7%	9.0%		0.6%	6.7%	6.2%	2.4%
2000		9.0%		7.5%	8.7%	8.9%		1.8%	6.7%	4.7%	2.5%
2001		8.7%		6.6%	8.2%	8.6%		2.0%	7.1%	6.0%	3.1%

~ Prices are for previous calendar year, e.g., CY 1993 prices are reported for FY 1994.
* University library periodicals index weights: 80 percent U.S. titles, 20 percent foreign titles.
^ College library periodicals index weights: 95 percent U.S. titles, 5 percent foreign titles.
** University library books and serials index weights: 35 percent books, 60 percent periodicals, 5 percent other serials.
^^College library books and serials index weights: 47 percent books, 48 percent periodicals, 5 percent other serials.
Sources: See text.

Table 12 / Academic Library Price Indexes, Non-Print Media and Electronic Services, FY 1992 to 2001

| 1992=100 | Microforms (microfilm) | Audio Recordings | | | | | Video | | |
Fiscal year	Index (AL5.1)	Tape cassette Price~	Index (AL5.2a)	Compact disc Price~	Index (AL5.2b)	Audio recordings index* (AL5.2)	VHS cassette Price~	Index (AL5.3a)	Video index (AL5.3)
1992	100.0	$12.18	100.0	n.a.	n.a.	100.0	$199.67	100.0	100.0
1993	104.3	11.73	96.3	n.a.		96.3	112.92	56.6	56.6
1994	107.9	8.20	67.3	$13.36	67.3	67.3	93.22	46.7	46.7
1995	110.6	8.82	72.4	14.80	74.6	73.5	84.19	42.2	42.2
1996	128.0	7.96	65.4	14.86	74.9	70.1	83.48	41.8	41.8
1997	132.9	8.13	66.7	16.43	82.8	74.8	82.10	41.1	41.1
1998	138.9	8.31	68.2	14.35	72.3	70.3	72.31	36.2	36.2
1999	142.9	8.20	67.3	12.65	63.7	65.5	77.85	39.0	39.0
2000	145.6	8.20	67.3	12.00	60.4	63.9	80.00	40.1	40.1
2001	145.7	8.20	67.3	12.00	60.4	63.9	85.00	42.6	42.6
1993	4.3%		-3.7%			-3.7%		-43.4%	-43.4%
1994	3.5%		-30.1%			-30.1%		-17.4%	-17.4%
1995	2.5%		7.6%		10.8%	9.2%		-9.7%	-9.7%
1996	15.7%		-9.8%		0.4%	-4.6%		-0.8%	-0.8%
1997	3.8%		2.1%		10.6%	6.6%		-1.7%	-1.7%
1998	4.5%		2.2%		-12.7%	-6.0%		-11.9%	-11.9%
1999	2.9%		-1.3%		-11.8%	-6.7%		7.7%	7.7%
2000	1.9%		0.0%		-5.1%	-2.5%		2.8%	2.8%
2001	0.1%		0.0%		0.0%	0.0%		6.3%	6.3%

~ Prices are for previous calendar year, e.g., CY 1993 prices are reported for FY 1994.
* Audio recordings index weights: 50 percent tape cassette, 50 percent compact disc.
Sources: See text.
n.a. = not available

Table 12A / Academic Library Price Indexes, Non-Print Media and Electronic Services, FY 1992 to 2001

1992=100 Fiscal year	Non-print Media			Non-print media index#	Electronic services index	Total Acquisitions Indexes		
	Graphic image (AL5.4)	Computer files (CD-ROM) Price~	Index (AL5.5)	(AL5.0)	(AL6.0)	University*	College^	All Institutions**
1992	100.0	$1,601	100.0	100.0	100.0	100.0	100.0	100.0
1993	97.3	1,793	112.0	98.7	101.9	104.6	105.6	104.9
1994	108.4	1,945	121.5	100.8	104.8	110.0	110.6	110.1
1995	111.3	1,930	120.5	101.5	108.5	113.9	112.7	113.5
1996	114.5	1,913	119.5	108.9	110.3	120.0	116.6	119.1
1997	126.5	1,988	124.2	113.3	110.3	132.2	126.9	130.7
1998	129.1	2,012	125.7	115.6	115.5	139.2	133.0	137.4
1999	124.5	2,007	125.4	117.3	119.2	147.5	140.2	145.5
2000	142.7	2,037	127.2	120.0	125.5	156.9	146.5	154.0
2001	168.8	2,085	130.2	122.7	131.2	167.2	154.6	163.7
1993	-2.7%		12.0%	-1.3%	1.9%	4.6%	5.6%	4.9%
1994	11.4%		8.5%	2.1%	2.8%	5.1%	4.7%	5.0%
1995	2.7%		-0.8%	0.7%	3.5%	3.6%	1.9%	3.1%
1996	2.9%		-0.9%	7.3%	1.7%	5.4%	3.5%	4.9%
1997	10.5%		3.9%	4.0%	0.0%	10.1%	8.8%	9.8%
1998	2.1%		1.2%	2.0%	4.7%	5.3%	4.9%	5.2%
1999	-3.6%		-0.2%	1.4%	3.2%	6.0%	5.4%	5.9%
2000	14.6%		1.5%	2.4%	5.3%	6.3%	4.5%	5.8%
2001	18.3%		2.4%	2.2%	4.5%	6.6%	5.5%	6.3%

~ Prices are for immediate preceding calendar year, e.g., CY 1993 prices are reported for FY 1994.

Non-print media index weights: 45 percent microforms, 5 percent audio recordings, 15 percent video, 5 percent graphic image, 30 percent computer materials.

* University total acquisitions 1992 weights: 81 percent books, 3 percent other printed material, 5 percent non-print media, and 11 percent electronic services.

^ College total acquisitions 1992 weights: 77 percent books, 2 percent other printed material, 10 percent non-print media, and 11 percent electronic services.

** All institutions total acquisitions weights: 72 percent university acquisitions, 28 percent college acquisitions.

Sources: See text.

Library Buildings 2002:
The Building Buck Doesn't Stop Here

Bette-Lee Fox

Managing Editor, *Library Journal*

Rumors to the contrary, the bucks for library capital improvement projects don't seem to be stopping anywhere or any time soon. The 212 U.S. public library building projects completed between July 1, 2001 and June 30, 2002 cost more than $788.4 million.

In many cases, we are seeing the results of previously approved bond issues. For instance, the Ypsilanti (Michigan) District Library ($15.1 million, 60,000 square feet), was financed by a $17 million bond issue referendum. Assistant Director Kathleen Evans Daly described the complex task of winning funds in her working-class community, generally lost in the shadow of more affluent Ann Arbor, and the pride residents feel in their new library.

The funding for the 101 new buildings and 111 addition/renovation projects featured here came predominantly from local sources, to the tune of $675.5 million, or 87 percent of total funding. Running a very distant second were charitable contributions/gift funds at $60 million, or 8 percent. Federal and state funds totaled 5 percent of funding.

Total Number Down

Though the money seems to be abundant, the number of public library projects ties the third lowest count in 14 years. Only fiscal year (FY) 1998 and FY 1999 had fewer total projects, with 197 and 195, respectively. Several large projects stand out this year, including the huge new central library of the Memphis and Shelby County (Tennessee) Public Library and Information Center ($65.3 million, 330,000 square feet). The Cerritos (California) Library, coming in at $47 million and 89,000 square feet, and the Berkeley (California) Central Library, addition/renovation at $38 million, 102,000 square feet, outpaced the Topeka and Shawnee County (Kansas) Public Library ($24.3 million, 178,600 square feet); Worcester (Massachusetts) Public Library ($23.3 million, 145,688 square feet); and Riverfront Branch, Yonkers (New York) Public Library ($22.8 million, 70,410 square feet).

When it comes to innovation, in terms of funding or construction, many of these projects excel. The Plymouth (Indiana) Public Library reaped the benefits of a state lottery. The Iberia Parish Library, New Iberia, Louisiana, used its former bookmobile garage as a room to house a music collection dedicated to early jazz trumpet/cornet player Willie "Bunk" Johnson. The new Rep. David J. Mayernik Avalon Public Library in Pennsylvania arose out of a converted church. Cooperative projects still satisfy the needs of many communities, with libraries cohabiting with town halls, schools, and firehouses.

Adapted from the December 2002 issue of *Library Journal,* which also lists architects' addresses.

Among the 34 academic projects featured here are the Library, Research, and Information Technology Center at Nova Southeastern University, Ft. Lauderdale, Florida ($44.3 million, 325,000 square feet); the E. B. House Undergraduate Library at the University of North Carolina–Chapel Hill ($11.8 million, 66,000 square feet); and the Brooklyn (New York) College addition/renovation ($72.5 million, 277,650 square feet).

While several capital projects across the country have been put on hold owing to overall budget constraints, many libraries reported approval of recent capital referenda. Nevertheless, the concerns of librarians and their communities do not stop at the threshold of a newly built or renovated structure. As many jurisdictions are now realizing, economics affects libraries beyond bricks and mortar. Municipalities have joined with libraries to create accessible facilities and must continue to work to keep them funded.

Table 1 / New Academic Library Buildings, 2002

Name of Institution	Project Cost	Gross Area	Sq. Ft. Cost	Construction Cost	Equipment Cost	Book Capacity	Architect
Library, Research, & Information Technology Center, Nova Southeastern University, Ft. Lauderdale, FL	$44,335,238	325,000	$109.94	$35,729,506	$4,263,339	1,400,000	Smallwood, Reynolds...
Veterinary Medicine Library, Ohio State University, Columbus	26,000,000	8,180 *	164.70	18,000,000	350,000	50,000	Braun & Steidl; Ballinger Architecture
Ames Library, Illinois Wesleyan University, Bloomington	23,000,000	103,000	174.75	18,000,000	n.a.	400,000	Shepley Bulfinch
ACES Library, Information & Alumni Center, University of Illinois at Urbana–Champaign	21,070,000	83,683	196.23	16,420,750	1,420,010	163,000	Woollen Molzan; Phillips Swager Assocs.
Washtenaw Community College Library, Ann Arbor, MI	21,000,000	62,000 **	133.00	16,200,000	1,500,000	80,000	Albert Kahn Assocs.
Biola University Library, La Mirada, CA	16,100,000	98,000	122.34	11,990,000	1,360,261	750,000	Gensler
Wayne G. Basler Library, Northeast State Technical Community College, Blountville, TN	10,990,000	58,745	173.26	10,178,000	812,000	65,000	Vaughn & Melton; Ken Ross Architects
Mission College Library, Santa Clara, CA	9,738,791	38,648	204.51	7,903,920	735,330	59,654	MBT Architecture
USM Gulf Coast Library, University of Southern Mississippi-Gulf Coast, Long Beach	8,477,308	54,836	139.90	7,671,308	806,000	75,000	Studio South Architects
Hugh & Edna White Library, Spring Arbor University, MI	6,560,000	38,500	137.66	5,300,000	1,260,000	160,500	TMP Assocs.
Benedictine University Library, Lisle, IL	n.a.	36,852	118.88	4,380,966	n.a.	n.a.	Prisco, Serena, Sturm
M.M. Bennett Library, St. Petersburg College, Palm Harbor, FL	2,942,397	15,602	145.07	2,263,382	346,340	60,000	Hoffman Architects
Music Library, Columbus State University, GA	644,040	3,740	121.00	452,540	191,500	16,212	Hecht, Burdeshaw...; Hardy, Holzman, Pfeiffer
ReCAP (Research Collections & Preservation Consortium, Columbia University, New York PL, Princeton University, NJ	n.a.	69,100	n.a.	n.a.	n.a.	7,000,000	Sasaki Assocs.; Russell, Scott, Steedle...
Engineering Library, Princeton University, NJ	n.a.	21,400	n.a.	n.a.	n.a.	130,000	Pei Cobb Freed

n.a. = not available
*Part of 109,292 sq. ft. Veterinary Medicine Academic Building
**Part of 131,000 sq. ft. project

Table 2 / Academic Library Buildings, Additions and Renovations, 2002

Name of Institution	Status	Project Cost	Gross Area	Sq. Ft. Cost	Construction Cost	Equipment Cost	Book Capacity	Architect
Brooklyn College Library, NY	Total	$72,524,000	277,650	$187.28	$51,998,712	$2,658,800	1,688,400	Shepley Bulfinch...; Buttrick, White, Burtis
	New	n.a.	105,000	n.a.	n.a.	n.a.	n.a.	
	Renovated	n.a.	172,650	n.a.	n.a.	n.a.	n.a.	
Walter Library/Digital Tech Center, University of Minnesota, Minneapolis	Total	54,600,000	260,500	165.96	43,232,000	1,900,000	500,000	Stageberg, Beyer, Sachs
	New	n.a.	79,750	n.a.	n.a.	n.a.	400,000	
	Renovated	n.a.	180,750	n.a.	n.a.	n.a.	100,000	
Charles V. Park Library, Central Michigan University, Mt. Pleasant	Total	50,000,000	316,000	91.66	28,963,900	10,286,600	1,319,250	URS, Inc.; Woollen Molzan Partners
	New	n.a.	128,000	116.48	14,909,000	n.a.	1,052,200	
	Renovated	n.a.	188,000	74.76	14,045,900	n.a.	267,050	
Mary Alice & Tom O'Malley Library, Manhattan College, Riverdale, NY	Total	18,000,000	81,000	182.22	14,760,000	870,000	220,300	Perkins Eastman; Edward I. Mills Assocs.
	New	12,500,000	45,000	227.78	10,250,000	n.a.	168,300	
	Renovated	5,500,000	36,000	125.28	4,510,000	n.a.	52,000	
DiMenna-Nyselius Library, Fairfield University, CT	Total	17,346,000	115,800	114.88	13,302,192	3,999,606	450,000	Stubbins Assocs.
	New	10,920,000	54,600	153.50	8,381,100	2,519,790	67,500	
	Renovated	6,426,000	61,200	80.41	4,921,092	1,479,816	382,500	
Anne Potter Wilson Music Library, Blair School of Music, Vanderbilt University, Nashville	Total	626,490	7,714	69.55	536,490	90,000	75,000	Street Dixon Rick
	New	490,000	4,100	100.00	410,000	80,000	20,000	
	Renovated	136,490	3,614	35.00	126,490	10,000	55,000	

n.a. = not available

Table 3 / Academic Library Buildings, Additions Only, 2002

Name of Institution	Project Cost	Gross Area	Sq. Ft. Cost	Construction Cost	Equipment Cost	Book Capacity	Architect
Wilson Library, Bethany College, Scotts Valley, CA	$130,000	1,600	$81.25	$130,000	$0	3,000	O/B

Table 4 / Academic Library Buildings, Renovations Only, 2002

Name of Institution	Project Cost	Gross Area	Sq. Ft. Cost	Construction Cost	Equipment Cost	Book Capacity	Architect
R. B. House Undergraduate Library, University of North Carolina at Chapel Hill	$11,800,000	66,000	$156.06	$10,300,000	$1,467,000	99,000	Perkins & Will
Mother Irene Gill Memorial Library, College of New Rochelle, NY	8,000,000	40,000	175.00	7,000,000	n.a.	335,400	Hillier
Engineering Library & Information Commons, University of Cincinnati	3,538,000	16,064	192.98	3,100,000	400,000	65,712	Michael Schuster Assocs.
University of Texas Southwestern Medical Center at Dallas Library	3,000,000	64,531	37.19	2,400,000	600,000	n.a.	Fred Alexander
Fong Optometry & Health Sciences Library, University of California–Berkeley	1,800,000	5,000	280.00	1,400,000	119,000	14,000	Noll & Tam Architects
Stanley Library, Ferrum College, VA	1,700,000	7,500	200.00	1,500,000	200,000	n.a.	Spectrum Assocs.
Ehrman Medical Library, New York University School of Medicine	850,000	9,077	62.25	565,000	0	n.a.	William N. Bernstein
Paul Laurence Dunbar Library, Wright State University, Dayton, OH	813,077	21,050	38.63	813,077	0	n.a.	LJB Inc.
Barnard College Library, New York	630,000	900	290.00	261,000	254,000	n.a.	Kostow Greenwood
Archives & Special Collections, MIT Libraries, Massachusetts Institute of Technology, Cambridge	331,000	2,400	91.88	220,500	0	0	Hallor Assocs.
E. H. Butler Library, State University of New York at Buffalo	177,870	3,000	44.09	132,270	45,600	n.a.	DiDonato Assocs.
Yale University/Branford & Saybrook Residential Colleges, New Haven, CT	n.a.	5,050	n.a.	n.a.	n.a.	n.a.	Perry Dean Rogers; Design Initiative

n.a. = not available

Table 5 / New Public Library Buildings, 2002

Community	Pop. ('000)	Code	Project Cost	Const. Cost	Gross Sq. Ft.	Sq. Ft. Cost	Equip. Cost	Site Cost	Other Costs	Volumes	Federal Funds	State Funds	Local Funds	Gift Funds	Architect
Alaska															
Big Lake	4	M	$1,392,765	$1,016,765	6,940	$146.50	$49,000	Owned	$327,000	27,294	$127,506	$793,282	$471,977	$0	Architects Alaska
Arizona															
Fountain Hills	21	B	3,665,186	2,261,492	20,000	113.07	393,753	Owned	1,009,941	72,900	0	0	3,565,186	100,000	HAD
Arkansas															
Bryant	10	B	1,308,732	946,426	6,589	143.64	137,684	130,000	94,622	35,820	0	0	1,168,732	140,000	Sims, Grisham, Blair
Little Rock	47	B	2,458,470	1,956,414	13,500	144.92	221,201	60,000	220,855	65,000	0	0	2,398,470	60,000	Fennell-Purifoy
California															
El Cajon	47	M	5,162,300	3,846,099	19,500	197.24	582,596	58,406	675,199	65,000	0	0	5,154,800	7,500	Carrier Johnson
Kerman	16	B	954,385	663,988	4,370	151.94	68,749	Leased	221,648	10,542	0	0	698,973	255,412	S.I.M. Architects
Los Angeles	67	B	4,998,106	3,619,944	12,000	301.66	183,445	840,717	354,000	40,251	1,250,000	0	3,748,106	0	Arch. Div. of L.A.
Los Angeles	98	B	3,771,025	3,222,319	11,300	285.16	177,036	Owned	371,670	33,850	270,000	0	3,501,025	0	Arch. Div. of L.A.
Menifee	22	B	975,000	790,000	5,000	158.00	125,000	Leased	60,000	15,000	0	0	975,000	0	WLC
San Diego	12	B	9,091,961	5,673,961	19,760	287.14	850,000	2,000,000	568,000	60,000	0	0	6,441,961	2,650,000	Wheeler•Wimer....
Westlake Village	10	B	4,524,100	3,828,000	10,250	373.46	264,900	Owned	431,200	55,000	0	0	4,524,100	0	Gonzalez Goodale
Colorado															
Denver	30	B	4,797,927	3,628,498	15,000	241.90	514,986	242,150	412,293	55,000	0	0	3,367,188	1,430,739	Brendle APV
Englewood	200	S	5,703,356	4,366,203	29,417	148.42	322,064	352,000	663,089	n.a.	0	0	5,703,356	0	Klipp, Colussy, Jenks...
Connecticut															
Cornwall	1	M	1,680,000	1,170,000	6,300	185.71	82,000	130,200	297,800	22,475	0	462,000	250,000	968,000	Amsler Woodhouse...
East Granby	5	M	2,744,621	2,077,000	12,000	173.08	228,000	Owned	439,621	39,013	0	500,000	925,000	1,319,621	Best Joslin
Stafford Springs	12	M	3,990,100	2,936,100	17,900	164.03	306,000	Owned	748,000	50,000	0	500,000	3,490,100	0	Schoenhardt Architects
Florida															
Astor	3	B	489,872	288,499	4,200	68.69	153,652	Owned	47,721	20,000	0	0	489,872	0	United Modular
Ft. Walton Beach	65	M	3,646,571	2,318,777	24,000	96.62	377,091	665,679	285,024	120,000	0	300,000	3,346,571	0	Harvard Jolly Clees...
Naples	60	MS	8,707,000	7,149,000	42,000	170.21	1,099,000	Owned	459,000	n.a.	0	0	8,607,000	100,000	Barany Schmitt...
Ocoee	120	B	2,277,952	1,780,000	12,500	142.40	123,940	276,412	97,600	100,000	0	300,000	1,977,952	0	Harvard Jolly Clees...
Paisley	6	B	534,395	325,063	4,200	77.40	161,611	Owned	47,721	20,000	0	0	534,395	0	United Modular
Sarasota	54	B	4,160,997	3,508,987	25,064	140.00	371,308	Owned	280,702	90,000	0	0	4,160,997	0	Hoyt Architects

Location		Symbol													Architect
Georgia															
Dawsonville	18	M	2,950,496	2,097,105	14,146	148.25	474,016	56,580	322,795	40,000	0	0	2,945,446	5,050	Lindsay, Pope…
Kennesaw	630	B	3,285,829	2,558,368	20,000	127.92	311,308	175,000	241,153	125,000	0	0	3,110,829	175,000	Perkins & Will
McDonough	120	B	3,529,970	2,604,184	18,000	144.68	750,000	Owned	175,786	67,990	0	550,000	2,979,970	0	Perkins & Will
Snellville	31	B	3,561,227	1,622,105	12,040	134.72	575,646	Owned	1,363,476	54,500	0	0	3,561,227	0	Ponder + Ponder
Yatesville	5	B	177,174	133,184	2,600	51.22	36,470	Owned	7,520	12,000	0	76,000	10,000	91,174	Juliana Jaramillo
Hawaii															
Kapolei	n.a.	M	8,687,000	7,170,000	34,000	210.88	525,000	Owned	992,000	70,000	n.a.	n.a.	n.a.	n.a.	CDS International
Illinois															
Algonquin	39	M	6,828,535	4,794,572	36,500	131.36	1,471,089	Leased	562,874	175,000	0	250,000	6,578,535	0	Burnidge Cassell
Auburn	4	M	736,693	575,872	7,056	81.61	18,921	65,000	76,900	38,000	0	550,000	186,693	0	Crawford, Murphy…
Batavia	26	M	11,397,600	7,897,000	54,000	146.24	806,347	1,000,000	1,694,253	190,000	0	75,000	11,322,600	0	Engberg Anderson
Biggsville	8	M	989,155	778,119	8,600	90.48	41,313	15,000	104,723	65,000	250,000	21,548	687,907	29,700	APACE Architects
Chicago	23	B	6,505,000	4,675,000	16,202	288.54	296,000	960,000	574,000	80,000	0	200,000	6,305,000	0	Antunovich Assocs.
Elmwood Park	25	M	7,285,425	4,105,000	38,500	106.62	620,000	1,700,000	860,425	n.a.	0	250,000	7,035,425	0	Charles E. Petrungaro
Harvard	8	M	3,052,806	2,570,427	18,015	142.68	136,420	60,000	285,959	71,200	0	265,000	2,000,000	787,806	RuckPate Architecture
Kankakee	5	M	619,969	484,003	5,962	81.18	49,537	53,400	33,029	28,000	0	250,000	309,153	60,816	Moline Architecture
Lake Zurich	33	M	13,902,000	10,507,102	71,603	146.74	2,026,000	615,000	753,898	280,000	0	0	13,902,000	0	Sente & Rubel
New Lenox	28	M	9,092,045	6,471,400	59,000	109.68	1,305,138	577,240	738,267	220,000	0	0	9,075,765	16,280	Burnidge Cassell
Indiana															
Auburn	n.a.	B	2,000,000	n.a.	9,200	n.a.	n.a.	n.a.	n.a.	n.a.	0	0	0	2,000,000	Design Collaborative
Fulton	5	B	424,500	314,000	3,481	90.20	40,000	35,500	35,000	30,000	5,000	0	409,500	10,000	H.L. Mohler
Kokomo	78	B	3,257,517	2,440,000	17,500	139.43	356,527	132,730	328,260	85,726	0	0	3,249,449	8,068	K.R. Montgomery
New Carlisle	5	M	5,000,000	3,170,000	25,920	122.30	535,000	169,000	1,126,000	70,128	0	0	4,998,500	1,500	not reported
Ridgeville	1	M	n.a.	n.a.	2,800	n.a.	n.a.	Leased	n.a.	20,000	0	475,000	n.a.	100,000	Brian Hostetler
Iowa															
Johnston	9	M	5,666,202	3,519,761	27,000	130.36	237,164	822,656	1,086,621	120,000	0	0	4,739,715	926,487	Michael Brendle; SVPA
Kentucky															
Elizabethtown	95	M	2,721,527	1,689,585	18,100	93.35	326,660	400,000	305,282	90,000	0	517,000	1,800,000	404,527	Louis & Henry Group
Richmond	72	BS	2,563,115	2,171,395	18,236	119.08	131,718	125,000	135,000	71,000	0	0	2,452,115	111,000	Brandstetter Carroll
Louisiana															
Baton Rouge	24	B	3,750,223	2,863,464	17,985	159.21	350,722	195,575	340,462	100,000	0	37,411	3,712,812	0	John J. Desmond
Baton Rouge	36	B	3,923,387	2,918,243	18,263	159.79	309,092	342,950	353,102	100,000	0	35,459	3,887,928	0	Grace & Hebert Archs.
Independence	2	B	307,109	242,847	2,500	97.14	32,975	10,000	21,287	15,000	0	29,595	267,514	10,000	Holly & Smith

Symbol Code: B—Branch Library; BS—Branch & System Headquarters; M—Main Library; MS—Main & System Headquarters; S—System Headquarters; n.a.—not available

Table 5 / New Public Library Buildings, 2002 *(cont.)*

Community	Pop. ('000)	Code	Project Cost	Const. Cost	Gross Sq. Ft.	Sq. Ft. Cost	Equip. Cost	Site Cost	Other Costs	Volumes	Federal Funds	State Funds	Local Funds	Gift Funds	Architect
Maine															
York	15	M	5,816,753	4,668,253	24,780	188.39	290,000	425,000	433,500	n.a.	0	0	1,300,000	4,516,753	Tappé Associates
Maryland															
Clear Spring	6	B	909,023	714,023	8,000	89.25	115,000	30,000	50,000	20,000	0	0	250,000	659,023	Bushey Feight Morin
Crofton	14	B	7,466,200	4,662,000	25,000	186.48	635,000	Owned	2,169,200	140,000	0	0	7,466,200	0	Grimm & Parker
Michigan															
Davisburg	14	M	7,638,166	6,333,833	31,500	201.07	472,700	744,000	87,633	50,000	0	0	7,633,166	5,000	Minoru Yamasaki
Dorr	7	M	667,352	542,391	7,100	76.39	105,562	Owned	19,399	35,000	0	0	667,352	0	Fifelsi Buildings Inc.
Grand Rapids	7	B	1,091,249	596,241	4,644	128.39	81,892	216,763	196,353	22,895	0	0	841,353	249,896	Fishbeck, Thompson...
Grayling	14	MS	1,760,000	1,110,000	10,868	102.13	350,000	20	299,980	40,000	0	0	1,500,000	260,000	Thomas I. O'Brien
Highland Twp.	20	M	6,415,888	5,045,445	25,050	201.41	710,474	Owned	659,969	68,500	0	0	6,349,869	66,019	David Osler Assocs.
Ypsilanti	72	M	15,103,821	11,786,702	60,000	196.45	1,609,141	Owned	1,707,978	300,000	0	0	14,985,913	117,908	David Milling & Assocs.
Minnesota															
Edina	47	B	3,400,000	n.a.	18,000	n.a.	706,000	Owned	n.a.	90,366	0	0`	3,400,000	0	Meyer, Scherer...
Mississippi															
Flowood	20	M	3,931,618	3,223,270	24,155	133.44	508,319	Owned	200,029	70,272	0	300,000	3,631,618	0	J H & H Architects
Nebraska															
Lincoln	250	B	7,007,000	4,011,446	31,400	127.75	2,370,469	208,853	416,232	110,000	0	0	7,007,000	0	Clark Enersen Ptnrs.
Lincoln	250	B	7,428,000	4,209,612	33,800	124.54	2,399,123	414,372	404,893	110,000	0	0	7,428,000	0	Clark Enersen Ptnrs.
Tilden	3	M	2,023,043	1,611,662	13,000	123.97	157,049	92,507	161,825	42,295	7,263	0	13,861	2,001,919	James Schmit Archs.
Nevada															
Henderson	80	MS	7,220,166	5,665,403	43,413	130.50	425,000	600,000	529,763	300,000	0	0	6,620,166	600,000	Dekker, Perich, Holmes
New Jersey															
Jackson	43	B	5,040,188	3,643,412	24,000	151.81	441,467	500,000	455,309	80,000	0	0	5,040,188	0	James W. Hyres
Pemberton Twp.	30	B	3,210,461	2,700,000	19,787	136.45	210,461	Owned	300,000	68,000	400,000	705,506	1,941,141	163,814	Regan Young England...
New York															
Burnt Hills	12	M	1,540,443	1,400,000	11,000	127.27	40,956	Owned	99,487	70,000	48,590	126,556	1,349,879	15,418	J.D. Smith Assocs.
Clarence	26	M	4,300,000	3,000,000	17,000	176.47	900,000	Owned	400,000	71,000	0	0	3,400,000	900,000	Wendel-Duchscherer
Collins	8	M	1,394,341	940,235	8,067	116.55	160,258	32,000	261,848	19,000	90,000	90,792	961,463	252,086	Habiterra Design
Newstead (Akron)	8	M	2,900,000	2,215,000	14,500	152.76	135,000	230,000	320,000	20,000	1,000,000	25,000	1,475,000	400,000	Hamilton Houston...

Location	No.	Sym.													Architect
North Carolina															
Harrisburg	n.a.	B	1,330,000	1,100,000	10,000	110.00	130,000	Owned	100,000	50,000	0	0	1,080,000	250,000	Overcash-Demmitt
Rocky Mount	106	M	8,565,000	6,255,000	60,000	104.25	1,335,000	500,000	475,000	250,000	0	20,000	6,445,000	2,100,000	J. Hyatt Hammond
Ohio															
Canton	81	B	994,494	651,099	4,607	141.33	41,906	130,574	170,915	27,602	0	0	994,494	0	Meehan; Lawrence…
Harrison	3	B	4,640,597	3,172,930	16,000	198.31	248,823	525,000	693,844	80,000	0	4,637,751	2,846	0	Champlin Haupt
Napoleon	1	B	398,000	275,000	1,700	161.76	25,000	70,000	28,000	15,000	0	0	398,000	0	Beilharz Architects
Oklahoma															
Allen	1	M	110,539	88,505	2,500	35.40	12,034	10,000	0	6,000	0	70,000	0	40,539	Patterson/Johnson
Owasso	19	B	655,126	532,655	8,800	60.53	66,734	Owned	55,737	35,693	0	0	655,126	0	Olsen Coffey
Sand Springs	17	B	913,477	740,013	5,300	139.63	107,844	Leased	65,620	29,352	0	0	813,477	100,000	Kinslow, Keith, & Todd
Oregon															
Fairview	n.a.	B	525,000	270,000	4,000	67.50	195,000	Leased	60,000	20,000	0	0	525,000	0	Group Mackenzie
Portland	n.a.	B	675,000	390,000	4,375	89.14	215,000	Leased	70,000	20,000	0	0	675,000	0	Waxman & Assocs.
Portland	n.a.	B	5,300,000	2,800,000	13,000	215.38	550,000	1,200,000	750,000	75,000	0	0	5,300,000	0	Thomas Hacker
White City	7	B	1,313,069	969,945	6,640	146.08	118,379	Owned	224,745	20,160	0	0	1,287,508	25,561	Fletcher Farr…; Skelton…
Pennsylvania															
Emporium	6	M	920,596	682,926	5,600	121.95	92,270	91,820	53,580	20,500	0	250,000	510,596	160,000	Larson Design
Plum Borough	27	M	1,115,000	871,000	7,000	124.43	167,000	Owned	77,000	n.a.	0	850,000	90,000	175,000	Richard Righter
Sunbury	16	M	3,190,979	2,545,134	25,230	100.88	365,919	Owned	279,926	95,000	0	50,000	402,102	2,738,877	Larson Design
South Carolina															
Fountain Inn	12	B	1,811,529	1,264,607	11,306	111.85	198,560	190,000	158,362	65,000	0	0	1,499,436	312,093	Tarleton-Tankersley
Tennessee															
Maryville	106	M	13,300,000	9,544,150	93,000	102.93	890,000	1,250,000	1,615,850	250,000	0	0	10,000,000	3,300,000	McCarty Holsaple…
Memphis	897	MS	65,364,000	42,850,000	330,000	129.85	5,734,000	7,041,000	9,739,000	1,200,000	0	0	60,892,000	4,472,000	Looney, Ricks, Kiss
Savannah	26	M	2,071,762	1,597,346	17,000	93.96	97,742	268,900	107,774	60,000	0	100,000	1,449,678	522,084	L Hughes & Assocs.
Texas															
Amarillo	80	B	2,981,349	2,352,000	20,000	117.60	259,533	Owned	369,816	130,000	0	0	2,972,349	9,000	WD Architects
Austin	45	MS	2,087,000	1,517,000	8,000	189.63	200,000	Owned	370,000	50,000	0	0	2,087,000	0	TeamHaas Architects
Beaumont	114	B	1,959,081	1,718,234	12,000	143.19	23,721	85,409	131,717	70,000	1,947,239	0		11,842	Architectural Alliance
Canyon	27	M	1,747,299	1,089,898	11,420	95.44	285,224	125,000	247,177	4,539	0	67,500	588,746	1,091,053	BGR Architects

Table 5 / New Public Library Buildings, 2002 (cont.)

Community	Pop. ('000)	Code	Project Cost	Const. Cost	Gross Sq. Ft.	Sq. Ft. Cost	Equip. Cost	Site Cost	Other Costs	Volumes	Federal Funds	State Funds	Local Funds	Gift Funds	Architect
Virginia															
Chesterfield County	30	B	4,158,300	3,304,000	15,500	213.16	366,400	200,000	287,900	117,600	0	0	4,158,300	0	Design Collaborative
Chesterfield County	44	B	5,591,600	3,184,200	20,000	159.21	431,200	1,021,100	955,100	139,200	0	0	5,591,600	0	Design Collaborative
Disputanta	8	B	179,121	173,333	1,200	144.44	5,788	Owned	0	16,000	0	0	159,121	20,000	Whitehead/Leach
Galax	34	M	2,488,500	2,242,000	15,000	149.46	135,500	55,000	56,000	75,000	0	0	1,000,000	1,500,000	Design Collaborative
Montross	6	B	483,496	325,496	3,500	93.00	140,000	Owned	18,000	25,000	0	0	433,496	50,000	dBF Assocs.
Richmond	96	B	3,679,620	2,612,830	15,044	173.68	591,514	Owned	475,276	56,000	0	0	3,679,620	0	Design Collaborative
West Virginia															
Poca	3	B	225,000	89,960	2,400	93.75	n.a.	Leased	n.a.	10,000	0	15,000	7,000	203,000	Appalachian Log
Wisconsin															
Franklin	30	M	5,500,000	4,250,000	40,000	106.25	575,000	Owned	675,000	n.a.	0	0	5,300,000	200,000	Eppstein Uhen

Symbol Code: B—Branch Library; BS—Branch & System Headquarters; M—Main Library; MS—Main & System Headquarters; S—System Headquarters; n.a.—not available

Table 6 / Public Library Buildings, Additions and Renovations, 2002

Community	Pop. ('000)	Code	Project Cost	Const. Cost	Gross Sq. Ft.	Sq. Ft. Cost	Equip. Cost	Site Cost	Other Costs	Volumes	Federal Funds	State Funds	Local Funds	Gift Funds	Architect
Alabama															
Centre	24	M	$278,750	$247,530	3,000	82.51	$13,970	Owned	$17,250	n.a.	$0	$100,000	$78,750	$100,000	Michael Page
Arkansas															
Little Rock	301	B	2,426,459	1,995,937	18,000	110.89	65,580	167,000	197,942	n.a.	0	0	2,376,459	50,000	Stocks-Mann...
California															
Berkeley	108	M	38,000,000	23,000,000	102,000	225.49	3,000,000	Owned	12,000,000	n.a.	0	0	35,000,000	3,000,000	Ripley-Boora
Bolinas	2	B	132,397	87,367	1,074	81.35	28,868	Leased	16,162	9,662	0	0	63,728	68,669	Turnbull Griffin...
Cerritos	51	M	47,050,000	32,300,000	89,000	362.92	8,050,000	Owned	6,700,000	300,000	0	0	47,050,000	0	CWA AIA, Inc.
Hayward	48	M	1,814,300	1,400,000	8,567	163.42	114,300	Owned	300,000	65,700	0	0	1,224,300	590,000	Noll & Tam Archs.
Los Angeles	91	B	7,965,348	3,696,919	20,000	184.85	273,651	3,686,158	308,620	75,625	3,026,000	0	4,939,348	0	Arch. Div. of L.A.
Montague	1	B	60,000	25,000	1,400	17.86	35,000	Owned	0	6,000	0	0	25,000	35,000	none
Riverside	15	B	121,000	24,000	2,100	11.43	95,000	Leased	2,000	12,000	0	0	121,000	0	none
Riverside	40	B	583,139	509,077	10,779	47.23	45,813	Owned	28,249	90,000	0	0	583,130	0	Kroh/Broeske Archs.
Colorado															
Estes Park	12	M	871,000	776,000	4,000	194.00	60,000	Owned	35,000	78,000	0	0	811,000	60,000	Thorp Assocs.
Parker	30	B	429,317	299,357	4,000	74.84	104,960	Owned	25,000	57,500	0	0	409,317	20,000	Humphries Poli
Connecticut															
Mansfield	13	M	1,856,000	1,646,000	16,735	98.35	100,000	Owned	110,000	57,025	0	282,380	1,573,620	0	Schoenhardt Archs.
North Haven	23	M	5,000,000	n.a.	29,250	n.a.	n.a.	Owned	n.a.	135,000	0	0	5,000,000	0	Fredricksen & Guido
Florida															
Englewood	30	B	1,768,927	1,389,016	17,777	78.14	82,841	171,621	125,449	85,000	0	300,000	1,309,937	159,000	James F. Soller
Sebastian	38	B	1,653,382	1,315,774	12,937	101.71	151,165	Owned	186,443	128,273	0	0	1,641,251	12,131	Edlund & Dritenbas
Illinois															
Rolling Meadows	25	M	311,250	145,200	30,000	4.84	156,050	Owned	10,000	210,000	0	0	311,250	159,000	Building Consultants
St. Charles	44	M	53,037	27,259	1,616	16.87	18,492	Owned	7,286	n.a.	0	0	53,037	0	WCT Architects

Symbol Code: B—Branch Library; BS—Branch & System Headquarters; M—Main Library; MS—Main & System Headquarters; S—System Headquarters; n.a.—not available

Table 6 / Public Library Buildings, Additions and Renovations, 2002 *(cont.)*

Community	Pop. ('000)	Code	Project Cost	Const. Cost	Gross Sq. Ft.	Sq. Ft. Cost	Equip. Cost	Site Cost	Other Costs	Volumes	Federal Funds	State Funds	Local Funds	Gift Funds	Architect
Indiana															
Anderson	75	M	1,719,611	1,484,348	78,637	18.88	124,093	Owned	111,170	300,000	0	0	1,719,611	0	K.R. Montgomery
Hammond	83	M	13,979,387	9,565,207	78,172	122.36	753,527	690,000	2,970,653	308,689	0	0	13,979,387	0	InterDesign
Muncie	72	BS	5,000,000	4,108,361	43,000	95.54	581,070	Owned	310,569	89,000	0	0	4,980,000	20,000	Woollen, Molzan...
Plymouth	18	M	1,543,000	1,158,000	18,000	64.33	100,000	210,000	75,000	200,000	0	120,000	1,223,000	200,000	B.A. Martin Archs.
Salem	10	M	1,978,906	1,639,027	14,348	114.23	107,129	Owned	232,750	50,000	450,000	200,000	1,095,000	233,906	Kovert-Hawkins
Iowa															
Dallas Center	2	M	377,242	291,550	4,580	63.66	12,968	Owned	72,724	24,000	0	0	2,769	374,473	Sires Architects
Winterset	5	M	2,853,400	1,755,440	17,000	103.26	416,580	130,000	551,380	50,939	0	0	2,753,400	100,000	FEH Inc.
Kansas															
Augusta	9	MS	1,587,200	1,278,879	15,262	83.80	72,000	140,000	96,321	54,396	0	0	1,500,000	87,200	William Morris
Marion	2	M	686,908	597,478	4,200	142.26	8,538	Owned	80,892	35,000	0	463,649	73,259	150,000	Pettijohn & Kinney
Topeka	167	M	24,300,651	15,510,746	178,600	86.85	5,678,775	1,249,457	1,861,673	650,000	0	0	24,300,651	0	Horst, Terrill & Karst
Kentucky															
Florence	22	B	1,150,000	789,900	12,765	61.88	236,287	Owned	123,813	125,000	0	0	1,150,000	0	Robert E. Hayes
Franklin	16	M	290,301	267,384	6,706	39.87	0	Owned	22,917	32,000	0	255,191	35,110	0	Trimble Dunaway
Louisiana															
Natchitoches	50	MS	2,129,499	1,132,308	15,128	74.84	264,954	575,000	157,237	90,000	0	0	2,129,499	0	Slack, Alost, McSwain
New Iberia	73	MS	441,747	371,580	12,413	29.93	18,160	Owned	52,007	262,100	0	0	441,747	0	Angelle Architects
Maine															
Springvale	20	M	1,266,500	1,090,000	12,300	88.61	70,500	Owned	106,000	35,000	0	0	0	1,266,500	Scott Simons Archs.
Maryland															
Aberdeen	n.a.	B	78,295	73,633	5,117	14.39	0	Owned	4,662	n.a.	0	0	78,295	0	Smith Architects
Frederick	200	MS	10,431,100	8,594,200	66,132	129.96	1,204,600	Owned	632,300	250,000	0	0	10,265,243	165,857	Lukmire Partnership
Joppa	n.a.	B	31,852	27,190	1,481	18.36	0	Owned	4,662	n.a.	0	0	31,852	0	Smith Architects
Silver Spring	60	B	1,980,000	1,187,000	21,000	56.52	300,000	213,000	280,000	80,000	0	0	1,980,000	0	Burt Hill Kosar...
Waldorf	129	B	1,500,000	1,000,000	14,300	69.93	500,000	Owned	0	60,000	0	0	1,500,000	0	R.L. Litten & Assocs.

Location	No.	Code	Value 1	Value 2	Sq Ft	Per	Value 3	Status	Value 4	Value 5					Architect
Massachusetts															
Methuen	43	M	8,503,868	5,019,411	39,520	127.00	531,913	Owned	1,452,544	130,000	0	2,003,868	6,300,000	200,000	Tappé Assocs.
Northampton	30	M	2,100,000	1,700,000	28,000	60.71	125,000	Owned	275,000	225,000	0	575,000	997,000	528,000	Arch. Resrcs. Camb.
Worcester	173	M	23,333,142	18,844,187	145,688	129.35	2,445,830	Owned	2,043,125	649,000	0	5,826,503	13,510,000	3,996,639	Tappé Assocs.
Michigan															
Grand Rapids	9	B	1,267,322	528,092	4,632	114.01	74,987	Owned	149,947	25,351	0	0	767,322	500,000	Fishbeck, Thompson…
Romeo	4	B	434,889	289,665	7,500	38.62	110,217	Owned	35,007	25,000	0	0	409,289	25,000	none
White Pigeon	5	M	426,944	335,096	6,400	52.36	52,193	Owned	39,655	27,000	0	0	426,944	0	Leedy, Cripe Archs.
Wyoming	69	B	7,550,000	6,135,210	47,862	128.19	467,873	Owned	946,917	124,500	0	0	7,000,000	550,000	Frye Gillan Molinaro
Minnesota															
St. Anthony	8	B	605,000	415,000	5,000	83.00	101,000	Leased	89,000	24,184	0	0	605,000	0	Hay Dobbs
St. Louis Park	44	B	n.a.	n.a.	15,166	n.a.	n.a.	Owned	n.a.	73,782	n.a.	n.a.	n.a.	n.a.	Hagen & McIlwain
Mississippi															
Clarksdale	30	M	357,200	287,500	20,000	14.39	42,500	Owned	27,200	60,000	0	214,500	142,700	0	Howorth & Assocs.
Crystal Springs	5	B	382,116	357,767	2,496	143.34	3,000	Owned	21,349	30,000	0	216,000	163,116	3,000	Carl Nobles
Mendenhall	3	M	200,000	190,000	2,400	79.17	0	Owned	10,000	n.a.	0	120,000	80,000	0	Gary Cahill
Missouri															
No. Kansas City	5	M	5,244,540	4,530,747	32,000	141.59	427,250	Owned	286,543	70,000	0	0	5,244,540	0	Rafael Architects
New Hampshire															
Tamworth	3	M	721,100	624,000	7,200	86.66	50,000	Owned	47,100	22,000	0	85,000	175,000	461,100	Dennis Mires
New Jersey															
Cranford	22	M	1,750,000	1,541,000	19,408	79.40	100,000	Owned	109,000	100,000	0	393,989	1,251,011	50,000	Vincentsen Assocs.
Hackensack	37	M	723,000	455,000	37,000	12.30	218,000	Owned	50,000	178,000	0	0	723,000	0	Arcari & Iovino
New Mexico															
Roswell	61	M	3,874,754	3,273,599	37,000	88.48	274,504	Owned	326,651	231,387	0	0	3,874,754	0	Rohde May Keller…
New York															
Canandaigua	2	M	37,600	36,000	600	60.00	1,600	Owned	0	3,560	0	200,000	35,000	2,600	Hanlon Architects
Bronx	43	B	1,702,516	1,387,246	12,283	112.94	112,000	Owned	203,270	56,678	366,938	0	1,135,578	0	Nobis; Tonetti
Bronx	53	B	355,000	239,500	6,895	34.74	64,000	Owned	51,500	42,000	0	0	355,000	0	Jennifer Nobis
Bronx	57	B	857,000	605,000	9,983	60.60	87,000	Owned	165,000	48,463	95,830	0	761,170	0	Jennifer Nobis
Brooklyn	n.a.	B	987,672	832,867	7,500	111.05	8,488	Owned	146,317	60,112	0	0	987,672	0	Sen Architects
Brooklyn	n.a.	B	1,522,633	998,679	12,380	80.67	232,792	Owned	291,162	61,135	0	0	1,522,633	0	Sen Architects
Forest Hills	50	B	694,200	637,000	3,400	187.35	0	Owned	57,200	195,000	0	0	694,200	0	Schaardt & Fullan
Highland Falls	5	M	1,135,902	878,000	13,500	65.04	113,092	Owned	144,810	59,000	0	91,268	523,834	520,800	Conrad Remick

Symbol Code: B—Branch Library; BS—Branch & System Headquarters; M—Main Library; MS—Main & System Headquarters; S—System Headquarters; n.a.—not available

Table 6 / Public Library Buildings, Additions and Renovations, 2002 (cont.)

Community	Pop. ('000)	Code	Project Cost	Const. Cost	Gross Sq. Ft.	Sq. Ft. Cost	Equip. Cost	Site Cost	Other Costs	Volumes	Federal Funds	State Funds	Local Funds	Gift Funds	Architect
New York (cont.)															
Marion	5	M	369,054	282,582	4,400	64.22	44,209	Owned	42,263	15,000	0	24,000	300,845	44,209	not reported
New York	30	B	1,875,000	1,449,000	6,960	208.18	273,000	Owned	153,000	n.a.	0	0	1,375,000	500,000	Macrae-Gibson
Pleasantville	33	M	230,579	186,000	1,888	98.52	20,579	Owned	24,000	140,000	0	37,250	64,329	129,000	Busing Assocs.
Valley Cottage	23	M	950,000	675,000	3,000	225.00	175,000	Owned	100,000	60,000	8,000	50,000	892,000	0	Michael Esmay
Webster	37	M	2,009,150	1,470,042	41,000	35.85	435,000	Leased	104,108	200,000	0	40,000	1,919,150	50,000	FJF Architects
Yonkers	200	M	22,875,000	19,025,000	70,410	270.20	1,350,000	Leased	2,500,000	258,830	0	1,350,000	21,525,000	0	Highland Assocs.
North Carolina															
Charlotte	700	MS	866,977	542,022	11,000	49.27	269,955	Owned	55,000	250	0	0	831,977	35,000	Adi Mistri
North Dakota															
Minot	37	M	2,568,550	2,289,985	37,140	61.66	120,000	Owned	158,565	200,000	0	0	2,200,000	368,550	Anderson, Wade...
Ohio															
Canton	234	MS	6,383,602	4,122,602	121,288	33.99	1,148,818	103,380	1,008,802	441,114	0	0	6,383,602	0	Harris Day Archs.
Canton	81	B	1,255,024	787,581	11,100	70.95	164,986	47,650	254,807	73,076	0	0	1,255,024	0	Meehan; Lawrence
Holland	28	B	808,202	671,785	2,395	280.49	75,006	Owned	61,411	114,000	0	0	808,202	0	The Collaborative Inc.
Perrysburg	17	M	8,542,998	6,709,069	62,685	107.03	856,831	Owned	977,098	127,500	0	0	8,252,170	290,828	Munger Munger
Poland	n.a.	B	8,213,558	6,914,918	35,610	194.18	573,977	225,543	499,120	71,000	0	0	7,231,086	982,472	4M Company
St. Marys	12	M	1,529,416	1,166,594	15,448	75.52	265,536	Owned	97,286	100,000	0	0	999,900	529,516	MKC Assocs.
Toledo	32	B	829,532	689,503	2,405	286.70	79,185	Owned	60,844	123,000	0	0	829,532	0	The Collaborative Inc.
Toledo	37	B	975,978	894,278	2,099	426.05	40,839	Owned	40,861	101,000	0	0	975,978	0	Vetter Design Group
Westlake	33	M	10,363,010	7,258,678	75,000	96.78	1,679,949	675,225	749,158	285,700	0	861,677	9,082,833	418,500	David Holzheimer
Oklahoma															
Geary	1	M	54,494	36,216	2,540	14.26	18,278	Owned	0	9,000	0	20,000	34,494	0	none
Skiatook	5	B	156,296	64,589	5,400	11.96	76,751	Owned	14,956	23,691	0	0	156,296	0	Woody Design
Tulsa	n.a.	B	1,986,106	1,495,439	29,708	50.34	349,443	Owned	141,224	91,979	0	0	1,986,106	0	Dewberry Design
Warner	2	B	163,145	149,545	2,900	51.57	8,600	Owned	5,000	16,000	0	146,000	8,811	8,334	Bill Stiger
Oregon															
Portland	n.a.	B	674,000	407,000	5,000	81.40	200,000	Leased	67,000	20,000	0	0	674,000	0	Holst Architecture
West Linn	23	M	3,900,000	3,037,640	27,000	112.51	239,255	Owned	623,105	200,000	0	0	3,900,000	0	SRG Partnership

Pennsylvania															
Avalon	12	M	1,650,291	1,185,291	7,787	152.21	87,000	230,000	148,000	25,000	0	1,100,000	550,291	0	Franus Architectural
Connellsville	38	M	128,379	77,785	452	172.09	23,022	Owned	27,572	2,260	50,000	0	2,915	75,464	Cochran Assocs.
Monroeville	30	M	95,885	74,166	300	247.22	8,412	Owned	13,307	n.a.	0	95,885	0	0	Design 3 Architecture
New Cumberland	7	M	1,179,733	1,026,356	6,600	155.51	55,039	Owned	98,338	77,477	0	355,000	131,701	693,032	Lenker Architects
Philadelphia	26	B	1,536,600	962,249	9,400	102.37	286,600	Owned	287,751	26,419	n.a.	n.a.	n.a.	n.a.	George Yu Architects
Warren	30	M	590,026	362,752	11,800	30.74	164,997	Owned	62,277	260,000	0	0	312,033	277,993	Habiterra Design
Rhode Island															
New Shoreham	1	M	1,791,991	1,527,442	9,445	161.72	68,000	Owned	196,549	28,500	0	797,995	481,862	512,134	Prout Robert & Elias
Portsmouth	17	M	718,785	512,807	13,316	38.51	112,743	Owned	93,235	81,265	0	338,149	117,043	263,593	Prout Robert & Elias
Woonsocket	43	M	3,895,442	3,201,614	25,899	123.62	358,633	Owned	335,195	145,000	0	1,920,153	1,160,750	814,539	Robinson, Green...
South Dakota															
Milbank	8	M	10,554	5,681	192	29.58	2,372	Owned	2,501	1,150	0	0	554	10,000	Schimmel Constr.
Tennessee															
Cleveland	88	M	625,869	428,220	5,000	85.64	165,130	Owned	32,519	40,000	100,000	20,000	405,869	100,000	Smith & Henderson
Madison	45	B	137,187	119,845	4,923	24.35	10,423	Owned	6,919	0	0	0	137,187	0	Gobbell Hayes
Martin	18	M	1,004,028	908,284	11,820	76.84	39,024	Owned	56,720	54,860	199,000	0	728,414	76,614	Anderson Vaughan
Nashville	7	B	68,689	59,798	606	98.68	1,479	Owned	7,412	10,000	0	0	68,689	0	Heery International
Texas															
Carrollton	113	B	6,812,989	3,700,000	37,000	100.00	237,989	2,500,000	375,000	151,483	0	120,000	6,692,989	0	F&S Partners
Grapevine	45	M	6,548,520	5,204,934	53,000	98.21	726,571	Owned	617,015	391,740	0	0	6,548,520	0	Phillips Swager
Utah															
Lehi	30	M	1,318,750	1,078,450	17,000	63.44	233,300	Owned	7,000	47,032	68,038	0	1,228,212	22,500	Wilson Mark
Vermont															
Montpelier	18	M	2,570,000	2,232,000	18,350	121.63	90,000	Owned	248,000	70,000	750,000	20,000	942,000	858,000	Gossens Bachman
Virginia															
Alexandria	25	B	815,330	520,280	9,870	52.71	223,500	Owned	71,550	40,056	0	0	815,330	0	Murray & Assocs.
Danville	50	B	17,154	17,154	1,500	11.44	0	Leased	0	10,000	0	0	17,154	0	not reported
Honaker	8	B	156,319	34,806	1,900	18.32	31,101	75,000	15,412	4,000	0	12,558	16,934	126,827	Lane Engineering
Marshall	11	B	163,624	131,818	3,200	41.19	17,500	Owned	14,306	14,000	0	0	158,624	5,000	SHW Group
Rohok Area	9	B	160,453	145,800	2,700	54.00	2,803	Owned	11,850	34,000	0	0	155,453	5,000	De Stefano Design
Rural Retreat	1	B	215,515	86,718	2,475	35.04	31,903	85,700	11,194	7,000	96,828	50,000	0	68,687	Cameron L. Wolfe Jr.
Virginia Beach	50	B	400,000	300,000	5,000	60.00	100,000	Leased	0	22,000	0	0	400,000	0	Lyall Design

Symbol Code: B—Branch Library; BS—Branch & System Headquarters; M—Main Library; MS—Main & System Headquarters; S—System Headquarters; n.a.—not available

Table 7 / Public Library Buildings, Six-Year Cost Summary

	Fiscal 1996	Fiscal 1997	Fiscal 1999*	Fiscal 2000	Fiscal 2001	Fiscal 2002
Number of new buildings	100	97	77	114	80	101
Number of ARRs[1]	145	128	118	127	132	111
Sq. ft. new buildings	2,002,067	2,153,203	1,555,583	1,752,395	1,924,548	2,144,185
Sq. ft. ARRs	2,315,523	2,710,599	2,188,221	2,272,684	2,215,702	2,351,100
New Buildings						
Construction cost	$286,141,319	$227,740,506	$192,319,192	$232,832,870	$275,404,635	$303,284,460
Equipment cost	57,222,035	35,983,384	25,382,314	36,127,111	51,445,962	44,985,041
Site cost	16,391,748	33,630,070	22,634,855	28,655,584	33,375,676	28,523,513
Other cost	49,498,901	40,060,597	43,631,263	39,878,940	39,511,803	48,115,515
Total—project cost	409,254,003	337,414,557	283,967,624	331,345,167	400,838,076	429,787,571
ARRs—project cost	314,191,342	324,762,086	280,604,091	301,200,950	285,583,407	358,658,087
New & ARR project cost	$723,445,345	$662,176,643	$564,571,715	$632,546,117	$686,421,483	$788,445,658
Fund Sources						
Federal, new buildings	$17,719,253	$4,572,130	$7,655,690	$7,598,492	$2,687,151	$5,395,598
Federal, ARRs	13,771,483	7,698,270	9,268,183	2,600,334	6,959,013	5,197,596
Federal, total	$31,490,736	$12,270,400	$16,923,873	$10,198,826	$9,646,164	$10,593,194
State, new buildings	$32,089,611	$73,081,134	$17,122,988	$12,456,471	$6,696,211	$13,745,400
State, ARRs	21,212,540	62,169,948	21,677,529	36,982,165	19,396,775	18,874,053
State, total	$53,302,151	$135,251,082	$38,800,517	$49,438,636	$26,092,986	$32,619,453
Local, new buildings	$301,996,679	$228,793,054	$226,616,333	$287,118,370	$356,563,114	$363,288,508
Local, ARRs	182,163,428	233,525,418	201,166,513	220,776,786	211,059,513	312,253,572
Local, total	$484,160,107	$462,318,472	$427,782,846	$507,895,156	$567,622,627	$675,542,080
Gift, new buildings	$57,478,470	$31,168,178	$32,563,613	$26,544,144	$34,923,118	$39,257,565
Gift, ARRs	97,019,403	21,345,010	48,614,252	33,309,803	43,344,138	20,795,667
Gift, total	$154,497,873	$52,513,188	$81,177,865	$59,853,947	$78,267,256	$60,053,232
Total Funds Used	$723,450,867	$662,353,142	$564,685,101	$627,386,565	$681,629,033	$778,807,959

[1] Additions, remodelings, and renovations. *Summary statistics were not kept for Fiscal 1998.

Book Trade Research and Statistics

Prices of U.S. and Foreign Published Materials

Sharon G. Sullivan
Chair, ALA ALCTS Library Materials Price Index Committee

The Library Materials Price Index Committee (LMPIC) of the American Library Association's Association for Library Collections and Technical Services continues to monitor library prices for a range of library materials from sources within North America and from other key publishing centers around the world. During 2001 price increases for library materials significantly exceeded the increase in the U.S. Consumer Price Index (CPI). However, the preliminary data for 2002 available at the time of publication suggested a return to the price levels of previous years. CPI data are obtained from the Bureau of Labor Statistics Web site at http://www.bls.gov/cpi/.

Some indexes have not been updated and are repeated from last year. Recent changes in the publishing and distribution world due to mergers and acquisitions have made it more difficult to determine what is published in a foreign country by "multinational" firms. Additionally, the conversion to the euro by several countries has affected our ability to obtain information from foreign agents and wholesalers. The conversion of pricing data from national currencies to the euro makes comparison from this year to prior years inconsistent. In other cases, the vendors were unable to provide data due to internal system migrations. The CD-ROM Price Inventory (former Table 10) is no longer being updated because the number of CD-ROM titles continues to decrease, with many of these publications migrating to Web-based publications.

Index	Percent Change				
	1997	1998/1999*	2000	2001	2002
CPI	1.7	2.7	2.7	1.6	2.4
Periodicals	10.3*	10.4	9.2	8.6	n.a.
Serials services	4.5*	5.6	5.3	5.8	n.a.
Hardcover books	-4.4	-1.9	-2.4	15.1	n.a.
Academic books	2.1	3.8	n.a.	0.4	-3.1
College books	2.7	-1.3	2.3	1.9	n.a.
Mass market paperbacks	1.7	3.5	2.3	9.4	n.a.
Trade paperbacks	1.1	6.5	-5.7	22.9	n.a.

*Payments made in 1997 for 1998 receipts.

n.a. = not available

U.S. Published Materials

Tables 1 through 9 indicate average prices and price indexes for library materials published primarily in the United States. These indexes include Periodicals (Table 1), Serials Services (Table 2), U.S. Hardcover Books (Table 3), North American Academic Books (Table 4), U.S. College Books (Table 5), U.S. Mass Market Paperback Books (Table 6), U.S. Trade Paperbacks (Table 7), U.S. Daily Newspapers and International Newspapers (Tables 8A and 8B), and U.S. Nonprint Media (Table 9).

Periodical and Serial Prices

The U.S. Periodicals Price Index (Table 1) and U.S. Serials Services Index (Table 2) are repeated from last year. The Library Materials Price Index Committee and divine/Faxon Academic Services, formerly the Faxon Company, jointly produced the U.S. Periodicals Price Index and the U.S. Serials Services Index for many years. Following the sale of the subscription services division of divine, the data from divine/Faxon were not available in usable form in time for publication. Alternate sources of periodical pricing data are being explored for next year.

The subscription prices shown are publishers' list prices, excluding publisher discount or vendor service charges. This report includes 2000, 2001, and 2002 data indexed to the base year of 1984. More extensive reports on the periodical price index are expected to be published later this year by the Association for Library Collections and Technical Services.

Compiled by Brenda Dingley and Barbara Albee, Table 1 shows that U.S. periodical prices, excluding Russian translations, increased by 7.9 percent from 2001 to 2002. This figure represents a 0.4 percent decrease in the overall rate of inflation from the 8.3 percent figure posted in 2001. Including the Russian translation category, the single-year increase was only slightly lower, at 7.6 percent for 2002. This figure is 1.0 percent lower than the rate of 8.6 percent for the entire sample in 2001. The multidisciplinary category of Russian translations again posted the highest percentage price increase (at 10.6 percent), while Sociology and Anthropology posted the highest increase of any single subject category (also at 10.6 percent). The subject category Political Science, which in 2001 had the highest increase of any single subject category, dropped to fifth place in 2002, with an 8.9 percent rise. No other subject category posted a double-digit increase in 2002.

Nancy Chaffin, compiler of the U.S. Serials Services Index (Table 2), noted that titles continued to experience migration from print to electronic format. As the index is built only of printed products, the e-only titles have been dropped from the various subject indexes. While some were converting to CD-ROM, there was a stronger movement toward Web-based delivery, especially in the Business category. U.S. Government Documents were also increasingly delivered only via the Web. As this trend continues, it becomes more difficult to identify new titles that are print subscriptions.

All areas of serials services saw increases in prices for 2002, with the highest in Law (6.8 percent) and the lowest (3.3 percent) in Business. The average

(text continues on page 502)

Table 1 / U.S. Periodicals: Average Prices and Price Indexes, 2000–2002
Index Base: 1984 = 100

Subject Area	1984 Average Price	2000 Average Price	2000 Index	2001 Average Price	2001 Index	2002 Average Price	2002 Index
U.S. periodicals excluding Russian translations	$54.97	$241.54	439.4	$261.56	475.8	$282.31	513.6
U.S. periodicals including Russian translations	72.47	311.37	429.7	338.25	466.7	363.77	502.0
Agriculture	24.06	92.72	385.4	102.57	423.6	109.11	453.5
Business and economics	38.87	142.08	365.5	152.79	393.1	164.70	423.7
Chemistry and physics	228.90	1,302.79	569.2	1,407.47	614.9	1,519.83	664.0
Children's periodicals	12.21	25.14	205.9	25.52	209.0	26.56	217.5
Education	34.01	124.23	365.3	135.72	399.1	146.98	432.2
Engineering	78.70	369.23	469.2	401.32	509.9	432.88	550.0
Fine and applied arts	26.90	56.51	210.1	59.17	220.0	62.33	231.7
General interest periodicals	27.90	44.48	159.4	45.96	164.7	47.57	170.5
History	23.68	63.12	266.6	67.06	283.2	72.23	305.0
Home economics	37.15	115.57	311.1	125.77	338.5	136.69	367.9
Industrial arts	30.40	110.83	364.6	112.57	370.3	122.70	403.6
Journalism and communications	39.25	116.17	296.0	122.44	311.9	128.96	328.6
Labor and industrial relations	29.87	114.84	384.5	127.02	425.2	135.74	454.4
Law	31.31	93.44	298.4	95.40	304.7	101.56	324.4
Library and information sciences	38.85	95.78	246.5	106.31	273.6	115.98	298.5
Literature and language	23.02	55.74	242.1	60.03	260.8	64.95	282.1
Mathematics, botany, geology, general science	106.56	516.70	484.9	559.23	524.8	603.11	566.0
Medicine	125.57	663.21	528.2	726.61	578.6	789.44	628.7
Philosophy and religion	21.94	58.54	266.8	62.43	284.5	67.11	305.9
Physical education and recreation	20.54	51.87	252.5	54.11	263.4	57.15	278.2
Political science	32.43	121.62	375.0	136.59	421.2	148.77	458.7
Psychology	69.74	319.46	458.1	355.63	509.9	387.15	555.1
Russian translations	381.86	1,575.51	412.6	1,774.85	464.8	1,962.39	513.9
Sociology and anthropology	43.87	182.56	416.1	197.24	449.6	217.37	495.5
Zoology	78.35	470.43	600.4	510.53	651.6	543.96	694.3
Total number of periodicals							
Excluding Russian translations	3,731	3,729		3,729		3,729	
Including Russian translations	3,942	3,935		3,928		3,919	

For further comments, see *American Libraries*, May 2000, May 2001, and May 2002.
Compiled by Barbara Albee, divine/Faxon Library Services, and Brenda Dingley, University of Missouri, Kansas City.

Table 2 / U.S. Serial Services: Average Price and Price Indexes 2000–2002
Index Base: 1984 = 100

Subject Area	1984 Average Price	2000 Average Price	2000 Index	2001 Average Price	2001 Percent Increase	2001 Index	2002 Average Price	2002 Percent Increase	2002 Index
U.S. serial services*	$295.13	$671.94	227.7	$711.07	5.80%	240.9	$747.16	5.10%	253.2
Business	437.07	820.73	187.8	822.48	0.20	188.2	849.65	3.30	194.4
General and humanities	196.55	503.98	256.4	538.68	6.90	274.1	569.02	5.60	289.5
Law	275.23	703.56	255.6	786.39	11.8	285.7	839.65	6.80	305.1
Science and technology	295.36	866.69	293.4	924.29	6.60	312.9	975.49	5.50	330.3
Social sciences	283.82	600.06	211.4	624.62	4.10	220.1	656.54	5.10	231.3
U.S. documents	97.37	195.16	200.4	197.26	1.10	202.6	202.60	2.70	208.1
Total number of services	1,537	1,294		1,302			1,311		

Compiled by Nancy J. Chaffin, Arizona State University (West) from data supplied by divine/Faxon Library Services, publishers' list prices, and library acquisitions records.

The definition of a serial service has been taken from *American National Standard for Library and Information Services and Related Publishing Practices—Library Materials—Criteria for Price Indexes* (ANSI Z39.20 - 1983).

* Excludes Wilson Index; excludes Russian translations as of 1988.

Table 3 / U.S. Hardcover Books: Average Prices and Price Indexes, 2000–2002

Index Base: 1997 = 100

Category	1997 Average Price	2000 Final Volumes	2000 Final Average Price	2000 Final Index	2001 Final Volumes	2001 Final Average Price	2001 Final Index	2002 Preliminary Volumes	2002 Preliminary Average Price	2002 Preliminary Index
Agriculture	$63.70	563	$66.52	104.4	582	$61.03	95.8	453	$63.88	100.3
Arts	55.99	2,447	50.31	89.9	2,586	56.00	100.0	2,195	53.86	96.2
Biography	54.78	2,017	45.31	82.7	2,385	53.05	96.8	2,444	44.00	80.3
Business	99.34	1,588	93.84	94.5	1,685	95.61	96.3	1,869	93.14	93.8
Education	85.74	1,107	62.23	72.6	1,328	72.55	84.6	1,202	55.22	64.4
Fiction	24.97	4,250	25.75	103.1	4,183	28.84	115.5	4,309	28.01	112.2
General works	108.87	639	165.39	151.9	693	167.40	153.8	699	155.05	142.4
History	62.81	4,137	54.01	86.0	4,514	61.21	97.5	3,122	54.44	86.7
Home economics	36.79	1,081	39.76	108.1	1,011	51.45	139.9	902	31.75	86.3
Juveniles	19.25	5,119	22.71	118.0	6,217	23.85	123.9	6,346	21.18	110.0
Language	71.9	1,143	57.27	79.7	1,243	73.96	102.9	936	66.12	92.0
Law	109.95	1,400	101.5	92.3	1,483	89.70	81.6	1,112	94.66	86.1
Literature	62.07	1,776	55.17	88.9	1,747	62.99	101.5	1,982	64.70	104.2
Medicine	111.88	2,845	90.32	80.7	2,864	99.62	89.0	2,652	95.52	85.4
Music	57.87	619	42.91	74.2	1,799	112.31	194.1	582	53.80	93.0
Philosophy, psychology	59.87	2,321	52.02	86.9	2,409	66.03	110.3	2,331	59.73	99.8
Poetry, drama	46.99	708	39.90	84.9	757	43.79	93.2	844	46.32	98.6
Religion	54.32	2,629	41.61	76.6	2,981	41.93	77.2	2,532	44.17	81.3
Science	103.54	5,222	90.11	87.0	5,060	100.61	97.2	4,098	96.35	93.1
Sociology, economics	79.32	6,981	66.79	84.2	8,220	94.80	119.5	6,786	68.29	86.1
Sports, recreation	46.97	1,254	40.64	86.5	1,289	41.63	88.6	1,219	41.85	89.1
Technology	133.58	3,449	102.4	76.7	3,262	99.93	74.8	2,799	88.16	66.0
Travel	44.87	652	40.27	89.8	664	67.88	151.3	483	41.71	93.0
Totals	$72.67	53,947	$60.84	83.7	58,962	$70.05	96.4	51,897	$59.80	82.3

Table 4 / North American Academic Books: Average Prices and Price Indexes 1999–2001
(Index Base: 1989 = 100)

Subject Area	LC Class	1989		1999		2000		2001			
		No. of Titles	Average Price	No. of Titles	Average Price	No. of Titles	Average Price	No. of Titles	Average Price	% Change 2000–2001	Index
Agriculture	S	897	$45.13	1,001	$64.90	1,152	$69.25	1,193	$72.76	5.1	161.2
Anthropology	GN	406	32.81	607	45.87	568	45.78	544	45.18	-1.3	137.7
Botany	QK	251	69.02	210	96.01	179	103.05	200	104.00	0.9	150.7
Business and economics	H	5,979	41.67	6,494	60.13	6,642	60.22	6,191	61.87	2.7	148.5
Chemistry	QD	577	110.61	592	132.46	515	143.81	505	133.92	-6.9	121.1
Education	L	1,685	29.61	2,377	41.39	2,623	44.29	2,413	42.31	-4.5	142.9
Engineering and technology	T	4,569	64.94	4,926	90.79	5,116	94.53	5,915	96.59	2.2	148.7
Fine and applied arts	M-N	3,040	40.72	3,655	46.21	3,955	45.84	4,243	63.42	38.4	155.7
General works	A	333	134.65	131	141.20	155	124.02	86	112.99	-8.9	83.9
Geography	G	396	47.34	693	59.29	633	60.85	722	58.99	-3.1	124.6
Geology	QE	303	63.49	220	87.77	229	81.05	287	105.50	30.2	166.2
History	C-D-E-F	5,549	31.34	6,396	39.91	7,078	43.22	7,530	40.48	-6.3	129.2
Home economics	TX	535	27.10	682	30.21	628	31.60	605	34.28	8.5	126.5
Industrial arts	TT	175	23.89	145	29.96	198	28.82	185	29.85	3.6	124.9
Law	K	1,252	51.10	1,717	71.42	1,679	74.48	1,804	68.93	-7.5	134.9

Subject	LC Class										
Library and information science	Z	857	44.51	639	57.29	608	68.44	630	64.31	-6.0	144.5
Literature and language	P	10,812	24.99	11,181	34.38	11,684	35.90	12,799	35.27	-1.8	141.1
Mathematics and computer science	QA	2,707	44.68	4,120	64.57	4,172	64.76	4,166	68.28	5.4	152.8
Medicine	R	5,028	58.38	6,175	73.20	5,832	74.51	5,526	73.50	-1.4	125.9
Military and naval science	U-V	715	33.57	529	66.61	548	62.03	538	55.84	-10.0	166.3
Philosophy and religion	B	3,518	29.06	4,760	42.94	5,046	45.52	4,863	44.65	-1.9	153.6
Physical education and recreation	GV	814	20.38	718	28.33	827	29.11	964	31.32	7.6	153.7
Physics and astronomy	QB	1,219	64.59	1,149	95.29	1,065	97.66	1,202	99.52	1.9	154.1
Political science	J	1,650	36.76	2,056	53.10	2,074	53.81	1,781	50.75	-5.7	138.1
Psychology	BF	890	31.97	1,337	49.79	1,173	47.04	1,089	44.69	-5.0	139.8
Science (general)	Q	433	56.10	313	71.09	324	70.58	357	83.51	18.3	148.9
Sociology	HM	2,742	29.36	3,815	44.99	3,886	46.53	3,886	46.76	0.5	159.3
Zoology	QH,L,P,R	1,967	71.28	1,927	86.84	1,951	86.54	2,065	84.13	-2.8	118.0
Average for all subjects		59,299	$41.69	68,565	$56.30	70,540	$57.42	72,289	$57.65	0.4	138.3

Compiled by Stephen Bosch, University of Arizona, from electronic data provided by Baker and Taylor, Blackwell North America, and Yankee Book Peddler. The data represent all titles (hardcover, trade, and paperback books, as well as annuals) treated for all approval plan customers serviced by the three vendors. Due to the merger between Yankee and Baker and Taylor, Baker and Taylor no longer services approval accounts, so the B&T data represent all 2001 imprints in their database. This table covers titles published or distributed in the United States and Canada during the calendar years listed.

This index does include paperback editions. The overall average price of materials is lower than if the index consisted only of hardbound editions.

Table 5 / U.S. College Books: Average Prices and Price Indexes, 1999–2001

(Index base for all years: 1983=100. 2000 also indexed to 1999; 2001 also indexed to 2000)

Choice Subject Categories	1983		1999			2000				2001			
	No. of Titles	Avg. Price Per Title	No. of Titles	Avg. Price Per Title	Prices Indexed to 1983	No. of Titles	Avg. Price Per Title	Prices Indexed to 1983	Prices Indexed to 1999	No. of Titles	Avg. Price Per Title	Prices Indexed to 1983	Prices Indexed to 2000
General	11	$24.91	23	$50.75	203.7	—	—	—	—	41	—	—	—
Humanities	40	$24.53	36	$45.73	186.4	43	$49.57	202.1	108.4	130	$48.69	198.5	98.2
Art and architecture	372	40.31	373	53.21	132.0	123	52.61	130.5	98.9	63	49.73	123.4	94.5
Communication	51	22.22	82	47.38	213.2	60	46.12	207.5	97.3	98	49.90	224.6	108.2
Language and literature	109	23.39	88	45.40	194.1	102	49.05	209.7	108.0	98	51.23	219.0	104.4
African and Middle Eastern [4]	—	—	26	37.94	—	25	51.31	—	135.2	30	44.89	—	87.5
Asian and Oceanian [4]	—	—	29	41.02	—	28	49.21	—	120.0	23	42.26	—	85.9
Classical	19	28.68	25	48.06	167.6	16	48.33	168.5	100.6	20	51.94	181.1	107.5
English and American	579	23.47	512	46.48	198.0	515	45.60	194.3	98.1	530	47.06	200.5	103.2
Germanic	53	20.45	41	42.90	209.8	25	50.51	247.0	117.8	42	46.39	226.8	91.8
Romance	93	20.47	89	42.43	207.3	106	46.61	227.7	109.9	86	46.80	228.6	100.4
Slavic	35	23.09	31	52.81	228.7	25	49.26	213.3	93.3	22	52.00	225.2	105.6
Performing arts	19	24.32	22	42.73	175.7	15	39.22	161.3	91.8	15	44.75	184.0	114.1
Film	67	24.81	79	48.72	196.4	110	47.60	191.8	97.7	90	50.46	203.4	106.0
Music	106	25.09	119	46.56	185.6	80	51.21	204.1	110.0	115	50.67	202.0	99.0
Theater and Dance [5]	51	23.18	43	45.01	194.2	50	47.63	205.5	105.8	53	50.94	219.8	107.0
Philosophy	155	26.27	177	47.83	182.1	155	46.43	176.7	97.1	158	45.80	174.3	98.6
Religion	196	19.33	209	38.95	201.5	149	40.37	208.9	103.6	222	37.94	196.3	94.0
Total Humanities [6]	2,038	$26.26	1,981	$46.74	178.0	1,932	$48.32	184.0	103.4	1,988	$48.05	183.0	99.4
Science/Technology	159	$36.11	88	$39.94	110.6	63	$38.50	106.6	96.4	55	$43.14	119.5	112.0
History of science/technology	56	28.45	79	46.32	162.8	70	41.25	145.0	89.0	75	47.06	165.4	114.1
Astronautics/astronomy	18	27.78	34	41.74	150.2	56	35.94	129.4	86.1	57	43.96	158.3	122.3
Biology	145	39.28	103	52.95	134.8	113	55.49	141.3	104.8	129	46.98	119.6	84.7
Botany	23	31.78	86	50.75	159.7	82	59.13	186.1	116.5	75	59.21	186.3	100.1
Zoology	38	44.21	79	47.10	106.5	70	53.93	122.0	114.5	71	56.62	128.1	105.0
Chemistry	30	48.57	64	99.32	204.5	35	109.93	226.3	110.7	47	82.99	170.9	75.5
Earth science	42	35.43	63	58.86	166.1	55	66.09	186.5	112.3	59	72.64	205.0	109.9
Engineering	154	44.88	70	76.12	169.6	78	82.37	183.5	108.2	70	77.66	173.0	94.3
Health sciences	121	24.45	124	41.91	171.4	124	53.09	217.1	126.7	138	49.67	203.1	93.6
Information/computer science	63	29.48	40	43.15	146.4	35	42.53	144.3	98.6	35	53.12	180.2	124.9
Mathematics	44	32.82	70	59.17	180.3	101	59.57	181.5	100.7	84	55.91	170.4	93.9
Physics	38	34.13	38	58.97	172.8	45	47.02	137.8	79.7	57	47.71	139.8	101.5
Sports/physical education	61	18.67	53	35.98	192.7	55	37.89	202.9	105.3	—	—	—	—
Total Science/Technology	992	$34.77	991	$53.22	153.1	982	$55.41	159.4	104.1	999	$54.51	156.8	98.4

Subject												
Social/Behavioral Sciences	173	$24.24	179.4	43.50	66	169.6	54	$41.11	94.5	86	52.42	216.2	127.5
Anthropology	98	26.68	192.4	51.33	162	190.8	147	50.91	99.2	152	50.52	189.4	99.2
Business management/labor	156	25.01	164.8	41.23	146	176.7	153	44.19	107.2	140	44.37	177.4	100.4
Economics	315	27.60	177.0	48.86	245	195.4	260	53.92	110.3	256	50.00	181.2	92.7
Education	120	20.23	216.2	43.74	204	213.8	153	43.25	98.9	162	47.61	235.3	110.1
History, geography/area studies	92	25.58	189.3	48.43	48	176.8	50	45.24	93.4	88	44.85	175.3	99.1
Africa	17	26.94	180.9	48.75	31	192.7	32	51.90	106.5	23	56.62	210.2	109.1
Ancient history	46	31.80	168.5	53.58	39	207.3	42	65.94	123.1	26	48.23	151.7	73.1
Asia and Oceania	58	25.55	195.5	49.95	61	194.1	65	49.60	99.3	80	49.27	192.8	99.3
Central and Eastern Europe [3]	—	—	—	50.76	44	—	54	51.21	100.9	61	46.41	—	90.6
Latin America and Caribbean	25	24.72	199.6	49.35	47	205.7	64	50.85	103.0	49	47.76	193.2	93.9
Middle East and North Africa	33	28.42	185.4	52.69	34	170.1	40	48.34	91.8	39	51.94	182.8	107.4
North America	274	24.42	162.8	39.76	430	156.1	431	38.11	95.8	364	40.33	165.2	105.8
United Kingdom [3]	—	—	—	52.90	124	—	113	53.60	101.3	104	55.81	—	104.1
Western Europe [3]	439	25.00	213.8	49.73	128	187.7	124	53.32	107.2	156	48.71	193.5	91.4
Political science	—	—	—	53.44	24	—	19	46.93	87.8	31	48.37	—	103.1
Comparative politics [2]	—	—	—	52.57	202	—	197	53.10	101.0	170	51.12	—	96.3
International relations [2]	—	—	—	50.28	137	—	142	50.74	100.9	160	50.78	—	100.1
Political theory [2]	—	—	—	40.08	59	—	50	50.78	126.7	55	48.90	—	96.3
U.S. politics [2]	—	—	—	42.78	166	—	183	45.05	105.3	146	42.43	—	94.2
Psychology	162	26.57	172.8	45.92	141	150.0	116	39.86	86.8	106	49.65	186.9	124.6
Sociology	244	24.38	192.9	47.02	132	187.2	156	45.63	97.0	193	50.61	207.6	110.9
Total Social/Behavioral Sciences	2,537	$25.81	180.5	$46.58	2,670	183.3	2,645	$47.31	101.6	2,647	$47.93	185.7	101.3
Total General, Humanities, Science/Technology, Social/Behavioral Sciences (excl. Reference) [6]	5,578	$27.57	173.4	$47.81	5,665	178.1	5,559	$49.10	102.7	5,634	$49.14	178.2	100.1
Reference	506	$44.75	—	$88.00	64	—	93	$73.74	—	109	$84.57	—	—
General [1]	—	—	—	97.60	185	—	199	89.33	83.8	177	94.47	—	114.7
Humanities [1]	—	—	—	97.50	73	—	91	85.67	91.5	82	103.90	—	105.8
Science/Technology [1]	—	—	—	94.03	236	—	243	97.96	87.9	266	107.83	—	121.3
Social/Behavioral [1]	—	—	—	—	—	—	—	—	104.2	—	—	—	110.1
Total Reference	506	$44.75	212.2	$94.98	558	200.7	626	$89.83	94.6	634	$99.59	222.6	110.9
Grand Total (incl. Reference) [6]	6,084	$29.00	179.5	$52.04	6,223	183.5	6,185	$53.22	102.3	6,268	$54.24	187.0	101.9

1 Began appearing as separate sections in July 1997.
2 Began appearing as separate sections in March 1988
3 Began appearing as separate sections, replacing Europe, in July 1997.
4 Began appearing as separate sections in September 1995.
5 Separate sections for Theater and Dance combined in September 1995.
6 1983 totals include Linguistics (incorporated into Language and Literature in 1985), Non-European/Other (replaced by African and Middle Eastern and Asian and Oceanian in September 1995), and Europe (replaced by Central and Eastern Europe, United Kingdom and Western Europe in July 1997).

Compiled by Donna Alsbury, Florida Center for Library Automation.

Table 6 / Mass Market Paperbacks Average Per-Volume Prices, 2000–2002

Category	1997 Average Prices	2000 Final Volumes	2000 Final Average Prices	2000 Final Index	2001 Final Volumes	2001 Final Average Prices	2001 Final Index	2002 Preliminary Volumes	2002 Preliminary Average Prices	2002 Preliminary Index
Agriculture	$7.50	8	$7.48	99.7	7	$5.96	79.5	1	$7.95	106.0
Arts	6.54	19	7.26	111.0	17	6.74	103.1	23	8.27	126.5
Biography	6.46	96	6.71	103.9	71	7.49	115.9	74	6.61	102.3
Business	6.51	20	8.41	129.2	64	9.51	146.1	6	7.80	119.8
Education	7.32	15	7.30	99.7	18	6.85	93.6	32	6.51	88.9
Fiction	5.40	4,020	5.78	107.0	3,498	6.29	116.5	2,384	6.81	126.1
General works	7.48	12	6.57	87.8	15	6.92	92.5	19	8.11	108.4
History	6.13	36	7.36	120.1	63	7.01	114.4	47	6.81	111.1
Home economics	6.89	48	7.07	102.6	82	7.89	114.5	24	7.69	111.6
Juveniles	4.69	2,358	5.21	111.1	1,972	5.49	117.1	2,183	5.72	122.0
Language	5.92	35	6.92	116.9	64	6.36	107.4	66	6.50	109.8
Law	6.69	5	8.77	131.1	4	6.73	100.6	3	7.66	114.5
Literature	6.72	64	6.71	99.9	74	7.06	105.1	62	7.94	118.2
Medicine	6.53	77	6.70	102.6	127	8.15	124.8	41	7.33	112.3
Music	7.97	17	7.24	90.8	2	6.97	87.5	11	7.52	94.4
Philosophy, psychology	6.52	127	7.24	111.0	188	7.43	114.0	112	7.41	113.7
Poetry, drama	6.41	39	6.09	95.0	22	6.17	96.3	17	7.23	112.8
Religion	6.99	85	8.16	116.7	188	7.77	111.2	111	8.40	120.2
Science	5.17	52	6.58	127.3	86	6.53	126.3	56	6.29	121.7
Sociology, economics	6.76	89	6.99	103.4	176	7.73	114.4	74	7.67	113.5
Sports, recreation	6.43	91	6.66	103.6	65	7.79	121.2	62	8.18	127.2
Technology	6.87	16	6.71	97.7	34	7.74	112.7	17	7.92	115.3
Travel	8.75	21	8.65	98.9	23	7.57	86.5	22	9.04	103.3
Totals	$5.36	7,350	$5.77	107.7	6,860	$6.31	117.7	5,447	$6.48	120.9

Table 7 / U.S. Paperbacks (Excluding Mass Market): Average Prices and Price Indexes, 2000–2002

Index Base: 1997 = 100

Category	1997 Average Price	2000 Final			2001 Final			2002 Preliminary		
		Volumes	Average Price	Index	Volumes	Average Price	Index	Volumes	Average Price	Index
Agriculture	$28.50	502	$41.31	145.0	606	$36.64	128.6	434	$26.31	92.3
Arts	27.78	2,514	26.96	97.1	2,726	30.49	109.8	2,265	27.23	98.0
Biography	19.83	1,786	19.47	98.2	2,438	20.33	102.5	2,534	21.55	108.7
Business	128.45	2,461	52.00	40.5	3,278	93.48	72.8	2,696	50.81	39.6
Education	27.41	2,257	28.43	103.7	2,575	29.08	106.1	2,424	29.20	106.5
Fiction	16.22	6,345	15.90	98.0	9,674	17.98	110.9	8,440	17.20	106.0
General works	199.57	667	39.84	20.0	844	118.76	59.5	752	46.25	23.2
History	26.24	3,758	27.24	103.8	4,454	24.38	92.9	3,658	25.44	97.0
Home economics	25.16	1,384	18.95	75.3	1,337	32.49	129.1	1,235	18.72	74.4
Juveniles	19.26	1,214	20.78	107.9	1,394	18.27	94.9	1,016	18.44	95.7
Language	28.98	1,357	26.52	91.5	1,648	27.49	94.9	1,418	30.92	106.7
Law	44.78	1,665	51.87	115.8	1,797	48.92	109.3	1,091	42.59	95.1
Literature	20.98	1,532	20.53	97.9	4,189	34.36	163.8	1,902	25.28	120.5
Medicine	47.25	3,313	35.72	75.6	4,087	48.86	103.4	3,256	44.16	93.5
Music	22.18	946	22.49	101.4	1,298	25.31	114.1	1,022	21.91	98.8
Philosophy, psychology	23.72	3,108	21.60	91.1	3,729	22.77	96.0	3,569	22.95	96.8
Poetry, drama	17.00	1,732	16.26	95.7	2,145	19.83	116.7	1,951	16.96	99.8
Religion	20.03	3,496	18.38	91.8	4,857	19.20	95.9	4,021	19.43	97.0
Science	48.57	3,191	40.29	83.0	3,787	45.11	92.9	2,889	45.51	93.7
Sociology, economics	31.23	7,839	41.22	132.0	8,180	36.38	116.5	6,969	29.53	94.6
Sports, recreation	23.56	2,138	20.76	88.1	2,435	21.05	89.4	2,288	20.81	88.3
Technology	69.52	5,117	56.22	80.9	6,070	100.59	144.7	5,110	54.40	78.3
Travel	20.13	2,498	22.45	111.5	2,435	22.12	109.9	1,822	19.52	97.0
Totals	$38.45	60,820	$31.07	80.8	75,983	$38.20	99.4	62,762	$29.42	76.5

(text continued from page 492)

increase was 5.1 percent for all subject categories. A more detailed article on serials services pricing appeared in the May 2001 issue of *American Libraries*.

Book Prices

Average book prices were mixed in 2001, with some subject categories showing price increases and others recording decreases. The overall average book price for hardcover books (Table 3) increased by $9.21 (15.14 percent) between 2000 and 2001, following a decline of $1.48 (2.37 percent) between 1999 and 2000. Preliminary prices for 2002, however, indicated that the final overall average price for hardcovers will show movement back toward the levels seen from 1998 to 2000.

In the North American Academic Books Index (Table 4), compiler Stephen Bosch finds the average price of North American Academic Books in 2001 (Table 4) increased by a very slim 0.4 percent in contrast to preceding years, which showed 2.0 percent and 3.8 percent increases in pricing. The data used for this index comprise titles treated by Blackwell North America and Yankee Book Peddler in their approval plans during the calendar years listed and titles treated by Baker and Taylor through all order types during the calendar years listed. It includes paperback editions as supplied by the vendors, and the recent increase in the number of these editions as part of the approval plans has clearly influenced the prices reflected in the index figures. Blackwell's showed an increase in the number of paperbacks—they now constitute 30 percent of the titles listed by Blackwell's. Paperbacks will continue to be a part of this index, as they are included in the approval plan data and represent a viable part of the North American book market. The true impact on inflation caused by hardback/paperback pricing continues to be unclear, although the modest increases in overall price inflation during the past year seem to parallel increases in paperback numbers. Other factors are also at work. Larger numbers of titles are being treated on approval plans. However, these increases are not due to an increase in output from traditional mainstream academic presses, but result from more titles coming from newer publishers that do not price books in the same range as the high-end academic presses. The preliminary prices for 2002 show a drop in price, and cost and coverage reports from vendors also reflect this decrease. But this does not mean that all academic libraries experienced a drop in their average purchase price.

Academic book price increases vary among subject categories. The largest price decrease was in Military and Naval Science with a 10 percent decrease continuing a trend over the past two years. Three categories—Fine Arts, Geology, and Science (General)—saw double-digit percent increases of 38.4 percent, 30.2 percent, and 18.3 percent, respectively. However, relatively few titles are published each year in the Geology and Science (General) categories, so a few expensive titles could affect the overall average price.

U.S. College Books (Table 5) could not be updated in time for publication and is repeated from last year. It contains information based on titles reviewed in *Choice* magazine, a publication of the Association of College and Research Libraries. The 2001 data showed a modest increase of only 1.9 percent across all categories. However, almost the entire increase came from the Reference category, which rose 10.9 percent. With the exception of Reference books, the average price remained almost flat.

The overall average price for mass market paperback books (Table 6) recorded an increase of 54 cents (9.36 percent) between 2000 and 2001, nearly four times the small increases registered in recent years. Preliminary figures for 2002 indicate a much lower rate of increase of only 17 cents (2.69 percent). Paperbacks other than mass market (Table 7) registered a huge increase of $7.13 (22.94 percent), reversing the 5.65 percent decline the previous year. Preliminary figures for 2002, however, indicate an equally significant shift toward lower average prices. The preliminary figures for 2002 indicate significant drops in Business and General Works. In the case of General Works, the price swings may reflect the publication of a few major works that skew the average prices in a given year.

Newspaper Prices

The indexes for U.S. (Table 8A) and international (Table 8B) newspapers showed larger percentage price increases, especially for international titles. The U.S. newspaper price increase of 3.6 percent is above inflation and the largest percentage increase in six years. The increase for international newspapers of 16.2 percent may reflect the increasing weakness of the U.S. dollar against most other major currencies during the past two years. This is the largest increase in the 10-year history of the index. Compilers Genevieve Owens and Wilba Swearingen anticipated this increase last year in light of higher postage rates. The high average costs of this material reflect the high frequency of publication and cost of timely shipment in the area of international newspapers. The figures reflect a

Table 8A / U.S. Daily Newspapers:
Average Prices and Price Indexes, 1990–2003
Index Base: 1990 = 100

Year	No. Titles	Average Price	Percent Increase	Index
1990	165	$189.58	0.0	100.0
1991	166	198.13	4.5	104.5
1992	167	222.68	12.4	117.5
1993	171	229.92	3.3	121.3
1994	171	261.91	13.9	138.2
1995	172	270.22	3.2	142.5
1996	166	300.21	11.1	158.4
1997	165	311.77	3.9	164.5
1998	163	316.60	1.5	167.0
1999	162	318.44	0.6	168.0
2000	162	324.26	1.8	171.0
2001	160	330.78	2.0	174.5
2002	158	340.38	2.9	179.5
2003	156	352.65	3.6	186.0

Compiled by Genevieve S. Owens, Williamsburg Regional Library, and Wilba Swearingen, Louisiana State University Health Sciences Center Library, from data supplied by EBSCO Subscription Services. We thank Kathleen Born of EBSCO for her assistance with this project.

Table 8B / International Newspapers:
Average Prices and Price Indexes, 1993–2003
Index Base: 1993 = 100

Year	No. Titles	Average Price	Percent Change	Index
1993	46	$806.91	0.0	100.0
1994	46	842.01	4.3	104.3
1995	49	942.13	11.9	116.3
1996	50	992.78	5.4	123.0
1997	53	1,029.49	3.7	127.6
1998	52	1,046.72	1.7	129.7
1999	50	1,049.13	0.2	130.0
2000	50	1,050.88	0.2	130.2
2001	50	1,038.26	-1.2	128.7
2002	49	1,052.69	1.4	130.5
2003	46	1,223.31	16.2	151.6

Compiled by Genevieve S. Owens, Williamsburg Regional Library, and Wilba Swearingen, Louisiana State University Health Sciences Center Library, from data supplied by EBSCO Subscription Services. We thank Kathleen Born of EBSCO for her assistance with this project.

decrease of two U.S. newspapers and three international newspapers. These titles are no longer available through EBSCO on a subscription basis. Data are provided with the assistance of EBSCO subscription services.

Prices of Other Media

The U.S. nonprint media index (former Table 9) does not appear this year. Those wishing historical information can find data for 1997 and 1998, indexed to a base of 1980, in the 2001 edition of the *Bowker Annual*. The database, compiled in previous years by Dana Alessi, collected information from titles reviewed in *Booklist, Library Journal, School Library Journal,* and *Video Librarian.*

The CD-ROM price inventory that formerly appeared as Table 10 has also been discontinued. As with U.S. Serials Services, many of the titles that were published in CD-ROM format have migrated to Web editions. Additionally, the changes from single workstation pricing to network pricing or site licenses made tracking of the prices for this category of material difficult to obtain.

Development of a price index for electronic journals has been discussed, but many factors have hindered progress in this area. The Association of Research Libraries is also considering ways to gather this important economic data for libraries.

Foreign Prices

In March 2003 the *Federal Reserve Bulletin* said the U.S. economy remained sluggish and forecast a strengthening of economic growth, combined with "well-contained" inflation pressures.

The adoption of the euro in January 2002 by most members of the European Union has complicated computations of the price fluctuations for foreign publications used by the compilers of the LMPIC indexes. Agents and wholesalers that supplied the data have converted to euros for ongoing operations, but not all historic data was converted. The exchange table below indicates that the Federal Reserve Board no longer tracks U.S. dollar exchange rates against individual European currencies. The exchange rates as of the end of 2002 are taken from the regional Federal Reserve Bank of St. Louis Web site (http://research.stlouisfed.org/fred/data/exchange.html) for all national currencies noted.

Dates	12/31/97	12/31/98	12/31/99	12/31/00	12/31/01	12/31/02
Canada	1.4261	1.5433	1.4722	1.5219*	1.5788	1.5592*
U.K.	1.6597	1.6708	1.6132	1.4629	1.4413	1.5863
Euro	n.a.	n.a.	1.0110*	0.8983*	0.8912*	1.0194*
Japan	129.73	117.07	102.58	112.21	127.59*	121.89*

* Data from the regional Federal Reserve Bank of St. Louis. Upon introduction of the euro on January 1, 1999, the Federal Reserve Board discontinued posting dollar exchange rates against the ECU and the currencies of the 11 countries participating in the European Economic and Monetary Union.

Price indexes include British Academic Books (Table 9, formerly Table 10), German Academic Periodicals (Table 10, formerly Table 12), Dutch English-Language Periodicals (Table 13, formerly Table 14), and Latin American Periodicals (Tables 14 A and 14 B, formerly Tables 15A and 15B).

British Prices

The price index for British academic books (Table 9) is compiled by Curt Holleman from information supplied by Blackwell Book Services. This table was not updated and is repeated from last year. The overall inflation rate for books showed a decrease of 5.1 percent. At the same time, the dollar remained strong against the British pound during 2001, experiencing a 1.5 percent increase during the year. These factors continued a trend noted in the past—that the cost for U.S. academic libraries to continue collecting British books at a pace similar to the prior year was falling.

German Prices

The price index for German academic books does not appear this year. Otto Harrassowitz, which provides the data, has been unable to supply prices for 1999 and more recent years due to system migration and conversion to the euro. Those wishing historical information will find data for 1996 through 1998, indexed to 1989, in the 2001 edition of the *Bowker Annual*.

The index for German Academic Periodicals (Table 10), compiled by Steven E. Thompson, is based on data provided by Otto Harrassowitz. This table is repeated once again for historical information. Conversion to the euro has made price comparisons with previous data impractical. Final 2000 data show an overall increase of 14.5 percent in the average price of this material. Preliminary 2001 periodical prices indicated a more moderate 4.8 percent increase. Looking at final 2000 data, only General Works, Library Science, and Psychology decreased in average price by more than 1 percent. However, periodicals in many of the sciences continued to show price increases well above 10 percent and even

(text continues on page 510)

Table 9 / British Academic Books: Average Prices and Price Indexes, 1999–2001

Index Base: 1985 = 100; prices listed are pounds sterling

Subject Area	1985		1999			2000			2001		
	No. of Titles	Average Price	No. of Titles	Average Price	Index	No. of Titles	Average Price	Index	No. of Titles	Average Price	Index
General works	29	£30.54	36	£37.84	123.9	27	£56.25	184.2	29	£35.89	117.5
Fine arts	329	21.70	387	32.78	151.1	420	34.86	160.6	427	34.93	161.0
Architecture	97	20.68	138	33.82	163.5	196	31.67	153.1	167	31.76	153.6
Music	136	17.01	129	37.00	217.5	134	54.33	319.4	143	38.71	227.6
Performing arts except music	110	13.30	151	34.08	256.2	225	29.48	221.6	204	31.32	235.5
Archaeology	146	18.80	148	42.16	224.3	218	37.15	197.6	112	41.95	223.1
Geography	60	22.74	18	50.80	223.3	55	42.13	185.3	54	42.24	185.6
History	1,123	16.92	902	33.39	197.3	968	36.21	214.0	738	32.05	189.4
Philosophy	127	18.41	228	42.12	228.8	281	47.12	255.9	283	39.52	214.7
Religion	328	10.40	401	31.11	299.1	595	29.32	281.9	588	33.06	317.9
Language	135	19.37	151	47.13	243.3	217	44.36	229.0	234	45.61	235.5
Miscellaneous humanities	59	21.71	34	37.24	171.5	36	45.83	211.1	249	38.36	176.7
Literary texts (excluding fiction)	570	9.31	325	17.16	184.3	485	15.29	164.2	548	15.79	169.6
Literary criticism	438	14.82	464	37.49	253.0	631	37.87	255.5	589	36.90	249.0
Law	188	24.64	350	52.09	211.4	521	52.40	212.7	511	55.28	224.4
Library science and book trade	78	18.69	64	34.27	183.4	77	48.43	259.1	59	35.08	187.7
Mass communications	38	14.20	92	37.30	262.7	122	32.28	227.3	113	34.53	243.2
Anthropology and ethnology	42	20.71	61	43.48	209.9	80	60.32	291.3	75	42.16	203.6
Sociology	136	15.24	205	43.35	284.4	237	43.58	286.0	265	42.80	280.8
Psychology	107	19.25	182	37.13	192.9	191	39.42	204.8	147	38.51	200.1
Economics	334	20.48	541	54.40	265.6	669	53.20	259.8	660	48.41	236.4
Political science, international relations	314	15.54	569	41.01	263.9	819	39.88	256.6	834	38.94	250.6
Miscellaneous social sciences	20	26.84	30	42.19	157.2	44	46.07	171.6	39	46.35	172.7
Military science	83	17.69	42	31.81	179.8	89	34.13	192.9	85	30.73	173.7
Sports and recreation	44	11.23	58	32.83	292.3	60	29.26	260.6	63	36.56	325.6
Social service	56	12.17	101	34.89	286.7	106	32.98	271.0	116	30.44	250.1
Education	295	12.22	316	39.25	321.2	401	34.34	281.0	385	34.97	286.2
Management and business administration	427	19.55	527	45.06	230.5	669	47.89	245.0	820	39.05	199.7
Miscellaneous applied social sciences	13	9.58	20	33.01	344.6	18	48.87	510.1	20	39.36	410.9
Criminology	45	11.45	65	40.89	357.1	79	37.71	329.3	101	34.13	298.1

Subject											
Applied interdisciplinary social sciences	254	14.17	559	43.22	305.0	674	39.34	277.6	637	40.73	287.4
General science	43	13.73	28	33.24	242.1	50	37.72	274.7	53	42.89	312.4
Botany	55	30.54	39	58.60	191.9	34	61.83	202.5	42	73.10	239.4
Zoology	85	25.67	59	55.59	216.6	76	55.53	216.3	66	58.88	229.4
Human biology	35	28.91	34	46.68	161.5	50	50.41	174.4	48	53.16	183.9
Biochemistry	26	33.57	35	61.39	182.9	48	84.18	250.8	40	63.73	189.8
Miscellaneous biological sciences	152	26.64	145	53.06	199.2	186	57.77	216.9	149	59.01	221.5
Chemistry	109	48.84	125	80.17	164.1	162	80.68	165.2	123	69.55	142.4
Earth sciences	87	28.94	102	65.44	226.1	140	63.30	218.7	110	61.29	211.8
Astronomy	43	20.36	44	53.61	263.3	80	35.81	175.9	78	40.16	197.2
Physics	76	26.58	207	62.91	236.7	327	57.17	215.1	269	62.75	236.1
Mathematics	123	20.20	178	48.23	238.8	308	44.78	221.7	288	47.85	236.9
Computer sciences	150	20.14	134	39.41	195.7	364	37.48	186.1	327	38.48	191.1
Interdisciplinary technical fields	38	26.14	67	55.43	212.1	154	44.16	168.9	126	42.38	162.1
Civil engineering	134	28.68	117	65.76	229.3	130	62.65	218.4	52	75.72	264.0
Mechanical engineering	27	31.73	21	111.38	351.0	42	83.63	263.6	16	60.92	192.0
Electrical and electronic engineering	100	33.12	74	66.46	200.7	105	59.42	179.4	142	54.56	164.7
Materials science	54	37.93	73	78.51	207.0	112	88.85	234.2	74	80.12	211.2
Chemical engineering	24	40.48	42	82.74	204.4	39	76.55	189.1	27	66.00	163.0
Miscellaneous technology	217	36.33	152	64.25	176.9	282	68.34	188.1	369	58.68	161.5
Food and domestic science	38	23.75	22	73.38	309.0	42	54.72	230.4	31	46.30	194.9
Non-clinical medicine	97	18.19	154	36.93	203.0	178	37.99	208.9	220	36.96	203.2
General medicine	73	21.03	63	53.93	256.4	101	62.24	296.0	12	50.08	238.1
Internal medicine	163	27.30	188	53.45	195.8	212	64.92	237.8	30	58.69	215.0
Psychiatry and mental disorders	71	17.97	142	36.90	205.3	167	35.16	195.7	34	46.11	256.6
Surgery	50	29.37	49	72.74	247.7	69	79.34	270.1	6	62.75	213.7
Miscellaneous medicine	292	22.08	256	45.39	205.6	348	47.04	213.2	725	49.94	226.2
Dentistry	20	19.39	14	29.83	153.8	10	31.87	164.4	15	48.62	250.7
Pharmacy*	n.a.	n.a.	n.a.	n.a.	n.a.	n.a.	n.a.	n.a.	20	53.02	n.a.
Nursing	71	8.00	74	22.68	283.5	91	24.09	301.1	96	25.96	324.5
Agriculture and forestry	78	23.69	51	50.47	213.0	71	55.87	235.8	67	59.93	253.0
Animal husbandry and veterinary medicine	34	20.92	41	45.72	218.5	48	60.57	289.5	48	45.39	217.0
Natural resources and conservation	58	22.88	41	47.38	207.1	53	49.74	217.4	68	41.37	180.8
Total, all books	9,049	£19.07	10,332	£42.54	223.1	13,847	£42.99	225.4	13,423	£40.81	214.0

Compiled by Curt Holleman, Southern Methodist University, from data supplied by B. H. Blackwell and the Library and Information Statistics Unit at Loughborough University.
* New category introduced in 2001.

Table 10 / German Academic Periodical Price Index, 1999–2001
Index Base: 1990 = 100: prices in Deutsche marks

Subject	LC Class	1990 Average Price	1999 No. of Titles	1999 Average Price	1999 Percent Increase	1999 Index	2000 Final No. of Titles	2000 Final Average Price	2000 Final Percent Increase	2000 Final Index	2001 Preliminary No. of Titles	2001 Preliminary Average Price	2001 Preliminary Percent Increase	2001 Preliminary Index
Agriculture	S	DM235.11	166	DM373.87	-1.1	159.0	161	DM456.89	22.2	194.3	173	DM497.04	8.8	211.4
Anthropology	GN	112.88	16	185.17	18.5	164.0	17	192.73	4.1	170.7	17	194.08	0.7	171.9
Botany	QK	498.79	16	994.49	20.5	199.4	17	1,017.94	2.4	204.1	17	1,057.11	3.8	211.9
Business and economics	H-HJ	153.48	260	255.01	10.5	166.2	212	254.14	-0.3	165.6	238	259.12	2.0	168.9
Chemistry	QD	553.06	52	2,737.38	27.0	495.0	50	3,315.49	21.1	599.5	52	3,535.08	6.6	639.2
Education	L	70.86	57	93.76	2.4	132.3	40	108.49	15.7	153.1	41	116.28	7.2	164.1
Engineering and technology	T-TT	239.40	332	415.79	10.3	173.7	290	474.13	14.0	198.0	306	495.69	4.5	207.1
Fine and applied arts	M-N	84.15	151	112.07	3.1	133.2	136	122.15	9.0	145.2	140	121.42	-0.6	144.3
General	A	349.37	68	432.15	-0.9	123.7	53	406.95	-5.8	116.5	54	405.08	-0.5	115.9
Geography	G	90.42	23	196.95	28.7	217.8	20	214.06	8.7	236.7	21	228.21	6.6	252.4
Geology	QE	261.30	36	637.44	22.3	243.9	30	788.26	23.7	301.7	30	828.03	5.0	316.9
History	C,D,E,F	66.09	147	103.00	6.2	155.8	143	104.18	1.1	157.6	143	103.13	-1.0	156.0
Law	K	193.88	155	350.81	8.5	180.9	137	364.11	3.8	187.8	142	372.32	2.3	192.0
Library and information science	Z	317.50	44	471.68	17.3	148.6	34	275.23	-41.6	86.7	36	653.98	137.6	206.0
Literature and language	P	102.69	176	155.44	9.0	151.4	160	159.37	2.5	155.2	163	151.99	-4.6	148.0
Mathematics and computer science	QA	1,064.62	62	1,370.49	5.8	128.7	51	1,734.75	26.6	162.9	54	1,670.88	-3.7	156.9
Medicine	R	320.62	337	756.80	23.1	236.0	343	796.83	5.3	248.5	365	811.90	1.9	253.2
Military and naval science	U-V	86.38	21	126.88	27.3	146.9	21	126.12	-0.6	146.0	21	127.31	0.9	147.4
Natural history	QH	728.36	47	1,774.61	29.0	243.6	52	1,784.22	0.5	245.0	55	1,867.72	4.7	256.4
Philosophy and religion	B	65.00	195	112.67	-1.5	173.3	195	115.13	2.2	177.1	194	114.46	-0.6	176.1
Physical education and recreation	GV	81.96	41	108.70	4.9	132.6	32	115.52	6.3	140.9	32	117.65	1.8	143.5
Physics and astronomy	QB-QC	684.40	50	2,472.22	30.1	361.2	54	2,716.26	9.9	396.9	54	2,916.39	7.4	426.1
Physiology	QM-QR	962.83	13	3,264.38	23.2	339.0	14	3,700.47	13.4	384.3	14	3,883.15	4.9	403.3
Political science	J	80.67	117	105.20	0.1	130.4	107	104.08	-1.1	129.0	107	104.55	0.5	129.6
Psychology	BF	94.10	33	189.71	19.4	201.6	30	184.77	-2.6	196.4	31	197.10	6.7	209.5
Science (general)	Q	310.54	24	602.08	16.3	193.9	21	736.25	22.3	237.1	21	736.25	0.0	237.1
Sociology	HM-HX	109.61	77	147.91	1.1	134.9	66	163.41	10.5	149.1	66	164.76	0.8	150.3
Zoology	QL	161.02	25	406.68	28.6	252.6	28	521.44	28.2	323.8	30	587.21	12.6	364.7
Totals and Averages		228.40	2,741	DM472.68	17.1	207.0	2,514	DM541.27	14.5	237.0	2,617	DM567.33	4.8	248.4

Data, supplied by Otto Harrassowitz, represent periodical and newspaper titles published in Germany; prices listed in marks.
Index is compiled by Steven E. Thompson, Brown University Library.

Table 11A / Latin American Periodical Price Index, 2001–2002
Country and Region Index

	Total Titles	Mean w/o newspapers	Index (1992 = 100)	Weighted mean w/o newspapers	Index (1992 = 100)
Country					
Argentina	144	$96.51	110	$82.11	114
Bolivia	7	61.54	141	114.28	329
Brazil	313	51.70	76	45.88	62
Caribbean	28	42.58	100	42.25	107
Chile	26	191.49	310	74.58	158
Colombia	58	79.00	172	104.37	224
Costa Rica	24	41.21	158	51.40	166
Cuba	18	54.17	153	53.66	141
Ecuador	18	66.51	191	80.91	244
El Salvador	9	54.33	286	64.10	414
Guatemala	12	140.00	183	175.93	202
Honduras	n.a.	n.a.	n.a.	n.a.	n.a.
Jamaica	19	46.49	144	56.26	178
Mexico	212	109.77	169	83.24	146
Nicaragua	7	24.65	81	23.84	77
Panama	13	35.92	135	34.81	137
Paraguay	5	2.40	15	305.20	1,368
Peru	52	124.67	124	108.61	99
Uruguay	21	85.70	257	60.21	184
Venezuela	33	105.96	104	98.02	207
Region					
Caribbean	46	47.11	127	48.34	132
Central America	65	58.42	161	75.04	182
South America	677	71.48	96	70.81	109
Mexico	213	109.77	169	83.24	146
Latin America	1,001	82.95	123	72.61	125

Subscription information provided by the Faxon Co., Library of Congress Rio Office, and the University of Texas. Index based on 1992 LAPPI mean prices. The 2000/2001 subscription prices were included in this year's index if a new subscription price was not available.
Compiled by Scott Van Jacob, University of Notre Dame.
n.a. = fewer than five subscription prices were found

Table 11B / Latin American Periodical Price Index, 2001–2002: Subject Index

Subjects	Mean	Index (1992 = 100)	Weighted mean	Index (1992 = 100)
Social Sciences	$93.02	143	$80.38	149
Humanities	45.40	121	43.68	120
Science/Technology	74.48	130	74.15	132
General	101.44	100	77.99	85
Law	98.10	87	81.58	95
Newspapers	587.78	120	600.86	148
Totals w/o newspapers	82.95	99	72.61	113
Total with newspapers	113.65	169	86.51	149
Total titles w/o newspapers = 1,001				
Total titles with newspapers = 1,067				

(text continued from page 505)

above 20 percent, including Agriculture (up 22.2 percent), Chemistry (up 21.1 percent), Geology (up 23.7 percent), Math and Computer Science (up 26.6 percent), Science (General) (up 22.3 percent), and Zoology (up 28.2 percent). The average prices noted are in German marks, so the relative strength of the U.S. dollar over this currency may have slightly reduced the impact of these increases.

Dutch Prices

The Dutch English-Language Periodical Index (former Table 13) is also omitted this year. Nijhoff, which provided this data in the past, has found it increasingly difficult to identify appropriate titles for this category. There are two reasons for this. It is hard to determine which periodicals are produced in the Netherlands as "multinational" Dutch publishers publish all over the world. And these materials tend to be priced in different currencies, making it difficult to establish consistent prices. The sale of Nijhoff to Swets Blackwell took place during 2001.

Latin American Prices

Scott Van Jacobs compiles the Latin American Periodicals indexes (Tables 11A and 11B, former Tables 14A and 14B) with prices provided by divine/Faxon, the Library of Congress, and the University of Texas, Austin. The most recent Latin American book price index was published in 1997. A new index based on data provided by Latin American book vendors is expected to replace that index, but is not yet available.

The weighted overall mean for Latin American periodicals including newspapers rose a moderate 3.7 percent in 2001/2002 over the previous two years. When newspapers are not included, the increase was only 1.6 percent. However, increases varied widely by region and especially by country. Overall prices in South America have declined by 16.1 percent over the past two years while the average price of materials from Mexico rose 37 percent. Currency fluctuations may well account for much of variation.

Using the Price Indexes

Librarians are encouraged to monitor trends in the publishing industry and changes in economic conditions when preparing budget forecasts and projections. The ALA ALCTS Library Materials Price Index Committee endeavors to make information on publishing trends readily available by sponsoring the annual compilation and publication of price data contained in Tables 1–11. The indexes cover newly published library materials and document prices and rates of percent changes at the national and international level. They are useful benchmarks against which local costs can be compared, but because they reflect retail prices in the aggregate, they are not a substitute for cost data that reflect the collecting patterns of individual libraries, and they are not a substitute for specific cost studies.

Differences between local prices and those found in national indexes arise partially because these indexes exclude discounts, service charges, shipping and handling fees, and other costs that the library might incur. Discrepancies may also relate to a library's subject coverage; mix of titles purchased, including both current and backfiles; and the proportion of the library's budget expended on domestic or foreign materials. These variables can affect the average price paid by an individual library, although the individual library's rate of increase may not differ greatly from the national indexes.

LMPIC is interested in pursuing studies that would correlate a particular library's costs with the national prices. The committee welcomes interested parties to its meetings at ALA Annual and Midwinter conferences.

Current Library Materials Price Index Committee members are Janet Belanger, Pamela Bluh, Mae Clark, Doina Farkas, Mary Fugle, Harriet Lightman, Merrill Smith, Roger Presley, and Sharon Sullivan (Chair). Consultants include Donna Alsbury, Catherine Barr, Ajaye Bloomstone, Stephen Bosch, Nancy Chaffin, Brenda Dingley, Virginia Gilbert, Curt Holleman, Genevieve Owens, Wilba Swearingen, Steven Thompson, and Scott van Jacob.

Book Title Output and Average Prices: 2001 Final and 2002 Preliminary Figures

Andrew Grabois

Senior Director for Publisher Relations & Content Development, R. R. Bowker

American book title output reached another new high of 141,703 titles in 2001, according to figures compiled by R. R. Bowker. This final total represents a staggering increase of 19,595 new titles and editions, or 16 percent, over the 122,108 titles reported for 2000. The 2000 total represented a 2.3 percent increase over the final figure for 1999. From the preliminary figures for 2002, we can confidently project that total title output will again top 140,000, achieving a positive but modest growth rate of 2 percent to 3 percent. The increases of the last two years would appear to indicate that the war on terror, which began during the fourth quarter of 2001, did not result in any long-lasting changes to either the volume or nature of U.S. title output. If the latest figures on book sales released by the American Association of Publishers are any indication, consumer purchasing rebounded as well.

Table 1 / American Book Production, 1999–2002

| | All Hard and Paper | | | |
Category	1999 Final	2000 Final	2001 Final	2002 Preliminary
Agriculture	1,037	1,073	1,195	888
Arts	4,795	4,980	5,324	4,481
Biography	4,051	3,899	4,887	5,049
Business	3,789	4,068	5,023	4,539
Education	3,408	3,378	3,914	3,652
Fiction	12,372	14,617	17,349	15,131
General works	1,456	1,318	1,553	1,468
History	7,486	7,931	9,028	6,818
Home economics	2,564	2,513	2,430	2,160
Juveniles	9,438	8,690	9,582	9,540
Language	2,565	2,536	2,954	2,419
Law	3,078	3,070	3,266	2,188
Literature	3,646	3,371	6,009	3,946
Medicine	6,153	6,234	7,080	5,933
Music	1,593	1,582	3,098	1,614
Philosophy, psychology	5,861	5,556	6,320	6,006
Poetry, drama	2,455	2,479	2,924	2,812
Religion	6,044	6,206	8,015	6,659
Science	7,862	8,464	8,928	7,032
Sociology, economics	14,579	14,908	16,555	13,804
Sports, recreation	3,252	3,483	3,789	3,569
Technology	8,896	8,582	9,359	7,888
Travel	2,977	3,170	3,121	2,327
Totals	119,357	122,108	141,703	119,923

As explained in the 2000 edition of the *Bowker Annual*, the title output and average price figures are now compiled from Bowker's *Books In Print* database, resulting in a more accurate and comprehensive portrayal of American book publishing.

Output by Format and by Category

Book title output for 2001 showed a significant increase for hardcover books, a decline for mass market paperbacks, and an extraordinary increase in trade and other paperbacks, fueled by the public's demand for more moderately priced editions of general adult trade titles and the wider availability of print-on-demand (POD) trade paper editions. Hardcover output (Table 2) increased by 5,015 titles (9.29 percent), mass market paperback output (Table 4) declined by 490 titles (6.67 percent), following the 11.24 percent decrease seen in 2000, and output of other paperbacks, including trade paperbacks (Table 5) increased by 15,163 titles (24.93 percent).

Nonfiction subject categories achieved positive growth in title output between 2000 and 2001, with only two categories, home economics and travel, showing small declines. The nonfiction categories that experienced the largest

Table 2 / Hardcover Average Per-Volume Prices, 2000–2002

Category	2000 Prices	2001 Final			2002 Preliminary		
		Vols.	$ Total	Prices	Vols.	$ Total	Prices
Agriculture	$66.52	582	$35,521.49	$61.03	453	$28,938.25	$63.88
Arts	50.31	2,586	144,818.23	56.00	2,195	118,226.50	53.86
Biography	45.31	2,385	126,527.67	53.05	2,444	107,543.18	44.00
Business	93.84	1,685	161,095.92	95.61	1,869	174,079.62	93.14
Education	62.23	1,328	96,351.07	72.55	1,202	66,375.56	55.22
Fiction	25.75	4,183	120,648.19	28.84	4,309	120,716.07	28.01
General works	165.39	693	116,007.95	167.40	699	108,381.01	155.05
History	54.01	4,514	276,318.48	61.21	3,122	169,959.91	54.44
Home economics	39.76	1,011	52,015.63	51.45	902	28,640.56	31.75
Juveniles	22.71	6,217	148,292.88	23.85	6,346	134,384.08	21.18
Language	57.27	1,243	91,931.20	73.96	936	61,889.41	66.12
Law	101.50	1,483	133,030.94	89.70	1,112	105,267.03	94.66
Literature	55.17	1,747	110,048.44	62.99	1,982	128,241.47	64.70
Medicine	90.32	2,864	285,316.63	99.62	2,652	253,307.21	95.52
Music	42.91	1,799	202,051.22	112.31	582	31,314.17	53.80
Philosophy, psychology	52.02	2,409	159,062.63	66.03	2,331	139,227.94	59.73
Poetry, drama	39.90	757	33,150.94	43.79	844	39,090.49	46.32
Religion	41.61	2,981	124,985.72	41.93	2,532	111,835.14	44.17
Science	90.11	5,060	509,079.48	100.61	4,098	394,852.65	96.35
Sociology, economics	66.79	8,220	779,295.73	94.80	6,786	463,412.73	68.29
Sports, recreation	40.64	1,289	53,667.04	41.63	1,219	51,017.76	41.85
Technology	102.40	3,262	325,968.93	99.93	2,799	246,754.28	88.16
Travel	40.27	664	45,071.74	67.88	483	20,147.53	41.71
Totals	$60.84	58,962	$4,130,258.15	$70.05	51,897	$3,103,602.55	$59.80

year-to-year increases in terms of titles were literature (including books on literary history and criticism, literary collections and anthologies, and some "literary" fiction) with an increase of 2,638 titles (78.26 percent), religion with an increase of 1,809 titles (29.15 percent), sociology and economics with an increase of 1,647 titles (11.05 percent), music with an increase of 1,516 titles (95.83 percent), and history with an increase of 1,097 titles (13.83 percent). Home economics (covering cookery, parenting and child rearing, and how-to titles) showed a slight decline of 83 titles (3.3 percent), and travel declined by only 49 titles (1.55 percent).

Fiction, an important measure of the overall health of the publishing industry, experienced an increase of 2,732 titles (18.69 percent) between 2000 and 2001, building on an 18.15 percent increase between 1999 and 2000. Virtually all of this increase was in trade and other paperbacks, with both mass market paperbacks and hardcovers registering declines. The preliminary 2002 figures would appear to indicate increases in fiction title output in both the hardcover and trade paper formats, and a marked decline in mass market paperbacks. The juveniles category (children's and young adult titles), also seen by the publishing industry as a barometer of healthy sales, registered an increase of 892 titles (10.26 percent) between 2000 and 2001, reversing the decline of 748 titles (7.93 percent) between 1999 and 2000. Preliminary figures for 2002 already show a total of

Table 3 / Hardcover Average Per-Volume Prices, Less Than $81, 2000–2002

Category	2000 Prices	2001 Final Vols.	2001 Final $ Total	2001 Final Prices	2002 Preliminary Vols.	2002 Preliminary $ Total	2002 Preliminary Prices
Agriculture	$35.04	448	$15,697.03	$35.04	332	$11,974.66	$36.07
Arts	40.32	2,287	93,461.09	40.87	1,946	79,511.64	40.86
Biography	33.22	1,999	65,376.74	32.70	2,196	72,307.16	32.93
Business	41.98	1,169	47,515.88	40.65	1,316	54,764.67	41.61
Education	45.62	1,072	46,804.72	43.66	1,017	42,725.81	42.01
Fiction	24.96	4,132	105,465.96	25.52	4,203	108,418.33	25.80
General works	41.13	378	14,622.49	38.68	394	17,035.23	43.24
History	39.73	3,693	153,259.90	41.50	2,709	108,721.89	40.13
Home economics	27.14	957	25,780.77	26.94	876	24,002.78	27.40
Juveniles	18.40	6,018	115,097.35	19.13	6,257	117,321.53	18.75
Language	42.14	931	39,926.73	42.89	699	30,580.55	43.75
Law	49.44	872	43,457.70	49.84	636	33,132.20	52.09
Literature	40.57	1,437	58,824.52	40.94	1,587	66,038.77	41.61
Medicine	41.76	1,637	72,281.81	44.16	1,474	66,246.00	44.94
Music	33.73	578	20,625.02	35.68	483	19,154.45	39.66
Philosophy, psychology	39.98	2,030	82,613.42	40.70	1,953	84,189.21	43.11
Poetry, drama	33.57	670	22,552.84	33.66	747	26,547.71	35.54
Religion	33.17	2,711	91,547.26	33.77	2,288	78,134.97	34.15
Science	41.69	2,711	112,723.67	41.58	2,287	94,810.60	41.46
Sociology, economics	45.64	5,806	274,435.47	47.27	5,391	260,566.57	48.33
Sports, recreation	33.27	1,209	40,709.30	33.67	1,137	39,554.36	34.79
Technology	46.63	1,853	85,882.19	46.35	1,547	72,495.41	46.86
Travel	32.17	599	19,921.66	33.26	443	14,185.39	32.02
Totals	$36.20	45,197	$1,648,583.52	$36.48	41,918	$1,522,419.89	$36.32

9,540 juvenile titles, indicating, in all likelihood, a final figure of more than 10,000 titles.

Average Book Prices

Average book prices were mixed in 2001, with some subject categories showing price increases and others recording decreases. The overall average book price for hardcover books (Table 2) increased by $9.21 (15.14 percent) between 2000 and 2001, following a decline of $1.48 (2.37 percent) between 1999 and 2000. Preliminary prices for 2002, however, strongly suggest that the final overall average price for hardcovers will be more in line with those registered from 1998 to 2000. Looking at just those hardcovers priced at less than $81 (Table 3), which constitute more than 75 percent of all hardcovers, there was much less price fluctuation. The average book price for these selected hardcovers increased by only 28 cents (0.76 percent) in 2001, coming on the heels of an equally modest increase of 24 cents (0.67 percent) in 2000.

The overall average price for mass market paperback books (Table 4) recorded an increase of 54 cents (9.36 percent) between 2000 and 2001, which is nearly four times the small average price increases seen in recent years. Paper-

Table 4 / Mass Market Paperbacks Average Per-Volume Prices, 2000–2002

Category	2000 Prices	2001 Final			2002 Preliminary		
		Vols.	$ Total	Prices	Vols.	$ Total	Prices
Agriculture	$7.48	7	$41.69	$5.96	1	$7.95	$7.95
Arts	7.26	17	114.63	6.74	23	190.10	8.27
Biography	6.71	71	531.68	7.49	74	489.49	6.61
Business	8.41	64	608.68	9.51	6	46.82	7.80
Education	7.30	18	123.38	6.85	32	208.20	6.51
Fiction	5.78	3,498	21,988.56	6.29	2,384	16,235.70	6.81
General works	6.57	15	103.83	6.92	19	154.12	8.11
History	7.36	63	441.82	7.01	47	320.29	6.81
Home economics	7.07	82	646.86	7.89	24	184.52	7.69
Juveniles	5.21	1,972	10,824.16	5.49	2,183	12,482.95	5.72
Language	6.92	64	406.98	6.36	66	428.77	6.50
Law	8.77	4	26.92	6.73	3	22.97	7.66
Literature	6.71	74	522.12	7.06	62	492.58	7.94
Medicine	6.70	127	1,035.18	8.15	41	300.45	7.33
Music	7.24	2	13.94	6.97	11	82.74	7.52
Philosophy, psychology	7.24	188	1,396.94	7.43	112	830.27	7.41
Poetry, drama	6.09	22	135.64	6.17	17	122.86	7.23
Religion	8.16	188	1,460.28	7.77	111	932.53	8.40
Science	6.58	86	561.33	6.53	56	352.09	6.29
Sociology, economics	6.99	176	1,359.72	7.73	74	567.62	7.67
Sports, recreation	6.66	65	506.39	7.79	62	507.43	8.18
Technology	6.71	34	263.03	7.74	17	134.65	7.92
Travel	8.65	23	174.18	7.57	22	198.98	9.04
Totals	$5.77	6,860	$43,287.94	$6.31	5,447	$35,294.08	$6.48

backs other than mass market (Table 5) registered a huge increase of $7.13 (22.94 percent), reversing the 5.65 percent decline recorded between 1999 and 2000.

The average book prices for fiction titles, usually considered a bellwether for book prices in the trade, increased across the board in 2001. Hardcover fiction titles rose $3.09 (12.09 percent), mass market 51 cents (8.75 percent), and trade and other paperbacks $2.08 (13.1 percent). In the preliminary numbers for 2002, only mass market fiction titles showed an increase in average price.

Hardcover children's books (juveniles) increased $1.14 (5.03 percent) in 2001, reversing the 35 cent decline (1.52 percent) recorded in 2000. Children's mass market paperbacks increased 28 cents, or 5.35 percent, while trade and other paperback children's titles registered a significant decline of $2.51 (12.07 percent).

Most of the other subject categories recorded mixed average prices in 2001, with many categories showing year-to-year price increases and decreases, varying by format. History, for example, shows an average price increase of $7.20 (13.34 percent) for hardcover titles, a decrease of 35 cents (4.71 percent) for mass market paperback titles, and a decrease of $2.86 (10.49 percent) for other paperback titles. Science recorded an average price increase of $10.50 (11.65 percent) for

Table 5 / Other Paperbacks Average Per-Volume Prices, 2000–2002

Category	2000 Prices	2001 Final			2002 Preliminary		
		Vols.	$ Total	Prices	Vols.	$ Total	Prices
Agriculture	$41.31	606	$22,201.63	$36.64	434	$11,416.82	$26.31
Arts	26.96	2,726	83,121.39	30.49	2,265	61,683.45	27.23
Biography	19.47	2,438	49,557.74	20.33	2,534	54,606.03	21.55
Business	52.00	3,278	306,425.00	93.48	2,696	136,992.90	50.81
Education	28.43	2,575	74,890.71	29.08	2,424	70,769.64	29.20
Fiction	15.90	9,674	173,971.75	17.98	8,440	145,143.56	17.20
General works	39.84	844	100,237.33	118.76	752	34,780.00	46.25
History	27.24	4,454	108,594.98	24.38	3,658	93,055.00	25.44
Home economics	18.95	1,337	43,442.18	32.49	1,235	23,114.04	18.72
Juveniles	20.78	1,394	25,472.40	18.27	1,016	18,731.74	18.44
Language	26.52	1,648	45,297.10	27.49	1,418	43,850.27	30.92
Law	51.87	1,797	87,913.07	48.92	1,091	46,466.91	42.59
Literature	20.53	4,189	143,942.26	34.36	1,902	48,079.56	25.28
Medicine	35.72	4,087	199,679.02	48.86	3,256	143,769.44	44.16
Music	22.49	1,298	32,850.37	25.31	1,022	22,393.38	21.91
Philosophy, psychology	21.60	3,729	84,913.62	22.77	3,569	81,918.23	22.95
Poetry, drama	16.26	2,145	42,541.42	19.83	1,951	33,087.77	16.96
Religion	18.38	4,857	93,238.20	19.20	4,021	78,117.17	19.43
Science	40.29	3,787	170,837.20	45.11	2,889	131,465.54	45.51
Sociology, economics	41.22	8,180	297,614.76	36.38	6,969	205,777.46	29.53
Sports, recreation	20.76	2,435	51,252.42	21.05	2,288	47,610.45	20.81
Technology	56.22	6,070	610,603.17	100.59	5,110	277,986.94	54.40
Travel	22.45	2,435	53,850.96	22.12	1,822	35,556.68	19.52
Totals	$31.07	75,983	$2,902,448.68	$38.20	62,762	$1,846,372.98	$29.42

hardcover titles, a decrease of 5 cents (0.8 percent) for mass market paperback titles, and an increase of $4.82 (11.97 percent) for other paperback titles.

Each of the 23 standard subject groups used here represents one or more specific Dewey Decimal Classification numbers, as follows: Agriculture, 630–699, 712–719; Art, 700–711, 720–779; Biography, 920–929; Business, 650–659; Education, 370–379; Fiction; General Works, 000–099; History, 900–909, 930–999; Home Economics, 640–649; Juveniles; Language, 400–499; Law, 340–349; Literature, 800–810, 813–820, 823–899; Medicine, 610–619; Music, 780–789; Philosophy, Psychology, 100–199; Poetry, Drama, 811, 812, 821, 822; Religion, 200–299; Science, 500–599; Sociology, Economics, 300–339, 350–369, 380–389; Sports, Recreation, 790–799; Technology, 600–609, 620–629, 660–699; Travel, 910–919.

Book Sales Statistics, 2002:
AAP Preliminary Estimates

Association of American Publishers

The industry estimates shown in the following table are based on the U.S. Census of Manufactures. However, book publishing is currently being transferred to the Economic Census, also called the Census of Information. Like the Census of Manufactures, this is a five-year census conducted in years ending in "2" and "7"; 1997 was a transition census with the data being collected and processed by the same government people as in prior years, but the forthcoming output will be under the auspices of the new census.

Between censuses, the Association of American Publishers (AAP) estimates are "pushed forward" by the percentage changes that are reported to the AAP statistics program, and by other industry data that are available. Some AAP data are collected in a monthly statistics program, and it is largely this material that is shown in this preliminary estimate table. More detailed data are available from, and additional publishers report to, the AAP annual statistics program, and this additional data will be incorporated into Table S1 that will be published in the AAP 2002 Industry Statistics.

Readers comparing the estimated data with census reports should be aware that the U.S. Census of Manufactures does not include data on many university presses or on other institutionally sponsored and not-for-profit publishing activities, or (under SIC 2731: Book Publishing) for the audiovisual and other media materials that are included in this table. On the other hand, AAP estimates have traditionally excluded "Sunday School" materials and certain pamphlets that are incorporated in the census data. These and other adjustments have been built into AAP's industry estimates.

As in prior reports, the estimates reflect the impact of industry expansion created by new establishments entering the field, as well as nontraditional forms of book publishing, in addition to incorporating the sales increases and decreases of established firms.

It should also be noted that the Other Sales category includes only incidental book sales, such as music, sheet sales (both domestic and export, except those to prebinders), and miscellaneous merchandise sales.

The estimates include domestic sales and export sales of U.S. product, but they do not cover indigenous activities of publishers' foreign subsidiaries.

Non-rack-size Mass Market Publishing is included in Trade—Paperbound. Prior to the 1988 AAP Industry Statistics, this was indicated as Adult Trade Paperbound. It is recognized that part of this is Juvenile (estimate: 20 percent), and adjustments have been made in this respect. AAP also notes that this area includes sales through traditional "mass market paperback channels" by publishers not generally recognized as being "mass market paperback" publishers.

Table 1 / Estimated Book Publishing Industry Sales, 1992, 1997, 2000–2002
(figures in millions of dollars)

	1992	1997	2000	% Change from 1999	2001	% Change from 2000	2002 Preliminary	% Change from 2001	Compound Growth Rate 1992–2002	Compound Growth Rate 1997–2002
Trade (total)	$4,661.6	$5,774.1	$6,540.8	-3.7	$6,369.9	-2.6	$6,929.8	8.8	4.0	3.7
Adult hardbound	2,222.5	2,663.6	2,685.9	-11.4	2,626.5	-2.2	2,935.5	11.8	2.8	2.0
Adult paperbound	1,261.7	1,731.7	1,900.7	-7.2	1,927.2	1.4	2,160.8	12.1	5.5	4.5
Juvenile hardbound	850.8	908.5	1,201.1	13.2	928.6	-22.7	957.2	3.1	1.2	1.0
Juvenile paperbound	326.6	470.3	753.1	16.4	887.6	17.9	876.3	-1.3	10.4	13.3
Religious (total)	907.1	1,132.7	1,246.9	2.5	1,305.1	4.7	1,262.2	-3.3	3.4	2.2
Bibles, testaments, hymnals, etc.	260.1	285.4	323.3	4.3	315.0	-2.6	329.2	4.5	2.4	2.9
Other religious	647.0	847.3	923.6	1.8	990.1	7.2	933.0	-5.8	3.7	1.9
Professional (total)	3,106.7	4,156.4	5,129.5	8.7	4,739.1	-7.6	5,140.1	8.5	5.2	4.3
Business	490.3	768.1	1,000.7	10.0	938.3	-6.2	n.a.	n.a.	n.a.	n.a.
Law	1,128.1	1,502.7	1,957.1	13.1	1,848.2	-5.6	n.a.	n.a.	n.a.	n.a.
Medical	622.7	856.5	995.8	1.3	886.3	-11.0	n.a.	n.a.	n.a.	n.a.
Technical, scientific, other prof'l	865.6	1,029.1	1,175.9	6.8	1,066.3	-9.3	n.a.	n.a.	n.a.	n.a.
Book clubs	742.3	1,143.1	1,291.6	1.5	1,334.5	3.3	1,463.3	9.7	7.0	5.1
Mail order publications	630.2	521	431.6	4.6	353.9	-18.0	333.5	-5.8	-6.2	-8.5
Mass market paperback, rack-sized	1,263.8	1,433.8	1,559.2	0.5	1,546.6	-0.8	1,726.8	11.7	3.2	3.8
University presses	280.1	367.8	402.0	-2.4	408.2	1.5	392.6	-3.8	3.4	1.3
Elementary, secondary (K–12 education)	2,080.9	3,005.4	3,881.2	13.3	4,289.8	10.5	4,073.3	-5.0	6.9	6.3
Higher education	2,084.1	2,669.7	3,237.1	3.5	3,468.9	7.2	3,898.2	12.4	6.5	7.9
Standardized tests	140.4	191.4	234.1	7.0	250.1	6.8	268.2	7.2	6.7	7.0
Subscription reference	572.3	736.5	809.1	2.6	819.4	1.3	797.0	-2.7	3.4	1.6
Other sales (incl. AV)	449.0	510.0	559.4	3.3	577.2	3.2	589.1	2.1	2.8	2.9
Total	$16,918.5	$21,641.9	$25,322.7	3.4	$25,462.7	0.6	$26,874.1	5.5	4.7	4.4

n.a. = not available
Source: Association of American Publishers

U.S. Book Exports and Imports: 2002

Albert N. Greco

Associate Professor
Fordham University
Graduate School of Business Administration
angreco@aol.com

U.S. Book Exports: 2002

The U.S. book industry sustained a 1.8 percent reduction in the value of export shipments in 2002, the second decline in as many years and the fourth since 1996. Compounding the problem was a plummet in exports as a percent of total publishers' shipments, hovering near the 6.4 percent mark in 2002, down from 6.9 percent in 2001 and a heady 9.1 percent in 1995.

Overall, these export totals, as reported by the U.S. Department of Commerce's International Trade Administration, could not come at a worse time for many publishers struggling with soft domestic sales, high return rates in the consumer book sector (adult trade hardcover book returns reached 32.6 percent while mass market paperbacks topped 41.8 percent in 2002), uncertainty about the U.S. economy, and war in the Middle East in 2003.

What makes these statistical indices even more disconcerting is the fact that English is, in many social and business sectors, the global language (Greco, 1997), a reason why U.S. fiction and nonfiction books traditionally posted strong sales tallies abroad. In addition, since the early 1990s, a majority of U.S. trade book publishers reconfigured their global business strategies, making sure sales representatives visited major foreign markets for American books, attended important international book fairs, and utilized global communications systems (e-mail, fax, and so forth) to keep in touch with clients. So any decline in export figures calls into question some highly visible and expensive foreign marketing strategies.

International Trade

What are the philosophical underpinnings behind international trade? Clearly, many of the world's economies realized after World War II that there was inexorable movement toward international trade. If trade barriers (i.e., tariffs) were reduced or discarded, or if free trade zones were crafted, then this newly configured environment had the potential to trigger sustained economic growth at home and abroad (Alesina and Spolaore, 1997; Armengol, 2002; Edwards, 1993; Frankel and Romer, 1999; Grossman and Helpman, 1991; Warner, 1994).

Yet doubts and controversy surrounded efforts to fashion workable trade and tariff agreements (Harrison and Hanson, 1999; Irwin, 2002), especially regarding the adverse impact of imports on domestic markets (Hiscox, 2002); other concerns centered on developing reasonable regional trading agreements (Breschi and Malerba, 2001; McCallum, 1995; Pomfret, 1998) and apprehension about globalization's impact on fragile economic structures in emerging nations (Bhagwati, 2002; Nordas, 2002; Sachs and Warner, 1995). However, many economists insisted that, in spite of certain short-term pitfalls related to globalization (Edwards, 1998), globalization and its emphasis on tariff reduction (especially after the 1980s) stimulated real economic growth and helped initiate effective reforms in developed and emerging countries, resulting in many instances of positive changes in the standards of living, wages, and political freedom for millions of people in these emerging nations.

While theories always work in econometric models, the harsh realities of international trade sometimes undermine theories and reveal what economics call "anomalies," unusual patterns that cannot be explained by the models. The year 2002 is a classic example of too many "anomalies" undermining theoretical representations, including: turmoil in the Middle East and North Korea; European Union (EU) nations hampered by flat economic growth and high wage costs (up 3.7 percent over 2001); deflationary pressures and banking crises in Japan; terrorist activities in certain parts of Asia (including the Philippines and Indonesia); downward shifts in tourism revenues in Thailand and Singapore; higher energy costs in China; and uncertainty in a few Latin American nations hammered with high unemployment rates (especially Argentina), external debt (Argentina and Brazil), and citizens living below the poverty line (primarily in Ecuador, Bolivia, Venezuela, and Argentina).

The Impact on Exports

The end result was that in 2002 seven of the eight major book categories posted declines in export revenues, with disconcerting results in the dictionaries and thesauruses category; only textbooks exhibited any strength in the global marketplace. Unit data were also unimpressive, although dictionaries and thesauruses posted a positive increase. Table 1 outlines these trends.

Table 1 / U.S. Exports of Books: 2002

Category	Value (millions of current $)	Percent Change 2001–2002	Units (millions of copies)	Percent Change 2001–2002
Dictionaries and thesauruses	2.5	-41.8	0.9	39.6
Encyclopedias	14.8	-5.2	3.5	-10.8
Textbooks	380.6	11.5	56.0	13.2
Religious books	73.9	-7.9	60.5	-4.3
Technical, scientific, and professional	376.6	-9.4	81.1	9.92
Art and pictorial books	20.7	-3.7	6.2	1.8
Hardcover books, n.e.s.	110.4	-16.9	31.8	-9.8
Mass market paperbacks	165.3	-13.8	99.3	-6.7
Total, all books	1,681.2	-1.8	967.4	1.7

n.e.s. = not elsewhere specified.

Individual shipments are excluded from the foreign trade data if valued under $2,500. All totals are rounded off to one decimal point. Data for individual categories may not add to totals due to statistical rounding.

Source: U.S. Department of Commerce, International Trade Administration

The top 25 countries buying U.S. books accounted for $1.58 billion (off 1.6 percent from 2001) and 93.95 percent of all exports. As expected, Canada remained the principal destination for exported books, accounting for 42.02 percent of all exports. The United Kingdom's market share was only 17.19 percent, although its tallies increased a sharp 8.2 percent over 2001. Other nations posting increases included Australia (up 7.3 percent, and 4.48 percent of the market); Hong Kong (up 7.3 percent, and a 2 percent share); India (up 22 percent, a 1.24 percent share); France (up 17.3 percent, but only a 0.78 percent share); and China (up 9.6 percent, a 0.74 percent share).

Deep losses were posted by the Republic of Korea, Germany, Taiwan, the Netherlands, Brazil, Nigeria, and Ireland. There are signs of potential economic uncertainty in those nations and these figures were quite possibly a harbinger of further declines in 2003. Table 2 outlines these trends.

Table 2 / U.S. Books Exports to 25 Principal Countries: 2002

Country	Value (millions of current $)	Percent change 2001–2002
Canada	742,619	2.1
United Kingdom	270,622	8.2
Japan	100,804	-22.0
Australia	70,806	7.3
Mexico	64,938	1.8
Singapore	49,570	1.2
Hong Kong	31,559	7.3
Korea (Republic of)	29,131	-17.9
Germany	29,081	-14.5
Taiwan	24,662	-14.6
Netherlands	22,901	-34.9
India	19,513	22.0
Philippines	15,331	-19.2
Belgium	12,826	11.8
France	12,370	17.3
South Africa	12,187	-18.3
China	11,739	9.6
Brazil	10,259	-46.3
Switzerland	9,727	-9.4
Nigeria	8,242	-33.9
Malaysia	7,709	6.5
New Zealand	6,775	9.1
Italy	6,448	-17.6
Ireland	5,138	-39.4
Ghana	4,552	134.0
Total, Top 25 countries	1,579,511	-1.6

Individual shipments are excluded from the foreign trade data if valued under $2,500.00. All totals are rounded off to one decimal point. Data for individual categories may not add to totals due to statistical rounding.

Source: U.S. Department of Commerce, International Trade Administration

An investigation of specific export categories revealed shifting interests in U.S. books abroad. The popular mass market paperback book (a rack-sized book) accounted for $165.3 million and 9.83 percent of all exports in 2002, down from $191.8 million in 2001. Canada's $81.6 million exceeded all nations and accounted for a hefty 49.36 percent of all mass market paperback exports, easily outpacing the United Kingdom's $21.2 million (a 12.83 percent market share) and Japan ($13.6 million, an 8.23 percent share). The remaining top 13 exports countries shared the remaining totals, all generating less than 5 percent in total market shares. Table 3 outlines these trends.

Table 3 / U.S. Book Exports of Mass Market Paperbacks (Rack-Sized), Top 15 Markets: 2002

Country	Value ($ million)	Quantity (millions)
Canada	81.6	56.9
United Kingdom	21.2	7.7
Japan	13.6	10.4
Australia	7.0	4.1
Singapore	5.0	2.5
South Africa	5.0	1.7
Netherlands	3.3	1.4
France	2.9	1.7
Brazil	2.8	1.8
Korea (Republic of)	2.5	1.7
Philippines	2.4	1.2
Taiwan	2.3	1.4
Germany	1.9	1.1
China	1.7	1.0
Israel	1.6	1.3

All totals are rounded off to one decimal point. Data for individual categories may not add to totals due to statistical rounding.
Source: U.S. Department of Commerce, International Trade Administration

The technical, scientific, and professional book niche underperformed in 2002; its $376.6 million represented a 9.41 percent decline from 2001's $415.7 million. Canada's $114.6 million accounted for 30.43 percent of exports in this category, with the United Kingdom (a 14.5 percent share) and a surging Japan (13.1 percent) trailing. While Mexico's dollar volume was only seventh, Mexico has the potential (so far clearly unrealized) to move up in the rankings because of its proximity to the United States. Table 4 outlines these trends.

Since the early to mid-1990s, the wide acceptance of the Internet, computers with CD-ROM disk drives (Lustig, 1997), and the introduction of inexpensive electronic encyclopedia products compelled many industry analysts to insist printed encyclopedias and serial installments were ultimately doomed for extinction (Getz, 1992). These dire predictions began to materialize around 2000, and by 2002 the beleaguered encyclopedia and serial installment niche unraveled. Total dollar exports were anemic, dropping from $15.6 million in 2001 to $14.8

**Table 4 / U.S. Exports of Technical, Scientific, and
Professional Books, Top 15 Markets: 2002**

Country	Value ($ million)	Units (million)
Canada	114.6	17.5
United Kingdom	54.6	10.0
Japan	49.2	5.3
Singapore	15.4	3.0
Australia	14.9	2.9
Germany	14.0	2.0
Mexico	12.5	17.5
Belgium	10.8	1.0
Netherlands	8.2	0.8
India	8.0	0.7
Hong Kong	7.9	1.3
Taiwan	7.5	0.8
Switzerland	5.8	1.1
Korea (Republic of)	5.3	1.1
France	5.3	1.1

All totals are rounded off to one decimal point. Data for individual categories may not add to totals due to statistical rounding.
Source: U.S. Department of Commerce, International Trade Administration

**Table 5 / U.S. Exports of Encyclopedias and Serial
Installments, Top 15 Markets: 2002**

Country	Value ($ million)	Units (million)
Mexico	3.5	1.6
United Kingdom	2.0	0.4
Canada	1.6	0.3
Japan	1.4	0.3
Australia	1.3	0.2
Venezuela	0.9	0.2
Switzerland	0.7	0.1
Philippines	0.5	0.1
South Africa	0.3	0.05
United Arab Emirates	0.3	0.03
Argentina	0.3	0.02
Germany	0.2	0.02
Brazil	0.2	0.04
Hong Kong	0.2	n.a.
India	0.1	0.03

n.a. = not available.
All totals are rounded off to one decimal point. Data for individual categories may not add to totals due to statistical rounding.
Source: U.S. Department of Commerce, International Trade Administration

million in 2002. Mexico was the leading export market in this category at $3.5 million (a total that paled in comparison with other book export niches).

It is likely that continued erosion in printed encyclopedias and serial installments will be evident between 2003 and 2005, with the possibility that this niche will no longer be tracked by the Commerce Department in the last half of this decade. Table 5 outlines this trend.

Textbook margins have been under pressure in recent years because of (1) the emergence of a viable, highly computerized, and international market for used textbooks, and (2) the impact of sophisticated book-pirating operations abroad. The Association of American Publishers, the largest book-publishing association in the United States, actively participates in the crackdown by the International Intellectual Property Alliance (IIPA) on pirating; pirating is estimated to cost U.S. publishers slightly more than $500 million annually in lost sales in almost every book category. Unfortunately, IIPA estimates that textbooks account for a significant portion of that $500 million.

While book pirates are difficult to find, and generally even more difficult to prosecute successfully, export textbook sales fortunately grew an impressive 11.5 percent between 2001 (when revenues reached $341.5 million) and 2002 (revenues $380.6 million). The United Kingdom set the pace in this category with $121.3 million in revenues and a 31.87 percent share of a growing market. Canada was firmly entrenched in second place with $66.4 million and a 17.44 percent share. Australia, Mexico, and Hong Kong rounded out the top five nations in this market sector.

However, concerns exist for the long-term growth of textbook exports if pirates and the used book market continue to cut deeply into sales. Table 6 outlines the trends in textbook exports.

Table 6 / U.S. Exports of Textbooks, Top 15 Markets: 2002

Country	Value ($ million)	Units (million)
United Kingdom	121.3	20.8
Canada	66.4	6.4
Australia	26.5	5.0
Mexico	24.8	3.9
Hong Kong	18.0	1.1
Singapore	16.3	2.9
Korea (Republic of)	15.3	3.1
Japan	12.7	2.0
Taiwan	10.4	1.9
Philippines	6.2	1.1
Netherlands	6.1	1.8
Germany	5.2	0.9
China	4.2	0.3
Ghana	3.2	0.8
Djibouti	3.2	0.8

All totals are rounded off to one decimal point. Data for individual categories may not add to totals due to statistical rounding.
Source: U.S. Department of Commerce, International Trade Administration

The Future of Book Exports

It is likely that exports will post total revenue declines in 2003 for a number of substantive reasons. First, the $45 trillion world economy is expected to grow a modest 3 percent in 2003. Second, war and unrest in the Middle East (and possibly in other parts of the world) could have a debilitating impact on economic stability, probably adversely affecting prices (especially oil), which can dampen economic growth in many parts of the world. Third, business investments in Europe, Japan, and parts of Asia remain listless, possibly limiting economic growth in those regions. Fourth, governmental budgets are mushrooming in the EU, which has mandatory policies limiting budgetary deficits to no more than 3 percent of a nation's gross domestic product (GDP). Fifth, since fluctuations are anticipated with the Euro, increases in the costs of exports for EU countries are consequently inevitable. Sixth, the United States remains the linchpin in the global economic superstructure because of its daunting $10 trillion economy, much to the chagrin of many foreign economists and politicians, and any economic slowdown or sluggishness in America inevitably spills over into other parts of the world.

The end result is pretty clear: Unless the U.S. economy grows in 2003, the rest of the world will probably languish, as will U.S. book exports.

U.S. Book Imports: 2002

Book imports are on the upswing. While they increased a modest 2.05 percent in 2002 (from $1.63 billion in 2001 to $1.67 billion in 2002), book imports surged 20.05 percent between 1998 and 2002. Exports, on the other hand, declined 8.72 percent during the same years. And the gap separating book exports from book imports—the pivotal balance of trade equation—was a wafer-thin 1.01 percent in 2002, with a negative balance of trade possible for 2003.

Table 7 / U.S. Imports of Books: 2002

Category	Value ($ million)	Percent Change 2001–2002
Dictionaries and thesauruses	2.1	58.5
Encyclopedias	1.5	174.9
Textbooks	79.2	17.3
Religious books	14.8	18.9
Technical, scientific, and professional	56.2	16.2
Art and pictorial books	5.9	65.5
Hardcover books, n.e.s.	145.7	1.7
Mass market paperbacks	13.1	52.8
Total, all books	1,661.2	2.1

n.e.s. = not elsewhere specified.

All totals are rounded off to one decimal point. Data for individual categories may not add to totals due to statistical rounding. Individual shipments are excluded from the foreign trade data if valued under $2,500.

Source: U.S. Department of Commerce, International Trade Administration

All eight of the important book import categories posted increases in 2002, with exceptional results in art and pictorial books, mass market paperbacks, and, ironically, dictionaries and thesauruses and encyclopedias (although their tallies were a bit modest). Table 7 outlines these growth trends.

Eleven of the top 25 nations supplying books for the U.S. market reported a growth in shipments, with exceptionally large increases posted by China, Colombia, and Malaysia. China accounted for 20.38 percent of all book imports, eclipsing the United Kingdom and Canada. It appears that prices related to printing, paper, and binding (which can account for about one-third of a publisher's overall budget) made these nations, all with low labor costs, attractive offshore suppliers of books. Some of the more traditional European industrialized nations (specifically Italy and Germany), bound by expensive labor contracts, might experience additional declines in the coming years. Table 8 outlines these trends.

Table 8 / U.S. Book Imports from 25 Principal Countries: 2002

Country	Value ($ million)	Percent Change 2001–2002
China	338.5	26.5
United Kingdom	267.8	-11.9
Canada	251.1	3.0
Hong Kong	223.4	-2.7
Singapore	100.6	4.1
Italy	83.4	-5.0
Germany	56.0	5.5
Spain	51.0	1.0
Japan	47.2	-5.5
Korea (Republic of)	40.5	13.8
Belgium	24.4	-15.0
France	22.9	-7.7
Mexico	18.6	-3.3
Netherlands	14.9	-22.7
Colombia	12.9	40.3
Israel	11.8	-8.5
Malaysia	11.6	49.8
Thailand	10.4	-4.8
Taiwan	9.9	59.3
Australia	8.7	-11.0
United Arab Emirates	5.9	-0.7
India	4.3	12.5
New Zealand	4.1	22.0
Russia	3.9	-3.5
Sweden	3.7	-12.7
Total, top 25 countries	1,627.5	2.5

All totals are rounded off to one decimal point. Data for individual categories may not add to totals due to statistical rounding. Individual shipments are excluded from the foreign trade data if valued under $2,500.

Source: U.S. Department of Commerce, International Trade Administration

Table 9 / U.S. Imports of Encyclopedias and Serial Installments, Top 15 Markets: 2002

Country	Value ($ million)	Units (million)
United Kingdom	1.5	0.2
Hong Kong	1.2	0.3
China	1.0	0.3
Italy	0.8	0.2
Spain	0.7	0.1
Germany	0.5	0.09
Singapore	0.5	0.1
Malaysia	0.3	0.04
Canada	0.3	0.02
Netherlands	0.3	0.03
Portugal	0.2	0.06
Slovakia	0.2	0.05
Mexico	0.09	0.004
Indonesia	0.08	0.04
Sweden	0.04	0.06

All totals are rounded off to one decimal point. Data for individual categories may not add to totals due to statistical rounding. Calculations used two decimal points because of the size of the totals.
Source: U.S. Department of Commerce, International Trade Administration

While interesting results were evident in the mercurial encyclopedias and serial installments category (see Table 9), the textbook sector generated some intriguing results.

The United Kingdom retained its preeminent position in the $162.7 million textbook sector, amassing a staggering 48.67 percent share of the market. This nation's long-standing strength in certain academic fields, notably in the humanities and the social sciences, allows it to dominate business in this growing, lucrative segment. Other nations able to penetrate sales in the next few years include low-cost producers Hong Kong and China. Mexico, on the other hand, seems unable to take advantage of either NAFTA or its proximity to the United States, languishing in this important book category. Table 10 outlines these textbook trends.

Sales of religious books (including Bibles, testaments, and prayer books) increased sharply in the United States in the 1990s, and imports of religious books reflected this trend.

For several years, the Republic of Korea, Belgium, and Israel dominated the religious-publishing niche, accounting for more than 45 percent of all shipments. While the emergence of China in this market in the late 1990s was a bit unexpected in light of its political and philosophical orientation, this nation continued to make inroads in this niche, reaching a 6.19 percent share by 2002. Continued Chinese growth patterns are anticipated for the next few years.

In spite of the growing Hispanic American population in the United States, Mexico failed to capitalize on these demographic trends, remaining 15th with a marginal 1.14 percent share of the market. Table 11 outlines these trends.

Table 10 / U.S. Imports of Textbooks,Top 15 Markets

Country	Value ($ million)	Units (million)
United Kingdom	79.2	7.3
Canada	15.9	5.7
Hong Kong	15.7	5.3
China	12.9	4.7
Mexico	6.1	0.8
Spain	4.8	1.0
Singapore	4.3	1.3
Italy	3.5	1.7
Germany	2.7	0.4
Colombia	2.4	0.5
New Zealand	2.0	1.1
Malaysia	1.5	0.5
United Arab Emirates	1.5	0.1
France	1.4	0.3
Australia	1.3	0.2

All totals are rounded off to one decimal point. Data for individual categories may not add to totals due to statistical rounding.
Source: U.S. Department of Commerce, International Trade Administration

Table 11 / U.S. Imports of Bibles, Testaments, Prayer Books, and Other Religious Books, Top 15 Markets: 2002

Country	Value ($ million)	Units (million)
Korea (Republic of)	14.8	4.3
Belgium	11.5	3.6
Israel	9.4	2.6
Colombia	5.8	6.2
United Kingdom	5.5	1.4
China	4.9	3.8
Hong Kong	3.7	4.2
France	3.3	4.2
Spain	3.2	1.3
Canada	2.8	3.0
Italy	1.8	0.7
Singapore	1.6	0.9
Germany	1.3	0.6
India	0.9	0.7
Mexico	0.9	0.6

All totals are rounded off to one decimal point. Data for individual categories may not add to totals due to statistical rounding.
Source: U.S. Department of Commerce, International Trade Administration

Clearly, the technical, scientific, and professional book area is highly specialized; the end result is that many nations, lacking a strong academic and research infrastructure in these sectors, find it exceptionally difficult to compete in this niche as producers of these books; printers in emerging countries, on the other hand, are essentially free from these impediments.

Canada, the United Kingdom, and Germany have exceptionally impressive scientific and professional universities and advanced research facilities, providing them with the needed foundation to generate technical, scientific, and professional books and carve out strong market shares in this area. Overall, they generated $119.6 million and a 63.25 percent market share. Japan and the Netherlands lagged in spite of their impressive technical research facilities and printing operations. The rest of the top 15 nations divided the remaining pieces of the market. Table 12 outlines these trends.

One of the most successful book categories in the United States is the mass market paperback book. Its appeal is simple: It is inexpensive (with a suggested retail price in the $4.99 to $8.99 range), portable, durable, and sold in a wide variety of retail establishments ranging from convenience stores to terminals. While one might assume that Canada and the United Kingdom would be major sources of these books, the niche leader was China, with an 18.71 percent share of the market, followed by the United Kingdom (18.14 percent), Hong Kong (15.71 percent), and Canada (14 percent). These four nations compose two-thirds of all market paperback book imports, and it is unlikely that any substantive shift in this market standing will occur in the next few years. Clearly, China is a major player in a number of key book categories, and its econometric structure makes it somewhat impervious to any significant business setbacks, unless energy costs soar. Table 13 outlines these trends.

Table 12 / U.S. Imports of Technical, Scientific, and Professional Books, Top 15 Markets: 2002

Country	Value ($ million)	Units (million)
Canada	56.2	15.5
United Kingdom	43.0	6.5
Germany	20.4	2.6
Japan	9.8	1.6
Netherlands	9.6	0.5
China	9.6	3.4
Hong Kong	7.3	2.1
Mexico	4.3	2.5
France	3.4	0.4
Belgium	3.2	0.3
Singapore	2.6	0.8
Italy	2.5	0.6
Taiwan	2.0	1.2
Korea (Republic of)	1.8	0.3
Sweden	1.8	0.4

All totals are rounded off to one decimal point. Data for individual categories may not add to totals due to statistical rounding.
Source: U.S. Department of Commerce, International Trade Administration

Table 13 / U.S. Imports of Mass Market Paperbacks
(Rack-Size), Top 15 Markets: 2002

Country	Value ($ million)	Units (million)
China	13.1	11.8
United Kingdom	12.7	3.6
Hong Kong	11.0	7.5
Canada	9.8	5.1
Singapore	4.9	2.8
Italy	4.8	2.4
Germany	2.9	1.0
Spain	2.3	1.8
Japan	1.7	0.2
Korea (Republic of)	1.0	0.7
Taiwan	1.0	0.4
Mexico	0.8	0.2
Thailand	0.8	0.2
France	0.5	0.2
Malaysia	0.5	0.3

All totals are rounded off to one decimal point. Data for individual categories may not add to totals due to statistical rounding.
Source: U.S. Department of Commerce, International Trade Administration

The Balance of Trade: Book Exports and Imports

In spite of sustained attacks on globalization, the United States and the majority of nations believe in the importance of international trade. A review of important econometric data released by the U.S. Department of Commerce's International Trade Administration revealed that the book industry's balance of trade sustained deep losses in 2001 and 2002.

The ratio between exports and imports stood at 1.65 in 1990, but exports lost ground throughout the 1990s, reaching 1.05 in 2001 and 1.01 in 2002. If this continues, books will become a negative balance-of-trade product in 2003, and publishers will scramble to craft new marketing strategies to increase export sales revenues, reach profitability goals, and maximize sell-through rates. This situation could become an exceptionally serious conundrum for publishers accustomed to an expanding foreign market for their books. Table 14 outlines this trend.

Equally unsettling is the sharp decline in the ratio between book exports and total U.S. dollar book shipment revenues. In 1990 the percentage stood at 9.4 percent; by 2002 it had declined to a paltry 6.4 percent, yet another sign of deep uncertainty in the entire export sector. Table 15 outlines this downward spiral.

Can the U.S. book industry initiate any policies to increase exports? Obviously, publishers active in the international marketplace have existing strategies. However, perhaps it is time for the entire book-publishing industry to consider a coordinated initiative to analyze the problem of declining exports on a macroeconomic level and then develop viable microeconomic stratagems (clearly within the spirit and the letter of antitrust laws; Hirschberg, Masoumi, Slottje, and Arize, 2003).

Table 14 / U.S. Trade in Books: 1970–2002

Year	U.S. Book Exports ($ million)	U.S. Book Imports ($ million)	Ratio: Exports/Imports
1970	174.9	92.0	1.90
1975	269.3	147.6	1.82
1980	518.9	306.5	1.69
1985	591.2	564.2	1.05
1990	1,415.1	855.1	1.65
1995	1,779.5	1,184.5	1.50
1996	1,775.6	1,240.1	1.43
1997	1,896.6	1,297.5	1.46
1998	1,841.8	1,383.7	1.33
1999	1,871.1	1,441.4	1.30
2000	1,877.0	1,590.5	1.18
2001	1,712.3	1,627.8	1.05
2002	1,681.2	1,661.2	1.01

All totals are rounded off to one decimal point. Data for individual categories may not add to totals due to statistical rounding. Due to changes in the classification of "U.S. traded products" and what constitutes products classified as "books," data prior to 1990 are not strictly comparable to data beginning in 1990.
Source: U.S. Department of Commerce, International Trade Administration

Table 15 / U.S. Book Industry Shipments Compared to U.S. Book Exports: 1970–2002

Year	Total Shipments ($ million)	U.S. Book Exports ($ million)	Exports as a Percentage of Total Shipments
1970	2,434.2	174.9	7.2
1975	3,536.5	269.3	7.6
1980	6,114.4	518.9	8.5
1985	10,165.7	591.2	5.8
1990	14,982.6	1,415.1	9.4
1995	19,471.0	1,779.5	9.1
1996	20,285.7	1,775.6	8.8
1997	21,131.9	1,896.6	9.0
1998	22,507.0	1,841.8	8.2
1999	23,263.9	1,871.1	8.2
2000	24,763.3	1,877.0	7.6
2001	24,885.5	1,712.3	6.9
2002	26,285.0	1,681.2	6.4

Source: U.S. Department of Commerce, International Trade Administration; and the Book Industry Study Group, Inc. (BISG). BISG's totals were used for shipments from 1985 through 2002. Commerce totals were used for 1970–1980. Due to changes in the classification of "U.S. traded products" and what constitutes products classified as "books," data prior to 1990 are not strictly comparable to data beginning in 1990. All totals are rounded off to one decimal point. Data for individual categories may not add to totals due to statistical rounding.

Independent empirical research is needed to determine (1) the changing markets for book exports and the viability of free trade agreements (King, 1998), (2) the elasticities of demand of book exports (Deppler, 1971, Erkel-Rousse and Mirza, 2002), (3) the preferences of various foreign markets for printed books and book content delivered electronically, and (4) the long-term "life span" of certain book formats.

To date, most publishers rarely develop empirical research on book exports. This means that whenever a foreign nation (or a region) sustains an economic slowdown, a decline in its GDP, or a surge in its inflation rate, publishers dependent on book-export revenues stand by helplessly and watch as unsettling events unfold, developments that adversely impact their bottom line.

In the current publishing environment where profit margins are critically important and conference calls with Wall Street analysts are now a fact of life, concrete knowledge about export trends will be indispensable in the coming years.

References

Adler, M. (1971). "Elasticities of Demand for U.S. Exports: A Reply." *Review of Economics & Statistics* 53(2): 203–204.

Alesina, A., and Spolaore, E. (1997). "On the Number and Size of Nations." *Quarterly Journal of Economics* 112(4): 1027–1056.

Armengol, M. O. I. (2002). *Strategic Trade Analysis.* Oxford University Press.

Bhagwati, J. (2002). *Free Trade Today.* Princeton University Press.

Breschi, S., and Malerba, F. (2001). "The Geography of Innovation and Economic Clustering: Some Introductory Notes." *Industrial and Corporate Change* 10(4): 817–833.

Deppler, M. C. (1971). "Elasticities of Demand for U.S. Exports: A Comment." *Review of Economics & Statistics* 53(2): 201–203.

Edwards, S. (1993). "Openness, Trade Liberalization, and Growth in Developing Countries." *Journal of Economic Literature* 31(3): 1358–1393.

Edwards, S. (1998). "Openness, Productivity, and Growth: What Do We Really Know?" *Economic Journal* 108(447): 383–398.

Erkel-Rousse, H., and Mirza, D. (2002). "Import Price Elasticities: Reconsidering the Evidence." *Canadian Journal of Economics* 35(2): 282–306.

Frankel, J. A., and Romer, D. (1999). "Does Trade Cause Growth?" *American Economic Review* 89(3): 379–399.

Getz, M. (1992). *Electronic Publishing: An Economic View."* Serials Review 18(1–2): 25–31.

Greco, A. N. (1997). *The Book Publishing Industry.* Allyn & Bacon.

Grossman, G., and Helpman, E. (1991). *Innovation and Growth in the Global Economy.* MIT Press.

Harrison, A., and Hanson, G. (1999). "Who Gains from Trade Reforms? Some Remaining Puzzles." *Journal of Development Economics* 48(3): 419–447.

Hirschberg, J. G., Maasoumi, E., Slottje, D., and Arize, A. C. (2003). "Antitrust Issues in International Comparisons of Market Structure." *Journal of Econometrics* 113(1): 129–158.

Hiscox, M. J. (2002). *International Trade and Political Conflict.* Princeton University Press.

Irwin, D. (2002). *Free Trade Under Fire.* Princeton University Press.

Janada, K. (1999). "Signaling and Underutilization of Import Quota." *Journal of International Trade & Economic Development* 11(4): 351–365.

King, D. W. (1998). "Some Economic Aspects of the Internet." *Journal of the American Society for Information Science,* 49(September): 990–1002.

Lustig, H. (1997). "Electronic Publishing: Economic Issues in a Time of Transition." *Astrophysics & Space Science* 247(1–2): 117–132.

McCallum, J. (1995). "National Borders Matter: Canada-U.S. Regional Trade Patterns." *American Economic Review* 85(3): 615–623.

Nordas, H. K. (2002). "Patterns of Foreign Direct Investment in Poor Countries." *Journal of International Trade & Economic Development* 11(3): 247–265.

Pomfret, R. (1998). *The Economics of Regional Trading Arrangements.* Oxford University Press.

Sachs, J., and Warner, A. (1995). "Economic Reform and the Process of Global Integration." *Brookings Papers on Economic Activity* 1: 1–118.

Warner, A. M. (1994). "Does World Investment Demand Determine U.S. Exports?" *American Economic Review* 84(5): 1409–1422.

Number of Book Outlets in the United States and Canada

The *American Book Trade Directory* (Information Today, Inc.) has been published since 1915. Revised annually, it features lists of booksellers, wholesalers, periodicals, reference tools, and other information about the U.S. and Canadian book markets. The data shown in Table 1, the most current available, are from the 2002–2003 edition of the directory.

The 27,182 stores of various types shown are located throughout the United States, Canada, and regions administered by the United States. "General" bookstores stock trade books and children's books in a general variety of subjects. "College" stores carry college-level textbooks. "Educational" outlets handle school textbooks up to and including the high school level. "Mail order" outlets sell general trade books by mail and are not book clubs; all others operating by mail are classified according to the kinds of books carried. "Antiquarian" dealers sell old and rare books. Stores handling secondhand books are classified as "used." "Paperback" stores have more than 80 percent of their stock in paperbound books. Stores with paperback departments are listed under the appropriate major classification ("general," "department store," "stationer," etc.). Bookstores with at least 50 percent of their stock on a particular subject are classified by subject.

Table 1 / Bookstores in the United States and Canada, 2002

Category	United States	Canada
Antiquarian General	1,574	117
Antiquarian Mail Order	486	12
Antiquarian Specialized	240	8
Art Supply Store	81	2
College General	3,372	186
College Specialized	119	10
Comics	249	23
Computer Software	987	0
Cooking	166	5
Department Store	1,973	0
Educational*	251	31
Federal Sites†	236	1
Foreign Language*	38	3
General	6,207	797
Gift Shop	211	16
Juvenile*	245	29
Mail Order General	282	20
Mail Order Specialized	656	23
Metaphysics, New Age, and Occult	244	24
Museum Store and Art Gallery	585	39
Nature and Natural History	190	6
Newsdealer	86	4
Office Supply	54	10

Table 1 / Bookstores in the United States and Canada, 2002 *(cont.)*

Category	United States	Canada
Other‡	2,023	270
Paperback§	226	11
Religious*	3,701	258
Self Help/Development	40	11
Stationer	10	10
Toy Store	44	20
Used*	561	99
Totals	25,137	2,045

* Includes Mail Order Shops for this topic, which are not counted elsewhere in this survey.

† National Historic Sites, National Monuments, and National Parks.

‡ Stores specializing in subjects or services other than those covered in this survey.

§ Includes Mail Order. Excludes used paperback bookstores, stationers, drugstores, or wholesalers handling paperbacks.

Review Media Statistics

Compiled by the staff of the *Bowker Annual*

Number of Books and Other Media
Reviewed by Major Reviewing Publications, 2001–2002

	Adult		Juvenile		Young Adult		Total	
	2001	2002	2001	2002	2001	2002	2001	2002
Appraisal[1]	16	n.a.	659	n.a.	165	n.a.	849	n.a.
Book[2]	281	261	44	32	—	—	325	293
Booklist[3]	4,772	5,095	2,884	3,999	—	—	8,652	9,094
Bulletin of the Center for Children's Books[4]	—	—	790	718	—	—	790	718
Chicago Sun Times	500	500	85	85	—	—	585	585
Chicago Tribune Sunday Book Section	650	600	275	275	15	25	940	900
Choice[5]	6,312	6,811	—	—	—	—	6,312	6,811
Horn Book Guide[6]	—	—	3,957	4,296	—	—	3,957	4,296
Horn Book Magazine	—	1	297	298	88	93	385	392
Kirkus Reviews[6]	3,930	2885	2,211	1,554	—	—	6,141	4,439
Library Journal[7]	6,237	6,117	—	—	—	—	6,237	6,117
Los Angeles Times	1,050	1,500	—	—	—	—	1,050	1,500
New York Times Sunday Book Review[6]	1,600	1,740	155	182	—	—	1,775	1,922
Publishers Weekly[8]	6,745	6,064	2,249	2,440	—	—	8,994	8,504
Rapport[9]	980	n.a.	—	—	—	—	980	n.a.
School Library Journal[10]	—	—	4,182,	4,321	—	—	4,182	4,321
Washington Post Book World	1,410	1,400	50	50	30	30	1,490	1,480

n.a.=not available

1 *Appraisal Science Books for Young People* reviews current science books for children and teenagers, plus teachers' resources for science. Since 2001, it has been published online only at http://www.appraisal.neu.edu.

2 YA books are included in the juvenile total.

3 All figures are for a 12-month period from September 1, 2001, to August 31, 2002 (vol. 98). YA books are included in the juvenile total. *Booklist* also reviewed 1,016 other media.

4 All figures are for 12-month period beginning September and ending July/August. YA books are included in the juvenile total. The *Bulletin* also reviewed 14 professional books.

5 All materials reviewed in *Choice* are scholarly publications intended for undergraduate libraries. Total includes 270 Internet sites and 29 CD-ROMs.

6 Juvenile figures include young adult titles.

7 In addition, *LJ* reviewed 360 audiobooks, 70 magazines, 356 videos, 401 books in "Collection Development," 142 Web sites, 162 online databases and CD-ROMs, and previewed 840 books in "Prepub Alert."

8 Total includes 393 reviews in the *Publishers Weekly* Web site "Review Annex."

9 Total includes 310 reviews of other media, including CDs.

10 Juvenile count includes YA titles. Total includes 67 books for professional reading, 82 December holiday books, 121 reference books, and 41 bilingual English/Spanish books.

Part 5
Reference Information

Bibliographies

The Librarian's Bookshelf

Cathleen Bourdon, MLS

Executive Director, Reference and User Services Association, American Library Association

Most of the books on this selective bibliography have been published since 2000; a few earlier titles are retained because of their continuing importance.

General Works

Alternative Library Literature, 2000/2001: A Biennial Anthology. Ed. by Sanford Berman and James P. Danky. McFarland, 2002. Paper $45.

Annual Review of Information Science and Technology (ARIST). Vol. 37. Ed. by Blaise Cronin. Information Today, Inc., 2003. $99.95.

American Library Directory, 2003–2004. 2 vols. Information Today, Inc., 2003. $299.

The Bowker Annual Library and Book Trade Almanac, 2003. Information Today, Inc., 2003. $199.

Introduction to Indexing and Abstracting. 3rd ed. By Donald and Ana Cleveland. Libraries Unlimited, 2000. $45.

Library and Information Science Annual. Vol. 7. Ed. by Bohdan S. Wynar. Libraries Unlimited, 1999. $65.

Library Literature and Information Science Index. H. W. Wilson, 1921. Also available online, 1984–.

The Whole Library Handbook: Current Data, Professional Advice, and Curiosa About Libraries and Library Services. 3rd ed. Comp. by George Eberhart. American Library Association, 2000. Paper $40.

Academic Libraries

ARL Statistics. Association of Research Libraries. Annual. 1964–. $120.

Academic Library Trends and Statistics, 2001. 3 vols. Association of College and Research Libraries/American Library Association, 2001. $240.

Academic Research on the Internet: Options for Scholars and Libraries. Ed. by Helen Laurence and William Miller. Haworth Press, 2001. Paper $49.95.

Books, Bytes, and Bridges: Libraries and Computer Centers in Academic Institutions. Ed. by Larry Hardesty. American Library Association, 2000. Paper $48.

CLIP (College Library Information Packet) Notes. Association of College and Research Libraries/American Library Association, 1980–. Most recent volume is No. 32, 2002. $29.

A Guide to the Management of Curriculum Materials Centers for the 21st Century: The Promise and the Challenge. Ed. by Jo Ann Carr. Association of College and Research Libraries/American Library Association, 2002. Paper $28.

Making the Grade: Academic Libraries and Student Success. Ed. by Maurie Caitlin

Kelly and Andrea Kross. Association of College and Research Libraries/American Library Association, 2002. Paper $18.

SPEC Kits. Association of Research Libraries. 1973–. 10/yr. $260.

Administration and Personnel

Advances in Library Administration and Organization. Ed. by Edward D. Garten and Delmus E. Williams. Elsevier Science, 2002. Most recent volume is No. 19. $86.

Coaching in the Library: A Management Strategy for Achieving Excellence. By Ruth F. Metz. American Library Association, 2001. Paper $45.

Developing a Compensation Plan for Your Library. By Paula M. Singer. American Library Association, 2002. Paper $38.

Get Them Talking: Managing Change Through Case Studies and Case Study Discussion. Ed. by Gwen Arthur. Reference and User Services Association/American Library Association, 2000. Paper $16.

The Library Meeting Survival Manual. By George J. Soete. Tulane Street Publications, 2000. Paper $29.95.

Management for Research Libraries Cooperation. Ed. by Sul H. Lee. Haworth Press, 2000. Paper $39.95.

Managerial Accounting for Libraries and Other Not-for-Profit Organizations. 2nd ed. By G. Stevenson Smith. American Library Association, 2002. Paper $55.

Powerful Public Relations: A How-To Guide for Librarians. Ed. by Rashelle S. Karp. American Library Association, 2002. Paper $32.

Practical Strategies for Library Managers. By Joan Giesecke. American Library Association, 2000. Paper $32.

Staff Development: A Practical Guide. 3rd ed. Ed. by Elizabeth Fuseler Avery, Terry Dahlin, Deborah A. Carver. American Library Association, 2001. Paper $40.

Staffing for Results: A Guide to Working Smarter. By Diane Mayo and Jeanne Goodrich. American Library Association, 2002. Paper $42.

Stop Talking, Start Doing! Attracting People of Color to the Library Profession. By Gregory L. Reese and Ernestine L. Haw-

kins. American Library Association, 1999. Paper $30.

Using Public Relations Strategies to Promote Your Nonprofit Organization. By Ruth Ellen Kinzey. Haworth Press, 2000. $59.95.

Bibliographic Instruction/Information Literacy

Becoming a Library Teacher. By Cheryl LaGuardia and Christine K. Oka. Neal-Schuman, 2000. Paper $49.95.

Hands-On Information Literacy Activities. By Jane Birks and Fiona Hunt. Neal Schuman, 2002. Paper and CD-ROM $75.

The Handy 5: Planning and Assessing Integrated Information Skills Instruction. Ed. by Robert Grover, Carol Fox, and Jacqueline McMahon Lakin. Scarecrow Press, 2002. Paper $22.50.

Information Literacy Toolkit: Grades Kindergarten–6; Information Literacy Toolkit: Grades 7 and Up; and *Research Projects: An Information Literacy Planner for Students*. By Jenny Ryan and Steph Capra. American Library Association, 2001. Paper with CD-ROM $45 for each toolkit, $20 for *Research Projects*.

Library Instruction: A Peer Tutoring Model. By Susan Deese-Roberts and Kathleen Keating. Libraries Unlimited, 2000. Paper $46.

Teaching Technology: A How-To-Do-It Manual for Librarians. By D. Scott Brandt. Neal-Schuman, 2002. Paper $55.

Web-Based Instruction: A Guide for Libraries. By Susan Sharpless Smith. American Library Association, 2001. Paper $40.

Cataloging and Classification

Anglo-American Cataloging Rules. 2nd ed. By Canadian Library Association, American Library Association, and the Chartered Institute of Library and Information Professionals. American Library Association, 2002. Loose-leaf and binder $87.

Cataloging the Web: Metadata, AACR and MARC 21. Ed. by Wayne Jones, Judith R.

Ahronheim, and Josephine Crawford. Scarecrow Press, 2002. Paper $39.50.

The Creation and Persistence of Misinformation in Shared Library Catalogs: Language and Subject Knowledge in a Technological Era. By David Blade. GLIS, University of Illinois, 2002. Paper $8.

The Evidence in Hand: Report of the Task Force on the Artifact in Library Collections. By Stephen G. Nichols and Abby Smith. Council on Library and Information Resources, 2001. Paper $20.

Guidelines on Subject Access to Individual Works of Fiction, Drama, Etc. By the Association for Library Collections and Technical Services. American Library Association, 2000. Paper $19.

Managing Cataloging and the Organization of Information: Philosophies, Practices and Challenges at the Onset of the 21st Century. Ed. by Ruth C. Carter. Haworth Press, 2001. Paper $39.95.

Maxwell's Guide to Authority Work. By Robert L. Maxwell. American Library Association, 2002. Paper $49.

Metadata and Organizing Educational Resources on the Internet. Ed. by Jane Greenberg. Haworth Press, 2000. Paper $39.95.

Papers of Sanford Berman, former cataloger at the Southdale Hennepin County Library in Minnesota. University of Illinois Library, 2001. http://web.library.uiuc.edu/ahx/ead/ala/9701040a/berman/intro.html.

Proceedings of the Bicentennial Conference on Bibliographic Control for the New Millennium: Confronting the Challenges of Networked Resources and the Web. Ed. by Ann M. Sandberg-Fox. Library of Congress, 2001. Paper $45.

Seymour Lubetzky: Writings on the Classical Art of Cataloging. Comp. by Elaine Svenonius and Dorothy McGarry. Libraries Unlimited, 2001. $67.50.

Small Library Cataloging. 3rd ed. By Herbert Hoffman. Scarecrow Press, 2002. $35.

Sorting Out the Web: Approaches to Subject Access. By Candy Schwartz. Ablex Publishing/Greenwood, 2001. Paper $32.95.

Standard Cataloging for Schools and Public Libraries. 3rd ed. By Sheila S. Intner and Jean Weihs. Libraries Unlimited, 2001. $45.

Wynar's Introduction to Cataloging and Classification. 9th ed. By Arlene G. Taylor. Libraries Unlimited, 2000. $65.

Children's and Young Adult Services and Materials

Bare Bones Children's Services: Tips for Public Library Generalists. By Anitra T. Steele. American Library Association, 2001. Paper $32.

Bare Bones Young Adult Services: Tips for Public Library Generalists. 2nd ed. By Renee J. Vaillancourt. American Library Association, 1999. Paper $32.

Best Books for Young Adults. 2nd ed. By Betty Carter, with Sally Estes, Linda Waddle, and the Young Adult Library Services Association. American Library Association, 2000. Paper $35.

Booktalks and Beyond: Thematic Learning Activities for Grades K–6. By Nancy J. Keane. Upstart Books, 2001. Paper $16.95.

Do it Right! Best Practices for Serving Young Adults in School and Public Libraries. By Patrick Jones and Joel Shoemaker. Neal-Schuman, 2001. Paper $45.

Excellence in Library Services to Young Adults. 3rd ed. By Mary K. Chelton. American Library Association, 2000. Paper $25.

Fun Reading Programs. By Kathryn Totten Fantastic. Upstart Books/Highsmith Press, 2001. Paper $16.95.

Keep Talking That Book! Booktalks to Promote Reading, Volume III. By Carol Littlejohn and Cathlyn Thomas. Linworth Publishing, 2001. Paper $36.95.

The New Books Kids Like. Ed. by Sharon Deeds and Catherine Chastain. American Library Association, 2001. Paper $32.

New Directions for Library Service to Young Adults. Ed. by Patrick Jones and Linda Waddle. American Library Association, 2002. Paper $32.

The Newbery and Caldecott Awards: A Guide to the Medal and Honor Books. By the Association for Library Service to Children (ALSC). American Library Association, 2002. Paper $19.

Something Funny Happened at the Library: How to Create Humorous Programs for

Children and Young Adults. By Rob Reid. American Library Association, 2002. Paper $32.

Story Programs: A Source Book of Materials. 2nd ed. By Carolyn Sue Peterson, Ann D. Fenton, and Stefani Koorey. Scarecrow Press, 2000. Paper $29.50.

A Storytime Year: A Month-To-Month Kit for Preschool Programming. By Susan M. Dailey, illus. by Nancy Carol Wagner. Neal-Schuman, 2000. Loose-leaf binder, $59.95.

Teen Spaces: The Step-By-Step Library Makeover. By Kimberly Bolan Taney. American Library Association, 2002. Paper $35.

Teens.library: Developing Internet Services for Young Adults. By Linda W. Braun. American Library Association, 2002. Paper $28.

25 Latino Craft Projects. By Ana-Elba Pavon and Diana Borrego. American Library Association, 2002. Paper $30.

Youth Development and Public Libraries: Tools for Success. Ed. by Kurstin Finch Gnehm. Urban Libraries Council, 2002. $20.

Collection Development

Creating New Strategies for Cooperative Collection Development. Ed. by Milton T. Wolf and Marjorie E. Bloss. Haworth Press, 2000. Paper $32.95.

Developing an Outstanding Core Collection: A Guide for Public Libraries. By Carol Alabaster. American Library Association, 2002. Paper $38.

Guide to User Needs Assessment for Integrated Information Resource Management and Collection Development. Ed. by Dora Biblarz, Stephen Bosch, and Chris Sugnet. Scarecrow Press, 2001. Paper $17.50.

Help Wanted: Job and Career Information Resources. Ed. by Gary W. White. Reference and User Services Association/American Library Association, 2003. Paper $25.

Selecting and Managing Electronic Resources: A How-To-Do-It Manual. By Vicki L. Gregory. Neal-Schuman, 2000. Paper $55.

Copyright

Commonsense Copyright: A Guide for Educators and Librarians. 2nd ed. By R. S. Talab. McFarland, 1999. Paper $39.95.

Copyright Essentials for Librarians and Educators. By Kenneth D. Crews. American Library Association, 2000. Paper $45.

Copyright in Cyberspace: Questions and Answers for Librarians. By Gretchen McCord Hoffmann. Neal-Schuman, 2001. Paper $55.

Copyright Plain and Simple. 2nd ed. By Cheryl Besenjak. Career Press, 2000. Paper $12.99.

Customer Service

Defusing the Angry Patron: A How-To-Do-It Manual for Librarians and Paraprofessionals. By Rhea Joyce Rubin. Neal-Schuman, 2000. Paper $45.

Delivering Satisfaction and Service Quality: A Customer-Based Approach for Libraries. By Peter Hernon and John R. Whitman. American Library Association, 2000. Paper $40.

Diversity in the Library: A Way of Life. Library Video Network, 2001. Video $99.

Face It! Using Your Face to Sell Your Message. By Arch Lustberg. Library Video Network, 2002. Video $75.

Distance Education

Attracting, Educating, and Serving Remote Users Through the Web: A How-To-Do-It Manual for Librarians. Ed. by Donnelyn Curtis. Neal-Schuman, 2002. Paper $55.

The Browsable Classroom: An Introduction to E-Learning. By Carolyn B. Noah and Linda W. Braun. Neal-Schuman, 2001. Paper $45.

Library Outreach, Partnerships, and Distance Education: Reference Librarians at the Gateway. Ed. by Wendi Arant and Pixey Anne Mosley. Haworth Press, 2000. Paper $24.95.

Library Services for Open and Distance Learning: The Third Annotated Bibliogra-

phy. By Alexander L. Slade and Marie A. Kascus. Libraries Unlimited, 2000. $75.

Off-Campus Library Services Ed. by Anne Marie Casey. Haworth Press, 2001. Paper $49.95.

The Electronic Library

Creating a Winning Online Exhibition: A Guide for Libraries, Archives and Museums. By Martin R. Kalfatovic. American Library Association, 2002. Paper $40.

Diffuse Libraries: Emergent Roles for the Research Library in the Digital Age. By Wendy Pratt Lougee. Council on Library and Information Resources, 2002. Paper $15.

Digital Content: A Practical Guide for Librarians. By Lesley Ellen Harris. American Library Association, 2002. Paper $45.

Digital Futures: Strategies for the Information Age. By Marilyn Deegan and Simon Tanner. Neal-Schuman, 2002. Paper $55.

Digital Libraries. By William Y. Arms. MIT Press, 2000. $45.

From Gutenberg to the Global Information Infrastructure: Access to Information in the Networked World. By Christine L. Borgman. MIT Press, 2000. $42.

Issues for Libraries and Information Science in the Internet Age. By Bruce A. Shuman. Libraries Unlimited, 2001. Paper $45.

Online Community Information: Creating a Nexus at Your Library. By Joan C. Durrance and Karen E. Pettigrew. American Library Association, 2002. Paper $42.

Strategies for Building Digitized Collections. By Abby Smith. Council on Library and Information Resources, 2001. Paper $20.

Evaluation of Library Services

An Action Plan for Outcomes Assessment in Your Library. By Peter Hernon and Robert E. Dugan. American Library Association, 2001. Paper $49.

Identifying and Analyzing User Needs: A Complete Handbook and Ready-To-Use Assessment Workbook with Disk. By Lynn

Westbrook. Neal-Schuman, 2000. Paper with CD-ROM $75.

Library Evaluation: A Casebook and Can-Do Guide. Ed. by Danny P. Wallace and Connie Van Fleet. Libraries Unlimited, 2000. Paper $45.

Measuring What Matters: A Library/LRC Outcomes Assessment Manual. By Bonnie Gratch Lindauer. Learning Resources Association, 2000. Three-ring binder $79.

Statistical Methods for the Information Professional: A Practical, Painless Approach to Understanding, Using and Interpreting Statistics. By Liwen Vaughan. Information Today, Inc., 2001. $39.50.

Usage and Usability Assessment: Library Practices and Concerns. By Denise Troll Covey. Council on Library and Information Resources, 2002. Paper $20.

Fund Raising

Becoming a Fundraiser: The Principles and Practice of Library Development. 2nd ed. By Victoria Steele and Stephen D. Elder. American Library Association, 2000. Paper $38.

Fundraising for Libraries: 25 Proven Ways to Get More Money for Your Library. By James Swan. Neal-Schuman, 2002. Paper $69.95.

Grantsmanship for Small Libraries and School Library Media Centers. By Sylvia D. Hall-Ellis, Doris Meyer, Frank W. Hoffman, and Ann Jerabek. Libraries Unlimited, 1999. Paper $32.50.

Legacies for Libraries: A Practical Guide to Planned Giving. By Amy Sherman Smith and Matthew D. Lehrer. American Library Association, 2000. $35.

Government Documents

Guide to Popular U.S. Government Publications. 5th ed. By Frank W. Hoffman and Richard J. Wood. Libraries Unlimited, 1998. $38.50.

Introduction to United States Government Information Sources. 6th ed. By Joe Morehead. Libraries Unlimited, 1999. Paper $65.

U.S. Government on the Web: Getting the Information You Need. 2nd ed. By Peter Hernon, Robert E. Dugan, and John A. Shuler. Libraries Unlimited, 2001. Paper $45.

Health Information, Medical Librarianship

Administration and Management in Health Sciences Libraries. Ed. by Rick B. Forsman. Scarecrow Press, 2000. $55.

Health Care Resources on the Internet: A Guide for Librarians and Health Care Consumers. Ed. by M. Sandra Wood. Haworth Press, 1999. Paper $24.95.

The Medical Library Association Guide to Managing Health Care Libraries. Ed. by Ruth Holst and Sharon A. Phillips. Neal-Schuman, 2000. Paper $75.

Information Science

Emerging Frameworks and Methods: Proceedings of the Fourth International Conference on Conceptions of Library and Information Science. Ed. by Harry Bruce, Raya Fidel, Peter Ingwersen, and Pertti Vakkari. Libraries Unlimited, 2002. Paper $40.

Intelligent Technologies in Library and Information Service Applications. By F. W. Lancaster and Amy Warner. Information Today, Inc. 2001. $39.50.

Introductory Concepts in Information Science. By Melanie J. Norton. Information Today, Inc. 2000. $39.50.

Knowledge and Knowing in Library and Information Science: A Philosophical Framework. By John M. Budd. Scarecrow Press, 2001. Paper $38.50.

Knowledge Management for the Information Professional. Ed. by T. Kanti Srikantaiah and Michael Koenig. Information Today, Inc., 2000. $44.50.

Preparing the Information Professional: An Agenda for the Future. By Sajjad ur Rehman. Greenwood, 2000. $60.

Techno-Human Mesh: The Growing Power of Information Technologies. By Cynthia K. West. Quorum Books, 2000. $62.50.

Super Searchers Go to the Source: The Interviewing and Hands-On Information Strategies of Top Primary Researchers, Online, on the Phone and in Person. By Risa Sacks. CyberAge Books/Information Today, Inc. Paper $24.95.

The Web of Knowledge: A Festshrift in Honor of Eugene Garfield. Ed. by Blaise Cronin and Helen Barsky Atkins. Information Today, Inc., 2000. $49.50.

Intellectual Freedom

Banned Books Resource Guide. Office for Intellectual Freedom/American Library Association, 2001. Paper $30.

Banned in the U.S.A.: A Reference Guide to Book Censorship in Schools and Public Libraries. By Herbert N. Foerstel. Greenwood, 2002. $54.95.

Censorship and Selection: Issues and Answers for Schools. 3rd ed. By Henry Reichman. American Library Association, 2001. Paper $35.

Hit List for Children 2: Frequently Challenged Books. By Beverley C. Becker and Susan M. Stan. American Library Association, 2002. Paper $25.

Hit List for Young Adults 2: Frequently Challenged Books. By Teri S. Lesesne and Rosemary Chance. American Library Association, 2002. Paper $25.

IFLA/FAIFE World Report on Libraries and Intellectual Freedom. IFLA/FAIFE, 2001. Paper $10.

Intellectual Freedom and Social Responsibility in American Librarianship, 1967–1974. By Toni Samek. McFarland, 2001. $35.

Intellectual Freedom Manual. 6th ed. ALA Office for Intellectual Freedom. American Library Association, 2001. Paper $45.

Libraries, First Amendment, and Cyberspace: What You Need to Know. By Robert S. Peck. American Library Association, 2000. Paper $32.

Teaching Banned Books: 12 Guides for Young Readers. By Pat R. Scales. American Library Association, 2001. Paper $28.

Interlibrary Loan, Document Delivery, and Resource Sharing

Interlibrary Loan and Document Delivery in the Larger Academic Library: A Guide for University, Research, and Larger Public Libraries. By Lee Andrew Hilyer. Haworth Press, 2002. Paper $24.95.

Interlibrary Loan Policies Directory. 7th ed. Ed. by Leslie R. Morris. Neal-Schuman, 2002. Paper $199.95.

Interlibrary Loan Practices Handbook. 2nd ed. By Virginia Boucher. American Library Association, 1996. Paper $45.

The Internet/Web

The Cybrarian's Manual 2. 2nd ed. By Pat Ensor. American Library Association, 2000. Paper $45.

A Digital Gift to the Nation: Fulfilling the Promise of the Digital and Internet Age. By Lawrence K. Grossman and Newton N. Minow. Brookings Institution, 2001. Paper $15.95.

Instant Web Forms and Surveys for Academic Libraries; Instant Web Forms and Surveys for Public Libraries; Instant Web Forms and Surveys for Children's/YA Services and School Libraries. By Gail Junion-Metz and Derrek L. Metz. Neal-Schuman, 2001. Paper and CD-ROM, $75 each.

The Invisible Web: Uncovering Information Sources Search Engines Can't See. By Chris Sherman and Gary Price. CyberAge Books/Information Today, Inc., 2001. Paper $29.95.

The Librarian's Internet Survival Guide. By Irene E. McDermott. Information Today, Inc., 2002. Paper $29.50.

Managing the Internet Controversy. Ed. by Mark Smith. Neal-Schuman, 2001. Paper $45.

Neal-Schuman Complete Internet Companion for Librarians. 2nd ed. By Allen C. Benson. Neal-Schuman, 2001. Paper and CD-ROM $79.95.

Open Source Software for Libraries: An Open Source for Libraries Collaboration. By Library and Information Technology Association/American Library Association, 2002. Paper $29.

The Role and Impact of the Internet on Library and Information Services. Ed. by Lewis-Guodo Liu. Greenwood, 2001. $64.95.

Simplify Web Site Management with Server-Side Includes, Cascading Style Sheets, and Perl. By Andrea Peterson. Library and Information Technology Association/American Library Association, 2002. Paper $29.

Teaching the Internet in Libraries. By Rachel Singer Gordon. American Library Association, 2001. Paper $38.

Usability Assessment of Library-Related Web Sites: Methods and Case Studies. Ed. by Nicole Campbell. Library and Information Technology Association/American Library Association, 2001. Paper $25.

Usability Testing for Library Web Sites: A Hands-On Guide. By Elaina Norlin and CM! Winters. American Library Association, 2001. Paper $32.

Librarians and Librarianship

The ALA Survey of Librarian Salaries 2002. Ed. by Mary Jo Lynch. American Library Association, 2002. Paper $56.

ARL Annual Salary Survey, 2000–2001. Association of Research Libraries, 2002. Paper $120.

Back Talk with Dr. Alan Sokoloff. By Alan Sokoloff. Library Video Network, 2002. Video $130.

Diversity in Libraries: Academic Residency Programs. Ed. by Raquel V. Cogell and Cindy A. Gruwell. Greenwood, 2001. $62.50.

Ethics and Librarianship. By Robert Hauptman. McFarland, 2002. Paper $35.

Getting Libraries the Credit They Deserve: A Festschrift in Honor of Marvin H. Scilken. Ed. by Loriene Roy and Antony Cherian. Scarecrow Press, 2002. Paper $26.50.

Handbook of Black Librarianship. 2nd ed. By E. J. Josey and Marva L. DeLoach. Scarecrow Press, 2000. $69.50.

The Information Professional's Guide to Career Development Online. By Sarah L.

Nesbeitt and Rachel Singer Gordon. Information Today, Inc., 2001. Paper $29.50.

Jump Start Your Career in Library and Information Science. By Priscilla K. Shontz. Scarecrow Press, 2002. Paper $22.50.

Leadership and Learning: Helping Libraries and Librarians Reach Their Potential. By Lyndon Pugh. Scarecrow Press, 2001. $35.

Leadership in the Library and Information Science Professions: Theory and Practice. Ed. by Mark D. Winton. Haworth Press, 2002. Paper $22.95.

Librarianship—Quo Vadis? Opportunities and Dangers as We Face the New Millennium. By Herbert S. White. Libraries Unlimited, 2000. $65.

Our Enduring Values: Librarianship in the 21st Century. By Michael Gorman. American Library Association, 2000. Paper $28.

Time Management, Planning and Prioritization for Librarians. By Judith A. Siess. Scarecrow, 2002. Paper $29.95.

Library Automation

Directory of Library Automation Software, Systems, and Services. Ed. by Pamela Cibbarelli. Information Today, Inc., 2002. Paper $89. Published biennially.

History of Telecommunications Technology: An Annotated Bibliography. By Christopher H. Sterling and George Shiers. Scarecrow Press, 2000. $65.

Library Automation in Transitional Societies: Lessons from Eastern Europe. Ed. by Andrew Lass and Richard E. Quandt. Oxford University Press, 2000. $55.

Neal-Schuman Library Technology Companion: A Basic Guide for Library Staff. By John J. Burke. Neal-Schuman, 2000. Paper $45.

System Analysis for Librarians and Information Professions. 2nd ed. By Larry N. Osborne and Margaret Nakamura. Libraries Unlimited, 2000. Paper $50.

Library Buildings and Space Planning

Building Libraries for the 21st Century: The Shape of Information. Ed. by T. D. Webb. McFarland, 2000. $55.

Checklist of Library Building Design Considerations. 4th ed. By William W. Sannwald. American Library Association, 2001. Paper $38.

Construction from a Staff Perspective. By Williamsburg (Virginia) Regional Library. McFarland, 2001. Paper $35.

Countdown to a New Library: Managing the Building Project. By Jeannette Woodward. American Library Association, 2000. Paper $48.

Energy Management Strategies in Public Libraries. By Edward Dean. Libris Design, 2002. Paper $35.

First a Dream: A Community Builds a Library. By Jo Ann Ridley. Vision Books International, 2001. $35.

Libraries Designed for Users: A 21st Century Guide. By Nolan Lushington. Neal-Schuman, 2002. Paper $99.95.

The Librarian's Facility Management Handbook. By Carmine J. Trotta and Marcia Trotta. Neal-Schuman, 2000. Paper $75.

When Change Is Set in Stone: An Analysis of Seven Academic Libraries Designed by Perry Dean Rogers and Partners, Architects. By Michael J. Crosbie and Damon D. Hickey. Association of College and Research Libraries/American Library Association, 2001. $60.

Library History

America's Library: The Story of the Library of Congress, 1800–2000. By James Conaway. Yale University Press, 2000. $39.95.

American Libraries Before 1876. By Haynes McMullen. Greenwood, 2000. $67.

Carnegie. By Peter Krass. Wiley, 2002. $35.

A History of the Farmington Plan. By Ralph D. Wagner. Scarecrow Press, 2002. $69.50.

Library History Research in America: Essays Commemorating the Fiftieth Anniversary of the Library History Round Table. Ed. by Andrew B. Wertheimer and Donald G. Davis, Jr. Oak Knoll Press, 2000. $35.

Winsor, Dewey, and Putnam: The Boston Experience. By Donald G. Davis, Jr., Kenneth E. Carpenter, Wayne A. Wiegand,

and Jane Aikin. GLIS Publications Office, University of Illinois, 2002. Paper $8.

Museums

Creating Web-Accessible Databases: Case Studies for Libraries, Museums, and Other Non-Profits. Ed. by Julie M. Still. Information Today, Inc., 2001. $39.50.

Libraries, Museums and Archives: Legal Issues and Ethical Challenges in the New Information Era. Ed. by Thomas A Lipinski. Scarecrow Press, 2002. $59.95.

Museum Librarianship. 2nd ed. By Esther Green Bierbaum. McFarland, 2000. Paper $39.95.

The New Museum: Selected Writings by John Cotton Dana. Ed. by William A. Peniston. American Association of Museums, 1999. Paper $28.

Preservation

Digital Preservation and Metadata: History, Theory, Practice. By Susan S. Lazinger. Libraries Unlimited, 2001. Paper $55.

Disaster Response and Planning for Libraries. 2nd ed. By Miriam B. Kahn. American Library Association, 2002. Paper $40.

Getting Ready for the Nineteenth Century: Strategies and Solutions for Rare Book and Special Collections Librarians. Ed. by William E. Brown, Jr., and Laura Stalker. Association of College and Research Libraries/American Library Association, 2000. Paper $18.

Handbook for Digital Projects: A Management Tool for Preservation. Ed. by Maxine Sitts. Northeast Document Conservation Center, 2000. $38.

Library Disaster Planning and Recovery Handbook. By Camila Alire. Neal-Schuman, 2000. Paper $75.

Moving Theory Into Practice: Digital Imaging for Libraries and Archives. By Anne R. Kenney and Oya Y. Rieger. Research Libraries Group, 2000. Paper $89.

An Ounce of Prevention: Integrated Disaster Planning for Archives, Libraries, and Record Centers. 2nd ed. By Johanna Wellheiser and Jude Scott. Scarecrow Press, 2002. Paper $30.

Preservation: Issues and Planning. Ed. by Paul N. Banks and Roberta Pilette. American Library Association, 2000. Paper $78.

The State of Digital Preservation: An International Perspective. By Council on Library and Information Resources, 2002. Paper $20.

The Storage of Art on Paper: A Basic Guide for Institutions. By Sherelyn Ogden. GLIS Publications Office, University of Illinois, 2001. Paper $8.

To Preserve and Protect: The Strategic Stewardship of Cultural Resources. Library of Congress Symposium. Superintendent of Documents, 2002. Paper $23.

Vandals in the Stacks? A Response to Nicholson Baker's Assault on Libraries. By Richard J. Cox. Greenwood, 2002. $64.95.

Public Libraries

Administration of the Small Public Library. 4th ed. by Darlene E. Weingand. American Library Association, 2001. Paper $45.

Adult Programs in the Library. By Brett W. Lear. American Library Association, 2001. Paper $40.

Civic Librarianship: Renewing the Social Mission of the Public Library. By Ronald B. McCabe. Scarecrow Press, 2001. $39.50.

Creating the Full-Service Homework Center in Your Library. By Cindy Mediavilla. American Library Association, 2001. Paper $32.

The Library Book Cart Precision Drill Team Manual. By Linda D. McCracken and Lynne Zeiher. McFarland, 2001. Paper $25.

Library Networks in the New Millennium: Top Ten Trends. Ed. by Sara Laughlin. Association of Specialized and Cooperative Library Agencies/American Library Association, 2000. Paper $25.

The New Planning for Results: A Streamlined Approach. By Sandra Nelson. American Library Association, 2001. Paper $55.

A Place at the Table: Participating in Community Building. By Kathleen de la Peña McCook. American Library Association, 2000. Paper $25.

Public Librarian's Human Resources Handbook. By David A. Baldwin. Libraries Unlimited, 2001. Paper $55.

Public Libraries in Africa: A Report and Annotated Bibliography. By Aissa Issak. INAS, 2000. Paper £15.

Public Library Data Service Statistical Report. Public Library Association/American Library Association, 2002. Paper $80.

The Public Library Service: IFLA/UNESCO Guidelines for Development. By Philip Gill on behalf of the IFLA Section on Public Libraries. K. G. Saur Verlag, 2001. $49.

The Responsive Public Library: How to Develop and Market a Winning Collection. 2nd ed. By Sharon L. Baker and Karen L. Wallace. Libraries Unlimited, 2002. Paper $46.

Small Libraries: A Handbook for Successful Management. 2nd ed. By Sally Gardner Reed. McFarland, 2002. Paper $35.

Statistics and Performance Measures for Public Library Networked Services. By John Carlo Bertot, Charles R. McClure, and Joe Ryan. American Library Association, 2000. Paper $38.

Readers' Advisory

ALA's Guide to Best Reading. American Library Association, 2002. Camera-ready lists of the year's best books for children, teens, and adults. Kit $34.95.

Christian Fiction: A Guide to the Genre. By John Mort. Libraries Unlimited, 2002. $55.

The Mystery Readers' Advisory: The Librarian's Clues to Murder and Mayhem. By John Charles, Joanna Morrison, and Candace Clark. American Library Association, 2001. Paper $30.

Readers' Advisor's Companion. Ed. by Kenneth D. Shearer and Robert Burgin. Libraries Unlimited, 2002. Paper $37.50.

The Reader's Advisory Guide to Genre Fiction. By Joyce G. Sarick. American Library Association, 2001. Paper $38.

The Science Fiction and Fantasy Readers' Advisory: The Librarian's Guide to Cyborgs, Aliens, and Sorcerers. By Derek M. Buker. American Library Association, 2002. Paper $38.

The Short Story Readers' Advisory: A Guide to the Best. By Brad Hooper. American Library Association, 2000. Paper $28.

Reference Services

Digital Reference Services in the New Millennium: Planning, Management and Evaluation. Ed. by R. David Lankes, John W. Collins, III, and Abby S. Kasowitz. Neal-Schuman, 2000. Paper $65.

Doing the Work of Reference: Practical Tips for Excelling as a Reference Librarian. Ed. by Celia Hales Mabry. Haworth Press, 2002. Paper $44.95.

Establishing a Virtual Reference Services. By Anne Grodzins Lipow and Steve Coffman. Library Solutions Press, 2001. $125.

Evaluating Reference Services: A Practical Guide. By Jo Bell Whitlatch. American Library Association, 2000. Paper $39.

Evolution in Reference and Information Services: The Impact of the Internet. Ed. by Di Su. Haworth Press, 2002. Paper $24.95.

Genealogical Research on the Web. By Diane K. Kovacs. Neal-Schuman, 2002. Paper $55.

New Technologies and Reference Services. Ed. by Bill Katz. Haworth Press, 2000. $39.95.

Reference and Information Services: An Introduction. 3rd ed. Ed. by Richard E. Bopp and Linda C. Smith. Libraries Unlimited, 2000. Paper $49.50.

Starting and Operating Live Virtual Reference Services: A How-To-Do-It Manual for Librarians. By Marc Meola and Sam Stormont. Neal-Schuman, 2002. Paper $59.95.

Statistics, Measures and Quality Standards for Assessing Digital Reference Library Services: Guidelines and Procedures. By Charles R. McClure, R. David Lankes, Melissa Gross, and Beverly Choltco-Devlin. ERIC Clearinghouse on Information and Technology, 2002. Paper $25.

The Virtual Reference Librarian's Handbook. By Anne Lipow. Neal-Schuman, 2002. Paper and CD-ROM $75.

Virtual Reference Services . . . What, Why and How. By College of DuPage. 3 Link Up, 2002. 2 videos, $345 each.

School Libraries/Media Centers

Battle of the Books and More: Reading Activities for Middle School Students. By Sybilla Cook, Frances Corcoran, and Beverley Fonnesbeck. Highsmith Press, 2000. Paper $19.95.

Curriculum Partner: Redefining the Role of the Library Media Specialist. By Carol A. Kearney. Greenwood, 2000. $39.95.

Designing a School Library Media Center for the Future. By Rolf Erikson and Carolyn Markuson. American Library Association, 2000. Paper $39.

The Information-Powered School. Ed. by Sandra Hughes-Hassell and Anne Wheelock. American Library Association, 2001. Paper $35.

Leadership in Today's School Library: A Handbook for the Library Media Specialist and the School Principal. By Patricia Potter Wilson and Josette Anne Lyders. Greenwood, 2001. $39.95.

Lesson Plans for the Busy Librarian: A Standards-Based Approach for the Elementary Library Media Center. By Joyce Keeling. Libraries Unlimited, 2002. Paper $30.

Power Research Tools: Learning Activities and Posters. By Joyce Kasman Valenza. American Library Association, 2002. Paper $55.

Premiere Events: Library Programs that Inspire Elementary School Patrons. By Patricia Potter Wilson and Roger Leslie. Libraries Unlimited, 2001. Paper $35.

School and Public Libraries: Developing the Natural Alliance. By Natalie Reif Ziarnik. American Library Association, 2002. Paper $32.

Technologies for Education: A Practical Guide. 4th ed. By Ann E. Barron, Gary W. Orwig, Karen S. Ivers, and Nick Lilavois. Libraries Unlimited, 2002. Paper $48.

Serials

Developing and Managing Electronic Journal Collections: A How-To-Do-It Manual for Librarians. By Donnelyn Curtis, Virginia M. Scheschy, and Adolfo Tarango. Neal-Schuman, 2000. Paper $55.

E-Serials Cataloging: Access to Continuing and Integrating Resources Via the Catalog and the Web. Ed. by Jim Cole and Wayne Jones. Haworth Press, 2002. Paper $39.95.

Journals of the Century. Ed. by Tony Stankus. Haworth Press, 2002. Paper $29.95.

Making Waves: New Serials Landscapes in a Sea of Change. Ed. by Joseph C. Harmon and P. Michelle Fiander. Haworth Press, 2001. Paper $44.95.

Managing Electronic Serials: Essays Based on the ALCTS Electronic Serials Institutes 1997–1999. Ed. by Pamela Bluh. Association of Library Collections and Technical Services/American Library Association, 2001. Paper $38.

Services for Special Groups

Adaptive Technologies for Learning and Work Environments. 2nd ed. By Joseph J. Lazzaro. American Library Association, 2001. Paper $48, CD-ROM, $35.

Adult Literacy Assessment Tool Kit. By Suzanne Knell and Janet Scrogins. American Library Association, 2000. Paper $35.

Blind to Failure. West Virginia Library Commission Television Network, 2001. Video $25.

The Functions and Roles of State Library Agencies. Comp. by Ethel E. Himmel and William J. Wilson. Association of Specialized and Cooperative Library Agencies/American Library Association, 2000. Paper $20.

Library Services to the Sandwich Generation and Serial Caregivers. Compiled by Linda Lucas Walling. Association of Specialized and Cooperative Library Agencies/American Library Association, 2001. Paper $20.

Literacy and Libraries: Learning from Case Studies. Ed. by GraceAnne A. DeCandido. ALA Office for Literacy and Outreach Services/American Library Association, 2001. Paper $40.

Planning for Library Services to People with Disabilities. By Rhea Rubin. Association of Specialized and Cooperative Library Agencies/American Library Association, 2001. Paper $30.

The Power of Language/El Poder de la Palabra: Selected Papers from the Second REFORMA National Conference. Ed. by Lillian Castillo-Speed. Libraries Unlimited, 2001. Paper $35.

Venture into Cultures: A Resource Book of Multicultural Materials and Programs. 2nd ed. Ed. by Olga R. Kuharets. American Library Association, 2001. Paper $38.

Technical Services

Book Repair: A How-To-Do-It Manual. 2nd ed. By Kenneth Lavender. Neal-Schuman, 2001. Paper $49.95.

Introduction to Technical Services for Library Technicians. By Mary L. Kao. Haworth Press, 2001. Paper $22.95.

Library Off-Site Shelving: Guide for High-Density Facilities. Ed. by Danuta A. Nitecki and Curtis L. Kendrick. Libraries Unlimited, 2001. Paper $60.

Managing Electronic Reserves. Ed. by Jeff Rosedale. American Library Association, 2001. Paper $42.

Managing Public Access Computers: A How-To-Do-It Manual for Librarians. By Donald Barclay. Neal-Schuman, 2000. Paper $59.95.

Volunteers

Managing Library Volunteers: A Practical Toolkit. By Preston Driggers and Eileen Dumas. American Library Association, 2002. Paper $38.

The Volunteer Library: A Handbook. By Linda S. Fox. McFarland, 1999. Paper $35.

Periodicals and Periodical Indexes

Acquisitions Librarian
Advanced Technology Libraries
Against the Grain
American Archivist
American Libraries
Behavioral and Social Sciences Librarian
Book Links
Book Report: Journal for Junior and Senior High School Librarians (see *Library Media Connection*)
Booklist

Bookmobile and Outreach Services
The Bottom Line
Cataloging and Classification Quarterly
Catholic Library World
CHOICE
Collection Management
College and Research Libraries
College and Undergraduate Libraries
Community and Junior College Libraries
Computers in Libraries
Criticas
DTTP: A Quarterly Journal of Government Information, Practice and Perspective
The Electronic Library
Government Information Quarterly
Information Technology and Libraries
Information Outlook (formerly *Special Libraries*)
Interface
Journal of Academic Librarianship
Journal of Education for Library and Information Science
Journal of Information Ethics
Journal of Interlibrary Loan, Document Delivery and Information Supply
Journal of Library Administration
Journal of the American Society for Information Science
Journal of the Medical Library Association
Knowledge Quest
Law Library Journal
Legal Reference Services Quarterly
Libraries & Culture
Library Administration and Management
Library and Archival Security
Library and Information Science Research (LIBRES)
Library Hi-Tech
Library Hotline
Library Issues: Briefings for Faculty and Academic Administrators
Library Journal
Library Media Connection (formerly *Book Report* and *Library Talk*)
Library Mosaics
The Library Quarterly
Library Resources and Technical Services
Library Talk: The Magazine for Elementary School Librarians (see *Library Media Connection*)
Library Technology Reports

Library Trends
Medical Reference Services Quarterly
MultiMedia Schools
Music Library Association Notes
Music Reference Services Quarterly
NetConnect
The One-Person Library
Portal: Libraries and the Academy
Progressive Librarian
Public Libraries
Public Library Quarterly
RBM: A Journal of Rare Books, Manuscripts, and Cultural Heritage
Reference and User Services Quarterly (formerly *RQ*)
Reference Librarian

Resource Sharing & Information Networks
RSR: Reference Services Review
Rural Libraries
School Library Journal
Science & Technology Libraries
Searcher
Serials Librarian
Serials Review
Shy Librarian
Technical Services Quarterly
Technicalities
Unabashed Librarian
Video Librarian
Voice of Youth Advocates (VOYA)
World Libraries
Young Adult Library Service

Ready Reference

How to Obtain an ISBN

Emery Koltay

Director Emeritus
United States ISBN Agency

The International Standard Book Numbering (ISBN) system was introduced into the United Kingdom by J. Whitaker & Sons Ltd., in 1967 and into the United States in 1968 by the R. R. Bowker Company. The Technical Committee on Documentation of the International Organization for Standardization (ISO TC 46) defines the scope of the standard as follows:

> . . . the purpose of this standard is to coordinate and standardize the use of identifying numbers so that each ISBN is unique to a title, edition of a book, or monographic publication published, or produced, by a specific publisher, or producer. Also, the standard specifies the construction of the ISBN and the location of the printing on the publication.
>
> Books and other monographic publications may include printed books and pamphlets (in various bindings), mixed media publications, other similar media including educational films/videos and transparencies, books on cassettes, microcomputer software, electronic publications, microform publications, braille publications and maps. Serial publications and music sound recordings are specifically excluded, as they are covered by other identification systems. [ISO Standard 2108]

The ISBN is used by publishers, distributors, wholesalers, bookstores, and libraries, among others, in 210 countries to expedite such operations as order fulfillment, electronic point-of-sale checkout, inventory control, returns processing, circulation/location control, file maintenance and update, library union lists, and royalty payments.

Construction of an ISBN

An ISBN consists of 10 digits separated into the following parts:

1 Group identifier: national, geographic, language, or other convenient group
2 Publisher or producer identifier
3 Title identifier
4 Check digit

When an ISBN is written or printed, it should be preceded by the letters *ISBN,* and each part should be separated by a space or hyphen. In the United States, the hyphen is used for separation, as in the following example: ISBN 1-879500-01-9. In this example, 1 is the group identifier, 879500 is the publisher identifier, 01 is the title identifier, and 9 is the check digit. The group of English-speaking countries, which includes the United States, Australia, Canada, New Zealand, and the United Kingdom, uses the group identifiers 0 and 1.

The ISBN Organization

The administration of the ISBN system is carried out at three levels—through the International ISBN Agency in Berlin, Germany; the national agencies; and the publishing houses themselves. Responsible for assigning country prefixes and for coordinating the worldwide implementation of the system, the International ISBN Agency in Berlin has an advisory panel that represents the International Organization for Standardization (ISO), publishers, and libraries. The International ISBN Agency publishes the *Publishers International ISBN Directory,* which is distributed in the United States by R. R. Bowker. As the publisher of *Books In Print,* with its extensive and varied database of publishers' addresses, R. R. Bowker was the obvious place to initiate the ISBN system and to provide the service to the U.S. publishing industry. To date, the U.S. ISBN Agency has entered more than 120,000 publishers into the system.

ISBN Assignment Procedure

Assignment of ISBNs is a shared endeavor between the U.S. ISBN Agency and the publisher. The publisher is provided with an application form and an instruction sheet. After an application is received and verified by the agency, an ISBN publisher prefix is assigned, along with a computer-generated block of ISBNs. The publisher then has the responsibility to assign an ISBN to each title, to keep an accurate record of the numbers assigned by entering each title in the ISBN Log Book, and to report each title to the *Books in Print* database. One of the responsibilities of the ISBN Agency is to validate assigned ISBNs and to retain a record of all ISBNs in circulation.

ISBN implementation is very much market-driven. Wholesalers and distributors, such as Baker & Taylor, Brodart, and Ingram, as well as such large retail chains as Waldenbooks and B. Dalton recognize and enforce the ISBN system by requiring all new publishers to register with the ISBN Agency before accepting their books for sale. Also, the ISBN is a mandatory bibliographic element in the International Standard Bibliographical Description (ISBD). The Library of Congress Cataloging in Publication (CIP) Division directs publishers to the agency to obtain their ISBN prefixes.

Location and Display of the ISBN

On books, pamphlets, and other printed material, the ISBN shall be on the verso of the title leaf or, if this is not possible, at the foot of the title leaf itself. It should also appear at the foot of the outside back cover if practicable and at the foot of the back of the jacket if the book has one (the lower right-hand corner is recommended). If neither of these alternatives is possible, then the number shall be printed in some other prominent position on the outside. The ISBN shall also appear on any accompanying promotional materials following the provisions for location according to the format of the material.

On other monographic publications, the ISBN shall appear on the title or credit frames and any labels permanently affixed to the publication. If the publication is issued in a container that is an integral part of the publication, the ISBN shall be displayed on the label. If it is not possible to place the ISBN on the item or its label, then the number should be displayed on the bottom or the back of the container, box, sleeve, or frame. It should also appear on any accompanying material, including each component of a multitype publication.

Printing of ISBN in Machine-Readable Coding

In the last few years, much work has been done on machine-readable representations of the ISBN, and now all books should carry ISBNs in bar code. The rapid worldwide extension of bar code scanning has brought into prominence the 1980 agreement between the International Article Numbering, formerly the European Article Numbering (EAN), Association and the International ISBN Agency that translates the ISBN into an ISBN Bookland EAN bar code.

All ISBN Bookland EAN bar codes start with a national identifier (00–09 representing the United States), *except* those on books and periodicals. The agreement replaces the usual national identifier with a special "ISBN Bookland" identifier represented by the digits 978 for books (see Figure 1) and 977 for periodicals. The 978 ISBN Bookland/EAN prefix is followed by the first nine digits of the ISBN. The check digit of the ISBN is dropped and replaced by a check digit calculated according to the EAN rules.

Figure 1 / Printing the ISBN in Bookland/EAN Symbology

The following is an example of the conversion of the ISBN to ISBN Bookland/EAN:

ISBN	1-879500-01-9
ISBN without check digit	1-879500-01
Adding EAN flag	978187950001
EAN with EAN check digit	9781879500013

Five-Digit Add-On Code

In the United States, a five-digit add-on code is used for additional information. In the publishing industry, this code can be used for price information or some other specific coding. The lead digit of the five-digit add-on has been designated a currency identifier, when the add-on is used for price. Number 5 is the code for the U.S. dollar; 6 denotes the Canadian dollar; 1 the British pound; 3 the Australian dollar; and 4 the New Zealand dollar. Publishers that do not want to indicate price in the add-on should print the code 90000 (see Figure 2).

Figure 2 / Printing the ISBN Bookland/EAN Number in Bar Code with the Five-Digit Add-On Code

978 = ISBN Bookland/EAN prefix
5 + Code for U.S. $
0995 = $9.95

90000 means no information
in the add-on code

Reporting the Title and the ISBN

After the publisher reports a title to the ISBN Agency, the number is validated and the title is listed in the many R. R. Bowker hard-copy and electronic publications, including *Books in Print, Forthcoming Books, Paperbound Books in Print, Books in Print Supplement, Books Out of Print, Books in Print Online, Books in Print Plus-CD ROM, Children's Books in Print, Subject Guide to Children's Books in Print, On Cassette: A Comprehensive Bibliography of Spoken Word Audiocassettes, Variety's Complete Home Video Directory, Software Encyclopedia, Software for Schools,* and other specialized publications.

For an ISBN application form and additional information, write to United States ISBN Agency, R. R. Bowker Company, 630 Central Ave., New Providence, NJ 07974, or call 877-310-7333. The e-mail address is ISBN-SAN@ bowker.com. The ISBN Web site is at http://www.ISBN.org.

How to Obtain an ISSN

National Serials Data Program
Library of Congress

In the early 1970s the rapid increase in the production and dissemination of information and an intensified desire to exchange information about serials in computerized form among different systems and organizations made it increasingly clear that a means to identify serial publications at an international level was needed. The International Standard Serial Number (ISSN) was developed and has become the internationally accepted code for identifying serial publications. The number itself has no significance other than as a brief, unique, and unambiguous identifier. It is an international standard, ISO 3297, as well as a U.S. standard, ANSI/NISO Z39.9. The ISSN consists of eight digits in arabic numerals 0 to 9, except for the last, or check, digit, which can be an X. The numbers appear as two groups of four digits separated by a hyphen and preceded by the letters ISSN—for example, ISSN 1234-5679.

The ISSN is not self-assigned by publishers. Administration of the ISSN is coordinated through the ISSN Network, an intergovernmental organization within the UNESCO/UNISIST program. The network consists of national and regional centers, coordinated by the ISSN International Centre, located in Paris. Centers have the responsibility to register serials published in their respective countries.

Because serials are generally known and cited by title, assignment of the ISSN is inseparably linked to the key title, a standardized form of the title derived from information in the serial issue. Only one ISSN can be assigned to a title; if the title changes, a new ISSN must be assigned. Centers responsible for assigning ISSNs also construct the key title and create an associated bibliographic record.

The ISSN International Centre handles ISSN assignments for international organizations and for countries that do not have a national center. It also maintains and distributes the collective ISSN database that contains bibliographic records corresponding to each ISSN assignment as reported by the rest of the network. The database contains more than 1 million ISSNs.

In the United States, the National Serials Data Program at the Library of Congress is responsible for assigning and maintaining the ISSNs for all U.S. serial titles. Publishers wishing to have an ISSN assigned should request an application form from the program, or download one from the program's Web site, and ask for an assignment. Assignment of the ISSN is free, and there is no charge for its use.

The ISSN is used all over the world by serial publishers to distinguish similar titles from each other. It is used by subscription services and libraries to manage files for orders, claims, and back issues. It is used in automated check-in systems by libraries that wish to process receipts more quickly. Copyright centers use the ISSN as a means to collect and disseminate royalties. It is also used as an identification code by postal services and legal deposit services. The ISSN is included as a verification element in interlibrary lending activities and for union catalogs as a collocating device. In recent years, the ISSN has been incorporated into bar codes for optical recognition of serial publications and into the standards for the identification of issues and articles in serial publications.

For further information about the ISSN or the ISSN Network, U.S. libraries and publishers should contact the National Serials Data Program, Library of Congress, Washington, DC 20540-4160; 202-707-6452; fax 202-707-6333; e-mail issn@loc.gov. ISSN application forms and instructions for obtaining an ISSN are also available via the Library of Congress World Wide Web site, http://lcweb.loc.gov/issn.

Non-U.S. parties should contact the ISSN International Centre, 20 rue Bachaumont, 75002 Paris, France; telephone (33-1) 44-88-22-20; fax (33-1) 40-26-32-43; e-mail issnic@issn.org; World Wide Web http://www.ISSN.org.

How to Obtain an SAN

Emery Koltay

Director Emeritus
United States ISBN/SAN Agency

SAN stands for Standard Address Number. It is a unique identification code for addresses of organizations that are involved in or served by the book industry, and that engage in repeated transactions with other members within this group. For purposes of this standard, the book industry includes book publishers, book wholesalers, book distributors, book retailers, college bookstores, libraries, library binders, and serial vendors. Schools, school systems, technical institutes, colleges, and universities are not members of this industry, but are served by it and therefore included in the SAN system.

The purpose of SAN is to facilitate communications among these organizations, of which there are several hundreds of thousands, that engage in a large volume of separate transactions with one another. These transactions include purchases of books by book dealers, wholesalers, schools, colleges, and libraries from publishers and wholesalers; payments for all such purchases; and other communications between participants. The objective of this standard is to establish an identification code system by assigning each address within the industry a discrete code to be used for positive identification for all book and serial buying and selling transactions.

Many organizations have similar names and multiple addresses, making identification of the correct contact point difficult and subject to error. In many cases, the physical movement of materials takes place between addresses that differ from the addresses to be used for the financial transactions. In such instances, there is ample opportunity for confusion and errors. Without identification by SAN, a complex record-keeping system would have to be instituted to avoid introducing errors. In addition, it is expected that problems with the current numbering system such as errors in billing, shipping, payments, and returns, will be significantly reduced by using the SAN system. SAN will also eliminate one step in the order fulfillment process: the "look-up procedure" used to assign account numbers. Previously a store or library dealing with 50 different publishers was assigned a different account number by each of the suppliers. SAN solved this problem. If a publisher indicates its SAN on its stationery and ordering documents, vendors to whom it sends transactions do not have to look up the account number, but can proceed immediately to process orders by SAN.

Libraries are involved in many of the same transactions as book dealers, such as ordering and paying for books and charging and paying for various services to other libraries. Keeping records of transactions, whether these involve buying, selling, lending, or donations, entails similar operations that require an SAN. Having the SAN on all stationery will speed up order fulfillment and eliminate errors in shipping, billing, and crediting; this, in turn, means savings in both time and money.

History

Development of the Standard Address Number began in 1968 when Russell Reynolds, general manager of the National Association of College Stores (NACS), approached the R. R. Bowker Company and suggested that a "Standard Account Number" system be implemented in the book industry. The first draft of a standard was prepared by an American National Standards Institute (ANSI) Committee Z39 subcommittee, which was co-chaired by Russell Reynolds and Emery Koltay. After Z39 members proposed changes, the current version of the standard was approved by NACS on December 17, 1979.

The chairperson of the ANSI Z39 Subcommittee 30, which developed the approved standard, was Herbert W. Bell, former senior vice president of McGraw-Hill Book Company. The subcommittee comprised the following representatives from publishing companies, distributors, wholesalers, libraries, national cooperative online systems, schools, and school systems: Herbert W. Bell (chair), McGraw-Hill Book Company; Richard E. Bates, Holt, Rinehart and Winston; Thomas G. Brady, The Baker & Taylor Companies, Paul J. Fasana, New York Public Library; Emery I. Koltay, R. R. Bowker Company; Joan McGreevey, New York University Book Centers; Pauline F. Micciche, OCLC, Inc.; Sandra K. Paul, SKP Associates; David Gray Remington, Library of Congress; Frank Sanders, Hammond Public School System; and Peter P. Chirimbes (alternate), Stamford Board of Education.

Format

The SAN consists of six digits plus a seventh *Modulus 11* check digit; a hyphen follows the third digit (XXX-XXXX) to facilitate transcription. The hyphen is to be used in print form, but need not be entered or retained in computer systems. Printed on documents, the Standard Address Number should be preceded by the identifier "SAN" to avoid confusion with other numerical codes (SAN XXX-XXXX).

Check Digit Calculation

The check digit is based on *Modulus 11*, and can be derived as follows:

1. Write the digits of the basic number.   2 3 4 5 6 7
2. Write the constant weighting factors associated
   with each position by the basic number.   7 6 5 4 3 2
3. Multiply each digit by its associated weighting factor.   14 18 20 20 18 14
4. Add the products of the multiplications. $14 + 18 + 20 + 20 + 18 + 14 = 104$
5. Divide the sum by *Modulus 11*
   to find the remainder. $104 \div 11 = 9$ plus a remainder of 5
6. Subtract the remainder from the *Modulus 11* to generate
   the required check digit. If there is no remainder,
   generate a check digit of zero. If the check digit is 10,

generate a check digit of X to represent 10,
since the use of 10 would require an extra digit. $11 - 5 = 6$

7. Append the check digit to create the standard
    seven-digit Standard Address Number.   SAN 234-5676

SAN Assignment

The R. R. Bowker Company accepted responsibility for being the central administrative agency for SAN, and in that capacity assigns SANs to identify uniquely
the addresses of organizations. No SANs can be reassigned; in the event that an
organization should cease to exist, for example, its SAN would cease to be in circulation entirely. If an organization using an SAN should move or change its
name with no change in ownership, its SAN would remain the same, and only the
name or address would be updated to reflect the change.

The SAN should be used in all transactions; it is recommended that the SAN
be imprinted on stationery, letterheads, order and invoice forms, checks, and all
other documents used in executing various book transactions. The SAN should
always be printed on a separate line above the name and address of the organization, preferably in the upper left-hand corner of the stationery to avoid confusion
with other numerical codes pertaining to the organization, such as telephone
number, zip code, and the like.

SAN Functions and Suffixes

The SAN is strictly a Standard Address Number, becoming functional only in
applications determined by the user; these may include activities such as purchasing, billing, shipping, receiving, paying, crediting, and refunding. Every
department that has an independent function within an organization could have a
SAN for its own identification. Users may choose to assign a suffix (a separate
field) to their SAN strictly for internal use. Faculty members ordering books
through a library acquisitions department, for example, may not have their own
separate SAN, but may be assigned a suffix by the library. There is no standardized provision for placement of suffixes. Existing numbering systems do not
have suffixes to take care of the "subset" type addresses. The SAN does not stan-
dardize this part of the address. For the implementation of SAN, it is suggested
that wherever applicable the four-position suffix be used. This four-position suffix makes available 10,000 numbers, ranging from 0000 to 9999, and will accommodate all existing subset numbering presently in use.

For example, there are various ways to incorporate an SAN in an order fulfillment system. Firms just beginning to assign account numbers to their customers will have no conversion problems and will simply use the SAN as the
numbering system. Firms that already have an existing number system can convert either on a step-by-step basis by adopting SANs whenever orders or payments are processed on the account, or by converting the whole file by using the
SAN listing provided by the SAN Agency. Using the step-by-step conversion,

firms may adopt SANs as customers provide them on their forms, orders, payments, and returns.

For additional information or suggestions, please write to Diana Luongo, SAN Coordinator, ISBN/SAN Agency, R. R. Bowker Company, 630 Central Ave., New Providence, NJ 07974, call 908-219-0283, or fax 908-219-0188. The e-mail address is ISBN-SAN@bowker.com. The SAN Web site is at http://www. ISBN.org.

Distinguished Books

Notable Books of 2002

The Notable Books Council of the Reference and User Services Association, a division of the American Library Association, selected these titles for their significant contribution to the expansion of knowledge or for the pleasure they can provide to adult readers.

Fiction

Auster, Paul. *Book of Illusions*. Holt (0-8050-5408-1).

Cisneros, Sandra. *Caramelo*. Random (Knopf) (0-679-43554-9).

Doerr, Anthony. *The Shell Collector*. Scribner (0-7432-1274-6).

Labiner, Norah. *Miniatures*. Coffee House Press (1-56689-136-1).

Lustig, Arnost. *Lovely Green Eyes*. Arcade (1-55970-629-5).

McEwan, Ian. *Atonement*. Random (Doubleday) (0-835-50395-4).

McGahern, John. *By the Lake*. Random (Knopf) (0-679-41914-4).

Merullo, Roland. *In Revere in Those Days*. Random (Crown) (0-609-61-32-5).

Mistry, Rohinton. *Family Matters*. Random (Knopf) (0-375-40373-6).

Oe, Kenzaburo. *Rouse Up, O Young Men of the New Age*. Grove (0-8021-1710-4).

Shteyngart, Gary. *The Russian Debutante's Handbook*. Penguin/Putnam (1-57322-213-5).

Slouka, Mark. *God's Fool*. Random (Knopf) (0-375-40216-0).

Nonfiction

Babel, Isaac. *Complete Works*. Norton (0-393-04846-2).

Berger, John. *Selected Essays*. Random (Pantheon) (0-375-42156-4).

Campbell, Greg. *Blood Diamonds: Tracing the Deadly Path of the World's Most Precious Stones*. HarperCollins (Westview) (0-8133-3939-1).

Caro, Robert A. *Master of the Senate: The Years of Lyndon Johnson*. Random (Knopf) (0-394-52836-0).

Gawande, Atul. *Complications: A Surgeon's Notes on an Imperfect Science*. Holt (0-8050-6319-6).

Gordon, Robert. *Can't Be Satisfied: The Life and Times of Muddy Waters*. Little, Brown (0-316-32849-9).

Morris, Edmund. *Theodore Rex*. Random (0-394-55509-0).

Preston, Diana. *Lusitania: An Epic Tragedy*. Walker (0-8027-1375-0).

Stiles, T. J. *Jesse James: Last Rebel of the Civil War*. Random (Knopf) (0-375-40583-6).

Stille, Alexander. *The Future of the Past*. Farrar, Strauss and Giroux (0-374-15977-7).

Wilson, Edward O. *The Future of Life*. Random (Knopf) (0-679-45078-5).

Poetry

Dugan, Alan. *Poems Seven: New and Complete Poetry*. Seven Stories Press (1-58322-265-0).

Hall, Donald. *The Painted Bed*. Houghton Mifflin (0-618-18789-8).

Tretheway, Natasha. *Bellocq's Ophelia*. Graywolf Press (1-55597-359-0).

Best Books for Young Adults

Each year a committee of the Young Adult Library Services Association (YALSA), a division of the American Library Association, compiles a list of the best fiction and nonfiction appropriate for young adults ages 12 to 18. Selected on the basis of each book's proven or potential appeal and value to young adults, the titles span a variety of subjects as well as a broad range of reading levels.

Fiction

Alvarez, Julia. *Before We Were Free.* Random House/Alfred A. Knopf, $15.95 (0-375-81544-9); library edition, $17.99 (0-375-91544-3).

Anderson, Laurie Halse. *Catalyst.* Penguin Putnam/Viking, $17.99 (0-670-03566-1).

Anderson, M. T. *Feed.* Candlewick Press, $16.99 (0-7636-1726-1).

Auch, Mary Jane. *Ashes of Roses.* Henry Holt & Co., $16.95 (0-8050-6686-1).

Bardi, Abby. *The Book of Fred: A Novel.* 2001 Pocket Books/Washington Square Press, $24.00 (0-7434-1193-5); library edition (0-7434-1194-3).

Barker, Clive. *Abarat.* HarperCollins/Joanna Cotler Books, $24.89 (0-06-028092-1); library edition (0-06-051084-6).

Bechard, Margaret. *Hanging on to Max.* Millbrook/Roaring Brook Press, $15.95 (0-7613-1579-9); library edition, $22.90 (0-7613-2574-3).

Black, Holly. *Tithe: A Modern Faerie Tale.* Simon & Schuster, $16.95 (0-689-84924-9).

Blackwood, Gary L. *Year of the Hangman.* Penguin Putnam/Dutton, $16.99 (0-525-46921-4).

Breslin, Theresa. *Remembrance.* Random House/Delacorte Press, $16.95 (0-385-73015-2); library edition, $18.99 (0-385-90067-8).

Chambers, Aidan. *Postcards from No Man's Land.* Penguin Putnam/Dutton, $19.99 (0-525-46863-3).

Clements, Andrew. *Things Not Seen.* Penguin Putnam/Philomel Books, $15.95 (0-399-23626-0).

Cohn, Rachel. *Gingerbread.* Simon & Schuster, $15.95 (0-689-84337-2).

Crowe, Chris. *Mississippi Trial, 1955.* Penguin Putnam/Phyllis Fogelman Books, $17.99 (0-8037-2745-3).

de Lint, Charles. *Seven Wild Sisters.* Illustrated by Charles Vess. Subterranean Press, $35.00 (1-931081-33-6).

Desai Hidier, Tanuja. *Born Confused.* Scholastic, $16.95 (0-439-35762-4).

Dessen, Sarah. *This Lullaby.* Penguin Putnam/Viking, $16.99 (0-670-03530-0).

Ellis, Deborah. *Parvana's Journey.* Groundwood/Douglas & McIntyre, $15.95 (0-88899-514-8).

Etchemendy, Nancy. *Cat in Glass and Other Tales of the Unnatural.* Illustrated by David Ouimet. Carus Publishing/Cricket Books, $15.95 (0-8126-2674-5).

Fama, Elizabeth. *Overboard.* Carus Publishing/Cricket Books, $15.95 (0-8126-2652-4).

Farmer, Nancy. *The House of the Scorpion.* Simon & Schuster/Atheneum/A Richard Jackson Book, $17.95 (0-689-85222-3).

Ferris, Jean. *Once Upon a Marigold.* Harcourt, $17.00 (0-15-216791-9).

Frank, E. R. *America.* Simon & Schuster/Atheneum/A Richard Jackson Book, $18.00 (0-689-84729-7).

Frank, Hillary. *Better Than Running at Night.* Houghton Mifflin, $17.00 (0-618-10439-9); library edition (0-618-25073-5).

Freymann-Weyr, Garret. *My Heartbeat.* Houghton Mifflin, $15.00 (0-618-14181-2).

Froese, Deborah. *Out of the Fire.* Sumach Press, $7.95 (1-894549-09-0).

Gaiman, Neil. *Coraline.* Illustrated by Dave McKean. HarperCollins, $15.99 (0-380-97778-8); library edition, $17.89 (0-06-623744-0).

Giff, Patricia Reilly. *Pictures of Hollis*

Woods. Random House/Wendy Lamb Books, $15.95 (0-385-32655-6); library edition, $17.99 (0-385-90070-8).

Giles, Gail. *Shattering Glass.* Millbrook Press/Roaring Brook Press, $15.95 (0-7613-1581-0); library edition, $17.99 (0-7613-2601-4).

Green Man: Tales from the Mythic Forest. Edited by Ellen Datlow and Terri Windling, illustrated by Charles Vess. Penguin Putnam/Viking, $18.99 (0-670-03526-2).

Grimes, Nikki. *Bronx Masquerade.* Penguin Putnam/Dial Books, $16.99 (0-8037-2569-8).

Halam, Ann. *Dr. Franklin's Island.* Random House/Wendy Lamb Books, $14.95 (0-385-73008-X); library edition, $16.99 (0-385-90056-2).

Hiaasen, Carl. *Hoot.* Random House/Alfred A. Knopf, $15.99 (0-375-82181-3); library edition, $17.99 (0-375-92181-8).

Holeman, Linda. *Search of the Moon King's Daughter.* Tundra Books, $17.95 (0-88776-592-0).

Jordan, Sherryl. *The Hunting of the Last Dragon.* HarperCollins, $15.95 (0-06-028902-3); library edition, $15.89 (0-06-028903-1).

Kidd, Sue Monk. *The Secret Life of Bees.* Penguin Putnam/Viking, $24.95 (0-670-89460-5).

Koertge, Ron. *Stoner & Spaz.* Candlewick Press, $15.99 (0-7636-1608-7).

Korman, Gordon. *Son of the Mob.* Hyperion Books for Children, $15.99 (0-7868-0769-5); library edition, $15.95 (0-7868-2616-9).

Lawrence, Iain. *The Lightkeeper's Daughter.* Random House/Delacorte Press, $16.95 (0-385-72925-1); library edition, $18.99 (0-385-90062-7).

Leavitt, Martine. *The Dollmage.* Red Deer Press, $8.95 (0-88995-233-7).

McCaughrean, Geraldine. *The Kite Rider.* HarperCollins, $15.95 (0-06-623874-9); library edition, $15.89 (0-06-623875-7).

Miller, Mary Beth. *Aimee.* Penguin Putnam/Dutton, $16.99 (0-525-46894-3).

Moore, Christopher. *Lamb: The Gospel According to Biff, Christ's Childhood Pal.* HarperCollins/William Morrow, $25.95 (0-380-97840-7).

Oates, Joyce Carol. *Big Mouth & Ugly Girl.* HarperCollins, $16.95 (0-06-623756-4); library edition, $16.89 (0-06-623758-0).

Park, Linda Sue. *When My Name Was Keoko: A Novel of Korea in World War II.* Houghton Mifflin/Clarion Books, $15.00 (0-618-13335-6).

Placide, Jaira. *Fresh Girl.* Random House/Wendy Lamb Books, $15.95 (0-385-32753-6).

Plum-Ucci, Carol. *What Happened to Lani Garver.* Harcourt, $17.00 (0-15-216813-3).

Powell, Randy. *Three Clams and an Oyster.* Farrar, Straus and Giroux, $16.00 (0-374-37526-7).

Rottman, S. L. *Stetson.* Penguin Putnam/Viking, $16.99 (0-670-03542-4).

Santana, Patricia. *Motorcycle Ride on the Sea of Tranquility.* University of New Mexico Press, $19.95 (0-8263-2435-5).

Savage, Deborah. *Kotuku.* Houghton Mifflin, $16.00 (0-618-04756-5).

Sebold, Alice. *The Lovely Bones: A Novel.* Little, Brown & Co., $21.95 (0-316-66634-3).

Shattered: Stories of Children and War. Edited by Jennifer Armstrong. Random House/Alfred A. Knopf, $15.95 (0-375-81112-5); library edition, $17.99 (0-375-91112-X).

Sheppard, Mary C. *Seven for a Secret.* Groundwood Books, $15.95 (0-88899-437-0).

Smith, Kevin, and Phil Hester. *Green Arrow: Quiver.* Illustrated by Ande Parks and Guy Major. Warner Books/DC Comics, $24.95 (1-56389-802-0); paperback, $17.95 (1-56389-887-X).

Smith, Sherri L. *Lucy the Giant.* Random House/Delacorte Press, $15.95 (0-385-72940-5); library edition, $17.99 (0-385-90031-7).

Tolan, Stephanie. *Surviving the Applewhites.* HarperCollins, $15.99 (0-06-623602-9); library edition, $17.89 (0-06-623603-7).

Toten, Teresa. *The Game.* Red Deer Press, $7.99 (0-88995-232-9).

Van Pelt, James. *Strangers and Beggars: Stories.* Fairwood Press, paperback, $17.99 (0-9668184-5-8).

Woodson, Jacqueline. *Hush.* Penguin Putnam/G. P. Putnam's Sons, $15.99 (0-399-23114-5).

Yolen, Jane, and Robert J. Harris. *Girl in a Cage*. Penguin Putnam/Philomel Books, $18.99 (0-399-23627-9).

Nonfiction

Bartoletti, Susan Campbell. *Black Potatoes: The Story of the Great Irish Famine, 1845–1850*. Houghton Mifflin, $18.00 (0-618-00271-5).

Fleischman, John. *Phineas Gage: A Gruesome But True Story About Brain Science*. Houghton Mifflin, $16.00 (0-618-05252-6).

Gantos, Jack. *Hole in My Life*. Farrar, Straus and Giroux, $16.00 (0-374-39988-3).

Hampton, Wilborn. *Meltdown: A Race Against Nuclear Disaster at Three Mile Island: A Reporter's Story*. Candlewick Press, $16.99 (0-7636-0715-0).

McPherson, James M. *Fields of Fury: The American Civil War*. Simon & Schuster/Atheneum, $22.95 (0-689-84833-1).

Nelson, Peter. *Left for Dead: A Young Man's Search for Justice for the USS Indianapolis*. Random House/Delacorte Press, $15.95 (0-385-72959-6); library edition, $17.99 (0-385-90033-3).

Nye, Naomi Shihab. *19 Varieties of Gazelle: Poems of the Middle East*. HarperCollins/Greenwillow, $16.95 (0-06-009765-5); library edition, $16.89 (0-06-009766-3).

Partridge, Elizabeth. *This Land Was Made For You and Me: The Life & Songs of Woody Guthrie*. Penguin Putnam/Viking, $21.99 (0-670-03535-1).

Philbrick, Nathaniel. *Revenge of the Whale: The True Story of the Whaleship Essex*. Penguin Putam/G. P. Putnam's Sons, $16.99 (0-399-23795-X).

Rall, Ted. *To Afghanistan and Back: A Graphic Travelogue*. Nantier Beall Minoustchine, $15.95 (1-56163-325-9).

Steinberg, Jacques. *The Gatekeepers: Inside the Admissions Process of a Premier College*. Penguin Putnam/Viking, $25.95 (0-670-03135-6).

Every five years, YALSA also produces a list of Outstanding Books for the College-Bound that includes books dating from the mid-19th century to the present. The most recent list appeared in the 2001 edition of the *Bowker Annual.*

Audiobooks for Young Adults

Each year a committee of the Young Adult Library Services Association, a division of the American Library Association, compiles a list of the best audiobooks for young adults ages 12 to 18. The titles are selected for their teen appeal and recording quality, and because they enhance the audience's appreciation of any written work on which the recordings may be based. While the list as a whole addresses the interests and needs of young adults, individual titles need not appeal to this entire age range but rather to parts of it.

All-American Girl, by Meg Cabot, read by Ariadne Meyers. Listening Library, 5 cassettes, 7 hours (0-8072-0902-3).

The Beetle and Me: A Love Story, by Karen Romano Young, read by Julie Dretzin. Recorded Books, 4 cassettes, 5 hours and 45 minutes (0-7887-5017-8).

Breathing Underwater, by Alex Flinn, read by Jon Cryer. Listening Library, 3 cassettes, 5 hours and 8 minutes (0-8072-0686-5).

Catalyst, by Laurie Halse Anderson, read by Samantha Mathis. Listening Library, 4 cassettes, 6 hours (0-8072-0940-6).

Devil's Island, by David Harris, read by Peter Hardy. Bolinda Audio, 2 cassettes, 2 hours and 30 minutes (1-74030-355-5).

Firehouse, by David Halberstam, read by Mel Foster. BrillianceAudio, 4 cassettes, 5 hours (1-59086-344-5).

Forged by Fire, by Sharon M. Draper, read by Thomas Penny. Recorded books, 3 cassettes, 3 hours and 45 minutes (1-4025-0892-1).

A Girl of the Limberlost, by Gene Stratton-Porter, read by Christina Moore. Recorded Books, 9 cassettes, 12 hours (0-7887-5106-9).

Hoot, by Carl Hiaasen, read by Chad Lowe. Listening Library, 4 cassettes, 6 hours and 30 minutes (0-8072-0923-6).

Lirael, by Garth Nix, read by Tim Curry. Listening Library, 9 cassettes, 14 hours and 44 minutes (0-8072-0564-8).

Make Lemonade, by Virginia Euwer Wolff, read by Heather Alicia Simms. Listening Library, 3 cassettes, 3 hours and 33 minutes (0-8072-0689-X).

Martin Luther King, Jr., by Marshall Frady, read by the author. Books on Tape, 5 cassettes, 7 hours and 30 minutes (0-7366-8491-3).

The Rag and Bone Shop, by Robert Cormier, read by Scott Shina. Recorded Books, 2 cassettes, 3 hours (01-4025-1028-4).

Sabriel, by Garth Nix, read by Tim Curry. Listening Library, 7 cassettes, 10 hours and 40 minutes (0-8072-0563-X).

The Secret Armies: Spies, Counterspies, and Saboteurs in World War II, by Albert Marrin, read by Johnny Heller. Recorded Books, 4 cassettes, 5 hours and 30 minutes (0-7887-5511-0).

The Seeing Stone, by Kevin Crossley-Holland, read by Michael Maloney. Listening Library, 6 cassettes, 7 hours and 51 minutes (0-8072-0546-X).

Seek, by Paul Fleischman, dramatized by Ben Fred, David Minnick, Kari Wishingrad, Vonya Morris, Richard Goodman, Randi Merzon, Anne Galjour, and Clark Taylor.

Listening Library, 2 cassettes, 2 hours and 42 minutes (0-8072-0821-3).

A Separate Peace, by John Knowles, read by Scott Snively. Audio Bookshelf, 4 cassettes, 6 hours (1-883332-49-4).

A Single Shard, by Linda Sue Park, read by Graeme Malcolm. Listening Library, 3 cassettes, 3 hours and 12 minutes (0-8072-0702-0).

Son of the Mob, by Gordon Korman, read by Max Casella. Listening Library, 3 cassettes, 4 hours and 36 minutes (0-8072-0971-6).

Spite Fences, by Trudy Krisher, read by Kate Forbes. Recorded Books, 6 cassettes, 8 hours and 30 minutes (0-7887-8971-6).

A Step from Heaven, by An Na, read by Jina Oh. Listening Library, 3 cassettes, 4 hours and 14 minutes (0-8072-0722-5).

Time Stops for No Mouse: A Hermux Tantamoq Adventure, by Michael Hoeye, read by Campbell Scott. Listening Library, 4 cassettes, 5 hours and 30 minutes (0-8072-0847-7).

Troy, by Adèle Geras, read by Miriam Margolyes. Listening Library, 6 cassettes, 10 hours and 6 minutes (0-8072-0599-0).

True Believer, by Virginia Euwer Wolff, read by Heather Alicia Simms. Listening Library, 3 cassettes, 3 hours and 45 minutes (0-8072-0692-X).

Whale Talk, by Chris Crutcher, read by Brian Corrigan. Listening Library, 4 cassettes, 6 hours and 31 minutes (0-8072-0709-8).

The Witch in the Lake, by Anna Fienberg, read by Melissa Eccleston. Louis Braille Audio, 5 compact discs (0-7320-2535-4).

Wolf on the Fold, by Judith Clarke, read by Dino Marnika. Bolinda Audio, 3 cassettes, 3 hours and 35 minutes (1-74030-622-8).

Zazoo, by Richard Mosher, read by Joanna Wyatt. Listening Library, 2002, 5 cassettes, 8 hours and 30 minutes (0-8072-0840-X).

Quick Picks for Reluctant Young Adult Readers

The Young Adult Library Services Association, a division of the American Library Association, annually chooses a list of outstanding titles that will stimulate the interest of reluctant teen readers. This list is intended to attract teens who, for whatever reason, choose not to read.

The list, compiled by an 11-member committee, includes 78 titles published from late 2001 through 2002. Thirty of the titles are fiction and 48 are nonfiction.

Atwater-Rhodes, Amelia. *Midnight Predator.* Random House/Delacorte Press, $9.95 (0-385-32794-3).

Basketball's Best Shots. Dorling Kindersley, $30.00 (0-7894-8914-7).

Beale, Fleur. *I Am Not Esther.* Hyperion, $15.99 (0-7868-0845-4).

Bechard, Margaret. *Hanging On to Max.* Roaring Book Press, $22.90 (0-7613-2574-3).

Cabot, Meg. *All-American Girl.* Harper-Collins, $15.99 (0-06-029470-1).

Cabot, Meg. *Princess Diaries, Volume III: Princess in Love.* HarperCollins, $15.95 (0-06-029467-1).

Clarkson, Mark. *Battlebots: The Official Guide.* McGraw Hill/Osbourne, paper $24.95 (0-07-222425-8).

Cobain, Kurt. *Journals: Kurt Cobain.* Riverhead/Penguin Putnam, $29.95 (1-57322-232-1).

Cohn, Rachel. *Gingerbread.* Simon and Schuster, $15.95 (0-689-84337-2).

Conniff, Richard. *Rats! The Good, the Bad, and the Ugly.* Crown Publishers/Random House, $15.95 (0-375-81207-5).

Dickey, Eric Jerome. *Thieves' Paradise.* Dutton/Penguin Putnam, $19.95 (0-525-94663-2).

Flinn, Alex. *Breaking Point.* HarperCollins, $15.95 (0-06-623847-1).

Fontaine, Smokey D. *E.A.R.L.: The Autobiography of DMX.* HarperEntertainment/HarperCollins, $24.95 (0-06-018826-X).

Fornay, Alfred. *Born Beautiful: The African American Teenager's Complete Beauty Guide.* Amber Books/John Wiley and Sons, $14.95 (0-471-40275-3).

Frank, E. R. *America.* Atheneum Books for Young Readers, $18.00 (0-689-84729-7).

Fujishima, Kosuke. *Oh My Goddess! Wrong Number.* Dark Horse Comics, $13.95 (1-56971-669-2).

Gaiman, Neil, et al. *9-11: September 11th, 2001 (Stories to Remember. Volume 2).* DC Comics, $9.95 (1-56389-878-0).

Gerard, Jim. *Celebrity Skin: Tattoos, Brands, and Body Adornments of the Stars.* Thunder's Mouth Press, paper $25.95 (1-56025-323-1).

Giles, Gail. *Shattering Glass.* Roaring Book Press, $15.95 (0-7613-1581-0).

Godfrey, Rebecca. *Torn Skirt.* HarperPerrenial, paper $11.95 (0-06-009485-0).

Goobie, Beth. *Sticks and Stones.* Orca Book Publishers, paper $7.95 (1-55143-213-7).

Grimes, Nikki. *Bronx Masquerade.* Dial/Penguin Putnam, $16.99 (0-8037-2569-8).

Groening, Matt. *Simpsons Comics Unchained.* HarperPerennial/HarperCollins, paper $14.95 (0-06-000797-4).

Haddix, Margaret Peterson. *Among the Betrayed.* Simon and Schuster, $15.95 (0-689-83905-7).

Hart, Christopher. *Anime Mania: How to Draw Characters for Japanese Animation.* Watson-Gupthill Publications, paper $19.95 (0-8230-0158-X).

Hart, Christopher. *Mecha Mania: How to Draw the Battling Robots, Cool Spaceships, and Military Vehicles of Japanese Comics.* Watson-Gupthill, paper $19.95 (0-8230-3056-3).

Hawk, Tony. *Between Boardslides and Burnout: My Notes From the Road.* Regan-Books/HarperCollins, paper $15.95 (0-06-0008631-9).

Hoffman, Mat with Mark Lewman. *The Ride of My Life.* ReganBooks/HarperCollins, $24.95 (0-06-009415-X).

Hogya, Bernie. *Milk Mustache Mania.* Scholastic, $9.95 (0-439-38889-9).

Horowitz, Anthony. *Point Blank: An Alex Rider Adventure*. Penguin Putnam/Philomel, $16.99 (0-399-23621-X).

Hrdlitschka, Shelley. *Dancing Naked*. Orca Book Publishers, paper $6.96 (1-55143-210-0).

Irons, Diane. *Teen Beauty Secrets: Fresh, Simple & Sassy Tips for Your Perfect Look*. Sourcebooks, paper $14.95 (1-57071-959-4).

Jemas, Bill. *Origin: The True Story of Wolverine*. Marvel Comics, $34.95 (0-7851-0866-1).

Johnson, Kathleen Jeffrie. *Parallel Universe of Liars*. Roaring Book Press, $15.95 (0-7613-2854-8).

Johnstone, Mike. *Nascar: The Need for Speed*. Lerner Sports/Lerner Publishing Group, $23.95 (0-8225-0389-1).

Jukes, Mavis. *The Guy Book: An Owner's Manual*. Crown/Random House, paper $12.95 (0-679-99028-3).

Kemp, Kristen. *I Will Survive*. Push/Scholastic, paper $6.99 (0-439-12195-7).

Kim: Empty Inside: Diary of an Anonymous Teenager. Edited by Beatrice Sparks. Avon/HarperCollins, paper $5.99 (0-380-81460-9).

Knapp, Jennifer. *Cheap Frills: Fabulous Facelifts for Your Clothes*. Chronicle Books, paper $18.95 (0-8118-3019-5).

Knowles, Beyonce. *Soul Survivors: The Official Autobiography of Destiny's Child*. ReganBooks/HarperCollins, $24.95 (0-06-009417-6).

Knowles, Tina. *Destiny's Style: Bootylicious Fashion, Beauty, and Lifestyle Secrets from Destiny's Child*. ReganBooks/HarperCollins, $24.95 (0-06-009777-9).

Koertge, Ron. *Stoner & Spaz*. Candlewick Press, $15.99 (0-7636-1608-7).

Korman, Gordon. *Son of the Mob*. Hyperion, $15.99 (0-7868-0769-5).

Krulik, Nancy. *Lisa Lopes*. Simon & Schuster, paper $4.99 (0-689-85690-3).

Lahaye, Tim, and Jerry Jenkins. *Left Behind: A Graphic Novel of Earth's Last Days*. Tyndale, paper $14.00 (0-8423-7395-0).

Mad About Super Heroes. Edited by Nick Meglin and John Ficarra. DC Comics, paper $9.95 (1-56389-886-1).

McCafferty, Megan. *Sloppy Firsts*. Crown/Random House, paper $10.95 (0-609-80790-0).

McDonnell, Nick. *Twelve*. Grove Press, $23.00 (0-8021-1717-1).

McPhee, Phoebe. *The Alphabetical Hookup List A–J*. MTV Books/Alloy/Pocket Books, paper $9.95 (0-7434-4842-1).

Manoy, Lauren. *Where to Park Your Broomstick: A Teen's Guide to Witchcraft*. Fireside, paper $13.00 (0-684-85500-3).

Marron, Maggie. *Stylin': Great Looks for Teens*. Friedman, paper $12.95 (1-58663-079-2).

Masoff, Joy. *Snowboard! Your Guide to Freeriding, Pipe and Park, Jibbing, Backcountry, Alpine, Boardercross and More*. National Geographic, $8.95 (0-7922-6740-0).

Milan, Garth. *Freestyle Motorcross 2 Air Sickness: More Jump Tricks for the Pros*. MBI, $19.95 (0-7603-1184-6).

MTV Photobooth. Universe, paper $17.95 (0-7893-0800-2).

Nathan, M. M. *Cribs: A Guided Tour Inside the Homes of Your Favorite Stars*. MTV/Pocket Books, paper $19.95 (0-7434-5174-0).

Odes, Rebecca, Esther Drill, and Heather McDonald. *The Looks Book: A Whole New Approach to Beauty, Body Image, and Style*. Penguin Putnam, paper $17.00 (0-14-200211-9).

Olmstead, Kathleen. *Girls' Guide to Tarot*. Sterling, paper $12.95 (0-8069-8072-9).

Paniccioli, Ernie. *Who Shot Ya? Three Decades of HipHop Photography*. HarperCollins, $29.95 (0-06-621168-9).

Pavanel, Jane. *The Sex Book: The Alphabet of Smarter Love*. Lobster Press, paper $14.95 (1-894222-30-X).

Philobus. *Twisted Yoga*. Sea Star Books/North-South Books, $9.95 (1-58717-136-8).

Pollack, Pamela. *Ski! Your Guide to Jumping, Racing, Skiboarding, Nordic, Backcountry, Aerobatics, and More*. National Geographic, $8.95 (0-7922-6738-9).

Rain, Gwinevere. *Spellcraft for Teens: A Magical Guide to Writing and Casting Spells*. Llewellyn, paper $12.95 (0-7387-0225-0).

Rennison, Louise. *Knocked Out by My Nunga Nungas: Further Further Confessions of*

Georgia Nicholson. HarperTempest/HarperCollins, $15.99 (0-06-623656-8).

Schatz, Howard. *Athlete.* HarperCollins, $59.95 (0-06-019553-3).

Seate, Mike. *Streetbike Extreme.* MBI, paper $19.95 (0-7603-1299-0).

Seckel, Al. *Great Book of Optical Illusions.* Firefly Books, $24.95 (1-55297-650-5).

Straczynski, J. Michael. *Amazing Spider-Man: Coming Home.* Marvel, paper $15.95 (0-7851-0806-8).

Tanzman, Carol. *Shadow Place.* Roaring Brook Press, $15.95 (0-7613-1588-8).

Thrasher Presents: How to Build Skateboard Ramps. Edited by Kevin Thatcher. High Speed Productions, Inc., paper $9.95 (0-9657271-4-9).

Traig, Jennifer. *Accessories: Things to Make and Do.* Chronicle, paper $12.95 (0-8118-3151-5).

Traig, Jennifer. *Crafty Girl: Slumber Parties: Things to Make and Do.* Chronicle, $12.95 (0-8118-3571-5).

Tucker, Reed. *Osbournes Unf***ingauthorized: The Completely Unauthorized and Unofficial Guide to Everything Osbourne.* Bantam Dell Publishing, paper $8.95 (0-553-37598-9).

Von Ziegesar, Cecily. *Gossip Girl.* Little, Brown, paper $8.95 (0-316-91033-3).

Von Ziegesar, Cecily. *You Know You Love Me: A Gossip Girl Novel.* 17th Street Productions/Little, Brown, paper $8.95 (0-316-91148-8).

Waid, Mark. *JLA: Tower of Babel.* DC Comics, paper $12.95 (1-56389-727-X).

Wilson, Jacqueline. *Girls in Love.* Random House Children's Books/Delacorte Press, $9.95 (0-385-90040-6).

Wittlinger, Ellen. *The Long Night of Leo and Bree.* Simon and Schuster, $15.00 (0-689-83564-7).

Worthington, Charles. *The Complete Book of Hairstyling.* Firefly Books, paper $19.95 (1-55297-576-2).

Notable Children's Books

A list of notable children's books is selected each year by the Notable Children's Books Committee of the Association for Library Service to Children, a division of the American Library Association. Recommended titles are selected by children's librarians and educators based on originality, creativity, and suitability for children. [See "Literary Prizes, 2002" later in Part 5 for Caldecott, Newbery, and other award winners—*Ed.*]

Books for Younger Readers

Carle, Eric. *"Slowly, Slowly, Slowly," Said the Sloth.* Putnam/ Philomel (0-399-23954-5).

Dillon, Leo, and Diane Dillon. *Rap a Tap Tap: Here's Bojangles—Think of That!* Scholastic/Blue Sky (0-590-47883-4).

Dunrea, Olivier. *Gossie & Gertie.* Houghton (0-618-17676-4).

Fleming, Candace. *Muncha! Muncha! Muncha!* Illus. by G. Brian Karas. Simon & Schuster/Atheneum (0-689-83152-8).

Fleming, Denise. *Alphabet Under Construction.* Holt (0-8050-6848-1).

Gerstein, Mordicai. *What Charlie Heard.* Farrar/Frances Foster (0-374-38292-1).

Johansen, Hanna. *Henrietta and the Golden Eggs.* Illus. by Käthi Bhend, trans. by John Barrett. David R. Godine (1-5679-2210-4).

Lowry, Lois. *Gooney Bird Greene.* Illus. by Middy Thomas. Houghton Mifflin/Walter Lorraine (0-618-23848-4).

McCarty, Peter. *Hondo & Fabian.* Holt (0-8050-6352-8).

McMullan, Kate. *I Stink!* Illus. by Jim McMullan. HarperCollins/Joanna Cotler (0-06-029848-0).

Mills, Claudia. *7 X 9 = Trouble!* Illus. by G. Brian Karas. Farrar (0-374-36746-9).

Paye, Won-Ldy, and Margaret H. Lippert. *Head, Body, Legs: A Story from Liberia.* Illus. by Julie Paschkis. Holt (0-8050-6570-9).

Rohmann, Eric. *My Friend Rabbit.* Millbrook Press/Roaring Brook Press (0-7613-1535-7).

Shannon, David. *Duck on a Bike.* Scholastic/Blue Sky (0-439-05023-5).

Sis, Peter. *Madlenka's Dog.* Farrar/Frances Foster (0-374-34699-2).

Thomas, Shelley Moore. *Get Well, Good Knight.* Illus. by Jennifer Plecas. Dutton (0-525-46914-1).

Wilson, Karma. *Bear Snores On.* Illus. by Jane Chapman. Simon & Schuster/Margaret K. McElderry (0-689-83187-0).

Winter, Jonah. *Frida.* Illus. by Ana Juan. Scholastic/Arthur A. Levine. (0-590-20320-7).

Books for Middle Readers

Andrews-Goebel, Nancy. *The Pot that Juan Built.* Illus. by David Diaz. Lee & Low (1-58430-038-8).

Bauer, Joan. *Stand Tall.* Putnam (0-399-23473-X).

Blake, Robert J. *Togo.* Putnam/Philomel (0-399-23381-4).

Creech, Sharon. *Ruby Holler.* HarperCollins/Joanna Cotler (0-06-027732-7).

Delano, Marfe Ferguson. *Inventing the Future: A Photobiography of Thomas Alva Edison.* National Geographic (0-7922-6721-4).

Denslow, Sharon Phillips. *Georgie Lee.* Illus. by Lynne Rae Perkins. Greenwillow (0-688-17940-1).

Ferris, Jean. *Once Upon a Marigold.* Harcourt (0-15-216791-9).

Fine, Anne. *Up on Cloud Nine.* Random House/Delacorte (0-385-73009-8).

Fradin, Dennis Brindell. *The Signers: The 56 Stories Behind the Declaration of Independence.* Illus. by Michael McCurdy. Walker (0-8027-8849-1).

Freedman, Russell. *Confucius: The Golden Rule.* Illus. by Frederic Clement. Scholastic/Arthur A. Levine (0-439-13957-0).

Funke, Cornelia. *The Thief Lord.* Trans. by Oliver Latsch. Chicken House/Scholastic Inc. (0-439-40437-1).

Gaiman, Neil. *Coraline.* Illus. by Dave McKean. HarperCollins (0-380-97778-8).

Giff, Patricia Reilly. *Pictures of Hollis Woods*. Random House/Wendy Lamb (0-385-32655-6).

Grimes, Nikki. *Talkin' About Bessie: The Story of Aviator Elizabeth Coleman*. Illus. by E. B. Lewis. Scholastic/Orchard (0-439-35243-6).

Ibbotson, Eva. *Journey to the River Sea*. Illus. by Kevin Hawkes. Penguin Putnam/Dutton (0-525-46739-4).

McKay, Hilary. *Saffy's Angel*. Simon & Schuster/Margaret K. McElderry (0-689-84933-8).

Mak, Kam. *My Chinatown: One Year in Poems*. HarperCollins (0-06-029190-7).

Martin, Ann. *A Corner of the Universe*. Scholastic (0-439-38880-5).

Old, Wendie. *To Fly: The Story of the Wright Brothers*. Illus. by Robert Andrew Parker. Clarion (0-618-13347-X).

Pinkney, Andrea Davis. *Ella Fitzgerald: The Tale of a Vocal Virtuosa*. Illus. by Brian Pinkney. Hyperion/Jump at the Sun (0-7868-0568-4).

Rubin, Susan Goldman. *Degas and the Dance: The Painter and the Petits Rats, Perfecting their Art*. Harry N. Abrams (0-8109-0567-1).

Ryan, Pam Muñoz. *When Marian Sang: The True Recital of Marian Anderson, The Voice of a Century*. Illus. by Brian Selznick. Scholastic (0-439-26967-9).

Stanley, Diane. *Saladin: Noble Prince of Islam*. HarperCollins (0-688-17135-4).

Testa, Maria. *Becoming Joe DiMaggio*. Illus. by Scott Hunt. Candlewick (0-7636-1537-4).

Tolan, Stephanie S. *Surviving the Applewhites*. HarperCollins (0-06-623602-9).

Walker, Sally M. *Fossil Fish Found Alive: Discovering the Coelacanth*. Carolrhoda (1-57505-536-8).

Books for Older Readers

Alvarez, Julia. *Before We Were Free*. Knopf (0-375-81544-9).

Avi. *Crispin: The Cross of Lead*. Hyperion (0-7868-0828-4).

Blumenthal, Karen. *Six Days in October: The Stock Market Crash of 1929*. Simon & Schuster/Atheneum (0-689-84276-7).

Colman, Penny. *Where the Action Was: Women War Correspondents in World War II*. Crown (0-517-80075-6).

Cooney, Caroline. *Goddess of Yesterday*. Delacorte (0-385-72945-6).

Farmer, Nancy. *The House of the Scorpion*. Simon & Schuster/Atheneum/Richard Jackson (0-689-85222-3).

Fleischman, John. *Phineas Gage: A Gruesome But True Story About Brain Science*. Houghton (0-618-05252-6).

Gantos, Jack. *Hole in My Life*. Farrar, Straus and Giroux (0-374-39988-3).

Giblin, James Cross. *The Life and Death of Adolf Hitler*. Clarion (0-395-90371-8).

Hiaasen, Carl. *Hoot*. Knopf (0-375-82181-3).

McCaughrean, Geraldine. *The Kite Rider*. HarperCollins (0-06-623875-7).

Nye, Naomi Shihab. *19 Varieties of Gazelle: Poems of the Middle East*. Greenwillow (0-06-009765-5).

Park, Linda Sue. *When My Name Was Keoko: A Novel of Korea in World War II*. Clarion (0-618-13335-6).

Partridge, Elizabeth. *This Land Was Made for You and Me: The Life and Songs of Woody Guthrie*. Viking (0-670-03535-1).

Books for All Ages

Fink, Sam. *The Declaration of Independence*. Scholastic (0-439-40700-1).

Greenberg, Jan, and Sandra Jordan. *Action Jackson*. Illus. by Robert Andrew Parker. Millbrook Press/Roaring Brook Press (0-7613-1682-5).

Howitt, Mary. *The Spider and the Fly*. Illus. by Tony DiTerlizzi. Simon & Schuster (0-689-85289-4).

Kalman, Maira. *Fireboat: The Heroic Adventures of the John J. Harvey*. Putnam (0-399-23953-7).

Karas, G. Brian. *Atlantic*. Putnam (0-399-23632-5).

Martin, Bill Jr., and Michael Sampson. *I Pledge Allegiance: The Pledge of Allegiance with Commentary*. Illus. by Chris Raschka. Candlewick (0-7636-1648-6).

Pinkney, Jerry. *Noah's Ark*. North-South/SeaStar (1-58717-201-1).

Zelinsky, Paul O. *Knick-Knack Paddywhack!* Dutton (0-525-46908-7).

Notable Children's Videos

These titles are selected by a committee of the Association for Library Service to Children, a division of the American Library Association. Recommendations are based on originality, creativity, and suitability for young children. The members select materials that respect both children's intelligence and imagination, exhibit venturesome creativity, and encourage the interest of users.

Company's Coming. 7 mins. Spoken Arts. Ages 5–8.

How Do Dinosaurs Say Good Night? 8 mins. Weston Woods. Ages 4–8.

The Hungry Squid. 14 mins. National Film Board of Canada. Age 7 and up.

I Love You Like Crazy Cakes. 8 mins. Weston Woods. Ages 4–8.

Martin's Big Words. 8 mins. Weston Woods. Ages 5–12.

Max (Reading Rainbow). 30 mins. GPN. Ages 5–8.

Merry Christmas, Space Case. 13 mins. Weston Woods. Ages 4–8.

Miss Twiggley's Tree. 22 mins. Bix Pix Entertainment. Age 8 and up.

Operation Cuckoo. 13 mins. National Film Board of Canada. Ages 4–10.

Our Big Home: An Earth Poem (Reading Rainbow). 30 mins. GPN. Ages 7–11.

So You Want to Be President? 27 mins. Weston Woods. Ages 6–12.

There Was an Old Lady Who Swallowed a Fly. 7 mins. Weston Woods. Ages 4–7.

Waiting for Wings. 7 mins. Weston Woods. Ages 2–6.

Notable Recordings for Children

This list of notable recordings for children was selected by the Association for Library Service to Children, a division of the American Library Association. Recommended titles, many of which are recorded books, are chosen by children's librarians and educators on the basis of their originality, creativity, and suitability.

"26 Fairmount Avenue: Books 1–4." 3 hrs., 3 cassettes or 4 CDs. Listening Library. Author-illustrator Tomie dePaola narrates this story of his childhood in suburban Connecticut in the 1930s.

"Beethoven's Wig." 35 mins., 1 CD. Rounder Records. Richard Perlmutter has written humorous lyrics to 11 well-known classical pieces. The orchestral versions are included, too.

"Boy." 4 hrs., 3 cassettes. Harper Children's Audio. Derek Jacobi reads stories by Roald Dahl.

"Clic, Clac, Muu—Vacas Escritoras." 7 mins., 1 cassette, sold separately or with hardcover book. Weston Woods. Jorge Pupo's reading in Spanish of the story "Click, Clack, Moo—Cows that Type."

"Coraline." 3 hrs., 2 cassettes or CDs. Harper Children's Audio. Neil Gaiman reads a spooky story, background music by the Gothic Archies.

"Everything on a Waffle." 3 hrs., 3 cassettes or 2 CDs. Listening Library. Kathleen McInerney reads Polly Horvath's book about Primrose Squarp.

"Feather Boy." 6 hrs., 4 cassettes. Listening Library. Nicky Singer's story is read by Philip Franks.

"Francie." 4 hrs. and 30 mins., 4 cassettes. Recorded Books. Sisi Aisha Johnson reads Karen English's story, set in rural Alabama during segregation.

"The Frogs Wore Red Suspenders." 50 mins., 1 cassette. Harper Children's Audio. Jack Prelutsky reads 28 of his own pieces.

"Good Night, Gorilla." 4 mins., 1 cassette or CD, sold separately or with paperback book. Weston Woods. Peggy Rathmann's tale of a late-night zoo outing is read by Anthony Edwards.

"The Grave." 6 hrs. and 30 mins., 5 cassettes. Recorded Books. Time travel is the theme of this story centered on the Irish potato famine, read by Gerard Doyle.

"How Do Dinosaurs Say Good Night?" 4 mins., 1 cassette or CD, sold separately or with hardcover book. Weston Woods. Jane Yolen reads her children's story.

"The Journey." 12 mins., 1 cassette and hardcover book. Live Oak Media. Sarah Stewart's story about a young Amish farm girl visiting the city is read by Daisy Egan.

"Latin Playground." 35 mins., 1 CD. Putumayo World Music. Eleven songs in Spanish, English, Maya, and Portuguese introduce Latin American culture.

"Love, Ruby Lavender." 3 hrs., 3 cassettes. Listening Library. Judith Ivey reads Deborah Wiles' story about nine-year-old Ruby.

"Maniac Magee." 4 hrs. and 30 mins., 3 cassettes or 4 CDs, or 3 cassettes and book. Listening Library. S. Epatha Merkerson is the reader of this story about challenging ignorance and racial prejudice in a segregated town.

"Martin's Big Words." 10 mins., 1 cassette or CD, sold separately or with hardcover book. Weston Woods. Martin Luther King, Jr.'s "big" words like *freedom* and *love* are the theme of Doreen Rappaport's story, read by Michael Clarke Duncan with music by Crystal Taliefero.

"More Tales of Uncle Remus." 3 hrs. and 15 mins., 3 cassettes. Recorded Books. Julius Lester adapts a collection of Brer Rabbit stories.

"Pictures of Hollis Woods." 3 hrs. and 18 mins., 2 cassettes. Listening Library. Hope Davis reads Patricia Reilly Giff's novel about runaway Hollis.

"Ruby Holler." 5 hrs., 3 cassettes. Harper Children's Audio. Sharon Creech's story is read by Donna Murphy.

"Saffy's Angel." 4 hrs. and 30 mins., 3 cassettes. Listening Library. Julia Sawalha's voice brings Hilary McKay's story to life.

"A Single Shard." 3 hrs., 3 cassettes or CDs. Listening Library. Graeme Malcolm interprets Linda Sue Park's story.

"So You Want to Be President?" 22 mins., 1 cassette or CD, sold separately or with hardcover book. Weston Woods. Stockard Channing reads this book about the U.S. presidency by Judith St. George.

"The Thief Lord." 8 hrs. and 30 mins., 5 cassettes. Listening Library. Simon Jones narrates Cornelia Funke's adventure tale.

"The Twits." 1 hr., 1 cassette. Harper Children's Audio. A Roald Dahl story read by Simon Callow.

"Why Don't You Get a Horse, Sam Adams?" 20 mins. (1 cassette) or 58 mins. (1 CD), sold separately or with paperback book. Voices and music enliven Jean Fritz's tale.

Notable Software for Children

This list is chosen by a committee of the Association for Library Service to Children, a division of the American Library Association. Titles are chosen on the basis of their originality, creativity, and suitability for young children.

Disney Learning Adventure: Search for the Secret Keys. Age 5 and up. Disney. Rescuing Mickey Mouse and friends from a haunted house involves math, reading, language arts, and logic. Windows/Macintosh.

Encarta Reference Library 2003. Age 8 and up. Microsoft. This 5-CD or 1-DVD set includes extensive multimedia content, an interactive atlas, and *Encarta Africana.* Windows.

Inspiration (Version 7). Age 10 and up. Inspiration Software, Inc. Students can create a graphic organizer with more than 50 templates on school-related subjects. Windows/Macintosh.

Math Arena Advanced. Age 12 and up. Sunburst Technology. Users practice advanced math skills including patterning, graphing, and solving for variables. Windows/Macintosh.

Moop and Dreadly in the Treasure on Bing Bong Island. Ages 5–10. Plaid Banana Entertainment. Recovering King Earwig's treasure involves solving basic logic problems. Windows/Macintosh.

Nancy Drew: Ghost Dogs of Moon Lake. Age 10 and up. Her Interactive. Logic and deductive reasoning are used in solving a mystery. Two levels of play. Windows.

The Powerpuff Girls: Mojo Jojo's Clone Zone. Ages 6–10. Learning Company/Riverdeep. The girls use math, logic, language arts, and geography skills to save Townsville. Five levels of activity. Windows/Macintosh.

PrintMaster Platinum 12. Age 9 and up. Broderbund. Thousands of new images and projects are included in this updated version of a popular graphics program. Windows.

Sesame Street Toddler. Ages 2–4. Encore Software. Big Bird, Elmo, and friends lead toddlers through simple activities with numbers, letters, and sorting. Windows.

Ultimate Ride Coaster Deluxe. Age 9 and up. Disney Interactive. Users create and ride a roller coaster using one of five track types and a variety of environments. Windows.

Zoombinis Island Odyssey. Age 8 and up. The Learning Company/Riverdeep. Math and logic problems incorporate science for the first time on Zoombini Isle. Windows/Macintosh.

Bestsellers of 2002

Hardcover Bestsellers: The Big Didn't Get Bigger

Daisy Maryles
Executive Editor, *Publishers Weekly*

Laurele Riippa
Editor, Adult Announcements, *Publishers Weekly*

No one will argue with the obvious—2002 was not the best year for the economy. America was still reeling from the September 11 terror attacks; stock market numbers were heading downward and consumer confidence was abysmal.

On the book front, a lot of ink was spilled about lower unit sales for books, even for the veteran authors who dominate the charts year after year; most of this brouhaha was reserved for fiction. Meanwhile, judging from our annual collation of the year-end bestsellers, it does not appear that this evaluation is totally supported by the information publishers submitted, especially when it comes to fiction. Eight fiction titles went over the 1-million mark—the highest number throughout the 1990s. In nonfiction, there were only two books with sales surpassing a million; the norm has been four to six nonfiction titles with sales of more than 1 million. The No. 1 nonfiction for 2001 was the *Prayer of Jabez*; it sold more than 8 million copies in 2002.

Still, in 2002 more new hardcovers went over the 100,000 mark than in the previous year. There were 125 new hardcover fiction titles that claimed sales of more than 100,000 in 2002; 130 new nonfiction tomes did the same. The 2001 figure for fiction was 110; in 2000 the number was 109. For nonfiction, the 2001 tally was 123; in 2000 it was 117.

Last year, an unprecedented number of debut novels sold more than 100,000—a total of 15; in 2001 there were only four. Two were among the top 15 bestsellers. Alice Sebold's *The Lovely Bones* sold more than 1.8 million copies in its first publication year; according to publisher Little, Brown, total sales are now over the 2 million mark. *The Nanny Diaries* by Emma McLauglin and Nicola Kraus, according to St. Martin's, racked up sales of about 850,000, and its tenure on our weekly charts was longer than any other novel, including John Grisham's *The Summons*, which was the No. 1-selling hardcover work last year, with about 2.6 million copies.

Even with the stellar performance of debut fiction, it is the veteran writers who continue to dominate these end-of-year charts. Grisham had two books on the top 15 list; James Patterson had three in the top 30, as did Danielle Steel. Stephen King, Janet Evanovich, and Nora Roberts each landed two in the top 30. In fact, just about all the newcomers to this list were debut novelists.

Did some veteran megaselling novelists falter in their unit sales last year? If we examine the "shipped and billed" numbers submitted by publishers, there is some evidence that this is true for a few authors. Grisham seems to be holding

Adapted from *Publishers Weekly,* March 24, 2003.

Publishers Weekly 2002 Bestsellers

FICTION

1. **The Summons** by John Grisham. Doubleday (2/02) **2,625,000
2. **Red Rabbit** by Tom Clancy. Putnam (8/02) 1,970,932
3. **Remnant** by Jerry B. Jenkins and Tim LaHaye. Tyndale (6/02) 1,880,549
4. **The Lovely Bones** by Alice Seybold. Little, Brown (6/02) 1,841,825
5. **Prey** by Michael Crichton. HarperCollins (11/02) 1,496,807
6. **Skipping Christmas** by John Grisham. Doubleday (11/01) **1,225,000
7. **The Shelters of Stone** by Jean M. Auel. Crown (4/02) 1,223,105
8. **Four Blind Mice** by James Patterson. Little, Brown (11/02) 1,060,470
9. **Everything's Eventual** by Stephen King. Scribner (3/02) **925,000
10. **The Nanny Diaries** by Emma McLaughlin and Nicola Kraus. St. Martin's (3/02) 852,021
11. **From a Buick 8** by Stephen King. Scribner (9/02) **840,000
12. **The Beach House** by James Patterson and Peter de Jonge. Little, Brown (6/02) 835,723
13. **Star Wars: Attack of the Clones** by R. A. Salvatore. Del Rey/LucasBooks (4/02) 784,750
14. **Nights in Rodanthe** by Nicholas Sparks. Warner (9/02) 744,543
15. **Answered Prayers** by Danielle Steel. Delacorte (10/02) **725,000

NONFICTION

1. **Self Matters** by Phillip C. McGraw. Simon & Schuster Source (11/01) **1,350,000
2. **A Life God Rewards** by Bruce Wilkinson with David Kopp. Multnomah (9/02) 1,186,000
3. **Let's Roll!** by Lisa Beamer with Ken Abraham. Tyndale (8/02) 958,208
4. **Guinness World Records 2003** by Guinness World Records Ltd. Guinness Publishing (8/02) 919,953
5. **Who Moved My Cheese?** by Spencer Johnson. Putnam (9/98) *850,000
6. **Leadership** by Rudolph W. Giuliani. Miramax (10/02) 801,470
7. **Prayer of Jabez for Women** by Darlene Wilkinson. Multnomah (9/02) 704,626
8. **Bush at War** by Bob Woodward. Simon & Schuster (11/02) **690,000
9. **Portrait of a Killer** by Patricia Cornwell. Putnam (11/02) 683,340
10. **Body for Life** by Bill Phillips. HarperCollins (5/99) *676,464
11. **I Hope You Dance** by Mark D. Sanders and Tia Sillers. Rutledge Hill (10/00) *648,021
12. **Stupid White Men** by Michael Moore. ReganBooks (3/02) 634,711
13. **Bringing Up Boys** by James Dobson. Tyndale (9/01) *612,109
14. **Good to Great** by Jim Collins. HarperBusiness (9/01) *528,031
15. **Get with the Program** by Bob Greene. Simon & Schuster (1/02) **490,000

Note: Rankings are determined by sales figures provided by publishers; the numbers generally reflect reports of copies "shipped and billed" in calendar year 2002 and publishers were instructed to adjust sales figures to include returns through January 31, 2003. Publishers did not at that time know what their total returns would be—indeed, the majority of returns occur after that cut-off date—so none of these figures should be regarded as final net sales. (dates in parentheses indicate month and year of publication.)

*Sales figures reflect books sold only in calendar year 2002.

**Sales figures were submitted to *PW* in confidence, for use in placing titles on the lists. Numbers shown are rounded down to the nearest 10,000 to indicate relationship to sales figures of other titles.

steady over the last nine years, although back in 1994, *The Chamber* sold more than 3 million copies. King's sales have dropped below the 1-million mark, while James Patterson's first hardcover million-copy seller is *Four Blind Mice*. HarperCollins's numbers for Michael Crichton's *The Prey* put him about 100,000 copies ahead of his 1999 bestseller, *Timeline*. Nicholas Sparks is up with *Nights in Rodanthe*. It's been 11 years since Jean Auel had a bestseller. Back in 1990, *The Plains of Passage* was the No. 1 bestseller for the year, with sales of more than 1.6 million; last year, sales of about 1.2 million for *The Shelters of Stone* made it the No. 7 fiction bestseller. (Keep in mind that all these figures are shipped and billed, meaning some of these books could wind up on the return shelves.) All the top 15 fiction titles enjoyed long tenures on the weekly charts, ranging from seven weeks for *Attack of the Clones* to 32 weeks for *The Nanny Diaries*.

In nonfiction, how-to and religion inspirational took up a large percentage of the top 15 slots—nine to be exact. The bestselling book to come out of 9/11 was *Let's Roll*; it did very well in all markets—general, Christian, and discount stores. September 11 also made Rudy Giuliani a national hero and certainly was a factor in selling an impressive 800,000-plus copies of his book *Leadership*—placing it in the No. 6 slot on the year-end nonfiction list. It's the fourth year for *Who Moved My Cheese?* on these year-end lists; it sold about 850,000 copies in 2002, and its sales since publication in September 1998 total more than 6.8 million.

Disclaimer: Net vs. Gross

As always, all our calculations are based on shipped and billed figures supplied by publishers for new books released in 2001 and 2002 (a few books issued earlier that continued their tenure on our 2002 weekly lists and/or our monthly religion lists are also included). These figures reflect only 2002 trade sales—publishers were specifically instructed not to include book club and overseas transactions. We also asked publishers to take into account returns through January 31. All sales figures in these pages should not be considered final net sales. For many of the books, especially those published in the latter half of the year, final returns are still to be calculated

Also note the tables "Who's on First?" and "What's on Second?" in which we compare *PW*'s top 15 rankings with how these books fared at selected independents, chains, and online booksellers. We lack information on how these titles fared at the price clubs, mass merchandisers, and in the gift retail market.

The Fiction Runners-Up

This second tier on our annual list is made up of well-known list veterans with strong sales—several with reported sales that are even higher than for their previous books. But these higher unit sales could not place them among the top 15. Jan Karon, Sue Grafton, and Mary Higgins Clark all slipped to the runners-up grouping. All the books in this group were on our weekly bestseller lists for four weeks or more.

16. *In This Mountain* by Jan Karon (Viking, 681,500)

17. *Q Is for Quarry* by Sue Grafton (Putnam, 665,558)

18. *Daddy's Little Girl* by Mary Higgins Clark (Simon & Schuster, *625,000)

19. *Chesapeake Blue* by Nora Roberts (Putnam, 616,000)

20. *The Christmas Train* by David Baldacci (Warner, 589,930)

21. *Reversible Errors* by Scott Turow (Farrar, Straus & Giroux, *581,000)

22. *Visions of Sugar Plums* by Janet Evanovich (St. Martin's, 580,321)

23. *2nd Chance* by James Patterson and Andrew Gross (Little, Brown, 575,992)

24. *Sunset in St. Tropez* by Danielle Steel (Delacorte, *525,000)

25. *The Janson Directive* by Robert Ludlum (St. Martin's, 511,290)

26. *The Cottage* by Danielle Steel (Delacorte, *510,000)

27. *Esther's Gift* by Jan Karon (Viking, 503,200)

28. *Three Fates* by Nora Roberts (Putnam, 500,000)

29. *Hard Eight* by Janet Evanovich (St. Martin's, 460,356)

30. *Fire Ice* by Clive Cussler with Paul Kemprecos (Putnam, 459,370)

More High Rollers Didn't Place

This year there were 15 novels with sales of more than 300,000 that did not make the top 30 list. That's more than the 10 books that shared the same state a year earlier. All but one—*The Secret Life of Bees* by Sue Monk Kidd—enjoyed runs on our weekly charts in 2002. Kidd's debut novel did very well at the independents and tracked for several weeks just below the top 15. *The Last Promise* by Richard Paul Evans appeared on the charts for one week, and *The Crush* by Sandra Brown had a three-week stint. The two Mattie J. T. Stepanek poetry collections and Stephen Carter's debut novel, *The Emperor of Ocean Park*, enjoyed double-digit runs on the weekly lists.

The three with 2002 sales of more than 400,000 copies are *Mortal Prey* by John Sandford (Putnam), *Quentins* by Maeve Binchy (Dutton), and *By the Light of the Moon* by Dean Koontz (Bantam).

In ranked order, the 12 titles with 300,000+ sales that did not make the top 30 annual list are *Hornet Flight* by Ken Follett (Dutton), *Journey Through Heartsongs* by Mattie J. T. Stepanek (Hyperion), *Up Country* by Nelson DeMille (Warner), *The Last Promise* by Richard Paul Evans (Dutton), *Hope Through Heartsongs* by Mattie J. T. Stepanek (Hyperion), *Blessings* by Anna Quindlen (Random House), *A Thousand Country Roads* by Robert James Waller (John M. Hardy), *The Murder Book* by Jonathan Kellerman (Ballantine), *The Crush* by Sandra Brown (Warner), *The Secret Life of Bees* by Sue Monk Kidd (Viking), *Eleventh Hour* by Catherine Coulter (Putnam), and *The Emperor of Ocean Park* by Stephen L. Carter (Knopf).

FICTION: Who's on First?

How *Publishers Weekly*'s bestsellers compared with the rankings
in major chains, wholesalers, and independents

	Sales Outlets											
PW Rankings	BN	B	W	I	O	DK	S	H	WS	TC	AM.c	BN.c
1. The Summons	2	2	2	8	9	18	2	3	3	10	3	2
2. Red Rabbit	4	5	4	6	4	25	4	4	4	23	5	8
3. The Remnant	11	12	9	21	—	—	—	1	8	—	15	12
4. The Lovely Bones	1	1	1	3	2	1	1	17	1	1	1	1
5. Prey	7	7	10	1	38	24	8	7	6	22	7	7
6. Skipping Christmas	17	8	6	—	—	31	7	8	57	—	32	23
7. The Shelters of Stone	5	4	3	13	29	17	9	2	9	8	6	4
8. Four Blind Mice	8	9	7	31	14	45	28	13	18	—	10	5
9. Everything's Eventual	14	11	8	36	—	—	31	5	10	—	16	16
10. The Nanny Diaries	3	3	14	2	3	2	3	38	2	5	2	3
11. From a Buick 8	23	25	5	—	—	—	—	6	37	—	26	15
12. The Beach House	6	6	13	9	—	14	16	25	5	—	11	6
13. Attack of the Clones	24	24	19	—	—	—	—	10	13	—	—	—
14. Nights in Rodanthe	10	22	11	40	—	39	39	12	15	—	—	24
15. Answered Prayers	—	—	12	—	—	—	—	19	—	—	—	—

NONFICTION: What's on Second?

How *Publishers Weekly*'s bestsellers compared with the rankings
in major chains, wholesalers, and independents

	Sales Outlets											
PW Rankings	BN	B	W	I	O	DK	S	H	WS	TC	AM.c	BN.c
1. Self Matters	1	1	1	5	—	11	4	1	6	7	—	6
2. A Life God Rewards	—	—	—	—	—	—	—	5	53	—	—	—
3. Let's Roll!	25	32	9	6	—	—	41	—	—	—	—	—
4. Guinness World Records 2003	—	—	22	—	—	—	41	—	—	—	—	—
5. Who Moved My Cheese?	2	2	2	2	26	37	23	4	1	4	2	1
6. Leadership	6	5	5	26	—	14	13	14	14	17	11	7
7. Prayer of Jabez for Women	—	—	—	29	—	—	—	15	64	—	—	—
8. Bush at War	9	7	6	17	16	17	11	34	19	24	16	22
9. Portrait of a Killer	17	17	8	35	—	41	24	25	—	—	41	23
10. Body for Life	3	3	4	22	—	21	35	3	23	10	15	15
11. I Hope You Dance	31	10	7	46	—	—	25	40	—	—	—	—
12. Stupid White Men	5	4	18	3	1	27	1	21	2	1	4	11
13. Bringing Up Boys	38	—	—	—	—	—	—	—	—	—	—	—
14. Good to Great	7	11	49	12	—	18	16	—	4	3	1	2
15. Get with the Program!	10	12	10	7	—	—	22	7	—	—	14	13

BN	= Barnes & Noble	B	= Borders
W	= Waldenbooks	I	= Ingram
O	= Olsson's	DK	= Davis Kidd
S	= Harry W. Schwartz	H	= Hastings
WS	= Waterstone's	TC	= Tattered Cover
AM.c	= Amazon.com	BN.c	= Barnes & Noble.com

A Higher Tally for 200,000+ Level

A handful of first-fiction titles, veteran list-makers, and some Christmas novels make up the group of books with sales of more than 200,000 that didn't get a shot at the top 30 charts. There were 17 books in this group, two more than in 2001.

Only *The Mitford Snowmen* by Jan Karon (Viking) did not land a slot on the top-15 weekly charts for 2002, although it did track among the top 25 for several weeks around the holiday season. NBCC's 2002 best-fiction choice, *Atonement* by Ian McEwan (Doubleday), was the only title in this group with a double-digit (12) run on the 2002 weekly charts.

Books in this group that appeared on the weekly charts for more than one month are *I Don't Know How She Does It* by Allison Pearson (Knopf), *Blackwood Farm* by Anne Rice (Knopf), *Dark Horse* by Tami Hoag (Bantam), *A Love of My Own* by E. Lynn Harris (Doubleday), *Standing in the Rainbow* by Fannie Flagg (Random House), *The Wailing Wind* by Tony Hillerman (HarperCollins), *City of Bones* by Michael Connelly (Little, Brown), and *The Cat Who Went Up the Creek* by Lilian Jackson Braun (Putnam).

Books on the list four weeks or more at this level are *Chasing the Dime* by Michael Connelly (Little, Brown), *Killjoy* by Julie Garwood (Ballantine), *The Christmas Shoes* by Donna VanLiere (St. Martin's), *No One to Trust* by Iris Johansen (Bantam), *Mission Compromised* by Oliver North with Joe Musser (Broadman & Holman), *Mount Vernon Love Story* by Mary Higgins Clark (Simon & Schuster), and *Midnight Runner* by Jack Higgins (Putnam).

The 150,000+ Group Is Also Big

The 2000 record of 24 books with sales over 150,000 that did not make the annual top 30 list still stands, but the 21 titles that did so this year is the second highest. Only two of these books—*Confessions of a Sociopathic Social Climber* by Adele Lang (St. Martin's) and *The Glorious Cause* by Jeff Shaara (Ballantine)—never made it to *PW*'s weekly top 15 hardcover list. There were also two—*The Dive from Clausen's Pier* by Ann Packer (Knopf) and *The Millionaires* by Brad Meltzer (Warner)—that had double-digit runs on the weekly charts.

Eight had bestseller runs of more than one month on the 2002 charts. They are *The Little Friend* by Donna Tartt (Knopf), *The Life of Pi* by Yann Martel (Harcourt), *Widow's Walk* by Robert B. Parker (Putnam), *Basket Case* by Carl Hiaasen (Knopf), *Sea Glass* by Anita Shreve (Little, Brown), *Voyage of the Jerle Shannara: Morgawr* by Terry Brooks (Del Rey), *Light in Shadow* by Jayne Ann Krentz (Putnam), and *Charleston* by John Jakes (Dutton).

Bestsellers in this category with runs of four weeks or less are *The Mulberry Tree* by Jude Deveraux (Atria), *Celebrate Through Heartsongs* by Mattie J. T. Stepanek (Hyperion), *Baudolino* by Umberto Eco (Harcourt), *The Short Forever* by Stuart Woods (Putnam), *Dying to Please* by Linda Howard (Ballantine), *Blood Orchid* by Stuart Woods (Putnam), *Body of Lies* by Iris Johansen (Bantam), *Tricky Business* by Dave Barry (Putnam), and *The Last Girls* by Lee Smith (Algonquin).

The 125,000+ Level

There were 16 fiction titles with sales of more than 125,000 that did not make the top 30 list. Only four books in this group did not appear on the weekly charts. They are *The Rana Look* by Sandra Brown (Bantam), *The Old Ace in the Hole* by Annie Proulx (Scribner), *Cape Light* by Thomas Kinkade (Berkley), and *Hot Ice* by Nora Roberts (Bantam). Both Brown's and Roberts's books were hardcover reissues of mass market originals published in the 1980s.

Only three books had runs of more than a month *The Last Jihad* by Joel C. Rosenberg (Forge), *The Stone Monkey* by Jeffery Deaver (Simon & Schuster), and *The Crimson Petal and the White* by Michael Faber (Harcourt).

The other books that sold more than 125,000 were on the lists from one to four weeks. They are *Thieves' Paradise* by Eric Jerome Dickey (Dutton), *Sin Killer* by Larry McMurtry (Simon & Schuster), *An Accidental Woman* by Barbara Delinsky (Simon & Schuster), *December 6* by Martin Cruz Smith (Simon & Schuster), *Stone Kiss* by Faye Kellerman (Warner), *Shrink Rap* by Robert B. Parker (Putnam), *Three Weeks in Paris* by Barbara Taylor Bradford (Doubleday), *Grave Secrets* by Kathy Reichs (Scribner), and *Star Wars: The Approaching Storm* by Alan Dean Foster (Del Rey/ LucasBooks).

A Look At the 100,000+

In 2002 there were 23 books with sales of more than 100,000 that did not make a top 30 list, two fewer that the record-setting 25 in 2001. Nine titles in this group have not landed on the weekly *PW* charts; two—*If Looks Could Kill* by Kate White (Warner) and *Hunting Season* by Nevada Barr (Putnam)—were on the list six and five weeks, respectively.

Books with four weeks or less were *Enemy Women* by Paulette Jiles (Morrow), *The Oath* by John Lescroart (Dutton), *The Apprentice* by Tess Gerritsen (Ballantine), *Dune: The Butlerian Jihad* by Brian Herbert and Kevin J. Anderson (Tor), *Star Wars: The New Jedi Order: Destiny's Way* by Walter Jon Williams (Del Rey/LucasBooks), *Thursday's Child* by Sandra Brown (Bantam), *Deadly Embrace* by Jackie Collins (Simon & Schuster), *McNally's Alibi* by Lawrence Sanders and Vincent Lardo (Putnam), *You Are Not a Stranger Here* by Adam Haslett (Doubleday), *Lullaby* by Chuck Palahniuk (Doubleday), *Partner in Crime* by J. A. Jance (Morrow), and *Courting Trouble* by Lisa Scottoline (HarperCollins).

The nine that did not appear on the weekly charts were *Three Junes* by Julia Glass (Pantheon), *Child of My Heart* by Alice McDermott (FSG), *I, Richard* by Elizabeth George (Bantam), *Miracle at St. Anna* by James McBride (Riverhead), *The Good Sister* by Diana Diamond (St. Martin's), *Wings of Fire* by Dale Brown (Putnam), *Jinxed* by Carol Higgins Clark (Scribner), *Sleep No More* by Greg Iles (Putnam), and *Everything Is Illuminated* by Jonathan Safran Foer (Houghton Mifflin). Several of these books, including those by Glass, McDermott, Iles and Foer, spent several weeks in the top 25.

The Nonfiction Runners-Up

Memoirs and self-help titles dominate these bestselling nonfiction runners-up. Two—*Way to Be* and *In Search of America*—have yet to hit *PW*'s weekly charts. All the others were on the charts for at least a month, and five had double-digit runs.

16. *Lucky Man* by Michael J. Fox (Hyperion, 476,493)
17. *Fish!* by Stephen Lundin, Harry Paul and John Christensen (Hyperion, 463,986 in 2002; total sales: 1,085,596)
18. *A Long Way from Home* by Tom Brokaw (Random House, 443,955)
19. *The Purpose-Driven Life* by Rick Warren (Zondervan, 438,749)
20. *My Losing Season* by Pat Conroy (Doubleday/Talese, **425,000)
21. *The Perricone Prescription* by Nicholas Perricone (HarperResource, 413,8530)
22. *Shadow Warriors* by Tom Clancy with Gen. Carl Stiner (Ret.) and Tony Koltz (Putnam, 404,089)
23. *Who Says Elephants Can't Dance?* by Louis Gerstner (HarperBusiness, 401,666)
24. *The Healthy Kitchen* by Andrew Weil and Rosie Daley (Knopf, 400,000)
25. *Way to Be* by Gordon B. Hinckley (Simon & Schuster, **394,000)
26. *Let Freedom Ring* by Sean Hannity (ReganBooks, 393,464)
27. *Journals* by Kurt Cobain (Riverhead, 385,000)
28. *The Power of Now* by Eckhart Tolle (New World Library, 381,423 in 2002; total sales: 679,000)
29. *The Sopranos Family Cookbook* by Artie Bucco (Warner, 374,376)
30. *In Search of America* by Peter Jennings and Todd Brewster (Hyperion, 369,059)

Big Numbers for 300,000+

While the seven nonfiction books with sales of more than 300,000 that did not make the top 30 annual bestseller list was not a record (there were nine in 1999), this was the first time books with sales of more than 350,000 did not get to the top 30.

Two books with reported sales of more than 300,000 did not make *PW*'s weekly charts; they are *Prescription for Nutritional Healing* by Phyllis A. Balch and James F. Balch, M.D. (Avery) and *The Bible Code II* by Michael Drosnin (Viking). Three enjoyed double-digit runs on the weekly charts: *Slander* by Ann Coulter (Crown), *A Mind at a Time* by Mel Levine (Simon & Schuster), and *The Right Words at the Right Time* by Marlo Thomas and Friends (Atria). *One Nation* by Life Magazine Editors (Little, Brown) was on our weekly list three times. *Everyday Grace* by Marianne Williamson (Riverhead) and *A Love Worth Giving* by Max Lucado (W Publishing) appeared on *PW*'s monthly religion lists several times.

The 200,000+ Tally

Just 10 years ago, selling more than 165,000 copies was enough to garner a slot among the top 30 nonfiction bestsellers; one year later, there were seven books that sold more than 200,000 and still did not make the top 30. In 2001 the record-setting number was 27; last year's tally was 23.

Three with reported sales of more than 200,000 did not make *PW*'s weekly charts. They are *Kitchen Privileges* by Mary Higgins Clark (Simon & Schuster), *Stand Up for Your Life* by Cheryl Richardson (Free Press), and *The New Sugar Busters! Cut Sugar to Trim Fat* by H. Leighton Steward et al. (Ballantine).

Most of these 200,000+ performers enjoyed runs of a month or more on *PW*'s weekly lists, and five had double-digit runs. Bernard Goldberg's *Bias*, from Regnery, turned in the strongest performance, with a 17-week run on last year's nonfiction list. The others with long tenure were *Sacred Contracts* by Caroline Myss (Harmony), *Execution* by Larry Bossidy (Crown Business), *Sandy Koufax* by Jane Leavy (HarperCollins), and *Master of the Senate* by Robert A. Caro (Knopf).

Ten books had runs of four to nine weeks: *Report from Ground Zero* by Dennis Smith (Viking), *Find Me* by Rosie O'Donnell (Warner), *Longitudes and Attitudes* by Thomas L. Friedman (FSG), *What We Saw* by CBS News with an introduction by Dan Rather (Simon & Schuster), *Sylvia Browne's Book of Dreams* by Sylvia Browne (Dutton), *You Cannot Be Serious* by John McEnroe (Putnam), *Live from New York* by Tom Shales and James Miller (Little, Brown), *Shakedown* by Ken Timmerman (Regnery), *Suzanne Somers' Fast and Easy* by Suzanne Somers (Crown), and *Knight* by Bob Knight with Bob Hammel (St. Martin's). *Wild at Heart* by John Eldredge (Thomas Nelson) was on *PW*'s monthly religion list 10 times in 2002.

Four landed just once on the weekly list. They are *The Sea Hunters II* by Clive Cussler (Putnam), *To America* by Stephen E. Ambrose (Simon & Schuster), *Hollywood Hulk Hogan* by Hulk Hogan (Pocket), and *10 Secrets for Success and Inner Peace* by Dr. Wayne W. Dyer (Hay House).

A Record 26 for 150,000+

In 2002 the tally for books with sales of 150,000 or more broke the 1999 record—26 books versus 23. In 2001 there were 18 books with sales at this level that didn't make the top 30.

Ten are no-shows on *PW*'s weekly lists. They are *What About the Big Stuff?* by Richard Carlson (Hyperion), *Anyway (The Paradoxical Commandments: Finding Personal Meaning in a Crazy World)* by Kent M. Keith and Spencer Johnson, M.D. (Putnam), *100 Years of Harley-Davidson* by Willie Davidson (Bulfinch), *Fish! Tales* by Stephen C. Lundin (Hyperion), *Now, Discover Your Strengths* by Marcus Buckingham and Donald O. Clifton (Free Press), *Dilbert and the Way of the Weasel* by Scott Adams (HarperBusiness), *Tim McGraw and the Dancehall Doctors* by Tim McGraw (Atria), *American: Beyond Our Grandest Notions* by Chris Matthews (Free Press), *Freedom: A History of US* by Joy Hakim (Oxford UP), and *George and Laura* by Christopher Andersen (Morrow).

Four books in this group were on the weekly lists for less than a month: *One Minute Millionaire* by Mark Victor Hansen (Harmony), *Above Hallowed Ground* by David Fitzpatrick (Viking Studio), *The Fat Flush Plan* by Ann Louise Gittleman (McGraw-Hill), and *Last Man Down* by FDNY Battalion Chief Richard Picciotto with Daniel Paisner (Berkley).

The rest spent a month or more on the weekly charts, or at least two months on *PW*'s religion list. This group is *Driver #8* by Dale Earnhardt, Jr., and J. Gurss (Warner), *Rich Dad's Prophecy* by Robert Kiyosaki and Sharon Lechter (Warner), *Abraham* by Bruce Feiler (Morrow), *Ten Stupid Things Couples Do to Mess Up Their Relationship* by Dr. Laura Schlessinger (HarperCollins), *The Conquerors* by Michael Beschloss (Simon & Schuster), *The Death of the West* by Patrick Buchanan (St. Martin's), *Indisputable Laws of Teamwork* by John Maxwell (Thomas Nelson), *Night Light for Parents* by James and Shirley Dobson (Multnomah), *The Road to Wealth* by Suze Orman (Riverhead), *The Wisdom of Menopause* by Christiane Northrup, M.D. (Bantam), *God's Leading Lady* by T. D. Jakes (Putnam), and *Odd Girl Out* by Rachel Simmons (Harcourt).

The 125,000+ Level

Sixteen books with sales of 125,000 and more did not make our top 30 list, four fewer than the 2001 tally. Only six made the weekly lists and only two in this group had runs of more than a month—*Satisfaction* by Kim Cattrall and Mark Levinson (Warner) was on the charts for nine weeks, one more than *The Lobster Chronicles* by Linda Greenlaw (Hyperion).

Four others spent a month or less on the weekly 2002 charts: *I May Be Wrong, but I Doubt It* by Charles Barkley (Random House), *What Went Wrong?* by Bernard Lewis (Oxford UP), *Demon in the Freezer* by Richard Preston (Random House), and *Nothing Is Impossible* by Christopher Reeve (Random House).

The 10 books that didn't make a *PW* weekly list in 2002 are *Whale Done!* edited by Ken Blanchard with Thad Lacinak, Chuck Tompkins, and Jim Ballard (Free Press), *A Man, a Can, a Plan* by David Joachim and the *Men's Health Magazine* Editors (Rodale), *Rolling with the Stones* by Bill Wyman and Richard Havers (DK), *Living Yoga* by Christy Turlington (Hyperion), *Barefoot Contessa Family Style* by Ina Garten (Clarkson Potter), *Primal Leadership* by Daniel Goleman (Harvard Business School), *Worth the Fighting For* by John McCain (Random House), *Top 10 of Everything 2003* by Russell Ash (DK), *The Lord of the Rings: The Two Towers Visual Companion* by Jude Fisher (Houghton Mifflin), and *Complete Home Bartender's Guide* by Salvatore Calabrese (Sterling).

A Record for 100,000+

In 2002 a total of 36 books reported 2002 sales of more than 100,000, just one less than the record set in 2000. In 2001 there were 28 books with sales of 100,000 or more that did not make the top 15.

About one-third (13 in all) of the titles in the 100,000+ group made one of *PW*'s weekly bestseller lists or our monthly religion charts. They are *A Song Flung Up from Heaven* by Maya Angelou (Random House), *How to Practice* by The Dalai Lama (Atria), *Breakdown* by Bill Gertz (Regnery), *Traveling Light* by Max Lucado (W Publishing), *Our Story* by the Quecreek Miners as told to Jeff

Goodell (Hyperion), *Take on the Street* by Arthur Levitt (Pantheon), *Dr. Shapiro's Picture Perfect Weight Loss 30-Day Plan* by Dr. Howard Shapiro (Rodale), *Firehouse* by David Halberstam (Hyperion), *The Universe in a Nutshell* by Stephen Hawking (Bantam), *Al Roker's Big Bad Book of Barbecue* by Al Roker (Scribner), *Small Wonder* by Barbara Kingsolver (HarperCollins), *Love, Greg & Lauren* by Greg Manning (Bantam), and *New York September 11* by Magnum Photographers (powerHouse).

The 23 no-shows are *Sex and the City: Kiss and Tell* by Amy Sohn and Melcher Media (Pocket), *From Conception to Birth* by Alexander Tsiaris (Doubleday), *The Merciful God of Prophecy* by Tim LaHaye (Warner), *My Heart's Cry* by Anne Graham Lotz (W Publishing), *Lidia's Italian-American Kitchen* by Lidia Matticchio Bastianich (Knopf, an additional 70,000 were sold in 2001), *The New Revelations* by Neale Donald Walsch (Atria), *Something Worth Leaving Behind* by Brett Beavers and Tom Douglas (Rutledge Hill), *Prescription for Herbal Healing* by Phyllis Balch (Avery), *A Family Christmas* by James Dobson (Multnomah), *I'm Just Here for the Food* by Alton Brown (Stewart, Tabori & Chang), *Secrets of the Baby Whisperer for Toddlers* by Tracy Hogg with Melinda Blau (Ballantine), *What's So Great About America* by Dinesh D'Souza (Regnery), *When I Was a Kid, This Was a Free Country* by G. Gordon Liddy (Regnery), *Happy Days with the Naked Chef* by Jamie Oliver (Hyperion), *Racing to Win* by Joe Gibbs (Multnomah), *Oh! The Things I Know!* by Al Franken (Dutton), *Mysterious Stranger* by David Blaine (Villard), *Common Sense* by Andy Rooney (Public Affairs), *Practicing the Power of Now* by Eckhart Tolle (New World Library, total with 2001 sales is about 147,000), *Jorge Cruise's 8 Minutes in the Morning* by Jorge Cruise (Rodale), *A Peanuts Christmas* by Charles M. Schulz (Ballantine), *Six Days of War* by Michael B. Oren (Oxford UP), and *Bobbi Brown Beauty Evolution* by Bobbi Brown (HarperResource).

Paperback Bestsellers: Playing the Numbers

Dermot McEvoy
Senior Editor, *Publishers Weekly*

Daisy Maryles
Executive Editor, *Publishers Weekly*

The biggest surprise in the 2002 annual trade bestsellers is that there was only one book that sold more than 1 million copies in the course of the year's 12 months. And that book wasn't a movie tie-in, a media book club pick, or written by a celebrity. The No. 1 book was *The Fix-It and Forget-It Cookbook: Feasting with Your Slow Cooker* by Dawn J. Ranck and Phyllis Pellman Good, from the Mennonite publishing house Good Books, based in Intercourse, Pa. It outsold all of the *Lord of the Rings* movie tie-ins by at least two to one. Sales of the book, published at the end of 2000, now total now more than 2.5 million; about 1.8 million sold last year. A follow-up book, *Fix-It and Forget-It Recipes for Entertaining*, was published in October of 2002; it finished the year with sales of more than 625,000 copies. Just two years earlier, there were 19 trade paperbacks with sales of one million or more. That 2000 list of winners included Oprah picks, six books from Tyndale's apocalyptic Left Behind series and three Chicken Soup titles. The Chicken Soup series had 14 books on the 2002 list, an excellent number considering the brand has been around since 1995; still, the highest sales were just over 600,000.

Publisher Merle Good (his wife is one of the books' authors and is the firm's senior editor; the coauthor is in its design department) put a lot of effort in getting the book distributed to a wide range of book and nonbook outlets without spending any advertising money in 2001. Last year Good allocated marketing money for positioning and endcaps in the stores; for Mother's Day 2003, there will be national advertising in *People* and *USA Today*. The book has enjoyed long stints on the national bestseller charts and also on the Book Sense list. Good estimates that about 50 percent of the two books' sales were through discount chains such as Sam's, Costco, and Wal-Mart. There was one offbeat sales venue. A publisher of a lot of quilting books, Good was always well represented by Checker Distributors, the largest distributor for quilt patterns and books to that specialty marketplace. Two of Good's hybrid quilt/cookbook titles—*A Quilter's Christmas Cookbook* and *Favorite Recipes for Quilters*—turned out to be good sellers for Checkers, so it took a gamble on the *Fix-It* cookbook. It was the wholesaler's bestselling book in 2002.

Back in 2001 there were seven books with annual sales of more than 1 million units; in 2000 there were 19 trade paperback with sales of more than 1 million. While annual sales in the higher ranges were down in trade paper, sales picked up in the 100,000-plus category. There were 92 trade paperbacks with annual sales over 100,000; that figure easily broke the record set just a year earlier, when 75 books sold 100,000 copies or more. Overall, the number of trade paperbacks that sell more than 100,000 copies has been heading upward. A total of 166 trade paperbacks had annual sales of more than 100,000 last year; that's twice as many as the 1995 figure of 83 books and quadruple the 39 trade paperback titles that sold more than 100,000 copies in 1980.

Trade paperback fiction bestsellers accounted for 65 of the 166 trade paperbacks that had sales over the 100,000 mark; 35 of these bestsellers were in the 200,000-copy-plus grouping.

Fiction Rules in Mass Market

No changes to report in the types of titles that made up the year's top mass market bestsellers. Only five of the books with sales of 500,000 or more were nonfiction. Reprints of hardcover bestsellers and original category (almost always romance) releases accounted for 102 fiction mass market top sellers.

In our 2002 calculations, we tracked mass market titles with sales of more than 500,000 for the first time. The decision was based on our observation that unit sales for this format have declined. Back in 1990, a total of 123 mass market titles enjoyed sales of one million or more copies; in 2002, 113 mass markets had sales of 500,000-plus, 52 of which sold more than 1 million copies.

Figuring 2002

Listed on the following pages are trade paperback and mass market titles published in 2001 and 2002; the rankings are based on 2002 sales only. To qualify, trade paperbacks had to have sold more than 100,000 copies in 2002; for mass markets, sales of more than 500,000 were required. A single asterisk (*) indicates the book was published in 2001; a double asterisk (**) means the book was published earlier but either remained or reappeared on the charts in the year 2002. Those reappearances were most often movie tie-ins. A pound symbol (#) indicates that the shipped and billed figure was rounded down to the nearest 25,000 to indicate its relationship to sales figures of other titles. The actual figures were given to *PW* in confidence for use in placing titles on these lists.

Trade Paperbacks

One Million+

**Fix-It and Forget-It Cookbook. Dawn J. Ranck and Phyllis Pellman Good. Orig. Good Books (1,806,379)

750,000+

The Two Towers. J. R. R. Tolkien. Movie tie-in. Houghton Mifflin (966,869)

The Lord of the Rings. J. R. R. Tolkien. Movie tie-in. Houghton Mifflin (871,276)

The Return of the King. J. R. R. Tolkien. Movie tie-in. Houghton Mifflin (799,123)

The Fellowship of the Ring. J. R. R. Tolkien. Movie tie-in. Houghton Mifflin (785,385)

What to Expect When You're Expecting, 3rd ed. Heidi Murkoff, Arlene Eisenberg, and Sandee Hathaway. Orig. Workman (769,416)

500,000+

***Sula.* Toni Morrison. Reissue. Plume (720,000)

Empire Falls. Richard Russo. Rep. Vintage (677,063)

**Fast Food Nation.* Eric Schlosser. Rep. Perennial (676,464)

The Last Time They Met. Anita Shreve. Rep. Little, Brown (652,315)

The Hobbit. J. R. R. Tolkien. Reissue. Houghton Mifflin (650,885)

A Common Life. Jan Karon. Rep. Penguin (650,000)

Suzanne's Diary for Nicholas. James Patterson. Rep. Warner (644,069)

**Chicken Soup for the Mother's Soul II.* Edited by Canfield & Hansen et al. Orig. HCI (631,000)

Fix-It and Forget-It Recipes for Entertaining. Phyllis Pellman Good and Dawn J. Ranck. Orig. Good Books (625,229)

Desecration: Antichrist Takes the Throne. Jerry B. Jenkins and Tim LaHaye. Tyndale (604,240)

White Oleander. Janet Fitch. Movie tie-in. Little, Brown (592,895)

Dangerous. Nora Roberts. Reissue. Harlequin (580,000)

***The Power of a Praying Wife.* Stormie Omartian. Rep. Harvest House (565,818)

**A Beautiful Mind.* Sylvia Nasar. Rep. Touchstone (554,600)

Good in Bed. Jennifer Weiner. Rep. Pocket (509,703)

John Adams. David McCullough. Rep. Touchstone (509,200)

***The Four Agreements.* Don Miguel Ruiz. Orig. Amber-Allen (506,867)

300,000+

Cordina's Royal Family. Nora Roberts. Reissue. Harlequin (495,000)

Seabiscuit. Laura Hillenbrand. Rep. Ballantine (491,672)

**Chicken Soup for the Father's Soul.* Edited by Canfield & Hansen et al. Orig. HCI (483,299)

Founding Brothers. Joseph J. Ellis. Rep. Vintage (453,409)

The Corrections. Jonathan Franzen. Rep. Picador USA (447,776)

***The Red Tent.* Anita Diamant. Rep. Picador USA (438,379)

Dr. Atkins' New Diet Revolution. Robert C. Atkins. Rep. Quill (435,657)

Bel Canto. Ann Patchett. Rep. Perennial (432,774)

**Chicken Soup for the Nurse's Soul.* Edited by Canfield & Hansen et al. Orig. HCI (420,726)

The Worst-Case Scenario Survival Handbook: Golf. David Borgenicht and Josh Piven. Orig. Chronicle (413,070)

Chicken Soup for the Soul of America. Edited by Canfield & Hansen et al. Orig. HCI (410,003)

Chicken Soup for the Teacher's Soul. Edited by Canfield & Hansen et al. Orig. HCI (389,516)

#*Tuesdays with Morrie.* Mitch Albom. Rep. Broadway (375,000)

The Worst-Case Scenario Survival Handbook: Holidays. David Borgenicht, Josh Piven and Jennifer Worick. Orig. Chronicle (356,587)

Nickel and Dimed. Barbara Ehrenreich. Rep. Holt (350,000)

**The Power of a Praying Husband.* Stormie Omartian. Orig. Harvest House (345,964)

**The Wrinkle Cure.* Nicholas Perricone, M.D. Rep. Warner (343,689)

Retire Young, Retire Rich. Robert T. Kiyosaki and Sharon L. Lechter. Orig. Warner (340,549)

Ghost Soldiers. Hampton Sides. Rep. Anchor (333,650)

Chicken Soup for the Sister's Soul. Edited by Canfield & Hansen et al. Orig. HCI (322,238)

Peace Like a River. Leif Enger. Rep. Grove (318,712)

Back When We Were Grownups. Anne Tyler. Rep. Ballantine (305,413)

About a Boy. Nick Hornby. Movie tie-in. Riverhead (303,129)

**It's Not About the Bike.* Lance Armstrong. Rep. Berkley (300,755)

200,000+

***The Power of a Praying Parent.* Stormie Omartian. Rep. Harvest House (293,903)

**Chicken Soup for the Gardener's Soul.* Edited by Canfield & Hansen et al. Orig. HCI (281,243)

Lucky. Alice Sebold. Rep. Little, Brown (276,069)

#*Shopaholic Takes Manhattan.* Sophie Kinsella. Orig. Dell (275,000)

The Grapes of Wrath. John Steinbeck. Reissue. Penguin (275,000)

How to Be Good. Nick Hornby. Riverhead (271,443)

Robert Ludlum's The Paris Option. Robert Ludlum and Gayle Lynds. Orig. St. Martin's (267,320)

The Hours. Michael Cunningham. Movie tie-in. Picador USA (260,521)

Chicken Soup for the Veteran's Soul. Edited by Canfield & Hansen et al. Orig. HCI (258,228)

#**Confessions of a Shopaholic.* Sophie Kinsella. Orig. Dell (255,000)

**The Courage to Be Rich.* Suze Orman. Rep. Riverhead (252,782)

Chicken Soup for the Grandparent's Soul. Edited by Canfield & Hansen et al. Orig. HCI (251,396)

The Darwin Awards. Wendy Northcutt. Rep. Plume (250,000)

Cane River. Lalita Tademy. Rep. Warner (239,534)

**Girl with a Pearl Earring.* Tracy Chevalier. Rep. Plume (230,000)

Theodore Rex. Edmund Morris. Rep. Modern Library (227,134)

Heartsongs. Mattie J. T. Stepanek. Rep. Hyperion (224,722)

Officially Osbourne. The Osbournes with Todd Gold. Orig. Pocket (220,545)

#*Catch Me if You Can.* Frank W. Abagnale with Stan Redding. Movie tie-in. Broadway (219,000)

The Beatles Anthology. The Beatles. Rep. Chronicle (215,361)

Chicken Soup for the Baseball Lover's Soul. Edited by Canfield & Hansen et al. Orig. HCI (215,145)

Balzac and the Little Chinese Seamstress. Dai Sijie. Rep. Anchor (212,915)

Honest Illusions. Nora Roberts. Reissue. Berkley (211,109)

Falling Angels. Tracy Chevalier. Rep. Plume (210,000)

#*A Girl Named Zippy*. Haven Kimmel. Orig. Broadway (202,000)

**Me Talk Pretty One Day*. David Sedaris. Rep. Little, Brown (201,538)

The Amazing Adventures of Kavalier and Clay. Michael Chabon. Rep. Picador USA (201,111)

150,000+

***The Case for Christ*. Lee Strobel. Orig. Zondervan (192,011)

**1001 PlayThinks*. Ivan Moscovich. Orig. Workman (187,659)

Portrait in Sepia. Isabelle Allende. Rep. Perennial (183,550)

Napalm and Silly Putty. George Carlin. Rep. Hyperion (181,457)

Raising Fences. Michael Datcher. Rep. Riverhead (180,212)

**We Were the Mulvaneys*. Joyce Carol Oates. Rep. Plume (180,000)

*How to Grill. Steven Raichlen. Orig. (177,222)

Crossing Over. John Edwards. Orig. Princess House (177,194)

The Fourth Hand. John Irving. Rep. Ballantine (176,576)

Chicken Soup for the Golfer's Soul 2. Edited by Canfield & Hansen et al. Orig. HCI (176,273)

*Help Yourself. Dave Pelzer. Rep. Plume (175,000)

My Dream of You. Nuala O'Faolain. Rep. Riverhead (172,113)

Year of Wonders. Geraldine Brooks. Rep. Penguin (170,000)

Black Hawk Down. Mark Bowden. Movie tie-in. Penguin (170,000)

Secrets of the Baby Whisperer. Tracy Hogg with Melinda Blau. Rep. Ballantine (167,629)

The Tipping Point. Malcolm Gladwell. Rep. Little, Brown (164,735)

Wild Blue. Stephen Ambrose. Rep. Touchstone (163,300)

Chicken Soup for the Christian Woman's Soul. Edited by Canfield & Hansen et al. Orig. HCI (161,655)

The Simpsons Beyond Forever. Matt Groening. Orig. Perennial (160,509)

**Left Behind. Jerry B. Jenkins and Tim LaHaye. Rep. Tyndale (160,420)

Killing Pablo. Mark Bowden. Rep. Penguin (160,000)

#*The O'Reilly Factor*. Bill O'Reilly. Rep. Broadway (160,000)

Top Secret Recipes. Todd Wilbur. Orig. Plume (160,000)

5 Quarters of the Orange. Joanne Harris. Rep. Perennial (158,868)

The Worst-Case Scenario Survival Handbook: Dating and Sex. David Borgenicht, Josh Piven and Jennifer Worick. Orig. Chronicle (158,021)

#*The Fiery Cross*. Diana Gabaldon. Rep. Dell (155,000)

**Relationship Rescue*. Dr. Phil McGraw. Rep. Hyperion (154,212)

The Weight of Water. Anita Shreve. Movie tie-in. Little, Brown (150,884)

100,000+

**Trust and Tragedy: Encountering God in Times of Crisis*. Tommy Tenney. Orig. Thomas Nelson (149,355)

*Drowning Ruth. Christina Schwartz. Rep. Ballantine (148,542)

The Rescue. Lori Wick. Rep. Harvest House (148,224)

Suze Orman's Financial Guidebook. Suze Orman. Rep. Three Rivers (147,961)

Big Cherry Holler. Adriana Trigiani. Rep. Ballantine (147,639)

For Better, for Worse. Carole Matthews. Orig. Avon (147,551)

The First American. H. W. Brands. Rep. Anchor (146,670)

**9-11*. Noam Chomsky. Orig. Seven Stories (145,000)

Tony Hawk. Tony Hawk. Rep. ReganBooks (144,394)

Even More Top Secret Recipes. Todd Wilbur. Orig. Plume (140,000)

**Windows XP for Dummies*. Andy Rathbone. Orig. Wiley (138,261)

The World Below. Sue Miller. Rep. Ballantine (137,972)

Good Harbor. Anita Diamant. Rep. Scribner Fiction (134,900)

Dare to Repair. Julie Sussman and Stephanie Glakas-Tenet. Orig. HarperResource (133,680)

The Lord of the Rings: The Making of the Movie Trilogy. Brian Sibley. Orig. Houghton Mifflin (132,291)

The Queen of Clean Conquers Clutter. Linda Cobb. Orig. Pocket (130,383)

Chicken Soup for the Traveler's Soul. Edited by Canfield & Hansen et al. Orig. HCI (129,938)

*Chicken Soup for the Jewish Soul. Edited by Canfield & Hansen et al. Orig. HCI (129,466)

Total Yu-Gi-Oh. Orig. Triumph (129,300)

Choke. Chuck Palahniuk. Rep. Anchor (129,082)

#Mr. Maybe. Jane Green. Rep. Broadway (127,000)

The Spongebob Squarepants Survival Guide. David Lewman. Orig. Pocket (126,325)

Blue Diary. Alice Hoffman. Rep. Berkley (125,646)

The Authorized Osbournes: TV's Favorite Outrageous Family. Orig. Triumph (125,500)

French Lessons. Peter Mayle. Rep. Vintage (125,239)

Churchill. Roy Jenkins. Rep. Plume (125,000)

*Cup of Comfort. Colleen Sell. Orig. Adams Media (123,965)

Prozac Nation. Elizabeth Wurtzel. Movie tie-in. Riverhead (123,025)

*Big Stone Gap. Adrianna Trigiani. Rep. Ballantine (122,510)

The Best American Short Stories 2002. Edited by Sue Miller. Orig. Houghton Mifflin (121,950)

*Real Estate Riches. Dolf Deroos. Orig. Warner (121,809)

Possession. A. S. Byatt. Movie tie-in. Vintage (121,325)

High Maintenance. Jennifer Belle. Rep. Riverhead (120,073)

Patches of Godlight. Jan Karon. Rep. Penguin (120,000)

Betty Crocker's Ultimate Cake Mix Cookbook. Betty Crocker editors. Orig. Wiley (119,593)

The Sex Chronicles. Zane. Orig. Pocket (119,564)

Botany of Desire: A Plant's-Eye View of the World. Michael Pollan. Rep. Random (118,385)

*A Heartbreaking Work of Staggering Genius. Dave Eggers. Rep. Vintage (117,765)

When Character Was King. Peggy Noonan. Rep. Penguin (115,000)

Lake Wobegon Summer 1956. Garrison Keillor. Rep. Penguin (115,000)

War Letters. Andrew Carroll. Rep. Pocket (114,738)

Walking the Bible. Bruce Feiler. Rep. Perennial (113,366)

The Onion Ad Nauseam. Onion editors. Rep. Three Rivers (112,534)

Chicken Soup for the Volunteer's Soul. Edited by Canfield & Hansen et al. Orig. HCI (112,432)

Get Clark Smart. Clark Howard and Mark Meltzer. Orig. Hyperion (112,281)

*Icy Sparks. Gwyn Rubio. Rep. Penguin (112,000)

Any Way the Wind Blows. E. Lynn Harris. Rep. Anchor (110,856)

*Bridget Jones: The Edge of Reason. Helen Fielding. Rep. Penguin (110,000)

#Diary of a Mad Bride. Laura Wolf. Rep. Dell (110,000)

*Death of Vishnu. Manil Suri. Rep. Perennial (109,255)

Boundaries. Henry Cloud and John Townsend. Orig. Zondervan (108,857)

*The Silmarillion. J. R. R. Tolkien. Reissue. Houghton Mifflin (106,858)

Justice. Dominick Dunne. Rep. Three Rivers (106,804)

Suze Orman's Protection Portfolio. Suze Orman. Orig. Hay House (105,859)

Betty Crocker's Cooky Book. Betty Crocker editors. Orig. Wiley (105,131)

Yoga: The Poetry of the Body. Rodney Yee with Nina Zolotow. Orig. St. Martin's (104,443)

Ten Stupid Things Couples Do to Mess Up Their Relationships. Dr. Laura Schlessinger. Rep. Quill (104,409)

April 1865. Jay Winik. Rep. Perennial (104,177)

From Beirut to Jerusalem. Thomas L. Friedman. Rep. Anchor (104,029)

*Prayers. Don Miguel Ruiz. Orig. Amber-Allen (104,013)

Hang 10. Detroit Free Press. Orig. Triumph (104,000)

*Rise of Theodore Roosevelt. Edmund Morris. Rep. Modern Library (103,762)

The Magical Worlds of Harry Potter. David Colbert. Rep. Berkley (102,103)

#*Smart Couples Finish Rich.* David Bach. Rep. Broadway (102,000)

Almanacs, Atlases, and Annuals

The World Almanac and Book of Facts 2003. Edited by Ken Park. Annual. World Almanac (993,647)

#*Guinness World Records 2002* edited by Antonia Cunningham. Revised. Bantam (510,000)

The World Almanac and Book of Facts 2002. Edited by Ken Park. Annual. World Almanac (262,773)

J. K. Lasser's Your Income Tax 2003. J. K. Lasser. Orig. Wiley (170,584)

The Ernst & Young Tax Guide 2003. Ernst & Young. Orig. Wiley (153,528)

AAA North American Road Atlas. Annual. AAA (131,342)

The World Almanac for Kids 2003. Edited by Kevin Seabrooke. Annual. World Almanac (121,704)

What Color Is Your Parachute 2003. Richard Nelson Bolles. Orig. Ten Speed (108,941)

Mass Market Paperbacks

Two Million+

#*The Summons.* John Grisham. Rep. Dell (3,965,000)

The Lord of the Rings: The Two Towers. J. R. R. Tolkien. Movie tie-in. Del Rey (2,828,087)

Face the Fire. Nora Roberts. Orig. Jove (2,700,269)

The Villa. Nora Roberts. Rep. Jove (2,204,755)

Midnight Bayou. Nora Roberts. Rep. Jove (2,034,602)

One Million+

On the Street Where You Live. Mary Higgins Clark. Rep. Pocket (1,796,342)

The Lord of the Rings: The Fellowship of the Ring. J. R. R. Tolkien. Movie tie-in. Del Rey (1,718,720)

The Hobbit. J. R. R. Tolkien. Movie tie-in. Del Rey (1,710,430)

1st to Die. James Patterson. Warner (1,710,323)

#*The Kiss.* Danielle Steel. Rep. Dell (1,610,000)

Violets Are Blue. James Patterson. Warner (1,605,733)

Isle of Dogs. Patricia Cornwell. Rep. Berkley (1,601,026)

Table for Two. Nora Roberts. Reissue. Harlequin (1,600,000)

The Lord of the Rings: The Return of the King. J. R. R. Tolkien. Movie tie-in. Del Rey (1,584,587)

The Black House. Stephen King and Peter Straub. Rep. Ballantine (1,555,038)

#*One Door Away from Heaven.* Dean Koontz. Rep. Bantam (1,535,000)

Chosen Prey. John Sandford. Rep. Berkley (1,500,936)

The Sum of All Fears. Tom Clancy. Movie tie-in. Berkley (1,404,592)

Summer Pleasures. Nora Roberts. Reissue. Harlequin (1,400,000)

#*Red Dragon.* Thomas Harris. Movie tie-in. Dell (1,375,000)

Valhalla Rising. Clive Cussler. Rep. Berkley (1,300,541)

#*A Painted House.* John Grisham. Rep. Dell (1,280,000)

Flesh and Blood. Jonathan Kellerman. Rep. Ballantine (1,258,152)

P Is for Peril. Sue Grafton. Rep. Ballantine (1,257,092)

Tom Clancy's Power Plays #6: Cutting Edge. Created by Tom Clancy and Martin Greenberg, written by Jerome Preisler. Orig. Berkley (1,240,000)

Purity in Death. J. D. Robb. Rep. Berkley (1,205,427)

The Scarlet Feather. Maeve Binchy. Rep. Signet (1,201,307)

Jackdaws. Ken Follett. Rep. Signet (1,200,037)

Hemlock Bay. Catherine Coulter. Rep. Jove (1,200,028)

The Summerhouse. Jude Deveraux. Rep. Pocket (1,155,400)

#*Lone Eagle.* Danielle Steel. Rep. Dell (1,150,000)

Last Man Standing. David Baldacci. Warner (1,122,525)

A Bend in the Road. Nicholas Sparks. Warner (1,116,110)

The Woman Next Door. Barbara Delinsky. Rep. Pocket (1,114,785)

The Divine Secrets of the Ya-Ya Sisterhood. Rebecca Wells. Orig. Avon (1,103,497)

The Jury. Steve Martini. Rep. Jove (1,102,725)

Reunion in Death. J. D. Robb. Orig. Berkley (1,101,122)

Tom Clancy's Op-Center IX: Men of Honor. Created by Tom Clancy and Steve Pieczenik, written by Jeff Rovin. Orig. Berkley (1,100,619)

*Pendragon. Catherine Coulter. Orig. Jove (1,100,161)

#Brazen Virtue. Nora Roberts. Reissue. Bantam (1,100,000)

The Bonesetter's Daughter. Amy Tan. Rep. Ballantine (1,093,711)

He Sees You When You're Sleeping. Mary and Carol Higgins Clark. Rep. Pocket (1,072,711)

#Final Target. Iris Johansen. Rep. Bantam (1,060,000)

#Leap of Faith. Danielle Steel. Rep. Dell (1,050,000)

The Sigma Protocol. Robert Ludlum. Rep. St. Martin's (1,049,603)

#Dust to Dust. Tami Hoag. Rep. Bantam (1,025,000)

Mercy. Julie Garwood. Rep. Pocket (1,002,704)

Shock. Robin Cook. Rep. Berkley (1,001,903)

The Penwyth Curse. Catherine Coulter. Orig. Jove (1,000,893)

750,000+

Forever. Jude Deveraux. Rep. Pocket (990,470)

*Dr. Atkins' New Diet Revolution. Robert C. Atkins. Rep. Avon (963,699)

Envy. Sandra Brown. Warner (958,781)

#Reap the Wind. Iris Johansen. Rep. Bantam (920,000)

The Manhattan Hunt Club. John Saul. Rep. Ballantine (913,735)

#The Smoke Jumper. Nicholas Evans. Rep. Dell (905,000)

Summer in Eclipse Bay. Jayne Ann Krentz. Orig. Jove (901,816)

Black Hawk Down. Mark Bowden. Movie tie-in. Signet (900,474)

Fall on Your Knees. Ann Marie MacDonald. Rep. Scribner Fiction (878,900)

Phantoms. Dean Koontz. Reissue. Berkley (875,580)

The Door to December. Dean Koontz. Reissue. Signet (875,183)

Willow. V. C. Andrews. Orig. Pocket (824,505)

Smoke in Mirrors. Jayne Ann Krentz. Rep. Jove (800,906)

Wicked Forest. V. C. Andrews. Orig. Pocket (796,449)

No Place Like Home. Fern Michaels. Orig. Pocket (796,350)

Every Breath You Take. Ann Rule. Rep. Pocket (786,490)

Millionaires. Brad Meltzer. Warner (780,687)

#The Pill Book, 10th Edition. Harold M. Silverman. Revised. Bantam (760,000)

Twisted Roots. V. C. Andrews. Orig. Pocket (758,119)

The Hearing. John Lescroart. Rep. Signet (751,345)

Cold Paradise. Stuart Woods. Rep. Signet (750,949)

500,000+

BradyGames Grand Theft Auto. Tim Bogenn. Orig. BradyGames (936,014)

Full House. Janet Evanovich and Charlotte Hughes. Orig. St. Martin's (821,316)

#Three Weeks in Paris. Barbara Taylor Bradford. Rep. Dell (740,000)

Dead Sleep. Greg Iles. Rep. Signet (726,963)

Edge of Danger. Jack Higgins. Rep. Berkley (726,100)

Open Season. Linda Howard. Rep. Pocket (721,534)

Hollywood Wives: The New Generation. Jackie Collins. Rep. Pocket (704,159)

Separation of Power. Vince Flynn. Rep. Pocket (701,296)

4 Blondes. Candace Bushnell. Rep. Signet (700,579)

Blue Nowhere. Jeffrey Deaver. Rep. Pocket (696,408)

#Once a Thief. Kay Hooper. Orig. Bantam (670,000)

Angels Everywhere. Debbie Macomber. Orig. Avon (669,234)

The Surgeon. Tess Gerritsen. Rep. Ballantine (669,225)

Speaking in Tongues. Jeffery Deaver. Rep. Pocket (660,967)

Strangers. Dean Koontz. Reissue. Berkley (650,453)

Seven Up. Janet Evanovich. Rep. St. Martin's (647,320)

#The Next Accident. Lisa Gardner. Rep. Bantam (645,000)

#*Whisper of Evil.* Kay Hooper. Orig. Bantam (620,000)

A Day Late and a Dollar Short. Terry McMillan. Rep. Signet (610,487)

Blood and Gold. Anne Rice. Rep. Ballantine (576,647)

Special Ops: A Brotherhood of War Novel. W. E. B. Griffin. Rep. Jove (576,575)

#*Looking Back.* Belva Plain. Rep. Dell (570,000)

#*True Blue.* Luanne Rice. Orig. Bantam (570,000)

#*Tell No One.* Harlan Coben. Rep. Dell (560,000)

Warrior Class. Dale Brown. Orig. Berkley (553,441)

The Cat Who Smelled a Rat. Lilian Jackson Braun. Rep. Jove (553,226)

Submarine. Tom Clancy. Reissue. Berkley (552,181)

Orchid Blues. Stuart Woods. Rep. Signet (550,255)

#*Summer Light.* Luanne Rice. Rep. Bantam (540,000)

#*Writ of Execution.* Perri O'Shaughnessy. Rep. Dell (530,000)

#*Thursday's Child.* Sandra Brown. Rep. Bantam (530,000)

Family. Mario Puzo. Rep. Avon (528,969)

Under Fire: A Corps Novel. W. E. B. Griffin. Rep. Jove (525,560)

Trust Fund. Stephen Frey. Rep. Ballantine (525,100)

Fatal Voyage. Kathy Reichs. Rep. Pocket (512,533)

Gangster. Lorenzo Carcaterra. Rep. Ballantine (511,681)

Rise to Rebellion. Jeff Shaara. Rep. Ballantine (510,097)

#*Dream Country.* Luanne Rice. Rep. Bantam (510,000)

Forgotten. Faye Kellerman. Rep. Avon (508,355)

Once Upon a Kiss. Nora Roberts. Orig. Jove (505,927)

Spider-Man. Peter David. Orig. Movie tie-in. Del Rey (505,021)

America. Stephen Coonts. Rep. St. Martin's (503,254)

Robert Ludlum's The Cassandra Compact. Robert Ludlum and Phillip Shelby. Rep. St. Martin's (502,460)

Children's Bestsellers: Big Names Top the Charts

Diane Roback

Senior Editor, Children's Books, *Publishers Weekly*

The numbers picked up a bit in 2002 from a slower 2001. Lemony Snicket's A Series of Unfortunate Events continued to entice millions of new readers, as did a certain bespectacled boy wizard; the lack of a new Harry Potter book didn't seem to hurt sales of the previous titles.

In hardcover fiction, new installments in established, bestselling series were the standouts, specifically: two Lemony Snicket titles; a new book in the If You Give a Mouse series by Laura Numeroff, illustrated by Felicia Bond; two Junie B. Jones books; a Fudge title by Judy Blume; plus new titles by such "brand names" as Jamie Lee Curtis and Jan Brett (not to mention a picture book by Vice-President Cheney's wife).

Sales in this category were brisker than the previous year; 21 titles sold more than 200,000 copies last year, compared with 15 in 2001, and there were 103 books (with sales of more than 75,000 copies) on this list, compared to 88 titles in 2001.

In hardcover backlist, Lemony Snicket, Harry Potter, and Dr. Seuss were the reigning champs. Four Series of Unfortunate Events titles were in the top 10, along with three Dr. Seuss stalwarts and *Harry Potter and the Goblet of Fire*. All told, eight Lemony Snicket titles made the backlist rankings (all nine in the series, plus the *Unauthorized Biography*, sold more than 3.3 million copies combined in 2002).

Two Harry Potter paperbacks were frontlist last year, and took No. 1 and No. 2 in their category, selling a combined 4 million copies (in all, the series sold more than 9.5 million in 2002, excluding boxed sets).

Clocking in at the half-million mark in paperback frontlist was a Chicken Soup for the Teenage Soul title, a Captain Underpants spinoff and the newest Magic Tree House entry. In all, there were 152 titles on the paperback frontlist charts last year, compared to 90 in 2001 (an increase of 69 percent).

However, paperback backlist experienced a bit of a slide, with 129 titles on the list in 2002, compared to 157 in 2001. The books at the top of this list don't change all that much from year to year: Harry Potter titles, *The Outsiders*, *Holes*, *Love You Forever*, *Number the Stars*. There's a slight sag in Captain Underpants, however: in 2001 the series nabbed four of the top 15 paperback backlist slots, compared to just one in 2002. But Junie B. Jones's backlist numbers continue to grow, an indication that strong frontlist sales (in hardcover and paperback) are giving a boost to the series's older titles as well.

Some sales figures were supplied to *Publishers Weekly* in confidence, for ranking purposes only.

Hardcover Frontlist

300,000+

1. *The Carnivorous Carnival (A Series of Unfortunate Events #9)*. Lemony Snicket, illus. by Brett Helquist. HarperCollins (726,543)
2. *If You Take a Mouse to School*. Laura Numeroff, illus. by Felicia Bond. HarperCollins/Geringer (526,008)
3. *America: A Patriotic Primer*. Lynne Cheney, illus. by Robin Preiss Glasser. Simon & Schuster (408,403)
4. *Double Fudge*. Judy Blume. Dutton (310,884)
5. *I'm Gonna Like Me: Letting Off a Little Self-Esteem*. Jamie Lee Curtis, illus. by Laura Cornell. HarperCollins/Cotler (310,246)
6. *Lemony Snicket: The Unauthorized Autobiography (A Series of Unfortunate Events)*. Lemony Snicket, illus. by Brett Helquist. HarperCollins (302,176)

200,000+

7. *Junie B., First Grader: Boss of Lunch*. Barbara Park, illus. by Denise Brunkus. Random (298,257)
8. *Scholastic Children's Dictionary (revised edition)*. Scholastic Reference (297,000)
9. *Who's That Knocking on Christmas Eve?* Jan Brett. Putnam (284,743)
10. *Junie B., First Grader: Toothless Wonder*. Barbara Park, illus. by Denise Brunkus. Random (284,444)

11. *Who Moved My Cheese? For Teens.* Spencer Johnson. Putnam (265,076)

12. *Artemis Fowl: The Arctic Incident.* Eoin Colfer. Hyperion/Miramax (258,602)

13. *The Night Before Christmas.* Clement C. Moore, illus. by Mary Engelbreit. HarperCollins (255,269)

14. *HarperCollins Treasury of Picture Book Classics.* HarperCollins (254,292)

15. *Let's Count (Bob the Builder).* Kelli Chipponeri, illus. by Vince Giarrano. Simon Spotlight (234,107)

16. *Spider-Man: The Ultimate Guide.* Tom DeFalco. DK (225,391)

17. *Emeril's There's a Chef in My Soup.* Emeril Lagasse, illus. by Charles Yuen. HarperCollins (212,398)

18. *Princess in Love (The Princess Diaries #3).* Meg Cabot. HarperCollins (208,163)

19. *God Made You Special.* Eric Metaxas. Zonderkidz/Big Idea (207,914)

20. *Disney's Lilo & Stitch: Read-Aloud Story Book.* Random/Disney (206,359).

21. *The Night Before Christmas.* Clement C. Moore, illus. by Robert Sabuda. Little Simon (201,010)

100,000+

22. *Bob's Busy Saw (Bob the Builder).* Kiki Thorpe, illus. by Barry Goldberg. Simon Spotlight (198,803)

23. *Neighborhood Animals (Baby Einstein).* Julie Aigner-Clark, illus. by Nadeem Zaidi. Hyperion (194,423)

24. *The McGraw-Hill Children's Dictionary.* McGraw-Hill (185,000)

25. *Bob's Busy Hammer (Bob the Builder).* Kiki Thorpe, illus. by Barry Goldberg. Simon Spotlight (181,029)

26. *Star Wars Attack of the Clones: The Visual Dictionary.* David West Reynolds. DK (172,150)

27. *Disney's Storybook Collection Volume 2.* Disney (169,995)

28. *Chicken Soup for the Soul Christmas Treasury for Kids.* Jack Canfield et al. HCI (168,826)

29. *The Thief Lord.* Cornelia Funke. Scholastic/Chicken House (167,000)

30. *Triss.* Brian Jacques. Philomel (164,936)

31. *Disney's Princess Music Box.* Disney (162,287)

32. *Let's Find Opposites (Bob the Builder).* Jenny Miglis, illus. by Vince Giarrano. Simon Spotlight (160,385)

33. *Hoot.* Carl Hiaasen. Knopf (157,537)

34. *Walt Disney's Classic Storybook.* Disney (153,978)

35. *Summerland.* Michael Chabon. Hyperion/Miramax (152,889)

36. *Disney Princess: A Read-Aloud Storybook.* Random/Disney (150,115)

37. *Abarat.* Clive Barker. HarperCollins/ Cotler (149,244)

38. *Giggle, Giggle, Quack.* Doreen Cronin, illus. by Betsy Lewin. Simon & Schuster (148,444)

39. *Thomas' Magnetic Play Book.* Illus. by Ted Gadecki. Random (147,219)

40. *Zathura.* Chris Van Allsburg. Houghton Mifflin (143,786)

41. *Mirror Me! (Baby Einstein).* Julie Aigner-Clark, illus. by Nadeem Zaidi. Hyperion (142,679)

42. *Olivia Counts.* Ian Falconer. Atheneum/Schwartz (142,186)

43. *Christmas in Camelot (Magic Tree House).* Mary Pope Osborne, illus. by Sal Murdocca. Random (136,127)

44. *Bob's Toolbox Mix-Up (Bob the Builder).* Kiki Thorpe, illus. by Cheryl Mendenhall. Simon Spotlight (135,607)

45. *Shel Silverstein: Poems and Drawings.* Shel Silverstein. HarperCollins (134,187)

46. *Junie B., First Grader (At Last!).* Barbara Park, illus. by Denise Brunkus. Random (130,992)

47. *Dora's Color Adventure (Dora the Explorer).* Phoebe Beinstein, illus. by Susan Hall. Simon Spotlight (127,137)

48. *The Water Hole.* Graeme Base. Abrams (127,072)

49. *Count with Dora! (Dora the Explorer).* Phoebe Beinstein, illus. by the Thompson Bros. Simon Spotlight (127,005)

50. *Olivia's Opposites.* Ian Falconer. Atheneum/Schwartz (126,764)

51. *All-American Girl.* Meg Cabot. HarperCollins (126,571)

52. *Daisy Comes Home.* Jan Brett. Putnam (123,186)

53. *Philadelphia Chickens.* Sandra Boynton. Workman (120,071)

54. *Eloise Takes a Bawth.* Kay Thompson with Mart Crowley, illus. by Hilary Knight. Simon & Schuster (119,318)

55. *Disney's Treasure Planet: Read-Aloud Storybook.* Random/Disney (118,261)

56. *Disney's Princess Treasury.* Disney (118,078)

57. *Disney's 5-Minute Princess Stories.* Disney (115,011)

58. *David Gets in Trouble.* David Shannon. Scholastic/Blue Sky (114,000)

59. *See and Spy Shapes (Baby Einstein).* Julie Aigner-Clark, illus. by Nadeem Zaidi. Hyperion (113,006)

60. *Bard's Rhyme Time (Baby Einstein).* Julie Aigner-Clark, illus. by Nadeem Zaidi. Hyperion (112,761)

61. *A Crack in the Track (Thomas the Tank Engine).* Jane Gerver, illus. by Tommy Stubbs. Random (109,161)

62. *Dora's Backpack Book (Dora the Explorer).* Simon Spotlight (108,745)

63. *Time Stops for No Mouse.* Michael Hoeye. Putnam (107,738)

64. *Draw with Jonah and Friends.* Cindy Kenney. Zonderkidz/Big Idea (106,958)

65. *"Slowly, Slowly, Slowly," Said the Sloth.* Eric Carle. Philomel (102,300)

66. *Barbie: The Nutcracker.* Random/Little Golden (102,074)

67. *My First Jumbo Book of Colors.* James Diaz and Melanie Gerth. Scholastic/Cartwheel (102,000)

68. *Elmo Loves You.* Sarah Albee, illus. by Maggie Swanson. Random/Sesame Workshop (101,880)

69. *Clifford's Christmas Presents.* Sonali Fry, illus. by John Kurtz. Scholastic/Cartwheel (101,000)

70. *Seven Little Postmen.* Margaret Wise Brown and Edith Thacher Hurd, illus. by Tibor Gergely. Random/Little Golden (100,314)

71. *Can You See What I See?* Walter Wick. Scholastic/Cartwheel (100,000)

75,000+

72. *Coraline.* Neil Gaiman. HarperCollins (98,795)

73. *Disney's Americana Storybook Collection.* Disney (97,583)

74. *The Veritas Project 2: Nightmare Academy.* Frank Peretti. Tommy Nelson (96,294)

75. *Halloween.* Jerry Seinfeld, illus. by James Bennett. Little, Brown (95,954)

76. *Barbie: Cinderella.* Random/Little Golden (94,616)

77. *Jane's Animal Expedition (Baby Einstein).* Julie Aigner-Clark, illus. by Nadeem Zaidi. Hyperion (93,666)

78. *Dora's Rainbow Surprise (Dora the Explorer).* Christine Ricci, illus. by Susan Hall. Simon Spotlight (93,297)

79. *Even Fish Slappers Need a Second Chance.* Eric Metaxas. Zonderkidz/Big Idea (93,274)

80. *Disney's Christmas Music Box.* Disney (92,953)

81. *Meet My Friends (SpongeBob SquarePants).* Tricia Boczkowski. Simon Spotlight (91,255)

82. *Corduroy's Merry Christmas.* Created by Don Freeman, illus. by Lisa McCue. Viking (87,918)

83. *Secrets of the Vine for Little Ones.* Bruce Wilkinson and Melody Carlson, illus. by Alexi Natchev. Tommy Nelson (87,208)

84. *Bob's Big Story Collection (Bob the Builder).* Simon Spotlight (83,531)

85. *See & Spy Counting (Baby Einstein).* Julie Aigner-Clark, illus. by Nadeem Zaidi. Hyperion (83,231)

86. *The Poky Little Puppy's First Christmas.* Justine Korman, illus. by Jean Chandler. Random/Little Golden (82,974)

87. *Babar's Yoga for Elephants.* Laurent de Brunhoff. Abrams (82,068)

88. *Merry Christmas, Big Hungry Bear!* Audrey and Don Wood, illus. by Don Wood. Scholastic/Blue Sky (82,000)

89. *Dora's Opposites/Opuestos de Dora (Dora the Explorer).* Phoebe Beinstein, illus. by Robert Roper. Simon Spotlight (81,764)

90. *A Present for Santa (Dora the Explorer).* Chris Gifford, illus. by Jason Fruchter. Simon Spotlight (81,687)

91. *Babies (Baby Einstein).* Julie Aigner-Clark, illus. by Nadeem Zaidi. Hyperion (80,821)

92. *Dogs (Baby Einstein).* Julie Aigner-Clark, illus. by Nadeem Zaidi. Hyperion (80,266)

93. *Knocked Out by My Nunga-Nungas.* Louise Rennison. HarperCollins (80,250)

94. *If Only I Had a Green Nose.* Max Lucado, illus. by Sergio Martinez. Crossway (79,721)

95. *Put Me in the Zoo (board book).* Robert Lopshire. Random (79,229)

96. *Martin's Big Words: The Life of Dr. Martin Luther King, Jr.* Doreen Rappaport, illus. by Bryan Collier. Hyperion/Jump at the Sun (78,523)

97. *Boots's Backpack Book (Dora the Explorer).* Simon Spotlight (78,149)

98. *The Grinch Pops Up!* Dr. Seuss. Random (77,947)

99. *Jonah and the Pirates Who (Usually) Don't Do Anything.* Eric Metaxas and Cindy Kenney. Zonderkidz/Big Idea (77,547)

100. *Auntie Claus and the Key to Christmas.* Elise Primavera. Harcourt/Silver Whistle (77,447)

101. *Monsters to Go.* Random/Disney (76,204)

102. *Kit's Home Run.* Valerie Tripp, illus. by Walter Rane. American Girls (75,903)

103. *Puzzling Shapes (Baby Einstein).* Julie Aigner-Clark, illus. by Nadeem Zaidi. Hyperion (75,418)

Hardcover Backlist

500,000+

1. *The Bad Beginning (A Series of Unfortunate Events #1).* Lemony Snicket, illus. by Brett Helquist. HarperCollins, 1999 (681,019)

2. *Harry Potter and the Goblet of Fire.* J. K. Rowling. Scholastic/Levine, 2000 (654,000)

3. *Goodnight Moon (board book).* Margaret Wise Brown, illus. by Clement Hurd. HarperCollins, 1991 (639,694)

4. *The Reptile Room (A Series of Unfortunate Events #2).* Lemony Snicket, illus. by Brett Helquist. HarperCollins, 1999 (504,964)

300,000+

5. *Green Eggs and Ham.* Dr. Seuss. Random, 1960 (497,772)

6. *Oh, the Places You'll Go!* Dr. Seuss. Random, 1990 (426,424)

7. *Five Little Monkeys Jumping on the Bed (board book).* Eileen Christelow. Houghton Mifflin, 1998 (412,000)

8. *The Wide Window (A Series of Unfortunate Events #3).* Lemony Snicket, illus. by Brett Helquist. HarperCollins, 2000 (409,909)

9. *Guess How Much I Love You (board book).* Sam McBratney, illus. by Anita Jeram. Candlewick, 1996 (408,232)

10. *The Miserable Mill (A Series of Unfortunate Events #4).* Lemony Snicket, illus. by Brett Helquist. HarperCollins, 2000 (396,098)

11. *The Cat in the Hat.* Dr. Seuss. Random, 1957 (376,314)

12. *The Ersatz Elevator (A Series of Unfortunate Events #6).* Lemony Snicket, illus. by Brett Helquist. HarperCollins, 2001 (367,395)

13. *The Austere Academy (A Series of Unfortunate Events #5).* Lemony Snicket, illus. by Brett Helquist. HarperCollins, 2000 (358,301)

14. *Harry Potter and the Chamber of Secrets.* J. K. Rowling. Scholastic/Levine, 1999 (357,000)

15. *The Very Hungry Caterpillar (board book).* Eric Carle. Philomel, 1981 (341,216)

16. *Brown Bear, Brown Bear, What Do You See? (board book).* Bill Martin, Jr., illus. by Eric Carle. Holt, 1996 (333,319)

17. *Disney's Princess Collection.* Disney, 1999 (331,119)

18. *Dr. Seuss's ABC (board book).* Dr. Seuss. Random, 1996 (330,428)

19. *One Fish Two Fish Red Fish Blue Fish.* Dr. Seuss. Random, 1960 (326,618)

20. *The Hostile Hospital (A Series of Unfortunate Events #8).* Lemony Snicket, illus. by Brett Helquist. HarperCollins, 2001 (324,106)

21. *Mr. Brown Can Moo, Can You? (board book).* Dr. Seuss. Random, 1996 (312,314)

22. *The Vile Village (A Series of Unfortunate Events #7).* Lemony Snicket, illus. by Brett Helquist. HarperCollins, 2001 (302,751)

200,000+

23. *Disney's Storybook Collection.* Disney, 1998 (293,034)

24. *Harry Potter Boxed Set 1.* J. K. Rowling. Scholastic/Levine, 2001 (287,000)

25. *Blessings Every Day.* Carla Barnhill, illus. by Elena Kucharik. Tyndale, 2001 (283,318)

26. *The Giving Tree.* Shel Silverstein. HarperCollins, 1964 (269,318)

27. *Harry Potter and the Prisoner of Azkaban.* J. K. Rowling. Scholastic/Levine, 1999 (261,000)

28. *A Single Shard.* Linda Sue Park. Clarion, 2001 (237,216)

29. *I Spy Treasure Hunt.* Jean Marzollo, illus. by Walter Wick. Scholastic/Cartwheel, 1999 (235,000)

30. *Hop on Pop.* Dr. Seuss. Random, 1963 (219,591)

31. *The Princess Collection Friendship Box.* Random/Disney, 2001 (205,548)

32. *The Polar Express.* Chris Van Allsburg. Houghton Mifflin, 1985 (202,500)

100,000+

33. *Disney's My Very First Winnie the Pooh: Growing Up Stories.* Disney, 1999 (193,294)

34. *Are You My Mother?* P. D. Eastman. Random, 1960 (191,609)
35. *Go, Dog. Go!* P. D. Eastman. Random, 1961 (191,600)
36. *The Poky Little Puppy.* Jane Sebring Lowrey. Random/Little Golden, 1942 (190,034)
37. *Dr. Seuss's ABC Book.* Dr. Seuss. Random, 1960 (189,176)
38. *The Foot Book (board book).* Dr. Seuss. Random, 1996 (189,086)
39. *Disney's My Very First Winnie the Pooh: More Growing Up Stories.* Disney, 2001 (173,271)
40. *Disney's Animal Stories.* Disney, 2000 (172,034)
41. *Fox in Socks.* Dr. Seuss. Random, 1965 (171,061)
42. *There's a Wocket in My Pocket! (board book).* Dr. Seuss. Random, 1996 (169,054)
43. *The Tower Treasure (Hardy Boys #1).* Franklin W. Dixon. Grosset & Dunlap, 1927 (167,272)
44. *Where the Sidewalk Ends.* Shel Silverstein. HarperCollins, 1974 (165,409)
45. *The Sisterhood of the Traveling Pants.* Ann Brashares. Delacorte, 2001 (163,347)
46. *I Spy Extreme Challenger.* Jean Marzollo, illus. by Walter Wick. Scholastic/Cartwheel, 2000 (163,000)
47. *If You Give a Mouse a Cookie.* Laura Numeroff, illus. by Felicia Bond. HarperCollins/Geringer, 1985 (162,450)
48. *Barnyard Dance!* Sandra Boynton. Workman, 1993 (162,345)
49. *The Secret of the Old Clock (Nancy Drew #1).* Carolyn Keene. Grosset & Dunlap, 1927 (157,428)
50. *Presents from Pooh.* Random/Disney, 2001 (155,677)
51. *The Runaway Bunny (board book).* Margaret Wise Brown, illus. by Clement Hurd. HarperCollins, 1991 (151,456)
52. *Disney's Adventure Stories.* Disney, 2001 (147,781)
53. *Polar Bear, Polar Bear, What Do You Hear? (board book).* Bill Martin, Jr., illus. by Eric Carle. Holt, 1997 (145,699)
54. *Grandmother's Memories to Her Grandchild.* Illus. by Thomas Kinkade. Tommy Nelson, 1999 (144,952)
55. *The Three Pigs.* David Wiesner. Clarion, 2001 (141,678)
56. *Mother's Memories to Her Child.* Illus. by Thomas Kinkade. Tommy Nelson, 2000 (134,448)
57. *Angelina Ballerina.* Katharine Holabird, illus. by Helen Craig. Pleasant Co., 2000 (133,889)
58. *Pajama Time!* Sandra Boynton. Workman, 2000 (133,654)
59. *The Going to Bed Book (board book).* Sandra Boynton. Little Simon, 1982 (133,175)
60. *Once Upon a Potty—Boy.* Alona Frankel. HarperCollins, 1999 (130,168)
61. *The Hidden Staircase (Nancy Drew #2).* Carolyn Keene. Grosset & Dunlap, 1930 (130,060)

62. *The Night Before Christmas.* Clement C. Moore, illus. by Christian Birmingham. Running Press, 1995 (128,046)

63. *Are You My Mother? (board book).* P. D. Eastman. Random, 1998 (127,051)

64. *Once Upon a Potty—Girl.* Alona Frankel. HarperCollins, 1999 (126,580)

65. *The Cat in the Hat Comes Back.* Dr. Seuss. Random, 1958 (125,855)

66. *Bob's Busy World (Bob the Builder).* Annie Auerback, illus. by Mel Grant. Simon Spotlight, 2001 (122,495)

67. *Ten Apples Up on Top (board book).* Dr. Seuss. Random, 1998 (121,410)

68. *Click, Clack Moo: Cows That Type.* Doreen Cronin, illus. by Betsy Lewin. Simon & Schuster, 2000 (121,308)

69. *Olivia.* Ian Falconer. Atheneum/ Schwartz, 2000 (119,589)

70. *The Bungalow Mystery (Nancy Drew #3).* Carolyn Keene. Grosset & Dunlap, 1930 (119,457)

71. *DK Merriam-Webster Children's Dictionary.* DK, 2000 (118,223)

72. *The Mystery at Lilac Inn (Nancy Drew #4).* Carolyn Keene. Grosset & Dunlap, 1930 (116,931)

73. *The Cheerios Play Book (board book).* Lee Wade. Little Simon, 1998 (115,929)

74. *The Secret of Shadow Ranch (Nancy Drew #5).* Carolyn Keene. Grosset & Dunlap, 1980 (114,377)

75. *The Little Engine That Could.* Watty Piper. Grosset & Dunlap, 1978 (109,679)

76. *I Love You As Much . . . (board book).* Laura Melmed, illus. by Henri Sorensen. HarperCollins, 1998 (109,630)

77. *If You Take a Mouse to the Movies.* Laura Numeroff, illus. by Felicia Bond. HarperCollins/Geringer, 2000 (107,890)

78. *Where the Wild Things Are.* Maurice Sendak. HarperCollins, 1963 (107,620)

79. *I Can Read with My Eyes Shut!* Dr. Seuss. Random, 1978 (107,194)

80. *The House on the Cliff (Hardy Boys #2).* Franklin W. Dixon. Grosset & Dunlap, 1927 (106,509)

81. *If You Give a Pig a Pancake.* Laura Numeroff, illus. by Felicia Bond. HarperCollins/Geringer, 1998 (105,610)

82. *The Secret at Red Gate Farm (Nancy Drew #6).* Carolyn Keene. Grosset & Dunlap, 1931 (105,578)

83. *You Are Special.* Max Lucado, illus. by Sergio Martinez. Crossway, 1997 (105,273)

84. *The Little Red Hen.* J. P. Miller. Random/Little Golden, 2001 (105,024)

85. *Olivia Saves the Circus.* Ian Falconer. Atheneum/Schwartz, 2001 (104,981)

86. *The Secret of the Old Mill (Hardy Boys #3).* Franklin W. Dixon. Grosset & Dunlap, 1927 (104,862)

87. *A Light in the Attic.* Shel Silverstein. HarperCollins, 1981 (104,354)

88. *James Bond: The Secret World of 007.* DK, 2000 (103,695)
89. *Put Me in the Zoo.* Robert Lopshire. Random, 1960 (102,894)
90. *Moo Baa La La La (board book).* Sandra Boynton. Little Simon, 1982 (102,467)
91. *Hand, Hand, Fingers, Thumb (board book).* Al Perkins. Random, 1998 (102,121)
92. *Hunting for Hidden Gold (Hardy Boys #5).* Franklin W. Dixon. Grosset & Dunlap, 1928 (101,830)
93. *The Missing Chums (Hardy Boys #4).* Franklin Dixon. Grosset & Dunlap, 1930 (100,966)
94. *Good Night, Gorilla (board book).* Peggy Rathmann. Putnam, 1996 (100,454)

75,000+

95. *I'm a Big Sister.* Joanna Cole, illus. by Maxie Chambliss. HarperCollins, 1997 (99,081)
96. *Time for Bed (board book).* Mem Fox, illus. by Jane Dyer. Harcourt/Red Wagon, 1997 (97,282)
97. *Go, Dog. Go! (board book).* P. D. Eastman. Random, 1997 (97,248)
98. *The Fire Engine Book.* Tibor Gergely. Random/Little Golden, 2001 (96,196)
99. *Walter the Farting Dog.* William Kotzwinkle and Glenn Murray, illus. by Audrey Colman. Frog/North Atlantic, 2001 (96,000)
100. *I Spy: A Book of Picture Riddles.* Jean Marzollo, illus. by Walter Wick. Scholastic/Cartwheel, 1992 (95,000)
101. *A Fish Out of Water.* Helen Palmer. Random, 1961 (94,849)
102. *I Spy Christmas.* Jean Marzollo and Carol Carson, illus. by Walter Wick. Scholastic/Cartwheel, 1992 (94,000)
103. *Potty Book for Her.* Alyssa Satin Capucilli, illus. by Dorothy Stott. Barron's, 2000
104. *Good Night Blue (Blue's Clues).* Angela Santomero, illus. by Jenine Pontillo. Simon Spotlight, 1999 (93,593)
105. *Barbie: Rapunzel.* Diane Muldrow. Random/Little Golden, 2001 (92,192)
106. *The Shore Road Mystery (Hardy Boys #6).* Franklin W. Dixon. Grosset & Dunlap, 1928 (91,378)
107. *Oh the Thinks You Can Think.* Dr. Seuss. Random, 1975 (90,133)
108. *The Alphabet Book (board book).* P. D. Eastman. Random, 2000 (88,312)
109. *Harry Potter and the Sorcerer's Stone.* J. K. Rowling. Scholastic/Levine, 1998 (88,000)
110. *Falling Up.* Shel Silverstein. HarperCollins, 1996 (87,501)
111. *I'm a Big Brother.* Joanna Cole, illus. by Maxie Chambliss. HarperCollins, 1997 (87,271)

112. *Harry Potter Charity Box Set.* J. K. Rowling. Scholastic/Levine, 2001 (87,000)

113. *Guess How Much I Love You.* Sam McBratney, illus. by Anita Jeram. Candlewick, 1995 (86,603)

114. *How the Grinch Stole Christmas.* Dr. Seuss. Random, 1957 (86,449)

115. *If You Give a Moose a Muffin.* Laura Numeroff, illus. by Felicia Bond. HarperCollins/Geringer, 1991 (86,137)

116. *I Am Not Going to Get Up Today!* Dr. Seuss, illus. by James Stevenson. Random, 1987 (85,925)

117. *Potty Book for Him.* Alyssa Satin Capucilli, illus. by Dorothy Stott. Barron's, 2000.

118. *Big Red Barn (board book).* Margaret Wise Brown, illus. by Felicia Bond. HarperCollins, 1995 (84,068)

119. *How Do Dinosaurs Say Good Night?* Jane Yolen, illus. by Mark Teague. Scholastic/Blue Sky, 2000 (84,000)

120. *The Very Hungry Caterpillar.* Eric Carle. Philomel, 1994 (83,798)

121. *Dream Snow.* Eric Carle. Philomel, 2000 (83,373)

122. *Walt Disney's Winnie the Pooh and His Friends: Friendship Box.* Random/Disney, 1997 (82,830)

123. *Chunky Farm Cow.* Illus. by Emily Bolam. Barron's, 2000

124. *Goodnight Moon.* Margaret Wise Brown, illus. by Clement Hurd. HarperCollins, 1947 (82,461)

125. *Just In Case You Ever Wonder (board book).* Max Lucado, illus. by Toni Goffe. Tommy Nelson, 2000 (82,350)

126. *Bob's White Christmas (Bob the Builder).* Alison Inches, illus. by Mel Grant. Simon Spotlight, 2001 (81,749)

127. *Prayers for Children.* Eloise Wilkin. Random/Golden, 1999 (80,835)

128. *Chunky Farm Pig.* Illus. by Emily Bolam. Barron's, 2000

129. *Chunky Safari Elephant.* Illus. by Emily Bolam. Barron's, 2001

130. *My First Book of Animal Sounds.* Marguerite Corsello. Random/Golden, 2000 (80,150)

131. *You Are My I Love You.* Maryann Cuismano. Philomel, 2001 (79,584)

132. *Chunky Safari Lion.* Illus. by Emily Bolam. Barron's, 2001

133. *Yay, You!* Sandra Boynton. Little Simon, 2001 (79,272)

134. *The Cheerios Animal Play Book (board book).* Lee Wade. Little Simon, 1999 (78,481)

135. *The Very Lonely Firefly (board book).* Eric Carle. Philomel, 1999 (76,298)

136. *Love You Forever.* Robert Munsch, illus. by Sheila McGraw. Firefly, 1986 (75,823)

137. *Today I Feel Silly & Other Moods That Make My Day.* Jamie Lee Curtis, illus. by Laura Cornell. HarperCollins/Cotler, 1998 (75,625)

138. *Barbie: The Special Sleepover.* Random/Golden, 2001 (75,151)

Paperback Frontlist

500,000+

1. *Harry Potter and the Goblet of Fire.* J. K. Rowling. Scholastic/Levine (2,810,000)
2. *Harry Potter and the Chamber of Secrets (mass market).* J. K. Rowling. Scholastic/Levine (1,217,000)
3. *Chicken Soup for the Teenage Soul: On Tough Stuff.* Jack Canfield et al. HCI (584,978)
4. *The Adventures of Super Diaper Baby.* Dav Pilkey. Scholastic/Blue Sky (512,000)

300,000+

5. *Good Morning, Gorillas (MTH #26).* Mary Pope Osborne, illus. by Sal Murdocca. Random (490,965)
6. *Gathering Blue.* Lois Lowry. Dell/Laurel-Leaf (469,292)
7. *Princess in the Spotlight (The Princess Diaries #2).* Meg Cabot. Harper-Trophy (423,122)
8. *Dora's Backpack (Dora the Explorer).* Sarah Willson, illus. by Robert Roper. Simon Spotlight (378,922)
9. *Go, Stitch, Go! (Lilo & Stitch)* Random/Disney (373,386)
10. *The Giver.* Lois Lowry. Dell/Laurel-Leaf, (347,540)
11. *Little Star (Dora the Explorer).* Sarah Willson. Simon Spotlight (337,351)
12. *Spider-Man: I Am Spider-Man.* Acton Figueroa. HarperFestival (321,559)
13. *Chicken Soup for the Teenage Soul on Love and Friendship.* Jack Canfield et al. HCI (317,426)
14. *Stage Fright on a Summer Night (MTH #25).* Mary Pope Osborne, illus. by Sal Murdocca. Random (317,227)
15. *The All New Captain Underpants Extra-Crunchy Book O'Fun #2.* Dav Pilkey. Scholastic/Blue Sky (317,000)

200,000+

16. *The Adventures of Spider-Man.* Michael Teitelbaum. HarperFestival (296,218)
17. *Thanksgiving on Thursday (MTH #27).* Mary Pope Osborne, illus. by Sal Murdocca. Random (291,778)
18. *Bud, Not Buddy.* Christopher Paul Curtis. Dell/Yearling (291,120)
19. *Artemis Fowl.* Eoin Colfer. Hyperion/Miramax (290,337)
20. *Disney's Return to Neverland.* Random/Disney (283,894)
21. *Junie B., First Grader (At Last!).* Barbara Park, illus. by Denise Brunkus. Random (274,927)
22. *Spider-Man: The Movie Storybook.* Shane Coll. HarperFestival (259,484)

23. *Spy Kids 2 Junior Novel.* Hyperion (256,767)
24. *Harry Potter #4 Paperback Box Set.* J. K. Rowling. Scholastic/Levine (254,000)
25. *Star Wars: Episode #2: Novelization.* Patricia Wrede. Scholastic (249,000)
26. *Dora's Treasure Hunt (Dora the Explorer).* Alison Inches, illus. by Susan Hall. Simon Spotlight (244,019)
27. *Arthur's Back to School Surprise.* Marc Brown. Random (239,338)
28. *Dora Saves the Prince (Dora the Explorer).* Alison Inches, illus. by Brian McGee. Simon Spotlight (230,659)
29. *Disney's Return to Neverland: Faith, Trust and Pixie Dust.* Random/Disney (225,350)
30. *Telling Christina Goodbye.* Lurlene McDaniel. Random/Bantam (225,095)
31. *Never Been Kissed (Mary-Kate & Ashley Sweet 16 #1).* Mary-Kate and Ashley Olsen. HarperEntertainment (223,802)
32. *Wishes and Dreams (Mary-Kate & Ashley Sweet 16 #2).* Mary-Kate and Ashley Olsen. HarperEntertainment (222,947)
33. *Spider-Man Saves the Day.* Acton Figueroa. HarperFestival (219,560)
34. *Star Wars Attack of the Clones: Anakin and Amidala.* Illus. by Scott Kolins. Random (217,693)
35. *Ice Age: Who You Callin' Extinct?* Judy Katschke. HarperEntertainment (215,925)
36. *Stargirl.* Jerry Spinelli. Knopf (213,995)
37. *Totally Crushed! (Lizzie McGuire #2).* Hyperion (210,122)
38. *Wee Sing 25th Anniversary Celebration.* Pamela Beall and Susan Nipp. Price Stern Sloan (209,524)
39. *Meet Kava.* Janet Shaw, illus. by Bill Farnsworth. Pleasant Co. (206,574)
40. *The Perfect Summer (Mary-Kate & Ashley Sweet 16 #3).* Mary-Kate and Ashley Olsen. HarperEntertainment (203,900)
41. *Spirit: Stallion of the Cimarron.* Mary Hogan. Price Stern Sloan (203,278)
42. *A Whale of a Time (The Little Mermaid).* Random/Disney (201,543)

100,000+

43. *Spider-Man: Spider Bite.* Leslie Goldman. HarperFestival (185,929)
44. *Star Wars Attack of the Clones: I Am a Jedi Apprentice.* Marc Cerasini, illus. by Jeff Albrecht. Random (184,914)
45. *Sammy Keyes and the Hollywood Mummy.* Wendelin Van Draanen. Dell/Yearling (182,384)
46. *Tuck Everlasting (movie tie-in).* Natalie Babbitt. FSG/Sunburst (177,901)
47. *How to Train a Boy (So Little Time #1).* Mary-Kate and Ashley Olsen. HarperEntertainment (177,092)
48. *Ice Age: The Classic Story.* Nancy Krulik. HarperEntertainment (175,252)
49. *Ice Age: The Movie Novel.* J. E. Bright. HarperEntertainment (173,536)

50. *The Case of the Mall Mystery (New Adventures of Mary-Kate & Ashley #28)*. Mary-Kate and Ashley Olsen. HarperEntertainment (173,058)

51. *Instant Boyfriend (So Little Time #2)*. Mary-Kate and Ashley Olsen. HarperEntertainment (168,929)

52. *New Disney's Treasure Planet: Space Case*. Random/Disney (164,924)

53. *Muck's Sleepover (Bob the Builder)*. Kiki Thorpe. Simon Spotlight (164,233)

54. *Your Friendly Neighborhood Spider-Man*. Kitty Richards. HarperFestival (163,308)

55. *Barbie as Rapunzel*. Merry North. Random/Golden (160,690)

56. *Say Cheese! (Lilo & Stitch)*. Random/ Disney (159,435)

57. *Kaya's Escape*. Janet Shaw, illus. by Bill Farnsworth. Pleasant Co. (158,486)

58. *The Cay*. Theodore Taylor. Dell/Yearling (157,457)

59. *What Janie Found*. Caroline B. Cooney. Dell/Laurel-Leaf (156,191)

60. *The New Adventures of Stuart Little*. Laura Hunt. HarperFestival (155,391)

61. *Pure Dead Magic*. Debi Gliori. Dell/ Yearling (152,042)

62. *Kaya's Hero*. Janet Shaw, illus. by Bill Farnsworth. Pleasant Co. (151,291)

63. *Kaya and the Lone Dog*. Janet Shaw, illus. by Bill Farnsworth. Pleasant Co. (150,958)

64. *Good Night, Dora! (Dora the Explorer)*. Christine Ricci, illus. by Susan Hall. Simon Spotlight (150,580)

65. *Star Wars: JQ #1: The Way of the Apprentice*. Jude Watson, illus. by David Mattingly. Scholastic (150,000)

66. *Stuart Little 2: The Movie Storybook*. Julie Michaels. HarperFestival (147,914)

67. *Ghost Boy*. Iain Lawrence. Dell/Laurel-Leaf (147,403)

68. *Brain Quest America*. Lynn St. Clair Strong with Joni Miller, illus. by Kimble Mead. Workman (146,969)

69. *Changes for Kaya*. Janet Shaw, illus. by Bill Farnsworth. Pleasant Co. (146,834)

70. *Powerpuff Girls Mad Libs*. Roger Price and Leonard Stern. Price Stern Sloan (145,401)

71. *The Case of the Game Show Mystery (Adventures of Mary-Kate & Ashley #27)*. Mary-Kate and Ashley Olsen. HarperEntertainment (144,104)

72. *Now You See Him, Now You Don't (Two of a Kind #21)*. Mary-Kate and Ashley Olsen. HarperEntertainment (143,876)

73. *Too Good to Be True (So Little Time #1)*. Mary-Kate and Ashley Olsen. HarperEntertainment (143,782)

74. *A Dangerous Plan (Left Behind: The Kids #20)*. Jerry B. Jenkins and Tim LaHaye. Tyndale (143,433)

75. *Bob's Halloween Party (Bob the Builder)*. Heather Feldman, illus. by Barry Goldberg. Simon Spotlight (142,477)

76. *Disney's Treasure Planet: Junior Novelization.* Random/Disney (141,410)
77. *Disney's The Lion King: The Brave Prince/A Princess Is Born.* Random/ Disney (140,383)
78. *Disney Treasure Planet: Pirates Attack!* Random/Disney (140,147)
79. *Getting There (Mary-Kate & Ashley Sweet 16 #4).* Mary-Kate and Ashley Olsen. HarperEntertainment (140,027)
80. *Dizzy and Muck Work It Out (Bob the Builder).* Adapted by Annie Auerback, illus. by Joe and Terri Chicko. Simon Spotlight (136,952)
81. *Disney Princess: A Pony for a Princess.* Andrea Posner-Sanchez, illus. by Francesc Mateu. Random/Disney (136,094)
82. *Kaya Shows the Way.* Janet Shaw, illus. by Bill Farnsworth. Pleasant Co. (135,312)
83. *Island Girls (Two of a Kind #23).* Mary-Kate and Ashley Olsen. HarperEntertainment (133,473)
84. *Recruited: An Alias Prequel Novel.* Lynn Mason. Random/Bantam (133,338)
85. *Harry Potter Poster Book #2.* Scholastic/Levine (133,000)
86. *Scooby-Doo (movie novelization).* Suzanne Weyn. Scholastic (132,000)
87. *Star Wars Attack of the Clones Movie Storybook.* Jane Mason and Sarah Hines Stephens. Random (131,263)
88. *The Case of the Candy Cane Clue (New Adventures of Mary-Kate & Ashley #32).* Mary-Kate and Ashley Olsen. HarperEntertainment (128,434)
89. *Bob's Snowy Day (Bob the Builder).* Annie Auerback, illus. by Barry Goldberg. Simon Spotlight (128,112)
90. *The Case of the Giggling Ghost (New Adventures of Mary-Kate & Ashley #31).* Mary-Kate and Ashley Olsen. HarperEntertainment (125,403)
91. *Lilo & Stitch Junior Novelization.* Random/Disney (125,340)
92. *Stuart Little 2: The Joke Book.* Catherine Hapka. HarperFestival (124,867)
93. *Walt Disney's Cinderella.* Random/ Disney (124,537)
94. *Star Wars: JQ #2: The Trail of the Jedi.* Jude Watson, illus. by David Mattingly. Scholastic (124,000)
95. *Walt Disney's Peter Pan.* Random/ Disney (122,262)
96. *World Almanac for Kids 2003.* Edited by Kevin Seabrooke. World Almanac (121,704)
97. *My Best Friend's Boyfriend (Mary-Kate & Ashley Sweet 16 #6).* Mary-Kate and Ashley Olsen. HarperEntertainment (121,598)
98. *Jack and Jill and Big Dog Bill.* Martha Weston. Random (121,083)
99. *The Berenstain Bears: Report Card Trouble.* Stan & Jan Berenstain. Random (120,398)
100. *Star Wars: Skywalker Family Album.* Alice Alfonsi. Random (120,370)
101. *E.T. The Extra-Terrestrial: A Friend for E.T.* Gail Herman. Simon Spotlight (120,343)
102. *The Perfect Gift (Two of a Kind #26).* Mary-Kate and Ashley Olsen. HarperEntertainment (119,838)

103. *The Case of Camp Crooked Lake (New Adventures of Mary-Kate & Ashley #30)*. Mary-Kate and Ashley Olsen. HarperEntertainment (119,784)
104. *Horsemen of Terror (Left Behind: The Kids #23)*. Jerry B. Jenkins and Tim LaHaye. Tyndale (119,626)
105. *Star Wars Attack of the Clones: Jango Fett: Bounty Hunter*. Eric Arnold, illus. by Valerie Reckert. Random (119,411)
106. *Escape from New Babylon (Left Behind: The Kids #22)*. Jerry B. Jenkins and Tim LaHaye. Tyndale (118,091)
107. *Secrets of New Babylon (Left Behind: The Kids #21)*. Jerry B. Jenkins and Tim LaHaye. Tyndale (117,777)
108. *Uplink from the Underground (Left Behind: The Kids #20)*. Jerry B. Jenkins and Tim LaHaye. Tyndale (116,225)
109. *Just Between Us (So Little Time #4)*. Mary-Kate and Ashley Olsen. HarperEntertainment (115,612)
110. *Disney's Beauty and the Beast*. Random/Disney (115,166)
111. *Monsters, Inc.: Boo on the Loose!* Random/Disney (115,073)
112. *I Was a Rat!* Philip Pullman, illus. by Kevin Hawkes. Dell/Yearling (114,934)
113. *George Washington and the General's Dog*. Frank Murphy, illus. by Richard Walz. Random (114,748)
114. *Men in Black II: The Movie Novel*. Michael Teitelbaum. HarperFestival (114,736)
115. *Secret Origins (Justice League #1)*. Michael Teitelbaum. Random/Bantam (113,631)
116. *Surf, Sand and Secrets (Two of a Kind #24)*. Mary-Kate and Ashley Olsen. HarperEntertainment (113,102)
117. *April Fools' Rules! (Two of a Kind #22)*. Mary-Kate and Ashley Olsen. HarperEntertainment (112,762)
118. *Secret Crush (So Little Time #6)*. Mary-Kate and Ashley Olsen. HarperEntertainment (112,762)
119. *No Biting!* Karen Katz. Grosset & Dunlap (112,529)
120. *Rescue: A Police Story*. Alison Hart, photos by Dennis Sutton. Random (112,435)
121. *Anyone But Me*. Nancy Krulik. Grosset & Dunlap. (112,382)
122. *On the Bright Side, I'm Now the Girlfriend of a Sex God*. Louise Rennison. HarperTempest (111,644)
123. *Star Wars: Jedi Training and Trails Quiz Book*. Jack Albrecht and Brandon McKinney. Random (111,604)
124. *Run-Away Roley (Bob the Builder)*. Adapted by Alison Inches, illus. by Art Ellis. Simon Spotlight (111,574)
125. *Makeup Shake-up (In Action #1)*. Mary-Kate and Ashley Olsen. HarperEntertainment (111,048)
126. *Pooh Loves You*. Random/Disney (111,030)

127. *The Case of the Weird Science Mystery (New Adventures of Mary-Kate & Ashley #29)*. Mary-Kate and Ashley Olsen. HarperEntertainment (110,672)

128. *E.T. The Extra-Terrestrial: Be Good Gertie!* Gail Herman. Simon Spotlight (110,669)

129. *Closer Then Ever (Two of a Kind #25)*. Mary-Kate and Ashley Olsen. HarperEntertainment (110,658)

130. *Star Wars Attack of the Clones Movie Scrapbook*. Ryder Windham. Random (110,248)

131. *The Dream Team (In Action #2)*. Mary-Kate and Ashley Olsen. HarperEntertainment (110,174)

132. *Stuart Little's Big Adventures*. Julia Richardson. HarperFestival (108,525)

133. *Hope Was Here*. Joan Bauer. Puffin (107,873)

134. *Spirit Junior Novelization*. Kathleen Duey. Puffin (107,799)

135. *Bible Heroes*. Random/Golden (107,742)

136. *Bible Stories*. Random/Golden (107,736)

137. *Star Wars Attack of the Clones: Anakin: Apprentice*. Marc Cerasini, illus. by Tommy Lee Edwards. Random (107,733)

138. *Stuart Little 2: Stuart's Wild Ride*. Patricia Lakin. HarperFestival (107,650)

139. *E.T. The Extra-Terrestrial (movie novelization)*. Terry Collins. Simon Spotlight (107,484)

140. *Stuart Little 2: Stuart Finds a Friend*. Patricia Lakin. HarperFestival (106,467)

141. *In Darkest Night (Justice League #2)*. Michael Jan Friedman. Random/Bantam (105,644)

142. *And the Phantom Cowboy (Scooby-Doo #3)*. Jesse Leon McCann, illus. by Duendes Del Sur. Scholastic (105,000)

143. *Fever 1793*. Laurie Halse Anderson. Aladdin (104,403)

144. *When in Rome (Mary-Kate & Ashley Starring in #5)*. Mary-Kate and Ashley Olsen. HarperEntertainment (104,138)

145. *Tell Me About It (So Little Time #5)*. Mary-Kate and Ashley Olsen. HarperEntertainment (104,102)

146. *Captain Underpants #1–#5 Box Set*. Dav Pilkey. Scholastic/Blue Sky (104,000)

147. *Memories of Summer*. Ruth White. Dell/Laurel-Leaf. (103,814)

148. *Bob's Egg Hunt (Bob the Builder)*. Annie Auerback, illus. by Barry Goldberg. Simon Spotlight (101,879)

149. *Where is Boots? (Dora the Explorer)*. Kiki Thorpe, illus. by Steve Savitsky. Simon Spotlight (101,787)

150. *Disney's 101 Dalmatians II: Patch's London Adventure*. Random/Disney (100,459)

151. *Spirit: A Friend in Rain*. Cathy Hapka. Puffin (100,159)

152. *Fubble Bubble Trouble (In Action #3).* Mary-Kate and Ashley Olsen. HarperEntertainment (100,060)

Paperback Backlist

300,000+

1. *Harry Potter and the Chamber of Secrets.* J. K. Rowling. Scholastic/Levine, 2000 (1,872,000)
2. *Harry Potter and the Prisoner of Azkaban.* J. K. Rowling. Scholastic/Levine, 2001 (1,275,000)
3. *Harry Potter and the Sorcerer's Stone.* J. K. Rowling. Scholastic/Levine, 1999 (990,000)
4. *When I Get Bigger.* Mercer Mayer. Random/Golden, 1999 (509,928)
5. *The Outsiders.* S. E. Hinton. Puffin, 1967 (506,171)
6. *Tales of a Fourth Grade Nothing.* Judy Blume. Dell/Yearling, 1976 (442,299)
7. *Holes.* Louis Sachar. Dell/Yearling, 2000 (439,993)
8. *Love You Forever.* Robert Munsch, illus. by Sheila McGraw. Firefly, 1986 (431,420)
9. *Junie B. Jones Is a Graduation Girl.* Barbara Park, illus. by Denise Brunkus. Random, 2001 (382,796)
10. *Number the Stars.* Lois Lowry. Dell/Yearling, 1990 (357,898)
11. *A Wrinkle in Time.* Madeleine L'Engle. Dell/Yearling, 1998 (339,000)
12. *Nate the Great.* Marjorie Weinman Sharmat. Dell/Yearling, 1997 (337,844)
13. *Dinosaurs Before Dark (MTH #1).* Mary Pope Osborne, illus. by Sal Murdocca. Random, 1992 (313,033)
14. *The Adventures of Captain Underpants.* Dav Pilkey. Scholastic/Blue Sky, 1997 (313,000)
15. *Island of the Blue Dolphins.* Scott O'Dell. Dell/Yearling 1971 (309,762)
16. *Junie B. Jones and the Stupid Smelly Bus.* Barbara Park, illus. by Denise Brunkus. Random, 1992 (308,410)
17. *The Giver.* Lois Lowry. Dell/Laurel-Leaf, 1994 (303,374)
18. *Captain Underpants and the Perilous Plot of Professor Poopypants.* Dav Pilkey. Scholastic/Blue Sky, 2000 (303,000)

200,000+

19. *Captain Underpants and the Invasion of the Incredibly Naughty Cafeteria Ladies from Outer Space.* Dav Pilkey. Scholastic/Blue Sky, 1999 (297,000)
20. *Frederick.* Leo Lionni. Dell/Dragonfly, 1973 (294,920)
21. *Captain Underpants and the Attack of the Talking Toilets.* Dav Pilkey. Scholastic/Blue Sky, 1999 (285,000)

22. *Captain Underpants and the Wrath of the Wicked Wedgie Woman.* Dav Pilkey. Scholastic/Blue Sky, 2001 (284,000)
23. *Junie B. Jones and Her Big Fat Mouth.* Barbara Park, illus. by Denise Brunkus. Random, 1993 (280,795)
24. *Wee Sing Children's Songs and Fingerplays.* Pamela Beall and Susan Nipp. Price Stern Sloan, 1977 (278,825)
25. *Charlie and the Chocolate Factory.* Roald Dahl. Puffin, 1998 (278,672)
26. *Junie B. Jones and a Little Monkey Business.* Barbara Park, illus. by Denise Brunkus. Random, 1993 (276,601)
27. *Junie B. Jones and Some Sneaky Peeky Spying.* Barbara Park, illus. by Denis Brunkus. Random, 1994 (274,483)
28. *Charlotte's Web.* E. B. White, illus. by Garth Williams. HarperTrophy, 1974 (263,757)
29. *Junie B. Jones Has a Monster Under Her Bed.* Barbara Park, illus. by Denise Brunkus. Random, 1997 (259,013)
30. *The Sign of the Beaver.* Elizabeth George Speare. Dell/Yearling, 1984 (249,358)
31. *Mummies in the Morning (MTH #3).* Mary Pope Osborne, illus. by Sal Murdocca. Random, 1993 (243,118)
32. *The Princess Diaries.* Meg Cabot. HarperTrophy, 2001 (241,765)
33. *The Knight at Dawn (MTH #2).* Mary Pope Osborne, illus. by Sal Murdocca. Random, 1993 (240,531)
34. *Roll of Thunder, Hear My Cry.* Mildred Taylor. Puffin, 1997 (236,867)
35. *Junie B. Jones Loves Handsome Warren.* Barbara Park, illus. by Denise Brunkus. Random, 1996 (232,994)
36. *The Lion, the Witch and the Wardrobe.* C. S. Lewis, illus. by Cliff Nielsen. HarperTrophy, 1994 (229,622)
37. *Because of Winn-Dixie.* Kate DiCamillo. Candlewick, 2001 (222,088)
38. *Junie B. Jones and the Mushy, Gushy Valentine.* Barbara Park, illus. by Denise Brunkus. Random, 1999 (220,001)
39. *Wee Sing Nursery Rhymes and Lullabies.* Pamela Beall and Susan Nipp. Price Stern Sloan, 1985 (212,893)
40. *Where the Wild Things Are.* Maurice Sendak. HarperTrophy, 1988 (210,996)
41. *Superfudge.* Judy Blume. Dell/Yearling, 1986 (210,176)
42. *The Chronicles of Narnia.* C. S. Lewis, illus. by Cliff Nielsen. HarperTrophy, 2001 (209,719)
43. *Pirates Past Noon (MTH #4).* Mary Pope Osborne, illus. by Sal Murdocca. Random, 1994 (206,717)
44. *Bob's Birthday (Bob the Builder).* Diane Redmond. Simon Spotlight, 2001 (206,673)
45. *Tuck Everlasting.* Natalie Babbitt. FSG/Sunburst, 1985 (205,135)
46. *Junie B. Jones and That Meanie Jim's Birthday.* Barbara Park, illus. by Denise Brunkus. Random, 1996 (202,759)

100,000+

47. *Where the Red Fern Grows.* Wilson Rawls. Dell/Laurel-Leaf, 1997 (199,289)

48. *Midnight on the Moon (MTH #8).* Mary Pope Osborne, illus. by Sal Murdocca. Random, 1996 (198,960)

49. *Junie B. Jones Is Almost a Flower Girl.* Barbara Park, illus. by Denise Brunkus. Random, 1999 (196,985)

50. *Night of the Ninjas (MTH #5).* Mary Pope Osborne, illus. by Sal Murdocca. Random, 1995 (196,633)

51. *Wee Sing Bible Songs.* Pamela Beall and Susan Nipp. Price Stern Sloan, 1986 (195,753)

52. *Speak.* Laurie Halse Anderson. Puffin, 2001 (193,088)

53. *James and the Giant Peach.* Roald Dahl, illus. by Lane Smith. Puffin, 1996 (191,770)

54. *Hatchet.* Gary Paulsen. Aladdin, 1995 (190,812)

55. *Afternoon on the Amazon (MTH #6).* Mary Pope Osborne, illus. by Sal Murdocca. Random, 1995 (190,491)

56. *Wee Sing Sing-Alongs.* Pamela Beall and Susan Nipp. Price Stern Sloan, 1982 (189,137)

57. *Junie B. Jones Is a Party Animal.* Barbara Park, illus. by Denise Brunkus. Random, 1997 (188,693)

58. *Junie B. Jones and the Yucky Blucky Fruitcake.* Barbara Park, illus. by Denise Brunkus. Random, 1995 (187,417)

59. *Bridge to Terabithia.* Katherine Paterson, illus. by Donna Diamond. HarperTrophy, 1987 (187,064)

60. *Freckle Juice.* Judy Blume. Dell/Yearling, 1978 (186,435)

61. *Wee Sing and Play.* Pamela Beall and Susan Nipp. Price Stern Sloan, 1981 (182,611)

62. *Dolphins at Daybreak (MTH #9).* Mary Pope Osborne, illus. by Sal Murdocca. Random, 1997 (178,922)

63. *Junie B. Jones Has a Peep in Her Pocket.* Barbara Park, illus. by Denise Brunkus. Random, 2000 (178,317)

64. *The Care and Keeping of You.* Pleasant Co., 1998 (175,323)

65. *Scoop Saves the Day (Bob the Builder).* Diane Redmond. Simon Spotlight, 2001 (169,694)

66. *Junie B. Jones Is Captain Field Day.* Barbara Park, illus. by Denise Brunkus. Random, 2001 (168,316)

67. *Sunset of the Sabertooth (MTH #7).* Mary Pope Osborne, illus. by Sal Murdocca. Random, 1996 (165,400)

68. *Junie B. Jones Smells Something Fishy.* Barbara Park, illus. by Denise Brunkus. Random, 1998 (164,090)

69. *Tonight on the Titanic (MTH #17).* Mary Pope Osborne, illus. by Sal Murdocca. Random, 1999 (163,592)

70. *Junie B. Jones Is Not a Crook.* Barbara Park, illus. by Denise Brunkus. Random, 1997 (162,544)

71. *The Captain Underpants Extra-Crunchy Book O'Fun #1.* Dav Pilkey. Scholastic/Blue Sky, 2001 (162,000)

72. *Walk Two Moons.* Sharon Creech. HarperTrophy, 1996 (159,244)

73. *The Magician's Nephew.* C. S. Lewis, illus. by Cliff Nielsen. HarperTrophy, 1994 (159,242)

74. *Junie B. Jones Is a Beauty Shop Guy.* Barbara Park, illus. by Denise Brunkus. Random, 1998 (158,234)

75. *Little House in the Big Woods.* Laura Ingalls Wilder, illus. by Garth Williams. HarperTrophy, 1971 (155,232)

76. *Dizzy's Bird Watch (Bob the Builder).* Alison Inches, illus. by Cheryl Mendenhall. Simon Spotlight, 2001 (154,359)

77. *Little House on the Prairie.* Laura Ingalls Wilder, illus. by Garth Williams. HarperTrophy, 1971 (152,983)

78. *Friends Are Sweet.* Random/Disney, 2001 (151,090)

79. *Wee Sing for Baby.* Pamela Beall and Susan Nipp. Price Stern Sloan, 1996 (150,390)

80. *Sarah, Plain and Tall.* Patricia MacLachlan. HarperTrophy, 1987 (145,445)

81. *The Watsons Go to Birmingham—1963.* Christopher Paul Curtis. Dell/Yearling, 1997 (144,417)

82. *The Cricket in Times Square.* George Selden, illus. by Garth Williams. Dell/Yearling, 1970 (144,404)

83. *Twister on Tuesday (MTH #23).* Mary Pope Osborne, illus. by Sal Murdocca. Random, 2001 (142,152)

84. *Frog and Toad Are Friends.* Arnold Lobel. HarperTrophy, 1979 (141,662)

85. *Biscuit.* Alyssa Satin Capucilli, illus. by Pat Schories. HarperTrophy, 1997 (140,698)

86. *Wendy Helps Out (Bob the Builder).* Alison Inches, illus. by Joe and Terry Chicko. Simon Spotlight, 2001 (140,349)

87. *Revolutionary War on Wednesday (MTH #22).* Mary Pope Osborne, illus. by Sal Murdocca. Random, 2000 (138,512)

88. *Amelia Bedelia.* Peggy Parish, illus. by Fritz Siebel. HarperTrophy, 1992 (138,433)

89. *The Boxcar Children.* Gertrude Chandler Warner. Albert Whitman, 1989 (138,329)

90. *The Original Mad Libs 1.* Roger Price and Leonard Stern. Price Stern Sloan, 1974 (137,372)

91. *Pat the Bunny.* Dorothy Kunhardt. Random/Golden, 2001 (134,289)

92. *Polar Bears Past Bedtime (MTH #12).* Mary Pope Osborne, illus. by Sal Murdocca. Random, 1998 (133,665)

93. *Goodnight Moon.* Margaret Wise Brown, illus. by Clement Hurd. HarperTrophy, 1977 (132,390)

94. *Vacation Under the Volcano (MTH #13)*. Mary Pope Osborne, illus. by Sal Murdocca. Random, 1998 (131,999)
95. *The Headless Horseman*. Natalie Standiford. Random, 1992 (131,148)
96. *Maniac Magee*. Jerry Spinelli. Little, Brown, 1990 (130,422)
97. *Fudge-a-Mania*. Judy Blume. Dell/ Yearling, 1991 (128,284)
98. *Go Ask Alice*. Anonymous. Aladdin, 1994 (128,195)
99. *Angus, Thongs and Full-Frontal Snogging*. Louise Rennison. HarperTempest, 2001 (127,966)
100. *Danny and the Dinosaur*. Syd Hoff. HarperTrophy, 1978 (127,769)
101. *Ramona Quimby, Age 8*. Beverly Cleary. HarperTrophy, 1992 (127,081)
102. *The Mighty Big Book of Riddles*. Craig Yoe. Price Stern Sloan, 2001 (126,712)
103. *The Westing Game*. Ellen Raskin. Puffin, 1997 (123,494)
104. *Frindle*. Andrew Clements. Aladdin, 1996 (123,355)
105. *Just Me and My Dad*. Mercer Mayer. Random/Golden, 2001 (123,103)
106. *My Side of the Mountain*. Jean Craighead George. Puffin, 2001 (123,025)
107. *The Monster Under the Shed (Thomas and Friends)*. Illus. by Richard Courtney. Random, 2001 (122,304)
108. *Little Engines Can Do Big Things (Thomas and the Magic Railroad)*. Britt Allcroft, illus. by Ted Gadecki. Random, 2000 (121,972)
109. *The Mouse and the Motorcycle*. Beverly Cleary. HarperTrophy, 1990 (121,817)
110. *Monster*. Walter Dean Myers. HarperTempest, 2001 (120,910)
111. *Ghost Town at Sundown (MTH #10)*. Mary Pope Osborne, illus. by Sal Murdocca. Random, 1997 (119,175)
112. *Johnny Tremain*. Esther Forbes. Dell/ Yearling, 1987 (118,659)
113. *Just Go to Bed*. Mercer Mayer. Random/Golden, 2001 (117,035)
114. *The Vanishings (Left Behind: The Kids #1)*. Jerry B. Jenkins and Tim LaHaye. Tyndale, 1998 (114,890)
115. *The New Baby*. Mercer Mayer. Random/Golden, 2001 (114,699)
116. *Tigers at Twilight (MTH #19)*. Mary Pope Osborne, illus. by Sal Murdocca. Random, 1999 (114,350)
117. *Just Me and My Mom*. Mercer Mayer. Random/Golden, 2001 (114,032)
118. *Catch Me, Catch Me!* Rev. W. Awdry, illus. by Owen Bell. Random, 1990 (114,018)
119. *Curious George Makes Pancakes*. In the style of Margret and H.A. Rey. Houghton Mifflin, 1998 (113,870)
120. *Stone Fox*. John Reynolds Gardiner, illus. by Marcia Sewall. HarperTrophy, 1983 (113,664)
121. *The Phantom Tollbooth*. Norton Juster. Dell/Yearling, 1988 (113,642)
122. *Civil War on Sunday (MTH #21)*. Mary Pope Osborne, illus. by Sal Murdocca. Random, 2000 (113,127)

123. *Out of the Dust.* Karen Hesse. Scholastic, 1999 (113,000)

124. *The Pigman.* Paul Zindel. Random/ Bantam, 1983 (112,206)

125. *Let Love Grow (Precious Moments).* Samuel J. Butcher. Random/Golden, 2001 (111,945)

126. *Day of the Dragon-King (MTH #14).* Mary Pope Osborne, illus. by Sal Murdocca. Random, 1998 (110,726)

127. *Lions at Lunchtime (MTH #11).* Mary Pope Osborne, illus. by Sal Murdocca. Random, 1998 (109,474)

128. *Corduroy's Best Halloween Ever.* Created by Don Freeman, illus. by Lisa McCue. Grosset & Dunlap, 2001 (109,079)

129. *Clifford's Happy Easter.* Norman Bridwell. Scholastic/Cartwheel, 1994 (109,000)

130. *Hour of the Olympics (MTH #19).* Mary Pope Osborne, illus. by Sal Murdocca. Random, 1998 (108,023)

131. *Shiloh.* Phyllis Reynolds Naylor. Aladdin, 1992 (107,664)

132. *Freak the Mighty.* Rodman Philbrick. Scholastic Signature, 2001 (106,000)

133. *The Little Prince.* Antoine de Saint-Exupéry. Harcourt/Harvest, 1942 (105,313)

134. *Ginger Pye.* Eleanor Estes. Harcourt Young Classics, 1951 (103,585)

135. *Alexander and the Terrible, Horrible, No Good, Very Bad Day.* Judith Viorst, illus. by Ray Cruz. Aladdin, 1972 (103,545)

136. *A Long Way from Chicago.* Richard Peck. Puffin, 2000 (103,171)

137. *Diesel 10 Means Trouble (Thomas and the Magic Railroad).* Illus. by Richard Courtney. Random, 2000 (102,790)

138. *Farewell to Manzanar.* Jeanne Houston. Dell/Laurel-Leaf, 1983 (102,637)

139. *The BFG.* Roald Dahl. Puffin, 1998 (102,316)

Literary Prizes, 2002

Gary Ink

Research Librarian, *Publishers Weekly*

Academy of American Poets Academy Fellowship. For distinguished poetic achievement. *Offered by*: Academy of American Poets. *Winner*: Ellen Bryant Voigt.

AJL Bibliography Book Award. *Offered by*: Assn. of Jewish Libraries. *Winner*: Robert Singerman for *Jewish Serials of the World: A Supplement to the Research Bibliography of Secondary Sources* (Greenwood Press).

AJL Reference Book Award. *Offered by*: Assn. of Jewish Libraries. *Winner*: Shmuel Spector and Geoffrey Wigoder, eds., for *The Encyclopedia of Jewish Life Before and During the Holocaust* (New York Univ. Press).

Ambassador Book Awards. To honor an exceptional contribution to the interpretation of life and culture in the United States. *Offered by*: English-Speaking Union. *Winners*: (fiction) Richard Russo for *Empire Falls* (Knopf); (poetry) Anthony Hecht for *The Darkness and the Light* (Knopf); (lifetime Achievement) Hortense Calisher.

American Academy of Arts and Letters Awards in Literature. To honor writers of exceptional achievement. *Offered by*: American Academy of Arts and Letters. *Winners*: (poetry) Linda Gregerson, Tony Hoagland, Stanley Plumly, James Richardson, Alan Shapiro; (fiction) Charles Johnson.

American Academy of Arts and Letters Rome Fellowships. For a one-year residency at the American Academy in Rome by young writers of promise. *Offered by*: American Academy of Arts and Letters. *Winners*: Jennifer Clarvoe, Peter Orner.

American Book Awards. For literary achievement by people of various ethnic backgrounds. *Offered by*: Before Columbus Foundation. *Winners*: (fiction) Tananarive Due for *The Living Blood* (Pocket Books); LeAnne Howe for *Shell Shaker* (Aunt Lute Books); Alex Kuo for *Lipstick and Other Stories* (Asia 2000); Rilla Askew for *Fire in Beulah* (Viking); (poetry) Aaron A. Abeyta for *Colcha* (Univ. Press of Colorado); Gloria Frym for *Homeless at Home* (Creative Arts); Dana Gioia for *Interrogations at Noon* (Graywolf); Al Young for *The Sound of Dreams Remembered* (Creative Arts); (nonfiction) Susanne Antonetta for *The Body Toxic* (Counterpoint); Michael N. Nagler for *The Search for a Nonviolent Future* (Berkley Hills); Donald Phelps for *Reading the Funnies* (Fantagraphics).

Hans Christian Andersen Awards. To an author and an illustrator whose body of work has made an important and lasting contribution to children's literature. *Offered by*: International Board on Books for Young People (IBBY). *Winners*: (author) Aidan Chambers (United Kingdom); (illustrator) Quentin Blake (United Kingdom).

Aventis Prize for Science Books (United Kingdom). For science writing that is accessible to the general reader. *Offered by*: Aventis Corp. *Winners*: (adult prize) Stephen Hawking for *The Universe in a Nutshell* (Bantam Press); (junior prize) Richard Walker for *The DK Guide to the Human Body* (Dorling Kindersley).

Bancroft Prizes. For books of exceptional merit and distinction in American history, American diplomacy, and the international relations of the United States. *Offered by*: Columbia University. *Winners*: David W. Blight for *Race and Reunion* (Harvard); Alice Kessler-Harris for *In Pursuit of Equity* (Oxford).

Barnes & Noble Discover Great New Writers Awards. To honor a first novel and a first work of nonfiction by American authors. *Offered by*: Barnes & Noble, Inc. *Winners*: (fiction) Manil Suri for *The Death of Vishnu* (Norton); (nonfiction) Hampton Sides for *Ghost Soldiers* (Doubleday).

Mildred L. Batchelder Award. For an American publisher of a children's book originally published in a foreign language in a foreign country and subsequently published in English in the United States. *Offered by*: American Library Association, Association for Library Service to Children. *Winner*: Karin Gundisch for *How I Became an American,* translated by James Skofield (Cricket Books).

Bellwether Prize for Fiction. For an unpublished manuscript that advocates social responsibility. *Offered by*: Barbara Kingsolver. *Winner:* Gayle Brandeis for *The Book of Dead Birds* (HarperCollins).

Pura Belpré Award. To a Latino/Latina writer and illustrator whose work best portrays, affirms, and celebrates the Latino cultural experience in an outstanding work of literature for children and youth. *Winners*: (narrative) Pam Munoz Ryan for *Esperanza Rising* (Scholastic Press); (Illustration) Susan Guevara for *Chato and the Party Animals* by Gary Soto (Putnam).

Curtis Benjamin Award for Creative Publishing. *Offered by*: Association of American Publishers. *Winner*: Barnet Rosset.

Helen B. Bernstein Award. For excellence in journalism. *Offered by*: New York Public Library. *Winner*: Nina Bernstein for *The Lost Children of Wilder* (Pantheon).

James Tait Black Memorial Prizes (United Kingdom). For the best novel and the best biography of the year. *Offered by*: University of Edinburgh. *Winners*: (novel) Sid Smith for *Something Like a House* (Picador); (biography) Robert Skidelsky for *John Maynard Keynes: Fighting for Britain, 1937–1946* (Macmillan).

Booker Prize. See Man Booker Prize.

BookSense Book of the Year Awards. To honor titles that member stores have most enjoyed handselling in the past year. *Offered by*: American Booksellers Association. *Winners*: (fiction) Leif Enger for *Peace Like a River* (Atlantic Monthly); (nonfiction) Laura Hillenbrand for *Seabiscuit* (Random House); (children's illustrated) Ian Falconer for *Olivia Saves the Circus* (Atheneum); (children's literature) Ann Brashares for *The Sisterhood of the Traveling Pants* (Delacorte); (rediscovery) Ruth Stiles Gannett for *My Father's Dragon* (Random House).

Boston Globe/Horn Book Awards. For excellence in children's literature. *Offered by*: *Boston Globe* and *Horn Book Magazine.* *Winners*: (fiction) Graham Salisbury for *Lord of the Deep* (Delacorte); (nonfiction) Elizabeth Partridge for *The Life and Songs of Woody Guthrie* (Viking); (picture book) Bob Graham for *Let's Get a Pup! Said Kate* (Candlewick).

William Boyd Literary Award. For a published work of fiction set in a period when the United States was at war. *Offered by*: American Library Association. *Winner*: Owen West for *Sharkman Six* (Simon & Schuster).

Michael Braude Award. For light verse. *Offered by*: American Academy of Arts and Letters. *Winner*: Henry Taylor.

British Academy Book Prize (United Kingdom). For a book in the humanities or social sciences that is both academically outstanding and accessible to the general reader. *Offered by*: British Academy. *Winner*: Stanley Cohen for *States of Denial: Knowing about Atrocities and Suffering* (Polity Press).

Witter Bynner Prize for Poetry. To support the work of emerging poets. *Offered by*: American Academy of Arts and Letters. *Winner*: Susan Wheeler.

Caldecott Medal. For the artist of the most distinguished picture book. *Offered by*: American Library Association, Association for Library Service to Children. *Winner*: David Wiesner for *The Three Pigs* (Clarion Books).

California Book Awards. To California residents to honor books of fiction and poetry published in the previous year. *Offered by*: Commonwealth Club of California. *Winners*: (Gold Medal for Poetry) Czeslaw Milosz for *New and Collected Poems: 1931–2001* (Ecco); (Gold Medal for Fiction) Susan Straight for *Highwire Moon* (Houghton Mifflin).

John W. Campbell Memorial Award. For science fiction writing. *Offered by*: Center for the Study of Science Fiction. *Winners*: Jack Williamson for *Terraforming Earth* (Tor); Robert Charles Wilson for *The Chronoliths* (Tor).

Truman Capote Award for Literary Criticism. Given in memory of Newton Arvin. *Offered by*: University of Iowa Writers Workshop. *Winner*: Declan Kieberd for *Irish Classics* (Harvard).

Carnegie Medal (United Kingdom). For the outstanding children's book of the year. *Offered by*: The Library Association. *Winner*: Terry Pratchett for *The Amazing Maurice and His Educated Rodents* (Doubleday).

Christopher Awards. To people in the media who have created works that affirm the highest values of the human spirit. *Offered by*: The Christophers. *Winners*: (adult books) Antoinette Bosco for *Choosing Mercy* (Orbis); Jimmy Carter for *An Hour Before Daylight* (Simon & Schuster); Barbara Ehrenreich for *Nickel and Dimed* (Metropolitan Books); David McCullough for *John Adams* (Simon & Schuster); Lynne Olson for *Freedom's Daughter* (Scribner); David Snowdon for *Aging with Grace* (Bantam); (young people's books) (preschool) Amy Hest for *Kiss Good Night* (Candlewick); (ages 6–8) Page McBrier for *Beatrice's Goat* (Atheneum/Schwartz); (ages 8–10) Sharon Creech for *Love That Dog* (HarperCollins/Cotler); (ages 10–12) Ralph Fletcher for *Uncle Daddy* (Henry Holt); (young adult) Karen Hesse for *Witness* (Scholastic); Don Wulffson for *Soldier X* (Viking).

Arthur C. Clarke Award (United Kingdom). For the best science fiction novel of the year. *Offered by*: British Science Fiction Association. *Winner*: Gwyneth Jones for *Bold as Love* (Gollancz).

Commonwealth Writers Prize (United Kingdom). To reward and encourage new Commonwealth fiction and ensure that works of merit reach a wider audience outside their country of origin. *Offered by*: Commonwealth Institute. *Winner*: Richard Flanagan for *Gould's Book of Fish* (Grove).

Thomas Cook/Daily Telegraph Travel Book Award (United Kingdom). For travel writing. *Offered by*: Booktrust. *Winner*: Ma Jian for *Red Dust* (Chatto & Windus).

Duff Cooper Prize (United Kingdom). For a literary work in the field of history, biography, politics, or poetry published in English or French and submitted by a recognized publisher. *Offered by*: Booktrust. *Winner*: Margaret MacMillan for *Peacemakers* (Murray).

Crime Writers' Association Awards (United Kingdom). For the best crime writing of the year. *Offered by*: Crime Writers' Association. *Winners*: (gold dagger for fiction) Jose Carlos Somoza for *The Athenian Murders* (Abacus); (silver dagger) James Crumley for *The Final Country* (HarperCollins); (Ian Fleming steel dagger) John Creed for *The Sirius Crossing* (Faber); (gold dagger for nonfiction) Lilian Pizzichini for *Dead Men's Wages* (Picador).

Crime Writers' Association Cartier Diamond Dagger for Lifetime Achievement (United Kingdom). *Offered by*: Crime Writers' Association. *Winner*: Sara Paretsky.

Philip K. Dick Award. For a distinguished science fiction paperback original published in the United States. *Offered by*: Norwescon. *Winner*: Richard Paul Russo for *Ship of Fools* (Ace).

Frederick Douglass Prizes. For nonfiction works on slavery, resistance, or abolition. *Offered by*: Gilder Lehrman Center for the Study of Slavery, Resistance and Abolition. *Winners*: Robert Harms for *The Diligent* (Basic Books); John Stauffer for *The Black Hearts of Men* (Harvard).

Encore Award (United Kingdom). For a second novel. *Offered by*: Society of Authors. *Winner*: Ali Smith for *Hotel World* (Hamish Hamilton).

Margaret A. Edwards Award. For lifetime contribution to writing for young adults. *Offered by*: American Library Association, Young Adult Library Services Association. *Winner*: Paul Zindel.

T. S. Eliot Prize (United Kingdom). For poetry. *Offered by*: Poetry Book Society. *Winner*: Anne Carson for *The Beauty of the Husband* (Cape).

Eleanor Farjeon Award (United Kingdom). For altering the public perception of children's books. *Offered by*: Children's Book Circle and Scholastic Corp. *Winner*: Philip Pullman.

E. M. Forster Award. To a young writer from England, Ireland, Scotland, or Wales for a stay in the United States. *Offered by*:

American Academy of Arts and Letters. *Winner*: Helen Simpson.

Frost Medal. To recognize achievement in poetry over a lifetime. *Offered by*: Poetry Society of America. *Winner*: Galway Kinnell.

Giller Prize (Canada). For the best novel or short story collection written in English. *Offered by*: Giller Prize Foundation. *Winner*: Austin Clarke for *The Polished Hoe* (Thomas Allen).

Golden Kite Awards. For children's books. *Offered by*: Society of Children's Book Writers and Illustrators. *Winners*: (fiction) Virginia Euwer Wolff for *True Believer* (Atheneum); (nonfiction) Susan Campbell Bartoletti for *Black Potatoes* (Houghton); (picture book text) J. Patrick Lewis for *The Shoe Tree of Chagrin*, illus. by Chris Sheban (Creative Co.); (picture book illustration) Jacqueline Briggs Martin for *The Lamp, the Ice, and the Boat Called Fish*, illus. by Beth Krommes (Houghton).

Kate Greenaway Medal (United Kingdom). For children's book illustration. *Offered by*: The Library Association. *Winner*: Chris Riddell for *Pirate Diary*, text by Richard Platt (Walker).

Griffin Poetry Prizes (Canada). For two books of poetry, one by a Canadian and one by an international poet or translator. *Offered by*: Griffin Trust for Excellence in Poetry. *Winners*: (Canadian prize) Christian Bok for *Eunoia* (Coach House); (international prize) Alice Notley for *Disobedience* (Penguin).

Guardian Children's Fiction Prize (United Kingdom). For an outstanding children's novel. *Offered by*: The Guardian. *Winner*: Sonya Hartnett for *Thursday's Child* (Walker).

Guardian First Book Award (United Kingdom). For recognition of a first book. *Offered by*: The Guardian. *Winner*: Jonathan Safran Foer for *Everything Is Illuminated* (Hamish Hamilton).

Guggenheim Literary Fellowships. For unusually distinguished achievement in the past and exceptional promise for future accomplishment. *Offered by*: Guggenheim Memorial Foundation. *Winners*: (poetry) Betty Adcock, Elizabeth Alexander, Peter Cole, Daniel Hall, Richard Jackson, Jane Mead, Mary Ruefle, Charlie Smith, Dean Young; (fiction) Rabih Alameddine, Donald Antrim, Mary Gaitskill, William Gay, Paul LaFarge, Jhumpa Lahiri, Claire Messud.

O. B. Hardison, Jr. Poetry Prize. For excellence in poetry and in the teaching of poetry. *Offered by*: Folger Shakespeare Library. *Winner*: Ellen Bryant Voight.

Drue Heinz Literature Prize. To recognize and encourage writing of short fiction. *Offered by*: Drue Heinz Foundation and the University of Pittsburgh. *Winner*: John Blair for *American Standard* (Univ. of Pittsburgh).

Ernest Hemingway Foundation Award. For a distinguished work of first fiction by an American. *Offered by*: PEN New England. *Winner*: Justin Cronin for *Mary and O'Neill* (Dial).

Hugo Awards. For outstanding science fiction writing. *Offered by*: World Science Fiction Convention. *Winners*: (best novel) Neil Gaiman for *American Gods* (Morrow); (best related book) Ron Miller and others *The Art of Chesley Bonestell* (Paper Tiger); (best editor) Ellen Datlow; (best artist) Michael Whelan.

IACP Cookbook Awards. For the best cookbooks of the year. *Offered by*: International Association of Culinary Professionals. *Winners*: (book of the year) Peter Reinhart for *The Bread Baker's Apprentice* (Ten Speed Press); (American) *The America's Test Kitchen Cookbook*, by the editors of *Cook's Illustrated* (Boston Common); (chefs & restaurants) Lidia Matticchio Bastianich for *Lidia's Italian-American Kitchen* (Knopf); (food reference/technical) Wayne Gisslen for *Professional Baking* (Wiley); (general) Sally Schneider for *A New Way to Cook* (Artisan); (health & special diet) Rozanne Gold for *Healthy 1-2-3* (Stewart, Tabori & Chang); (international) Julie Sahni for *Savoring Indian* (Weldon Owen); (literary) Susan Herrmann Loomis for *On Rue Tatin* (Broadway); (single subject) Steven Raichlen for *How to Grill* (Workman); (wine, beer, and spirits) Stephen Brook for *Bordeaux* (Mitchell Beazley); (first book) Barbara Shinn and David Page for *Recipes from*

Home (Artisan); (Jane Grigson Award for Distinguished Scholarship) Diane Kochilas for *The Glorious Foods of Greece* (Morrow), Stephen Brook for *Bordeaux* (Mitchell Beazley); (design) Birgitta Ralston for *Van Gogh's Table at the Auberge Ravoux* (Artisan).

IMPAC Dublin Literary Award (Ireland). For a book of high literary merit written in English or translated into English. *Offered by*: IMPAC Corp. and the City of Dublin. *Winners*: Michel Houellebecq for *The Elementary Particles* (Knopf); (translator award) Frank Wynne.

International Horror Guild Awards. To recognize outstanding achievements in the field of horror and dark fantasy. *Offered by*: International Horror Guild. *Winners*: (novel) Caitlin R. Kieman for *Threshold* (Roc); (first novel) David Searcy for *Ordinary Horror* (Viking); (collection) David B. Silva for *Through Shattered Glass* (Gauntlet Press); (anthology) Richard Chizmar, ed., for *Night Visions 10* (Subterranean Press); (living legend award) William F. Nolan.

Jewish Quarterly/Wingate Literary Prizes (United Kingdom). To recognize the contribution authors can make to thinking about issues related to Jews and Judaism. *Offered by*: Harold Hyam Wingate Foundation. *Winners*: (fiction) W. G. Sebald for *Austerlitz* (Hamish Hamilton); (nonfiction) Oliver Sacks for *Uncle Tungsten* (Picador).

Samuel Johnson Prize for Nonfiction (United Kingdom). For an outstanding work of nonfiction. *Offered by*: an anonymous donor. *Winner*: Margaret MacMillan for *Peacemakers* (John Murray).

Sue Kaufman Prize for First Fiction. For a first novel or collection of short stories. *Offered by*: American Academy of Arts and Letters. *Winner*: Donald Lee for *Yellow* (Norton).

Coretta Scott King Awards. For works that promote the cause of peace and brotherhood. *Offered by*: American Library Association, Social Responsibilities Roundtable. *Winners*: (author) Mildred D. Taylor for *The Land* (Penguin Putnam); (illustrator) Jerry Pinkney for *Goin' Someplace Special,* text by Patricia McKissack (Atheneum); (new talent award) Jerome Lagarrigue for *Freedom Summer,* text by Deborah Wiles (Atheneum).

Coretta Scott King/John Steptoe Award for New Talent. For an outstanding book designed to bring visibility to a black writer or artist at the beginning of his or her career. *Winner*: Jerome Lagarrigue, illus., for *Freedom Summer* by Deborah Wiles (Atheneum).

Kiriyama Pacific Rim Book Prizes. For a book of fiction and a book of nonfiction that best contribute to fuller understanding among the nations and peoples of the Pacific Rim. *Offered by*: Kiriyama Pacific Rim Institute. *Winners*: (fiction) Rohinton Mistry for *Family Matters* (Knopf); (nonfiction) Pascal Khoo Thwe for *From the Land of Green Ghosts* (HarperCollins).

Robert Kirsch Award. To a living author whose residence or focus is the American West , and whose contributions to American letters clearly merit body-of-work recognition. *Offered by*: *Los Angeles Times*. *Winner*: Jonathan Kirsch.

Koret Jewish Book Awards. To underline the centrality of books in Jewish culture and to encourage serious readers to seek the best of Jewish books. *Offered by*: Koret Foundation. *Winners*: (fiction) Natalie Babel, ed., for *The Complete Works of Isaac Babel* (Norton); (special award for literature) W. G. Sebald for *Austerlitz* (Random House); (Jewish philosophy and thought) Samuel Heilman for *When a Jew Dies* (Univ. of California), Ken Koltun-Fromm for *Moses Hess and Modern Jewish Identity* (Indiana Univ.); (biography/autobiography) Dorothy Gallagher for *How I Came into My Inheritance and Other True Stories* (Random House); (history) Eli Lederhendler for *New York Jews and the Decline of Urban Ethnicity, 1950–1970* (Syracuse Univ.).

Harold Morton Landon Translation Award. For a book of verse translated into English by a single translator. *Offered by*: Academy of American Poets. *Winner*: David Ferry for *The Epistles of Horace* (Farrar Straus & Giroux).

James Laughlin Award. To commend and support a second book of poetry. *Offered by*: Academy of American Poets. *Winner*: Karen Volkman for *Spar* (Univ. of Iowa).

Ruth Lily Poetry Fellowships. To help aspiring writers to continue their study and practice of poetry. *Offered by*: Modern Poetry Association. *Winners*: Ilya Kaminsky, Brady Udall.

Ruth Lily Poetry Prize. To a United States poet whose accomplishments warrant extraordinary recognition. *Offered by*: Modern Poetry Association. *Winner*: Lisel Mueller.

Locus Awards. For science fiction writing. *Offered by*: Locus Publications. *Winners*: (best novel) Connie Willis for *Passage* (Bantam); (best fantasy novel) Neil Gaiman for *American Gods* (Morrow); (best first novel) Jacqueline Carey for *Kushiel's Dart* (Tor); (best nonfiction book) Michael Swanwick for *Being Gardner Dozois* (Old Earth Books); (best art book) Cathy and Arnie Fenner, eds., for *Spectrum 8: The Best in Contemporary Fantastic Art* (Underwood Books); (best collection) Ursula K. Le Guin for *Tales from Earthsea* (Harcourt); (best anthology) Gardner Dozois, ed., for *The Year's Best Science Fiction: Eighteenth Annual Collection* (St. Martin's); (best editor) Gardner Dozois; (best artist) Michael Whelan; (best publisher) Tor.

Los Angeles Times Book Prizes. To honor literary excellence. *Offered by*: Los Angeles Times. *Winners*: (fiction) Mary Robinson for *Why Did I Ever?* (Counterpoint); (biography) Edmund Morris for *Theodore Rex* (Random House); (current interest) Barbara Ehrenreich for *Nickel and Dimed* (Metropolitan Books); (history) Rick Perlstein for *Before the Storm* (Hill & Wang); (poetry) Anne Carson for *The Beauty of the Husband* (Knopf); (mystery) T. Jefferson Parker for *Silent Joe* (Hyperion); (science and technology) Richard Hamblyn for *The Invention of Clouds* (Farrar Straus & Giroux); (young adult fiction) Mildred D. Taylor for *The Land* (Phyllis Fogelman Books); (Art Seidenbaum Award for first fiction) Rachel Seiffert for *The Dark Room* (Pantheon).

Amy Lowell Poetry Travelling Scholarship. To a U.S. poet to spend one year outside North America in a country the recipeint feels will most advance his or her work. *Offered by*: Amy Lowell Poetry Travelling Scholarship. *Winner*: Rick Hilles.

J. Anthony Lukas Prizes. For nonfiction writing that demonstrates literary grace, serious research, and concern for an important aspect of American social or political life. *Offered by*: Columbia University Graduate School of Journalism and the Nieman Foundation. *Winners*: (book prize) Diane McWhorter for *Carry me Home* (Simon & Schuster); (work-in-progress) Jacques Leslie for *On Dams* (Farrar Straus & Giroux).

Mark Lynton History Prize. For history writing that demonstrates literary grace and serious research. *Offered by*: Columbia University Graduate School of Journalism and the Nieman Foundation. *Winner*: Mark Roseman for *A Past in Hiding* (Metropolitan Books).

Man Booker Prize (United Kingdom). For the best novel written in English by a Commonwealth author. *Offered by*: Booktrust and the Man Group. *Winner*: Yann Martel for *Life of Pi* (Harcourt).

Lenore Marshall Poetry Prize. For an outstanding book of poems published in the United States. *Offered by*: Academy of American Poets. *Winner*: Madeline DeFrees for *Blue Dusk* (Copper Canyon).

Somerset Maugham Awards (United Kingdom). For young British writers to gain experience in foreign countries. *Offered by*: Society of Authors. *Winner*: Charlotte Hobson for *Black Earth City* (Granta); Marcel Theroux for *The Paperchase* (Abacus).

McKitterick Prize (United Kingdom). For a first novel by a writer over the age of 40. *Offered by*: Society of Authors. *Winner*: Manil Suri for *The Death of Vishnu* (Bloomsbury).

Addison Metcalf Award for Literature. To a young writer of great promise. *Offered by*: American Academy of Arts and Letters. *Winner*: Claire Messud.

National Arts Club Medal of Honor for Literature. *Offered by*: National Arts Club. *Winner*: Edna O'Brien.

National Book Awards. For the best books of the year published in the United States. *Offered by*: National Book Foundation. *Winners*: (fiction) Julia Glass for *Three Junes* (Pantheon); (poetry) Ruth Stone for *In the Next Galaxy* (Copper Canyon); (nonfiction) Robert A. Caro for *Master of the Senate* (Knopf); (young people's literature) Nancy Farmer for *The House of the Scorpion* (Richard Jackson/Atheneum); (Distinguished Contribution to American Letters) Philip Roth.

National Book Critics Circle Awards. For literary excellence. *Offered by*: National Book Critics Circle. *Winners*: (fiction) W. G. Sebald for *Austerlitz* (Random House); (general nonfiction) Nicholson Baker for *Double Fold* (Random House); (poetry) Albert Goldbarth for *Saving Lives* (Ohio State Univ.); (biography/autobiography) Adam Sisman for *Boswell's Presumptuous Task* (Farrar Straus & Giroux); (criticism) Martin Amis for *The War Against Cliché* (Talk Miramax); (Nona Balakian Citation for Excellence in Reviewing) Michael Gorra; (Ivan Sandrof Lifetime Achievement Award) Jason Epstein.

Nebula Awards. For the best science fiction writing. *Offered by*: Science Fiction Writers of America. *Winner*: (best novel) Catherine Asaro for *The Quantum Rose* (Tor).

John Newbery Medal. For the most distinguished contribution to literature for children. *Offered by*: American Library Association, Association for Library Service to Children. *Winner*: Linda Sue Park for *A Single Shard* (Clarion Books).

Nobel Prize in Literature (Sweden). For the total literary output of a distinguished career. *Offered by*: Swedish Academy. *Winner*: Imre Kertesz.

Flannery O'Connor Awards for Short Fiction. For collections of short fiction. *Offered by*: PEN American Center. *Winners*: Jennifer Davis for *Her Kind of Want* (Univ. of Georgia); Laura Valeri for *The Kind of Things Saints Do* (Univ. of Georgia).

Orange Prize for Fiction (United Kingdom). For the best novel written by a woman and published in the United Kingdom. *Offered by*: Orange plc. *Winner*: Ann Patchett for *Bel Canto* (HarperPerennial).

PEN Award for Poetry in Translation. *Offered by*: PEN American Center. *Winner*: Anne Twitty for *Islandia* by Maria Negroni (Barrytown Ltd.).

PEN/Martha Albrand Award for the Art of the Memoir. *Offered by*: PEN American Center. *Winner*: Paula Fox for *Borrowed Finery* (Holt).

PEN/Martha Albrand Award for First Nonfiction. *Offered by*: PEN American Center. *Winner*: Nina Bernstein for *The Lost Children of Wilder* (Pantheon).

PEN/Robert Bingham Fellowships. For debut fiction authors. *Offered by*: PEN American Center. *Winners*: Carolyn Cook, Matthew Klam, Manil Suri.

PEN/Book-of-the-Month Club Translation Award. *Offered by*: PEN American Center. *Winners*: Richard Pevear and Larissa Volokhonsky for *Anna Karenina* by Leo Tolstoy (Viking).

PEN/Faulkner Award for Fiction. To honor the best work of fiction published by an American. *Offered by*: PEN American Center. *Winner*: Ann Patchett for *Bel Canto* (HarperCollins).

PEN/Nabokov Award. To celebrate the accomplishments of a living author whose body of work, either written in English or translated into English, represents achievement in a variety of literary genres and is of enduring originality and consummate craftsmanship. *Offered by*: PEN American Center. *Winner*: Mario Vargas Llosa.

PEN/Phyllis Naylor Working Writer Fellowship. To provide the financial support to enable the completion of a book. *Offered by*: PEN American Center. *Winner*: Lori Aurelia Williams.

PEN/Spielvogel-Diamonstein Essay Award. For an outstanding book of essays by an American writer. *Offered by*: PEN American Center. *Winner*: David Bromwich for *Skeptical Music* (Univ. of Chicago).

PEN/Voelcker Award for Poetry. To an American poet at the height of his or her powers. *Offered by*: PEN American Center. *Winner*: Frederick Seidel.

Edgar Allan Poe Awards. For outstanding mystery, suspense, and crime writing. *Offered by*: Mystery Writers of America. *Winners*: (novel) T. Jefferson Parker for *Silent Joe* (Hyperion); (first novel) David Ellis for *Line of Vision* (Putnam); (paperback original) Daniel Chavaria for *Adios Muchacho* (Akashic Books); (critical/biographical) Dawn Sova for *Edgar Allan Poe* (Facts on File); (fact crime) Kent Walker for *Son of a Grifter* (Morrow); (young adult) Tim Wynne-Jones for *The Boy in the Burning House* (Farrar Straus & Giroux); (Mary Higgins Clark Award) Judith Kelman for *Summer of Storms* (Putnam).

Katherine Anne Porter Award. To a prose writer of demonstrated achievement. *Offered by*: American Academy of Arts and Letters. *Winner*: Lynn Freed.

Michael L. Printz Award. For excellence in literature for young adults. *Offered by*: American Library Association, Association for Library Service to Children. *Winner*: An Na for *A Step from Heaven* (Front Street Books).

Pulitzer Prizes in Letters. To honor distinguished work by American writers, dealing preferably with American themes. *Offered by*: Columbia University Graduate School of Journalism. *Winners*: (fiction) Richard Russo for *Empire Falls* (Knopf); (general nonfiction) Diane McWhorter for *Carry Me Home* (Simon & Schuster); (biography) David McCullough for *John Adams* (Simon & Schuster); (history) Louis Menand for *The Metaphysical Club* (Farrar Straus & Giroux); (poetry) Carl Dennis for *The Practical Gods* (Penguin).

Quality Paperback Book Club New Visions Award. For the most distinct and promising work of nonfiction by a new writer offered by the club each year. *Offered by*: Quality Paperback Book Club. *Winner*: Andrew Solomon for *The Noonday Demon* (Simon & Schuster).

Quality Paperback Book Club New Voices Award. For the most distinct and promising work of fiction by a new writer offered by the club each year. *Offered by*: Quality

Paperback Book Club. *Winner*: Brady Udall for *The Miracle Life of Edgar Mint* (Norton).

Raiziss/De Palchi Translation Award. For a translation into English of a significant work of modern Italian poetry by a living translator. *Offered by*: Academy of American Poets. *Winner*: Stephen Sartarelli for *Songbook: The Selected Poems of Umberto Saba* (Sheep Meadow Press).

Rea Award for the Short Story. To honor a living writer who has made a significant contribution to the short story as an art form. *Offered by*: Dungannon Foundation. *Winner*: Mavis Gallant.

Arthur Rense Poetry Prize. Given every few years to an exceptional poet who may not have received due recognition over the course of a long career. *Offered by*: Academy of American Poets. *Winner*: B. H. Fairchild.

John Llewellyn Rhys Memorial Award (United Kingdom). For fiction writers under the age of 35. *Offered by*: The Mail on Sunday. *Winner*: Susanna Jones for *The Earthquake Bird* (Picador).

Richard and Hinda Rosenthal Foundation Award. For a work of fiction that is a considerable literary achievement though not necessarily a commercial success. *Offered by*: American Academy of Arts and Letters. *Winner*: Amy Wilentz for *Martyrs' Crossing* (Simon & Schuster).

Juan Rulfo International Latin American and Caribbean Prize for Literature (Mexico). To a writer of poetry, novels, short stories, drama, or essays who is a native of Latin America or the Caribbean, and who writes in Spanish, Portuguese, or English. *Offered by*: Juan Rulfo Award Committee. *Winner*: Cintio Vitier.

Runciman Award (United Kingdom). For a book about Greece or the Hellenic scene, published in the United Kingdom. *Offered by*: Booktrust. *Winner*: James Whitley for *The Archaeology of Ancient Greece* (Cambridge).

Sagittarius Prize (United Kingdom). For a first novel by a writer over the age of 60. *Offered by*: Society of Authors. *Winner*: Svi Jagendorf for *Wolfy and the Strudelbakers* (Dewi Lewis).

Scottish Book of the Year (Scotland). *Offered by*: Scottish Arts Council. *Winner*: Ali Smith for *Hotel World* (Penguin).

Scottish Children's Book of the Year (Scotland). *Offered by*: Scottish Arts Council. *Winner*: Alison Prince for *Oranges and Murder* (Oxford).

Shamus Awards. For crime and mystery writing. *Offered by*: Private Eye Writers of America. *Winners*: (best novel) S. J. Rozan for *Reflecting the Sky* (St. Martin's); (best Paperback original) Lyda Morehouse for *Archangel Protocol* (ROC/NAL); (best first novel) David Fulmer for *Chasing the Devil's Tail* (Poisoned Pen); (lifetime achievement) Lawrence Block.

Shelley Memorial Award. To a poet living in the United States who is chosen on the basis of genius and need. *Offered by*: Poetry Society of America. *Winners*: Angela Jackson, Marie Ponsot.

Robert F. Sibert Award. For the most distinguished informational book for children. *Offered by*: American Library Association, Association for Library Service to Children. *Winner*: Susan Campbell Bartoletti for *Black Potatoes* (Houghton Mifflin).

Smarties Book Prizes (United Kingdom). To encourage high standards and to stimulate interest in books for children. *Offered by*: Booktrust and Nestlé Rowntree. *Winners*: (ages 9–11) Philip Reeve for *Mortal Engines* (Scholastic); (ages 6–8) Richard Platt and Chris Riddell for *Pirate Diary* (Walker); (ages 0–5) Lucy Cousins for *Jazzy in the Jungle* (Walker).

W. H. Smith Literary Awards. *Winners*: (fiction) Nick Hornby for *How to Be Good* (Penguin); (children's) Eoin Colfer for *Artemis Fowl* (Puffin); (biography) Pamela Stephenson for *Billy* (HarperCollins); (literary fiction) Ian McEwan for *Atonement* (Cape); (general knowledge) Alastair Fothergill and others for *The Blue Planet* (BBC Books); (home and leisure) Nigella Lawson for *Nigella Bites* (Chatto).

Sydney Taylor Children's Book Awards. *Offered by*: Assn. of Jewish Libraries. *Winners*: (older readers) *Hana's Suitcase: A True Story* by Karen Levine (Second Story Press); (younger readers) *Chicken Soup By Heart* by Esther Hershenhorn, illus. by Rosanne Litzinger (Simon & Schuster).

Sydney Taylor Manuscript Award. *Offffered by*: Assn. of Jewish Libraries. *Winner*: Karen Schwabach for *A Pickpocket's Tale*.

Templeton Prize for Progress in Religion. To honor a person judged to have contributed special insights to religion and spirituality. *Offered by*: Templeton Foundation. *Winner*: John C. Polkinghorne.

Betty Trask Awards (United Kingdom). For works of a romantic or traditional nature by writers under the age of 35. *Offered by*: Society of Authors. *Winners*: (first novel) Hari Kunzru for *The Impressionist* (Hamish Hamilton); Rachel Seiffert for *The Dark Room* (Heineman); Shamim Sarif for *The World Unseen* (Women's Press); Helen Cross for *My Summer of Love* (Bloomsbury); Susanna Jones for *The Earthquake Bird* (Picador); Chloe Hooper for *A Child's Book of True Crime* (Cape); Gwendoline Riley for *Cold Water* (Cape).

Kate Frost Tufts Discovery Award. For a first or very early book of poetry by an emerging poet. *Offered by*: Claremont Graduate School. *Winner*: Cate Marvin for *World's Tallest Disaster* (Sarabande).

Kingsley Tufts Poetry Award. For a book of poetry by a mid-career poet. *Offered by*: Claremont Graduate School. *Winner*: Carl Phillips for *The Tether* (Farrar Straus & Giroux).

Harold D. Vursell Memorial Award. For writing that merits recognition for the quality of its prose style. *Offered by*: American Academy of Arts and Letters. *Winner*: Freeman House.

Washington Post/Children's Book Guild Nonfiction Award. To an author or illustrator whose total body of work has contributed significantly to the quality of nonfiction for children. *Offered by*: Children's Book Guild. *Winner*: George Ancona.

Whitbread Literary Prizes (United Kingdom). For literature of merit that is readable on a wide scale. *Offered by*: Booksellers Association of Great Britain. *Winners*: (novel) Michael Frayn for *Spies* (Faber); (first novel) Norman Lebrecht for *The Song of Names* (Review); (poetry) Paul Farley for *The Ice Age* (Picador); (biography) Claire

Tomalin for *Samuel Pepys* (Viking); (children's) Hilary McKay for *Saffy's Angel* (Hodder).

Whiting Writer's Awards. For emerging writers of exceptional talent and promise. *Offered by*: Mrs. Giles Whiting Foundation. *Winners*: (poetry) Elizabeth Arnold, David Gewanter, Joshua Weiner; (fiction) Jeffrey Renard Allen, Justin Cronin, Kim Edwards, Michelle Huneven, Danzy Senna.

Walt Whitman Award. For Poetry. *Offered by*: Academy of American Poets. *Winner*: Sue Kwok Kim for *Notes from the Divided Country* (Louisiana State Univ.).

Helen and Kurt Wolf Translator's Prize. For an outstanding translation from German into English, published in the United States. *Offered by*: Goethe Institut Inter Nationes Chicago. *Winner*: Anthea Bell for *Austerlitz* by W. G. Sebald (Random House).

World Fantasy Convention Awards. For outstanding fantasy writing. *Offered by*: World Fantasy Convention. *Winners*: (novel) Ursula K. Le Guin for *The Other Wind* (Harcourt); (anthology) Dennis Etchison, ed., *The Museum of Horrors* (Leisure Books); (collection) Nalo Hopkinson for *Skin Folk* (Warner); (lifetime achievement) George Scithers, Forrest J. Ackerman.

Young Lions Fiction Award. For a novel or collection of short stories by an American under the age of 35. *Offered by*: Young Lions of the New York Public Library. *Winner*: Colson Whitehead for *John Henry Days* (Doubleday).

Morton Dauwen Zabel Award in Poetry. To writers of experimental and progressive tendencies. *Offered by*: American Academy of Arts and Letters. *Winner*: Ronald Sukenick.

Part 6
Directory of Organizations

Directory of Library and Related Organizations

Networks, Consortia, and Other Cooperative Library Organizations

This list is taken from the 2002–2003 edition of *American Library Directory* (Information Today, Inc.), which includes additional information on member libraries and primary functions of each organization.

United States

Alabama

Alabama Health Libraries Association, Inc. (ALHeLa), Univ. of Southern Alabama, Medical Center Lib., Mobile 36617. SAN 372-8218. Tel. 251-471-7855, fax 251-471-7857. *Dir.* Tom Williams.

Jefferson County Hospital Librarians Association, Brookwood Medical Center, Birmingham 35209. SAN 371-2168. Tel. 205-877-1131, fax 205-877-1189.

Library Management Network, Inc., 110 Johnston St. S.E., Decatur 35601. SAN 322-3906. Tel. 256-308-2529, fax 256-308-2533. *System Coord.* Charlotte Moncrief.

Marine Environmental Sciences Consortium, Dauphin Island Sea Lab, Dauphin Island 36528. SAN 322-0001. Tel. 251-861-2141, fax 251-861-4646, e-mail disl@disl.org. *Dir.* George Crozier.

Network of Alabama Academic Libraries, c/o Alabama Commission on Higher Education, Montgomery 36130-2000. SAN 322-4570. Tel. 334-242-2164, fax 334-242-0270. *Dir.* Sue Medina.

Alaska

Alaska Library Network (ALN), 344 W. Third Ave., Suite 125, Anchorage 99501. SAN 371-0688. Tel. 907-269-6570, fax 907-269-6580, e-mail aslanc@eed.state.ak.us.

Arizona

Maricopa County Community College District Library Technical Services, 2411 W. 14 St., Tempe 85281-6942. SAN 322-0060. Tel. 480-731-8774, fax 480-731-8787. *Head of Technical Services* Vince Jenkins.

Arkansas

Arkansas Area Health Education Center Consortium (AHEC), Sparks Regional Medical Center, Forth Smith 72901-4992. SAN 329-3734. Tel. 501-441-5337, fax 501-441-5339. *Dir.* Grace Anderson.

Arkansas Independent Colleges and Universities, 1 Riverfront Place, Suite 610, North Little Rock 72114. SAN 322-0079. Tel. 501-378-0843, fax 501-374-1523. *Pres.* Kearney Dietz.

Northeast Arkansas Hospital Library Consortium, 223 E. Jackson, Jonesboro 72401. SAN 329-529X. Tel. 870-972-1290, fax 870-931-0839. *Dir.* Karen Crosser.

South Arkansas Film Coop., 301 S. Main St., Malvern 72104-3738. SAN 321-5938. Tel. 501-332-5442, fax 501-332-6679, e-mail hotspringcountylibrary@yahoo.com.

California

Bay Area Library and Information Network (BAYNET), 672 Prentiss St., San Francisco 94110-6130. SAN 371-0610. Tel. 415-826-2464, e-mail infobay@baynetlibs.org.

Central Association of Libraries (CAL), 605 N. El Dorado St., Stockton 95202-1999. SAN 322-0125. Tel. 209-937-8649, fax 209-937-8292. *Dir.* Darla Gunning.

Consortium for Open Learning, 3841 N. Freeway Blvd., Suite 200, Sacramento 95834-1948. SAN 329-4412. Tel. 916-565-0188, fax 916-565-0189, e-mail cdl@calweb.com. *Exec. Dir.* Jerome Thompson.

Consumer Health Information Program and Services (CHIPS), County of Los Angeles Public Lib., Carson 90745. SAN 372-8110. Tel. 310-830-0909, fax 310-834-4097, e-mail chips@colopl.org. *Libn.* Scott Willis.

Dialog Corporation, 2440 El Camino Real, Mountain View 94040. SAN 322-0176. Tel. 650-254-7000, fax 650-254-8093.

Educational Resources Information Center (ERIC) Clearinghouse for Community Colleges (JC), 3051 Moore Hall, 405 Hilgard Ave., UCLA, Los Angeles 90095. SAN 322-0648. Tel. 310-825-3931, fax 310-206-8095, e-mail ericcc@ucla.edu. *Dir.* Art Cohen.

Gold Coast Library Network, 4882 McGrath St., Suite 230, Ventura 93003-7721. Tel. 805-477-0390, fax 805-477-0521, e-mail goldcln@rain.org. *Dir.* Vince Schmidt.

Golden Gateway Library Network (GGLN), 2471 Flores St., San Mateo 94403. Tel. 650-349-5538, fax 650-349-5089. *Pres., Exec. Dir.* Linda Crowe.

Hewlett-Packard Library Information Network, 1501 Page Mill Rd., Palo Alto 94304. SAN 375-0019. Tel. 650-857-3091, 857-6620, fax 650-852-8187. *Dir.* Eugenie Prime.

Kaiser Permanente Library System—Southern California Region (KPLS), Health Sciences Lib., San Diego 92120. SAN 372-8153. Tel. 619-528-7323, fax 619-528-3444. *Dir.* Sheila Latus.

Metropolitan Cooperative Library System (MCLS), 3675 E. Huntington Dr., Suite 100, Pasadena 91107. SAN 371-3865. Tel. 626-683-8244, fax 626-683-8097, e-mail mclshq@mcls.org. *Exec. Dir.* Barbara Custen.

National Network of Libraries of Medicine—Pacific Southwest Region (NN-LM PSR), Louise M. Darling Biomedical Lib., Los Angeles 90095-1798. SAN 372-8234. Tel. 310-825-1200, fax 310-825-5389, e-mail psr-nnlm@library.ucla.edu. *Dir.* Alison Bunting.

Nevada Medical Library Group (NMLG), Barton Memorial Hospital Lib., South Lake Tahoe 96150. SAN 370-0445. Tel. 530-542-3000, ext. 2903, fax 530-541-4697. *In Charge* Laurie Anton.

Northern California Association of Law Libraries (NOCALL), c/o Santa Clara Univ., Santa Clara 95053. SAN 323-5777. E-mail admin@nocall.org. *Pres.* Ellen Platt.

Northern California Consortium of Psychology Libraries (NCCPL), Alliant International Univ., Alameda 94501. SAN 371-9006. Tel. 510-523-2300, ext. 185, fax 510-523-5943. *Dir.* Deanna Gaige.

OCLC Western Service Center, 3281 E. Quasti Rd., Suite 560, Ontario 91761. SAN 370-0747. Tel. 909-937-3300, fax 909-937-3384. *Dir.* Pamela Bailey.

Peninsula Libraries Automated Network (PLAN), 2471 Flores St., San Mateo 94403-4000. SAN 371-5035. Tel. 650-358-6714, fax 650-358-6715. *Database Manager* Susan Yasar.

Research Libraries Group, Inc. (RLG), 1200 Villa St., Mountain View 94041-1100. SAN 322-0206. Tel. 800-537-7546, fax 650-964-0943, e-mail bl.ric@rlg.org. *Pres.* James Michalko.

San Bernardino, Inyo, Riverside Counties United Library Services (SIRCULS), 3581 Mission Inn Ave., Riverside 92501-3377. SAN 322-0222. Tel. 909-369-7995, fax

909-784-1158, e-mail sirculs@inlandlib. org. *Exec. Dir.* Kathleen Aaron.

San Diego and Imperial Counties College Learning Resources Cooperative (SDICC-CL), Palomar College, San Marcos 92069-1487. SAN 375-006X. Tel. 760-744-1150, ext. 2848, fax 760-761-3500. *Dir.* George Mozes.

San Francisco Biomedical Library Network (SFBLN), H. M. Fishbon Memorial Lib., UCSF-Mount Zion, San Francisco 94115. SAN 371-2125. Tel. 415-885-7378, fax 415-776-0689, e-mail fishbon@itsa.ucfs. edu. *Dir.* Gail Sorrough.

Santa Clarita Interlibrary Network (SCIL-NET), 21726 W. Placerita Canyon Rd., Santa Clarita 91321. SAN 371-8964. Tel. 661-259-3540, fax 661-222-9159. *Libn.* John Stone.

Serra Cooperative Library System, 5555 Overland Ave., Bldg. 15, San Diego 92123. SAN 372-8129. Tel. 858-694-3600, fax 858-495-5905, e-mail hq@serralib.org. *System Coord.* Susan Swisher.

Smerc Library, 101 Twin Dolphin Dr., Redwood City 94065-1064. SAN 322-0265. Tel. 650-802-5655, fax 650-802-5665. *Libn.* Karol Thomas.

Southnet, c/o Silicon Valley Lib. System, San Jose 95113. SAN 322-4260. Tel. 408-294-2345, fax 408-295-7388, e-mail srch @ix.netcom.com.

Substance Abuse Librarians and Information Specialists (SALIS), Box 9513, Berkeley 94709-0513. SAN 372-4042. Tel. 510-642-5208, fax 510-642-7175, e-mail salis @arg.org. *Chair* Virginia Sanchez.

Colorado

American Gas Association—Library Services (AGA-LSC), c/o Excel Energy, Denver 80202. SAN 371-0890. Tel. 303-294-2620, fax 303-294-2799. *Libn.* Maryanne Hamm.

Arkansas Valley Regional Library Service System (AVRLSS), 635 W. Corona, Suite 113, Pueblo 81004. SAN 371-5094. Tel. 719-542-2156, fax 719-542- 3155. *Chair* Dorothy Cowgill.

Bibliographical Center for Research, Rocky Mountain Region, Inc. (BCR), 14394 E. Evans Ave., Aurora 80014-1478. SAN 322-0338. Tel. 303-751-6277, fax 303-751-9787, e-mail admin@bcr.org. *Exec. Dir.* David Brunell.

Central Colorado Library System (CCLS), 4350 Wadsworth Blvd., Suite 340, Wheat Ridge 80033-4634. SAN 371-3970. Tel. 303-422-1150, fax 303-431-9752. *Dir.* Gordon Barhydt.

Colorado Alliance of Research Libraries, 3801 E. Florida Ave., Suite 515, Denver 80210. SAN 322-3760. Tel. 303-759-3399, fax 303-759-3363.

Colorado Association of Law Libraries, Box 13363, Denver 80201. SAN 322-4325. Tel. 303-492-7312. *Pres.* Druet Klugh.

Colorado Council of Medical Librarians (CCML), Box 101058, Denver 80210-1058. SAN 370-0755. Tel. 303-450-3568, fax 303-560-4504.

Colorado Library Resource Sharing and Information Access Board, c/o Colorado State Lib., Denver 80203-1799. SAN 322-3868. Tel. 303-866-6900, fax 303-866-6940. *Dir.* Brenda Bailey.

High Plains Regional Library Service System, 800 Eighth Ave., Suite 209, Greeley 80631. SAN 371-0505. Tel. 970-356-4357, fax 970-353-4355. *Chair* Laura Roth.

Peaks and Valleys Library Consortium, c/o Arkansas Valley Regional Lib. Service System, Pueblo 81004. SAN 328-8684. Tel. 719-542-2156, fax 719-542-3155. *Dir.* Donna Morris.

Southwest Regional Library Service System (SWRLSS), Drawer B, Durango 81302. SAN 371-0815. Tel. 970-247-4782, fax 970-247-5087. *Exec. Dir.* Judith Griffiths.

Three Rivers Regional Library Service System, 1001 Grand Ave., Suite 205, Glenwood Springs 81601. SAN 301-9934. Tel. 970-945-2626, fax 970-945-9396. *Dir.* Sandra Scott.

Connecticut

Capital Area Health Consortium, 270 Farmington Ave., Suite 352, Farmington 06032-1994. SAN 322-0370. Tel. 860-676-1110, fax 860-676-1303.

Capitol Region Library Council, 599 Matianuck Ave., Windsor 06095-3567. SAN 322-0389. Tel. 860-298-5319, fax 860-

298-5328, e-mail office@crlc.org. *Exec. Dir.* Dency Sargent.

Council Of State Library Agencies in the Northeast (COSLINE), Connecticut State Lib., Hartford 06106. SAN 322-0451. Tel. 860-757-6510, fax 860-757-6503.

CTW Library Consortium, Olin Memorial Lib., Wesleyan Univ., Middletown 06457-6065. SAN 329-4587. Tel. 860-685-3889, fax 860-685-2661. *Dir.* Alan Hagyard.

Eastern Connecticut Libraries (ECL), ECSU Lib., Rm. 134, Willimantic 06226. SAN 322-0478. Tel. 860-465-5001, fax 860-465-5004. *Dir.* Christine Bradley.

Hartford Consortium for Higher Education, 1800 Asylum Ave., West Hartford 06117. SAN 322-0443. Tel. 860-236-1203, fax 860-233-9723. *Exec. Dir.* Rosanne Druckman.

LEAP (Library Exchange Aids Patrons), 110 Washington Ave., North Haven 06473. SAN 322-4082. Tel. 203-239-1411, fax 203-239-9458. *Exec. Dir.* Diana Sellers.

Libraries Online, Inc. (LION), 123 Broad St., Middletown 06457. SAN 322-3922. Tel. 860-347-1704, fax 860-346-3707. *Exec. Dir.* Edward Murray.

New England Law Library Consortium, Inc. (NELLCO), Yale Law School, Lillian Goldman Lib., New Haven 06520-8215. SAN 322-4244. Tel. 203-777-6599, fax 203-624-8811. *Exec. Dir.* Tracy Thompson.

North Atlantic Health Sciences Libraries, Inc. (NAHSL), Medial Lib. CB-3, Hartford 06102. SAN 371-0599. Tel. 508-856-6099, fax 508-856-5899. *Chair* Edward Donnald.

Southern Connecticut Library Council, 2911 Dixwell Ave., Suite 201, Hamden 06518-3130. SAN 322-0486. Tel. 203-288-5757, fax 203-287-0757, e-mail office@sclc.org. *Dir.* Marlene Palmquist.

Western Connecticut Library Council, Inc., 530 Middlebury Rd., Suite 210B, Middlebury 06762. SAN 322-0494. Tel. 203-577-4010, fax 203-577-4015. *Exec. Dir.* Anita Barney.

Delaware

Central Delaware Library Consortium, Dover Public Lib., Dover 19901. SAN 329-3696.

Tel. 302-736-7030, fax 302-736-5087. *Dir.* Sheila Anderson.

Delaware Library Consortium (DLC), Delaware Academy of Medicine, Wilmington 19806. SAN 329-3718. Tel. 302-656-6398, fax 302-656-0470. *Pres.* Gail P. Gill.

Wilmington Area Biomedical Library Consortium (WABLC), Christiana Care Health System, Newark 19718. SAN 322-0508. Tel. 302-733-1116, fax 302-733-1365, e-mail ccw@christianacare.org. *Pres.* Christine Chastain-Warheit.

District of Columbia

CAPCON Library Network, 1990 M St. N.W., Suite 200, Washington 20036-3430. SAN 321-5954. Tel. 202-331-5771, fax 202-331-5788, e-mail capcon@capcon.net. *Exec. Dir.* Robert A. Drescher.

Council for Christian Colleges and Universities, 321 Eighth St. N.E., Washington 20002. SAN 322-0524. Tel. 202-546-8713, fax 202-546-8913, e-mail council@cccu.org. *Pres.* Robert Andringa.

District of Columbia Area Health Science Libraries (DCAHSL), American College of Obstetrics and Gynecology Resource Center, Washington 20024. SAN 323-9918. Tel. 202-863-2518, fax 202-484-1595, e-mail resources@acog.org. *Dir.* Mary Hyde.

Educational Resources Information Center (ERIC), U.S. Dept. of Education, Office of Educational Research and Improvement, Washington 20202. SAN 322-0567. Tel. 202-219-1001, fax 202-219-0958, e-mail library@ed.gov. *Dir.* Sheila McGarr.

Educational Resources Information Center (ERIC) Clearinghouse on Higher Education (HE), George Washington Univ., Washington 20036-1183. SAN 322-0621. Tel. 202-296-2597, ext. 217, fax 202-452-1844, e-mail eric-he@eric-he.edu. *Reference Services* Shannon Loane.

Educational Resources Information Center (ERIC) Clearinghouse on Languages and Linguistics (FL), Center for Applied Linguistics, Washington 20016-1859. SAN 322-0656. Tel. 202-362-0700, fax 202-363-7204, e-mail eric@cal.org. *Dir.* Joy Peyton.

Educational Resources Information Center (ERIC) Clearinghouse on Teaching and Teacher Education (SP), American Assn. of Colleges for Teacher Education, Washington 20005-4701. SAN 322-0702. Tel. 202-293-2450, fax 202-457-8095. *Dir.* Mary Dilworth.

EDUCAUSE, c/o 1150 18th St. N.W., Suite 1010, Washington 20036. SAN 371-487X. Tel. 202-872-4200, fax 202-872-4318. *Pres.* Brian Hawkins.

FEDLINK (Federal Library and Information Network), c/o Federal Lib. and Information Center Committee, Washington 20540-4935. SAN 322-0761. Tel. 202-707-4800, fax 202-707-4818, e-mail flicc@loc.gov. *Exec. Dir.* Susan Tarr.

National Library Service for the Blind and Physically Handicapped, Library of Congress, 1291 Taylor St. N.W., Washington 20542. SAN 370-5870. Tel. 202-707-5100, fax 202-707-0712, e-mail nls@loc.gov. *Dir.* Frank Cylke.

Transportation Research Board, 2001 Wisconsin Ave. N.W., GR146, Washington 20007. SAN 370-582X. Tel. 202-334-2990, fax 202-334-2527. *Dir.* Barbara Post.

Veterans Affairs Library Network (VALNET), Lib. Programs Office 19E, Washington 20420. SAN 322-0834. Tel. 202-273-8523, 202-273-8522, fax 202-273-9125.

Washington Theological Consortium, 487 Michigan Ave. N.E., Washington 20017-1585. SAN 322-0842. Tel. 202-832-2675, fax 202-526-0818, e-mail wtconsort@aol.com. *Dir.* John Crossin.

Florida

Central Florida Library Cooperative (CFLC), 431 E. Horatio Ave., Suite 230, Maitland 32751. SAN 371-9014. Tel. 407-644-9050, fax 407-644-7023. *Exec. Dir.* Marta Westall.

Florida Library Information Network, c/o Bureau of Lib. and Network Services, State Lib. of Florida, Tallahassee 32399-0250. SAN 322-0869. Tel. 850-245-6600, fax 850-488-2746, e-mail library@mail.dos.state.fl.us. *Research* Betsy Kallenberger.

Palm Beach Health Sciences Library Consortium (PBHSLC), c/o Good Samaritan Medical Center Medical Lib., West Palm Beach 33402. SAN 370-0380. Tel. 561-650-6315, fax 561-650-6417.

Panhandle Library Access Network (PLAN), 5 Miracle Strip Loop, Suite 8, Panama City Beach 32407-3850. SAN 370-047X. Tel. 850-233-9051, fax 850-235-2286. *Exec. Dir.* William Conniff.

Southeast Florida Library Information Network, Inc. (SEFLIN), 100 S. Andrews Ave., Fort Lauderdale 33301. SAN 370-0666. Tel. 954-357-7345, fax 954-357-6998. *Pres.* Brian Kelley.

Southwest Florida Library Network, 24311 Walden Center Dr., Suite 100, Bonita Springs 34134. Tel. 941-948-1830, fax 941-948-1842. *Exec. Dir.* Barbara Stites.

Tampa Bay Library Consortium, Inc., 1202 Tech Blvd., Suite 202, Tampa 33619. SAN 322-371X. Tel. 813-740-3963, fax 813-628-4425.

Tampa Bay Medical Library Network (TABAMLN), Lakeland Regional Medical Center, Lakeland 33805. SAN 322-0885. Tel. 863-687-1176, fax 863-687-1488, e-mail jan.booker@lrmc.com.

Georgia

Association of Southeastern Research Libraries (ASERL), c/o SOLINET, Atlanta 30309-2955. SAN 322-1555. Tel. 404-892-0943, fax 404-892-7879. *Dir.* Robert Hulshof-Schmidt.

Atlanta Health Science Libraries Consortium, St. Joseph's Health System Lib., Atlanta 30342. SAN 322-0893. Tel. 770-793-7178, fax 770-793-7956. *Pres.* Brenda Curry-Kimberly.

Atlanta Regional Consortium for Higher Education, 50 Hurt Plaza, Suite 735, Atlanta 30303-2923. SAN 322-0990. Tel. 404-651-2668, fax 404-651-1797, e-mail arche@atlantahighered.org. *Pres.* Michael Gerber.

Biomedical Media, 1712 Upper Gate Dr., Suite 18, Atlanta 30322. SAN 322-0931. Tel. 404-727-9797, fax 404-727-9798. *Dir.* Chuck Bogle.

Georgia Interactive Network for Medical Information (GAIN), c/o Medical Lib., School of Medicine, Mercer Univ., Macon 31207. SAN 370-0577. Tel. 478-301-

2515, fax 478-301-2051. *Dir.* Jan La-Beause.

Georgia Online Database (GOLD), c/o Public Lib. Services, Atlanta 30345-4304. SAN 322-094X. Tel. 404-982-3560, fax 404-982-3563. *Dir.* Lamar Veach.

Metro Atlanta Library Association (MALA), c/o Atlanta Fulton Public Lib., Atlanta 30303-1089. SAN 378-2549. Tel. 404-730-1961, fax 404-730-1988. *Pres.* Andrea Akiti.

Southeastern Library Network (SOLINET), 1438 W. Peachtree St. N.W., Suite 200, Atlanta 30309-2955. SAN 322-0974. Tel. 404-892-0943, fax 404-892-7879. *Exec. Dir.* Kate Nevins.

SWGHSLC, Colquitt Regional Medical Center Health Sciences Lib., Moultrie 31776. SAN 372-8072. Tel. 229-890-3460, fax 229-891-9345. *Libn.* Susan Leik.

Hawaii

Hawaii-Pacific Chapter of the Medical Library Association (HPC-MLA), 1221 Punchbowl St., Honolulu 96813. SAN 371-3946. Tel. 808-536-9302, fax 808-524-6956. *Chair* Christine Sato.

Idaho

Boise Valley Health Sciences Library Consortium (BVHSLC), Health Sciences Lib., Boise 83706. SAN 371-0807. Tel. 208-367-3993, fax 208-367-2702. *Libn.* Sandra Hight.

Canyon Owyhee Library Group, 203 E. Idaho Ave., Homedale 83628. Tel. 208-337-4613, fax 208-337-4933, e-mail stokes@sd370.k12.id.us.

Catalyst, c/o Boise State Univ., Albertsons Lib., Boise 83707. SAN 375-0078. Tel. 208-426-4024, fax 208-426-1885.

Cooperative Information Network (CIN), 8385 N. Government Way, Hayden 83835-9280. SAN 323-7656. Tel. 208-772-5612, fax 208-772-2498. *In Charge* John Hartung.

Eastern Idaho Library System, 457 Broadway, Idaho Falls 83402. SAN 323-7699. Tel. 208-529-1450, fax 208-529-1467.

Gooding County Library Consortium, c/o Gooding High School, Gooding 83330. SAN 375-0094. Tel. 208-934-4831, fax 208-934-4347. *Head Libn.* Cora Caldwell.

Grangeville Cooperative Network, c/o Grangeville Centennial Lib., Grangeville 83530-1729. SAN 375-0108. Tel. 208-983-0951, fax 208-983-2336, e-mail library@grangeville.us.

Idaho Health Information Association (IHIA), Kootenai Medical Center, W. T. Wood Medical Library, Coeur d'Alene 83814. SAN 371-5078. Tel. 208-666-3498, fax 208-666-2854. *Dir.* Marcie Horner.

Lynx, c/o Boise Public Lib., Boise 83702-7195. SAN 375-0086. Tel. 208-384-4238, fax 208-384-4025. *Dir.* Marilyn Poertner.

Southeast Idaho Document Delivery Network, c/o American Falls District Lib., American Falls 83211-1219. SAN 375-0140. Tel. 208-226-2335, fax 208-226-2303, e-mail amlib@dcdi.net. *Head Libn.* Margaret McNamara.

Valnet, Lewis Clark State College Lib., Lewiston 83501. SAN 323-7672. Tel. 208-792-2227, fax 208-792-2831.

Illinois

Alliance Library System, Business Office, Pekin 61554. SAN 371-0637. Tel. 309-353-4110, fax 309-353-8281. *Exec. Dir.* Valerie Wilford.

American Theological Library Association (ATLA), 250 S. Wacker Dr., Suite 1600, Chicago 60606-5834. SAN 371-9022. Tel. 312-454-5100, fax 312-454-5505, e-mail atla@atla.com. *Exec. Dir.* Dennis Norlin.

Areawide Hospital Library Consortium of Southwestern Illinois (AHLC), c/o St. Elizabeth Hospital Health Sciences Lib., Belleville 62222. SAN 322-1016. Tel. 618-234-2120, ext. 1181, fax 618-222-4620, e-mail campese@exl.com, campese @apci.net. *Dir.* Michael Campese.

Association of Chicago Theological Schools (ACTS), McCormick Seminary, Chicago 60637. SAN 370-0658. Tel. 773-947-6300, fax 773-288-2612. *Pres.* Cynthia Campbell.

Capital Area Consortium, Decatur Memorial Lib.–Health Science Lib., Decatur 62526.

Tel. 217-876-2940, fax 217-876-2945. *Coord.* Karen Stoner.

Center for Research Libraries, 6050 S. Kenwood, Chicago 60637-2804. SAN 322-1032. Tel. 773-955-4545, fax 773-955-4339. *Pres.* Bernard Reilly.

Chicago and South Consortium, Governors State Univ. Lib., University Park 60466. SAN 322-1067. Tel. 708-534-5000, ext. 5142, fax 708-534-8454.

Chicago Library System (CLS), 224 S. Michigan, Suite 400, Chicago 60604. SAN 372-8188. Tel. 312-341-8500, fax 312-341-1985.

Consortium of Museum Libraries in the Chicago Area, c/o Morton Arboretum, Sterling Morton Lib., Lisle 60532-1293. SAN 371-392X. Tel. 630-719-7932, fax 630-719-7950. *Chair* Michael Stieber.

Council of Directors of State University Libraries in Illinois (CODSULI), Univ. of Illinois at Springfield, Springfield 62794. SAN 322-1083. Tel. 217-206-6597, fax 217-206-6354.

East Central Illinois Consortium, Carle Foundation Hospital Lib., Urbana 61801. SAN 322-1040. Tel. 217-383-3456, fax 217-383-3452. *Manager* Gerald Dewitt.

Educational Resources Information Center (ERIC) Clearinghouse on Elementary and Early Childhood Education (PS), Univ. of Illinois at Urbana-Champaign, Champaign 61820-7469. SAN 322-0591. Tel. 217-333-1386, fax 217-333-3767, e-mail ericeece@uiuc.edu. *Dir.* Lilian Katz.

Fox Valley Health Science Library Consortium, Central DuPage Hospital Medical Lib., Winfield 60190. SAN 329-3831. Tel. 630-681-4535, 630-933-1600, fax 630-682-0028.

Heart of Illinois Library Consortium, Galesburg Cottage Hospital, Galesburg 61401. SAN 322-1113. Tel. 309-345-4237. *Dir.* Michael Wold.

Illinois Library and Information Network (ILLINET), c/o Illinois State Lib., Springfield 62701-1796. SAN 322-1148. Tel. 217-782-2994, fax 217-785-4326. *Dir.* Jean Wilkins.

Illinois Library Computer Systems Organization (ILCSO), Univ. of Illinois, Lib. and Information Sciences Bldg., Suite 228,

Champaign 61820-6211. SAN 322-3736. Tel. 217-244-7593, fax 217-244-7596, e-mail oncall@listserv.ilcso.uiuc.edu. *Dir.* Kristine Hammerstrand.

Illinois Office of Educational Services, 2450 Foundation Dr., Suite 100, Springfield 62703-5464. SAN 371-5108. Tel. 217-786-3010, fax 217-786-3020, e-mail oesiscc@siu.edu.

Libras, Inc., Dominican Univ., River Forest 60305. SAN 322-1172. Tel. 708-524-6875, ext. 6889, fax 708-366-5360. *Dir.* Inez Ringlend.

Metropolitan Consortium of Chicago, Weiss Memorial Hospital Medical Lib., Chicago 60640. SAN 322-1180. Tel. 773-564-5820, fax 773-564-5821, e-mail libsch@interaccess.com. *Dir.* Connie Gibbons.

National Network of Libraries of Medicine—Greater Midwest Region (NN-LM GMR), c/o Lib. of the Health Sciences, Univ. of Illinois at Chicago, Chicago 60612-4330. SAN 322-1202. Tel. 312-996-2464, fax 312-996-2226, e-mail gmr@uic.edu. *Dir.* Susan Jacobson.

Private Academic Libraries of Illinois (PALI), c/o Wheaton College Lib., Franklin and Irving, Wheaton 60187. SAN 370-050X. E-mail crflatzkehr@curf.edu. *Pres.* P. Snezek.

Quad Cities Libraries in Cooperation (QUAD-LINC), 220 W. 23 Ave., Coal Valley 61240. SAN 373-093X. Tel. 309-799-3155, fax 309-799-5103. *Head of Automation* MaryAnne Stewart.

Quad City Area Biomedical Consortium, Perlmutter Lib., Silvis 61282. SAN 322-435X. Tel. 309-792-4360, fax 309-792-4362. *Coord.* Barbara Tharp.

River Bend Library System (RBLS), 220 W. 23 Ave., Coal Valley 61240-9624. SAN 371-0653. Tel. 309-799-3155, fax 309-799-7916.

Sangamon Valley Academic Library Consortium, MacMurray College, Henry Pfeiffer Lib., Jacksonville 62650. SAN 322-4406. Tel. 217-479-7110, fax 217-245-5214, e-mail mjthomas@mac.edu.

Shabbona Consortium, c/o Illinois Valley Community Hospital, Peru 61354. SAN 329-5133. Tel. 815-223-3300, ext. 502, fax 815-224-1747. *In Charge* Sheila Brolley.

Upstate Consortium, c/o Menbota Community Hospital, Menbota 61342. SAN 329-3793. Tel. 815-539-7461, ext. 305.

Indiana

American Zoo and Aquarium Association (AZA-LSIG), Indianapolis Zoo, Indianapolis 46222. SAN 373-0891. Tel. 317-630-5110, fax 317-630-5114. *Manager of Lib. Services* Susan Braun.

Central Indiana Health Science Libraries Consortium, Indiana Univ. School of Medicine Lib., Indianapolis 46202. SAN 322-1245. Tel. 317-274-2292, fax 317-278-2349. *Pres.* Peggy Richwine.

Collegiate Consortium of Western Indiana, c/o Cunningham Memorial Lib., Terre Haute 47809. SAN 329-4439. Tel. 812-237-3700, fax 812-237-3376. *Acting Dean* Elizabeth Hine.

Educational Resources Information Center (ERIC) Clearinghouse for Social Studies—Social Science Education (SO), Indiana Univ., Social Studies Development Center, Bloomington 47408-2698. SAN 322-0699. Tel. 812-855-3838, fax 812-855-0455, e-mail ericso@indiana.edu. *Dir.* Jane Henson.

Educational Resources Information Center (ERIC) Clearinghouse on Reading, English, and Communication (CS), Indiana Univ., Smith Research Center, Bloomington 47408-2698. SAN 322-0664. Tel. 812-855-5847, fax 812-856-5512, e-mail ericcs@indiana.edu. *Dir.* Carl Smith.

Evansville Area Library Consortium, 3700 Washington Ave., Evansville 47750. SAN 322-1261. Tel. 812-485-4151, fax 812-485-7564. *Coord., Libn.* Jane Saltzman.

Indiana Cooperative Library Services Authority (INCOLSA), 6202 Morenci Trail, Indianapolis 46268-2536. SAN 322-1296. Tel. 317-298-6570, fax 317-328-2380.

Indiana State Data Center, Indiana State Lib., Indianapolis 46204-2296. SAN 322-1318. Tel. 317-232-3733, fax 317-232-3728. *Coord.* Roberta Brooker.

Northeast Indiana Health Science Libraries Consortium (NEIHSL), Univ. of Saint Francis Health Sciences Lib., Fort Wayne 46808. SAN 373-1383. Tel. 219-434-7691, fax 219-434-7695. *Coord.* Lauralee Aven.

Northwest Indiana Health Science Library Consortium, c/o Northwest Center for Medical Education, Gary 46408-1197. SAN 322-1350. Tel. 219-980-6852, fax 219-980-6566.

Society of Indiana Archivists, University Archives, 201 Bryan Hall, Bloomington 47405. SAN 329-5508. Tel. 812-855-5897, fax 812-855-8104. *Dir.* Philip Bantin.

Iowa

Consortium of College and University Media Centers, Instructional Tech Center, Iowa State Univ., Ames 50011-3243. SAN 322-1091. Tel. 515-294-1811, fax 515-294-8089, e-mail ccumc@ccumc.org. *Exec. Dir.* Don Rieck.

Dubuque (Iowa) Area Library Information Consortium, c/o Wahlert Memorial Lib., Loras College, Dubuque 52001. Tel. 563-588-7009, 563-588-7189, fax 563-588-7292. *Pres.* Robert Klein.

Iowa Private Academic Library Consortium (IPAL), c/o Buena Vista University Lib., Storm Lake 50588. SAN 329-5311. Tel. 712-749-2127, fax 712-749-2059. *Dir.* Jim Kennedy.

Linn County Library Consortium, National Czech and Slovak Museum and Lib., Cedar Rapids 52402. SAN 322-4597. Tel. 319-352-8500, fax 319-363-2209. *Pres.* David Muhlena.

Polk County Biomedical Consortium, c/o Cowles Lib., Drake Univ., Des Moines 50311. SAN 322-1431. Tel. 515-271-4819, fax 515-271-3933. *Dir.* Rod Hemshaw.

Sioux City Library Cooperative (SCLC), c/o Sioux City Public Lib., Sioux City 51101-1203. SAN 329-4722. Tel. 712-255-2933, ext. 251, fax 712-279-6432.

State of Iowa Libraries Online Interlibrary Loan (SILO-ILL), State Lib. of Iowa, Des Moines 50319. SAN 322-1415. Tel. 515-281-4105, fax 515-281-6191. *State Libn.* Mary Wegne.

Kansas

Associated Colleges of Central Kansas, 210 S. Main St., McPherson 67460. SAN 322-

1474. Tel. 620-241-5150, fax 620-241-5153.

Dodge City Library Consortium, c/o Dodge City Public Lib., Dodge City 67801. SAN 322-4368. Tel. 620-225-0248, fax 620-225-0252. *Dir.* Rosanne Goble.

Kansas Library Network Board, 300 S.W. Tenth Ave., Rm. 343 N., Topeka 66612-1593. SAN 329-5621. Tel. 785-296-3875, fax 785-296-6650, e-mail eric@kslib.org. *Exec. Dir.* Eric Hansen.

Mid-America Law School Library Consortium (MALSLC), Washburn Univ. School of Law Lib., Topeka 66621. SAN 371-6813. Tel. 785-231-1088. *Chair* John Christensen.

Kentucky

Association of Independent Kentucky Colleges and Universities, 484 Chenault Rd., Frankfort 40601. SAN 322-1490. Tel. 502-695-5007, fax 502-695-5057. *Pres.* Gary Cox.

Eastern Kentucky Health Science Information Network (EKHSIN), c/o Camden-Carroll Lib., Morehead 40351. SAN 370-0631. Tel. 606-783-2610, fax 606-783-2799. *Dir.* Larry VeSant.

Kentuckiana Metroversity, Inc., 200 W. Broadway, Suite 700, Louisville 40202. SAN 322-1504. Tel. 502-897-3374, fax 502-895-1647.

Kentucky Health Science Libraries Consortium, VA Med Center, Lib. Services 142D, Louisville 40206-1499. SAN 370-0623. Tel. 502-894-6240, fax 502-894-6134. *Head Libn.* Gene Haynes.

State Assisted Academic Library Council of Kentucky (SAALCK), c/o Steely Lib., Highland Heights 41099. SAN 371-2222. Tel. 859-572-5483, fax 859-572-6181. *In Charge* Arne Almquist.

Theological Education Association of Mid America (TEAM-A), c/o Southern Baptist Theological Seminary, Louisville 40280-0294. Tel. 502-897-4807, fax 502-897-4600. *Libn.* Bruce Keisling.

Louisiana

Baton Rouge Hospital Library Consortium, Earl K. Long Hospital, Baton Rouge 70805. SAN 329-4714. Tel. 225-358-1089, 225-358-1000, fax 225-358-1240. *Dir.* Mary DeFoe.

Central Louisiana Medical Center Library Consortium, VA Medical Center 142D, Alexandria 71306. Tel. 318-619-9102, fax 318-619-9144, e-mail clmlc@yahoo.com. *Coord.* Miriam Brown.

Health Sciences Library Association of Louisiana Medical Library, LSU Health Sciences Lib., New Orleans 70112-7021. SAN 375-0035. Tel. 504-568-6100, fax 504-568-7720. *Chair* Carolyn Bridgewater.

Loan SHARK, State Lib. of Louisiana, Baton Rouge 70802. SAN 371-6880. Tel. 225-342-4918, 225-342-4920, fax 225-219-4725. *Coord.* Virginia Smith.

Louisiana Government Information Network (LaGIN), c/o State Lib. of Louisiana, Baton Rouge 70802. SAN 329-5036. Tel. 225-342-4920, e-mail lagin@pelican.state. lib.la.us. *Coord.* Virginia Smith.

New Orleans Educational Telecommunications Consortium, 2 Canal St., Suite 2038, New Orleans 70130. SAN 329-5214. Tel. 504-524-0350, fax 504-524-0327, e-mail noetcinc@excite.com. *Chair* Gregory O'Brien.

Maine

Health Science Library Information Consortium (HSLIC), Husson College, Bangor 04401-2999. SAN 322-1601. Tel. 207-743-5933, ext. 323, fax 207-743-2378. *Dir.* Amy Averre.

Maryland

Educational Resources Information Center ACCESS ERIC, Aspen Systems Corp., Rockville 20850-3172. SAN 375-6084. Tel. 301-519-5157, fax 301-519-6760, e-mail accesseric@accesseric.org. *Dir.* Lynn Smarte.

Educational Resources Information Center (ERIC) Clearinghouse on Assessment and Evaluation (TM), Univ. of Maryland, College Park 20742. SAN 322-0710. Tel. 301-405-7449, fax 301-405-8134, e-mail feedback3@ericae.net. *Dir.* Lawrence Rudner.

Educational Resources Information Center (ERIC) Processing and Reference Facility,

Computer Sciences Corp., 4483-A Forbes Blvd., Lanham 20706. SAN 375-6068. Tel. 301-552-4200, fax 301-552-4700, e-mail info@ericfac.piccard.csc.com. *Dir.* Donald Frank.

ERIC Processing and Reference Facility, 4483-A Forbes Blvd., Lanham 20706. SAN 322-161X. Tel. 301-497-4080, fax 301-552-4700, e-mail ericfac@inet.ed. gov. *Dir.* Donald Frank.

Library Video Network (LVN), 320 York Rd., Towson 21204. SAN 375-5320. Tel. 410-887-2090, fax 410-887-2091, e-mail lvn@bcpl.net.

Maryland Association of Health Science Librarians (MAHSL), Carroll County General Hospital, Westminster 21157. SAN 377-5070. Tel. 410-871-7065, fax 410-871-6987. *Manager, Lib. Services* Vicky Spitalnick.

Maryland Interlibrary Loan Organization (MILO), c/o Enoch Pratt Free Lib., Baltimore 21201-4484. SAN 343-8600. Tel. 410-396-5498, fax 410-396-5837, e-mail milo@epfl.net. *Manager* Sharon Smith.

Metropolitan Area Collection Development Consortium (MCDAC), c/o Carrol County Public Lib., Westminster 21157. SAN 323-9748. Tel. 410-386-4500, ext. 144, fax 410-386-4509. *Dir.* Linda Mielke.

National Network of Libraries of Medicine (NN-LM), National Lib. of Medicine, Bethesda 20894. SAN 373-0905. Tel. 301-496-4777, fax 301-480-1467. *Dir.* Angela Ruffin.

National Network of Libraries of Medicine—Southeastern Atlantic Region (NN/LM SE/A), Univ. of Maryland Health Sciences and Human Services Lib., Baltimore 21201-1512. SAN 322-1644. Tel. 410-706-2855, fax 410-706-0099. *Dir.* Frieda Weiss.

Regional Alcohol and Drug Abuse Resource Network (RADAR), National Clearinghouse for Alcohol and Drug Information, Rockville 20852-3007. SAN 377-5569. Tel. 301-468-2600, fax 301-468-6433, e-mail info@health.org. *Coord.* John Noble.

Washington Research Library Consortium (WRLC), 901 Commerce Dr., Upper Marlboro 20774. SAN 373-0883. Tel. 301-390-2031, fax 301-390-2020. *Exec. Dir.* Lizanne Payne.

Massachusetts

Boston Area Music Libraries (BAML), Bakalar Lib., Cambridge 02138. SAN 322-4392. Tel. 617-876-0956, fax 617-354-8841. *Coord.* Roy Rudolph.

Boston Biomedical Library Consortium (BBLC), c/o Percy R. Howe Memorial Lib., Boston 02115. SAN 322-1725. Tel. 617-262-5200, ext. 244, fax 617-262-4021. *Chair* Susan Orlando.

Boston Library Consortium, 700 Boylston St., Rm. 317, Boston 02117. SAN 322-1733. Tel. 617-262-0380, fax 617-262-0163. *Exec. Dir.* Barbara Preece.

Boston Theological Institute Library Program, 99 Brattle St., Cambridge 02138. SAN 322-1741. Tel. 617-349-3602, ext. 315, fax 617-349-3603, e-mail btilibrary@edswjst.org. *Dir.* Esther Griswold.

Cape Libraries Automated Materials Sharing (CLAMS), 270 Communication Way, Unit 4E-4F, Hyannis 02601. SAN 370-579X. Tel. 508-790-4399, fax 508-771-4533. *Dir.* Monica Grace.

Catholic Library Association, 100 North St., Suite 224, Pittsfield 01201-5109. SAN 329-1030. Tel. 413-443-2252, fax 413-442-2252, e-mail cla@cathla.org. *Exec. Dir.* Jean Bostley, SSJ.

Central Massachusetts Consortium of Health Related Libraries (CMCHRL), c/o Medical Lib., Univ. of Massachusetts Memorial Healthcare, Worcester 01605. SAN 371-2133. Tel. 508-334-6421, fax 508-334-6527. *In Charge* Andrew Dzaugis.

Consortium for Information Resources, Emerson Hospital, John Cuming Bldg., 3rd fl., Concord 01742. SAN 322-4503. Tel. 978-287-3090, fax 978-287-3651.

Cooperating Libraries of Greater Springfield (CLIC), Springfield College, Springfield 01109. SAN 322-1768. Tel. 413-748-3502, fax 413-748-3631. *Acting Dir.* Andrea Taupier.

CW Mars (Central-Western Massachusetts Automated Resource Sharing), 1 Sunset Lane, Paxton 01612-1197. SAN 322-3973. Tel. 508-755-3323, fax 508-755-3721.

Fenway Libraries Online (FLO), Wentworth Institute of Technology, Boston 02115. SAN 373-9112. Tel. 617-442-2384, fax 617-442-1519. *Dir.* Jamie Ingram.

Fenway Library Consortium, Simmons College, Beatly Lib., Boston 02115. SAN 327-9766. Tel. 617-521-2741, 617-573-8536, fax 617-521-3093. *Dir.* Robert Dugan.

Massachusetts Health Sciences Libraries Network (MAHSLIN), c/o Beverly Hospital Medical Lib., Beverly 01915. SAN 372-8293. Tel. 978-922-3000, ext. 2920, fax 978-922-3000, ext. 2273. *Pres.* Ann Tomes.

Merrimack Valley Library Consortium, 123 Tewksbury St., Andover 01810. SAN 322-4384. Tel. 978-475-7632, fax 978-475-7179. *Exec. Dir.* Lawrence Rungren.

Metrowest Massachusetts Regional Library System (METROWEST), 135 Beaver St., Waltham 02452. Tel. 781-398-1819, fax 781-398-1821. *Admin.* Sondra Vandermark.

Minuteman Library Network, 10 Strathmore Rd., Natick 01760-2419. SAN 322-4252. Tel. 508-655-8008, fax 508-655-1507. *Exec. Dir.* Carol Caro.

National Network of Libraries of Medicine— New England Region (NN-LM NER), Univ. of Massachusetts Medical School, Shrewsbury 01545. SAN 372-5448. Tel. 508-856-5979, fax 508-856-5977. *Dir.* Ralph Arcari.

NELINET, Inc., 153 Cordaville Rd., Southborough 01772. SAN 322-1822. Tel. 508-460-7700, ext. 1934, fax 508-460-9455. *Exec. Dir.* Arnold Hirshon.

North of Boston Library Exchange, Inc. (NOBLE), 26 Cherry Hill Dr., Danvers 01923. SAN 322-4023. Tel. 978-777-8844, fax 978-750-8472. *Exec. Dir.* Ronald Gagnon.

Northeast Consortium of Colleges and Universities in Massachusetts (NECCUM), Northern Essex Community College, Haverhill 01830. SAN 371-0602. Tel. 978-556-3400, fax 978-556-3738. *Dir.* Linda Hummel-Shea.

Northeastern Consortium for Health Information (NECHI), Anna Jaques Hospital, Medical Lib., Newburyport 01950. SAN 322-1857. Tel. 978-463-2480, fax 978-463-1286. *Dir.* Florence Mereer.

Sails, Inc., 547 W. Groves St., Suite 4, Middleboro 02346. SAN 378-0058. Tel. 508-946-8600, fax 508-946-8605. *Pres.* Patricia Lambirth.

Southeastern Massachusetts Consortium of Health Science Libraries (SEMCO), South Shore Hospital, South Weymouth 02190. SAN 322-1873. Tel. 781-340-8528, fax 781-331-0834. *Dir.* Kathy McCarthy.

Southeastern Massachusetts Cooperating Libraries (SMCL), c/o Wheaton College, Norton 02766-0849. SAN 322-1865. Tel. 508-285-8225, fax 508-286-8275. *Dir.* Terry Metz.

Southeastern Massachusetts Library System (SEMLS), 10 Riverside Dr., Lakeville 02347. Tel. 508-923-3531, fax 508-923-3539. *Admin.* Cynthia Roach.

West of Boston Network (WEBNET), Horn Lib., Babson College, Babson Park 02457. SAN 371-5019. Tel. 781-239-4308, fax 781-239-5226. *Pres.* Hope Tillman.

Western Massachusetts Health Information Consortium, c/o Holyoke Hospital Medical Lib., Holyoke 01040. SAN 329-4579. Tel. 413-534-2500, ext. 5282, fax 413-534-2710. *Dir.* Mary Caraker.

Worcester Area Cooperating Libraries (WACL), Gordon Lib., Worcester 01609. SAN 322-1881. Tel. 508-754-3964, fax 508-831-5829. *In Charge* Gladys Wood.

Michigan

Berrien Library Consortium, c/o William Hessel Lib., Benton Harbor 49022-1899. SAN 322-4678. Tel. 616-927-8605, fax 616-927-6656. *In Charge* Diane Baker.

Detroit Area Consortium of Catholic Colleges, c/o Sacred Heart Seminary, Detroit 48206. SAN 329-482X. Tel. 313-883-8500, fax 313-868-6440. *Dir.* Karen Mehaffey.

Detroit Associated Libraries Region of Cooperation (DALROC), Detroit Public Lib., Detroit 48202. SAN 371-0831. Tel. 313-833-4835, fax 313-832-0877.

Kalamazoo Consortium for Higher Education (KCHE), Kalamazoo College, Kalamazoo 49006. SAN 329-4994. Tel. 269-337-7220, fax 269-337-7219. *Pres.* James Jones.

Lakeland Library Cooperative, 4138 Three Mile Rd. N.W., Grand Rapids 49544. SAN 308-132X. Tel. 616-559-5253, fax 616-559-4329. *Dir.* Dan Siebersma.

Michigan Association of Consumer Health Information Specialists (MACHIS), Bronson Methodist Hospital, Kalamazoo 49007. SAN 375-0043. Tel. 616-341-8627, fax 616-341-8828. *Dir.* Marge Kars.

Michigan Health Sciences Libraries Association (MHSLA), Genesys Regional Medical Center, Grand Blanc 48439-1477. SAN 323-987X. Tel. 810-606-5261, fax 810-606-5270, e-mail glauet@com.msu.edu. *Dir.* Doris Blauet.

Michigan Library Consortium (MLC), 1407 Rensen St., Suite 1, Lansing 48910-3657. SAN 322-192X. Tel. 517-394-2420, fax 517-394-2096, e-mail reception@mlcnet. org.

Northland Interlibrary System (NILS), 316 E. Chisholm St., Alpena 49707. SAN 329-4773. Tel. 989-356-1622, fax 989-354-3939. *Dir.* Bryon Sitler.

Southeastern Michigan League of Libraries (SEMLOL), Lawrence Technological Univ., Southfield 48075. SAN 322-4481. Tel. 248-204-3009, fax 248-204-3005. *Chair* Gretchen Weiner.

Southern Michigan Region of Cooperation (SMROC), 415 S. Superior, Suite A, Albion 49224-2135. SAN 371-3857. Tel. 517-629-9469, fax 517-629-3812.

Southwest Michigan Library Cooperative (SMLC), 305 Oak St., Paw Paw 49079. SAN 371-5027. Tel. 616-657-4698, fax 616-657-4494. *Dir.* Alida Geppert.

Suburban Library Cooperative (SLC), 16480 Hall Rd., Clinton Township 48038. SAN 373-9082. Tel. 586-286-5750, fax 586-286-8951. *Dir.* Tammy Turgeon.

The Library Network (TLN), 13331 Reeck Rd., Southgate 48195. SAN 370-596X. Tel. 734-281-3830, fax 734-281-1905, 734-281-1817. *Dir.* A. Deller.

Upper Peninsula of Michigan Health Science Library Consortium, c/o Marquette Health System Hospital, Marquette 49855. SAN 329-4803. Tel. 906-225-3429, fax 906-225-3524. *In Charge* Janis Lubenow.

Upper Peninsula Region of Library Cooperation, Inc., 1615 Presque Isle Ave., Mar-

quette 49855. SAN 329-5540. Tel. 906-228-7697, fax 906-228-5627. *Dir.* Suzanne Dees.

Valley Library Consortium, 3210 Davenport Ave., Saginaw 48602-3495. Tel. 989-497-0925, fax 989-497-0918. *Exec. Dir.* Karl Steiner.

Minnesota

Arrowhead Health Sciences Library Network, Lib., St. Luke's Hospital, Duluth 55805. SAN 322-1954. Tel. 218-726-5320, fax 218-726-5181. *Libn.* Doreen Roberts.

Capital Area Library Consortium (CALCO), c/o Minnesota Dept. of Transportation, Lib. MS155, Saint Paul 55155. SAN 374-6127. Tel. 651-296-5272, fax 651-297-2354. *Libn.* Shirley Sherkow.

Central Minnesota Libraries Exchange (CMLE), Miller Center, Rm. 130-D, Saint Cloud 56301-4498. SAN 322-3779. Tel. 320-255-2950, fax 320-654-5131. *Dir.* Patricia Peterson.

Community Health Science Library, c/o Saint Francis Medical Center, Breckenridge 56520. SAN 370-0585. Tel. 218-643-7542, fax 218-643-7452. *Dir.* Karla Lovaasen.

Cooperating Libraries in Consortium (CLIC), 1619 Dayton Ave., Suite 204A, Saint Paul 55104. SAN 322-1970. Tel. 651-644-3878, fax 651-644-6258. *Exec. Dir.* Chris Olson.

Metronet, 1619 Dayton Ave., Suite 314, Saint Paul 55104. SAN 322-1989. Tel. 651-646-0475, fax 651-649-3169, e-mail info@metronet.lib.mn.us.

Metropolitan Library Service Agency (MELSA), 1619 Dayton Ave., No. 314, Saint Paul 55104-6206. SAN 371-5124. Tel. 651-645-5731, fax 651-649-3169, e-mail melsa@melsa.lib.mn.us.

MINITEX Library Information Network, c/o 15 Andersen Lib., Univ. of Minnesota, Minneapolis 55455-0439. SAN 322-1997. Tel. 612-624-4002, fax 612-624-4508. *Dir.* William DeJohn.

Minnesota Department of Human Services Library, DHS Lib. and Resource Center, 444 Lafayette, Saint Paul 55155-3820. SAN 371-0750. Tel. 651-297-8708, 651-

296-6627, fax 651-282-5340. *Libn.* Kate Nelson.

Minnesota Theological Library Association (MTLA), c/o Luther Seminary Lib., Saint Paul 55108. SAN 322-1962. Tel. 651-641-3202, fax 651-641-3280. *Pres.* Sandy Oslund.

North Country Library Cooperative, 5528 Emerald Ave., Mountain Iron 55768-2069. SAN 322-3795. Tel. 218-741-1907, fax 218-741-1908. *Dir.* Linda Wadman.

Northern Lights Library Network, 103 Graystone Plaza, Detroit Lakes 56501-3041. SAN 322-2004. Tel. 218-842-2825, fax 218-847-1461, e-mail nloffice@nlln.org. *Dir.* Ruth Solie.

Smile (Southcentral Minnesota Inter-Library Exchange), 1400 Madison Ave., Suite 622, Mankato 56001. SAN 321-3358. Tel. 507-625-7555, fax 507-625-4049, e-mail smile @tds.lib.mn.us. *Dir.* Nancy Steele.

Southeast Library System (SELS), 2600 19th St. N.W., Rochester 55901-0767. SAN 322-3981. Tel. 507-288-5513, fax 507-288-8697.

Southeastern Libraries Cooperating (SELCO), 2600 19th St. N.W., Rochester 55901-0767. SAN 308-7417. Tel. 507-288-5513, fax 507-288-8697. *Exec. Dir.* Ann Hutton.

Southwest Area Multicounty Multitype Interlibrary Exchange (SAMMIE), BA 282 Southwest State Univ., Marshall 56258. SAN 322-2039. Tel. 507-532-9013, fax 507-532-2039. *Dir.* Robin Chaney.

Twin Cities Biomedical Consortium, c/o Health East St. Joseph's Hospital Lib., Saint Paul 55102. SAN 322-2055. Tel. 651-232-3193, fax 651-232-3296. *Chair* Karen Brudvig.

Valley Medical Network, Lake Region Hospital Lib., Fergus Falls 56537. SAN 329-4730. Tel. 218-736-8158, fax 218-736-8731. *Dir.* Connie Schulz.

Waseca Interlibrary Resource Exchange (WIRE), c/o Waseca High School, Waseca 56093. SAN 370-0593. Tel. 507-835-5470, ext. 218, fax 507-835-1724, e-mail tlol@waseca.k12.mn.us.

West Group, Box 64526, Saint Paul 55164-0526. SAN 322-4031. Tel. 651-687-7000, fax 651-687-5614, e-mail webmaster@ westgroup.com.

Mississippi

Central Mississippi Library Council (CMLC), c/o Hinds Commercial College Lib., Raymond 39154-1100. SAN 372-8250. Tel. 601-857-3255, fax 601-857-3293. *Dir.* Juanita Flanders.

Mississippi Biomedical Library Consortium, c/o College of Veterinary Medicine, Mississippi State Univ., Mississippi State 39762. SAN 371-070X. Tel. 662-325-1240, fax 662-325-1141, e-mail library@ cvm.msstate.edu. *Reference (Info. Services)* John Cruickshank.

Missouri

Health Sciences Library Network of Kansas City, Inc. (HSLNKC), Univ. of Missouri Health Sciences Lib., Kansas City 64108-2792. SAN 322-2098. Tel. 816-235-1880, fax 816-235-5194.

Kansas City Metropolitan Lib. and Information Network, 15624 E. 24 Hwy., Independence 64050. SAN 322-2101. Tel. 816-521-7257, fax 816-461-0966. *Exec. Dir.* Susan Burton.

Kansas City Regional Council for Higher Education, Park Univ., Parkville 64152-3795. SAN 322-211X. Tel. 816-741-2816, fax 816-741-1296, e-mail kcrche@kc.rr. com. *Pres.* Ron Doering.

Library Systems Service, Washington Univ. —Bernard Becker Medical Lib., Saint Louis 63110. SAN 322-2187. Tel. 314-362-2778, fax 314-362-0190. *Manager* Russ Monika.

Missouri Library Network Corp., 8045 Big Bend Blvd., Suite 202, Saint Louis 63119-2714. SAN 322-466X. Tel. 314-918-7222, fax 314-918-7727, e-mail sms@mlnc.org. *Exec. Dir.* Susan Singleton.

Saint Louis Regional Library Network, 341 Sappention Rd., Saint Louis 63122. SAN 322-2209. Tel. 314-965-1305, fax 314-965-4443.

Nebraska

Eastern Library System (ELS), 11929 Elm St., Suite 12, Omaha 68144. SAN 371-506X. Tel. 402-330-7884, fax 402-330-1859.

Lincoln Health Sciences Library Group (LHSLG), Univ. of Nebraska, Lincoln 68588-4100. SAN 329-5001. Tel. 402-472-2554, fax 402-472-5131.

Meridian Library System, 3519 Second Ave., Suite B, Kearney 68847. SAN 325-3554. Tel. 308-234-2087, fax 308-234-4040, e-mail sosenga@nol.org. *Pres.* Joan Davis.

NEBASE, c/o Nebraska Lib. Commission, Lincoln 68508-2023. SAN 322-2268. Tel. 402-471-2045, fax 402-471-2083.

Northeast Library System, 3038 33rd Ave., Columbus 68601-2334. SAN 329-5524. Tel. 402-564-1586.

Southeast Nebraska Library System, 5730 R St., Suite C-1, Lincoln 68505. SAN 322-4732. Tel. 402-467-6188, fax 402-467-6196.

Western Council of State Libraries, Inc., Nevada State Lib. and Archives, Carson City 89701. SAN 322-2314. Tel. 775-684-3360, fax 775-684-3330. *Admin. Dir.* Sarah Jones.

Nevada

Information Nevada, Interlibrary Loan Dept., Nevada State Lib. and Archives, Carson City 89701-4285. SAN 322-2276. Tel. 775-684-3325, fax 775-684-3330.

New Hampshire

Carroll County Library Cooperative, Box 240, Madison 03849. SAN 371-8999. Tel. 603-367-8545.

Hillstown Cooperative, 3 Meetinghouse Rd., Bedford 03110. SAN 371-3873. Tel. 603-472-2300, fax 603-472-2978.

Librarians of the Upper Valley Coop. (LUV Coop), Box 1580, Grantham 03753. SAN 371-6856. Tel. 603-863-2172, fax 603-863-2172, e-mail dunbarlib@adelphia.net. *Dir., Libn.* Carla Boyington.

Merri-Hill-Rock Library Cooperative, c/o Hampstead Public Lib., Hampstead 03841. SAN 329-5338. Tel. 603-329-6411, fax 603-329-6036. *Chair* Judi Crowley.

New Hampshire College and University Council, 3 Barrell Court, Suite 100, Concord 03301-8543. SAN 322-2322. Tel. 603-225-4199, fax 603-225-8108. *Exec. Dir.* Thomas Horgan.

Nubanusit Library Cooperative, c/o Peterborough Town Lib., Peterborough 03458. SAN 322-4600. Tel. 603-924-8040, fax 603-924-8041.

Scrooge and Marley Cooperative, 310 Central St., Franklin 03235. SAN 329-515X. Tel. 603-934-2911. *Dir.* Rob Sargent.

Seacoast Coop. Libraries, North Hampton Public Lib., North Hampton 03862. SAN 322-4619. Tel. 603-964-6326, fax 603-964-1107, e-mail coop@hampton.lib.nh.us. *Dir.* Pamela Schwotzer.

New Jersey

Bergen County Cooperative Library System, 810 Main St., Hackensack 07601. SAN 322-4546. Tel. 201-489-1904, fax 201-489-4215, e-mail bccls@bccls.org. *Exec. Dir.* Robert White.

Bergen Passaic Health Sciences Library Consortium, c/o Englewood Hospital and Medical Center, Health Sciences Lib., Englewood 07631. SAN 371-0904. Tel. 201-894-3069, fax 201-894-9049, e-mail lia.sabbagh@ehmc.com.

Central Jersey Health Science Libraries Association, Saint Francis Medical Center Medical Lib., Trenton 08629. SAN 370-0712. Tel. 609-599-5068, fax 609-599-5773. *Libn.* Donna Barlow.

Central Jersey Regional Library Cooperative, 4400 Route 9 S., Freehold 07728-1383. SAN 370-5102. Tel. 732-409-6484, fax 732-409-6492. *Dir.* Connie Paul.

Cosmopolitan Biomedical Library Consortium, Medical Lib., East Orange General Hospital, East Orange 07019. SAN 322-4414. Tel. 973-672-8400. *In Charge* Peggy Dreker.

Health Sciences Library Association of New Jersey (HSLANJ), Saint Michael's Medical Center, Newark 07102. SAN 370-0488. Tel. 973-877-5471, fax 973-877-5378. *Dir.* Larry Dormer.

Highlands Regional Library Cooperative, 66 Ford Rd., Suite 124, Denville 07834. SAN 329-4609. Tel. 973-664-1776, fax 973-664-1780, e-mail help@hrlc.org.

INFOLINK Eastern New Jersey Regional Library Cooperative, Inc., 44 Stelton Rd., Suite 330, Piscataway 08902. SAN 371-5116. Tel. 732-752-7720, 973-673-2343, fax 973-673-2710, 732-752-7785. *Exec. Dir.* Charles Dowlin.

Integrated Information Solutions, 600 Mountain Ave., Rm. 6A-200, Murray Hill 07974. SAN 329-5400. Tel. 908-582-4840, fax 908-582-3146, e-mail libnet@library.lucent.com. *Information Services* Bridget Bailey.

LMX Automation Consortium, 1030 Saint George, Suite 203, Avenel 07001. SAN 329-448X. Tel. 732-750-2525, fax 732-750-9392.

Monmouth-Ocean Biomedical Information Consortium (MOBIC), Community Medical Center, Toms River 08755. SAN 329-5389. Tel. 732-557-8117, fax 732-557-8354. *Libn.* Reina Reisler.

Morris Automated Information Network (MAIN), Box 900, Morristown 07963-0900. SAN 322-4058. Tel. 973-631-5353, fax 973-631-5366.

Morris-Union Federation, 214 Main St., Chatham 07928. SAN 310-2629. Tel. 973-635-0603, fax 973-635-7827.

New Jersey Health Sciences Library Network (NJHSN), Mountainside Hospital, Montclair 07042. SAN 371-4829. Tel. 973-429-6240, fax 973-680-7850, e-mail pat.regenberg@ahsys.org.

New Jersey Library Network, Lib. Development Bureau, Trenton 08625. SAN 372-8161. Tel. 609-984-3293, fax 609-633-3963.

South Jersey Regional Library Cooperative, Paint Works Corporate Center, Gibbsboro 08026. SAN 329-4625. Tel. 856-346-1222, fax 856-346-2839. *Exec. Dir.* Karen Hyman.

Virtual Academic Library Environment (VALE), William Paterson Univ. Lib., Wayne 07470-2103. Tel. 973-720-2113, fax 973-720-3171. *Exec. Dir.* John Gaboury.

New Mexico

Alliance for Innovation in Science and Technology Information (AISTI), 369 Montezuma Ave., No. 156, Santa Fe 87501. Fax 505-992-2728. *Exec. Dir.* Corinne Machado.

New Mexico Consortium of Academic Libraries, Dean's Office, Albuquerque 87131-1466. SAN 371-6872. Tel. 505-277-5057, fax 505-277-6019, 505-277-7288. *Dean* Camila Alire.

New Mexico Consortium of Biomedical and Hospital Libraries, c/o Lovelace Medical Lib., Albuquerque 87108. SAN 322-449X. Tel. 505-262-7158, fax 505-262-7897. *Libn.* Linda Davis.

New York

Academic Libraries of Brooklyn, Long Island Univ. Lib.–LLC 517, Brooklyn 11201. SAN 322-2411. Tel. 718-488-1081, fax 715-780-4057. *Dean* Constance Woo.

American Film and Video Association, Cornell Univ. Resource Center, Ithaca 14850. SAN 377-5860. Tel. 607-255-2090, fax 607-255-9946, e-mail resctr@cornell.edu. *Audio Visual* Richard Gray.

Associated Colleges of the Saint Lawrence Valley, State Univ. of New York College at Potsdam, Potsdam 13676-2299. SAN 322-242X. Tel. 315-267-3331, fax 315-267-2389. *Exec. Dir.* Anneke Larrance.

Brooklyn-Queens-Staten Island Health Sciences Librarians (BQSI), Saint John's Episcopal Hospital, South Shore Div. Medical Lib., Far Rockaway 11691. SAN 370-0828. Tel. 718-869-7699, fax 718-869-8528. *Libn.* Desai Kalpana.

Capital District Library Council for Reference and Research Resources, 28 Essex St., Albany 12206. SAN 322-2446. Tel. 518-438-2500, fax 518-438-2872, e-mail info@cdlc.org. *Exec. Dir.* Jean Sheviak.

Central New York Library Resources Council (CLRC), 6493 Ridings Rd., Syracuse 13206-1195. SAN 322-2454. Tel. 315-446-5446, fax 315-446-5590, e-mail mclane@clrc.org. *Exec. Dir.* Michael McLane.

Consortium of Foundation Libraries, c/o Carnegie Corporation of New York, New York 10022. SAN 322-2462. Tel. 212-207-6245, fax 212-838-6109, e-mail rs@carnegie.org. *Libn.* Ron Sexton.

Council of Archives and Research Libraries in Jewish Studies (CARLJS), 330 Seventh Ave., 21st fl., New York 10001. SAN 371-053X. Tel. 212-629-0500, fax 212-629-0508, e-mail nfjc@jewishculture.org. *In Charge* Dana Schneider.

Educational Film Library Association, c/o AV Resource Center, Cornell Univ., Ithaca 14850. SAN 371-0874. Tel. 607-255-2090, fax 607-255-9946, e-mail resctr@cornell.edu. *Audio Visual* Richard Gray.

Educational Resources Information Center (ERIC) Clearinghouse on Information and Technology (IR), Syracuse Univ., Syracuse 13244-4292. SAN 322-063X. Tel. 315-443-3640, fax 315-443-5448, e-mail eric@ericir.syr.edu. *Dir.* R. Lankes.

Educational Resources Information Center (ERIC) Clearinghouse on Urban Education (UD), Columbia Univ. Teachers College Inst. of Urban and Minority Education, New York 10027-6696. SAN 322-0729. Tel. 212-678-3433, fax 212-678-4012, e-mail eric-cue@columbia.edu. *Dir.* Erwin Flaxman.

Library Consortium of Health Institutions in Buffalo, 155 Abbott Hall, SUNY at Buffalo, Buffalo 14214. SAN 329-367X. Tel. 716-829-3900, ext. 143, fax 716-829-2211. *Exec. Dir.* Martin Mutka.

Long Island Library Resources Council (LILRC), Melville Lib. Bldg., Suite E5310, Stony Brook 11794-3399. SAN 322-2489. Tel. 631-632-6650, fax 631-632-6662. *Dir.* Herbert Biblo.

Manhattan-Bronx Health Sciences Libraries Group, c/o KPR Medical Lib., New York 10016. SAN 322-4465. Tel. 212-856-8743, fax 212-856-8892. *Research* Ilene Somin.

Medical Library Center of New York, 5 E. 102 St., 7th fl., New York 10029. SAN 322-3957. Tel. 212-427-1630, fax 212-876-6697. *Dir.* William Self.

Medical and Scientific Libraries of Long Island (MEDLI), c/o Palmer School of Lib. and Information Science, Brookville 11548. SAN 322-4309. Tel. 516-299-2866, fax 516-299-4168. *Pres.* Ellen Maleszewski.

Metropolitan New York Library Council (METRO), 57 E. 11 St., 4th fl., New York 10003-4605. SAN 322-2500. Tel. 212-228-2320, ext. 12, fax 212-228-2598. *Exec. Dir.* Dottie Hiebing.

Middle Atlantic Region National Network of Libraries of Medicine, New York Academy of Medicine, New York 10029-5293.

SAN 322-2497. Tel. 212-822-7396, fax 212-534-7042, e-mail rml@nyam.org. *Dir.* Mary Mylenski.

National Network of Libraries of Medicine— Mid Atlantic Region (NN-LM MAR), 1216 Fifth Ave., New York 10029-5293. Tel. 212-822-7396, fax 212-534-7042. *Associate Dir.* Mary Mylenki.

New York State Interlibrary Loan Network (NYSILL), c/o New York State Lib., Albany 12230. SAN 322-2519. Tel. 518-474-5129, fax 518-474-5786, e-mail ill@nysl.nysed.gov.

Northeast Foreign Law Cooperative Group, Fordham Univ., New York 10023. SAN 375-0000. Tel. 212-636-6900, fax 212-636-7357, 212-977-2662. *Dir.* Janet Tracey.

Northern New York Library Network, 6721 U.S. Hwy. 11, Potsdam 13676. SAN 322-2527. Tel. 315-265-1119, fax 315-265-1881, e-mail nnyln@northnet.org. *Exec. Dir.* John Hammond.

Research Library Association of South Manhattan, New York Univ., Bobst Lib., New York 10012. SAN 372-8080. Tel. 212-998-2477, fax 212-995-4366. *Dean of Lib.* Carol Mandel.

Rochester Regional Library Council, 390 Packetts Landing, Fairport 14450. SAN 322-2535. Tel. 585-223-7570, fax 585-223-7712, e-mail rrlc@rrlc.org. *Exec. Dir.* Kathleen Miller.

South Central Regional Library Council, 215 N. Cayuga St., Ithaca 14850. SAN 322-2543. Tel. 607-273-9106, fax 607-272-0740, e-mail scrlc@lakenet.org. *Exec. Dir.* Jean Currie.

Southeastern New York Library Resources Council (SENYLRC), 220 Route 299, Highland 12528. SAN 322-2551. Tel. 845-691-2734, fax 845-691-6987. *Exec. Dir.* John Shaloiko.

State University of New York–NYLINK, SUNY System Admin., Albany 12246. SAN 322-256X. Tel. 518-443-5444, fax 518-432-4346, e-mail nylink@nylink.suny.edu. *Exec. Dir.* Mary-Alice Lynch.

United Nations System Consortium, c/o Dag Hammarskjold Lib., Rm. L-166A, New York 10017. SAN 377-855X. Tel. 212-963-7394, fax 212-963-2388. *Head Libn.* Phyliss Dickstein.

Western New York Library Resources Council, 4455 Genesee St., Buffalo 14225. SAN 322-2578. Tel. 716-633-0705, fax 716-633-1736. *Exec. Dir.* Gail Staines.

North Carolina

Cape Fear Health Sciences Information Consortium, Southeastern Regional Medical Center, Lumberton 28359. SAN 322-3930. Tel. 910-671-5000, fax 910-671-4143.

Consortium of South Eastern Law Libraries, Duke Univ. Law Lib., Durham 27708-0361. SAN 372-8277. Tel. 919-613-7113, fax 919-613-7237.

Educational Resources Information Center (ERIC) Clearinghouse on Counseling and Student Services (CG), Univ. of North Carolina at Greensboro, Greensboro 27412-5001. SAN 322-0583. Tel. 336-334-4114, fax 336-334-4116, e-mail ericcass@uncg.edu. *Dir.* Jeanne Bleyer.

Microcomputer Users Group for Libraries in North Carolina (MUGLNC), Catawba College, Salisbury 28144. Fax 704-637-4304. *Dir.* John Harer.

NC Area Health Education Centers, Health Sciences Lib., CB 7585, Chapel Hill 27599-7585. SAN 323-9950. Tel. 919-962-0700, fax 919-966-5592. *In Charge* Diana McDuffee.

North Carolina Community College System, 200 W. Jones St., Raleigh 27603-1379. SAN 322-2594. Tel. 919-733-7051, fax 919-733-0680. *Dir.* Pamela B. Doyle.

North Carolina Library and Information Network, State Lib., Raleigh 27699-4640. SAN 329-3092. Tel. 919-733-2570, fax 919-733-8748. *State Libn.* Sandra Cooper.

Northwest AHEC Library at Salisbury, c/o Rowan Regional Medical Center, Salisbury 28144. SAN 322-4589. Tel. 704-210-5069, fax 704-636-5050.

Northwest AHEC Library Information Network, Northwest Area Health Education Center—Carpenter Lib., Winston-Salem 27157-1069. SAN 322-4716. Tel. 336-713-7115, fax 336-713-7028.

Unifour Consortium of Health Care and Educational Institutions, c/o Northwest AHEC Lib. at Hickory, Hickory 28602. SAN 322-4708. Tel. 828-326-3662, fax 828-326-3484. *Dir.* Stephen Johnson.

Western North Carolina Library Network (WNCLN), Univ. of North Carolina at Asheville, Asheville 28804-3299. SAN 376-7205. Tel. 828-232-5095, fax 828-232-5137. *Dir.* Richard Moul.

North Dakota

Dakota West Cooperating Libraries (DWCL), Mandan County Lib., Mandan 58554. SAN 373-1391.

Tri-College University Libraries Consortium, 209 Engineering Technology, Fargo 58105. SAN 322-2047. Tel. 701-231-8170, fax 701-231-7205.

Ohio

Central Ohio Hospital Library Consortium, Mount Carmel, Columbus 43222-1560. SAN 371-084X. Tel. 614-234-5214, fax 614-234-1257. *Dir.* Rebecca Ayers.

Cleveland Area Metropolitan Library System (CAMLS), 20600 Chagrin Blvd., Suite 500, Shaker Heights 44122-5334. SAN 322-2632. Tel. 216-921-3900, fax 216-921-7220, e-mail camls@oplin.lib.oh.us. *Exec. Dir.* Michael Snyder.

Columbus Area Library and Information Council of Ohio (CALICO), c/o Westerville Public Lib., Westerville 43081. SAN 371-683X. Tel. 614-882-7277, fax 614-882-5369.

Consortium of Popular Culture Collections in the Midwest (CPCCM), c/o Popular Culture Lib., Bowling Green 43403-0600. SAN 370-5811. Tel. 419-372-2450, fax 419-372-7996. *Chair* Peter Berg.

Educational Resources Information Center (ERIC) Clearinghouse for Science, Mathematics, and Environmental Education (SE), Ohio State Univ., Columbus 43210-1080. SAN 322-0680. Tel. 614-292-6717, fax 614-292-0263, e-mail ericse@osu.edu. *Dir.* David Haury.

Educational Resources Information Center (ERIC) Clearinghouse on Adult, Career, and Vocational Education (CE), Ohio State Univ., Columbus 43210-1090. SAN 322-0575. Tel. 614-292-7069, fax 614-292-1260, e-mail ericacve@osu.edu. *Dir.* Susan Imel.

Greater Cincinnati Library Consortium, 2181 Victory Pkwy., Suite 214, Cincinnati 45206-2855. SAN 322-2675. Tel. 513-751-4422, fax 513-751-0463, e-mail gclc @gclc-lib.org. *Exec. Dir.* Michael McCoy.

Molo Regional Library System, 1260 Monroe Ave., New Philadelphia 44663-4147. SAN 322-2705. Tel. 330-364-8535, fax 330-364-8537, e-mail molo@tusco.net.

NEOUCOM Council of Associated Hospital Librarians, Oliver Ocasek Regional Medical Info. Center, Rootstown 44272. SAN 370-0526. Tel. 330-325-6616, 330-325-6600, fax 330-325-0522, e-mail lsc@ neoucom.cdu. *Dir.* Onadell Bly.

NOLA Regional Library System, 4445 Mahoning Ave. N.W., Warren 44483. SAN 322-2713. Tel. 330-847-7744, fax 330-847-7704, e-mail nola@nolanet.org. *Dir.* Paul Pormen.

Northwest Library District (NORWELD), 181 ½ S. Main St., Bowling Green 43402. SAN 322-273X. Tel. 419-352-2903, fax 419-353-8310. *Dir.* Allan Gray.

OCLC Online Computer Library Center, Inc., 6565 Frantz Rd., Dublin 43017-3395. SAN 322-2748. Tel. 614-764-6000, fax 614-764-6096, e-mail oclc@oclc.org. *Pres.* Jay Jordan.

Ohio Library and Information Network (Ohio LINK), 2455 N. Star Rd., Suite 300, Columbus 43221. SAN 374-8014. Tel. 614-728-3600, fax 614-728-3610, e-mail info@ohiolink.edu. *Exec. Dir.* Thomas Sanville.

Ohio Network of American History Research Centers, Ohio Historical Society Archives/ Lib., Columbus 43211-2497. SAN 323-9624. Tel. 614-297-2510, fax 614-297-2546, e-mail ohsaef@ohiohistory.org. *Research* Louise Jones.

OHIONET, 1500 W. Lane Ave., Columbus 43221-3975. SAN 322-2764. Tel. 614-486-2966, fax 614-486-1527. *Exec. Dir.* Michael Butler.

Southwestern Ohio Council for Higher Education, 3155 Research Blvd., Suite 204, Dayton 45420-4014. SAN 322-2659. Tel. 937-258-8890, fax 937-258-8899, e-mail soche@soche.org.

Oklahoma

Greater Oklahoma Area Health Sciences Library Consortium (GOAL), VA Medical Center—Medical Lib., Oklahoma City 73104. SAN 329-3858. Tel. 405-270-0501, ext. 3688, fax 405-270-5145. *Pres.* Sara Hill.

Metropolitan Libraries Network Of Central Oklahoma, Inc. (MetroNetwork), 131 Dean A. McGee Ave., Oklahoma City 73102. SAN 372-8137. Tel. 405-231-8602, 733-7323, fax 405-236-5219.

Oklahoma Health Sciences Library Association (OHSLA), Univ. of Oklahoma, Bird Health Science Lib., Oklahoma City 73190. SAN 375-0051. Tel. 405-271-2285, fax 405-271-3297.

Oregon

Chemeketa Cooperative Regional Library Service, c/o Chemeketa Community College, Salem 97309-7070. SAN 322-2837. Tel. 503-399-5105, fax 503-589-7628, e-mail cocl@chemeketa.edu. *Coord.* Linda Cochrane.

Coos County Library Service District, Extended Service Office, Tioga 104, 1988 Newmark, Coos Bay 97420. SAN 322-4279. Tel. 541-888-7260, fax 541-888-7285. *Dir.* Mary Fisher.

Educational Resources Information Center (ERIC) Clearinghouse on Educational Management (EA), Univ. of Oregon, Eugene 97401-5207. SAN 322-0605. Tel. 541-346-5043, fax 541-346-2334, e-mail ssmith@eric.uoregon.edu. *Dir.* Phil Piele.

Library Information Network of Clackamas County, 16239 S.E. McLoughlin Blvd., Suite 208, Oak Grove 97267-4654. SAN 322-2845. Tel. 503-723-4888, fax 503-794-8238.

Northwest Association of Private Colleges and Universities Libraries (NAPCUL), 500 N. Willamette Blvd., Portland 97203. SAN 375-5312. *Pres.* Votaw Floyd.

Orbis, 1501 Kincaid, No. 4, Eugene 97401-4540. SAN 377-8096. Tel. 541-346-1832, fax 541-346-1968, e-mail orbis@oregon. uoregon.edu. *Chair* Patricia Cutright.

Oregon Health Sciences University Association (OHSLA), Oregon Health and Science Univ. Lib., Portland 97201-3098. SAN 371-2176. Tel. 503-494-3462, fax 503-494-3322, e-mail lib@oshu.edu. *Dir.* James Morgan.

Southern Oregon Library Federation, c/o Klamath County Lib., Klamath Falls 97601. SAN 322-2861. Tel. 541-882-8894, fax 541-882-6166. *Dir.* Andy Swanson.

Washington County Cooperative Library Services, 111 N.E. Lincoln St., MS No. 58, Hillsboro 97124-3036. SAN 322-287X. Tel. 503-846-3222, fax 503-846-3220. *Manager* Eva Calcagno.

Pennsylvania

Associated College Libraries of Central Pennsylvania, c/o Penn State Harrisburg Lib., Middletown 17057-4850. Tel. 717-948-6079, fax 717-948-6757. *Pres.* Harold Shill.

Basic Health Sciences Library Network, Latrobe Area Hospital Health Sciences Lib., Latrobe 15650-1096. SAN 371-4888. Tel. 724-537-1275, fax 724-537-1890. *Manager* Marilyn Daniels.

Berks County Library Association (BCLA), Albright College Lib., Reading 19612-5234. SAN 371-0866. Tel. 610-921-7211.

Berks County Public Libraries (BCPL), Agricultural Center, 1238 County Welfare Rd., Leesport 19533. SAN 371-8972. Tel. 610-378-5260, fax 610-378-1525, e-mail bcpl@epix.net.

Central Pennsylvania Consortium, Dickinson College, Carlisle 17013-2896. SAN 322-2896. Tel. 717-245-1515, fax 717-245-1807, e-mail cpc@dickinson.edu.

Central Pennsylvania Health Science Library Association (CPHSLA), Lois High Berstler Community Health Lib., Hershey 17033-2003. SAN 375-5290. Tel. 717-531-4032, fax 717-531-5942, e-mail pmhall@psu.edu.

Consortium for Health Information and Library Services, One Medical Center Blvd., Upland 19013-3995. SAN 322-290X. Tel. 610-447-6163, fax 610-447-6164, e-mail ch1@hslc.org. *Exec. Dir.* Barbara R. Devlin.

Cooperating Hospital Libraries of the Lehigh Valley Area, Lehigh Valley Hospital–Muhlenberg, Bethlehem 18017-7384. SAN 371-0858. Tel. 610-861-2237, fax 610-861-0711.

Delaware Valley Information Consortium, c/o Health Sciences Lib., St. Mary Medical Center, Langhorne 19047. Tel. 215-750-2012, fax 215-891-6453. *Dir.* Ann Laliotes.

Eastern Mennonite Associated Libraries and Archives (EMALA), 2215 Millstream Rd., Lancaster 17602. SAN 372-8226. Tel. 717-393-9745, fax 717-393-8751. *Chair* Edsel Burdge.

Erie Area Health Information Library Cooperative (EAHILC), Northwest Medical Center Medical Lib., Franklin 16323. SAN 371-0564. Tel. 814-437-7000, ext. 5331, fax 814-437-4538, e-mail nwmc@mail.cosmosbbs.com. *Chair, Dean* Ann Lucas.

Greater Philadelphia Law Library Association (GPLLA), Box 335, Philadelphia 19105-0335. SAN 373-1375. Tel. 215-963-5764, e-mail gplla-l@hslc.org. *Pres.* Kristin Foster.

Health Sciences Libraries Consortium, 3600 Market St., Suite 550, Philadelphia 19104-2646. SAN 323-9780. Tel. 215-222-1532, fax 215-222-0416, e-mail support@hslc.org. *Exec. Dir.* Joseph Scorza.

Interlibrary Delivery Service of Pennsylvania (IDS), c/o Bucks County IU, No. 22, Doylestown 18901. SAN 322-2942. Tel. 215-348-2940, ext. 1620, fax 215-348-8315, e-mail ids@bucksiu.org. *Admin. Dir.* Beverly Carey.

Keystone Library Network, Educational Resources Group, Harrisburg 17110-1201. Tel. 717-720-4088, fax 717-720-4453. *Coord.* Mary Sonden.

Laurel Highlands Health Sciences Library Consortium, Owen Lib., Rm. 209, Johnstown 15904. SAN 322-2950. Tel. 814-269-7280, fax 814-266-8230. *Dir.* Heather Brice.

Lehigh Valley Association of Independent Colleges, 130 W. Greenwich St., Bethlehem 18018. SAN 322-2969. Tel. 610-625-7888, fax 610-625-7891. *Exec. Dir.* Tom Tenges.

Northeastern Pennsylvania Library Network, c/o Marywood Univ. Lib., Scranton 18509-1598. SAN 322-2993. Tel. 570-348-6260, fax 570-961-4769. *Dir.* Catherine Schappert.

Northwest Interlibrary Cooperative of Pennsylvania (NICOP), Edinboro Univ., Edinboro 16444. SAN 370-5862. Tel. 814-732-1534, fax 814-732-2883. *Chair* Christine Troutman.

PALINET, 3401 Market St., Suite 262, Philadelphia 19104. SAN 322-3000. Tel. 215-382-7031, fax 215-382-0022, e-mail palinet@palinet.org. *Exec. Dir.* Bernadette Freedman.

Pennsylvania Citizens for Better Libraries (PCBL), 806 West St., Homestead 15120. SAN 372-8285. Tel. 412-461-1322, fax 412-461-1250, e-mail tsimain@transitional services.org. *Dir.* Sharon Alberts.

Pennsylvania Community College Library Consortium, 1333 S. Prospect St., Nanticoke 18634. SAN 329-3939. Tel. 570-740-0415, fax 570-735-6130. *Pres.* Mary Stubbs.

Pennsylvania Library Association, 3905 N. Front St., Harrisburg 17110. SAN 372-8145. Tel. 717-233-3113, fax 717-233-3121. *Exec. Dir.* Glenn Miller.

Philadelphia Area Consortium of Special Collections Libraries (PACSCL), Rare Books Dept., Free Library of Philadelphia, Philadelphia 19103. SAN 370-7504. Tel. 215-686-5322, fax 215-563-3628. *Pres.* William Lang.

Southeastern Pennsylvania Theological Library Association (SEPTLA), c/o St. Charles Borromeo Seminary, Wynnewood 19096-3012. SAN 371-0793. Tel. 610-667-3394, fax 610-664-7913. *Head of Technical Services* Christine Schwartz.

State System of Higher Education Library Cooperative (SSHELCO), c/o Bailey Lib., Slippery Rock 16057. Tel. 724-738-2630, fax 724-738-2661. *Dir.* Barbara Farah.

Susquehanna Library Cooperative, Harvey A. Andruss Lib., Bloomsburg Univ., Bloomsburg 17815-1301. SAN 322-3051. Tel. 570-389-4224. *Chair* John Pitcher.

Tri-County Library Consortium, c/o New Castle Public Lib., New Castle 16101.

SAN 322-306X. Tel. 724-658-6659, fax 724-658-9012. *Dir.* Susan E. Walls.

Tri-State College Library Cooperative (TCLC), c/o Rosemont College Lib., Rosemont 19010-1699. SAN 322-3078. Tel. 610-525-0796, fax 610-525-1939, e-mail tclc@hslc.org. *Coord.* Ellen Gasiewski.

Rhode Island

Cooperating Libraries Automated Network (CLAN), 600 Sandy Lane, Warwick 02886. SAN 329-4560. Tel. 401-738-2200, fax 401-736-8949. *Chair* Deborah Barchi.

Library of Rhode Island (LORI), c/o Office of Lib. and Info. Services, Providence 02908-5870. SAN 371-6821. Tel. 401-222-2726, fax 401-222-4195. *Information Services* Barbara Weaver.

South Carolina

Charleston Academic Libraries Consortium (CALC), Trident Technical College, Charleston 29423. SAN 371-0769. Tel. 843-574-6088, fax 843-574-6484. *Chair* Drucie Raines.

Columbia Area Medical Librarians' Association (CAMLA), Professional Lib., Columbia 29202. SAN 372-9400. Tel. 803-898-1735, fax 803-898-1712. *Coord.* Neeta Shah.

South Carolina AHEC, c/o Medical Univ. of South Carolina, Charleston 29425. SAN 329-3998. Tel. 843-792-4431, fax 843-792-4430. *Exec. Dir.* Stoney Abercombie.

South Carolina Library Network, 1500 Senate St., Columbia 29211. SAN 322-4198. Tel. 803-734-8666, fax 803-734-8676. *State Libn.* James Johnson.

South Dakota

South Dakota Library Network (SDLN), 1200 University, Unit 9672, Spearfish 57799-9672. SAN 371-2117. Tel. 605-642-6835, fax 605-642-6472. *Dir.* Gary Johnson.

Tennessee

Association of Memphis Area Health Science Libraries (AMAHSL), c/o Univ. of Tennessee Health Sciences Lib., Lamar Alexander Bldg., Memphis 38163. SAN 323-9802. Tel. 901-448-5635, fax 901-448-6855, e-mail lbellamy@utmem.edu. *Associate Prof.* Lois Bellamy.

Consortium of Southern Biomedical Libraries (CONBLS), Meharry Medical College, Nashville 37208. SAN 370-7717. Tel. 615-327-6728, fax 615-321-2932. *Dir.* Rosalind Lett.

Knoxville Area Health Sciences Library Consortium (KAHSLC), Univ. of Tennessee Medical Center, Knoxville 37920. SAN 371-0556. Tel. 865-544-9525. *In Charge* Doris Prichard.

Mid-Tennessee Health Science Librarians Association, VA Medical Center, Murfreesboro 37129. SAN 329-5028. Tel. 615-867-6142, fax 615-867-5778.

Tennessee Health Science Library Association (THeSLA), Holston Valley Medical Center Health Sciences Lib., Kingsport 37662. SAN 371-0726. Tel. 423-224-6870, fax 423-224-6014, e-mail sharon_m_brown@wellmont.org.

Tri-Cities Area Health Sciences Libraries Consortium, East Tennessee State Univ., James H. Quillen College of Medicine, Johnson City 37614. SAN 329-4099. Tel. 423-439-6252, fax 423-439-7025. *Dir.* Biddanda Ponnappa.

West Tennessee Academic Library Consortium, Loden-Daniel Lib., Freed-Hardeman Univ., Henderson 38340-2399. SAN 322-3175. Tel. 731-989-6067, fax 731-989-6065, e-mail library@fhu.edu. *Chair* Hope Shull.

Texas

Abilene Library Consortium, 241 Pine St., Suite 15C, Abilene 79601. SAN 322-4694. Tel. 915-672-7081, fax 915-672-7084. *Exec. Dir.* Robert Gillette.

AMIGOS Library Services, Inc., 14400 Midway Rd., Dallas 75244. SAN 322-3191. Tel. 972-851-8012, fax 972-991-6061, e-mail amigos@amigos.org. *Exec. Dir.* Bonnie Juergens.

APLIC International Census Network, c/o Population Research Center, Austin 78712.

SAN 370-0690. Tel. 512-471-5514, fax 512-471-4886.

Council of Research and Academic Libraries (CORAL), Box 290236, San Antonio 78280-1636. SAN 322-3213.

Del Norte Biosciences Library Consortium, c/o Reference Dept. Lib., El Paso 79968. SAN 322-3302. Tel. 915-747-6714, 915-747-5683, fax 915-747-5327. *Libn.* Barbara Campbell.

Harrington Library Consortium, 2201 Washington, Amarillo 79109. SAN 329-546X. Tel. 806-371-5135, fax 806-371-5119.

Health Library Information Network, John Peter Smith Hospital Lib., Fort Worth 76104. SAN 322-3299. Tel. 817-921-3431, ext. 5088, fax 817-923-0718. *Dir.* Leslie Herman.

Houston Area Research Library Consortium (HARLiC), c/o Houston Public Lib., Houston 77002. SAN 322-3329. Tel. 713-247-2700, fax 713-247-1266.

National Network of Libraries of Medicine, South Central Region (NNLM SCR), c/o HAM-TMC Lib., Houston 77030-2809. SAN 322-3353. Tel. 713-799-7880, fax 713-790-7030, e-mail nnlmscr@library.tmc.edu. *Associate Dir.* Renee Bougard.

Northeast Texas Library System (NETLS), 625 Austin, Garland 75040-6365. SAN 370-5943. Tel. 972-205-2566, fax 972-205-2767. *Dir.* Claire Bausch.

Piasano Consortium, Victoria College, Univ. of Houston, Victoria Lib., Victoria 77901-5699. SAN 329-4943. Tel. 361-570-4848, fax 361-570-4155. *Coord.* Joe Dahlstrom.

South Central Academic Medical Libraries Consortium (SCAMEL), c/o Lewis Lib./UNTHSC, Fort Worth 76107. SAN 372-8269. Tel. 817-735-2380, fax 817-735-5158. *Dir. of Lib. Services* Bobby Carter.

Texas Council of State University Librarians, Univ. of Texas—Health Science Center at San Antonio, San Antonio 78229-3900. SAN 322-337X. Tel. 210-567-2400, fax 210-567-2490, e-mail info.blis@uthscsa.edu. *Dir.* Virginia Bowden.

Texnet, Box 12927, Austin 78711. SAN 322-3396. Tel. 512-463-5406, fax 512-936-2306. *In Charge* Dayna Jones.

Utah

Forest Service Library Network, Rocky Mountain Research Station, Ogden 84401. SAN 322-032X. Tel. 801-625-5445, fax 801-625-5129, e-mail rmrs_library@fs.fed.us.

National Network of Libraries of Medicine— Midcontinental Region (NN-LM MCR), Univ. of Utah, Spencer S. Eccles Health Science Lib., Salt Lake City 84112-5890. SAN 322-225X. Tel. 801-587-3412, fax 801-581-3632. *Dir.* Wayne Peay.

Utah Academic Library Consortium (UALC), Univ. of Utah, J. Willard Marriott Lib., Salt Lake City 84112-0860. SAN 322-3418. Tel. 801-581-8558, fax 801-581-3997. *Chair* Wayne Peay.

Utah Health Sciences Library Consortium, c/o Univ. of Utah, Spencer S. Eccles Health Science Lib., Salt Lake City 84112. SAN 376-2246. Tel. 801-581-8771, fax 801-581-3632.

Vermont

Health Science Libraries of New Hampshire and Vermont (HSL-NH-VT), c/o Archivist, Dana Medical Lib., Univ. of Vermont, Burlington 05405-0068. SAN 371-6864. Tel. 802-656-2200, fax 802-656-0762. *Dir.* Marianne Burke.

Vermont Resource Sharing Network, c/o Vermont Dept. of Libs., Montpelier 05609-0601. SAN 322-3426. Tel. 802-828-3261, fax 802-828-2199. *Dir. of Lib. Services* Marjorie Zunder.

Virginia

American Indian Higher Education Consortium (AIHEC), 121 Oronoco St., Alexandria 22314. SAN 329-4056. Tel. 703-838-0400, fax 703-838-0388, e-mail aihec@aihec.org. *Pres.* James Shanley.

Defense Technical Information Center, 8725 John J. Kingman Rd., Suite 1948, Fort Belvoir 22060-6218. SAN 322-3442. Tel. 703-767-9100, fax 703-767-9183. *Admin.* Kurt Molholm.

Educational Resources Information Center (ERIC) Clearinghouse on Disabilities and Gifted Education (EC), Council for Exceptional Children, Arlington 22201-5704. SAN 322-0613. Tel. 703-264-9474, fax 703-620-4334, e-mail ericec@cec.sped.org. *Dir.* Cassandra Peters-Johnson.

Educational Resources Information Center (ERIC) Document Reproduction Service (EDRS), Dyn EDRS Inc., Springfield 22153-2852. SAN 375-6076. Tel. 703-440-1400, fax 703-440-1408, e-mail service@edrs.com. *Dir.* Peter M. Dagutis.

Lynchburg Area Library Cooperative, Bedford Public Lib., Bedford 24523. SAN 322-3450. Tel. 540-586-8911, fax 540-586-7280. *Associate Dir.* Steve Preston.

Lynchburg Information Online Network (LION Consortium of Virginia), 2315 Memorial Ave., Lynchburg 24503. SAN 374-6097. Tel. 434-381-6311, fax 434-381-6173. *Dir.* John Jaffe.

NASA Libraries Information System—NASA Galaxie, NASA Langley Research Center, Hampton 23681-2199. SAN 322-0788. Tel. 757-864-2356, 757-864-2392, fax 757-864-2375. *In Charge* Carolyn Helmetsie.

Richmond Academic Library Consortium, Virginia Commonwealth Univ., 901 Park Ave., Box 2033, Richmond 23284-2033. Tel. 804-828-1107, fax 804-828-0151. *Pres.* John E. Ulmschneider.

Southside Virginia Library Network (SVLN), Longwood College, Farmville 23909-1897. SAN 372-8242. Tel. 434-395-2633, fax 434-395-2453. *Dir.* Calvin Boyer.

Southwestern Virginia Health Information Librarians (SWVAHILI), Box 800722, Health System, Charlottesville 22908. SAN 323-9527. Tel. 804-799-4418, fax 804-799-2255. *Chair* Elaine Banner.

United States Army Training and Doctrine Command (TRADOC) Lib. Program Office, ATBO-FL, Bldg. 5A, Rm. 102, Fort Monroe 23651-1048. SAN 322-418X. Tel. 757-788-4096, fax 757-788-5300. *Dir.* Janet Scheitle.

Virginia Independent College and University Lib. Association, c/o Mary Helen Cochran Lib., Sweet Briar 24595. SAN 374-6089. Tel. 434-381-6138, fax 434-381-6173. *Dir.* John Jankey.

Virginia Tidewater Consortium for Higher Education, 1417 43rd St., Norfolk 23529-0293. SAN 329-5486. Tel. 757-683-3183, fax 757-683-4515, e-mail lgdotolo@aol. com. *Pres.* Lawrence Dotolo.

Virtual Library of Virginia (VIVA), George Mason Univ., Fairfax 22030-4444. Tel. 703-993-4652, fax 703-993-4662. *Chair* Ralph Alberico.

Washington

Consortium for Automated Library Services (CALS), Evergreen State College Lib. L2300, Olympia 98505. SAN 329-4528. Tel. 360-866-6000, ext. 6260, fax 360-866-6790. *Dean* Lee Lyttle.

Inland Northwest Health Sciences Libraries (INWHSL), Box 10283, Spokane 99209-0283. SAN 370-5099. Tel. 509-324-7344, fax 509-324-7349.

National Network of Libraries of Medicine— Pacific Northwest Region (NN-LM PNR), Univ. of Washington, Seattle 98195-7155. SAN 322-3485. Tel. 206-543-8262, fax 206-543-2469, e-mail nnlm@u.washington. edu. *Dir.* Sherrilynne Fuller.

OCLC Lacey Product Center, 4224 Sixth Ave. S.E., Bldg. 3, Lacey 98503. SAN 322-3507. Tel. 360-923-4000, fax 360-923-4009. *Dir.* Scott Barringer.

Palouse Area Library Information Services (PALIS), c/o Neill Public Lib., Pullman 99163. SAN 375-0132. Tel. 509-334-3595, fax 509-334-6051. *Dir.* Mike Pollastro.

Washington Idaho Network (WIN), Foley Center, Gonzaga Univ., Spokane 99258. Tel. 509-323-6545, fax 509-323-5904. *Dean of Lib.* Eileen Bell-Garrison.

West Virginia

Educational Resources Information Center (ERIC) Clearinghouse on Rural Education and Small Schools (RC), Appalachia Educational Laboratory (AEL), Charleston 23501-2326. SAN 322-0672. Tel. 304-347-0400, fax 304-347-0467, e-mail ericrc @ael.org. *Dir.* Pat Hammer.

Huntington Health Science Library Consortium, Marshall Univ. Health Science Libs., Huntington 25701-3655. SAN 322-4295. Tel. 304-691-1753, fax 304-691-1766. *Dir.* Edward Dzierzak.

Mid-Atlantic Law Library Cooperative (MALLCO), West Virginia Univ., College of Law Lib., Morgantown 26506. SAN 371-0645. Tel. 304-293-7641, 304-293-7775, fax 304-293-6020. *Dir.* Camille Riley.

Mountain States Consortium, c/o Alderson Broaddus College, Philippi 26416. SAN 329-4765. Tel. 304-457-1700, fax 304-457-6239. *Pres.* Stephen Markwood.

Wisconsin

Fox River Valley Area Library Consortium, Moraine Park Technical College, Fond Du Lac 54935. SAN 322-3531. Tel. 920-924-3112, 920-922-8611, fax 920-924-3117. *In Charge* Charlene Pettit.

Fox Valley Library Council (FVLC), c/o Owls, Fox Valley Lib. Council, Appleton 54911. SAN 323-9640. Tel. 920-832-6190, fax 920-832-6422. *Pres.* Cheryl Gage.

Library Council of Metropolitan Milwaukee, Inc., 814 W. Wisconsin Ave., Milwaukee 53233-2309. SAN 322-354X. Tel. 414-271-8470, fax 414-286-2798, e-mail lcomm @execpc.com. *Exec. Dir.* Susie Just.

North East Wisconsin Intertype Libraries, Inc. (NEWIL), 515 Pine St., Green Bay 54301. SAN 322-3574. Tel. 920-448-4412, fax 920-448-4420. *Coord.* Terrie Howe.

Northwestern Wisconsin Health Science Library Consortium, Wausau Hospital Center, Joseph F. Smith Medical Lib., Wausau 54401. Tel. 715-847-2121, 715-847-2184, fax 715-847-2183. *In Charge* Jan Kraus.

South Central Wisconsin Health Science Library Consortium, c/o FAMHS Medical Lib., Fort Atkinson 53538. SAN 322-4686. Tel. 920-568-5194, fax 920-568-5195. *Coord.* Carrie Garity.

Southeastern Wisconsin Health Science Library Consortium, Convenant Healthcare Systems Lib., Milwaukee 53210. SAN 322-3582. Tel. 414-447-2194, fax 414-447-2128. *Dir.* Sunja Shaikh.

Southeastern Wisconsin Information Technology Exchange, Inc. (SWITCH), 6801 N. Yates Rd., Milwaukee 53217-3985. SAN 371-3962. Tel. 414-351-2423, fax 414-228-4146. *Exec. Dir.* Jack Fritts.

University of Wisconsin System School Library Education Consortium (UWSSLEC), Graduate and Continuing Education, Whitewater 53190. Tel. 262-472-5208, fax 262-472-5210, e-mail lenchoc@mail.uww.edu. *Coord., Associate Prof.* E. Zarinnia.

Wisconsin Area Research Center Network, Wisconsin Historical Society, Madison 53706. SAN 373-0875. Tel. 608-264-6477, fax 608-264-6486. *Head of Public Services* Richard Pifer.

Wisconsin Library Services, 728 State St., Rm. 464, Madison 53706-1494. SAN 322-3612. Tel. 608-263-4962, fax 608-292-6067. *Dir.* Kathryn Michaelis.

Wisconsin Valley Library Service (WVLS), 300 N. First St., Wausau 54403. SAN 371-3911. Tel. 715-261-7250, fax 715-261-7259. *Dir.* Heather Eldred.

WISPALS Library Consortium, c/o Gateway Technical College, Kenosha 53144-1690. Tel. 262-564-2602, fax 262-564-2787. *Coord.* Ellen Pedraza.

Wyoming

University of Wyoming Information Network Plus, Univ. of Wyoming Libs. (UWIN Plus), 112 Coe Lib., Laramie 82071. SAN 371-4861. Tel. 307-766-6537, fax 307-766-5368, e-mail uwin-plus@uwyo.edu. *Coord.* Mary Henning.

WYLD Network, c/o Wyoming State Lib., Cheyenne 82002-0060. SAN 371-0661. Tel. 307-777-6339, fax 307-777-6289. *State Libn.* Lesley Boughton.

Virgin Islands

VILINET (Virgin Islands Lib. and Information Network), c/o Division of Libs., Museums and Archives, Saint Thomas 00802. SAN 322-3639. Tel. 340-774-3407, fax 340-775-1887. *Dir.* Sharlene Harris.

Canada

Alberta

Alberta Association of College Librarians (AACL), Lakeland College, Learning Resources Centre, Vermillion T9X 1K5. SAN 370-0763. Tel. 780-853-8468, fax 403-849-2570. *Chair* Mircea Panciuk.

Alberta Government Libraries Council (AGLC), 10025 Jasper Ave., Edmonton T5J 2N3. SAN 370-0372. Tel. 780-415-0228, fax 780-422-9694. *In Charge* Peggy Yeh.

Northern Alberta Health Libraries Association (NAHLA), 2100 Research Transition Facility, Edmonton T6G 2E1. SAN 370-5951. *Pres.* Tanya Voth.

British Columbia

BC Electronic Library Network (ELN), 4355 Mathissi Pl., Burnaby V5G 4S8. Tel. 604-431-3020, fax 604-431-3381, e-mail eln@ola.bc.ca. *Manager* Anita Cocchia.

British Columbia College and Institute Library Services, Langara College Lib., Vancouver V5Y 2Z6. SAN 329-6970. Tel. 604-323-5237, fax 604-323-5544, e-mail cils@langara.bc.ca. *Dir.* Mary Epp.

Manitoba

Manitoba Government Libraries Council (MGLC), c/o 250-240 Graham Ave., Winnipeg R3C 4B3. SAN 371-6848. Tel. 204-984-0779, fax 204-983-3852. *Dir.* John Giesbrecht.

Manitoba Library Consortium, Inc. (MLCI), c/o Lib. Admin., Univ. of Winnipeg, Winnipeg R3B 2E9. SAN 372-820X. Tel. 204-945-1413, fax 204-783-8910. *Chair* Betty Dearth.

New Brunswick

Maritimes Health Libraries Association (MHLA-ABSM), c/o Region 7 Hospital Corp., Miramich E1V 3G5. SAN 370-0836. Tel. 506-623-3215, fax 506-623-3280. *Pres.* Nancy McAllister.

Nova Scotia

NOVANET, 1550 Bedford Hwy., No. 501, Bedford B4A 1E6. SAN 372-4050. Tel. 902-453-2461, fax 902-453-2369. *Exec. Dir.* William Birdsall.

Ontario

Bibliocentre, 80 Cowdray Court, Scarborough M1S 4N1. SAN 322-3663. Tel. 416-289-5151, fax 416-299-4841. *Exec. Dir.* Janice Hayes.

Canadian Agriculture Library System, Sir John Carling Bldg., Ottawa K1A 0C5. SAN 377-5054. Tel. 613-759-7068, fax 613-759-6627, e-mail cal-bca@agr.gc.ca. *Dir.* Victor Desroches.

Canadian Association of Research Libraries (Association des Bibliothèques de Recherche du Canada), Morisset Hall, Rm. 239, Ottawa K1N 9A5. SAN 323-9721. Tel. 613-562-5385, fax 613-562-5195, e-mail carladm@uottawa.ca. *Exec. Dir.* Timothy Mark.

Canadian Health Libraries Association (CHLA-ABSC), Office of Secretariat, 3324 Yonge St., Toronto M4N 3R1. SAN 370-0720. Tel. 416-485-0377, fax 416-485-6877, e-mail info@chla-absc.ca. *Pres.* Catherine Rayment.

Hamilton and District Health Library Network, c/o St. Joseph's Hospital, Hamilton L8N 4A6. SAN 370-5846. Tel. 905-522-1155, ext. 3410, fax 905-540-6504. *Coord.* Jean Maragno.

Health Science Information Consortium of Toronto, c/o Gerstein Science Information Center, Univ. of Toronto, Toronto M5S 1A5. SAN 370-5080. Tel. 416-978-6359, fax 416-971-2637, e-mail laurie.scott@utoronto.ca.

Ontario Health Libraries Association (OHLA), Lib., Sarnia General Hospital, Sarnia N7T 6H6. SAN 370-0739. Tel. 519-464-4500, ext. 5251, fax 519-464-4511.

Ontario Library Consortium (OLC), Owen Sound and North Grey Union Public Lib., Owen Sound N4K 4K4. *Pres.* Judy Armstrong.

Shared Library Services (SLS), South Huron Hospital, Exeter N0M 1S2. SAN 323-9500. Tel. 519-235-4002, ext. 249, fax 519-235-4476, e-mail shha.sls@hphp.org.

Sheridan Park Association, Lib. and Info. Science Committee (SPA-LISC), 2275 Speakman Dr., Unit 6, Mississauga L5K 1B1. SAN 370-0437. Tel. 905-823-6160, ext. 221, fax 905-823-6161, e-mail spamgr@interlog.com. *Manager* Cindy Smith.

Toronto Health Libraries Association (THLA), 3324 Yonge St., Toronto M4N 3R1. SAN 323-9853. Tel. 416-485-0377, fax 416-485-6877, e-mail medinfoserv@rogers.com.

Toronto School of Theology, 47 Queen's Park Crescent E., Toronto M5S 2C3. SAN 322-452X. Tel. 416-978-4039, fax 416-978-7821. *Chair* Noel McFerran.

Quebec

Association des Bibliothèques de la Santé Affiliées à l'Université de Montréal (ABSAUM), c/o Health Lib., Univ. of Montreal, Montreal H3C 3J7. SAN 370-5838. Tel. 514-343-6826, fax 514-343-2350. *Dir.* Diane Raymond.

Canadian Heritage Information Network (CHIN), 15 Eddy St., 4th fl., Hull K1A 0M5. SAN 329-3076. Tel. 819-994-1200, fax 819-994-9555, e-mail service@chin.gc.ca. *Libn.* Vicki Davis.

Saskatchewan

Saskatchewan Government Libraries Council (SGLC), c/o Saskatchewan Agriculture and Food Lib., Regina S4S 0B1. SAN 323-956X. Tel. 306-787-5152, 306-787-5140, fax 306-787-0216. *Info. Specialist* Olive McDonald.

National Library and Information-Industry Associations, United States and Canada

American Association of Law Libraries

Executive Director, Susan E. Fox
53 W. Jackson Blvd., Suite 940, Chicago, IL 60604
312-939-4764, fax 312-431-1097
World Wide Web http://www.aallnet.org

Object

The American Association of Law Libraries (AALL) is established for educational and scientific purposes. It shall be conducted as a nonprofit corporation to promote and enhance the value of law libraries to the public, the legal community, and the world; to foster the profession of law librarianship; to provide leadership in the field of legal information; and to foster a spirit of cooperation among the members of the profession. Established 1906.

Membership

Memb. 5,000+. Persons officially connected with a law library or with a law section of a state or general library, separately maintained. Associate membership available for others. Dues (Indiv., Indiv. Assoc., and Inst.) $145; (Inst. Assoc.) $256 times the number of members; (Retired) $36; (Student) $36; (SIS Memb.) $12 each per year. Year. July 1–June 30.

Officers

Pres. Carol Avery Nicholson, Asst. Dir. for Bibliographic and Collection Resources, Univ. of North Carolina at Chapel Hill, CB 3385, 100 Ridge Rd., Chapel Hill, NC 27599. E-mail carol_nicholson@unc.edu; *V.P.* Janis Johnston; *Past Pres.* Barbara Bintliff; *Secy.* Catherine Lemann; *Treas.* Anne C. Matthewman.

Executive Board

James E. Duggan (2004), Ann Fessenden (2005), Karl C. Gruben (2003), Sarah G. Holterhoff (2003), Nina Platt (2005), Alvin M. Podboy, Jr. (2004).

Committees

Access to Electronic Legal Information.
AALL LexisNexis Call for Papers Committee.
AALLNET (Advisory).
Annual Meeting Program.
Authentication and Preservation of Digital Law (Special).
Awards.
Bylaws.
Citation Formats.
Copyright.
Relations with Information Vendors.
Develop Performance Measurements for Law Librarians (Special).
Diversity.
Economic Study (Advisory).
Election Procedures (Special).
Executive Board Finance and Budget.
Executive Board Governance.
Executive Board Strategic Planning.
Fair Business Practices (Special).
Future of Law Libraries in the Digital Age (Special).
Government Relations.
Grants.
Indexing of Periodical Literature (Advisory).
Membership and Retention.
Nominations.

Placement.
Price Index for Legal Publications.
Professional Development.
Public Relations.

Publications.
Recruitment to Law Librarianship.
Research.
Scholarships.

American Library Association

Executive Director, Keith Michael Fields
50 E. Huron St., Chicago, IL 60611
800-545-2433, 312-280-1392, fax 312-944-3897
World Wide Web http://www.ala.org

Object

The mission of the American Library Association (ALA) is to provide leadership for the development, promotion, and improvement of library and information services and the profession of librarianship in order to enhance learning and ensure access to information for all. Founded 1876.

Membership

Memb. (Indiv.) 58,562; (Inst.) 4,885; (Corporate) 249; (Total) 63,696 (as of August 31, 2002). Any person, library, or other organization interested in library service and librarians. Dues (Indiv.) 1st year, $50; 2nd year, $75, 3rd year and later, $100; (Trustee and Assoc. Memb.) $45; (Student) $25; (Foreign Indiv.) $60; (Other) $35; (Inst.) $110 and up, depending on operating expenses of institution.

Officers (2002–2003)

Pres. Maurice J. "Mitch" Freedman, Westchester Lib. System, 410 Saw Mill River Rd., Ardsley, NY 10549. Tel. 914-231-3223, fax 914-674-4193, e-mail freedman@wlsmail. org; *Pres.-Elect* Carla D. Hayden, Dir., Enoch Pratt Free Lib., 400 Cathedral St., Baltimore, MD 21201-4401. Tel. 410-396-5395, fax 410-396-1321, e-mail chayden@epfl.net;

Immediate Past Pres. John W. Berry, Exec. Dir., NILRC, Box 390, Sugar Grove, IL 60554. Tel. 708-366-0667, fax 708-366-0728, e-mail jberry@psinet.com; *Treas.* Lizbeth Bishoff, Colorado Digitization Project, Univ. of Denver, Penrose Lib., 2150 E. Evans Ave., Denver, CO 80208-2007. Tel. 303-871-2006, fax 303-871-2290, e-mail liz@bishoff.com; *Exec. Dir.* Keith Michael Fiels, ALA Headquarters, 50 E. Huron St., Chicago, IL 60611. Tel. 312-280-1392, fax 312-944-3897, e-mail kfiels@ala.org.

Executive Board

Camila A. Alire (2003), Kathleen E. Bethel (2005), Nancy Davenport (2005), Ken Haycock (2003), Kenton L. Oliver (2004), Mary E. "Molly" Raphael (2003), Barbara K. Stripling (2005), Patricia M. Wong (2004).

Endowment Trustees

Robert R. Newlen, Rick J. Schwieterman, Carla J. Stoffle; *Exec. Board Liaison* Lizbeth Bishoff; *Staff Liaison* Gregory L. Calloway.

Divisions

See the separate entries that follow: American Assn. of School Libns.; Assn. for Lib. Collections and Technical Services; Assn. for

Lib. Service to Children; Assn. for Lib. Trustees and Advocates; Assn. of College and Research Libs.; Assn. of Specialized and Cooperative Lib. Agencies; Lib. Admin. and Management Assn.; Lib. and Info. Technology Assn.; Public Lib. Assn.; Reference and User Services Assn.; Young Adult Lib. Services Assn.

New Members. Joseph Yue (Michael Dowling).

Social Responsibilities. Rory Litwin (Satia Orange).

Staff Organizations. Earl Houser, Jr. (Lorelle R. Swader).

Video. Michael Boedicker (Danielle M. Alderson).

Publications

ALA Handbook of Organization (ann.).
American Libraries (11 a year; memb.; organizations $60; foreign $70; single copy $6).
Book Links (6 a year; U.S. $27.95; foreign $35; single copy $6).
Booklist (22 a year; U.S. and possessions $79.95; foreign $95; single copy $6).

Round Table Chairpersons

(ALA staff liaison is given in parentheses.)
Continuing Library Education Network and Exchange. Cheryl M. Rogers (Lorelle R. Swader).
Ethnic and Multicultural Information Exchange. John H. Barnett (Satia Orange).
Exhibits. John E. Ison (Deidre Ross).
Federal and Armed Forces Libraries. Jennifer Bushong (Patricia May, Reginald Scott).
Gay, Lesbian, Bisexual, Transgendered. Anne L. Moore, Stephen E. Stratton (Satia Orange).
Government Documents. William E. Sudduth (Patricia May, Reginald Scott).
Intellectual Freedom. Michael B. Wessells (Don Wood).
International Relations. Karen J. Starr (Michael Dowling).
Library History. Christine Jenkins (Mary Jo Lynch).
Library Instruction. Anne M. Houston (Lorelle R. Swader).
Library Research. Marie Radford (Mary Jo Lynch).
Library Support Staff Interests. Carolyn Tate (Lorelle R. Swader).
Map and Geography. Mary McInroy (Danielle M. Alderson).

Committee Chairpersons

(ALA staff liaison is given in parentheses.)
Accreditation (Standing). Carla J. Stoffle (Ann L. O'Neill).
American Libraries Advisory (Standing). Marcia G. Schneider (Leonard Kniffel).
Appointments (Standing). Carla D. Hayden (Elizabeth Dreazen, Lois Ann Gregory-Wood).
Awards (Standing). Leslie B. Burger (Cheryl Malden).
Budget Analysis and Review (Standing). Patricia H. Smith (Gregory Calloway).
Chapter Relations (Standing). Charles E. Beard (Michael Dowling).
Committee on Committees (Elected Council Committee). Carla D. Hayden (Elizabeth Dreazen, Lois Ann Gregory-Wood).
Conference Committee (Standing). Dottie R. Hiebing (Deidre Ross).
Conference Program Coordinating Team, 2003. Sarah E. Hamrick (Mary W. Ghikas, Deidre Ross).
Conference Program Coordinating Team, 2004. Carolyn P. Giambra (Mary W. Ghikas, Deidre Ross).
Constitution and Bylaws (Standing). Norman Horrocks (Letitia Earvin).
Council Orientation (Standing). Carol A. Brey (Lois Ann Gregory-Wood).
Diversity (Standing). Rhea Brown Lawson (Wendy Prellwitz).
Education (Standing). Lorna Peterson (Lorelle R. Swader).
Election (Standing). Sheryl J. Nichin-Keith (Al Companio).
Human Resource Development and Recruitment (Standing). Kay A. Cassell (Lorelle R. Swader).
Information Technology Policy Advisory. Linda D. Crowe (Frederick Weingarten).

Intellectual Freedom (Standing). Nancy C. Kranich (Judith F. Krug).

International Relations (Standing). Betty J. Turock (Michael Dowling).

Legislation (Standing). Bernadine Abbott Hoduski (Lynne E. Bradley).

Literacy (Standing). William B. Hawk (Dale P. Lipschultz).

Literacy and Outreach Services Advisory (Standing). Clara M. Chu (Satia Orange).

Membership (Standing). J. Linda Williams (Gerald G. Hodges).

Nominating 2003 Election (Special). Anne C. Sparanese (Elizabeth Dreazen).

Organization (Standing). James R. Rettig (Lois Ann Gregory-Wood).

Orientation, Training and Leadership Development. Irene M. Percelli (Dorothy A. Ragsdale).

Pay Equity (Standing). Michael Gorman (Lorelle R. Swader).

Policy Monitoring (Standing). Stephen L. Matthews (Lois Ann Gregory-Wood).

Professional Ethics (Standing). Sarah M. Pritchard (Beverley Becker, Judith F. Krug).

Public Awareness Advisory (Standing). Patricia Glass Schuman (Mark R. Gould).

Publishing (Standing). Amy K. Small (Donald Chatham).

Research and Statistics (Standing). Daniel O. O'Connor (Mary Jo Lynch).

Resolutions. Monika J. Antonelli (Lois Ann Gregory-Wood).

Spectrum Scholarship Program (Special Presidential Task Force) Christine Parke Booth (Wendy Prellwitz).

Standards Review (Standing). Rhea Joyce Rubin (Mary Jo Lynch).

Status of Women in Librarianship (Standing). Diane Gordon Kadanoff (Lorelle R. Swader).

Web Advisory. Rory Litwin (Sherri Vanyek, Karen Muller).

Joint Committee Chairpersons

American Federation of Labor/Congress of Industrial Organizations–ALA, Library Service to Labor Groups, RUSA. Dan D. Golodner (ALA); Anthony Sarmiento (AFL/CIO).

Anglo-American Cataloguing Rules Principals. Mary W. Ghikas (ALA).

Association of American Publishers–ALA. Maurice J. Freedman (ALA); to be appointed (AAP).

Association of American Publishers–ALCTS. Sheryl J. Nichin-Keith (ALCTS); Athena S. Michael (AAP).

Children's Book Council–ALA. Judith Rovenger (ALA); Jeanne McDermott (CBC).

Society of American Archivists–ALA (Joint Committee on Library-Archives Relationships). David W. Carmicheal (ALA); Charlotte B. Brown (SAA).

American Library Association
American Association of School Librarians

Executive Director, Julie A. Walker
50 E. Huron St., Chicago, IL 60611
312-280-4386, 800-545-2433 ext. 4386, fax 312-664-7459
E-mail AASL@ala.org, World Wide Web http://www.ala.org/aasl

Object

The American Association of School Librarians (AASL) is interested in the general improvement and extension of library media services for children and young people.

AASL has specific responsibility for planning a program of study and service for the improvement and extension of library media services in elementary and secondary schools as a means of strengthening the educational program; evaluation, selection, interpretation, and utilization of media as they are used in the context of the school program; stimulation of continuous study and research in the library field and establishing criteria of evaluation; synthesis of the activities of all units of the American Library Association in areas of mutual concern; representation and interpretation of the need for the function of school libraries to other educational and lay groups; stimulation of professional growth, improvement of the status of school librarians, and encouragement of participation by members in appropriate type-of-activity divisions; conducting activities and projects for improvement and extension of service in the school library when such projects are beyond the scope of type-of-activity divisions, after specific approval by the ALA Council. Established in 1951 as a separate division of ALA.

Membership

Memb. 9,403. Open to all libraries, school library media specialists, interested individuals, and business firms with requisite membership in ALA.

Officers (2002–2003)

Pres. Nancy Zimmerman, Univ. of South Carolina College of Lib. and Info. Science, 217 Davis College, Columbia, SC 29208. Tel. 803-777-1215, fax 803-777-7938, e-mail nzimmerman@gwm.sc.edu; *Pres.-Elect* Frances Roscello, New York State Educ. Dept., Albany, NY 12234; *Treas./Financial Officer* Carolyn S. Hayes, Lakeshore, FL 33854; *Past Pres.* Helen R. Adams, Rosholt Public Schools, Rosholt, WI 54473-9547.

Board of Directors

Officers; James Carey, LuAnn L. Cogliser, Diane Durbin, Nancy Everhart, Lesley S. J. Farmer, Jody Gehrig, Carol A. Gordon, Liz Gray, Bonnie J. Grimble, Eugene Hainer, Elizabeth Haynes, Erlene Bishop Killeen, Toni Negro, Elaine Twogood, Donna Shannon, Julie A. Walker (ex officio).

Publications

Knowledge Quest (5 a year; memb.; nonmemb. $40). *Ed.* Debbie Abilock, Nueva School, 6565 Skyline Blvd., Hillsborough, CA 94010-6221. E-mail dabilock@pacbell.net.

School Library Media Research (nonsubscription electronic publication available to memb. and nonmemb. at http://www.ala.org/aasl/SLMR). *Ed.* Daniel Callison, School of Lib. and Info. Sciences, 10th and Jordan, Indiana Univ., Bloomington, IN 47405. E-mail callison@indiana.edu.

Committee Chairpersons

AASL @ Your Library Special Committee. Harriet Selverstone.

AASL/ACRL Joint Information Literacy Committee. Allison Kaplan, Adis Beesting.

AASL/ELMS Executive Committee. Judy Repman.

AASL/Highsmith Research Grant. To be announced.

AASL/ISS Executive Committee. Karen Phillips.

AASL/SPVS Executive Committee. Martha Alewine.

ABC/CLIO Leadership Grant. Pamela Chesky.

Affiliate Assembly. Cynthia Phillip.

Alliance for Association Excellence. Carolyn S. Hayes.

American Univ. Press Book Selection. To be annunced.

Annual Conference. Carolyn Giambra, Shirley Tastad, Merchuria Williams.

Appointments. Barbara Weathers.

Awards. Hilda Weisburg.

Bylaws and Organization. Carolyn Cain.

Collaborative School Library Media Award. To be announced.

Distinguished School Administrator Award. To be announced.

Distinguished Service Award. To be announced.

Frances Henne Award. To be announced.

ICONnect FamiliesConnect. Sally Trexler.

ICONnect Online Courses. To be announced.

Information Technology Pathfinder Award. To be announced.

Institute Planning. Deborah Levitov.

Intellectual Freedom. Sandra Dobbins Andrews.

Intellectual Freedom Award. To be announced.

International Relations Committee. To be announced.

Knowledge Quest Editorial Board. Debbie Abilock.

Leadership Forum Planning. Gail K. Dickinson.

Legislation. Dennis J. LeLoup, John McGinnis.

National Conference, 2003. Cassandra Barnett, Floyd Pentlin.

National School Library Media Program of the Year Award. Blanche Woolls.

NCATE Coordinating Committee. To be announced.

Publications. Judy King.

Reading for Understanding Special Committee. Sharon Coatney.

Recruitment for the Profession Task Force. Eileen E. Schroeder.

Research/Statistics. June Kahler Berry.

School Librarians Workshop Scholarship. To be announced.

SLMR Electronic Editorial Board. Daniel J. Callison.

Teaching and Instruction Special Committee. Linda Corey.

Virtual Participation Task Force. Pam Berger.

Vision Expansion Special Committee. Carrie Gardner.

Web Advisory. Sandra Jane Scroggs.

Association for Library Collections and Technical Services

Executive Director, Charles Wilt
50 E. Huron St., Chicago, IL 60611
800-545-2433 ext. 5030, fax 312-280-5033
E-mail cwilt@ala.org
World Wide Web http://www.ala.org/alcts

Object

ALCTS envisions an environment in which traditional library roles are evolving. New technologies are making information more fluid and raising expectations. The public needs quality information anytime, anyplace. ALCTS provides frameworks to meet these information needs.

ALCTS provides leadership to the library and information communities in developing principles, standards, and best practices for creating, collecting, organizing, delivering, and preserving information resources in all forms. It provides this leadership through its members by fostering educational, research, and professional service opportunities. ALCTS is committed to quality information, universal access, collaboration, and life-long learning.

Standards: Develop, evaluate, revise, and promote standards for creating, collecting, organizing, delivering, and preserving information resources in all forms.

Best practices: Research, develop, evaluate, and implement best practices for creating, collecting, organizing, delivering, and preserving information resources in all forms.

Education: Assess the need for, sponsor, develop, administer, and promote educational programs and resources for life-long learning.

Professional development: Provide opportunities for professional development through research, scholarship, publication, and professional service.

Interaction and information exchange: Create opportunities to interact and exchange information with others in the library and information communities.

Association operations: Ensure efficient use of association resources and effective delivery of member services.

Established 1957; renamed 1988.

Membership

Memb. 5,091. Any member of the American Library Association may elect membership in this division according to the provisions of the bylaws.

Officers (2002–2003)

Pres. Olivia M. A. Madison, Iowa State Univ. Lib., 302 Parks Lib., Ames, IA 50011-2140. Tel. 515-294-1443, fax 515-294-2112, e-mail omadison@iastate.edu; *Pres.-Elect* Brian E. C. Schottlaender, Univ. of California at San Diego Lib., 9500 Gilman Dr., 0175G, La Jolla, CA 92093-0175. Tel. 858-534-3060, fax 858-534-6193, e-mail becs@ucsd.edu; *Past Pres.* Bill Robnett, California State Univ.–Monterey, 100 Campus Center Bldg. 12, Seaside, CA 93955. Tel. 831-582-4448, fax 831-582-3354, e-mail bill_robnett@csumb.edu; *Councilor* Bruce Chr. Johnson, Cataloging Distribution Service, Lib. of Congress, Washington, DC 20540-0001. Tel. 202-707-1652, fax 202-707-3959, e-mail bjoh@loc.gov.

Address correspondence to the executive director.

Board of Directors

Rosann Bazirjian, Mary Case, Carol Pitts Diedrichs, Bruce Chr. Johnson, Bonnie MacEwan, Olivia M. A. Madison, Carolynne Myall, Judith Niles, Miriam W. Palm, Sharon A. Roberts, Bill Robnett, Brian E. C. Schottlaender, Laura Sill, Julian Stam, Jane Treadwell, Charles Wilt.

Publications

ALCTS Newsletter Online (q.; free). *Ed.* Miriam W. Palm, 2185 Waverley St., Palo Alto, CA 94301. Tel./fax 650-327-8989, e-mail Miriam.Palm@stanford.edu. Posted to http://www.ala.org/alcts/alcts_news.

Library Resources & Technical Services (q.; memb.; nonmemb. $55). *Ed.* John M. Budd, School of Info. Science and Learning Technologies, Univ. of Missouri–Columbia, 221M Townsend Hall, Columbia, MO 65211. Tel. 573-882-3258, fax 573-884-4944, e-mail buddj@missouri.edu.

Section Chairpersons

Acquisitions. Rosann Bazirjian.
Cataloging and Classification. Mary Dabney Wilson.
Collection Management and Development. Bonnie MacEwan.
Preservation and Reformatting. Julian Stam.
Serials. Carolynne Myall.

Committee Chairpersons

Hugh C. Atkinson Memorial Award (ALCTS/ACRL/LAMA/LITA). Janet Swan Hill.
Association of American Publishers/ALCTS Joint Committee. Athena Michael, Sheryl Nichin-Keith.
Paul Banks and Carolyn Harris Preservation Award. Wesley Boomgaarden.
Best of *LRTS* Award. Sandra Beehler.
Blackwell's Scholarship Award. Sharon Bonk.
Budget and Finance. Judith Niles.
Catalog Form and Function. Melinda Reagor-Flannery.
Commercial Technical Services. Lynda Kresge.
Education. Peggy Johnson.
Fund Raising. Pamela M. Bluh.
International Relations. Edward Swanson.
Leadership Development. Brad Eden.
Legislation. Bernard Karon.
Library Materials Price Index. Sharon G. Sullivan.
LRTS Editorial Board. John M. Budd.
MARBI. Thomas Saudargas.
Media Resources. Miriam Palm.
Membership. Manuel Urrizola.
Networked Resources and Metadata. Mary Woodley.
Nominating. Carlen Ruschoff.
Organization and Bylaws. Ann Swartzell, Bill Robnett.
Esther J. Piercy Award Jury. D. E. Perushek.
Planning. Laura Sill.

Program. Helen Reed.

Publications. Genevieve Owens.

Publisher/Vendor Library Relations. Robert Nardini.

Research and Statistics. Cindy Hepfer.

Discussion Groups

Authority Control in the Online Environment (ALCTS/LITA). Ann Della Porta.

Automated Acquisitions/In-Process Control Systems. Michael Kaplan.

Creative Ideas in Technical Services. Katia Roberto, Frances Krempasky.

Electronic Resources. Tina Shrader.

MARC Formats (ALCTS/LITA). Laura Sill, Marc Truitt.

Newspaper. Jessica Albano, Sharon E. Clark.

Out of Print. Narda Tafuri.

Pre-Order and Pre-Catalog Searching. Daniel Cromwell.

Role of the Professional in Academic Research Technical Service Departments. Wanda Brown.

Scholarly Communications. Anne McKee, Maria Sitko.

Serials Automation. Carol Trinchitella.

Technical Services Administrators of Medium-Sized Research Libraries. Jack Hall.

Technical Services Directors of Large Research Libraries. Sally Sinn.

Technical Services in Public Libraries. Ross McLachlan.

Technical Services Workstations. David Banush.

American Library Association
Association for Library Service to Children

Executive Director, Malore I. Brown
50 E. Huron St., Chicago, IL 60611
312-280-2162, 800-545-2433 ext. 2162
E-mail mbrown@ala.org
World Wide Web http://www.ala.org/alsc

Object

Interested in the improvement and extension of library services to children in all types of libraries. Responsible for the evaluation and selection of book and nonbook materials for, and the improvement of techniques of, library services to children from preschool through the eighth grade or junior high school age, when such materials or techniques are intended for use in more than one type of library. Founded 1901.

Membership

Memb. 3,712. Open to anyone interested in library services to children. For information on dues, see ALA entry.

Address correspondence to the executive director.

Officers

Pres. Barbara Genco; *V.P./Pres.-Elect* Cynthia K. Richey; *Past Pres.* Carole D. Fiore.

Directors

Carolyn Brodie, Floyd Dickman, Randall Enos, Kathleen Horning, Debra McLeod, Carolyn Noah, Judith Rovenger, Bessie Condos Tichauer, Sue Zeigler.

Publication

Children and Libraries: The Journal of the Association for Library Service to Children (JOYS) (q.; memb.; nonmemb. $40; foreign $50).

Committee Chairpersons

Priority Group I: Child Advocacy

Consultant. Kelly Jennings.
Intellectual Freedom.
International Relations.
Legislation.
Library Service to Special Population Children and their Caregivers.
Preschool Services and Parent Education.
Preschool Services Discussion Group.
Public Library-School Partnership Discussion Group.
School-Age Programs and Service.
Social Issues Discussion Group.

Priority Group II: Evaluation of Media

Consultant. Barbara Barstow.
Great Web Sites.
Notable Children's Books.
Notable Children's Recordings.
Notable Children's Videos.
Notable Computer Software for Children.

Priority Group III: Professional Awards and Scholarships

Consultant. Virginia McKee.
ALSC/Book Wholesalers Summer Reading Program Grant and Reading Program.
ALSC/Econo-Clad Literature Program Award.
Arbuthnot Honor Lecture.
Louise Seaman Bechtel Fellowship.
Distinguished Service Award.
Penguin Putnam Books for Young Readers Award.
Scholarships: Melcher and Bound to Stay Bound.

Priority Group IV: Organizational Support

Consultant. Linda Perkins.
Local Arrangements.
Membership.

Nominating.
Organization and Bylaws.
Planning and Budget.
Preconference Planning.

Priority Group V: Projects and Research

Consultant. Kathy Toon.
Collections of Children's Books for Adult Research (Discussion Group).
National Planning of Special Collections.
Oral History.
Publications.
Research and Development.

Priority Group VI: Award Committees

Consultant. Jan Moltzan.
Mildred L. Batchelder Award Selection.
Pura Belpré Award.
Randolph Caldecott Award.
Andrew Carnegie Award.
John Newbery Award.
Sibert Informational Book Award.
Laura Ingalls Wilder Award.

Priority Group VII: Partnerships

Consultant. Katherine Todd.
Liaison with National Organizations Serving Children and Youth.
Public Library-School Partnerships Discussion Group.
Quicklists Consulting Committee.

Priority Group VIII: Professional Development

Consultant. Marie Orlando.
Children and Technology.
Children's Book Discussion Group.
Education.
Managing Children's Services.
Managing Children's Services Discussion Group.
Storytelling Discussion Group.

American Library Association
Association for Library Trustees and Advocates

Executive Director, Kerry Ward
50 E. Huron St., Chicago, IL 60611-2795
312-280-2161, 800-545-2433 ext. 2161, fax 312-944-7671
World Wide Web http://www.ala.org/alta

Object

The Association for Library Trustees and Advocates (ALTA) is interested in the development of effective library service for all people in all types of communities and in all types of libraries; it follows that its members are concerned, as policymakers, with organizational patterns of service, with the development of competent personnel, the provision of adequate financing, the passage of suitable legislation, and the encouragement of citizen support for libraries. ALTA recognizes that responsibility for professional action in these fields has been assigned to other divisions of ALA; its specific responsibilities as a division, therefore, are

1. A continuing and comprehensive educational program to enable library trustees to discharge their grave responsibilities in a manner best fitted to benefit the public and the libraries they represent

2. Continuous study and review of the activities of library trustees

3. Cooperation with other units within ALA concerning their activities relating to trustees

4. Encouraging participation of trustees in other appropriate divisions of ALA

5. Representation and interpretation of the activities of library trustees in contacts outside the library profession, particularly with national organizations and governmental agencies

6. Promotion of strong state and regional trustee organizations

7. Efforts to secure and support adequate library funding

8. Promulgation and dissemination of recommended library policy

9. Assuring equal access of information to all segments of the population

10. Encouraging participation of trustees in trustee/library activities, at local, state, regional, and national levels

Organized 1890. Became an ALA division in 1961.

Membership

Memb. 1,150. Open to all interested persons and organizations. For dues and membership year, see ALA entry.

Officers (2002–2003)

Pres. Dale H. Ross; *1st V.P./Pres.-Elect* Shirley Bruursema; *2nd V.P.* Marguerite E. Ritchey; *Councilor* Wayne Coco; *Past Pres.* Gail Dysleski.

Board of Directors

Officers; *Council Administrators* Ruth Newell, Jane Rowland, Sharon Saulmon, Carol K. Vogelman; *Regional V.P.s* Gloria Aguilar, Alma Denis, Lillian Edelmann, Elizabeth Joyner, Ellen Miller, Robert Petrulis, Francis Picart, Donald L. Roalkvam, Anne D. Sterling.

Staff

Exec. Dir. Kerry Ward; *Program Officer* Gretchen Kalwinski.

Publication

The Voice (q.; memb.). *Ed.* Sharon Saulmon.

American Library Association
Association of College and Research Libraries

Executive Director, Mary Ellen K. Davis
50 E. Huron St., Chicago, IL 60611-2795
312-280-2523, 800-545-2433 ext. 2523, fax 312-280-2520
E-mail mdavis@ala.org
World Wide Web http://www.ala.org/acrl

Object

The Association of College and Research Libraries (ACRL) provides leadership for development, promotion, and improvement of academic and research library resources and services to facilitate learning, research, and the scholarly communication process. ACRL promotes the highest level of professional excellence for librarians and library personnel in order to serve the users of academic and research libraries. Founded 1938.

Membership

Memb. 11,297. For information on dues, see ALA entry.

Officers

Pres. Helen H. Spalding, Assoc. Dir. of Libs., Univ. of Missouri–Kansas City, 5100 Rockhill Rd., Kansas City, MO 64110-2446. Tel. 816-235-1558, fax 816-333-5584, e-mail spaldingh@umkc.edu; *Pres.-Elect* Tyrone H. Cannon, Lib. Dean, Univ. of San Francisco, 2130 Fulton St., San Francisco, CA 94117. Tel. 415-422-6167, fax 415-422-5949; *Past Pres.* Mary Reichel, Univ. Libn., Carol Grotnes Belk Lib., Appalachian State Univ., Boone, NC 28608. Tel. 828-262-2188, fax 828-262-3001, e-mail reichelml@appstate. edu; *Budget and Finance Chair* Erika C. Linke, Assoc. Univ. Libn., Hunt Lib., Carnegie Mellon Univ., 4909 Frew St., Pittsburgh, PA 15213-3890. Tel. 412-268-7800, fax 412-268-2793, e-mail erika.linke@cmu. edu; *ACRL Councilor* Patricia A. Wand, Univ. Libn., American Univ., 4400 Massachusetts Ave. N.W., Washington, DC 20016-8046.

Board of Directors

Officers; Theresa S. Byrd, Lois H. Cherepon, Deborah B. Dancik, Rita Jones, Patricia Kreitz, W. Bede Mitchell, Robert F. Rose, Pamela Snelson.

Publications

Choice (11 a year; $237; foreign $287). *Ed.* Irving Rockwood.

Choice Reviews-on-Cards ($317; foreign $377).

ChoiceReviews.online ($270).

College & Research Libraries (6 a year; memb.; nonmemb. $60). *Ed.* Donald E. Riggs.

College & Research Libraries News (11 a year; memb.; nonmemb. $40). *Ed.* Stephanie D. Orphan.

Publications in Librarianship (formerly *ACRL Monograph Series*) (occasional). *Ed.* John M. Budd.

RBM: A Journal of Rare Books, Manuscripts, and Cultural Heritage (2 a year; $35). *Eds.* Lisa M. Browar, Marvin J. Taylor.

List of other publications and rates available through the ACRL office.

Committee and Task Force Chairpersons

Academic/Research Librarian of the Year Award Selection. Susan K. Nutter.

ACRL @ Your Library. Kenneth E. Marks.

ACRL Friends Fund. John Popko.

ACRL/Harvard Leadership Institute Advisory. Maureen Sullivan.

Appointments. Kathleen M. Carney.

Association of the Future. Maureen Sullivan.

Hugh C. Atkinson Memorial Award. Janet Swan Hill.

Budget and Finance. Erika C. Linke.

Bylaws. Collen Cuddy.

Choice Editorial Board. Craig S. Likness.

Colleagues. Charles Beard, Charles Kratz.

College & Research Libraries Editorial Board. William Gray Potter.

College & Research Libraries News Editorial Board. Brian Coutts.

College & Research Libraries Standards. Barton M. Lessin.

Conference Program Planning, Toronto (2003). Helen H. Spalding.

Copyright. Jeanne E. Boyle.

Council of Liaisons. Mary Ellen K. Davis.

Doctoral Dissertation Fellowship. Kathryn Blackmer-Reyes.

Effective Practices Review Committee. Gordon J. Aamot.

Ethics. Frances J. Maloy.

Excellence in Academic Libraries Award (Nominations). Lori Arp.

Excellence in Academic Libraries Award (Selection). Betsy Wilson.

Focus on the Future. W. Lee Hisle.

Government Relations. Cheryl S. McCoy.

Information Literacy Advisory. To be announced.

Institute for Information Literacy Executive. Thomas Kirk.

Intellectual Freedom. Robert P. Holley.

International Relations. Priscilla Yu.

Samuel Lazerow Fellowship. George L. Abbott.

Membership. Susanna Boylston.

National Conference Executive Committee, Charlotte, 2003. Larry Hardesty.

New Publications Advisory. Gary B. Thompson.

Nominations. Albie Johnson.

President's Program Planning Committee, Toronto, 2003. Charles E. Kratz, Jr.

President's Program Planning Committee, Orlando, 2004. Julie S. Alexander.

Professional Development. Sally Kalin.

Publications. Jamie A. Gill.

Publications in Librarianship Editorial Board. John M. Budd.

Racial and Ethnic Diversity. Loanne L. Snavely.

Rare Books and Manuscripts Librarianship

Editorial Board. Lisa M. Browar, Marvin J. Taylor.

Recruitment to the Profession, ACRL/ARL. Shirley K. Baker, Hannelore B. Rader.

Research. Mary K. Sellen.

Review and Revision of the Guidelines for the Preparation of Policies on Library Access. Susan M. Maltese.

K. G. Saur Award for Best *College & Research Libraries* Article. Norma Kobzina.

Scholarly Communications. Ray English.

Spectrum Scholar Mentor. Theresa S. Byrd.

Standards and Accreditation. Paul J. Beavers.

Statistics. William Miller.

Status of Academic Librarians. William Neal Nelson.

Supplemental Funding Models. Barbara Baxter Jenkins.

Discussion Group Chairpersons

Alliances for New Directions in Teaching/Learning. Mark Horan.

Australian-Canadian-New Zealand Studies. Bradd Burningham.

Consumer and Family Studies. Priscilla C. Geahigan.

Criminal Justice/Criminology. Deborah Schaeffer.

Electronic Reserves. Rebecca Martin, Leah G. McGinnis.

Electronic Text Centers. Michael S. Seadle.

Exhibits and Displays in College Libraries. Michael M. Miller.

Fee-Based Information Service Centers in Academic Libraries. J. Yem Fong.

Heads of Public Services. Cheryl C. Albrecht.

Librarians and Information Science. Cathy D. Rentschler.

Library Development. Samuel T. Huang.

Media Resources. Jill W. Ortner.

Medium-Sized Libraries. Joann Michalak, Daniel A. Ortiz.

MLA International Bibliography. Robert S. Means.

Personnel Administrators and Staff Development Officers. Shelley Elizabeth Phipps, Keith W. Russell.

Philosophical, Religious, and Theological Studies. J. Doreen Simonsen.

Popular Cultures. Paul A. Kauppila.

Research. Darrell L. Jenkins.

Sports and Recreation. Mila C. Su.

Team-Based Organizations. Robert Patrick Mitchell.

Undergraduate Librarians. Ree DeDonato.

Section Chairpersons

Afro-American Studies Librarians. Raquel Cogell.

Anthropology and Sociology. Royce D. Kurtz.

Arts. Ann M. Lindell.

Asian, African, and Middle Eastern. Jung-ran Park.

College Libraries. Mark E. Cain.

Community and Junior College Libraries. Cynthia K. Steinhoff.

Distance Learning. Maryhelen W. Jones.

Education and Behavioral Sciences. Katherine Ann Corby.

Instruction. Trudi E. Jacobson.

Law and Political Science. Barbara P. Norelli.

Literatures in English. Michaelyn Burnette.

Rare Books and Manuscripts. Daniel J. Slive.

Science and Technology. Barton M. Lessin.

Slavic and East European. Jared S. Ingersoll.

University Libraries. Louise S. Sherby.

Western European Studies. Gordon B. Anderson.

Woman's Studies. Connie L. Phelps.

American Library Association
Association of Specialized and Cooperative Library Agencies

Executive Director, Cathleen Bourdon
50 E. Huron St., Chicago, IL 60611-2795
312-280-4398, 800-545-2433 ext. 4398, fax 312-944-8085
World Wide Web http://www.ala.org/ascla

Object

Represents state library agencies, specialized library agencies, multitype library cooperatives, and independent librarians. Within the interests of these types of library organizations, the Association of Specialized and Cooperative Library Agencies (ASCLA) has specific responsibility for

1. Development and evaluation of goals and plans for state library agencies, specialized library agencies, and multitype library cooperatives to facilitate the implementation, improvement, and extension of library activities designed to foster improved user services, coordinating such activities with other appropriate ALA units

2. Representation and interpretation of the role, functions, and services of state library agencies, specialized library agencies, multitype library cooperatives, and independent librarians within and outside the profession, including contact with national organizations and government agencies

3. Development of policies, studies, and activities in matters affecting state library agencies, specialized library agencies, multitype library cooperatives and independent librarians relating to (a) state and local library legislation, (b) state grants-in-aid and appropriations, and (c) relationships among state, federal, regional, and local governments, coordinating such activities with other appropriate ALA units

4. Establishment, evaluation, and promotion of standards and service guidelines relating to the concerns of this association

5. Identifying the interests and needs of all persons, encouraging the creation

of services to meet these needs within the areas of concern of the association, and promoting the use of these services provided by state library agencies, specialized library agencies, multitype library cooperatives, and independent librarians

6. Stimulating the professional growth and promoting the specialized training and continuing education of library personnel at all levels in the areas of concern of this association and encouraging membership participation in appropriate type-of-activity divisions within ALA

7. Assisting in the coordination of activities of other units within ALA that have a bearing on the concerns of this association

8. Granting recognition for outstanding library service within the areas of concern of this association

9. Acting as a clearinghouse for the exchange of information and encouraging the development of materials, publications, and research within the areas of concern of this association

Membership

Memb. 992.

Board of Directors (2002–2003)

Pres. Ethel E. Himmel; *Pres.-Elect* Tom W. Sloan; *Past Pres.* Jerome W. Krois; *Dirs.-at-Large* Cheryl G. Brown, Judith A. Gibbons,

Patrcia L. Owens, Linda Lucas Walling; *Div. Councilor* Marilyn M. Irwin; *Newsletter Editor* Sara G. Laughlin; *Section Reps.* Barbara Land, Carol A. Nersinger, Ruth J. Nussbaum, Diana Reese, Mary Ellen Tyckoson.

Executive Staff

Exec. Dir. Cathleen Bourdon; *Deputy Exec. Dir.* Lillian Lewis.

Publications

Interface (q.; memb.; single copies $7). *Ed.* Sara G. Laughlin, 1616 Treadwell La., Bloomington, IN 47408. Tel. 812-334-8485.

Committee Chairpersons

ADA Assembly. Rhea Joyce Rubin.
American Correctional Association/ASCLA Joint Committee on Institution Libraries. Vibeke Lehmann.
Awards. James H. Kirks, Jr.
Conference Program Coordination. Jeanette P. Smithee.
Legislation. Janice Ison.
Library Personnel and Education. Cheryl G. Bryan.
Membership Promotion. Marshall Alex Shore.
Organization and Bylaws. Naomi K. Angier.
Planning and Budget. Jerome W. Krois, Tom W. Sloan.
Publications. Sondra Vandermark.
Research. Barbara W. Cole.
Standards Review. John M. Day.

American Library Association
Library Administration and Management Association

Executive Director, Lorraine Olley
50 E. Huron St., Chicago, IL 60611
312-280-2156, 800-545-2433 ext. 2156, fax 312-280-5033
E-mail Lolley@ala.org
World Wide Web http://www.ala.org/lama

Object

The Library Administration and Management Association (LAMA) provides an organizational framework for encouraging the study of administrative theory, for improving the practice of administration in libraries, and for identifying and fostering administrative skill. Toward these ends, the division is responsible for all elements of general administration that are common to more than one type of library. These may include organizational structure, financial administration, personnel management and training, buildings and equipment, and public relations. LAMA meets this responsibility in the following ways:

1. Study and review of activities assigned to the division with due regard for changing developments in these activities
2. Initiating and overseeing activities and projects appropriate to the division, including activities involving bibliography compilation, publication, study, and review of professional literature within the scope of the division
3. Synthesizing the activities of other ALA units that have a bearing upon the responsibilities or work of the division
4. Representing and interpreting library administrative activities in contacts outside the library profession
5. Aiding the professional development of librarians engaged in administration and encouraging their participation in appropriate type-of-library divisions
6. Planning and developing programs of study and research in library administrative problems that are most needed by the profession

Established 1957.

Membership

Memb. 4,941.

Officers (July 2002–July 2003)

Pres. Linda Sue Dobb; *Pres.-Elect* Paul M. Anderson; *Past Pres.* Joan R. Giesecke; *Dirs.-at-Large* Joyce Taylor, Eva D. Poole; *Div. Councilor* Charles E. Kratz; *COLA Chair* Nicky Stanke; *Budget and Finance Chair* Rod MacNeil; *Section Chairs* Marsha Joan Stevenson (BES), Pamela Gay Bonnell (FRFDS), Teri R. Switzer (HRS), M. Sue Baughman (LOMS), Judith Lin Hunt (MAES), Marcia Schneider (PRMS), Gregg E. Sapp (SASS); *Ex officio* Cheryl C. Albrecht, Virginia C. Branch, Mary Frances Burns, Eric C. Shoaf, Wicky Sleight, Virginia Steel, Deborah G. Tenofsky, Susan M. Weaver, Robert F. Moran, Jr., Marta Deyrup.

Address correspondence to the executive director.

Publications

Library Administration and Management (q.; memb.; nonmemb. $55; foreign $65). *Ed.* Robert F. Moran, Jr.; *Assoc. Ed.* Marta Deyrup.

LEADS from LAMA (approx. weekly; free through Internet). *Ed.* Lorraine Olley. To subscribe, send to listproc@ala.org the message *subscribe lamaleads [first name last name].*

Committee Chairpersons

Budget and Finance. Roderick MacNeil.
Certified Public Library Administrator Certification, LAMA/PLA/ASCLA. Joyce Taylor.
Council of LAMA Affiliates. Nicky Stanke.
Cultural Diversity. Jennifer R. Wright.
Editorial Advisory Board. Amy K. Weiss.
Education. Mary Genther.
Governmental Affairs. Philip Tramdack.
Leadership Development. Janice Flug.
Membership. Cathy Miesse.
National Institute Planning. Rod Henshaw.
Nominating, 2003 Elections. Thomas E. Schneiter.
Organization. Virginia Steel.
President's Program 2003. Caryn J. Carr, Vera J. Weisskopf.
Program. Paul Anderson.
Publications. Barbara G. Preece.
Recognition of Achievement. Judith Adams-Volpe.
Research. Carolyn A. Snyder.
Small Libraries Publications Series. Sondra Vandermark.

Special Conferences and Programs. Robert Smith.
Strategic Planning Implementation. Catherine Murray-Rust.

Section Chairpersons

Buildings and Equipment. Marsha Joan Stevenson.
Fund Raising and Financial Development. Pamela Gay Bonnell.
Human Resources. Teri Switzer.
Library Organization and Management. M. Sue Baughman.
Measurement, Assessment, and Evaluation. Judith Lin Hunt.
Public Relations and Marketing. Marcia Schneider.
Systems and Services. Gregg E. Sapp.

Discussion Group Chairpersons

Assistants-to-the-Director. Carol J. Lang.
Diversity Officers. Laura K. Blessing, Laura Bayard.
Library Storage. Christine Brennan.
Middle Management. Rebecca L. Mugridge, Joan Reyes.
Women Administrators. Elizabeth A. Avery, Meg K. Scharf.

American Library Association
Library and Information Technology Association

Executive Director, Mary C. Taylor
50 E. Huron St., Chicago, IL 60611
312-280-4270, 800-545-2433
E-mail mtaylor@ala.org
World Wide Web http://www.lita.org

Object

The Library and Information Technology Association (LITA) envisions a world in which the complete spectrum of information technology is available to everyone—in libraries, at work, and at home. To move toward this goal, LITA provides a forum for discussion, an environment for learning, and a program for actions on many aspects of information technology for both practitioners and managers.

LITA educates, serves, and reaches out to its members, other ALA members and divisions, and the entire library and information community through its publications, programs, and other activities designed to promote, develop, and aid in the implementation of library and information technology. LITA is concerned with the planning, development, design, application, and integration of technologies within the library and information environment, with the impact of emerging technologies on library service, and with the effect of automated technologies on people.

Membership

Memb. 4,800.

Officers (2002–2003)

Pres. Pat Ensor; *V.P./Pres.-Elect* Thomas C. Wilson; *Past Pres.* Flo Wilson.

Directors

Officers; Karen Cook, Thomas Dowling, James R. Kennedy, Scott Muir, Patrick J. Mullin, Bonnie Postlethwaite, Colby M. Riggs; *Councilor* Barbra Higginbotham; *Bylaws and Organization* Susan Jacobson; *Exec. Dir.* Mary C. Taylor.

Publication

Information Technology and Libraries (*ITAL*) (q.; memb.; nonmemb. $55; single copy $20). *Ed.* Dan Marmion. For information or to send manuscripts, contact the editor.

Committee Chairpersons

Budget Review. Flo Wilson.
Bylaws and Organization. Susan Jacobson.
Committee Chair Coordinator. Michele Newberry.
Education. Catherine L. Wilkinson.
Executive. Pat Ensor.
International Relations. Dennis C. Tucker.
ITAL Editorial Board. Dan Marmion.
Legislation and Regulation. Buckley Barry Barrett.
LITA/Endeavor Student Writing Award. Jane B. Mandelbaum.
LITA/Gaylord Award. Diana Joy Davis.
LITA/Library Hi Tech Award. Margaret E. Craft.
LITA/LSSI and LITA/OCLC Minority Scholarships. Laura J. Tull.
LITA National Forum 2003. Debra S. Shapiro.
LITA/OCLC Kilgour Award. Lawrence A. Woods.
LITA/Sirsi and LITA/Christian Larew Scholarships. Jonathan Rothman.
Membership Development. Navjit K. Brar.
Nominating. Barbra Higginbotham.
Program Planning. John W. Forys, Jr.
Publications. Melinda S. Stowe.
Regional Institutes. Lynne Lysiak.
Technology and Access. Ellen Parravano.
TER Board. Adriene Lim.
Top Technology Trends. David Ward.
Web Coordinating. Michelle L. Frisque.

Interest Group Chairpersons

Interest Group Coordinator. Susan Logue.
Authority Control in the Online Environment (LITA/ALCTS). Ann Della Porta.
Digital Library Technologies. Catherine Mary Jannik.
Distance Learning. Howard Carter.
Electronic Publishing/Electronic Journals. Lloyd Davidson.
Emerging Technologies. Sharon Clapp.
Heads of Library Technology. Byron Mayes.
Human/Machine Interface. Nicole M. Campbell.
Imagineering. Richard J. Kuster.
Internet Portals. Stephen F. Mitchell.
Internet Resources. Juan Carlos Rodriguez.
Library Consortia/Automated Systems. Jon Mark Bolthouse.
MARC Formats (LITA/ALCTS). Lara A. Sill.
Microcomputer Users. Henry Harken, Jr.
Secure Systems and Services. Beth W. Helsel.
Serials Automation (LITA/ALCTS). Carol Trinchitella.
Standards. Krisellen Maloney.
Technical Services Workstations (LITA/ALCTS). David Banush.
Technology and the Arts. Mary M. LaMarca.

American Library Association
Public Library Association

Executive Director, Greta K. Southard
50 E. Huron St., Chicago, IL 60611
312-280-5752, 800-545-2433 ext. 5752, fax 312-280-5029
E-mail pla@ala.org
World Wide Web http://www.pla.org

Object

The Public Library Association (PLA) has specific responsibility for

1. Conducting and sponsoring research about how the public library can respond to changing social needs and technical developments
2. Developing and disseminating materials useful to public libraries in interpreting public library services and needs
3. Conducting continuing education for public librarians by programming at national and regional conferences, by publications such as the newsletter, and by other delivery means
4. Establishing, evaluating, and promoting goals, guidelines, and standards for public libraries
5. Maintaining liaison with relevant national agencies and organizations engaged in public administration and human services, such as the National Association of Counties, the Municipal League, and the Commission on Post-Secondary Education
6. Maintaining liaison with other divisions and units of ALA and other library organizations, such as the Association of American Library Schools and the Urban Libraries Council
7. Defining the role of the public library in service to a wide range of user and potential user groups
8. Promoting and interpreting the public library to a changing society through legislative programs and other appropriate means
9. Identifying legislation to improve and to equalize support of public libraries

PLA enhances the development and effectiveness of public librarians and public library services. This mission positions PLA to

- Focus its efforts on serving the needs of its members
- Address issues that affect public libraries
- Promote and protect the profession
- Commit to quality public library services that benefit the general public

The goals of PLA are

Advocacy and recognition. Public libraries will be recognized as the destination for a wide variety of valuable services and their funding will be a community priority.

A literate nation. PLA will be a valued partner of public library initiatives to create a nation of readers.

Staffing and recruitment. Public libraries will be recognized as exciting places to work and will be staffed by skilled professionals who are recognized as the information experts, are competitively paid, and reflect the demographics of their communities.

Training and knowledge transfer. PLA will be nationally recognized as the leading source for continuing education opportunities for public library staff and trustees.

Membership

Memb. 9,000+. Open to all ALA members interested in the improvement and expansion of public library services to all ages in various types of communities.

Officers (2002–2003)

Pres. Jo Ann Pinder, Gwinnett County Public Lib., 1001 Lawrenceville Hwy., Lawrenceville, GA 30045. Tel. 770-822-5321, fax 770-822-5379, e-mail jap@gwinnettpl.org; *V.P./ Pres.-Elect* Luis Herrera, Pasadena Public Lib., 285 E. Walnut St., Pasadena, CA 91101. E-mail lherrera@ci.pasadena.ca.us; *Past Pres.* Toni Garvey, Phoenix Public Lib., 1221 N. Central Ave., Phoenix, AZ 85004. E-mail tgarvey1@ci.phoenix.az.us.

Publication

Public Libraries (bi-m.; memb.; nonmemb. $50; foreign $60; single copy $10). *Managing Ed.* Kathleen Hughes, PLA, 50 E. Huron St., Chicago, IL 60611.

Cluster Chairpersons

Issues and Concerns Steering Committee. Ken Yamashita.
Library Development Steering Committee. Raymond Santiago.
Library Services Steering Committee. Carol Starr.

Committee Chairs

Issues and Concerns Cluster

Intellectual Freedom. Mary Scott Wallace.
Legislation. Anne Marie Gold.
Library Confidentialty Task Force. Carol Sheffer.
Public Policy in Public Libraries. Carol French Johnson.
Recruitment of Public Librarians. Lynn Wheeler.
Research and Statistics. Robert Belvin.
Workload Measures and Staffing Patterns. Susan Hildreth.

Library Development Cluster

Branch Libraries. Karen Vargas.
Marketing Public Libraries. Marilyn Barr.
Metropolitan Libraries. Miriam Morris.

Practical Applications of Technology in Public Libraries. Bruce Ziegman.
Public Library Systems. Lorraine Lessey.
Rural Library Services. Eric Hansen.
Small and Medium-Sized Libraries. Kendi Kelley.
Technology in Public Libraries. Dan Walters.

Library Services Cluster

Adult Continuing and Independent Learning Services. Kathleen Degyansky.
Audiovisual. Judy Napier.
Basic Education and Literarcy Services. Sandra Newell.
Career and Business Services. Shelley Bennett.
Cataloging Needs of Public Libraries. Heeja Chung.
Collection Management Committee. Margaret Thompson, Susan Pober.
Community Information Services. Gregory Kallenberg.
Reader's Advisory. Penelope Hamblin.
Resources for the Adult New Reader. Maureen O'Connor.
Services to Elementary School-Age Children and Their Caregivers. Barbara Fischer.
Services to Multicultural Populations. Oksara Kraus.
Services to Preschool Children and Their Caregivers. Wendy Wilson.

Business Committees

2004 National Conference. Clara Nailli Bohrer.
2004 National Conference (Program). Neel Parikh.
2004 National Conference (Local Arrangements). Nancy Pearl.
Awards. Sue Epstein.
Awards, Advancement of Literacy Award Jury. Catharine Cook.
Awards, Baker & Taylor Entertainment Audio/Music/Video Product Award Jury. David Macksam.
Awards, Demco Creative Merchandising Grant Jury. Lace Keaton.
Awards, Excellence in Small and/or Rural Public Library Service Award Jury. Deborah Pawlik.
Awards, Highsmith Library Innovation Award

Jury. Anne Marie Gold.

Awards, Allie Beth Martin Award Jury. Gail Rogers.

Awards, New Leaders Travel Grant Jury. Micki Freeny.

Awards, Charlie Robinson Award Jury. Susan Studebaker.

Budget and Finance. Kathy Ames.

Bylaws and Organization. Eva Poole.

Certified Public Library Administrator (PLA/LAMA/ASCLA) Implementation Task Force. Judith Drescher.

Leadership Development 2004. Beth Walker.

Membership. Lynn Wheeler.

PLA Partners. David Paynter.

President's Events 2003. Claudia Sumler.

President's Events 2004. Kathleen Reif.

Publications, Electronic Communications Advisory. Sue Calbreath.

Publications, PLA Monographs. Larry Neal.

Publications, *Public Libraries* Advisory. Victor Kralisz.

Publications, *Statistical Report* Advisory. Irene Blalock.

Publications, University Press Books for Public Libraries. Rex Miller.

State Relations. Susan Odencrantz.

Task Force on Preschool Literacy Initiatives (joint with ALSC). Harriet Henderson, Elaine Meyers.

American Library Association
Reference and User Services Association

Executive Director, Cathleen Bourdon
50 E. Huron St., Chicago, IL 60611-2795
312-280-4398, 800-545-2433 ext. 4398, fax 312-944-8085
E-mail rusa@ala.org
World Wide Web http://www.ala.org/rusa

Object

The Reference and User Services Association (RUSA) is responsible for stimulating and supporting in every type of library the delivery of reference/information services to all groups, regardless of age, and of general library services and materials to adults. This involves facilitating the development and conduct of direct service to library users, the development of programs and guidelines for service to meet the needs of these users, and assisting libraries in reaching potential users.

The specific responsibilities of RUSA are

1. Conduct of activities and projects within the association's areas of responsibility

2. Encouragement of the development of librarians engaged in these activities, and stimulation of participation by members of appropriate type-of-library divisions

3. Synthesis of the activities of all units within the American Library Association that have a bearing on the type of activities represented by the association

4. Representation and interpretation of the association's activities in contacts outside the profession

5. Planning and development of programs of study and research in these areas for the total profession

6. Continuous study and review of the association's activities

Membership

Memb. 4,909. For information on dues, see ALA entry.

Officers (July 2002–June 2003)

Pres. Cindy Stewart Kaag; *Pres.-Elect* Nancy Huling; *Past Pres.* Carol M. Tobin; *Secy.* Kathy L. Tomajko.

Directors-at-Large

Emily Batista, Elliot Jay Kanter, Kathleen M. Kluegel, Pamela C. Sieving, David A. Tyckoson, Carol Z. Womack; *Councilor* Julia M. Rholes; *Eds.* Connie Van Fleet, Danny P. Wallace; *Ex Officio* Suzanne Sweeney; *Exec. Dir.* Cathleen Bourdon.

Address correspondence to the executive director.

Publication

RUSQ (q.; memb. $50, foreign memb. $60, single copies $15). *Eds.* Connie J. Van Fleet, Danny P. Wallace.

Section Chairpersons

Business Reference and Services. Lydia La Faro.

Collection Development and Evaluation. Muzette Z. Diefenthal.

History. Nancy M. Godleski.

Machine-Assisted Reference. Leilani S. Freund.

Management and Operation of User Services. Diana D. Shonrock.

Committee Chairpersons

Access to Information. Rosanne M. Cordell.

AFL/CIO Joint Committee on Library Services to Labor Groups. Dan D. Golodner, Anthony R. Sarmiento.

Awards Coordinating. Caroline C. Long.

Conference Program. Betty A. Gard.

Conference Program Coordinating. Carla Rickerson.

Dartmouth Medal. Teresa Portilla Omidsalar.

Gale Research Award for Excellence in Reference and Adult Services. Betty A. Gard.

Membership. Nancy E. Bodner.

Margaret E. Monroe Library Adult Services Award. Eugenia D. Bryant.

Isadore Gilbert Mudge/R. R. Bowker Award. Richard Bleiler.

Nominating 2003. Corinne M. Hill.

Organization. Denise Beaubien Bennett.

Organizational Structure (Task Force). Carol Mary Tobin.

Planning and Finance. Carol Mary Tobin.

Professional Competencies (ad hoc). Jo Bell Whitlatch.

Professional Development. Merle L. Jacob.

Publications. Susan C. Awe.

Reference Services Press Award. Lynn K. Chmelir.

(John) Sessions Memorial Award. Harriet Helen Gottfried.

(Louis) Shores/Oryx Press Award. Pamela T. Harris.

Standards and Guidelines. Gale S. Etchmaier.

American Library Association
Young Adult Library Services Association

Executive Director, Julie A. Walker
50 E. Huron St., Chicago, IL 60611
312-280-4390, 800-545-2433 ext. 4390, fax 312-664-7459
E-mail yalsa@ala.org
World Wide Web http://www.ala.org/yalsa

Object

In every library in the nation, quality library service to young adults is provided by a staff that understands and respects the unique informational, educational, and recreational needs of teenagers.

Equal access to information, services, and materials is recognized as a right, not a privilege. Young adults are actively involved in the library decision-making process. The library staff collaborates and cooperates with other youth-serving agencies to provide a holistic, community-wide network of activities and services that support healthy youth development. To ensure that this vision becomes a reality, the Young Adult Library Services Association (YALSA)

1. Advocates extensive and developmentally appropriate library and information services for young adults, ages 12 to 18

2. Promotes reading and supports the literacy movement

3. Advocates the use of information and communications technologies to provide effective library service

4. Supports equality of access to the full range of library materials and services, including existing and emerging information and communications technologies, for young adults

5. Provides education and professional development to enable its members to serve as effective advocates for young people

6. Fosters collaboration and partnerships among its individual members with the library community and other groups involved in providing library and information services to young adults

7. Influences public policy by demonstrating the importance of providing library and information services that meet the unique needs and interests of young adults

8. Encourages research and is in the vanguard of new thinking concerning the provision of library and information services for youth

Membership

Memb. 3,320. Open to anyone interested in library services and materials for young adults. For information on dues, see ALA entry.

Officers (July 2002–July 2003)

Pres. Caryn Sipos, Three Creeks Community Lib., Vancouver, Washington. Tel. 360-571-9696, e-mail csipos@fvrl.org; *V.P/Pres.-Elect* Audra Caplan, Harford County Public Lib., Belcamp, Maryland. Tel. 410-273-5601, e-mail caplan@harf.lib.md.us; *Past Pres.* Bonnie Kunzel, Princeton (New Jersey) Public Lib. Tel. 609-924-9529, e-mail bkunzel@aol.com; *Div. Councilor* Catherine Clancy, Boston (Massachusetts) Public Lib. Tel. 617-536-5400, e-mail cclancycat@aol.com; *Fiscal Officer* C. Allen Nichols, Wadsworth-Ella M. Everhard Public Lib., Wadsworth, Ohio. Tel. 330-335-1299, e-mail allen@wadsworth.lib.oh.us.

Directors

Officers; Amy Alessio (2004), Sheila B. Anderson (2004), Linda Braun (2005), Sara Ryan (2003), Kevin Scanlon (2005), Edward Sullivan (2003); *Chair, Organization and Bylaws* Monique LeConge; *Chair, Strategic Planning* Connie Adams Bush.

Publication

Young Adult Library Services (s. ann.) (memb.; nonmemb. $40; foreign $50). *Ed.* Jana Fine.

Committee Chairpersons

Alex Awards. Deborah Taylor, David Mowery.
Audio Books and Media Exploration. Francisca Goldsmith.
Best Books for Young Adults 2003. Cindy Dobrez.
Conference Toronto 2003 Local Arrangements. Susan Riley.
Cultural Diversity Task Force. Adela Peskorz.
Division and Membership Promotion. Erminia Mina Gallo.
Margaret A. Edwards Award 2003. Rosemary Chance.
Margaret A. Edwards Award 2004. Francisca Goldsmith.
Intellectual Freedom. James Cook.
Legislation. Gail Tobin.
Literacy Task Force. Daphne Daly.
Nominating. Susan Riley.

Organization and Bylaws. Monique Le Conge.
Outreach to Young Adults with Special Needs. Kevin Scanlon.
Outstanding Books for the College-Bound. Mary Arnold.
Partnerships Advocating for Teens. Shawn Thrasher.
Popular Paperbacks for Young Adults 2003. Dawn Rutherford.
Preconference Planning 2003. Jana Fine.
President's Program 2003 Planning. Amy Alessio
Michael L. Printz Award 2004. Pam Spencer Holley.
Michael L. Printz Award 2003. Joel Shoemaker.
Professional Development. John Bradford.
Program Planning Clearinghouse and Evaluation. Sarah Cornish.
Publications. Leslie Farmer.
Publishers Liaison. Judy Nelson.
Quick Picks for Reluctant Young Adult Readers. Melanie Rapp-Weiss.
Research. Melanie Kimball.
Selected DVDs and Videos for Young Adults. Josephine Caisse.
Serving Young Adults in Large Urban Populations Discussion Group. Susan Raboy.
Strategic Planning. Connie Adams Bush.
Teaching Young Adult Literature Discussion Group. Adela Peskorz.
Technology for Young Adults. Ian Rosenior.
Teen Read Week Work Group. Stephen Crowley.
Teen Web Site Advisory Committee. Tracey Firestone.
Web Site Review Task Force. Linda Braun.
Youth Participation. Bonnie Herrage.

American Merchant Marine Library Association

(An affiliate of United Seamen's Service)
Executive Director, Roger T. Korner
20 Exchange Place, Suite 2901, New York, NY 10005
212-269-0714, e-mail ussammla@ix.netcom.com
World Wide Web http://uss-ammla.com

Object

Provides ship and shore library service for American-flag merchant vessels, the Military Sealift Command, the U.S. Coast Guard, and other waterborne operations of the U.S. government. Established 1921.

Officers (2002–2003)

Pres. Talmage E. Simpkins; *Chair, Exec.*

Committee Edward R. Morgan; *Honorary Chair* Capt. William G. Schubert; *V.P.s* John M. Bowers, Capt. Timothy A. Brown, James Capo, David Cockroft, Ron Davis, Capt. Remo Di Fiore, John Halas, Sakae Idemoto, Rene Lioeanjie, Michael R. McKay, George E. Murphy, Capt. Gregorio Oca, Michael Sacco, John J. Sweeney; *Secy.* Donald E. Kadlac; *Treas.* William D. Potts; *Gen. Counsel* John L. DeGurse, Jr.; *Community Relations Dir.* Eileen Horan; *Exec. Dir.* Roger T. Korner.

American Society for Information Science and Technology

Executive Director, Richard B. Hill
1320 Fenwick Lane, Suite 510, Silver Spring, MD 20910
301-495-0900, fax 301-495-0810, e-mail ASIS@asis.org

Object

The American Society for Information Science and Technology (ASIS&T) provides a forum for the discussion, publication, and critical analysis of work dealing with the design, management, and use of information, information systems, and information technology.

Membership

Memb. (Indiv.) 3,500; (Student) 800; (Inst.) 250. Dues (Indiv.) $115; (Student) $30; (Inst.) $650 and $800.

Officers

Pres. Trudi Bellardo Hahn, Univ. of Maryland; *Pres.-Elect* Samantha Hastings, Univ.

of North Texas; *Treas.* Cecelia Preston, Preston and Lynch; *Past Pres.* Donald Kraft, Louisiana State Univ.

Address correspondence to the executive director.

Board of Directors

Dirs.-at-Large Allison Brueckner, Dudee Chiang, Beverly Colby, Andrew Dillon, Abby Goodrum, Karen Howell, Michael Leach, Gretchen Whitney; *Deputy Dirs.* Vicki Gregory, Beata Panagopoulos; *Exec. Dir.* Richard B. Hill.

Publications

Advances in Classification Research, vols. 1–10. Available from Information Today,

Inc., 143 Old Marlton Pike, Medford, NJ 08055.

Annual Review of Information Science and Technology. Available from Information Today, Inc.

ASIS Thesaurus of Information Science and Librarianship. Available from Information Today, Inc.

Bulletin of the American Society for Information Science and Technology. Available from ASIST.

Editorial Peer Review: Its Strengths and Weaknesses by Ann C. Weller. Available from Information Today, Inc.

Electronic Publishing: Applications and Implications. Eds. Elisabeth Logan and Myke Gluck. Available from Information Today, Inc.

Evaluating Networked Information Services: Techniques, Policy and Issues by Charles R. McClure and John Carlo Bertot. Available from Information Today, Inc.

From Print to Electronic: The Transformation of Scientific Communication. Susan Y. Crawford, Julie M. Hurd, and Ann C. Weller. Available from Information Today, Inc.

Historical Studies in Information Science. Eds. Trudi Bellardo Hahn and Michael Buckland. Available from Information Today, Inc.

Information Management for the Intelligent Organization: The Art of Environmental Scanning, 2nd edition, by Chun Wei Choo, Univ. of Toronto. Available from Information Today, Inc.

Intelligent Technologies in Library and Information Service Applications by F. W. Lancaster and Amy Warner. Available from Information Today, Inc.

Introductory Concepts in Information Science by Melanie J. Norton. Available from Information Today, Inc.

Journal of the American Society for Information Science and Technology. Available from John Wiley and Sons, 605 Third Ave., New York, NY 10016.

Knowledge Management for the Information Professional. Eds. T. Kanti Srikantaiah and Michael Koenig. Available from Information Today, Inc.

Knowledge Management: The Bibliography. Compiled by Paul Burden. Available from Information Today, Inc.

Proceedings of the ASIST Annual Meetings. Available from Information Today, Inc.

Scholarly Publishing: The Electronic Frontier. Eds. Robin P. Peek and Gregory B. Newby. Available from MIT Press, Cambridge, Massachusetts.

Statistical Methods for the Information Professional by Liwen Vaughan. Available from Information Today, Inc.

Studies in Multimedia. Eds. Susan Stone and Michael Buckland. Based on the Proceedings of the 1991 ASIS Mid-Year Meeting. Available from Information Today, Inc.

The Web of Knowledge: A Festschrift in Honor of Eugene Garfield. Eds. Blaise Cronin and Helen Barsky Atkins. Available from Information Today, Inc.

Committee Chairpersons

Awards and Honors. Linda Smith.
Budget and Finance. Cecilia Preston.
Constitution and Bylaws. Norman Horrocks.
Education. June Lester.
Leadership Development. Penny O'Connor.
Membership. Steven Hardin.
Nominations. Donald Kraft.
Standards. Mark Needleman.

American Theological Library Association

250 S. Wacker Dr., Suite 1600, Chicago, IL 60606-5889
Tel. 888-665-2852, 312-454-5100, fax 312-454-5505
E-mail atla@atla.com
World Wide Web http://www.atla.com

Object

To bring its members into close working relationships with each other, to support theological and religious librarianship, to improve theological libraries, and to interpret the role of such libraries in theological education, developing and implementing standards of library service, promoting research and experimental projects, encouraging cooperative programs that make resources more available, publishing and disseminating literature and research tools and aids, cooperating with organizations having similar aims, and otherwise supporting and aiding theological education. Founded 1946.

Membership

Memb. (Inst.) 269; (Indiv.) 625; (affiliates) 50. Membership is open to persons engaged in professional library or bibliographical work in theological or religious fields and others who are interested in the work of theological librarianship. Dues (Inst.) $75 to $750, based on total library expenditure; (Indiv.) $15 to $150, based on salary scale. Year. Sept. 1–Aug. 31.

Officers

Pres. Eileen K. Saner, Associated Mennonite Biblical Seminary Lib., 3003 Benham Ave., Elkhart, IN 46517-1999. Tel. 574-296-6233, fax 574-295-0092, e-mail esaner@ambs.edu; *V.P.* Paul Schrodt, Methodist Theological School in Ohio, John W. Dickhaut Lib., 3081 Columbus Pike, Box 8004, Delaware, OH 43015-8004. Tel. 740-362-3435, fax 740-362-3456, e-mail pschrodt@mtso.edu; *Secy.* Paul F. Stuehrenberg, Yale Univ. Divinity School Lib., 409 Prospect St., New Haven,

CT 06511. Tel. 203-432-5292, fax 203-432-3906, e-mail paul.stuehrenberg@yale.edu; *Past Pres.* Sharon Taylor, Trask Lib., Andover Newton Theological School, 169 Herrick Rd., Newton Centre, MA 02459. Tel. 617-964-1100 ext. 259, fax 617-965-9751, e-mail staylor@ants.ed.

Board of Directors

Officers; Milton J. "Joe" Coalter, Stephen Crocco, D. William Faupel, Bill Hook, Mary Martin, Sara Myers, Susan Sponberg, Christine Wenderoth; *Exec. Dir.* Dennis A. Norlin; *Dir. of Electronic Products and Services* Tami Luedtke; *Dir. of Finance* Pradeep Gamadia; *Dir. of Indexes* Cameron Campbell; *Dir. of Member Services* Karen L. Whittlesey.

Publications

ATLA Indexes in MARC Format (semi-ann.).
ATLA Religion database on CD-ROM, 1949–.
Biblical Studies on CD-ROM (ann.).
Catholic Periodical and Literature Index on CD-ROM (ann.).
Index to Book Reviews in Religion (ann.).
Newsletter (q.; memb.; nonmemb. $50). *Ed.* Margaret Tacke.
Old Testament Abstracts on CD-ROM (ann.).
Proceedings (ann.; memb.; nonmemb. $50). *Ed.* Margaret Tacke.
Religion Index One: Periodicals (semi-ann.).
Religion Index Two: Multi-Author Works (ann.).
Religion Indexes: RIO/RIT/IBRR 1975– on CD-ROM.
Research in Ministry: An Index to Doctor of Ministry Project Reports (ann.).
Latin American Subset on CD-ROM (ann.).

Committee Chairpersons and Other Officials

Annual Conference. Roger Loyd.

Archives. Joan S. Clemens.

Collection Evaluation and Development. Cheryl L. Adams.

College and University. Melody Layton McMahon.

Education. Jeffery L. Brigham, Saundra Lipton.

Judaica. Kirk Moll.

Newsletter. Johnathan West.

Nominating. D. William Faupel.

Proceedings. Jonathan West.

Professional Development. David R. Stewart.

Public Services. Douglas R. Gragg.

Special Collections. Jefferson P. Webster.

Technology. Douglas J. Fox.

Archivists and Librarians in the History of the Health Sciences

President, Jodi Koste
Archivist, Tompkins-McCaw Library
Virginia Commonwealth University
Box 980582, Richmond, VA 23298-0582
804-828-9898

Object

This association was established exclusively for educational purposes to serve the professional interests of librarians, archivists, and other specialists actively engaged in the librarianship of the history of the health sciences by promoting the exchange of information and by improving the standards of service.

Membership

Memb. 170. Dues $15 (Americas), $21 (other countries).

Officers (May 2002–May 2003)

Pres. Jodi Koste, Archivist, Tompkins-McCaw Lib., Box 980582, Richmond, VA 23298-0582. Tel. 804-828-9898, fax 804-828-6089, e-mail jlkoste@vcu.edu; *Secy.-Treas.* Micaela Sullivan-Fowler, Libn./Curator, Health Sciences Lib., Univ. of Wisconsin, 1305 Linden Dr., Madison, WI 53706. Tel. 608-262-2402, fax 608-262-4732; e-mail micaela@library.wisc.edu.

Publication

Watermark (q.; memb.). *Ed.* Lilli Sentz, Historical Lib., Harvey Cushing/John Hay Whitney Medical Lib., Yale Univ., 333 Cedar St., New Haven, CT 06520-8014. Tel. 203-483-8404, fax 203-483-5037, e-mail lsentz@email.msn.com.

ARMA International–The Association for Information Management Professionals

Executive Director/CEO, Peter R. Hermann
13725 W. 109 St., Suite 101, Lenexa, KS 66215
800-422-2762, 913-341-3808, fax 913-341-3742
E-mail hq@arma.org, World Wide Web http://www.arma.org

Object

To advance the practice of records and information management as a discipline and a profession; to organize and promote programs of research, education, training, and networking within that profession; to support the enhancement of professionalism of the membership; and to promote cooperative endeavors with related professional groups.

Membership

Annual dues $115 for international affiliation. Chapter dues vary. Membership categories are Chapter Member ($115 plus chapter dues), Student Member ($15), and Unaffiliated Member.

Officers (July 2002–June 2003)

Pres. Juanita M. Skillman, Records Management, Orange County Sanitation Dist., 10844 Ellis Ave., Fountain Valley, CA 92728. Tel. 714-593-7129, fax 714-962-0356, e-mail jskillman@ocsd.com; *Pres.-Elect* Gisele L. Crawford, City of Edmonton, Corp. Records, City Hall, 1 Sir Winston Churchill Sq., Edmonton, AB T5J 2R7, Canada. Tel. 780-496-8001, fax 780-496-7817, e-mail Gisele. Crawford@edmonton.ca; *Immediate Past Pres. and Board Chair* Terrence J. Coan, Accutrac Software, Inc., 350 S. Figueroa St., Suite 141, Los Angeles, CA 90071. Tel. 213-626-3000, fax 213-229-9095, e-mail tcoan@accutrac.com; *Treas.* Cheryl L. Pederson,

Cargill, Inc., Box 5716, Minneapolis, MN 55440-5716. Tel. 952-742-6363, fax 952-742-4467, e-mail cheryl_pederson@cargill.com; *Dirs.* Carol E. B. Choksy, Barbra L. Cooper, Patrick Cunningham, John P. Frost, James A. Long, III, Gail Ann McCreary, Susan McKinney, Fred A. Pulzello, Claudette E. Samuels, Rick Alexander Stirling, Helen M. Streck, Susan B. Whitmire.

Publication

Information Management Journal. Exec. Ed. J. Michael Pemberton, School of Info. Sciences, Univ. of Tennessee at Knoxville, 804 Volunteer Blvd., Knoxville, TN 37996-4330. E-mail jpembert@utkux.utcc.utk.edu.

Committee Chairpersons

Awards. Juanita M. Skillman.
Canadian Legislative and Regulatory Affairs (CLARA). Peter Shewchenko.
Education Development. Julie A. Gee.
Election Management. Terrence J. Coan.
International Relations. Claudette E. Samuels.
Industry Specific Groups. Penny J. Quirk.
Member Relations. Helen M. Streck.
Publications Editorial Board. Jean K. Brown.
Standards Development. Sandra Williamson.
Technology Advisory Council. Carol E. B. Choksy.
U.S. Government Relations (GRECO). Rae Cogar.

Art Libraries Society of North America

Executive Director, Elizabeth Clarke
329 March Rd., Suite 232, Box 11, Kanata, ON K2K 2E1, Canada
800-817-0621, 613-599-3074, fax 613-599-7027
E-mail arlisna@igs.net
World Wide Web http://www.arlisna.org

Object

To foster excellence in art librarianship and visual resources curatorship for the advancement of the visual arts. Established 1972.

Membership

Memb. 1,100. Dues (Inst.) $135; (Indiv.) $65–$135; (Business Affiliate) $135; (Student) $40; (Retired/Unemployed) $50; (Sustaining) $250; (Sponsor) $500; (Overseas) $90. Year. Jan. 1–Dec. 31. Membership is open and encouraged for all those interested in visual librarianship, whether they be professional librarians, students, library assistants, art book publishers, art book dealers, art historians, archivists, architects, slide and photograph curators, or retired associates in these fields.

Officers (2003)

Pres. Daniel Starr, Thomas J. Watson Lib., Metropolitan Museum of Art, 1000 Fifth Ave., New York, NY 10028-1198. Tel. 212-650-2582, fax 212-570-3847, e-mail daniel.starr@metmuseum.org; *V.P./Pres.-Elect* Allen Townsend, Philadelphia Museum of Art, Box 7646, Philadelphia, PA 19101-7651. Tel. 215-684-7651, fax 215-236-0534, e-mail aktownsend@philamuseum.org; *Past Pres.* Ted Goodman, Avery Architectural and Fine Arts Lib., Columbia Univ., 1172 Amsterdam Ave., MC 0301, New York, NY 10027. Tel. 212-854-8407, fax 212-854-8904, e-mail goodman@columbia.edu; *Secy.* Norine Duncan, List Art Center, Brown Univ., Box 1855, Providence, RI 02912. Tel. 401-863-3082, fax 401-863-9589, e-mail Norine_Duncan@Brown.edu; *Treas.* Phillip Heagy, The

Menil Collection, 1511 Branard St., Houston, TX 77006. Tel. 713-525-9426, fax 713-525-9444, e-mail pheagy@menil.org.

Address correspondence to the executive director.

Executive Board

Officers; *Regional Reps.* (Northeast) Laurie Whitehill Chong, (South) Laura Schwartz, (Midwest) Ursula Kolmstetter, (West) Kay Teel, (Canada) Irene Pulchalski.

Publications

ARLIS/NA Update (bi-m.; memb.).
Art Documentation (semi-ann.; memb., subsc.).
Handbook and List of Members (ann.; memb.).
Occasional Papers (price varies).
Miscellaneous others (request current list from headquarters).

Committee Chairpersons

AWS Advisory. Lorna Corbetta Noyes.
Cataloging (Advisory). Elizabeth O'Keefe.
Collection Development. Nancy Pistorius.
Conference Planning. Daniel Starr.
Development. Gregory Most.
Distinguished Service Award. Rosemary Haddad.
Diversity. Marilyn Russell-Bogle, Lucie Stylianopoulos.
Finance. Trudy Jacoby.
International Relations. Susana Tejada.
Membership. Leslie Lowe Preston.
Gerd Muehsam Award. Paula Gabbard.
Nominating. Roger Lawson.
North American Relations. Paula Gabbard.

Professional Development. Tom Greives.
Public Policy. James Mitchell, Barbara Rock-
enbach.
Publications. Betsy Peck Learned.
Research. Thomas Riedel.

Standards. David Austin.
Travel Awards. Carole Ann Fabian.
Visual Resources Advisory. Mary S. Wasser-
man.
George Wittenborn Award. Nancy Norris.

Asian/Pacific American Librarians Association

Executive Director, Ling Hwey Jeng
Tel. 859-257-5679, e-mail lhjeng00@uky.edu.
World Wide Web http://www.uic.edu/depts/lib/projects/resources/apala

Object

To provide a forum for discussing problems
and concerns of Asian/Pacific American
librarians; to provide a forum for the exchange of ideas by Asian/Pacific American
librarians and other librarians; to support and
encourage library services to Asian/Pacific
American communities; to recruit and support Asian/Pacific American librarians in the
library/information science professions; to
seek funding for scholarships in library/infor-
mation science programs for Asian/Pacific
Americans; and to provide a vehicle whereby
Asian/Pacific American librarians can cooperate with other associations and organizations having similar or allied interests. Founded 1980; incorporated 1981; affiliated with
American Library Association 1982.

Membership

Open to all librarians and information specialists of Asian/Pacific descent working in
U.S. libraries and information centers and
other related organizations, and to others who
support the goals and purposes of APALA.
Asian/Pacific Americans are defined as those
who consider themselves Asian/Pacific
Americans. They may be Americans of
Asian/Pacific descent, Asian/Pacific people

with the status of permanent residency, or
Asian/Pacific people living in the United
States. Dues (Inst.) $50; (Indiv.) $20; (Stu-
dents/Unemployed Librarians) $10.

Officers (July 2002–June 2003)

Pres. Gerardo "Gary" Colmenar, Asian
American Studies Libn., Reference Services,
Davidson Lib., Univ. of California, Santa
Barbara, CA 93106-9010; *Pres.-Elect* Yvonne
Chen; *Treas.* Heawon Paick; *Past Pres.*
Tamiye Meehan.

Publication

APALA Newsletter (q.). *Ed.* Kenneth Yama-
shita, Lib. Div. Mgr., Stockton-San
Joaquin City Public Lib., 1209 W. Downs
St., Stockton, CA 95207.

Committee Chairs

Constitution and Bylaws. Ben Wakashige.
Membership and Recruitment. Sunnie Kim.
Newsletter and Publications. Kenneth Yama-
shita.
Nomination. Tamiye Meehan.
Program. Yvonne Chen.
Web. May Chang.

Association for Information and Image Management (AIIM International)

President, John F. Mancini
1100 Wayne Ave., Suite 1100, Silver Spring, MD 20910
301-587-8202, fax 301-587-2711
E-mail aiim@aiim.org, World Wide Web http://www.aiim.org
European Office: The IT Centre, 8 Canalside, Lowesmoor Wharf, Worcester WR1 2RR,
England. Tel. 44-1905-727600, fax 44-1905-727609, e-mail info@aiim.org.uk

Object

AIIM is a global industry association that connects the users and suppliers of document and business process management technologies and services. Founded 1943.

Officers

Chair Reynolds Bish, Captiva Software Corp. San Diego, CA 92121; *V. Chair* Martyn Christian, FileNET Corp., Costa Mesa, CA; *Treas.* M. S. Lee, HF Inc., Costa Mesa, CA.

Publication

e-doc Magazine (bi-m.; memb.).

Association for Library and Information Science Education

Executive Director, Maureen Thompson
703-243-4146, fax 703-435-4390, e-mail alise@drohanmgmt.com
World Wide Web http://www.alise.org

Object

The Association for Library and Information Science Education (ALISE) is devoted to the advancement of knowledge and learning in the interdisciplinary field of information studies. Established 1915.

Membership

Memb. 500. Dues (Inst.) for ALA-accredited programs, sliding scale; (International Affiliate Inst.) $125; (Indiv.) $90; (Retired or Student) $40. Year. January–December. Any library/information science school with a program accredited by the ALA Committee on Accreditation may become an institutional member. Any school that offers a graduate degree in librarianship or a cognate field but whose program is not accredited by the ALA Committee on Accreditation may become an institutional member at a lower rate. Any school outside the United States and Canada offering a program comparable to that of institutional membership may become an international affiliate institutional member. Any organizational entity wishing to support LIS education may become an associate institutional member. Any faculty member, administrator, librarian, researcher, or other individual employed full time may become a personal member. Any retired or part-time faculty member, student, or other individual employed less than full time may become a personal member. Any student may become a member at a lower rate.

Officers (2002–2003)

Pres. Prudence Dalrymple, Dominican Univ. E-mail pdalrymple@email.dom.edu; *V.P./ Pres.-Elect* Elizabeth Aversa, Univ. of Tennessee. E-mail aversa@utk.edu; *Secy.-Treas.* Pat Feehan, Univ. of South Carolina. E-mail pfeehan@qwm.sc.edu. *Past Pres.* James Matarazzo, Simmons College. E-mail james.matarazzo@simmons.edu.

Directors

Officers; Louise S. Robbins, Univ. of Wisconsin–Madison. E-mail LRobbins@macc.wisc.edu; Ann Curry, Univ. of British Columbia. E-mail ann.curry@ubc.ca; Diane Barlow, Univ. of Maryland. E-mail dbarlow@umd.edu; *Co-Eds.* Joseph Mika, Wayne State Univ. E-mail jmika@cms.cc.wayne.edu; Ronald W. Powell, Wayne State Univ. E-mail rpowell@cms.cc.wayne.edu; *Exec. Dir.* Maureen Thompson. E-mail mthomson@drohanmgmt.com.

Publications

ALISE Library and Information Science Education Statistical Report (ann.; $65).
Journal of Education for Library and Information Science (4 a year; $78; foreign $88).

Membership Directory (ann.; $55).

Committee Chairpersons

Awards and Honors. Mary Brown, Southern Connecticut State Univ.
Conference Planning. Elizabeth Aversa, Univ. of Tennessee.
Editorial Board. Joe Mika, Wayne State Univ.
Government Relations. Betty Turock, Rutgers Univ.
International Relations. Ismail Abdullahi, Clark Atlanta Univ.
LIS Education Statistical Report Project. Evelyn Daniel, Jerry Saye, Univ. of North Carolina.
Membership. Stephen Bajjaly, Univ. of South Carolina.
Nominating. Gretchen Whitney, Univ. of Tennessee.
Organization and Bylaws. Heidi Julien, Dalhousie Univ.
Recruitment. Ling Hwey Jen, Univ. of Kentucky.
Research. Rebecca Watson-Boone, CSIP.
Tellers. Sue Easun, Scarecrow Press.

Association of Academic Health Sciences Libraries

Executive Director, Shirley Bishop
2150 N. 107, Suite 205, Seattle, WA 98133
206-367-8704, fax 206-367-8777
E-mail aahsl@shirleybishopinc.com.

Object

The Association of Academic Health Sciences Libraries (AAHSL) is composed of the directors of libraries of 142 accredited U.S. and Canadian medical schools belonging to the Association of American Medical Colleges. Its goals are to promote excellence in academic health science libraries and to ensure that the next generation of health practitioners is trained in information-seeking skills that enhance the quality of health care delivery, education, and research. Founded 1977.

Membership

Memb. 142. Dues $1,500. Regular membership is available to nonprofit educational institutions operating a school of health sciences that has full or provisional accreditation by the Association of American Medical Colleges. Regular members shall be represented by the chief administrative officer of the member institution's health sciences library. Associate membership (and nonvoting representation) is available at $600 to organizations having an interest in the purposes and activities of the association.

Officers (2002–2003)

Pres. David Ginn, Alumni Medical Lib., Boston Univ.; *Pres.-Elect* J. Roger Guard, Univ. of Cincinnati; *Secy.-Treas.* Holly Shipp Buchanan, Health Sciences Center Lib., Univ. of New Mexico; *Past Pres.* Rick Forsman, Charles Denison Memorial Lib., Univ. of Colorado.

Association of Independent Information Professionals (AIIP)

8550 United Plaza Blvd., Suite 1001, Baton Rouge, LA 70809
225-408-4400, fax 225-922-4611, e-mail info@aiip.org
World Wide Web http://www.aiip.org

Membership

Memb. 750+.

Officers (2002–2003)

Pres. Pam Wegmann, Information Matters, LLC. Tel. 504-738-0070, e-mail pam@info-matters.com.

Object

AIIP's members are owners of firms providing such information-related services as online and manual research, document delivery, database design, library support, consulting, writing, and publishing. The objectives of the association are

- To advance the knowledge and understanding of the information profession
- To promote and maintain high professional and ethical standards among its members
- To encourage independent information professionals to assemble to discuss common issues
- To promote the interchange of information among independent information professionals and various organizations
- To keep the public informed of the profession and of the responsibilities of the information professional

Publications

Connections (q.).
Membership Directory (ann.).
Professional Paper series.

Association of Jewish Libraries

15 E. 26 St., Rm. 1034, New York, NY 10010
212-725-5359, e-mail ajl@jewishbooks.org
World Wide Web http://www.jewishlibraries.org

Object

To promote the improvement of library services and professional standards in all Jewish libraries and collections of Judaica; to provide professional development opportunities for Judaic librarians; to promote quality Judaic literature and reference materials; to select and publicize quality Judaic children's literature; to serve as a center of dissemination of Jewish bibliographic information and guidance; to encourage the establishment of Jewish libraries and collections of Judaica; to promote publication of literature that will be of assistance to Judaic librarianship; to encourage people to enter the field of librarianship. Organized in 1965 from the merger of the Jewish Librarians Association and the Jewish Library Association.

Membership

Memb. 1,100. Dues $50; (Foreign) $75; (Student/Retired) $30; Year. July 1–June 30.

Officers (June 2002–June 2004)

Pres. Pearl Berger, Yeshiva Univ. Libs., New York; *Past Pres.* Toby Rossner, Providence, R.I.; *V.P./Pres.-Elect* Ronda Rose, Kosofsky Lib., Temple Emanuel, Beverly Hills; *V.P., Memb.* Joseph Galron, Ohio State Univ., Columbus; *V.P., Publications* Elana Gensler, Hebrew Academy of Long Beach (New York); *Treas.* Laurel Wolfson, Hebrew Union College–JIR, Cincinnati; *Recording Secy.* Elliot H. Gertel, Univ. of Michigan, Ann Arbor; *Corresponding Secy.* Noreen Wachs, Ramaz Middle School, New York.

Address correspondence to the association.

Publications

AJL Newsletter (q.). *General Ed.* Barbara Sutton, Lawrence Family Jewish Community Center, 4126 Executive Drive, San Diego, CA 92037.

Judaica Librarianship (irreg.). *Ed.* Linda Lerman, Bobst Lib., New York Univ., 70 Washington Sq. S., New York, NY 10012.

Division Presidents

Research and Special Library. Rita Saccal.
Synagogue, School, and Center Libraries. Susan Dubin.

Association of Research Libraries

Executive Director, Duane E. Webster
21 Dupont Circle N.W., Suite 800, Washington, DC 20036
202-296-2296, fax 202-872-0884
E-mail arlhq@arl.org, World Wide Web http://www.arl.org

Object

The mission of the Association of Research Libraries (ARL) is to shape and influence forces affecting the future of research libraries in the process of scholarly communication. ARL's programs and services promote equitable access to and effective use of recorded knowledge in support of teaching, research, scholarship, and community service. The association articulates the concerns of research libraries and their institutions, forges coalitions, influences information policy development, and supports innovation and improvement in research library operations. ARL is a not-for-profit membership organization comprising the libraries of North American research institutions and operates as a forum for the exchange of ideas and as an agent for collective action.

Membership

Memb. 124. Membership is institutional. Dues $19,000.

Officers (Oct. 2002–Oct. 2003)

Pres. Fred Heath, Texas A&M; *V.P./Pres.-Elect* Sarah Thomas, Cornell; *Past Pres.* Paula Kaufman, Univ. of Illinois.

Board of Directors

Nancy Baker, Univ. of Iowa; Joseph Branin, Ohio State Univ.; Frances Groen, McGill Univ.; Fred Heath, Texas A&M; Paula Kaufman, Univ. of Illinois; Sarah Michalak, Univ. of Utah; Rush Miller, Univ. of Pittsburgh; Sherrie Schmidt, Arizona State Univ.; Brian Schottlaender, Univ. of California–San Diego; Sarah Thomas, Cornell; Paul Willis, Univ. of South Carolina; Ann Wolpert, Massachusetts Inst. of Technology.

Publications

ARL: A Bimonthly Report on Research Libraries Issues and Actions from ARL, CNI, and SPARC (bi-m.).
ARL Academic Law and Medical Library Statistics (ann.).
ARL Annual Salary Survey (ann.).
ARL Preservation Statistics (ann.).
ARL Statistics (ann.).
ARL Supplementary Statistics (ann.).
SPEC Kits (6 a year).

Committee and Work Group Chairpersons

Access to Information Resources. Sarah Thomas, Cornell.
Diversity. Stella Bentley, Auburn.
Information Policies. Lance Query, Tulane.
Membership. Kenneth Frazier, Univ. of Wisconsin.
Preservation of Research Library Materials. Nancy Gwinn, Smithsonian.
Research Collections. Merrily Taylor, Brown.
Research Library Leadership and Management. Joan Giesecke, Univ. of Nebraska.
Scholarly Communication. Marianne Gaunt, Rutgers.
SPARC Steering Committee. James Neal, Columbia.
Statistics and Measurement. Carla Stoffle, Univ. of Arizona.
Working Group on Portal Applications. Sarah Michalak, Univ. of Utah.

ARL Membership

Nonuniversity Libraries

Boston Public Lib., Canada Inst. for Scientific and Technical Info., Center for Research Libs., Lib. of Congress, National Agricultural Lib., National Lib. of Canada, National Lib. of Medicine, New York Public Lib., New York State Lib., Smithsonian Institution Libs.

University Libraries

Alabama, Alberta, Arizona, Arizona State, Auburn, Boston College, Boston Univ., Brigham Young, British Columbia, Brown, California–Berkeley, California–Davis, California–Irvine, California–Los Angeles, California–Riverside, California–San Diego, California–Santa Barbara, Case Western Reserve, Chicago, Cincinnati, Colorado, Colorado State, Columbia, Connecticut, Cornell, Dartmouth, Delaware, Duke, Emory, Florida, Florida State, George Washington, Georgetown, Georgia, Georgia Inst. of Technology, Guelph, Harvard, Hawaii, Houston, Howard, Illinois–Chicago, Illinois–Urbana, Indiana, Iowa, Iowa State, Johns Hopkins, Kansas, Kent State, Kentucky, Laval, Louisiana State, Louisville, McGill, McMaster, Manitoba, Maryland, Massachusetts, Massachusetts Inst. of Technology, Miami (Florida), Michigan, Michigan State, Minnesota, Missouri, Montreal, Nebraska–Lincoln, New Mexico, New York, North Carolina, North Carolina State, Northwestern, Notre Dame, Ohio, Ohio State, Oklahoma, Oklahoma State, Oregon, Pennsylvania, Pennsylvania State, Pittsburgh, Princeton, Purdue, Queen's (Kingston, ON, Canada), Rice, Rochester, Rutgers, Saskatchewan, South Carolina, Southern California, Southern Illinois, Stanford, SUNY–Albany, SUNY–Buffalo, SUNY–Stony Brook, Syracuse, Temple, Tennessee, Texas, Texas A&M, Texas Tech, Toronto, Tulane, Utah, Vanderbilt, Virginia, Virginia Tech, Washington, Washington (Saint Louis, Mo.), Washington State, Waterloo, Wayne State, Western Ontario, Wisconsin, Yale, York.

Association of Vision Science Librarians

Chair 2002–2003, Maureen Watson
Ferris State University, Michigan College of Optometry Reading Rm., 1310 Cramer Circle, Big Rapids, MI 49307-2738. Tel. 231-591-2124, e-mail watsonm@ferris.edu

Object

To foster collective and individual acquisition and dissemination of vision science information, to improve services for all persons seeking such information, and to develop standards for libraries to which members are attached. Founded 1968.

Publications

Guidelines for Vision Science Libraries.
Opening Day Book, Journal and AV Collection—Visual Science.
Ph.D. Theses in Physiological Optics (irreg.).
Standards for Vision Science Libraries.
Union List of Vision-Related Serials (irreg.).

Meetings

Annual meeting held in December in connection with the American Academy of Optometry; midyear mini-meeting with the Medical Library Association.

Membership

Memb. (U.S.) 85; (Foreign) 35.

Beta Phi Mu
(International Library and Information Studies Honor Society)

Executive Director, Jane Robbins
School of Information Studies, Florida State University,
Tallahassee, FL 32306-2100
850-644-3907, fax 850-644-9763
E-mail beta_phi_mu@lis.fsu.edu
World Wide Web http://www.beta-phi-mu.org

Object

To recognize and encourage scholastic achievement among library and information studies students and to sponsor appropriate professional and scholarly projects. Founded at the University of Illinois in 1948.

Membership

Memb. 23,000. Open to graduates of library school programs accredited by the American Library Association who fulfill the following requirements: complete the course requirements leading to a fifth year or other advanced degree in librarianship with a scholastic average of 3.75 where A equals 4 points (this provision shall also apply to planned programs of advanced study beyond the fifth year that do not culminate in a degree but that require full-time study for one or more academic years) and in the top 25 percent of their class; receive a letter of recommendation from their respective library schools attesting to their demonstrated fitness for successful professional careers.

Officers (2001–2003)

Pres. Robert S. Martin, Institute of Museum and Lib. Services, 1100 Pennsylvania Ave. N.W., Washington, DC 20506. Tel. 202-606-4649, fax 202-606-8591, e-mail rmartin@imls.gov; *V.P./Pres.-Elect* W. Michael Havener, Univ. of Rhode Island, Grad. School of Lib. and Info. Studies, Rodman Hall, 94 W. Alumni Ave., Suite 2, Kingston, RI 02881. Tel. 401-874-4641, fax 401-874-4964, e-mail mhavener@uri.edu; *Past Pres.* Barbara Immroth, Graduate School of Lib. and Info. Science, Univ. of Texas at Austin; *Treas.* Robin

Gault, College of Law Lib., Florida State Univ., Tallahassee, FL 32306-1600. Tel. 850-644-7487, fax 850-644-5216, e-mail rgault@law.fsu.edu; *Exec. Dir.* Jane Robbins, School of Info. Studies, Florida State Univ., Tallahassee, FL 32306-2100. Tel. 850-644-3907, fax 850-644-9763, e-mail beta_phi_mu@lis.fsu.edu.

Directors

Susan M. Agent, Nicholas C. Burckel, Michael Carpenter, Louise S. Robbins, Vicky Schmarr, Sue Stroyan, Danny P. Wallace.

Publications

Beta Phi Mu Monograph Series. Book-length scholarly works based on original research in subjects of interest to library and information professionals. Available from Greenwood Press, 88 Post Rd. W., Box 5007, Westport, CT 06881-9990.

Chapbook Series. Limited editions on topics of interest to information professionals. Call Beta Phi Mu for availability.

Newsletter. (2 a year). *Ed.* Lynne Barrett.

Chapters

Alpha. Univ. of Illinois, Grad. School of Lib. and Info. Science, Urbana, IL 61801; *Beta.* (Inactive). Univ. of Southern California, School of Lib. Science, Univ. Park, Los Angeles, CA 90007; *Gamma.* Florida State Univ., School of Lib. and Info. Studies, Tallahassee, FL 32306; *Delta* (Inactive). Loughborough College of Further Educ., School of Libnship., Loughborough, England; *Epsilon.*

Univ. of North Carolina, School of Lib. Science, Chapel Hill, NC 27599; *Zeta.* Atlanta Univ., School of Lib. and Info. Studies, Atlanta, GA 30314; *Theta.* Pratt Inst., Grad. School of Lib. and Info. Science, Brooklyn, NY 11205; *Iota.* Catholic Univ. of America, School of Lib. and Info. Science, Washington, DC 20064; Univ. of Maryland, College of Lib. and Info. Services, College Park, MD 20742; *Kappa.* (Inactive). Western Michigan Univ., School of Libnship., Kalamazoo, MI 49008; *Lambda.* Univ. of Oklahoma, School of Lib. Science, Norman, OK 73019; *Mu.* Univ. of Michigan, School of Lib. Science, Ann Arbor, MI 48109; *Xi.* Univ. of Hawaii, Grad. School of Lib. Studies, Honolulu, HI 96822; *Omicron.* Rutgers Univ., Grad. School of Lib. and Info. Studies, New Brunswick, NJ 08903; *Pi.* Univ. of Pittsburgh, School of Lib. and Info. Science, Pittsburgh, PA 15260; *Rho.* Kent State Univ., School of Lib. Science, Kent, OH 44242; *Sigma.* Drexel Univ., School of Lib. and Info. Science, Philadelphia, PA 19104; *Tau.* (Inactive). State Univ. of New York at Genesee, School of Lib. and Info. Science, Genesee, NY 14454; *Upsilon.* (Inactive). Univ. of Kentucky, College of Lib. Science, Lexington, KY 40506; *Phi.* Univ. of Denver, Grad. School of Libnship. and Info. Mgt., Denver, CO 80208; *Chi.* Indiana Univ., School of Lib. and Info. Science, Bloomington, IN 47401; *Psi.* Univ. of Missouri at Columbia, School of Lib. and Info. Sciences, Columbia, MO 65211; *Omega.* (Inactive). San Jose State Univ., Div. of Lib. Science, San Jose, CA 95192; *Beta Alpha.* Queens College, City College of New York, Grad. School of Lib. and Info. Studies, Flushing, NY 11367; *Beta Beta.* Simmons College, Grad. School of Lib. and Info. Science, Boston, MA 02115; *Beta Delta.* State Univ. of New York at Buffalo, School of Info. and Lib. Studies, Buffalo, NY 14260; *Beta Epsilon.* Emporia State Univ., School of Lib. Science, Emporia, KS 66801; *Beta Zeta.* Louisiana State Univ., Grad. School of Lib. Science, Baton Rouge, LA 70803; *Beta Eta.* Univ. of Texas at Austin, Grad. School of Lib. and Info. Science, Austin, TX 78712; *Beta Theta.* (Inactive). Brigham Young Univ., School of Lib. and Info. Science, Provo, UT 84602; *Beta Iota.* Univ. of Rhode Island, Grad. Lib. School, Kingston, RI 02881; *Beta Kappa.* Univ. of Alabama, Grad. School of Lib. Service, University, AL 35486; *Beta Lambda.* North Texas State Univ., School of Lib. and Info. Science, Denton, TX 76203; Texas Woman's Univ., School of Lib. Science, Denton, TX 76204; *Beta Mu.* Long Island Univ., Palmer Grad. Lib. School, C. W. Post Center, Greenvale, NY 11548; *Beta Nu.* Saint John's Univ., Div. of Lib. and Info. Science, Jamaica, NY 11439. *Beta Xi.* North Carolina Central Univ., School of Lib. Science, Durham, NC 27707; *Beta Omicron.* (Inactive). Univ. of Tennessee at Knoxville, Grad. School of Lib. and Info. Science, Knoxville, TN 37916; *Beta Pi.* Univ. of Arizona, Grad. Lib. School, Tucson, AZ 85721; *Beta Rho.* Univ. of Wisconsin at Milwaukee, School of Lib. Science, Milwaukee, WI 53201; *Beta Sigma.* (Inactive). Clarion State College, School of Lib. Science, Clarion, PA 16214; *Beta Tau.* Wayne State Univ., Div. of Lib. Science, Detroit, MI 48202; *Beta Upsilon.* (Inactive). Alabama A&M Univ., School of Lib. Media, Normal, AL 35762; *Beta Phi.* Univ. of South Florida, Grad. Dept. of Lib., Media, and Info. Studies, Tampa, FL 33647; *Beta Psi.* Univ. of Southern Mississippi, School of Lib. Service, Hattiesburg, MS 39406; *Beta Omega.* Univ. of South Carolina, College of Libnship., Columbia, SC 29208; *Beta Beta Alpha.* Univ. of California at Los Angeles, Grad. School of Lib. and Info. Science, Los Angeles, CA 90024; *Beta Beta Gamma.* Rosary College, Grad. School of Lib. and Info. Science, River Forest, IL 60305; *Beta Beta Delta.* Univ. of Cologne, Germany; *Beta Beta Epsilon.* Univ. of Wisconsin at Madison, Lib. School, Madison, WI 53706; *Beta Beta Zeta.* Univ. of North Carolina at Greensboro, Dept. of Lib. Science and Educational Technology, Greensboro, NC 27412; *Beta Beta Theta.* Univ. of Iowa, School of Lib. and Info. Science, Iowa City, IA 52242; *Beta Beta Iota.* State Univ. of New York, Univ. at Albany, School of Info. Science and Policy, Albany, NY 12222; *Beta Beta Kappa.* Univ. of Puerto Rico Grad. School of Info. Sciences and Technologies, San Juan, PR 00931-1906; *Pi Lambda Sigma.* Syracuse Univ., School of Info. Studies, Syracuse, NY 13210.

Bibliographical Society of America

Executive Secretary, Michele E. Randall
Box 1537, Lenox Hill Station, New York, NY 10021
212-452-2500 (tel./fax), e-mail bsa@bibsocamer.org
World Wide Web http://www.bibsocamer.org

Object

To promote bibliographical research and to issue bibliographical publications. Organized 1904.

Membership

Memb. 1,200. Dues $50. Year. Jan.–Dec.

Officers

Pres. Hope Mayo; *V.P.* John Bidwell; *Treas.* R. Dyke Benjamin; *Secy.* Claudia Funke.

Council

Susan Allen (2003), Anna Lou Ashby (2004), Eric Holzenberg (2004), Marie E. Korey (2003), Mark Samuels Lasner (2003), Katharine Kyes Leab (2004), Justin G. Schiller (2004), Elizabeth Witherell (2003).

Publication

Papers (q.; memb.). *Ed.* Trevor Howard-Hill, Thomas Cooper Lib., Univ. of South Carolina, Columbia, SC 29208. Tel./fax 803-777-7046, e-mail RalphCrane@msn.com.

Committee Chairpersons

Delegate to American Council of Learned Societies. Marcus McCorison.
Fellowship. Bruce Whiteman.
Finance. William P. Barlow.
Publications. John Bidwell.
Program. Marie Korey.

Canadian Association for Information Science (Association Canadienne des Sciences de l'Information)

University of Toronto, Faculty of Information Studies,
140 Saint George St., Toronto, ON M5S 3G6, Canada
416-978-7111, fax 416-971-1399

Object

To promote the advancement of information science in Canada and encourage and facilitate the exchange of information relating to the use, access, retrieval, organization, management, and dissemination of information.

Membership

Institutions and individuals interested in information science and involved in the gathering, organization, and dissemination of information (such as information scientists, archivists, librarians, computer scientists, documentalists, economists, educators, journalists, and psychologists) who support CAIS's objectives can become association members.

Dues (Inst.) $165; (Personal) $75; (Student) $40.

Publication

Canadian Journal of Information and Library Science (q.; memb.).

Canadian Library Association

Executive Director, Don Butcher
328 Frank St., Ottawa, ON K2P 0X8
613-232-9625 ext. 306, fax 613-563-9895
E-mail dbutcher@cla.ca
World Wide Web http://cla.ca

Object

To promote, develop, and support library and information services in Canada and to work in cooperation with all who share our values in order to present a unified voice on issues of mutual concern. The association offers library school scholarship and book awards, carries on international liaison with other library associations, makes representation to government and official commissions, offers professional development programs, and supports intellectual freedom. Founded in 1946, CLA is a nonprofit voluntary organization governed by an elected executive council.

Membership

Memb. (Indiv.) 2,500; (Inst.) 600. Open to individuals, institutions, and groups interested in librarianship and in library and information services.

Officers

Pres. Wendy Newman, CEO, Brantford Public Lib., 173 Colbourne St., Brantford, ON N3T 2G8. Tel. 519-756-2223 ext. 4, fax 519-756-4979, e-mail wnewman@brantford. library.on.ca; *V.P.* Madeleine J. Lefebvre, Univ. Libn., Saint Mary's Univ., Patrick Power Lib., Halifax, NS B3H 3C3. Tel. 902-420-5532, fax 902-491-8698; *Treas.* Kathryn Arbuckle, Law Libn., Univ. of Alberta, John A. Weir Memorial Law Lib., Edmonton, AB T6G 2H5. Tel. 780-492-3717, fax 780-492-7546, e-mail kathryn.arbuckle@ualberta.ca; *Past Pres.* Margaret Law, Coord., Post Secondary Libs., The Alberta Lib., 7 Sir Winston Churchill Sq., Room 6-14, Edmonton, AB T5J 2V5. Tel. 780-414-0805, fax 780-414-0806, e-mail mlaw@thealbertalibrary.ab.ca.

Publication

Feliciter: Linking Canada's Information Professionals (6 a year; newsletter).

Division Representatives

Canadian Association of College and University Libraries (CACUL). E. Jane Philipps, Head, Queen's Univ. Engineering and Science Lib., Douglas Lib., Kingston, Ontario K7L 5C4. Tel. 613-533-6846, fax 613-545-2684, e-mail phillipj@post.queensu.ca.

Canadian Association of Public Libraries (CAPL). Rick Walker, Mgr. of Lib. Services, Winnipeg Public Lib., 251 Donald St., Winnipeg, MB R3C 3P5. Tel. 204-986-6472, fax 204-942-5671, e-mail rwalker@city.winnipeg.mb.ca.

Canadian Association of Special Libraries and Information Services (CASLIS). Tracey Palmer, Mgr., Knowledge Management, Research in Motion, RIM 5, 156 Columbia St., Waterloo, ON N2L 3L3. Tel. 519-888-7465 ext. 5716, fax 519-746-0474, e-mail traceypalmer_mist@yahoo.com.

Canadian Library Trustees' Association (CLTA). Ernest Neumann, Trustee, Burnaby Public Lib., 6100 Willdon Ave., Burnaby, BC V5H 4N5. Tel. 604-421-3559, fax 604-421-7883, e-mail ernest.neumann@hotmail.com.

Canadian School Library Association (CSLA). Karin Paul, 4291 Caen Rd., Victoria, BC V8X 3S5. Tel. 250-479-1414, fax 250-479-5356, e-mail kepaul@shaw.ca.

Catholic Library Association

Executive Director, Jean R. Bostley, SSJ
100 North St., Suite 224, Pittsfield, MA 01201-5109
413-443-2252, fax 413-442-2252, e-mail cla@cathla.org
World Wide Web http://www.cathla.org

Object

The promotion and encouragement of Catholic literature and library work through cooperation, publications, education, and information. Founded 1921.

Membership

Memb. 1,000. Dues $45–$500. Year. July–June.

Officers (2003–2005)

Pres. M. Dorothy Neuhofer, OSB, St. Leo Univ., Box 6665 MC 2128, Saint Leo, FL 33574-6665. Tel. 352-588-8260, fax 352-588-8484, e-mail dorothy.neuhofer@saintleo.edu; *V.P./Pres.-Elect* Kenneth G. O'Malley, CP, Paul Bechtold Lib., Catholic Theological Union, 5401 S. Cornell Ave., Chicago, IL 60615-5698. Tel. 772-753-5322, fax 773-753-5440, e-mail omalleyk@ctu.lib.il.us; *Past Pres.* Sally Anne Thompson, Pope John XXIII Catholic School Community, 16235 N. 60 St., Scottsdale, AZ 85254-7323. Tel. 480-905-0939, fax 480-905-0955, e-mail desertsat@aol.com.

Address correspondence to the executive director.

Executive Board

Officers; Kathy C. Born, 1120 Hickory Lake Dr., Cincinnati, OH 45233; John R. Edson, Hamburg Public Lib., 102 Buffalo St., Hamburg, NY 14075; Anne LeVeque, U.S. Conference of Catholic Bishops, 3211 4th St. N.E., Washington, DC 20017; Maxine C. Lucas, St. Mel School, 20874 Ventura Blvd., Woodland Hills, CA 91364; Nancy K. Schmidtmann, 174 Theodore Dr., Coram, NY 11727; Cecil R. White, St. Patrick's Seminary, 320 Middlefield Rd., Menlo Park, CA 94025.

Publications

Catholic Library World (q.; memb.; nonmemb. $60). *General Ed.* Mary E. Gallagher, SSJ; *Production Ed.* Allen Gruenke.
Catholic Periodical and Literature Index (q.; $400 calendar year; abridged ed., $100 calendar year; *CPLI* on CD-ROM, inquire. *Ed.* Kathleen Spaltro.

Section Chairpersons

Academic Libraries/Library Education. Herman A. Peterson.
Children's Libraries. Chrys Rudnik.
High School Libraries. Lisa Valerio-Nowc.
Parish/Community Libraries. Marie Sivak.

Committee Chairpersons

Catholic Library World Editorial. Nancy K. Schmidtmann.
Catholic Periodical and Literature Index. Cecil R. White.
Constitution and Bylaws. Sara Baron.
Coordinator of Chapters, Sections, and Round Tables. Kathy C. Born.
Elections. Eileen Franke.
Finance. Kenneth G. O'Malley, CP.
Grant Development. Jean R. Bostley, SSJ.
Membership Development. To be appointed.
Nominations. To be appointed.
Publications. Paul E. Pojman.
Scholarship. Sandra Silber.

Special Appointments

American Friends of the Vatican Library Board. Jean R. Bostley, SSJ.
American Theological Library Association. Kenneth G. O'Malley, CP.

Convention Program Coordinator. Jean R. Bostley, SSJ.

National Catholic Educational Association. Jean R. Bostley, SSJ.

Parliamentarian. Rev. Jovian Lang, OFM.

Chief Officers of State Library Agencies

167 W. Main St., Suite 600, Lexington, KY 40507
859-231-1925, fax 859-231-1928, e-mail ttucker@amrinc.net

Object

To provide a means of cooperative action among its state and territorial members to strengthen the work of the respective state and territorial agencies, and to provide a continuing mechanism for dealing with the problems faced by the heads of these agencies, which are responsible for state and territorial library development.

Membership

Chief Officers of State Library Agencies (COSLA) is an independent organization of the men and women who head the state and territorial agencies responsible for library development. Its membership consists solely of the top library officers of the 50 states, the District of Columbia, and the territories, variously designated as state librarian, director, commissioner, or executive secretary.

Officers (2002–2004)

Pres. GladysAnn Wells, Dir., State Lib. of Arizona, State Capitol, 1700 W. Washington, Rm. 200, Phoenix, AZ 85007. Tel. 602-542-4035, fax 602-542-4972, e-mail gawells@lib. az.us; *V.P./Pres.-Elect* J. Gary Nichols, State Libn., Maine State Lib., 64 State House Sta., Augusta, ME 04333. Tel. 207-287-5600, fax 207-287-5615, e-mail gary.nichols@state.me. us; *Secy.* Suzanne Miller, State Libn., South Dakota State Lib., 800 Governors Dr., Pierre, SD 57501-2294. Tel. 605-773-3131, fax 605-773-4950, e-mail suzanne.miller@state.sd.us; *Treas.* Lesley Boughton, Wyoming State Libn., 2301 Capitol Ave., Cheyenne, WY 82002. Tel. 307-777-7283, fax 307-777-6289, e-mail lbough@state.wy.us; *Past Pres.* Karen Crane, Dir., Alaska Libs., Archives and Museums, Box 110571, Juneau, AK 99811-0571. Tel. 907-465-2910, fax 907-465-2151, e-mail Karen_Crane@eed.state.ak. us; *Dirs.* Sybil McShane, Vermont State Libn., Dept. of Libs., 109 State St., Montpelier, VT 05609-3261. Tel. 802-828-3265, fax 802-828-2199, e-mail sybil.mcshane@dol. state.vt.us; Lamar Veatch, Dir., State of Georgia Public Lib. Services, 1800 Century Place, Suite 150, Atlanta, GA 30345. Tel. 404-982-3560, fax 404-982-3563, e-mail lveatch@state.lib.ga.us; *Assn. Dir.* Tracy Tucker. Tel. 859-514-9210, e-mail ttucker@ amrinc.net.

Chinese American Librarians Association

Executive Director, Sally C. Tseng
949-552-5615, fax 949-857-1988, e-mail sctseng888@yahoo.com
World Wide Web http://www.cala-web.org

Object

To enhance communications among Chinese American librarians as well as between Chinese American librarians and other librarians; to serve as a forum for discussion of mutual problems and professional concerns among Chinese American librarians; to promote Sino-American librarianship and library services; and to provide a vehicle whereby Chinese American librarians may cooperate with other associations and organizations having similar or allied interests.

Membership

Memb. 770. Open to anyone who is interested in the association's goals and activities. Dues (regular) $30; (student/nonsalaried) $15; (inst.) $100; (life) $400.

Officers

Pres. Angela Yang. E-mail AYang@ac library.org; *V.P./Pres.-Elect* Amy Tsiang. E-mail ctsiang@library.ucla.edu; *Treas.* Dora Ho. E-mail doraho@yahoo.com; *Past Pres.* Liana Hong Zhou. E-mail zhoul@indiana. edu.

Publications

Journal of Library and Information Science (2 a year; memb.; nonmemb. $15). *Ed.* Mengxiong Liu. E-mail mliu@mail.sjsu. edu.

Membership Directory (memb.).

Newsletter (3 a year; memb.; nonmemb. $10). *Ed.* Haipeng Li. E-mail pli@oberlin.edu.

Committee Chairpersons

Awards. Mengxiong Liu, Xiwen Zhang.
Constitution and Bylaws. Susana Liu, Carl Chen.
Finance. Peter Wang.
International Relations. Cathy Yang, Harriet Ying.
Membership. Lisa Zhao.
Nominating. Liana Zhou.
Public Relations/Fund Raising. Diana Wu, Esther Lee.
Publications. Zhijia Shen.
Scholarship. Yu-Lan Chou, Wen-Ling Liu.
Conference Program Committee. Amy Tsiang.
Webmaster. Shixing Wen.

Chapter Presidents

California. Diana Wu.
Florida. Ying Zhang.
Greater Mid-Atlantic. Zhangjun Yan.
Midwest. Haipeng Li.
Northeast. Janey Chao.
Southwest. Jiun Kuo.

Church and Synagogue Library Association

Box 19357, Portland, OR 97280-0357
503-244-6919, 800-542-2752, fax 503-977-3734
E-mail CSLA@worldaccessnet.com.
World Wide Web http://www.worldaccessnet.com/~CSLA

Object

To act as a unifying core for the many existing church and synagogue libraries; to provide the opportunity for a mutual sharing of practices and problems; to inspire and encourage a sense of purpose and mission among church and synagogue librarians; to study and guide the development of church and synagogue librarianship toward recognition as a formal branch of the library profession. Founded 1967.

Membership

Memb. 1,900. Dues (Inst.) $175; (Affiliated) $70; (Church/Synagogue) $45 ($50 foreign); (Indiv.) $25 ($30 foreign). Year. July–June.

Officers (July 2002–June 2003)

Pres. Helen Zappia; *Pres.-Elect* Naomi Kauffman; *2nd V.P.* Dorothy Lewis; *Treas.* Warren Livingston; *Admin.* Judith Janzen; *Past Pres.* Barbara May; *Ed., Church and*

Synagogue Libraries Karen Bota, 490 N. Fox Hills Dr., No. 7, Bloomfield Hills, MI 48304; *Book Review Ed.* Charles Snyder, 213 Lawn Ave., Sellersville, PA 18960.

Executive Board

Officers; committee chairpersons.

Publications

Bibliographies (1–5; price varies).
Church and Synagogue Libraries (bi-mo.; memb.; nonmemb. $35; Canada $45).
CSLA Guides (1–17; price varies).

Committee Chairpersons

Awards. Barbara Graham.
Conference. Alice Hamilton.
Finance. Warren Livingston.
Library Services. Judy Livingston.
Nominations and Elections. JoMae Spoelhof.
Publications. Carol Campbell.

Coalition for Networked Information (CNI)

Executive Director, Clifford A. Lynch
21 Dupont Circle, Suite 800, Washington, DC 20036
202-296-5098, fax 202-872-0884
E-mail info@cni.org, World Wide Web http://www.cni.org

Mission

The Coalition for Networked Information (CNI) is an organization to advance the transformative promise of networked information technology for the advancement of scholarly communication and the enrichment of intellectual productivity.

Membership

Memb. 210. Membership is institutional. Dues $5,560. Year. July–June.

Officers (July 2002–June 2003)

Duane Webster, Exec. Dir., Association of Research Libraries; Brian Hawkins, Pres., EDUCAUSE.

Steering Committee

Richard P. West, California State Univ. (*Chair*); Gregory Crane, Tufts Univ; Nancy Eaton, Pennsylvania State Univ.; Peter Graham, Syracuse Univ.; Brian L. Hawkins, EDUCAUSE; Charles Henry, Rice Univ.; Lawrence M. Levine, Dartmouth College; Clifford Lynch, CNI; Susan Lane Perry, Andrew W. Mellon Foundation and Council on Lib. and Info. Resources; Donald J. Waters, Andrew Mellon Foundation; Duane Webster, ARL.

Publication

CNI-Announce (subscribe by e-mail to List proc@CNI.org)

Council on Library and Information Resources

1755 Massachusetts Ave. N.W., Suite 500, Washington, DC 20036-2124
202-939-4750, fax 202-939-4765
World Wide Web http://www.clir.org

Object

In 1997 the Council on Library Resources (CLR) and the Commission on Preservation and Access (CPA) merged and became the Council on Library and Information Resources (CLIR). The mission of the council is to identify and define the key emerging issues related to the welfare of libraries and the constituencies they serve, convene the leaders who can influence change, and promote collaboration among the institutions and organizations that can achieve change. The council's interests embrace the entire range of information resources and services from traditional library and archival materials to emerging digital formats. It assumes a particular interest in helping institutions cope with the accelerating pace of change associated with the transition into the digital environment. The council pursues this mission out of the conviction that information is a public good and has great social utility.

The term *library* is construed to embrace its traditional meanings and purposes and to encompass any and all information agencies and organizations that are involved in gathering, cataloging, storing, preserving, and distributing information and in helping users meet their information requirements.

While maintaining appropriate collaboration and liaison with other institutions and organizations, the council operates independently of any particular institutional or vested interests.

Through the composition of its board, it brings the broadest possible perspective to bear upon defining and establishing the priority of the issues with which it is concerned.

Membership of Board

CLIR's board of directors is limited to 18 members.

Officers

Chair Stanley Chodorow; *Pres.* Deanna B. Marcum. E-mail dmarcum@CLIR.org; *Treas.* Dan Tonkery.

Address correspondence to headquarters.

Publications

Annual Report.
CLIR Issues.
CLIRinghouse (bi-mo.).
Technical reports.

Federal Library and Information Center Committee

Executive Director, Susan M. Tarr
Library of Congress, Washington, DC 20540-4935
202-707-4800
World Wide Web http://www.loc.gov/flicc

Object

The Federal Library and Information Center Committee (FLICC) makes recommendations on federal library and information policies, programs, and procedures to federal agencies and to others concerned with libraries and information centers. The committee coordinates cooperative activities and services among federal libraries and information centers and serves as a forum to consider issues and policies that affect federal libraries and information centers, needs and priorities in providing information services to the government and to the nation at large, and efficient and cost-effective use of federal library and information resources and services. Furthermore, the committee promotes improved access to information, continued development and use of the Federal Library and Information Network (FEDLINK), research and development in the application of new technologies to federal libraries and information centers, improvements in the management of federal libraries and information centers, and relevant education opportunities. Founded 1965.

Membership

Libn. of Congress, Dir. of the National Agricultural Lib., Dir. of the National Lib. of Medicine, Dir. of the National Lib. of Educ., representatives of each of the cabinet-level executive departments, and representatives of each of the following agencies: National Aeronautics and Space Admin., National Science Foundation, Smithsonian Institution, U.S. Supreme Court, National Archives and Records Admin., Admin. Offices of the U.S. Courts, Defense Technical Info. Center, Government Printing Office, National Technical Info. Service (Dept. of Commerce), Office of Scientific and Technical Info. (Dept. of Energy), Exec. Office of the President, Dept. of the Army, Dept. of the Navy, Dept. of the Air Force, and chair of the FEDLINK Advisory Council. Fifteen additional voting member agencies shall be selected on a rotating basis by the voting members of FEDLINK. These rotating members will serve a three-year term. One representative of each of the following agencies is invited as an observer to committee meetings: General Accounting Office, General Services Admin., Joint Committee on Printing, National Commission on Libs. and Info. Science, Office of Mgt. and Budget, Office of Personnel Mgt., and U.S. Copyright Office.

Officers

Chair James H. Billington, Libn. of Congress; *Chair Designate* Beacher Wiggins, Acting Assoc. Libn. for Lib. Services, Lib. of Congress; *Exec. Dir.* Susan M. Tarr.

Address correspondence to the executive director.

Publications

FEDLINK Technical Notes (every other month.).
FLICC Newsletter (q.).

Federal Publishers Committee

Chair, Glenn W. King
Bureau of the Census, Washington, DC 20233
301-457-1171, fax 301-457-4707
E-mail glenn.w.king@census.gov

Object

To foster and promote effective management of data development and dissemination in the federal government through exchange of information, and to act as a focal point for federal agency publishing.

Membership

Memb. 500. Membership is available to persons involved in publishing and dissemination in federal government departments, agencies, and corporations, as well as independent organizations concerned with federal government publishing and dissemination. Some key federal government organizations represented are the Joint Committee on Printing, Government Printing Office, National Technical Info. Service, National Commission on Libs. and Info. Science, and the Lib. of Congress. Meetings are held monthly during business hours.

Officers

Chair Glenn W. King; *V. Chair, Programs* Sandra Smith; *Dirs.* John Ward, Pat Woods.

Publication

Guide to Federal Publishing (occasional).

Lutheran Church Library Association

Interim Executive Director, Sue Benish
122 W. Franklin Ave., No. 604, Minneapolis, MN 55404
612-870-3623, fax 612-870-0170
E-mail ContactUs@lclahq.org
World Wide Web http://www.lclahq.org

Object

To promote the growth of church libraries by publishing a quarterly journal, *Lutheran Libraries*; furnishing recommended-book lists; assisting member libraries with technical problems; and providing workshops and meetings for mutual encouragement, guidance, and exchange of ideas among members. Founded 1958.

Membership

Memb. 1,800 churches, 250 personal. Dues $28, $40, $55, $70, $75, $100, $500, $1,000. Year. Jan.–Jan.

Officers (2003)

Pres. Bonnie McLellan; *V.P.* Barbara Livdahl; *Secy.* Brenda Langerud; *Treas.* Dale Kennen.

Address correspondence to the executive director.

Directors

Betty Bender, Gerrie Buzard, Mildred Herder, Una Lamb, Helen Shoup.

Publication

Lutheran Libraries (q.; memb.; nonmemb. $30).

Board Chairpersons

Advisory. Mary Jordan.
Finance. To be announced.
Library Services. Marlys Johnson.
Publications. David Halaas.
Telecommunications. Elaine Hanson.

Medical Library Association

Executive Director, Carla Funk
65 E. Wacker Place, Suite 1900, Chicago, IL 60601-7298
312-419-9094, fax 312-419-8950
E-mail info@mlahq.org, World Wide Web http://mlanet.org

Object

MLA is a nonprofit, educational organization of more than 1,100 institutions and 3,600 individual members in the health sciences information field, committed to educating health information professionals, supporting health information research, promoting access to the world's health sciences information, and working to ensure that the best health information is available to all.

Membership

Memb. (Inst.) 1,100; (Indiv.) 3,800. Institutional members are medical and allied scientific libraries. Individual members are people who are (or were at the time membership was established) engaged in professional library or bibliographic work in medical and allied scientific libraries or people who are interested in medical or allied scientific libraries. Dues (Student) $30; (Emeritus) $50; (International) $90; (Indiv.) $135; (Lifetime) $2,540; and (Inst.) $210–$495, based on the number of the library's periodical subscriptions. Members may be affiliated with one or more of MLA's 23 special-interest sections and 14 regional chapters.

Officers

Pres. Linda A. Watson, Claude Moore Health Sciences Lib., Univ. of Virginia Health System, Box 800722, 1300 Jefferson Park Ave., Charlottesville, VA 22908-0722; *Pres.-Elect* Patricia L. Thibodeau, Duke Univ. Medical Center Lib., Box 3702, DUMC, 103 Seeley G. Mudd Bldg., Durham, NC 27710; *Past*

Pres. Carol Jenkins, Health Sciences Lib., Univ. of North Carolina–Chapel Hill, Box 7585, Chapel Hill, NC 27599-7585.

Directors

Diana J. Cunningham (2004), Lynn M. Fortney (2003), Mark E. Funk (2003), Norma F. Funkhouser (2004), Ruth Holst (2004), Michelynn McKnight (2005), Linda G. Markwell (2004), Gerald J. Perry (2005), Neil Rambo (2005).

Publications

Journal of the Medical Library Association (q.; $136).

MLA News (10 a year; $48.50).

Miscellaneous (request current list from association headquarters).

Music Library Association

8551 Research Way, Suite 180, Middleton, WI 53562
608-836-5825
World Wide Web http://www.musiclibraryassoc.org

Object

To promote the establishment, growth, and use of music libraries; to encourage the collection of music and musical literature in libraries; to further studies in musical bibliography; to increase efficiency in music library service and administration; and to promote the profession of music librarianship. Founded 1931.

Membership

Memb. 1,197. Dues (Inst.) $90; (Indiv.) $75; (Retired) $45; (Student) $35. Year. July 1–June 30.

Officers

Pres. James P. Cassaro, Music Lib., B-30 Music Bldg., Univ. of Pittsburgh, Pittsburgh, PA 15260. Tel. 412-624-4130, fax 412-624-4180, e-mail cassaro+@pitt.edu; *Vice Pres.* Laura Dankner, 708 Hesper Ave., Metairie, LA 70005. Tel. 504-837-8399, fax 504-837-7945, e-mail dankner@bellsouth.net; *Rec. Secy.* Michael Colby, Catalog Dept., Shields Lib., 100 N. West Quad, Univ. of California–Davis, Davis, CA 95616-5292. Tel. 530-752-0931, fax 530-754-8785, e-mail mdcolby@ucdavis.edu; *Treas./Exec. Secy.* Nancy B. Nuzzo, Music Lib., Univ. at Buffalo, 104 Baird Hall, Buffalo, NY 14260. Tel. 716-645-2924, fax 716-645-3906, e-mail nuzzo@buffalo.edu.

Members-at-Large

Joseph Boonin, New York Public Lib. of the Performing Arts; Virginia Danielson, Harvard Univ.; Alan Green, Ohio State Univ.; Neil Hughes, Univ. of Georgia; Deborah Pierce, Univ. of Washington; Michael Rogan, Tufts Univ.

Special Officers

Advertising Mgr. Susan Dearborn, 1572 Massachusetts Ave., No. 57, Cambridge, MA 02138. Tel. 617-876-0934; *Business Mgr.* Jim Zychowicz, 8551 Research Way, Suite 180, Middleton, WI 53562. Tel. 608-836-5825; *Convention Mgr.* Gordon Rowley, Box 395, Bailey's Harbor, WI 54202. Tel. 920-839-2444, e-mail baileysbreeze@itol.com; *Asst. Convention Mgr.* Annie Thompson, 435 S. Gulfstream Ave., Apt. 506, Sarasota, FL 34326. Tel. 941-955-5014, fax 941-316-0468, e-mail figarotu@msn.com; *Placement* Renee McBride, A1538 Young Research Lib., UCLA, Box 951575, Los Angeles, CA 90095-1575. Tel. 310-206-5853, fax 310-206-4974, e-mail rmcbride@library.ucla.edu; *Publicity* Alan Karass, College of the Holy Cross, Music Lib., Worcester, MA 01610. Tel. 508-793-2295, e-mail akarass@holy cross.edu.

Publications

MLA Index and Bibliography Series (irreg.; price varies).
MLA Newsletter (q.; memb.).
MLA Technical Reports (irreg.; price varies).
Music Cataloging Bulletin (mo.; $25).
Notes (q.; indiv. $70; inst. $80).

Committee and Roundtable Chairpersons

Administration. Robert Acker, DePaul Univ.
Bibliographic Control. Matthew Wise, New York Univ.
Development. Ruthann McTyre, Univ. of Iowa.
Education. Deborah Pierce, Univ. of Washington.
Finance. Neil Hughes, Univ. of Georgia.
Legislation. Bonna Boettcher, Bowling Green State Univ.
Membership. Sarah Dorsey, Univ. of North Carolina, Greensboro.
Preservation. Alice Carli, Eastman School of Music.
Public Libraries. Steven Landstreet, Free Lib. of Philadelphia.
Publications. Karen Little, Univ. of Louisville.
Reference and Public Service. Kathleen Abromeit, Oberlin College.
Resource Sharing and Collection Development. Mark Germer, Univ. of the Arts.

National Association of Government Archives and Records Administrators

48 Howard St., Albany, NY 12207
518-463-8644, fax 518-463-8656
E-mail nagara@caphill.com
World Wide Web http://www.nagara.org

Object

Founded in 1984, the association is successor to the National Association of State Archives and Records Administrators, which had been established in 1974. NAGARA is a growing nationwide association of local, state, and federal archivists and records administrators, and others interested in improved care and management of government records. NAGARA promotes public awareness of government records and archives management programs, encourages interchange of information among government archives and records management agencies, develops and implements professional standards of government records and archival administration, and encourages study and research into records management problems and issues.

Membership

Most NAGARA members are federal, state, and local archival and records management agencies.

Officers

Pres. Terry B. Ellis, County Records Mgr., Salt Lake County Records Mgt. and Archives, 2001 S. State St. N4400, Salt Lake City, UT 84190-3000. Tel. 801-468-2332, fax 801-468-3987, e-mail tellis@co.slc.ut.us; *V.P.* Timothy A. Slavin, Delaware Public

Archives, 121 Duke of York St., Dover, DE 19901. Tel. 302-739-5318, fax 302-739-2578, e-mail tslavin@state.de.us; *Secy.* Robert Horton, State Archivist, Minnesota Historical Society, 345 Kellogg Blvd. W., St. Paul, MN 55102. Tel. 651-215-5866, fax 651-296-9961, e-mail robert.horton@mnhs. org; *Treas.* John Stewart, National Archives and Records Admin., Great Lakes Region, 7358 S. Pulaski Rd., Chicago, IL 60629-5898. Tel. 773-581-7816, fax 312-886-7883, e-mail john.stewart@nara.gov.

Directors

Kent Carter, National Archives and Records Admin., Southwest Region; Nancy Fortna, National Archives and Records Admin., Washington, D.C.; Mary Beth Herkert, Oregon State Archives; C. Preston Huff, Lib. of Virginia; Kay Lanning Minchew, Troup County (Georgia) Archives; Richard Roberts, City of Hollywood (Florida); Jeanne Young, Board of Governors of the Federal Reserve System.

Publications

Clearinghouse (q.; memb.).
Crossroads (q.; memb.).
Government Records Issues (series).
Preservation Needs in State Archives (report).
Program Reporting Guidelines for Government Records Programs.

NFAIS

Executive Director, Bonnie Lawlor
1518 Walnut St., Suite 307, Philadelphia, PA 19102
215-893-1561, fax 215-893-1564
E-mail nfais@nfais.org
World Wide Web http://www.nfais.org

Object

NFAIS (formerly the National Federation of Abstracting and Information Services) is an international, nonprofit membership organization comprised of leading information providers. Its membership includes government agencies, nonprofit scholarly societies, and private-sector businesses. NFAIS serves groups that aggregate, organize, or facilitate access to information. To improve members' capabilities and to contribute to their ongoing success, NFAIS provides a forum to address common interests through education and advocacy. Founded 1958.

Membership

Memb. 50+. Full members: regular and government organizations that provide information services, primarily through organizing, compiling, and providing access to original or source materials. Examples of full members: organizations that assemble tables of contents, produce abstract and indexing services, provide library cataloging services, or generate numeric or factual compilations.

Associate members: organizations that operate or manage online information services, networks, in-house information centers, and libraries; undertake research and development in information science or systems; are otherwise involved in the generation, promotion, or distribution of information products under contract; or publish original information sources.

Corporate affiliated members: another member of the corporation or government agency must already be a NFAIS member paying full dues.

Officers (2002–2003)

Pres. Michael W. Dennis; *Pres.-Elect* Marjorie M. K. Hlava; *Past Pres.* R. Paul Ryan.

Directors

Barbara T. Bauldock, Linda A. Beebe, Mary Berger, Kevin A. Bouley, David Brown, Terence Ford, Lucian A. Parziale, Linda Sacks, Sally Sinn.

Staff

Exec. Dir. Bonnie Lawlor. E-mail blawlor@nfais.org; *Dir., Planning and Communications* Jill O'Neill. E-mail jilloneill@nfais.org; *Customer Service* Margaret Manson. E-mail mmanson@nfais.org.

Publications

NFAIS Newsletter (mo.; North America $120; elsewhere $135).

For a detailed list of NFAIS publications, see the NFAIS Web site (http://www.nfais.org).

National Information Standards Organization

Executive Director, Patricia R. Harris
4733 Bethesda Ave., Suite 300, Bethesda, MD 20814
301-654-2512, fax 301-654-1721
E-mail nisohq@niso.org, World Wide Web http://www.niso.org

Object

To initiate, develop, maintain, and publish technical standards for information services, libraries, publishers, and others involved in the business of the creation, storage, preservation, sharing, accession, and dissemination of information. Experts from their respective fields volunteer to lend their expertise in the development of NISO standards. The standards are approved by the consensus body of NISO's voting membership, which consists of 70+ voting members representing libraries, government, associations, and private businesses and organizations. NISO is supported by its membership and corporate grants. Formerly a committee of the American National Standards Institute (ANSI), NISO, formed in 1939, was incorporated in 1983 as a nonprofit educational organization. NISO is accredited by ANSI and serves as the U.S. Technical Advisory Group to ISO/TC 46.

Membership

Memb. 70+. Open to any organization, association, government agency, or company willing to participate in and having substantial concern for the development of NISO standards.

Officers

Chair Beverly P. Lynch, Univ. of California, Los Angeles, CA 90095; *V. Chair/Chair-Elect* Jan Peterson, V.P., Content Development, Infotrieve, 10850 Wilshire Blvd., Los Angeles, CA 90024; *Secy.* Patricia R. Harris, NISO, 4733 Bethesda Ave., Suite 300, Bethesda, MD 20814; *Treas.* Carl Grant, Pres., ExLibris (USA), Inc., Chicago, IL 60614; *Past Chair* Donald J. Muccino, Dublin, OH 43017.

Publications

Information Standards Quarterly (q.; $85; foreign $125).

NISO published standards are available free of charge as downloadable PDF files from the NISO Web site (http://www.niso.org). Standards in hard copy are available for sale on the Web site. The *NISO Annual Report* is available on request.

REFORMA (National Association to Promote Library Services to Latinos and the Spanish-Speaking)

President, Ben Ocón
Day-Riverside Library, 1575 W. 1000 North
Salt Lake City, UT 84116

Object

Promoting library services to the Spanish-speaking for more than 30 years, REFORMA, an affiliate of the American Library Association, works in a number of areas: to promote the development of library collections to include Spanish-language and Latino-oriented materials; the recruitment of more bilingual and bicultural professionals and support staff; the development of library services and programs that meet the needs of the Latino community; the establishment of a national network among individuals who share our goals; the education of the U.S. Latino population in regard to the availability and types of library services; and lobbying efforts to preserve existing library resource centers serving the interest of Latinos.

Membership

Memb. 700. Any person who is supportive of the goals and objectives of REFORMA.

Officers

Pres. Ben Ocón, Salt Lake City Public Lib. Tel. 801-594-8632, email bocon@mail.sclpl. lib.ut.us; *Pres.-Elect* Linda Chavez-Doyle, County of Los Angeles Public Lib. Tel. 310-830-0231, e-mail lcdoyle@lhqsmpt.colapl. org; *Past Pres.* Susana Hinojosa, Doe Lib., Univ. of California at Berkeley. Tel. 510-643-9347, e-mail shinojos@library.berkeley. edu; *Treas.* Ramona Grijalva, Tucson Lib. Tel. 520-791-4791, e-mail Rgrijal1@ci. tucson.az.us; *Secy.* Diana Morales, Houston Public Lib. Tel. 832-393-1720, e-mail Diana. Morales@cityofhouston.net; *Newsletter Ed.* Pedro Reynoso. Tel. 909-607-1298, e-mail pedro.reynoso@libraries.claremont.edu; *Ar-*

chivist Sal Guereña. Tel. 805-893-8563, e-mail guerena@library.ucsb.edu.

Publication

REFORMA Newsletter (q.; memb.). Ed. Pedro Reynoso, Honnold/Mudd Lib., Claremont Colleges, 800 N. Dartmouth Ave., Claremont, CA 91711. Tel. 909-607-1298, e-mail pedro.reynoso@libraries. claremont.edu.

Committees

Pura Belpré Award. Rose Treviño.
Children's and Young Adult Services. Maria Mena, Rose Treviño.
Education. Sonia Ramirez-Wohlmuth.
Finance. Susana Hinojosa.
Fund-raising. Ben Ocón.
Information Technology. Lily Castillo-Speed.
International Relations. Hector Marino.
Joint Ethnic Caucus Conference. John Ayala, Toni Bissessar.
Legislative. Jacqueline Ayala.
Librarian of the Year. Rafaela Castro.
Member at Large. Michael Shapiro.
Membership. Derrie Perez.
Mentoring Committee. Beckie Brazell.
Nominations. Ina Rimpau.
Organizational Development. Bob Diaz.
Program Committee. Linda Chavez-Doyle.
Public Relations. Adalin Torres-Zayas.
Scholarship. Jose Aguiñaga.

Meetings

General membership and board meetings take place at the American Library Association's Midwinter Meeting and Annual Conference.

RLG
(formerly Research Libraries Group)

Manager of Corporate Communications, Jennifer Hartzell
1200 Villa St., Mountain View, CA 94041-1100
650-691-2207, fax 650-964-0943
E-mail jlh@notes.rlg.org
World Wide Web http://www.rlg.org

Object

Founded as the Research Libraries Group in 1974, RLG is a not-for-profit membership corporation of universities, national libraries, archives, and other memory institutions with remarkable collections for research and learning. RLG and its members collaborate on standards and specific projects to bring these collections online, help deliver them around the world, and support their preservation in digital form. As part of this work, RLG offers Internet-based services to institutions and individuals for improving information discovery and use. RLG's main classes of information, available over the Web, are *RLG Library Resources* (international union catalogs), *RLG Citation Resources* (article- and chapter-level indexing), *RLG Archival Resources* (full-text finding aids and archival collections cataloging), and *RLG Cultural Resources* (such as the RLG Cultural Materials digitized objects database and the AMICO Library of high-quality art multimedia and descriptions, created by the Art Museum Image Consortium). *RLG's ILL Manager* is peer-to-peer PC-based software for handling an institution's interlibrary loan traffic. CJK, Eureka, Marcadia, and RLIN are registered trademarks of the Research Libraries Group, Inc. AMICO Library is a trademark of the Art Museum Image Consortium.

Membership

Memb. 160+. Membership is open to any nonprofit institution with an educational, cultural, or scientific mission. There are two membership categories: general and special. General members are institutions that serve a clientele of more than 5,000 faculty, academic staff, research staff, professional staff, students, fellows, or members. Special members serve a similar clientele of 5,000 or fewer.

Directors

RLG has a 19-member board of directors, comprising 12 directors elected from and by RLG's member institutions, up to six at-large directors elected by the board itself, and the president. Theirs is the overall responsibility for the organization's governance and for ensuring that it fulfills its purpose and goals. Annual board elections are held in the spring. In 2003 the board's chair is Reg Carr, director of University Library Services at the University of Oxford and Bodley's Librarian. For a current list of directors, see the Web site http://www.rlg.org/boardbio.html.

Staff

Pres. and CEO James Michalko; *Dir., Integrated Information Services* Susan Yoder; *Dir., Member Programs and Initiatives* Linda West; *Dir., Customer and Operations Support* Jack Grantham; *Dir., Computer Development* David Richards; *Dir., Finance and Administration, and CFO* John Sundell. There are approximately 100 staff, headquartered in Mountain View, California, with a second office in New York City.

Publications

RLG regularly issues Web-based informational, research, and user publications, and more publishes in print. See http://www.rlg.org, or contact RLG for more information. RLG newsletters comprise:

NewsScan Daily (daily; sponsored online summary of information technology news).

RLG News (2 a year; 20-page magazine).

RLG DigiNews (bi-m.; Web-based newsletter to help keep pace with preservation uses of digitization).

RLG Focus (bi-m.; Web-based user services newsletter).

ShelfLife (weekly; online executive news summary for information professionals that provides context for RLG's major initiatives).

Scholarly Publishing and Academic Resources Coalition (SPARC)

Enterprise Director, Richard Johnson
21 Dupont Circle, Suite 800, Washington, DC 20036
202-296-2296, fax 202-872-0884
E-mail sparc@arl.org
World Wide Web http://www.arl.org/sparc

Mission

SPARC (the Scholarly Publishing and Academic Resources Coalition) is an alliance of academic and research libraries and organizations founded as an initiative of the Association of Research Libraries to correct market dysfunctions in the scholarly publishing system. These dysfunctions have driven up the cost of scholarly journals (especially in science, technology, and medicine) to unsupportable high levels that inhibit the advancement of scholarship and are at odds with fundamental needs of scholars and the academic enterprise.

SPARC is a catalyst for action. Its pragmatic agenda stimulates the emergence of new systems that expand dissemination of research and reduce financial pressures on libraries. Action by SPARC in concert with other stakeholders will help unleash the promise of the networked digital environment to serve scholarship.

Because of the complex nature of scholarly communication across many disciplines with widely varying traditions, SPARC promotes and supports experimentation with several promising scenarios. It focuses on linking broad advocacy of change with real-world demonstrations of how change might actually work. Three key strategies form the basis of SPARC activity:

- *Expand competition in the journals marketplace.* SPARC seeks to introduce new competitive forces in the journals market as a means of controlling prices. The strategy promotes more-effective journal price signaling to faculty and supports the start-up of affordable alternative journals.

- *Introduce alternatives to the subscription model.* The access-restricting subscription model of financing publication of research is an artifact of the print environment. SPARC encourages new business models that support open electronic access to research by recovering publication costs via means other than subscriptions (such as publication fees).

- *Disaggregate the core functions of scholarly publication.* As a means of squeezing cost inefficiencies out of the publishing process, this strategy envisions the logical separation of scholars' articles and the discreet services that enhance their value. SPARC supports the development of interoperable "open archives" of articles (e.g., institutional or disciplinary repositories) that interact with value-adding services such as peer review, linking, and searching as a new framework for scholarly communications with attractive long-term potential.

These strategies are advanced via several types of SPARC activity:

- *Incubation of alternative publishing ventures and initiatives.* SPARC reduces the risk faced by alternative publications and models via publisher partnership programs that marshal library support of innovative new journal publishing programs, and business planning services that help nonprofit ventures organize for sustainability.
- *Advocacy of fundamental changes in the system and the culture of scholarly communication.* This encompasses outreach to various stakeholder groups (e.g., librarians, faculty, editorial boards, higher education administrators, research funding agencies) and ongoing communications activities that build support for expanded institutional and scholarly community roles in and control over the scholarly communication process.
- *Education activities aimed at enhancing public awareness of scholarly communication issues and options.*

Membership

Memb. 198, with eight affiliates. Membership is institutional. Full member dues $5,000 a year, with $7,500 purchase commitment. Other membership categories are available.

SPARC Europe members are listed at http://www.sparceurope.org.

Steering Committee (2003)

Sherrie Bergman, Bowdoin College; Ray English, Dir. of Libs., Oberlin College; Kenneth Frazier, Dir. of Libs., Univ. of Wisconsin–Madison; Sarah Michalak, Dir., Univ. of Utah Lib.; James Neal, V.P. for Info. Services and Univ. Libn., Columbia Univ.; *Liaison to SPARC Europe Steering Committee* J. S. M. (Bas) Savenije, Univ. Libn., Utrecht Univ. (Netherlands).

Publications

SPARC Institutional Repository Checklist and Resource Guide (http://www.arl.org/sparc/IR/IR_Guide.html).

The Case for Institutional Repositories: A SPARC Position Paper (http://www.arl.org/sparc/IR/ir.html).

SPARC e-news (subscribe by sending name, title, organization and e-mail address to kerri@arl.org).

Declaring Independence: A Guide to Creating Community-Controlled Science Journals (http://www.arl.org/sparc/di).

Gaining Independence: A Manual for Planning the Launch of an Electronic Publishing Venture (http://www.arl.org/sparc/GI).

Media Map: Charting a Media Relations Strategy (http://www.arl.org/MediaMap.pdf).

Society for Scholarly Publishing

Executive Directors, Francine Butler, Jerry Bowman
10200 W. 44 Ave., Suite 304, Wheat Ridge, CO 80033
303-422-3914, fax 303-422-8894
E-mail ssp@resourcenter.com
World Wide Web http://www.sspnet.org

Object

To draw together individuals involved in the process of scholarly publishing. This process requires successful interaction of the many functions performed within the scholarly community. The Society for Scholarly Publishing (SSP) provides the leadership for such interaction by creating opportunities for the exchange of information and opinions among scholars, editors, publishers, librarians, printers, booksellers, and all others engaged in scholarly publishing.

Membership

Memb. 800. Open to all with an interest in the scholarly publishing process and dissemination of information. Dues (Indiv.) $105; (Supporting) $1,000; (Sustaining) $2,500. Year. Jan. 1–Dec. 31.

Executive Committee (2002–2003)

Pres. Ed Barnas, Cambridge Univ. Press; *Pres.-Elect* Margaret Reich, American Physiological Society; *Past Pres.* Bill Kasdorf, Impressions Book and Journal Services; *Secy.-Treas.* Ray Fastiggi, Rockefeller Univ. Press.

Meetings

An annual meeting is conducted in late May/June; the location changes each year. Additionally, SSP conducts several seminars throughout the year and a Top Management Roundtable each fall.

Society of American Archivists

Interim Executive Co-Directors, Carroll Dendler, Debbie Nolan
527 S. Wells St., Fifth fl., Chicago, IL 60607
312-922-0140, fax 312-347-1452
World Wide Web http://www.archivists.org

Object

Provides leadership to ensure the identification, preservation, and use of records of historic value. Founded 1936.

Membership

Memb. 3,600. Dues (Indiv.) $70–$170, graduated according to salary; (Assoc.) $70, domestic; (Student) $40; (Inst.) $225; (Sustaining) $440.

Officers (2002–2003)

Pres. Peter Hirtle; *V.P.* Tim Ericson; *Treas.* Elizabeth Adkins.

Council

Thomas Battle, Dana Bell-Russel, Frank Boles, Tom Connors, Jackie Dooley, Elaine Engst, David Haury, Richard Pearce-Moses, Megan Sniffin-Marinoff, Joel Wurl.

Staff

Interim Co-Exec. Dirs. Carroll Dendler, Debbie Nolan; *Memb. Services Coord.* Jeanette Spears; *Publishing Dir.* Teresa Brinati; *Dir. of Finance* Carroll Dendler; *Educ. Dirs.* Solveig Desutter, Patricia O'Hara; *Program Coord.* Carlos Salgado.

Publications

American Archivist (q.; $85; foreign $90). *Ed.* Philip Eppard; *Managing Ed.* Teresa Brinati. Books for review and related correspondence should be addressed to the managing editor.

Archival Outlook (bi-m.; memb.). *Ed.* Teresa Brinati.

Software and Information Industry Association

1090 Vermont Ave. N.W., Washington, DC 20005
Tel. 202-289-7442, fax 202-289-7097
World Wide Web http://www.siia.net

Membership

Memb. 1,200 companies. Formed January 1, 1999, through the merger of the Software Publishers Association (SPA) and the Information Industry Association (IIA). Open to companies involved in the creation, distribution, and use of software information products, services, and technologies. For details on membership and dues, see the SIIA Web site.

Staff

Pres. Kenneth Wasch. E-mail kwasch@siia.net; *Exec. V.P.* Lauren Hall. E-mail lhall@siia.net.

Board of Directors

Robert Antonucci, Riverdeep Interactive Learning; Graham Beachum, II, Edge Technology Group; Daniel Cooperman, Oracle Corp.; Robert Firestone, Dow Jones Electronic Publishing; Elizabeth Frazee, AOL Time Warner; Edward A. Friedland, Thomson Corp.; Dale Fuller, Borland Software Corp.; Glenn Goldberg, McGraw-Hill Companies; Traver Gruen-Kennedy, Citrix Systems; Kathy Hurley, NetSchools Corp.; R. Douglas Kemp, Bloomberg L.P.; Kelly Jo MacArthur, RealNetworks; Steve Manzo, Reed Elsevier; Robert Merry, Congressional Quarterly; Michael Morris, Sun Microsystems; Gary Schuster, Novell; Michael Wheeler, Westerly Partners; Kenneth Wasch, SIIA.

Special Libraries Association

Acting Executive Director, Lynn K. Smith
1700 18th St. N.W., Washington, DC 20009-2514
202-234-4700, fax 202-265-9317
E-mail sla@sla.org, World Wide Web http://www.sla.org

Mission

To advance the leadership role of special librarians in putting knowledge to work in the information- and knowledge-based society. The association offers myriad programs and services designed to help its members serve their customers more effectively and succeed in an increasingly challenging environment of information management and technology.

Membership

Memb. 13,500. Dues (Sustaining) $500; (Indiv.) $125; (Student) $35. Year. July–June.

Officers (July 2002–June 2003)

Pres. William Fisher; *Pres.-Elect* Cynthia Hill; *Treas.* Richard G. Geiger; *Chapter Cabinet Chair* Stephanie D. Tolson; *Chapter Cabinet Chair-Elect* Davenport Robertson; *Div. Cabinet Chair* Karen Kreizman-Reczek; *Div. Chapter Chair-Elect* Pam Rollo; *Past Pres.* Hope N. Tillman.

Directors

Officers; Marjorie M. K. Hlava, Christine De Bow Klein, Jesus Lau, Dee Magnoni, Barbara Spiegelman, David Stern.

Publication

Information Outlook (mo.) (memb., nonmemb. $125/yr.)

Committee Chairpersons

Association Office Operations. Bill Fisher.
Awards and Honors. Donna Scheeder.
Bylaws. Marilyn Bromley.
Cataloging. Jian Qin.
Committees. Richard Wallace.
Conference Plan (2003). Agnes Mattis.
Consultation Service. Gail Stahl.
Diversity Leadership Development. Jacqueline Cenacveira.
Finance. Richard Geiger.
International Relations. Nancy Stewart.
Nominating. Sandy Spurlock.
Professional Development. Lynne McCay.
Public Policy. Pat Wilson.
Public Relations. Ellen Cartledge.
Research. Roberta Brody.
SLA Endowment Fund Grants. Lorri Zipperer.
SLA Scholarship. Rebecca Vargha.
Strategic Planning. Christine De Bow Klein.
Student and Academic Relations. Claire McInerney.
Technical Standards. Marcia Lei Zeng.

Theatre Library Association

c/o The Shubert Archive, 149 W. 45 St., New York, NY 10036
212-944-3895, fax 212-944-4139
World Wide Web http://tla.library.unt.edu

Object

To further the interests of collecting, preserving, and using theater, cinema, and performing-arts materials in libraries, museums, and private collections. Founded 1937.

Membership

Memb. 500. Dues (Indiv./Inst.) $30. Year. Jan. 1–Dec. 31.

Officers

Pres. Kevin Winkler, New York Public Lib. for the Performing Arts; *V.P.* Martha S. LoMonaco, Fairfield Univ.; *Exec. Secy.* Camille Croce Dee, independent researcher; *Treas.* Paul Newman, private collector.

Executive Board

Pamela Bloom, Maryann Chach, Annette Fern, Mary Ann Jensen, Florence M. Jumonville, Brigitte J. Kueppers, Mark Maniak, Annette Marotta, Robert W. Melton, Karen Nickeson, Kenneth Schlesinger, Daniel J. Watermeier, *Honorary* Paul Myers; *Historian* Louis A. Rachow; *Legal Counsel* Madeleine Nichols.

Publications

Broadside (q.; memb.). *Ed.* Ellen Truax.
Performing Arts Resources (occasional; memb.).
Membership Directory. Ed. Maryann Chach.

Committee Chairpersons

Finance. Paul Newman.
Membership. Paul Newman, Maryann Chach, Kenneth Schlesinger.
Nominating. Bob Taylor.
Professional Award. Nena Couch, Camille Croce Dee.
Programs. Kevin Winkler.
Strategic Planning. Martha S. LoMonaco.
TLA/Freedley Awards. Richard Wall.

Urban Libraries Council

President, Eleanor Jo Rodger
1603 Orrington Ave., Suite 1080, Evanston, IL 60201
847-866-9999, fax 847-866-9989
E-mail info@urbanlibraries.org
World Wide Web http://www.urbanlibraries.org

Object

To identify and make known the opportunities for urban libraries serving cities of 100,000 or more individuals, located in a Standard Metropolitan Statistical Area; to provide information on state and federal legislation affecting urban library programs and systems; to facilitate the exchange of ideas and programs of member libraries and other libraries; to develop programs that enable libraries to act as a focus of community development and to supply the informational needs of the new urban populations; to conduct research and educational programs that will benefit urban libraries and to solicit and accept grants, contributions, and donations essential to their implementation.

ULC currently receives core funding from membership dues. Current major projects supported by grant funding from a variety of sources include: Community Partnerships for Informal Lifelong Learning (funded by a research grant from the Institute for Museum and Library Services), and the Executive Leadership Institute (funded by the Institute for Museum and Library Services, the Bill and Melinda Gates Foundation, and the W. K. Kellogg Foundation). ULC is a 501(c)(3) not-for-profit corporation based in the state of Illinois.

Membership

Membership is open to public libraries serving populations of 100,000 or more located in a Standard Metropolitan Statistical Area and to corporations specializing in library-related materials and services. Annual dues are based on the size of the library's operating budget, according to the following schedule: under $2 million to $10 million, $3,000; over $10 million, $5,000. In addition, ULC member libraries may choose Sustaining or Contributing status (Sustaining, $12,000; Contributing, $7,000). Corporate membership dues are $5,000.

Officers (2002–2003)

Chair Jim Fish, Dir., Baltimore County Public Lib., 320 York Rd., Towson, MD. Tel. 410-887-6160; *Vice-Chair/Chair-Elect* Duncan Highsmith, Pres., Highsmith, Inc., W5527 Hwy. 106, Box 800, Fort Atkinson, WI 53538. Tel. 920-563-9571; *Secy./Treas.* Donna Nicely, Dir., Nashville Public Lib., 615 Church St., Nashville, TN 37219. Tel. 615-862-5760.

Officers serve one-year terms, members of the executive board two-year terms. New officers are elected and take office at the summer annual meeting of the council.

Executive Board

Dianne Campbell. E-mail diannescampbell@hotmail.com; Mary Dempsey. E-mail mdempsey@chipublib.org; Herb Elish. E-mail elishh@carnegielibrary.org; Jim Fish. E-mail jfish@mail.bcpl.net; Diane Frankel. E-mail dfrankel@irvine.org; Duncan Highsmith. E-mail dhighsmith@highsmith.com; Charles Higueras. E-mail chigueras@ghcp.com; Laura Isenstein. E-mail lisenstein@ci.sat.tx.us; Wai-Fong Lee. E-mail wflee@sccd.ctc.edu; Jenny McCurdy. E-mail jenny.mccurdy@gbhcs.org; Michael Morand. E-mail michael.morand@yale.edu; Donna Nicely. E-mail donna_nicely@metro.nashville.org; Pamela J. Seigle. E-mail pseigle@wellesley.edu.

Key Staff

Pres. Eleanor Jo "Joey" Rodger; *Senior V.P., Admin./Member Services* Bridget A. Bradley; *V.P., Program/Development.* Danielle Milam.

State, Provincial, and Regional Library Associations

The associations in this section are organized under three headings: United States, Canada, and Regional. Both the United States and Canada are represented under Regional associations.

United States

Alabama

Memb. 1,200. Term of Office. Apr. 2002–Apr. 2003. Publication. *The Alabama Librarian* (q.).

Pres. Paulette Williams, Shelby County Schools, 36 Sixth Ave. S.E., Alabaster 35007. Tel. 205-682-5921, fax 205-682-5925, e-mail pwilliams@shebyed.k12.al.us; *Pres.-Elect* Juanita Owes, Montgomery Public Lib., Box 1950, Montgomery 36102. Tel. 334-240-4300, fax 334-240-4977, e-mail jowes@mccpl.lib.al.us; *Past Pres.* Henry Stewart, Dean, Lib. Services, Wallace Hall, Troy State Univ., Troy 36082. Tel. 334-670-3263, fax 334-670-3694, e-mail hstewart@troyst.edu; *Exec. Dir.* Sara Warren, Alabama Lib. Assn., 400 S. Union St., Suite 395, Montgomery 36104. Tel. 334-263-1272, fax 334-265-1281, e-mail psgllc@bellsouth.net.

Address correspondence to the executive director.

World Wide Web http://allaonline.home.mindspring.com.

Alaska

Memb. 463. Publication. *Newspoke* (bi-mo.).

Pres. Patricia Linville. E-mail plinville@cityofseward.net; *V.P./Committees* Greg Hill. E-mail greg.hill@fnsb.lib.ak.us; *V.P./Conference* Deborah Mole. E-mailafdlm2@uaa.alaska.edu; *Secy.* Freya Anderson. E-mail freya_anderson@eed.state.ak.us; *Treas.* Diane Ruess. E-mail ffder@aurora.uaf; *Exec. Officer* Mary Jennings. E-mail exec_officer@akla.org.

Address correspondence to the secretary, Alaska Lib. Assn., Box 81084, Fairbanks 99708. Fax 877-863-1401, e-mail akla@akla.org.

World Wide Web http://www.akla.org.

Arizona

Memb. 1,000. Term of Office. Nov. 2002–Dec. 2003. Publication. *AzLA Newsletter* (mo.).

Pres. Brenda Brown, Peoria Public Lib. Tel. 623-773-7557, e-mail brendab@peoriaaz.com; *Pres.-Elect* Betsy Stunz-Hall, Tucson Pima Public Lib. Tel. 520-791-4391, fax 520-791-3213, e-mail bstunz1@ci.tucson.az.us; *Past Pres.* Robert Shupe, Mohave Community College. Tel. 928-757-0802, fax 757-08871, e-mail robshu@mohave.edu; *Treas.* Carol Damaso, Scotttsdale Public Lib./Mustang. Tel. 480-312-6031, fax 480-312-6084, e-mail cdamaso@ci.scottsdale.az.us; *Secy.* Louis Howley, Phoenix Public Lib./Cholla. Tel. 602-534-3775, e-mail lhowley@mindspring.com; *Exec. Secy.* Jean Johnson, 14449 N. 73 St., Scottsdale 85260-3133. Tel. 480-998-1954, fax 480-998-7838, e-mail meetmore@aol.com.

Address correspondence to the executive secretary.

Arkansas

Memb. 600. Term of Office. Jan.–Dec. 2003. Publication. *Arkansas Libraries* (bi-mo.).

Pres. Dwain Gordon, Central Arkansas Lib. System, 100 Rock St., Little Rock 72201. Tel. 501-918-3053, fax 501-375-7451, e-mail dwain@cals.lib.ar.us; *V.P./Pres.-Elect* Loretta Edwards, Univ. of Arkansas for Medical Sciences, 4301 W. Markham, Slot 586, Little Rock 72205. Tel. 501-686-6752, fax 501-686-6745, e-mail edwards lorettaj@uams.edu; *Secy.-Treas.* Sandy Olson, Univ. of Central Arkansas, 201 Donaghey Ave., Conway 72035. Tel. 501-450-5210, fax 501-450-3234, e-mail sandyo@mail.uca.edu; *Past Pres.* Barbie James, Forrest City H.S., 467 Victoria St., Forrest City 72335. Tel. 870-633-1464 ext. 12, fax 870-

261-1844, e-mail jamesb@fcsd.grsc.k12.ar.
us; *Exec. Dir.* Jennifer Coleman, Arkansas
Lib. Assn., 9 Shackleford Plaza, Suite 1, Little Rock 72211. Tel. 501-228-0775, fax 501-
228-5535, e-mail JCole10145@aol.com or
arlassociation@aol.com.

Address correspondence to the executive
director.

World Wide Web http://www.arlib.org.

California

Memb. 2,500. Publication. *California Libraries* (mo., except July/Aug., Nov./Dec.).
Pres. Les Kong, CSU–San Bernardino.
Tel. 909-880-5111, e-mail lkong@csusb.edu;
V.P./Pres.-Elect Susan Hildreth, San Francisco Public Lib. Tel. 415-557-4232, e-mail
shildreth@sfpl.org; *Treas.* Karen Bosch
Cobb, Fresno County Public Lib. Tel. 559-
488-3438, e-mail karen.bosch.cobb@fresno
library.org; *Past Pres.* Anne M. Turner,
Santa Cruz City-County Lib. System. Tel.
831-420-5600, e-mail turnera@santacruzpl.
org; *Exec. Dir./Secy.* Susan E. Negreen, California Lib. Assn., 717 20th St., Suite 200,
Sacramento 95814. Tel. 916-447-8541, fax
916-447-8394, e-mail info@cla-net.org.

Address correspondence to the executive
director.

World Wide Web http://www.cla-net.org.

Colorado

Memb. 1,100. Term of Office. Oct. 2002–
Oct. 2003. Publication. *Colorado Libraries*
(q.). *Co-Eds.* Janet Lee, Dayton Memorial
Lib., D-20, Regis Univ., 3333 Regis Blvd.,
Denver 80221. Tel. 303-458-3552, fax 303-
964-5497, e-mail jlee@regis.edu; Eileen
Dumas, Aurora Public Lib., 14949 E. Alameda Dr., Aurora 80012. Tel. 303-739-6637, fax
303-739-6579, e-mail edumas@ci.aurora.
co.us.
Pres. Donna Jones Morris, Arkansas Valley Regional Lib. Service System, 635 W.
Corona, Suite 113, Pueblo 81004. Tel. 719-
524-2156 ext. 101, e-mail dmorris@avrlss.
org; *V.P./Pres.-Elect* Paul Paladino, Montrose Lib. District, 343 S. First St., Montrose
81401. Tel. 970-249-9656, fax 970-240-
1901, e-mail ppaladin@colosys.net; *Treas.*

George Jaramillo, Colorado State Univ.
Libs., 110 Morgan Lib., Fort Collins 80523-
1019. Tel. 970-491-1836, fax 970-491-1195,
e-mail gjaramil@manta.colostate.edu; *Secy.*
Linda Van Wert, Gambro, Inc., 10811 W.
Collins Ave., Lakewood 80215. Tel. 303-
231-4159, fax 303-239-2115, e-mail linda.
vanwert@gambrobct.com; *Past Pres.* Lorena
Mitchell, Plains and Peaks Regional Lib. Service System, 530 Communications Circle,
No. 205, Colorado Springs 80905. Tel. 719-
473-3417, e-mail lorenamitchell@earthlink.
net; *Exec. Dir.* Kathleen Sagee.

Address correspondence to the executive
director, Colorado Assn. of Libs., 4350
Wadsworth Blvd., Suite 340, Wheat Ridge
80033. Tel. 303-463-6400, fax 303-431-
9752, e-mail kathleen@cal-webs.org.

World Wide Web http://www.cal-webs.
org.

Connecticut

Memb. 1,100. Term of Office. July 2002–
June 2003. Publication. *Connecticut Li-
braries* (11 a year). *Ed.* David Kapp, 4 Llyn-
wood Dr., Bolton 06040. Tel. 203-647-0697.
Pres. Karen McNulty, Avon Free Public
Lib., 281 Country Club Rd., Avon 06001.
Tel. 860-673-9712; *V.P./Pres.-Elect* Les
Kozerowitz, Norwalk Public Lib., 1 Belden
Ave., Norwalk 06850. Tel. 203-899-2780;
Treas. Veronica Stevenson-Moudamane,
Danbury Public Lib., Danbury 06810. Tel.
203-797-4505; *Past Pres.* Mary Engels, Mid-
dletown Lib. Service Center, 786 S. Main St.,
Middletown 06457. Tel. 860-344-2972;
Admin. Karen Zoller, Connecticut Lib. Assn.,
Box 85, Willimantic 06226. Tel. 860-465-
5006, e-mail kzoller@ecl.org.

Address correspondence to the administrator.

World Wide Web http://cla.uconn.edu.

Delaware

Memb. 300. Term of Office. Apr. 2002–Apr.
2003. Publication. *DLA Online Bulletin*
(http://www.dla.lib.de.us/bulletin.shtml).
Pres. Win Rosenberg, Rehoboth Beach
Public Lib., 226 Rehoboth Ave., Rehoboth
Beach 19971. Tel. 302-227-8044, fax 302-

227-0597, e-mail wrosenberg@delaware.net; V.P./Pres.-Elect Suzanne Smith, Dickinson H.S. Lib.,1801 Milltown Rd., Wilmington 19808-4099. Tel. 302-992-5500, e-mail suzanne.smith@redclay.k12.de.us; Treas. Nick Chiarkas, Univ. of Delaware Lib., Newark 19717-5267. Tel. 302-831-0234, fax 302-831-1046, e-mail chiarkas@udel.edu; Secy. Shelia Anderson, Dover Public Lib., 45 S. State St., Dover 19901. Tel. 302-736-7030, e-mail sanderso@kentnet.dtcc.edu. Address correspondence to the association, Box 816, Dover 19903-0816. E-mail dla@dla.lib.de.us.

World Wide Web http://www.dla.lib.de.us/aboutus.html.

District of Columbia

Memb. 300. Term of Office. July 2002–June 2003. Publication. *Intercom* (mo.).

Pres. Andrea Gruhl. Tel./fax 301-596-5460, e-mail andreagruhl@aol.com; *V.P./Pres.-Elect* Jean Craigwell. Tel. 202-458-6172, e-mail jcwell@juno.com; *Secy.* Barbara Conaty, Lib. of Congress. Tel. 202-707-2715, fax 202-707-0810, e-mail bcon@loc.gov; *Treas.* William L. Turner, Catholic Univ. of America School of Lib. and Info. Science. Tel. 202-319-5085, fax 202-319-5574, e-mail turnerjr@cua.edu.

Address correspondence to the association, Box 14177, Benjamin Franklin Sta., Washington, DC 20044.

World Wide Web http://www.dcla.org.

Florida

Memb. (Indiv.) 1,300+. Term of Office. July 2002–June 2003. Publication. *Florida Libraries* (bi-ann.). *Ed.* Gloria Colvin, Strozier Lib., Florida State Univ., Tallahassee 32306. Tel. 850-644-5211, fax 850-644-5016, e-mail gcolvin@mailer.fsu.edu.

Pres. Marta Westall, Central Florida Lib. Cooperative. Tel. 407-644-9050, fax 407-644-7023, e-mail mwestall@cflc.net; *V.P./Pres.-Elect* John Szabo, St. Petersburg Public Lib. E-mail jszabo@clearwater-fl.com; *Secy.* Rob Lenholt, DuPont Ball Lib., Stetson Univ. Tel. 904-822-7181, fax 904-822-7199, e-mail rlenholt@stetson.edu; *Treas.* Charlie Parker,

State Lib. of Florida. E-mail cparker@mail.dos.state.fl.us; *Past Pres.* Betty D. Johnson, Dupont-Ball Lib., Stetson Univ. E-mail betty.johnson@stetson.edu; *Exec. Secy.* Marjorie Stealey, Florida Lib. Assn., 1133 W. Morse Blvd., Winter Park 32789. Tel. 407-647-8839, fax 407-629-2502, e-mail mjs@crowsegal.com.

Address correspondence to the executive secretary.

World Wide Web http://www.flalib.org.

Georgia

Memb. 1,080. Term of Office. Dec. 2002–Dec. 2003. Publication. *Georgia Library Quarterly. Ed.* Susan Cooley, Sara Hightower Regional Lib., 205 Riverside Pkwy., Rome 30161. Tel. 706-236-4621, fax 706-236-4631, e-mail cooleys@mail.floyd.public.lib.ga.us.

Pres. Gordon N. Baker, Coord. of Instructional Technology, Henry County Schools, Dept. of Technical Services, 396 Tomlinson St., McDonough 30253. Tel. 770-957-6601 ext. 147, fax 678-583-4974, e-mail gnbaker@henry.k12.ga.us; *1st V. P./Pres.-Elect* George Gaumond, Dir., Odum Lib., Valdosta State Univ., Valdosta 31698. Tel. 229-333-5860, fax 229-259-5055, e-mail ggaumond@valdosta.edu; *2nd V.P.* Jane Richards, DeKalb County Public Lib., 3560 Kensington Rd., Decatur 30032. Tel. 404-508-7190 ext. 38; fax 404-508-7184, e-mail richardsj@dekalblibrary.org; *Secy.* Callie McGinnis, Dir., Simon Schwob Memorial Lib., Columbus State Univ., 4225 University Ave., Columbus 31907. Tel. 706-562-1494, e-mail mcginnis_callie@colstate.edu; *Treas.* Robert E. Fox, Jr., Dir. Lib. Services, Clayton College and State Univ., Box 285, Morrow 30260. Tel. 770-961-3520, fax 770-961-3712, e-mail bobfox@mail.clayton.edu; *ALA Councillor* Ann Hamilton, Zach Henderson Lib., Georgia Southern Univ., Box 8074, Statesboro 30460-8074. Tel. 912-681-5115, fax 912-681-0093, e-mail ahamilton@gasou.edu; *Past Pres.* Tom Budlong, 949 Rupley Dr. N.E., Atlanta 30306-3818. Tel 404-874-7483, e-mail tbudlong@bellsouth.net.

Address correspondence to the president.

World Wide Web http://wwwlib.gsu.edu/gla.

Hawaii

Memb. 320. Publications. *HLA Newsletter* (3 a year).

Pres. Cora Nishimura Eggerman. E-mail coran@lib.state.hi.us; *V.P.* Vacant.

Address correspondence to the association, Box 4441, Honolulu 96812-4441.

World Wide Web http://www.hlaweb.org.

Idaho

Memb. 500. Term of Office. Oct. 2002–Oct. 2003.

Pres. Vicki Kreimeyer, Boise Public Lib., 715 S. Capitol Blvd., Boise 83702. Tel. 208-384-4341, e-mail vkreimeyer@cityofboise.org; *V.P./Pres.-Elect* Vacant; *Secy.* LaRita Shandorff, 1108 Standford, Nampa 83686. Tel. 520-467-8606, e-mail llschandorff@nnu.edu; *Treas.* Pam Bradshaw, Idaho State Lib., 325 W. State St., Boise 82702. Tel. 208-334-2150, e-mail pbradsha@isl.state.id.us; *Past Pres.* Marlene Earnest, 15335 David St., Caldwell 83607. Tel. 208-454-9253 ext. 301, e-mail mearnest@sd139.k12.id.us.

Address correspondence to the president.

World Wide Web http://www.idaho libraries.org.

Illinois

Memb. 3,000. Term of Office. July 2002–July 2003. Publication. *ILA Reporter* (bi-mo.).

Pres. Sylvia Murphy Williams, Dundee Township Public Lib. District, 555 Barrington Ave., Dundee 60118-1422. Tel. 847-428-3661, fax 847-428-0521, e-mail smwill@nslsilus.org; *V.P./Pres.-Elect* Nancy Gillfillan, Fondulac District Lib., 140 E. Washington St., East Peoria 61611-2526; *Treas.* Robert McKay, River Bend Lib. System, 220 W. 23 Ave., Box 125, Coal Valley 61240-9651; *Past Pres.* Arthur P. Young, Univ. Libs., Northern Illinois Univ., De Kalb 60115-2868; *Exec. Dir.* Robert P. Doyle, 33 W. Grand Ave., Suite 301, Chicago 60610-4306. Tel. 312-644-1896, fax 312-644-1899, e-mail ila@ila.org.

Address correspondence to the executive director.

World Wide Web http://www.ila.org.

Indiana

Memb. 3,000+. Term of Office. March 2002–April 2003. Publications. *Focus on Indiana Libraries* (11 a year), *Indiana Libraries* (s. ann.). *Ed.* Patricia Tallman.

Pres. Patricia Steele. Tel. 812-855-0294, fax 812-855-6077, e-mail steele@indiana.edu; *1st V.P.* Nancy McGriff. Tel. 219-767-2263 ext. 389, fax 219-767-2260, e-mail nmcgriff @scentral.k12.in.us; *2nd V.P.* John M. Robson. Tel. 812-877-8365, fax 812-877-8175, e-mail john.robson@rose-hulman.edu; *Secy.* Rhonda Hill. Tel. 317-835-3000 ext. 373, fax 317-835-3012, e-mail rhill@indy.net; *Treas.* Connie Mitchell. Tel. 317-846-7712 ext. 1513, fax 317-571-4066, e-mail cmitchel@ccs.k12.in.us; *Past Pres.* Connie A. Patsiner. Tel./fax 317-329-9163, e-mail iaudio@indy.net; *Exec. Dir.* Linda Kolb. E-mail lkolb@ilfonline.org.

Address correspondence to Indiana Lib. Federation, 941 E. 86 St., Suite 260, Indianapolis 46240. Tel. 317-257-2040, fax 317-257-1389, e-mail ilf@indy.net.

World Wide Web http://www.ilfonline.org.

Iowa

Memb. 1,700. Term of Office. Jan.–Dec. Publication. *The Catalyst* (bi-mo.). *Ed.* Laurie Hews.

Pres. Betty J. Rogers, Stewart Memorial Lib., Coe College, Cedar Rapids 52402. Tel. 319-399-8017, e-mail brogers@coe.edu; *V.P./Pres.-Elect* Kay Weiss, Burlington Public Lib., 501 N. Fourth St., Burlington 52601-5279. Tel. 319-753-1647, e-mail kweiss@aea16.k12.ia.us; *Secy.* Marilyn Murphy. Tel. 319-363-8213 ext. 1244, e-mail marilyn@mmc.mtmercy.edu; *Exec. Dir.* Laurie Hews. Tel. 515-273-5322, fax 515-273-5323, e-mail ialib@mcleodusa.net.

Address correspondence to the association, 3636 Westown Pkwy., Suite 202, West Des Moines 50266.

World Wide Web http://www.iowalibrary association.org.

Kansas

Memb. 1,718. Term of Office. July 2002–June 2003. Publications. *KLA Newsletter* (q.); *KLA Membership Directory* (ann.).

Pres. Robert Walter, Axe Lib., Pittsburg State Univ., Pittsburg 66762. Tel. 620-235-4878, fax 620-235-4090, e-mail bwalter@mail.pittstate.edu; *1st V.P.* Debra Ludwig, Anschutz Lib., Rm. 424A, Univ. of Kansas, 1301 Hoch Auditoria Dr., Lawrence 66045. Tel. 785-864-1376, fax 785-864-5380, e-mail dludwig@ku.edu; *2nd V.P.* Patti Butcher, NEKLS, 3300 Clinton Pkwy., No. 100, Lawrence 66047. Tel. 785-838-4090, fax 785-838-3989, e-mail pbutcher@nekls.org; *Secy.* Barbara Dew, Ottawa Lib., 105 S. Hickory, Ottawa 66067. Tel. 785-242-3080, fax 785-242-8789, e-mail bdew52@yahoo.com; *Past Pres.* Karyl Buffington, Coffeyville Public Lib., 311 W. Tenth St., Coffeyville 67337. Tel. 620-252-1370, fax 620-251-1612, e-mail kbuffington@terraworld.net; *Exec. Dir.* Rosanne Goble, Kansas Library Assn., 1020 Washburn, Topeka, 66604. Tel. 866-552-4636 (toll-free), 785-235-1383, fax 785-663-9506, e-mail kansaslibraryassociation@yahoo.com.

Address correspondence to the executive director.

World Wide Web http://skyways.lib.ks.us/KLA.

Kentucky

Memb. 1,900. Term of Office. Oct. 2002–Oct. 2003. Publication. *Kentucky Libraries* (q.).

Pres. Sue Burch, Univ. of Kentucky, 128 Law Lib., Lexington 40506-0048. Tel. 859-257-8351, fax 859-323-4906, e-mail sburch@uky.edu; *V.P./Pres.-Elect* Carol Nutter, Camden-Carroll Lib., Morehead State Univ., Morehead 40351. Tel. 606-783-5110, fax 606-783-2799, e-mail c.nutter@morehead state.edu; *Secy.* Linda Kompanik, Logan County Public Lib., 201 W. Sixth St., Russellville 42276. Tel. 270-726-6129, fax 270-726-6127, e-mail lindak@loganlibrary.org; *Past Pres.* Terri Kirk, Reidland H.S., 5349 Benton Rd., Paducah 42003. Tel. 270-538-4225, fax 270-538-4211, e-mail tkirk@mccracken.k12.ky.us; *Exec. Secy.* Tom Underwood, 1501 Twilight Trail, Frankfort 40601. Tel. 502-223-5322, fax 502-223-4937, e-mail kylibasn@mis.net.

Address correspondence to the executive secretary.

World Wide Web http://www.kylibasn.org.

Louisiana

Memb. (Indiv.) 1,170; (Inst.) 56. Term of Office. July 2003–June 2004. Publication. *Louisiana Libraries* (q.).

Pres. Charlene Cain. Tel. 225-578-4957, fax 225-578-5773, e-mail llcain@lsu.edu; *Past Pres.* Angelle Deshautelles. Tel. 225-647-8924, fax 225-644-0063, e-mail adeshaut@pelican.state.lib.la.us; *Exec. Dir.* Beverly E. Laughlin, Louisiana Lib. Assn., 421 S. Fourth St., Eunice 70535. Tel. 337-550-7890, fax 337-550-7846, e-mail lalibassoc@yahoo.com.

World Wide Web http://www.llaonline.org.

Maine

Memb. 950. Term of Office. (Pres., V.P.) spring 2002–spring 2004. Publications. *Maine Entry* (q.), *Maine Memo* (mo.).

Pres. Anne Davis, Gardiner Public Lib., 152 Water St., Gardiner 04345. Tel. 207-582-3312, e-mail staff@gpl.lib.me.us; *V.P.* Steve Norman, Belfast Free Lib., 106 High St., Belfast 04915. Tel. 207-338-3884; *Secy.* Vaughan Gagne, Wilton Free Public Lib., Box 454, 6 Goodspeed St., Wilton 04294-0454. Tel. 207-645-4831, e-mail vgagne@wilton-free.lib.me.us; *Treas.* Donna Rasche, Turner Memorial Lib., 39 Second St., Presque Isle 04769-2677. Tel. 207-764-2571, fax 207-768-5756, e-mail drasche@presqueisle.lib.me.us; *Past Pres.* Jay Scherma, Thomas Memorial Lib., 6 Scott Dyer Rd., Cape Elizabeth. Tel. 207-799-1720, e-mail jscherma@thomas.lib.me.us.

Address correspondence to the association, 60 Community Dr., Augusta 04330. Tel. 207-623-8428, fax 207-626-5947.

World Wide Web http://mainelibraries.org.

Maryland

Memb. 1,300. Term of Office. July 2002–July 2003. Publications. *Happenings* (mo.), *The Crab* (q.).

Pres. Dolores Maminski, C. Burr Artz Central Lib., 110 E. Patrick St., Frederick. Tel. 301-694-1613, fax 301-631-3789; *Past Pres.* Karen Trennepohl, Howard County Lib., Savage Branch, 9525 Durness Lane, Laurel 20723. Tel. 410-880-5990, fax 410-880-5999; *Exec. Dir.* Margaret Carty.

Address correspondence to the association, 1401 Hollins St., Baltimore 21223. Tel. 410-947-5090, fax 410-947-5089, e-mail mla@mdlib.org.

World Wide Web http://mdlib.org.

Massachusetts

Memb. (Indiv.) 950; (Inst.) 100. Term of Office. July 2002–June 2003. Publication. *Bay State Libraries* (10 a year).

Pres. Krista McLeod, Nevins Memorial Lib., 305 Broadway, Methuen 01844-6898. Tel. 978-686-4080, fax 978-686-8669, e-mail kristamcleod1@aol.com; *V.P./Pres.-Elect* Barbara Flaherty. Tel. 978-671-0949 ext. 101, fax 978-670-9493, e-mail bflaherty@mailserv.mvlp.lib.ma.us; *Secy.* Meg Clancy. Tel. 413-538-5045, fax 413-539-9250, e-mail mclancy@cwmars.org; *Treas.* Patricia T. Cramer. Tel. 413-568-7833, fax 413-568-1558, e-mail pcramer@exit3.com; *Past Pres.* James Sutton. Tel. 978-623-8401, fax 978-623-8407, e-mail jsutton@mhl.org; *Exec. Secy.* Barry Blaisdell, Massachusetts Lib. Assn., 14 Pleasant St., Gloucester 01930. Tel. 978-282-0415, fax 978-282-1304, e-mail info@masslib.org.

Address correspondence to the executive secretary.

World Wide Web http://www.masslib.org.

Michigan

Memb. (Indiv.) 1,850; (Inst.) 375. Term of Office. July 2002–June 2003 Publications. *Michigan Librarian Newsletter* (6 a year), *Michigan Library Association Forum* e-journal (2 a year).

Pres. Phyllis Jose, Oakland County Lib., Dept. 481, 1200 N. Telegraph Rd., Pontiac 48341-0481. Tel. 248-858-0380, fax 248-858-1234, e-mail pjose@tln.lib.mi.us; *Pres.-Elect* Marcia Warner, Public Libs. of Saginaw. E-mail mwarner@vlc.lib.mi.us; *Secy.* Louise Bugg, Wayne State Univ. E-mail ac3731@wayne.edu; *Treas.* Leslee Nietham-

mer, Saline District Lib., 555 N. Maple Rd., Saline 48176. Tel. 734-429-2313, fax 734-944-0600, e-mail leslee@saline.lib.mi.us; *Past Pres.* Elaine Didier, Kresge Lib., Oakland Univ., 13060 Beacon Hill Dr., Plymouth 48170-6502. Tel. 248-370-2486, fax 248-370-2474, e-mail didier@oakland.edu; *Exec. Dir.* Stephen A. Kershner, Michigan Lib. Assn., 1407 Rensen St., Lansing 48910. Tel. 517-394-2774, fax 517-394-2675, e-mail kershner@mlc.lib.mi.us.

Address correspondence to the executive director.

World Wide Web http://www.mla.lib.mi.us.

Minnesota

Memb. 1,200. Term of Office. (Pres., Pres.-Elect) Jan.–Dec. 2003; (Treas.) Jan. 2001–Dec. 2003; (Secy.) Jan. 2002–Dec. 2003. Publication. *MLA Newsletter* (6 a year).

Pres. Melissa Brechon. Tel. 612-448-9595, fax 612-448-9392, e-mail mbrechon@co.carver.mn.us; *Pres.-Elect* Bill Sozanski. Tel. 218-726-8102, fax 218-726-8019, e-mail bsozansk@d.umn.edu; *Secy.* Michelle Twait. Tel. 507-933-7563, fax 507-933-6292, e-mail mtwait@gac.edu; *Treas.* Sandy Walsh. Tel. 651-486-2301, fax 651-486-2313, e-mail swalsh@ramsey.lib.mn.us; *Past Pres.* Chris Olson. Tel. 651-644-3878, fax 651-644-6258, e-mail olsonc@macalester.edu; *Exec. Dir.* Alison Johnson, Minnesota Lib. Assn., 1619 Dayton Ave., Suite 314, Saint Paul 55104. Tel. 651-641-0982, fax 651-641-3169, e-mail alison@mnlibraryassociation.org.

Address correspondence to the executive director.

World Wide Web http://www.mnlibrary association.org.

Mississippi

Memb. 700. Term of Office. Jan.–Dec. 2003. Publication. *Mississippi Libraries* (q.).

Pres. Prima Plauché, Hancock County Lib. System, 312 Hwy. 90, Bay St. Louis 39520-2595. Tel. 228-467-6836, fax 228-467-5503, e-mail pplauche@hancock.lib.ms.us; *V.P./Pres.-Elect* Juanita Flanders, Hinds Community College, Box 1100, Raymond 39154-1100. Tel. 601-857-3380, fax 601-857-3293, e-mail hjflanders@hinds.cc.ms.us; *Secy.* Sara Morris, Mitchell Memorial Lib., Mississippi

State Univ., Drawer 5408, Mississippi State 39762. Tel. 662-325-9347, fax 662-325-9131, e-mail smorris@library.msstate.edu; *Past Pres.*Terry S. Latour, W. B. Roberts Lib., Delta State Univ., Cleveland 38733. Tel. 662-846-4440, fax 662-846-4443, e-mail tlatour@merlin.deltast.edu; *Exec. Secy.* Mary Julia Anderson, Box 20448, Jackson 39289-1448. Tel. 601-352-3917, fax 601-352-4240, e-mail mla@meta3.net.

Address correspondence to the executive secretary.

World Wide Web http://www.lib.usm.edu/~mla/org/main.html.

Missouri

Memb. 825. Term of Office. Jan.–Dec. 2003. Publication. *MO INFO* (bi-mo.). *Ed.* Jean Ann McCartney.

Pres. Karen Hicklin, Dir., Livingston County Lib., 450 Locust St., Chillicothe 64601. Tel. 660-646-0547, fax 660-646-5504, e-mail ugy001@mail.connect.more. net; *Pres.-Elect* Victor Gragg, Trustee, Mid-Continent Public Lib., 15616 E. 24 Hwy., Independence 64050. Tel. 816-796-4408, fax 816-521-7253, e-mail vgragg@juno.com; *Exec. Dir.* Jean Ann McCartney, Missouri Lib. Assn., 1306 Business 63 S., Suite B, Columbia 65201. Tel. 573-449-4627, fax 573-449-4655, e-mail jmccartn@mail.more. net.

Address correspondence to the executive director.

World Wide Web http://www.molib.org.

Montana

Memb. 600. Term of Office. July 2002–June 2003. Publication. *Montana Library Focus* (bi-mo.). *Ed.* Pam Henley, Bozeman Public Lib., 220 E. Lamme, Bozeman 59715-3579.

Pres. Coby Johnson, UM–Mansfield Lib., 32 Campus Dr., No. 9936, Missoula 59812-9936. Tel. 406-243-4729, fax 406-243-2060, e-mail ml_cry@selway.umt.edu; *V.P./Pres.-Elect* John Finn, Great Falls Public Lib, 301 2nd Ave. N., Great Falls 59401-2593. Tel. 406-453-0349, fax 406-453-0181, e-mail jfinn@mtlib.org; *Secy./Treas.* Susan Howe, Bozeman Public Lib., 220 E. Lamme, Bozeman 59715-3579. Tel. 406-582-2405, fax 406-582-2424, e-mail showe@mtlib.org;

Exec. Dir. Karen A. Hatcher, 510 Arbor, Missoula 59802-3126. Tel. 406-721-3347, fax 406-243-2060, e-mail hatcher@montana. com.

Address correspondence to the executive director.

Nevada

Memb. 450. Term of Office. Jan.–Dec. 2003. Publication. *Nevada Libraries* (q.).

Pres. Holly Van Valkenburgh, Nevada State Lib. and Archives, 100 N. Stewart St., Carson City 89701-4285. Tel. 775-684-3322, fax 775-684-3311, e-mail hvanvalk@clan.lib. nv.us; *V.P./Pres.-Elect* Felton Thomas, Las Vegas/Clark County Lib. District, West Las Vegas Lib. E-mail thomasf@lvccld.org; *Treas.* Ken Bierman, Univ. of Nevada, Las Vegas. E-mail kbierman@ccmail.nevada.edu; *Past Pres.*Tom Fay, Henderson District Public Libs. E-mail tffay@hdpl.org; *Exec. Secy.* Amie Maurins. E-mail amaurins@mail.co. washoe.nv.us.

Address correspondence to the executive secretary.

World Wide Web http://www.nevada libraries.org.

New Hampshire

Memb. 700. Publication. *NHLA News* (bi-mo.).

Pres. Rob Sargent, Franklin Public Lib., 310 Central St., Franklin 03235. E-mail rob.sargent@franklin.lib.nh.us; *V.P.* Andrea Thorpe, Richards Free Lib., 58 N. Main St., Newport 03773. E-mail athorpe@newport. lib.nh.us; *Secy.* Jennifer Bone, Keene Public Lib., 60 Winter St., Keene 03431. E-mail jbone@ci.keene.nh.us; *Past Pres.* Lesley Gaudreau, Wiggin Memorial Lib., Bunker Hill Ave., Stratham 03885. E-mail lesley@ WigginML.org.

Address correspondence to the association, Box 2332, Concord 03302.

World Wide Web http://webster.state.nh. us/nhla.

New Jersey

Memb. 1,700. Term of Office. July 2002–June 2003. Publication. *New Jersey Libraries Newsletter* (mo.).

Pres. Karen Avenick, Camden County Lib., 203 Laurel Rd., Voorhees 08043. Tel. 856-772-1636 ext. 3328, fax 856-772-6105, e-mail karen@camden.lib.nj.us; *V.P.* Patricia Ann Hannon, Emerson Public Lib., 20 Palisade Ave., Emerson 07630. Tel. 201-261-5569, fax 201-262-7999, e-mail pahannon@verizon.net; *2nd V.P.* Carol Phillips, East Brunswick Public Lib., 2 Jean Walling Civic Center, East Brunswick 08816. Tel. 732-390-6789, fax 732-390-6796, e-mail cphillips@ebpl.org; *Secy.* Heidi Cramer, Newark Public Lib., 5 Washington St., Box 630, Newark 07101. Tel. 973-733-7837, fax 973-733-8539, e-mail hcramer@npl.org; *Treas.* Keith McCoy, Roselle Free Public Lib., 104 W. 4 Ave., Roselle 07203. Tel. 908-245-5809, fax 908-298-8881, e-mail wkmccoy@lmxac.org; *Past Pres.* Leslie Burger, Princeton Public Lib., 65 Witherspoon St., Princeton 08542. Tel. 609-924-8822 ext. 253, fax 609-924-7937, e-mail burger@princetonlibrary.org; *Exec. Dir.* Patricia Tumulty, New Jersey Lib. Assn., Box 1534, Trenton 08607. Tel. 609-394-8032, fax 609-394-8164, e-mail ptumulty@njla.org.

Address correspondence to the executive director, Box 1534, Trenton 08607.

World Wide Web http://www.njla.org.

New Mexico

Memb. 550. Term of Office. Apr. 2002–Apr. 2003. Publication. *New Mexico Library Association Newsletter* (6 a year). *Ed.* Lorie Mitchell. Tel. 505-887-9538, e-mail loriem1970@hotmail.com.

Pres. Earl Phillips, 6050 Shadow Hills Rd., Las Cruces 88012. Tel. 505-527-6065, e-mail ephillip@lcps.k12.nm.us; *V.P.* Eileen Longsworth, Alb/Bernalillo, 501 Copper N.W., Albuquerque 87102. Tel. 505-898-3660, fax 505-768-5191, e-mail elongsworth@cabq.gov; *Secy.* Susan Magee, UNM Parish Business Lib., Albuquerque 87131. Tel. 505-277-4909, e-mail smagee@unm.edu; *Treas.* Kathryn Albrecht, NM Tech, 801 Leroy Place, Socorro 87801. Tel. 505-835-5201, e-mail kalbrecht@admin.nmt.edu; *Past Pres.* Kay Krehbiel, NM Tech, Campus Sta., Socorro 87801. Tel. 505-835-5615, e-mail kkrehbie@admin.nmt.edu.

Address correspondence to the association, Box 26074, Albuquerque 87125. Tel. 505-899-7600, e-mail nmla@rt66.com.

World Wide Web http://lib.nmsu.edu/nmla.

New York

Memb. 3,000. Term of Office. Oct. 2002–Nov. 2003. Publication. *NYLA Bulletin* (6 a year). *Ed.* David Titus.

Pres. Diane Courtney. Tel. 914-834-2281, e-mail courtney@wlsmail.org; *Treas.* Mary Brown. Tel. 518-563-5190, e-mail mabrown@northnet.org; *Exec. Dir.* Susan Lehman Keitel, New York Lib. Assn., 252 Hudson Ave., Albany 12210. Tel. 518-432-6952, e-mail nyladirector@pobox.com.

Address correspondence to the executive director.

World Wide Web http://www.nyla.org.

North Carolina

Memb. 1,100. Term of Office. Oct. 2001–Oct. 2003. Publication. *North Carolina Libraries* (q.). *Ed.* Plummer Alston Jones, Jr., Assoc. Professor, Dept. of Libnship., Educ. Technology, and Distance Learning, East Carolina Univ., 122 Joyner E., Greenville 27858-4353. Tel. 252-328-6803, fax 252-328-4368, e-mail jonesp@mail.ecu.edu.

Pres. Ross Holt, Randolph County Public Lib., 201 Worth St., Asheboro 27203. Tel. 336-318-6806, fax 336-318-6823, e-mail rholt@ncsl.dcr.state.nc.us; *V.P./Pres.-Elect* Pauletta Bracy, North Carolina Central Univ., SLIS, Box 19586, Durham 27707. Tel. 919-560-6485, fax 919-560-6402, e-mail pbracy@slis.nccu.edu; *Secy.* Martha Davis, 5002 Marigold Way, Greensboro 27410. Tel. 336-855-0853, e-mail mdavis92627@yahoo.com; *Treas.* Diane Kester, Dept. of Broadcasting, Libnship., and Educ. Technology, 102 Joyner E., Greenville 27858-4353. Tel. 252-328-6621, fax 252-328-4368, e-mail kesterd@mail.ecu.edu; *Admin. Asst.* Caroline J. Walters, North Carolina Lib. Assn., 4646 Mail Service Center, Raleigh 27699-4646. Tel. 919-839-6252, fax 919-839-6253, e-mail nclaonline@ibiblio.org.

Address correspondence to the administrative assistant.

World Wide Web http://www.nclaonline.org.

North Dakota

Memb. (Indiv.) 400; (Inst.) 18. Term of Office. Sept. 2002–Sept. 2003. Publication. *The Good Stuff* (q.). *Ed.* Marlene Anderson, Bismarck State College Lib., Box 5587, Bismarck 58506-5587. Tel. 701-224-5578.

Pres. Kaaren Pupino, Thormodsgard Law Lib., Univ. of North Dakota, Box 9004, Grand Forks 58202-9004. Tel. 701-777-2486, fax 701-777-2217, e-mail Kaaren.Pupino@ thor.law.und.nodak.edu; *Pres.-Elect* Pamela Drayson, Dir., North Dakota State Univ. Libs., Box 5599, Fargo 58205-5599. Tel. 701-231-8887, fax 701-231-6128, e-mail Pamela.Drayson@ndsu.nodak.edu; *Secy.* Marlene Anderson, Bismarck State College Lib., Box 5587, Bismarck 58506-5587. Tel. 701-224-5578, 701-224-5551, e-mail Marlene. Anderson@bsc.nodak.edu; *Treas.* Michael Safratowich, Harley French Lib. of the Health Sciences, Univ. of North Dakota, Box 9002, Grand Forks 58202-9004. Tel. 701-777-2602, fax 701-777-4790, e-mail msafratmedicine. nodak.edu.

Address correspondence to the president.

World Wide Web http://ndsl.lib.state.nd. us/ndla.

Ohio

Memb. 3,400+. Term of Office. Jan.–Dec. 2003. Publications. *Access* (mo.), *Ohio Libraries* (q.).

Chair Meribah Mansfield, Worthington Public Lib., 820 High St., Worthington 43085-4108. Tel. 614-645-2620 ext. 239, fax 614-645-2642, e-mail meribah@worthington libraries.org; *V. Chair* Jack Burtch, 1959 W. Lane Ave., Columbus 43221. Tel. 614-488-9619, e-mail jburtch@baker-hostetler.com; *Secy.* Dave Lehtoma, 37210 Beech Hills Dr., Willoughby Hills 44094. Tel. 440-946-5699, e-mail dlehtoma@wepl.lib.oh.us; *Treas.* Thomas Adkins, Garnet A. Wilson Public Lib. of Pike County, 207 N. Market St., Waverly 45690-1176. Tel. 740-947-4921, fax 740-947-2918, e-mail dirgaw@oplin.lib.oh. us; *Past Chair* JoAnn Scanlon, 2335 Abington Rd., Columbus 43221. Tel. 614-486-3906, e-mail jvsohio@columbus.rr.com; *Exec. Dir.* Douglas S. Evans.

Address correspondence to the executive director, OLC, 35 E. Gay St., Suite 305, Columbus 43215. Tel. 614-221-9057, fax 614-231-6234, e-mail olc@olc.org.

World Wide Web http://www.olc.org.

Oklahoma

Memb. (Indiv.) 1,050; (Inst.) 60. Term of Office. July 2002–June 2003. Publication. *Oklahoma Librarian* (bi-mo.). *Ed.* Pat Williams. E-mail pwilliams@oltn.odl.state.ok.us.

Pres. Kathryn Roots Lewis. E-mail klewis @norman.k12.ok.us; *V.P./Pres.-Elect* Anne Prestamo. E-mail prestamo@att.net; *Secy.* Pauline Boyer Rodriguez. E-mail prodriguez @mls.lib.ok.us; *Treas.* Anne R. Hsieh. E-mail ahsieh@mls.lib.ok.us; *Past Pres.* Wayne Hanway. E-mail whanway@sepl.lib. ok.us; *Exec. Dir.* Kay Boies, 300 Hardy Dr., Edmond 73013. Tel. 405-348-0506, fax 405-348-1629, e-mail kboies@coxinet.net or kboies@ionet.net.

Address correspondence to the executive director.

World Wide Web http://www.oklibs.org.

Oregon

Memb. (Indiv.) 1,049. Publications. *OLA Hotline* (bi-w.), *OLA Quarterly.*

Pres. Connie Bennett, Eugene Public Lib. Tel. 541-682-5363, e-mail connie.j.bennet@ ci.eugene.or.us; *V.P./Pres.-Elect* Faye Chadwell, Univ. of Oregon Lib. Tel. 541-346-1819, e-mail chadwell@uoregon.edu; *Secy.* Steve Skidmore, Siuslaw Public Lib. Tel. 541-997-3132, e-mail skidmore@siuslaw.lib. or.us.

Address correspondence to John McCulley, OLA, Box 2042, Salem OR 97308. Tel. 503-370-7019, e-mail ola@olaweb.org.

World Wide Web http://www.olaweb.org.

Pennsylvania

Memb. 1,800. Term of Office. Jan.–Dec. 2003. Publication. *PaLA Bulletin* (10 a year).

Pres. Olga F. Conneen, Dir., Northampton Community College, 3835 Green Pond Rd., Bethlehem 18020. Tel. 610-861-5358, fax 610-861-5373, e-mail oconneen@northampton. edu; *1st V.P.* Jonelle Prether Darr, Exec. Dir.,

Cumberland County Lib. System. E-mail jdarr@ccpa.net; *2nd V.P.* Marilyn Jenkins, Exec. Dir., Allegheny County Lib. Assn. E-mail jenkinsm@einetwork.net; *Past Pres.* Mary Elizabeth Colombo, Dir., B. F. Jones Memorial Lib., 663 Franklin Ave., Aliquippa 15001. Tel. 724-375-2900, fax 724-375-3274, e-mail bfjones@shrsys.hslc.org; *Exec. Dir.* Glenn R. Miller, Pennsylvania Lib. Assn., 3905 N. Front St., Harrisburg 17110. Tel. 717-233-3113, 800-622-3308 (Pennsylvania only), fax 717-233-3121, e-mail glenn @palibraries.org.

Address correspondence to the executive director.

World Wide Web http://www.palibraries. org.

Rhode Island

Memb. (Indiv.) 349; (Inst.) 59. Term of Office. June 2001–June 2003. Publication. *Rhode Island Library Association Bulletin.* *Ed.* Leslie McDonough.

Pres. David Macksam, Cranston Public Lib., 140 Sockanosset Cross Rd., Cranston 02920. Tel. 401-943-9080, fax 401-946-5079, e-mail davidmm@lori.state.ri.us; *Secy.* Joyce May, East Providence Public Lib., 41 Grove St., East Providence 02914. Tel. 401-434-2453, e-mail mayjoyb@aol.com; *Clerk* Jane Granatino. Tel. 401-568-0369, e-mail jgranati@providence.edu. Address correspondence to the secretary.

World Wide Web http://www.uri.edu/ library/rila/rila.html.

South Carolina

Memb. 557. Term of Office. Jan.–Dec. 2003. Publication. *News and Views.*

Pres. Tom Gilson, Robert Scott Small Lib., College of Charleston, 66 George St., Charleston 29424. Tel. 843-953-8014, fax 843-953-8019, e-mail gilsont@cofc.edu; *V.P./Pres.-Elect* Marilyn Tisirigotis, Dir., Harvin Clarendon County Lib., 215 N. Brooks St., Clarendon 29102. Tel. 803-435-8633, fax 803-435-8101, e-mail marilynt@infoave.net; *2nd V.P. for Membership* Peg Tyler, R. M. Cooper Lib., Clemson Univ., Box 343001, Clemson 29634-3001. Tel. 864-656-6375, fax 864-656-7608, e-mail ptyler@clemson.

edu; *Secy.* Camille McCutcheon, USC Spartanburg Lib., 800 University Way, Spartanburg 29303. Tel. 864-503-5612, fax 864-503-5601, e-mail cmccutcheon@uscs.edu; *Treas.* Quincy Pugh, Richland County Public Lib., 1431 Assembly St., Columbia 29201. Tel. 803-929-3449, fax 803-929-3448, e-mail qpugh@richland.lib.sc.us; *Past Pres.* Jeanette Bergeron, Crumley Lutheran Archives, 4201 N. Main St., Columbia 20203. Tel. 803-787-8840, fax 803-787-8840, e-mail bergeron@ conterra.com; *Exec. Dir.* Laura Stuckey, SCLA, Box 1763, Columbia 29202. Tel. 803-252-1087, fax 803-252-0589, e-mail scla@ capconsc.com.

Address correspondence to the executive director.

World Wide Web http://www.scla.org.

South Dakota

Memb. (Indiv.) 497; (Inst.) 54. Term of Office. Oct. 2002–Oct. 2003. Publication. *Book Marks* (bi-mo.).

Pres. Jeanne Conner. Tel. 605-647-2203, e-mail jeanne.conner@k12.sd.us; *Secy.* Pam Lingor, Alexander Mitchell Public Lib., Aberdeen 57104; *Treas.* Elizabeth Fox, South Dakota State Univ., Brookings 57007; *ALA Councillor* Joe Edelen, ID Weeks Lib., Univ. of South Dakota, Vermillion 57069; *MPLA Rep.* Suzanne Miller, South Dakota State Lib., Pierre 57501; *Exec. Secy.* Brenda Hemmelman, SDLA, Box 1212, Rapid City 57709-1212. Tel. 605-786-0324, fax 605-394-1256, e-mail bkstand@rap.midco.net.

Address correspondence to the executive secretary.

World Wide Web http://www.usd.edu/ sdla.

Tennessee

Memb. 646. Term of Office. July 2002–June 2003. Publications. *Tennessee Librarian* (q.), *TLA Newsletter* (bi-mo.).

Pres. Biddanda Suresh Ponnappa, Medical Lib., James H. Quillen College of Medicine, East Tennessee State Univ., Johnson City 37614. E-mail ponnappa@etsu.edu; *V.P./ Pres.-Elect* Kathryn Pagles, Dir., Blount County Lib., 508 N. Cusick St., Maryville 37804. E-mail kathryn.pagles@state.tn.us; *Record-*

ing Secy. Susan N. Rogers, Dir., Reelfoot Regional Lib., Box 168, 736 Elm St., Martin 38237. E-mail susan.rogers@state.tn.us; *Past Pres.* Faith Holdredge, Dir., Caney Fork Regional Lib., 25 Rhea St., Sparta 38583. Tel. 931-836-2209, e-mail fholdred@mail. state.tn.us; *Exec. Dir.* Annelle R. Huggins, Tennessee Lib. Assn., Box 241074, Nashville 38124. Tel. 901-485-6952, e-mail ahuggins@ midsouth.rr.com.

Address correspondence to the executive director.

World Wide Web http://tnla.org.

Texas

Memb. 7,300. Term of Office. Apr. 2002– Apr. 2003. Publications. *Texas Library Journal* (q.), *TLACast* (9 a year).

Pres. Barry Bishop, Spring Branch ISD, Box 19432, Houston 77224. Tel. 713-365- 5580, fax 713-365-4330, e-mail bishopb@ springbranchisd.com; *Pres.-Elect* Eva Poole, Dir., Denton Public Lib., 502 Oakland St., Denton 76201-3102. Tel. 940-349-7735, fax 940-349-8260, e-mail eva.poole@cityof denton.com; *Treas.* S. Joe McCord, 1302 W. Castlewood Ave., Friendswood 77546-5222. Tel. 281-992-5527, e-mail mccord@cl.uh. edu; *Exec. Dir.* Patricia H. Smith, 3355 Bee Cave Rd., Suite 401, Austin 78746-6763. Tel. 512-328-1518, fax 512-328-8852, e-mail pats@txla.org.

Address correspondence to the executive director.

World Wide Web http://www.txla.org.

Utah

Memb. 650. Term of Office. May 2002–May 2003. Publication. *UTAH Libraries News* (bi-mo.) (electronic at http://www.ula.org/news letter).

Pres. Kayla Willey, 6721 Harold B. Lee Lib., Brigham Young Univ., Provo 84602. Tel. 801-378-6766, e-mail kayla_willey@byu. edu; *V.P./Pres.-Elect* David Hales, Giovale Lib., Westminster College of Salt Lake City, 1840 S 13 E., Salt Lake City 84105. Tel. 801-832-2256, e-mail dhales@westminster college.edu; *Treas./Exec. Secy.* Christopher R. Anderson.

Address correspondence to the executive secretary, Box 970488, Orem 84097-0488. Tel. 801-378-4433, e-mail cranders@ xmission.com.

World Wide Web http://www.ula.org.

Vermont

Memb. 400. Publication. *VLA News* (6 a year).

Pres. Karen Lane, Aldrich Public Lib., 6 Washington St., Barre 05644-4227. Tel. 802- 476-7550 ext. 307, e-mail aldrich@helicon. net; *V.P./Pres.-Elect* Ellen F. Hall, Kreitzberg Lib., Norwich Univ., 23 Harmon Dr., Northfield 05663. Tel. 802-485-2169, e-mail ehall@norwich.edu; *Secy.* Daisy Benson, Bailey/Howe Lib., Univ. of Vermont, Burlington 05405. Tel. 802-656-0636; *Treas.* Krista W. Ainsworth, Kreitzberg Lib., Norwich Univ., 158 Harmon Dr., Northfield 05663. Tel. 802-485-2183, e-mail kainswor @norwich.edu; *Past Pres.* Trina Magi, Bailey/Howe Lib., Univ. of Vermont, Burlington 05405. Tel. 802-656-5723, e-mail tmagi@ zoo.uvm.edu.

Address correspondence to VLA, Box 803, Burlington 05402.

World Wide Web http://www.vermont libraries.org.

Virginia

Memb. 1,200. Term of Office. Oct. 2002– Oct. 2003. Publications. *Virginia Libraries* (q.). *Co.-Eds.* Barbie Selby. Tel. 423-924- 3504, e-mail bselby@virginia.edu; Earlene Viano. Tel. 757-727-1312, e-mail eviano@ hampton.gov; *VLA Newsletter* (10 a year). *Ed.* Helen Q. Sherman, 4369 Wiltshire Place, Dumphries 22026. E-mail hsherman@dtic. mil.

Pres. Morel Fry, Perry Lib., Old Dominion Univ., Norfolk 23529-0256. Tel. 757-683- 4143, fax 757-683-5767, e-mail mfry@odu. edu; *Pres.-Elect* Sam Clay, Fairfax County Public Lib., 1200 Gov. Center Pkwy., Suite 324, Fairfax 22035-0059. Tel. 703-324-8308, fax 703-222-3193, e-mail edwin.clay@co. fairfax.va.us; *2nd V.P.* Harriett Edmunds, Lib. of Virginia, 800 E. Broad St., Richmond 23219. Tel. 804-692-3727, fax 804-692- 3736, e-mail hedmunds@lva.lib.va.us; *Secy.*

Susan Paddock, Virginia Beach Public Lib., 4100 Virginia Beach Blvd., Virginia Beach 23452. Tel. 757-431-3014, fax 757-431-3022, e-mail spaddock@vbgov.com; *Treas.* Andrew Morton, Boatwright Memorial Lib., Univ. of Richmond, Richmond 23173. Tel. 804-287-6047, fax 804-287-1840, e-mail amorton@richmond.edu; *Exec. Dir.* Linda Hahne, Box 8277, Norfolk 23503-0277. Tel. 757-583-0041, fax 757-583-5041, e-mail lhahne@coastalnet.com.

Address correspondence to the executive director.

World Wide Web http://www.vla.org.

Washington

Memb. 1,200. Term of Office. Apr. 2001–Apr. 2003. Publications. *ALKI* (3 a year), *WLA Link* (5 a year).

Pres. Carol Gill Schuyler, Kitsap Regional Lib., 1301 Sylvan Way, Bremerton 98310-3498. Tel. 360-405-9127, fax 360-405-9128, e-mail carol@krl.org; *V.P./Pres.-Elect* John Sheller, Federal Way 320th/KCLS, 848 S. 320, Federal Way 98003. Tel. 253-839-0257, fax 206-296-5053, e-mail jsheller@kcls.org; *Secy.* Liz Hawkins, Everett Public Lib., 2702 Hoyt Ave., Everett 98201. Tel. 425-257-8270, fax 425-257-8265, e-mail lhawkins@ci.everett.wa.us; *Treas.* Monica Weyhe, Yakima Valley Regional Lib., 102 N. Third St., Yakima 98901. Tel. 509-452-8541 ext. 702, fax 509-575-2093, e-mail mweyhe@yvrls.lib.wa.us; *Assn. Coord.* Gail E. Willis.

Address correspondence to the association office, 4016 First Ave. N.E., Seattle 98105-6502. Tel. 800-704-1529, 206-545-1529, fax 206-545-1543, e-mail washla@wla.org.

World Wide Web http://www.wla.org.

West Virginia

Memb. 668. Term of Office. Dec. 2002–Nov. 2003. Publication. *West Virginia Libraries* (6 a year). *Ed.* Jennifer Soule, South Charleston Public Lib., 312 Fourth Ave., South Charleston 25303. Tel. 304-744-6561, fax 304-744-8808, e-mail souleja@scpl.wvnet.edu.

Pres. Julie Spiegler, Kanawha County Public Lib., 123 Capitol St., Charleston 25301. Tel. 304-343-4646 ext. 284, fax 304-348-6530, e-mail julie.spiegler@kanawha.

lib.wv.us; *1st V.P./Pres.-Elect* Charley Hively, Parkersburg/Wood County Public Lib. E-mail hivelyc@park.lib.wv.us; *2nd V.P.* Judy Gunsaulis, Fayette County Public Lib. E-mail gunsaulj@raleigh.lib.wv.us; *Secy.* Judith Duncan, St. Albans Public Lib. E-mail judith.duncan@kanawha.lib.wv.us; *Treas.* Steve Christo, Cabell County Public Lib. E-mail schristo@cabell.lib.wv.us; *Past Pres.* Sharon Saye, Bridgeport Public Lib., 1200 Johnson Ave., Bridgeport 26330. E-mail saye@bridgeportwv.com.

Address correspondence to the president.

World Wide Web http://www.wvla.org.

Wisconsin

Memb. 1,800. Term of Office. Jan.–Dec. 2003. Publication. *WLA Newsletter* (quarterly).

Pres. Peter Gilbert, Mudd Lib., Lawrence Univ., Box 599, Appleton 54911-5683. Tel. 920-832-6700, fax 920-832-6967, e-mail peter.j.gilbert@lawrence.edu; *Pres.-Elect* Nancy McClements, Memorial Lib., UW–Madison, 728 State St., Madison 53706. Tel. 608-262-8271, fax 608-262-8569, e-mail nmcclements@library.wisc.edu; *Secy.* Kathy Schmidt, Manitowoc Public Lib., N6193 Woodland Meadows Dr., Sheboygan 53083-3347. Tel. 920-683-4863 ext. 329, e-mail kschmidt@mcls.lib.wi.us; *Treas.* Michael Cross, Div. for Libs., Technology, and Community Learning. Tel. 608-267-9225, fax 608-267-1052, e-mail michael.cross@dpi.state.wi.us; *Exec. Dir.* Lisa Strand. Tel. 608-245-3640, fax 608-245-3646, e-mail strand@scls.lib.wi.us.

Address correspondence to the association, 5250 E. Terrace Dr., Suite A1, Madison 53718-8345.

World Wide Web http://www.wla.lib.wi.us.

Wyoming

Memb. (Indiv.) 425; (Inst.) 21. Term of Office. Oct. 2002–Oct. 2003.

Pres. Kay Carlson, Northwest College, 231 W. Sixth St., Powell 82435. Tel. 307-754-6527, fax 307-754-6010, e-mail carlsonk@northwestcollege.edu; *V.P./Pres.-Elect* Carey Hartmann, Laramie County Lib. System, 2800 Central Ave., Cheyenne 82001. Tel. 307-635-1032, fax 307-634-2082, e-mail chartmann@larm.lib.wy.us; *Past Pres.* Trish Palluck, Wyoming State Lib., Supreme Court Bldg., Cheyenne 82002. Tel. 307-777-5913, fax 307-777-6289, e-mail tpallu@state.wy. us; *Exec. Secy.* Laura Grott, Box 1387, Cheyenne 82003. Tel. 307-632-7622, fax 307-638-3469, e-mail grottski@aol.com.

Address correspondence to the executive secretary.

World Wide Web http://www.wyla.org.

Canada

Alberta

Memb. 500. Term of Office. May 2001–Apr. 2002. Publication. *Letter of the LAA* (5 a year).

Pres. Pat Cavill, Pat Cavill Consulting, Box 43036, Calgary T2J 7A7. Tel. 403-278-1630, fax 403-278-1612, e-mail pcavill@telusplanet.net; *1st V.P.* Michael Perry, Univ. of Lethbridge, 4401 University Dr., Lethbridge T1K 3M4. Tel. 403-329-2272, fax 403-329-2022, e-mail perrmw@uleth.ca; *2nd V.P.* Myra Skaronski, EPL Lessard Branch, 6104 172 St., Edmonton T6M 1G9. Tel. 780-496-7078, fax 780-496-7087, e-mail mskaronski@epl.ca; *Past Pres.* Rick Leech, Provincial Court Lib. System, 5th fl. North, Law Courts, 1A Sir Winston Churchill Sq., Edmonton T5J 0R2. Tel. 780-427-3247, fax 780-427-0481, e-mail rick.leech@just.gov. ab.ca; *Exec. Dir.* Christine Sheppard, 80 Baker Crescent N.W., Calgary T2L 1R4. Tel. 403-284-5818, fax 403-282-6646, e-mail shepparc@cadvision.com.

Address correspondence to the executive director.

World Wide Web http://www.laa.ab.ca.

British Columbia

Memb. 750. Term of Office. May 2003–June 2004. Publication. *BCLA Reporter.* *Ed.* Ted Benson.

Pres. Carol Elder; *V.P./Pres.-Elect* Alison Nussbaumer; *Exec. Dir.* Michael Burris.

Address correspondence to the association, 150-900 Howe St., Vancouver V6Z 2M4.

Tel. 604-683-5354, fax 604-609-0707, e-mail office@bcla.bc.ca.

Manitoba

Memb. 500. Term of Office. May 2001–May 2002. Publication. *Newsline* (mo.).

Pres. Janice Linton, Aboriginal Health Libn., Univ. of Manitoba, Winnipeg R3E 0W3. Tel. 204-789-3878, fax 204-789-3923, e-mail lintonjs@ms.umanitoba.ca; *V.P./Pres.-Elect* Theresa Yauk, Branch Head, Sir William Stevenson Branch Lib., 765 Keewatin Ave., Winnipeg R2X 3B9. Tel. 204-986-7156, fax 204-986-7201, e-mail tyauk1 @city.winnipeg.mb.ca; *Secy.* Irmy Nikkel, Head of Cataloging, Winnipeg Public Lib., 251 Donald St., Winnipeg R3C 3P5. Tel. 204-986-6485, fax 204-942-5671, e-mail inikkel@city.winnipeg.mb.ca; *Past Pres.* Mark Leggott, Univ. Libn., Univ. of Winnipeg Lib., 515 Portage Ave., Winnipeg R3B 2E9. E-mail mleggott@uwinnipeg.ca.

Address correspondence to the association, 606-100 Arthur St., Winnipeg R3B 1H3. Tel. 204-943-4567, fax 204-942-1555, e-mail mla@uwinnipeg.ca.

World Wide Web http://www.mla.mb.ca.

Ontario

Memb. 4,000. Term of Office. Jan. 2003–Jan. 2004. Publications. *Access* (q.), *Teaching Librarian* (q.), *Accessola.com* (q.).

Pres. Elizabeth Kerr, Kawartha Pine Ridge District School Board. Tel. 705-742-9773, fax 705-760-8698, e-mail sabram@micro media.on.ca; *V.P.* Ken Roberts, Hamilton Public Lib. Board. Tel. 905-546-3215, fax 90-546-3202, e-mail kroberts@hpl.ca; *Treas.* Roderick McLean, Teck Centennial Public Lib. Board. Tel. 416-363-3388, fax 416-941-9581; *Past Pres.* Stephen Abram, Micromedia ProQuest. Tel. 416-369-2594, fax 416-362-1699, e-mail sabram@micromedia.on.ca; *Exec. Dir.* Larry Moore.

Address correspondence to the association, 100 Lombard St., Suite 303, Toronto M5C 1M3. Tel. 416-363-3388, fax 416-941-9581, e-mail info@accessola.com.

World Wide Web http://www.accessola. com.

Quebec

Memb. (Indiv.) 125; (Inst.) 13; (Commercial) 2. Term of Office. June 2002–May 2003. Publication. *ABQ/QLA Bulletin* (3 a year).

Pres. Rosemary Cochrane; *Exec. Secy.* Cheryl McDonell, Box 1095, Pointe-Claire H9S 4H9. Tel. 514-421-7541, e-mail abqla@abqla.qc.ca.

Address correspondence to the executive secretary.

World Wide Web http://www.abqla.qc.ca.

Saskatchewan

Memb. 225. Term of Office. June 2002–May 2003. Publication. *Forum* (5 a year).

Pres. Michelle Splitter, John M. Cuelenaere Lib., 125 12th St. E., Prince Albert S6V 1B7. E-mail splitter@jmc.panet.pa.sk.ca; *V.P.* Gregory Salmers, Estevan Public Lib., 701 Souris Ave., Estevan S4A 2T1. E-mail greg@southeast.lib.sk.ca; *Exec. Dir.* Judith Silverthorne, Box 3388, Regina S4P 3H1. Tel. 306-780-9413, fax 306-780-9447, e-mail slaexdir@sasktel.net.

Address correspondence to the executive director.

World Wide Web http://www.lib.sk.ca/sla.

Regional

Atlantic Provinces: N.B., N.L., N.S., P.E.

Memb. (Indiv.) 215; (Inst.) 24. Term of Office. May 2002–May 2003. Publications. *APLA Bulletin* (bi-mo.), *Membership Directory* (ann.).

Pres. Elaine MacLean, Head, Technical Services, Angus L. Macdonald Lib., St. Francis Xavier Univ., Antigonish, NS B2W 2W5. Tel. 902-867-2221, fax 902-867-5153, e-mail emaclean@stfx.ca; *V.P./Pres.-Elect* Laurette Mackey, York Lib. Region, New Brunswick Public Lib. Service, 4 Carleton, Fredericton, NB E3B 5P4. Tel. 506-453-5380, fax 506-457-4878, e-mail laurette.mackey@gnb.ca; *Secy.* Gwendolyn MacNairn, Killam Lib., Dalhousie Univ., 6225 University Ave., Halifax, NS B3H 4H8. Tel. 902-494-1320, fax 902-494-2062, e-mail g.macnairn@dal.ca;

Treas. Denise Corey-Fancy, Mount Saint Vincent Univ. Lib. Tel. 902-457-6025, fax 902-457-6445, e-mail dcorey@msvu1.msvu.ca; *Past Pres.* Norine Hanus, Collections Libn., Robertson Lib., UPEI, Charlottetown, PE C1A 4P3. Tel. 902-566-0479, fax 902-628-4305, e-mail nhanus@upei.ca.

Address correspondence to Atlantic Provinces Lib. Assn., c/o School of Lib. and Info. Studies, Dalhousie Univ., Halifax, NS B3H 4H8.

World Wide Web http://www.apla.ca.

Mountain Plains: Ariz., Colo., Kan., Mont., Neb., Nev., N.Dak., N.M., Okla., S.Dak., Utah, Wyo.

Memb. 820. Term of Office. One year. Publications. *MPLA Newsletter* (bi-mo.), *Ed. and Adv. Mgr.* Lisa Mecklenberg Jackson, Montana Legislative Reference Center, Box 201706, Helena, MT 59620-1706. Tel. 406-444-2957, e-mail ljackson@state.mt.us; *Membership Directory* (ann.).

Pres. Jean Hatfield, Johnson County Lib., Box 2933, Shawnee Mission, KS 66201-1333, e-mail hatfield@jcl.lib.ks.us; *V.P./Pres.-Elect* Carol Hammond, International Business Info. Center–Thunderbird,15249 N. 59 Ave., Glendale, AZ 85306. Tel. 602-978-7234, fax 602-978-7762, e-mail hammondc@t-bird.edu; *Exec. Secy.* Joe Edelen, I. D. Weeks Lib., Univ. of South Dakota, Vermillion, SD 57069. Tel. 605-677-6082, fax 605-677-5488, e-mail jedelen@usd.edu.

Address correspondence to the executive secretary, Mountain Plains Lib. Assn.

World Wide Web http://www.usd.edu/mpla.

New England: Conn., Maine, Mass., N.H., R.I., Vt.

Memb. (Indiv.) 1,300; (Inst.) 100. Term of Office. Nov. 2002–Oct. 2004 (Treas., Dirs., and Secy., two years). Publication. *New England Libraries* (bi-mo.). *Ed.* Patricia Holloway. E-mail holloway@crlc.org.

Pres. Karen Valley, Portland Public Lib., 5 Monument Sq., Portland, ME 04101. Tel. 207-871-1716, fax 207-871-1703, e-mail valley@portland.lib.me.us; *V.P./Pres.-Elect* John

Barrett, Nesmith Lib., 8 Fellows Rd., Windham, NH 03087. Tel. 603-432-7154, e-mail jbarrett@library.windham.nh.us; *Secy.* Alicia Antone, East Providence Public Lib., Riverside Branch, 100 Bullock Point Ave., East Providence, RI 02915. Tel. 401-433-6284, e-mail aliciaae@lori.state.ri.us; *Treas.* Peter Blodgett, Thetford Town Lib., Latham Memorial Lib., and Peabody Lib., Box 240, Thetford, VT 05074. Tel. 802-785-4361, e-mail peter.blodgett@valley.net; *Past Pres.* Cheryl Bryan, 10 Riverside Dr., Lakeville, MA 02347. Tel. 508-923-3531, fax 508-923-3539, e-mail cbryan@semls.org; *Exec. Secy.* Barry Blaisdell, New England Lib. Assn., 14 Pleasant St., Gloucester, MA 01930. Tel. 972-282-0787, e-mail info@nelib.org.

Address correspondence to the executive secretary.

World Wide Web http://www.nelib.org.

Pacific Northwest: Alaska, Idaho, Mont., Ore., Wash., Alberta, B.C.

Memb. (Active) 550; (Subscribers) 100. Term of Office. Aug. 2002–Aug. 2003. Publication. *PNLA Quarterly.*

Pres. Daniel Masoni, Unalaska Public Lib., Box 1370, Unalaska, AK 99685. Tel. 907-581-5060, fax 907-581-5266, e-mail sandy@krl.org; *1st V.P./Pres.-Elect* Mary DeWalt, Ada Community Lib., 10664 W. Victory Rd., Boise, ID 83709. Tel. 208-362-0181, fax 208-362-0303, e-mail akunak@ci.unalaska.ak.us; *2nd V.P.* Christine Sheppard, Lib. Assn. of Alberta, 80 Baker Crescent N.W., Calgary, AB T2L 1R4. Tel. 403-284-5818, e-mail christine.shepard@shaw.ca; *Secy.* Carolynn Avery, Oregon State Lib., 250 Winter St. N.E., Salem, OR 97301. Tel. 503-378-4243 ext. 269, e-mail averyc@pioneer.net; *Treas.* Robert Hook, Univ. of Idaho Lib., Moscow, ID. E-mail rdhook@uidaho.edu.

Address correspondence to the president, Pacific Northwest Lib. Assn.

World Wide Web http://www.pnla.org.

Southeastern: Ala., Ark., Fla., Ga., Ky., La., Miss., N.C., S.C., Tenn., Va., W.Va.

Memb. 500. Term of Office. Oct. 2002–Oct. 2004. Publication. *The Southeastern Librarian* (q.).

Pres. Ann H. Hamilton, Assoc. Dean of Libs., Georgia Southern Univ., 211 Wendwood Dr., Statesboro, GA 30458-5075. Tel. 912-681-5115, fax 912-681-0093, e-mail ahamilton@gasou.edu; *V.P./Pres.-Elect* Judith Gibbons, Dir., Field Services Div., Kentucky Dept. for Libs. and Archives, Box 537, Frankfort, KY 40602-0537. Tel. 502-564-8300, fax 502-564-5773, e-mail judith.gibbons@kdla.net; *Secy.* Faith Line, Dir., Sumter County Lib., 111 N. Harvin St., Sumter, SC 29150. Tel. 803-773-7273, fax 803-773-4875, e-mail linef@infoave.net; *Treas.* Diane Baird, User Services Libn., Circulation, Middle Tennessee State Univ., 425 E. Main, Apt. A, Murfreesboro, TN 37130. Tel. 615-898-2539, fax 615-904-8225, e-mail dbaird@ulibnet.mtsu.edu.

State and Provincial Library Agencies

The state library administrative agency in each of the U.S. states will have the latest information on its state plan for the use of federal funds under the Library Services and Technology Act (LSTA). The directors and addresses of these state agencies are listed below.

Alabama

Rebecca Mitchell, Dir., Alabama Public Lib. Service, 6030 Monticello Dr., Montgomery 36130. Tel. 334-213-3902, fax 334-213-3993, e-mail rmitchell@apls.state.al.us.

Alaska

George Smith, Acting Dir., Div. of Libs., Archives, and Museums, Box 110571, Juneau 99811-0571. Tel. 907-465-2911, fax 907-465-2151, e-mail george_smith@eed.state.ak.us.

Arizona

GladysAnn Wells, State Libn., 1700 W. Washington, Phoenix 85007-2896. Tel. 602-542-4035, fax 602-542-4972, e-mail gawells @lib.az.us.

Arkansas

Jack C. Mulkey, State Libn., Arkansas State Lib., 1 Capitol Mall, Little Rock 72201. Tel. 501-682-1526, fax 501-682-1899, e-mail jmulkey@asl.lib.ar.us.

California

Kevin Starr, State Libn., California State Lib., Box 942837, Sacramento 94237. Tel. 916-654-0174, fax 916-654-0064, e-mail kstarr@library.ca.gov.

Colorado

Nancy Bolt, State Libn. and Asst. Commissioner, Dept. of Educ., State Lib., 201 E. Colfax Ave., Denver 80203. Tel. 303-866-6900, fax 303-866-6940, e-mail nancybolt@earthlink.net.

Connecticut

Kendall F. Wiggin, State Libn., Connecticut State Lib., 231 Capitol Ave., Hartford 06106. Tel. 860-757-6510, fax 860-757-6503, e-mail kwiggin@cslib.org.

Delaware

Anne Norman, Dir. and State Libn., Div. of Libs., 43 S. DuPont Hwy., Dover 19901. Tel. 302-739-4748, fax 302-739-6787, e-mail norman@lib.de.us.

District of Columbia

Mary E. "Molly" Raphael, Dir. and State Libn., Dist. of Columbia Public Lib., 901 G St. N.W., Suite 400, Washington 20001. Tel. 202-727-1101, fax 202-727-1129, e-mail molly.raphael@dc.gov.

Florida

Debra Sears, Bureau Chief, Bureau of Lib. and Network Services, R. A. Gray Bldg., 500 S. Bronough St., Tallahassee 32399-0250. Tel. 850-245-6600, fax 850-488-2746, e-mail dsears@mail.dos.state.fl.us.

Georgia

Lamar Veatch, State Libn., Georgia Public Lib. Service, 1800 Century Place, Suite 150, Atlanta 30345. Tel. 404-982-3569, fax 404-982-3563, e-mail lveatch@state.lib.ga.us.

Hawaii

Virginia Lowell, State Libn., State Public Lib. System, 465 S. King St., Rm. B1, Honolulu 96813. Tel. 808-586-3704, fax 808-586-3715, e-mail stlib@lib.state.hi.us.

Idaho

Charles Bolles, State Libn., Idaho State Lib., 325 W. State St., Boise 83702. Tel. 208-334-2150, fax 208-334-4016, e-mail cbolles@isl.state.id.us.

Illinois

Jean Wilkins, Dir., Illinois State Lib., 300 S. 2 St., Springfield 62701-1796. Tel. 217-782-2994, fax 217-785-4326, e-mail jwilkins@ilsos.net.

Indiana

Ray Ewick, Dir., Indiana State Lib., 140 N. Senate Ave., Indianapolis 46204. Tel. 317-232-3692, fax 317-232-0002, e-mail ewick@statelib.lib.in.us.

Iowa

Mary Wegner, State Libn., State Lib. of Iowa, 1112 E. Grand Ave., Des Moines 50319. Tel. 515-281-4105, fax 515.281.6191, e-mail Mary.Wegner@lib.state.ia.us.

Kansas

Duane Johnson, State Libn., Kansas State Lib., State Capitol, 3rd fl., Topeka 66612. Tel. 785-296-3296, fax 785-296-6650, e-mail duanej@kslib.info.

Kentucky

James A. Nelson, State Libn./Commissioner, Kentucky Dept. for Libs. and Archives, 300 Coffee Tree Rd., Frankfort 40601. Tel. 502-564-8300 ext. 312, fax 502-564-5773, e-mail jim.nelson@kdla.net.

Louisiana

Thomas F. Jaques, State Libn., State Lib. of Louisiana, Box 131, Baton Rouge 70821-0131. Tel. 225-342-4923, fax 225-219-4804, e-mail tjaques@pelican.state.lib.la.us.

Maine

J. Gary Nichols, State Libn., Maine State Lib., 64 State House Sta., Augusta 04333. Tel. 207-287-5600, fax 207-287-5615, e-mail gary.nichols@state.me.us.

Maryland

Irene Padilla, Asst. State Superintendent for Lib. Development and Services, Maryland State Dept. of Educ., 200 W. Baltimore St., Baltimore 21201. Tel. 410-767-0435, fax 410-333-2507, e-mail ipadilla@msde.state.md.us.

Massachusetts

Robert C. Maier, Dir., Massachusetts Board of Lib. Commissioners, 648 Beacon St., Boston 02215. Tel. 617-267-9400, fax 617-421-9833, e-mail robert.maier@state.ma.us.

Michigan

Christie Pearson Brandau, State Libn., Lib. of Michigan, 702 W. Kalamazoo, Box 30007, Lansing 48909-7507. Tel. 517-373-7513, fax 517-373-5815, e-mail cbrandau@michigan.gov.

Minnesota

Bruce Pomerantz, Coord., Office of Lib. Development and Services, 1500 Hwy. 36 West, Roseville 55113. Tel. 651-582-8722, fax 651-582-8897, e-mail bruce.pomerantz@state.mn.us.

Mississippi

Sharman B. Smith, Exec. Dir., Mississippi Lib. Commission, 1221 Ellis Ave., Box 10700, Jackson 39289-0700. Tel. 601-961-4039, fax 601-354-6713, e-mail sharman@lc.lib.ms.us.

Missouri

Sara Parker, State Libn., Secy. of State's Office, Kirkpatrick State Info. Center, 600 W. Main, Box 387, Jefferson City 65102-0387. Tel. 573-751-2751, fax 573-751-3612, e-mail parkes@sosmail.state.mo.us.

Montana

Karen Strege, State Libn., Montana State Lib., 1515 E. 6 Ave., Box 201800, Helena

59620-1800. Tel. 406-444-3115, fax 406-444-5612, e-mail kstrege@state.mt.us.

Nebraska

Rod Wagner, Dir., Nebraska Lib. Commission, 1200 N St., Suite 120, Lincoln 68508. Tel. 402-471-4001, fax 402-471-2083, e-mail rwagner@nlc.state.ne.us.

Nevada

Sara Jones, Admin. and State Libn., Nevada State Lib. and Archives, 100 N. Stewart St., Carson City 89710. Tel. 775-684-3315, fax 775-684-3311, e-mail sfjones@clan.lib.nv.us.

New Hampshire

Michael York, State Libn., New Hampshire State Lib., 20 Park St., Concord 03301-6314. Tel. 603-271-2392, fax 603-271-6826, e-mail myork@library.state.nh.us.

New Jersey

Norma Blake, State Libn., New Jersey State Lib., 185 W. State St., Trenton 08625-0520. Tel. 609-292-6201, fax 609-292-2746, e-mail rpallante@njstatelib.org.

New Mexico

Benjamin Wakashige, State Libn., New Mexico State Lib., Aquisitions Section, 1209 Camino Carlos Rey, Santa Fe 87505. Tel. 505-476-9762, fax 505-476-9761, e-mail ben@stlib.state.nm.us.

New York

Janet M. Welch, State Libn./Asst. Commissioner for Libs., New York State Lib., 10C34 Cultural Educ. Center, Albany 12230. Tel. 518-474-5930, fax 518-486-6880, e-mail jwelch2@mail.nysed.gov.

North Carolina

Sandra M. Cooper, State Libn., State Lib. of North Carolina, 4640 Mail Service Center, Raleigh 27699-4640. Tel. 919-733-2570, fax 919-733-8748, e-mail scooper@library.dcr.state.nc.us.

North Dakota

Doris Ott, State Libn., North Dakota State Lib., 604 E. Boulevard Ave., Bismarck 58505-0800. Tel. 701-328-2492, fax 701-328-2040, e-mail dott@state.nd.us.

Ohio

Michael S. Lucas, State Libn., State Lib. of Ohio, 274 E. 1 Ave., Columbus 43201. Tel. 614-644-7041, fax 614-466-3584, e-mail mlucas@sloma.state.ohio.us.

Oklahoma

Susan McVey, Dir., Oklahoma Dept. of Libs., 200 N.E. 18 St., Oklahoma City 73105. Tel. 405-521-3173, fax 405-525-7804, e-mail smcvey@oltn.odl.state.ok.us.

Oregon

Jim Scheppke, State Libn., Oregon State Lib., 250 Winter St. N.E., Salem 97301-3950. Tel. 503-378-4367, fax 503-585-8059, e-mail jim.b.scheppke@state.or.us.

Pennsylvania

Gary D. Wolfe, Deputy Secy. of Educ. and Commissioner for Libs., State Lib. of Pennsylvania, Box 1601, Harrisburg 17105-1601. Tel. 717-787-2646, fax 717-772-3265, e-mail gwolfe@state.pa.us.

Rhode Island

Anne T. Parent, Chief of Lib. Services, Office of Lib. and Info. Services, 1 Capitol Hill, Providence 02908-5870. Tel. 401-222-5763, fax 401-222-2083, e-mail annept@gw.doa.state.ri.us.

South Carolina

James B. Johnson, Jr., Dir., South Carolina State Lib., Box 11469, Columbia 29211. Tel. 803-734-8656, fax 803-734-8676, e-mail jim@leo.scsl.state.sc.us.

South Dakota

Suzanne Miller, State Libn., South Dakota State Lib., 800 Governors Dr., Pierre 57501-

2294. Tel. 605-773-3131, fax 605-773-4950, e-mail suzanne.miller@state.sd.us.

Tennessee

Edwin S. Gleaves, State Libn./Archivist, Tennessee State Lib. and Archives, 403 Seventh Ave. N., Nashville 37243-0312. Tel. 615-741-7996, fax 615-532-9293, e-mail edwin.gleaves@state.tn.us.

Texas

Peggy D. Rudd, Dir./State Libn., Texas State Lib. and Archives Commission, Box 12927, Capitol Sta., Austin 78711-2927. Tel. 512-463-5460, fax 512-463-5436, e-mail peggy.rudd@tsl.state.tx.us.

Utah

Amy Owen, Dir., Utah State Lib. Div., 250 N. 1950 W., Suite A, Salt Lake City 84115-7901. Tel. 801-715-6770, fax 801-715-6767, e-mail aowen@utah.gov.

Vermont

Sybil Brigham McShane, State Libn., Vermont Dept. of Libs., 109 State St., Montpelier 05609. Tel. 802-828-3265, fax 802-828-2199, e-mail sybil.mcshane@dol.state.vt.us.

Virginia

Nolan T. Yelich, Libn. of Virginia, Lib. of Virginia, 800 E. Broad St., Richmond 23219. Tel. 804-692-3535, fax 804-692-3594, e-mail nyelich@lva.lib.va.us.

Washington

Jan Walsh, State Libn., Washington State Lib. Div., Office of the Secy. of State, 6880 Capitol Blvd., Tumwater 98501. Tel. 360-704-5253, fax 360-586-7575, e-mail jwalsh@secstate.wa.gov.

West Virginia

James D. Waggoner, Secy., West Virginia Lib. Commission, 1900 Kanawha Blvd. E., Charleston 25305. Tel. 304-558-2041, fax 304-558-2044, e-mail waggoner@wvlc.lib.wv.us.

Wisconsin

Calvin Potter, Asst. Superintendent, Div. for Libs., Technology and Community Learning, Dept. of Public Instruction, Box 7851, Madison 53707-7841. Tel. 608-266-2205, fax 608-267-1052, e-mail calvin.potter@dpi.state.wi.us.

Wyoming

Lesley Boughton, State Libn., Wyoming State Lib., 2301 Capitol Ave., Cheyenne 82002. Tel. 307-777-7283, fax 307-777-6289, e-mail lbough@missc.state.wy.us.

American Samoa

Cheryl Morales, Territorial Libn., Feleti Barstow Public Lib., Box 997687, Pago Pago, AS 96799. Tel. 684-633-5816, fax 684-633-5213, e-mail feletibarstow@yahoo.com.

Federated States of Micronesia

Eliuel K. Pretrick, Secy., Dept. of Health, Educ., and Social Affairs, FSM Div. of Educ., Box PS 70, Palikir Sta., Pohnpei, FM 96941. Tel. 691-320-2619, fax 691-320-5500, e-mail fsmhealth@mail.fm.

Guam

Christine K. Scott-Smith, Dir./Territorial Libn., Guam Public Lib. System, 254 Martyr St., Agana 96910-0254. Tel. 671-475-4753, fax 671-477-9777.

Northern Mariana Islands

Joseph McElroy, Commonwealth Libn. and Dir., Joeten-Kiyu Public Lib., Box 1092, Commonwealth of the Northern Mariana Islands, Saipan 96950. Tel. 670-235-7322, fax 670-235-7550, e-mail jklibrary@saipan.com.

Palau (Republic of)

Mario Katosang, Minister of Educ., Republic of Palau, Box 7080, Koror, PW 96940. Tel.

680-488-2973, fax 680-488-2930, e-mail mariok@palaumoe.net.

Puerto Rico

Cesar A. Rey Hernandez, Secy. of Educ., Puerto Rico Dept. of Educ./Public Lib. Programs, Box 190759, San Juan, PR 00919-0759. Tel. 787-759-2004, fax 787-250-0275, e-mail Rey_CE@de.gobierno.pr.

Republic of the Marshall Islands

Frederick deBrum, Secy., Internal Affairs, Marshall Islands, Box 629, Majuro, MH 96960. Tel. 692-625-3372, fax 692-625-3226, e-mail rmihpo@ntamar.com.

Virgin Islands

Sharlene Harris, Dir. of Libs./Territorial Libn., Div. of Libs., Archives, and Museums, 23 Dronningens Gade, St. Thomas, VI 00802. Tel. 340-774-3407, fax 809-775-1887.

Canada

Alberta

Punch Jackson, Dir., Strategic Info. and Libs., Alberta Community Development, 901 Standard Life Centre, 10405 Jasper Ave., Edmonton T5J 4R7. Tel. 780-415-0284, fax 780-422-9132, e-mail pjackson@mcd.gov.ab.ca.

British Columbia

Barbara Greeniaus, Dir., Lib. Services Branch, Ministry of Municipal Affairs, Box 9490 Sta. Prov. Govt., Victoria V8W 9N7. Tel. 250-356-1795, fax 250-953-3225, e-mail bgreeniaus@hq.marh.gov.bc.ca.

Manitoba

Will Enns, Acting Dir., Public Library Services, Manitoba Dept. of Culture, Heritage and Citizenship, Unit 200, 1525 1 St., Brandon R7A 7A1. Tel. 888-603-8131, fax 204-726-6868, e-mail wenns@gov.mb.ca.

New Brunswick

Sylvie Nadeau, Exec. Dir., New Brunswick Public Lib. Service, Box 6000, Fredericton E3B 5H1. Tel. 506-453-2354, fax 506-444-4064, e-mail Sylvie.Nadeau@gnb.ca.

Newfoundland and Labrador

Shawn Tetford, Exec. Dir., Provincial Info. and Lib. Resources Board of Newfoundland and Labrador, 48 St. George's Ave., Stephenville A2N 1K9. Tel. 709-643-0901, fax 709-643-0925, e-mail shawntetford@publib.nf.ca, World Wide Web http://www.publib.nf.ca.

Northwest Territories

Sandy MacDonald, Territorial Libn., Northwest Territories Public Lib. Services, 75 Woodland Dr., Hay River X0E 1G1. Tel. 867-874-6531, fax 867-874-3321, e-mail sandy_macdonald@gov.nt.ca.

Nova Scotia

Elizabeth Armstrong, Acting Provincial Libn., Nova Scotia Provincial Lib., 3770 Kempt Rd., Halifax B3K 4X8. Tel. 902-424-2455, fax 902-424-0633, e-mail armstreh@gov.ns.ca.

Ontario

Michael Langford, Dir., Heritage and Libs. Branch, Ontario Government Ministry of Citizenship, Culture, and Recreation, 400 University Ave., 4th fl., Toronto M7A 2R9. Tel. 416-314-7342, fax 416-314-7635, e-mail Michael.Langford@mczcr.gov.on.ca.

Prince Edward Island

Allan Groen, Provincial Libn., P.E.I. Provincial Lib. Service, 89 Red Head Rd., Box 7500, Morrell COA 1S0. Tel. 902-961-7320, fax 902-961-7322, e-mail plshq@gov. pe.ca.

Quebec

André Couture, Dir., Direction des Politiques et de la Coordination des Programmes, 225 Grande Allée Est, Quebec G1R 5G5. Tel.

418-644-0485, fax 418-643-4080, e-mail andre.couture@mcc.gouv.qc.ca.

Saskatchewan

Joylene Campbell, Provincial Libn., Saskatchewan Provincial Lib., 1352 Winnipeg St., Regina S4P 3V7. Tel. 306-787-2972, fax 306-787-2029, e-mail campbell@prov.lib.sk.ca.

Yukon Territory

Linda Johnson, Dir., Libs. and Archives Div., Dept. of Educ., Box 2703, Whitehorse Y1A 2C6. Tel. 867-667-5309, fax 867-393-6253, e-mail Linda.Johnson@gov.yk.ca.

State School Library Media Associations

Alabama

Children's and School Libns. Div., Alabama Lib. Assn. Memb. 650. Publication. *The Alabama Librarian* (q.).

Chair Jane Garret, 466 Bowling Green Dr., Montgomery 36109. Tel. 334-269-3918; *Exec. Dir.* Virginia Lott, ALLA, 400 S. Union St., Suite 395, Montgomery 36104. Tel. 334-263-1272, fax 334-265-1281, e-mail psgllc@bellsouth.net.

Address correspondence to the executive director.

World Wide Web http://allaonline.home.mindspring.com.

Alabama Instructional Media Assn. Memb. 400. Term of Office. July 2002–June 2003.

Pres. Tywanna B. Burton, Vestavia Hills Elementary West, 1965 Merryvale Rd., Vestavia Hills 35216. Tel. 205-402-5159, e-mail tburton@vestavia.k12.al.us; *V.P./Pres.-Elect* Linda Parker, Shades Valley H.S. Tel. 205-956-3482, e-mail Lkparker6250@yahoo.com; *Secy.* Ann Mixon, Highlands Elementary. Tel. 256-428-7206, e-mail cmlib3453@aol.com; *Treas.* Cynthia Sankey, McIntyre Middle School. Tel. 334-263-7167, e-mail cmlib3453@aol.com; *Past Pres.* Ann Marie Pipkin, Hoover H.S. Tel. 205-439-1242, e-mail apipkin@hoover.k12.al.us.

Address correspondence to the president.

World Wide Web http://www.alaima.org.

Alaska

Alaska Assn. of School Libns. Memb. 200+. Term of Office. March 2002–Feb. 2003. Publication. *Puffin* (3 a year).

Pres. Cathy Boutin. E-mail boutinc@jsd.k12.ak.us; *Pres.-Elect* Bob VanDerWege. E-mail rvdw@kpbsd.k12.ak.us; *Secy.* Darla Grediagin. E-mail jelinek121@gci.net; *Treas.* Karen Joynt. E-mail joynt@alaska.net; *Past Pres.* Tiki Levinson. E-mail tlevinson@nnk.gcisa.net; *School Lib. Coord. for Alaska State Lib.* Sue Sherif. E-mail sue_sherif@eed.state.ak.us.

World Wide Web http://www.akla.org/akasl.

Arizona

Teacher-Librarian Div., Arizona Lib. Assn. Memb. 1,000. Term of Office. Dec. 2002–Dec. 2004. Publication. *AZLA Newsletter.*

Chair Judi Moreillon, Sabino H.S. Tel. 520-749-8359, e-mail storypower@theriver.com; *Chair-Elect* Ann Dutton, Cholla Middle School. Tel. 602-509-3156, e-mail adutton1@cox.net.

Address correspondence to the chairperson.

World Wide Web http://www.azla.org/tld/index.html.

Arkansas

Arkansas Assn. of School Libns. Term of Office. Jan.–Dec. 2003.

Chair Diane Hughes, Lake Hamilton Junior H.S., 281 Wolf St., Pearcy 71964. Tel. 501-767-2731, fax 501-767-1711, e-mail diane.hughes@lh.dsc.k12.ar.us.

Address correspondence to the chairperson.

California

California School Lib. Assn. Memb. 2,200. Publication. *CSLA Journal* (2 a year). *Ed.* Lesley Farmer.

Pres. Linda Jewett, Sacramento City Unified School Dist., 5735 47th St., Sacramento 95824. Tel. 916-643-9091, e-mail Lindaje@sac-city.k12.ca.us; *Pres.-Elect* Susan Maass, Chaffey Joint Union H.S. Dist., 11801 Lark Dr., Rancho Cucamonga 91701. Tel. 909-989-1600 ext. 2065, e-mail susan_maass@cjuhsd.k12.ca.us; *Secy.* Kathryn L. Matlock, Jehue Middle School, 1500 Eucalyptus Ave., Colton 92376. Tel. 909-421-7377 ext. 1115, e-mail kmatlock@realto.k12.ca.us; *Past Pres.* Jeanne V. Nelson, Murrieta Valley Unified School Dist., 26396 Beckman Ct., Murrieta 92562. Tel. 909-696-1600 ext. 1027, e-mail jnelson@murrieta.k12.ca.us *Office Mgr.* Carol Clayton, 717 K St., Suite 515, Sacramento 95814. Tel. 916-447-2684, e-mail csla@pacbell.net.

World Wide Web http://www.schoolibrary.org.

Address correspondence to the office manager.

Colorado

Colorado Assn. of School Libns. (successor
to Colorado Educational Media Assn.).
Memb. 500. Term of Office. Feb. 2002–Feb.
2003. Publication. *The Medium* (5 a year).
  Pres. Judy Barnett, Wasson H.S., 35 Lake
Ave., Colorado Springs 80906. Tel. 719-328-
2024, fax 719-328-2058, e-mail barnejm@
d11.org; *V.P./Pres.-Elect* David Sanger,
Baker Middle School, 574 W. Sixth Ave.,
Denver 80204. Tel. 303-629-6906, fax 303-
825-3012, e-mail Dave_Sanger@dpsk12.org;
Secy. Jacque Ossian, Cottonwood Creek Elementary, 11200 E. Orchard Ave., Englewood
80111. Tel. 303-773-1453, e-mail jossian@
mail.ccsd.k12.co.us; *Exec. Dir., CAL* Kathleen Sagee.
  Address correspondence to Colorado Assn.
of School Libns., c/o Colorado Assn. of
Libs., 4350 Wadsworth Blvd., No. 340,
Wheat Ridge 80033. Tel. 303-463-6400, fax
303-431-9752, e-mail officemanager@cal-
webs.org.
  World Wide Web http://www.cal-webs.
org.

Connecticut

Connecticut Educational Media Assn. Memb.
550. Term of Office. July 2002–June 2003.
Publications. *CEMA Update* (q.), *CEMA
Gram* (mo.).
  Pres. Rebecca Hickey, 14 Boston Post
Road Place, Old Saybrook 06457. E-mail
bukgrl@yahoo.com; *V.P.* Jerilyn Van Leer,
213 Cotton Hill Rd., New Hartford 06057.
Tel. 860-489-3767, e-mail jeri_VanLeer@
whps.org; *Secy.* Julia Wiggins-Strada, 12
Prospect St., Chester 06412. E-mail wiggins
strada@yahoo.com; *Treas.* Sewell Pruchnik,
85 Benson Rd., Bridgewater 06752. Tel. 860-
355-2693, e-mail spruchnik@snet.net; *Past
Pres.* Irene Kwidzinski, 293 Pumpkin Hill
Rd., New Milford 06776. Tel. 203-355-0762,
e-mail kwidzinskii.nor-po@new-milford.k12.
ct.us; *Admin. Secy.* Anne Weimann, 25 Elm-
wood Ave., Trumbull 06611. Tel. 203-372-
2260, e-mail aweimann@snet.net.
  Address correspondence to the administrative secretary.
  World Wide Web http://www.ctcema.org.

Delaware

Delaware School Lib. Media Assn., Div. of
Delaware Lib. Assn. Memb. 100+. Term of
Office. Apr. 2002–Apr. 2003. Publications.
DSLMA Newsletter (irreg.), column in *DLA
Bulletin* (3 a year).
  Pres. Allison G. Kaplan. Tel. 302-831-
1584, fax 302-831-8404, e-mail akaplan@
udel.edu; *V.P.* Barbara Ruszkowski. Tel.
302-421-3739; *Secy.* Christine Kutcher. Tel.
302-832-1343, e-mail cakutcher@yahoo.
com; *Past Pres.* Elizabeth S.Tiffany. E-mail
etiffany@irsd.k12.de.us.
  Address correspondence to the president.
  World Wide Web http://www.udel.edu/
educ/slms/dslma.html.

District of Columbia

District of Columbia Assn. of School Libns.
Memb. 35. Publication. *Newsletter* (4 a year).
  Pres. André Maria Taylor, Wheaton,
Maryland. E-mail divalibrarian2@aol.com.

Florida

Florida Assn. for Media in Education. Memb.
1,450. Term of Office. Nov. 2002–Oct. 2003.
Publication. *Florida Media Quarterly. Ed.*
Linda Miller. E-mail miller_12@firn.edu
(advertising inquiries to FAME, 407 Wekiva
Springs Rd., Suite 241, Longwood 32779. E-
mail fame@amni.net).
  Pres. Kathryn "Ginger" Klega. Tel. 407-
905-2400 ext. 2682, fax 407-905-2400 ext.
2703, e-mail klegag@ocps.k12.fl.us; *Pres.-
Elect* Sandra McMichael. Tel. 904-610-4903,
fax 904-858-3880; e-mail sandymc@
bellsouth.net; *V.P.* Vic Burke. Tel. 352-671-
4104, fax 352-671-4108, e-mail burke_v@
firn.edu; *Secy.* Leslie Miller. Tel. 850-492-
6136 ext. 233, e-mail miller3@aol.com;
Treas. Judy Coon. Tel. 561-564-4193, fax
561-564-4215, e-mail judycoon11@hotmail.
com; *Exec. Dir.* Jo Sienkiewicz, AMNI Association Management Network. Tel. 407-834-
6688, fax 407-834-4747, e-mail fame@amni.
net.
  Address correspondence to the executive
director.
  World Wide Web http://www.firn.edu/
fame.

Georgia

Georgia Lib. Media Assn. Memb. 200. Term of Office. Jan. 2002–Jan. 2003. *Pres.* Kathi L. Vanderbilt. E-mail klv@mindspring.com; *Pres.-Elect* Millicent D. Norman. E-mail mkdnorman@juno.com; *Secy.* Priscilla Stewart. E-mail prissystewart @yahoo.com; *Treas.* Lynn Strickland. E-mail lstrickland@paulding.k12.ga.us; *Past Pres.* Barbara C. Hallstrom. E-mail caenet@mindspring.com.

World Wide Web http://www.glma-inc.org.

Georgia Independent School Library Media Group.
Pres. Robin Tanis, St. Pius X Catholic H.S. E-mail rtanis@spx.org; *Pres.-Elect/ Treas.* Debbi Carlisi, Wesleyan School. E-mail dcarlisi@wesleyanschool.org; *Secy.* Myra Morrison, Trinity School. E-mail mmorrison@trinityatl.org.

World Wide Web http://www.lovett.org/libraryweb/gisl.htm.

Hawaii

Hawaii Assn. of School Libns. Memb. 216. Term of Office. June 2002–May 2003. Publication. *HASL Newsletter* (4 a year).
Pres. Jo-An Goss, Hawaiian Studies and Language Programs Section. E-mail gossj002 @hawaii.rr.com; *V.P., Programming* Fran Corcoran, St. Andrew's Priory School; *V.P., Membership* Grace Omura, Kamehameha Schools. E-mail gomura@ksbe.edu.

Address correspondence to the association, Box 235019, Honolulu 96823.

World Wide Web http://www.k12.hi.us/~hasl.

Idaho

Educational Media Div., Idaho Lib. Assn. Memb. 125. Term of Office. Oct. 2001–Oct. 2003 Publication. Column in *The Idaho Librarian* (q.).
Chair Penni Cyr, Moscow Senior H.S., Moscow 83843 Tel. 208-882-2591, e-mail cpenni@SD281.k12.id.us.

Address correspondence to the chairperson.

Illinois

Illinois School Lib. Media Assn. Memb. 1,100. Term of Office. July 2002–June 2003. Publications. *ISLMA News* (5 a year), *ISLMA Membership Directory* (ann.).
Pres. Katherine Oberhardt, University H.S., Illinois State Univ., Normal 61790-7100. Tel. 309-438-5520, fax 309-438-5250, e-mail koberhar@ilstu.edu; *Pres.-Elect* Leslie Forsman, Triopia CUSD No. 27, RR 1, Box 141A, Concord 62631. Tel. 217-457-2284 or 217-457-2281, fax 217-457-2277, e-mail lforsman@hotmail.com; *Past Pres.* Pam Storm. Tel. 217-345-2768, e-mail pstorm@charleston.k12.il.us; *Exec. Secy.* Kay Maynard, ISLMA, Box 598, Canton 61520, Tel. 390-649-0911, e-mail ISLMA@aol.com.

World Wide Web http://www.islma.org.

Indiana

Assn. for Indiana Media Educators. Term of Office. May 2002–Apr. 2003. Publications. *FOCUS on Indiana Libraries* (mo.), *Indiana Libraries* (q.).
Pres. Ann Abel, Maple Crest Middle School, Kokomo. E-mail aabel@kokomo. k12.in.us; *Pres.-Elect* Leslie Preddy, Perry Meridian Middle School, Indianapolis. E-mail lpreddy@msdpt.k12.in.us.

Address correspondence to the association, 941 E. 86 St., Suite 260, Indianapolis 46240. Tel. 317-257-2040, fax 317-257-1389, e-mail ilf@indy.net.

World Wide Web http://ilfonline.org.

Iowa

Iowa Educational Media Assn. Memb. 400. Term of Office. Apr. 2002–Apr. 2003. Publication. *Iowa Media Message* (4 a year). *Ed.* Becky Stover, 415 17th St. S.E., Cedar Rapids 52403.
Pres. Rick Valley. E-mail rvalley@rconnect.com; *V.P./Pres.-Elect* Dale Vande-Haar. E-mail dale.vandehaar@dmps.k12.ia. us; *Secy.* Kelly Diller. E-mail kelly.diller@uni.edu; *Treas.* Mia Beasley; *Exec. Secy.* Paula Behrendt, 2306 6th, Harlan 51537. Tel./fax 712-755-5918, e-mail paulab@harlannet.com.

Address correspondence to the executive secretary.

World Wide Web http://www.iema-ia.org.

Kansas

Kansas Assn. of School Libns. Memb. 700. Term of Office. Aug. 2002–July 2003. Publication. *KASL Newsletter* (s. ann.).

Pres. Jane Barnard. Tel. 316-776-3391; *Pres.-Elect* Susan Ryan. Tel. 785-379-5950; *Secy.* Marge Loyd. Tel. 785-271-3765; *Treas.* Teresa MacKay. Tel. 316-747-3356; *Exec. Secy.* Judith Eller, 8517 W. Northridge, Wichita 67205. Tel. 316-773-6723, e-mail judy.eller@wichita.edu.

Address correspondence to the executive secretary.

World Wide Web http://www.skyways.org/KASL.

Kentucky

Kentucky School Media Assn. Memb. 620. Term of Office. Oct. 2002–Oct. 2003. Publication. *KSMA Newsletter* (q.).

Pres. Tammy Rich, Adair County Middle School, 322 Gen. John Adair Dr., Columbia 42728. Tel. 270-384-5308, e-mail trich@adair.k12.ky.us; *Pres.-Elect* Crystal Smallwood, Dorton Elementary, Box 249, Dorton 41520. Tel. 606-639-9842, e-mail csmallwood@pike.k12.ky.us; *Secy.* Jennifer Richard, Saint Charles Middle School, 1155 Hwy. 327, Lebanon 40033. Tel. 270-692-4576, e-mail jrichard@marion.k12.ky.us; *Treas.* Lisa Hughes, Heath High School, 4330 Metropolis Lake Rd., West Paducah 42086. Tel. 270-538-4104, fax 270-538-4091, e-mail lhughes@paducah.k12.ky.us; *Past Pres.* Margaret Roberts, Scott County H.S., 1080 Cardinal Dr., Georgetown 40324. Tel. 502-863-4131 ext. 1200, e-mail mroberts@scott.k12.ky.us.

Address correspondence to the president.
World Wide Web http://www.kysma.org.

Louisiana

Louisiana Assn. of School Libns. Memb. 300+. Term of Office. July 2002–June 2003.

Pres. Jerilyn Woodson. Tel. 225-273-2972, e-mail jwoodson@lsvi.org; *1st V.P.* Linda Lingefelt. Tel. 337-828-3714, e-mail llingefelt@stmary.k12.la.us; *2nd V.P.* Linda

Holmes. Tel. 225-635-6820, e-mail holmesl@wfpsb.org; *Secy.* Jennifer Lovitt. Tel. 337-988-6911, e-mail jklovitt@lft.k12.la.us; *Past Pres.* Betty Brackins. Tel. 225-819-2313, e-mail bbrackins@ebrschools.org.

Address correspondence to the association, c/o Louisiana Lib. Assn., 421 S. Fourth St., Eunice 70535. Tel. 337-550-7890, fax 337-550-7846, e-mail lalibassoc@yahoo.com.

World Wide Web http://www.llaonline.org/lasl.

Maine

Maine School Lib. Assn. Memb. 350. Term of Office. May 2000–May 2002. Publication. *Maine Entry* (with the Maine Lib. Assn.; q.).

Pres. Nancy B. Grant, Penquis Valley H.S. E-mail nbgrant@prexar.com; *1st V.P.* Pam Goucher, Freeport Middle School. E-mail Pam_Goucher@coconetme.org; *Secy.* Margaret McNamee, Biddeford H.S. E-mail margaretmc@lamere.net; *Treas.* Donna Chale, Warsaw Middle School. E-mail dchale@midmaine.com.

Address correspondence to the president.
World Wide Web http://www.maslibraries.org.

Maryland

Maryland Educational Media Organization. Term of Office. July 2002–June 2003.

Pres. Jay Bansbach, Lib. Media Services, Anne Arundel County Public Schools, 188 Green St., Annapolis 21401. E-mail cjbansbach@yahoo.com; *Past Pres.* Elizabeth Harwood, Frederick Douglass H.S., Upper Marlboro 20772. E-mail eharwood@pgcps.org.

Address correspondence to the association, Box 21127, Baltimore 21228.

World Wide Web http://www.tcps.k12.md.us/memo/memo.html.

Massachusetts

Massachusetts School Lib. Media Assn. Memb. 700. Term of Office. June 2002–May 2003. Publication. *Media Forum* (q.).

Pres. Dorothy McQuillan, Newton South H.S. Tel. 617-552-7539, fax 617-552-7078, e-mail Dorothy_McQuillan@newton.mec.

edu; *Pres.-Elect* Ann Perham, Needham H.S. Tel. 781-455-0800 ext. 1708, e-mail Ann_ Perham@needham.k12.ma.us; *Secy.* Phyllis Robinson. Tel. 781-380-0170 ext. 1112, e-mail prob@bhs.ssec.org; *Treas.* Thelma Dakubu, Chelsea H.S. Tel. 617-889-4868, fax 617-889-8468, e-mail tdakubu@yahoo. com; *Exec. Dir.* Doris Smith, MSLMA, Box 25, Three Rivers 01080-0025. Tel./fax 413-283-6675, e-mail dorsmith43@yahoo.com; *Admin. Assistant* Deb McDonald. E-mail mslma@samnet.net.

Address correspondence to the administrative assistant.

World Wide Web http://www.mslma.org.

Michigan

Michigan Assn. for Media in Education. Memb. 1,400. Term of Office. Jan.–Dec. 2002. Publications. *Media Spectrum* (3 a year), *MAME Newsletter* (4 a year).

Pres. Karen Lemmons, Howe Elementary School, 2600 Garland, Detroit 48214. Tel. 313-642-4801 ext. 109, fax 313-642-4802, e-mail Camaralfe@aol.com; *Pres.-Elect* Diane Nye, E. P. Clarke Elementary, 515 E. Glenlord Rd., St. Joseph 49085. Tel. 269-982-4633, fax 269-429-6355, e-mail dnye@ remc11.k12.mi.us; *Secy.* Joanne Steckling, Sashabaw Middle School, 5565 Pine Knob La., Clarkston 48346. Tel. 248-623-4261, fax 248-623-4262, e-mail jms7639@qix.net; *Treas.* Bruce Popejoy, East Jackson Middle School, 4340 Walz Rd., Jackson 49201. Tel. 517-764-6010, fax 517-764-6081, e-mail booken2@aol.com; *Past Pres.* Ginger Sisson, Grandville H.S., 4700 Canal S.W., Grandville 49418. Tel. 616-261-6450, fax 616-261-6501, e-mail gsisson@gpsk12.net; *Exec. Dir.* Roger Ashley, MAME, 1407 Rensen, Suite 3, Lansing 48910. Tel. 517-394-2808, fax 517-394-2096, e-mail ashleymame@aol.com.

Address correspondence to the executive director.

World Wide Web http://www.mame.gen. mi.us.

Minnesota

Minnesota Educational Media Organization. Memb. 750. Term of Office. (Pres.) July 2002–July 2003. Publications. *Minnesota Media, ImMEDIAte, MEMOrandom, MTNews.*

Co-Pres. Gay Galles, 447 Clearview Ct., Moorhead 56560. Tel. 218-284-2339, 218-233-2307, e-mail ggalles@moorhead.k12. mn.us; Becky Beck, 18560 Everglade Dr., Wyoming 55092. Tel. 763-502-5430, 763-434-9801, e-mail Becky.Beck@Fridley.k12. mn.us; *Pres.-Elect* Doug Johnson, 46813 Cape Horn Rd., Cleveland 56017. Tel. 507-387-7698, 507-931-0077, e-mail djohns1@ isd77.k12.mn.us; *Secy.* Douglas A. Howard, 613 Fifth St. N., New Ulm 56073. Tel. 507-359-7431, e-mail dhoward@newulm.k12.mn. us; *Treas.* Kelly Sharkey, 501 E. Main St., New Prague 56071. Tel. 612-708-1693 or 888-815-8052, e-mail ksharkey@bevcomm. net; *Admin. Asst.* Deanna Sylte, Box 130555, Roseville 55113. Tel. 651-340-0696, fax 651-340-0700, e-mail dsylte@tcq.net.

World Wide Web http://memoweb.org.

Mississippi

School Section, Mississippi Lib. Assn. Memb. 1,300.

Chair Dee Dee Long, Pearl Lower Elementary School. Tel. 601-932-7980, e-mail readingrules@yahoo.com; *V. Chair* Donna Harrison, Washington County Schools. Tel. 662-335-8418, e-mail wharrison@tecinfo. com; *Exec. Dir., MLA* Mary Julia Anderson.

Address correspondence to the association, c/o Mississippi Lib. Assn., Box 20448, Jackson 39289-1448. Tel. 601-352-3917, fax 601-352-4240, e-mail mla@meta3.net.

World Wide Web http://www.misslib.org.

Missouri

Missouri Assn. of School Libns. Memb. 1,129. Term of Office. June 2002–May 2003. Publications. *Media Horizons* (ann.), *Connections* (q.).

Pres. Karen Vialle; *1st V.P./Pres.-Elect* Cheryl Hoemann; *2nd V.P.* Patricia Bibler; *Secy.* Susan Webb; *Treas.* Robin Gibbons; *Past Pres.* Marianne Fues.

Address correspondence to the association, 3912 Manorwood Dr., St. Louis 63125-4335. Tel./fax 314-416-0462, e-mail masl@i1.net.

World Wide Web http://maslonline.org.

Montana

Montana School Lib. Media Div., Montana Lib. Assn. Memb. 200+. Term of Office. July 2002–June 2003. Publication. *FOCUS* (published by Montana Lib. Assn.) (q.).

Chair Steve White, Frenchtown H.S. Lib., Box 117, Frenchtown 59834. Tel. 406-626-5222, fax 406-626-4355, e-mail whites@frenchtown.k12.mt.us.

World Wide Web http://www.mtlib.org/slmd/slmd.html.

Nebraska

Nebraska Educational Media Assn. Memb. 370. Term of Office. July 2002–June 2003. Publication. *NEMA News* (q.).

Pres. Becky Pasco, 6217 Tanglewood Circle, Lincoln 68510. Tel. 402-554-2119, fax 402-554-2125, e-mail rpasco@mail.unomaha.edu; *Exec. Secy.* Joie Taylor, 2301 31st St., Columbus 68601. Tel. 402-564-1781, fax 402-563-8185, e-mail jtaylor@esu7.org.

Address correspondence to the executive secretary.

World Wide Web http://nema.k12.ne.us.

Nevada

Nevada School and Children's Lib. Section, Nevada Lib. Assn. Memb. 120.

Chair Robbie Nickel, Elko County School District. E-mail rnickel@nsn.k12.nv.us; *Exec. Secy.* Arnie Maurins. E-mail amaurins@mail.co.washoe.nv.us.

Address correspondence to the executive secretary.

New Hampshire

New Hampshire Educational Media Assn., Box 418, Concord 03302-0418. Memb. 265. Term of Office. June 2002–June 2003. Publication. *On line* (5 a year).

Pres. Jean Newcomb, Fairgrounds Junior H.S., Nashua 03064. Tel 603-594-4393, e-mail newcombj@nashua.edu; *V.P./Pres.-Elect* Becky Albert, Tilton School, 30 School St., Tilton 03276. Tel. 603-286-1752, e-mail BAlbert@tiltonschool.org; *V.P.-Elect* Karin Kell-Deyo, Merrimack Valley H.S. E-mail kkell-deyo@mv.k12.nh.us; *Treas.* Jeff Kent,

Dewey School, 38 Liberty St., Concord 03301. Tel. 603-225-0833, e-mail jkent@csd.k12.nh.us; *Recording Secy.* Mimi Crowley, Amherst Street School, 71 Amherst St., Nashua 03064, e-mail crowleym@nashua.edu or mimic@crowley.mv.com; *Past Pres.* Gail Shea Grainger, Chesterfield School, Box 205, Chesterfield 03443. E-mail ggrainger@deweybrowse.org.

Address correspondence to the president.

World Wide Web http://www.nhema.net.

New Jersey

Educational Media Assn. of New Jersey. Memb. 1,100. Term of Office. Aug. 2001–July 2003. Publication. *Bookmark* (mo).

Pres. Susan Heinis, West Essex Senior H.S., 65 W. Greenbrook Rd., North Caldwell 07006. Tel. 973-228-1200 ext. 252, e-mail sheinis@westex.org; *Pres.-Elect* Cathie Miller, Princeton Day School, Box 75, Great Rd., Princeton 08542. Tel. 609-924-6700 ext. 242, e-mail cmiller@pds.org; *V.P.* Mary Lewis, David Brearley Middle/H.S., 401 Monroe Ave., Kenilworth 07033. Tel. 908-931-9696, fax 908-931-1618, e-mail mary.lewis@erols.com.

Address correspondence to the president-elect.

Association office Box 610, Trenton 08607. Tel. 609-394-8032.

World Wide Web http://www.emanj.org.

New York

School Lib. Media Section, New York Lib. Assn., 252 Hudson St., Albany 12210. Tel. 518-432-6952, 800-252-6952. Memb. 880. Term of Office. Oct. 2002–Oct. 2003. Publications. *SLMSGram* (q.); participates in *NYLA Bulletin* (mo. except July and Aug.).

Pres. Rosina Alaimo, Williamsville Central School District, Maple West Elementary, 851 Maple Rd., Williamsville 14221. Tel. 716-626-8846, fax 716-626-8859, e-mail ralaimo@williamsvillek12.org; *V.P. Conferences* Patricia Shanley; *V.P. Communications* Christine Betz; *Secy.* Marcia Eggleston; *Treas.* Sally Koes; *Past Pres.* Cathie Marriott.

Address correspondence to the president.

World Wide Web http://www.slms-nyla.org.

North Carolina

North Carolina School Lib. Media Assn. Memb. 749. Term of Office. Oct. 2002–Oct. 2003.

Pres. Rusty Taylor, Media Services, Wake County Public Schools, 4401 Atlantic Ave., Raleigh 27604. Tel. 919-431-8081, fax 919-431-8077, e-mail jtaylor@wcpss.net; *V.P./Pres.-Elect* Edna Cogdell, Dir. Media Services, Cumberland County Public Schools, 734 Ashburton Dr., Fayetteville 28301. Tel. 910-678-2614, fax 910-678-2641, e-mail ednac@ccs.k12.nc.us; *Secy.* Libby Oxenfeld, Lib. Media Services, Guilford County Public Schools, 3904 Watauga Dr., Greensboro 27410. Tel. 336-370-2310, e-mail oxenfee@guilford.k12.nc.us; *Treas.* Diane Averett, Kerr Vance Academy, 700 Vance Academy Rd., Henderson 27536. Tel. 252-492-0018, fax 252-438-4652, e-mail daverett@kerr vance.com; *Past Chair* Karen Gavigan, Teacher Educ. Resource Center, Univ. of North Carolina–Greensboro, Box 26171, Greensboro 27402. Tel. 336-334-4035, fax 336-334-4120, e-mail karen_gavigan@uncg.edu.

Address correspondence to the chairperson.
World Wide Web http://www.ncslma.org.

North Dakota

School Lib. and Youth Services Section, North Dakota Lib. Assn. Memb. 100. Term of Office. Sept. 2002–Sept. 2003. Publication. *The Good Stuff* (q).

Chair Konnie Wightman, Lib. Media Office, Hughes Educ. Center, 806 N. Washington St., Bismarck 58501. Tel. 701-355-3076, e-mail konda_wightman@educ8.org.

Address correspondence to the chairperson.

Ohio

Ohio Educational Lib. Media Assn. Memb. 1,200. Publication. *Ohio Media Spectrum* (q.).

Pres. Suellyn Stotts. E-mail stotts_suellyn @msmail.dublin.k12.oh.us; *V.P.* Joanna McNally. E-mail joanna.mcnally@lnoca.org;

Past Pres. Linda Cornette. E-mail lcornett@columbus.rr.com; *Exec. Assistant* Kate Brunswick, 17 S. High St., Columbus 43215. Tel. 614-221-1900, fax 614-221-1989, e-mail oelma@mecdc.org.

Address correspondence to the executive assistant.
World Wide Web http://www.oelma.org.

Oklahoma

Oklahoma Assn. of School Lib. Media Specialists. Memb. 3,000+. Term of Office. July 2001–June 2002. Publication. *Oklahoma Librarian.*

Chair Lily Kendall; *Chair-Elect* Jayme Seat; *Secy.* Joan Sizemore; *Treas.* Sue Jenkins; *AASL Delegate* Buffy Edwards; *Past Chair* Sandy Austin.

Address correspondence to the chairperson, c/o Oklahoma Lib. Assn., 300 Hardy Dr., Edmond 73013. Tel. 405-348-0506.

World Wide Web http://www.oklibs.org/oaslms.

Oregon

Oregon Educational Media Assn. Memb. 600. Term of Office. July 2002–June 2003. Publication. *INTERCHANGE.*

Pres. Kelly Kuntz. E-mail kelly_kuntz@beavton.k12.or.us; *Pres.-Elect* Linda Ague. E-mail ague@4j.lane.edu; *Past Pres.* Jeri Petzel. E-mail jpetzel@canby.com; *Exec. Dir.* Jim Hayden, Box 277, Terrebonne 97760. Tel./fax 541-923-0675, e-mail jhayden@bendnet.com.

Address correspondence to the executive director.
World Wide Web http://www.OEMA.net.

Pennsylvania

Pennsylvania School Libns. Assn. Memb. 1,565. Term of Office. July 2002–June 2004. Publication. *Learning and Media* (q.).

Pres. Geneva Reeder. E-mail greeder@dejazzd.com; *V.P./Pres.-Elect* Anita Vance. E-mail alv@lion.crsd.k12.pa.us; *Secy.* Debra Gniewek; *Treas.* Connie Roupp.

Address correspondence to the president.
World Wide Web http://www.psla.org.

Rhode Island

Rhode Island Educational Media Assn. Memb. 398. Term of Office. June 2002–May 2003.

Pres. Holly Barton. E-mail bartonh@ride. ri.net; *V.P.* Phyllis Humphrey. E-mail rid04893 @ride.ri.net; *Secy.* Sue Fleisig. E-mail sue fleisig@aol.com; *Treas.* Judi O'Brien. E-mail obrienj@ride.ri.net; *Past Pres.* Connie Zack. E-mail ride0276@ride.ri.net.

Address correspondence to the association, Box 470, East Greenwich 02818.

World Wide Web http://www.ri.net/ RIEMA.

South Carolina

South Carolina Assn. of School Libns. Memb. 1,100. Term of Office. June 2002–May 2003. Publication. *Media Center Messenger* (4 a year).

Pres. Janet Boltjes. E-mail jboltjes@ lexington1.net; *V.P./Pres.-Elect* Martha Taylor. E-mail MarthaTaylor@anderson5.net; *Secy.* Jennifer Garrett; *Treas.* Judy Thomas. E-mail jthomas@clover.k12.sc.us; *Past Pres.* Claudia Myers. E-mail claudiamyers@ berkeley.k12.sc.us.

Address correspondence to the president. World Wide Web http://www.scasl.net.

South Dakota

South Dakota School Lib. Media Assn., Section of the South Dakota Lib. Assn. and South Dakota Education Assn. Memb. 140+. Term of Office. Oct. 2002–Oct. 2003.

Chair Dianne Hemminger, Wolsey Schools. E-mail dianne.hemminger@k12.sd.us.

Tennessee

Tennessee Assn. of School Libns. Memb. 450. Term of Office. Jan. –Dec. 2003. Publication. *Footnotes* (q.).

Pres. Nancy Dickinson, Hillsboro Elementary School, 284 Winchester Hwy., Hillsboro 37342. E-mail fsufan@dtccom.net; *V.P./ Pres.-Elect* Diane Chen, Hickman Elementary School, 112 Stewart's Ferry Park, Nashville 37214; *Secy.* Wanda Powell, Dresden H.S., 7150 Hwy. 22, Dresden 38225; *Treas.* Vicki Randolph, Springfield Middle School, 715 Fifth Ave. W., Springfield 37172. E-mail randolphv@k12tn.net; *Past Pres.* Janette Lambert, Pearl-Cohn H.S., 904 26th Ave. N., Nashville 37208. E-mail tasl2002@aol.com.

Address correspondence to the president. World Wide Web http://www.korrnet.org/ tasl.

Texas

Texas Assn. of School Libns. (Div. of Texas Lib. Assn.). Memb. 4,051. Term of Office. Apr. 2002–Apr. 2003. Publication. *Media Matters* (3 a year).

Chair Susan Meyer, 2309 Covington, Plano 75023. E-mail pmkmtx@attbi.com; *Chair-Elect* Janice Richardson, 18215 Lura Lane, Jonestown 78645-3426. Tel. 512-434-7840, e-mail janice.richardson@leander.isd. tenet.edu.

Address correspondence to the association, 3355 Bee Cave Rd., Suite 401, Austin 78746. Tel. 512-328-1518, fax 512-328-8852, e-mail tla@txla. org.

World Wide Web http://www.txla.org/ groups/tasl/index.html.

Utah

Utah Educational Lib. Media Assn. Memb. 390. Term of Office. Mar. 2002–Feb. 2003. Publication. *UELMA Newsletter* (4 a year).

Pres. Diane Stokoe, Olympus H.S., 4055 S. 2300 E., Salt Lake City 84124. Tel. 801-273-2000, fax 801-273-2021, e-mail diane. stokoe@granite.k12.ut.us; *Pres.-Elect* Burke Belknap, Snow Canyon H.S., 1385 N. Lava Flow Dr., St. George 84770. Tel. 435-634-1967, fax 435-634-1130, e-mail burke@ admin.schs.wash.k12.ut.us; *Secy.* Althea Bennett, Wasatch Junior High, 3750 S. 3100 E., Salt Lake City 84109. Tel. 801-273-2115, fax 801-273-2012, e-mail althea.bennett@ granite.k12.ut.us; *Past Pres.* Paula Zsiray, Mountain Crest H.S., 255 S. 800 E., Hyrum 84319. Tel. 435-245-6093, fax 435-345-3818, e-mail paula.zsiray@cache.k12.ut.us; *Exec. Dir.* Larry Jeppesen, Cedar Ridge Middle School, 65 N. 200 W., Hyde Park 84318. Tel. 435-563-6229, fax 435-563-3914, e-mail. ljeppese@crms.cache.k12.ut.us.

Address correspondence to the executive director.

World Wide Web http://www.uelma.org.

Vermont

Vermont Educational Media Assn. Memb. 226. Term of Office. May 2002–May 2003. Publication. *VEMA News* (q.).

Pres. Christine Varney, Hinesburg Community School, 10888 Rte. 116, Hinesburg 05461. Tel. 802-482-6288, e-mail varney@ hcsvt.org; *Pres.-Elect* Rebecca Brown, People's Academy, 202 Copley Ave., Morrisville 05661. E-mail Rebecca.Brown@morrisville. org; *Secy.* Joanne Axelrod; *Treas.* Merlyn Miller.

Address correspondence to the president.
World Wide Web http://www.vemaonline. org.

Virginia

Virginia Educational Media Assn. Memb. 1,450. Term of Office. (Pres., Pres.-Elect) Nov. 2002–Nov. 2003; (other offices 2 years in alternating years). Publication. *Mediagram* (q.).

Pres. Roxanne Mills, Chesapeake Public Schools. E-mail millsrwe@cps.k12.va.us; *Pres.-Elect* Betsy Davis, Norfolk Public Schools. E-mail bdavis@nps.k12.va.us; *Exec. Dir.* Jean Remler. Tel./fax 703-764-0719, e-mail jremler@pen.k12.va.us.

Address correspondence to the association, Box 2743, Fairfax 22031-0743.
World Wide Web http://vema.gen.va.us.

Washington

Washington Lib. Media Assn. Memb. 1,200. Term of Office. Oct. 2002–Oct. 2003. Publications. *The Medium* (3 a year), *The Message* (2 a year).

Pres. Sally Lancaster. E-mail slancaster@ everett.wednet.edu; *Pres.-Elect* Andrea Hynes. E-mail ahynes@seanet.com; *V.P.* Linda Collins. E-mail lcollins@upsd.wednet. edu; *Treas.* Kathy Kugler. E-mail kkugler@ mindspring.com; *Secy.* MarieAnne Hunter. E-mail mhunter@nthurston.k12.wa.us.

Address correspondence to the association, Box 50194, Bellevue 98015-0194. E-mail wlma@wlma.org.
World Wide Web http://www.wlma.org.

West Virginia

West Virginia Technology, Education, and Media Specialists (WVTEAMS). Memb. 200. Term of Office. Aug. 2002–July 2003.

Pres. Susan Danford. E-mail sdanford@ access.k12.wv.us; *Pres.-Elect* Richard Skinner. E-mail spirit@access.mountain.net; *Secy.* Shannon Carnes; *Treas.* June Geiger. E-mail jgeiger@access.k12.wv.us; *Past Pres.* Ann Skinner. E-mail spirit@access.mountain. net.

Address correspondence to the president.
World Wide Web http://www.wvteams.org.

Wisconsin

Wisconsin Educational Media Assn. Memb. 1,122. Term of Office. Apr. 2002–Apr. 2003. Publication. *Dispatch* (7 a year).

Pres. Mary Lou Zuege. E-mail zuegmar@ sdmf.k12.wi.us; *Pres.-Elect* Kate Bugher. E-mail kbugher@madison.k12.wi.us; *Secy.* Becki George. E-mail bageorge@chibardun. net; *Treas.* Mike Webber. E-mail weber@ hartfordjt1.k12.wi.us; *Past Pres.* Jim Bowen. E-mail Bowenjm@netnet.net.

Address correspondence to the president or the secretary.
World Wide Web http://www.wemaonline. org/ab.main.cfm.

Wyoming

Section of School Library Media Personnel, Wyoming Lib. Assn. Memb. 91. Term of Office. Oct. 2002–Oct. 2003. Publications. *WLA Newsletter, SSLMP Newsletter.*

Chair Val Roady, Dist. Lib. Media Specialist, Big Horn County Dist. 4. E-mail roady@bgh4.k12.wy.us; *Chair-Elect* Mary Lou Bowles-Banks, District Libn., Dubois School Libs. E-mail maryloub@rams. fremont2.k12.wy.us; *Secy.* Georgia Lundquist, Lib. Media Specialist, Campbell County H.S. Media Center. E-mail glundquist@ccsd.k12. wy.us; *Past Chair* Lisa Smith, Lib. Media Specialist, Tongue River H.S., Box 408, Dayton 83836. Tel. 306-655-2236, fax 307-655-9897, e-mail lisa@sheridank12.net.

Address correspondence to the chairperson.

International Library Associations

International Association of Agricultural Information Specialists (IAALD)

c/o Pamela Q. Andre, Acting President
Box 218, 5863 Lilac Circle
St. Leonard, MD 20685
410-586-1274
E-mail pamandre@hotmail.com
World Wide Web http://www.iaald.org

Object

The association facilitates professional development of and communication among members of the agricultural information community worldwide. Its goal is to enhance access to and use of agriculture-related information resources. To further this mission, IAALD will promote the agricultural information profession, support professional development activities, foster collaboration, and provide a platform for information exchange. Founded 1955.

Membership

Memb. 600+. Dues (Inst.) US$95; (Indiv.) $45.

Officers

Acting Pres. Pamela Q. Andre, Box 218, 5863 Lilac Circle, St. Leonard, MD 20685; *Secy.-Treas.* Margot Bellamy, 14 Queen St., Dorchester-on-Thames, Wallingford, Oxon OX10 7HR, England. Tel. 44-1865-340054, e-mail margot.bellamy@fritillary.demon.co.uk.

Publications

Quarterly Bulletin of the IAALD (memb.).
World Directory of Agricultural Information Resource Centres.

International Association of Law Libraries

Box 5709, Washington, DC 20016-1309
Tel. 804-924-3384, fax 804-924-7239
World Wide Web http://www.iall.org

Object

IALL is a worldwide organization of librarians, libraries, and other persons or institutions concerned with the acquisition and use of legal information emanating from sources other than their jurisdictions, and from multinational and international organizations.

IALL's basic purpose is to facilitate the work of librarians who must acquire, process, organize, and provide access to foreign legal materials. IALL has no local chapters but maintains liaison with national law library associations in many countries and regions of the world.

Membership

More than 800 members in more than 50 countries on five continents.

Officers (2001–2004)

Pres. Holger Knudsen (Germany); *1st V.P.* Jules Winterton (Great Britain); *2nd V.P.* Marie-Louise H. Bernal (USA); *Secy.* Ann Morrison (Canada); *Treas.* Gloria F. Chao (USA).

Board Members

Jennefer Aston (Ireland); Joan A. Brathwaite (Barbados); James Butler (Australia); Richard A. Danner (USA); Halvor Kongshavn (Norway); Jarmila Looks (Switzerland); Lis-beth Rasmussen (Denmark); Silke A. Sahl (USA).

Publications

International Journal of Legal Information (3 a year; US$65 for individuals; $95 for institutions).

Committee Chairpersons

Communications. Richard A. Danner (USA).

International Association of Music Libraries, Archives and Documentation Centres (IAML)

c/o Alison Hall, Secretary-General
Cataloging Dept., Carleton University Library
1125 Colonel By Drive, Ottawa, ON K1S 5B6, Canada
Tel. 613-520-2600 ext. 8150, fax 613-520-2750, e-mail Alison_Hall@Carleton.ca
World Wide Web http://www.cilea.it/music/iaml/iamlhome.htm

Object

To promote the activities of music libraries, archives, and documentation centers and to strengthen the cooperation among them; to promote the availability of all publications and documents relating to music and further their bibliographical control; to encourage the development of standards in all areas that concern the association; and to support the protection and preservation of musical documents of the past and the present.

Membership

Memb. 2,000.

Board Members (2002–2004)

Pres. John H. Roberts, Music Lib., 240 Morrison Hall, Univ. of California, Berkeley, Berkeley, CA 94720. Tel. 510-642-2428, fax 510-642-8237, e-mail jroberts@library. berkeley.edu; *Past Pres.* Pamela Thompson, Royal College of Music Lib., Prince Consort Rd., London SW7 2BS, England; *V.P.s* Dominique Hausfater, Mediathèque Hector Berlioz, Conservatoire National Supérieur de Musique et de Danse de Paris, 209 Ave. Jean-Jaurès, F-75019 Paris, France. Tel. 33-1-40-40-46-28, fax 33-1-40-40-45-34, e-mail dhausfater@cnsmdp.fr; Ruth Hellen, Audio Visual Services, Enfield Libs., Town Hall, Green Lane, London N13 4XD, England. Tel. 44-208-379-2760, fax 44-208-379-2761, e-mail r-hellen@msn.com; Federica Riva, Bibliotecario del Conservatorio Sezione Musicale della Biblioteca Palatina, Nel Conservatorio di Musica Arrigo Boito, via Conservatorio 27/a, I-43100 Parma, Italy. Tel. 39-0521-381-958, fax 39-0521-200-398, e-mail f.riva @agora.it; Kirsten Voss-Eliasson, Astershaven 149, DK-2765 Smorum, Denmark. E-mail kvoss@worldonline.dk; *Secy.-Gen.* Alison Hall, Cataloging Dept., Carleton Univ. Lib., 1125 Colonel By Dr., Ottawa, ON K1S 5B6; *Treas.* Martie Severt, MCO Muziekbibliotheek, Postbus 125, NL-1200

AC Hilversum, Netherlands. E-mail m.severt @mco.nl.

Publication

Fontes Artis Musicae (4 a year; memb.). *Ed.* John Wagstaff, Music Faculty Lib., Oxford Univ., St. Aldate's, Oxford OX1 1DB, England.

Professional Branches

Archives and Documentation Centres. Judy Tsou, Univ. of Washington, Seattle, WA 98145.

Broadcasting and Orchestra Libraries Jutta Lambrecht, Westdeutscher Rundfunk, Dokumentation und Archive, Appellhof-platz 1, D-50667 Köln, Germany.

Libraries in Music Teaching Institutions. Anne Le Lay, Bibliothèque du CNR, 22 rue de la Belle Feuille, F-92100 Boulogne-Billancourt, France.

Public Libraries. Kirsten Husted, Biblioteket for Vejle By og Amt, Willy Sørensen Plads 1, Vejle, Denmark.

Research Libraries. Joachim Jaenecke, Staats-bibliothek zu Berlin, 10102 Berlin, Germany.

International Association of School Librarianship

Penny Moore, Executive Director
Box 34069, Dept. 962, Seattle, WA 98124-1069
Tel. 604-925-0266, fax 604-925-0566
E-mail iasl@rockland.com or penny.moore@xtra.co.nz
World Wide Web http://www.iasl-slo.org

Object

The objectives of the International Association of School Librarianship are to advocate the development of school libraries throughout all countries; to encourage the integration of school library programs into the instructional and curriculum development of the school; to promote the professional preparation and continuing education of school library personnel; to foster a sense of community among school librarians in all parts of the world; to foster and extend relationships between school librarians and other professionals connected with children and youth; to foster research in the field of school librarianship and the integration of its conclusions with pertinent knowledge from related fields; to promote the publication and dissemination of information about successful advocacy and program initiatives in school librarianship; to share information about programs and materials for children and youth throughout the international community; and to initiate and coordinate activities, conferences, and other projects in the field of school librarianship and information services. Founded 1971.

Membership

Memb. 850.

Officers and Executive Board

Pres. Peter Genco, USA; *V.P.s* Helle Barrett, Sweden; Sandy Zinn, South Africa; James Henri, Hong Kong; *Financial Officer* Kathy Lemaire, United Kingdom; *Dirs.* Eleanor Howe, USA; Sandra Hughes, Canada; Constanza Mekis, Latin America; John Royce, North Africa/Middle East; Monica Milsson, Europe; Margaret Balfour-Awuah, Africa–Sub-Sahara; Gail Parr, Asia; Sandra Lee, East Asia; Elizabeth Greef, Oceania; Colleen MacDonell, International Schools.

Publications

Selected Papers from Proceedings of Annual Conferences (all $25).
21st Annual Conference, 1992, Belfast, Northern Ireland. Toward the 21st Century: Books and Media for the Millennium.
22nd Annual Conference, 1993, Adelaide, Australia. Dreams and Dynamics.

23rd Annual Conference, 1994, Pittsburgh. Literacy: Traditions, Cultures, Technology.
24th Annual Conference, 1995, Worcester, England. Sustaining the Vision.
25th Annual Conference, 1996, Ocho Rios, Jamaica. School Libraries Imperatives for the 21st Century.

International Association of Technological University Libraries

c/o President, Michael Breaks, Heriot-Watt Univ. Lib., Edinburgh EH14 4AS, Scotland
Tel. 44-131-451-3570, fax 44-131-451-3164, e-mail m.l.breaks@hw.ac.uk
World Wide Web http://www.iatul.org

Object

To provide a forum where library directors can meet to exchange views on matters of current significance in the libraries of universities of science and technology. Research projects identified as being of sufficient interest may be followed through by working parties or study groups.

Membership

Ordinary, associate, sustaining, and honorary. Membership fee is 107 Euros a year, sustaining membership 500 Euros a year. Memb. 232 (in 42 countries).

Officers and Executives

Pres. Michael Breaks, Heriot-Watt Univ. Lib., Edinburgh EH14 4AS, Scotland. Tel. 44-131-351-3570, fax 44-131-451-3164, e-mail m.l.breaks@hw.ac.uk; *1st V.P.* C. Lee Jones, Linda Hall Lib., 5109 Cherry St., Kansas City, MO 64110. Tel. 816-926-8742, fax 816-926-8790, e-mail leejones@linda hall.org; *2nd V.P.* Gaynor Austen, Queensland Univ. of Technology, GPO Box 2434, Brisbane, Qld. 4001, Australia. Tel. 61-7-3864-2560, fax 61-7-3864-1823, e-mail g.austen@qut.edu.au; *Secy.* Judith Palmer, Radcliffe Science Lib., Oxford Univ., Parks Road, Oxford OX1 3QP, England. E-mail judith.palmer@bodley.ox.ac.uk; *Treas.* Maria Heijne, Delft Univ. of Technology Lib. (DUTL), Postbus 98, 2600 MG Delft, Netherlands. Tel. 31-15-278 56 56, fax 31-15-257 20 60, e-mail M.A.M.Heijne@library.tudelft.nl; *Membs.* Murray Shepherd, Canada; Marianne Nordlander, Sweden; Anna Azevedo, Portugal; Cathy Matthews, Canada; Matjaz Zaucer, Slovenia.

Publications

IATUL Proceedings on CD-ROM (ann.).

International Council on Archives

Joan van Albada, Secretary-General
60 Rue des Francs-Bourgeois, F-75003 Paris, France
Tel. 33-1-40-27-63-06, fax 33-1-42-72-20-65, e-mail ica@ica.org
World Wide Web http://www.ica.org

Object

To establish, maintain, and strengthen relations among archivists of all lands, and among all professional and other agencies or institutions concerned with the custody, organization, or administration of archives, public or private, wherever located. Established 1948.

Membership

Memb. c. 1,700 (representing c. 180 countries and territories).

Officers

Secy.-Gen. Joan van Albada; *Deputy Secy.-*

Gens. Perrine Canavaggio, Marcel Caya.

Publications

Comma (memb.).

Guide to the Sources of the History of Nations (Latin American Series, 11 vols. pub.; African South of the Sahara Series, 20 vols. pub.; North Africa, Asia, and Oceania, 15 vols. pub.)

Guide to the Sources of Asian History (English language series—India, Indonesia, Korea, Nepal, Pakistan, Singapore—14 vols. pub.; National Language Series—Indonesia, Korea, Malaysia, Nepal, Thailand—6 vols. pub.; other guides, 3 vols. pub.)

International Federation of Film Archives (FIAF)

Secretariat, 1 Rue Defacqz, B-1000 Brussels, Belgium
Tel. 32-2-538-3065, fax 32-2-534-4774, e-mail info@fiafnet.org
World Wide Web http://www.fiafnet.org

Object

Founded in 1938, FIAF brings together institutions dedicated to rescuing films both as cultural heritage and as historical documents. FIAF is a collaborative association of the world's leading film archives whose purpose has always been to ensure the proper preservation and showing of motion pictures. A total of 126 archives in more than 60 countries collect, restore, and exhibit films and cinema documentation spanning the entire history of film.

FIAF seeks to promote film culture and facilitate historical research, to help create new archives around the world, to foster training and expertise in film preservation, to encourage the collection and preservation of documents and other cinema-related materials, to develop cooperation between archives, and to ensure the international availability of films and cinema documents.

Officers

Pres. Ivan Trujillo Bolio; *Secy.-Gen.* Steven Ricci; *Treas.* Karl Griep; *Members* Adriano Apra, Claude Bertemes, Hong-Teak Chung, Stefan Droessler, Vera Gyurey, Vigdis Lian,

Susan Oxtoby, Roger Smither, Paolo Cherchi Usai.

Address correspondence to Christian Dimitriu, Senior Administrator, c/o the Secretariat. E-mail info@fiafnet.org.

Publications

Journal of Film Preservation.
International Filmarchive CD-ROM.
For other FIAF publications, see the Web site http://www.fiafnet.org.

International Federation of Library Associations and Institutions (IFLA)

Box 95312, 2509 CH The Hague, Netherlands
Tel. 31-70-314-0884, fax 31-70-383-4827
E-mail ifla@ifla.org, World Wide Web http://www.ifla.org

Object

To promote international understanding, cooperation, discussion, research, and development in all fields of library activity, including bibliography, information services, and the education of library personnel, and to provide a body through which librarianship can be represented in matters of international interest. Founded 1927.

Membership

Memb. (Lib. Assns.) 153; (Inst.) 1,116; (Aff.) 430; Sponsors: 34. Membs. represent 153 countries.

Officers and Governing Board

Pres. Christine Deschamps, Bibliothèque de l'Université de Paris V–René Descartes, Paris, France; *Pres.-Elect* Kay Raseroka, Univ. Lib. of Botswana, Gaborone, Botswana; *Treas.* Derek Law, Univ. of Strathclyde, Glasgow, Scotland; *Governing Board* Alex Byrne, Univ. of Technology, Sydney, Australia; Sissel Nilsen, National Lib. of Norway, Oslo Div.; Sally McCallum, Lib. of Congress, Washington, D.C.; Ellen Tise, Univ. of the Western Cape, Bellville, South Africa; Ingrid Parent, National Lib. of Canada, Ottawa; Claudia Lux, Zentral- und Lan-

desbibliothek Berlin, Berlin, Germany; Jianzhong Wu, Shanghai Lib., Shanghai, China; Ana Maria Peruchena Zimmermann, ABGRA, Buenos Aires, Argentina; Wanda V. Dole, Washburn Univ., Topeka, Kansas; Ia McIlwaine, Dir., School of Lib., Archive, and Info. Studies, Univ. College, London, England; John Meriton, National Art Lib., Victoria and Albert Museum, London, England; Marian Koren, NBLC, The Hague, Netherlands; Mary E. Jackson, Assn. of Research Libs., Washington, D.C.; John M. Day, Gallaudet Univ. Lib., Washington, D.C.; Winston Tabb, Lib. of Congress; Cristobal Pasadas Urena, Universidad de Granada Biblioteca, Granada, Spain; Rashidah Begun bt. Fazal Mohamed, Lib., Universiti Malaysia; *Secy.-Gen.* Ross Shimmon; *Coord. Professional Activities* Sjoerd M. J. Koopman; *IFLA Office for Universal Bibliographic Control and International MARC Program Dir.* Marie-France Plassard, Deutsche Bibliothek, Frankfurt am Main, Germany; *IFLA Office for Preservation and Conservation Program Dir.* M. T. Varlamoff, Bibliothèque Nationale de France, Paris; *IFLA Office for the Advancement of Librarianship Dir.* Birgitta Sandell, Uppsala Univ. Lib., Uppsala, Sweden; *IFLA Committee on Copyright and Other Legal Matters Chair* Marianne Scott; *IFLA Committee on Freedom of Access to Information and Freedom of Expression (FAIFE) Chair* Alex Byrne.

Publications

IFLA Annual Report
IFLA Directory (bienn.).
IFLA Journal (6/yr.).
IFLA Professional Reports.
IFLA Publications Series.
International Cataloguing and Bibliographic Control (q.).
International Preservation News.

American Membership

American Assn. of Law Libs.; American Lib. Assn.; Art Libs. Society of North America; Assn. for Lib. and Info. Science Education; Assn. of Research Libs.; International Assn. of Law Libs.; International Assn. of School Libns.; Medical Lib. Assn.; Special Libs. Assn. *Institutional Membs.* There are 143 libraries and related institutions that are institutional members or consultative bodies and sponsors of IFLA in the United States (out of a total of 1,167), and 105 personal affiliates (out of a total of 361).

International Organization for Standardization (ISO)

ISO Central Secretariat, 1 rue de Varembé, Case Postale 56,
CH-1211 Geneva 20, Switzerland
41-22-749-0111, fax 41-22-733-3430, e-mail central@iso.org
World Wide Web http://www.iso.org

Object

Worldwide federation of national standards bodies, founded in 1947, at present comprising some 145 members, one in each country. The object of ISO is to promote the development of standardization and related activities in the world with a view to facilitating international exchange of goods and services, and to developing cooperation in the spheres of intellectual, scientific, technological, and economic activity. The scope of ISO covers international standardization in all fields except electrical and electronic engineering standardization, which is the responsibility of the International Electrotechnical Commission (IEC). The results of ISO technical work are published as International Standards.

Officers

Pres. Oliver R. Smoot, USA; *V.P. (Policy)* Torsten Bahke, Germany; *V.P. (Technical Management)* Ross Wraight, Australia;

Secy.-Gen. Alan Bryden.

Technical Work

The technical work of ISO is carried out by some 190 technical committees. These include:

ISO/TC 46–Information and documentation (Secretariat, Association Française de Normalization, 11 Ave. Francis de Pressensé, 93571 Saint-Denis La Plaine, Cedex, France). Scope: Standardization of practices relating to libraries, documentation and information centers, indexing and abstracting services, archives, information science, and publishing.

ISO/TC 37–Terminology and other languages resources (Secretariat, INFOTERM, Aichholzgasse 6/12, 1120, Vienna, Austria). Scope: Standardization of principles, methods, and applications relating to terminology and other language resources.

ISO/IEC JTC 1–Information technology (Secretariat, American National Standards Institute, 25 W. 43 St., 4th fl., New York, NY

10036). Scope: Standardization in the field of information technology.

Publications

ISO Annual Report.

ISO Bulletin (mo.).
ISO Catalogue (ann.).
ISO International Standards.
ISO Management Systems (bi-mo.).
ISO Memento (ann.).
ISO Online information service on World Wide Web (http://www.iso.org).

Foreign Library Associations

The following is a list of regional and national library associations around the world. A more complete list can be found in *International Literary Market Place* (Information Today, Inc.).

Regional

Africa

Standing Conference of Eastern, Central, and Southern African Lib. and Info. Assns., c/o Lib. and Info. Assn. of South Africa, National Office, Box 1598, Pretoria 0001, South Africa. Tel: 27-012-481-2871, fax 27-012-481-2873, e-mail liasa@liasa.org.za.

The Americas

Asociación de Bibliotecas Universitarias, de Investigación e Institucionales del Caribe (Assn. of Caribbean Univ., Research, and Institutional Libs.), Box 23317, UPR Sta., San Juan, Puerto Rico 00931-3317. Tel. 787-790-8054, fax 787-764-2311, e-mail acuril@rrpac.upr.clu.edu or acuril@coqui.net, World Wide Web http://www.acuril.rrp.upr.edu. *Exec. Secy.* Oneida R. Ortiz.

Seminar on the Acquisition of Latin American Lib. Materials, c/o *Exec. Secy.* Laura Gutiérrez-Witt, SALALM Secretariat, Benson Latin American Collection, Sid Richardson Hall 1.109, Univ. of Texas, Austin, TX 78713. Tel. 512-495-4471, fax 512-495-4488, e-mail Sandyl@mail.utexas.edu, World Wide Web http://www.lib.utexas.edu/benson/secretariat.

Asia

Congress of Southeast Asian Libns. (CONSAL), c/o *Secy.-Gen.* R. Ramachandran, CONSAL Secretariat, c/o National Lib. Board, 1 Temasek Ave., No. 06-00, Millenia Tower, Singapore 039192. Tel. 65-332-3600, fax 65-332-3616, e-mail secretariat@consal.org.sg, World Wide Web http://www.consal.org.sg.

The Commonwealth

Commonwealth Lib. Assn., Bridgetown Campus, Univ. of the West Indies, Learning Resources Centre, Box 64, Bridgetown, Barbados. Tel. 246-417-4291, fax 246-424-8944, e-mail watsone@uwichill.edu.bb. *Pres.* Elizabeth Watson.

Standing Conference on Lib. Materials on Africa, Commonwealth Secretariat, Marlborough House, Pall Mall, London SW14 5HX, England. Tel. 207-747-6164, fax 207-747-6168, e-mail scolma@hotmail.com. *Chair* Sheila Allcock; *Secy.* David Blake.

Europe

Ligue des Bibliothèques Européennes de Recherche (LIBER) (Assn. of European Research Libs.), c/o Erland Kolding Nielsen, Dir. Gen., Royal Lib., Box 2149, DK-1016 Copenhagen. Tel. 45-33-47-4301, fax 45-33-32-98-46, e-mail ekn@kb.dk, World Wide Web http://www.kb.dk/guests/intl/liber.

National

Argentina

Asociación de Bibliotecarios Graduados de la República Argentina (ABGRA) (Assn. of Graduate Libns. of Argentina), Tucuman 1424, 8 piso D, 1050 Buenos Aires. Tel./fax 1-373-0571, e-mail postmaster@abgra.org.ar. *Pres.* Ana Maria Peruchena Zimmermann; *Exec. Secy.* Rosa Emma Monfasani.

Australia

Australian Lib. and Info. Assn., Box E 441, Kingston, ACT 2600. Tel. 6-285-1877, fax

6-282-2249, e-mail enquiry@alia.org.au. *Pres.* Joyce Kirk; *Exec. Dir.* Jennifer Nicholson.

Australian Society of Archivists, POB 83, O'Connor, ACT 2602. E-mail asa@asap. unimelb.edu.au, World Wide Web http:// www.archivists.org.au. *Pres.* Stephen Yorke; *Secy.* Annabel Lloyd.

Council of Australian State Libs., c/o State Lib. of New South Wales, Macquarie St., Sydney, NSW. Tel. 2-9273-1414, fax 7-3846-2421. *Chair* D. H. Stephens.

Austria

Österreichische Gesellschaft für Dokumentation und Information (Austrian Society for Documentation and Info.), c/o TermNet, Simmeringer Hauptstr. 24, A-1110 Vienna. Tel. 1-7404-0280, fax 1-7404-0281, e-mail oegdi@oegdi.at, World Wide Web http://www.oegdi.at. *Pres.* Gerhard Richter.

Vereinigung Österreichischer Bibliothekarinnen und Bibliothekare (Assn. of Austrian Libns.), c/o Voralberger Landesbibliothek, Fluherstr. 4, A-6900 Bregenz. Tel. 43-5574-511, fax 43-5574-511, e-mail harald. weigel@vlr.gv.at, World Wide Web http:// voeb.uibk.ac.at. *Pres.* Harald Weigel; *Secy.* Werner Schlacher.

Bangladesh

Lib. Assn. of Bangladesh, c/o Safia Kanal National Public Lib. Bldg., Shahbagh, Ramna, Dacca 1000. Tel. 2-504-269, e-mail msik@icddrb.org. *Pres.* M. Shamsul Islam Khan; *Gen. Secy.* Kh. Fazlur Rahman.

Barbados

Lib. Assn. of Barbados, Box 827E, Bridgetown. *Pres.* Shirley Yearwood; *Secy.* Hazelyn Devonish.

Belgium

Archives et Bibliothèques de Belgique/ Archief- en Bibliotheekwezen in België (Archives and Libs. of Belgium), 4 Blvd. de l'Empereur, B-1000 Brussels. Tel. 2-

519-5351, fax 2-519-5533, e-mail wim. devos@kbr.be. *Gen. Secy.* Wim De Vos.

Association Belge de Documentation/Belgische Vereniging voor Documentatie (Belgian Assn. for Documentation), Chaussée de Wavre 1683, Waversesteenweg, B-1160 Brussels. Tel. 2-675-5862, fax 2-672-7446, e-mail abdbvd@abd-bvd.be, World Wide Web http://www.abd-bvd.be. *Pres.* Philippe Laurent.

Association Professionnelle des Bibliothécaires et Documentalistes (Assn. of Libns. and Documentation Specialists), 30 ave. Rêve d'Or, 7100 La Louvière. Tel. 064-21-51-76, fax 064-21-28-50, e-mail jean_ claude.trefois@hainaut.be, World Wide Web http://www.apbd.be. *Pres.* Jean-Claude Tréfois; *Secy.* Laurence Hennaux.

Vlaamse Vereniging voor Bibliotheek-, Archief-, en Documentatiewezen (Flemish Assn. of Libns., Archivists, and Documentalists), Statiestraat 179, B-2600 Berchem, Antwerp. Tel. 3-281-4457, fax 3-218-8077, e-mail vvbad@vvbad.be, World Wide Web http://www.vvbad.be. *Pres.* Geert Puype; *Exec. Dir.* Marc Storms.

Belize

Belize Lib. Assn., c/o Central Lib., Bliss Inst., Box 287, Belize City. Tel. 2-7267. *Pres.* H. W. Young; *Secy.* Robert Hulse.

Bolivia

Asociación Boliviana de Bibliotecarios (Bolivian Lib. Assn.), c/o Biblioteca y Archivo Nacional, Calle Bolivar, Sucre. *Dir.* Gunnar Mendoza.

Bosnia and Herzegovina

Drustvo Bibliotekara Bosne i Hercegovine (Libns. Society of Bosnia and Herzegovina), Zmaja od Bosne 8B, 71000 Sarajevo. Tel./fax 71-212-435, e-mail nevenka@ utic.net.ba. *Pres.* Nevenka Hajdarovic.

Botswana

Botswana Lib. Assn., Box 1310, Gaborone. Tel. 31-355-2295, fax 31-357-291, e-mail mbangiwa@noka.ub.bw. *Chair* F. M. Lamusse; *Secy.* A. M. Mbangiwa.

Brazil

Associação dos Arquivistas Brasileiros (Assn. of Brazilian Archivists), Rua da Candelária, 9-Sala 1004, Centro, Rio de Janeiro RJ 20091-020. Tel./fax 21-233-7142. *Pres.* Lia Temporal Malcher; *Secy.* Laura Regina Xavier.

Brunei Darussalam

Persatuan Perpustakaan Kebangsaan Negara Brunei (National Lib. Assn. of Brunei), c/o Language and Literature Bureau Lib., Jalan Elizabeth II, Bandar Seri Begawan. Tel. 2-235-501. *Contact* Abu Bakar Bin.

Cameroon

Association des Bibliothécaires, Archivistes, Documentalistes et Muséographes du Cameroun (Assn. of Libns., Archivists, Documentalists, and Museum Curators of Cameroon), Université de Yaoundé, Bibliothèque Universitaire, B.P. 337, Yaoundé. Tel. 220-744, fax 221-320.

Canada

Association for Teacher-Librarianship in Canada (ATLC), Box 9, Pouch Cove, NF A0A 3L0. Tel. 709-335-2978, World Wide Web http://www.atlc.ca.

Bibliographical Society of Canada/La Société Bibliographique du Canada, Box 575, Postal Sta. P, Toronto, ON M5S 2T1. E-mail mcgaughe@yorku.ca, World Wide Web http://www.library.utoronto.ca/bsc. *Pres.* Gwendolyn Davies; *Secy.* Anne McGaughey.

Canadian Assn. for Info. Science/Association Canadienne de Sciences de l'Information, c/o CAIS Secretariat, Univ. of Toronto, 140 St. George St., Toronto, ON M5S 1A1. *Pres.* Kirsti Nilsen, Faculty of Information and Media Studies, Middlesex College, Univ. of Western Ontario, London, ON N6A 5B7. Tel. 519-661-2111 ext. 88480, fax 519-661-3506, e-mail knilsen@uwo.ca.

Canadian Association of Research Libraries/Association des Bibliothèques de Recherche du Canada (CARL/ABRC), Univ. of Ottawa, 65 University St., Rm. 239, Ottawa, ON K1N 9A5. World Wide Web http://www.uottawa.ca/library/carl.

Canadian Lib. Assn., c/o *Exec. Dir.* Don Butcher, 328 Frank St., Ottawa, ON K2P 0X8. Tel. 613-232-9625, fax 613-563-9895, e-mail dbutcher@cla.ca. (For detailed information on the Canadian Lib. Assn. and its divisions, see "National Library and Information-Industry Associations, United States and Canada." For information on the library associations of the provinces of Canada, see "State, Provincial, and Regional Library Associations.")

Chile

Colegio de Bibliotecarios de Chile AG (Chilean Lib. Assn.), Diagonal Paraguay 383, Depto. 122, Santiago 3741. Tel. 2-222-5652, fax 2-635-5023, e-mail cbc@uplink.cl, World Wide Web http://www.bibliotecarios.cl. *Pres.* Marcia Marinovic Simunovic; *Secy.* Ana María Pino Yañez.

China

China Society for Lib. Science, 39 Bai Shi Qiao Rd., Beijing 100081. Tel. 10-684-15566, ext. 5563, fax 10-684-19271. *Secy.-Gen.* Liu Xiangsheng.

Colombia

Asociación Colombiana de Bibliotecarios (Colombian Lib. Assn.), Calle 10, No. 3-16, Apdo. Aéreo 30883, Bogotá. Tel. 1-269-4219. *Pres.* Saul Sanchez Toro.

Congo, Democratic Republic

Association Zaïroise des Archivistes, Bibliothécaires et Documentalistes (Zaire Association of Archivists, Librarians, and Documentalists), BP 805, Kinshasa X1. Tel. 012-30123. *Exec. Secy.* E. Kabeba-Bangasa.

Costa Rica

Asociación Costarricense de Bibliotecarios (Costa Rican Assn. of Libns.), Apdo. 3308, San José. *Secy.-Gen.* Nelly Kopper.

Croatia

Hrvatsko Knjiznicarsko Drustvo (Croation Lib. Assn.), Ulica Hrvatske bratske zajednice 4, 10000 Zagreb. Tel. 41-616-4037, fax 41-616-4186, e-mail hbd@nsk.hr, World Wide Web http://pubwww.srce.hr/hkd. *Pres.* Dubravka Stancin-Rosic; *Secy.* Dunja Marie Gabriel.

Cuba

Lib. Assn. of Cuba, Biblioteca Nacional José Marti, Apdo. 6881, Ave. de Independencia e/20 de Mayo y Aranguren, Plaza de la Revolución, Havana. Tel. 7-708-277. *Dir.* Marta Terry González.

Cyprus

Kypriakos Synthesmos Vivliothicarion (Lib. Assn. of Cyprus), Box 1039, Nicosia. *Pres.* Costas D. Stephanov; *Secy.* Paris G. Rossos.

Czech Republic

Svaz Knihovniku Informachnich Pracovniku Ceske Republiky (Assn. of Lib. and Info. Professionals of the Czech Republic), National Lib., Klementinum 190, 11000 Prague. Tel. 2-2166-3338, fax 2-2166-3175, e-mail vit.richter@mkp.cr, World Wide Web http://www.nkp.cz. *Pres.* Vit Richter.

Denmark

Arkivforeningen (Archives Society), c/o Landsarkivet for Sjaelland, jagtvej 10, 2200 Copenhagen K. Tel. 3139-3520, fax 3315-3239. *Pres.* Tyge Krogh; *Secy.* Charlotte Steinmark.

Danmarks Biblioteksforening (Danish Lib. Assn.), Vesterbrogade 20/5, 1620 Copenhagen V. Tel. 3325-0935, fax 3325-7900. *Dir.* Winnie Vitzansky.

Danmarks Forskningsbiblioteksforening (Danish Research Lib. Assn.), Postboks 2149, 1016 Copenhagen K. Tel. 3393-6222, fax 3391-9596, e-mail df@kb.dk. *Pres.* Erland Kolding; *Secy.* D. Skovgaard.

Kommunernes Skolebiblioteksforening (formerly Danmarks Skolebiblioteksforening) (Assn. of Danish School Libs.), Vesterbro-

gade 20, DK-1620, Copenhagen V. Tel. 3325-3222, fax 3325-3223, e-mail komskolbib@internet.dk, World Wide Web http://www.ksbk.dk. *Chief Exec.* Paul Erik Sorensen.

Dominican Republic

Asociación Dominicana de Bibliotecarios (Dominican Assn. of Libns.), c/o Biblioteca Nacional, Plaza de la Cultura, Cesar Nicolás Penson 91, Santo Domingo. Tel. 809-688-4086. *Pres.* Prospero J. Mella-Chavier; *Secy.-Gen.* V. Regús.

Ecuador

Asociación Ecuatoriana de Bibliotecarios (Ecuadoran Lib. Assn.), c/o Casa de la Cultura Ecuatoriana Benjamin Carrión, Apdo. 67, Ave. 6 de Diciembre 794, Quito. Tel. 2-528-840, 2-263-474. *Pres.* Eulalia Galarza.

Egypt

Egyptian Assn. for Lib. and Info. Science, c/o Dept. of Archives, Librarianship, and Info. Science, Faculty of Arts, Univ. of Cairo, Cairo. Tel. 2-567-6365, fax 2-572-9659. *Pres.* S. Khalifa; *Secy.* Hosam El-Din.

El Salvador

Asociación de Bibliotecarios de El Salvador (El Salvador Lib. Assn.), c/o Biblioteca Nacional, 8A Avda. Norte y Calle Delgado, San Salvador. Tel. 216-312.

Asociación General de Archivistas de El Salvador (Assn. of Archivists of El Salvador), Archivo General de la Nación, Palacio Nacional, San Salvador. Tel. 229-418.

Ethiopia

Ye Ethiopia Betemetshaft Serategnoch Mahber (Ethiopian Lib. and Info. Assn.), Box 30530, Addis Ababa. Tel. 1-518-020, fax 1-552-544. *Pres.* Mulugeta Hunde; *Secy.* Girma Makonnen.

Finland

Suomen Kirjastoseura (Finnish Lib. Assn.), Vuorkatu 22 A18, FIN-00100 Helsinki.

Tel. 9-622-1399, fax 9-622-1466, e-mail fla@fla.fi. *Pres.* Kaarina Dromberg; *Secy.- Gen.* Sinikka Sipila.

France

Association des Archivistes Français (Assn. of French Archivists), 60 rue des Francs-Bourgeois, F-75141 Paris Cedex 3. Tel. 1-40-27-60-00. *Pres.* Jean-Luc Eichenlaub; *Secy.* Jean LePottier.

Association des Bibliothécaires Français (Assn. of French Libns.), 31 rue de Chabrol, F-75010 Paris. Tel. 1-55-33-10-30, fax 1-55-30-10-31, e-mail abf@abf.asso.fr, World Wide Web http://www.abf.asso.fr. *Pres.* Gérard Briand; *Gen. Secy.* Jean-François Jacques.

Association des Professionnels de l'Information et de la Documentation (Assn. of Info. and Documentation Professionals), 25 rue Claude Tillier, 75012 Paris. Tel. 1-43-72-25-25, fax 1-43-72-30-41, e-mail adbs@adbs.fr, World Wide Web http://www.adbs.fr. *Pres.* Florence Wilhelm.

Germany

Arbeitsgemeinschaft der Spezialbibliotheken (Assn. of Special Libs.), c/o Forschungszentrum, Jülich GmbH, Zentralbibliothek, 52426 Jülich. Tel. 2461-61-2907, fax 2461-61-6103, e-mail e.salz@fz-juelich. de. *Chair* Rafael Ball; *Secretariat Dir.* Edith Salz.

Berufsverband Information Bibliothek (formerly Verein der Bibliothekare und Assisten) (Assn. of Info. and Lib. Professionals), Postfach 1324, 72703 Reutlingen. Tel. 7121-34910, fax 7121-300-433, e-mail mail@bib-info.de, World Wide Web http://www.bib-info.de. *Pres.* Klaus Peter Bottger; *Secy.* Katharina Boulanger.

Deutsche Gesellschaft für Informationswissenschaft und Informationspraxis eV (German Society for Info. Science and Practice), Ostbahnhofstr. 13, 60314 Frankfurt-am-Main 1. Tel. 69-430-313, fax 69-490-9096, e-mail zentrale@dgi-info.de, World Wide Web http://www.dgi-info.de. *Pres.* Gabriele Beger.

Deutscher Bibliotheksverband eV (German Lib. Assn.), Strasse des 17 Juni 114, 10623 Berlin. Tel. 30-3900-1480, fax 30-3900-1484, e-mail dbv@bdbibl.de, World Wide Web http://www.bdbibl.de/dbv. *Pres.* Christof Eichert.

Verband Deutscher Archivarinnen und Archivare (Assn. of German Archivists), Postfach 2119, 99402 Weimar. Tel. 03643-870-235, fax 03643-870-164, e-mail info @vda.archiv.net, World Wide Web http:// www.vda.archiv.net. *Chair* Volker Wahl.

Verein der Diplom-Bibliothekare an Wissenschaftlichen Bibliotheken (Assn. of Certified Libns. at Academic Libs.), c/o Universitätsbibliothek, Am Hubland 97074, Würzburg. Tel. 221-574-7161, fax 221-574-7110. *Chair* Marianne Saule.

Verein Deutscher Bibliothekare (Assn. of German Libns.), Krummer Timpen 3-5, 48143 Münster. Tel. 251-832-4032, fax 251-832-8398. *Pres.* Klaus Hilgemann. E-mail hilgema@ui-muenster.de; *Secy.* Lydia Jungnickel.

Ghana

Ghana Lib. Assn., Box 4105, Accra. Tel. 2-668-731. *Pres.* E. S. Asiedo; *Secy.* A. W. K. Insaidoo.

Greece

Enosis Hellinon Bibliothekarion (Greek Lib. Assn.), Themistocleus 73, 10683 Athens. Tel. 1-322-6625. *Pres.* K. Xatzopoulou; *Gen. Secy.* E. Kalogeraky.

Guyana

Guyana Lib. Assn., c/o National Lib., Church St. and Ave. of the Republic, Georgetown. Tel. 2-62690, 2-62699. *Pres.* Hetty London; *Secy.* Jean Harripersaud.

Honduras

Asociación de Bibliotecarios y Archiveros de Honduras (Assn. of Libns. and Archivists of Honduras), 11a Calle, 1a y 2a Avdas., No. 105, Comayagüela DC, Tegucigalpa. *Pres.* Fransisca de Escoto Espinoza; *Secy.- Gen.* Juan Angel R. Ayes.

Hong Kong

Hong Kong Lib. Assn., GPO 10095, Hong Kong. E-mail hklib@hklib.org.hk, World

Wide Web http://www.hklib.org.hk. *Pres.* Tommy Yeung.

Hungary

Magyar Könyvtárosok Egyesülete (Assn. of Hungarian Libns.), Hold u 6, H-1054 Budapest. Tel./fax 1-311-8634, e-mail mke@oszk.hu, World Wide Web http://www.mke.oszk.hu. *Pres.* Zoltan Ambrus; *Gen. Secy.* Katalin Haraszti.

Iceland

Bókavardafélag Islands (Icelandic Lib. Assn.), Box 1497, 121 Reykjavik. Tel. 564-2050, fax 564-3877. *Pres.* H. A. Hardarson; *Secy.* A. Agnarsdottir.

India

Indian Assn. of Academic Libns., c/o Zakir Husein Lib., Jamia Milia Islamia Univ., Jamia Nagar, New Delhi 110025. Tel. 11-683-1717. *Secy.* M. M. Kashyap.

Indian Assn. of Special Libs. and Info. Centres, P-291, CIT Scheme 6M, Kankurgachi, Calcutta 700054. Tel. 33-334-9651.

Indian Lib. Assn., c/o Mukerjee Nagar, A/40-41, Flat 201, Ansal Bldg., Delhi 110009. Tel. 11-711-7743. *Pres.* P. S. G. Kumar.

Indonesia

Ikatan Pustakawan Indonesia (Indonesian Lib. Assn.), Jalan Merdeka Selatan No. 21, Box 3624, 10002 Jakarta, Pusat. Tel. 21-342-529, fax 21-310-3554. *Pres.* S. Kartosdono.

Iraq

Iraqi Lib. Assn., c/o National Lib., Bab-el-Muaddum, Baghdad. Tel. 1-416-4190. *Dir.* Abdul Hameed Al-Alawchi.

Ireland

Cumann Leabharlann Na h-Eireann (Lib. Assn. of Ireland), 53 Upper Mount St., Dublin. Tel. 1-661-9000, fax 1-676-1628, World Wide Web http://www.library association.ie. *Pres.* Marjory Sliney; *Hon. Secy.* Geraldine McHugh.

Israel

Israel Libns. and Info. Specialists Assn., Box 238, 91001 Jerusalem. Tel. 2-6207-2868, fax 2-625-628. *Pres.* Benjamin Schachter.

Israel Society of Libs. and Info. Centers, POB 28273, 91281 Jerusalem. Tel./fax 2-624-9421, e-mail asmi@asmi.org.il, World Wide Web http://www.asmi.org.il. *Chair* Shoshana Langerman.

Italy

Associazione Italiana Biblioteche (Italian Lib. Assn.), C.P. 2461, I-00100 Rome A-D. Tel. 6-446-3532, fax 6-444-1139, e-mail aib@aib.it, World Wide Web http://www.aib.it. *Pres.* I. Poggiali; *Secy.* A. Paoli.

Jamaica

Jamaica Lib. Assn., Box 58, Kingston 5. Tel. 876-63310, fax 876-62188. *Pres.* P. Kerr; *Secy.* F. Salmon.

Japan

Joho Kagaku Gijutsu Kyokai (Info. Science and Technology Assn.), Sasaki Bldg., 5-7 Koisikawa 2, Bunkyo-ku, Tokyo. *Pres.* T. Gondoh; *Gen. Mgr.* Yukio Ichikawa.

Nihon Toshokan Kyokai (Japan Lib. Assn.), 1-11-14 Shinkawa, Chuo-ku, Tokyo 104 0033. Tel. 3-3523-0841, fax 3-3421-7588, e-mail info@jla.or.jp. *Secy.-Gen.* Reiko Sakagawa.

Senmon Toshokan Kyogikai (Japan Special Libs. Assn.), c/o Japan Lib. Assn., Bldg. F6, 1-11-14 Shinkawa, Chuo-ku, Tokyo 104 0033. Tel. 3-3537-8335, fax 3-3537-8226, e-mail jsla@jsla.or.jp, World Wide Web http://www.jsla.or.jp. *Pres.* Kousaku Inaba; *Exec. Dir.* Fumihisa Nakagawa.

Jordan

Jordan Lib. Assn., Box 6289, Amman. Tel. 6-629-412. *Pres.* Anwar Akroush; *Secy.* Yousra Abu Ajamieh.

Kenya

Kenya Lib. Assn., Box 46031, Nairobi. Tel. 2-214-917, fax 2-336-885, e-mail jwere@

ken.healthnet.org. *Chair* Jacinta Were; *Secy.* Alice Bulogosi.

Korea (Republic of)

Korean Lib. Assn., 60-1 Panpo Dong, Seocho-ku, Seoul. Tel. 2-535-4868, fax 2-535-5616, e-mail klanet@hitel.net *Pres.* Ki Nam Shin; *Exec. Dir.* Won Ho Jo.

Laos

Association des Bibliothécaires Laotiens (Assn. of Laotian Libns.), c/o Direction de la Bibliothèque Nationale, Ministry of Info. and Culture, B.P. 122, Vientiane. Tel. 21-212-452, fax 21-213-029, e-mail pfd-mill@pan.laos.net.la. *Dir.* Somthong.

Latvia

Lib. Assn. of Latvia, Latvian National Lib., Kr. Barona iela 14, 1423 Riga. Tel. 132-728-98-74, fax 132-728-08-51, e-mail lnb@com.latnet.lv. *Pres.* Aldis Abele.

Lebanon

Lebanese Lib. Assn., c/o American Univ. of Beirut, Univ. Lib./Serials Dept., Box 113/5367, Beirut. Tel. 1-374-374 ext. 2606. *Pres.* Fawz Abdalleh; *Exec. Secy.* Rudaynah Shoujah.

Lesotho

Lesotho Lib. Assn., Private Bag A26, Maseru. *Chair* S. M. Mohai; *Secy.* N. Taole.

Lithuania

Lithuanian Libns. Assn., Sv. Ignoto 6-108, LT-2600, Vilnius. Tel./fax 2-750-340, e-mail lbd@vpu.lt, World Wide Web http://www.lbd.lt.

Macedonia

Bibliotekarsko Drustvo na Makedonija (Union of Libns.' Assns. of Macedonia), Box 566, 91000 Skopje. Tel. 91-212-736, fax 91-232-649, e-mail mile@nubsk.edu.mk or bmile47@yahoo.com. *Pres.* Mile Boseki; *Secy.* Poliksena Matkovska.

Malawi

Malawi Lib. Assn., Box 429, Zomba. Tel. 50-522-222, fax 50-523-225. *Chair* Joseph J. Uta; *Secy.* Vote D. Somba.

Malaysia

Persatuan Perpustakaan Malaysia (Lib. Assn. of Malaysia), Box 12545, 50782 Kuala Lumpur. Tel. 3-273-114, fax 3-273-1167. *Pres.* Chew Wing Foong; *Secy.* Leni Abdul Latif.

Mali

Association Malienne des Bibliothécaires, Archivistes et Documentalistes (Mali Assn. of Libns., Archivists, and Documentalists), c/o Bibliothèque Nationale du Mali, BP 159, Bamako. Tel. 224-963. *Dir.* Mamadou Konoba Keita.

Malta

Malta Lib. and Info. Assn. (MaLIA), c/o Univ. Lib., Msida MSD 06. Tel. 356-213-2024, World Wide Web http://www.malia-malta.org. *Chair* Joseph R. Grima; *Secy.* Robert Mizzi.

Mauritania

Association Mauritanienne des Bibliothécaires, Archivistes et Documentalistes (Mauritanian Assn. of Libns., Archivists, and Documentalists), c/o Bibliothèque Nationale, B.P. 20, Nouakchott. *Pres.* O. Diouwara; *Secy.* Sid'Ahmed Fall dit Dah.

Mauritius

Mauritius Lib. Assn., c/o The British Council, Royal Rd., POB 111, Rose Hill. Tel. 454-9550, fax 454-9553, e-mail bcouncil @intnet.mu, World Wide Web http://www.britishcouncil.org/mauritius. *Pres.* K. Appadoo; *Secy.* S. Rughoo.

Mexico

Asociación Mexicana de Bibliotecarios (Mexican Assn. of Libns.), Apdo. 80-065, Admin. de Correos 80, México D.F. 06001. Tel. 5-575-1135, e-mail ambac@solar.sar.

net. *Pres.* Filiberto Felipe Martínez Arellano; *Secy.* Elías Cid Ramírez.

Myanmar

Myanmar Lib. Assn., c/o National Lib., Strand Rd., Yangon. *Chief Libn.* U Khin Maung Tin.

Nepal

Nepal Lib. Assn., c/o National Lib., Harihar Bhawan, Pulchowk Lib., Box 2773, Kathmandu. Tel. 1-521-132. *Libn.* Shusila Dwivedi.

The Netherlands

Nederlandse Vereniging voor Beroepsbeofenaren in de Bibliotheek-Informatie-en Kennissector (Netherlands Libns. Society), NVB-Verenigingsbureau, Nieuwegracht 15, 3512 LC Utrecht. Tel. 30-231-1263, fax 30-231-1830, e-mail nvbinfo@wxs.nl, World Wide Web http://www.nvb-online. nl. *Pres.* J. S. M. Savenije.

New Zealand

Lib. and Info. Assn. of New Zealand, Old Wool House, Level 5, 139-141 Featherston St., Box 12-212, Wellington. Tel. 4-473-5834, fax 4-499-1480, e-mail steve@lianza. org.nz.

Nicaragua

Asociación Nicaraguense de Bibliotecarios y Profesionales a Fines (Nicaraguan Assn. of Libns.), Apdo. Postal 3257, Managua. *Exec. Secy.* Susana Morales Hernández.

Nigeria

Nigerian Lib. Assn., c/o National Lib. of Nigeria, Gidan Isa, Festival Rd., Garki District, Area 10, Abuja. Tel. 1-260-0220, fax 1-631-563. *Pres.* A. O. Banjo; *Secy.* D. D. Bwayili.

Norway

Arkivarforeningen (Assn. of Archivists), c/o Riksarkivet, Folke Bernadottes Vei 21, Postboks 10, N-0807 Oslo. Tel. 22-022-600, fax 22-237-489.

Norsk Bibliotekforening (Norwegian Lib. Assn.), Malerhaugveien 20, N-0661 Oslo. Tel. 2-268-8550, fax 2-267-2368. *Dir.* Berit Aaker.

Pakistan

Pakistan Lib. Assn., c/o Pakistan Inst. of Development Economics, Univ. Campus, Box 1091, Islamabad. Tel. 51-921-4041, fax 51-921-0886, e-mail naqvizj@ hotmail.com. *Pres.* Sain Malik; *Secy.-Gen* Atta Ullah.

Panama

Asociación Panameña de Bibliotecarios (Panama Lib. Assn.), c/o Biblioteca Interamericana Simón Bolivar, Estafeta Universitaria, Panama City. *Pres.* Bexie Rodriguez de León.

Paraguay

Asociación de Bibliotecarios del Paraguay (Assn. of Paraguayan Libns.), Casilla 910, 2064 Asunción. *Pres.* Gloria Ondina Ortiz; *Secy.* Celia Villamayor de Diaz.

Peru

Asociación de Archiveros del Perú (Peruvian Assn. of Archivists), Archivo Central Salaverry, 2020 Jesús Mario, Universidad del Pacifico, Lima 11. Tel. 1-471-2277, fax 1-265-0958, e-mail dri@u8p.edu.pe. *Pres.* José Luis Abanto Arrelucea.

Asociación Peruana de Bibliotecarios (Peruvian Assn. of Libns.), Bellavista 561 Miraflores, Apdo. 995, Lima 18. Tel. 1-474-869. *Pres.* Martha Fernandez de Lopez; *Secy.* Luzmila Tello de Medina.

Philippines

Assn. of Special Libs. of the Philippines, Rm. 301, National Lib. Bldg., T. M. Kalaw St., Manila. Tel./fax 2-590-177. *Pres.* Zenaida F. Lucas; *Secy.* Socorro G. Elevera.

Bibliographical Society of the Philippines, National Lib. of the Philippines, T. M. Kalaw St., 1000 Ermita, Box 2926, Manila. Tel. 2-583-252, fax 2-502-329, e-mail amb@max.ph.net. *Secy.-Treas.* Leticia R. Maloles.

Philippine Libns. Assn., c/o National Lib. of the Philippines, Rm. 301, Box 2926, T. M. Kalaw St., Manila. Tel. 2-590-177. *Pres.* Antonio M. Sontos; *Secy.* Rosemarie Rosali.

Poland

Stowarzyszenie Bibliotekarzy Polskich (Polish Libns. Assn.), 8-10 Czerwca, 2001 Warsaw-Miedzeszyn. Tel. 22-823-0270, fax 22-822-5133. *Chair* Stanislaw Czajka; *Secy.-Gen.* Janina Jagielska.

Portugal

Associação Portuguesa de Bibliotecários, Arquivistas e Documentalistas (Portuguese Assn. of Libns., Archivists, and Documentalists), R. Morais Soares, 43C-1 DTD, 1900-341 Lisbon. Tel. 1-815-4479, fax 1-815-4508, e-mail badbn@mail.telepac.pt. *Pres.* Ernestina de Castro.

Puerto Rico

Sociedad de Bibliotecarios de Puerto Rico (Society of Libns. of Puerto Rico), Apdo. 22898, Universidad de Puerto Rico Sta., San Juan 00931. Tel. 787-764-0000 ext. 5204, fax 787-763-5685, e-mail vtorres@upracd.upr.clu.edu. *Pres.* Aura Jiménez de Panepinto; *Secy.* Olga L. Hernández.

Romania

Asociaţia Bibliotecarilor din Bibliotecile Publice-România (Assn. of Public Libns. of Romania), Strada Ion Ghica 4, Sector 3, 79708 Bucharest. Tel. 1-614-2434, fax 1-312-3381, e-mail bnr@ul.ici.ro. *Pres.* Gheorghe-Iosif Bercan; *Secy.* Georgeta Clinca.

Russia

Lib. Council, State V. I. Lenin Lib., Prospect Kalinina 3, Moscow 101000. Tel. 95-202-4656. *Exec. Secy.* G. A. Semenova.

Senegal

Association Sénégalaise des Bibliothécaires, Archivistes et Documentalistes (Senegalese Assn. of Libns., Archivists, and Documentalists), BP 3252, Dakar. Tel. 246-981, fax 242-379. *Pres.* Mariétou Diongue Diop; *Secy.* Emmanuel Kabou.

Sierra Leone

Sierra Leone Assn. of Archivists, Libns., and Info. Scientists, c/o Sierra Leone Lib. Board, Box 326, Freetown. Tel. 223-848. *Pres.* Deanna Thomas.

Singapore

Lib. Assn. of Singapore, c/o Bukit Merah Central, Box 0693, Singapore 9115. *Hon. Secy.* Siti Hanifah Mustapha.

Slovenia

Zveza Bibliotekarskih Društev Slovenije (Union of Assns. of Slovene Libns.), Turjaška 1, 1000 Ljubljana. Tel. 61-200-1193, fax 61-251-3052, World Wide Web http://193.2.8.11. *Pres.* Irena Sešek. E-mail Irena.Sesek@nuk.uni-lj.si. *Secy.* Lijana Hubej.

South Africa

Lib. and Info. Assn. of South Africa (formerly African Lib. Assn. of South Africa), c/o South African Institute for Libnship. and Info. Science, Box 1598, Pretoria 0001. Tel. 12-481-2870, fax 12-481-2873, e-mail liasa@liasa.org.za, World Wide Web http://www.liasa.org.za. *Exec. Dir.* Gwenda Thomas.

Spain

Asociación Española de Archiveros, Bibliotecarios, Museólogos y Documentalistas (Spanish Assn. of Archivists, Libns., Curators, and Documentalists), Recoletos 5, 28001 Madrid. Tel./fax 1-575-1727. *Pres.* Julia M. Rodrigez Barrero.

Sri Lanka

Sri Lanka Lib. Assn., Professional Center, 275/75 Bauddhaloka Mawatha, Colombo 7. Tel. 1-589-103, e-mail postmast@slla.ac.lk. *Pres.* Harrison Perera.

Swaziland

Swaziland Lib. Assn., Box 2309, Mbabane. Tel. 43101, fax 42641. *Chair* L. Dlamini; *Secy.* P. Muswazi.

Sweden

Svenska Arkivsamfundet (Swedish Assn. of Archivists), Malmtorgsg 3, S-10339 Stockholm. Tel. 8-405-100, fax 8-657-9564, e-mail berndt.fredriksson@foreign.ministry.se, World Wide Web http://www.arkivsanfundet. org. *Pres.* Berndt Fredriksson.

Sveriges Allmanna Biblioteksförening (Swedish Lib. Assn.), Box 3127, S-103 62 Stockholm. Tel. 8-5451-3230, fax 8-5451-3231, e-mail christina.stenberg@sab.se, World Wide Web http://www.sab.se. *Secy.-Gen.* Christina Stenberg.

Switzerland

Association des Bibliothèques et Bibliothécaires Suisses/Vereinigung Schweizerischer Bibliothekare/Associazione dei Bibliotecari Svizzeri (Assn. of Swiss Libs. and Libns.), Effingerstr. 35, CH-3008 Bern. Tel. 31-382-4240, fax 31-382-4648, e-mail bbs@bbs.ch, World Wide Web http://www.bbs.ch. *Gen. Secy.* Marianne Tschäppät.

Schweizerische Vereinigung für Dokumentation/Association Suisse de Documentation (Swiss Assn. of Documentation), Schmidgasse 4, Postfach 601, CH-6301 Zug. Tel. 41-726-4505, fax 41-726-4509, World Wide Web http://www.svd-asd.org. *Secy.* H. Schwenk.

Verein Schweizerischer Archivarinnen und Archivare (Assn. of Swiss Archivists), Schweizerisches Bundesarchiv, Archivstr. 24, 3003 Bern. Tel. 21-316-3711, e-mail andreas.kellerhals@bar.admin.ch, World Wide Web http://www.staluzern.ch/vsa. *Pres.* Andreas Kellerhals.

Taiwan

Lib. Assn. of China, c/o National Central Lib., 20 Chungshan S. Rd., Taipei 100-01. Tel. 2-2331-2475, fax 2-2370-0899, e-mail lac@msg.ncl.edu.tw, World Wide Web http://www.lac.ncl.edu.tw. *Pres.* Huang Shih-wson; *Secy.-Gen.* Teresa Wang Chang.

Tanzania

Tanzania Lib. Assn., POB 2645, Dar es Salaam. Tel. 51-402-6121. *Chair* T. E. Mlaki; *Secy.* A. Ngaiza.

Thailand

Thai Lib. Assn., 1346 Akarnsongkrau Rd. 5, Klongchan, Bangkapi, Bangkok 10240. Tel. 662-734-8022-3, fax 662-734-8024, World Wide Web http://tla.tiac.or.th. *Pres.* Khunying Maenmas Chawalit, *Exec. Secy.* Vorrarat Srinamngern.

Trinidad and Tobago

Lib. Assn. of Trinidad and Tobago, Box 1275, Port of Spain. Tel. 868-687-0194, e-mail secretary@latt.org.tt. *Pres.* Gemma Crichton; *Secy.* Ernesta Greenidge.

Tunisia

Association Tunisienne des Documentalistes, Bibliothécaires et Archivistes (Tunisian Assn. of Documentalists, Libns., and Archivists), B.P. 380, 1015 Tunis. *Pres.* Ahmed Ksibi.

Turkey

Türk Küüphaneciler Dernegi (Turkish Libns. Assn.), Elgün Sok-8/8, 06440 Yenisehir, Ankara. Tel. 312-230-1325, fax 312-232-0453. *Pres.* A. Berberoglu; *Secy.* A. Kaygusuz.

Uganda

Uganda Lib. Assn., Box 5894, Kampala. Tel. 141-285-001 ext. 4. *Chair* Elisam Naghra; *Secy.* Charles Batembyze.

Ukraine

Ukrainian Lib. Assn., 14 Chyhorin St., Kiev 252042. Tel. 380-44-268-2263, fax 380-44-295-8296. *Pres.* Valentyna S. Pashkova.

United Kingdom

ASLIB (Assn. for Info. Management), Temple Chambers, 3-7 Temple Ave, London, EC4Y 0HP, England. Tel. 1-207-583-8900, fax 1-207-583-8401, email aslib@

aslib.com. World Wide Web http://www.
aslib.co.uk. *Dir.* R. B. Bowes.

Bibliographical Society, c/o Welcome Lib.,
Victoria & Albert Museum, 183 Euston
Rd., London NW1 2BE, England. Tel. 20-
7611-7244, fax 20-7611-8703, e-mail
d.pearson@welcome.ac.uk. *Hon. Secy.*
David Pearson.

Chartered Institute of Lib. and Info. Professionals (formerly the Lib. Assn.), 7 Ridg-
mount St., London WC1E 7AE, England.
Tel. 20-7255-0500, fax 20-7255-0501,
e-mail info@cilip.org.uk, World Wide
Web http://www.cilip.org.uk. *Chief Exec.*
Bob McKee.

School Lib. Assn., Unit 2, Lotmead Business
Village, Lotmead Farm, Wanborough,
Swindon, Wilts. SN4 0UY, England. Tel.
1793-791-787, fax 1793-791-786, e-mail
info@sla.org.uk, World Wide Web http://
www.sla.org.uk. *Pres.* Frank N. Hogg;
Chief Exec. Kathy Lemaire.

Scottish Lib. Assn., 1 John St., Hamilton
ML3 7EU, Scotland. Tel. 1698-458-888,
fax 1698-458-899, e-mail sla@slainte.
org.uk, World Wide Web http://www.
slainte.org.uk. *Dir.* Robert Craig.

Society of Archivists, 40 Northampton Rd.,
London EC1R 0HB, England. Tel. 20-7278-
8630, fax 20-7278-2107, e-mail societyof
archivists@archives.org.uk, World Wide
Web http://www.archives.org.uk. *Exec.
Secy.* P. S. Cleary.

Society of College, National, and Univ. Libs
(SCONUL) (formerly Standing Confer-
ence of National and Univ. Libs.), 102
Euston St., London NW1 2HA, England.
Tel. 20-7387-0317, fax 20-7383-3197.
Exec. Secy. A. J. C. Bainton.

Welsh Lib. Assn., c/o Publications Office,
Dept. of Info. and Lib. Studies, Llanbadarn
Fawr, Aberystwyth, Dyfed SY23 3AS,
Wales. Tel. 1970-622-174, fax 1970-622-
190, e-mail hle@aber.ac.uk. *Exec. Officer*
Huw Evans.

Uruguay

Agrupación Bibliotecológica del Uruguay

(Uruguayan Lib. and Archive Science
Assn.), Cerro Largo 1666, 11200 Montev-
ideo. Tel. 2-400-57-40. *Pres.* Luis Alberto
Musso.

Asociación de Bibliotecólogos del Uruguay,
Eduardo V. Haedo 2255, CC 1315, Box
1315, 11000 Montevideo. Tel./fax 2-499-
989, e-mail ABU@adinet.com.uy. *Pres.*
Eduardo Correa.

Vatican City

Biblioteca Apostolica Vaticana, Cortile del
Belvedere, 00120 Vatican City, Rome.
Tel. 6-6988-3302, fax 6-6988-4795, e-mail
bav@librsbk.vatlib.it. *Prefect* Don Raf-
faele Farina.

Venezuela

Colegio de Bibliotecólogos y Archivólogos
de Venezuela (Venezuelan Lib. and Archives Assn.), Apdo. 6283, Caracas. Tel.
2-572-1858. *Pres.* Elsi Jimenez de Diaz.

Vietnam

Hôi Thu-Vien Viet Nam (Vietnamese Lib.
Assn.), National Lib. of Vietnam, 31
Trang Thi, 10000 Hanoi. Tel. 4-825-2643.

Yugoslavia

Jugoslovenski Bibliografsko-Informacijski
Institut (Yugoslav Institute for Bibliography and Info.), Terazije 26, 11000 Bel-
grade. Tel. 11-687-836, fax 11-687-760.
Dir. Radomir Glavicki.

Zambia

Zambia Lib. Assn., Box 32839, Lusaka.
Chair C. Zulu; *Hon. Secy.* W. C. Mulalami.

Zimbabwe

Zimbabwe Lib. Assn., Box 3133, Harare.
Chair Driden Kunaka; *Hon. Secy.* Albert
Masheka.

Directory of Book Trade and Related Organizations

Book Trade Associations, United States and Canada

For more extensive information on the associations listed in this section, see the annual edition of *Literary Market Place* (Information Today, Inc.).

American Booksellers Assn., 828 S. Broadway, Tarrytown, NY 10591. Tel. 800-637-0037, 914-591-2665, fax 914-591-2724, World Wide Web http://www.bookweb.org. *Pres.* Ann Christophersen, Women & Children First, 5233 N. Clark St., Chicago, IL 60640-2122. Tel. 773-769-9299, fax 773-769-6729, e-mail achristophersen@sprintmail.com; *V.P./Secy.* Mitchell Kaplan, Books & Books, 296 Aragon Ave., Coral Gables, FL 33134-5009. E-mail mitchell@booksandbooks.com; *Chief Exec. Officer* Avin Mark Domnitz.

American Institute of Graphic Arts, 164 Fifth Ave., New York, NY 10010. Tel. 212-807-1990, fax 212-807-1799, e-mail aiga@aiga.org, World Wide Web http://www.aiga.org. *Exec. Dir.* Richard Grefé. E-mail grefe@aiga.org.

American Literary Translators Assn. (ALTA), Univ. of Texas–Dallas, MC35, Box 830688, Richardson, TX 75083-0688. Tel. 972-883-2093, fax 972-883-6303, e-mail ert@utdallas.edu, World Wide Web http://www.literarytranslators.org. *Exec. Dir.* Eileen Tollett.

American Medical Publishers Assn., 14 Fort Hill Rd., Huntington, NY 11734. Tel./fax 631-423-0075, e-mail jillrudansky-ampa@email.msn.com, World Wide Web http://www.ampaonline.org. *Exec. Dir.* Jill Rudansky.

American Printing History Assn., Box 4922, Grand Central Sta., New York, NY 10163-4922. *Pres.* Martin Antonetti; *Exec. Secy.* Stephen Crook. E-mail scrook@printinghistory.org, World Wide Web http://www.printinghistory.org.

American Society of Indexers, 10200 W. 44 Ave., Suite 304, Wheat Ridge, CO 80033. Tel 303-463-2887, fax 303-422-8894, e-mail info@asindexing.org, World Wide Web http://www.asindexing.org/site. *Pres.* Kate Mertes; *Pres.-Elect* Frances Lennie; *Exec. Dir.* Jerry Bowman.

American Society of Journalists and Authors, 1501 Broadway, Suite 302, New York, NY 10036. Tel. 212-997-0947, fax 212-768-7414, e-mail execdir@asja.org, World Wide Web http://www.asja.org. *Pres.* Lisa Collier Cool; *Exec. Dir.* Brett Harvey.

American Society of Media Photographers, 150 N. 2 St., Philadelphia, PA 19106. Tel. 215-451-2767, fax 215-451-0880, e-mail mopsik@asmp.org, World Wide Web http://www.asmp.org. *Pres.* Stanley Rowin; *Exec. Dir.* Eugene Mopsik.

American Society of Picture Professionals, 409 S. Washington St., Alexandria, VA 22314. Tel./fax 703-299-0219, e-mail aspp1@idsonline.com, World Wide Web http://www.aspp.com. *Exec. Dir.* Cathy Sachs. E-mail cathy@aspp.com.

American Translators Assn., 225 Reinekers Lane, Suite 590, Alexandria, VA 22314. Tel. 703-683-6100, fax 703-683-6122, e-mail ata@atanet.org, World Wide Web http://www.atanet.org. *Pres.* Thomas L. West, III; *Pres.-Elect* Scott Brennan; *Secy.* Courtney Searls-Ridge; *Treas.* Jiri Stejskal; *Exec. Dir.* Walter W. Bacak, Jr. E-mail walter@atanet.org.

Antiquarian Booksellers Assn. of America, 20 W. 44 St., 4th fl., New York, NY 10036-6604. Tel. 212-944-8291, fax 212-944-8293, e-mail inquiries@abaa.org, World Wide Web http://www.abaa.org. *Exec. Dir.* Liane Thomas Wade. E-mail lwade@abaa.org.

Assn. of American Publishers, 71 Fifth Ave., New York, NY 10003. Tel. 212-255-0200, fax 212-255-7007. *Washington Office* 50 F St. N.W., Washington, DC 20001-1564. Tel. 202-347-3375, fax 202-347-3690. *Pres./CEO* Patricia S. Schroeder; *V.P.s* Allan Adler, Kathryn Blough, Barbara Meredith; *Dir., Communications and Public Affairs* Judith Platt; *Exec. Dir., School Division* Stephen D. Driesler; *Chair* Robert Evanson, McGraw Hill; *V. Chair* Jane Friedman, HarperCollins.

Assn. of American Univ. Presses, 71 W. 23 St., Suite 901, New York, NY 10010. Tel. 212-989-1010, e-mail info@aaupnet.org, World Wide Web http://aaupnet.org. *Pres.* Peter Milroy; *Exec. Dir.* Peter Givler; *Admin. Mgr.* Linda McCall. Address correspondence to the executive director.

Assn. of Authors' Representatives, Box 237201, Ansonia Sta., New York, NY 10023. Tel. 212-252-3695, e-mail aarinc@mindspring.com, World Wide Web http://aar-online.org. *Pres.* Gail Hochman; *Admin. Secy.* Leslie Carroll.

Assn. of Canadian Publishers, 110 Eglinton Ave. W., Suite 401, Toronto, ON M4R 1A3. Tel. 416-487-6116, fax 416-487-8815, e-mail info@canbook.org, World Wide Web http://www.publishers.ca. *Exec. Dir.* Monique Smith. Tel. 416-487-6116 ext. 222, e-mail monique_smith@canbook.org. Address correspondence to the executive director.

Assn. of Educational Publishers (AEP), 510 Heron Dr., Suite 309, Logan Township, NJ 08085. Tel. 856-241-7772, fax 856-241-0709, e-mail mail@edpress.org, World Wide Web http://www.edpresss.org. *Exec. Dir.* Charlene F. Gaynor. E-mail cgaynor@edpress.org.

Assn. of Graphic Communications, 330 Seventh Ave., 9th fl., New York, NY 10001-5010. Tel. 212-279-2100, fax 212-279-5381, World Wide Web http://www.agcomm.org. *Pres.* Susan Greenwood. E-mail susie@agcomm.org.

Book Industry Study Group, 19 W. 21 St., Suite 905, New York, NY 10010. Tel. 646-336-7141, fax 646-336-6214, e-mail bisg-info@bisg.org, World Wide Web http://www.bisg.org.

Book Manufacturers Institute, 65 William St., Suite 300, Wellesley, MA 02481-3800. Tel. 781-239-0103, fax 781-239-0106, e-mail info@bmibook.com, World Wide Web http://www.bmibook.org. *Pres.* Bruce W. Smith, R. R. Donnelley & Sons Co.; *V.P.* David N. Mead, Banta Book Group; *Exec. V.P.* Stephen P. Snyder. Address correspondence to the executive vice president.

Book Publicists of Southern California, 6464 Sunset Blvd., Suite 755, Hollywood 90028. Tel. 323-461-3921, fax 323-461-0917, e-mail bookpublicists@aol.com. *Pres.* Ernie Weckbaugh; *V.P.* Patty Weckbaugh; *Treas.* Lynn Walford.

Book Publishers of Texas, 6387 B Camp Bowie No. 340, Fort Worth, TX 76116. Tel. 817-247-6016, e-mail bookpublishersoftexas@att.net, World Wide Web http://www.bookpublishersoftexas.com.

Bookbuilders of Boston, 26 Bates Way, Hanover, MA 02339. Tel. 781-878-5868, fax 866-820-0469, e-mail office@bbboston.org, World Wide Web http://www.bbboston.org. *Pres.* Sarah Bodden Kopec, Houghton Mifflin; *1st V.P.* Carol Heston, Victor Graphics; *2nd V.P.* Edda Sigurdardottir, Houghton Mifflin; *Treas.* Larry Bisso, Edwards Brothers; *Secy.* Amy Fleischer, Addison-Wesley Professional.

Bookbuilders West, Box 7046, San Francisco, CA 94120-9727. Tel. 415-273-5790, World Wide Web http://www.bookbuilders.org; *Pres.* Michele Bisson Savoy, Quebecor World; *1st V.P.* Mary Lou Goforth, Banta Book Group; *Secy.* Ramona Beville, Sheriden Books; *Treas.* Michael O'Brien, GTS Companies.

Canadian Booksellers Assn.,789 Don Mills Rd., Suite 700, Toronto, ON M3C 1T5. Tel. 416-467-7883, fax 416-467-7886, e-mail enquiries@cbabook.org, World Wide

Web http://www.cbabook.org. *Pres.* Todd Anderson, Univ. of Alberta Bookstore. E-mail todd.anderson@ualberta.ca; *V.P.* Suzanne Brooks, Gulliver's. E-mail gulliver @mail.efni.com; *Gen. Mgr.* Susan Dayus. E-mail sdayus@cbabook.org.

Canadian ISBN Agency, c/o Acquisitions and Bibliographic Services Branch, National Library of Canada, 395 Wellington St., Ottawa, ON K1A 0N4. Tel. 819-994-6872, 877-896-9481 (toll-free), fax 819-997-7517, e-mail isbn@nlc-bnc.ca.

Canadian Printing Industries Association, 75 Albert St., Suite 906, Ottawa, ON K1P 5E7. Tel. 613-236-7208, fax 613-236-8169, World Wide Web http://www.cpia-aci.ca. *Pres.* Pierre Boucher; *Chair* Bob Kadis; *V. Chair* Blair Fraser.

Catholic Book Publishers Assn. 8404 James-port Dr., Rockford, IL 61108. Tel. 815-332-3245, e-mail cbpa3@aol.com, World Wide Web http://cbpa.org; *Pres.* John D. Wright; *V.P.* Kay Weiss; *Secy.* Thomas R. Artz; *Treas.* Jean Larkin; *Exec. Dir.* Terry Wessels.

Chicago Book Clinic, 5443 N. Broadway, Suite 101, Chicago, IL 60640. Tel. 773-561-4150, fax 773-561-1343, e-mail kg boyer@ix.netcom.com, World Wide Web http://www.chicagobookclinic.org. *Pres.* Cheryl Horch, McGraw-Hill Higher Educ., 2460 Kerper Blvd., Dubuque, IA 52001. Tel. 563-589-2915, fax 563-589-4751, e-mail cheryl_horch@mcgraw-hill.com; *V.P.* Tammy Levy, Scott Foresman, 1900 E. Lake Ave., Glenview, IL 60025. Tel. 847-486-2354, fax 847-486-3718, e-mail tammy.levy@scottforesman.com; *Exec. Dir.* Kevin G. Boyer.

Children's Book Council, 12 W. 37 St., 2nd fl., New York, NY 10018-7480. Tel. 212-966-1990, fax 212-966-2073, e-mail info@ cbcbooks.org, World Wide Web http:// www.cbcbooks.org. *Chair* Mark Vineis; *V. Chair* Alan Smagler; *Secy.* Virginia Duncan; *Treas.* Lori Benton.

Copyright Society of the USA. *Pres.* Maria A. Danzilo; *V.P.* Barry Slotnick; *Secy.* Donna DeGrandi; *Treas.* Gary Roth; *Admin.* Barbara S. Pannone. E-mail barpan @rcn.com.

Council of Literary Magazines and Presses, 154 Christopher St., Suite 3C, New York, NY 10014. Tel. 212-741-9110, fax 212-741-9112, e-mail info@clmp.org, World Wide Web http://clmp.org. *Exec. Dir.* Jeffrey Lependorf.

Educational Paperback Assn. *Pres.* Thomas J. Milano; *V.P.* Dick Tinder; *Treas.* Jennifer Carrico. World Wide Web http:// www.edupaperback.org. *Exec. Secy.* Marilyn Abel, Box 1399, East Hampton, NY 11937. Tel. 212-879-6850, e-mail edu paperback@aol.com.

Evangelical Christian Publishers Assn., 1969 E. Broadway Rd., Suite 2, Tempe, AZ 85282. Tel. 480-966-3998, fax 480-966-1944, e-mail dross@ecpa.org, World Wide Web http://www.ecpa.org. *Pres./CEO* Doug Ross; *Chair* Lillian Miao, Paraclete Press; *V. Chair* Mark D. Taylor, Tyndale House Publishers; *Secy.* Robert A. Fryling, InterVarsity Press.

Friendship Press, 475 Riverside Dr., Suite 880, New York, NY 10115-0050. Tel. 212-870-2896, fax 212-870-2030, e-mail sbates@ncccusa.org, World Wide Web http://www.ncccusa.org/friend/fphome. html.

Graphic Artists Guild, 90 John St., Suite 403, New York, NY 10038. Tel. 212-791-3400, fax 212-792-0333, e-mail admin@gag.org, World Wide Web http://www.gag.org. *Deputy Exec. Dir.* Ammon Turner.

Great Lakes Booksellers Assn., c/o *Exec. Dir.* Jim Dana, Box 901, 208 Franklin St., Grand Haven, MI 49417. Tel. 616-847-2460, fax 616-842-0051, e-mail glba@ books-glba.org, World Wide Web http:// www.books-glba.org. *Pres.* Dave Kaverman, Little Professor Book Company, Fort Wayne, Indiana. E-mail davek@million storybuilding.com; *V.P.* Becky Anderson Wilkin, Anderson's Bookshops, Naperville, Illinois.

Guild of Book Workers, 521 Fifth Ave., New York, NY 10175. Tel. 212-292-4444, World Wide Web http://palimpsest. stanford.edu/byorg/gbw. *Memb. Secy.* Bernadette Callery. E-mail bcallery@ flounder.com.

International Association of Printing House Craftsmen (IAPHC), 7042 Brooklyn Blvd.,

Minneapolis, MN 55429. Tel. 800-466-4274, 612-560-1620, fax 612-560-1350, World Wide Web http://www.iaphc.org. *Chair* Howard Drayson. E-mail dbmman@aol.com; *V. Chair* Bill Orr. E-mail billyo@excelonline.com; *Pres./CEO* Kevin Keane. E-mail kkeane1069@aol.com.

International Standard Book Numbering U.S. Agency, 630 Central Ave., New Providence, NJ 07974. Tel. 877-310-7333, fax 908-219-0188, e-mail ISBN-SAN@bowker.com, World Wide Web http://www.ISBN.org. *Chair* Michael Cairns; *Dir.* Doreen Gravesande; *Industry Relations Mgr.* Don Riseborough; *SAN Mgr.* Diana Luongo.

Jewish Book Council, 15 E. 26 St., 10th fl., New York, NY 10010. Tel. 212-532-4949 ext. 297, fax 212-481-4174, World Wide Web http://www.jewishbookcouncil.org. *Exec. Dir.* Carolyn Starman Hessel.

Library Binding Institute, 70 E. Lake St., Suite 300, Chicago, IL 60601. Tel. 312-704-5020, fax 312-704-5025, e-mail info@lbibinders.org, World Wide Web http://www.lbibinders.org. *Pres.* Gary Wert; *V.P.* John Salistean; *Treas.* Jay B. Fairfield; *Exec. Dir.* Joanne Rock.

Magazine Publishers of America, 919 Third Ave., 22nd fl., New York, NY 10022. Tel. 212-872-3700, fax 212-888-4217, e-mail mpa@magazine.org, World Wide Web http://www.magazine.org. *Pres.* Nina Link. Tel. 212-872-3710, e-mail president@magazine.org; *Chair* Daniel B. Brewster, Jr.; *V. Chair* Thomas O. Ryder.

Midwest Independent Publishers Assn., Box 581432, Minneapolis, MN 55458-1432. Tel. 651-917-0021, World Wide Web http://www.mipa.org; *Pres.* Sybil Smith. E-mail smitheprs@aol.com; *V.P. Memb.* Pat Bell. E-mail patjbell@aol.com.

Miniature Book Society, c/o *Pres.* Neale M. Albert, 815 Park Ave., New York, NY 10021. Tel. 212-861-9093, fax 212-772-9905, e-mail nalbert@paulweiss.com; *V.P.* Jon Mayo, Box 74, North Clarendon, VT 05759. Tel. 802-773-9695, fax 802-773-1493, e-mail microbib@sover.net; *Secy.* Patricia Pistner, 10 Seagate Dr. PH 1N, Naples, FL 34103. Tel. 941-263-6005, fax 941-263-4544, e-mail pistner@mediaone.

net; *Exec. Secy.* Mark Palcovic, 620 Clinton Springs Ave., Cincinnati, OH 45229-1325. Tel. 513-861-3554, fax 513-556-2113, World Wide Web http://www.mbs.org.

Minnesota Book Publishers Roundtable. *Pres.* Jim Cihlar, Redleaf Press, 450 N. Syndicate Ave., No. 5, St. Paul 55104. Tel. 651-641-6629, fax 651-645-0990, e-mail jcihlar@redleafpress.org; *V.P.* Tricia Theurer, Voyageur Press, 123 N. 2 St., Stillwater 55082. Tel. 651-430-2210, fax 651-430-2211, e-mail ttheurer@voyageur press.com; *Secy.* Hilary Reeves, Milkweed Editions, 1011 Washington Ave. South, No. 300, Minneapolis 55415. Tel. 612-332-3192, e-mail Hilary_Reeves@milkweed.org; *Treas.* Brad Vogt, Bradley & Assoc., 40214 Wallaby Rd., Rice 56367. Tel. 320-260-3594, fax 320-656-9520, e-mail bvogt@cloudnet.com. World Wide Web http://www.publishersroundtable.org. Address correspondence to the vice president.

Mountains and Plains Booksellers Assn., 19 Old Town Sq., Suite 238, Fort Collins, CO 80524. Tel. 970-484-5856, fax 970-407-1479, e-mail lknudsen@mountainsplains.org, World Wide Web http://www.mountainsplains.org. *Exec. Dir.* Lisa Knudsen.

National Assn. for Printing Leadership, 75 W. Century Rd., Paramus, NJ 07652. Tel. 201-634-9600, 800-642-6275, fax 201-634-0324, e-mail napl@napl.org, World Wide Web http://www.napl.org. *Pres./CEO* Joseph P. Truncale.

National Assn. of College Stores, 500 E. Lorain St., Oberlin, OH 44074-1294. Tel. 440-775-7777, fax 440-775-4769, e-mail info@nacs.org, World Wide Web http://www.nacs.org. *Chief Exec. Officer* Brian Cartier.

National Assn. of Independent Publishers, Box 430, Highland City, FL 33846. Tel./fax 863-648-4420, e-mail NAIP@aol.com. World Wide Web http://www.publishers report.com.

National Coalition Against Censorship (NCAC), 275 Seventh Ave., 20th fl., New York, NY 10001. Tel. 212-807-6222, fax 212-807-6245, e-mail ncac@ncac.org,

World Wide Web http://www.ncac.org.
Exec. Dir. Joan E. Bertin.

New Atlantic Independent Booksellers Assn., 2667 Hyacinth St., Westbury, NY 11590. Tel. 516-333-0681, fax 516-333-0689, e-mail info@naiba.com. *Pres.* Sheilah Egan, A Likely Story Children's Books, 1555 King St., Alexandria, VA 22314. Tel. 703-836-2498, 703-836-5949, e-mail alikely@bellatlantic.net; *Exec. Dir.* Eileen Dengler.

New England Booksellers Assn., 1770 Massachusetts Ave., Suite 332, Cambridge, MA 02140. Tel. 800-466-8711, fax 617-576-3091, e-mail rusty@neba.org, World Wide Web http://www.newenglandbooks.org. *Pres.* Linda Ramsdell; *V.P.* Susan Novotny; *Treas.* Peter Sevenair; *Exec. Dir.* Wayne A. Drugan, Jr.

New Mexico Book League, 8632 Horacio Place N.E., Albuquerque, NM 87111. Tel. 505-299-8940, fax 505-294-8032. *Ed., Book Talk* Carol A. Myers.

North American Bookdealers Exchange, Box 606, Cottage Grove, OR 97424. Tel. 541-942-7455, fax 561-258-2625, e-mail nabe@bookmarketingprofits.com, World Wide Web http://bookmarketingprofits.com. *Dir.* Al Galasso.

Northern California Independent Booksellers Assn., The Presidio, 37 Graham St., Suite 210, Box 29169, San Francisco, CA 94129. Tel. 415-561-7686, fax 415-561-7685, e-mail office@nciba.com, World Wide Web http://www.nciba.com. *Pres.* Karen Pennington; *Exec. Dir.* Hut Landon.

Pacific Northwest Booksellers Assn., 317 W. Broadway, Suite 214, Eugene, OR 97401-2890. Tel. 541-683-4363, fax 541-683-3910, e-mail info@pnba.org. *Pres.* Holly Myers, Elliott Bay Book Co., 101 S. Main St., Seattle, WA 98104-2581. Tel. 206-624-6600, fax 206-903-1601, E-mail hmyers@elliottbaybook.com; *Exec. Dir.* Thom Chambliss.

PEN American Center, Div. of International PEN, 568 Broadway, New York, NY 10012. Tel. 212-334-1660, fax 212-334-2181, e-mail pen@pen.org, World Wide Web http://www.pen.org.

Periodical and Book Assn. of America, 481 Eighth Ave., Suite 803, New York, NY 10001. Tel. 212-563-6502, fax 212-563-4098, e-mail info@pbaa.net, World Wide Web http://www.pbaa.net. *Pres.* William Michalopoulos. E-mail william_michalopoulos@businessweek.com; *Exec. Dir.* Lisa W. Scott. E-mail lscott@pbaa.net.

Philadelphia Book Clinic, c/o *Secy.* Thomas Colaiezzi, 136 Chester Ave., Yeadon, PA 19050-3831. Tel. 610-259-7022, fax 610-394-9886.

Publishers Marketing Assn., 627 Aviation Way, Manhattan Beach, CA 90266. Tel. 310-372-2732, fax 310-374-3342, e-mail info@pma-online.org, World Wide Web http://www.pma-online.org. *Pres.* Don Tubesing; *Exec. Dir.* Jan Nathan.

Research and Engineering Council of the Graphic Arts Industry, Box 1086, White Stone, VA 22578. Tel. 804-436-9922, fax 804-436-9511, e-mail recouncil@rivnet.net, World Wide Web http://www.recouncil.org. *Pres.* Laura Gale; *Exec. V.P./Secy.* Jeffrey White; *Exec. V.P./Treas.* Lynn Poretta; *Managing Dir.* Ronald Mihills.

Romance Writers of America, 3707 FM 1960 W., Suite 555, Houston, TX 77068. Tel. 281-440-6885, fax 281-440-7510, e-mail info@rwanational.com, World Wide Web http://www.rwanational.com. *Pres.* Shirley Hailstock; *Pres.-Elect* Patricia Potter; *Secy.* Nancy Fraser; *Treas.* Connie Newman.

Science Fiction and Fantasy Writers of America, Box 877, Chestertown, MD 21620. E-mail execdir@sfwa.org, World Wide Web http://www.sfwa.org. *Pres.* Sharon Lee; *V.P.* Catherine Asaro; *Secy.* ElizaBeth Gilligan; *Treas.* Chuck Rothman; *Exec. Dir.* Jane Jewell.

Small Press Center, 20 W. 44 St., New York, NY 10036. Tel. 212-764-7021, fax 212-354-5365, World Wide Web http://www.smallpress.org. *Exec. Dir.* Karin Taylor.

Small Publishers Assn. of North America (SPAN), Box 1306-W, Buena Vista, CO 81211-1306. Tel. 719-395-4790, fax 719-395-8374, e-mail SPAN@SPANnet.org, World Wide Web http://www.SPANnet.org. *Exec. Dir.* Marilyn Ross.

Society of Children's Book Writers & Illustrators (SCBWI), 8271 Beverly Blvd., Los Angeles, CA 90048. Tel. 323-782-1010, fax 323-782-1892, e-mail stephenmooser

@scbwi.org, World Wide Web http://www.scbwi.org. *Pres.* Stephen Mooser; *Exec. Dir.* Lin Oliver.

Society of Illustrators (SI), 128 E. 63 St., New York, NY 10021. Tel. 212-838-2560, fax 212-838-2561, e-mail SI1901@aol.com, World Wide Web http://www.society illustrators.org.

Society of National Association Publications (SNAP), 8405 Greensboro Dr., Suite 800, McLean, VA 22102. Tel. 703-506-3285, fax 703-506-3266, e-mail snapinfo@snaponline.org, World Wide Web http://www.snaponline.org. *Pres.* Fred Haag; *V.P.* John Grady; *Treas.* Peter Banks.

Technical Assn. of the Pulp and Paper Industry, 15 Technology Pkwy. South Norcross, GA 30092 (postal address Box 105113, Atlanta, GA 30348). Tel. 770-446-1400, fax 770-446-6947, World Wide Web http://www.tappi.org. *Pres.* Kathleen M. Bennett, Georgia-Pacific; *V.P.* Willis J. Potts, Inland Paperboard & Packaging; *Exec. Dir.* W. H. Gross.

Western Writers of America, c/o *Secy./Treas.* James Crutchfield, 1012 Fair St., Franklin, TN 37064. World Wide Web http://www.westernwriters.org. *Pres.* Paul Andrew Hutton; *V.P.* Rita Cleary; *Exec. Dir.* Karin Taylor.

Women's National Book Assn., c/o Susannah Greenberg Public Relations, 26 W. 17 St., Suite 504, New York, NY 10011. Tel. 212-727-7271, fax 212-20804629, e-mail publicity@bookbuzz.com, World Wide Web http://www.wnba-books.org/index.html. *Pres.* Margaret E. Auer, Dean of Univ. Libs., Univ. of Detroit Mercy, Box 19900, Detroit, MI 48219-0900. Tel. 313-993-1090, fax 313-993-1780, e-mail auerme@udmercy.edu; *V.P./Pres.-Elect* Jill A. Tardiff, Bamboo River Assocs., 625 Madison St., Unit B, Hoboken, NJ 07030. Tel. 201-656-7220, fax 201-792-0254, e-mail jtardiff-wnbanyc@worldnet.att.net.

International and Foreign Book Trade Associations

For Canadian book trade associations, see the preceding section, "Book Trade Associations, United States and Canada." For a more extensive list of book trade organizations outside the United States and Canada, with more detailed information, consult *International Literary Market Place* (Information Today, Inc.), which also provides extensive lists of major bookstores and publishers in each country.

International

African Publishers' Network, 18 Van Praagh Ave., Milton Park, Harare, Zimbabwe. Tel. 4-708-418, fax 4-708-413, e-mail apnet@mango.zw, World Wide Web http://www.africanpublishers.org. *Chair* Mamadou Aliou Sow.

Afro-Asian Book Council, 4835/24 Ansari Rd., Daryaganj, New Delhi 110002, India. Tel. 11-326-1487, fax 11-326-7437, e-mail sdas@ubspd.com. *Secy.-Gen.* Sukumar Das; *Dir.* Abul Hasan.

Centre Régional pour la Promotion du Livre en Afrique (Regional Center for Book Promotion in Africa), Box 1646, Yaoundé, Cameroon. Tel. 22-4782. *Secy.* William Moutchia.

Centro Régional para el Fomento del Libro en América Latina y el Caribe (CERLALC) (Regional Center for Book Promotion in Latin America and the Caribbean), Calle 70, No. 9-52, Apdo. Aeréo 57348, Santafé de Bogotá 2, Colombia. Tel. 1-249-5141, fax 1-255-4614, e-mail cerlalc@impsat. net.co. *Dir.* Carmen Barvo.

Federation of European Publishers, Ave. de Tervueren 204, B-1150, Brussels, Belgium. Tel. 2-770-1110, fax 2-771-2071, e-mail fep.Alemann@brutele.be, World Wide Web http://editeur.org/FEP.html. *Pres.* Michael Gill; *Dir.* Mechtild Von Alemann.

International Board on Books for Young People (IBBY), Nonnenweg 12, Postfach, CH-4055 Basel, Switzerland. Tel. 61-272-2917, fax 61-272-2757, e-mail ibby@eye. ch, ibby@ibby.org. *Dir.* Leena Maissen.

International Booksellers Federation, Rue de Grand Hospice 34A, B1000 Brussels, Belgium. Tel. 2-223-4940, fax 2-223-4941, e-mail eurobooks@skynet.be. *Pres.* Yvonne Steinberger; *Gen. Secy.* Christiane Vuidar.

International Assn. of Scientific, Technical and Medical Publishers (STM), Muurhuisen 165, 3811 EG Amersfoort, Netherlands. Tel. 33-465-6060, fax 33-465-6538, e-mail lefebvre@stm.nl, World Wide Web http:/www.stm-assoc.org. *Secy.* Lex Lefebvre.

International League of Antiquarian Booksellers, 400 Summit Ave., Saint Paul, MN 55102. Tel. 800-441-0076, 612-290-0700, fax 612-290-0646, e-mail rulon@ winternet.com, World Wide Web http:// www.ilab.org. *Secy. Gen.* Rob Rulon-Miller.

International Publishers Assn. (Union Internationale des Editeurs), Ave. Miremont 3, CH-1206 Geneva, Switzerland. Tel. 22-346-3018, fax 22-347-5717, e-mail secretariat @ipa-uie.org, World Wide Web www. ipa-uie.org. *Pres.* Pere Vicens; *Secy.-Gen.* Benoît Muller.

National

Argentina

Cámara Argentina de Publicaciones (Argentine Publications Assn.), Lavalle 437, 6 D-Edif. Adriático, 6 piso, 1047 Buenos Aires. Tel./fax 011-4394-2892, e-mail publicaciones@icatel.net, World Wide Web http://www.publicaciones.org. *Pres.* Agustin dos Santos.

Cámara Argentina del Libro (Argentine Book Assn.), Avda. Belgrano 1580, 4 piso, 1093 Buenos Aires. Tel. 1-4381-8383, fax 1-4381-9253, e-mail caarlibro@impsatl. com.ar, World Wide Web http://www. editores.com. *Dir.* Norberto J. Pou.

Fundación El Libro (Book Foundation), Hipolito Yrigoyen 1628, 5 piso, 1344 Buenos Aires. Tel. 1-4374-3288, fax 1-4375-0268, e-mail fund@libro.satlink.net, World Wide Web http://www.el-libro.com.ar. *Pres.* Jorge Naveiro; *Dir.* Marta V. Diaz.

Australia

Australian and New Zealand Assn. of Antiquarian Booksellers, 69 Broadway, Nedlands, WA 6009. Tel. 618-9386-5842, e-mail admin@anzaab.com, World Wide Web http://www.anzaab.com.au. *Pres.* Robert Muir.

Australian Booksellers Assn., 136 Rundle Mall, Adelaide, SA 5000. Tel. 3-9663-7888, fax 3-9663-7557. *Pres.* Tim Peach; *Exec. Dir.* Celia Pollock.

Australian Publishers Assn., Suite 60, 89 Jones St., Ultimo, NSW 2007. Tel. 2-9281-9788, fax 2-9281-1073, e-mail apa@publishers.asn.au, World Wide Web http://www.publishers.asn.au. *Pres.* Greg Browne; *Chief Exec.* Susan Bridge.

National Book Council, 71 Collins St., Melbourne, Vic. 3000. Tel. 3-663-8043, fax 3-663-8658. *Pres.* Michael G. Zifcak; *Exec. Dir.* Thomas Shapcott.

Austria

Hauptverband des Österreichischen Buchhandels (Austrian Publishers and Booksellers Assn.), Grünangergasse 4, A-1010 Vienna. Tel. 1-512-1535, fax 1-512-8482, World Wide Web http://www.buecher.at. *Pres.* Anton C. Hilscher.

Verband der Antiquare Österreichs (Austrian Antiquarian Booksellers Assn.), Grünangergasse 4, A-1010 Vienna. Tel. 1-512-1535, fax 1-512-8482, e-mail sekretariat@hvb.at. *Pres.* Hans-Dieter Paulusch.

Belarus

National Book Chamber of Belarus, 31a Very Khoruzhey St., 220002 Minsk. Tel./fax 172-289-3396, fax 172-2893-3863, e-mail palata@palata.belpak.minsk.by. *Contact* Anatoli Voronko.

Belgium

Vlaamse Boekverkopersbond (Flemish Booksellers Assn.), Hof ter Schriecklaan 17, 2600 Berchem/Antwerp. Tel. 3-239-5740, fax 3-230-8835, e-mail vvb@boek.be, World Wide Web http://www.boek.be. *Gen. Secy.* Luc Tessens.

Bolivia

Cámara Boliviana del Libro (Bolivian Booksellers Assn.), Casilla 682, Calle Capitan Ravelo No. 2116, La Paz. Tel./fax 2-327-039, e-mail cabolib@ceibo.entelnet.bo. *Pres.* Rolando S. Condori; *Secy.* Teresa G. de Alvarez.

Brazil

Cámara Brasileira do Livro (Brazilian Book Assn.), AlSantos 1000, CEP 01418-100 São Paulo. Tel./fax 11-3147-0870, e-mail cbl@cbl.org.br, World Wide Web http://www.cbl.org.br. *Pres.* Raul Wasserman; *Gen. Mgr.* Aloysio T. Costa.

Sindicato Nacional dos Editores de Livros (Brazilian Publishers Assn.), SDS, Edif. Venancio VI, Loja 9/17, 70000 Brasilia, Brazil. Tel. 21-233-6481, fax 21-253-8502. *Pres.* Sérgio Abreu da Cruz Machado; *Exec. Secy.* Henrique Maltese.

Chile

Cámara Chilena del Libro AG (Chilean Assn. of Publishers, Distributors, and Booksellers), Casilla 13526, Santiago. Tel. 2-698-9519, fax 2-698-9226, e-mail camlibro@reuna.cl, World Wide Web http://www.camlibro.cl. *Mgr.* Carlos Franz.

Colombia

Cámara Colombiana del Libro (Colombian Book Assn.), Carrera 17A, No. 37-27, Apdo. Aéreo 8998, Santafé de Bogotá. Tel. 1-288-6188, fax 1-287-3320.

Czech Republic

Svaz ceskych knihkupcu a nakladetelu (Czech Publishers and Booksellers Assn.), Jana Masaryka 56, 120 00 Prague 2. Tel. 224-219-944, fax 224-219-942, e-mail sckn@

sckn.cz, World Wide Web http://www. sckn.cz. *Chair* Jitka Undeova.

Denmark

Danske Boghandlerforening (Danish Booksellers Assn.), Siljangade 6.3, DK 2200 Copenhagen S. Tel. 3254-2255, fax 3254-0041, e-mail ddb@bogpost.dk, World Wide Web http://www.bogguide.dk. *Pres.* Jesper Moller.

Danske Forlaeggerforening (Danish Publishers Assn.), 18/1 Kompagnistr. 1208, Copenhagen K. Tel. 3315-6688, fax 3315-6588, e-mail publassn@webpartner.dk. *Dir.* Tune Olsen.

Ecuador

Cámara Ecuatoriana del Libro, Núcleo de Pichincha, Avda. Eloy Alfaro No. 355, piso 9, Casilla 17-01, Quito. Tel. 2-553-311, fax 2-222-150, e-mail celnp@hoy. net. *Pres.* Luis Mora Ortega.

Egypt

General Egyptian Book Organization, Corniche El-Nil-Boulaq, Cairo. Tel. 2-775-371, 2-775-649, fax 2-754-213. *Chair* Ezz El Dine Ismail.

Estonia

Estonian Publishers Assn., Box 3366, EE0090 Tallinn. Tel. 2-443-937, fax 2-445-720. *Dir.* A. Tarvis.

Finland

Kirjakauppaliitto Ry (Booksellers Assn. of Finland), Eerikinkatu 15-17 D 43-44, FIN-00100 Helsinki. Tel. 9-6859-9110, fax 9-6859-9119, e-mail toimisto@kirjakauppaliitto.fi. *Chief Exec.* Olli Erakivi.

Suomen Kustannusyhdistys (Finnish Book Publishers Assn.), Box 177, FIN-00121 Helsinki. Tel. 9-2287-7250, fax 9-612-1226, World Wide Web http://www.skyry. net. *Dir.* Veikko Sonninen.

France

Cercle de la Librairie (Circle of Professionals of the Book Trade), 35 Rue Grégoire-de-Tours, F-75006 Paris. Tel. 1-44-41-28-00, fax 1-44-41-28-65. *Pres.* Charles Henri Flammarion.

Fédération Française des Syndicats de Libraires (FFSL) (French Booksellers Assn.), 43 Rue de Châteaudun, F-75009 Paris. Tel. 1-42-82-00-03, fax 1-42-82-10-51. *Pres.* Jean-Luc Dewas.

France Edition, 115 Blvd. Saint-Germain, F-75006 Paris. Tel. 1-44-41-13-13, fax 1-46-34-63-83, e-mail info@franceedition.org, World Wide Web http://www.france edition.org. *Chair* Liana Levi. *New York Branch* French Publishers Agency, 853 Broadway, New York, NY 10003-4703. Tel. 212-254-4520, fax 212-979-6229.

Syndicat National de la Librairie Ancienne et Moderne (National Assn. of Antiquarians and Modern Booksellers), 4 Rue Git-le-Coeur, F-75006 Paris. Tel. 1-43-29-46-38, fax 1-43-25-41-63, e-mail slam@worldnet. fr, World Wide Web http://www.slam-livre.fr. *Pres.* Alain Marchiset.

Syndicat National de l'Edition (National Union of Publishers), 115 Blvd. Saint-Germain, F-75006 Paris. Tel. 1-44-41-40-50, fax 1-44-14-077. *Pres.* Serge Eyrolles.

Union des Libraires de France, 40 Rue Grégoire-de-Tours, F-75006 Paris. Tel./fax 1-43-29-88-79. *Pres.* Eric Hardin; *Gen. Delegate* Marie-Dominique Doumenc.

Germany

Börsenverein des Deutschen Buchhandels e.V. (Stock Exchange of German Booksellers), Postfach 100442, 60004 Frankfurt-am-Main. Tel. 69-1306-0, fax 69-1306-201, World Wide Web http://www. boersenverein.de. *Gen. Mgr.* Harald Heker.

Verband Deutscher Antiquare e.V. (German Antiquarian Booksellers Assn.), Seeblick 1, 56459 Elbingen. Tel. 06435-90-91-47, fax 06435-90-91-48, e-mail buch@ antiquare.de, World Wide Web http:// www.antiquare.de. *Pres.* Ulrich Hobbeling.

Ghana

University Bookshop (formerly West African University Booksellers Assn.), Univ. of Ghana, Box LG 1, Legon. Tel. 21-500-

398, fax 21-500-774, e-mail bookshop@ug.edu.gh. *Mgr.* E. H. Tonyigah.

Great Britain

See United Kingdom

Greece

Hellenic Federation of Publishers and Booksellers, Themistocleous 73, 10683 Athens. Tel. 1-330-0924, fax 1-330-1617, e-mail poev@otenet.gr. *Pres.* Georgios Dardanos.

Hungary

Magyar Könyvkiadók és Könyvterjesztök Egyesülése (Assn. of Hungarian Publishers and Booksellers), POB 130, 1367 Budapest. Tel. 1-343-2540, fax 1-343-2541. *Pres.* István Bart; *Secy.-Gen.* Péter Zentai.

Iceland

Félag Islenskra Bókaútgefenda (Icelandic Publishers Assn.), Baronsstig 5, 101 Reykjavik. Tel. 511-8020, fax 511-5020, e-mail baekur@mmedia.is, World Wide Web http://www.bokautgefa.is. *Chair* Sigurdur Svavarsson; *Gen. Mgr.* Vilborg Hardardóttir.

India

Federation of Indian Publishers, Federation House, 18/1-C Institutional Area, JNU Rd., Aruna Asaf Ali Marg, New Delhi 110067. Tel. 11-696-4847, 685-2263, fax 11-686-4054. *Pres.* Shri R. C. Govil; *Exec. Secy.* S. K. Ghai.

Indonesia

Ikatan Penerbit Indonesia (Assn. of Indonesian Book Publishers), Jl. Kalipasir 32, Jakarta 10330. Tel. 21-314-1907, fax 21-314-6050. *Pres.* Arselan Harahap; *Secy. Gen.* Robinson Rusdi.

Ireland

CLE: The Irish Book Publishers Assn., 43/44 Temple Bar, Dublin 2. Tel. 1-670-7393, fax 1-670-7642, e-mail info@publishingireland.com, World Wide Web http://www.publishingireland.com. *Contact* Orla Martin.

Israel

Book and Printing Center, Israel Export Institute, 29 Hamered St., Box 50084, Tel Aviv 68125. Tel. 3-514-2916, fax 3-514-2881, e-mail israeli@export.gov.il, World Wide Web http://www.export.gov.il. *Dir.* Ronit Adler.

Book Publishers Assn. of Israel, Box 20123, Tel Aviv 67132. Tel. 3-561-4121, fax 3-561-1996, e-mail tbpai@netvision.net.il. *Managing Dir.* Amnon Ben-Shmuel.

Italy

Associazione Italiana Editori (Italian Publishers Assn.), Via delle Erbe 2, 20121 Milan. Tel. 2-86-46-3091, fax 2-89-01-0863, e-mail aie@aie.it, World Wide Web http://www.aie.it. *Dir.* Ivan Cecchini.

Associazione Librai Antiquari d'Italia (Antiquarian Booksellers Assn. of Italy), Via Jacopo Nardi 6, I-50132 Florence. Tel./fax 55-24-3253, e-mail alai@dada.it, World Wide Web http://www.dada.it/alai. *Pres.* Giuliano Gallini; *Secy.* Francesco Scala.

Jamaica

Booksellers' Assn. of Jamaica, c/o Novelty Trading Co. Ltd., Box 80, Kingston. Tel. 876-922-5883, fax 876-922-4743. *Pres.* Keith Shervington.

Japan

Japan Assn. of International Publications (formerly Japan Book Importers Assn.), Chiyoda Kaikan 21-4, Nihonbashi 1-chome, Chuo-ku, Tokyo 103. Tel. 3-3271-6901, fax 3-3271-6920, World Wide Web http://www.jaip.gr.jp. *Chair* Seishiro Murata; *Secy. Gen.* Hiroshi Takahashi.

Japan Book Publishers Assn., 6 Fukuro-machi, Shinjuku-ku, Tokyo 162. Tel. 3-3268-1301, fax 3-3268-1196. *Pres.* Kunizo Asakura; *Exec. Dir.* Tadashi Yamashita.

Kenya

Kenya Publishers Assn., c/o Phoenix Publishers Ltd., Box 18650, Nairobi. Tel. 2-22-

2309, 2-22-3262, fax 2-33-9875. *Secy.* Stanley Irura.

Korea (Republic of)

Korean Publishers Assn., 105-2 Sagan-dong, Jongro-gu, Seoul 110-190. Tel. 2-735-2702, fax 2-738-5414, e-mail kpa@kpa21. or.kr, World Wide Web http://www.ifrro. org/members/kpa.html. *Pres.* Choon Ho Na; *Secy.-Gen.* Jong Jin Jung.

Latvia

Latvian Publishers Assn., K Barona iela 36-4, 1011 Riga. Tel. 371-728-2392, fax 371-728-0549, e-mail lga@gramatizdeveji.lv, World Wide Web http://www.gramatizdeveji.lv. *Exec. Dir.* Dace Pugaca.

Lithuania

Lithuanian Publishers Assn., Z Sierakausko 15, 62600 Vilnius. Tel. 2-332-943, fax 2-330-519. *Pres.* Aleksandras Krasnovas.

Malaysia

Malaysian Book Publishers' Assn., c/o Penerbit UKM, Paras 3, Univ. Kebansaan Malaysia, 43600 UKM Bangi Selangor Darul Ehsan. Tel. 3-829-2840, fax 3-825-4515. *Hon. Secy.* Thomas Soh.

Mexico

Cámara Nacional de la Industria Editorial Mexicana (Mexican Publishers' Assn.), Holanda No. 13, CP 04120, Mexico 21. Tel. 5-604-5338, fax 5-604-3147. *Co-Pres.* A. H. Gayosso, J. C. Cramerez.

The Netherlands

KVB (formerly Koninklijke Vereeniging ter Bevordering van de Belangen des Boekhandels) (Royal Dutch Book Trade Assn.), Postbus 15007, 1001 MA Amsterdam. Tel. 20-624-0212, fax 20-620-8871, e-mail info@kvb.nl, World Wide Web http://www.kvb.nl. *Exec. Dir.* C. Verberne.

Nederlands Uitgeversverbond (Royal Dutch Publishers Assn.), Postbus 12040, 1100 AA Amsterdam. Tel. 20-430-9150, fax 20-430-9179, e-mail info@uitgeversverbond. nl, World Wide Web http://www. uitgeversverbond.nl. *Pres.* Henk J. L. Vonhoff.

Nederlandsche Vereeniging van Antiquaren (Netherlands Assn. of Antiquarian Booksellers), Postbus 364, 3500 AJ, Utrecht. Tel. 30-231-9286, fax 30-234-3362, e-mail bestbook@wxs.nl, World Wide Web http:// nvva.nl. *Pres.* F. W. Kuyper; *Secy.* Gert Jan Bestebreurtje.

Nederlandse Boekverkopersbond (Dutch Booksellers Assn.), Postbus 32, 3720 AA Bilthoven. Tel. 70-228-7956, fax 70-228-4566, World Wide Web http://www.boek bond.nl. *Pres.* W. Karssen; *Exec. Secy.* A. C. Doeser.

New Zealand

Booksellers New Zealand, Box 11-377, Wellington. Tel. 4-472-8678, fax 4-472-8628. *Chair* Tony Moores.

Nigeria

Nigerian Publishers Assn., GPO Box 2541, Ibadan. Tel. 2-496-3007, fax 2-496-4370. *Pres.* V. Nwankwo.

Norway

Norske Bokhandlerforening (Norwegian Booksellers Assn.), Øvre Vollgate 15, 0158 Oslo 1. Tel. 22-396-800, fax 22-396-810, e-mail firmapost@bokhandlerfor.no, World Wide Web http://www.bokhandler for.no. *Dir.* Randi Øgrey.

Norske Forleggerforening (Norwegian Publishers Assn.), Øvre Vollgate 15, 0158 Oslo 1. Tel. 22-007-580, fax 22-333-830, e-mail dfn@forleggerforeningen.no, World Wide Web http://www.forleggerforeningen. no. *Dir.* Kristin Slordahl.

Peru

Cámara Peruana del Libro (Peruvian Publishers Assn.), Ave. Abancay cdra 4 s/n, Lima 1. Tel. 428-7630, fax 427-7331, e-mail jefatura@binape.gob.pe, World Wide Web http://www.binape.gob.pe. *Pres.* Julio César Flores Rodriguez; *Exec. Dir.* Loyda Moran Bustamente.

Philippines

Philippine Educational Publishers Assn., 84 P. Florentino St., 3008 Quezon City. Tel. 2-740-2698, fax 2-711-5702, e-mail dbuhain @cnl.net. *Pres.* D. D. Buhain.

Poland

Polskie Towarzystwo Wydawców Ksiazek (Polish Society of Book Editors), ul. Mazowiecka 2/4, 00-048 Warsaw. Tel./fax 22-826-0735. *Pres.* Janusz Fogler; *Gen. Secy.* Donat Chruscicki.

Stowarzyszenie Ksiegarzy Polskich (Assn. of Polish Booksellers), ul. Mokotowska 4/6, 00-641 Warsaw. Tel. 32-219-2393. *Pres.* Tadeusz Hussak.

Portugal

Associação Portuguesa de Editores e Livreiros (Portuguese Assn. of Publishers and Booksellers), Largo de Andaluz, 16-7 Esq., 1000 Lisbon. Tel. 1-556-241, fax 1-315-3553. *Pres.* Francisco Espadinha; *Secy. Gen.* Jorge de Carvalho Sá Borges.

Russia

All-Union Book Chamber, Kremlevskaja nab 1/9, 121019 Moscow. Tel. 95-203-4653, fax 95-298-2576, e-mail chamber@aha.ru, World Wide Web http://www.bookchamber. ru. *Dir.-Gen.* Boris Lenski.

Publishers Assn., B. Nikitskaya St. 44, 121069 Moscow. Tel. 95-202-1174, fax 95-202-3989. *Contact* M. Shishigin.

Singapore

Singapore Book Publishers Assn., c/o Cannon International, 86 Marine Parade Centre, No. 03-213, Singapore 440086. Tel. 65-344-7801, fax 65-447-0897. *Pres.* Wu-Cheng Tan.

Slovenia

Zdruzenie Zaloznikov in Knjigotrzcev Slovenije Gospodarska Zbornica Slovenije (Assn. of Publishers and Booksellers of Slovenia), Dimiceva 13, 1504 Ljubljana. Tel. 386-1-58-98-277, fax 386-1-58-98-

200, e-mail irena.brolez@gzs.si, World Wide Web http://www.gzs.si.

South Africa

Publishers Assn. of South Africa, Box 116, 7946 St. James. Tel. 21-788-6470, fax 21-788-6469, e-mail pasa@icon.co.za, World Wide Web http://www.icon.co.za/~pasa. *Chair* Basil Van Rooyen.

South Africa Booksellers Assn. (formerly Associated Booksellers of Southern Africa), Box 870, Bellville 7530. Tel. 21-918-8616, fax 21-951-4903, e-mail fnel@ naspers.com, World Wide Web http:// sabooksellers.com. *Pres.* Guru Redhi; *Secy.* Peter Adams.

Spain

Federación de Gremios de Editores de España (Federation of Spanish Publishers Assns.), Cea Bermudez 44-2 Dehe, 28003 Madrid. Tel. 91-534-5195, fax 91-535-2625, e-mail fgee@fge.es, World Wide Web http:// www.federacioneditores.org. *Pres.* Emiliano Martinez; *Exec. Dir.* Antonio Auila.

Sri Lanka

Sri Lanka Assn. of Publishers, 112 S. Mahinda Mawatha, Colombo 10. Tel. 1-695-773, fax 1-696-653, e-mail dayawansajay@ hotmail.com. *Pres.* Dayawansa Jayakody.

Sudan

Sudanese Publishers Assn., c/o Institute of African and Asian Studies, Khartoum Univ., Box 321, Khartoum 11115. Tel./fax 249-11-77820.

Sweden

Svenska Förlaggareföreningen (Swedish Publishers Assn.), Drottninggatan 97, S-11360 Stockholm. Tel. 8-736-1940, fax 8-736-1944, e-mail svf@forlagskansli.se. *Dir.* Kristina Ahlinder.

Switzerland

Schweizerischer Buchhandler- und Verleger-Verband (Swiss German-Language Booksellers and Publishers Assn.), Postfach 9045, 8050 Zurich. Tel. 1-318-6430, fax 1-318-6462, e-mail sbvv@swissbooks.ch, World Wide Web http://www.swissbooks.ch. *Exec. Dir.* Martin Dann.

Société des Libraires et Editeurs de la Suisse Romande (Assn. of Swiss French-Language Booksellers and Publishers), Case Postale 1215, 1001 Lausanne. Tel. 21-796-3300, fax 21-796-3311, e-mail aself@centrepatronal.ch. *Dir.* François Perret. E-mail fperret@centrepatronal.ch.

Thailand

Publishers and Booksellers Assn. of Thailand, 320 Lat Phrao 94-aphat Pracha-u-thit Rd., Bangkok 10310. Tel. 2-559-2642, fax 2-559-2643.

Uganda

Uganda Publishers and Booksellers Assn., Box 7732, Kampala. Tel. 41-259-163, fax 41-251-160. *Contact* Martin Okia.

United Kingdom

Antiquarian Booksellers Assn., Sackville House, 40 Piccadilly, London W1V 9PA, England. Tel. 20-7439-3118, fax 20-7439-3119. *Administrators* Philippa Gibson, Deborah Stratford.

Assn. of Learned and Professional Society Publishers, Sentosa Hill Rd., Fairlight, Hastings, East Sussex TN35 4AE, England. Tel. 1424-812-353, fax 181-663-3583, e-mail donovan@alpsp.demon.co.uk. *Secy.-Gen.* B. T. Donovan.

Booktrust, 45 East Hill, Wandsworth, London SW18 2QZ, England. Tel. 20-8516-2977, fax 20-8516-2978, World Wide Web http://www.booktrust.org.uk.

Educational Publishers Council, 1 Kingsway, London WC2B 6XF, England. Tel. 20-7565-7474, fax 20-7836-4543, e-mail mail@publishers.org.uk, World Wide Web http://www.publishers.org.uk. *Chair* Philip Walters; *Dir.* Graham Taylor.

Publishers Assn., 29B Montague St., London WC1B 5BH, England. Tel. 20-7691-9191, fax 20-7691-9199, e-mail mail@publishers.org.uk, World Wide Web http://www.publishers.org.uk. *Pres.* Anthony Forbes-Watson; *Chief Exec.* Ronnie Williams.

Scottish Book Trust, Scottish Book Centre, 137 Dundee St., Edinburgh EH11 1BG, Scotland. Tel. 131-229-3663, fax 131-228-4293, e-mail info@scottishbooktrust.com.

Scottish Publishers Assn., Scottish Book Centre, 137 Dundee St., Edinburgh EH11 1BG, Scotland. Tel. 131-229-3663, fax 131-228-4293, World Wide Web http://www.scottishbooks.org. *Dir.* Lorraine Fannin; *Chair* Peter Mackenzie.

Welsh Books Council (Cyngor Llyfrau Cymru), Castell Brychan, Aberystwyth, Ceredigion SY23 2JB, Wales. Tel. 1970-624-455, fax 1970-625-506, e-mail castelbrychan@cllc.org.uk, World Wide Web http://www.cllc.org.uk. *Dir.* Gwerfyl Pierce Jones.

Uruguay

Cámara Uruguaya del Libro (Uruguayan Publishers Assn.), Juan D. Jackson 1118, 11200 Montevideo. Tel. 2-241-4732, fax 2-241-1860.

Venezuela

Cámara Venezolana del Libro (Venezuelan Publishers Assn.), Ave. Andrés Bello, Torre Oeste 11, piso 11, Of. 112-0, Apdo. 51858, Caracas 1050-A. Tel. 212-793-1347, fax 212-793-1368, e-mail cavelibro@cantv.net. *Dir.* M. P. Vargas.

Zambia

Booksellers and Publishers Assn. of Zambia, Box 31838, Lusaka. Tel. 1-225-195, fax 1-225-282; *Exec. Dir.* Basil Mbewe.

Zimbabwe

Zimbabwe Book Publishers Assn., 12 Selous Ave., Harare Causeway, Harare. Tel 4-750-282, fax 4- 751-202.

National Information Standards Organization (NISO) Standards

Information Retrieval

Z39.2-1994 (R 2001) Information Interchange Format
Z39.47-1993 Extended Latin Alphabet Coded Character Set for Bibliographic Use (ANSEL)
Z39.50-2003 Information Retrieval (Z39.50) Application Service Definition and Protocol Specification
Z39.53-2001 Codes for the Representation of Languages for Information Interchange
Z39.64-1989 (R 2002) East Asian Character Code for Bibliographic Use
Z39.76-1996 (R 2002) Data Elements for Binding Library Materials
Z39.84-2000 Syntax for the Digital Object Identifier

Library Management

Z39.7-1995* Library Statistics
Z39.20-1999 Criteria for Price Indexes for Print Library Materials
Z39.71-1999 Holdings Statements for Bibliographic Items
Z39.73-1994 (R 2001) Single-Tier Steel Bracket Library Shelving

Preservation and Storage

Z39.32-1996 (R 2002) Information on Microfiche Headers
Z39.48-1992 (R 2002) Permanence of Paper for Publications and Documents in Libraries and Archives
Z39.62-2000 Eye-Legible Information on Microfilm Leaders and Trailers and on Containers of Processed Microfilm on Open Reels
Z39.74-1996 (R 2002) Guides to Accompany Microform Sets
Z39.77-2001 Guidelines for Information About Preservation Products
Z39.78-2000 Library Binding
Z39.79-2001 Environmental Conditions for Exhibiting Library and Archival Materials

Publishing and Information Management

Z39.9-1992 (R 2001) International Standard Serial Numbering (ISSN)
Z39.14-1997 (R 2002) Guidelines for Abstracts

Z39.18-1995*	Scientific and Technical Reports—Elements, Organization, and Design
Z39.19-1993*	Guidelines for the Construction, Format, and Management of Monolingual Thesauri
Z39.23-1997 (R 2002)	Standard Technical Report Number Format and Creation
Z39.26-1997 (R 2002)	Micropublishing Product Information
Z39.41-1997 (R 2002)	Printed Information on Spines
Z39.43-1993 (R 2001)	Standard Address Number (SAN) for the Publishing Industry
Z39.56-1996 (R 2002)	Serial Item and Contribution Identifier (SICI)
NISO/ANSI/ISO 12083 (R 2002)	Electronic Manuscript Preparation and Markup
Z39.82-2001	Title Pages for Conference Publications
Z39.85-2001	Dublin Core Metadata Element Set

In Development

Networked Reference Services
OpenURL: A Transport Mechanism for Content Objects
Technical Metatdata for Digital Still Images
U.S. National Profile for Library Applications

NISO Technical Reports and Other Publications

Environmental Guidelines for the Storage of Paper Records (TR-01-1995)
Guidelines for Indexes and Related Information Retrieval Devices (TR-02-1997)
A Guide to Alphanumeric Arrangement and Sorting of Numerals and Other Symbols (TR-03-1999)
Information Standards Quarterly (*ISQ*) (NISO quarterly newsletter)
Metadata Made Simpler
The RFP Writer's Guide to Standards for Library Systems
Up and Running: Implementing Z39.50—Proceedings of a Symposium Sponsored by the State Library of Iowa
Z39.50: A Primer on the Protocol
Z39.50 Implementation Experiences

*These standards are being reviewed by NISO's Standards Development Committee or are under revision. For further information, please contact NISO, 4733 Bethesda Ave., Suite 300, Bethesda, MD 20814. Tel. 301-654-2512, fax 301-654-1721, e-mail nisohq@niso.org, World Wide Web http://www.niso.org.

Calendar, 2003–2012

The list below contains information on association meetings or promotional events that are, for the most part, national or international in scope. State and regional library association meetings are also included. To confirm the starting or ending date of a meeting, which may change after *Bowker Annual* has gone to press, contact the association directly. Addresses of library and book trade associations are listed in Part 6 of this volume. For information on additional book trade and promotional events, see *Literary Market Place* and *International Literary Market Place*, published by Information Today, Inc., and other library and book trade publications such as *Library Journal, School Library Journal,* and *Publishers Weekly.*

2003

June

2–6	International Assn. of Technological University Libraries	Edinburgh, Scotland
2–8	Assn. of Caribbean University Research and Institutional Libraries (ACURIL)	San Juan, Puerto Rico
7–12	Special Libraries Assn.	New York
8–16	Crimea 2002, "Libraries and Associations in the Transient World: New Technologies and New Forms of Cooperation"	Sudak, Crimea
12–13	Rhode Island Library Assn.	Smithfield
14–18	Assn. of Jewish Libraries	Denver
18–21	American Theological Library Assn.	Portland, OR
19–25	American Library Assn. Annual Conference, Canadian Library Assn. Annual Conference	Toronto, ON
23–27	Jerusalem International Book Fair	Jerusalem, Israel
25–28	American Theological Library Assn.	Portland, OR

July

12–16	American Assn. of Law Libraries	Seattle
23–28	Hong Kong Book Fair	Hong Kong

August

1–9	International Federation of Library Assns. and Institutions (IFLA) General Conference	Berlin, Germany

August 2003 *(cont.)*

6–9	Pacific Northwest Library Assn.	Boise, ID
9–25	Edinburgh International Book Festival	Edinburgh, Scotland

September

23–26	North Carolina Library Assn.	Winston-Salem
24–26	Minnesota Library Council	Rochester
25–27	North Dakota Library Assn.	Minot
27–1/10	Arkansas Library Assn.	Ft. Smith

October

1–3	Library and Information Technology Assn.	Norfolk, VA
1–3	Missouri Library Assn.	Springfield
1–4	Idaho Library Assn.	Post Falls
1–4	Wyoming Library Assn.	Sheridan
2–5	Pennsylvania Library Assn.	Pittsburgh
3–5	LITA National Forum	Norfolk, VA
8–11	Kentucky Library Assn.	Louisville
8–13	Frankfurt Book Fair	Frankfurt, Germany
14–16	KMWorld & Intranets 2003	Santa Clara, CA
14–18	Illinois Library Assn.	Springfield
15–17	Iowa Library Assn.	Cedar Rapids
15–17	South Dakota Library Assn.	Sioux Falls
19–21	New England Library Assn.	Manchester, NH
19–22	ARMA International	Boston
20–23	American Society for Information Science and Technology	Long Beach, CA
22–24	Georgia Library Assn.	Jekyll Island
22–24	Nebraska Educational Media Assn.	Omaha
22–26	American Assn. of School Librarians	Kansas City, MO
22–26	Assn. for Educational Communications and Technology	Anaheim, CA
26–28	New England Library Assn.	Manchester, NH
27–30	Wisconsin Library Assn.	Milwaukee
28–31	Michigan Library Assn.	Lansing

November

3–5	Internet Librarian	Monterey, CA
3–7	REFORMA	Lake Tahoe, NV
5–7	Virginia Library Assn., Virginia Assn. of Law Libraries	Hot Springs
5–8	American Translators Assn.	Phoenix
5–8	Mountain Plains Library Assn., Nevada Library Assn. joint conference	North Lake Tahoe, NV
5–8	New York Library Assn.	Saratoga Springs
6–8	Illinois School Library Media Assn.	Decatur

| 14–17 | California Library Assn., California School Library Assn. | Ontario |
| 19–21 | Ohio Library Council | Cleveland |

December

| 3–5 | West Virginia Library Assn. | Greenbrier |

2004

January

| 6–9 | Assn. for Library and Information Science Education (ALISE) | San Diego |
| 9–14 | American Library Assn. Midwinter Meeting | San Diego |

February

| 24–28 | Public Libraries Assn. | Seattle |

March

14–16	London Book Fair	London, England
15–20	Texas Library Assn.	San Antonio
16–18	Louisiana Library Assn.	Monroe

April

14–16	Oregon Library Assn.	Eugene
18–24	National Library Week	
20–23	Alabama Library Assn.	Montgomery
21–23	Oklahoma Library Assn.	Tulsa

June

| 4–6 | BookExpo America 2004 | Chicago |
| 24–30 | American Library Assn. Annual Conference | Orlando |

July

| 10–15 | American Assn. of Law Libraries | Boston |

August

| 18–21 | Pacific Northwest Library Assn. | Pasco, WA |

September

| 28–2/10 | Illinois Library Assn. | Chicago |

October

| 6–9 | Idaho Library Assn. | Boise |

October 2004 *(cont.)*

6–11	Frankfurt Book Fair	Frankfurt, Germany
8–10	Library and Information Technology Assn. (LITA)	St. Louis
13–15	Iowa Library Assn.	Sioux City
20–22	New England Library Assn.	Manchester, NH

November

2–5	Wisconsin Library Assn.	Lake Geneva
3–6	Illinois School Library Media Assn.	Arlington

2005

January

14–19	American Library Assn. Midwinter Meeting	Boston

March

13–15	London Book Fair	London, England

April

7–10	Assn. of College and Research Libraries	Minneapolis
10–16	National Library Week	
11–16	Texas Library Assn.	Dallas
20–23	Washington Library Assn.	Spokane

June

3–5	BookExpo America 2005	New York
23–29	American Library Assn. Annual Conference	Chicago

July

16–21	American Assn. of Law Libraries	San Antonio

September

20–23	North Carolina Library Assn.	Winston-Salem
30–2/10	Library and Information Technology Assn. (LITA)	San Jose, CA

October

5–8	Idaho Library Assn.	Pocatello
16–18	New England Library Assn.	Worcester, MA
19–24	Frankfurt Book Fair	Frankfurt, Germany
25–28	Wisconsin Library Assn.	Lacrosse
27–29	Illinois School Library Media Assn.	Decatur

2006

January

20–25   American Library Assn. Midwinter Meeting   San Antonio

March

20–25   Public Library Assn.   Boston

April

2–8   National Library Week
24–29   Texas Library Assn.   Houston

June

22–28   American Library Assn. Annual Conference   New Orleans

July

15–20   American Assn. of Law Libraries   St. Louis

October

4–9   Frankfurt Book Fair   Frankfurt, Germany

2007

January

19–24   American Library Assn. Midwinter Meeting   Seattle

March

12–17   Texas Library Assn.   San Antonio

April

15–21   National Library Week

June

21–27   American Library Assn. Annual Conference   Washington, DC

July

14–18   American Assn. of Law Librarians   New Orleans

2008

January

11–16   American Library Assn. Midwinter Meeting   Philadelphia

April 2008

1–5	Public Library Assn.	Minneapolis
7–12	Texas Library Assn.	Dallas

June

26–2/7	American Library Assn. Annual Conference	Anaheim

2009

January

23–28	American Library Assn. Midwinter Meeting	Denver

April

20–25	Texas Library Assn.	Houston

July

9–15	American Library Assn. Annual Conference	Chicago

2010

January

15–20	American Library Assn. Midwinter Meeting	Boston

April

12–16	Texas Library Assn.	San Antonio

June

24–30	American Library Assn. Annual Conference	Orlando

2011

January

28–2/2	American Library Assn. Midwinter Meeting	Chicago

June

23–29	American Library Assn. Annual Conference	New Orleans

2012

January

20–25	American Library Assn. Midwinter Meeting	San Antonio

June

21–27	American Library Assn. Annual Conference	Anaheim

Acronyms

A

AALL. American Association of Law Libraries

AAP. Association of American Publishers

AASL. American Association of School Librarians

AAUP. Association of American University Presses

ABA. American Booksellers Association

ABFFE. American Booksellers Foundation for Free Expression

ACRL. Association of College and Research Libraries

AgNIC. Agriculture Network Information Center

AIIP. Association of Independent Information Professionals

AJL. Association of Jewish Libraries

ALA. American Library Association

ALCTS. Association for Library Collections and Technical Services

ALIC. Archives Library Information Center

ALS. Academic Libraries Survey

ALSC. Association for Library Service to Children

ALTA. Association for Library Trustees and Advocates

AMMLA. American Merchant Marine Library Association

AMS. Advanced Marketing Services

APALA. Asian/Pacific American Librarians Association

ARL. Association of Research Libraries

ARLIS/NA. Art Libraries Society of North America

ASCLA. Association of Specialized and Cooperative Library Agencies

ASIS&T. American Society for Information Science and Technology

ASM. American Society of Microbiology

ATLA. American Theological Library Association

B

BEA. BookExpo America

BSA. Bibliographical Society of America

C

CAIS. Canadian Association for Information Science

CALA. Chinese-American Librarians Association

CD-ROM. Compact Disc Read-Only Memory

CIPA. Children's Internet Protection Act

CLA. Canadian Library Association; Catholic Library Association

CNI. Coalition for Networked Information

COPA. Child Online Protection Act

COPPA. Children's Online Privacy Protection Act

COSLA. Chief Officers of State Library Agencies

COUNTER. Internet/Web, Counting Online Usage of NeTworked Electronic Resources

CPPA. Child Pornography Prevention Act

CRS. Congressional Research Service

CSLA. Church and Synagogue Library Association

CTEA. Copyright Term Extension Act

D

DARPA. Defense Advanced Research Projects Agency

DLF. Digital Library Federation

DMCA. Digital Millennium Copyright Act

DMCRA. Digital Media Consumers' Rights Act

DOD. Defense, U.S. Department of

DOE. Education, U.S. Department of

DOI. Digital reference, digital object identifier

DRM. Digital rights management

E

E-FDLP. Federal depository libraries, Electronic Federal Depository Library Program

E-SPY. American Library Association, E-SPY

EAR. National Technical Information Service, Export Administration Regulations

ECAR. EDUCAUSE Center for Applied Research

EDB. Energy, Science and Technology Database

EDRS. Educational Resources Information Center, ERIC Document Reproduction Service

EDVAPS. Educational Resources Information Center, ERIC Data Validation and Processing System

EMIERT. American Library Association, Ethnic Material and Information Exchange Round Table

EPA. Environmental Protection Agency

ERIC. Educational Resources Information Center

F

FAFLRT. American Library Association, Federal and Armed Forces Librarians Round Table

FBI. Federal Bureau of Investigation

FDLP. Government Printing Office, Federal Depository Library Program

FEDRIP. National Technical Information Service, FEDRIP (Federal Research in Progress Database)

FIAF. International Federation of Film Archives

FLICC. Federal Library and Information Center Committee

FOIA. Freedom of Information Act

FOLUSA. Friends of Libraries U.S.A.

FPC. Federal Publishers Committee

G

GATS. General Agreement on Trade in Services

GLBT. American Library Association, Gay, Lesbian, Bisexual, and Transgendered Round Table

GLIN. Global Legal Information Network

GODORT. American Library Association, Government Documents Round Table

GPEA. Government Paperwork Elimination Act

GPO. Government Printing Office

GRC. National Technical Information Service, GOV.Research Center

I

IAALD. International Association of Agricultural Information Specialists

IALL. International Association of Law Libraries

IAML. International Association of Music Libraries, Archives, and Documentation Centres

IASL. International Association of School Librarianship

IATUL. International Association of Technological University Libraries

IDLH. Databases, Immediately Dangerous to Life or Health Concentrations Database

IFLA. International Federation of Library Associations and Institutions

IFRT. American Library Association, Intellectual Freedom Round Table

ILL/DD. Interlibrary loan/document delivery

IMAA. Instructional Materials Accessibility Act

IMLS. Institute of Museum and Library Services

ISBN. International Standard Book Number

ISO. International Organization for Standardization

ISSN. International Standard Serial Number

ITAA. Information Technology Association of America

L

LAMA. Library Administration and Management Association

LHRT. American Library Association, Library History Round Table

LIS. Library of Congress, Legislative Information System; Library/information science

LITA. Library and Information Technology Association

LPS. Government Printing Office (GPO), Library Programs Service

LRRT. American Library Association, Library Research Round Table

LSCA. Library Services and Construction Act

LSP. National Center for Education Statistics, Library Statistics Program

LSTA. Library Services and Technology Act

M

MAGERT. American Library Association, Map and Geography Round Table

MHC. McGraw-Hill Companies

MLA. Medical Library Association; Music Library Association

N

NACS. National Association of College Stores

NAGARA. National Association of Government Archives and Records Administrators

NAL. National Agricultural Library

NARA. National Archives and Records Administration

NASTA. National Association of Textbook Administrators

NCBI. National Center for Biotechnology Information

NCES. National Center for Education Statistics

NCIPA. Neighborhood Children's Internet Protection Act

NCLIS. National Commission on Libraries and Information Science

NDIIPP. National Digital Information Infrastructure and Preservation Program

NEDRC. National Education Data Resource Center

NEH. National Endowment for the Humanities

NEN. National Education Network

NHES. National Center for Education Statistics, National Household Education Survey

NHPRC. National Archives and Records Administration, National Historical Publications and Records Commission

NIOSH. National Institute for Occupational Safety and Health

NISO. National Information Standards Organization

NIST. National Institute of Standards and Technology

NLC. National Library of Canada

NLE. National Library of Education

NLM. National Library of Medicine

NMRT. American Library Association, New Members Round Table

NPG. National Institute for Occupational Safety and Health, NIOSH Pocket Guide to Chemical Hazards (NPG)

NTIS. National Technical Information Service

P

PGW. Publishers Group West

PLA. Public Library Association

R

RPAC. Association of American Publishers, Rights and Permissions Advisory Committee

RTECS. Registry of Toxic Effects of Chemical Substances

RUSA. Reference and User Services Association

S

SAA. Society of American Archivists

SAN. Standard Address Number

SLA. Special Libraries Association

SPARC. Scholarly Publishing and Academic Resources Coalition

SRIM. National Technical Information Service, Selected Research in Microfiche

SRRT. American Library Association, Social Responsibilities Round Table

SSP. Society for Scholarly Publishing

StLA. State libraries and library agencies; NCES State Library Agencies survey

T

TIPS. Homeland security, Operation TIPS (Terrorism, Terrorism Information and Prevention System)

TLA. Theatre Library Association

U

UCITA. Uniform Computer Information Transactions Act

ULC. Urban Libraries Council

USPS. Postal Service, U.S.

V

VRD. LSSI, Virtual Reference Desk

W

WNC. World News Connection

Y

YALSA. Young Adult Library Services Association

Index of Organizations

Please note that many cross-references refer to entries in the Subject Index.

MINERVA, 31
NAL, 54, 55, 57–58
NARA, 90, 101
NLM, 59–61
OCLC, 50
Online Lyceum, 180
plagiarism, 14
portals, *see* Portals (library); Portals (insti-
tutional)
privacy issues, 259–262
Profiles in Science, 61
PubSCIENCE, 311
removal of information, 233–235
school libraries and, 11–12
Shibboleth, 272
standards, 415–416
state library agencies, 434–435
terrorist attacks of 9/11 and, 25
Tox Town, 61
under Homeland Security Act, 233–235
Whois database legislation, 331–332
See also Children's Internet Protection Act;
Digital rights management; Dot Kids
Implementation and Efficiency Act;
E-government; main entries, e.g.,
MEDLINE
InterTrust Technologies, 16
ISBN, *see* International Standard Book Num-
ber
IUniverse.com, 19

L

Library Administration and Management
Association (LAMA), 670–671
awards, 402
Library of Congress, 6, 23–36
acquisitions, 30–31
American Folklife Center
Veterans History Project, 35
American Memory, 28–29
Beginnings: World Treasures of the Library
of Congress, 33
budget, 26
cataloging, 30
collections, 29–31
Congressional Relations Office, 28
Copyright Office, 28, 32
digital projects/planning, 27, 28–29, 31
election reform and, 27
fund-raising activities, 26–27
Global Gateway, 29

Integrated Library System (ILS), 23, 29–30
Internet resources, 28
September 11 Web Archive, 25
Jefferson Library Project, 30
John W. Kluge Center, 32–33
Legislative Information System (LIS), 27
legislative support to Congress, 27–28
National Book Festival, 23–24
National Digital Information Infrastructure
and Preservation Program (NDIIPP),
28
National Film Registry, 35–36
preservation activities, 33–36
publications, 33–34
Rare Book Forum, 41
reference service, 31
security measures, 24, 25–26
storage, secondary, 30
symposia, 34
telephone numbers, 36
terrorism, response to, 24–25, 27, 30, 32
THOMAS, *see* THOMAS
See also Center for the Book; Congressional Research Service; National Audio-
Visual Conservation Center
Library and Information Technology Association (LITA), 671–672
awards, 402–403, 421
Lightning Source, 19
LPC Group, 15
Lutheran Church Library Association, 703

M

McGraw-Hill Companies (MHC), 19
Massachusetts Institute of Technology
(MIT), 238
Medical Library Association (MLA),
703–704
awards, 410–411
grants, 425
MEDLINE, 59–60
MEDLINEplus, 60–61
Andrew W. Mellon Foundation, 174
Music Library Association (MLA), 704–705

N

National Agricultural Library (NAL), 54–58
collection, 55–56
DigiTop, 58

Subject Index

Please note that many cross-references refer to entries in the Index of Organizations.

A

Academic books
  prices and price indexes, 465,
      498–499(table)
    British averages, 506–507(table)
    North American, 496–497(table)
    U.S. college books, 471(table), 472(table)
  sales, 22
  See also Association of American Publishers, Professional/Scholarly Publishing; Association of American University Presses; Society for Scholarly Publishing; Textbooks
Academic journals, 8–9
  German periodicals, 508(table)
Academic libraries, *see* Academic Libraries Survey; College and research libraries
Academic Libraries Survey (ALS), 99
Academic publishing, 19, 236
Academic resources, 193–194
Acquisitions
  expenditures, 439–447
    academic libraries, 442–443(table)
    government libraries, 446–447(table)
    public libraries, 440–441(table)
    special libraries, 444–445(table)
  prices and price indexes, 456(table), 462,
      467(table)
    major components, 457(table)
  See also specific types of libraries, e.g.,
      Public libraries
Adults, services for
  NCES survey, 97
  readers' advisory; bibliography for librarians, 550
  See also Literacy programs; Reference and User Services Association
Agencies, library, *see* Library associations and agencies

Agricultural libraries, *see* International Association of Agricultural Information Specialists; National Agricultural Library
Alabama
  library associations, 718
  networks and cooperative library organizations, 631
  school library media associations, 739
Alaska
  library associations, 718
  networks and cooperative library organizations, 631
  school library media associations, 739
Almanacs, bestselling, 594
Anticounterfeiting Amendments, 327–328
Archives
  acquisition expenditures
    academic libraries, 442–443(table)
    government libraries, 446–447(table)
    public libraries, 440–441(table)
    special libraries, 444–445(table)
  electronic/digital, 25, 69
  mammography, digital, 64
  See also Archives Library Information Center; National Archives and Records Administration
Arizona
  library associations, 718
  networks and cooperative library organizations, 631
  school library media associations, 739
Arkansas
  library associations, 718–719
  networks and cooperative library organizations, 631–632
  school library media associations, 739
Armed forces libraries, number of, 426–427
Armey, Dick, 240
Artists, freelance, 334

Canadian, 427–428

construction, *see* Library buildings

funding, anticipated, 449(table)

grants, 450

Internet use and, 448, 450–451

LJ budget report, 448–454, 449(table)

NCES survey, 95–99, 429–431, 435

number of, 426, 427

prices and price indexes, 455, 461–463

  books and serials, 459(table)

  major component subindexes, 457(table)

  non-print media and electronic services, 460(table)

  operating expenses, 461(table), 563

  personnel compensation, 458(table)

research on, 417–419

services to young adults, 418–419

staffing, 448

use of, 417, 448

See also Collection development; Electronic resources; Funding for libraries; Library buildings; Public Library Association, and specific states

Public relations for school librarians, 13–14

Public schools, *see* No Child Left Behind; School libraries; School library media centers and services

Publishers and publishing

AAP activities

academic, 19

antipiracy efforts, 525

digital, 7

education, 19

government, *see* Government Printing Office

legislation, *see* Legislation affecting publishing

mergers and acquisitions, 17–18

NISO standards, 781–782

prices and price indexes, *see* under Academic books; Audiovisual materials; Books; CD-ROM; Hardcover books; Microforms; Newspapers; Paperback books; Periodicals and serials; Videocassettes

sales, *see* Book sales

staffing, 16–17, 18–19

terrorism and, 16

Turkish, 159

See also Association of American Publishers; Digital Millennium Copyright Act; E-books; Federal Publishers Committee, and names of specific countries, e.g., Germany

Publishers Weekly (*PW*)

bestseller lists, 578–617

  children's, 596–617

  hardcover, 578–588

  paperback, 588–596

R

Random House v. *Rosetta Books*, 20

Raseroka, Kay, 205, 206

Readers' advisory; bibliography for librarians, 550

Recordings for children, notable, 576–577

Records management, *see* National Association of Government Archives and Records Administrators

Reference services

bibliography for librarians, 550

e-reference, *see* Digital reference

Library of Congress, 31

See also Reference and User Services Association

Religious books

sales, 22

U.S. imports, 529(table)

Religious libraries, *see* American Theological Library Association; Association of Jewish Libraries; Catholic Library Association; Church and Synagogue Library Association; Lutheran Church Library Association

Research libraries, *see* College and research libraries

Rhode Island

library associations, 727

networks and cooperative library organizations, 650

school library media associations, 746

Ridge, Tom, 241

Roberts, Nora, 578

Rosset, Barney, 148

Russia, 40

S

Safire, William, 240

Salaries, 296–297, 372–385

2001 U.S. graduates, 373(table), 382–383(table)